4th Annual International Conference on Information Technology and Applications (ITA 2017)

ITM Web of Conferences Volume 12 (2017)

Guangzhou, China
26 - 28 May 2017

Editors:

Li Long
Yongjun Li
Xzaolong Li
Yonghui Dai
Hui Yang

ISBN: 978-1-5108-4742-2

Printed from e-media with permission by:

Curran Associates, Inc.
57 Morehouse Lane
Red Hook, NY 12571

proceedings.com

Some format issues inherent in the e-media version may also appear in this print version.

Printed by Curran Associates, Inc. (2017)

For additional information, please contact EDP Sciences – Web of Conferences at the address below.

EDP Sciences – Web of Conferences
17, Avenue du Hoggar
Parc d'Activité de Courtabœuf
BP 112
F-91944 Les Ulis Cedex A
France

Phone: +33 (0) 1 69 18 75 75
Fax: +33 (0) 1 69 28 84 91

contact-edps@webofconferences.org

Additional copies of this publication are available from:

Curran Associates, Inc.
57 Morehouse Lane
Red Hook, NY 12571 USA
Phone: 845-758-0400
Fax: 845-758-2633
Email: curran@proceedings.com
Web: www.proceedings.com

TABLE OF CONTENTS

Preface

ITA 2017

4th Annual International Conference on Information Technology and Application (ITA 2017) was held in guangzhou, China, from 26-28 May 2017. ITA 2017 is to offer scholars, professionals, academics and graduate students to present, share, and discuss their studies from various perspectives in the aspects of Information Technology and Applications. These proceedings tend to collect the up-to-date, comprehensive and worldwide state-of-art knowledge on information technology and application. All accepted papers were subjected to strict peer-reviewing by expert referees. The papers have been selected for this proceedings based on originality, significance, and clarity for the purpose of the conference. The selected papers and additional late-breaking contributions to be presented will make an exciting technical program on conference. The conference program is extremely rich, featuring high impact presentation. We hope this conference will not only provide the participants a broad overview of the latest research results on information technology, but also provide the participants a significant platform to build academic connections.

The Technical Program Committee worked very hard to have all papers reviewed before the review deadline. The final technical program consists of 97 papers. There is four keynote speech and nine invited sessions. The keynote speakers are internationally recognized as a leading expert in the research field of information technology who has demonstrated outstanding proficiency and has achieved distinction in his profession. The proceedings were published as a volume in by EDP science.

We would like to express our sincere gratitude to all the members of Technical Program Committee and organizers for their enthusiasm, time, and expertise. Our deep thanks also go to many volunteers and staffs for the long hours and hard work they have generously given to ITA 2017. Finally, we would like to thank all the authors, speakers, and participants of this conference for their contributions to ITA 2017, and also looks forward to welcoming you to ITA 2018.

Prof. Ting Yang

Program Chair
Prof. Yanghua Xiao, Fudan University, China
Prof. Yinghua Zhou, Chongqing University of Posts and Telecommunications, China

Editor
Professor, Yongjun LI, Northwestern Polytechnical University, China
Prof. Lei Zhang, College of Communication Engineering, Chongqing University, Chongqing, China）
Prof. Hong-Can Yan, North China University of Science and Technology, China

Co-Chair
Professor, Qiang Yang, College of Electrical Engineering, Zhejiang University, Hangzhou, China
Prof. Farn Wang, National Taiwan University, Taiwan
Prof. Tsung-Han Tsai, National Central University, Taiwan
Prof. Tao Gong, Donghua University, China

Technical Program Committee
Dr. Raza Hasan, Middle East College, Pakistani
Dr. li long, State Key Laboratory of High-end Server & Storage Technology, Inspur Group, China
Dr. Yonghui Dai, Information Building, Shanghai University of International Business and Economics, China
Dr. Yongjun LI, Northwestern Polytechnical University, China
Dr. Hui Yang, Beijing University of Posts and Telecommunications, China
Dr. Liu Jianwei, Department of Automation,College of Geophysics and Information Engineering, China
Dr. Hui Zhang, Nankai University, China
Professor, Yan-Fei Jing, University of Electronic Science and Technology of China (UESTC), China
Professor, Liangxiao Jiang, Department of Computer Science,China University of Geosciences, China
Professor, Weidong Qiu, School of Information Security Engineering,Shanghai Jiaotong Universigy, China
Dr. Guoqing Xiao, Hunan University (HNU) College of Computer Science and Electronic Engineering, China
Dr. Ximing Fu, Tsinghua University, China
Dr. Qiang Yang, College of Electrical Engineering,Zhejiang University, Hangzhou, China
Professor, Tao Gong, College of Information S.& T., Donghua University, China, China

Kastoria, Greece
Dr., Kuan Chee, University of Nottingham Ningbo China, Ningbo, China
Dr., Hyun Sung Kim, Kyungil University, Kyungbuk, Korea
Dr., Oskars Ozolins, Acreo Swedish ICT AB, Kista, Sweden
Dr., Quan Zhou, Nanjing University of Posts and Telecommunictions, Nanjing, China
Dr., Jian Wei Liu, China University of Petroleum, Beijing, China
Dr., Bin Liu, Uber, San Francisco, USA
Dr., Galar Idoate, Mikel, Public University of Navarra, Navarra, Spain
Dr., Dariusz Grabowski, Silesian University of Technology, Gliwice, Poland
Dr., P. M. Meshram, Yeshwantrao Chavan College of Engineering, Nagpur, India
Dr., Yun Kai Liu, Gannon University, Erie, USA
Dr., Lee Tian Soon, Multimedia University, Melaka, Malaysia
Prof., Alexandru Woinaroschy, University Politehnica of Bucharest, Bucharest, Romania
Dr., Indrajit De, Mckv Institute of Engineering, Howrah, India
Dr., OzgurOzdemir, Selcuk University, Konya, Turkey
Dr., Ahmet Sayar, Kocaeli University, Izmit, Turkey
Dr., Wuyi Yue, Konan University, Japan
Dr., Manu Pratap Singh, Ambedkar University, Agra, India
Dr., Manik Sharma, DAV University, Jalandhar, India
Dr., Mahdi Salman Mohammad Alshamasin, Al-Balqa' Applied University, Amman, Jordan
Dr., Karen Miranda, Universidad AutónomaMetropolitana, Mexico City, Mexico
Dr., Zhe Chen, Dalian University of Technology, Dalian, China
Dr., Teodor Lucian Grigorie, Ecole de TechnologieSuperieure in Montreal, Quebec, Canada
Dr., S.Muthusundari, R.M.D Engineering College, Tamil Nadu, India
Dr., BrahimAïssa, Hamad Bin Khalifa University, Doha, Qatar
Dr., FatmaTangour, National Institute of Applied Sciences and Technology,Tunis
Dr., DongbingGu, University of Essex, Colchester, UK
Dr., Yilun Shang, Tongji University, Shanghai, China
Dr. Gursharanjeet Singh Kalra, Lovely Professional University, Jalandhar, India
Dr. WeiQing Sun, University of Toledo, Toledo, USA
Dr. SamanShojaeChaeikar, IAU University, Iran
Prof., Syed Afzal Murtaza Rizvi, Central University, New Delhi, India Prof., Yi Xin Gao, The Johns Hopkins University, USA
Prof., Xun Wei Zhou, Beijing Union University, Beijing, China
Dr., Jun Guo, East China Normal University, Shanghai, China
Dr., Yuexin Mao, University of Connecticut, Storrs, USA

Program Chair & Keynote Prof. Yang-Hua Xiao

Department of computer science, Fudan University, China

Yanghua Xiao got his PHD degree in software theory from Fudan University, Shanghai, China, in 2009. He now is an associate professor of computer science at Fudan University. He is one of young 973 scientists. His research interest includes big data management and mining, graph database, knowledge graph. He was a visiting professor of Human Genome Sequencing Center at Baylor College Medicine, and visiting researcher of Microsoft Research Asia. He won the Best PhD ThesisNomination of CCF (Chinese Computer Federation) in year 2010, CCF2014 Natural Science Award (second level), ACM (CCF) Shanghai distinguished young scientists nomination award. Recently, he has published 50+ papers in international leading journal and top conferences, including Pattern Recognition, Physical Review E,Plos One, Information System, Computers & Mathematics with Applications, BCM Systems Biology, Physica A; SIGMOD,VLDB, ICDE, IJCAI, AAAI, EDBT, ICSE,OOPSLA, WWW, ICDM, CIKM, SDM, ECML/PKDD, ICWS, ICSM, DASFAA,COMPSAC, SSDBM, etc.

Program Chair Prof. Ying-Hua Zhou,

Chongqing University of Posts and Telecommunications, China

His Research included Computer Algorithms, Artificial Intelligence, Data Mining & Big Data Analysis, Computational Intelligence, He working as Associate professor in Posts and Telecommunications, China, he has published many articles, and participated in many international conferences.

Editor Prof. Jian-Wei Liu

Jianwei Liu, received the BSc, MSc and PhD degrees from Nanjing Universi ty of Science and Technology, Beijing University of Chemical Technology, Donghua University, China, in 1997, 2000 and 2006, respectively. He joined Department of Automation, College of Geophysics and Information Engine ering, China University of Petroleum, Beijing in 2006. His main research int erests cover analysis of the algorithm and the design, intelligent information processing; machine learning; analysis, prediction, controlling of complicate d nonlinear system. In these areas he has published over 140 papers in intern ational journals or conference proceedings.

Editor Hong-Can Yan

Professor of North China University of Technology, Ph.D., master tutor, Hebei province science and technology experts, she is the second Hebei province higher school teaching instruction committee candidate, Chinese information society member (E221501404M), Computer Science journal review expert

The main research directions is Web semantic retrieval and knowledge discovery, data mining and intelligent computing, in recent years engaged in particle computing model in the field of artificial intelligence applications, published more than 40 academic papers, including core papers and three major papers nearly 20 , Published monograph 2; main research National Natural Fund 1, the provincial Natural Fund 3, of which two were awarded the third prize of scientific and technological progress in Hebei Province and Tangshan City Science and Technology Progress Award.

Co-Chair Dr Qiang Yang

Dr. Qiang Yang obtained the BS degree (first class honors) in Electrical Engineeringin 2001, and received the M.Sc. (with distinction) and Ph.D. degree both in Electronic Engineering and Computer Science from Queen Mary, University of London, London, U.K., in 2003 and 2007, respectively. He has worked as a Postdoctoral Research Associate at the Department of Electrical and Electronic Engineering, Imperial College London, U.K., from 2007 to 2010 and involved in a number of high-profile U.K. EPSRC and European IST research projects. Currently he is an Associate Professor at College of Electrical Engineering, Zhejiang University, China, and has published more than 100 technical papers, co-authored 2books and holds 5 national patents. His research interests over the years include communication networks, smart energy systems, and large-scale complex network modeling, control, optimization, and simulation. He is the member of various international academic bodies including IEEE, IET and IEICE as well as the Senior Member of China Computer Federation (CCF).

Co-Chiar Prof. Farn Wang,

National Taiwan University, Taiwan

Department of Electrical Engineering Graduate Institute of Electronic Engineering, National Taiwan University, got Ph.D. Computer Science, in The University of Texas at Austin, 1993, working as Associate professor in National Taiwan University, 2002-2005, Published many books, Participated in many international conferences.

Co-Chiar & Editor & Keynote Prof. Tao Gong

Prof. Tao Gong received the MS degree in Pattern Recognition and Intelligent Systems and PhD degree in Computer Science from the Central South University respectively in 2003 and 2007. He is an associate professor of immune computation at Dong hua University, China, and he was a visiting scholar at Department of Computer Science and CERIAS, Purdue University, USA. He is the General Editors-in-Chief of the first leading journal Immune Computation in its field, and an editorial board member of some international journals.

Co-Chiar &Keynote Prof. Tsung-Han Tsai

Department of Electrical Engineering, Director of Intelligent Chip and System Center, National Central University, Chung-Li, 320, Taiwan

Tsung-Han Tsai received the B.S., M.S., and Ph.D. degrees in electrical engineering from the National Taiwan University, Taipei, Taiwan, in 1990, 1994, and 1998 respectively. From 1999 to 2000, he was an Associate Professor of electronic engineering at Fu Jen University. He joined National Central University in 2000. Since 2008 he was a full Professor in the department of electrical engineering at National Central University. Currently he is also the director of Intelligent Chip and System Center in National Central University, and also serves as the Principal Investigator of the National Program for Intelligent Electronics. Dr. Tsai has been awarded more than 40 patents and 230 refereed papers published in international journals and conferences. Dr. Tsai received the Industrial Cooperation Award in 2003 from the Ministry of Education, Taiwan. He has been an IEEE member for over 15 years, and serves as Technical Program Committee member or Session Chair of several international conferences. His research interests include VLSI signal processing, video/audio coding algorithms, DSP architecture design, wireless communication and System-On-Chip design.

Keynote Prof. Ting Yang

School of Electrical Engineering and Automation, Tianjin University,
Tianjin, China

Dr. Ting Yang is currently a Chair professor of Theory and Advanced Technology of Electrical Engineering, at the School of Electrical Engineering and Automation, Tianjin University, China. He was the cooperative research staff of Imperial College London (2008), University of Sydney, Australia (2011, 2015). Prof. Yang is the winner of the "New Century Excellent Talents in University Award" from Chinese Ministry of Education. He is the leader of tens of research grant projects, including the International S&T Cooperation Program of China, the National High-Tech Research and Development Program of China (863 Program), the National Natural Science Foundation of China, and so on. Prof. Yang is the chairman of two workshops of IEEE International Conference, and the editor in Chief of one of Special Issues of the international journal of DSN. He is the author/co-author of four books, more than one hundred publications in internationally refereed journals and conferences. Prof. Yang is a senior member of the Chinese Institute of Electronic, the fellow of Circuit and System committee, the fellow of Theory and Advanced Technology of Electrical Engineering, and the member of International Society for Industry and Applied Mathematics. His research fields include Smart Grid, advanced metering infrastructure, and information and communication technologies in electric power system.

Editor& Keynote Prof. Lei Zhang

Lei Zhang received his Ph.D degree in Circuits and Systems from the College of Communication Engineering, Chongqing University, Chongqing, China, in 2013. He was selected as a Hong Kong Scholar in China in 2013, and worked as a Post-Doctoral Fellow with The Hong Kong Polytechnic University, Hong Kong, from 2013 to 2015. He is currently a Professor/Distinguished Research Fellow with Chongqing University. He has authored more than 50 scientific papers in top journals, including the IEEE Transactions on Neural Networks and Learning Systems, the IEEE Transactions on Image Processing, the IEEE Transactions on Multimedia, the IEEE Transactions on Instrumentation and Measurement, the IEEE Transactions on Systems, Man, and Cybernetics: Systems, the IEEE Sensors Journal, Information Fusion, Sensors & Actuators B, and Analytica Chimica Acta. His current research interests include machine learning, pattern recognition, computer vision, electronic olfaction and intelligent systems.

Keynote Prof. Hui Zhang

Hui Zhang received the B.S. degree and PhD. degree respectively in 2005 and 2010, both from Beijing University of Posts and Telecommunications. In 2010, he became a faculty member in the School of Information Science in Nankai University, Tianjin, China. From 2013-2014, he was a postdoctoral research fellow respectively in University of Southampton and Korea Advanced Institute of Science and Technology. He is currently an associated professor in Nankai University. His research interests are in the areas of Wireless Networks, Visible Light Communication, Social Networks, Energy Internet, etc. Currently He is the reviewer for the following journals: IEEE Transactions on Wireless Communication, IEEE Transactions on Mobile Computing, IEEE Transactions on Vehicular Technology, EURASIP Journal on Wireless Communications and Networking, IEEE Globecom, IEEE VTC, Chinese Journal of Electronics.

Keynote Prof. Hui Zhang

Dr. Ning Zhang, male, Professor, Beijing Union University, China. Ning Zhang received the MS degree in Physics science from Hefei University of Technology in 1992, and the PhD degree in Optics science from the department of Optics Engineering, University of Tianjin in 2002. From 2002-2004, as a postdoctoral research fellow, he worked in Beijing University of Posts and Telecommunications. He is currently a professor in Beijing Union University. His research interests are in the areas of Communication Science, Computer Network Technology, Information Systems, Software Engineering, Education Management, etc.
Dr. Ning Zhang, is invited reviewer for the following international journals: Chinese Journal of Electronics (China, SCI), Mathematical Problems in Engineering (USA.SCI), Optics Communications (USA. SCI), etc. Areas of Interest: Communication Science, Computer Network Technology.

Keynote Prof .Wei-Ming Zeng

He received Ph.D degree in Biomedical Engineering, Southeast University, China, in 2005. From April 2006 to May 2008, he was a postdoctoral research fellow at F. M. Kirby Center for Functional Brain Imaging, Johns Hopkins University. Now he is working in Shanghai Maritime University as a full professor, director of the Lab of Digital Imaging and Intelligent Computation, and vice dean of College of Information Engineering. He is a professor of Special Appointment at Shanghai Institutions of Higher Learning (Eastern Scholar). He is senior member of IEEE and senior member of CCF. His research interests focus on brain functional connectivity detection, Medical Image Processing, Artificial Intelligence and Pattern Recognition. In recent years, he undertook about 20 projects including 2 National Natural Science Foundation projects, one key Funded project of Shanghai Science and Technology Commission of Shanghai Municipality, and other provincial projects.

Keynote Prof. Wen-Tsai Sung

Department of Electrical Engineering, National Chin-Yi University of Technology, Taiwan

Wen-Tsai Sung is working with the Department of Electrical Engineering, National Chin-Yi University of Technology as a professor and Vice-Dean of Academic Affairs. He received a PhD and MS degree from the Department of Electrical Engineering, National Central University, Taiwan in 2007 and 2000. He has won the 2009 JMBE Best Annual Excellent Paper Award and the dragon thesis award that sponsor is Acer Foundation. His research interests include Wireless Sensors Network, Data Fusion, System Biology, System on Chip, Computer-Aided Design for Learning, Bioinformatics, and Biomedical Engineering. He has published a number of international journal and conferences article related to these areas. Currently, he is the chief of Wireless Sensors Networks Laboratory. At present, he serves as the Editor-in-Chief in three international journals: International Journal of Communications (IJC), Communications in Information Science and Management Engineering (CISME) and Journal of Vibration Analysis, Measurement, and Control (JVAMC), he also serves as the other international journals in Associate-Editor and Guest Editor (IET Systems Biology).

Keynote Prof. Xun-Wei Zhou

Institute of Information Technology, College of Information, Beijing Union University, Beijing, China.

Professor Zhou received B.E. from Department of Automation, Beijing University of Technology in 1982. He was lecturer in Department of Computer Science, Beijing University of Technology from 1987 to 1992, associate professor in College of Information, Beijing Union University from 1992 to 2005, professor in Institute of Information Technology, College of Information, Beijing Union University from 2005 to 2012, professor emeritus in Institute of Information Technology, College of Information, Beijing Union University since 2012. He construct mutually-inversistic logic and apply it to the fields of computer science, artificial intelligence, and automation, such as automatic theorem proving, logic programming, planning and scheduling, expert systems, semantic network, program verification, natural language understanding, hardware verification, machine learning, data mining, uncertainty reasoning, program refinement, many-valued computer, modern control theory, etc. He published about 80 papers, authored 4 monographs on them. He is a senior member of China Computer Federation, a member of Technical Committer of Artificial Intelligence Theory of Chinese Association for Artificial Intelligence, a director of Beijing Logical Association.

Keynote I

Prof.WeimingZeng
brain functional connectivity detection, Medical Image Processing, Artificial Intelligence and Pattern Recognition.
Shanghai Maritime University

Speaker'sBio

He received Ph.D degree in Biomedical Engineering, Southeast University, China, in 2005. From April 2006 to May 2008, he was a postdoctoral research fellow at F. M. Kirby Center for Functional Brain Imaging, Johns Hopkins University. Now he is working in Shanghai Maritime University as a full professor, director of the Lab of Digital Imaging and Intelligent Computation, and vice dean of College of Information Engineering. He is a professor of Special Appointment at Shanghai Institutions of Higher Learning (Eastern Scholar). He is senior member of IEEE and senior member of CCF. His research interests focus on brain functional connectivity detection, Medical Image Processing, Artificial Intelligence and Pattern Recognition. In recent years, he undertook about 20 projects including 2 National Natural Science Foundation projects, one key Funded project of Shanghai Science and Technology Commission of Shanghai Municipality, and other provincial projects.

Keynote2

Prof.Ning Zhang
Communication Science,Computer Network Technology,Information Systems,Software Engineering,Education Management,Signal Process
Beijing Union University, China

Speaker'sBio

Dr.NingZhang, male, Professor, Beijing Union University, China. Ning Zhang received the MS degree in Physics science from Hefei University of Technology in 1992, and the PhD degree in Optics science from the department of Optics Engineering, University of Tianjin in 2002. From 2002-2004, as a postdoctoral research fellow, he worked in Beijing University of Posts and Telecommunications. He is currently a professor in Beijing Union University. His research interests are in the areas of Communication Science, Computer Network Technology, Information Systems, Software Engineering, Education Management, etc.

Dr. NingZhang, is invited reviewer for the following international journals: Chinese Journal of Electronics (China, SCI), Mathematical Problems in Engineering (USA.SCI), OpticsCommunications (USA. SCI),etc.Areas of Interest:Communication Science, Computer Network Technology.

Keynote 3

Prof.Ting Yang
Key Laboratory of Smart Grid of Ministry of Education
School of Electrical Engineering and Automation
Tianjin University

Speaker'sBio

Dr. Ting Yang is currently a Chair professor of Theory and Advanced Technology of Electrical Engineering, at the School of Electrical Engineering and Automation, Tianjin University, China. He was the cooperative research staff of Imperial College London (2008), University of Sydney, Australia (2011, 2015). Prof. Yang is the winner of the "New Century Excellent Talents in University Award" from Chinese Ministry of Education. He is the leader of tens of research grant projects, including the International S&T Cooperation Program of China, the National High-Tech Research and Development Program of China (863 Program), the National Natural Science Foundation of China, and so on. Prof. Yang is the chairman of two workshops of IEEE International Conference (the 6th IEEE International Conference on Cloud Computing Technology and Science–IEEE CloudCom, the 18th IEEE International Conference on Parallel and Distributed Systems–IEEE ICPADS), and the editor in Chief of the Special Issues "Ubiquitous Data-Centric Sensor Networks" of the international journal of DSN.

Keynote 4

Prof.Lei Zhang
College of Communication Engineering, Chongqing University,
Chongqing, China

Speaker'sBio

Lei Zhang received his Ph.D degree in Circuits and Systems from the College of Communication Engineering, Chongqing University, Chongqing, China, in 2013. He was selected as a Hong Kong Scholar in China in 2013, and worked as a Post-Doctoral Fellow with The Hong Kong Polytechnic University, Hong Kong, from 2013 to 2015. He is currently a Professor/Distinguished Research Fellow with Chongqing University. He has authored more than 50 scientific papers in top journals, including the IEEE Transactions on Neural Networks and Learning Systems, the IEEE Transactions on Image Processing, the IEEE Transactions on Multimedia, the IEEE Transactions on Instrumentation and Measurement, the IEEE Transactions on Systems, Man, and Cybernetics: Systems, the IEEE Sensors Journal, Information Fusion, Sensors & Actuators B, and AnalyticaChimicaActa. His current research interests include machine learning, pattern recognition, computer vision, electronic olfaction and intelligent systems.

Keynote 5

Prof. Hui Zhang
Wireless Networks, Visible Light Communication, Social Networks, Energy Internet
Nankai University, China

Speaker's Bio

Hui Zhang received the B.S. degree and PhD. degree respectively in 2005 and 2010, both from Beijing University of Posts and Telecommunications. In 2010, he became a faculty member in the School of Information Science in Nankai University, Tianjin, China. From 2013-2014, he was a postdoctoral research fellow respectively in University of Southampton and Korea Advanced Institute of Science and Technology. He is currently an associated professor in Nankai University. His research interests are in the areas of Wireless Networks, Visible Light Communication, Social Networks, Energy Internet, etc. Currently He is the reviewer for the following journals: IEEE Transactions on Wireless Communication, IEEE Transactions on Mobile Computing, IEEE Transactions on Vehicular Technology, EURASIP Journal on Wireless Communications and Networking, IEEE Globecom, IEEE VTC, Chinese Journal of Electronics.

Keynote 6

Prof.Tsung-Han Tsai
Department of Electrical Engineering, Director of Intelligent Chip and System Center, National Central University, Chung-Li, 320, Taiwan

Speaker's Bio

Tsung-Han Tsai received the B.S., M.S., and Ph.D. degrees in electrical engineering from the National Taiwan University, Taipei, Taiwan, in 1990, 1994, and 1998 respectively. From 1999 to 2000, he was an Associate Professor of electronic engineering at Fu Jen University. He joined National Central University in 2000. Since 2008 he was a full Professor in the department of electrical engineering at National Central University. Currently he is also the director of Intelligent Chip and System Center in National Central University, and also serves as the Principal Investigator of the National Program for Intelligent Electronics. Dr. Tsai has been awarded more than 40 patents and 230 refereed papers published in international journals and conferences. Dr. Tsai received the Industrial Cooperation Award in 2003 from the Ministry of Education, Taiwan. He has been an IEEE member for over 15 years, and serves as Technical Program Committee member or Session Chair of several international conferences. His research interests include VLSI signal processing, video/audio coding algorithms, DSP architecture design, wireless communication and System-On-Chip design.

Keynote 7

Prof.Wen-Tsai Sung
Department of Electrical Engineering, National Chin-Yi University of Technology, Taiwan

Speaker's Bio

Wen-Tsai Sung is working with the Department of Electrical Engineering, National Chin-Yi University of Technology as a professor and Vice-Dean of Academic Affairs. He received a PhD and MS degree from the Department of Electrical Engineering, National Central University, Taiwan in 2007 and 2000. He has won the 2009 JMBE Best Annual Excellent Paper Award and the dragon thesis award that sponsor is Acer Foundation. His research interests include Wireless Sensors Network, Data Fusion, System Biology, System on Chip, Computer-Aided Design for Learning, Bioinformatics, and Biomedical Engineering. He has published a number of international journal and conferences article related to these areas. Currently, he is the chief of Wireless Sensors Networks Laboratory. At present, he serves as the Editor-in-Chief in three international journals: International Journal of Communications (IJC), Communications in Information Science and Management Engineering (CISME) and Journal of Vibration Analysis, Measurement, and Control (JVAMC), he also serves as the other international journals in Associate-Editor and Guest Editor (IET Systems Biology).

Keynote 8

Prof.Yanghua Xiao
Department of computer science, Fudan University, China

Speaker's Bio

Yanghua Xiao got his PHD degree in software theory from FudanUniversity,Shanghai, China, in 2009. He now is an associate professor of computer science at Fudan University. He is one of young 973 scientists. His research interest includes big data management and mining, graph database, knowledge graph. He was a visiting professor of Human Genome Sequencing Center at Baylor College Medicine,and visiting researcher of Microsoft Research Asia. He won the Best PhD ThesisNomination of CCF (Chinese Computer Federation) in year 2010, CCF2014 Natural Science Award (second level), ACM (CCF) Shanghai distinguished young scientists nomination award. Recently, he has published 50+ papers in international leading journal and top conferences, including Pattern Recognition, Physical Review E,Plos One, Information System, Computers & Mathematics with Applications, BCM Systems Biology, Physica A; SIGMOD,VLDB, ICDE, IJCAI, AAAI, EDBT, ICSE,OOPSLA, WWW, ICDM, CIKM, SDM, ECML/PKDD, ICWS, ICSM, DASFAA,COMPSAC, SSDBM, etc.

Keynote 9

Prof. Xun-Wei Zhou
Institute of Information Technology, College of Information, Beijing Union University, Beijing, China.

Speaker's Bio

Professor Zhou received B.E. from Department of Automation, Beijing University of Technology in 1982. He was lecturer in Department of Computer Science, Beijing University of Technology from 1987 to 1992, associate professor in College of Information, Beijing Union University from 1992 to 2005, professor in Institute of Information Technology, College of Information, Beijing Union University from 2005 to 2012, professor emeritus in Institute of Information Technology, College of Information, Beijing Union University since 2012. He construct mutually-inversistic logic and apply it to the fields of computer science, artificial intelligence, and automation, such as automatic theorem proving, logic programming, planning and scheduling, expert systems, semantic network, program verification, natural language understanding, hardware verification, machine learning, data mining, uncertainty reasoning, program refinement, many-valued computer, modern control theory, etc. He published about 80 papers, authored 4 monographs on them. He is a senior member of China Computer Federation, a member of Technical Committee of Artificial Intelligence Theory of Chinese Association for Artificial Intelligence, a director of Beijing Logical Association.

Keynote10

Prof.Tao Gong
Department of immune computation, Donghua University, China

Speaker's Bio

Prof. Tao Gong received the MS degree in Pattern Recognition and Intelligent Systems and PhD degree in Computer Science from the Central South University respectively in 2003 and 2007. He is an associate professor of immune computation at Donghua University, China, and he was a visiting scholar at Department of Computer Science and CERIAS, Purdue University, USA. He is the General Editors-in-Chief of the first leading journal Immune Computation in its field, and an editorial board member of some international journals. He was a Technical Committee Chair of ISEEIP 2012, and a Publicity Chair of ISA 2012 and ICSI3 2015. He was Invited Speaker for some conferences such as SecTech 2012, ICAMR 2014, ITA 2016 and CSA 2016. He was also a program committee member of some international conferences such as IEEE ICNC 2011, IEEE BMEI 2011, WMSE 2011, ICARIS 2012, AITS 2012, CCA 2012, ASP 2012, IST 2012, ISA 2012 and SIS2013 etc.

edp sciences

ITM Web of Conferences

Statement of Peer review

In submitting conference proceedings to ITM Web of Conferences, I certify to the Publisher that I adhere to the **Policy on Publishing Integrity** of the journal in order to safeguard good scientific practice in publishing.

1. All articles have been subjected to peer review administered by the proceedings editors.
2. Reviews have been conducted by expert referees, who have been requested to provide unbiased and constructive comments aimed, whenever possible, at improving the work.
3. Proceedings editors have taken all reasonable steps to ensure the quality of the materials they publish and their decision to accept or reject a paper for publication has been based only on the merits of the work and the relevance to the journal.

Title, date and place of the conference

The 4th International Conference on Information Technology and Applications
May 26-28, 2017
Guangzhou, China

Proceedings editor(s):

Li Long, Yongjun Li, XIAOLONG Li, Yonghui Dai, Hui Yang

Date and editor's signature

P300-Based Chinese Speller: A Systematic Summary

Xiang-Qian Liu[1,*], Min Jiang[1,**], Fei Chao[1,***], Chang-Le Zhou[1,****], Ming-Hui Shi[1,*****]

[1]*Department of Cognitive Science, School of Information Science and Engineering, Xiamen University, Xiamen 361005, China;*
Fujian Key Laboratory of Brain-inspired Computing Technique and Applications (Xiamen University), Xiamen 361005, China
**31520151154115@stu.xmu.edu.cn, **minjiang@xmu.edu.cn, ***fchao@xmu.edu.cn, ****dozero@xmu.edu.cn, *****smh@xmu.edu.cn*

Abstract: Evoked by the oddball events, P300 potential is closely related to the advanced psychological activities of human beings, and plays a significant role in the electroencephalogram (EEG)-based brain-computer interface (BCI) systems. Utilizing the principle of eliciting P300, we can implement BCIs to input characters, which enable people to express their intentions directly by brain. In recent years, P300-based English speller (P300ES) has been widely studied while P300-based Chinese speller (P300CS) has been far less fully investigated, owing to the complexity of sinograms. This paper aims at making a systematic summary of the current P300CS systems, and showing that P300CS would be a promising research field deserving of further researches in the furture.

1. Introduction

The ability to communicate with other people is one of the main factors that makes our lives meaningful. However, patients suffering from amyotrophic lateral sclerosis (ALS) or brainstem damage may lose control over voluntary muscles and require assistive technologies to help them communicate.

Brain-computer interfaces (BCIs) provide a promising means to fulfill basic communication needs for such people. A brain-computer interface is a system which uses brain signals to establish direct communication pathways between human brains and external devices, without the involvement of peripheral nerves and muscles [1].

Depending on the brian signals used, there are many types of BCIs, such as: electroencephalogram (EEG)-based BCI, magnetoencephalogram (MEG)-based BCI, functional magnetic resonance imaging (fMRI)-based BCI, functional near infrared spectroscopy (fNIRS)-based BCI. EEG is the general term for various electrical activities induced by cortical neurons, and it can be sensed through a set of electrodes placed on the scalp of subjects. Due to the superiority of high time resolution and low-cost acquisition devices, EEG has been the most commonly used brain signal in noninvasive BCIs at present [2].

As a well-known component of endogenous EEG, P300 was firstly discovered by Sutton et al in 1965 [3]. It is a positive peak in the EEG signals, appearing approximately 300 ms after the presentation of infrequent task-relevant stimuli [4]. To evoke a P300 potential, subjects are required to observe a random sequence of stimuli which the task-relevant stimulus (oddball event) appears only rarely, while the other stimuli (normal events) appear more often. By determining the occurrence time of P300 response, P300-based BCIs can identify which stimulus is task-relevant.

P300-based BCIs have been applied in many aspects, such as recognizing traffic lights [5], dialing phone numbers [6], moving cursors [7], or even controlling a robotic prosthesis [8]. However, the most popular application of P300-based BCIs is spelling [9-12], which enable users to input characters directly by brain. The original P300-based speller was proposed by Farwell and Donchin in 1988 [13]. In their speller, users were presented with a 6×6 matrix containing 36 characters. The rows and columns of the matrix were flashed in random order. Users were required to concentrate exclusively on the desired character while ignoring others. In this case, P300 could be elicited by the flashing of the row and column containing the desired character, and the desired character was identified as the intersection of the above row and column.

Most of the researches on P300-based spellers are focused on the input of English or other languages written using letters. Few studies have examined the efficacy of spellers for inputting languages that use "strokes", such as Chinese. This is because the number of sinograms is too numerous (more than 11000) for a reasonably sized matrix. Therefore, P300-based Chinese spller (P300CS) is more

DOI: 10.1051/itmconf/20171201001

difficult to actualize than P300-based English speller (P300ES).

This article is a systematic summary of the current P300CS systems, the remainder of this paper is organized as follows: Section 2 introduces the implementation methods of P300CS; Section 3 discusses the existing problems and outlines possible lines of future developments of this field; Section 4 concludes the paper.

2. Implementation Methods of P300CS

2.1 Stroke-Based Method

Sinograms are made up of hierarchical arrangements of strokes, a P300CS could be developed that allow users to input sinograms stroke-by-stroke (stroke-based method).

Employing the stroke-based method, Wu et al proposed the first P300CS in 2009, using five basic stroke items (—, 丨, 丿, 丶, ⌒) and two control items [14]. The items flicked one by one (Fig. 1(a)). When the target item flicked, the P300 response could be evoked in users' EEG signals.

Based on the same method, in 2010, Jin et al developed a more sophisticated P300CS which can send messages on a cell phone [15]. In this speller, a 4×4 matrix containing five stroke items, eight number items (1-8) and three control items was used to allow sinogram input with P300 (Fig. 1(b)).

However, for traditional Chinese (used in Hongkong and Taiwan), a sinogram may consists of twenty or more strokes, greatly limiting the efficiency of such a P300CS. In 2010, Minett et al presented a novel matrix devoted to speed up selection process of stroke-based method [16]. In the novel matrix, each item represents a subcharacter comprising multiple strokes (Fig. 1(c)), users can make smaller number of selections by inputting sinograms subcharacter-by-subcharacter. The subcharacter-by-subcharacter approach could be seen as an improvement of stroked-based method.

2.2 Phonetics-Based Method

Each sinogram has its own pronunciation, P300CS could also be exploited to allow sinogram input with phonetics (phonetics-based method). There are two types of phonetics used in China: Zhuyin (used in Taiwan) and Pinyin (used in maninland). Correspondingly, phonetics-based method can be divided into the Zhuyin-based method and the Pinyin-based method.

In 2011, Sun et al reported the first phonetics-based P300CS adopting Zhuyin [17]. This BCI constructed a 3×4 matrix containing 11 groups of Zhuyin items and one control item (Fig. 2(a)), a whole row or column of the matrix was intensified at a time. The speller attained acceptable results, and proved the feasibility of phonetics-based method.

Another P300CS based on phonetics (Pinyin) was proposed by Xu et al in 2015 [18], their work can be seen in Fig. 2(b).

Compared with stroke-based method, phonetics-based method is more in line with people's inputting habits. However, it can't cover up the reality that the same phonetics generally correspond to several different sinograms, which means phonetics-based method might result in many optional sinograms.

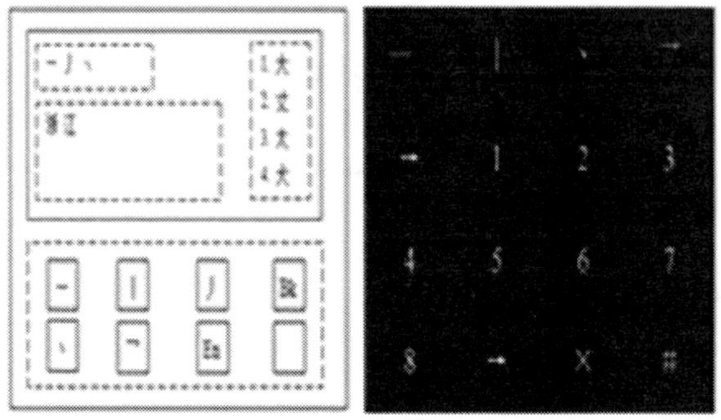

(a) (adapt from [14]) (b) (adapt from [15])

一	丨	丿	㇏	乙	紅
孖	彳	儿	扌	八	力
打	口	厂	白	中	王
火	言	日	鉄	寺	草
們	江	木	天	大	女
二	十	石	悱	山	←

(c) (adapt from [16])

Figure1. Stroke-based method display.

(a) (adapt from [17])

(b) (adapt from [18])

Figure2. Phonetics-based method display.

3. Discussion

P300CS systems are normally characterized by low rates of accuracy and information transfer [19], and there are several problems in the current research.

First, most of the current works on P300CS are intended to prove the feasibility of their solutions, not to provide a practicable system. Then, most of the current approaches employed in P300CS are modeled on P300ES, without considering the uniqueness of sinograms. In addition, the experimens are mostly peroformed only on the healthy students in college, the very limited range of subjects may lead to unrepresentative results.

Regarding the future research of P300CS, the development trends of this research field are discussed in this section too.

First, P300CS should be more user-friendly. P300-based BCIs are required to present many repetitive stimuli during use, which will inevitably lead to the problem of fatigue. How to improve the comfort degree of system is a issue deserves more research. Then, the non-P300 components could be taken in account. P300-based BCIs typically rely on not only the P300, but also other EEG components such as N100, N200, N400 and P600. For example, Scholars found that the face paradigm (items are transparently overlaid with human faces) could accentuated the N170 and N400 which had a high signal to noise ratio and significantly improved the classification accuracy [20, 21]. Finally, P300CS could be enhanced by adding a statistical language model. Most of the current P300CS treat sinogram selections as an independent process with no prior information. The statistical language model could provide the function of language prediction, which means the subsequent target sinograms are more likely to be selected utilizing the information information of sinograms inputted previously. For instance, a P300-based speller conjunction with a statistical language model was tested in [22], its high performance had showed the efficiency of language prediction function.

4. Conclusion

P300CS allows for sinogram input directly by brain. A systematic summary of the current P300CS systems is made in this paper. Firstly, the implementation methods (stroke-based method and phonetics-based method) of P300CS is introduced. Then, the existing problems and the future development directions of this field are discussed. Although there have been several works tentative to explore the P300CS, it is not enough. It is sincerely hoped that more in-depth studies can be conducted in this research field in the future.

Acknowledgment

The project was supported by the Natural Science Foundation of Fujian Province of China (No.2017J01128 and 2017J01129) and by the National Natural Science Foundation of China (No.61673322 and 61673328).

References

[1] J. R. Wolpaw and D. J. McFarland, "Brain-computer interfaces for communication and control," Clinical Neurophysiology, vol. 113, pp. 767-791, 2002.

[2] E. C. Leuthardt, G. Schalk, J. R. Wolpaw, and J. G. Ojemann, "A brain-computer interface using electrocorticographic signals in humans," Journal of Neural Engineeringy, vol. 1, pp. 63-71, 2004.

[3] S. Sutton, M. Braren, J. Zubin, and E. R. John, "Evoked-potential correlates of stimulus uncertainty," Science, vol. 150, pp. 1187-1188, 1965.

[4] J. Polich, "On the relationship between EEG and P300: Individual differences, aging, and ultradian rhythms," International Journal of Psychophysiology, vol. 26, pp. 299-317, 1997.

[5] J. D. Bayliss and D. H. Ballard, "Single trial P3 epoch recognition in a virtual environment," Neurocomputing, vol. 32, pp. 637-642, 2000.

[6] A. R. Miller, J. P. Rosenfeld, M. Soskins, and M. Jhee, "P300 Amplitude and topography in an autobiographical oddball paradigm involving simulated amnesia," International Journal of Psychophysiology, vol. 16, pp. 1-11, 2002.

[7] J. R. Wolpaw, D. J. McFarland, G. W. Neat, and C. A. Forneris, "An EEG-based brain-computer interface for cursor control," Electroencephalography and clinical neurophysiology, vol. 78, pp. 252-259, 1991.

[8] R. T. Lauer, P. H. Peckham, K. L. Kilgore, and W. J. Heetderks, "Applications of cortical signals to neuroprosthetic control: A critical review," IEEE Transactions on Rehabilitation Engineering, vol. 8, pp. 205-208, 2000.

[9] B. Z. Allison and J. A. Pineda, "ERPs evoked by different matrix sizes: implications for a brain computer interface (BCI) system," IEEE Transactions on Neural Systems and Rehabilitation Engineering, vol. 11, pp. 110-113, 2003.

[10] E. W. Sellers and D. J. McFarland, "Toward enhanced P300 speller performance," Journal of Neuroscience Methods, vol. 167, pp. 15-21, 2008.

[11] N. Xu, X. Gao, and B. Hong, "BCI Competition 2003-Data set IIb: enhancing P300 wave detection using ICA based subspace projections," IEEE Transactions on Bio-medical Engineering, vol. 51, pp. 1067-1072, 2004.

[12] R. Fazel-Rezai and K. Abhari, "A region-based P300 speller for brain-computer interface," Canadian Journal of Electrical and Computer Engineering, vol. 34, pp. 81-85, 2009.

[13] L. A. Farwell and E. Donchin, "Talking off the top of your head: Toward a mental prosthesis utilizing event-related brain potentials," Electroencephalography and clinical neurophysiology, vol. 70, pp. 510-523, 1988.

[14] B. Wu, Y. Su, J. Zhang, and X. Li, "A Virtual Chinese Keyboard BCI System Based on P300 Potentials," Acta Electronica Sinica, vol. 37, pp. 1733-1738, 2009.

[15] J. Jin, B. Z. Allison, C. Brunner, and B. Wang, "P300 Chinese input system based on Bayesian LDA," Biomedizinische Technik Biomedical Engineering, vol. 55, pp. 5-18, 2010.

[16] J. Minett, G. Peng, L. Zhou, H. Y. Zheng, and S. Wang, "An Assistive Communication Brain-Computer Interface for Chinese Text Input," 4th International Conference on Bioinformatics and Biomedical Engineering, Jun. 2010.

[17] K. T. Sun, T. W. Huang, and M. C. Chen, "Design of Chinese Spelling System Based on ERP," 11th International Conference on Bioinformatics and Bioengineering, vol. 1997, pp. 310-313, Jun. 2010.

[18] X. Xu and H. J. Fang, "A P300-based BCI system for Online Chinese input," Journal of Huaqiao University (Natural Science), vol. 36, pp. 269-274, 2015.

[19] T. W. Huang, Y. H. Tai, Y. J. Tian, and K. T. Sun, "The fastest BCI for writing Chinese characters using brain waves," 4th Global Congress on Intelligent Systems, pp. 346-349, 2013.

[20] T. Kaufmann, S. M. Schulz, C. Grünzinger, and A. Kübler, "Flashing characters with famous faces improves ERP-based brain-computer interface performance," Journal of Neural Engineering, vol. 8, pp. 173-178, 2011.

[21] Y. Zhang, Q. Zhao, J. JIn, and X. Wang, "A novel BCI based on ERP components sensitive to configural processing of human faces," Journal of Neural Engineering, vol. 9, pp. 26018-26030, 2012.

[22] D. B. Ryan, G. E. Frye, G. Townsend, D. R. Berry, and S. Mesag, "Predictive spelling with a P300-based brain-computer interface: Increasing the rate of communication," International journal of human-computer interaction, vol. 27, pp. 69-84, 2011.

A Novel Coverage Pattern Mining Method for Unordered Tree

Ying Xia[1a], Hong-Xu Li[2b]

[1] Research Center of Spatial Information System Chongqing University of Posts and Telecommunications Chongqing, China
[2]Research Center of Spatial Information System
Chongqing University of Posts and Telecommunications Chongqing, China
[a] xiaying@cqupt.edu.cn, [b]565268915@qq.com

Abstract: Unordered tree is widely used for semi-structured data modeling, coverage pattern mining on it has benefit for finding frequent subtrees without redundant information, so that improve the efficiency of subsequent knowledge discovering. A coverage pattern mining method MCRP is proposed. Firstly, all candidate subtrees are generated on the basis of maximum prefix coding and edge extension.Then coverage patterns are output by introducing δ'- coverage concept. Compared with traditional algorithms such as mining frequent closed tree patterns and maximal frequent tree patterns, the proposed method can output fewer frequent subtrees in the case of preserving all the frequent subtree information, and has a certain superiority in processing efficiency.

1. Introduction

With the development of Internet, a large number semi-structured data such as Web pages and XML documents continuous emerged. Modeling these data with unordered tree and mining frequent subtrees can effectively find the hidden knowledge. At present, many frequent subtree mining algorithms have been proposed, such as FP-tree tree [1] and PFP-tree[2] mine frequent subtrees based on the idea of projection, while EvoMiner [3] and MCFP-tree[4] adopt the ideas of Apriori. However, these algorithms usually output large scale frequent subtrees with redundant information which affect the efficiency of subsequent processing. In order to reduce the output scale of frequent subtrees, FBMiner[5] is proposed to mine frequent closed tree and MFTM[6] is presented to mine maximal frequent subtree. Although these algorithms can effectively reduce the output scale of frequent subtrees, they lose some structure information of frequent subtrees.

Aiming at the shortcomings of traditional methods, this paper proposes MCRP algorithm for mining the coverage pattern. MCRP first encodes an unordered tree by code rule based on width and number of children (WANOC), which will improves the computational efficiency of subtree support degree. On the basis of WANOC, MCRP uses edge extension method based on maximum prefix coding sequence to generate candidate subtrees, which ensures that all the frequent subtrees can be found without information omitted. In addition, a new concept of δ'- coverage is proposed based on δ-coverage[7] to judge whether a subtree is satisfied the requirement of coverage pattern for output.

The paper is outlined as follows: Section 1 introduces encoding rule of WANOC. Section 2 gives detailed description of MCRP algorithm. Section 3 presents the experimental results. Conclude is drawn in Section 4.

2. Encoding Rule of Wanoc

Defination1. Tree Support Degree And Frequent Subtree

Suppose that $D = \{T1, T2...Tn\}$ is a set of unordered tree. Given a unordered tree T, the support degree of T is as follows:

$$\mathrm{Dsupp(T)} = \frac{|\{T'|T \subseteq T', T' \in D\}|}{|D|}$$

|D| represents the size of the tree set. Given a minimum support threshold $\mathrm{min\_sup} \in [0,1]$, if $\mathrm{Dsupp(T)} \geq \mathrm{min\_sup}$, then T is a frequent subtree on D.

In order to improve the computational efficiency of subtree support degree, an encoding rule named WANOC (the code of width and number of children) is proposed based on traditional string coding[8]. In the rule, each tree node is denoted by a triplet (index(v), range(v), tag(v)), index(v) denotes the position of node v in the width-first sequence of a tree, range(v) denotes the position range of the children of node v, tag(v) denotes the label of node v. By breadth-first traveling of tree, we can get the code of width and number of children of a tree.

Due to the disorder between the brothers in an unordered tree, we order nodes with sibling relationship by the dictionary order of their tag in order to make WANOC more standardized. For the sample tree T and t in Figure I, their WANOC codes are shown in TABLE I. By matching the WANOC code of given subtree with all existing trees, it is easy to count the frequency of subtree, so that calculate the subtree support degree. For example, when detecting wether tree t is included in T, we firstly find node A in WANOC code of T, and then search wether node C and D are included in range(A) , it is unnecessary to match each node one by one.

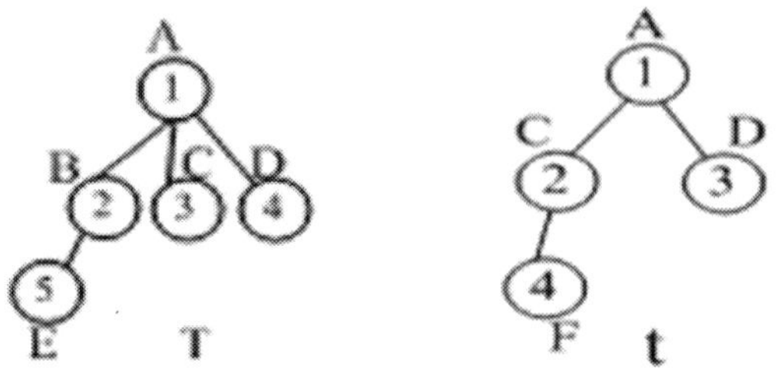

Figure I. Sample trees

Table 1 The wanoc code of sample trees

Tree	the WANOC code
T	(1,(2,4),A)-(2,(5),B)-(3,(),C)-(4,(),D)-(5,(),E)
t	(1,(2,3),A)-(2,(4),C)-(3,(),D)-(4,(),F)

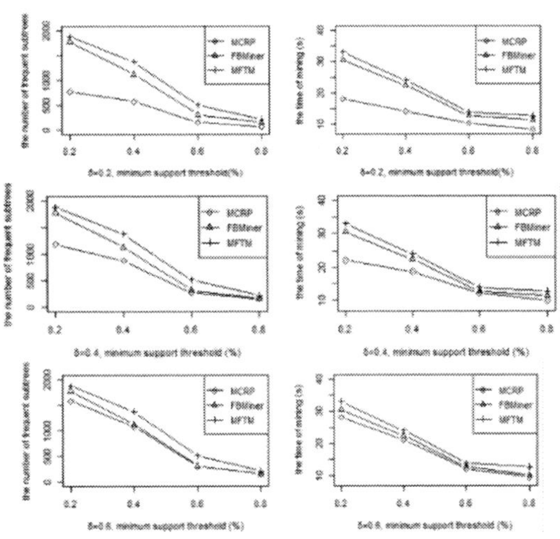

Figure 2. Experiment result

3. Mcrp Algorithm

Defination 2. Maximum Prefix Coding

Suppose an unordered tree is encoded by WANOC, the code of remaining nodes after the last one is removed is called maximum prefix encoding of the tree.

Defination 3. δ'-Coverag

Assuming that T and T' are both frequent tree, stipulating T is δ'-covered by T' if $T \subseteq T'$, the Jaccard distance [9] between T and T' is less than δ', $H(T') \leq H(T) + 1$ and $W(T') \leq W(T) + 1$. H (T) and W (T) denote the height and width of T respectively. The Jaccard distance formula is as follows:

$$D(T, T') = 1 - \frac{|S(T) \cap S(T')|}{|S(T) \cup S(T')|}$$

S(T) represents the numbers of T in D.

The algorithm includes two core steps. The first step is to generate the candidate subtrees using the edge extension method based on the maximum prefix encoding and to determine whether the candidate subtrees are frequent subtrees. In the second step, the algorithm outputs coverage patterns that are satisfied with the condition of δ'-coverageon the basis of the frequent subtrees.

2.1 Edge Extension Based On Maximum Prefix Coding

Generating candidate subtrees usually adopts the edge extension method. Traditional methods generate candidate subtrees based on the most right path to expand [10] need to find the most right path in advance, which will affect the efficiency. According to edge extension based on maximal prefix coding rule, two subtrees with the same maximum prefix coding can be combined. The more candidate subtrees are generated, the more original data information is retained. It is useful for some real applications to generate all candidate subtrees. Edge extension based on maximum prefix coding can generate all candidate subtrees. And, it can improve the time efficiency and reduce the omission of the information.

The topologies of two tree with the same maximal prefix coding may be the same or different. There are two cases for generating candidate subtrees. In the first case, the last node of two trees with the same topologies are on the same layer, if combining them, the last node of each tree might be sibling or parent-child relationship in the candidate subtree. In the second case, the last node of two trees with the different topologies might be on the same layer or not, if combine them, overlapping maximum prefix coding of two trees and the last node of the two tree keep the relative position unchanged.

2.2 Output Coverage Pattern

In order to reduce the output scale of frequent subtrees and improve the efficiency of subsequent operations, all frequent subtree patterns can summarized by a small set of coverage patterns. Domain experts only need to analyze this small set of coverage patterns to gain all information in the data set. If tree T is δ'-covered by tree T' , the algorithm will only output T' instead of T.

The coverage pattern is on the basis of concept of δ'-coverage. In order to make the topology of coverage pattern as similar as possible, stipulated that the absolute value of the difference of node number between the coverage pattern and its corresponding covered pattern can not exceed 1. If the height of T' is greater than the height of T by 1, the algorithm adds the label 'H' to the front of the coding of T', this means that T' covered a tree with the height of 1 smaller than its own. Domain experts can restore the T that is not exported by removing the last node of the last layer of the

DOI: 10.1051/itmconf/20171201002

T'. If the weight of T′ is greater than the weight of T by 1, the algorithm adds the label 'W' to the front of the coding of T′, this means that T' covered a tree with the weight of 1 smaller than its own. Domain experts can restore the T that is not exported by removing the most right node of T'. In the same way, if the width and height of T' was larger than that of T by 1, we label on the front of the coding of T' with 'HW'.

2.3 Pseudo Code Of Algorithm Mcrp

Algorithm MCRP(D, min_sup, δ')
Input: data set D, min_sup, Jaccard distance threshold δ'
Output: coverage pattern set of frequent subtrees CS
//S^k denotes a set of the frequent subtrees with k nodes
//$L(S^1)$ denotes the size of S^1
//$S^1(i)$ denotes the i-th tree of S^1
//countNum(T) is used to count the frequency of T
1 Traverse the data set D, count the frequency of each node and M which denotes the max node number of tree in D, put frequent nodes in S1.
2 for(int i=0; i<L(S1)-1; i++) // get all 2-frequdent subtrees
3 for(int j=i; j<L(S1)-1; j++)
4 the candidate subtree T obtained by combining S1 (i) and S1 (j)
5 if(countNum(T)/|D| $\geq$ min_sup)
6 S2←T;
7 end for
8 end for
9 for (int i=2; i<=M; i++) // get all frequent subtrees
10 CS←GenerateCorageTree(Si, δ');
11end for
12 return CS;

Function GenerateCorageTree(Sk, δ')
1 if (L(Sk)>= 2)
2 for (int i=0; i<L(Sk)-1; i++)
3 for (int j=i+1; j<L(Sk); j++)
4 if (Sk(i) and Sk(j) have the same maximum prefix

coding)
5 if (Sk(i) and Sk(j) have the same topologies)
6 the candidate subtree T obtained by combining Sk (i) and Sk(j)
7 else
8 the candidate subtree T obtained by overlaping the maximum prefix coding of S1(i) and S1(j)
9 end if
10 if(countNum(T)/|D| $\geq$ min_sup)
11 Sk+1←T;
12 if $(1-|\{Tr|(T \subseteq Tr)\ \&(\ Sk(e) \subseteq Tr), Tr \in D\}|/|\{Tr|(T \subseteq Tr)\ |\ (Sk(e) \subseteq Tr), Tr \in D\}| \geq \delta')$ //e=i, j
13 if(H(T)>H(Sk(e)))
14 CSK←Tag('H', T); // Tag('H',T) denotes that the result of add the label 'H' in the front of the code(T)
15 else if(W(T)>W(Sk(e)))
16 CSK←Tag('W', T);
17 else if(H(T)>H(Sk(e)) && W(T)>W(Sk(e)))
18 CSK←Tag('HW', T);
19 end if
20 end if
21 end for
22 end for
23 return CSK;

The most time-consuming part of algorithm MCRP is the process of generating frequent subtrees and outputting the coverage pattern. In order to check all the possible generating of candidate subtrees, function GenerateCorageTree (S^i,δ') needs to traverse k-frequent subtrees when generated (k+1)-candidate subtrees. But in practice, the time complexity of MCRP algorithm is not so high because that not any two k-frequent subtrees satisfies the conditional to generate (k+1)-candidate subtrees.

4. Experiment Result

In the experiment, we compared MCRP algorithm to FBMiner that is used to mining requent closed tree and MFTM that is used to mining maximal frequent subtrees respectively. Experimental data comes from the website (http://more.datatang.com/data/12122), which includes 5000 XML documents. All experiments were done on the environment ,which is shown in TABLE II. As what shown in Figure 2, the left column of the following experimental chart shows the number of frequent subtrees that the above three algorithms outputs in case of different support thresholds min_sup when the Jaccard distance threshold δ' is 0.2 , 0.4 and 0.6 respectively. The right column corresponds to the calculation time of three algorithms on the basis of the different δ'. Experimental results show that both the output scale of frequent subtrees and consuming time of MCRP algorithm are less than FBMiner and MFTM.

Table2 Experimental environment

Operating Ssytem	Windows 8.1
CPU	Intel Core I7
RAM/Hard Disk	8GB/1TB
DB/Drawing Tool	MYSQL/R
XML Parsing Tool	DOM4J
Programming Langue	JAVA

5. Conclusion

This paper focuses on the method of mining frequent subtrees on unordered trees. Firstly, an encoding method named WANOC is proposed, which keeps the position information of nodes and their children's nodes, so that the efficiency is improved when the subtree support degree is calculated. And then, the maximum prefix coding is proposed to generate all the candidate subtrees on the basis of WANOC, which avoids the omission of frequent subtree information. In the end, in order to avoid outputing frequent subtrees in large scale and affecting the efficiency of subsequent operations , the coverage patterns is output on the basis of δ'coverage concept. Experimental results show that the MCRP algorithm is effective in the frequent subtree output scale and time cost.

References

[1] Yakop, M.A.M., S. Mutalib and S. Abdul-Rahman, Data Projection Effects in Frequent Itemsets Mining. 2015: Springer Singapore. 23-32.

[2] Malviya, J., A. Singh and D. Singh, An FP Tree based Approach for Extracting Frequent Pattern from Large Database by Applying Parallel and Partition Projection. International Journal of Computer Applications, 2015. 114(18): p. 1-5.

[3] Deepak, A., et al., EvoMiner: frequent subtree mining in phylogenetic databases. Knowledge and Information Systems, 2014. 41(3): p. 559-590.

[4] Wu Qian , Luo Jianxu, An Improved Search Algorithm for Compressed FP-Tree.Computer Engineering and Design, 2015 (7): 1771-1777.

[5] Feng, B., et al. A new method of mining frequent closed trees in data streams. in International Conference on Fuzzy Systems and Knowledge Discovery, Fskd 2010, 10-12 August 2010, Yantai, Shandong, China. 2010.

[6] Yang Pei , Tan Qi, Maximal Frequent Subtree Mining and its Application, in Computer Science, 2008.35 (2): 150-153.

[7] D. Xin, J. Han, X. Yan, et al. Mining Compressed Frequent Pattern Sets[C]//31th International Conference on Very Large Data Bases (VLDB). Santiago de Chile,Chile:VLDB Endowment,2005:709–720.

[8] Liu, L. and J. Liu. Mining Frequent Embedded Subtree From Tree-Like Databases. in International Conference on Internet Computing & Information Services. 2011.

[9] A. K. Jain, R. C. Dubes. Algorithms for Clustering Data[M]. 1st ed., Prentice Hall,1998:366–367

[10] Han, K., et al. Constrained Frequent Subtree Mining Method. in International Conference on Digital Home. 2014.

Design and Implementation of Agriculture Industrialization APP Based on Industrial 4

Yan-Fei Sun[1], Peng Wu[2]

[1]*ZIBO Vocational Institute, Zibo, Shan Dong, 255000, P.R. China*
[2]*ZIBO Vocational Institute Zibo, Shan Dong, 255000, P.R. China*
1s_sailing@sina.com, 2 erlangwu@qq.com

Abstract; This paper designs and implements a wisdom agriculture platform client based on Android. According to the need of wisdom agriculture and achieve goal of agricultural industrialization, combined with mode of operation of agricultural production, this paper analyses agricultural production related business processes and information systems process from services provided the supplier's perspective. The system realizes the data synchronization between server and client and the real-time monitoring and control of the production condition of each greenhouse. At the same time it provides real-time production of the majority farmers for agricultural experts and leadership and improves the efficiency of agricultural management.

1. Introduction

With the integration of information technology and industrial technology, the Deep interleaving of Network, computer technology, information technology, software and automation technology to create a new value model. We call the virtual network - physical system industry 4.The system is associated with resource, information, goods and people. It will promote the formation of a new platform for information and physical systems. The new information system platform can connect all the people, objects and systems. It will provide a comprehensive, fast, safe and reliable service and application business processes. And it will support the mobile terminal devices and the collaborative manufacturing, service, analysis and forecasting processes of the business networks.

In the new era, the goal of agricultural industrialization is to make agricultural production and management intelligent, convenient, scientific and efficient. It can provide farmers with agricultural production related information, so as to establish market-oriented, specialized agriculture, improve the efficiency of agricultural production, and realize the modernization of agriculture. As a large agricultural country, it is important to make full use of the limited resources to develop the agricultural industry and improve the grain yield.

Our government attaches great importance to the development of agriculture in our country. With the continuous development of the Internet of things technology, more and more technology is also applied to agricultural production. At present intelligent agriculture has achieved the monitoring of the various indicators of agricultural greenhouses, and it promotes the development of agricultural industry. However, these platforms transmit to the farmer's information in a single, fragmented and so on, and they cannot provide a strong guidance to farmers. So the role of intelligent agriculture will be greatly reduced. Therefore, a rapid configuration, rapid implementation, rapid application, rapid and effective agricultural information technology application platform will be very obvious advantages.

2. System Framework Design

The so-called wisdom agricultural solutions is the system can automatically open or close the specified equipment by collecting the environmental parameters such as temperature, soil temperature, CO2 concentration, humidity signal, illumination, humidity and dew point temperature. It can be processed at any time according to user needs. It provides a scientific basis for the automatic monitoring of ecological information, the automatic control and intelligent management of the environment. And it can realize remote control of temperature and humidity in greenhouse by collecting data such as temperature sensor and transmitting data through wireless signal transceiver module.

From the need of wisdom agriculture and the goal of agricultural industrialization, combined with mode of operation of agricultural production, it analysis agricultural production related business processes and information systems process from the perspective of the service provider. At the same time it takes into account

Foundation items: Zibo science and technology development project (No. 2015kj010047)

DOI: 10.1051/itmconf/20171201003

the actual demand of agriculture and information transfer between the two sides of the supply and demand in the planning of its management system, and it highlights the business characteristics of wisdom agriculture.

The whole system framework as shown below:

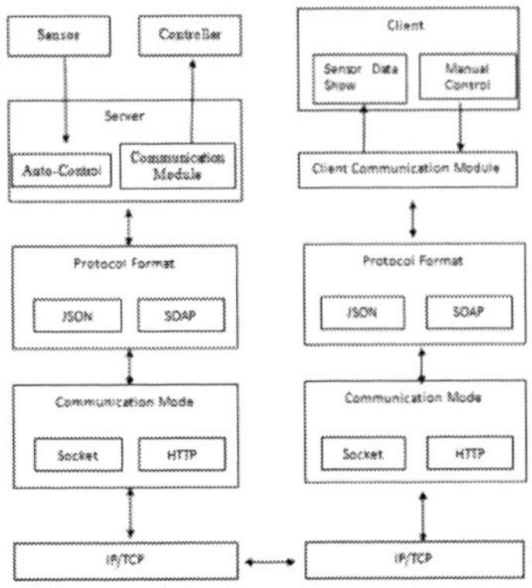

Figure 1. System Framework

Server: It is mainly responsible for the management of the system users, the current data collection. it is responsible for adapting the protocol connection between various clients, and It can feed the data which the client needs back to the client through the protocol interface. It can also receive control information from the client and control the corresponding control unit.

Client: It is responsible for displaying and controlling the data and status of the system, including the implementation of data curve charts, historical data show and manual control.

The communication protocol format: It includes JSON and SOAP two data format protocol. This has nothing to do with the specific communication mode.

Communication mode: It includes HTTP and SOCKET two communication modes.

The log module: The log function of server is used to record the information of client, operation type, operation time and other relevant information. It can also browse logs.

3. The Design of The Server Module

The design of the server module as shown below: This paper focuses on the design and implementation of the client, so the server part is not the focus of this paper.

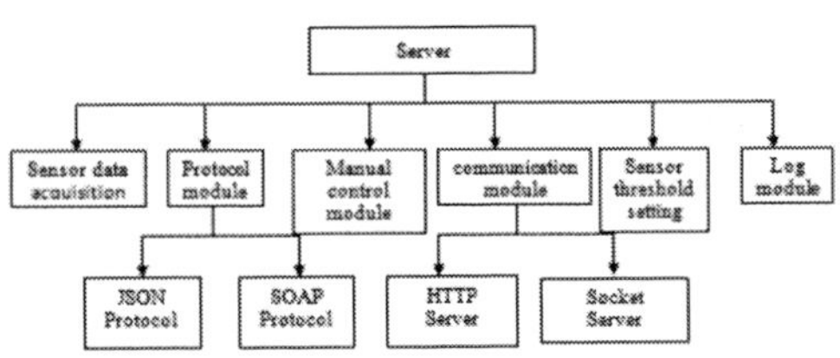

Figure 2. the Server Module

4. The Design Of The Client Module

The design of the client module as shown below:

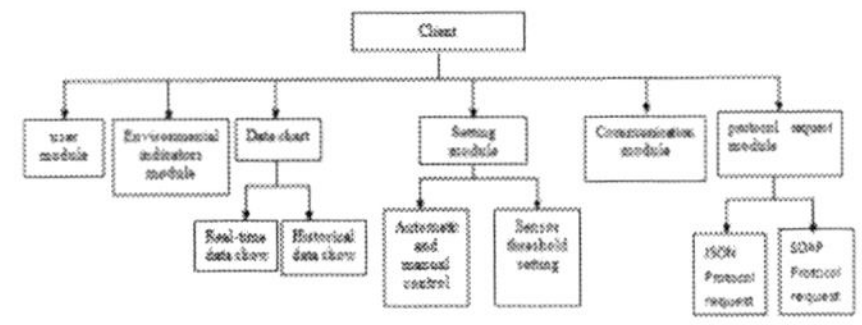

Figure 3. the ClientModule

4.1 Functional Design

The user module: This includes user registration, login, etc.

Administrator permissions: It can be manually controlled and finish each sensor's threshold setting.

Environmental indicators: It can display the current value of all sensor data in real time, and it can be judged that an alarm is needed according to each sensor threshold.

The data chart: This includes real-time data show and historical data show.

Automatic and manual control switch: it provides two control modes, one is automatic control and the other is manual control. The function can be set in the system settings.

Sensor threshold setting: The client can set the maximum and minimum values for each sensor. The system will be based on the threshold to judge whether to enter the alarm state.

The communication module: The client can choose to communicate with the server using HTTP or SOCKET.

The protocol request module: The client can choose to interact with the server using the JSON or SOAP data format protocol.

4.2 The Protocol Interface Design

Communication between the client and the server uses the answer mode. That is, the client sends a request, the server receives it and it responds based on query results.

For example, in the HTTP communication mode, the SOAP request content of the user login should be:

Url:http://192.168.1.119:8890/type/soap/action/login
<? xml version="1.0" encoding="utf-8"? >
<soap:Envelopxmlns:xsi="http://www.w3.org/2001/XMLSchem-instnce"
xmlns:xsd="http://www.w3.org/2001/XMLSchema"
xmlns:soap="http://schemas.xmlsoap.org/soap/envelop/">
<soap:Body>
<username>admin</username>
<pssword>admin</password>
</soap:Envelop>

The response of the server:

```
<? xml version=\"1.0\" encoding=\"utf-8\"? >
<soap:Envelopxmlns:xsi="http://www.w3.org/2001/XMLSchem-instnce"
xmlns:xsd="http://www.w3.org/2001/XMLSchema"
xmlns:soap="http://schemas.xmlsoap.org/soap/envelop/">
<soap:Body>
<result>ok</result>
</soap:Body>
</soap:Envelop>
```

This indicates a successful login.

```
<? xml version=\"1.0\" encoding=\"utf-8\"? >
<soap:Envelopxmlns:xsi="http://www.w3.org/2001/XMLSchem-instnce"
xmlns:xsd="http://www.w3.org/2001/XMLSchema"
xmlns:soap="http://schemas.xmlsoap.org/soap/envelop/">
<soap:Body>
<result>failed</result>
</soap:Body>
</soap:Envelop>
```

This indicates a failed login.

For example, in the HTTP communication mode, the JSON request content of the user login should be:

```
Url:http://192.168.1.119:8890/type/soap/action/login
Body:{'username':'admin','password':'admin'}
```

At this time if the server's response is {'result':'ok'} which indicates a successful login. If the server's response is {'result':'failed'} which indicates a failed login.

5. Client Implementation

The client APP is developed by Android language. For example, we read the sensor data from the client in real time, the relevant code is as follows:

```
/**
 * Set up and start the thread to get the current value of the sensor
 *
 */
private void setGetSenosorThread() {
mSensorThread = new RequestThread(this, mApp.getHandler());
mSensorThread.setLoop(true, 1500);
mSensorRequest = new GetSensorRequest("");
mSensorRequest.setSensorValue(mApp.getCurSensorValue());
mSensorRequest
.setOnResponseEventListener(new OnResponseEventListener() {
@Override
public void onResponse(BaseRequest requestRequestResult result) {
mUpDate.upDate();
}
});
mSensorThread.setRequest(mSensorRequest);
mSensorThread.start();
}
/**
 * Update data
 *
 */
public void upDateView() {
mList.clear();
SensorBeanmBean;
SensorValuemValue = mApp.getCurSensorValue();
SensorConfigmConfig = mApp.getSensorConfig();
// Set CO2 sensor data
mBean = new SensorBean(mStrings[0]);
mBean.setMaxValue(mConfig.maxCo2);
mBean.setMinValue(mConfig.minCo2);
mBean.setValue(mValue.getCo2());
mList.add(mBean);
// Set light sensor data
mBean = new SensorBean(mStrings[1]);
mBean.setMaxValue(mConfig.maxLight);
mBean.setMinValue(mConfig.minLight);
mBean.setValue(mValue.getLight());
mList.add(mBean);
// Set air temperature sensor data
mBean = new SensorBean(mStrings[2]);
mBean.setMaxValue(mConfig.maxAirTemperature);
mBean.setMinValue(mConfig.minAirTemperature);
mBean.setValue(mValue.getAirTemper());
mList.add(mBean);
// Set air humidity sensor data
mBean = new SensorBean(mStrings[3]);
mBean.setMaxValue(mConfig.maxAirHumidity);
mBean.setMinValue(mConfig.minAirHumidity);
mBean.setValue(mValue.getAirHumid());
mList.add(mBean);
// Set the soil temperature sensor data
mBean = new SensorBean(mStrings[4]);
mBean.setMaxValue(mConfig.maxSoilTemperature);
mBean.setMinValue(mConfig.minSoilTemperature);
mBean.setValue(mValue.getSoilTemper());
mList.add(mBean);
// Set the soil humidity sensor data
mBean = new SensorBean(mStrings[5]);
mBean.setMaxValue(mConfig.maxSoilHumidity);
mBean.setMinValue(mConfig.minSoilHumidity);
mBean.setValue(mValue.getSoilHumid());
mList.add(mBean);
mAdpater.notifyDataSetChanged();
}
```

After analyzing and testing, the system runs stably and smoothly. The system realizes the data synchronization between server and client and the real-time monitoring and control of the production condition of each greenhouse. At the same time it provides real-time production of the majority farmers for agricultural experts and leadership and improves the efficiency of agricultural management.

6. Conclusion

With the rapid development of industry 4, mobile Internet and big data, it is very important for making use of intelligent mobile phone real-time access to agricultural monitoring data and the guidance of the development of intelligent agriculture. This paper hopes to make up for the deficiency of the existing market products, at the same time, it is close to the actual needs of the agricultural industry, and it can effectively promote the process of the intelligent agricultural development and promote the rapid development of the agricultural industry management, production, transportation, processing.

Acknowledgment

Foundation items: Zibo science and technology development project (No. 2015kj010047)

References

[1] Sun Yanfei,WuPeng.On implementation scheme of agriculture industrialization APP based on industrial 4[J]. Advances in Social Science, Education and Humanities Research. 2016,10.

[2] Yuan Xiaomin. Industrial structure upgrading in the era of big data[J]. Market Modernization. 2015,(3).

[3] Huang Chaoqiong, Wang Dabao, Chen Chao,Zhang Li. Design and implementation of intelligent agriculture APP based on Android[J]. Software Guide, 2015(1).

[4] Zhang Shujuan. Design and implementation of enterprise information management system based on BPM[J]. Journal of Hubei University of Science and Technology.2014,34(3).

[5] Yang Darong. Development strategy of China's intelligent agricultural industry[J]. Jiangsu Agricultural Sciences,2014(4).

[6] Sun Zhongfu,Du Keming,Zheng Feixiang,Yin Shouyi. Perspectives of Research and Application of Big Data on Smart Agriculture[J]. Journal of Agricultural Science and Technology.2013,15(6):63-71.

[7] Yan Zhangpeng,Peng Cheng.On implementation scheme of the Internet of things technology in wisdom agriculture[J]. Journal of Xi'an University of Posts and Telecommunications,2013,18(4).

[8] Xu Haibin,Wang Hongxiang,Yang Xiaolin,Cao Jiwen. Current situation and Prospect of the application of Internet of things in modern agriculture[J]. Jiangsu Agricultural Sciences. 2013(05).

[9] Ma Guojun. The core technology of Internet of things and its application in agriculture[J]. Jiangsu Agricultural Sciences. 2012(11).

[10] Zhu Hongbo,Yang Longxiang,Zhu Qi. Survey on the Internet of Things[J]. Journal of Nanjing University of Posts and Telecommunications(Natural Science Edition). 2011(01).

Research on Joint Torque Optimization Method of Redundant Space Manipulators with Vibration Suppression

Xin Gao [1]., Ming-Tao Du [2], Lin Zhai [3], Yan-heng Zhang [4], Han-Xu Sun [5], Xin-Ping Diao [6]

[1]*School of Automation Beijing University of Posts and Telecommunications, Beijing, China*
[2]*School of Automation Beijing University of Posts and Telecommunications, Beijing, China*
[3]*School of Automation Beijing University of Posts and Telecommunications, Beijing, China*
[4]*School of Automation Beijing University of Posts and Telecommunications, Beijing, China*
[5]*School of Automation Beijing University of Posts and Telecommunications, Beijing, China*
[6]*School of Automation Beijing University of Posts and Telecommunications, Beijing, China*
[1]xlhhh74@bupt.edu.cn, [2]dmt2013@bupt.edu.cn, [3] zhailin0522@sina.com, [4] zyh620@bupt.edu.cn, [5] hxsun@bupt.edu.cn, [6] dxp0724@163.com

Abstract: The space manipulator can exert its advantages of high efficiency and low cost, which can assist or even replace astronauts to complete a variety of space operations. However, the research has less consideration on joint torque optimization method with considering the influence of flexible factors on the manipulator. A joint torque optimization method of redundant space flexible manipulator with vibration suppression is proposed in this paper. The bending deformation of flexible connecting rod is described by the assumed mode method and the dynamic model of space flexible manipulator system is derived by the Lagrange method. On the basis of decomposing the dynamic equation of the flexible redundant manipulator, the joint torque is optimized as well as restraining the terminal vibration through introducing the Lagrange multiplier. Finally, simulation result shows that the increase rate of joint torque is not very obvious based on the Particle Swarm Optimization algorithm compared with the experiment without vibration suppression. The forward torque of first joint increases 20.2% and that of second joint only increases 4.1% while the backward torque of both two joints decrease obviously. Meanwhile, the running trajectory has excellent effect on vibration suppression of end effector of flexible manipulators. The terminal deformation in two directions is reduced by 21.3% and 78.6%. The decline of vibration deformation of end effector is obviously larger than the rise of joint torque, which verifies the feasibility and effectiveness of the algorithm.

1. Introduction

Redundant space manipulator, an advanced manipulator system, has been invented as the development of space technology and higher demands of advanced manufacturing technology [1-2].Redundant manipulator refers to the kind of mechanical arm with more than the minimum number of degree of freedom (DOF) required to complete the task. The particular self-motion ability of redundant manipulator can overcome the weaknesses of general ones, such as poor flexibility, poor dynamic performance, limited joints, and poor obstacle avoidance, and it can also ensure the completion of actuator tasks and optimize every system performance index [3-4].

It is one of important performance indexes to optimize dynamics of redundant manipulator for the purpose of rational allocation of joint torque, and its premise is to satisfy the limit of the manipulator joint torque. The research at the present stage mainly focuses on two aspects: on the premise of meeting mission requirements, scientists often take action to minimize joint torque and reduce system energy consumption [5-7]. The method proposed by Hollerbach et al [8] and by Osumi et al[9] is typical method of joint torque local optimization and global optimization for redundant manipulator. The former may lead to local optimal solution, while when the dynamic performance is optimized in global method; the control equation will be so complex that the optimization process is very complicated. However, the research has less consideration on joint torque optimization method with considering the influence of flexible factors on the manipulator [10].

The joint optimization of space flexible manipulators in the condition of vibration suppression is mainly based on the following two aspects: 1)from the perspective of safety of working process, the end-effector will cause joints severe jitter if vibrating violently in the process of task execution, which may degrade dynamic performance, fail algorithm or even damage the manipulator itself. Reducing the terminal vibration can improve the stability and tracking accuracy of manipulators movement; reduce the wear and resonance of manipulators; delay the attenuation rate of mechanical structure caused by severe changes in the joint stress; reduce the use cost of the manipulator and prolong its service life. 2) We hope the torque of each manipulator joint becomes small when it finishes the prescribed procedures and we also hope to reduce energy consumption improving the situation of limitation of fuel supply. Thus, it has important theoretical value and practical significance to carry out the research on joint torque optimization method of space flexible manipulator in the condition of vibration suppression, and it has a very wide application prospect.

A joint torque optimization method of redundant manipulator with vibration suppression is proposed in this paper. The bending deformation of flexible connecting rod is described by the assumed mode method and the dynamic model of space flexible manipulator system is derived by the Lagrangian formulation. On the basis of decomposing the dynamic equation of the flexible redundant manipulator, the joint torque is optimized as well as restraining the terminal vibration through introducing the Lagrange multiplier. Simulation shows its feasibility and effectiveness.

2. Research on the Optimization Method of Joint Torque of Space Manipulator Considering Flexibility

The deformation description of flexible manipulator during working process is the fundamental for model construction and operation. To reduce the model complexity, combined with the structure character of the target itself, this paper only considers the flexibility of the connecting rod. In this part, assumed modes method was used to approximately describe the deformation of connecting rod, regardless the vibration mode at higher-order. Then we use Lagrange method to analyze the kinetic characteristics of the flexible manipulator. Accompanied with system momentum conservation, kinetic model of the flexible manipulator system can be inferred. Further, inhibiting the vibration of terminal effector and optimizing the joint torque can be implemented, which is based on splitting the kinetic equation of the flexible manipulator, through introducing the Lagrange multiplier.

2.1 Establishment of Dynamic Model of Flexible Manipulator

The assumed mode method was used to describe the deformation caused by the flexibility of the manipulator. For flexible manipulator with multiple connection rods, to describe the deformation accurately, following assumptions were made [11-12]:

- The length-to-diameter ratio for each rod is higher enough to neglect the transverse force and rotary inertia
- Deformation can only occurred within the motor level of each rod.
- Each rod had higher rigid level so that the deflection of each rod can be ignored.
- The vibration and joint torque of each rod do not affect others' vibration frequency and modal shape.
- The orthogonality of the vibration function is independent on external force and other factors.

The description of the deformed flexible manipulator in inertial frame is shown in Fig.1.

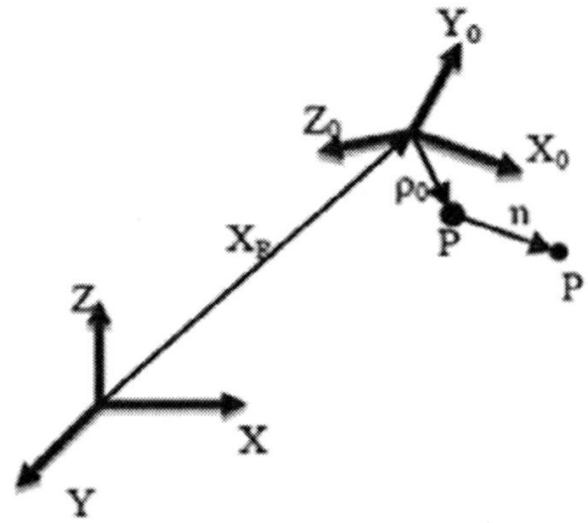

Figure 1. Description of Flexible Body in Inertial Coordinate System

In Fig.1, point P move to P' after the deformation. The pose, after shape changing, of P in inertial frame can be expressed as:

$$r_{p'} = X_R + \rho_0 + \eta \tag{1}$$

where, X_R is the pose of FM according to the original point in inertial frame; ρ_0 is the pose of P in its own coordinate system; η is the elastic deformation vector of P.

Taking the derivative of type (1) with respect to time, the velocity of any point on flexible manipulator can be obtained in the inertial frame.

$$V = \frac{dr_{p'}}{dt} = V_R + \omega\times(\rho_0\times\eta) + \dot{\rho}_0 + \dot{\eta} \tag{2}$$

The kinetic energy of a typical flexible manipulator is:

$$T = \frac{1}{2}\int_V V^T \cdot V dm \tag{3}$$

Bring type (2) into type (3)

$$T = \frac{1}{2}\int_V \{V_R\cdot V_R + [\omega\times(\rho_0+\eta)]\cdot[\omega\times(\rho_0+\eta)] + \dot{\eta}\cdot\dot{\eta} + 2V_R\cdot[\omega\times(\rho_0+\eta)] + 2V_R\cdot\dot{\eta} + 2[\omega\times(\rho_0+\eta)]\cdot\dot{\eta}\}dm \tag{4}$$

Then, we solve the kinetic energy of the flexible manipulator in Space rectangular coordinate system.

DOI: 10.1051/itmconf/20171201004

Before this, we definite a form of expression, that is, we use $\Phi_k\dot{\varsigma}_\kappa$ to express $\sum_{k=1}^{N}\Phi_k\dot{\varsigma}_\kappa$.

The kinetic energy of the flexible manipulator can be expressed in quadratic form of generalized velocity:

$$T=\frac{1}{2}U^T MU \tag{5}$$

According to the previous conclusions, the kinetic energy can be expressed with generalized coordinates as:

$$T=\frac{1}{2}\dot{q}^T(H^T MH)\dot{q}=\frac{1}{2}\dot{q}^T\tilde{M}\dot{q} \tag{6}$$

As the space manipulator works in the microgravity environment, the influence of its own gravity can be neglected. The elastic potential energy produced by the flexible deformation of the manipulator is the only potential energy on the system. According to the theory of mechanics of materials, the elastic potential energy can be expressed as:

$$V=\frac{1}{2}\xi^T K\xi \tag{7}$$

Where, K is modal stiffness matrix of the manipulator; ω_i is the corresponding frequency of ith-order natural vibration ξ is modal displacement matrix, $\xi=[\xi_1\ \ \xi_2\ \ \xi_3]^T$

The kinetic energy and potential energy required for solving the dynamic equations of the manipulator system have been obtained in former two sections. At the same time, the expression forms of the generalized coordinates of the system kinetic energy and potential energy have been obtained through the transformation of the corresponding matrix. Then, the dynamic equations of a single flexible body can be obtained and its matrix form is shown as follows:

$$\tilde{M}\ddot{q}+\tilde{C}\dot{q}+\tilde{K}q=Q+\lambda\alpha-\dot{\tilde{M}}\dot{q}+\frac{1}{2}\dot{q}^T\frac{\partial\tilde{M}}{\partial q}\dot{q} \tag{8}$$

So far, dynamic differential equation has been established. We can draw a conclusion from the derivation of the equations that on account of considering the elastic deformation, the dynamic equations of flexible body become a nonlinear strong coupling differential equation set.

If n、nr、$nf(n=nr+nf)$ are respectively total degree of freedom, rigid degree of freedom and flexible degree of freedom of the manipulator, The dynamic equation of the flexible manipulator is shown as follows:

$$M(\theta,q)\begin{bmatrix}\ddot{\theta}\\ \ddot{q}\end{bmatrix}+D(\theta,q)\begin{bmatrix}\dot{\theta}\\ \dot{q}\end{bmatrix}+K(\theta,q)\begin{bmatrix}\theta\\ q\end{bmatrix}+Q=I\tau \tag{9}$$

where M、D、$K\in R^{n\times n}$ is respectively the generalized mass matrix, the damping matrix and the stiffness matrix; Q is n order column vector which is the sum of gravity, centrifugal force and Coriolis force etc.; $\tau\in R^{nr}$ is control torque on joint; I is nr dimension of the unit matrix; $\theta\in R^{nr}$ is column vector of joint angle; $q\in R^{nf}$ is generalized coordinates matrix of flexible deformation.

$$\mathrm{M}=\begin{bmatrix}M_{rr} & M_{fr}\\ M_{rf} & M_{ff}\end{bmatrix}$$

Where $M_{rr}\in R^{nr\times nf}$, $M_{fr}\in R^{nf\times nr}$ and $M_{ff}\in R^{rf\times nf}$ are respectively sub block matrix of M. Similarly, we divide the matrix D and K into blocks. $Q=[Q_r\ \ Q_f]^T$, $Q_r\in R^{nr}$, $Q_f\in R^{nf}$ are respectively sub block matrix of Q. Thus, the above formula can be decomposed as follows:

$$M_{rr}\ddot{\theta}+M_{rf}\ddot{q}+Q_r=\tau \tag{10}$$

$$M_{ff}\ddot{q}+D_{ff}\dot{q}+K_{ff}q=-M_{fr}\ddot{\theta}-Q_f \tag{11}$$

The above two types are dynamic equations of the flexible redundant manipulator, where type (10) is torque control equation of space manipulator and type (11) is vibration equation of manipulator system.

2.2 The Algorithm of Joint Torque Optimization for Flexible Space Manipulator with Vibration Suppression

We assumed m is dimension of working space of the manipulator; n、nr、$nf(n=nr+nf)$ are respectively total degree of freedom, rigid degree of freedom and flexible degree of freedom of the manipulator; $X\in R^m$ is the vector of position and pose of effector. Thus, the following relationship is established for the flexible manipulator:

$$X=f(\theta,q) \tag{12}$$

Taking the derivative of type (12), the equation of velocity and acceleration between Rectangular Coordinates and generalized coordinates (including joint displacement coordinates and flexible deformation coordinates)can be obtained as follows:

DOI: 10.1051/itmconf/20171201004

$$\dot{X} = J_r\dot{\theta} + J_f\dot{q}$$
$$\ddot{X} = J_r\ddot{\theta} + J_f\ddot{q} + \dot{J}_r\dot{\theta} + \dot{J}_f\dot{q}$$

(13)

Where, $J_r = \partial f / \partial\theta \in R^{m\times nr}, J_f = \partial f / \partial q \in R^{m\times nf}$ is respectively Jacobian matrix of rigid and flexible motion of the manipulator. The rigid motion and flexible motion are coupled, but the amplitude of the flexible motion is relatively small, which can be regarded as a disturbance to the rigid motion. The influence of the flexible motion is usually neglected in the trajectory planning and the inverse kinematics solution and the error is eliminated with vibration suppression. Thus, the above formula can be simplified as:

$$\ddot{X} = J_r\ddot{\theta} + \dot{J}_r\dot{\theta}$$

(14)

As for redundant manipulator, θ has infinite solution on non-singular position ($rank(J_r) = m < n$) which can be optimized. Then, the complex modal excitation force of the vibration of flexible manipulator can be obtained through complex modal transformation of the dynamic equations.

$$Q_e = V_{\mathrm{RHL}}^{\mathrm{T}} M_{ff}^{-1} f_e = V_{\mathrm{RHL}}^{\mathrm{T}} M_{ff}^{-1}[-M_{fr}\ddot{\theta} - Q_f]$$

(15)

Where, $V_{RHL} \in R^{nf\times nf}$ is real part of left modal matrix.

We can make the exciting force become small or even zero via reasonably selecting the self-motion variables of the manipulator, which can restrain the vibration of the terminal manipulator. Now, we want to optimize the joint torque on the basis of vibration suppression. Thus, the optimization problem becomes as follows:

$$min(Z) = min(\tau^{\mathrm{T}}\tau + Q_e^{\mathrm{T}}Q_e)$$
$$s.t. \quad J_r\ddot{\theta} + \dot{J}_r\dot{\theta} - \ddot{X} = 0$$

(16)

By introducing Lagrange multiplier, we can obtain:

$$Z = \tau^{\mathrm{T}}\tau + Q_e^{\mathrm{T}}Q_e + \lambda^{\mathrm{T}}(J_r\ddot{\theta} + \dot{J}_r\dot{\theta} - \ddot{X})$$

(17)

$$A = -2M_{rr}^{\mathrm{T}}M_{rr} - 2\left[(V_{\mathrm{RHL}}^{\mathrm{T}}M_{ff}^{-1}M_{fr})^{\mathrm{T}}(V_{\mathrm{RHL}}^{\mathrm{T}}M_{ff}^{-1}M_{fr})\right],$$
$$B = 2M_{rr}^{\mathrm{T}}$$

$(M_{rf}\ddot{}$ ... $+ 2(V_{\mathrm{RHL}}^{\mathrm{T}}M_{ff}^{-1}M_{fr})^{\mathrm{T}}(V_{\mathrm{RHL}}^{\mathrm{T}}M_{ff}^{-1}Q_f)$ and solve the following conditions:

$$\frac{\partial Z}{\partial\ddot{\theta}} = 0$$
$$\frac{\partial Z}{\partial\lambda} = 0$$

(18)

We can obtain:

$$\ddot{\theta} = A^{-1}B + A^{-1}J_r^{\mathrm{T}}\lambda$$
$$J_r\ddot{\theta} + \dot{J}_r\dot{\theta} - \ddot{X} = 0$$

(19)

Then, the simultaneous equation can be obtained from type (24)

$$\ddot{\theta} = D(\ddot{X} - \dot{J}_r\dot{\theta}) + (I - DJ_r)A^{-1}B$$

(20)

Where $D = A^{-1}J_r^T(J_rA^{-1}J_r^T)^{-1}$. It's easy to verify $J_rD = I$, so D is right inverse of J_r.

Until now, we have accomplished the optimization of the dynamic equation. Then, we can realize the corresponding control algorithm. Comparing with the pseudo-inverse method, the above algorithm can optimize joint torque of redundant space manipulator on the basis of vibration suppression with complex modal method.

2.3 Numerical Simulation

To verify the feasibility and efficiency of the upper algorithm, we use a two-link flexible manipulator to do numerical simulation research. We assumed that the mass of two connecting rods are m1=m2=10kg, the concentrated mass at the end of two connection rod are m1=50kg, m2=1000kg, the length of two rods are l1=l2=3m, the elastic parameter of flexible rod is EI=1200, the density of the rods is p=2.7*103kg/m3, the cross-sectional area is $A = 1.2\times10^{-4}m^2$. The initial angles of given configuration are θ_{ini} = [0°, 0°] and the termination angles are θ_{des} = [45°, 45°]. The planning time is t = [0, 10s] and the limitation of two joint angles is $\theta \in [-180°, 180°]$. Specific value of each parameter in given particle swarm optimization algorithm is as follows: the velocity range of particles is limited to $v \in [-5, 5]$; the maximum update iteration is $max\_length = 80$;the number of particles is $Popnum = 30$; the inertial factor is gradually fading from 0.8 to 0.2.

Cubic spline curve was used to trace the moving trajectory of the manipulator and the middle node of the spline curve can be regarded as the control parameter of the optimal computing. Finally, we got the optimal solution by using PSO algorithm. The cubic spline curve of two joint angles of the manipulator is shown in Fig 2; Fig 3-4 reflects its torque changing and terminal deformation caused by vibration. To evaluate the test result, another manipulator, whose joint torque was optimized only, was designed under the same circumstance, regardless of the inhibition of its terminal vibration. Its changing curve of the joint angle is shown in Fig 5. Fig 6-7 reflects its torque changing and terminal deformation caused by vibration.

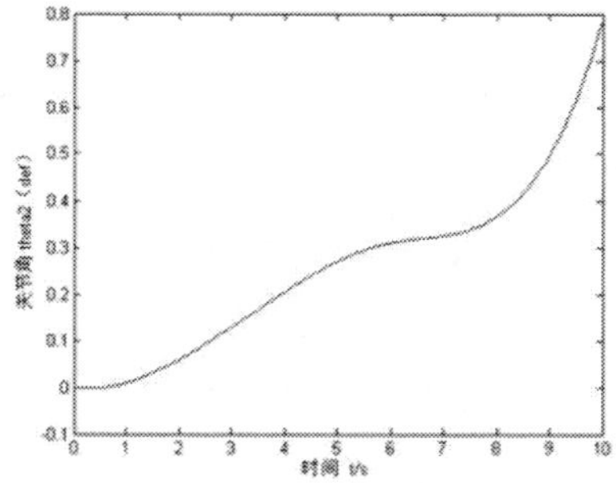

(a)

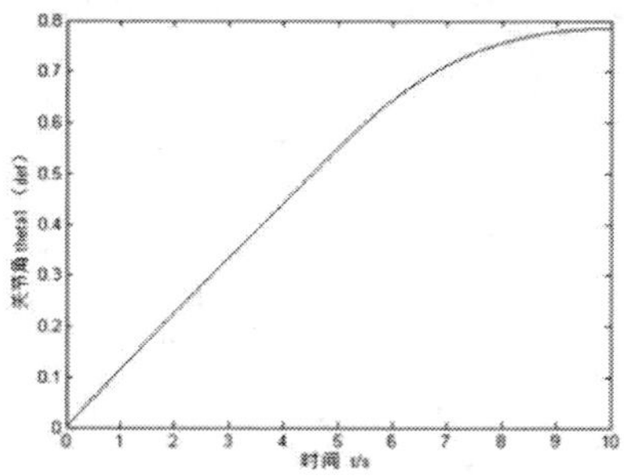

(b)

Figure 2. Cubic Spline Curve of Two Joint Angles of the Manipulator

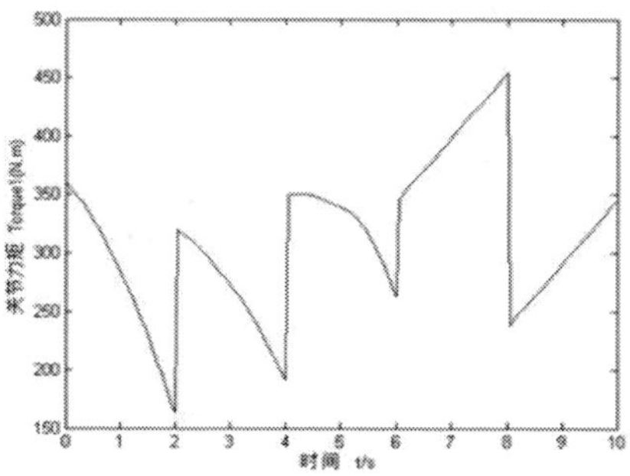

(a)

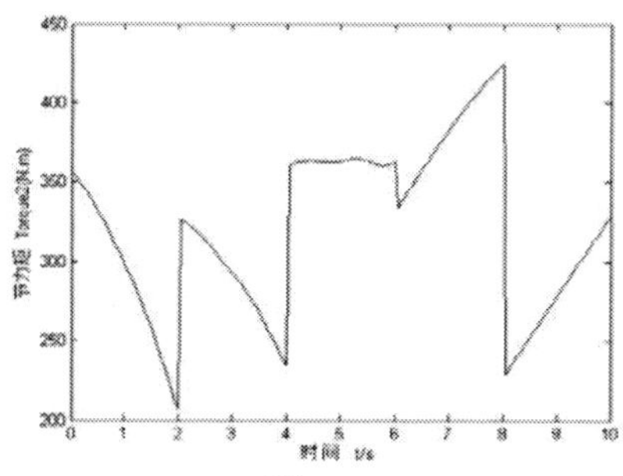

(b)

Figure 3.Variation Curve of Two Joint Torque of the Manipulator

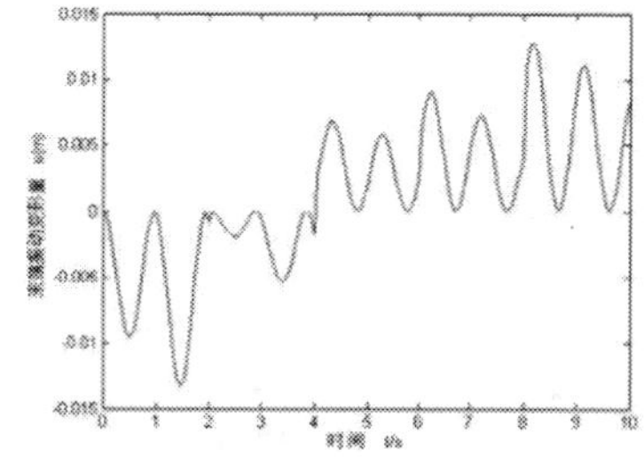

Figure 4.The variation curve of Terminal Vibration Deformation of the Manipulator

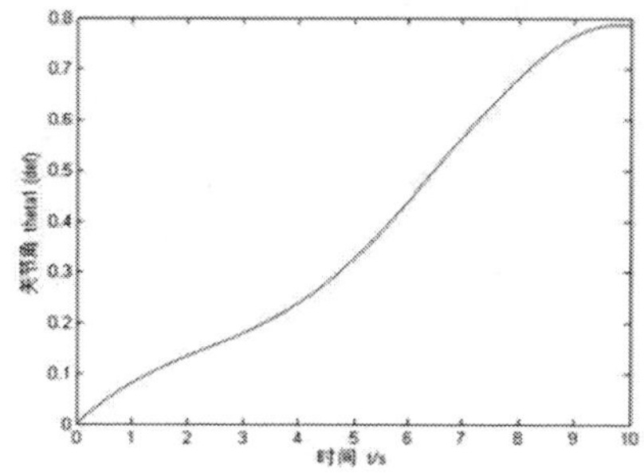

(a)

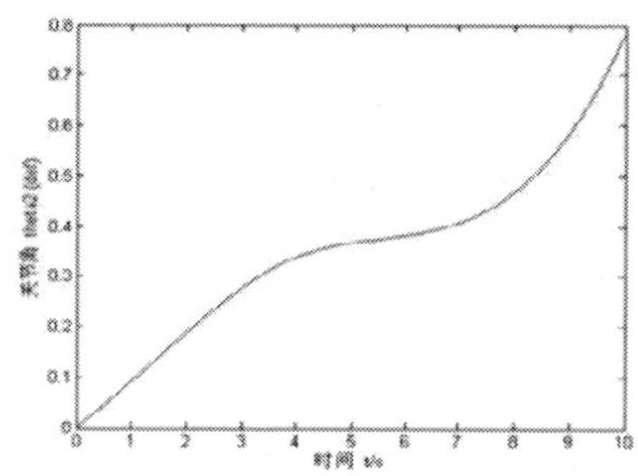

(b)

Figure 5. The Variation Curve of Two Joint Angles of the Manipulator in Contrast Experiment

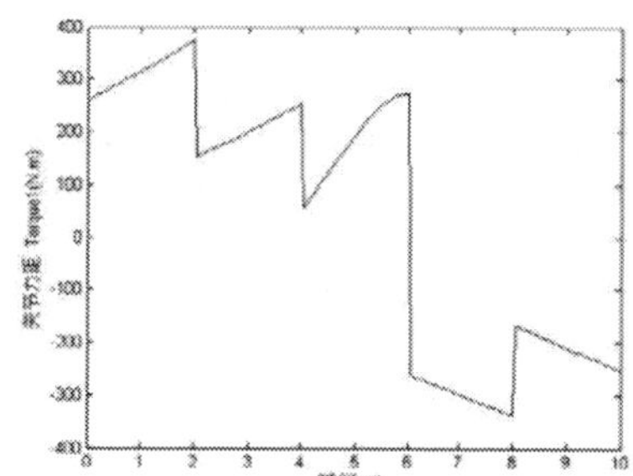

(a)

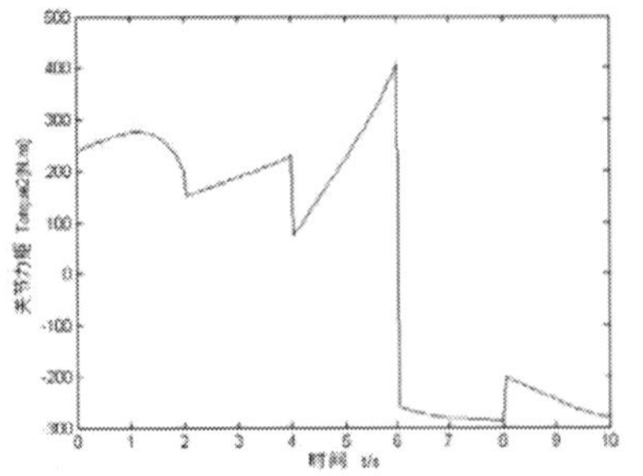

(b)

Figure 6.The variation Curve of Two Joint Torque of the Manipulator in Contrast Experiment

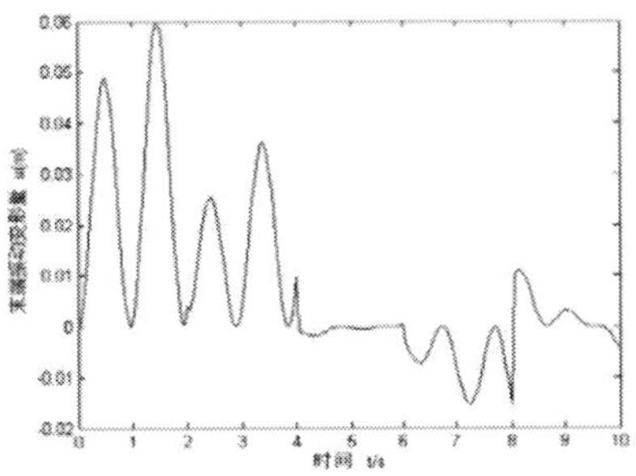

Figure 7.The Variation Curve of Terminal Vibration Deformation of the Manipulator in Contrast Experiment

From the simulation result, after doing the interpolation calculation towards the joint angle via cubic spline, and doing the practical swarm optimization, the trajectory of the manipulator can be obtained. The amplitude of variation of its two joint torques are $Torque1 \in [163.5\text{Nm}, 451.1\text{Nm}]$, $Torque2 \in [207.7\text{Nm}, 424.3\text{Nm}]$ respectively, while in the same lab environment, when optimizing the joint torque of the connection rod itself without considering the inhibition of the endpoint vibration, the amplitude of variation of its two joint torque is [illegible] $[-337.8\text{Nm}, 375.2\text{Nm}]$, [illegible] $[-288.8\text{Nm}, 407.7\text{Nm}]$ respectively. Further, the terminal vibration amplitude of the manipulator whose trajectory was optimized by PSO is [-0.0122m, 0.0128m], while that of the control group is [-0.0155m, 0.0599m].

From the numerical simulation result, we can inferred that, comparing with experiment that only optimizing the joint torque while neglect the inhibiting of terminal vibration, the increase of joint torque when applying the PSO algorithm is quite negligible. The first forward joint torque increased 20.2%, and the second forward joint torque increased only 4.1%, however, the backward of two joint torque dropped significantly. But, when it comes to the operation trajectory and its inhibiting towards the terminal vibration, PSO is quite obvious when applying to manipulator. Its terminal deformation decrease 78.6% and 21.3% in two directions respectively. The decrease of terminal deformation is significantly larger than the increase of its joint torque, which verifies the feasibility and efficiency of this algorithm.

3. Conclusion

We have carried out the research on joint torque optimization method of space flexible manipulator and we have proposed an algorithm with vibration suppression. First of all, the bending deformation of the flexible rod is approximated by the assumed mode method. Then, using Lagrange method to derive the dynamic equations of flexible manipulator and separate the rigid and flexible terms from the dynamic equation, the vibration excitation of the manipulator was obtained. The weighted sum of joint torque and terminal deformation are objective functions of the particle swarm optimization algorithm. At last, we use cubic spline curve to describe the trajectory of space manipulator in joint coordinate system and the middle control node of spline curve is chosen as control parameters of optimization. The research realizes restraining the terminal vibration as well as optimizing the joint torque based on Particle Swarm Optimization algorithm and the simulation has verified its feasibility and effectiveness.

Acknowledgment

The authors would like to thank their colleagues from the Robotics Research Group for helpful discussions and comments on this paper. This work is supported in part by Key Project of Chinese National Programs for Fundamental Research and Development (973 program) (No. 2013CB733000), National Natural Science Foundation of China (No. 61573066) and National Natural Science Foundation of China (No. 61403038).

References

[1] Jürgen Hes, Gian Diego Tipaldi and Wolfram Burgard, "Null Space Optimization for Effective Coverage of 3D Surfaces Using Redundant Manipulators", IEEE/RSJ International Conference on Intelligent Robots and Systems, pp1923-1928, Oct, 2012

[2] Apoorva D. Kapadia and Ian D. Walker, "Self-motion Analysis of Extensible Continuum Manipulators", IEEE International Conference on Robotics and Automation, pp1988-1994, May, 2013

[3] Arne Wahrburg, Johannes Boes, Bjoern Matthias, Fan Dai and Hao Ding, "Sensorless Null-Space Admittance Control for Redundant Manipulators", Proceedings of 47st International Symposium on Robotics, Munich, Germany, pp1-7, Jun, 2016

[4] Junghwan Lee, Sung-eui Yoon, "Productive Regions Oriented Task Space Path Planning for Hyper-redundant Manipulators", IEEE International Conference on Robotics and Automation, pp6491-6498, May, 2014

[5] FabrizioFlacco, Alessandro De Luca, "Discrete-time Velocity Control of Redundant Robots with Acceleration/Torque Optimization Properties", IEEE

International Conference on Robotics and Automation, pp5139-5144, May, 2014

[6] Yang Yang, Xiaoyu Shang, Hui Li, “Joint Torque Optimization Method for Space Manipulator”, IEEE International Conference on Information and Automation, pp1233-1238, July, 2014

[7] Xin Gao, , Mingtao Du, Haoxin Wu, Hanxu Sun, Qingxuan Jia, Gang Chen, Yifan Wang, “A joint torque optimization method for space manipulators considering the in-orbit motion reliability”, Journal of Astronautics,pp784-794, July, 2016

[8] Sartaj Singh, Babu D Jadhav and K Madhava Krishna, “Posture Control of a Three-segmented Tracked Robot with Torque Minimization During Step Climbing”, IEEE International Conference on Robotics and Automation, pp4200-4207, May, 2014

[9] Osumi H, Yokohama K, Takeuchi K etc,“Time Optimal Control for Quadruped Robots by Using Torque Redundancy”, IEEE International Conference on Intelligent Robots and Systems, pp1853-1858, Oct,2012

[10] Xin Gao, Haoxin Wu, Mingtao Du, Gang Chen, Hanxu Sun, Qingxuan Jia, Yifan Wang, "Research on the operational reliability system control methodology and its application for aerospace mechanism" International Journal of Advanced Robotic Systems, 2016.

[11] Natraj Mishra, S. P. Singh and B. C. Nakra, “Dynamic Analysis of a Single Link Flexible Manipulator Using Lagrangian-assumed Modes Approach”, International Conference on Industrial Instrumentation and Control”, pp1144-1149, May, 2015

[12] Xinxin Yang and Shuzhi Sam Ge, “Dynamics and Tracking Control for a Free-flying Space Robot with Rigid-flexible Links”, IEEE International Conference on Information and Automation, pp394-399, July, 2014

Facial Expression Recognition Based on TensorFlow Platform

Xiao-Ling Xia [1], Cui Xu*[2], Bing Nan[3]

*College of computer science. Donghua University, Shanghai, China
[1]College of computer science. Donghua University, Shanghai, China
[2]College of computer science. Donghua University, Shanghai, China
[1]sherlysha@dhu.edu.cn, [2] 2151547@mail.dhu.edu.cn

Abstract--Facial expression recognition have a wide range of applications in human-machine interaction, pattern recognition, image understanding, machine vision and other fields. Recent years, it has gradually become a hot research. However, different people have different ways of expressing their emotions, and under the influence of brightness, background and other factors, there are some difficulties in facial expression recognition. In this paper, based on the Inception-v3 model of TensorFlow platform, we use the transfer learning techniques to retrain facial expression dataset (The Extended Cohn-Kanade dataset), which can keep the accuracy of recognition and greatly reduce the training time.

1. Introduction

Facial expression recognition is an important part of human emotion recognition, which is widely used in human-computer interaction, pattern recognition, image understanding, machine vision and other fields. There are more than 10 thousand kinds of expressions, and different people have different ways to express their emotions. In 1971, Paul Ekman [23] the famous psychologist in American proposed that the facial expressions of people from different cultures are much in common, the expression of the six basic emotions of happiness, anger, sadness, disgust, surprise and fear are very similar in many cultures.

Early facial expression recognition is mainly use the common methods in face recognition to classify and recognize facial expressions. Usually, SVM, LBP and Gabor are used to classify and recognize facial expressions according to the features of Haar, Adaboost and neural network. For example, Kobayashi et al. [21] realized the classification and recognition of basic facial expressions based on neural network. Caifeng Shan et al. using SVM classifier based on the LBP features to achieve facial expression recognition [18]. Ioan Buciu et al. using SVM classifier based on ICA and Gabor features for facial expression classification, the facial expression recognition system realized by combining Gabor wavelet and SVM classifier can achieve a higher recognition rate [20]. Xia Mao et al. [17] realized robust facial expression recognition based on RPCA and AdaBoost. Early facial expression recognition methods lack analysis of the unique features of facial expression.

In recent years, as a new recognition method combining artificial neural network and depth learning theory, convolutional neural network has made great progress in the field of image classification. This method uses local receptive field, weights sharing and pooling technology and makes the training parameters greatly reduced compared to the neural network. It also has a certain degree of translation, rotation and distortion invariance of image. It has been widely used in speech recognition, face recognition, handwriting recognition and other applications. Compared with traditional methods, it has higher recognition rate and wider application.

TensorFlow [1] is the second generation of artificial intelligence research and development system developed by Google, which supports convolutional neural network (CNN) [3], recurrent neural network (RNN) and other depth neural network model. This system is widely used in Google's products and services, it has been deployed in more than and 100 machine learning projects, involving more than a dozen field of speech recognition, computer vision, robotics, information retrieval, information extraction, natural language processing, drug testing.

This paper implements an effective facial expression recognition model based on Inception-v3 [8] model under the TensorFlow [1] platform. In this paper, we use the transfer learning technique to retrain the Inception-v3 [8] model on the facial expression dataset, which can reduce the training time as much as possible. The rest of this paper is organized as follows. Section II introduces the related work on facial expression recognition. In section III, we introduce the construction process of facial expression classification model. We prove the validity of the model through experiments in section IV.

2. Related Work

In 1971, Paul [23] from the psychological point of view proposed that there are six basic emotions (happiness, sadness, anger, disgust, surprise and fear) across cultures. In 1978, Ekman et al. [22] developed the facial action coding system (FACS) to describe facial expressions. Nowadays, most of the facial expression recognition work is done on the basis of the above work, this paper also chose the six basic emotions and neutral emotions as the standard of facial expression classification.

Lu Guanming et al. [2] proposed a convolutional neural network for facial expression recognition, and the dropout strategy and the dataset expansion strategy are adopted to solve the problem of insufficient training data and the problem of overfitting. C. Shan et al. [16] uses LBP and SVM algorithm to classify facial expressions with 95.10% accuracy. Andre Teixeira Lopes et al. [7] used a depth convolution neural network to classify facial expression, the accuracy reached 97.81%. However, in terms of the convolutional neural network algorithm, low level network model achieves low accuracy, the deep network models often has some problems, such as lack of data, easy to over fitting, long training time and so on.

In the traditional classification and learning, in order to ensure the accuracy and reliability of the classification model trained, need to meet two basic assumptions: the first is the training samples and test samples meet with independent distribution; the second is that it need enough training data. However, in many cases, these two conditions are difficult to meet. The most likely scenario is that the training data is out of date. This often requires us to relabel a large number of training data to meet the needs of our training, but it is very expensive to label new data, which requires a lot of manpower and material resources.

Transfer learning is a new machine learning method based on existing knowledge to solve different but related problems. The goal of transfer learning is to apply the knowledge learned from an environment into a new environment. Compared with the traditional machine learning, transfer learning relaxes the requirements of the two basic assumptions, it cannot require a large amount of training data, or only a small amount of data can be labeled. Transfer learning does not have to be like the traditional machine learning as the training samples and test samples need to be independent and identically distributed. At the same time, compared with the traditional network with random initialization, the learning speed of transfer learning is much faster.

3. Construction of Facial Expression Classification Model

This section focuses on the construction process of facial expression classification model. The process of facial expression can be divided into four steps: image preprocessing, training, validation and testing. The basic steps of facial expression classification model are shown in figure 1.

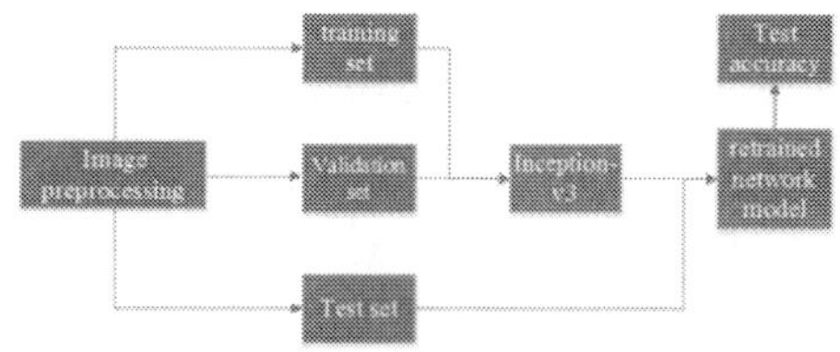

Figure1. Facial expression classification model.

3.1 Image Preprocessing

In order to improve the effect of image classification, image preprocessing is a very important stage. The target image preprocessing includes image format conversion, image clipping.

Image format conversion. Using Python image processing library PIL to achieve the conversion of different image formats.

Image clipping. In order to improve the accuracy of image classification and reduce the interference of other non target information on image classification, the target image can be cut in the process of image preprocessing.

3.2 Inception-v3

Inception-v3 [8] is a network model of Google after Inception-v1 [13], Inception-v2 [9] in 2015. It is a rethinking for the initial structure of computer vision.

Inception-v3 [8] model is mainly based on the basic principles of network design of the Inception structure changes, the main methods are: large size filter convolution decomposition, additional classifier, reduce the size of the feature map, etc.

The Inception-v3 [8] model is trained on the ImageNet datasets (1 million 200 thousand training set, validation set 50000, 100000 test set), containing the information that can identify 1000 classes in ImageNet, the error rate of top-5 is 3.5%, the error rate of top-1 dropped to 17.3%.

3.3 Transfer Learning

Inception-v3 network model is a complex network, it will cost at least a few days or even a few day time if we train the model directly. By using the method of transfer learning, the parameters of the previous layer are unchanged, but only the last layer is trained. The last layer is a softmax classifier. This classifier is 1000 output nodes in the original network (ImageNet has 1000 classes), so we need to remove the last network layer, and then retrain the last layer. The reason for retraining the last layer is to work on the new object class. As a result, identifying 1000 classes of information in the ImageNet is also useful for identifying new classes.

4. Experiment

This experiment is based on the Inception-v3 [8] model of TensorFlow [1] platform, the hardware platform is MacBook Pro: processor 2.9GHz Intel i7, memory 8GB 1600MHz DDR3. The use of the experimental dataset is CK+ facial expression dataset (The Extended Cohn-Kanade dataset [15], CK+). We select 1004 images of facial expression image, which contains 7 basic facial expressions: happiness (158), sad (155), anger (103), disgust (146), surprised (161), fear (137) and neutral (144)

In this section, the following part is as follows: first, we make a simple introduction on the dataset; then, we introduce the process of the experiment in detail; finally, we verify the effectiveness of the method through the comparison experiment.

4.1 Dataset

The CK+ dataset [15], was released in 2010 and is based on the CK dataset. The image data collected from 210 adults, aged 18-50, of which women accounted for 69%, 81% of Europe and the United States, more than 13% of African Americans. The dataset contains 123 items, 593 image sequences, including 327 image sequences with emotional labels. The dataset is a common dataset for facial expression recognition.

4.2 Experimental Procedure

Image preprocessing. First, the Inception-v3 [8] model is the image of JPG or JPEG format for training, and the image format in the dataset for the PNG format, so to convert image format to PNG format images converted to jpg format. Secondly, because the image in the dataset is the facial expression image captured by the digital camera, and some of the color image, and some gray image, so the image must be converted to grayscale image. Finally, in order to remove the interference of the background and hair improve the accuracy of image classification, we should cut out the face region in the image, and use the clipping image for training, verification and testing.

The Inception-v3 [8] network model is a very complex network, it will cost a lot of time if we train the model directly, and the data of CK+ dataset in [15] is relatively small, the training data is insufficient. Therefore,we use transfer learning technology to retrain the Inception-v3 [8] model.

The last layer of the Inception-v3 [8] model is a softmax classifier, because there are 1000 classes in the ImageNet dataset, so the classifier has 1000 output nodes in the original network. Here, we need to delete the last layer of the network, put the number of output nodes to 7 (the number of facial expressions), and then retrain the network model.

The last layer of the model is trained by back propagation algorithm, and the cross entropy cost function is used to adjust the weight parameter by calculating the error between the output of the softmax layer and the label vector of the given sample category.

4.3 Control Experiment

In order to verify the effectiveness of the proposed method, experiments are carried out to compare the facial expression classification algorithm based on MLP [2], CNN +AD [2], LBP+SVM [16] and CNN [7], and the results are shown in Table I.

Table1. Classification performance comparison of different algorithms in CK+ dataset

Method	*Performance*
MLP[2]	81.11%
CNN+AD[2]	84.55%
LBP+SVM[16]	95.10%
CNN[7]	97.81%
Our Method	97%

From the experimental results of Table I, we can see that the classification accuracy of this method is higher than that of MLP [2], CNN+AD [2] and LBP+SVM [16] algorithm, but it is less than CNN [7].

Table II shows the number of training layers in CNN [7] and our method.

Table2. The Number of Training Layers

Method	*Layers*
CNN[7]	5
Our Method	1

We know that the training time will be increased dramatically when we increase one layer. Compared with the method used in CNN [7], our method need to train fewer layers. So Compared with the method used in CNN [7], our method can greatly reduce the training time.

5. Conclusion

In this paper, based on the Inception-v3 model of Tensor Flow platform, we use the transfer learning technology to train a new facial expression classification model in CK+ dataset. The classification accuracy of the model is 97%, which is higher than that of MLP, LBP and low-level network model. Compared with some deep network models, this paper takes less time. The future work is to study and develop a facial expression recognition model based on dynamic sequences.

References

[1] Martín Abadi, Ashish Agarwal, et al: TensorFlow: Large-Scale Machine Learning on Heterogeneous Distributed Systems. CoRR abs/1603.04467 (2016)

[2] Lu Guanming, Shi Wanwan, Li Xu, et al: A kind of convolution neural network for facial expression recognition [J]. Journal of Nanjing University of Posts and Telecommunications (NATURAL SCIENCE EDITION). 2016 (01)

[3] Abhineet Saxena: Convolutional neural networks: an illustration in TensorFlow. ACM Crossroads 22(4): 56-58 (2016)

[4] Bo-Kyeong Kim, Jihyeon Roh, Suh-Yeon Dong, Soo-Young Lee: Hierarchical committee of deep convolutional neural networks for robust facial expression recognition. J. Multimodal User Interfaces 10(2): 173-189 (2016)

[5] Zhenhai Liu, Hanzi Wang, Yan Yan, Guanjun Guo: Effective Facial Expression Recognition via the Boosted Convolutional Neural Network. CCCV (1) 2015: 179-188

[6] Mao Xu, Wei Cheng, Qian Zhao, Li Ma, Fang Xu: Facial expression recognition based on transfer learning from deep convolutional networks. ICNC 2015: 702-708

[7] Andre Teixeira Lopes, Edilson de Aguiar, Thiago Oliveira-Santos: A Facial Expression Recognition System Using Convolutional Networks. SIBGRAPI 2015: 273-280

[8] Christian Szegedy, Vincent Vanhoucke, et at: Rethinking the Inception Architecture for Computer Vision. arXiv:1512.00567, 2015.

[9] Sergey Ioffe, Christian Szegedy, et al: Batch Normalization: Accelerating Deep Network Training by Reducing Internal Covariate Shift. ICML2015: 448-456, 2015.

[10] Andre Teixeira Lopes, Edilson de Aguiar, Thiago Oliveira-Santos: A Facial Expression Recognition System Using Convolutional Networks. SIBGRAPI 2015: 273-280

[11] Zhuang Fuzhen, Luoping, Heqing, history Zhongzhi: Transfer learning progress of [J]. Journal of software 2015 (01).

[12] Andre Teixeira Lopes, Edilson de Aguiar, Thiago Oliveira-Santos: A Facial Expression Recognition System Using Convolutional Networks. SIBGRAPI 2015: 273-280

[13] Christian Szegedy, Wei Liu, et al: Going Deeper with Convolutions. arXiv:1409.4842, 2014.

[14] Alex Krizhevsky, Ilya Sutskever, Geoffrey E. Hinton: ImageNet Classification with Deep Convolutional Neural Networks. NIPS 2012: 1106-1114

[15] P. Lucey, J. F. Cohn, T. Kanade, J. Saragih, Z. Ambadar, and I. Matthews, "The extended cohn-kanade dataset (ck+): A complete dataset for action unit and emotion-specified expression,"in Computer Vision and Pattern Recognition Workshops (CVPRW), 2010 IEEE Computer Society Conference on. IEEE, 2010, pp. 94–101.

[16] C. Shan, S. Gong, and P. W. McOwan: "Facial expression recognition based on local binary patterns: A comprehensive study," Image and Vision Computing, vol. 27, no. 6, pp. 803–816, 2009.

[17] Xia Mao, Yu-Li Xue, Zheng Li, Kang Huang, ShanWei Lv: Robust facial expression recognition based on RPCA and AdaBoost. WIAMIS 2009: 113-116

[18] Caifeng Shan, Tommaso Gritti: Learning Discriminative LBP-Histogram Bins for Facial Expression Recognition. BMVC 2008: 1-10

[19] Sung-Oh Lee, Yong-Guk Kim, Gwi-Tae Park: Facial Expression Recognition Based upon Gabor-Wavelets Based Enhanced Fisher Model. ISCIS 2003: 490-496

[20] Ioan Buciu, Constantine Kotropoulos, Ioannis Pitas: ICA and Gabor representation for facial expression recognition. ICIP (2) 2003: 855-858

[21] Kobayashi H, Hara F: The recognition of basic facial expression by neutral network. [C], International Joint Conference on Neural Network. 1991:460-466.

[22] E. Friesen and P. Ekman: "Facial action coding system: a technique for the measurement of facial movement," Palo Alto, 1978.

[23] P. Ekman: "Universals and cultural differences in facial expressions of emotion."in Nebraska symposium on motivation. University of Nebraska Press, 1971.

Ship Detection Using Transfer Learned Single Shot Multi Box Detector

Gu-Hong Nie[1], Peng Zhang[2], Xin Niu[3], Yong Dou[4], Fei Xia [5]

[1]*National Lab for Parallel and Distributed Processing, National University of Defense Technology, Changsha, China*
[2]*National Lab for Parallel and Distributed Processing, National University of Defense Technology, Changsha, China*
[3]*National Lab for Parallel and Distributed Processing, National University of Defense Technology, Changsha, China*
[4]*National Lab for Parallel and Distributed Processing, National University of Defense Technology, Changsha, China*
[5] *Institute of Electronic Information Warfare, Naval University of Engineering, Wuhan, China*
[1] nieguhong15@nudt.edu.cn,[2] zhangpeng14f@nudt.edu.cn, [3]niuxin@nudt.edu.cn, [4]yongdou@nudt.edu.cn, [5] xcyphoenix@nudt.edu.cn

Abstract: Ship detection in satellite images is a challenging task. In this paper, we introduce a transfer learned Single Shot MultiBox Detector (SSD) for ship detection. To this end, a state-of-the-art object detection model pre-trained from a large number of natural images was transfer learned for ship detection with limited labeled satellite images. To the best of our knowledge, this could be one of the first studies which introduce SSD into ship detection on satellite images. Experiments demonstrated that our method could achieve 87.9% AP at 47 FPS using NVIDIA TITAN X. In comparison with Faster R-CNN, 6.7% AP improvement could be achieved. Effects of the observation resolution has also been studied with the changing input sizes among 300 x 300, 600 x 600 and 900 x 900. It has been noted that the detection accuracy declined sharply with the decreasing resolution that is mainly caused by the missing small ships.

1. Introduction

Ship detection from satellite imagery plays an important role in the maritime surveillance, e.g. traffic monitoring, fishing management, oil pollution control etc. In the past few years, with the development of remote sensing technologies, the optical satellites can provide optical imagery with high resolution, making ship detection in optical satellite images a hotspot. There is some prior knowledge about the ships in satellite images: (1) the shape of ship is rectangle, with small width and large height, (2) the length of ships is in large various, (3) complex surroundings, including open water and harbor, (4) ship directions are almost in a circle unit. All the above make the ship detection become a challenging task.

The object detection task is usually composed of feature extraction and classification. Like other object detection tasks, the ship detection performance is proportional to the description ability of ship features. According to the feature extraction method, the previous work on ship detection can be classified into two groups, handcraft feature and machine learning feature.

Over the handcraft feature, researchers proposed some adaptive feature extraction methods according to the expert knowledge about the ship in satellite imagery. Some ships are just a few pixels in size in satellite images, and the ships may be highly blurred, leaving only object outlines as differentiable. So the handcraft feature approaches for ship detection are often based on shape, edge, and texture features [1]. However, the description ability of the handcraft feature is limited to the human cognition. There are still many deviations in the human cognition over the underlying feature. Besides, the hand-craft feature approaches have poor generalization ability. When the application scene is not uniform or the images are polluted by noise, the detection performance may be affected. The HOG-based classifiers [2] [3] [4] may break down in crowded or complex scenes. Due to the variety of ship size, the handcraft feature approaches may also lead to poor performance for ship detection.

On the other side, machine learning feature makes a great profit for object detection. These approaches take advantage of some prior knowledge, automatically learn image features, and find potential object characters and the distribution rules over the object which cannot be described by human cognition. Recent years, the machine learning has opened up prospects for superior image classification and detection, especially the success of deep CNN since 2012 [5]. Zhu et al. [6] explored orientation robust features from combined layers of DCNN for object detection in aerial image. Tang and Deng et al. [7] proposed compressed domain ship detection system using deep neural network and extreme learning machine (ELM) [8]. However, the existing ship detection methods using DNN utilize the features from top layer. While the ships are only a few pixels in size or blurred, the model may

DOI: 10.1051/itmconf/20171201006

generate false candidates confused by small islands, harbors etc.

The deep learning (DL) algorithm automatically extracts the representative and discriminative feature from bottom level (e.g. edge and texture) to top level (underlying feature) in a hierarchical manner and turns to be a hotspot in machine learning [9]. Current state-of-the-art object detection systems using deep learning are variants of the following approach: hypothesize bounding boxes, resample pixels or features for each box, and apply a high quality classifier. The methods of generating candidate boxes in Region-Based Convolutional Networks (R-CNN) [10] can be Selective Search [11], EdgeBox [12] or BING [13], but they are similar to sliding window essentially. Though SPP-NET [14], Fast R-CNN [15] and Faster R-CNN [16] extract features from convolutional layer and avoid the large amount of repeated convolution computation for every candidate region. There are still many unnecessary search, resulting in a large amount of computation. The Fast and Faster R-CNN adapt regression learning method to amend the object position. YOLO [17] and SSD [18] generate object position and category from the network directly.

There are some differences between satellite images and natural images. Firstly, the range of satellite images usually covers a large area, which is much larger than natural images, and the object size in the satellite images is much smaller. Secondly, the satellite images are simpler. The satellite images are taken in nearly constant zenith view angle along with simple surroundings. Besides, the direction of objects in satellite images is in circle. Nevertheless, the optical satellite images still share common visual features in low and middle abstract levels with natural images.

SSD, a fully convolutional network, discretizes the output space of bounding boxes into a set of default boxes over different aspect ratios and scales per feature map location [18]. The SSD achieved state-of-the-art detection performance on the PASCAL VOC, MS COCO, and ILSVRC datasets. During the ship detection task, the shape of ships is simple, but the size scale is large. Combined with the feature map from different layers, we can project the ship feature to different layers according to the ship size automatically.

To the best of our knowledge, this could be one of the first studies which introduce SSD into ship detection on satellite images. The rest of this paper is organized as follows. In section II, we detail the ship detection methodology. In Section III, Experiments and analysis are shown. Finally, we conclude this paper in section IV.

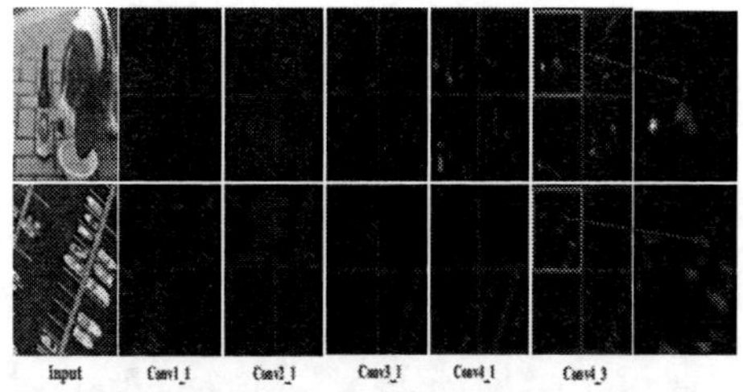

Figure 1. Feature maps from low to middle layers for natural and satellite image using pre-trained VGG-16

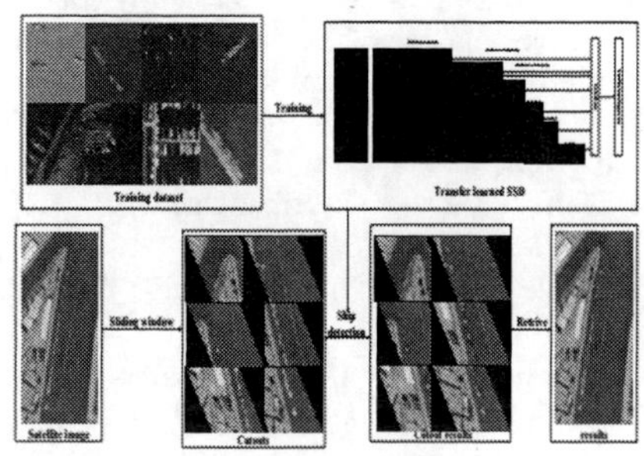

Figure 2. Framework of the ship detection

Figure 3. Transfer learned SSD architecture

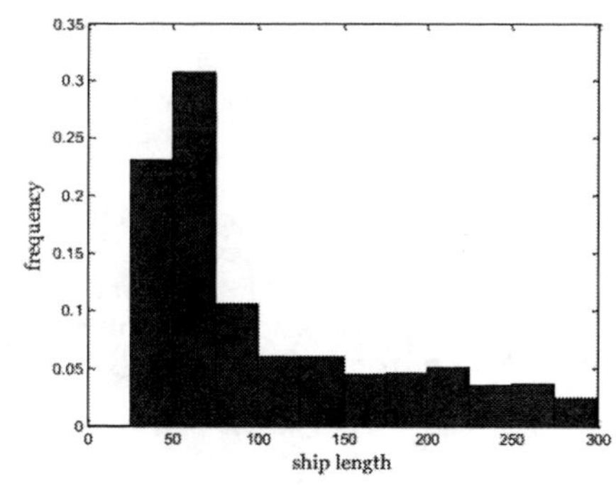

Figure 4. statistic of the ship length in satellite images.

2. Methodlogy

2.1 Framework

Though the satellite images are abundant, the original images are usually megapixel and the ships are small compared to the image range, which makes labeling work complex and complicated. Training an effective DNN model means to estimate millions of parameters, which requires a large number of labeled data. There is a fact that the convolutional neural networks provide means to learn rich low and middle level features transferrable to a variety of visual recognition tasks [19]. As is shown in Fig. 1, there are feature maps among conv1_1, con2_1, con3_1, con4_1 and conv4_3 for natural image and satellite image, using the pre-trained VGG-16 [21] model. We hypothesize that there are many common low and middle level visual features between satellite images and natural images. Transfer learning aims to transfer knowledge between related source and target domains [20]. Therefore, we transfer the SSD from natural images to satellite images domain. We use the transfer learned SSD for ship detection. The framework is shown in Fig. 2. The details of the transfer learned SSD are described later.

2.2 Details

As is shown in Fig. 3, our transfer learned SSD architecture is based on a feed-forward CNN. The number of labeled satellite images is limit and is not sufficient to train an effective DNN. We extract the low and middle level visual feature with the pre-trained base network of VGG-16. Fig. 4 shows the statistic on ship length in the satellite images. The size of ships is multi-scale. We concatenate the end of truncated base network with convolutional feature layers, which decrease in size. The reception filed of those layers is different. The multi-scale problem can be solved by utilizing the feature map from different layers. For each Extra feature layer (or the top layer in the base network), we can produce a fixed set of detection prediction, including the scores for each class, and the offsets of the bounding boxes, using a set of small convolutional filters. In the architecture, the filter size is 3 x 3. For a layer with m x n x p feature map, a 3 x 3 x p small kernel can produce a score for a class or the bounding box offset. The ships in the satellite images usually moored in a circle unit. We choose some default aspect ratios for ship detection. As is shown in Fig. 3, we use Conv4_3, Conv6 (FC6), Conv7 (FC7), Conv8_2, Conv9_2, Conv10_2 and pool11 to generate the ship confidence and offsets relative to the default box. In the end, we use the non-maximum suppression (NMS) step to produce the final detections.

3. Experiment

Our database contains 206 images covering the harbor or open water. All the satellite images were collected from Google Earth with 0.54m ground sample distance (GSD). And the images are taken near the Pacific and the Atlantic States. The image size is various, ranging from 900 x 900 to 3600 x 5400. For each of the original satellite images, we cut it in a fixed size using sliding window. A total of 138 original images and 3898 ships were used as a training set. A total of 34 original images and 1265 ships were used as the validation set. The others containing 34 original images and 1383 ships were used as the test set.

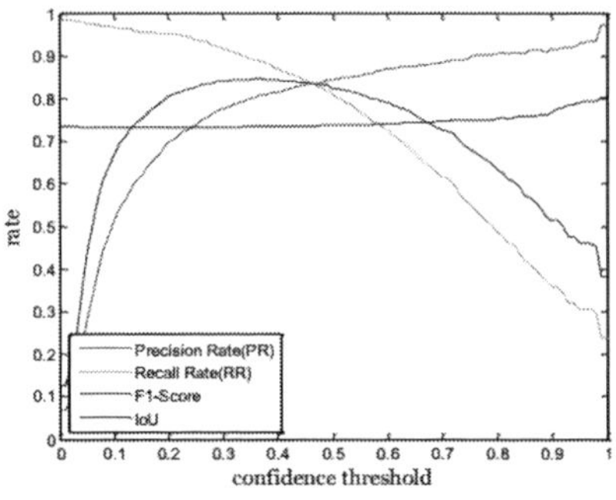

Figure 5. Ship detection result in our ship test set with original pixel.

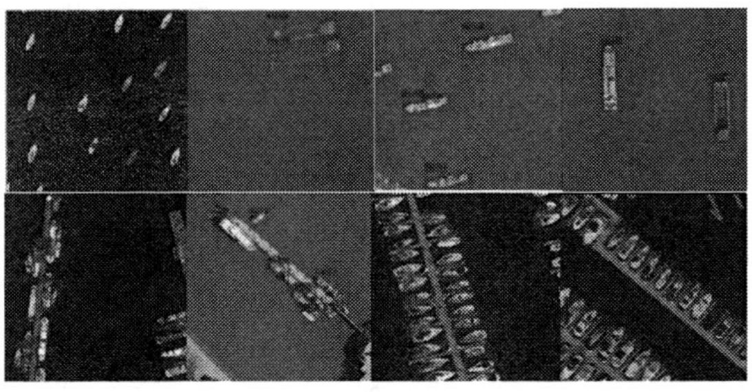

Figure 6. Some detection result by transfer learned SSD in open water

and harbor. The four images in the first row are the detection results in the open water, and the other four images in the second row is the detection results in the harbor.

Table1. Detection Result Using Transfer Learned Ssd

Detection result	Given Recall Rate					
	95.0 %	*90.0 %*	*85.0 %*	*80.0 %*	*75.0 %*	*70.0 %*
Precision Rate	71.0 %	79.2 %	82.6 %	84.5 %	85.9 %	87.5 %
F1-Score	0.813	0.843	0.838	0.822	0.801	0.778
IOU	0.732	0.734	0.736	0.737	0.739	0.743

3.1 Ship Detection Using Transfer Learned SSD

The input size of the transfer learned SSD in our framework is 300 x 300. All the input images in our framework will be resized to the fixed size. We use the original image pixels and cut the satellite images with 300 x 300 scale using sliding window method. The precision rate (PR), recall rate (RR) and F1-Score are defined as (1).

$$\begin{cases} PR = \frac{number\ of\ detected\ ships}{number\ of\ detected\ objects} \\ RR = \frac{number\ of\ detected\ ships}{number\ of\ ships} \\ F1 - Score = \frac{2\times PR\times RR}{PR+RR} \end{cases} \quad (1)$$

A ship is detected when the intersection-over-union (IoU) between candidate bounding box and the actual object rectangle is bigger than 0.45. Fig. 5 shows the ship detection results in the test set, including precision rate, recall rate, F1-Score and IoU. The IoU is high, which is above 0.73. Given the confidence threshold = 0.45, we have PR = 82.8%, RR = 84.9%, F1-Score = 0.838 and IOU = 0.736. Fig. 6 shows some detection results by our transfer learned SSD in open water and harbor. Table I lists the details of the detection results given the recall rate.

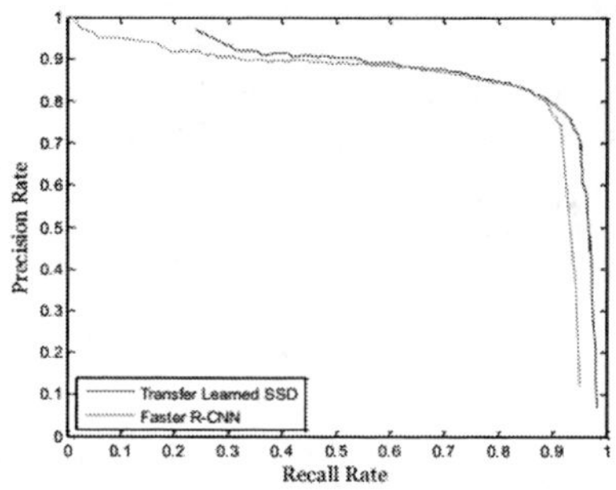

Figure 7. The Recall-Precision-Curves (RPC) of Transfer learned SSD and Faster R-CNN in our ship test set.

Table2. Detection Results of Transfer Learned Ssd and Faster R-Cnn

Method	AP	FPS
Transfer learned SSD	87.9%	47
Faster R-CNN	81.2%	6

Fig. 6 shows the Recall-Precision-Curve of Faster R-CNN and Transfer learned SSD in our ship test set. Table II shows the comparison between transfer learned SSD and Faster R-CNN. Both methods use the VGG-16 as base network. Our computing platform consists of a CPU of Intel i7-4970K and a GPU of NVIDIA TITAN X. In our experiment, our transfer learned SSD method outperformed the Faster R-CNN in both accuracy and speed. Our transfer learned SSD achieved 87.9% average performance (AP) at 47 FPS. In comparison with Faster R-CNN, 6.7% AP improvement could be achieved.

For the ship detection task in the satellite images, the ship size is varied, and a large number of ships are only a few pixels in size. Faster R-CNN only uses the feature map from the top layer. Because of the pooling and up-sampling, the information of small ship may vanish and be lost, leading to some missing detections. On the contrary, our framework utilizes the feature map from multi-layers and deals well with the multi-scale problem. The faster R-CNN framework is composed of region proposal generation, feature extraction, classification and location refine. Our framework eliminates the proposal generation, pixel resampling or feature resampling stage, and utilizes small convolutional filter to predict category and offsets of the default bounding boxes, which reduce the computation.

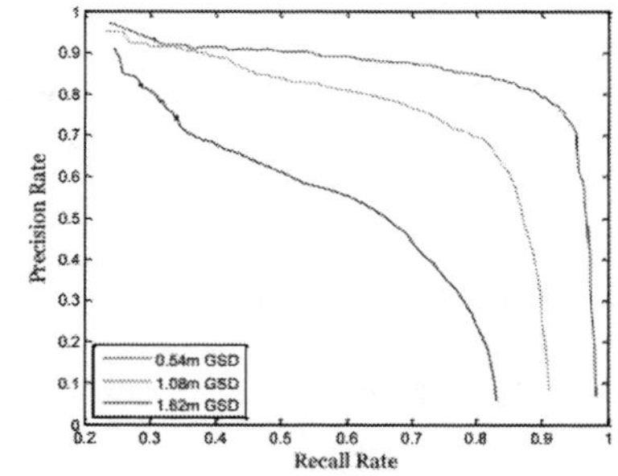

Figure 8. The Recall-Precision-Curves (RPC) of Transfer learned SSD with images in different spatial resolution.

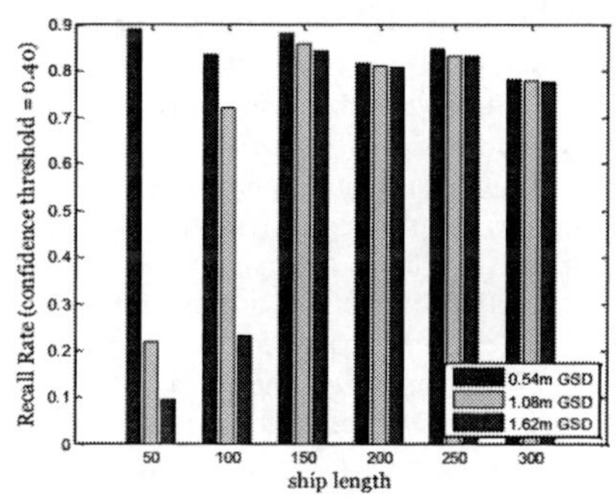

Figure 9. Given the confidence threshold = 0.40, the recall rate for each ship group in different resolution.

Table3. The ap in different spatial resolution

Detection result	0.54m GSD	1.08m GSD	1.62m GSD
AP	87.9%	72.6%	57.9%

3.2 Effect of Resolution on Ship Detection Accuracy

The input size of the transfer learned SSD in our framework is 300 x 300. All the input images will resize to the fixed size. In order to examine the effect of resolution on ship detection, we form the database by cutting the original satellite image with the size with 300 x 300, 600 x 600 and 900 x 900 individually. The original collected images are 0.54m GSD. Thus, after the resize operation, the 600 x 600 and 900 x 900 cutouts are 1.08m and 1.62m GSD individually. Fig. 7 shows the Recall-Precision-Curve (RPC) of our ship detection framework with images in different resolution. Table III shows the AP of ship detection in different spatial resolution. The detection accuracy declined sharply with the decreasing resolution. In order to further explore this phenomenon, we divided the ships into 6 groups according to the ship length, and then count recall rate for each group. Fig. 8 shows the comparison of recall rate for each group in different spatial resolution. From the chart, we can see that the recall rate declines sharply when the ship length is less than 100 and declines gradually when the ship length is over 100. Though our method predicts the category and offsets of bounding box with the feature map from different layers, the lowest layer for prediction is Conv_4_3 and the feature map size is 38 x 38 x 512. The reception field in this layer is 92 x 92. The ship size declines with decreasing resolution. The visual feature of ships with few pixels may vanish and lose when it passes through many layers, resulting in low recall rate.

4. Conclusions

This paper introduces a transfer learned SSD that transfers visual knowledge between natural image and satellite image. We use the feature map from different layers to predict category and offsets of default box, which deals well with the multi-scale problem. Compared with some other DNN methods, our framework leverages a fully convolutional network and eliminates the proposal generation, pixel resampling or feature resampling stage, which reduces the computation. Experiments demonstrated that our method achieved state-of-the-art ship detection performance and could satisfy the real-time requirements. We investigated the effects of resolution on ship detection performance. There is a sharp degradation for small ships and almost no change for big ships.

Acknowledgment

We acknowledge support by the National Natural Science Foundation of China under Grants of U1435219 and 61402507.

References

[1] C. Zhu, H. Zhou, R. Wang, and J. Guo, "A novel hierarchical method of ship detection from spaceborne optical image based on shape and texture features," Geoscience and Remote Sensing, IEEE Transactions on, vol. 48, no. 9, pp. 3446–3456, 2010.

[2] N. Dalal and B. Triggs, "Histograms of oriented gradients for human detection," in Computer Vision and Pattern Recognition, 2005. CVPR 2005. IEEE Computer Society Conference on, vol. 1. IEEE, 2005, pp. 886–893.

[3] X. X. Bao, S. S. Zinger, D. P. P. With, R. R. Wijnhoven, and J. J. Han, "Water region and multiple ship detection for port surveillance," in Proc. the 33rd WIC Symposium on Information Theory in the Benelux, 2012.

[4] Gan, Lu, P. Liu, and L. Wang. "Rotation Sliding Window of the Hog Feature in Remote Sensing Images for Ship Detection," International Symposium on Computational Intelligence and Design IEEE, 2015:401-404.

[5] Krizhevsky, Alex, I. Sutskever, and G. E. Hinton. "ImageNet classification with deep convolutional neural networks," International Conference on Neural Information Processing Systems Curran Associates Inc. 2012:1097-1105.

[6] Zhu, H., et al. "Orientation robust object detection in aerial images using deep convolutional neural network," IEEE International Conference on Image Processing IEEE, 2015:3735-3739.

[7] J. Tang, C. Deng, and G. B. Huang. "Compressed-Domain Ship Detection on Spaceborne Optical Image Using Deep Neural Network and Extreme Learning Machine," IEEE Transactions on Geoscience & Remote Sensing 53.3(2015):1174-1185.

[8] G. B. Huang, Q. Y. Zhu, and C. K. Siew, "Extreme learning machine: Theory and applications," Neurocomputing, vol. 70, no. 1–3, pp. 489–501, Dec. 2006.

[9] L. Zhang, L. Zhang, and B. Du. "Deep Learning for Remote Sensing Data: A Technical Tutorial on the State of the Art," IEEE Geoscience & Remote Sensing Magazine 4.2(2016):22-40.

[10] R. Girshick, J. Donahue, T. Darrell, et al. "Region-Based Convolutional Networks for Accurate Object Detection and Segmentation," IEEE Transactions on Pattern Analysis & Machine Intelligence 38.1(2016):142-158.

[11] J. Uijlings, K. van de Sande, T. Gevers, and A. Smeulders. "Selective Search for Object Recognition[J]," International Journal of Computer Vision, 2013, 104(2):154-171.

[12] C. L. Zitnick and P. Dollár. "Edge Boxes: Locating Object Proposals from Edges," 8693(2014):391-405.

[13] M. M. Cheng, Z. Zhang, W. Y. Lin, et al. Cheng, Ming Ming, et al. "BING: Binarized Normed Gradients for Objectness Estimation at 300fps," (2014):3286-3293.

[14] K. He, X. Zhang, S. Ren, et al. "Spatial Pyramid Pooling in Deep Convolutional Networks for Visual Recognition," He, Kaiming, et al. "Spatial Pyramid Pooling in Deep Convolutional Networks for Visual Recognition." IEEE Transactions on Pattern Analysis & Machine Intelligence 37.9(2015):1904-1916.

[15] R. Girshick. "Fast R-CNN," Proceedings of the IEEE International Conference on Computer Vision. 2015: 1440-1448.

[16] S. Ren, K. He, R . Girshick, et al. "Faster R-CNN: Towards Real-Time Object Detection with Region Proposal Networks[J]," Computer Science, 2015:1-1.

[17] J. Redmon, S. Divvala, R. Girshick, et al. "You Only Look Once: Unified, Real-Time Object Detection[J]," Computer Science, 2015.

[18] W. Liu, D. Anguelov, D. Erhan, et al. "SSD: Single Shot MultiBox Detector[J]. 2016. "SSD: Single Shot MultiBox Detector[J]," (2016).

[19] M. Oquab, L. Bottou, I. Laptev, and J. Sivic, "Learning and transferring mid-level image representations using convolutional neural networks," in Proc. IEEE Comput. Vis. Pattern Recog., 2014, pp. 1717–1724.

[20] S. Pan and Q. Yang. "A survey on transfer learning. Knowledge and Data Engineering," IEEE Transactions on, 22(10):1345–1359, 2010. 2

[21] K. Simonyan, A. Zisserman. "Very deep convolutional networks for large-scale image re

[22] cognition," Computer Science, 2015.

A Role Based Framework for Robot Sensor Management

Ran WANG[1], Xiao-Dong LV[2], Dian-Xi SHI[3], Zhe-Hang TONG[4]

[1]*National Lab for Parallel and Distributed Processing, National University of Defense Technology, Changsha, China*
[2]*National Lab for Parallel and Distributed Processing, National University of Defense Technology, Changsha, China*
[3]*National Lab for Parallel and Distributed Processing, National University of Defense Technology, Changsha, China*
4National Lab for Parallel and Distributed Processing, National University of Defense Technology, Changsha, China
[1]*532576041@qq.com,* [2]*lxdnogfly@sina.com,* [3]*dxshi@nudt.edu.cn,* [4]*zhehangt@163.com*

Abstract: Sensors play an important role in the execution of robot tasks as an important component of understanding the world. In this paper, we propose a role-based sensor management framework on ROS (Robot Operating System), in which the role is a set of information needed for robot sensor development. Firstly, we develop a sensor management interface to facilitate the development of sensor applications on robot. And a subscriber module is proposed to shield the details of the sensor driver and the communication between processes, the sensor drivers on the robot are effectively managed. Robot sensors have different executive ability in different situations when robot performing tasks. For example, we know that RGB camera can collect a clear image when the light is strong, while generate a blurred image in weak light environment. Secondly, we propose an environment based sensor role dynamic evaluation mechanism to get the confidence of sensor in a certain environment. The confidence represents the executive ability of sensor when performing tasks. The confidence provides the basis for switching the task schemes. In the mechanism we can dynamically configure the environment information and confidence calculation method. In the experiment phase, we verify the effectiveness of the framework through a robot patrol task. Experiment results show that our framework can effectively manage the robot sensors with a certain environmental adaptability.

1. Introduction

With the rapid development of robot technology, different types of robots in different platforms emerge in an endless stream. Robots are used in different fields, such as industry, education, entertainment, service and so on [1]. Sensors play an important role in the execution of robot tasks as an important component of understanding the world. The development of sensor technology have greatly improved the perception ability of robot. Intelligent robots are often equipped with a large number of different types of sensors to detect the environments and collect the data. It is of great significance for development of robot sensor application to manage sensors on the robot effectively. Robot needs an intelligent sensor interface for gathering the data [2]. As the most popular robot operating system, ROS (robot operating system) [3] [4] provides a unified communication architecture for heterogeneous sensors data acquisition. However, as far as the author knows, ROS does not provide a unified management method or framework for different robot sensors. We do not know a lot of information for the development of sensor applications, such as sensors the robot has, related information of sensors, sensors that are performing tasks and so on. In ROS, the process of inter-process communication is carried out through the publish/subscribe mode to get the sensor data. The developer needs to know the related topics and messages of the hardware driver. Different sensors have different hardware drivers and publish different topics and messages. Sensors of the same type may also publish different topics due to different manufacturers and driver developers. We need to understand information of underlying drivers to obtain the sensor information and data. It is advisable for developers to get sensor information directly without knowing the details of the inter-process communication. Shielding details of hardware driver and communication between processes are critical to a sensor management framework. We present the concept of sensor roles to represent the set of information needed in the development of robot sensors applications and a subscriber module to shield the sensor hardware driver details.

The environments in which the robot performs the task are complex. In the real world, it is necessary to take into account the robot's attributes and environmental uncertainties [5]. Task execution ability of sensors varies in different environments [6] [7]. For example, when robot performs patrol and reconnaissance tasks, in the case of adequate light the RGB camera has a strong task execution ability and can collect better data; while in the case of insufficient light, it is better to use infrared camera to collect data. In order to express the task execution ability of sensor in a certain environment, sensor confidence is added to the sensor role. The confidence information can provides basis for switching task schemes and multi-sensor data fusion.

In this paper, we propose a role-based sensor management framework on ROS, which shields the details of sensor hardware drivers and the inter-process communication. In order to facilitate the development of sensor applications we present the concept of sensor role which is a set of information for sensor development. In order to express the capability of task execution, confidence information is added to the sensor role. This paper designs a sensor dynamic evaluation mechanism, which can obtain the real time role confidence by configuring the related environment information and the confidence calculation function in the confidence rule file. The structure of this paper is as follows: Section 1 introduces the research background and organizational structure; Section 2 analyzes the related work; Section 3 outlines the overall design of this framework; Section 4 details the relevant modules of this framework; Section 5 verifies the effectiveness of the framework by a robot patrol task; Section 6 summarizes the thesis.

2. Related Work

2.1 ROS

ROS is the most popular open source robot operating system, the emergence of ROS has greatly promoted the research of robot and code reuse in robot application development. Process exists as a node in ROS and the communications infrastructure of ROS provides the ability to communicate across processes for nodes. A robot system consists of multiple nodes, and the most common communication pattern between nodes is publish/subscribe mode, as shown in Figure 1. For sensor data acquisition, the sensor drivers are equivalent to the Pub nodes and the applications are equivalent to the Sub nodes. In addition, ROS also provides a service communication mechanism which is similar to RPC (remote procedure call).

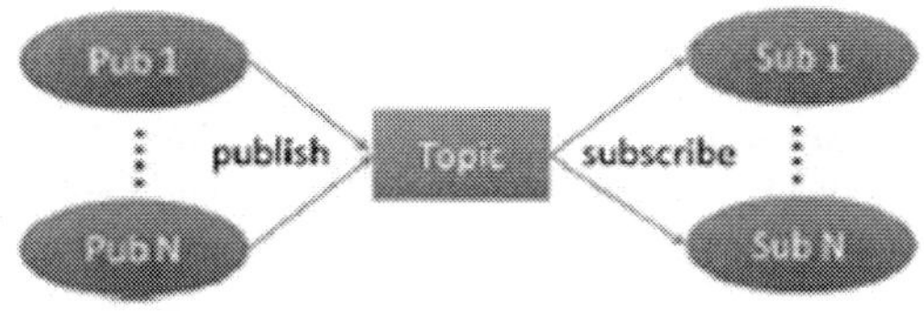

Figure 1. Publish subscribe communication

2.2 Android Sensor Management

Android as the most popular portable device operating system provides a good manner to get the sensor information for different hardware devices. And android provides a unified user access interface [8]. Figure 2 shows a very simplified sensor management architecture in android. Android shields the hardware heterogeneity through HAL layer (hardware abstraction layer). The well-established sensor architecture makes Android a robust platform for perceptual applications.

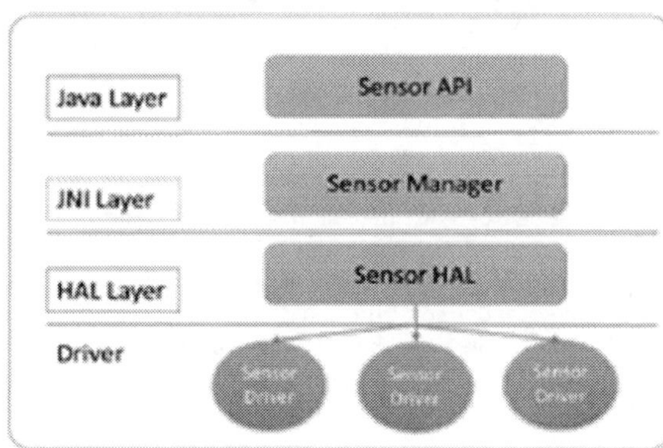

Figure 2. Publish subscribe communication

2.3 Classic Sensor Management

A good sensor management system can dynamically manage the sensor resources and change sensor configuration through the results of sensing [9]. There are many methods for sensor management. In [10] and [11], the temporal characteristics of sensor management are presented and the sequence decision process is described as a general Markov process. In [12], a sensor management framework for mobile robot is established using Bayesian Confidence Network and decision theory. In [13], the Boolean matrix is defined based on the sensor capability and effectiveness, and predict the task performance using the sensor performance model and then select the sensor model beneficial to the goal. In [14], knowledge reasoning and fuzzy theory are applied to sensor management which achieve some effects. There are many classic sensor management methods, and the goal of sensor management system is to complete the task effectively and improve the accuracy of the information fusion system [15]. We have done the following work with reference to the idea of Android sensor management architecture and the classic sensor management methods: (1) we provide a subscriber module to shield sensor hardware driver details on ROS; (2) the sensor confidence is introduced to represent the task execution ability of the sensor; (3) an environment based sensor dynamic evaluation mechanism is designed to obtain the confidence.

3. Overall Framework Design

3.1 Role Definition

In order to provide a general sensor management framework for robots, we present the concept of sensor role. Sensor role is a set of information needed for robot sensor application development and we introduce confidence to sensor role to express the task execution capability of sensor. Sensor role is dynamic and environment related. Sensor role contains five parts, namely, attributes, capabilities, platform, configuration information and confidence, as shown in Figure 3. The role attributes are inherent information of sensor, including sensor name, identifier, device manufacturer, version, and encapsulated sensor topic with corresponding message. The role ability represent the function and strength of sensor, including sensor type, detection range, maximum sampling frequency, maximum resolution and power. The role platform represents the platform where the sensor performs the task, including land, sea and air. The role configuration information represents the configuration parameter for data acquisition, including sampling frequency and resolution. The role confidence indicates the task execution capability of the sensor in the current environment which includes the confidence value and the name of confidence rule file. The confidence rule file includes the name of environment information and confidence calculation method. The sensor role has two states, the development state and running state. The sensor role exists in the form of XML file during developing state and in the form of object during running state. The sensor role file corresponds to the sensor on the robot.

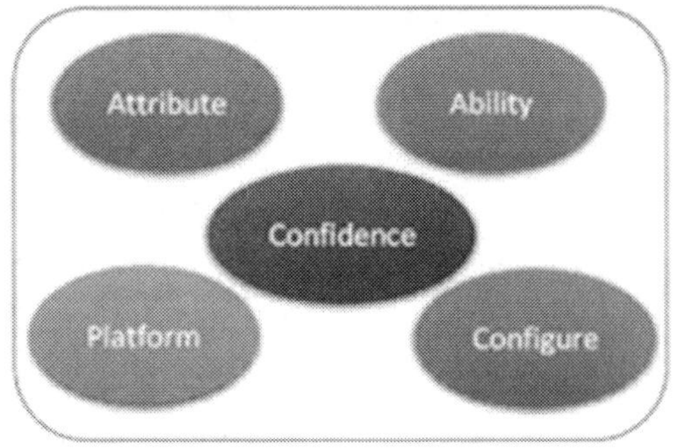

Figure 3. Sensor role definition

3.2 Overall Architecture Design

The overall architecture of the role-based robot sensor management framework is shown in Figure 4. The framework includes three parts, role catalog module, sensor manager module and dynamic evaluation mechanism module. Role catalog module is responsible for three parts, conversion between role file and role object, management of the sensor role object and roles in performing the task. All the role objects are added to the role list. And sensors that need to acquire the data are added to the task list. We manage the sensor role object and roles in performing the task through processing these lists.

Sensor manager module directly interacts with the application layer, and with this module developers can easily get the role-related information. Sensor manager provide four kinds of operations, including get the information about the sensor, register and unregister the sensor, select the sensor to be evaluated, and set the environment monitoring frequency. If we select the role to be evaluated, the dynamic role evaluation mechanism will be activated, and then we can get the real time confidence of the sensor. We can set the environment monitoring frequency, this frequency indicates how long it will take to reevaluate the sensor.

The dynamic evaluation mechanism includes two parts, role evaluation module and environment monitor. Role evaluation module is used to calculate the confidence of the sensor. And environment monitor is a thread, which is used to inform the role evaluation module to reevaluate the sensor at a fix frequency. Role evaluation involves two aspects, environment abstract and confidence rules. Environment abstract module is used to get the value of the concrete environment information. For example how much Lux is the light intensity, how high is the barometric altitude. The confidence rules include what environment information and confidence calculation method we need to calculate the confidence of the sensor. The developer can customize the environment information and confidence calculation method. In Section 4 we will detail the implementation of related modules.

 DOI: 10.1051/itmconf/20171201007

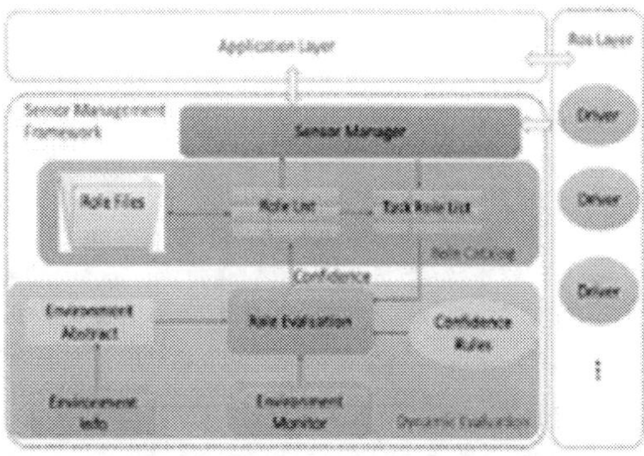

Figure 4. Overall architecture of the framework

4. Implementation Details

In this section we will detail the implementation of the framework. The whole framework is written in Python.

4.1 Role Catalog Module

Role catalog is responsible for three parts, conversion between role file and role object, management of the role list and management about the task role list. In the framework initialization phrase, role catalog module will resolve the role files and convert the files to objects. Developers can easy get the information of sensors with the object. The role list contains the objects of all the sensors on the robot. Once the developer set the sensor role needed to be evaluated, the object of the sensor role will be added to the task role list. The role evaluation related module will get the list, and makes a corresponding evaluation.

4.2 Sensor MANAGER

Sensor manager module is the unified interface interact with the application layer. The architecture of sensor manager is shown in figure 5. Sensor manager include three parts: unified info manager, subscribe module and the evaluation switch. The unified info manager can get the sensor related information from the role list, such as attributes, ability, confidence, and so on. Subscriber module is responsible for generate and start the subscribe thread and get the sensor data. Developer can use evaluation switch to get the sensor role evaluated. If we open the switch of the role sensor, the role will be added to the task role list. And roles in the task list will be evaluated. When we need to get data, we just need to register sensor with the sensor name and the callback function pointer without caring about the topic name and message of the sensor driver. We don't need to change the code of data acquisition when the hardware driver changes. The timing diagram of data acquisition is shown in Figure 6. When we initialize the framework, at first the unified info manager will inform the catalog module to create the role object collection. Then the unified info manager will get the topic and message from the sensor object, subscriber module will generate the subscriber thread object with the topic and other parameters configured. At last of the initialization phrase the unified info will get the role subscriber thread objects of all sensor roles on the robot. When we register the sensor, the unified info manager will set the listener which is the pointer of callback function, and then start the subscriber thread. The subscriber module will get the sensor data from the topic and pass it to the listener.

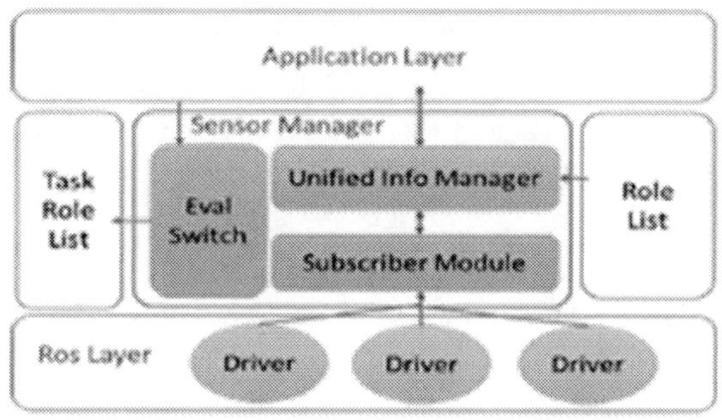

Figure 5. Sensor manager architecture

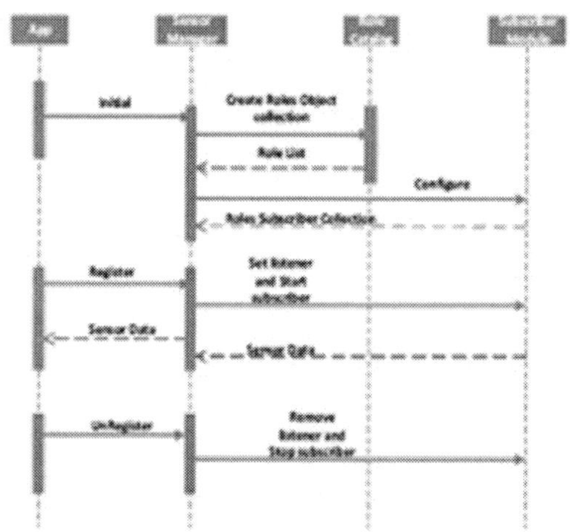

Figure 6. Timing diagram of data acquisition

4.3 Dynamic Evaluation Mechanism

The evaluation mechanism is a real time mechanism because we are monitoring the environment and constantly reevaluate the sensor. This mechanism includes two parts: sensor role evaluation and environment monitor. The process of role evaluation is as follows, at first the role evaluation module will get the sensor to be evaluated from the task role list and then get the name of confidence rule file. In order to dynamically change the environment information and confidence methods, we use XML file to define the confidence rules. The role evaluation module will analyzes the file and get the environment name and the confidence method name. And then the role evaluation module will find the related functions with these names. Functions about environment information acquisition are in the environment abstract module and confidence calculation methods are in the role evaluation module. After get the related function, the role evaluation module can get the environment value from the environment abstract module, and then input the environment value to the confidence calculation method to get the confidence. If the framework have integrated enough environment abstract and confidence calculation methods, the developer could get the evaluation results just through configuring the confidence rule file. By now we have developed some related method for some tasks. For example, related methods about collecting image data under different illumination conditions and high accuracy height measurement of low level UAV (unmanned aerial vehicle).

5. Experiments and Results

In the experiment phrase, we verify the effectiveness of the framework through a robot patrol and image collection task.

5.1 Experiment Setup

There are three equipment in the experiment, a Turtlebot robot equipped with a Kinect, a laptop with ROS installed, and an android phone. The model of the android is Samsung galaxy S5. The experimental scenario is shown in Figure 7. In the room, the light intensity is strong in one side and weak in the other side. Smartphone has equipped with a lot of sensors, in this experiment we will use some sensor of the smartphone to sensing the environment.

Figure 7. Experimental scenario

5.2 Experiment Deatails

The robot will patrol to collect image data in the room. The robot will collect RGB image with RGB camera in the side where the light intensity is strong and disparity map with depth camera in the other side.

In the development phrase, at first we need to configure the environment information and confidence calculation method in the confidence rule file. The confidence rule file of RGB camera is shown in Figure 8. By now, we just use light information to evaluate the camera. And the light data is sent by the phone with standard ROS message format. Our core work is not to study specific evaluation algorithms, therefore our evaluation method is relatively simple. In confidence calculation method, we take 24 Lux as the threshold of light intensity. When the light intensity is higher than the threshold, we will set the confidence of RGB camera to 1.0, and otherwise the confidence will be set to 0.0. The depth camera is just opposite. We will get the data and other information with the unified sensor manager interface. The collected image data is shown in Figure 9.

Results of the experiment show that our sensor manager framework could effectively facilitate the development of sensor application.

DOI: 10.1051/itmconf/20171201007

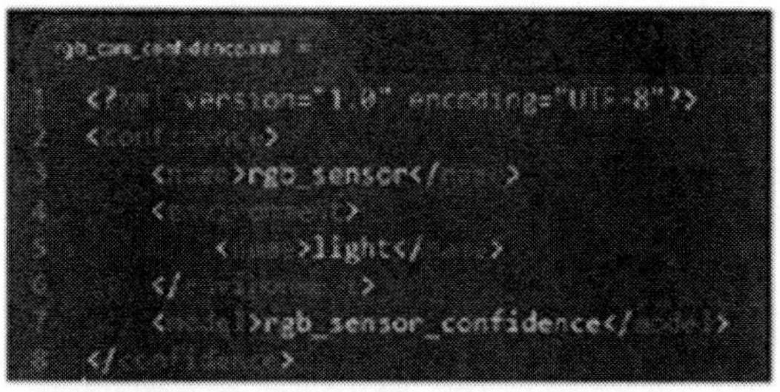

Figure 8. Confidence rule file of RGB camera

Figure 9. (a)RGB image

Figure 9. (b) Disparity map

6. Conclusions and Future Work

This paper proposed a role-based unified sensor management framework on ROS to facilitate the development of sensor applications. We propose the concept of sensor role to represent the set of information needed for the development of the robot sensor. Developers can get the related information through the unified interface named sensor manager. We proposed a subscriber module to shield the details of topic and message. Developers can use the same data acquisition code without caring the type of the driver and the topics. We introduce confidence to represent the task execution ability of the sensor and propose an environment-related dynamic evaluation mechanism to get the real time confidence of the sensor. We development some functions of evaluation abstraction and confidence calculation, developers can use different confidence calculation function just through configuring the confidence rule file. We have verified the effectiveness of the framework through a robot patrol task. In the future, we will develop more experiment abstraction and confidence calculation functions to support more tasks.

References

[1] Al-Razgan M, Alfallaj L F, Alsarhani N S, et al. Systematic Review of Robotics Use Since 2005[J]. International Journal of Mechanical Engineering and Robotics Research, 2016, 5(2): 129.

[2] Kumar Y B, Ilaiyaraja S. Smart interface for sensors in robot[C]// Sixth International Conference on Advanced Computing. IEEE, 2014:145-149.

[3] Quigley M, Conley K, Gerkey B, et al. ROS: an open-source Robot Operating System[C]//ICRA workshop on open source software. 2009, 3(3.2): 5

[4] "ROS" [Online]. Available: Available: http://www.ros.org

[5] Suzuki S, Habib M K, Iijima J, et al. How to describe the mobile robot's sensor-based behavior?[J]. Robotics & Autonomous Systems, 2015, 7(2-3):227-237.

[6] Murphy T B, Morison A. Affordances as a Means to Assess Human-Sensor-Robot Performance[C]// Human Factors and Ergonomics Society Meeting. 2016:1610-1611.

[7] Tsung T T, Hoai N. Dynamic Performance Measurement of Proximity Sensors for a Mobile Robot[J]. Key Engineering Materials, 2014, 625(625):683-688.

[8] Yan Y, Cosgrove S, Blantont E, et al. Real-Time Sensing on Android[C]// International Workshop on Java Technologies for Real-Time and Embedded Systems. ACM, 2014:67.

[9] Hero A O, Cochran D. Sensor Management: Past, Present, and Future[J]. IEEE Sensors Journal, 2011, 11(12):3064-3075.

[10]Malhotra R. Temporal considerations in sensor management[J]. 1995, 1:86-93 vol.1.

[11]Meier L, Peschon J, Dressler R. Optimal control of measurement subsystems[J]. IEEE Transactions on Automatic Control, 1967, 12(5):528-536.

[12]Schenker P S. Sensor models and a framework for sensor management[J]. Proceedings of SPIE - The International Society for Optical Engineering, 1993.

[13]Rothman P L, Bier S G. Evaluation of sensor management systems[C]// Aerospace and Electronics Conference, 1989. NAECON 1989. Proceedings of the IEEE 1989 National. IEEE, 1989:1747-1752 vol.4.

[14]Molina Lopez J M, Jimenez Rodriguez S J, Corredera J R C. Fuzzy reasoning for multisensor management[C]// IEEE International Conference on Systems, Man and Cybernetics, 1995. Intelligent Systems for the, Century. IEEE Xplore, 1995:1398-140

[15]Xiong N, Svensson P. Multi-sensor management for information fusion: issues and approaches[J]. Inf

[16]ormation Fusion, 2002, 3(2):163-186.

ITM Web of Conferences 12, 01008 (2017) DOI: 10.1051/itmconf/20171201008
ITA 2017

The Study of Graininess for Tibetan Named Entity Recognition

Fei-Fei Liu[1,2,a], Zhi-Juan Wang[1,2,b*]

[1]*School of Information Engineering, Minzu University of China, Beijing, China*
[2]. *National Language Resource Monitoring & Research Center of Minority Languages, Beijing, China*
[1]*Liufeifei_muc@163.com,* [2]*wangzj_muc@126.com*

Abstract: Tibetan named entity recognition (NER), which is a fundamental part in Tibetan natural language processing, is the important subtask of Information extraction. In this paper, we surveyed the methods, effect and problems of Tibetan NER. And we discussed which kind of tokens that should be taken as the graininess for Tibetan NER task. The paper used two kinds of different graininess in a comparative experiment for Tibetan person names, location names and organization names, based on syllables, or based on words. From the result, we know that the person names based on syllable have better result than that based on words. Location names have small difference while species differ. But the organization names are more suitable based on words.

1. Introduction

Named entity recognition (NER) (also known as entity identification, entity chunking and entity extraction) is a subtask of information extraction that seeks to locate and classify named entities in text into pre-defined categories such as the names of persons, locations, organizations, expressions of times, quantities, monetary values, percentages, etc. Tibetan NER is the fundamental and key subtask for Tibetan information extraction and text mining in Tibetan natural language processing.

Nowadays, named entity recognition had achieved good results in various languages, such as English. State-of-the-art NER systems for English produce near-human performance. For example, the best system entering MUC-7 scored 93.39% of F-measure while human annotators scored 97.60% and 96.95%. However, Tibetan NER started late. It has yielded a great number of positive results, but is still a new study field in which there are series of problems.

This paper will summarize the present situation of Tibetan NER, introduce the existing research methods, the results obtained and the existing problems. By summarizing the results of studies, we find out that there are two kinds of graininess for Tibetan NER, including syllables, and words. Syllables are the basic units in Tibetan, and words created by syllables based on word segmentation.

Then the paper discusses the granularity problem in Tibetan NER by a comparative experiment. In addition to the graininess, syllables or words, all attributes are the same for Tibetan person names, location names and organization names. By comparing the accuracy, recall, F-score, we will get the conclusion that which graininess is more suitable.

The rest of the paper is organized as follows: In section 2, we briefly describe the background of Tibetan NER, including current situation, difficulties, methods, problems and improvement direction. In section 3, we introduce the algorithm of Tibetan named entity recognition based on conditional random field(CRF), this method is used in our comparative experiments about graininess. We report in section 4 our experimental results and give our conclusions on this work in section 5.

2. Tibetan Named Entity Recognition

The basic work of Tibetan natural language processing (NLP) includes Tibetan word segmentation, Tibetan POS tagging and named entity recognition. Nowadays, there are many practical methods in Tibetan word segmentation, such as automatic Tibetan word segmentation scheme based on lattice auxiliary word and continuation feature [3], Tibetan language word segmentation system [4], SegT [5], Yangjin [6], TIP-LAS [7], but for Tibetan NER, the research conclusions are immature. As the fundamental part in Tibetan NLP, there are many aspects of the need for further study and improve in Tibetan NER.

2.1 Introduction to Tibetan

Tibetan (བོད་ཡིག) refers to the use of Tibetan language Tibetan. The glyph structure is a letter as the core, the rest of the letters are based on this before and after the

DOI: 10.1051/itmconf/20171201008

additional and overlapping from top to bottom, combined into a complete word table structure. Writing habits from left to right. The font is divided into "head" and "headless" two categories.

Tibetan is a phonetic alphabet, with 30 consonants and 4 vowels. One Tibetan syllable can have 1 to 7 basic characters, if you consider Sanskrit, characters may be more. The seven basic characters have a base character and a vowel, the other characters were added to the base word, the up, down, front, back, and then back[1][2].

There are fewer types of punctuation in Tibetan .Tibetan various syllables separate with a small point, this point named the syllable node (་).In addition to the syllable node, the most common punctuation is a single vertical line (།), as a full stop, colon and other situations. And the paragraph ends with a double vertical line (༎).

2.2 Methods of Tibetan NER

The methods of Tibetan NER can be divided into rule-based methods and based on supervised machine learning methods.

Rule-based methods

In the early days, the study of Tibetan NER was based on a rule-based approach. Yu et al. used a rule-based model based on case-auxiliary word and lexicon, and also adapt boundary information list static from large corpus to improve recognition. And experiments shows that recall rate and precise rate are respectively 90.13% and 94.02% in the newspaper corpus, 85.67% and 88.20% in the website text. Sun et al. used the internal features of names, contextual features and boundary features of names, and establishes the dictionary and feature base of Tibetan names. The results prove the algorithm is effective with 0.8391 F-score. Dou et al. used the Statistical Method of Mutual Information to, combining the rules of lattice auxiliary and the dictionary of person names, F value in the test can be up to 93.55%.

Supervised machine learning methods

After 2014, supervised machine learning methods are increasingly applied to Tibetan NER. Jia et al. came up with Maximum entropy (ME) and conditional random field(CRF), and the F-score of the recognition of names can be 92.08%. Hua et al. proposed a syllable features with Perceptron training model to identify Tibetan name entity with detail analysis NE structure rule and word segmentation ambiguity. The F-score of NE identification is 86.03% for the testset. Kang et al. defined a feature tag set to fit in with the characters of Tibetan names, used CRF as tagging model to train and test corpus data. The highest F-score obtained in the experiment can reach 94.31%. Zhu et al. studied Tibetan name recognition technology using conditional random fields (CRF) principle， focuses on analysis of the internal structure of the Tibetan names, contextual features, feature selection and data preprocessing, etc. and evaluated the effectiveness of different features through experiments. The recognition rate of Tibetan names can reach 80% of F-score.

2.3 Difficulties in Tibetan NER

Tibetan belongs to the Sino-Tibetan language family. In theory, the natural language processing methods used in Chinese can be used in Tibetan information processing. But in practice, it must be considered in the specific problems. The main difficulties in Tibetan NER are as follows:

Tibetan is a complex system of phonetic logic. The basic unit of the sentence is syllable. Syllables are separated by syllable node. One syllable or more syllables constitute words. There is no obvious mark between the word and next word. The boundaries of named entities are difficult to determine. And too few punctuation types, just single vertical line (།) and double vertical line (༎), will make the too long analysis object length, increasing the difficulty of recognition algorithm.

There is no morphological difference between named entities and unnamed entities in Tibetan. Unlike English, the person names, location names and organization names in English with the capitalized first letter, are easy to extract. And compared to Chinese person name, most of the Tibetans do not have the family name and the length of the name which can be from single syllable to twenty-six syllables.

The name dictionary, the labeled corpus and other related resources is insufficient. Nowadays, the main method of Tibetan Named Entity Recognition is supervised learning algorithms which require large-scale of labeled corpus. But Tibetan resource is not easy to obtain.

2.4 Summary of Tibetan NER

All kinds of methods are proven the feasibility and accuracy in the Tibetan NER. However, due to the different corpus of different methods, we cannot judge which method is better based on the experimental results alone. Today, the problems in Tibetan NER: the conflicts between Tibetan names and ordinary words, the misinterpretation of translations, and the difficulties in identifying Tibetan NE boundaries.

In the future, building a large amount of manually annotated training data is urgent for improving effect. It is necessary to improve the recognition accuracy of Tibetan named entities by using syntactic information, extending boundary information, making full use of boundary information, expanding the translation of the thesaurus, and testing other possible recognition models such as Support Vector Machine (SVM).

3. Tibetan NER based on CRF

3.1 Description

CRFs are a type of discriminative undirected probabilistic graphical model. It is used to encode known relationships between observations and construct consistent interpretations. It is often used for labeling or parsing of sequential data, such as natural language text.

Specifically, CRFs find applications in shallow parsing, named entity recognition.

Lafferty, McCallum and Pereira define a CRF on observations X and random variables Y as follows:

Let G = (V , E) be a graph such that Y=(Yv)v∈V, so that Y is indexed by the vertices of G. Then (X,Y) is a conditional random field when the random variables Yv , conditioned on X, obey the Markov property with respect to the graph: p(Yv |X, Yw ,w≠v)=p(Yv |X, Yw ,w~v), where w~v means that w and v are neighbors in G.

What this means is that a CRF is an undirected graphical model whose nodes can be divided into exactly two disjoint sets X and Y, the observed and output variables, respectively; the conditional distribution p(Y|X) is then modeled.

By now, CRF has become a widely used technique which is applied in named entity recognition on low resource language [17], such as Hindi, Bengali, Tamil, and Telugu [18].

3.2 Tibetan NER based on CRF

Tibetan NER can be defined as a sequence labeling problem for determining whether a observations belongs to a labeled set of markers. Suppose that a given marker sequence y= (y_1, y_2..., y_n) is labeled, n is the length of the sequence. The sequence of Tibetan NE is represented as w= (w_1, w_2,⋯,w_m),m is the length of the NE. The model of CRF is defined as follows:

$$p(y|w) = \frac{1}{Z(w)} \exp\left(\sum_i \sum_k \lambda_k f_k(y_i, y_{i-1}, w)\right)$$

Z (w) is normalization factor, determined by the observation sequence.

$$Z(w) = \sum_y \exp\left[\sum_k \lambda_k f_k(y_i, y_{i-1}, w)\right]$$

λ_k is the weight of the k-th function, f_k (y_i,$y_{(i-1)}$,w) is a characteristic function.

$$f_k(y_i, y_{i-1}, w) = \begin{cases} 1, \text{if } y_i = u, \text{and } y_{i-1} = v \\ 0, \text{otherwise} \end{cases}$$

3.3 Design of Feature Template

The use of the CRF model for a feature set is defined by a fixed pattern of feature templates, by a feature template to get features in a context (or window). The larger the window is, the better the relationship between the current word and the context can be observed, and the long distance dependency can be found in the text. But when the window is too large, the model will take a long time. This will lead to a decline in overall performance.

Considering the relationship between the Tibetan NE and its context correlation, the length of the window is set to 5, which can achieve a balance between training time and recognition effect.

The characteristics of the template used in the experiment shown in Figure 1.

```
#Unigram
U00:%x[-2,0]
U01:%x[-1,0]
U02:%x[0,0]
U03:%x[1,0]
U04:%x[2,0]

U05:%x[-2,0]/%x[-1,0]
U06:%x[-1,0]/%x[0,0]
U07:%x[0,0]/%x[1,0]
U08:%x[1,0]/%x[2,0]
U09:%x[-1,0]/%x[1,0]

#Bigram
B
```

Figure 1. Feature Template of CRF

4. Comparison Experiment for Graininess

4.1 Corpus Pretreatment

In the experiment, the corpora which built from text of the Tibetan version of People's Daily online website published. The train data is 5.97M and the test data is about 700K, which were included 2546 person names, 6469 location names, 4049 organization names.

In order to examine the effect of different graininess on Tibetan NER， We designed a comparative experiment used CRF on Tibetan person names, location names and organization names , based on syllables, or based on words. The syllable-based markers : B-PER(person names' first syllable),I-PER(syllable in person names' but not the first syllable),B-LOC(location names' first syllable),I-LOC(syllable in location names' but not the first syllable),B-ORG(organization names' first syllable),I-ORG(syllable in organization names' but not the first syllable),O(remaining syllables). The word-based markers: PER (person names), LOC (location names), ORG (organization names), O (remaining words).

We use Precision (P), Recall (R), F1 to evaluate the performance of each graininess, which are very common in NLP evaluation.

P= (number of correctly identified NE) / (number of identified NE)

R= (number of correctly identified NE) / (number of all NE)

F1= (2*P*R) / (P+R)

4.2 Result and Analysis

The result of the experiment is in table 1. We labeled "Words as the graininess" as group A, and" Syllables as the graininess" as group B.

Table1 Evaluation result for experiment

Tibetan NE	Words as the graininess(A)			Syllables as the graininess(B)		
	P	*R*	*F1*	*P*	*R*	*F1*
PER	87.72	34.25	49.26	76.95	77.74	77.34
LOC	97.57	74.31	84.36	88.38	82.84	85.52
ORG	92.11	71.92	80.77	88.66	58.90	70.78

As can be seen from the experimental results in Table 1, we get the following several conclusions.

The precision of group A is higher than that of group B. But its recall is short of group B, except in ORG. Compared F1, which considered as comprehensive effect, differs greatly in PER and ORG. For PER, the score of group B is 28.08% higher than that of group A. But for ORG, B is 9.99% less than A. It can be considered that the granularity of the syllable is small, more data can be obtained, which has a great influence on the recall rate. This also shows that the syllables-based approach because of the smaller particle size, can partially solve the problem of data sparseness.

For PER, although the Precision of group A is significantly higher than group B, but the recall is serious losses, resulting in poor F, while the results of group B were stable. This means that the identification of Tibetan person names should be based on syllables to achieve good results without Tibetan word segmentation.

For LOC, the Precision of group A is better than B, but the Recall is less. However, the F1 is slight difference between A and B. So, we can get conclusions that the identification of Tibetan location names can use both methods. But based on syllables, Tibetan word segmentation can be omitted.

For ORG, all the evaluation results in a group A are higher than those in group B. It indicates that the better results can be achieved by Tibetan word segmentation for organization names. Based on the analysis, we think organization names are complex, nesting and more syllables. These lead to difficulties in boundary identification based on syllables. But the boundary is confirmed on the method based on words.

5. Conclusions

In this paper, to get which kind of tokens that should be taken as the graininess for Tibetan NER, we did a comparison experiment for graininess. The paper used two different graininess, syllables or words, for identification of three kinds of named entities, including Tibetan person names, location names and organization names. From the result, we know that the method which syllable as graininess for person names is better. But the organization names are more suitable based on words. And both are fit into location names. In other words, identification of person names and location names can achieve very good results without Tibetan segmentation. But it is inconformity for organization names.

Acknowledgment

The project was supported by Key Program of National Natural Science Foundation of China (Grant No. 61331013), National Language Committee of China (Grant No. WT125-46), Minzu University of China Tier-1 Universities and Tier-1 Subjects Graduate independent research projects (Grant No. 10301-0170040601-184).

References

[1] LIU Huidan Rui Jianwu, Wu Jian. Encoding Detection and Conversion of Tibetan Web Pages [C] // 25th Anniversary Conference of Chinese Information Society of China.

[2] Wu Jian, Rui Jianwu, Liu Huidan. Tibetan web page and its code identification method: CN, CN 101055593 A[P]. 2007.

[3] Chen YZ, Li BL, Yu SW. The Design and Implementation of a Tibetan Word Segmentation System[J]. Journal of Chinese Information Processing, 2003.

[4] Cai Z J, Cai R. Design of a Tibetan Word Segmentation System[J]. Computer Engineering & Science, 2011, 33(5):151-154.

[5] Liu H, Minghua N, Zhao W, et al. SegT:A Practical Tibetan Word Segmentation System[J]. Journal of Chinese Information Processing, 2012, 26(1):97-103.

[6] Shi XD, Lu YJ. A Tibetan Segmentation System—Yangjin[J]. Journal of Chinese Information Processing, 2011, 25(4):54-56.

[7] Li YC,Jiang J, Jia YJ, Yu HZ.TIP-LAS: TIP-LAS: An Open Source Toolkit for Tibetan Word Segmentation and POS Tagging [J]. Journal of Chinese Information Processing, 2015, 29(6):203-207.

[8] Li YC, Jia YJ, Zong CQ, Yu HZl. Research and Implementation of Tibetan Automatic Word Segmentation Based on Conditional Random Field[J]. Journal of Chinese Information Processing, 2013, 27(4):52-58.

[9] Sun Z, Wang. Overview on the Advance of the Research on Named Entity Recognition[J]. New Technology of Library & Information Service, 2010.

[10] Yu HZ, Jiang T, Ma N.Named Entity Recognition for Tibetan Texts[J].Lecture Notes in Engineering and Computer Science,2010,2180.

[11] Dou R, Jia YJ, Huang W.Automatic recognition of tibetan name with the combination of statistics and regular. Journal of Changchun Institute of Technology (Social Science Edition), 11 (2) 113-115.,2010.2:113-115.

[12] Sun Y, Yan X, Zhao X, et al. Research on automatic recognition of Tibetan personal names based on multi-features[C]// International Conference on Natural Language Processing and Knowledge Engineering. IEEE, 2010:1-5.

[13] Jia Y, Yachao L I, Zong C, et al. A Hybrid Approach to Tibetan Person Name Identification by Maximum Entropy Model and Conditional Random Fields[J]. Journal of Chinese Information Processing, 2014.

[14] Hua Q, Jiang W, Zhao H, et al. Tibetan name entity recognition with perceptron model[J]. Computer Engineering & Applications, 2014.

[15] Kang C, Long C, Jiang D. Tibetan names recognition research based on CRF[J]. Computer Engineering and Applications, 2015.

DOI: 10.1051/itmconf/20171201008

[16] Zhu J, Li T, Liu S. Research on Tibetan name recognition technology under CRF[J]. Journal of Nanjing University, 2016.

[17] Hänig C, Bordag S, Thomas S. Modular classifier ensemble architecture for named entity recognition on low resource systems[C]//Workshop Proceedings of the 12th Edition of the KONVENS Conference. 2014: 113-116.

[18] Das A, Garain U. CRF-based Named Entity Recognition @ICON 2013[J]. Computer Science, 2014

Image Quality Assessment Based on Contourlet and ESD Method

Shuang Liang[1], Guan-Xiang Wang[2], Lei Sun[3]

[1]*School of Mathematical Science, Peking University, Beijing P.R. China*
[2]*School of Mathematical Science, Peking University, Beijing P.R. China*
[3]*Army Aviation Institute, Beijing P.R. China*
[1] *liangshuang12@pku.edu.cn*, [2]*gxwang@math.pku.edu.cn*, [3]*waterprison@163.com*

Abstract: In recent years, the development of the digital image processing promotes the research of the image quality assessment (IQA). A novel metric for full-reference image quality assessment is presented. The metric combined the contourlet transform with the energy of structural distortion (ESD), namely the CT-ESD. The calculation of the ESD is carried out in each subband of the contourlet transform. Then the comparisons between the reference and the distorted images on each subband are integrated by weighting sum. The superiority of the contourlet transform integrates well into new IQA metric. Experiments performed on the database TID2013 demonstrate that the CT-ESD can achieve high consistency with the subjective evaluation.

1. Introduction

Digital images are experiencing a tremendous growth in both theoretical developments and sophisticated applications. The primary issue in digital image processing is the image quality assessment (IQA) [1]. Image quality assessment is the procedure mapping the changes of the images to corresponding visual preference. It can be divided into subjective evaluation and objective evaluation. Obviously, humans, as the ultimate receivers of the images, are the best candidate to assess the quality of images. Nevertheless, the inconvenience and huge consumption of subjective evaluation leads to its less favor. And the objective image quality assessment has attracted increasing attentions from more and more researchers.

According to the dependence of the reference image, the objective image quality can fall into three categories: full-reference (FR), reduced-reference (RR) and no-reference (NR). Full-reference image quality assessment algorithms has the strongest dependence on the reference image. They take both a reference image and a distorted image as input and produce a scalar which measure the quality of the distorted image. Reduced-reference image quality assessment algorithms has less dependence on reference images. Instead of reference images, certain features of reference images are available to evaluate the quality. No-reference image quality assessment (also known as blind image quality assessment) algorithms perform image quality estimation with no reference image information but only the distorted images. In this paper we focus on the full-reference image quality assessment.

Conventional full-reference image quality assessment algorithms calculate the pixel-wise difference between a distorted image and its corresponding reference image, for example, the mean-squared error (MSE) and the peak signal-to-noise ratio (PSNR). Despite its intensive usage, these metrics are not preferable choice because they correlate poorly with human visual subjectivity.

More FR image quality assessment algorithms have been developed these years. As the ultimate objective of IQA is human visual preference, it is taken for granted to combine the characteristics of human visual system (HVS) with the IQA. The easy way to combine with HVS is weighting the frequency domain error with a contrast sensitivity function (CSF), which is called the weighting signal-to-noise ratio (WSNR) [2]. N. Damera Venkata et al. proposed the noise quality measure (NQM) which consists of the contrast pyramid processing and the signal-to-noise ratio computation [3]. Karen Egizarian et al. presented the IQA metric named as PSNR-HVS [4]. It removes the mean shift and then stretches the contrast by a scanning window before the calculation of the modified PSNR. The modification of PSNR is taking HVS into account when in the calculation of the MSE in PSNR. In the next year, these researchers proposed the PSNR-HVS-M metric [5] based on PSNR-HVS. The new metric is based on model of inter-coefficient masking of DCT basis functions and the modifications version of PSNR. Damon M. Chandler and Sheila S. Hemami presented an IQA metric based on near-threshold and suprathreshold properties of human vision called the visual signal-to-noise ratio (VSNR) [6].

HVS-based IQA metrics have a high dependence on the accuracy on the models of HVS. So many researchers employ other models such as image statistics. Hamid Rahim Sheikh et al. took the IQA problem as an information fidelity problem. They proposed a new metric named as information fidelity criterion (IFC) [7] which measured the statistical information that a distorted image had of the reference image. Similarly, Hamid Rahim Sheikh and Alan C. Bovik presented visual information fidelity (VIF) [8] which was derived from a statistical model for natural scenes, a model for image distortions and a HVS model. In the other direction, Zhou Wang and Qiang Li found a novel weighting approach based on a Gaussian scale mixture (GSM) model. It had pretty well and consistent performance improvement of both PSNR and SSIM based IQA named as information content weighted PSNR (IW-PSNR) and SSIM (IW-SSIM) respectively [9].

Besides HVS and statistics based IQA, there are structure based IQA metrics. Though ‘image structure’ remains non uniform definition, this class of metric is of more preference. Among these metrics, the universal image quality index (UQI) [10] and the structural similarity index (SSIM) [11] are of essential importance. The UQI employs cross-correlation and measures of luminance and contrast differences to estimate quality. The SSIM is actually the extended version of the UQI. The difference is that the SSIM added small constants to the numerator and the denominator of each measure. There are a lot of IQA metrics based on SSIM. Take CW-SSIM [12] as an example, it combines a complex wavelet with the SSIM and it is insensitive to translation, scaling and rotation of images in comparison with SSIM. Except for these SSIM based metrics, there are other structure based IQA. The energy of structural distortion (ESD) [13] is an IQA metric of this kind. Cailing Wang et al. extended ESD to the spectral image in spectrum aspect and spatial aspect [14].

In this paper, we proposed a full-reference image quality assessment metric based on the contourlet transform and the energy of structural distortion (ESD). Section II presents the background knowledge of the contourlet transform and the ESD. Section III presents our proposed IQA metric named as contourlet transform based ESD (CT-ESD). Section IV presents the subjective validation details. Then we conclude the paper in Section V.

2. Theory Basis

It is known to all that 2-D wavelet transform is short of efficiency for image representation in spite of its excellent performance for 1-D signal processing. Therefore, to develop multiscale geometric analysis is necessary. Contourlet transform [15] is an attractive alternative. It is constructed originally in discrete domain, meanwhile, it has a precise connection with continuous domain expansions. Contourlet transform allows for a different number of directions at different scale while achieve nearly critical sampling. Its implement based on iterated filter banks leads to computationally efficient. Moreover, Contourlet transform can provide a sparse representation for natural images with smooth contours. It possesses the qualities of directionality and anisotropy which are important for image representations. Thus we applied Contourlet transform in IQA metric design.

Contourlet transform is actually a double filter bank structure. The first filter bank is Laplacian pyramid (LP). It is aimed at capture the point discontinuities. Here we focus on the decomposition of LP. At each level, the input image is filtered by lowpass analysis filter H and downsampled by sampling matrix M to generate a lowpass version of the input. At the same time, a bandpass image is obtained by the subtraction between the input at this level and the prediction. The prediction is the lowpass version mentioned above with sequentially upsampling and filtering. The sampling matrix in upsampling is M and the filter is synthesis filter G. The second filter bank is directional filter bank (DFB). This filter bank links point discontinuities into linear structures. It decomposes the bandpass image from LP into 2^l subbands via l-level binary tree. Each subband has a wedge-shaped frequency partitioning. DFB has two building blocks: two-channel quincunx filter bank and shearing operator. The former one divides a 2-D spectrum into horizontal and vertical directions while the latter reorder the image samples. The combination of these two building blocks can leads to the desired 2-D spectrum division. The Fig 1 shows this two steps procedure of the contourlet transform. The contourlet transform has been applied to image quality assessment before, for example, in [16].

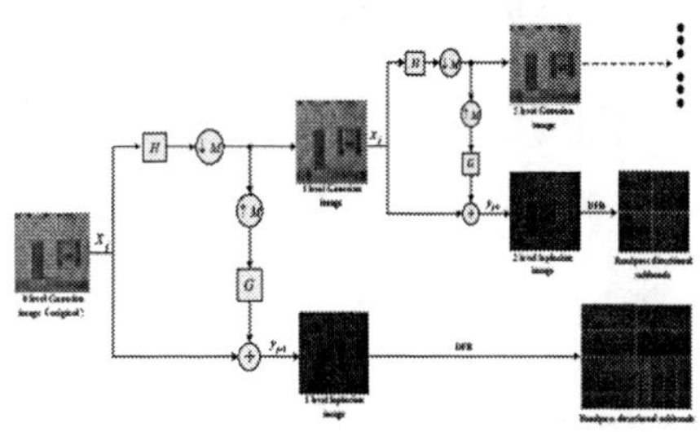

Figure 1. The flow diagram of the contourlet transform. First, the LP is employed to decompose the image into multiscale. Then in each bandpass channel, the DFB divides it into different directional subbands.

After we learn about the contourlet transform, we will continue to introduce the energy of structural distortion (ESD) [13].

The reference and distorted image are divided into blocks with size $H \times L$. The blocks are actually 2D vectors denoted by b_i and b_i' respectively for the reference and distorted image. The element of b_i is defined as $P_i(x, y)$. The structural characterization S_i of b_i is defined as

$$S_i = \frac{b_i}{\sqrt{\sum_{x,y} P_i(x,y)^2}} \tag{1}$$

It is noticeable that the square of S_i is 1, in other words, the energy of S_i is 1.

The inner product is set to be the simplest one. When $V=\{v_{i,j}|i=1,...,H,j=1,...,L\}$ and $W=\{w_{i,j}|i=1,...,H,j=1,...,L\}$, the inner product of them is

$$\langle V,W\rangle=\langle W,V\rangle=\sum_{i,j} v_{i,j}*w_{i,j}, i=1,...,H, j=1,...,L$$

Based on the inner product, we obtain the energy of structural information E_i of b_i by the following formula,

$$E_i=\langle b_i,S_i\rangle \quad (2)$$

The energy of structural information E_i' corresponding to b_i' in distorted image is calculated the same way as follows:

$$E_i'=\langle b_i',S_i\rangle \quad (3)$$

It should be noted that in the calculation of E_i', the object in the inner product is S_i.

The final score of ESD is defined as

$$ESD=\log\left(\sqrt{\sum_{i=1}^{K}(E_i-E_i')^2}\right) \quad (4)$$

in which K is the number of blocks. The lower the score of ESD is, the higher image quality is. The fact that the distorted image is identical to the reference one will result in the value of ESD being negative infinity. So we insist that the calculation of ESD should add a small constant before the logarithm operation.

3. Metric Proposed

The ultimate objective of IQA is to obtain an evaluation of image quality which approximate the perception by human visual system (HVS). The multi-resolution, directionality, and anisotropy are characteristics possessed both by HVS and Contourlet transform. Moreover, the Contourlet transform is sparse and effective for image representation which is fundamental to IQA. Subsequently, it is naturally inclined to employ the Contourlet transform into the IQA metric. We propose an IQA metric combined the Contourlet transform and the energy of structural distortion (CT-ESD). The procedures are list below.

Input the distorted image I_D and the corresponding reference image I_R. These two images are decomposed by the Contourlet transform to get the coefficients $\{c_{j,k}^D\}$ and $\{c_{j,k}^R\}$. The superscript D indicates the distorted image and R indicates the reference image. The subscript j represents the scale index and k means the orientation index. For example, $c_{j,k}^D$ denotes the Contourlet coefficients of the distorted image at the j_{th} level in the k_{th} direction. And the low frequency subband has no direction division.

The Contourlet coefficients $\{c_{j,k}^D\}$ and $\{c_{j,k}^R\}$ are divided into blocks $\{b_{i;j,k}^D\}$ and $\{b_{i;j,k}^R\}$ with the size $H\times L$ (in this paper 8×8). The index i denotes the block index. Then obtain the structural characterization $\{S_{i;j,k}\}$ as the same way as the equation (1).

Calculate the energy of structural information of the distorted image and the reference image which are denoted as $\{E_{i;j,k}^D\}$ and $\{E_{i;j,k}^R\}$ respectively.

$$\{E_{i;j,k}^D\}=\langle b_{i;j,k}^D,S_{i;j,k}\rangle,\{E_{i;j,k}^R\}=\langle b_{i;j,k}^R,S_{i;j,k}\rangle \quad (5)$$

It should be noted that each subband of Contourlet transform generates an energy value matrix.

At each scale j, the variance of the energy is calculated

$$EV_j=\sum_{k=1}^{K}\sum_{i=1}^{N}\left(E_{i;j,k}^R-E_{i;j,k}^D\right)^2, j=1,...,J \quad (6)$$

The sum ensures EV_j is a scalar.

The final metric proposed is defined as

$$ESD=\log\left(\sqrt{\sum_j^J w_j*EV_j}+\alpha\right) \quad (7)$$

in which α is a constant to avoid the logarithm of zero and small enough to have no influence on the result. w_j is the weighting coefficient of the EV_j at scale j. Moreover, the sum of all the w_j is one ($\sum_j^J w_j=1$). For different scale, its weighting coefficient can change according to its contribution to the HVS.

The flow chat of the CT-ESD is in Figure 2.

4. Experiments

At the beginning of this section, we need to introduce the image database briefly. According to [1] there are over twenty publicly available image databases. In consideration of the diversity of distortion patterns and the challenge of the database, we choose the image database TID 2013[17]. It is intended for analysis and verification of full-reference image quality assessment metrics. Actually the image database TID 2013 is the successor of the image database TID2008. Compared to TID2008, new types and one new level of distortions have been added to TID2013. In general, TID2013 contains 25 reference color images. It involves 24 types of image distortion in which 7 types are new. And 5 levels of distortion are in the database approximately corresponding to the PSNR equal to 21,24,27,30, and 33dB respectively. In [17] the distorted images of TID2013 can be divided into six subsets: Noise, Actual, Simple, Exotic, New, and Color. These subsets depend upon different applications. For example, the subset 'Noise' excludes the images distorted by the type of noise in conventional image processing. Other details about the subsets and TID2013 can refer to [17]

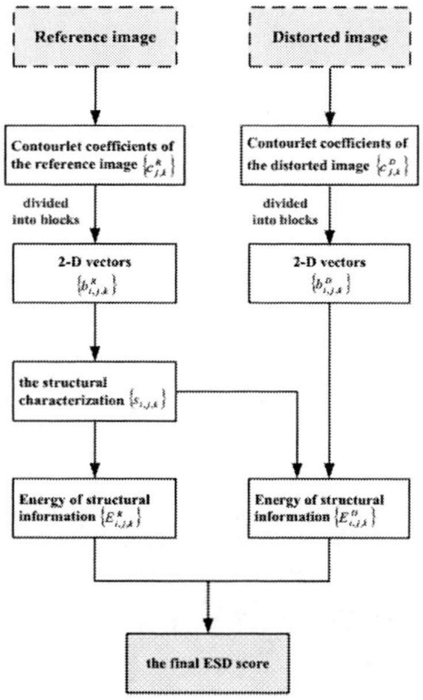

Figure 2. The flow chart of the IQA metric combined the Contourlet transform and the energy of structural distortion (CT-ESD).

In this paper, we choose the Spearman rank-order correlation coefficient (SROCC) and the Kendall rank-order correlation coefficient (KROCC) just as the authors of TID2013 do. They prefer to employ rank order correlation coefficients to avoid fitting procedures which may be not unique.

The value of the SROCC and the KROCC between the mean opinion score (MOS) and the proposed metric score is expected to be high which implies the new metric is a good substitution for HVS.

As there are there are parameters $w_j, j=1,2,...,J$ in our proposed metric, we choose the w_j which can lead to higher SROCC and KROCC. Experiments prove that high parameter corresponding to medium frequency subband can lead to high rank-order correlation coefficients. This phenomenon is essentially in agreement with the charac-teristic of HVS. In this paper we choose 3 level Laplacian decomposition in the contourlet. It produces coefficients of four cells corresponding to one low frequency subband and three pyramidal levels. And each pyramidal level contains 2^3 frequency bands. Here, we set the parameters as follows: $w_1=0.01$, $w_2=0.93$, $w_3=0.03$, $w_4=0.03$. They were assigned to the low frequency subband and three pyramidal levels. Obviously, w_2 is the biggest one which means the weighting coefficient of the medium frequency subband is the biggest.

The performance of the proposed CT-ESD metric will be validated and compared with some representative IQA metrics of the HVS based, statistics based and structural based IQA metrics respectively. These metrics are NQM [3], PSNR-HVS [4], VSNR[6], UQI[10], SSIM[11], IFC[7], VIF[8], IW-PSNR[9], and ESD [13]. And the comparisons to the conventional IQA such as PSNR and MSE are meaningful and necessary. The data is provided in [17] for most of these metrics. And it also can be calculated by Metrix MUX Visual Quality Assessment Package [18].

The following two tables show the SROCC and KROCC between the metrics and the MOS respectively for each subset. In the tables, each column represents a subset of the database TID2013 except for the last column. The last column 'Full' means the whole set of the database TID2013. Each row represents a metric. For example, in the Table 1, the value at the row 'CT-ESD' and the column 'Full' is 0.7250. It indicates that the metric CT-ESD gets 0.7250 for the SROCC with the MOS on the whole set. As a result of the challenging difficulty of the database TID2013, the values of the SROCC and KROCC have not appear the high values very close to 1.

From the tables, we can conclude that CT-ESD outperforms the other metrics in the table on the whole distorted images set. Though the CT-ESD fails to outperform the others on each subset, its performance is more evenly in different subset. Especially, the 'Exotic' subset contains distortions types which are not happen frequently but among the most difficult ones for IQA. In this subset the CT-ESD has the highest KROCC value 0.5021 of that column in the Table 2. In Table 1, the CT-ESD is 0.6894, only lower than the VSNR 0.7064 on this subset. On the 'New' subset and the 'Color' subset, which drag down the rank-order correlation coefficient for most metrics, the CT-ESD has preferable performance. It gets 0.6776 and 0.6021 for the SROCC which are both ahead in the corresponding column.

It is noteworthy that compared to ESD, CT-ESD is better on the subsets 'Noise', 'Actual', and 'Exotic'. These three subset relate to distortion types most common and difficult respectively. And CT-ESD has a significant improvement on the subset 'Exotic'. Together these subsets, CT-ESD outperforms the ESD in the full database TID2013. Whether the SROCC or the KROCC, it wins the other metrics at the 'Full' column with the highest values 0.7250 and 0.5514 respectively.

In Figure 3 we can see the scatter plot between the MOS and the metrics. From Figure 3(a) and (b), it is easy to conclude that the scatters in (b) are more compact and have more apparent tendency. Figure 3(b) represents the scatter plot between the MOS and the CT-ESD. So this means the CT-ESD has better evaluation of the image quality. Figure 3(c) and (d) show that different metrics may lead to the scatter plot into different shapes. From them we can know that the CT-ESD has better performance as it performs better on the compactness and tendency.

Table 1 the SROCC values of the metrics for the database TID2013

Metric	Noise	Actual	Simple	Exotic	New	Color	Full
PSNR	0.8217	0.8246	0.9134	0.5968	0.6190	0.5387	0.6395
MSE	0.7855	0.8048	0.8785	0.5468	0.7210	0.6696	0.6724
NQM	0.8362	0.8572	0.8752	0.5891	0.6258	0.5418	0.6349
PSNR-HVS	0.9172	0.9257	0.9507	0.6006	0.6471	0.5589	0.6536
VSNR	0.8691	0.8817	0.9121	0.7064	0.5888	0.5122	0.6809
UQI	0.6482	0.6904	0.7575	0.5313	0.4935	0.4440	0.5444
SSIM	0.7574	0.7877	0.8371	0.6320	0.5801	0.5057	0.6370
IFC	0.7218	0.7608	0.7792	0.3610	0.5444	0.4449	0.5400
VIF	0.8420	0.8589	0.9321	0.6282	0.5930	0.5210	0.6770
IW-PSNR	0.8961	0.9097	0.9237	0.6510	0.6470	0.5533	0.6888
ESD	0.7402	0.7893	0.8796	0.3438	0.7813	0.7719	0.5753
CT-ESD	0.8681	0.8698	0.8661	0.6894	0.6776	0.6021	0.7250

Table 2 the KROCC values of the metrics for the database TID2013

Metric	Noise	Actual	Simple	Exotic	New	Color	Full
PSNR	0.6236	0.6242	0.7452	0.4254	0.4728	0.4156	0.4700
MSE	0.5793	0.6007	0.6984	0.3822	0.5319	0.4874	0.4870
NQM	0.6413	0.6665	0.6812	0.4120	0.4831	0.4087	0.4662
PSNR-HVS	0.7547	0.7661	0.8092	0.4356	0.5169	0.4486	0.5077
VSNR	0.6761	0.6908	0.7312	0.5193	0.4374	0.3788	0.5077
UQI	0.4601	0.4976	0.5499	0.3776	0.3529	0.3154	0.3906
SSIM	0.5515	0.5768	0.6286	0.4548	0.4226	0.3823	0.4636
IFC	0.5273	0.5630	0.5740	0.2579	0.3982	0.3209	0.3959
VIF	0.6590	0.6729	0.7694	0.4634	0.4474	0.3998	0.5148
IW-PSNR	0.7240	0.7465	0.7705	0.4606	0.5185	0.4349	0.5250
ESD	0.5409	0.5935	0.7081	0.2364	0.5856	0.5673	0.4175
CT-ESD	0.6899	0.6916	0.6748	0.5021	0.5194	0.4509	0.5514

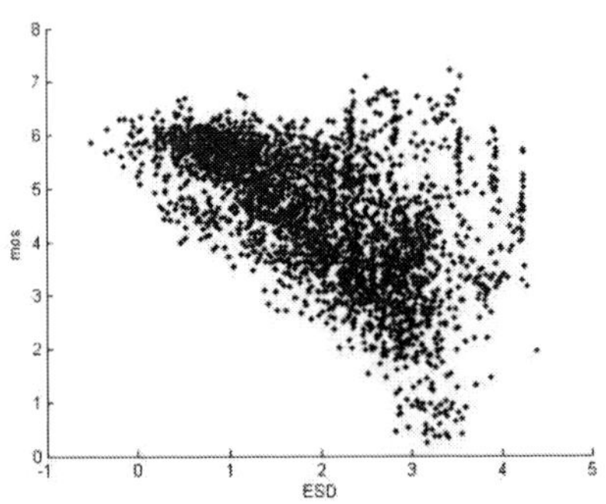

(a)

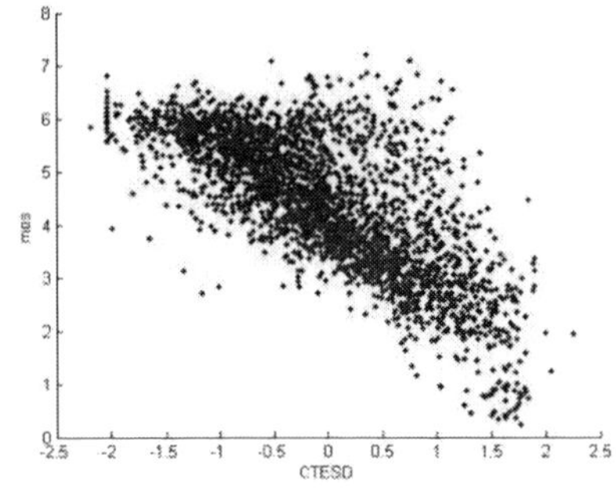

(b)

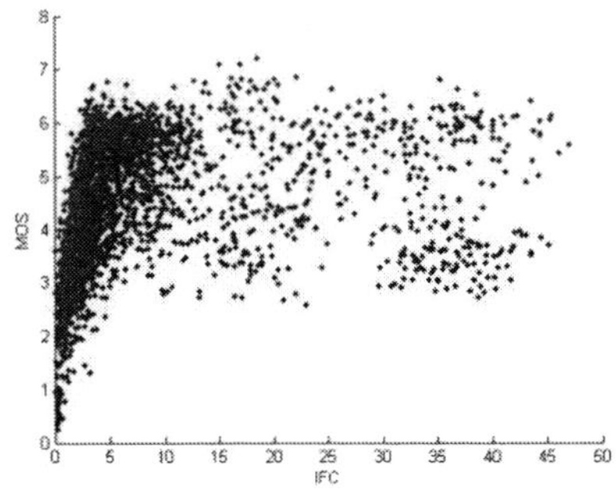

(c)

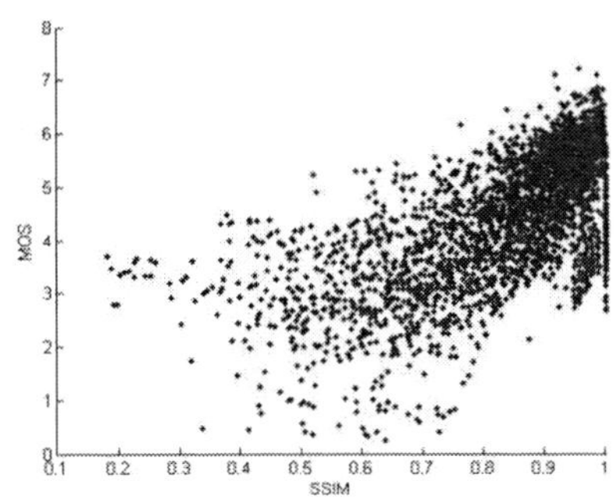

(d)

Figure 3. The scatter plot between the MOS and some metrics. (a) the plot between the MOS and the ESD;(b) the plot between the MOS and the CT-ESD;(c) the plot between the MOS and the IFC;(d) the plot between the MOS and the SSIM.

The data and the charts above show that it is meaningful to introduce the contourlet transform into the IQA metric. We attribute the preferable performance of the CT-ESD to the attendance of the contourlet transform. The multi-resolution and the sparse representation of the contourlet transform make the IQA metric more effective and more similarity to the HVS. These advantages lead to the success of the IQA.

5. Discussions

In this paper, we proposed a novel full-reference IQA combined the ESD with the contourlet transform named as CT-ESD. It is a structural based IQA metric which measures the loss of the structure information to evaluate the image quality. The attendance of the contourlet lead to the improvement of the ESD image quality assessment. Moreover, its preferable performance on the database TID2013 proves its validity and practicability, especially for the 'Exotic' type distortions. Our proposed metric still has the potential of improvement. We will focus on the utilization of the multi-direction of the contourlet in the IQA and the IQA metric aimed at the 'Color' type distortion. We insist that the contourlet transform as a 'real' two dimensional transform will be a powerful tool in the IQA.

References

[1] Dammon M.Chandler, Seven Challenges in Image Quality Assessment: Past, Present, and Future Research, ISRN Signal Processing, volume 2013

[2] T.Mitsa, K.L.Varkur, Evaluation of contrast sensitivity functions for the formulation of quality measures incorporated in halftoning algorithms, in IEEE International Conference on Acoustics, Speech, and Signal Processing(ICASSP), Minneapolis,USA,1993,pp.301-304

[3] Niranjan Damera-Venka, Thomas D.Kite, Wilson S.Geisler, Brian L.Evans, and Alan C.Bovik, Image Quality Assessment Based on a Degradation Model, IEEE Transactions on Image Processing, Vol.9, No.4, 2000

[4] K.Egiazarian, J.Astola, N.Ponomarenko, V.Lukin, F.Battisti, M.Carli, New full-reference quality metrics based on HVS, in Second International Workshop on Video Processing and Quality Metrics, Scottsdale, USA, 2006,pp.1-4

[5] N.Ponomarenko, F.Silvestri, K.Egizarian, M.Carli,J.Astola,V.Lukin, On between-coefficient contrast masking of DCT basis functions, in Third International Workshop on Video Processing and Quality metrics, Scottsdale, USA,2007,pp.1-4

[6] Damon M.Chandler, Sheila S.Hemami, VSNR: A Wavelet-Based Visual Signal-to-Noise Ratio for Natural Images, IEEE Transactions on Image Processing, Vol.16, No.9, 2007

[7] Hamid Rahim Sheikh, Alan Conrad Bovik, Gustavo de Veciana, An Information Fidelity Criterion for Image Quality Assessment Using Natural Scene Statistics, in IEEE Transaction on Image Processing, Vol.14,No.12,2005

[8] Hamid Rahim Sheikh and Alan C.Bovik, Image information and visual quality, in IEEE Transactions on Image Processing, Vol.15,No.2,2006

[9] Zhou Wang, Qiang Li, Information Content Weighting for Perceptual Image Quality Assessment, in IEEE Transactions on Image Processing , Vol.20, No.5, 2011

[10] Zhou Wang, Alan C.Bovik, A Universal Image Quality Index, in IEEE Signal Processing Letters, Vol.9, No.3, 2002

[11] Zhou Wang, Alan C.Bovik, Hamid Rahim Sheikh, Eero P.Simoncelli, Image Quality Assessment: From Error Visibility to Structural Similarity, in IEEE Transaction on Image Processing, Vol.13, No.4,2004

[12] Zhou Wang, E.P.Simoncelli, Translation insensitive image similarity in complex wavelet domain, in IEEE International Conference on Acoustics, Speech, and Signal Processing(ICASSP'05), Philadelphia, USA,2005,pp.573-576

[13] Jianxin Pang, Rong Zhang, Lu Lu, Zhengkai Liu, Image Quality Assessment Based on Energy of Structural Distortion, Advances in Multimedia Information Processing-PCM 2007,pp785-793

[14] Cailing Wang, Xuebin Liu, Bingliang Hu, A New Spectral Image Assessment Based on Energy of Structural Distortion, in 2009 International Conference on Image Analysis and Signal Processing(IASP),2009

[15] Minh N.Do and Martin Vetterli, The Contourlet Transform: An Efficient Directional multiresolution Image Representation, in IEEE Transactions on Image Processing, Vol.14,No.12,2005

[16] Bin Wang, Image Quality Assessment Method Based on Contourlet Transform and Generalized Gamma Distribution, in 3rd International Conference on Material, Mechanical and Manufacturing Engineering (IC3ME2015), 2015

[17] Nikolay Ponmarenko, Lina Jin, Oleg Ieremeiev, Vladimir Lukin, Karen Egiazarian, Jaakko Astola, Benoit Vozel, Kacem Chehdi, Marco Carli, Federica Battisti, C.-C. Jay Kuo, Image database TID2013: Peculiarities, results, and perspectives, in Signal Processing: Image Communication 30(2015),pp.57-77, 2015

[18] M.Gaubatz, Metrix MUX Visual Quality Assessment Package, in http://foulard.ece.cornell.edu/gaubatz/metrix_mux/, 27 March 2014.

Generating Algorithm for High Order Curve Based on ACO

Zhi-Jie Li[1], Xiao-Dong Duan[2], Bo Lu[3], Jian Yun[4]

[1]*School of Computer Science and Engineering, Dalian Minzu University, Dalian, China*
[2]*School of Computer Science and Engineering, Dalian, Minzu University, Dalian, China*
[3]*School of Computer Science and Engineering, Dalian Minzu University, Dalian, China*
[4]*School of Computer Science and Engineering, Dalian Minzu University, Dalian, China*
[1] *lizhijie@dlnu.edu.cn*

Abstract: A generating algorithm for parametric curve based on ant colony optimization is proposed in this paper. In order to produce the maximum step efficiently, the ant colony optimization is used to search the optimal step of curve in forward. Based on ant colony optimization, curve generating algorithm can search for the optimal step of parametric curve with any order quickly. Comparison of optimal step value between the proposed algorithm and other methods is also performed. Simulation results show the effectiveness of the proposed method. Since there is no restriction on control point position and curve order, the algorithm can be extended easily to other parametric curves besides Bézier curves.

1. Introduction

Parameter curve1 is the most common one in the research area of computer graphics and CAD. Up to now, raster graphics display monitor is widely used. Raster display can be viewed as a pixel matrix. So, any curve on the raster display is actually a collection of pixels. As the number and size of pixels is limited, the raster curve is only similar to the actual curve. How to make raster curve approximate to the real curve fast and perfectly is a problem to be deeply studied. The non-regularity of curve direction makes the point-to-point drawing for parameter curve difficult. Currently, very effective generating algorithm has not been found. The existing studies about curve generating algorithms can be classified into two different types. One is the traditional algorithms that focus on the interpolation method. Disadvantage of this interpolation approach is that it is difficult to determine the size of the step. Moreover, operations of multiplication and division are used several times, which limits the algorithm efficiency. The other is focus on the derivative method. For example, literature 5 presents an integer algorithm for generating implicit function curve, but for high-order parametric curves, the generation becomes complex. Literature6 contributes a quick generating algorithm for parameter polynomial curve, which determine the maximum step size according to the upper bound of the derivative value. However, the step size produced by the quick algorithm still not achieves the best value. Literature 7 calculates the optimal step by deriving the least upper bound of the derivative value according to the extreme point. Yet, the optimal step size for curve with more than four orders is not considered. Since the parametric curves of high-order have more control points, the derivation of multiple extreme points become very complex.

Based on the above considerations, a simple and very effective search algorithm using ant colony optimization is proposed. The concept of ant colony optimization (ACO), inspired by the behavior of real ants, was initially introduced by Colorni, Dorigo and Maniezzo. The principles of the algorithm can be illustrated by examining the food-searching process of an ant colony. Along their way from the food source to the nest, ants communicate with one another by means of pheromone. As the ants move, a certain amount of pheromone is deposited on their path and the pheromone gradually evaporates. The ants, then, determine their movements by judging the pheromone density on a path. This process can be described as a loop of positive information feedback, in which the more the ants follow a given trail, the more the pheromone is left, and the higher the probability that this trail will be followed by other ants. This selection process is the result of the ant's self-catalyzing activities. Ant colony optimization is capable to solve many complex problems, which require sophisticated planning. Hence, utilizing ant colony optimization the optimal step size for generating parameter curve with arbitrary order can be solved in a short time. Not only the continuity of the curve is guaranteed, but also unnecessary computation is reduced.

2. Step Solving in Curve Generating

Currently, the basic method for drawing parametric curves effectively is as follows. Because the coordinates of parametric curves is determined by the parametric equation, a forward extent of parameter (i.e. step size *1/n*) is supposed to be determined first. Then, the approximate pixels are calculated and drawn according to the parameter equation of curve and forward step. Many pixels together form a curve. In general, the quick criteria to determine step is that: selecting the largest possible step size under the condition that the forward extend not exceed one pixel. Many algorithms estimate n value from the curve length. The specific method is that let n = max (n_x, n_y), n_x and n_y is the n value corresponding to x-axis and y-axis. The calculation equation is as follows.

$$n_x = \sqrt{2} \cdot m \cdot \max_{0 \le i \le m-1} |X_{i+1} - X_i| \quad (1)$$

$$n_y = \sqrt{2} \cdot m \cdot \max_{0 \le i \le m-1} |Y_{i+1} - Y_i| \quad (2)$$

Where m is order of curve, (X_i, Y_i) is the coordinate of the i-th control points. However, the n value calculated by this traditional method is too large, which lead to the points too dense when drawing. Therefore, literature[6] gives a smaller n value calculation method. It's basic idea is let parametric curve equation as

$$x = f(t), \quad y = g(t), \quad t \in [0,1] \quad (3)$$

The units of x and y is pixels. Then the best value n = max (n_x, n_y), where n_x, n_y is given by

$$n_x = \max_{0 \le t \le 1}(|f'(0)|, |f'(1)|, |f'(t)|), t \in \{t \mid f'(t) = 0\} \quad (4)$$

$$n_y = \max_{0 \le t \le 1}(|g'(0)|, |g'(1)|, |g'(t)|), t \in \{t \mid g'(t) = 0\} \quad (5)$$

Considering the above mentioned method, literature 7 describes the derivation of the optimal value of n based on cubic Bézier curve. Also, the calculation method for the optimal n of quartic curve is given. But for curve more than four orders, there exists no effective method to solve the optimal n. For more than four orders, derivative becomes more complex due to the increased control points. In the range of argument t, more extreme points often appear. The increasing order of curve makes the derivation to obtain extreme become more and more difficult. Especially for arbitrary order Bézier curve, an effective way to solve the extreme of derivative function is needed. Ant Colony Optimization (ACO) is suitable for solving such non-linear and multi-peak optimization of complex issues. The advantage of ACO is that it can deal with some examples that traditional methods can't handle. The following will details how to use ACO for solving the optimal step-size.

3. Optimal Step Based on ACO

3.1 Basic ACO Algorithm

We describe the basic framework of ant colony algorithm taking TSP (Traveling Salesman Problem) as an example. Suppose there are l cities and m ants. d_{ij} (i,j=1,2,…,l) denotes the distance between city i and city j. The city transition is probabilistic. The probability of ant k transferring from city i to city j at time t is given by:

$$P_{ij}^k(t) = \begin{cases} \tau_{ij}^{\alpha}(t)\eta_{ij}^{\beta} \Big/ \sum_{r \in allowed_k} (\tau_{ir}^{\alpha}(t)\eta_{ir}^{\beta}), & j \in allowed_k \\ 0, & \text{otherwise} \end{cases} \quad (6)$$

Where τ_{ij}(t) denotes the intensity of pheromone between city i and city j at time t. Pheromone is used to simulated the real ant secretions. In the motion process, ant k determines the next path according to the pheromone on each path. η_{ij}^{β} is the expectation degree and can be set as $1/d_{ij}$. α and β are control parameters. By $allowed_k$ we present the set of accessible city for ant k. The amount of information τ_{ij}(t) will gradually decay over time. 1-ρ is used to denote the pheromone evaporation. A cycle of ACO algorithm is completed when every ant has constructed a solution. At the end of each cycle, the intensity of pheromone is updated by a pheromone trail updating rule:

$$\tau_{ij}(t+1) = \rho \cdot \tau_{ij}(t) + \sum_{k=1}^{m} \Delta\tau_{ij}^k \quad (7)$$

Where $\Delta\tau_{ij}^k$ is the amount of pheromone laid between city i and j by the kth ant and could be given by:

$$\Delta\tau_{ij}^k = \begin{cases} Q/L_k, & \text{if city } i \text{ and } j \text{ is traversed by the } k\text{th ant} \\ 0, & \text{otherwise} \end{cases} \quad (8)$$

Where L_k is the length of the walking path by the kth ant in this cycle and Q is a constant. The end of the algorithm could be achieved by a predefined number of cycles, or the maximal number of cycles between two improvements of the global best solution.

The following specific example demonstrates the working principle of ant colony optimization (shown as Fig. 1).

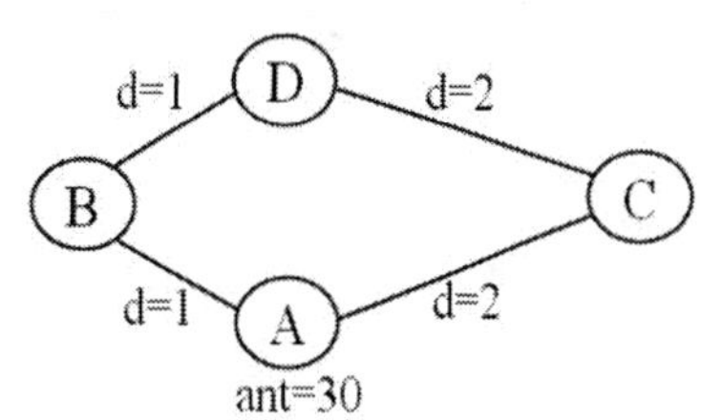

(a) Path length

DOI: 10.1051/itmconf/20171201010

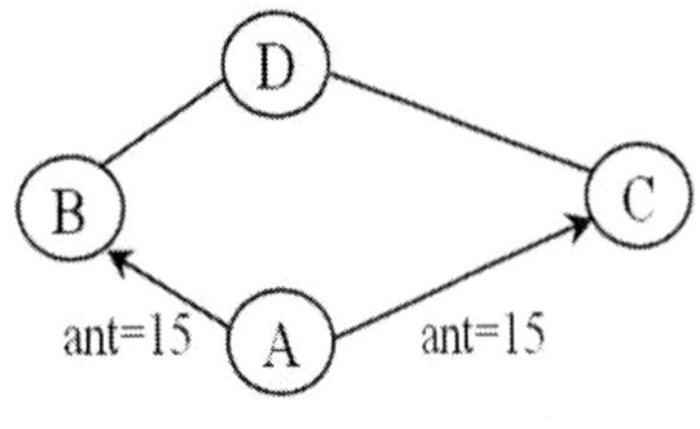

(b) First cycle

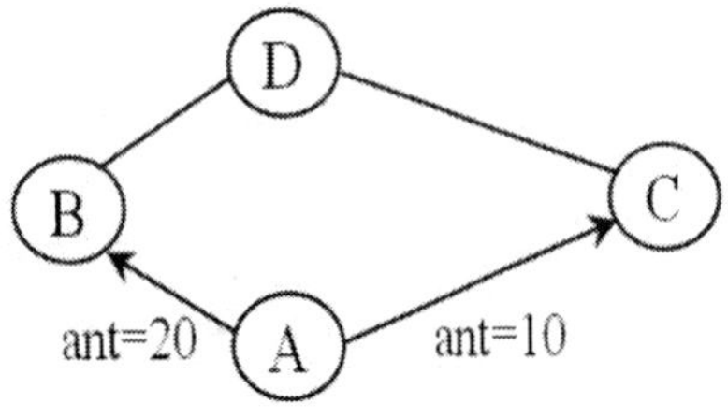

(c) Second cycle

Fig. 1. Illustration of ant colony optimization

Suppose node A and D are nest and food source, respectively. Path ABD and ACD is different in the path length. At beginning, path AB and AC have the same intensity of pheromone. That means the probability of each ant transferring from A to B and from A to C is the same. So, there are 15 ants select path AB, and 15 ants select path AC. After the first cycle, all ants return to nest A. According to equation (7) and (8), the intensity of pheromone of AB and AC is different, and the ratio of A and B is about 2:1. According to equation (6), in the second cycle, ants will move from A to B with probability 2/3 and from A to C with probability 1/3. Therefore, ants will prefer B with increasing probability than C. Finally, all ants select the short path ABD.

3.2 Continuous ACO for Optimal Step

The technology of ant colony optimization is initially used to solve discrete network routing problem. Since each ant always has limited choices at each stage, ant colony optimization is applicable to the discrete optimization problem, but not to optimization problem of continuous space, such as linear and nonlinear programming. We improve the search strategy of ant colony algorithm based on literatures 11. The solution space is divided into several sub-domains. During each iteration, ant colony algorithm first solves the possible sub-domain that contains optimal solution according to pheromone, then root around within this sub-domain to determine the optimal solution.

In the ant colony optimization, the region of each ant position corresponds to a region of possible optimal solution. For the extremum problem of derivative curve $|f'(t)|$, the representation of ant is relative simple, namely, one-dimensional vector $X_i = (x_i)$, where element x_i denotes an equal division region in the solution interval [0,1]. During each iteration, the region with larger objective function value has higher intensity of pheromone, which attracting more ants moving towards it. After positioning an optimal region x_i, ant colony algorithm will search the parameter t within region x_i for the optimal value $|f'(t)|$.

Suppose there are l regions and m ants. Let S be the region set $\{1,2,...l\}$. For continuous ant colony optimization, the probability of ant k transferring from region i to region j at time t is given by:

$$P_{ij}^k(t)=\begin{cases}\tau_j^{\alpha}(t)\eta_{ij}^{\beta}\Big/\sum_{r\in S,r\neq i}(\tau_r^{\alpha}(t)\eta_{ir}^{\beta}), & \eta_{ij}>0 \\ 0, & \eta_{ij}\le 0\end{cases} \quad i,j\in S,\ i\neq j \tag{9}$$

Where $\tau_j(t)$ denotes the pheromone intensity of region j at time t. η_{ij} is defined as $\eta_{ij} = f_{j\max} - f_{i\max}$, namely, the difference of max objective function value between region i and j. At the end of each cycle, the intensity of pheromone is updated by an updating rule:

$$\tau_j(t+1) = \rho\cdot\tau_j(t) + \sum_{k=1}^{m}\Delta\tau_j^k \tag{10}$$

Where the definition of $\Delta\tau_j^k$ is given by $\Delta\tau_j^k = Qf_{j\max}^k$.

4. Experiments

4.1 Configuration

Suitable algorithm parameters are determined based on experience. α and β control the relative importance of intensity of pheromone versus visibility. Therefore, as a result of high values for α, ants tend to choose regions previously have been chosen by other ants, where low values of α make the algorithm similar to stochastic algorithms. Parameters of our optimal algorithm that will be estimated through experiments are listed in Table I.

Table1. Experimental parameters for ACO based algorithm

Number	Parameter	Value
1	m	40
2	l	10
3	α	1
4	β	1
5	ρ	0.7
6	Q	1

We use the Bézier curve to verify the effectiveness of proposed ACO algorithm for solving the optimal curve step. Bézier curve is a kind of parametric polynomial curves. It uses Bernstein polynomial as basis function, which makes it easy to represented and possess many beautiful properties. The definition of Bézier curve is as follows:

Let P_0, P_1, P_2,, P_n be the control points of curve with n-order, then the Bézier curve is defined as

$$P(t)=\sum_{i=0}^{n} P_i \cdot B_{i,n}(t), \quad t\in[0,1] \tag{11}$$

Where $B_{i,n}(t)=C_n^i\cdot(1-t)^{n-i}\cdot t^i$ is the Bernstein basis function. Bézier curve is exactly the linear combination of Bernstein basis and control points. The form of Bézier curve is simple and intuitive, and has geometric invariance, symmetry and many other beautiful natures. Equation (11) is called Bernstein-Bézier curve defined by control polynomial P_0, P_1, P_n. It can also be referred to as Bézier curve. For the two-dimensional Bézier function, the parametric function is usually given by

$$\begin{cases} x=f(t)=\sum_{i=0}^{n} X_i\cdot C_n^i\cdot(1-t)^{n-i}\cdot t^i \\ y=g(t)=\sum_{i=0}^{n} Y_i\cdot C_n^i\cdot(1-t)^{n-i}\cdot t^i \end{cases} \quad t\in[0,1] \tag{12}$$

Where (X_0,Y_0), (X_1,Y_1),..., (X_n,Y_n) is the coordinates the of control points. For example, the Bézier curve in Fig. 2 is drawn by a polynomial with 12 control points. Any change of control points will result the shape change of the curve.

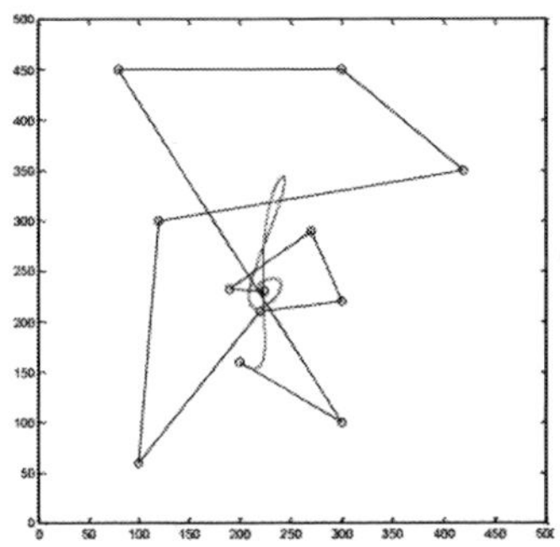

Fig. 2. Bézier curve with 11-order and its control points

In this paper, function of Bézier curve with order from 2 to 10 will be discussed, as well as derivatives of x-axis and y-axis. Also, the comparison results of optimal step between ACO and existing algorithms are summarized. Since the parameter function of x-axis and y-axis is the same except the coefficient, only the parameter functions of x-axis are listed below.

4.2 Results

In this section, the effectiveness of the suggested algorithm is validated using experimental data. The Bézier curve with order from 2 to 10 are generated on the basis of the continuous ACO algorithm. The first raw shows the Bézier curve using ACO algorithm. Second raw shows the x-axis derivative curve $|f'(t)|$. Third raw shows the y-axis derivative curve $|g'(t)|$. The maximum of absolute derivative is solved as value n based on the derivatives of x-axis and y-axis. Then, the corresponding Bézier curve is drawn point-to-point taking the reciprocal of n as the step size. From Table II, we can see that Bézier curve shows a more complex graphics with the increase of order. Especially for more than four order, curve shape tends to be more irregular due to the increase of control points. In order to generate curve with least pixels and without breakpoints, the minimize upper bound of absolute curve derivative ($|f'(t)|$ or $|g'(t)|$) needs to be found. Therefore, the way that only using deduction method to obtain the extreme derivative becomes increasingly difficult with the rise of curve order. This paper utilizes ACO algorithm to search the extreme point of curve derivative. In this way, Bézier curve can be drawn without breakpoint, and achieve the maximize step size compared with other algorithms.

Table2. Bézier and its derivative curve with order from 8 to 10

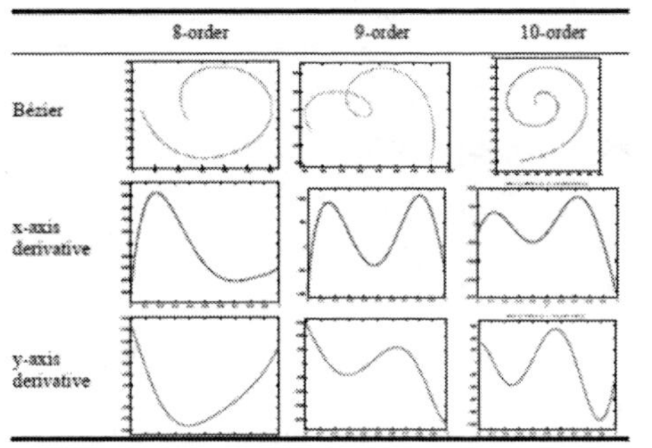

Fig. 3 compares the values of n between the ACO algorithm and other algorithms based on the Bézier curves with order from 2 to 10. From the comparison results, we can see that the value of n in different algorithm presents a rising tendency with the increase of curve order. Except quadratic Bézier curves, the value of n using ACO algorithm is the smallest of the three methods. It is known that the value of n determines the forward step size that affects the cycle times. Therefore, the smaller the n value, the faster the algorithm. For a Bézier curve with determined order, just one search for n is needed using ACO algorithm. Therefore, ACO will not affect the speed of curve generating.

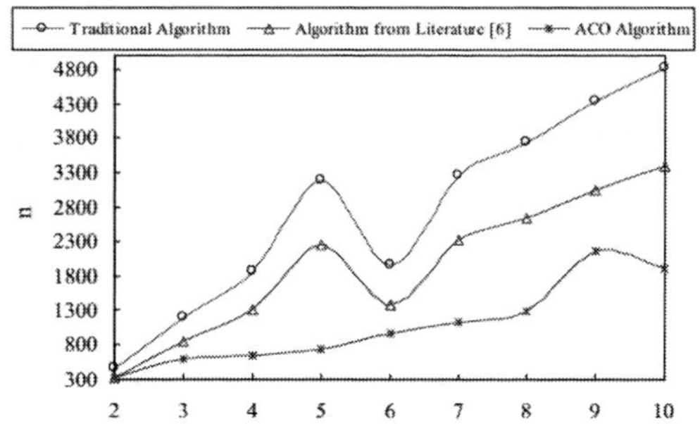

Fig. 3. Comparison of n using three algorithms

5. Conclusion

This paper presents a common algorithm for generating parametric curves on graphical display device. Ant colony optimization is utilized to search the extreme point of curve derivation. The maximum value of absolute derivative is used as the reciprocal of step to generate parametric curve. Searching the optimal step based on the proposed algorithm is simple and effective, without adding too much computation. As the Bézier curve is relatively stable and easily calculated, the algorithm is tested based on Bézier curve from low order to high order. Experimental results show that the algorithm could generate curve without break, and achieve the maximum step size in comparison with other methods. In addition, the algorithm is not limited by the location of control point and order of curve, and hence achieves good generality.

Acknowledgment

This work is supported by the National Natural Science Foundation of China under Grant No.61370146, No.61040054, No.61602085, the Fundamental Research Funds for the Central Universities under Grant (No.DC201502030203, No.DC201502030403, No.DC201501030401), and the National Social Science Foundation of China under Grant No. 16BMZ010.

References

[1] F.H. Guo. Optimal Parameterization of Parametric Curves [J]. Journal of Computer-Aided Design & Computer Graphics, 2007, 19(4): 464-467.

[2] S.L. Lien, M. Shantz, V. Pratt. Adaptive forward differencing for rendering curves and surfaces [J]. Computer Graphics, 1987, 21(4): 111-118.

[3] S.L. Chang, M. Shantz, R. Rocchetti. Rendering cubic curves and surfaces with integer adaptive forward differencing [J]. Computer Graphics, 1989, 23(3): 157-166.

[4] R.V. Klassen. Integer forward differencing of cubic polynomials: Analysis and algorithms [J]. ACM Transactions on Graphics, 1991, 10(2): 152-181.

[5] Y.K. Liu, J.Y. Shi. An All-Integer Arithmetic Algorithm for Drawing Curves [J]. Chinese Journal of Computers, 1998, 21(3): 270-280.

[6] Y.D. Huang, G.Q. Zhu. A Fast Point-by-Point Generating Algorithm for Polynomial Parametric Curve [J]. Chinese Journal of Computers, 2000, 23(4): 393-397.

[7] Y.K. Liu, X.M. Zhou. Pixel-Level Double-Step Algorithm for Rasterizing Parametric Curve [J]. Journal of Computer-Aided Design & Computer Graphics. 2002, 14(7): 619-623.

[8] D.W. Crowder, A.R. Horowitz, P.J.D. Barro, et al. Mating behaviour, life history and adaptation to insecticides determine species exclusion between whiteflies. Journal of Animal Ecology 2010, 79(3): 563-570.

[9] D. Merkle, M. iddendorf, H. Schmeck. Ant Colony Optimization for Resource-Constrained Project Scheduling. IEEE Transactions on Evolutionary Computation. 2002, 6(4): 333-345.

[10] M. Dorigo, C. Blum. Ant colony optimization theory: A survey. Theoretical Computer Science. 2005, 344(2-3): 243-278.

[11] L. Cheng, J. Shen, L. Qin. A Method for Solving Optimization Problem in Continuous Space by Using Ant Colony Algorithm. Journal of Software, 2002, 13(12): 2317-2323.

[12] X.Q. Wu, X.L. Han. Extension of Cubic Bézier Curve [J]. Journal of Engineering Graphics, 2005, (6): 98-102.

[13] J. Chen, G.J. Wang. Optimal Parameterizations of the Degree 2 Rational Bézier Curves [J]. Journal of Computer Research and Development, 2008, 45(9): 1601-1604.

 DOI: 10.1051/itmconf/20171201011

Research on Sliding Mode Control for Steer-by-Wire System in Forklift

Jun-Jie HUANG[1], Ben-Xian XIAO[2], Yang LIU[3], Yi-Gang HE[4]

[1]*Institute of Industry & Equipment Technology, School of Electrical Engineering and Automation, Hefei University of Technology, Hefei, P.R .China*
[2]*School of Electrical Engineering and Automation, Hefei University of Technology, Hefei, P.R. China*
[3]*Institute of Industry & Equipment Technology, Hefei University of Technology, Hefei, P.R. China*
[4]*School of Electrical Engineering and Automation, Hefei University of Technology, Hefei, P.R. China*
[1]*1114738405@qq.com,* [2]*xiaobenxian@126.com,* [3]*yangly11@163.com,* [4]*18655136887@163.com*

Abstract: Aiming at steering stability and wheel angle tracking of steer-by-wire (SBW) three wheeled forklift, steering dynamic model and SBW system mathematical model of three wheeled forklift are established. A control strategy for the ideal transmission ratio is introduced based on this model, which ensures forklift steering gain invariant. A sliding mode controller can then be designed based on the bound information of uncertain system parameters, uncertain self-aligning torque, and external disturbances. The results of simulation show the control strategies above can effectively reduce the sideslip angle when the forklift is steering and improve the sensitivity and stability of the steering forklift; at the same time can effectively restrain the parameter perturbation of internal system and external disturbance, which improves the tracking performance of the wheel angle.

1. Introduction

The forklift usually works in small working space to handle cargo with low speed, so more need to ensure the steering maneuverability and handling stability [1]. The three wheeled forklift has the characteristic of small size, it uses advanced dual-front technology and rear wheel active steering technology, can achieve 90-degree steering, has advantage of small turning radius, more effort to operate, so very suitable for working in narrow space.

Conventional forklifts, which are mechanical steering, can't take the initiative to control the angular transmission characteristics and force transfer characteristics of the steering system. The Steer-by-Wire (SBW) system eliminates the mechanical connection between steering handle and steering wheels in a conventional steering system and transmits the control signals via electrical signals, so that can be freely designed[2-5].

Nowadays, the research on the vehicle steering system is mostly based on the variable transmission ratio and the strategy of yaw stability control, and does not take into account the tracking performance of the wheel angle of SBW system. In this paper, for the three wheeled forklift equipped with SBW system, the stability of the steering forklift and the problem of wheel angle tracking are considered. Based on the ideal transmission ratio control which the yaw rate gain is fixed, sliding mode angle tracking controller based on variable parameters is designed. Through simulation experiments, it is verified that the proposed scheme can improve the stability of the steering forklift and the tracking performance of wheel angle.

2. Modeling of SBW System for Three Wheeled Forklift

In this paper, a three wheel steering model with 2DOF (which are lateral and yaw) was established.

2.1 Three Wheeled Forklift Steering Dynamics Model Based on Ground Coordinate System

As shown in Fig.1, o' is the steering center of the forklift, O is the centroid of forklift. The parameters of rear wheel steering dynamic model of three wheeled forklift are shown as follows: u is the longitudinal velocity of the vehicle centroid (m/s), v is the lateral velocity of the vehicle centroid (m/s), β is the sideslip angle at the centroid (rad). ω_r is the yaw rate(rad/s), δ is the angle of steering rear wheel(rad), α_1 and α_2 are the sideslip angle of left front wheel and right front wheel respectively(rad), α_3 is the sideslip angle of rear wheel (rad), F_{y1} and F_{y2} are the lateral force of left front wheel and right front wheel respectively(N), F_{y3} is the lateral force of rear wheel(N), a and b are the distance from centroid to front axle and rear axle respectively(m), L is the distance from front wheel center to rear wheel center(m), c is the center distance between the left front wheel and the right front wheel(m), M is the mass of the whole forklift (kg).

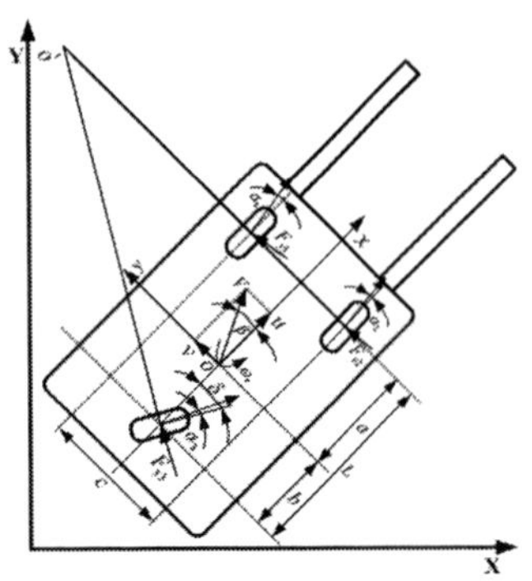

Figure 1. Dynamic model of rear wheel steering of forklift

According to the Fig.1, the resultant force along the y-axis and the torque around the centroid when the forklift is steering are shown below:

$$\begin{cases} Mu(\dot{\beta}+\omega_r)=F_{y1}+F_{y2}+F_{y3}\cos\delta \\ J_z\dot{\omega}_r=-aF_{y1}-aF_{y2}+bF_{y3}\cos\delta \end{cases} \tag{1}$$

Where, the sideslip angle at the centroid $\beta \approx \tan\beta = v/u$. When a forklift is steering, the transformation of its rear wheel angle is slow, so in the moment of steering, it can be considered that $\cos\delta \approx 1$. J_z is the moment of inertia of the vehicle around the z-axis ($kg\cdot m^2$), so (1) can be written as:

$$\begin{cases} Mu(\dot{\beta}+\omega_r)=M(\dot{v}+u\omega_r)=F_{y1}+F_{y2}+F_{y3} \\ J_z\dot{\omega}_r=-aF_{y1}-aF_{y2}+bF_{y3} \end{cases} \tag{2}$$

When the sideslip angle is less than 5°, the lateral force of the tire is linearly related to the sideslip angle[4], so the lateral force of three wheels are:

$$F_{y1}=-C_1\alpha_1 \text{ , } F_{y2}=-C_2\alpha_2 \text{ , } F_{y3}=-C_3\alpha_3 \tag{3}$$

Where, C_1 and C_2 are the cornering stiffness of left front wheel and right front wheel, C_3 is the cornering stiffness of rear wheel.

According to the relative motion principle:

$$\begin{cases} \alpha_1=\dfrac{v-a\omega_r}{u+\dfrac{c}{2}\omega_r}\approx\beta-\dfrac{a\omega_r}{u},\alpha_2=\dfrac{v-a\omega_r}{u-\dfrac{c}{2}\omega_r}\approx\beta-\dfrac{a\omega_r}{u} \\ \alpha_3=\dfrac{v+b\omega_r}{u-\dfrac{c}{2}\omega_r}-\delta\approx\beta+\dfrac{b\omega_r}{u}-\delta \end{cases}$$

(4)

According to (2), (3), (4), the 2DOF state space equation of rear wheel steering of three wheel forklift is:

$$\begin{bmatrix}\dot{\beta}\\ \dot{\omega}_r\end{bmatrix}=\begin{bmatrix}a_{11} & a_{12}\\ a_{21} & a_{22}\end{bmatrix}\begin{bmatrix}\beta\\ \omega_r\end{bmatrix}+\begin{bmatrix}b_1\\ b_2\end{bmatrix}\delta \tag{5}$$

Where:

$$a_{11}=\frac{-(C_1+C_2+C_3)}{Mu}\text{, } a_{12}=\frac{aC_1+aC_2-bC_3}{Mu^2}-1$$
$$a_{21}=\frac{aC_1+aC_2-bC_3}{J_z}\text{, } a_{22}=-\frac{a^2C_1+a^2C_2+b^2C_3}{J_z u}$$
$$b_1=\frac{C_3}{Mu}\text{, } b_2=\frac{bC_3}{J_z}.$$

2.2 Dynamics Model of Steering Executive Mechanism for SBW System

The dynamics model of steering handle (i.e. the steering handle of forklift) can be described by the following equation:

$$J_h\ddot{\theta}_h+B_h\dot{\theta}_h+C_h\theta_h=\tau_h-\tau_f \tag{6}$$

Where, J_h , B_h and C_h are the moment of inertia of steering handle, the viscous friction coefficient and the torsional stiffness of steering shaft respectively; θ_h is the angle of steering handle, τ_h is the input hand torque of driver. τ_f is the feedback resistance moment which transfers to the steering shaft through the road feeling motor and deceleration mechanism.

Due to the SBW system eliminates the mechanical connection between steering handle and steering wheels, it is not necessary to consider the influence of road impact on steering system. The road feeling is totally produced by the simulation of road feeling motor [4-6]. In order to simplify the calculation, τ_f is designed as:

$$\tau_f=\tau_e/(r_p\cdot G_1) \tag{7}$$

Where, τ_e is the self-aligning torque of rear wheel, r_p is the transmission ratio of steering gear, G_1 is the reduction ratio of deceleration mechanism of road feeling motor.

The actual torque is generated by steering motor, and the rear wheel is rotated by steering gear. The model of steering motor is described by the following second-order equation:

$$J_{sm}\ddot{\theta}_{sm} + B_{sm}\dot{\theta}_{sm} + \tau_{12} = \tau_{sm} \tag{8}$$

Where, J_{sm} and B_{sm} are the moment of inertia and the viscous friction coefficient of steering motor respectively, θ_{sm} is the axial angle of steering motor, τ_{12} is the torque which the steering rear wheel applies to the motor shaft through the steering gear, τ_{sm} is the torque control input of steering motor, i.e. the electromagnetic torque of motor.

The steering rear wheel is used as driving load of steering motor, which rotates around the vertical axis through the wheel center. Therefore, the rotation of the steering rear wheel satisfies the following kinetic equation:

$$J_{rw}\ddot{\delta} + B_{rw}\dot{\delta} + \tau_e = \tau_s \tag{9}$$

Where, J_{rw} and B_{rw} are the moment of inertia and the viscous friction coefficient of steering rear wheel respectively, τ_s is the torque exerted by the steering motor on the steering shaft through the steering gear.

Where, the relationship of θ_{sm}, δ is:

$$\frac{\theta_{sm}}{\delta} = \frac{\dot{\theta}_{sm}}{\dot{\delta}} = \frac{\ddot{\theta}_{sm}}{\ddot{\delta}} = G_2 = \frac{\tau_s}{\tau_{12}} \tag{10}$$

G_2 is the transmission ratio of the steering motor to the steering shaft through the deceleration mechanism.

Linking (8), (9) and (10), it can be obtained that:

$$J_{eq}\ddot{\delta} + B_{eq}\dot{\delta} + \tau_e = \tau_{eq} \tag{11}$$

Where,

$$J_{eq} = J_{rw} + G_2^2 J_{sm} \tag{12}$$

$$B_{eq} = B_{rw} + G_2^2 B_{sm} \tag{13}$$

Then the equivalent driving torque of steering electromotor is:

$$\tau_{eq} = G_2 \tau_{sm} \tag{14}$$

It can be seen from (11) that the SBW system from the steering motor to the steering rear wheel is equivalent to a second-order direct drive system. Although the moments of inertia J_{sm} and J_{rw}, and the viscous friction coefficient B_{sm} and B_{rw} are unknown, they have the following bounded conditions: $0 \le J_{rw0} \le J_{rw} \le J_{rw1}$, $0 \le B_{rw} \le B_{rw1}$, $0 \le B_{sm} \le B_{sm1}$, $0 \le J_{sm0} \le J_{sm} \le J_{sm1}$.

Besides the uncertainties above, another significant amount of uncertainty in the executive mechanism of steering system is self-aligning torque τ_e in the steering rear wheel, which is generated by the lateral force that suffered by the rear wheel when the forklift is steering[2-4].

$$\tau_e = (l_m + l_p) F_{y3} \tag{15}$$

In the (15), l_p is the pneumatic trail, l_m is mechanical trail. Combining (3) and (4), the total self-aligning torque of the tire is:

$$\tau_e = -C_3 \cdot (l_m + l_p) \cdot \left(\beta + \frac{b\omega_r}{u} - \delta \right) \tag{16}$$

For the design of sliding mode controller in the next section, the upper bound on the self-aligning torque τ_e of tire is estimated as follows:

$$|\tau_e| \le \bar{\tau}_e \tag{17}$$

Where, $\bar{\tau}_e = \bar{C}_3 \cdot (\bar{l}_m + \bar{l}_p) \cdot \left| \beta + \frac{b\omega_r}{u} - \delta \right|$, $\bar{l}_m$ and $\bar{l}_p$ are the upper bound of l_p and l_m, $\bar{C}_3$ is the upper bound of C_3.

3. Steady State Control of Steering Gain for Three Wheeled Forklift

3.1 Description of Steering Characteristic

When the three wheeled forklift is steering, the ratio of the steering handle angle θ_h to the rear wheel angle of the forklift δ is defined as the steering ratio i [7, 8],

$$i = \theta_h / \delta \tag{18}$$

By changing the transmission ratio, the SBW makes the steering characteristics exhibit a fixed proportional relationship, which is independent of the vehicle speed, In this paper, the ideal transmission ratio of SBW for forklift is determined based on yaw rate gain invariant [7, 8].

3.2 Design of Ideal Transmission Ratio for Three Wheeled Forklift

After a step angle input, 2DOF vehicle model of rear wheel steering three wheeled forklift achieves steady state which is the constant-speed circumference. At steady state, the yaw rate ω_r is constant, so $\dot{v}=0$, $\dot{\omega}_r=0$, $C_1=C_2$, linking (2) and (5), we can get the yaw rate as follows:

$$\omega_r=\frac{2u/L}{\frac{Mu^2}{L^2}\left(\frac{2a}{C_3}-\frac{b}{C_1}\right)+2}\delta=\frac{2u/L}{Ku^2+2}\delta \tag{19}$$

In (19), K (s^2/m^2) is defined as the stability factor of three wheeled forklift, $K=M\left(2a/C_3-b/C_1\right)/L^2$.

Therefore, the desired yaw rate gain K_s (s^{-1}) is:

$$K_s=\frac{\omega_r}{\theta_h}=\frac{2u/L}{Ku^2+2}\cdot\frac{\delta}{\theta_h} \tag{20}$$

Then, basing on the premise that the desired yaw rate gain remains constant, the ideal transmission ratio of the three wheeled forklift is shown as follow:

$$i=\frac{\theta_h}{\delta}=\frac{2u/L}{Ku^2+2}\cdot\frac{1}{K_s} \tag{21}$$

3.3 Determination of Ideal Transmission Ratio for Three Wheeled Forklift

In order to ensure that forklift increases the steering sensitivity at low speed , increases the stability at high speed, and to ensure the yaw rate remains constant for the steering handle angle in the steering process, the change of ideal transmission ratio of three wheeled forklift with vehicle speed is designed as followed.

When the speed is below the set value u_0 , the transmission ratio of the SBW system is fixed; thus the ideal transmission ratio i of steering system is set as follow:

$$i=\begin{cases} i_{\min}=1 & (u\le u_0) \\ \dfrac{2u/L}{Ku^2+2}\cdot\dfrac{1}{K_s} & (u>u_0) \end{cases} \tag{22}$$

When i is fixed, the transition speed u_0 can be obtained according to (21):

$$u_0=\frac{1\pm\sqrt{1-2i_{\min}{}^2K_s{}^2L^2K}}{iLK_sK} \tag{23}$$

There is no standardized method for the selection of the yaw rate gain value up to now. According to the research and statistics of modern car: the yaw rate gain value of car is 0.16~0.33 s^{-1} [7, 8]. In this paper, four values which meet the steering characteristics for forklift are chosen as: 0.21, 0.22, 0.23, 0.24 s^{-1} , these values are used as the quantitative analysis, the corresponding transition speeds are 0.40, 0.42, 0.44, 0.46 m/s respectively. Through the above method, curves of the ideal transmission ratio with the vehicle speed are shown in Fig.2.

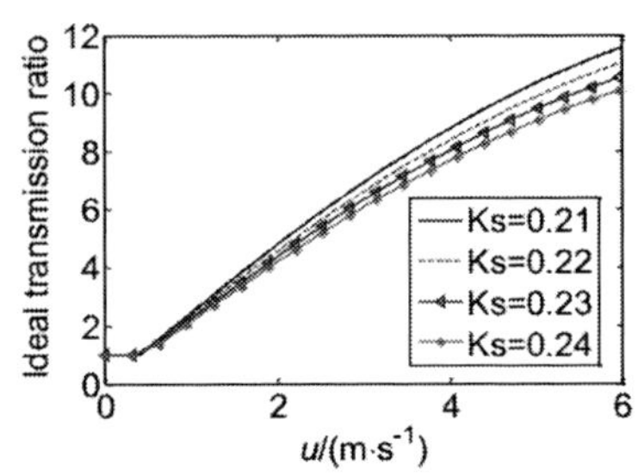

Figure 2. Variation curves of ideal transmission ratio with vehicle speed under different K_s

4. Design of Sliding Mode Controller for Steering Executive mechanism

The uncertain parameters in (11) makes the establishment of accurate mathematical model becomes difficult, or even destroys the tracking performance of system[9]. For the bounded information of uncertain parameters existing in (11) and the self-aligning torque in (16), the sliding mode controller is designed in this section, which makes tracking error of steering executive mechanism converge to zero gradually.

4.1 The Mathematical Model of Steering Executive Mechanism Control System

According to the bounded information of uncertain parameters τ_e, J_{eq} and B_{eq} , let:

$P_a=-\frac{B_{eq}}{J_{eq}}$, $P_b=\frac{1}{J_{eq}}$, $P_d=-\frac{\tau_e}{J_{eq}}$, $P_{a0}=-\frac{B_{eq1}}{J_{eq0}+J_{eq1}}$,

$P_{b0}=\frac{2}{J_{eq0}+J_{eq1}}$, $\Delta P_a=P_a-P_{a0}$, $\Delta P_b=P_b-P_{b0}$, $\Delta P_d=P_d$;

and the (11) can be rewritten as:

$$\ddot{\delta} = P_{a0}\dot{\delta} + P_{b0}\tau_{eq} + \Delta P_a\dot{\delta} + \Delta P_b\tau_{eq} + \Delta P_d \tag{24}$$

And:
$|\Delta P_a| \le \zeta$, $|\Delta P_b / P_{b0}| \le \xi$, $|\Delta P_d| \le \eta$, $(\xi+1)(2\xi+1)^{-1} \le P_b / P_{b0}$.

Where, $\zeta = \dfrac{B_{eq1}J_{eq1}}{J_{eq0}(J_{eq0}+J_{eq1})}$, $\xi = \dfrac{J_{eq1}-J_{eq0}}{2J_{eq0}}$, $\eta = \dfrac{\overline{\tau}_e}{J_{eq0}}$.

4.2 Design of Sliding Mode Control Law

Let δ_d as the target rear wheel angle, the tracking error of rear wheel angle is $e = \delta - \delta_d$; then it can be obtained that $\dot{e} = \dot{\delta} - \dot{\delta}_d$, $\ddot{e} = \ddot{\delta} - \ddot{\delta}_d$

Using the law of sliding mode control, the switching function is defined as $s = \dot{e} + \lambda e$, where $\lambda > 0$. The law of control is defined as $\tau_{eq} = \tau_{eq0} + \tau_{eq1}$, where τ_{eq0} is the equivalent control, the purpose is to keep the state of the system staying on the sliding mode hyperplane. τ_{eq1} is used to overcome the influence of uncertainties and make the system state meet the reachability condition of sliding mode. Taking the derivative s with respect to time, it can be obtained that $\dot{s} = \ddot{e} + \lambda\dot{e} = \ddot{\delta} - \ddot{\delta}_d + \lambda(\dot{\delta} - \dot{\delta}_d)$; taking (24) into the above equation.

$$\begin{aligned}\dot{s} &= (P_{a0}\dot{\delta} + P_{b0}\tau_{eq} + \Delta P_a\dot{\delta} + \Delta P_b\tau_{eq} + \Delta P_d) \\ &\quad - \ddot{\delta}_d + \lambda(\dot{\delta} - \dot{\delta}_d)\end{aligned} \tag{25}$$

Taking the equivalent control:

$$\tau_{eq0} = -P_{b0}^{-1}\mu' \tag{26}$$

Where, $\mu' = P_{a0}\dot{\delta} - \ddot{\delta}_d + \lambda(\dot{\delta} - \dot{\delta}_d)$;In order to make the system state meet the reachability condition of sliding mode, the sliding mode control is designed as follow:

$$\tau_{eq1} = -P_{b0}^{-1}k\,\mathrm{sgn}(s) \tag{27}$$

Where $k = (2\xi+1)(\xi+1)^{-1}\left[\zeta\dot{\delta} + \eta + \xi|\mu'| + \varepsilon\right]$; $\varepsilon > 0$, and it is a selectable constant.

4.3 Proof of Stability

Constructing Lyapunov function as $V = s^2/2$, differentiating V respect to time, and taking into account (25), (26) and (27), it can be obtained that:

$$\begin{aligned}\dot{V} &= s\cdot\dot{s} \\ &= s\cdot[P_b\tau_{eq1} + \Delta P_a\dot{\delta} + \Delta P_b\tau_{eq0} + \Delta P_d] \\ &= s\cdot[-P_bP_{b0}^{-1}k\,\mathrm{sgn}(s) + \Delta P_a\dot{\delta} - \Delta P_bP_{b0}^{-1}\mu' + \Delta P_d] \\ &\le -P_bP_{b0}^{-1}k\cdot|s| + |s|\cdot|\Delta P_a\dot{\delta} - \Delta P_bP_{b0}^{-1}\mu' + \Delta P_d| \\ &\le |s|\{-P_bP_{b0}^{-1}k + |\Delta P_a|\dot{\delta} + |\Delta P_bP_{b0}^{-1}|\cdot|\mu'| + |\Delta P_d|\} \\ &\le |s|\{-(\xi+1)(2\xi+1)^{-1}k + \zeta\cdot\dot{\delta} + \xi\cdot|\mu'| + \eta\} \\ &= -\varepsilon|s|\end{aligned}$$

Due to $\varepsilon > 0$, it can be obtained that $\dot{V} < 0\,(|s| \ne 0)$, the sliding mode is asymptotically reachable and the system is stable. The tracking error between the actual rear wheel angle and the target rear wheel angle can converge to zero asymptotically.

4.4 Suppression of Buffeting

Because of the symbol function $\mathrm{sgn}(s)$ in (27), sliding mode control in the switching action of the switching surface causes control discontinuity and result in chattering. For this problem, the saturated function $sat(s)$ is used instead of $\mathrm{sgn}(s)$ in the sliding mode controller, to ensure the smooth continuity of the controlled input in the vicinity of the switching surface. Saturated function sat(s) is:

$$sat(s) = \begin{cases}\mathrm{sgn}(s) & |s| > \phi \\ s/\phi & |s| \le \phi\end{cases} \tag{28}$$

Where, ϕ is the boundary layer.

5. Simulation and Analysis

5.1 Simulation Environment

The design parameters of SBW system are shown in Table 1, parameters of three wheeled forklift dynamic model are shown in Table 2. In the simulation test, boundary conditions of uncertain parameters in SBW system are set as follows:

$0.015\ \mathrm{kg\cdot m^2} \le J_{sm} \le 0.028\ \mathrm{kg\cdot m^2}$, $0 < B_{sm} \le 0.045\ \mathrm{Nms/rad}$
$0 < B_{rw} \le 0.5\ \mathrm{Nms/rad}$, $0.0040\ \mathrm{kg\cdot m^2} \le J_{rw} \le 0.0048\ \mathrm{kg\cdot m^2}$

$\overline{l}_m = 0.02\ \mathrm{m}$, $\overline{l}_p = 0.03\ \mathrm{m}$, $\overline{C}_3 = 160000\ \mathrm{N/rad}$.

Table.1 Nominal Parameters Of SBW System

DOI: 10.1051/itmconf/20171201011

parameters	*values*
J_h, C_h ($kg \cdot m^2$)	0.0791, 0.2
B_h (Nms/rad)	0.15
G_1, G_2	16.5, 30
K_s (s^{-1})	0.23
r_p, ϕ	20, 0.05
λ, ε	1, 0.01

Table.2 Parameters of Three Wheeled Forklift Dynamics

Parameters	*Values*
M (kg)	2937
a, b, c (m)	1.408, 0.512, 1.88
L (m)	1.92
Wet asphalt pavement ($C_1 = C_2$, C_3 (N/rad))	43000,80000
Dry asphalt pavement ($C_1 = C_2$, C_3 (N/rad))	77850,153840
J_z ($kg \cdot m^2$)	50
l_m, l_p (m)	0.016,0.023

Simulation environment is set as follows:

(1) Using two different road environments, the first 10s is set to wet asphalt pavement, the second 10s is set to dry asphalt pavement.

(2) The speed of forklift is: $u = 10 km/h \approx 2.78 m/s$.

(3) The driver input torque is set to sinusoidal continuous input to examine the stability and the tracking performance, which is $\tau_h = 0.5\sin(1.9t)$ N·m.

5.2 Simulation Results

The 30° step signal of steering handle is simulated and analyzed. The simulation results are shown in Fig.4, Fig.5.

It can be seen from Fig.3 and Fig.4 that when using conventional fixed transmission ratio to control, the sideslip angle and yaw rate gain change greatly with the speed of forklift, when using ideal transmission ratio to control, the yaw rate response of the forklift does not vary with vehicle speed, which is good for improving steering performance; and the sideslip angle is obviously reduced relative to the fixed transmission ratio, which makes the forklift has better steering stability.

It can be seen from Fig.5 (a) and Fig.5 (b) that, for the steering angle tracking sliding mode control of SBW system based on ideal transmission ratio, although there are uncertain parameters exist in the system, the rear wheel angle of forklift can closely follow the change of the target rear wheel angle through the sliding mode control. Although the road environment changes at 10s, the SBW system is still able to meet good steering performance, which shows the strong robustness of the sliding mode control to the external conditions. Fig. 5 (c) shows the motor equivalent control torque, Fig. 5 (d) shows the uncertain self-aligning torque of the wheel and its upper bound during the process of forklift moving.

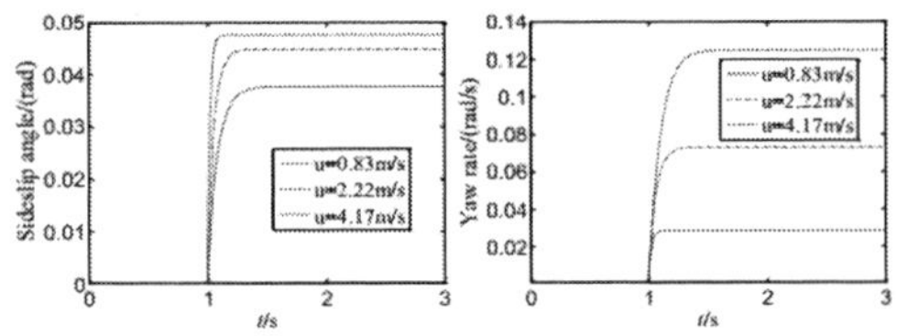

Figure 3. The step response of the steering performance when the transmission ratio is fixed to 8

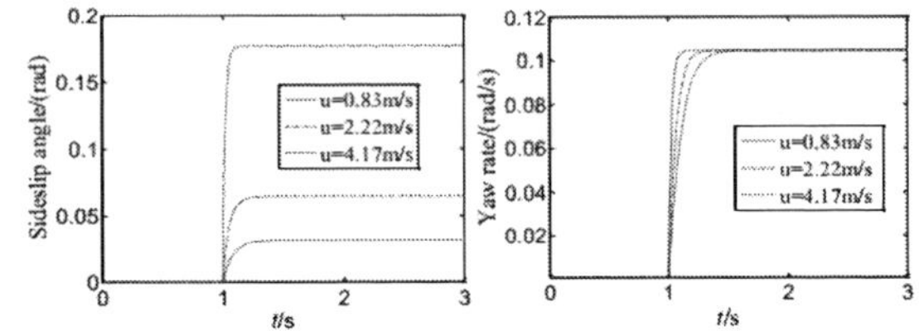

Figure 4. The step response of the steering performance under the ideal transmission ratio

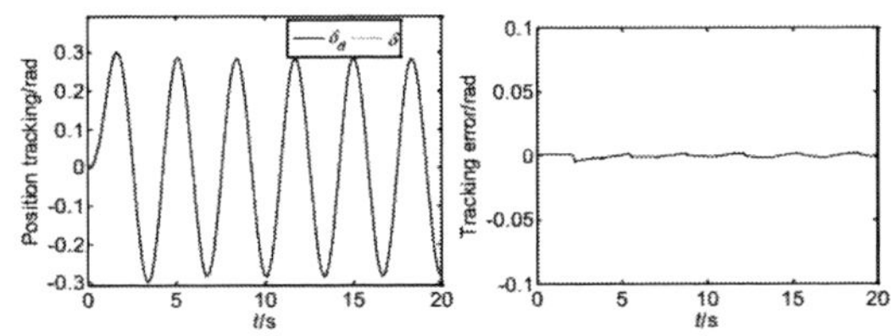

(a) Position tracking (b) Tracking error

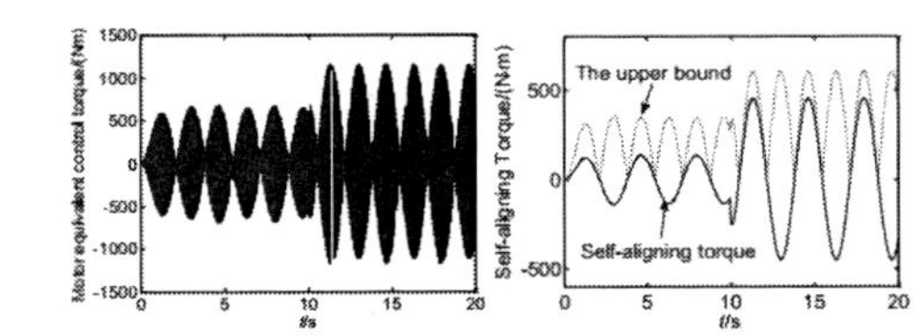

(c) Motor equivalent control torque (d) Self-aligning torque

Figure 5. Sliding mode control for SBW

The simulation results of boundary layer sliding mode control is shown in Fig. 6.It can be seen from Fig. 6 (a) and Fig. 6 (b) that the SBW system exhibits good tracking performance under the boundary layer sliding mode control. Although the angle position tracking error has increased, by a reasonable choice of the thickness of the boundary layer, the position tracking error can be suppressed small enough to meet the requirements of actual operation of forklift SBW system. As shown in Fig. 6 (c), by using the boundary layer sliding mode to control, not only the chattering in the motor drive torque is effectively restrained, but also the amplitude of the equivalent drive torque is greatly reduced.

DOI: 10.1051/itmconf/20171201011

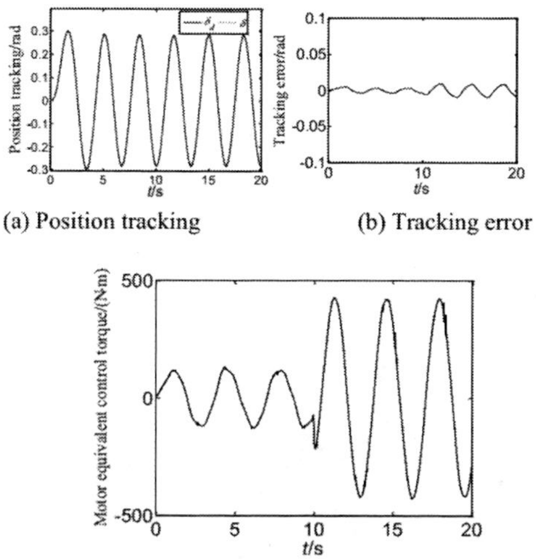

(a) Position tracking (b) Tracking error

(c) Motor equivalent control torque

Figure 6. The boundary layer sliding mode control for SBW

6. Conclusions

Based on the structural characteristics of SBW system for three wheeled forklift, the 2DOF dynamic model and steering executive mechanism dynamic model of SBW system are deduced. A steering control strategy combining ideal variable transmission ratio and sliding mode control algorithm is proposed. The simulation results show that the steering stability of forklift can be improved by using the steering control strategy. The strategy is robust to parameter uncertainties, which makes the tracking errors converge quickly to achieve satisfactory tracking performance.

Acknowledgment

This work was supported by the National Natural Science Foundation of China under Grant No.51577046, the State Key Program of National Natural Science Foundation of China under Grant No.51637004, the national key research and development plan "important scientific instruments and equipment development" Grant No.2016YFF0102200.

References

[1] X. Lei, D. Zhang, Y. Jin, "Research on vibration suppression of the Forklift Steering System based on finite element modal analysis and pole placement," Robotics and Manufacturing Automation (ROMA), 2014 IEEE International Symposium on. IEEE Press, 2014,pp. 46-51.

[2] B. Zheng, S. Anwar, "Yaw stability control of a steer-by-wire equipped vehicle via active front wheel steering," Mechatronics, vol.19, 2009, pp. 799-804.

[3] N. Matsunaga, J. Im, S. Kawaji, "Control of steering-by-wire system of electric vehicle using bilateral control designed by passivity approach," Journal of System Design and Dynamics, vol.4, 2010, pp. 50-60.

[4] H. Wang, H. Kong, Z. Man, Z. Cao, DM Tuan, "Sliding mode control for steer-by-wire systems with AC motors in road vehicles," IEEE transactions on Industrial Electronics, vol 61, 2014, pp. 1596-1611.

[5] D. Bernardiniy, S. Di Cairanoz, A. Bemporad, H. Tsengz, "Drive-by-wire vehicle stabilization and yaw regulation: A hybrid model predictive control design," in Proceedings of the 48th IEEE Conference on. IEEE Press, 2009, pp.7621-7626.

[6] A. Rodriguez-Angeles, JA. Garcia-Antonio, "Active disturbance rejection control in steering by wire haptic systems," ISA transactions, vol. 53, 2014, pp. 939-946.

[7] C. Wang, T. Cui, W. Zhao, J. Chen, "Active front wheel steering control based on ideal transmission ratio," Transactions of the Chinese Society of Agricultural Engineering, vol. 31, 2015, pp. 85-90.

[8] H. Zheng, C. Zong, C. Tian, Z.Cheng, T. Zhu, Y. Dong, et al, "Control algorithm for steer-by-wire system with ideal steering ratio, "Journal of Jilin University (Engineering and Technology Edition), vol.37, 2007,pp. 1229-1235.

[9] D. Ren, S. Cui, J. Zhang, "Quasi-Sliding mode control for lane keeping with bounded and varying parameters," Transactions of Beijing Institute of Technology, vol.31, 2011, pp. 69-73.

ITM Web of Conferences 12, 01012 (2017) DOI: 10.1051/itmconf/20171201012
ITA 2017

To Classify Spontaneous Motion Intention of Step Size by Using Cerebral Hemoglobin Information

Kai Zhu[1], Chun-Guang Li*[2], Hedian Jin[3], Juan Li[4], Haiyan Hu[5] and Lining Sun[6], Wei Qu[7]

[2]*Key Laboratory of Robotics and System of Jiangsu Province, School of Mechanical and Electric Engineering, Soochow University, Suzhou, China*
7 ECOVACS Robotics (Suzhou) Co. Ltd, China
[2] lichunguang@suda.edu.cn, [7]quw0219@foxmail.com

Abstract: To improve the effect of walking-assistive devices, there is a need for it to develop devices controlled by spontaneous intention of patients. In recent study, we identified spontaneous motion intention of walking step based on cerebral hemoglobin information. Twenty healthy subjects performed walking tasks in three levels of step size (small, normal and large). According to distribution features of signals' power spectral-density, six frequency bands (0-0.18Hz with an interval of 0.03Hz for each band width) divided by applying wavelet packets decomposition were mainly analyzed. Feature vectors were extracted from the difference between oxygenated hemoglobin (oxyHb) and deoxygenated hemoglobin (dexoyHb) in different measuring channels in the six frequency bands. Support vector machine (SVM) method was utilized to classify the three levels of step sizes. Mean recognition accuracy achieved up to 83.3%. The result indicated that it is possible to identify spontaneous walking by using cerebral hemoglobin information. This is helpful for enhancing the intelligence of walking-assistive devices and motivating the active control of patients, which further is profitable for enhancing self-confidence of patients.

1. Introduction

A variety of accidents, injuries and diseases make many people disabled. And the aging of population results in many people unable to walk. So it is necessary and meaningful to develop walking-assistive devices for the elderly or disabled people. At the same time, walking-assistive devices have been becoming more and more intelligent with the development of measuring technique and pattern recognition. What we need is not a robot which has flexible commands controlled by buttons, voice and so on. Assistive robots are further expected to achieve different functions based on the spontaneous intention of patients.

Among the various brain-signal acquisition methods (fNIRS[1, 2], EEG [3, 4], MRI [5, 6], EMG [7], etc.), functional near-infrared spectroscopy (fNIRS) is portable, quiet, accurate and not too sensitive to the motion of objects. fNIRS measures oxygenated hemoglobin (oxyHb) and deoxygenated hemoglobin (dexoyHb) concentration changes by shining near-infrared light into the head (with three wavelengths of 780nm, 805nm, and 830nm) and measuring the diffusively reflected light changes that originate from physiological changes in the skin and cortex [8]. Compared to EEG and MEG, fNIRS technology has a better spatial resolution. So it guarantees the accuracy of different measuring channels. At the same time, fNIRS technology has a better time sampling rate than MRI. Therefore, it can detect complete physiological signal, which is helpful for removing noise interference [9]. In addition, it can also realize real-time measurement. Currently, fNIRS technology has been widely used in disease monitoring [10], cognitive research [11], and brain activity imaging [12, 13]. Previous studies have also explored the functional neural correlates of gait during dynamic tasks [14]. In sum, fNIRS is suitable for the study of identifying walking step. However, regions were often used to identify step size in previous studies [15]. At the same time, the motion of walking was mostly unnatural and not controlled by spontaneous intention [16]. These factors were not advantageous for the study of step size.

Our project proposed a method to identify walking step by using fNIRS technology. All the motions during the experiments were controlled by spontaneous intention. In the present work, the fNIRS signals in 22 channels were studied to seek for appropriate features. Wavelet packets decomposition and SVM were used to identify different step size. It is expected that the identified walking step could be applied in controlling walking-assistive devices.

2. Material and Methods

2.1Subjects

A total of twenty healthy subjects (21±1years old, 17 male and 3 female) participated in our experiment. None of them had a history of any psychiatric or neurological disorder. The experimental procedure was explained to all of them in detail before they provided their verbal informed consent.

2.2 Signal Acquisition

2.2.1 Measuring Instrument

Figureure.1 Experimental diagram

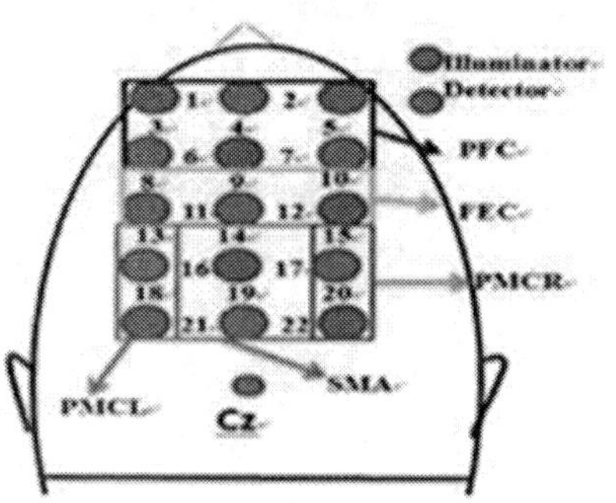

Figure.2 Diagram of measurement channels

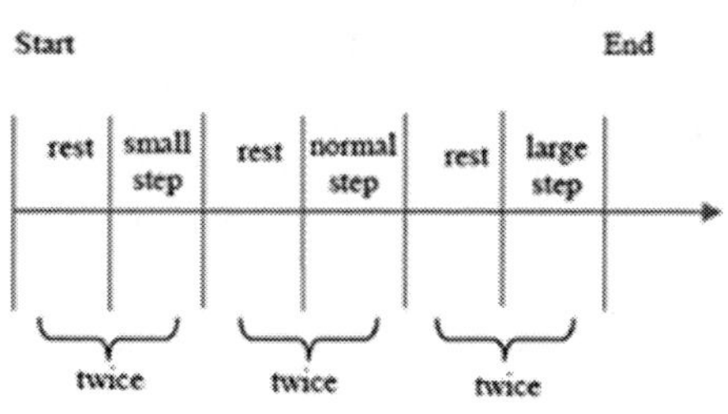

Figure.3 The procedure of first group's experiment. The sequence of the first group was small, normal and large step size, while the sequence of the second group was large, normal and small step size.

In this study, a FORIE-3000 optical topography system (Shimadzu Corporation, Kyoto, Japan) [17] was used to measure concentration changes of oxygenated hemoglobin, deoxygenated hemoglobin, and total hemoglobin (totalHb) (Figure. 1). The raw fNIRS signals were acquired at a sampling period of 0.13s.

2.2.2 Optode Arrangement

One set of 3×5 parietal flash holder was applied to fix emitters and detectors. The arrangement of optodes are shown in the Figure. 2. The number of measurement channels was 22. The measured regions included prefrontal cortex(PFCL: channels 1, 3, 4, 6 in the left hemisphere; PFCR: channels 2, 4, 5, 7 in the right hemisphere), premotor cortices(PMCL: channels 13, 18 in the left hemisphere; PMCR: channels 15, 20 in the right hemisphere), supplementary motor areas(SMAL: channels 14, 16, 19, 21 in the left hemisphere; SMAR: channels 14, 17, 19, 22 in the right hemisphere), frontal eye field (FECL: channels 8, 9, 11 in the left hemisphere; FECR: channels 9, 10, 12 in the right hemisphere). These areas have been confirmed to play an important role on regulating of walking [18].

2.3 Experimental Procedure

To eliminate the effects of experimental sequence, twenty participants were classified into two groups. The two groups were asked to perform experiments in a reverse motion sequence. The first group performed the walking tasks with a small, normal and large step size, while the second group performed the task with large, normal and small step size. In order to avoid the influence of dandruff, all the subjects were asked to wash hair one day before the experiment. During the experiment, all the motions were controlled by the subjects themselves without any implication or stimulation. That is, the start and the period of each task, as well as the period of each rest were all controlled by themselves. Cerebral hemoglobin information corresponding with spontaneous intention is preferable for enhancing application value of identification results.

The detailed procedure is shown in Figure. 3. Subjects were asked to walk in a fixed distance. The rest time was about 30s and each level of step size was repeated twice. The marks of the start and end of one task were signed by an experiment operator. Before the experiment, all the tasks and rest were performed twice by the subjects to acquaint themselves with the tasks. During the experiment, they were asked to rest enough without any counting.

3. Results

In the first time of walking, there was some kind of nervous for the most subjects. Therefore, only the tasks performed in the second time were analyzed. 18 subjects (9 subjects of the first group and 9 subjects of the second group) were used to select features. And the two other subjects were used to verify. In our study, the difference between oxyHb and deoxyHb was mainly analyzed as the following steps.

3.1 Data Preprocessing

3.1.1 Power Spectrum Density

As the frequency band showed, the main power was distributed below 0.18Hz. So the raw signals were firstly low-pass filtered at 0.18Hz to eliminate the effects of all kinds of noises. To confirm the correct division of wavelet packets decomposition, we analyzed the peak and valley values of power spectrum density. As shown in Figure. 4, the interval between the peak and valley values was around 0.03Hz. Therefore, as for the following wavelet packets decomposition, frequency band was divided into six parts (0-0.03Hz, 0.03-0.06Hz, 0.06Hz-0.09Hz, 0.09-0.12Hz, 0.12Hz-0.15Hz, 0.15Hz-0.18Hz).

3.1.2 Wavelet Packets Decomposition

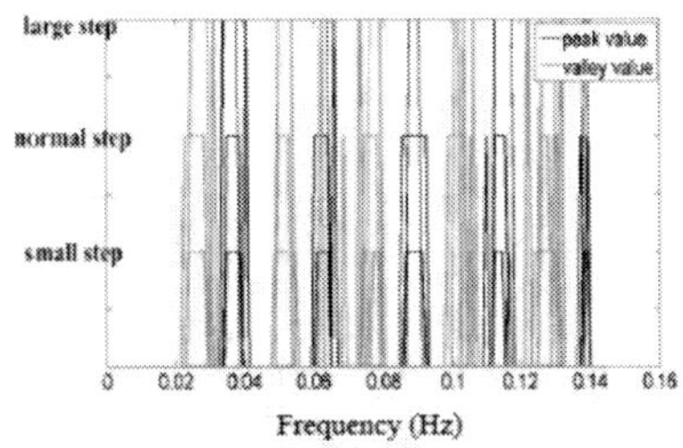

Figure.4 The peak values and valley values of power spectrum density. The green lines represent the peak values and the black lines denote the valley values. Frequency ranges of the peak or valley value observed from different subjects are shown on the vertical axis. And the three levels of walking step are shown on the horizontal axis.

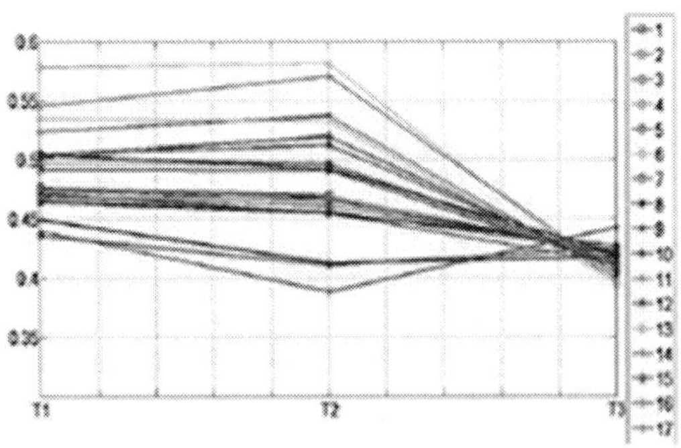

Figure.5 Line chart of different channels in the three time periods. CWP: Coefficient of wavelet packet reconstruction. T1: The means of the 8 points before the start marks. T2: The means of the 8 points after the start marks. T3: The means of the 9th-16th points after the start marks. Different colors represented 22 channels.

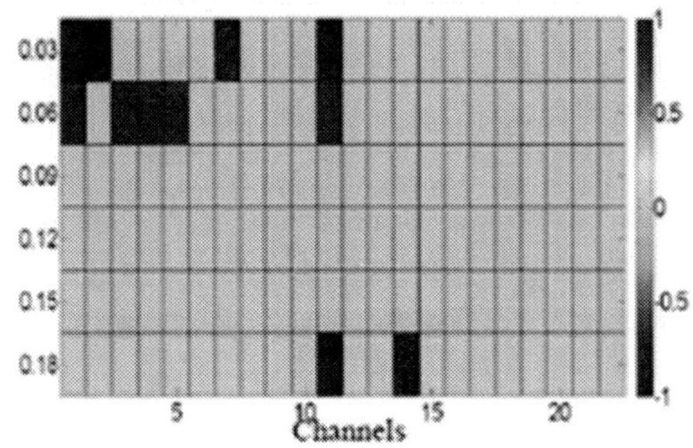

Figure.6 The results of statistical analysis. The red regions represent the values in the channels and frequency bands belonging to the top 30%, and the blue regions represent the bottom 30%.

First, 300 sampling points were truncated (180 sampling points before the start marks and 120 sampling points after the start marks) for the tasks in each step size. Second, the 300 sampling points subtracted their average value so as to reduce the effect of direct component. Third, the data was decomposed and reconstructed by 7-dimension wavelet packet algorithm [19-22]. If so, each frequency band was 0.03Hz corresponding with the result of power spectrum density.

3.2 Feature Extraction

24 sampling points which show the best information of movement were further selected. The means of the 8 points before the start marks were recorded as T1; the means of the 8 points after the start marks were recorded as T2 and the means of the 9th-16th points after the start marks were recorded as T3. After that, means of the subjects calculated for T1, T2, and T3. In order to reduce the influence of individual difference in the two groups, the averages of the two groups were calculated respectively. Then, common features were selected based on the results of the two groups.

As for the measured 22 channels, each channel has three mean values of T1, T2, and T3 in each frequency band, and there were six frequency bands. Analyses were performed in both the time domain and frequency domain. As for the time domain, signal variation following as time (T1, T2, and T3) was observed for six frequency band. One of six frequency bands was taken for example in Figure. 5. If the values in one channel were distinctly larger or smaller than those in the other channels, or the values in one channel were obviously changed, the channel was selected as an important one. As for the frequency domain, information difference among the frequency bands was observed for each time period (T1, T2 and T3). It was the most obvious in T3.

To guarantee the correctness and universality of feature vectors, statistics method was applied to seek for important channels and frequency bands. For the values in the 22 channels in the 6 frequency bands, if the value in some channel and frequency band was the top or bottom 30 percent, and the same conclusion was obtained for 78% (14 subjects) of the 18 subjects, the corresponding channel in that frequency band was selected as one feature vector. One level of step size was taken as an example in Figure. 6.

3.3 Identification of Step Size

Since the features were much more obvious in T3 than those in T1 and T2. Thereby, the features in T3 were applied. Combining the features in the time domain and frequency domain, all the feature vectors were listed in Table 1. Finally these feature vectors were used to classify three levels of walking step by SVM [23]. Most features were concentrated in the regions of PMC and SMA. It suggested that the regions of SMA and PMC had a huge impact on controlling step size.

For SVM, among the 18 subjects whose data were used to extract features, 14 subjects' data were adopted as training set. Two subjects whose features were not obvious were removed. The data of the rest two subjects and two other subjects who were not used for feature extraction were used to verify the algorithm. Each subject performed three levels of step size. A classification accuracy of 83.3% was achieved.

Tabel 1. Features Vectors Used For Identifying Step Size

Frequency	Channels(T3)
0-0.03Hz	16
0.03-0.06Hz	12,13
0.06-0.09Hz	1,11
0.09-0.12Hz	19
0.12-0.15Hz	8,14,15,17,18
0.15-0.18Hz	17,18,20,21

4. Conclusion

The present study demonstrated a new method to classify three levels of walking step, which was controlled by the subjects' spontaneous intention. And the classification accuracy of 83.3% was achieved. Spontaneous motion intentions are important in the control of walking-assistive devices. The proposed method had brighter prospects for realizing the intelligent control of walking assistive robots.

However, our study still had some limitations to solve before being applied in actual. First, the feature vectors were obtained in the time period of T3. Though the highest classification accuracy was achieved in T3, it resulted in a time delay of about 2s for classification. Much more appropriate features should be found before the start of movement. In the following researches, we will try to apply the rate of cerebral hemoglobin change as features to eliminate the delay. The improvements of wavelet algorithm which are suitable for real-time application would also be considered. Further experiments and analyses would be performed on more subjects.

Moreover, current data was obtained from healthy subjects rather than paraplegics. However, our study is designed to be applied in paraplegics. Though their brains are normal, more and more patients would be analyzed in the near future.

Acknowledgment

This study was supported by the grants from the national high technology research and development program, China (863 Program: 2015AA042301) and Postdoctoral Science Foundation (2015M580461).

References

[1] M. Cope, "Methods of Quantitating Cerebral Near Infrared Spectroscopy Data." Advances in Experimental Medicine & Biology, vol. 222, pp.183-189, 1988.

[2] F.F. Jobsis, "Noninvasive, infrared monitoring of cerebral and myocardial oxygen sufficiency and circulatory parameters." Science, vol. 198, no. 4323, pp.1264-1267, 1977.

[3] Giuseppe, Lisi, and M. Jun. "EEG Single-Trial Detection of Gait Speed Changes during Treadmill Walk." PLOS One, 2015, 10(4): e0125479.

[4] Joseph T Gwin* and Daniel P Ferris. "An EEG-based study of discrete isometric and isotonic human lower limb muscle contractions." Journal of neuroengineering and rehabilitation, 2012, 9:35.

[5] Agnew, A. John, T. A. Zeffiro, and G. F. Eden. "Left hemisphere specialization for the control of voluntary movement rate." Neuroimage, vol. 22, no. 1, pp.289-303, 2004.

[6] Chan, C.K. Raymond, J. Huang, and X. Di. "Dexterous movement complexity and cerebellar activation: A meta-analysis." Brain Research Reviews, vol. 59, no. 2, pp. 316-323, 2009.

[7] S. Lee, and Y. Sankai, "Power assist control for walking aid with HAL-3 based on EMG and impedance adjustment around knee joint." Intelligent Robots and Systems, vol. 2, pp.1499-1504, 2002.

[8] Scholkmann F, Kleiser S, Metz A J, Zimmermann R, Mata Pavia J, Wolf U and Wolf M. "A review on continuous wave functional near-infrared spectroscopy and imaging instrumentation and methodology." Neuroimage, vol. 6, no, 27, pp.85, 2014.

[9] Yamamoto, Toru, and T. Kato. "Paradoxical correlation between signal in functional magnetic resonance imaging and deoxygenated hemoglobin content in capillaries: a new theoretical explanation." Physics in Medicine & Biology 2.6195, pp.938-938, 1979.

[10] Chen, W.G., et al., "Ischemic and bleeding disease monitoring with fNIRS imager." One case report,

in Saratov Fall Meeting '98: Light Scattering Technologies for Mechanics, Biomedicine, and Material Science, V.V. Tuchin, V.P. Ryabukho, and D.A. Zimnyakov, Editors. Spie-Int Soc Optical Engineering: Bellingham. pp. 540-544, 1999.

[11] Kwee, I.L. and T. Nakada, "Dorsolateral prefrontal lobe activation declines significantly with age – Functional NIRS study." Journal of Neurology, vol. 250, no. 5, pp. 525-529. 2003.

[12] Hoshi, Y., S.J. Chen, and M. Tamura, "Spatiotemporal imaging of human brain activity by functional near-infrared spectroscopy." American Laboratory, vol. 33, no. 20, pp. 35, 2001.

[13] Schroeter, M.L., et al., "Towards a standard analysis for functional near-infrared imaging." Neuroimage, vol. 21, no. 1, pp. 283-290, 2004.

[14] Blumen HM, Holtzer R, Brown LL, Gazes Y, Verghese J, Behavioral and neural correlates of imagined walking and walking-while-talking in the elderly. Hum Brain Mapp, 2014.

[15] Pietro Caliandro, Mariano Serrao, Luca Padua, Gabriella Silvestri, Chiara Iacovelli, Chiara Simbolotti , Silvia Mari, Giuseppe Reale, Carlo Casali and Paolo M. Rossini," Prefrontal cortex as a compensatory network in ataxic gait: A correlation study between cortical activity and gait parameters." Restorative Neurology and Neuroscience, vol. 33, pp. 177–187, 2015.

[16] Lukas Jaeger, Laura Marchal-Crespo, Peter Wolf, Andreas R. Luft, Robert Riener, Lars Michels, Spyros Kollias," On the Modulation of Brain Activation During Simulated Weight Bearing in Supine Gait-Like Stepping." Brain Topogr, vol. 29, pp. 193–205, 2016.

[17] Shimadzu Corporation, Kyoto, Japan, Instruction manual for functional optical imaging system FOIRE-3000 series, Manual No : M587-E005, Rev. B, Oct. 2010.

[18] Picard, Nathalie, and P. L. Strick. "Imaging the premotor areas." Current Opinion in Neurobiology, vol. 11, no. 6, pp.663-672, 2001.

[19] Zengyong, Li, "Wavelet analysis of skin blood oscillations in persons with spinal cord injury and able-bodied subjects." Archives of Physical Medicine & Rehabilitation, vol. 87, no. 11, pp.7-8, 2007.

[20] Dario Farina, Omar Feix do Nascimento, Marie-Franc¸ oise Lucas, Christian Doncarli. "Optimization of wavelets for classification of movement-related cortical potentials generated by variation of force-related parameters." Journal of Neuroscience Methods, vol. 162, pp.357–363, 2007.

[21] Abry P, Aldroubi A. "Designing multiresolution analysis-type wavelets and their fast algorithms." J Fourier Anal Appl, vol. 2, pp. 135–159, 1995.

[22] Aldroubi A, Abry P, Unser M. "Construction of biorthogonal wavelets starting from any two resolutions." IEEE Trans Sig Proc, vol. 46, pp. 1130–1133, 1998.

[23] V.N. Vapnik, "An overview of statistical learning theory." IEEE Transactions on Neural Networks, vol. 10, no. 10, pp.988-99, 1999.

LSTM-Based Temperature Prediction for Hot-Axles of Locomotives

Can LUO, Di YANG, Jin HUANG, Yang-Dong DENG

School of Software, Tsinghua University, Beijing, China
luocan14 mails.tsinghua.edu.cn, yangd15@mails.tsinghua.edu.cn, huangjin@tsinghua.edu.cn, dengyd@tsinghua.edu.cn

Abstract: The reliability of locomotives plays a central role for the smooth operation of railway systems. Hot-axle failures are one of the most commonly found problems leading to locomotive accidents. Since the operating status of the locomotive axle bearings can be distinctly reflected by the axle temperatures, online temperature monitoring has become an essential way to detect hot-axle failures. In this work, we explore the feasibility of predict the hot-axle failures by identifying the temperature from predicted nominal values. We propose a data-driven approach based on the Long Short-Term Memory (LSTM) network to predict the sensor temperature for axle bearings. The effectiveness of the prediction model was validated with operation data collected from commercial locomotives. With a prediction accuracy is within a few percent, the proposed techniques can be used as a dynamic reference for hot-axle monitoring.

1. Introduction

With the fast-growing trend of the global industrialization and urbanization, the railway transportation plays an increasingly important role in modern society since it's the most energy-efficient and environment-friendly means of mass transportation. As the major asset of the railway transportation, locomotives have become highly complex machines involving the synergy of components from many different domains. Among various components, axle bearings are safety-critical and their failures can lead to disastrous accidents. The temperatures of the axle bearings are usually considered to be one of the most important health indicators. High-speed rotation of the bearings will cause the rise of the temperatures due to the mechanical friction. As a result, the respective failures are designated as hot-axles. Figure 1 shows an example of the accident caused by hot-axle failures.

Today the temperature based detection of hot-axle is becoming popular in the railway industry. However, there is a strong demand for predicting hot-axle failures so as to further improve the safety of locomotives and optimize the maintenance cost.

Because the temperature rising can be rather abrupt after the happening of hot-axles, an early failure warning solution is to forecast the nominal temperature given the environmental and operational information and then detect the deviation of the measured data from temperature sensors. However, it is rather a difficult task for such predictions due to the complex working environmental factors of the locomotives. In fact, the sensor data for axles are determined by a large number of factors including the operation modes of locomotives, the geographical situation of current route, the environment, and the disturbances from various sources. The hardship in building the analytical physical model enhanced such difficulties.

Figure1. An accident caused by a hot-axle failure

Due to the criticality of hot-axles, many researchers and engineers have been dedicated to develop fast and accurate systems to monitor the temperatures of axle bearings [1] [2]. The rapid development of machine learning and artificial intelligence in recent years has provided a new perspective for the temperature prediction of the hot-axle problem. Many researchers begin to use statistical learning methods to study the early warnings signals of the hot-axle based on the historical temporal data [3] [4]. Ma et al. use the stepwise regression analysis (SRA) to predict the train axle temperature to avoid possible failures [5]. Chen et al. apply the spectral based techniques in wheel-bearings defect detection problem

[6]. Brockwell et al. adapted the ARIMA model for single time series analysis, Lütkepohl uses the Vector Auto-Regression (VAR) model for multivariate time series analysis, while both got reasonable results for the state prediction problems [7] [8].

The fast-growing machine learning techniques provide feasible and powerful solutions to improve the safety of industrial equipment in the application of Prognostics and Health Management (PHM) [9]. Under such practical needs, in this paper, we propose a temperature prediction framework for the hot-axle problem based on the Long Short-Term Memory (LSTM) networks. The data driven approach avoids the modeling of the potential physical mechanisms and focus on predicting according to the relevant historical time series data. After training with the practical running data of the locomotives, the LSTM-based model can predict the temperatures at different points of the axle rapidly with acceptable accuracy. This work shows that the LSTM network is a promising method to deal with the temperature prediction of the hot-axle problem and make an important reference for avoiding the hot-axle failures, which can further support the repair and maintenance process of the locomotives.

The paper is organized as follows. Section II describes the hot-axle problem and introduces the LSTM model for the time-series prediction. Section III proposes the prediction framework for the temperature of the hot-axles of locomotives. In Section IV, we implement the experiments and evaluate the results. Section V then follows with the conclusion of the paper.

2. Problem Formulation and the LSTM Model

2.1 The Temperature Prediction Problem

The axle bearings are the main parts that bears the loads of a locomotive, and the temperature distribution is one of the most important indicators of the state of the axle bearings. Since the temperature distribution is determined by many factors, such as the ratio between axle and wheel diameters, loading of the axle, locomotive speed, friction factor, the heat capacity, etc. [10], it is difficult to get the analytical temperature distribution.

A common solution is to deploy temperature sensors at the key points of the axle bearings. There are usually eight temperature sensors on each of the six axles of a locomotive, two of which are placed on the endpoints of the axle to gather environment temperatures and the remaining six are evenly locate at the two bearings attached to the axle with each bearing has three sensors positioned on the upper left, upper, and upper right side, respectively. The deployment is shown in Figure 2. The meanings of sensors are in Table I.

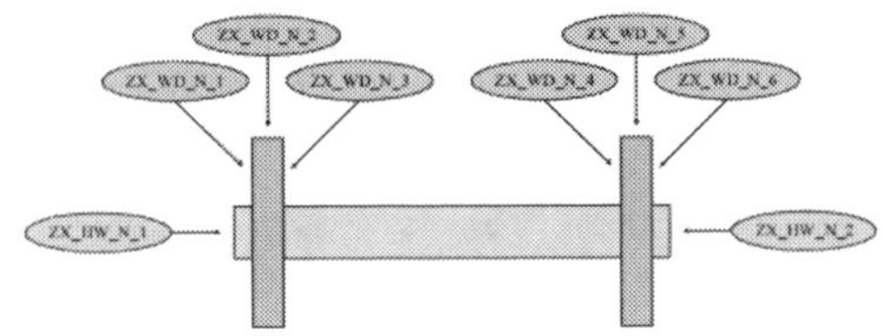

Figure2. Temperature sensors deployment on an axle bearing

In this work, we endeavor to build a LSTM model to predict the temperatures at the point 1 to 6 and compare them with the monitored temperatures by the sensors ZX_WD_N_1 to ZX_WD_N_6.

2.2 The LSTM Model

Recurrent neural networks (RNN) are feedforward neural networks with edges that span adjacent time steps introduces the time series features to the model. The recurrent edges that connect adjacent time steps may form cycles. At time step t, hidden node values $\boldsymbol{h}^{(t)}$ with recurrent edges receive the input from the current data point $\boldsymbol{x}^{(t)}$ and also from the hidden node values $\boldsymbol{h}^{(t-1)}$ at the previous time step. The output $\hat{\boldsymbol{y}}^{(t)}$ at time step t is computed according to the hidden node values $\boldsymbol{h}^{(t)}$. The input at the previous time step can influence the output $\hat{\boldsymbol{y}}^{(t)}$ at current time step by the recurrent edges. A simple RNN model is shown in Figure 3. It is because the recurrent edges that make the RNN has the ability to model the time series features. The long time steps dependence can be passed along the recurrent edges.

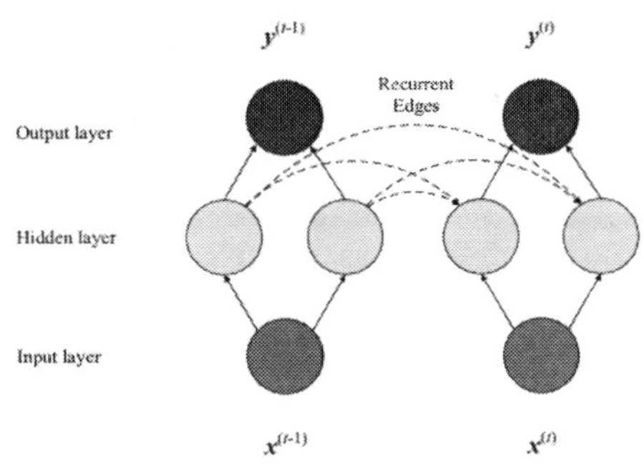

Figure3. A simple RNN model

The LSTM is one of the most successful modern RNN architectures for sequence learning tasks. The memory cell is introduced in [11] and replaces traditional nodes in the hidden layer of RNN. A memory cell is a composite unit, built form simpler nodes in a specific connectivity pattern, and the design of the unit can ensure that the gradient can pass across many time steps without vanishing or exploding.

In recent years, the LSTM networks have achieved great success dealing with sequential data in a range of different fields, including video analysis [12], information retrieval [13], natural language translation [14], and handwriting recognition [15]. Many studies have been done according to different tasks. Malhotra et al. [16] use the stacked LSTM network to detect the anomaly points in time series. Lipton et al. [17] apply the LSTM network on the clinical time series data to solve the problem of phenotyping critical care patients. ElSaid et al. [18] predict the excess vibration events in aircraft engines with LSTM recurrent neural networks.

Although many variations have been proposed to optimize the design of the LSTM unit in view of the connectivity pattern and the activation functions since the original LSTM was introduced, all of them have explicit memory nodes for storing information for long time steps.

In this paper, we select the LSTM unit introduced by Zaremba et al. [19] for the temperature prediction of hot-axles of locomotives. This model is very successful and gain good performance on a variety of tasks, including language modeling, speech recognition, image caption generation, and machine translation. The graphical representation of the LSTM memory cell is shown in Figure 4.

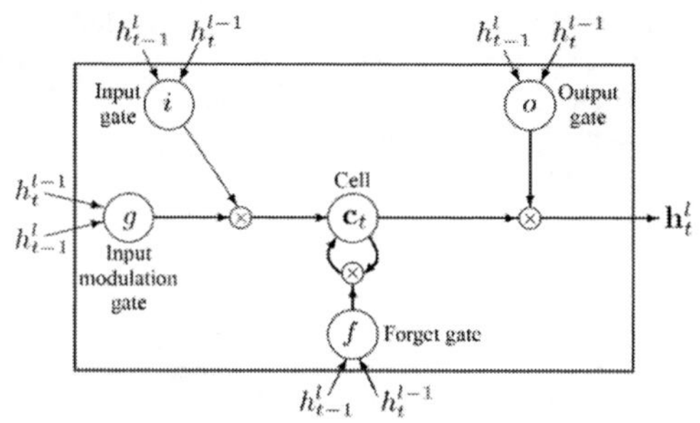

Figure 1. The graphical representation of LSTM memory cell for the tempreture prediction

The $h_t^l \in R^n$ represents the state of the LSTM memory cell in the hidden layer l at time step t. Since the h_t^l is determined by h_{t-1}^l and h_t^{l-1}, this LSTM unit can be applied to deep LSTM networks with multiple hidden layers. In general, we denote the h_t^0 as the input point $x^{(t)}$ and the h_t^L as the prediction point $\hat{y}^{(t)}$, where L is the number of layers of the LSTM network.

The state transition equations of the above LSTM unit defined are as follows [19]:

$$\text{LSTM}: h_t^{l-1}, h_{t-1}^l, c_{t-1}^l \rightarrow h_t^l, c_t^l$$

$$\begin{pmatrix} i \\ f \\ o \\ g \end{pmatrix} = \begin{pmatrix} sigm \\ sigm \\ sigm \\ tanh \end{pmatrix} T_{2n,4n} \begin{pmatrix} D(h_t^{l-1}) \\ h_{t-1}^l \end{pmatrix}$$

$$c_t^l = f \odot c_{t-1}^l + i \odot g$$

$$h_t^l = o \odot tanh(c_t^l)$$

Where $\odot$ is element-wise multiplication, $sigm$ and $tanh$ are applied element-wisely, and D is the dropout operator.

3. LSTM-Based Temperature Prediction Framework

As shown in Figure 5, our axle temperature prediction framework is mainly composed of three parts, a data preprocessing module, a core LSTM-based prediction module, and an assistant warning module. When the prediction module gets possible indicators for the system failure, the assistant warning module will be activated to remind the drivers for proper operations. Here we only introduce the data preprocessing and the prediction parts in details.

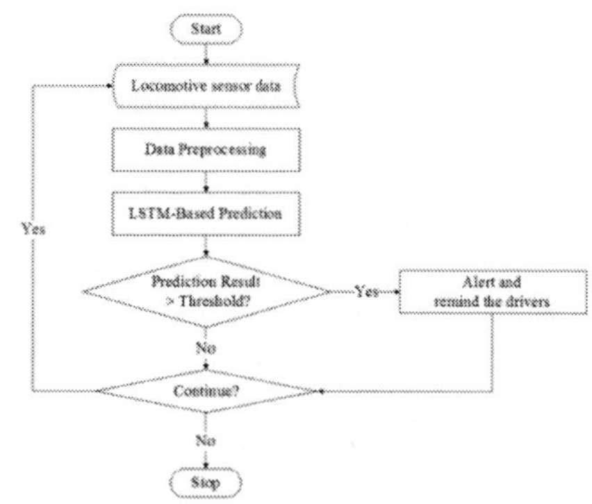

Figure 2. Overview of our prediction framework

3.1 Data Preprocessing

The temperatures at different positions of the axle are determined by many factors, e.g., the physical states of the locomotives including the running speed and the traction level, the route characteristics including the altitude and the slopes, the environmental temperature and other environmental parameters, as well as the disturbances from various sources. We select some main parameters and collect the time series data from the data sensors deployed at different positions of the locomotives. Table I lists the data sensors of relevant physical variables that we need.

Table1. Data sensors in the hot-axle prediction

Data sensors	*Description*
ZD_LCG	The train pip pressure
ZD_TFG	Park cylinder pressure
ZD_JHG	Balance cylinder pressure
ZD_LLJ	The train pipe flow
ZD_SPEED	Locomotive's running speed
ZX_HW_N_1	Left side environment temperature of axle N
ZX_HW_N_2	Right side environment temperature of axle N
ZX_WD_N_1	Temperature for point 1 of axle N
ZX_WD_N_2	Temperature for point 2 of axle N
ZX_WD_N_3	Temperature for point 3 of axle N
ZX_WD_N_4	Temperature for point 4 of axle N
ZX_WD_N_5	Temperature for point 5 of axle N
ZX_WD_N_6	Temperature for point 6 of axle N

The data collected by the sensors are usually with much noise, the data preprocessing step is thus needed to improve the quality of data. Here we removed the redundant data and obvious external interferences first, then a resampling process was carried out on the input

DOI: 10.1051/itmconf/20171201013

time series so that the data can be sampled at a fixed interval (10s in our experiments). During the resampling process, irregularities may present due to the multiple measurements, making the interpolation or sophisticated methods be needed to reconstruct the data. We select the linear interpolation technique since it is simple and efficient for the LSTM-based prediction in the next subsection.

3.2 LSTM Network Architecture

The input of the LSTM-based prediction model is a time series $\mathbf{x} = \{\mathbf{x}^{(1)}, \mathbf{x}^{(2)}, \dots, \mathbf{x}^{(T)}\}$, where the T is the input window size. Each point $\mathbf{x}^{(t)} \in R^n$ is an n-dimensional vector $\{x_1^{(t)}, x_2^{(t)}, \dots, x_n^{(t)}\}$. Here we choose n as 13 so that each element in $\mathbf{x}^{(t)}$ corresponds to one data sensor in Table I.

The output $\hat{\mathbf{y}}^{(T+k)} \in R^m$, the future temperatures to be predicted for point 1 to 6 of the axle after k time steps, where m = 6.

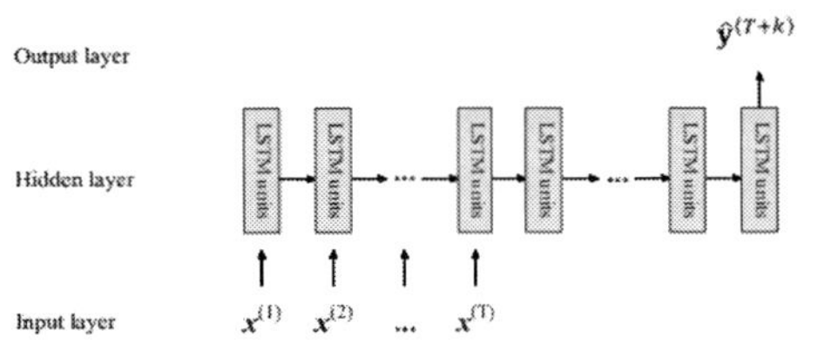

Figure 3. The architecture of the LSTM network

The LSTM network architecture is shown in Figure 6. The input layer has T input points, where each input point is 13-dimentional vector. The output layer has only one unit of a 6-dimentional vector. A hidden layer with LSTM units are connected to the input and output layer. There are 64 LSTM units in the hidden layer at each time step.

We set k = 1, 6, 12, so as to predict the results every 10 seconds, 1 minute, and 2 minutes, respectively. The time window size T is set to 16 empirically according to the experiment results.

4. Experiments

4.1 Experiment Design

We use Tensorflow to implement and train our LSTM networks. Tensorflow is an open-source software library developed by Google for numerical computation and is widely used in machine learning and deep learning tasks. Data flow graphs are used in Tensorflow to represent the architecture of networks. With the Tensorflow API, we can perform the computation on one or more CPUs or GPUs in the platform.

We deploy the LSTM networks on a high performance server equipped with two Intel(R) Xeon(R) E5-2609 v3 CPU and 256 GB of DDR3 main memory. Two Nvidia GTX Titan X (Pascal) GPUs are added to the motherboard as co-processor to accelerate the computation in Tensorflow. We run the experiments on CentOS 7.0 with Tensorflow v1.0 and CUDA 8.0. The configuration of the hardware and software platform is outlined in Table II.

Table2. Hardware and software configuration

Parameters	*Description*
CPU	Intel(R) Xeon(R) E5-2609 v3 @ 1.90GHz
RAM	256GB
GPU	NVIDIA GTX Titan X (Pascal)
OS	CentOS 7.0
CUDA version	8.0
Tensorflow version	v1.0

We collect the raw sensor data from 10 locomotives of the same type running in the same route. After preprocessing, ten continuous resampling data with each has about 5500 sampling points were generated. We randomly select nine of them as the training data and the last one as the test data. We segment the continuous sampling data to coordinate with the input time window size and the time steps in the prediction and feed the segments to the LSTM networks defined in Tensorflow.

The Mean Squared Error (MSE) is selected as the cost function to train the LSTM networks as it provides a smoother optimization results. The Adam optimizer [20] was employed in training the LSTM networks as it is a simple and computationally efficient algorithm for gradient-based optimization. Additionally, the training batch size is set to be 10 and the learning rate is set to be 0.0001.

4.2 Results and Evaluation

We evaluate the max prediction error $\mathbf{e}^{(t+k)}$ on the test set where $e_i^{(t+k)} = |y_i^{(t+k)} - \hat{y}_i^{(t+k)}|, i = 1, 2, \dots, 6$. Here $y_i^{(t+k)}$ represent the true value of the temperature at the point i of the axle collect by the sensor ZD_WD_i at the time step t + k, while $\hat{y}_i^{(T+k)}$ represent the prediction value of the temperature at the point *i* of the axle output by the LSTM network according to the input time series $\{\mathbf{x}^{(t-T+1)}, \mathbf{x}^{(t-T+2)}, \dots, \mathbf{x}^{(t)}\}$

The number of iteration steps is chosen as 100000 and the corresponding training time is about 2 hours. The max prediction errors of different prediction time step on the test set are listed in Table 3

Tanle3. Prediction errors

Axle Position	Max Prediction Errors(℃)		
	k = 1	*k = 6*	*k = 12*
Point 1	1.19	1.58	1.87
Point 2	1.17	1.61	1.74
Point 3	0.98	1.22	1.68
Point 4	1.04	1.36	1.66
Point 5	1.05	1.45	1.65
Point 6	1.12	1.55	1.74

From the results we can see that the max prediction error does not exceed 1.2℃, 1.7℃, 1.9℃ while k = 1, 6, 12. That means we can predict temperatures of the axle two minutes ahead and the prediction error of any points does not exceed 1.9℃.

In the practical application, the prediction values are acceptable as they serve as a reference temperature under normal operation. A significant deviation of the observed sensor data from the referenced prediction value can be considered as a potential danger and trigger a warning notification to the driver and locomotive monitoring center. Therefore, the prediction errors are acceptable and the LSTM-based prediction framework is effective in the hot-axle prediction problem.

5. Conclusions and Discussion

The temperature prediction is useful in predicting the failure of the hot-axles in the PHM system of the locomotives. This paper developed a temperature prediction framework for hot-axle problem in the locomotives with a core component of the LSTM-based model. The prediction errors are acceptable and the results provide a reference for capturing abnormal trend of the axle's temperatures. The effectiveness of the prediction model is validated on the practical running data of a locomotive. Experiment results shows the acceptable accuracy and effectiveness of the temperature prediction of the hot-axle problem in engineering practice.

Acknowledgment

The research is sponsored in part by NSFC Program (No. 61527812), National Science and Technology Major Project (No. 2016ZX01038101), MIIT IT funds (Research and application of TCN key technologies) of China, and The National Key Technology R&D Program (No. 2015BAG14 B01-02).

References

[1] R. W. Ngigi, C. Pislaru, A. Ball, and F. Gu, "Modern techniques for condition monitoring of railway vehicle dynamics", In Journal of Physics: Conference Series, vol. 364, no. 1, p. 012016. IOP Publishing, 2012.

[2] S. D. Milic, "A stationary system of noncontact temperature measurement and hotbox detecting", IEEE Transactions on Vehicular Technology 57, no. 5 (2008): 2684-2694.

[3] A. Amini, M. Entezami, and M. Papaelias, "Onboard detection of railway axle bearing defects using envelope analysis of high frequency acoustic emission signals", Case Studies in Nondestructive Testing and Evaluation Volume 6, Part A, pp. 8–16, 2016.

[4] W. Ma, S. Tan, X. Hei, J. Zhao and G. Xie, "A Prediction Method Based on Stepwise Regression Analysis for Train Axle Temperature", 12th International Conference on Computational Intelligence and Security (CIS) IEEE Computer Society, pp.386-390, 2016.

[5] W. Ma, S. Tan, X. Hei, J. Zhao, and G. Xie, "A Prediction Method Based on Stepwise Regression Analysis for Train Axle Temperature", In Computational Intelligence and Security (CIS), 2016 12th International Conference on, pp. 386-390. IEEE, 2016.

[6] B. Chen, Z. Yan, and W. Chen, "Defect Detection for Wheel-Bearings with Time-Spectral Kurtosis and Entropy." Entropy, vol. 16, pp. 607-626. 2014.

[7] P. J. Brockwell, and R. A. Davis, "Introduction to Time Series and Forecasting". springer, 2016.

[8] H. Lütkepohl, "New Introduction to Multiple Time Series Analysis", Springer Science & Business Media, 2005.

[9] J. Lee, E. Lapira, B. Bagheri and H. A. Kao, "Recent advances and trends in predictive manufacturing systems in big data environment", Manufacturing Letters, vol.1, pp.38–41, 2013.

[10] D. Chen, "Study of the Rule of Train Axle Temperature and Infrared Detection Mode of Axle Temperature", Harbin Engineering University, 2003.

[11] S. Hochreiter, and J. Schmidhuber, "Long short-term memory", Neural computation 9, no. 8, 1735-1780. 1997.

[12] N. Srivastava, E. Mansimov, and R. Salakhudinov, "Unsupervised learning of video representations using lstms", In International Conference on Machine Learning, pp. 843-852. 2015.

[13] H. Palangi, L. Deng, Y. Shen, J. Gao, X. He, J. Chen, X. Song, and R. Ward, "Deep sentence embedding using long short-term memory networks: Analysis and application to information retrieval", IEEE/ACM Transactions on Audio, Speech and Language Processing (TASLP) 24, no. 4, 694-707. 2016.

[14] I. Sutskever, O. Vinyals, and Q. V. Le, "Sequence to sequence learning with neural networks", In Advances in neural information processing systems, pp. 3104-3112. 2014.

[15] V. Pham, T. Bluche, C. Kermorvant, and J. Louradour, "Dropout improves recurrent neural networks for handwriting recognition", In Frontiers in Handwriting Recognition (ICFHR), 2014 14th

DOI: 10.1051/itmconf/20171201013

International Conference on, pp. 285-290. IEEE, 2014.

[16] P. Malhotra, L. Vig, G. Shroff, and P. Agarwal, "Long short term memory networks for anomaly detection in time series", In Proceedings, p. 89. Presses universitaires de Louvain, 2015.

[17] Z. C. Lipton, D. C. Kale, and R. C. Wetzell, "Phenotyping of Clinical Time Series with LSTM Recurrent Neural Networks", arXiv preprint arXiv:1510.07641. 2015.

[18] A. ElSaid, B. Wild, J. Higgins, and T. Desell, "Using LSTM recurrent neural networks to predict excess vibration events in aircraft engines", In e-Science (e-Science), 2016 IEEE 12th International Conference on, pp. 260-269. IEEE, 2016.

[19] W. Zaremba, I. Sutskever, and O. Vinyals, "Recurrent neural network regularization", arXiv preprint arXiv:1409.2329. 2014.

[20] D. Kingma, and J. Ba, "Adam: A method for stochastic optimization", arXiv preprint arXiv:1412.6980 (2014).

Top-k Keyword Search Over Graphs Based On Backward Search

Jia-Hui Zeng, Jiu-Ming Huang, Shu-Qiang Yang

1College of Computer National University of Defense Technology, Changsha, China
2College of Computer National University of Defense Technology, Changsha, China
3College of Computer National University of Defense Technology, Changsha, China
jhzeng93@foxmail.com

Abstract: Keyword search is one of the most friendly and intuitive information retrieval methods. Using the keyword search to get the connected subgraph has a lot of application in the graph-based cognitive computation, and it is a basic technology. This paper focuses on the top-k keyword searching over graphs. We implemented a keyword search algorithm which applies the backward search idea. The algorithm locates the keyword vertices firstly, and then applies backward search to find rooted trees that contain query keywords. The experiment shows that query time is affected by the iteration number of the algorithm.

1. Introduction

Graphs are applied in many areas. For example, RDF (Resource Description Framework) data model is a graph-shaped data model. Keyword search is a useful tool when searching large graph data. It is a user-friendly way to retrieve graphs because it does not require users to know the structure of the graph and the syntax of the query language.

In this paper, we focus on top-k ranked keyword searching on vertex-labelled graphs. Each vertex in the graph can contain multiple keywords. Given a query list with multiple keywords, we want to find out the subgraph that contains all query keywords. There may be multiple subgraphs that meet the requirement in the graph. It is time-consuming to find all such subgraphs. Moreover, users usually want to obtain the most relevant results with the query. So an evaluation function is needed to assess and sort the results. The evaluation function will be discussed in section 2.

For its convenience, keyword search has been adopted in many situations. Keyword search can be used to query XML data, and there is a lot of works focusing on this problem (e.g., [3] [4] [5] [6] [7]).

Keyword search in relational databases also attracts the attention of many researchers. [8] [9] [10] [11] [12] are related works about keyword search in relational databases.

There are many studies about keyword search over graphs. [13] [14] [2] [15] [16] are well known methods about keyword search over graphs. With the development of Semantic Web, a large amount of RDF data is distributed to the Internet. There has been increasing interest in keyword queries over RDF data recently. Because RDF is a kind of graph-shaped data, keyword search can be used to search RDF data. Related work includes [17] [18] [19] [1] [21]. A recent survey about keyword search over XML data, relational databases and graphs can be found in [22].

The rest of the paper is organized as follows. Section 2 defines the problem to be solved in this paper. Section 3 describes the data structure used in the search algorithm. Section 4 describes the detailed implementation of the algorithm. Section 5 discusses the experimental results. Section 6 concludes the paper.

2. Problem Definition

We are concerned with querying the directed graph $G = (V, E)$. Because the undirected graph is a special directed graph, the algorithm in this paper can be applied to undirected graphs. We follow the problem definition in [2]. Each vertex can contain multiple keywords and each keyword can be contained by multiple vertices. We use $W(v)$ to represent all keywords that contained by v. Given a query q with m keywords $\{w_1, w_2, \dots, w_m\}$, $\{r, v_1, v_2, \dots, v_m\}$ is called a candidate answer $A(q)$ if it meets the requirements below:

For each w_i, $w_i \in W(v_i)$.

For each v_i, a path can be found in G from r to v_i.

Each element in $A(q)$ is a vertex and r is called the root of $A(q)$. There may be a lot of candidate answers for the query q in G. So the definition above can be extended to the top-k version. The quality of a candidate answer is measured by the evaluation function. Equation (1) is the evaluation function used in this paper.

$$Score(A(q)) = \sum_{i=1}^{m} d(r, v_i) \quad (1)$$

In Equation (1), $d(r, v_i)$ denotes the shortest path from r to v_i. In our definition, the smaller the score, the higher the quality of the answer. When all answers for q in G are sorted in ascending order based on the scores, we use $A(q, i)$ to represent the ith candidate answer. Given a query q, the goal of top-k keyword search is to find out $\{A(q,1), A(q,2), \ldots, A(q,k)\}$. Moreover, the root of each $A(q, i)$ is not the same.

3. Data Structure Used In Algorithm

The algorithm mentioned in this paper applies the backward search idea. It starts to search simultaneously at all vertices that contain any keyword of q and expand to their neighboring vertices recursively. If a vertex connecting all query keywords of q was found, this vertex would be the root of a candidate answer. The termination condition determines when to stop the iteration process. We first introduce the data structure used in the algorithm.

3.1 Structure Table

The structure table is used to store the adjacent information of the graph. Assume that $u, v \in G$ and there is an edge from u to v in G. Then we call u is the upper vertex of v. We use $Upper(v)$ to indicate the collection of all upper vertices of v. The structure table is a two-column table in the database. The first column is used to store vertices in G. And the second column stores $Upper(v)$ of corresponding v in the first column. The data type of the second column is array. Taking Figure 1 as an example, the structure table of Figure 1 is shown in Table 1. Because v_5 has no upper vertex, there is no corresponding row in Table 1.

3.2 Inverted Index Table

A keyword can be contained by multiple vertices. The inverted index table is used to record the distribution of keywords. We use W_i to denote the collection of vertices containing the keyword w_i. The inverted index table is a two-column table in the database. The first column is used to store keywords. And the second column is used to store vertices that contain the corresponding keyword. For example, the inverted index table of Figure 1 is shown in Table 2.

3.3 Iteration List

The algorithm is based on the BFS (Breadth-First Search). A lot of vertices will be visited in the process of search. The iteration list is used to record vertices visited in each step. It is dynamically changing with the iteration process. In each element of iteration list, we store a list of m sets. We use $IL[i][j]$ to indicate the jth set in ith element of iteration list. The content of $IL[i+1][j]$ is shown in Equation (2).

$$IL[i+1][j] = \cup_{v \in IL[i][j]} Upper(v) - \cup_{p=0}^{i} IL[p][j] \quad (2)$$

In Equation (2), the range of values for i is $[0, +\infty)$ and for j is $[1, m]$. $IL[i][j]$ indicates the collection of vertices that can reach any vertex containing w_j in i hops. So $IL(0, j)$ is the same as W_j. For any $v \in w_j$, i is the length of shortest path from v to w_j, or more precisely, the length of shortest path from v to any vertex in W_j. Therefore, if $v \in IL[i][j]$, v would not be contained in $IL[i+\alpha][j]$ for $\alpha \in N^*$.

3.4 Shortest Path Map

In the process of search, the length of shortest path between two vertices will be recorded. We maintain a set of elements in a map and one for distinct vertex which has been visited in the process of search. We use $SP[v]$ to indicate the entry for v in the map. An array is stored in $SP[v]$. The length of the array is $m+2$. We use $SP[v][j]$ to denote the jth element in $SP[v]$. $SP[v][j+2]$ represents the length of shortest path from v to w_j for $j \in [1, m]$. $SP[v][0]$ indicates the sum of known shortest path length of v and $SP[v][1]$ denotes the number of keywords in q that have not been reached by v so far.

4. Algorithm Details

Given a query q, the purpose of the algorithm is to find out k top ranked candidate answers. The algorithm consists of two parts. One is used to find roots of candidate answers and the other is used to build paths from the root to query keywords. The algorithm detail of finding roots appears in Algorithm 1.

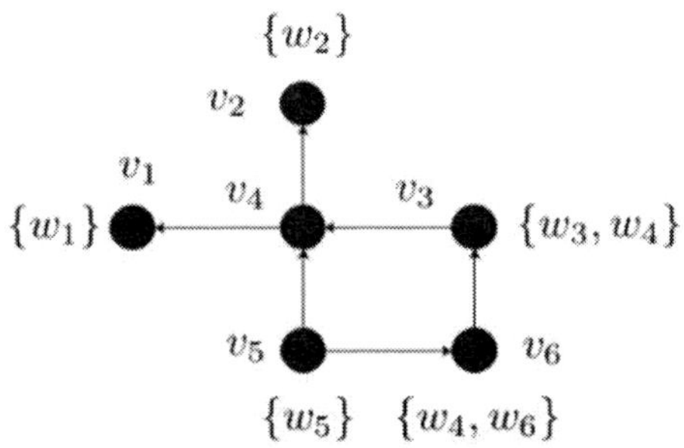

Figure 1. A sample graph

Table1. The structure table of the sample graph

Vertex	Upper Vertices
v_1	$\{v_4\}$
v_2	$\{v_4\}$
v_3	$\{v_6\}$
v_4	$\{v_3, v_5\}$
v_6	$\{v_5\}$

Table2. The inverted index table of the sample graph

Keyword	Vertices
w_1	$\{v_1\}$
w_2	$\{v_2\}$
w_3	$\{v_3\}$
w_4	$\{v_3, v_6\}$
w_5	$\{v_5\}$
w_6	$\{v_6\}$

Algorithm 1 Root Finding

Input: a query with m keywords $\{w_1, w_2, \ldots, w_m\}$
Output: roots and scores of top-k answers
1: Initialize IL and SP to empty sets;
2: Initialize $WV[i]$ to an empty set for $i \in [1, m]$;
3: $step \leftarrow 0$;
4: **for** each $i \in [1, m]$ **do**
5: search for W_i from the inverted index;
6: add W_i to $IL[0][i]$;
7: **for** each $v \in W_i$ **do**
8: update $SP[v]$;
9: add v to $WV[i]$;
10: **end for**
11: **end for**
12: **if** $\bigcap_{i=1}^{m} WV[i] \neq \emptyset$ **then**
13: **for** each $v \in \bigcap_{i=1}^{m} WV[i]$ **do**
14: add v and $SP[v][0]$ to AS;
15: remove $SP[v]$ from SP;
16: **end for**
17: **end if**
18: **while** termination condition is not satisfied **do**
19: **for** each $i \in [1, m]$ **do**
20: $temp[i] \leftarrow \emptyset$;
21: **for** each $v \in IL[step][i]$ **do**
22: search for $Upper(v)$ from the database or NH;
23: add $Upper(v)$ to $temp[i]$;
24: **end for**
25: $temp[i] \leftarrow temp[i] - WV[i]$;
26: $WV[i] \leftarrow WV[i] \cup temp[i]$;
27: **for** each $v \in temp[i]$ **do**
28: update $SP[v]$;
29: **end for**
30: **end for**
31: $step \leftarrow step + 1$;
32: add $temp$ to $IL[step]$;
33: **if** $\bigcap_{i=1}^{m} WV[i] - AS \neq \emptyset$ **then**
34: **for** each $v \in \bigcap_{i=1}^{m} WV[i] - AS$ **do**
35: add v and $SP[v][0]$ to AS;
36: remove $SP[v]$ from SP;
37: **end for**
38: **end if**
39: $\tau_{stop} \leftarrow$ the kth smallest score of answers in AS;
40: **end while**
41: **return** AS;

In Algorithm 1, $WV[i]$ is used to store vertices that can reach w_i. AS represents the answer set. There are many entries in AS and each entry is a pair $(root, score)$. $root$ denotes the root of a candidate answer and $score$ is the score of this candidate answer according to Equation (1).

In line 22, NH denotes a data structure which is used to store $Upper(v)$ in memory. The structure of NH is similar to the structure table. All adjacency information of $v \in G$ is stored in the structure table, which is a table in the database. The presence of adjacency information in the database can facilitate the storage of large graphs. Moreover, the indexing mechanism of the database can speed up the retrieval of $Upper(v)$. But in the search process, the operation of finding adjacency information is very frequent. So we set up NH to store part of adjacency information in memory. When searching for $Upper(v)$, we first look from NH. If v existed in the NH, then the algorithm would read $Upper(v)$ from NH. If v did not exist in the NH, then the algorithm would read $Upper(v)$ from the structure table and put v and $Upper(v)$ in NH. In this way, it is not necessary to access the database repeatedly when searching for $Upper(v)$ of a same v.

$SP[v]$ records the length of shortest paths from v to query keywords. If the shortest path from v to w_j was found, then the length of this path would be stored in $SP[v][j+2]$. If not, $SP[v][j+2]$ would remain null.

The meaning of Algorithm 1 is as follows. Firstly, initialize the variables used in the algorithm. Then search for W_i from the inverted index in the database. Next put W_i in $IL[0][i]$. For each vertex v in W_i, update the corresponding values of $SP[v]$. For example, if $SP[v]$ existed and $SP[v][i]$ was null, then we would assign $step$ to $SP[v][i]$. If $SP[v]$ did not exist, then we would create an entry $SP[v]$ and assign $step$ to $SP[v][i]$. If $SP[v]$ existed and $SP[v][i]$ was not null, then we would not make any changes. Afterwards, update $SP[v][0]$ and $SP[v][1]$. Next, put v in $WV[i]$. That means v has been visited. Then check if the intersection of $WV[i]$ is empty. If not, that means there are vertices containing all query keywords. Then put these vertices with corresponding scores in AS and remove them from SP. Next, determine whether the termination condition is satisfied. If not, start the iteration process. For each $v_i \in IL[step][i]$, search for $Upper(v_i)$ from the database or NH and put $Upper(v_i)$ in $temp[i]$. In that way, what $temp[i]$ stores is upper vertices of $v \in IL[step][i]$. Remove the vertices that have already been visited from $temp[i]$ and put the remaining vertices in $WV[i]$. Next, update the $SP[v]$ for $v \in temp[i]$. Afterwards, add 1 to $step$ and put $temp$ in $IL[step]$. Next determine whether new roots of candidate answers are found. When new roots are found, put these vertices with corresponding scores in AS and remove them from SP. After that, choose the k th smallest score of answers in AS as threshold τ_{stop}. Then continue determining the termination condition. Lastly, return AS in which the first k vertices are roots of $\{A(q,1), A(q,2), \ldots, A(q,k)\}$.

We used two termination conditions. The first termination condition is $\tau_{stop} \geq step$. When $\tau_{stop} \geq step$, it is impossible to find a better answer. For a possible candidate answer rooted at v that has not been put in the answer set, there is at least one keyword that has not been reached by v yet. So the length of shortest path from v to w must be greater than $step$. That means the score of this possible candidate answer must be greater than the kth smallest score of answers in the answer set. So it is impossible to find a better answer when this condition is satisfied. The second termination condition is $\tau_{stop} \geq minScore(SP)$. $minScore(SP)$ is used to calculate the lower bound of each possible answer's score which is rooted at v, and select the smallest lower bound. The calculation method is shown in Equation (3).

$$B_l(v) = \sum_{j=1}^{m} f(v,j)SP[v][j+2] + (1 - f(v,j))(step + 1) \qquad (3)$$

If v can reach w_j, then $f(v,j)$ equals 1. Otherwise, $f(v,j)$ equals 0. If the kth smallest score of candidate answers in AS is no greater than $minScore(SP)$, then the iteration process can be terminated because the candidate answer with smaller score cannot be found any more. Assume that there is a candidate answer $A(q)$ rooted at v with smaller score when $minScore(SP)$ is less than the kth smallest score. In that case, the root of $A(q)$ does not exist in the AS. That means that there is at least one keyword w_j that has not been reached by v yet. Then the length from v to w_j is at least $step + 1$. So it is impossible for $A(q)$ to be a top-k answer. This termination condition can help find the top-k answers for the query.

After getting k roots, paths from each root to w_j can be constructed by searching IL, SP and the structure table. The detailed description of the algorithm is shown in Algorithm 2.

Algorithm 2 returns the path from $root$ to w_j. Assume that $u, v \in G$ and there is an edge from v to u in G. We call u is the lower vertex of v. We use $Lower(v)$ to denote all lower vertices of v. $queue_i$ is a queue in which vertices can be reached by $root$ in i hops. $queue_i.removeAll$ means to clear all elements in $queue_i$. There may be multiple shortest paths, and the Algorithm 2 only returns one of them.

The top-k answers for keyword search over the graph can be found by combining Algorithm 1 and Algorithm 2.

Algorithm 2 Path Building

Input: $root, w_j$
Output: a path from $root$ to w_j

$i \leftarrow 0$;
$length \leftarrow SP[root][j+2]$;
$v \leftarrow root$;
$path[0] \leftarrow v$;
while $i < length$ **do**
  if v is not null **then**
    if $Lower(v) \cap IL[length - i - 1][j] \neq \emptyset$ **then**
      $queue_{i+1}.removeAll$;
      $queue_{i+1}.add(Lower(v) \cap IL[length - i - 1][j])$;
      $i \leftarrow i + 1$;
    end if
  else
    $i \leftarrow i - 1$;
  end if
  $v \leftarrow pop(queue_i)$;
  $path[i] \leftarrow v$;
end while
return $path$;

5. Experimental Results

The vertex-labelled graph used in experiments is randomly generated. It includes 1000000 vertices and 1000000 keywords. We use different integers to represent different keywords. The DBMS used in the experiment is PostgreSQL.

We carried out Algorithm 1 under different termination conditions on a randomly generated graph with 1000000 vertices. We randomly select some integers as query keywords. Table 3 lists eight queries. Figure 2 shows the time Algorithm 1 takes to find roots of top 2 answers under two termination conditions and Figure 3 shows the number of iterations in different conditions. The unit of time is milliseconds.

From Figure 2, we can see that the query time under Termination 2 is shorter than that of Termination 1. Moreover, when the number of query keywords increases, the difference between the query time of two conditions also increases. From the Figure 3, we can see that the number of iterations under Termination 2 is no greater than the number of iterations under Termination 1. That means Termination 2 can terminate the Algorithm 1 in fewer steps. By comparing two figures, we can see that the query time decreases as the number of iterations decreases. In query Q3, the iteration number of Termination 1 is the same as that of Termination 2 and the query time is not much different. And in other queries, we can see that as the difference between iteration numbers increases, the difference between query times also increases. So Termination 2 can terminate the Algorithm 1 more quickly than Termination 1 because the iteration number under Termination 2 is less than that of Termination 1. Moreover, the number of query keywords also has an impact on query time. The iteration number of Q4 under Termination 1 is the same as the iteration number of Q7

DOI: 10.1051/itmconf/20171201014

under Termination 2. But the query time of Q4 under Termination 1 is shorter than the query time of Q7 under Termination 2. So the number of query keywords can also have an impact on the query time. The more query keywords, the longer the query time.

In a word, Termination 2 can terminate the algorithm more quickly than Termination 1 because Termination 2 has less number of iterations than Termination 1. Moreover, the number of keywords is positively correlated with the query time.

Table3. Queries

Queries	Keyword vertices
Q_1	(1,2)
Q_2	(10,26598)
Q_3	(11,3299)
Q_4	(666,888)
Q_5	(3976,644)
Q_6	(987,25267)
Q_7	(550560,402060,200442)
Q_8	(12013,172248,281573)

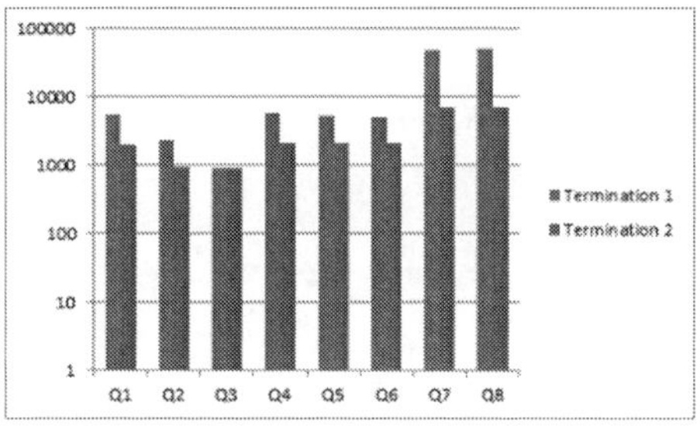

Figure 2. Query time under different termination conditions

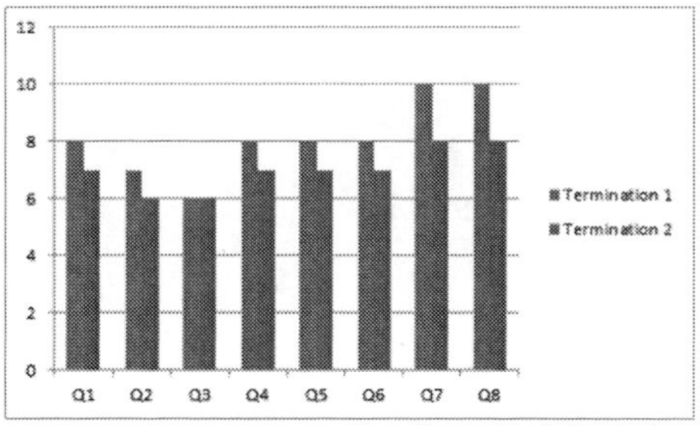

Figure 3. Comparing the number of iterations

6. Conclusion

In this paper, we implemented a method that addresses the issue of top-k keyword search over graphs. For each query keyword w_i, we first find vertices which contain w_i. Then using BFS to extend each keyword vertex. If a vertex that can reach all query keywords was found, this vertex would be the root of a candidate answer. The algorithm will terminate when the termination condition is satisfied. When the algorithm stops, it will return top-k answers and each answer is a rooted tree. We compared the query time and iteration numbers when using different termination conditions. And the experiment shows that the second termination is better than the first one, because it has fewer numbers of iterations than the first termination condition.

Acknowledgment

The work described in this paper is supported by National Basic Research Program of China (973 Program) granted No.2013CB329601, The National Key Research and Development Program of China (2016QY03D0601, 2016QY03D0603) and National Natural Science Foundation of China (No.61502517, No.61672020, No.61662069).

References

[1] W. Le, F. Li, A. Kementsietsidis, and S. Duan, Scalable Keyword Search on Large RDF Data, IEEE Transactions on Knowledge and Data Engineering, vol. 26, no. 11, pp. 2774–2788, 2014.

[2] H. He, H. Wang, J. Yang, and P. S. Yu, BLINKS: Ranked Keyword Searches on Graphs, ACM SIGMOD International Conference on Management of Data, pp. 305-316, 2007.

[3] D. Florescu, D. Kossmann, and I. Manolescu, Integrating Keyword Search into XML Query Processing, international world wide web conferences, vol. 33, no. 1, pp. 119–135, 2000.

[4] S. Cohen, J. Mamou, Y. Kanza, and Y. Sagiv, XSEarch: A Semantic Search Engine for XML, Very Large Data Bases, pp. 45-56, 2003.

[5] L. Guo, F. Shao, C. Botev, and J. Shanmugasundaram, XRANK: Ranked Keyword Search over XML Documents, ACM SIGMOD International Conference on Management of Data ACM, pp. 16-27, 2003.

[6] R. Kaushik, R. Krishnamurthy, J. F. Naughton, and R. Ramakrishnan, On the Integration of Structure Indexes and Inverted Lists, pp. 779–790, 2004.

[7] Y. Li, C. Yu, and H. V. Jagadish, Schema-Free XQuery, Very Large Data Bases, pp. 72–83, 2004.

[8] S. Agrawal, S. Chaudhuri, and G. Das, DBXplorer: A System for Keyword-Based Search over Relational Databases, International Conference on Data Engineering, 2002.

[9] G. Bhalotia, A. Hulgeri, C. Nakhe, S. Chakrabarti, and S. Sudarshan, Keyword Searching and Browsing in Databases using BANKS, pp. 431–440, 2002.

[10] V. Hristidis, and Y. Papakonstantinou, DISCOVER: Keyword Search in Relational Databases, Very Large Data Bases, pp. 670-681, 2002.

[11] V. Hristidis, L. Gravano, and Y. Papakonstantinou, Efficient IR-Style Keyword Search over Relational Databases, Very Large Data Bases, pp. 850–861, 2003.

[12] F. Liu, C. Yu, W. Meng, and A. Chowdhury, Effective Keyword Search in Relational Databases, pp. 563–574, 2006.

[13] V. Kacholia, S. Pandit, S. Chakrabarti, S. Sudarshan, R. Desai, and H. Karambelkar, Bidirectional Expansion For Keyword Search on Graph Databases, Very Large Data Bases, pp. 505–516, 2005.

[14] B. Ding, J. X. Yu, S. Wang, L. Qin, X. Zhang, and X. Lin, Finding Top-k Min-Cost Connected Trees in Databases, pp. 836–845, 2007.

[15] B. Dalvi, M. Kshirsagar, and S. Sudarshan, Keyword Search on External Memory Data Graphs, Proceedings of The Vldb Endowment, vol. 1, no. 1, pp. 1189–1204, 2008.

[16] J. Shi, D. Wu, and N. Mamoulis, Top-k Relevant Semantic Place Retrieval on Spatial RDF Data, pp. 1977–1990, 2016.

[17] S. Elbassuoni and R. Blanco, Keyword Search over RDF Graphs, pp. 237–242, 2011.

[18] T. Tran, H. Wang, S. Rudolph, and P. Cimiano, Top-k Exploration of Query Candidates for Efficient Keyword Search on Graph-Shaped (RDF) Data, pp. 405–416, 2009.

[19] X. Lian, E. De Hoyos, A. Chebotko, B. Fu, and C. F. Reilly, k-nearest keyword search in RDF graphs, Journal of Web Semantics, vol. 22, no. 0, pp. 40–56, 2013.

[20] C. Halaschek, B. Alemanmeza, I. B. Arpinar, and A. P. Sheth, Discovering and Ranking Semantic Associations over a Large RDF metabase, Very Large Data Bases, pp. 1317–1320, 2004.

[21] H. Fu and K. Anyanwu, Effectively Interpreting Keyword Queries on RDF Databases with a Rear View, pp. 193–208, 2011.

[22] H. Wang, and C. C. Aggarwal, A Survey of Algorithms for Keyword Search on Graph Data, Managing and Mining Graph Data. Springer US, pp. 249-273, 2010.

3D Path Planning of UAV Based on Improved A * Algorithm

Zhe-Tong Tian, Yan Ding[a], Jian-Mei Song, Liang-Jin Zhao, and Yu-Tong Zhang

Key laboratory of dynamics and control of flight vehicle, Beijing Institute of Technology, Beijing, China
[a] *dingyan@bit.edu.cn*

Abstract: A 3D path planning method based on A* algorithm is proposed. This method introduces the constraints of UAV and line-of-sight communication with ground stations, and it combines the UAV's maneuverability, mission requirements and terrain information and other constraints together to avoid terrain and threat. The method of extending the child nodes to the 3D detailed position calculation is also provided. The simulation is realized by Unity 3D software, and the simulation results show that the proposed method can be used to plan the 3D path of UAV which meets UAV constraints.

1. Introduction

The third-rate army follows the war, the second-rate army replies the war, and the first-rate army designs the war [1]. In the modern battlefield environment, in order to give full play to the UAV's advantages such as zero casualties, high mobility, low cost and so on, to complete the task of searching, locating, tracking and attacking targets accurately and efficiently, the UAV path planning is essential. The core content of path planning is to select the optimal or feasible path to meet a series of constraints and performance indexes, so that the UAV can arrive at the task area in a safe and timely manner, and as far as possible to maximize the effectiveness to complete the specified tasks [1].

Aiming at the problem of path planning, scholars have put forward many algorithms to solve the problem. The A* algorithm is widely used for its high efficiency, less memory requirement and easy code implementation. In 2000, Szczerba [2] proposed an improved A* algorithm, called Sparse A* Search(SAS), which combines the path constraints to reduce the search space for 2D path planning effectively. In 2002, Li Chunhua, Zheng Changwen [3] extended the path planning to 3D based on SAS, it makes full use of the planning environment of three-dimensional information, and can effectively avoid terrain and threat. In 2003, Zheng Changwen [4] proposed a dynamic sparse A* search (Dynamic Sparse A* Search, DSAS) algorithm. This method can realize the online real-time re-planning of the path in the flight environment with unknown threat. In 2011, Wu Jian and Yu Yuhua [5] proposed a variable step size A* method, but only for two dimensional path planning. In this paper, we add the constraint condition of UAV and ground station line-of-sight communication based on the sparse A* algorithm, and elaborate the calculation of extended child nodes coordinates. The experiment results show that this method can effectively realize 3D path planning.

2. Path Planning Constraints

Based on UAV's own physical constraints, the combat environment and other needs, UAVs need to meet certain basic constraints in the flight process. Specifically, the common constraints that should be considered in path planning mainly include the following contents:

2.1 Maximum Course Angle α

Restricting the expansion of child nodes in the UAV course angle and effectively cutting off the search space for algorithm to generate the path.

2.2 The Maximum Pitch Angle β

Restricting the expansion of the child nodes in the UAV pitch angle and effectively cutting off the search space for algorithm to generate the path.

2.3 Minimum Path Length l

Restricting the minimum distance of each path point and reflecting the shortest distance that the UAV must flight before changing the flight attitude. It is also defined as the minimum step size of the UAV and we extend the child nodes by using this step size.

2.4 Fixed Direction of Destination Approaching

Restricting the path's predetermined direction to approach the destination position. Assume that the angle between the fixed direction and the north direction is φ.

2.5 The Total Length of the Path L_{max}

Restricting the length of the path must be less than or equal to a pre-set maximum distance. Considering the maneuvering, speed, wind resistance and other effects, the fuel consumption calculation is complex. This maximum path length constraint can be considered as a simplification of the maximum fuel consumption constraint.

2.6 Flight Height Constraint

Restricting the range of UAV flight height. This constrain is defined by balancing two aspects, one of which is the probability decrease of being detected by using terrain mask, and the other one is the avoidance of crash when the flight height is too low. Assuming that the path height is H, the minimum flight height is H, the constraint can be expressed as: $H \geq H_{min}$.

2.7 Line-of-sight Communication with Ground Station Constraint

Restricting the path to be generated in the effective Fresnel zone of the ground station. This constraint ensures the line-of-sight communication of UAVs with the ground station can complete the assigned task normally. As shown in Fig. 1, assuming that the ground base station coverage is d, the distance between the path detection point and the ground base station is d_t, and the coverage boundary is d_r. Ground base station height is h_t, and minimum height of the receiving point at the coverage boundary is h_r (minimum flight height H_{min}). The transmit signal frequency of ground station is f (MHz), so the path detection point of the smallest Fresnel zone radius is h_0:

$$h_0 = 0.577\sqrt{\frac{\lambda d_t d_r}{d}} = 0.577\sqrt{\frac{c(m/s)d_t(km)d_r(km)}{f(MHz)d(km)}} \quad (2.1)$$

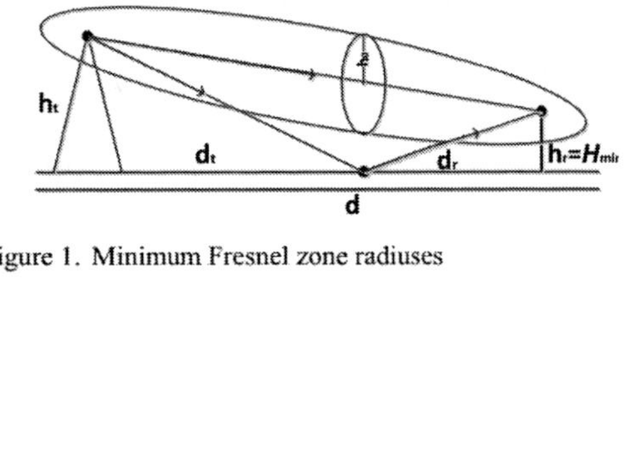

Figure 1. Minimum Fresnel zone radiuses

2.8 Meteorological Conditions Constraints

Restricting the path generation space, so that UAV can avoid rain, snow, fog and other adverse weather conditions, and ensure the safety and communication stability.

These constraints are not fixed and may change during the execution of the task. To obtain the required path, these different constraints are combined into the A * algorithm to get a search method that can be used for 3D path planning. The method can effectively reduce the search space and improve the efficiency of the search so that the algorithm can converge to the feasible solution in real time.

3. Path Planning Based on Sparse A * Search Algorithm

A * algorithm is a heuristic search algorithm which is widely used in artificial intelligence. SAS is an improved A * algorithm and its cost function is:

$$f(x) = g(x) + h(x) \quad (3.1)$$

The $g(x)$ is the actual cost from the starting node to the current node, in other words it is the distance of the path being through. The $h(x)$ means that the estimate cost from the current node to the destination node and the A* algorithm will select child nodes in accordance with the $f(x)$ value.

3.1 Selection of the Cost Function

The flight status (speed, height, maneuvering, etc.) of UAV, the probability of crash or being detected and other factors are mutual coupled, the following cost function can be used:

$$C = \sum_{i=1}^{n}(\omega_1 l_i^2 + \omega_2 h_i^2 + \omega_3 T_i) \quad (3.2)$$

In the formula (3.2), C is the Path planning cost function, n is the total number of path segments, l_i means the length of path segment No.i, T_i means the threat index of the path segment No.i, $\omega_1, \omega_2, \omega_3$ are the three kinds weight coefficient of cost value. In this article, the child nodes are expanded by a fixed step length (minimum path length). The minimum threat threshold is set, and the threat index which is under the threshold can be ignored. The safe distance can be calculated by these. Without taking the breakthrough defense into consideration, the length l_i in formula (3.3) can be replaced by l, $D(x)$ means the real distance that x walked through from the start node to the current node, and the threat index T_i equals to 0. So the cost function can be simplified to:

$$C = \sum_{i}^{n} \omega h_i^2 + D(x) \quad (3.3)$$

3.2 The Application of Constraints

3.2.1 Extension Constrains (Incorporating Constraints Into Child Nodes Extension Methods):

Minimum path length l, maximum course angle α, maximum trim angle β constrains: Assuming that the UAV's position coordinates and velocity direction are known, and ignore other interference, the place which the UAV can fly to in the next moment is on a sphere of a spherical rectangular pyramid which edge-lengths is l, pan range is 2α ,vertical angle is 2β, and this sphere is tangent with the speed direction of UAV. In order to save resources and increase the speed of planning, we divide the spherical rectangular pyramid equally into M layers according to its vertical angle and divide it equally into N regions according to its pan angle. Now the (M+1) (N+1) intersections on the sphere can be used to expand and calculate the cost value as the child nodes. The values of M and N generally take 2 - 4. As shown in the Fig. 2.

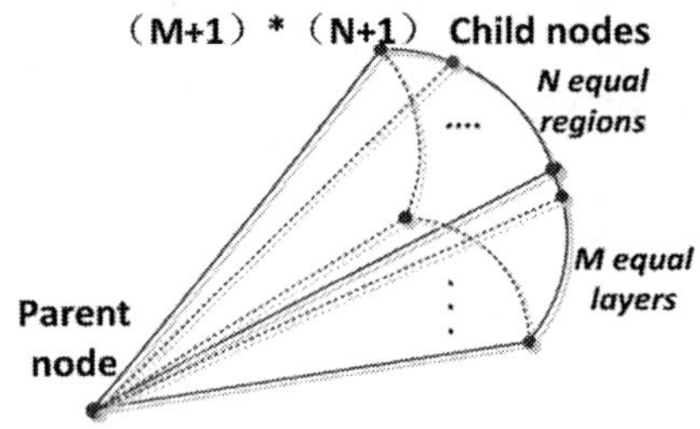

Figure 2. Schematic diagram of single-step extended node area (spherical rectangular pyramid)

3.2.2 Fixed Direction of the Destination Entrance Constraint:

The A * algorithm can be extended toward the starting node along the opposite direction of the fixed entry direction from the destination point.

3.2.3 Judgement Constraints:

The total length of the path L_{max} : Judge that whether the current extended child node x is satisfied with formula (3.4).

$$D(x) + SL(x) \le L_{max} \quad (3.4)$$

$D(x)$ means the real distance that x walked through from the start node to the current node, and $SL(x)$ means the linear distance from node x to the destination node. Retain this child node if it meets the condition in formula (3.4); otherwise remove it from the OPEN list.

Flight height, Line-of-sight communication with ground station: Judge that whether the current child node, the 1/4, 1/2, 3/4 path points from the parent node to the child node, of which the heights H can be satisfied with the formula $H \ge H_{min}$, and whether they are in the smallest Fresnel zone. If so, this child node can be retained, otherwise remove it from the OPEN list.

Threat source, meteorological conditions: To simplify the calculation, we consider the range of threat source as a hemisphere, the poor weather conditions as cylinders. Judge whether the distance between the current extended child node and the threat center or the horizontal meteorological center is greater than the safety distance (the threat radius). This child node can be retained if it is satisfied, otherwise remove it from the OPEN list.

3.3 The Coordinate Calculation of the Extended Child Node

A main difficulty in the proposed path planning algorithm is to calculate the coordinate of the expanded child nodes, the solution process will be described in detail.

3.3.1 Known Conditions:

The world coordinate system in Unity 3D is the left hand coordinate system, as shown in Fig. 3.

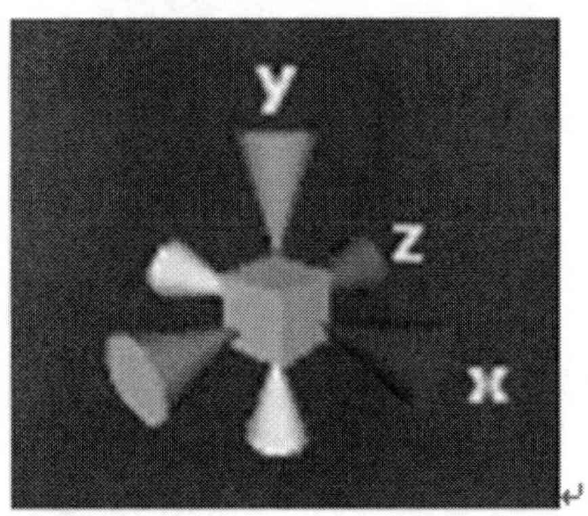

Figure 3. World coordinate system in Unity 3D

The world coordinates of the destination node is (x_0, y_0, z_0).

The angle between the fixed destination and the north direction is φ, and the positive direction is from the Z-axis to the X-axis direction;

Minimum step size is l ; Minimum flight height is H_{min} ;

As described above, the expansion of child node is a (M+1)×(N+1) dot matrix, and we'll give an example of a 3 × 3 dot matrix for derivation here;

The maximum course angle is α and the maximum trim angle is β.

3.3.2 Solving Process:

Set up the UAV body coordinate system: The speed direction is Z-axis positive direction, and the X-axis positive direction is from the left of the wings to the right, perpendicular to the XOZ plane upward is the Y-axis positive direction. Think of UAV as a mass point, and ignore its roll gesture. So the body coordinate system's ZOY plane and the world coordinate system's XOZ plane are perpendicular to each other.

In order to make the derivation process more general and representative, we set the destination node on the ground, instead of being at the height $H_{\min}$ from the ground. As shown in Fig. 4 and Fig. 5, expand the child nodes along the opposite direction of the fixed entrance direction from the destination node toward the starting node, and then we can get the inclination θ between the initial path and ground, and the second point which called the sub-destination node is $(x_0 + l\sin\varphi\cos\theta, y_0 + H_{\min}, z_0 + l\cos\varphi\cos\theta)$.

$$\angle\theta = \arcsin\theta(\frac{H_{\min}}{l}) \quad (3.5)$$

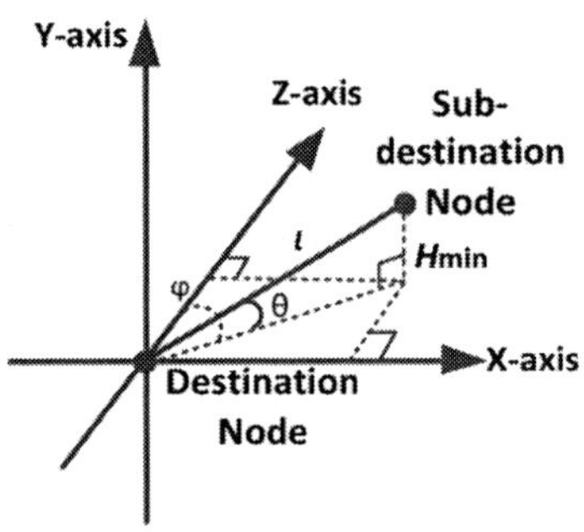

Figure 4. Determination of sub-destination node

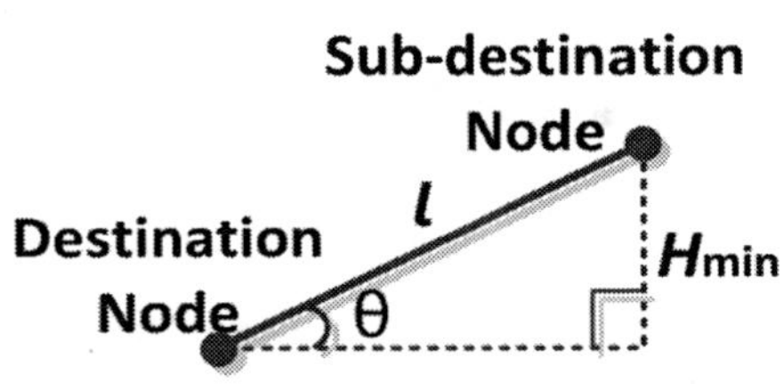

Figure 5. Inclination θ between the initial path and ground

Take the direction of ligature from destination node to the sub-destination node as the UAV body coordinate system's Z-axis positive direction, so we can get nine extended child nodes of the sub-destination node in the body of the body coordinate system as shown in Figure. 6. The nine nodes in the figure are located in the same plane which parallel to the XOY plane, and the distance between the two planes is l, the point 5 is on the Z-axis.

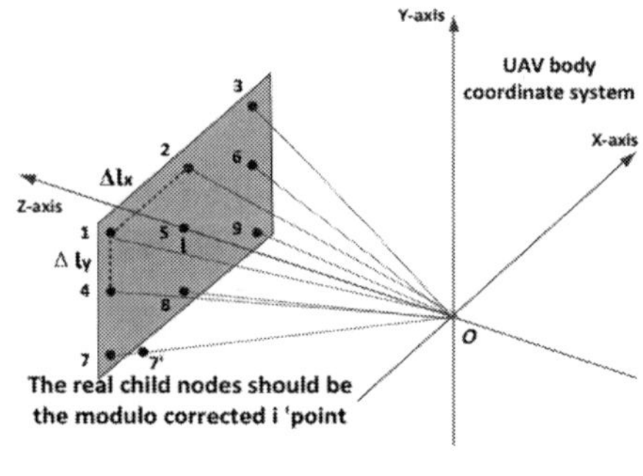

Figure 6. Mode of child node extension

Assume that the unit vector matrix of the UAV body coordinate system is $\left[\vec{b}_1, \vec{b}_2, \vec{b}_3\right]$, so the vectors of the nine expanded child nodes in the body coordinate system are:

$$\vec{r}_{ib} = \begin{bmatrix} \pm\Delta l_x, 0 \\ \pm\Delta l_y, 0 \\ l \end{bmatrix} \frac{l}{\sqrt{l^2 + (\Delta l_x)^2 + (\Delta l_y)^2}} \quad (3.6)$$

In formula (3.6), $\Delta l_x = l \cdot \tan\alpha$, $\Delta l_y = l \cdot \tan\beta$. The real expanded child nodes are located on a spherical quadrangular pyramid, as shown in Fig. 2, so we need use the length correctional formula (3.7) to correct the length of the child nodes' vectors.

$$\frac{l}{\sqrt{l^2 + (\Delta l_x)^2 + (\Delta l_y)^2}} \quad (3.7)$$

Assume that the unit vector matrix of the world coordinate system is $\left[\vec{g}_1, \vec{g}_2, \vec{g}_3\right]$. Therefore, the conversion matrix can be assumed as C_{gb}, and we can get:

$$\left[\vec{g}_1, \vec{g}_2, \vec{g}_3\right] \cdot C_{gb} = \left[\vec{b}_1, \vec{b}_2, \vec{b}_3\right] \quad (3.8)$$

Assume $\vec{r}_i$ to be $\vec{r}_{ig}$ when it is in the world coordinate system and $\vec{r}_{ib}$ when it is in the body coordinate system. The body coordinate system has the same origin point with the world coordinate system.

$$\vec{r}_i = \left[\vec{g}_1, \vec{g}_2, \vec{g}_3\right] \cdot \vec{r}_{ig} = \left[\vec{b}_1, \vec{b}_2, \vec{b}_3\right] \cdot \vec{r}_{ib} \quad (3.9)$$

Substituting formula (3.8) into formula (3.9), and we can obtain:

$$\vec{r_{ig}} = C_{gb} \cdot \vec{r_{ib}} \quad (3.10)$$

So we only need to calculate the conversion matrix C_{gb}. Firstly, as shown in Fig. 7, make the body coordinate system rotate φ degrees around the Y-axis, and we can get the first rotated matrix $C_{gb'}$:

$$C_{gb'} = \begin{bmatrix} \cos\varphi & 0 & \sin\varphi \\ 0 & 1 & 0 \\ -\sin\varphi & 0 & \cos\varphi \end{bmatrix} \quad (3.11)$$

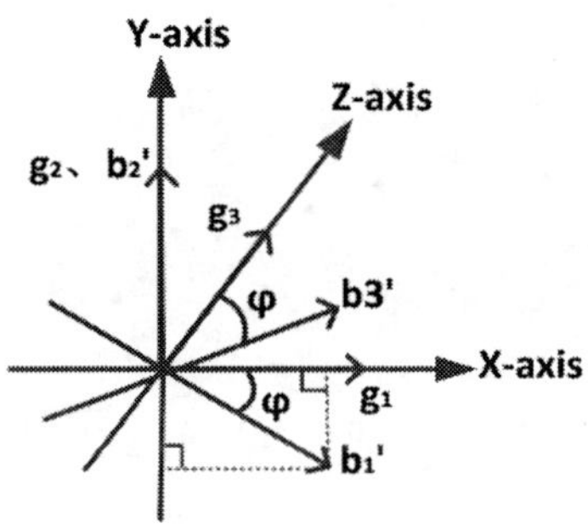

Figure 7. Rotate around the Y-axis

Secondly, as shown in Fig. 8, make the body coordinate system rotate θ degrees around the X-axis, and we can get the second rotated matrix $C_{b'b}$:

$$C_{b'b} = \begin{bmatrix} 1 & 0 & 0 \\ 0 & \cos\theta & \sin\theta \\ 0 & -\sin\theta & \cos\theta \end{bmatrix} \quad (3.12)$$

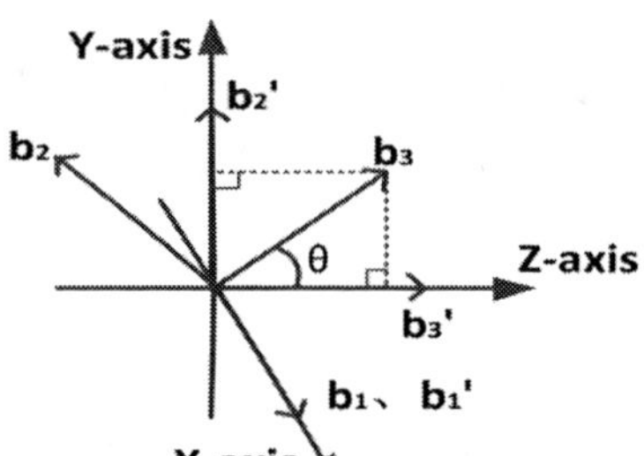

Figure 8. Rotate around the X-axis

Then the conversation matrix C_{gb} can be calculated:

$$C_{gb} = \begin{bmatrix} \cos\varphi & -\sin\varphi\sin\theta & \sin\varphi\cos\theta \\ 0 & \cos\theta & \sin\theta \\ -\sin\varphi & -\cos\varphi\sin\theta & \cos\varphi\cos\theta \end{bmatrix} \quad (3.13)$$

$$\vec{r_{ig}} = C_{gb} \cdot \vec{r_{ib}} \quad (3.14)$$

Now, the body coordinate system is parallel to the world coordinate system after twice rotations. In formula (3.14), $\vec{r_{ig}}$ is the vector of the expanded child nodes which expressed in the new body coordinate system.

$$\vec{P_{ig}} = \vec{R_g} + \vec{r_{ig}} \quad (3.15)$$

In formula (3.15), $\vec{P_{ig}}$ is the vector of the extended child nodes which expressed in the world coordinate system. The vector of the body system's origin point in the world coordinate system is $\vec{R_g}$.

3.4 Algorithm Description

The following steps show the 3D path planning algorithm's specific process:

Step 1: After the calculation, we put the sub-destination node into the OPEN list, and empty the CLOSED.

Step 2: If the OPEN list is empty, the path search fails. And we need to increase the value of M, N appropriately to re-planning.

Step 3: Remove the least costly node from the OPEN list, take it as the current node and place it into the CLOSED list.

Step 4: If the distance between the current node and the starting point is less than l, the parent node pointer of the starting node points to the current node, the path search ends. Along the direction of the pointer, from the starting node back to the destination node, we can get the minimum cost path.

Step 5: Extending the child nodes of the current node.

Construct the UAV body coordinate system by using the current node and its parent node, Z-axis positive direction is the direction of the extension. Take the Z-axis as the center benchmark, and make a quadrangular pyramid of which the horizontal section angle is 2 times of the maximum course angle, the vertical section angle is 2 times of the maximum pitch angle and the height is l. Divide the bottom of quadrangular pyramid into M regions in the vertical direction, and N regions in the horizontal direction equally (M, N generally takes 2 to 4), we can obtain (M + 1) (N + 1) child nodes. Then perform length correction to make the distance between the child nodes and the origin of the coordinate system equal to l. So we can get the world coordinates of the extended child nodes.

Calculate the substitution value of the remaining extended child nodes according to formula (3.3) and place the child nodes, according to the value from small to large, into the OPEN list.

Judge that whether each extended child node satisfies the total length constraint of the path, and then calculate the four quarter points coordinate information of the ligature between the parent node and each extended

DOI: 10.1051/itmconf/20171201015

child node to determine whether the flight height constraint and the Line-of-sight communication constraint are satisfied. If all these constraints are met, put the child node's parent node pointer towards the current node; otherwise remove it from the OPEN list.

Step 6: Return to step 3.

Along the direction of the pointer, from the starting node back to the destination node, we can get the minimum cost path.

4. Simulation and Implementation

For now, the mainstream of the path planning simulation research is carried out in the MATLAB software. Because of the limitation of the software performance, the planning space is usually represented as a grid in the planning process, the terrain and threat data are discretized in advance. These make the path planning extended to 3D space and the computation process complicated. In this paper, we will explore the path planning based on the Unity 3D software and the existing artificial intelligence. We simplify the terrain greatly, especially the complexity of the real terrain by making full use of its rich plug-in resources. We also make the interface much friendlier, and improve the visibility and operability a lot.

The simulation is carried out by C#, which is based on the real terrain of 2.6 * 2.4 km in a certain area of Taiwan province and the threat models which are generated by simulation. In the simulation experiment, the parameters are: $\omega = 1$, $M = 3$, $N = 3$, $l = 10$, $L_{max} = 5km$, $\alpha = 45^{\circ}$, $\beta = 45^{\circ}$, $\varphi = 145^{\circ}$, $H = 100m$, $d = 400m$. The Fig. 9 shows the results of the method. The left group of pictures is the result of no weather conditions. The right group of pictures is based on the experimental results of the left and the weather condition constraint is added. The red hemispheres are threat areas; the gray hemispheres are the line-of-sight communication coverage areas of the ground station; the yellow cylinders are adverse weather areas; the green line is the planned path line. The bottom left is the starting point and the right upper is the destination point. The Fig. 9A1 and Fig. 9A2 show the path display in top view. The Fig. 9B1 and Fig. 9B2 show the path display in side view. The Fig. 9C1 and Fig. 9C2 show the path display in three-dimension view.

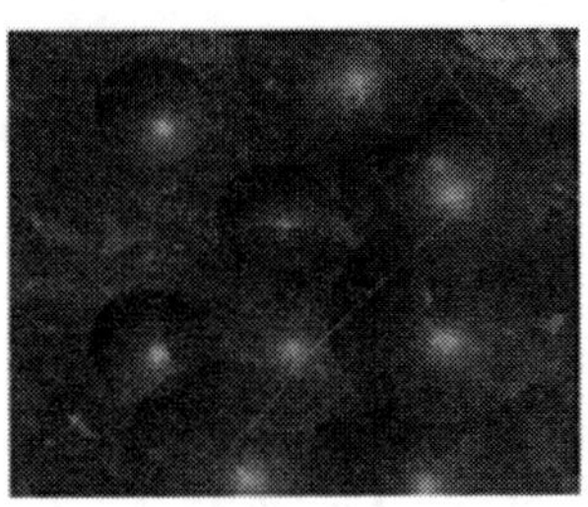

Figure 9. Figure 9A1. Top view

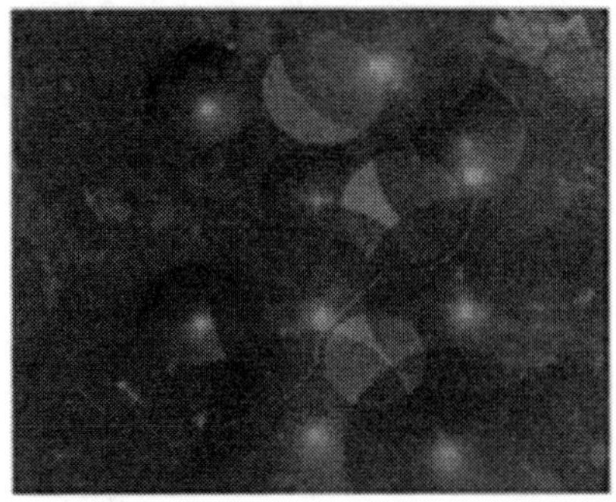

Figure 9A2. Top view

Figure 9B1. Side view

Figure 9B2. Side view

Figure 9C1. Three-dimension view

Figure 9C2. Three-dimension view

Figure 9. Two groups of pictures about experimental result

The experimental results show that the proposed method based on Unity 3D simulation is a fast and effective method. Under the premise of satisfying many constraints, it has obvious improvement effect on the interface friendliness, visibility and operability.

5. Concluding

In recent years, with the development of artificial intelligence, Unity 3D becomes a very popular game development engine, which plays an important role in the exploitation of AI. Because of the gradual enrichment of artificial intelligence resources and the gradual maturity of the algorithm, certain tasks in the military field which require preciseness, efficiency and high feasibility, for example, UAV path planning, helicopter rescue etc. can be simulated and developed by using the Unity 3D totally.

References

[1] Mao Hongbao, Tian Song, Chao Ainong. UAV mission planning [M]. Beijing: National Defense Industry Press, 2015.

[2] Szczerba R J. Robust algorithm for rea-l time route planning[J].IEEE Transactions on Aerospace and Electronic Systems,2000,36(3):869-878.

[3] Li Chunhua, Zheng Changwen, et al. A new method for fast 3D path searching [J]. Journal of Astronautics, 2002,23 (3): 12-17.

[4] Zheng Changwen. Research on flight path planning method [D]. Huazhong University of Science and Technology, 2003

[5] Wu Jian, Yu Yuhua, Zhou Jiqiang, Huang Yimin. Variable step size A* algorithm for path planning of UAV [J]. electro-optic and control, 2011, (05): 1-6+10.

The Discussion of the Effects of Linear and Nonlinear Algorithms on Emotional Evaluation

Yang Wu[1], Yu Nie[2], Guang-Zhi Sun[3], Zhong-Yao Yang4

1Software College of Jilin University, Changchun China
2Software College of Jilin University, Changchun China
3Software College of Jilin University, Changchun China
4Software College of Jilin University, Changchun China
[1]albertwyjoy@gmail.com, [2]13943186112@163.com, [3]2238284250@qq.com, [4]819462206@qq.com

Abstract: With the continuous development of brain-computer interface technology, as a typical brainwave signal carrying brain state information, has entered the researcher's point of view. Brain waves carry detailed information about the state of the brain. [1]Therefore, the use of computers to collect and analyze EEG signals play an important role in the study of artificial intelligence. In this paper, the EEG signal of positive and negative emotions is taken as the research object.[2] Firstly, the present situation of brain wave research is introduced, and the image is experimented with the Chinese emotional image system (CAPS) of Chinese Academy of Sciences. Based on the previous work of "Emotional Evaluation Based on SVM", further data analysis was carried out using support vector machines (SVM) and linear machines with linear and nonlinear cores, and 49.2% to 62.4% accuracy were obtained respectively. This paper provides a feasible solution for the study of EEG in the field of emotional analysis.Finally, through the accuracy of the linear algorithm and the nonlinear algorithm on the data, we find that the EEG data are non-linear separable.

1. Introduction

Since the last century, James, Connon and other scholars found that: emotions is a change in their own body of a feeling, first physical changes, only emotional perception, any emotional generation must be accompanied by some changes in the body [3]. This is the earliest definition of emotion. Moreover, the emotional generation is determined by the hypothalamus [4]. At present, a large number of neurological and cognitive science-related research results show that emotional production and physiological activities, especially with the cortex activity is closely related to the study by the cerebral cortex activity analysis and identification of human emotional state provides a theoretical basis [6].

It is of great significance to study emotional recognition. Artificial intelligence in an indicator is to understand the human emotions, so the emotional identification of related research will promote the development of artificial intelligence. In terms of human-computer interaction, let the machine understand human emotions, will make it more accurate understanding of human intent, so as to better help humans. Emotional recognition of the application there are many, such as driver fatigue testing and cardiac care and so on.

Emotional classification, such as emotions, has not yet formed a unified theoretical understanding. Researchers through further research, found that there is still a certain correlation between emotions, such as anger and aversion sometimes appear at the same time, so there Lange two-dimensional emotional classification model [7]. The model is also the most common classification model, the use of vertical coordinates of the mood of pleasure, never like to gradually over to like; use the abscissa that the state of excitement, from the downturn to excitement.

There are two major categories of common emotion recognition methods. The first category is based on the recognition of nonphysiological signals, which include recognition of facial expressions and recognition of speech tones. The advantage is that the data acquisition is relatively simple, do not need special equipment; shortcomings cannot guarantee the reliability of emotional recognition, because it will be subjective factors. The second category is based on physiological signal recognition. At present, the physiological signals adopted at home and abroad mainly include electrooculogram (EOG), Galvanic Skin Response (GSR), Blood Volume Pulse (BVP), Electromyogram (EMG), EEG (EEG), electrocardology (Electrocardiogram, ECG) and so on.

At present, there are many studies on emotional recognition based on EEG signals [8, 9]. In the emotional mode of learning and classification stage, the algorithm used at home and abroad is mainly to support the vector machine. The academic community has now been able to achieve 75% of the emotional classification by some data analysis methods [10].

The main steps of emotion recognition based on EEG include: emotional induction; collection of EEG signals; pretreatment of EEG signals; feature extraction; feature dimensionality reduction; learning and classification of emotional patterns. This paper mainly through the use of machine learning in two different ways to human brain waves.

2. Experiment

After being processed by pretreatment algorithm such as low-pass filtering algorithm, the EEG data obtained from the psychological experiment became 8-dimensional data. Before classification, we should analysis the degree of linear correlation between data in the different dimension. We used the linear correlation coefficients to quantify it. As shown in figure 1, there were different degrees of relevance between data in the different dimension. Therefore, we considered using dimension reduction algorithm. On one hand, the dimensions would be lower which made it more convenient to observe the data and because data in different dimension were not independent, we removing some features from the data through the dimension reduction algorithm would not decrease the accuracy of classification too much.

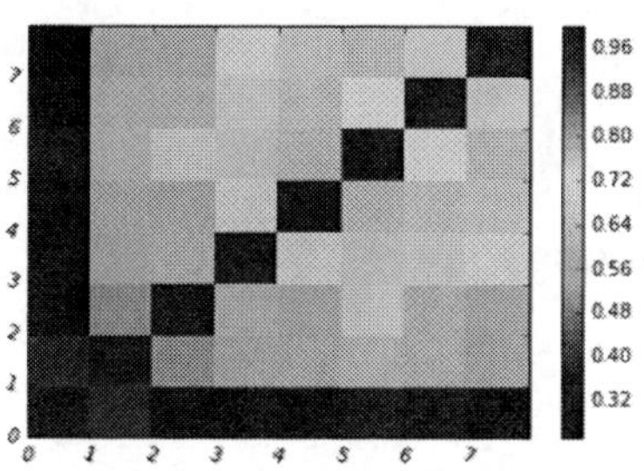

Figure 1

Before beginning our experiment, we need to observe the data distribution, so we could get a preliminary understanding. The method was that we used PCA algorithm to process the dimensional data from which we could get 3 or 2-dimensional data and we display the data in coordinates as shown in Figure 2, Figure 3 and Figure 4.

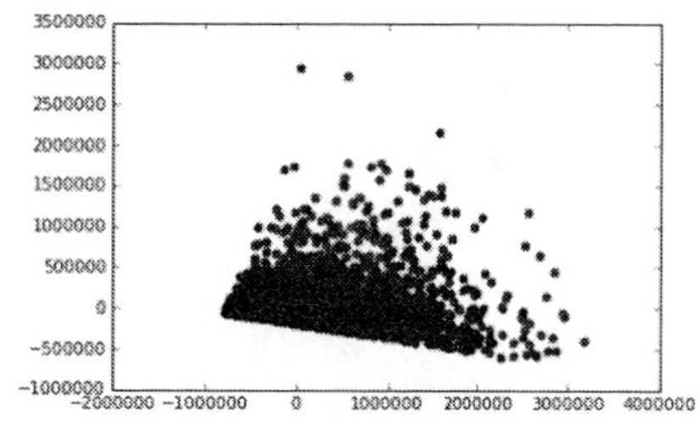

Figure 2

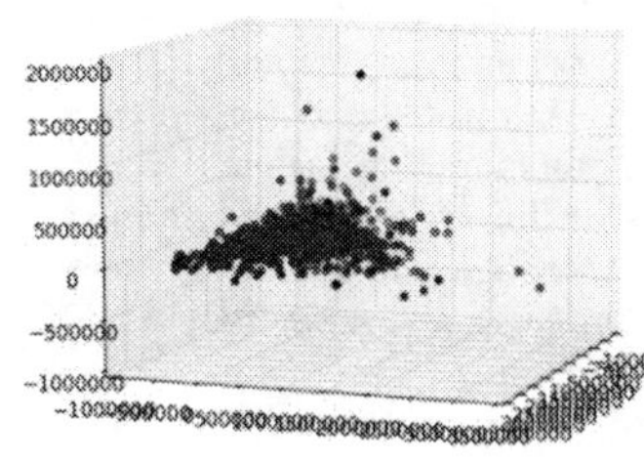

Figure 3

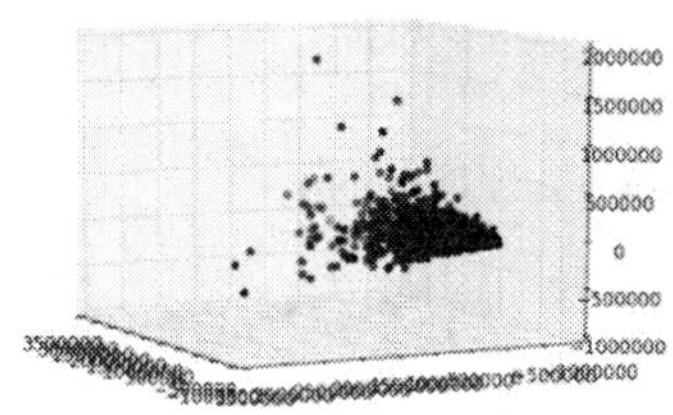

Figure 4

We found that Figure 2 could be seen as a projection from three-dimensional space to two-dimensional space of Figure 3 or Figure 4 and also know that the distribution of data was non-linear which caused the data was hard to classify. Through observed Figure 3 and Figure 4, we found the two kinds data cannot be split by a plane. Just observing more carefully, we could know the data were split by the graph like shown in Figure 5, the red point on the inside and blue point on the outside.

DOI: 10.1051/itmconf/20171201016

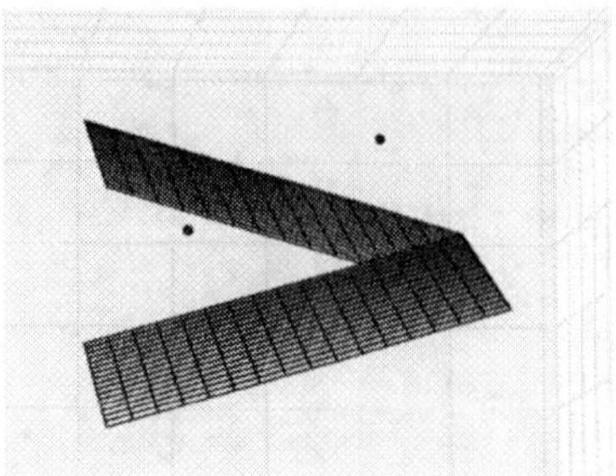

Figure 5

Based on the distributions of two-dimensional data and three-dimensional data, we estimated that the EEG data was nonlinear separable. Therefore, the classification result would not be good when we used the linear classifying algorithm such as perceptron algorithm and SVM with linear kernel algorithm. However, the classification result would be better when we used the no-linear classifying algorithm such as SVM with the no-linear kernel.

We used perceptron algorithm, SVM with linear kernel algorithm and SVM with nonlinear kernel (RBF) algorithm for experiments. We did our experiments on two sets of data. One was 8-dimensional data (the EEG data). The other was 3-dimensional data obtained through PCA algorithm. Considering the SVM algorithm, we set the parameter γ to different values 1,10 and 20. The accuracy of classification of SVM with nonlinear kernel (RBF) algorithm on data was shown in Table 1. The accuracy of classification of SVM with linear kernel algorithm on data was shown in Table 2. As for perceptron algorithm, we set the iterative number to different values 10,100 and 1000. The accuracy of perceptron was shown in Table 3.

Table 1

γ	SVM RBF(8)	SVM RBF (3)
1	0.570	0.511
10	0.624	0.561
20	0.623	0.568

Table 2

γ	SVM linear(8)	SVM linear (3)
1	0.506	0.497
10	0.506	0.497
20	0.506	0.497

Table 3

n	Perceptron(8)	Perceptron(3)
10	0.511	0.511
100	0.490	0.506
1000	0.492	0.520

Though the experimental data shown in the Table1, Table 2 and Table 3, we could find on both 8-dimensional data and 3-dimensional data the accuracy of classification of SVM with nonlinear kernel (RBF) algorithm is highest among the three algorithms. And SVM with linear kernel algorithm considered, its performance on 8-dimensional data was better than 3-dimensional data. The accuracy of the linear algorithm was about 50%. We could find the reason of it in the distribution of data. The distribution of 3-dimensional data could be seen as shown in Figure 5. The two kinds data was split by the graph. Whatever the plan decided by the algorithm was the upper plane or the lower plane or any plane, there would be many points which were classified wrongly. However, the no-linear algorithm mapped nonlinear data into high-dimensional space which made it easier to classify.

3. Conclusion

In this study, we obtained the EEG data and did experiments on it. Firstly, we analyzed the degree of linear correlation between data in the different dimension and we found here were different degrees of relevance between data in the different dimension. But the accuracy of SVM with nonlinear kernel (RBF) algorithm on 8-dimensional data was higher than 3-dimensional data which indicated even if the data in different dimension were independent, the information in the data would lose after reducing the dimension of data. To sum up, though observing the distribution of the data and the results of experiments the accuracy of the linear algorithm was lower than that of the no-linear algorithm, we concluded that the EEG data is nonlinear separable.

References

[1] W. James. Mind 34 (1884): 188-205.

[2] W.B. Cannon. The American journal of psychology 39.1/4 (1927): 106-124.

[3] T. Dalgleish. Nature Reviews Neuroscience 5.7 (2004): 583-589.

[4] P.J. Lang, M.M. Bradleyand B.N. Cuthbert. "International affective picture system (IAPS): Technical manual and affective ratings." Gainesville, FL: The Center for Research in Psychophysiology, University of Florida (1999).

[5] H.H. Jasper. Electroencephalography and clinical neurophysiology 10 (1958): 371-375.

[6] C. Peacock. "Interfacing the standard parallel port." (1998).

[7] K. Schaaffand T. Schultz. "Towards emotion recognition from electroencephalographic signals." 2009 3rd International Conference on Affective Computing and Intelligent Interaction and Workshops. IEEE, 2009.

[8] A. Jain, K.Nandakumarand A. Ross. Pattern recognition 38.12 (2005): 2270-2285.

[9] B. Kahn. Electroencephalogram (EEG) signal processing, wave identification, and emotion recognition. Diss. California State University, Northridge, 2015.

[10] R.M. Mehmoodand H.J. Lee. Int. J. Bio-Sci. Bio-Technol. 7 (2015): 23-32.

Multimodal Path Optimization and Logistics Distribution of Military Transportation

Shu-Xin Wang, Jin Zhang

Zhenjiang Watercraft College, Zhenjiang, Jiangsu, China
* *doc.wsx@163.com*

Abstract. The problem of route optimization of large volume and long distance material distribution is carried out from the rear strategic logistics center to the front line distribution center, researched by turning into multimodal transport problems, and a single-path multimodal transport path optimization model is established. Decision variables about stage safety probability are introduced; the nonlinear model is simplified into a second-order programming model, by changing the probability of task safety and simplified the model to a linear programming model by using the monotonicity of logarithmic functions. An example is presented to solve the simulation with LINGO software, made a reference plan under different constraints, the correctness of the model is verified.

1. Introduction

Logistics distribution is the important content of military traffic transport, is shouldering the important combat goods delivery to combat troop's task, and it is the link that transforms logistics support into operational capability. Under large-scale combat conditions, military transport are the characteristics of great material consumption, the transport mission is large, the transport scope is wide, and the tasks have a variety of forms; The timeliness of transport is high and the persistent requirements also high, the transport environment is poor and the hidden defense is difficult. So it is difficult to improve the coordination of military transport organization, the requirement of the loading and unloading and the plan of transportation guarantee.

The paper studied the problem of route optimization of railway, highway, waterway and aviation in the context of large-scale operation, a scientific and rational path optimization model is established, by reasonable selecting the running line and transport tools, accurate and efficient delivery plan can be developed.

2. Research Status of Multimodal Transport and Shortest Path Problems

2.1 The Research Status of Multimodal Transport Problem

There is little research on multimodal military transport at home and abroad at present, Xi-rui Yang based on Lagrangian relaxation method, decomposed the problem of multimodal military transport into two sub-problems: cargo flow and vehicle flow, the two subproblems are solved separately; Jiaying Zhang has set up a multimodal military transport model, which take time and cost as the target, and time and capacity as constraints, and solved the problem by Genetic algorithm and Matlab software.

2.2 Research Status of the Shortest Path Problem

The shortest path problem researched the single objective optimization problem of the single-attribute network, for example, the fastest path problem is to use time as the network property, the proposed model is generally unconstrained 0-1 programming model, Dijkstra, Ford, Floyd and other precise algorithms can be used to obtain the optimal solution directly. The constraint path optimization problem is the extension of the shortest path problem, mainly studies the multi-attribute network path optimization problem, consider a target, multiple attribute constraints, the proposed model is a constrained 0-1 nonlinear programming model, it can be solved by heuristic algorithm or improved algorithm.

2.3 Research Status of Path Optimization Algorithm

The research of path optimization is mainly focused on the precise algorithm at first, the accurate algorithm can solve the global optimal solution theoretically, but the disadvantage is that it is computationally intensive, it's easy to be constrained by problem size. LINGO software is able to obtain the global optimal solution for large-scale linear programming problem, Thus, this NP problem can be solved which considered the tolerability of calculating time and optimality of solution.

3. Single Path Multi-Modal Transport Path Optimization Model

Depending on the mode of transport, large-scale combat logistics distribution problems can be divided into multi-modal transport problems and vehicle path problems, as shown in figure 1. According to the transport task style, the problem of large-scale combat logistics distribution can be divided into multi-modal transport problems and vehicle routing problems, as shown in figure 1. The distribution to front distribution center or force user from rear logistics centre or strategic warehouse is usually a long-distance transport, which requires a variety of modes of transport, its multi-modal transport. The distribution from forward distribution centre to force users is generally a vehicle path problem. Multimodal transport is a form of transport organization with multiple modes of transport; it can significantly improve transport efficiency, optimize transport structure, and enhance the rationality and economy of transportation. This paper mainly studies the optimization model of single-path multimodal transport path and its solution.

Fig.1 Large-scale combat Military Transportation logistics problems

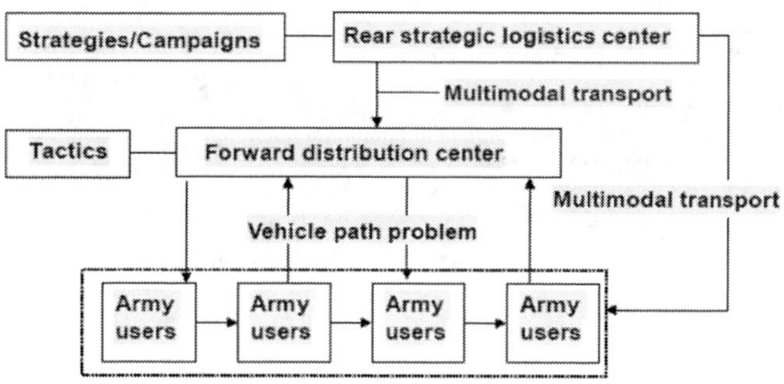

3.1 Determination of the Value of the Intermodal Property

In this paper, we choose to construct a two-dimensional uncoupled transport network with a directed graph $G(V,E,T,C,P)$, V is the point set, the total number is n, $v_i \in V$ is the point in the graph, $v_i = [1,2,3,4,5,6]$ represent logistics centers, railway stations, bus stations, airports, ports and military users respectively; E is the edge set, $e_{ij} \in E$ indicates the path v_i connected to v_j, T is the time attribute matrix of E, $t_{ij} \in T$, C is the cost attribute matrix of E, $c_{ij} \in C$ indicates the cost required for transport v_i to v_j, P is the safety attribute matrix of E, $p_{ij} \in P$ is the safety probability of road e_{ij}.

If $e_{ij} \notin E$, make $t_{ij} = +\infty$, $c_{ij} = +\infty$, $p_{ij} = 1$; Introduce the homogeneous judgment matrix $B = [b_{ij}]_{n \times n}$:

$$b_{ij} = \mathrm{sgn}\left[(v_i - v_j)^2\right] \forall i, j \in [1,2,\cdots,n] \quad (1)$$

$\mathrm{sgn}[\ ]$ is symbolic function, When transported homogeneity, $v_i = v_j$, $b_{ij} = 0$, When transported non-homogeneous, $v_i \neq v_j$, $b_{ij} = 1$.

3.1.1 Time Property

t_{ij} is the time property of e_{ij}, which Indicates the time interval between the arrival of the first vehicle v_i and the departure of the first vehicle v_j, when transported homogeneity:

$$t_{ij} = s_{ij} / \mu_{ij} \quad (2)$$

s_{ij} is the mileage of e_{ij}, if $e_{ij} \notin E$ or $e_{ij} \in E$, But in the event of an attack, $s_{ij} = +\infty$, μ_{ij} is the Average speed of e_{ij}.

When transported non-homogeneous:

$$t_{ij} = \alpha_i g_i + s_{ij} / \mu_{ij} + \beta_j \cdot \min\{d_j, M\} \quad (3)$$

α_i and β_j represented the uninstall time factor v_i and loading time factor of v_j, g_i is the standard load for transit vehicles of v_i, M is the total amount of delivery (the unit is ton), The volume is calculated according to the relevant standards when transporting the light cargo, d_j is the standard load for a single vehicle of v_j.

When loading is faster than uninstalling,

$$t_{ij} = \alpha_i \cdot \min\{d_j, M\} + s_{ij} / \mu_{ij} + \beta_j \cdot g_i \quad (4)$$

$$t_{ij} = s_{ij} / \mu_{ij} + b_{ij}\left[\min\{\alpha_i, \beta_j\} \cdot g_i + \max\{\alpha_i, \beta_j\} \cdot \min\{d_j, M\}\right] \forall i, j \in [1,2,\cdots,n] \quad (5)$$

3.1.2 Cost Attributes

Cost attributes c_{ij} showed the direct economic cost of the shipping and loading process e_{ij}, the cost included of, loading and unloading cost, transportation cost consisted of the start-up cost and the running cost. If homogeneous transport c_{ij} is made up of running expenses only, it has to do with transport distance and volume.

$$c_{ij} = \gamma_{ij} \cdot s_{ij} \cdot M \quad (6)$$

γ_{ij} is run base price, unit is Yuan/ ton per kilometer.

If it's Non-homogeneous transport, c_{ij} including transportation charges in transit, loading and unloading fees, start-up cost of transportation tools in v_j.

$$c_{ij} = (\eta_i + \gamma_{ij} \cdot s_{ij} + \lambda_j + \theta_j)M \quad (7)$$

η_i is the unloading cost coefficient of v_i(Yuan/ ton), λ_j is the loading cost coefficient of v_j (Yuan/ ton), θ_j is the delivery price (Yuan/ ton). The computational formula for the cost is:

$$c_{ij} = \left[\gamma_{ij} \cdot s_{ij} + b_{ij}(\eta_i + \lambda_j + \theta_j)\right]M$$
$$\forall i, j \in [1,2,\cdots,n] \quad (8)$$

3.1.3 Transport Properties

If e_{ij} is Non-homogeneous transport, the capacity constraint consists of the following three components:

d_j is the standard load of means of transportation in v_j, d_j not less than the minimum unit of distribution m, $d_j \geq m$;

The length/width/height ($l_j^1 / l_j^2 / l_j^3$) of the conveyance in v_j must be bigger than the length/width/height ($l^1 / l^2 / l^3$) of the unit of the minimum unit of distribution, so $l_j^1 > l^1$, $l_j^2 > l^2$, $l_j^3 > l^3$;

D_j is the total load weight of all means of transportation in v_j, which not less than the total weight of the distribution M, so $D_j \geq M$.

3.2 Established the Single Path Multi-Modal Transport Path Optimization Model

If the war zone distribute the total amount of material M from strategic logistics center v_1 to forward distribution center or military user v_n, satisfying three conditions, that are the total delivery time *TIME* no more than W_t, total cost *COST* no more than W_c, the probability of safety *SAFETY* no less than W_p.

When the path Γ is chosen for transport only, it is a single path multi-modal transport path optimization problem. Set up target function with the total time TIME, total cost COST, Total safety probability SAFETY individually, established a multi-objective multimodal transport path optimization model.

$$Min \quad TIME = \sum_{i=1}^{n} \sum_{j=1}^{n} t_{ij} x_{ij} \quad (9)$$

$$Min \quad COST = \sum_{i=1}^{n} \sum_{j=1}^{n} c_{ij} x_{ij} \quad (10)$$

$$max \quad SAFETY = \prod_{i=1}^{n} \prod_{j=1}^{n} q_{ij} \quad (11)$$

$$s.t \quad x_{ij} = \begin{cases} 0 & if \quad e_{ij} \notin \Gamma \\ 1 & if \quad e_{ij} \in \Gamma \end{cases}$$
$$\forall i, j \in [1,2,\cdots,n] \quad (12)$$

$$\sum_{j=1}^{n} x_{1j} = 1 \quad \forall j \in [2,3,\cdots,n] \quad (13)$$

$$\sum_{i=1}^{n} x_{in} = 1 \quad \forall i \in [1,2,\cdots,n-1] \quad (14)$$

$$\sum_{i=1}^{n} x_{ik} = \sum_{j=1}^{n} x_{kj} \quad \forall k \in [2,3,\cdots,n-1] \quad (15)$$

$$u_i - u_j + n \cdot x_{ij} \le n-1 \quad \forall i,j \in [1,2,\cdots,n] \tag{16}$$

$$v_i \in [1,2,3,4,5,6] \quad \forall i \in [1,2,\cdots,n] \tag{17}$$

$$b_{ij} = \mathrm{sgn}\left[(v_i - v_j)^2\right] \quad \forall i,j \in [1,2,\cdots,n] \tag{18}$$

$$t_{ij} = s_{ij} / \mu_{ij} + b_{ij}\left[\min\{\alpha_i, \beta_j\} \cdot g_i + \max\{\alpha_i, \beta_j\} \cdot \min\{d_j, M\}\right] \quad \forall i,j \in [1,2,\cdots,n]$$
(19)

$$c_{ij} = \left[\gamma_{ij} \cdot s_{ij} + b_{ij}(\eta_i + \lambda_j + \theta_j)\right]M \quad \forall i,j \in [1,2,\cdots,n] \tag{20}$$

$$(m - d_j)\sum_{i=1}^{n}(b_{ij}x_{ij}) \le 0 \quad \forall j \in [1,2,\cdots,n-1] \tag{21}$$

$$(M - D_j)\sum_{i=1}^{n}(b_{ij}x_{ij}) \le 0 \quad \forall j \in [1,2,\cdots,n-1] \tag{22}$$

$$(l^k - l_j^k)\sum_{i=1}^{n}(b_{ij}x_{ij}) \le 0 \quad \forall j \in [1,2,\cdots,n-1]; \quad \forall k \in [1,2,3] \tag{23}$$

$$q_{ij} = \left[(p_{ij} - 1)x_{ij} + 1\right] \quad \forall i,j \in [1,2,\cdots,n]$$
(24)

$$TIME \le W_t \tag{25}$$

$$COST \le W_c \tag{26}$$

$$SAFETY \ge W_p \tag{27}$$

Introduction the decision variable p_j, which is a stage safety probability, stand for the safety probability on the distribution path Γ from the starting point v_1 to v_j.

$$p_1 = 1, \quad p_j = \sum_{i=1}^{n} p_i p_{ij} x_{ij} \quad \forall j \in [2,3,\cdots,n]$$

(28)

So the *SAFETY* can be expressed in another form.

$$SAFETY = \sum_{i=1}^{n} p_i p_{in} x_{in} \tag{29}$$

This simplified the 0-1 nonlinear programming model to the 0-1 linear programming model.

$$\ln(SAFETY) = \ln\left(\prod_{i=1}^{n}\prod_{j=1}^{n} q_{ij}\right) = \sum_{i=1}^{n}\sum_{j=1}^{n}(x_{ij}\ln p_{ij})$$

(30)

$$q_{ij} = \exp(x_{ij} \cdot \ln p_{ij}) \quad \forall i,j \in [1,2,\cdots,n] \tag{31}$$

3.3 Model Solution Method

The problem of single path multi-modal transport path optimization is linear programming; these planning issues involve more variables, the constraint expression is more complex, In this paper, LINGO software for nonlinear programming is selected to programming and solving, it can be greatly improved the speed of the solution, the global optimal solution can be obtained conveniently.

4. Simulation Analysis and Solution Of The Model

4.1 Transportation Task

The superior ordered the X Military Region to have a reasonable distribution plan, and organize transportation delivering 40 tons goods to the front distribution center of an island in the Taiwan Strait from a strategic logistics center near the base of Wuhan within 40 hours.

4.2 Implementation Plan

Selected different optimization targets and setting different constraints, Using LINGO software, the model of single path multi-modal transport path optimization is analyzed, made a reference plan as shown in table 1 (assuming that 120 km/h of railway transportation, unloading at the rate of 200 tons per hour; 90 km/h of road transportation, transit transportation 60 km/h; 25 km/h of carrier, loading and unloading speed per hour 150 tons; 800 km/h of air transport, loading and unloading rate of 100 tons per hour. Basic price of railway transport is 10.4 Yuan/ton, basic price of road transport is 0.45 Yuan/ton per kilometers, loading of the goods is 2 Yuan/ton, unloading of the goods is 1.5 Yuan/ton, shipping prices is 5 Yuan/ton, loading and unloading price of 20 Yuan/ton; air transport price is 1097 Yuan/ton, running basic price is 1.628 Yuan/ton per kilometers, loading and unloading price is 500 Yuan/ton). From table1:

Table.1 Multimodal transport network simulation and optimization plan

Reference plan	Constraint conditions	Distance/km	Time/h	Cost/THY*	Safety probability
The most economical solution	Γ_1 : Without constraints	1839	79.77	17.95	0.808
	Γ_2 : $TIME < 40h$,	1548	36.11	18.18	0.727
	Γ_3 : $TIME < 30h$	1234	28.45	47.82	0.583
The fastest solution	Γ_4 : Without constraints	1086	23.58	342.74	0.613
	Γ_5 ; $COST < 50$ THY	1234	28.45	47.82	0.583
	Γ_6 ; $COST < 50$ THY	1548	36.11	18.18	0.727
The safest solution	Γ_7 : Without constraints	2196	44.35	446.05	0.808
	Γ_8 : $TIME < 30h$, $COST < 350$	1192	28.98	338.95	0.767
	Γ_9 : $TIME < 40h$, $COST < 100$	1548	36.11	18.18	0.727

*THY stand for Ten thousand Yuan

If cost is the optimal target, Γ_1 is the most economic plan, which is water transport after the goods delivery, transport along the Yangtze river from Wuhan to Shanghai, then delivery to the specified location on the island; Γ_2 is the most economic plan meet the conditions of $TIME < 40h$ and $SAFETY > 0.7$, which transport from Wuhan to Wenzhou by railway , then turn to the destination by water transportation; Γ_3 is the most economic plan meet the condition of $TIME < 30h$, which transport directly to Fuzhou via the highway and then transport to the destination by water.

If time is the optimal goal, Γ_4 is the quickest plan, which transport directly to Fuzhou by air and transferred to the destination by water. Γ_5 is the quickest plan if $COST < 50$ THY, which the same as Γ_3; Γ_6 is the quickest plan meet the conditions of $COST < 50$ THY and $SAFETY > 0.7$,which the same as Γ_2.

If the objective is to optimize the safety probability, Γ_7 is the safest plan, obtained the maximum safety probability is 0.808, which is to determine the maximum safe probability of unconstrained conditions; Γ_8 is the safest plan $TIME < 30h$ and $COST < 350$ THY, which transport to Wenzhou by air then transported to the destination by water. Γ_9 is the safest plan meet the condition of $TIME < 40h$ and $COST < 100$ THY, which the same as Γ_2.

5. Conclusion

In this paper, a single-path multi-objective multimodal transport path optimization model is established; the model of the n^2 order characteristic is simplified to a 0-1 linear programming model by simplifying. The solution time is greatly reduced, the global optimal solution is also easy to obtain, and the model is verified by an example. The optimal distribution plan can be developed according to different constraints, the simulation results show that the model is reasonable; it can provide theoretical support for fast accurate and efficient transportation, it can realize the optimal allocation of multi-modal transport resources and capacity of military transport. The next step is to optimize the multi-path multimodal transport path optimization model, and improve the logistics distribution capacity of our military.

Reference

1. IBRAHIM A. BARBAROS C T. Optimization of Transportation Requirements in the Deployment of Military Units [J]. Computers & Operations Research, 2007(34):1158-1176.
2. UGUR Z Y, BARBAROS C T, IHSAN S. A Multi-modal Discrete-event Simulation Model for Military Deployment [J]. Simulation Modeling Practice and Theory, 2009(17):597-611.
3. YANG Xi-rui , SONG Chuan-ping. Optimizing Model Design for Military Transportation Based on Multimode Transportation [J] Journal of academy of military transportation, 2008, 10(6):65-69.
4. LIU Hua-xia,YANG Xi-long,ZHANG Chong-bo.Application of Multimodal Transportation in Military Transportation under the Military Logistical Environment[J]. Logistics Management, 2010(12):111-112.
5. PAYMAN J, ROBERT C L. A Supply-chain Optimization Model of the Allocation of Containerized Imports from Asia to the United States [J]. Transportation Research Part E, 2011(47): 609-622.
6. CHANG Tsungsheng. Best Routs Selection in International Intermodal Networks. Cmoputers & Operational Research, 2008 ,3 5(9):2877-2891.
7. CARAMIA M, GUERIERO F. A Heuristic Approach to Long-haul Freight Transportation with Multiple Objective Functions. The International Journal of Management Science, 2009(37):600-614.
8. CHEN Shaokuan, PENG Hongqin, LIU Shuang, Yang Yuanzhou. A Multimodal Hierarchical-based Assignment Model for Integrated Transportation Networks [J]. Journal of Transportation Systems Engineering and Information Technology, 2009,

9(6):130-135.

9. ZHANG Jin, WANG Shuxin, SHEN Jun et al. A Study on Path Optimization of Multimodal Military Transportation Based on Road Transfer[C]. Proceedings of the 32nd Chinese Control Conference, Xi'an, China, July 26-28, 2013: 8097-8101.

3D Reconstruction from a Single Still Image Based on Monocular Vision of an Uncalibrated Camera

Tao Yu[1], Jian-Hua Zou[2], Qin-Bao Song[3]

[1,2]*Systems Engineering Institute, School of Electronic & Information Engineering, Xi'an JiaoTong University, 28 Xian-Ning West Road, Xi'an city, Shaanxi Province, 710049, P R China*
[1,2]*State key laboratory for systems engineering, Xi'an Jiaotong University, 28 Xian-Ning West Road, Xi'an city, Shaanxi Province, 710049, P R China*
[1,3] *Dept. of Computer Science & Technology, School of Electronics & Information Engineering, Xi'an Jiaotong University, 28 Xian-Ning West Road Xi'an city, Shaanxi Province, 710049, P R China*
[1]*yvt9399@stu.xjtu.edu.cn,* [2]*jhzou@sei.xjtu.edu.cn,* [3]*qbsong@mail.xjtu.edu.cn*

Abstract: we propose a framework of combining Machine Learning with Dynamic Optimization for reconstructing scene in 3D automatically from a single still image of unstructured outdoor environment based on monocular vision of an uncalibrated camera. After segmenting image first time, a kind of searching tree strategy based on Bayes rule is used to identify the hierarchy of all areas on occlusion. After superpixel segmenting image second time, the AdaBoost algorithm is applied in the integration detection to the depth of lighting, texture and material. Finally, all the factors above are optimized with constrained conditions, acquiring the whole depthmap of an image. Integrate the source image with its depthmap in point-cloud or bilinear interpolation styles, realizing 3D reconstruction. Experiment in comparisons with typical methods in associated database demonstrates our method improves the reasonability of estimation to the overall 3D architecture of image's scene to a certain extent. And it does not need any manual assist and any camera model information.

1. Introduction

We all know that the 3D scene has more valuable information than 2D scene because of including the depth information. However, the acquisition for 3D scene is usually complex and difficult. It often needs many cameras to take pictures at multi-view angles and needs the techniques of camera's calibration, image matching etc or needs the complex sophisticated depth sensor instruments to realize.

In reality, sometimes, we cannot acquire many images from different view angles to reconstruct 3D scenes because of the limited conditions, such as the vehicles in the distance, ships in the sea, or the stars in the interstellar space etc, but we are still interested in understanding the hierarchy relationships of front and back among the objects. At these situations, we only can hope to utilize the information from monocular vision to recover or approximate the real 3D effects directly.

Recently, many investigations attempting to reconstruct 3D scenes from monocular vision directly involve mainly two types: from videos [1-5] and from a still image. Among the latter: some demand camera calibration in advance[6-8], some need manual assistance[9-11], some recur to auxiliary accurate sensors[12], some use the means of camera's focus[13, 14], some append a few extra constrained conditions[15-17].

At present, with the rapid development of Machine Learning, some investigators utilize these theories for training associated models such as Bayes[18, 19], Adaboost[20-23] and Markov random field(MRF)[24-26] etc to estimate the structural information of scenes. However, pure machine learning often brings the problem of under-fitting or over-fitting, which often leads to incorrect or inaccurate estimation for the whole 3D structure of scenes. To make up the deficiency, since optimization's theory and methods can deal with selecting the best alternative in the sense of the given objective function, we consider of introducing the strategy of optimization upon the Machine Learning for estimating the final whole 3D structure of scenes.

In this paper, a method of combining Machine Learning with Dynamic Optimization is used to reconstruct 3D scene directly from a single still image based on monocular vision of an uncalibrated camera. It improves the reasonability of estimation to the whole 3D structure of images' scenes to a certain extent and doe not need any manual assist and any camera model information.

The remainder of this paper is arranged as follows. Section 2 interprets the principle of 3D reconstruction from a single still image based on monocular vision of an uncalibrated camera; Section 3 provides relative experiment and results analysis; Section 4 concludes this paper.

2. The Principle of 3D Reconstruction From A Single Still Image Based on Monocular Vision of An Uncalibrated Camera

2.1 Global Principle

Comparing with 3D image, the monocular vision produces 2D image, which has only the information at orientations of X and Y, without Z. That is to say, it has not the depth information. So, in order to realize 3D reconstruction, we need to estimate the depth information from 2D image.

If we close our one eye, with the other one open to see a picture, we still can feel the relationship of different parts' back and forth to the object in image. To the complex image, according to some rules, we often can also infer its relationship of back or forth with other objects around and further infer the whole architecture of depth from an image. These phenomena provide us with some possibilities for the 3D reconstruction of the scene from monocular image. Here, we think that the perception above maybe some past experience and the rules above maybe some kind of optimization. So, this paper will attempt to combine Machine Learning with Dynamic Optimization for the computer to solve this problem automatically.

In a picture, usually we will see some familiar or unfamiliar object, which involves shape, material, texture, color, and the effect of illumination. And we usually can also accept the inferences that:

A. For a familiar object, if it only can be seen part shape, it is usually sheltered by something.

B. For the material, the part near to us is usually clearer and rougher than the part in distance.

C. For the texture, usually, the near part presents sparser, however, the part in distance presents denser.

D. For the effect of lighting, the part near light source is usually brighter than the part far away.

E. For the color, it usually changes with different objects or different parts of one object or even different lighting sources etc.

According to the experiences above: we can use some samples owning different depth levels for the material, texture and brightness of pictures respectively to train the relative learning machines; then we use some priority to infer the depth level of some area in image and for some objects with familiar shapes, we can use some decision algorithm to infer the possible existed occlusions; finally, to the whole image, we can use optimization algorithm to integrate with all the inferences above; thus, we will acquire multi-possible architectures of depths for an image and we will select the most possible one as the final result according to the computational optimal value or the biggest probability value. In addition, because we do not use any camera's model information, here, the depths studied are not real absolute depths, but the relative depths of the different components in an image.

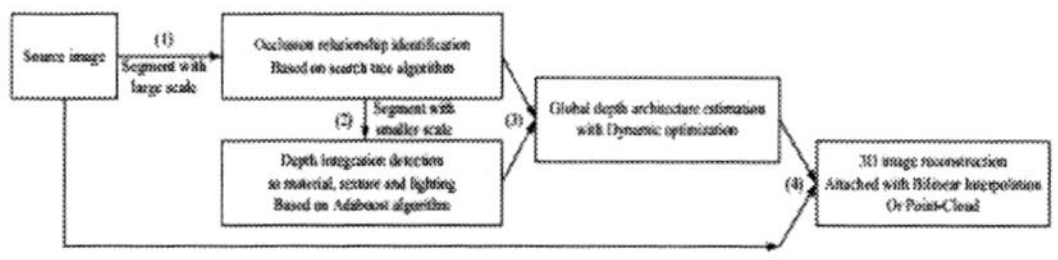

Fig.1 the principle of the 3D reconstruction

Fig.1 gives this paper' main principle of the 3D reconstruction directly from monocular 2D image, in which: the source image is segmented with bigger scale and smaller scale in turn, to make occlusion identification and depth integration detection on material, texture and lighting; then the global depth architecture is estimated with dynamic optimization based on the two stages' results above; at last, combining the global depth architecture with source image, the 3D image reconstruction attached with bilinear interpolation or point-cloud is realized. Next, we will describe each part of the principle in detail.

2.2 Implementation

To estimate the depth structure reasonably, the key is need to make correct image representation as much as possible to the image's important information. Image representation is usually hierarchical, so it is carried on the basis of the image segmentation in different scales [27, 28], in which the image's different components represent different meanings.

2.2.1 Occlusion Identification

First, we segment the image in bigger scale with method in Ref. [27] to acquire familiar objects and identify the associated occlusions. Here, the occluding phenomenon is defined as: when object A can only be seen in partial shape and the other area where should be embodied as the rest shape of A, is occupied by object B, then we think that object A is occluded by object B, or B is in front of A. The occluded areas' divisions refer to [29]. The related principle is as Eqs. (2-1) displaying, in which M, N are two neighboring objects in an image; X represents the associated traits; Y is the associated prior knowledge for familiar objects and Q is the number of objects in an image. According to Bayesian rule, the more remarkable the traits information P(X/(M, N)) and the prior information P(Y/(M, N, X)) are, the bigger the value of posterior probability function P((M, N)/(X, Y)) on occlusion will be.

$$P\left((M,N)/(X,Y)\right)=\frac{P\left(Y/(M,N,X)\right)P\left(X/(M,N)\right)}{\sum_{M\neq N\in Q}\left[P\left(Y/(M,N,X)\right)P\left(X/(M,N)\right)\right]} \qquad (2-1)$$

To find out all the familiar objects' occlusive relationships in an image, we adopt a kind of searching tree algorithm. The searching process is just as Fig.2, in which all the familiar objects' relative occlusive relationships of each other are inferred by the principle of Eqs. (2-1) and at last, relative different number is used to represent different depth hierarchy. Of course, there exists the likelihood of inferring error on the occluding problem. It relies on whether the prior information on the familiar objects' understanding is reliable. And the more reliable the prior knowledge is, the more accurate the inference is.

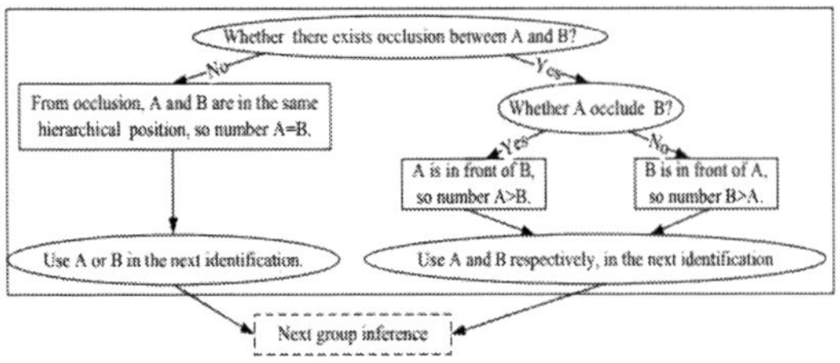

Fig.2 the search strategy on occlusion in one image

2.2.2 Depth Integration Detection to Material, Texture and Lighting

After the occlusion identification is over, then, the image will be segmented again in smaller scale with method in Ref. [27] to acquire the superpixels, each of which represents a coherent region with similar properties such as lighting, texture, material or colors. Fig.3 displays an example of segmenting image, in which there are two grades of segmentation with yellow color and red color describing respectively.

3-a Source image 3-b Superpixel segmenting image

Fig.3 An example of segmenting image

Next, we process the superpixels' image above from the aspects of lighting, texture and material to extract more depth information. Here, before further depth identification, we predefine multiple depth classes according to different changing extent of lighting, texture and material with depth changing. We use the logistic regression version of AdaBoost algorithm in Ref. [30] to train each class of depth samples and acquire relative detector. At each class of depth, the relative detector based on textural or material traits' weighting is trained and the relative lighting model is also trained. In identifying, according to some priority order, we integrate the detectors to acquire the integration depth on material, texture and lighting. Fig.4 displays the associated detecting principle, in which the property of AdaBoost that uses weak classifiers to construct strong classifiers is applied for both the single depth class detection and the integration depth detection.

On the selection of associated traits: the textural energy which are computed from Law's masks in Refs. [31, 32] act as textural features to embody the extent of textural denseness at different depths; the Haar-like traits in Ref. [33] act as material features to describe the extent of material smoothness and ambiguity with depth changing; the lighting model on depth refers to [34, 35], in which the distance from light source to viewer is regarded as the relative depth herein, then image's other components are assigned to corresponding lighting categorical depth classes and model parameters in turn.

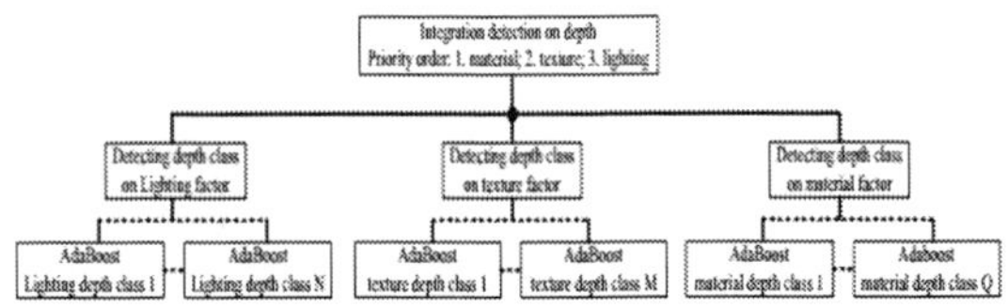

Fig.4. The principle of integration detection to the depth of lighting, texture and material

2.2.3 Global Depth Architecture

To acquire the final global depth architecture of an image, we combine with all the inferences of the factors above and apply a kind of dynamic optimization with constrain conditions to solve the problem. In addition, image's gray values usually reflect some depth information, so it will also be regarded as one base applied in the estimation for the final global depth architecture. The corresponding formula is Eqs. (2-2), where: m, n represents two neighboring areas in an image; g(m,n,d) is the depth mapping function between neighboring area m and n corresponding to the constrains above. Herein: q=1, base on gray image; q=2, base on lighting; q=3, base on texture; q=4, base on material; q=5, base on occluding; λ and μ are associated Lagrange multipliers; L is the total number of correlations corresponding to neighboring areas in an image; d is the final depth correlation to be established for all the smaller areas of an image; c is introduced slack variable used to transform the inequality constrains above to equality constrains.

$$\arg\min_{d,c}\left(\sum_{p=1}^{L}\left\| d_p-\sum_{q=1}^{5}\left(\lambda_{pq}\cdot\left(g_q\left(m_p,n_p,d_p\right)-c_{pq}\right)\right)+\frac{1}{2\mu_p}\cdot\sum_{q=1}^{5}\left(\left(g_q\left(m_p,n_p,d_p\right)-c_{pq}\right)^2\right)\right\|\right) \quad (2\text{-}2)$$

From optimization theory in Ref. [36], we can infer optimal

the value of c_{pq} as Eqs. (2-3)

$$c_{pq}=\max\left(g_q\left(m_p,n_p,d_p\right)-\mu_p\cdot\lambda_{pq},0\right) \quad (2\text{-}3)$$

Combing Eqs. (2-2) with (2-3), we can construct the augmented Lagrangian function (2-4).

$$LA(d,\lambda,\mu)\overset{def}{=}\sum_{p=1}^{L}\left\| \begin{array}{l} d_p-\sum_{q=1}^{5}\left(\lambda_{pq}\cdot\left(g_q\left(m_p,n_p,d_p\right)-\max\left(g_q\left(m_p,n_p,d_p\right)-\mu_p\cdot\lambda_{pq},0\right)\right)\right) \\ +\frac{1}{2\mu_p}\cdot\sum_{q=1}^{5}\left(\left(g_q\left(m_p,n_p,d_p\right)-\max\left(g_q\left(m_p,n_p,d_p\right)-\mu_p\cdot\lambda_{pq},0\right)\right)^2\right) \end{array}\right\| \quad (2\text{-}4)$$

Thus the problem (2-2) above is transformed into formula (2-5).

$$\min_d\left(LA(d,\lambda,\mu)\right) \quad (2\text{-}5)$$

Referring to [37], the specific solving procedures on problem

the above are as follow:

Given $\mu_0 > 0$, tolerance $\varepsilon > 0$, starting points $\mathbf{d}^{s0}$ and $\boldsymbol{\lambda}^0$;

for k = 0, 1, 2, . . .

Find an approximate minimizer $\mathbf{d}^k$ of LA($\bullet,\boldsymbol{\lambda}^k;\boldsymbol{\mu}^k$), starting at $\mathbf{d}^{sk}$,

and terminating when $\|\nabla_d LA(\mathbf{d}^k, \boldsymbol{\lambda}^k;\boldsymbol{\mu}^k)\| \leq \varepsilon$;

if final convergence test for formula (2-5) is satisfied

Stop with approximate solution $\mathbf{d}^k$;

end(if)

Update Lagrange multipliers using Eqs. (2-6) to obtain $\boldsymbol{\lambda}^{k+1}$;

$$\lambda^{k+1} = \max\left(\lambda^k - g\left(m,n,d^k\right)/\mu^k, 0\right); \quad (2\text{-}6)$$

Choose new penalty parameter $\boldsymbol{\mu}^{k+1} \geq \boldsymbol{\mu}^k$;

Set starting point for the next iteration to $\mathbf{d}^{s(k+1)} = \mathbf{d}^k$;

end (for)

According to the method described above, the vector **d**, **λ** and **μ** are integrated updating until convergence. Note that the vector **d** refers to relative depth, not absolute depth.

Fig.5 illustrates an example of the estimation to an image's global depth architecture with the method of this paper, in which the different gray levels indicate different depths.

Fig.5 An example of the estimation to the global depth architecture of an image

2.2.4 3D Reconstruction Realization

At last, after acquiring the complete depthmap of an image, we combine the depthmap with its source image to reconstruct the 3D image. And here, two kinds of methods are used to process the voxels in 3D image: to the images distributed mainly with continuous qualities, the bilinear interpolation method is applied to complementing and smoothing the color area among the reconstructed 3D pixel points; to the images distributed mainly with discrete qualities, the point-cloud method is applied directly to the reconstruction of the 3D image's voxels. In addition, during the course of 3D image reconstruction, to the borderlines of the segmentation before, we use the corresponding pixels in original image to replace them. Fig.6 gives an example of reconstructed 3D images viewed in different visual angles from a single 2D source image. From different view angles, we can see that they all approximate the usual real objects and scenes.

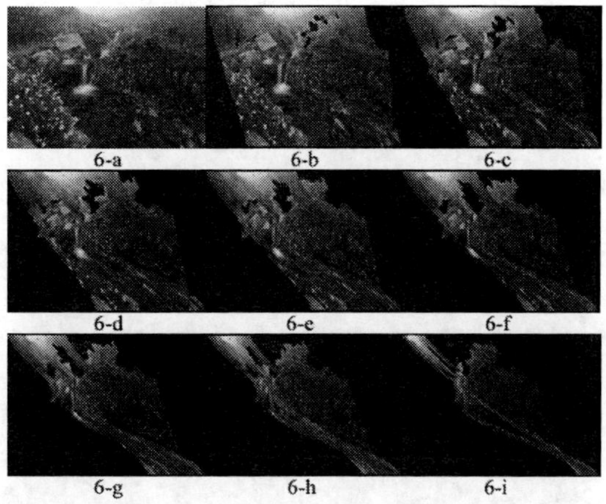

a-frontal image; b- right rotation 10。; c- right rotation 20。; d- right rotation 30。; e- right rotation 40。; f- right rotation 50。; g- right rotation 60。; h- right rotation 70。; i- right rotation 80。;

Fig.6 Example of 3D reconstruction from single image

3. Experiment

3.1 Testing Environment

In order to prove the ability of the application in general environment for the method proposed in this paper, all the experiments are conducted in the environment of Microsoft visual c++ 6.0 at the platform of Pentium 1.73GHz personal computer.

The framework of 3D reconstruction from monocular vision proposed by this paper is tested with the Make3D Range Image Data' dataset1[24, 25], which consists of 534 image+depthmap pairs, with an image resolution of 2272×1704 and a depthmap resolution of 55×305. In our experiment, 400 of the images/depthmaps are used for training associated detectors and the remaining 134 for testing. At the same time, we will compare the experimental results with typical Saxena[24] method and HEH[23] method. And for fairness, their depthmaps are scaled and shifted before computing the errors to match the global scale of our test images.

3.2 Testing Results and Analysis

Fig.7 gives some examples of real effects for contrasting typical methods —Saxena[24] and HEH[23] with ours. In comparisons: HEH's generating a popup effect by folding the images at "ground-vertical" boundaries is not feasible for all the images. Especially for multy non-ground and discontinuous areas with front and back relationships in an image, it often fails to describe these scenes' structure correctly, such as fig.7-b1, 7-b2. Saxena's using Markov Random Field (MRF) to infer both 3D location and orientation of the patches in an image without any explicit assumptions about the structure of the scene makes it generalize well, even to scenes with significant nonvertical structure. The deficiency exists in that at the aspect of the whole structural reconstruction, it lacks the comprehensive considering for many factors, so its global 3D structural estimation is sometimes inaccurate, such as fig. 7-c3. Our algorithm's global dynamic optimization seems to be more reasonable and feasible for the whole 3D architectural reconstruction to a certain extent, producing better effects although a few small local parts in images are estimated somewhat coarsely.

a-Source image; b-HEH' algorithm; c-Saxena's algorithm; d-our algorithm

Fig.7 Examples of 3D reconstruction from single image with different algorithms

Table.1 and Fig.8 give the final statistical results for the testing comparisons of our algorithm with the two typical algorithms above, in which: whether 'Depth error' or 'Relative Depth error' are both averaged over all pixels in the hold-out test set; 'Correct rate' means percent of models qualitatively correct; 'Planes Correct rate' is percent of major planes correctly identified. Combing with the analysis before, we can see that from the whole testing data, Saxena's method is a little better than ours probably because of our method's accumulated several local small estimation errors during the course of computation and our method outperforms HEH mainly for HEH' sometimes failed estimation for the whole structure of scenes, all of which verifies our algorithm's feasibility and rationality further.

Table.1 comparisons with typical methods

Method	Depth error $\lvert \log_{10} d - \log_{10} \hat{d} \rvert$	Relative Depth error $\lvert d-\hat{d} \rvert / d$	Correct rate (%)	Planes Correct rate (%)
HEH	0.320	0.423	33.1	50.3
Saxena	0.187	0.370	64.9	71.2
Ours	0.253	0.382	52.5	69.4

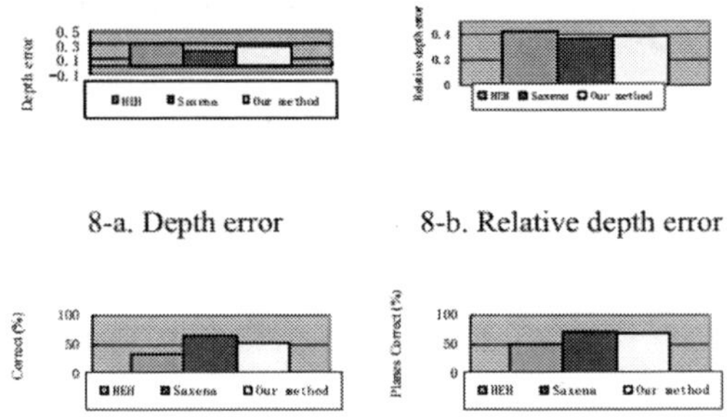

8-a. Depth error 8-b. Relative depth error

8-c. Correct rate 8-d. Planes correct rate

Fig.8 comparisons with typical methods.

4. Conclusion

This paper mainly proposes a framework of 3D reconstruction from a single still image of unstructured outdoor environment based on monocular vision of an uncalibrated camera. It integrates machine's learning for each factor with dynamic optimization's considering comprehensively for multy-factors to estimate scene's 3D structure and does not need any manual assist, any camera model information. In experiment, we use Make3D Range Image Data to compare it with typical methods of HEH and Saxena. The results basically confirm our method's reasonability and feasibility for image scene's global architectural 3D reconstruction to a certain extent.

In the next work, our investigation will manage to improve the accuracy of estimation not only for the scene's local patches especially, but also for the global structure further. Meanwhile, whether this paper's method can apply to other databases needs new testing. In addition, we will investigate the real-time 3D reconstruction from a single still image, which needs paralleled mechanism and improving our algorithm's speed furtherly.

Acknowledgment

The authors thank to Computer Science Department, Stanford University for supplying investigators with the free Make3D Range Image Data and thank for being supported by the National Natural Science Foundation of China (50177025).

References

1. Jebara, T., A. Azarbayejani, and A. Pentland, 3D structure from 2D motion. Signal Processing magazine, 1999. **16**(3): p. 66-84.
2. Po, L.-M., et al., Automatic 2D-to-3D video conversion technique based on depth-from-motion and color segmentation, in Signal Processing (ICSP), 2010 IEEE 10th International Conference

DOI: 10.1051/itmconf/20171201018

on. 2010, IEEE. p. 1000-1003.

3. Bok, Y., Y. Hwang, and I.S. Kweon, Accurate motion estimation and high-precision 3d reconstruction by sensor fusion, in Robotics and Automation, 2007 IEEE International Conference on. 2007, IEEE. p. 4721-4726.
4. Cao, X., Z. Li, and Q. Dai, Semi-automatic 2D-to-3D conversion using disparity propagation. IEEE TRANSACTIONS ON BROADCASTING, 2011. **57**(2): p. 491-499.
5. Hertzmann, A. and S.M. Seitz, Example-based photometric stereo: Shape reconstruction with general, varying brdfs. IEEE TRANSACTIONS ON PATTERN ANALYSIS AND MACHINE INTELLIGENCE, 2005. **27**(8): p. 1254-1264.
6. Guillou, E., et al., Using vanishing points for camera calibration and coarse 3D reconstruction from a single image. The Visual Computer, 2000. **16**(7): p. 396-410.
7. Wilczkowiak, M., E. Boyer, and P. Sturm. Camera calibration and 3D reconstruction from single images using parallelepipeds. in Computer Vision, 2001. ICCV 2001. Proceedings. Eighth IEEE International Conference on. 2001. IEEE.
8. Wang, G., et al., Camera calibration and 3D reconstruction from a single view based on scene constraints. Image and Vision Computing, 2005. **23**(3): p. 311-323.
9. Criminisi, A., I. Reid, and A. Zisserman, Single View Metrology. International Journal of Computer Vision, 2000. **40**(2): p. 123-148.
10. Barinova, O., et al., Fast automatic single-view 3-d reconstruction of urban scenes, in Computer Vision-ECCV 2008. 2008, Springer. p. 100-113.
11. Sturm, P. and S. Maybank. A method for interactive 3d reconstruction of piecewise planar objects from single images. in The 10th British Machine Vision Conference (BMVC'99). 1999. The British Machine Vision Association (BMVA).
12. Willneff, J., J. Poon, and C. Fraser, Single-image high-resolution satellite data for 3D information extraction. International Archives of Photogrammetry, Remote Sensing and Spatial Information Sciences, 2005. **36**(1/W3): p. 1-6.
13. Namboodiri, V.P. and S. Chaudhuri, Recovery of relative depth from a single observation using an uncalibrated (real-aperture) camera, in Computer Vision and Pattern Recognition, CVPR. IEEE Conference on. 2008, IEEE. p. 1-6.
14. Zhuo, S. and T. Sim, On the recovery of depth from a single defocused image, in Computer Analysis of Images and Patterns. 2009, Springer. p. 889-897.
15. Van den Heuvel, F.A., 3D reconstruction from a single image using geometric constraints. ISPRS Journal of Photogrammetry and Remote Sensing, 1998. **53**(6): p. 354-368.
16. El-Hakim, S.F. A flexible approach to 3D reconstruction from single images. in ACM SIGGRAPH. 2001. Citeseer.
17. Wang, G., et al., Single view metrology from scene constraints. Image and Vision Computing, 2005. **23**(9): p. 831-840.
18. Delage, E., H. Lee, and A.Y. Ng, A dynamic bayesian network model for autonomous 3d reconstruction from a single indoor image, in Computer Vision and Pattern Recognition, 2006 IEEE Computer Society Conference on. 2006, IEEE. p. 2418-2428.
19. Han, F. and S.-C. Zhu. Bayesian reconstruction of 3d shapes and scenes from a single image. in Higher-Level Knowledge in 3D Modeling and Motion Analysis, 2003. HLK 2003. First IEEE International Workshop on. 2003. IEEE.
20. Hoiem, D., A.A. Efros, and M. Hebert, Recovering surface layout from an image. International Journal of Computer Vision, 2007. **75**(1): p. 151-172.
21. Hoiem, D., A.A. Efros, and M. Hebert, Closing the loop in scene interpretation, in Computer Vision and Pattern Recognition. CVPR. IEEE Conference on. 2008, IEEE. p. 1-8.
22. Hoiem, D., A.A. Efros, and M. Hebert, Automatic photo pop-up. ACM Transactions on Graphics (TOG), , 2005. **24**(3): p. 577-584.
23. Hoiem, D., A.A. Efros, and M. Hebert, Geometric context from a single image, in Computer Vision. ICCV 2005. Tenth IEEE International Conference on. 2005, IEEE. p. 654-661.
24. Saxena, A., M. Sun, and A.Y. Ng, Make3d: Learning 3d scene structure from a single still image. IEEE TRANSACTIONS ON PATTERN ANALYSIS AND MACHINE INTELLIGENCE, 2009. **31**(5): p. 824-840.
25. Saxena, A., S.H. Chung, and A.Y. Ng, Learning depth from single monocular images, in Advances in Neural Information Processing Systems(NIPS). 2005. p. 1161-1168.
26. Delage, E., H. Lee, and A.Y. Ng, Automatic single-image 3d reconstructions of indoor manhattan world scenes, in Robotics Research. 2007, Springer. p. 305-321.
27. Levinshtein, A., et al., Turbopixels: Fast superpixels using geometric flows. 2009, IEEE TRANSACTIONS ON PATTERN ANALYSIS AND MACHINE INTELLIGENCE,. p. 2290-2297.
28. Felzenszwalb, P.F. and D.P. Huttenlocher, Efficient graph-based image segmentation, in International Journal of Computer Vision. 2004, Springer. p. 167-181.
29. Hoiem, D., et al., Recovering occlusion boundaries from a single image, in Computer Vision, 2007. ICCV 2007. IEEE 11th International Conference on. 2007, IEEE. p. 1-8.
30. Collins, M., R.E. Schapire, and Y. Singer, Logistic regression, AdaBoost and Bregman distances, in Machine Learning. 2002, Springer. p. 253-285.
31. Davies, E.R., Laws' texture energy in texture. 1997, Machine vision: theory, algorithms, practicalities.

32. Laws, K.I., Rapid texture identification, in 24th Annual Technical Symposium. 1980, International Society for Optics and Photonics. p. 376-381.
33. Lienhart, R., A. Kuranov, and V. Pisarevsky, Empirical analysis of detection cascades of boosted classifiers for rapid object detection, in Pattern Recognition. 2003, Springer. p. 297-304.
34. Klassen, R.V., Modeling the effect of the atmosphere on light. 1987, ACM. p. 215-237.
35. Narasimhan, S.G. and S.K. Nayar, Shedding light on the weather, in Computer Vision and Pattern Recognition, 2003. Proceedings. 2003 IEEE Computer Society Conference on. 2003, IEEE. p. I-665-I-672 vol. 1.
36. Nocedal, J. and S.J. Wright, Numerical Optimization. Springer, 2006. **9**(4): p. 1556-1556.
37. Nocedal, J. and S.J. Wright, Numerical Optimization Second Edition. 1999..

A Review on Fatigue Driving Detection

Sheng-Yang Shi[1], Wen-Zhong Tang[1] and Yan-Yang Wang[2,a]

[1]*School of Computer Science and Engineering, Beihang University, 100191 HaiDian District, Beijing, China*
[2]*School of Aeronautic Science and Engineering, Beihang University, 100191 HaiDian District, Beijing, China*

Abstract: The socialization of automobile development has brought great convenience to people's travel. However, the rapid increase in the number of vehicles has also caused a series of problems. The increase in traffic accidents has brought great social casualties and economic losses. Fatigue driving, which is an important factor in the traffic accident, has aroused people's attention. This paper reviews all kinds of fatigue driving detection methods at present; compares various fatigue driving detection methods in terms of accuracy, real-time and cost; analyses the advantages and disadvantages of various methods; introduces the application of fatigue detection system in automobile; summarizes the current deficiencies and future development trends in the field of fatigue driving detection. The future research of this field will be more to the data fusion, computer vision and deep learning.

1 Introduction

The number of cars is increasing rapidly in recent years, which has led to an increase in the number of traffic accidents. Frequent traffic accidents have brought a lot of casualties and economic losses and become a serious problem around the world [1-3]. It is an important task for people to determine the causes of traffic accidents and to find suitable methods to reduce the incidence of accidents. Fatigue driving is one of the most important factors of traffic accidents. According to the statistical data of the China National Bureau of statistics [4], there were 1029735 traffic accident in the past 5 years, causing 304671 deaths and direct economic loss of 5 billion 294 million yuan. The traffic accidents caused by fatigue driving accounted for 20% of the total number of accidents and more than 30% of highway traffic accidents. Fatigue driving refers to the driver's mental or physical disorders due to lacking of sleep or long time driving, which results in the decreased control of the vehicles [5]. Therefore, it will be able to effectively reduce the probability of traffic accidents by finding out the causes and characteristics of fatigue driving and proposing an effective fatigue driving detection method. At present, more and more researchers focused on fatigue driving detection method [6].

The main methods of fatigue driving detection can be divided into subjective detection methods and objective detection methods [7-8]. The subjective detection methods require the driver to determine their degree of fatigue by checking the driving record sheet and their own physiological response. The objective detection methods extract the characteristic parameters related to driving with special equipment, and then evaluate the driver's fatigue degree based on the model build with the extracted parameters.

Subjective fatigue detection methods are simple and easy. But their accuracy and real-time performance is very poor because these methods require driver to test their own fatigue level. This approach will be affected by driver's individual differences. The objective detection methods are more reliable and accurate because they use special model or algorithm to analyze the driver's fatigue degree with the characteristic parameters related to driving. The driver only needs to focus on driving the vehicle. However, the current fatigue driving detection systems have not been widely used because they need special equipment to collect data, which need high cost. In addition, these current algorithms still have room for improvement in accuracy.

Although current methods have various drawbacks, they have great potential in reducing the incidence of traffic accidents. So in this paper, all kinds of popular objective fatigue driving detection technology are summarized and sorted out, which can lay a solid foundation for the future research of fatigue driving detection technology.

2 Method

Objective detection methods use various sensors or image acquisition equipment to collect physiological parameters, driver behavior parameters, vehicle parameters and other kinds of parameters. The collected parameters are used as input of the analysis model to evaluate the fatigue degree of driver. This kind of method is more objective and reliable than the subjective detection methods. Therefore, the objective fatigue detection methods have been

DOI: 10.1051/itmconf/20171201019

referred to as the research focus in the field of scientific research and engineering application. This paper focuses on objective detection methods. As shown in Figure 1, the objective detection method can be divided into three types: driver physiological parameters based detection method, driver facial features based detection method, and the vehicle driving parameters based detection method.

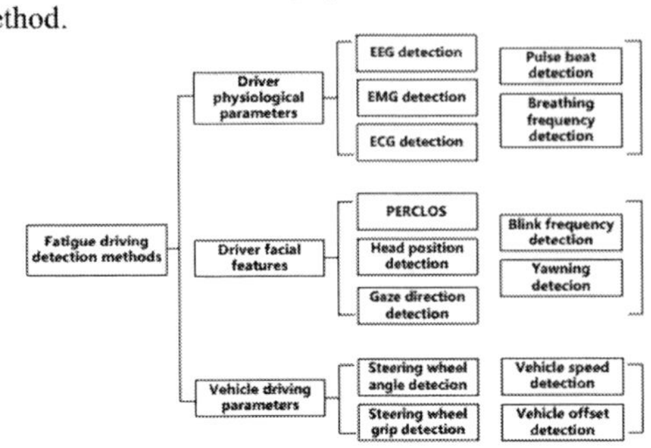

Figure 1. Fatigue detection methods.

2.1 Driver Physiological Parameters Based Detection Method

Related studies showed that [9], when a driver is in the state of fatigue, his physiological response will become slow, his body's response to stimulation appears to be delay, his physiological indicators will deviate from the normal state. Therefore, driver's physiological parameters collected by physiological sensors can be used to determine whether the driver is in the fatigue state. At present, there are many mature detection methods, such as the methods based on the detection of EEG (electroencephalogram), EMG(electromyography), ECG(electrocardiogram), pulse beat and respiratory frequency [10-12].

2.1.1 EEG Detection

Brain waves are fluctuations in the potential of synchronous changes in nerve cells in the brain. The change of EEG reflects the change of human brain. There are four kinds of wave in the human brain, delta wave, theta wave, alpha wave and beta wave. The delta wave and theta wave increase while the alpha wave and beta wave decrease when the driver changes from a state of consciousness to a state of fatigue [13]. Based on the relationship between the change of band signal and degree of driver fatigue, detection algorithm is able to use the real-time EEG signals to make accurate judgments on the degree of driver fatigue. EEG signals is the most important and reliable index for fatigue detection [13].

Mohammedabubasim developed an auxiliary driving system based on the EEG signals [14]. They first collected the real-time EEG signals by sensors. Then they processed the signals by Gobar filter and the linear SVM classifier and get the analysis result. At last they send alarm messages to drivers falling into fatigue state.

EEG signal detection has high reliability and sensitivity, strong anti-interference ability. But its cost is high because the structure of the instrument is complex and sophisticated. In addition, it may affect the driver's operation because the sensors directly contact with the driver.

2.1.2 EMG Detection

EMG is the superposition of action potential of motor unit in time and space. SEMG is a comprehensive effect of superficial muscle electrical signals and electrical activity on the skin surface, which can reflect the neuromuscular activity to some extent [15]. When the driver's fatigue degree deepens, the frequency of EMG signal will continue to decline, the amplitude gradually increased [16]. Therefore, the analysis of EMG signals can achieve the purpose of the driver's fatigue level. In general, the evoked potential method is used to measure the EMG signal, it uses an electrode fixed on the muscle surface of the driver to collect the signals.

HONG et al. [15] judged the driver's fatigue based on the driver's EMG signals. They used sensors to collect the EMG signal of the driver, processed the original signals with the FastICA algorithm and digital filter. The processed results were classified using the Mahalanobis distance and classification results were used to judge the degree of driver fatigue.

The detection method based on EMG signal is objective and true, but it has some invasion to the driver's skin, which is not conducive to the driver's safe driving.

2.1.3 ECG Detection

The ECG is produced by the weak current in the process of cardiac excitation. When the driver is tired, the ECG signal will show a significant regularity decline [17]. The heart rate (HR) index and heart rate variability (HRV) index are the important indexes to judge the degree of fatigue.

Sangeetha et al. [18] developed a vehicle mounted fatigue driving detection system. The system collected the driver's ECG signal and compared it with the stored fatigue driving ECG signal. The system sent driver an alarm message when the similarity between the two signals reached the threshold.

ECG detection method has the characteristics of easy to carry and easy to operate. However, its sensitivity is poor. And because of the individual differences of drivers, their heart rate change is different, which results in the high false positive rate of this method.

2.1.4 Pulse Beat Detection

Pulse beat can also reflect the degree of driver fatigue. When the driver is tired, the intensity and frequency of the pulse gradually decrease. Japanese Convenience Computer Company [19], collected real-time driver pulse signal parameters by sensors mounted on the steering wheel, and used algorithm model to analysis the signal parameters. The analysis result was used to judge the fatigue degree of the driver.

This method is simple and easy. However, the direct contact of the sensor to the driver will make the driver feel uncomfortable. Besides, due to the different pulse changes of different drivers, this method is not accurate enough. Therefore this method is best used as an adjunct to other methods.

2.1.5 Breathing Frequency Detection

Similar to the pulse signal, when the driver enters the fatigue driving state, the breathing frequency tends to be gentle. In this way, the driver needs to wear the respiratory frequency sensor, which will affect the driver's normal driving. Therefore, the method is also suitable for use as an auxiliary method for other methods.

2.2 Driver Facial Features Based Detection Method

When the driver is in a state of fatigue, the facial features of the driver will be different from that of the conscious state. Therefore, it is an effective method to detect fatigue driving in real time by continuously collecting and analysing the driver's facial features data [20]. The changes in the head and face features are more obvious and most easily detected, thus the research hotspot at present also gathered in this part. The major methods of detection include PERCLOS, head position detection, gaze direction detection, blink frequency detection and mouth state detection [21-23].

2.2.1 Perclos

Carnegie Mellon University Driving Research Center developed PERCLOS system [24] in 1998. This system was based on the theory that the reflection ability of retina to infrared light of different wavelengths is different in the same illumination. It located the retina according to the difference of image formed by different wavelength, analysed the size and position of the eyes, and finally determined the eyes closed according to the image of eye region.

The experiment shows that there is a close relationship between the length of the eyes closed and the degree of fatigue. The longer the eyes are closed, the more serious the degree of fatigue. The PERCLOS method is used to evaluate the driver's fatigue degree by comparing the percentage of eye closure time per unit time.

The PERCLOS method has the advantages of high accuracy, real-time and non-contact. It is the most widely used detection method in the market currently. However, this method is easy to be affected by light, occlusion, driver's glasses and other factors. It still has room for improvement in robustness.

2.2.2 Head Position Detection

In the course of driving, the position of the head is different when the driver is awake and tired. Therefore, it is feasible to determine whether the driver is in a state of fatigue by detecting the driver's head position. Reference [25] proposed a method to detect fatigue by the change of head acceleration. It collected the head acceleration parameters by setting the three axis acceleration sensor ADXL330 on the driver's seat behind his head, which was based on the Micro-Electro-Mechanical Systems (MEMS).

The advantages of this method are real-time and reliable. The disadvantages are high cost, low sensitivity and immunity. So it is not suitable as the main judging parameter, but as an auxiliary parameter.

2.2.3 Gaze Direction Detection

The sight line of awake driver will be in front of the vehicle and move fast. The sight line of fatigued driver will deviate from the normal direction and move slow. Inho Choi et al. [26] used the CDF analysis method to locate the driver's pupil position, and then to detect the gaze direction of the driver's sight line and the changing frequency of the sight line. These two indicators were used to estimate the driver's fatigue level.

The equipment of gaze direction detection is simple and cheap. But the reliability and sensitivity of this method is poor. It is suitable to be used in combination with other detection methods.

2.2.4 Blink Frequency Detection

Blink frequency refers to the number of blink times per unit time. When the driver is tired, the blink frequency will be higher than the normal value. Sigari et al. [27] used the computer vision technology to extract the driver's eye information and calculated the blink frequency. The calculated blink frequency was used to analyse the driver's fatigue.

Blink frequency detection method has the characteristics of real-time and high accuracy. Its robustness is poor because it is easy to be affected by occlusion, driver's glasses and other factors. With the development of computer vision technology, this problem can be overcome [28]. Therefore, blink frequency is an important fatigue evaluation index.

2.2.5 Yawning Detection

Yawning is one of the most important and obvious facial features of fatigue driving. Many researchers have detected the fatigue degree by extracting the characteristics of the driver's mouth [29-30]. Based on the image recognition technology, researchers extracted and analysed the mouth features of driver to judge whether the driver was yawning. They evaluated driver's fatigue degree based on the number of driver yawn per unit time and the mouth opening degree when driver yawns. This method is easy to go wrong when the driver is just talking rather than yawning. In order to solve this problem, the researchers [31] used hidden Markov model to analyse the driver's mouth characteristics, and successfully separated the two characteristics of talk and yawning. The method of yawning detection has the advantages of real-time and high accuracy, which is suitable to be used as an auxiliary method for fatigue detection.

2.3 Vehicle Driving Parameters Based Detection Method

With the deepening of fatigue, the driver's ability to perceive the surrounding environment, judge the situation and control the vehicle will decline. This change makes driver's control precision reduced, which can be reflected by the abnormal fluctuation of vehicle driving parameters. Compared to the acquisition of various parameters for the driver, the acquisition of vehicle driving parameters is simpler. Current vehicles are equipped with various types of sensors, which are used to collect the real-time parameters of vehicle speed, fuel consumption and engine speed [32]. It is possible to indirectly detect the driver's fatigue degree through the modeling of these data.

Therefore, the detection methods of fatigue driving based on the vehicle driving parameters also receive a lot of attention in research field. The popular methods include steering wheel angle detection method, steering wheel grip detection method, vehicle speed detection method, vehicle offset detection method, brake pedal force detection method and the accelerator pedal force detection method [33-35].

2.3.1 Steering Wheel Angle Detection

When the driver is tired, his ability to control the car will fall. The amplitude of the steering wheel will increase, and then the value of steering wheel angle does not change significantly in the next period of time, the operation of the steering frequency decreases. It is a common method to determine the fatigue driving by collecting and analysing the parameters of the steering wheel angle in time, amplitude and frequency from steering wheel sensors. The researchers used method of sample entropy to analyse steering wheel rotation characteristics [34]. They found the sample entropy under the normal state is greater than the sample entropy under fatigue state. So they developed the method to determine driver fatigue based on rotation angle of steering wheel detection.

The steering wheel angle detection method can easily collect the precise data from sensors without affecting the driver's normal driving. But its accuracy is not enough because the driver's driving habits, cars and driving environment are different.

2.3.2 Steering Wheel Grip Detection

When the driver is in the state of fatigue, the steering wheel grip will gradually decrease. Based on this characteristic, researchers proposed an algorithm to analyze the change rule of the driving steering wheel grip [35]. The data was collected by the force sensor installed on the steering wheel.

Just like the steering wheel angle detection method, the detection signal parameters are easy to obtain by the sensors embedded in the steering wheel. And this method has no effect on the driver. But the accuracy is still not enough.

2.3.3 Vehicle Speed Detection

The vehicle speed detection method mainly uses the CCD camera and the vehicle mounted sensor to detect the vehicle's speed, lateral acceleration, lateral displacement and other parameters. In reference [36], the parameters of vehicle driving were obtained by simulation driving. After being denoised, the processed parameters were used to train a classifier for distinguishing driver's awake state and fatigue state.

The vehicle speed detection method can easily collect the precise speed parameters of vehicle with low cost. However, the change of vehicle speed is difficult to accurately reflect the driver's fatigue degree. This method can only be used as an auxiliary parameter.

2.3.4 Vehicle Offset Detection

The vehicle offset detection method mainly monitors the vehicle's travel path by using the computer vision technology to identify the lane. It sends the driver alarm messages when the vehicle is found to deviate from the lane. AutoVue system [37] developed by American Iteris, detects the driver's track by the image data collected by a front facing CCD camera in the car. The system will alarm when it finds vehicle lane departure caused by fatigue driving.

The advantages of vehicle offset detection include high accuracy and non-contact detection. The problem is that it is easily affected by weather, road conditions and other factors. In addition, it is too late for fatigue driving detection when the vehicle is out of control.

2.4 Summary

These common fatigue detection methods have their own advantages and disadvantages. As shown in Table 1, the three kinds of fatigue detection methods are compared in terms of accuracy, sensitivity, contact, anti-jamming and cost. On the whole, the fatigue detection method based on driver facial features is a promising method.

Table 1. Method comparison

Detection parameter	accuracy	sensitivity	contact	Anti-jamming	cost
Driver physiological parameters	high	high	yes	strong	high
Driver facial features	high	common	no	Weak	common
Vehicle driving parameters	low	common	no	common	common

The advantage of the fatigue detection method based on driver physiological parameters is that it can objectively and accurately reflect the degree of driver fatigue. The disadvantages are that data acquisition equipments are complex and expensive; the equipment contact the driver's body directly, which affects the normal operation of the driver and the traffic safety. Therefore, the application of this method to the actual driver fatigue detection is limited.

The advantage of the fatigue detection method based on driver facial features is intuitive and obvious. It can more accurately determine the degree of driver fatigue. Besides, it realizes the feature extraction of non-contact, which does not affect the normal driving of the driver. The disadvantages are that the recognition algorithm is complex, the feature extraction is difficult, and the detection results are easily affected by the illumination and occlusion factors. But in recent years, image recognition, machine learning techniques have made great progress. Especially the deep learning technology has made remarkable achievements in the field of computer vision. Method based on convolutional neural network (CNN) can quickly and accurately extract useful features from the images for analysis. Therefore, the driver fatigue detection method based on driver facial features is the mainstream direction in the future development of this field.

Fatigue detection method based on vehicle driving parameters has the advantage of simple and real-time data acquisition. The disadvantages are that its analysis result is easily influenced by personal driving habits, the weather, traffic conditions and other external factors, the accuracy is not enough; moreover, the method can detect the abnormality only when the driver is about to have an accident, which is not safe for driver. Therefore, the analysis result of this method is better to be used as an auxiliary detection indicator rather than the main detection indicators.

3 Application of Fatigue Driving Detection Technology

After a long period of development, the fatigue driving detection technology has been gradually transferred from the field of research to the field of industrial applications. However, due to the low detection accuracy and high cost, fatigue detection products are far from universal but only appear in some high-end vehicles. The representative products are as follows.

Attention assist system equipped with Benz [38], which uses 71 sensors to collect parameters of vehicle steering wheel angle, acceleration, accelerator pedal, brake pedal and various external environmental parameters. These parameters are used to conduct a scientific analysis of the driver's driving behavior. The system alerts when the driver is in a state of fatigue.

The European Union has launched a comprehensive monitoring system for driving behavior called "AWAKE" project [39]. The system collects driving data with a variety of sensors of image, pressure and speed. The collected data include parameters like eye movement, gaze direction, steering wheel grip, and driving speed, which are used to analyse the driver and vehicle behavior. The driver's fatigue degree is divided into wakefulness, fatigue and deep fatigue. The system improves the driver's alertness by acoustic optic stimulation and seat belt dithering.

Volvo automobile is equipped with a driver safety warning system (DAC) [40]. The system uses a camera to collect driver's facial feature data and use sensors to collect the parameters of the vehicle movement. The comprehensive analysis result of these two kinds of data is used judge the fatigue state of driver. The system warns the driver who is in a state of fatigue by displaying the warning text on the dashboard and making a sound in the vehicle.

Most of the existing fatigue driving detection productions judge the fatigue state of driver based on multi characteristic parameters, which guarantees the accuracy of analysis result. At present, the production cost of this kind of detection equipment is high, which leads to the failure of wide application of the fatigue detection system. The market now needs low cost and high accuracy products. Fatigue detection method based on driver facial feature will be promising. It only needs special camera to collect the facial features of driver, the cost is low. With the development of deep learning, the ability of the machine to extract features from a picture will be enhanced and the accuracy of fatigue analysis by machine will be improved.

4 Future Works

The driver fatigue detection system needs to detect the driver's fatigue accurately and in real time without affecting the driver's normal driving and comfort. This section analyses the current problems and future development trend of fatigue driving detection technology. The future works will be focused on two aspects: detection technology research and engineering implementation.

4.1 Detection Technology Research

Fatigue detection technology research includes research fields of the data sources selection, data collection and data analysis. Problems existing in these fields can be summarized as follows.

4.1.1 Data Sources Selection

Current fatigue detection methods are based on one single kind of parameters like driver physiological parameters, driver facial features and vehicle driving parameters. The driving behavior of driver cannot be represented completely by a single kind of feature parameters, which only contain limited information. So the present methods need to be improved both in accuracy and robustness. Method based on multiple kinds of parameters is able to obtain more credible analysis result. Therefore, how to integrate multiple kinds of parameters for fatigue detection is a problem need to be solved.

From this point of view, the data fusion technology is helpful to detect fatigue driving, which integrates a variety of parameters of driver and vehicle to judge the fatigue driving. Any single detection method has its own disadvantages, so the accuracy of method which is based on one single parameter is not enough. With the development of information fusion technology, many researchers try to integrate the driver's physiological parameters, driver facial features and the running parameters of the vehicle to judge the fatigue state of the driver. Considering all kinds of factors, this method can effectively improve the accuracy of the results, and reduce the probability of false alarm.

From the present point of view, fatigue detection method based on driver facial features works best overall. By means of data fusion, a new method with higher accuracy and stronger robustness can be obtained by analysing the driver facial features and vehicle related parameters.

4.1.2 Data Collection

Driver's facial image data and Vehicle driving parameters are able to be collected by camera and vehicle sensor easily. Driver physiology parameters are hard to be collected because current sensors need to be in contact with the human body, which will affect the normal driving. This is the reason why the method based on driver physiological parameters has not been widely used, although the driver physiological parameters are the most reliable parameters to measure the fatigue degree.

There are two ways to improve the sensor, non-contact sensor and wearable sensor. Non-contact sensor can be deployed to the vehicle and collect various kinds of driver's physiological parameters. With these data, computer can analyse and obtain most reliable fatigue state of the driver. But the point is the manufacturing cost, and if the costs of sensors are too high, then this method will be meaningless. In recent years, wearable mobile device like Apple Watch and Mi Band have emerged. These kinds of devices are able to collect the wearer's physiological parameters without making him uncomfortable. Wearable sensor is a better choice for fatigue detection. Compared to the traditional sensor, wearable sensor will not affect the normal driving.

4.1.3 Data Analysis

Most fatigue detection methods are based on traditional machine learning algorithms for data analysis. Traditional machine learning algorithms require manually designed features. The abstraction degree of these kinds of features is low, so their representation power is weak. Therefore, the analysis results of current fatigue detection methods are easily affected by light, shadow, driving habits, weather environment and other factors. Getting a feature with high abstraction degree and strong representation power is the work to be done.

Combining the deep learning technology, the more robust feature extraction models are able to be trained. In recent years, the deep learning develops rapidly, which has achieved good results in research fields like image analysis, video analysis and NLP（Natural Language Processing）. It is able to learn and extract more abstract and robust features from the input, which has stronger representation power. Therefore, driving fatigue detection method based on deep learning is also a hot research field in the future.

4.2 Engineering Implementation

Engineering implementation refers to the method of applying technology to the industrial field. In the field of fatigue driving detection, the current approach is to deploy data acquisition devices, data analysis equipment, and alarm devices to the vehicle. The advantage is that the vehicle has become an independent system and it does not need to communicate with other systems. But the problem is that the data analysis requires on-board embedded system with high processing capacity because real-time performance is essential. This has led to a high cost of the entire fatigue driving detection system, which is the reason why the current fatigue detection system only appeared in high-end vehicles. Therefore, how to apply the fatigue detection technology to the vehicle at lower cost is also a problem to be considered.

"Internet of Vehicles" based on big data processing technology is a solution that can be considered [41-42]. In the system of "Internet of Vehicles", the vehicle is responsible for data acquisition, transmission and analysis results reception while the big data processing system is responsible for data processing and analysis [43-44]. In this way, the purpose of real time can be achieved under the premise of satisfying accuracy. This solution reduces the cost of on-board embedded system because the most onerous work is done by the "Cloud". It should be noted that this solution requires bandwidth and stability of mobile networks. But with the development of mobile networks, solutions based on "Internet of Vehicles" are the future trend.

5 Conclusions

The increase in the number of cars will lead to an increase in the number of traffic accidents. Fatigue driving is one of the most important factors in traffic accidents. Therefore, it is of great significance to study the fatigue detection methods with high accuracy, real-time and strong anti-interference. One single kind of parameters is not accurate enough to determine the fatigue state of driver. Fatigue detection methods based on data fusion technology judge the fatigue driving by the fusion data of parameters related to vehicle and driver. This is an important research direction; In addition, fatigue detection methods analysing fatigue state by deep learning are able to get more robust detection result. This is a hot research field; finally, the "Internet of Vehicles" is the development trend of intelligent transportation. It is a good solution to combine "Internet of Vehicles" and driver fatigue detection. The strong data transmission and analytical capabilities will make a great contribution to the accuracy and real-time performance of fatigue driving detection.

References

1. B. Leard, K. Roth, others, Resources For the Future Discussion Paper, 15–19 (2015)
2. M. Bhagyaiah, B. Shrinagesh, IOP:EES. **20**, 12026 (2014)
3. R. Kakkar, P. Aggarwal, M. Kakkar, K. Deshpande, D. Gupta, (2014)
4. N. B. of S. of China, China Statistical Yearbook (http://www.stats.gov.cn/english/)
5. Q. I. Ji-Yan, AMST (2011)
6. Q. Wang, J. Yang, M. Ren, Y. Zheng, *Intelligent Control and Automation, 2006. WCICA 2006. The Sixth World Congress on (IEEE, 2006)*, **2**, 8587–8591 (2006)
7. Y. Dong, Z. Hu, K. Uchimura, N. Murayama, IEEE Trans. Intell. Transp. Syst. **12**, 596–614 (2011)
8. M.-H. Sigari, M.-R. Pourshahabi, M. Soryani, M. Fathy, (2014)
9. K. Sun et al., *Multimedia, Communication and Computing Application: Proceedings of the 2014 International Conference on Multimedia, Communication and Computing Application (MCCA 2014), Xiamen, China, October 16-17, 2014 (CRC Press, 2015)*, 269 (2015)
10. F. Wang, H. Wang, X. Luo, J NORTHEAST UNIV. **35**, 175–178 (2014)
11. Z. Yangyan, AMM (2015)
12. R. Fu, H. Wang, Int. J. Neural Syst. **24**, 1450006 (2014)
13. S. Kar, M. Bhagat, A. Routray, Transp. Res. Pt. F-Traffic Psychol. **13**, 297–306 (2010)
14. N. Mohammedabubasim, P. Sathyabalan, P. Suresh, Int. J. Comput. Appl. **115**, 9–14 (2015)
15. R. Fu, H. Wang, W. Zhao, Expert Syst. Appl. **63**, 397–411 (2016)
16. V. Balasubramanian, K. Adalarasu, JBMT. **11**, 151–158 (2007)
17. Q. Wu, Y. Zhao, X. Bi, **2**, 544–547 (2012)
18. M. Sangeetha. Driver Fatigue Management System using Embedded ECG Sensor
19. S. Jung, H. Shin, W. Chung, IET Intell. Transp. Syst. **8**, 43–50 (2014)
20. M. F. Khan, F. Aadil, IJITM. **3**, 480 (2012)
21. Y. LI, C. ZHANG, L. MENG, JTIS. **5**, 21 (2014)
22. X.-Y. Gao, Y.-F. Zhang, W.-L. Zheng, B.-L. Lu, *Neural Engineering (NER), 2015 7th International IEEE/EMBS Conference on (IEEE, 2015)*, 767–770 (2015)
23. L. F. Ibrahim et al., Multimed. Tools Appl. **71**, 1857–1877 (2014)
24. R. Grace et al., A drowsy driver detection system for heavy vehicles, 2 (1998)
25. Z. Wang, C. H. Sun, Y. Cao, L. H. Wang, DIMEP (2010)
26. I.-H. Choi, Y.-G. Kim, *Big Data and Smart Computing (BIGCOMP), 2014 International Conference on (IEEE, 2014)*, 241–244 (2014)
27. M. Sigari, M. Fathy, M. Soryani, IJVT. 2013, 1–11 (2013)
28. Y. Li, F. You, K. Chen, L. Huang, J. Xu, **39**, 1–12 (2016)
29. S. Abtahi, B. Hariri, S. Shirmohammadi, IEEE Trans. Instrum. Meas, 1–4 (2011)
30. R. Putta, G. Shinde, P. Lohani, Int. J. Comput. Appl. **95**, 28–34 (2014)
31. H. Li, *Intelligent Multimedia, Video and Speech Processing, 2001. Proceedings of 2001 International Symposium on (IEEE, 2001)*, 490–493 (2001)
32. D. Nandhini, G. Nandhini, M. Nandhini, R. Vidhya, IJARCET. **3** (2014)
33. W. Hailin, L. Hanhui, S. Zhumei, *Optoelectronics and Image Processing (ICOIP), 2010 International Conference on (IEEE, 2010)*, **1**, 549–552 (2010)
34. Z. L. Li, X. Jin, B. J. Wang, X. H. Zhao, AMM, 2001–2005 (2015)
35. K. LEE, S.-A. HYUN, S. OAH, IJOC. 12 (2016)
36. M. Mao, L. Du, *Vehicular Electronics and Safety, 2007. ICVES. IEEE International Conference on (IEEE, 2007)*, 1–4 (2007)
37. M. I. Chaconmurguia, C. Prietoresendiz, IEEE CEM. **4**, 107–119 (2015)
38. M. H. Abdullah et al., ICISA, 269–278 (2016)
39. T. Brandt, R. Stemmer, A. Rakotonirainy, **7**, 6451–6456 (2004)
40. L. Jakobsson, A. Axelson, M. Bjrklund, P. Nilsson, T. Victor, *24th International Technical Conference on the Enhanced Safety of Vehicles (ESV)* (2015)
41. Z. Sitavancova, M. Hajek, Thematic Research Summary: Intelligent Transport Systems, (2010)
42. S. Ma, JNW. **7**, 305–310 (2012)
43. M. Gerla, E. Lee, G. Pau, U. Lee, 241–246 (2014)
44. C. Jiacheng et al., JCMIMNW. **1**, 14–26 (2016)

DOI: 10.1051/itmconf/20171201020

Double HEVC Compression Detection with Different Bitrates Based on Co-occurrence Matrix of PU Types and DCT Coefficients

Zhao-Hong Li[1], Rui-shi Jia[1], Zhen-Zhen Zhang[1,a], Xiao-Yun Liang[1], Jin-Wei Wang[2]

[1]School of Electronic and Information Engineering, Beijing Jiaotong University, Beijing, 100044
[2]College of Computer and Software, Nanjing University of Information Science and Technology, Nanjing, 210044, China

Abstract. Detection of double video compression is of particular importance in video forensics, as it reveals partly the video processing history. In this paper, a double compression method is proposed for HEVC–the latest video coding standard. Firstly, four 5×5 co-occurrence matrixes were derived from DCT coefficients along four directions respectively, i.e., horizontal, vertical, main diagonal and minor diagonal. Then four 4×4 co-occurrence matrixes were derived from PU types which are innovative features of HEVC and rarely been utilized by researchers. Finally, these two feature set are combined and sent to support vector machine (SVM) to detect re-compressed videos. In order to reduce the feature dimension, only the co-occurrence matrixes of DCT coefficients and PU types in horizontal direction are adopted to identify whether the video has undergone double compression. Experimental results show the effectiveness and the robustness against frame deletion of the proposed scheme.

1 Introduction

Nowadays due to the rapid development of network and the popularity of multimedia technology, digital videos have been widely used in many fields. Meanwhile, with the wide spreading of powerful and easy-to-use video editing software, digital videos are exposed to vigorous possible forgery kinds which destroyed the authenticity and integrity of videos. Therefore, video forensics technology is becoming a hot topic in information security field. Generally, due to the large amount of video data and strong correlation between them, digital videos are stored and transmitted in the form of compression. However, the video tampering process has to be operated on uncompressed domain. Namely, tampering with video often involves decoding the video streams into image sequences and then recoding the tampered video into compressed ones. Thus, double compression is necessary for video tampering process, and it plays an important role in revealing the tampering possibility.

The study of video recompression forensics began in 2006. As an important detection means of video forensics, there are various kinds of methods effective for double compression detection. Chen et al. [1] distinguished double compression by judging whether the probability distribution of the first digits of the non-zero MPEG quantized AC coefficients would be disturbed. In Ref [2] Liao introduced that the probability distribution of quantized nonzero AC coefficients would be obviously disturbed only when the QP used in the second compression is smaller than that in the first compression. Ref [3] introduced the sequence of average residual of P-frames (SARP) and used its time- and frequency-domain features to classify the tampered videos and original videos. Sun and Xu in [4-5] detected double compression for MPEG videos by studying the distribution of quantized DCT coefficients. In Ref [6], a method based on the statistical feature of macroblock mode (MBM) which consists of macroblock type and motion vector in P-frames was proposed to detect double MPEG compression. Wang et al. [7] proposed a detection method based on the indication that in doubly MPEG compressed videos, the distribution of the doubly quantized DCT coefficients contains empty bins when the second quantization step is smaller than the first one. Ref [8] detected doubly-compressed MPEG video sequence by the presence of specific static and temporal statistics. In Ref [9], 162-D Markov statistical characteristic based DCT coefficient were adopted to distinguish double MPEG-4 compression artefacts.

The detection algorithms of double compression above are all based on the video coding standards which precede the latest high efficient video coding (HEVC). For instance, Ref [1, 4-9] studied the double compression for MPEG videos and ref [2-3] aims at H.264 videos. As the latest generation of coding standards, HEVC provides lower video data rate. Compared with H.264/AVC, it improves compression efficiency of high-resolution and high-fidelity videos. There is no doubt that it will play an important role in the applications of high definition and ultra-high-definition videos. Therefore, double HEVC compression detection is of significance. But only a few of works have been done on this issue. Huang et al.[10] proposed a method by constructing co-occurrence matrix of DCT coefficients to detect double compression. In ref [11], before and after tampering, the PU type of I-frame will change. In one of our previous works, we use this phenomenon as a breakthrough, and make the best of the standard deviation of 4×4 PU blocks difference (SDoPU) to capture this change. This statistical features based on the same QP indicates the occurrence of double compression. Both [10] and [11] discussed detection of double compression for HEVC videos based on the quantization parameter. There are few studies detecting double HEVC compression with different bit rates. Motivated by this phenomenon, a new method based on Co-occurrence Matrix of PU types and DCT coefficients was presented in this paper to detect double HEVC compression with different bitrates. The experimental results show that the proposed method has high classification accuracy and strong robustness against frame-deletion attack.

The rest of this paper is organized as follows. Section 2 gives an interpretation of the error analysis for double HEVC compression, and then introduces the PU types and quantized DCT coefficient. In section 3 gives an introduction of Co-occurrence matrix and detailed procedures of deriving Co-occurrence Matrix from PU types and DCT coefficients. In section 4, we present experimental results and discussion, followed by conclusions and future work in section 5.

2 The Analysis of DCT Coefficients and PU Types

2.1 Error Analysis of I Frame for Double HEVC Compression

HEVC video compression is widely used in the field of multimedia, it achieves better image quality while ensuring high compression rate. The traditional prediction, transformation, quantization, entropy coding and other links is still used for HEVC. But it also uses a more flexible coding block partition structure [12]. The main generation procedure of singly-compressed video and re-compressed video is shown in Fig.1. Letting V_{ori} represents the uncompressed YUV video and R_2 represents the target bit rate.

Fig.1 (a) shows the construction of singly-compressed video. After the coding process of Fig.1 (a), a singly-compressed video is obtained, $\boldsymbol{S}_{\text{R}_2}$ represents the bit stream corresponding to the singly-compressed video. Then decoding will be done and the re-construction video V_{R_2} of V_{ori} is achieved. During the decoding process, the PU partition type $\boldsymbol{P}_{\text{R}_2}$ in each CTU of the I frame and the quantized DCT coefficients $\boldsymbol{D}_{\text{R}_2}$ of the I frame can be extracted. Fig.1 (b) describes the construction of the re-compressed video. Firstly, the bit stream $\boldsymbol{S}_{\text{R}_1}$ is obtained with the bitrate of R_1 according to the coding process of Fig.1 (a), and the rebuilt video V_{R_1} is achieved by decoding $\boldsymbol{S}_{\text{R}_1}$. Then, recompressing V_{R_1} with the bitrate R_2 and the re-compressed video can be achieved, $\boldsymbol{C}_{\text{R}_2}$ represents its bit stream. And then decoding $\boldsymbol{C}_{\text{R}_2}$ we can get the reconstructed video V'_{R_2}. During the recompressing process, the PU partition type $\boldsymbol{P}'_{\text{R}_2}$ and the quantized DCT $\boldsymbol{D}'_{\text{R}_2}$ coefficients can be extracted.

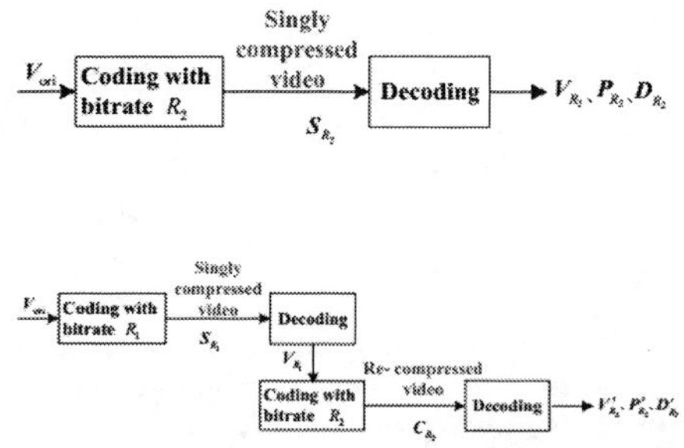

(a)

(b)

Figure 1. The generation procedure of singly-compressed video and re-compressed video (a) Singly-compressed video (b) Re-compressed video

During the above-mentioned process, discrete cosine transform (DCT) coefficients are achieved, then those DCT coefficients are quantized according to the given QP value, and this process will produce a Quantization error. Besides, when the video is reconstructed, it will result in rounding errors and truncation errors. In summary, there is irreversible quantization error and reconstruction error in the coding process of HEVC videos, which makes $V_{\text{R}_1} \neq V_{\text{ori}}$. Besides, the rate control algorithm regulates the QP and PU division types, so that the value of QP used for re-compressed video will be different from the singly-compressed video, which further affects the quantized DCT coefficients, resulting in the change of quantized DCT coefficients and PU divisions for singly-compressed video and re-compressed video, then we will give a detailed analysis and discussion of DCT coefficients and PU types as follows.

2.2 The Interpretation of DCT Coefficients

DCT is the main transform way from space domain to frequency domain for HEVC. Eq.(1) illustrate how the residual pixels of a specific N×N TU are transformed into corresponding DCT coefficients in the frequency domain, where $c(k)=c(l)=\begin{cases}1/\sqrt{N}, & k,l=0\\ \sqrt{2/N}, & k,l\neq 0\end{cases}$, $\boldsymbol{E}_{(n,m)}$ indicates the i th row and j th column residual pixel in N×N TU, denotes the n th DCT coefficient in the m th row of transform matrix.

$$Y_{(n,m)}(k,l)=c(k)c(l)\sum_{i=0}^{N-1}\sum_{j=0}^{N-1}\boldsymbol{E}_{(n,m)}(i,j)\cos\frac{(2i+1)k\pi}{2N}\cos\frac{(2j+1)l\pi}{2N} \quad (1)$$
$$k,l=0,1,\cdots$$

DOI: 10.1051/itmconf/20171201020

The traditional scalar quantization is used to all of DCT coefficients, and quantized DCT coefficients are calculated by Eq. (2),

$$Q_{(n,m)}(i,j)=floor(\frac{Y_{(n,m)}(i,j)}{Q_{step}}+f) \quad (2)$$

where $Y_{(n,m)}$ represents DCT coefficient, $Q_{(n,m)}$ marks the quantized DCT coefficient; f is the variable of round offset; $floor(\cdot)$ defines a down integer function; Q_{step} is the quantization step, which is related to quantization parameter (QP). The value of Q_{step} is doubled if QP is increased by 6. For HEVC video compression coding, there are 52 quantization parameters which range from 0 to 51.

After the transformation and quantization, most of DCT coefficients are fallen into a small interval and obey the Laplace distribution with the mean of 0 [13]. Further, according to our statistical analysis for HEVC videos, the histogram can reflect the overall distribution of the quantized DCT coefficients, and Fig.2 shows that the probability of DCT coefficients in a fixed interval [-4, 4] is about 99%.

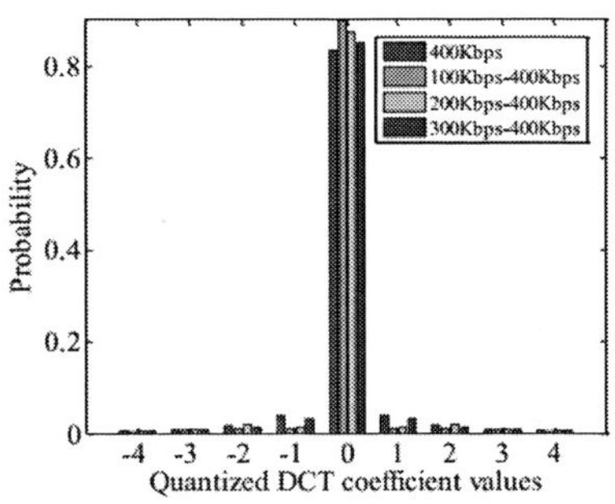

Figure 2. Histogram of quantized DCT coefficients

Fig.2 shows that the purple bar represents the probability distribution of DCT coefficients for the singly-compressed video with the bitrate of 400Kbps, the blue, orange and green columns denotes the probability for the re-compressed video with the bitrate of 100Kbps-400Kbps, 200Kbps-400Kbps and 300Kbps-400Kbps. As can be seen from Fig.2, the probability values of quantized DCT coefficients of singly-compressed videos is lower than that of re-compressed videos and the distribution of it has a big difference, which indicates that we can use the probability distributions of DCT coefficients to detect re-compressed video. The gray level co-occurrence matrix is defined by the joint probability density of the pixels pairs with different direction and interval. It often used as a common way to describe the texture by studying the spatial correlation of gray, which can reveal the distribution characteristics of the entire data and also illustrate the dependence very well. So we will extract the co-occurrence of DCT coefficients as the classification feature to distinguish the re-compressed videos from singly-compressed videos.

2.3 The Analysis of PU Types

As the latest generation of video coding standard, HEVC still adopts the traditional hybrid coding framework. However, it gives up the concept of macro-block utilized in H.264/AVC but introduces three basic units, i.e., coding unit (CU), prediction unit (PU) and transform unit (TU), which makes it more flexible compared with the previous video compression coding standard. CU is a root unit for HEVC compression, its size sets to 8×8, 16×16, 32×32 and 64×64. Assuming that the size of the coding unit CU is $2N\times2N$, $N\in\{4\ 8\ 16\ 32\}$, the CU can be subdivided into one or multiple prediction unit PU depending on the prediction mode. HEVC provides eight kinds of PU division structure as shown in Fig.3.

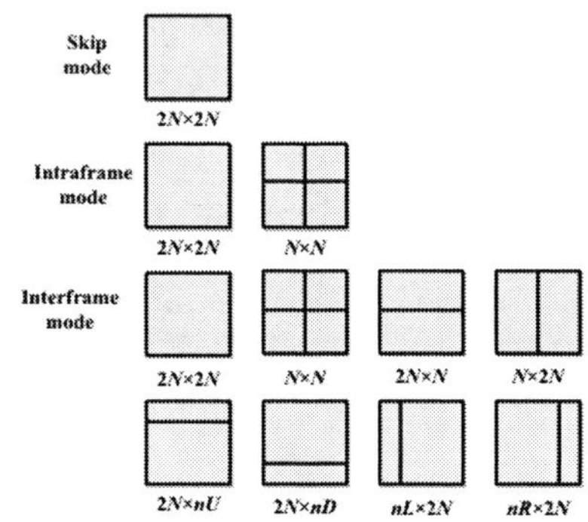

Figure 3. PU types under different prediction modes.

PU blocks carry abundant prediction information which indicates how CU is predicted. Fig. 4 shows the PU partition types of the first I frame in the singly-compressed video and the re-compressed video. Singly-compressed video (Fig.4 (a)) is obtained by compressing YUV video akiyo directly with the bitrate of 200Kbps. Re-compressed video (Fig.4 (b)) is obtained by compressing akiyo with the bitrate of 100Kbps and then with the bitrate of 200Kbps. Among them, the boundary of the thick solid lines show the maximum size (64×64) of CU, and so on, the dotted line denotes the smallest size (4×4) for PU blocks. It is indicated that for the same I frame, PU types delicately vary before and after re-compressed. Tab. 1 shows the number of each PU type for Fig. 4(a) and Fig. 4(b).

It is observed that the number of 4×4 PU blocks for the first I-frame of singly-compressed and re-compressed video is 680 and 568, and the number of 8×8 PU type and 16×16 PU type has varied. Besides that, the PU partition type and its neighbour relationship have also changed, for example, there are one 16×16 PU block for singly-compressed video in the lower left corner while four 8×8 PU blocks for re-compressed video, in the upper right corner it is different too, and so on. So we can extract the co-occurrence of PU types as another classification feature to reveal the changes of video statistical data.

(a)

(b)

Figure 4. The PU types of the first I frame of singly-compressed video and doubly-compressed video (a)The PU types of singly-compressed video (b)The PU types of re-compressed video

Table 1. Number of each PU type for Fig. 4(a) and Fig. 4(b)

PU type	PU number	
	Fig.4 (a)	Fig.4 (b)
4×4	680	568
8×8	166	182
16×16	15	18

3 The Proposed Scheme of Double HEVC Compression Detection

3.1 The Introduction of Co-Occurrence Matrix

The gray level co-occurrence matrix is the joint probability of pixel pairs with different direction and interval. Owing to the strong relevance between neighbouring image data (such as pixels or coefficients), co-occurrence matrix is widely used in image classification and image recognition. Suppose the size of coefficients matrix $\boldsymbol{C}$ of an image is $M \times N$, the co-occurrence matrix of which can be defined as follows:

$$\boldsymbol{P}_h(a,b) = \frac{\sum_{x=1}^{M}\sum_{y=1}^{N-d}\delta(\boldsymbol{C}(x,y)=a, \boldsymbol{C}(x,y+d)=b)}{M\times(N-d)} \quad (3)$$

$$\boldsymbol{P}_v(a,b) = \frac{\sum_{x=1}^{M-d}\sum_{y=1}^{N}\delta(\boldsymbol{C}(x,y)=a, \boldsymbol{C}(x+d,y)=b)}{(M-d)\times N} \quad (4)$$

$$\boldsymbol{P}_d(a,b) = \frac{\sum_{x=1}^{M-d}\sum_{y=1}^{N-d}\delta(\boldsymbol{C}(x,y)=a, \boldsymbol{C}(x+d,y+d)=b)}{(M-d)\times (N-d)} \quad (5)$$

$$\boldsymbol{P}_m(a,b) = \frac{\sum_{x=d+1}^{M}\sum_{y=1}^{N-d}\delta(\boldsymbol{C}(x,y)=a, \boldsymbol{C}(x-d,y+d)=b)}{(M-d)\times (N-d)} \quad (6)$$

where $\delta(X=a, Y=b)=\begin{cases}1, X=a, Y=b\\ 0, else\end{cases}$; the parameter d denotes the distance of the selected adjacent element pairs, and is given by 1 in this paper; $\boldsymbol{P}_h$, $\boldsymbol{P}_v$, $\boldsymbol{P}_d$, $\boldsymbol{P}_m$ represent the co-occurrence matrix in horizontal, vertical, major diagonal and minor diagonal direction respectively; $\boldsymbol{P}_h(a,b)$, $\boldsymbol{P}_v(a,b)$, $\boldsymbol{P}_d(a,b)$, $\boldsymbol{P}_m(a,b)$ are corresponding to the probability of adjacent coefficient pairs with values (a,b).

3.2 Co-Occurrence Matrix of DCT Coefficients and PU Types

As described in Section 2, it is investigated that DCT coefficients and PU types have been changed after re-compressing HEVC videos with different bitrates. The neighboring DCT coefficients and PU types have a certain correlation more or less, but it will vary with compression times. The co-occurrence matrix can well capture this change. Therefore, we first combine the co-occurrence matrix of DCT coefficients (CMoDCTCs) and the co-occurrence matrix of PU Types (CMoPUTs) to form a joint feature, and then send the joint feature into SVM for video classification. The extraction of the joint feature is divided into two parts, namely, the extraction of CMoDCTCs and the extraction of CMoPUTs.

3.2.1 The Extraction of CMoDCTCs

We first extract the quantized DCT coefficients in CTUs for given video during the decoding process, then set a threshold T=4 to truncate it and take the absolute value of it. Then all DCT coefficients of CTUs are arranged one after the other in a two-dimensional matrix $\boldsymbol{C}$ defined as Eq.(7), where $\boldsymbol{C}_i$ represents DCT coefficients of the i th CTU; q is the number of CTUs in one video with N frames; $\lceil X \rceil$ is a ceiling function. The value of q changes with the resolution of the given video. For example, $q = N\times\left\lceil\frac{176}{64}\right\rceil\times\left\lceil\frac{144}{64}\right\rceil = N\times 3\times 3 = 9N$, if the resolution is 176×144.

 DOI: 10.1051/itmconf/20171201020

$$C=\begin{pmatrix} C_1 \\ C_2 \\ \cdots \\ C_i \\ \cdots \\ C_q \end{pmatrix}, C_i=\begin{bmatrix} DCT_{i,1,1} & DCT_{i,1,2} & \cdots & DCT_{i,1,64} \\ DCT_{i,2,1} & DCT_{i,2,2} & \cdots & DCT_{i,2,64} \\ \cdots & \cdots & \cdots & \cdots \\ DCT_{i,64,1} & DCT_{i,64,2} & \cdots & DCT_{i,64,64} \end{bmatrix} \quad (7)$$

Once the DCT coefficients matrix C is got, we can calculate the 5×5 probability co-occurrence matrix of it in horizon, vertical, major diagonal and minor diagonal according to Eq. (3) to Eq. (6) in Section 3.1, and then four corresponding 25-dimensional features are achieved in four directions. Finally, the 25-dimensional co-occurrence matrices of the four directions are combined to form a 100-dimensional quantized DCT coefficient co-occurrence matrix CMoDCTCs.

3.2.2 The Extraction of CMoPUTs

We first extract the declared bit rate R of the given video during the decoding process and use the open source HEVC stream analysis software GitlHEVC Analyzer [14] to get PU partition of each I frame. Then let 8×8 image block to be one basic unit to mark PU types and calculate its frequency matrix in horizon, vertical, major diagonal and minor diagonal. Fig.5 (a) shows an example of how to mark PU types in one image. We mark 4×4 PU type, 8×8 PU type, 16×16 PU type, 32×32 PU type as 0, 1, 2, 3 separately.

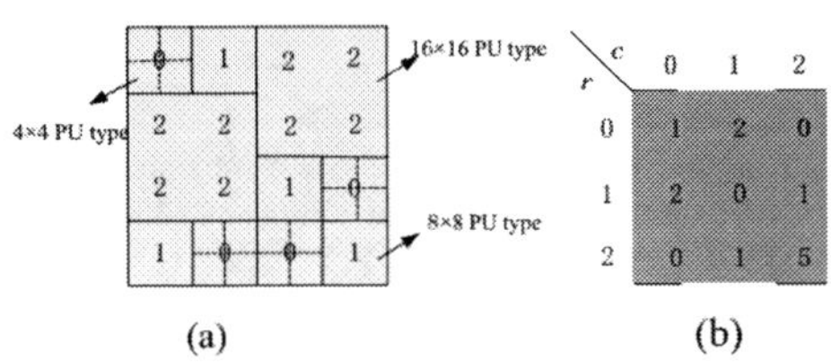

Figure 5. An example for calculating frequency matrix of PU-type pair (a) The Mark of PU types in one image. (b) Horizontal frequency matrix of PU-type pair

Fig.5 (b) shows the horizontal frequency matrix of Fig.5 (a), where r, c denote the PU types of the PU-type pair; the number in each cell means the times of the PU-type pair occurs with the interval d=1 in horizontal direction. Once the frequency matrix is achieved, we can calculate the 4×4 probability co-occurrence matrix of it in horizon, vertical, major diagonal and minor diagonal according to Eq. (3) to Eq. (6) in Section 3.1. Thus, four 16-dimensional features can be built correspondingly. Finally, the 16-dimensional co-occurrence matrices of the four directions are combined to form a 64-dimensional PU Types co-occurrence matrix CMoPUTs.

4 Experiments and Discussion

4.1 Video Database

In our experiments, 17 widely known YUV sequences [15] were selected as source sequences, these videos are QCIF format (with the resolution of 176×144) and have various kinds of content, such as people, scene, news, etc. In order to increase sample quantity, each video was split into non-overlapped clips with length of 100 frames. Finally, 36 QCIF video clips were generated in total.

HM10.0 [16] with encoder_lowdelay_P_main configuration file was adopted to conduct HEVC encoding and decoding process, we set the frame rate to 30 f/s and the GOP structure as IPPP. For QCIF video clips, the values of compressed bitrates B_1 and B_2 are selected from {100, 200, 300} (kbps) and {200, 300, 400} (kbps), respectively. For the sake of the video sample library consists of singly-compressed and re-compressed videos. All of 36 video clips (original standard YUV sequences) are first compressed with the bitrates of B_1. Then each compressed HEVC video streams is decoded and recoded with different bitrates B_2. Thus, 36 groups of datasets are generated in total.

4.2 Experimental Results and Discussion

For each combination of (B_1, B_2), LIBSVM [17] with PolySVC kernel was selected as classifier to distinguish original videos with bitrate B_2 from re-compressed ones with B_1 followed by B_2. 30 originals videos and 30 re-compressed ones were randomly chosen for training a classification model, and the rest were used for testing. AR was adopted as the evaluation metric of the proposed method and was calculated as follows:

$$AR=(TPR+TNR)/2 \quad (8)$$

Where $TPR=TP/(TP+FN)\times100\%$ and $TNR=TN/(TN+FP)\times100\%$. TP and TN represent true positive rate (the rate that re-compressed videos were labelled as re-compressed) and true negative rate (the rate that singly-compressed videos were labelled as singly-compressed), respectively; FP and FN represent false positive rate (the rate that singly-compressed videos were labelled as re-compressed) and false negative rate (the rate that re-compressed videos were labelled as singly-compressed), respectively. Due to the contingency, the entire experimental procedure is repeated for 20 times by randomly choosing training samples for each combination (B_1, B_2), and the average of AR is treated as the final detection accuracy.

In this paper, we first combine CMoDCTCs and CMoPUTs as effective 164-dimensional features to detect HEVC double compression. Table 2 gives the detection results. It can be observed that classification rates of distinguishing the re-compressed videos from singly-compressed ones are all 1, which demonstrate that the proposed method works well for detecting re-compressed videos.

In order to reduce the joint feature dimension and the computational complexity, we combine PhoDCT and PhoPUTs to form 41-dimensional features to detect HEVC double compression. Table 3 gives the detection results of distinguishing re-compressed videos from original ones. We can see that the classification rates are above 0.9 in all cases. Among them, four video groups' detection rate reached 1, and the lowest *AR* has reached 0.9667. A conclusion is summarized that our method can also achieve good classification ability after reducing the joint feature dimension.

Table 2. AR of distinguishing re-compressed videos from original ones based on mixed feature (164-D)

$B_1 \setminus B_2$	200k	300k	400k
100k	1	1	1
200k	--	1	1
300k	--	--	1

Table 3. AR of distinguishing re-compressed videos from original ones based on mixed feature (41-D)

$B_1 \setminus B_2$	200k	300k	400k
100k	1	1	1
200k	--	0.9875	1
300k	--	--	0.9667

Frame-deletion is another common forgery type for digital videos. Hence, the robustness of the proposed method against it is tested in this section. 10-frames-deleted videos, 30-frames-deleted videos and 50-frames-deleted videos are constructed, and the classification rate between each of them and original videos are displayed in Table 4 - Table 6. We can see that the classification rates are all above 0.8 except two detection rate which are expressed in bold in Table 5 and Table 6. Furthermore, there are four video groups' classification rate are above 0.9 in each table of Tabl4 4 – Table 6. The results demonstrate that the combined feature set of the proposed method is robust against frame deletion.

Table 4. AR of distinguishing re-compressed videos undergone 10 frames deletion from original ones based on mixed feature (41-D)

$B_1 \setminus B_2$	200k	300k	400k
100k	0.9708	1	1
200k	--	0.8709	0.95
300k	--	--	0.8084

Table 5. AR of distinguishing re-compressed videos undergone 30 frames deletion from original ones based on mixed feature (41-D)

$B_1 \setminus B_2$	200k	300k	400k
100k	0.9709	0.975	0.9834
200k	--	0.8917	0.9333
300k	--	--	**0.7709**

Table 6. AR of distinguishing re-compressed videos undergone 50 frames deletion from original ones based on mixed feature (41-D)

$B_1 \setminus B_2$	200k	300k	400k
100k	0.9775	1	0.975
200k	--	0.8459	0.9667
300k	--	--	0.7667

5 Conclusions

With the development of the advanced video editor, the authenticity and integrity of the videos can't be guaranteed anymore. In this paper, an effective method to detect double HEVC compression based on different bitrates is proposed. We extract the DCT coefficient and PU types of the original videos and the re-compressed ones, and then model co-occurrence matrixes based on DCT coefficient and PU types to reveal the artefacts. Experimental results show that the proposed algorithm performs well when the first compressed bitrates B1 is lower than the second compressed bitrates B2 for HEVC compression coding. Our future work will focus on how to detect double compression videos with the same compressed bitrates and the first compressed bitrates higher than the second ones.

Acknowledgement

This work was supported in part by the Fundamental Research Funds for the ROCS, SEM (W15C300020), in part by A Project Funded by the Priority Academic Program Development of Jiangsu Higher Education Institutions (PAPD), and in part by Jiangsu Collaborative Innovation Center on Atmospheric Environment and Equipment Technology (CICAEET).

References

1. Chen W, Shi Y Q. Detection of Double MPEG Compression Based on First Digit Statistics[C]// Digital Watermarking, International Workshop, IWDW 2008, Busan, Korea, November 10-12, 2008. Selected Papers. 2009:16-30.
2. Liao D, Yang R, Liu H. Double H.264/AVC compression detection using quantized non-zero AC coefficients[J]. Proceedings of SPIE - The International Society for Optical Engineering, 2011, 7880(2):78800Q-78800Q-10.
3. Liu H, Li S, Bian S. Detecting Frame Deletion in H.264 Video[M]// Information Security Practice and Experience. 2014:262-270.
4. Sun T, Wang W, Jiang X. Exposing video forgeries by detecting MPEG double compres-sion[C]// IEEE International Conference on Acoustics, Speech and Signal Processing. IEEE, 2012:1389-1392.
5. JUNYU XU, YUTING SU, QINGZHONG LIU. DETECTION OF DOUBLE MPEG-2

DOI: 10.1051/itmconf/20171201020

COMPRESSION BASED ON DISTRIBUTIONS OF DCT COEFFICIENTS[J]. Interna-tional Journal of Pattern Recognition & Artificial Intelligence, 2013, 27(1):1354001.

6. Chen J, Jiang X, Sun T, et al. Detecting double MPEG compression with the same quantiser scale based on MBM feature[C]// IEEE International Conference on Acoustics, Speech and Signal Processing. IEEE, 2016:2064-2068.
7. Wang, W., Farid, H.: 'Exposing Digital Forgeries in Video by Detecting Double Quantization', Proc of the 11th ACM workshop on Multimedia and security (MM&Sec), ACM, New York, USA, 2009, pp. 39-48
8. Wang W, Farid H. Exposing digital forgeries in video by detecting double MPEG compression[J]. Proceedings of the Multimedia and Security Workshop. Geneva, Switzerland: ACM, 2006: 37-47.
9. Jiang X, Wang W, Sun T, et al. Detection of Double Compression in MPEG-4 Videos Based on Markov Statistics[J]. IEEE Signal Processing Letters, 2013, 20(5):447-450.
10. Huang M, Wang R, Xu J, et al. Detection of Double Compression for HEVC Videos Based on the Co-occurrence Matrix of DCT Coefficients[M]// Digital-Forensics and Watermarking. Springer International Publishing, 2015.
11. Jia R S, Li Z H, Zhang Z Z, et al. Double HEVC Compression Detection with the Same QPs Based on the PU Numbers[J]. Information Technology and Applications. 2016,02010(7):1-4.
12. B. Bross, W.J. Han, J.R. Ohm, G.J. Sullivan, T. Wiegand, High efficiency video coding (HEVC) text specification draft 10, document JCTVC-L1003 (2013).
13. Lam E Y, Goodman J W. A mathematical analysis of the DCT coefficient distributions for images.[J]. IEEE Transactions on Image Processing, 2000, 9(10):1661-1666.
14. SourceForge.net,"GtilHEVCAnalyzer",https://sourceforge.net/projects/gtilhevcanalyzer/
15. 'YUV video sequences', http://www.trace.eas.asu.edu/yuv/index.html,accessed 2 August 2015.
16. JVT-VC Reference Software version HM-10.0 Available on http://download.csdn.net/detail/amymayadi/7903385
17. Chang, C., Lin, C.: 'LIBSVM: a library for support vector machines', ACM Trans. Intell. Syst. Technol., 2011, 2, (3), pp. 35–38 Software available at: http://www.csie.ntu.edu.tw/~cjlin/libsvm, accessed 2 August 2015.

Automated Brunnstrom Assessment for Home Rehabilitation Based on GRNN Model

Ji-Ping Wang[1], Li-Quan Guo[1], Tian-Yu Sheng[1,2], Da-Xi Xiong[1]

[1]*Suzhou Institute of Biomedical Engineering and Technology Chinese Academy of Sciences, 215163 Suzhou, China*
[2]*Shanghai University, 200444, Shanghai*
[1]*wangjp@sibet.ac.cn*

Abstract. To realize the upper extremity rehabilitation assessment for post-stroke intelligently, a new movement assessment model is established in this paper. A WBSN system consisted of two inertial sensors is employed to acquisit patients' rehabilitation data. The data is stored in both local and server database. An intelligent Brunnstrom assessment based on GRNN model is built on the server. In order to test the accuracy and reliability of the model, twenty patients and four physicians were chosen as volunteers to finish a standard rehabilitation action – touching shoulder with affected hand. The accuracy of the assessment model can be 93.6%. The purpose to build an intelligent assessment is achieved. It makes patients train in the home setting and community possible.

1. Introduction

With the improvement of people's living standards, cerebrovascular diseases have become a major cause of people's death worldwide. Stroke is one of top three cause of death in them [1]. 70-85% of first-ever strokes are accompanied by hemiplegia [2]. According to the epidemiological statistics [3], over 1.6 million people died from stroke each year, about 157 per 100,000, in china and there are more than 2 million new stroke patients survived. It costs over 20 billion Chinese Yuan each year.

With the aggravating trend of aging population in china, hospital costs increase sharply. Therefore, during past decades, many researches focus on finding a method to improve rehabilitation effectiveness and reduce the costs. It is reported that home-based rehabilitation performs as well as hospital care [4]. Patients can practise under their personal training schedules with fewer constraint on time and location. However, patients cannot assess their training effect by themselves in the home setting without physician's help. It is difficult for the popular application of home-based rehabilitation [5]. Brunnstrom stage standard table is widely used in the clinical practice to assess rehabilitation stage for stoke patients' motor function [7-8]. Patients' motor function is classified into 6 stages by evaluating the accomplishment quality of standard actions listed in the table. It is difficult to be carried out in home settings and community because of its cost of time and need of physicians at hand [9]. An objective, quantitative and intelligent unsupervised assessment is required.

With the development of science and technology, wearable body sensor network systems (WBSNs) – especially inertial sensors that include accelerometers, gyroscopes, and magnetometers – can assess the type, intensity, duration, frequency, and quality of various motion-related functional activities [9-10]. Patel et al. [11] have proposed a method based on Random. Forests algorithm to monitor rehabilitation outcomes in stroke patients with sensors attached to the hand, arm and trunk. 8 tasks were chosen from the Wolf Motor Function Test (WMFT) to estimate the total Functional Ability Scale (FAS) score. A wearable body sensor network system was developed and applied well in several hospitals and communities. However, the system could not provide an assessment of patients' motion function recovery.

Based on the works finished and the shortcomings of the system, a GRNN based motion function assessment model was proposed in this paper to assess the Brunnstrom stage for home-based rehabilitation.

2. Methodolory

2.1 System

The remote quantitative assessment system consists of three parts: the patient client, physician client, and web server. At the patient client side, patients will wear the sensors on the arm and wrist first and then finish the

DOI: 10.1051/itmconf/20171201021

rehabilitation prescriptions which were made by the physicians in advance. During their training process, the wearable sensors will record the movement information in real time and wirelessly transmit the data to the computer and then upload to the web server database through Internet. Besides the storage function, another important function of web server is to analyse the movement data and give an assessment of Brunnstrom stage. According to the assessment, physicians can adjust the individualized rehabilitation prescriptions on time. The system can be used in the home setting and community anytime.

2.2 Grnn Theory

Generalized regression neural network (GRNN) is a variation to radial basis neural networks. It was suggested by D.F. Specht in 1991 [12]. It is similar to RBF neural network in structure. It consists of four parts (as shown in Figure 1): input layer, pattern layer summation layer and output layer (shown in Figure 1). Given a datasheet X=[x1, x2 , … ,xn]T, the corresponding target is Y=[y1,y2, … , yn]T.

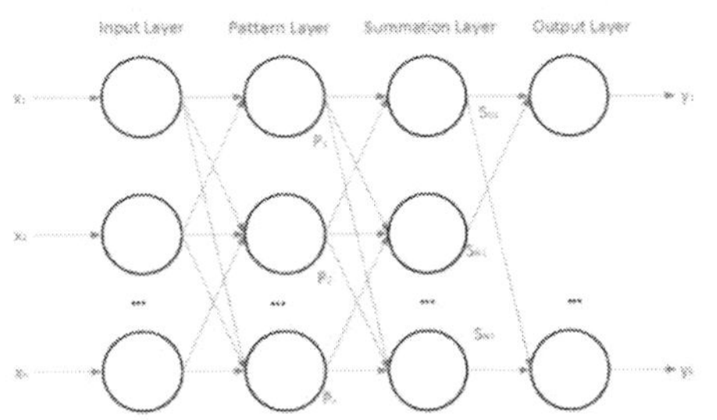

Figure 1 The structure of generalized regression neural network (GRNN)

The basic theory of GRNN is nonlinear regression analysis. Actually, the analysis of the dependent variable Y related to the independent variable x is to compute a maximum probability value – y. the joint density function between x and y is supposed as f(x,y), then the conditional mean can be descript as function (1):

$$\hat{Y} = E(y/X) = \frac{\int_{-\infty}^{\infty} y f(X,y) dy}{\int_{-\infty}^{\infty} f(X,y) dy} \quad (1)$$

Nonparametric estimation Parazen considered, sample datasheet $\{x_i, y_i\}_{i=1}^{n}$ supposed, the density function $\hat{f}(X,y)$ is that:

$$\hat{f}(X,y) = \frac{1}{n(2\pi)^{\frac{p+1}{2}}\sigma^{p+1}} \sum_{i=1}^{n} \exp[-\frac{(X-X_i)^T(X-X_i)}{2\sigma^2}] \exp[-\frac{(X-Y_i)^2}{2\sigma^2}] \quad (2)$$

$\int_{-\infty}^{\infty} z e^{-z^2} dz = 0$, the output $\hat{Y}(X)$ is that:

$$\hat{Y}(X) = \frac{\sum_{i=1}^{n} Y_i \exp[-\frac{(X-X_i)^T(X-X_i)}{2\sigma^2}]}{\sum_{i=1}^{n} \exp[-\frac{(X-X_i)^T(X-X_i)}{2\sigma^2}]} \quad (3)$$

$\hat{Y}(X)$ is the weighted mean of the sample observations. While the smoothness factor σ is very big, $\hat{Y}(X)$ will be very close to the dependent mean of all samples. While the smoothness factor σ approaches zero, $\hat{Y}(X)$ will be close to the sample. In a word, when the factor σ is an appropriate value, the dependent variable of all training samples is considered, the dependent variable of the point close to the predicted point will be given more weights.

3. Experimental Configurations

3.1 Experimental Setup

The experiment was carried out in the Rehabilitation Medical centre of the 2nd Hospital in Jiaxing, China. Twenty patients and four physicians were chosen as volunteers. The Brunnstrom stages of the patients were in the range II to V(estimated by the physicians). While patients in Brunnstrom stage VI perform no difference from the healthy people. The physicians served as the patients in Brunnstrom stage VI. All the patients attended in the test were listed in Table 1. There were eleven male patients and nine female patients, aged from 49 to 79, involved in the experiment.

Table 1 the information of patients

Brunnstrom Stage	case	Gender M/F	Age	Paraplegia side left/right
II	2	0/2	59.0±1.0	2/0
III	8	4/4	56.3±7.3	4/4
IV	4	3/1	66.6±10.1	1/3
V	6	4/2	65.6±7.5	2/4

According to the Brunnstrom scale, the motion range of elbow, shoulder and forearm is a very important index to classify the stage of patient rehabilitation status. A standard motion, touching shoulder with affected hand, which can descript the index well was employed.

A WBSN system consisted of two inertial sensors was employed to collect patients' training data. The placements of sensors were shown in Figure 2, it is clear that the sensors were placed at the volunteer's forearm and the center of upper limb respectively with x-axis of sensor parallel to the arm. The volunteers were required to finish the selected action five times and the action should be finished in 10s with no pause. The data collected were stored in both local and server database. The assessment of the volunteers were given on server. The physicians, patients and their guardians have permission to check training data and the assessment on the web or mobile devices.

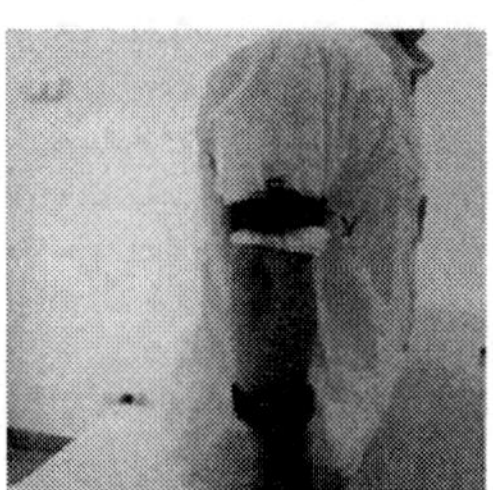

Figure 2 the sensors placed on arm

3.2 Feature Extraction

The raw data was seen noisy due to sensor sample noise which reduced the data accuracy. A median filter was employed and works well in this paper. The raw data and denoised data were shown in Figure 3. It is observed that after filtering, the denoised data were smoother than raw data and the outliers caused by packet loss during transmission were removed.

Five types of feature were extracted (AMP, MEAN, RMS, JERK, and ApEn) during rehabilitation. Each inertial sensor has 3 axis and two sensors were employed, then there were total 30 features extracted. Besides, the energy, maximum of velocity, mean of velocity, std, entropy and maximum angle features were extracted too. These 42 features as shown in Table 2 were employed to assess the Brunnstrom stage of patients.

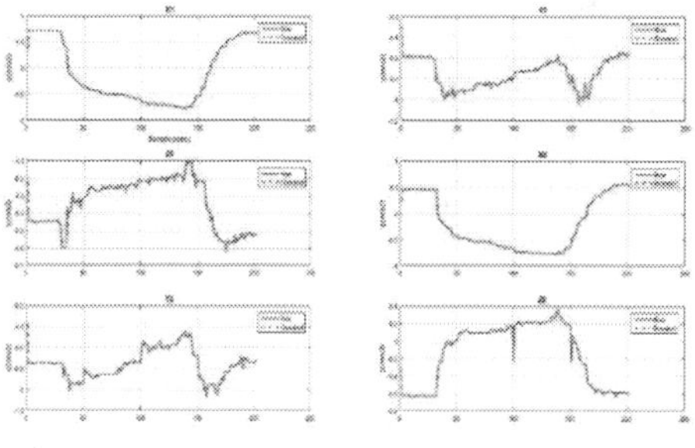

Figure 3 raw and denoised data of rehabilitation training

Table 2 features extracted from the rehabilitation data

Feature	Number of features for each instance
Maximum magnitude of data(AMP)	2×3
Root mean square value of data(RMS)	2×3
Root mean square value of the derivative of data (JERK)	2×3
Mean value of data(MEAN)	2×3
Approximate entropy of data (ApEn)	2×3
Energy (ENE)	2
Maximum of the velocity(V max)	2
Mean value of the velocity (V mean)	2
STD of the velocity(V std)	2
Approximate entropy of the velocity (V ApEn)	2
Maximum angle (ANGLE max)	2

4. Results and Discussion

4.1 Results

The predicted result of test sample is shown in Figure 4 . A sample in Brunnstrom stage III is predicted as stage IV; a sample in Brunnstrom stage IV is predicted as stage III; a sample in Brunnstrom stage V is predicted as stage IV. The predictive accuracy of samples is that the accuracy in stage II at 100%, the accuracy in stage III at 93.8%, the accuracy in stage IV at 90.0%, the accuracy in stage V at 90.0%, the accuracy in stage VI at 100%. The study found that the errors might be cause by the factors listed below. Firstly, the lack of training samples used during the progress of building prediction model lead to an inaccurate model. Secondly, the patients performed well when their condition were comfortable and vice versa. In conclusion, the predictive accuracy of all test sample is 93.6%. It means that the Brunnstrom assessment model based on GRNN has the extensive applicability.

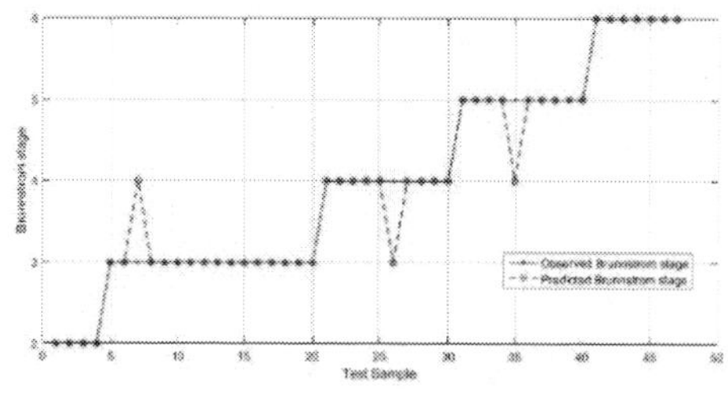

Figure 4 Observed results and predicted of the test samples

4.2 Discussion

An automated Brunnstrom assessment based on GRNN model is proposed to assess patients' motion function recovery in this paper. It can give the Brunnstrom stage of patients and help patients finish their assessment in home setting and community. An experiment was designed and carried in the rehabilitation center of 2rd hospital in Jiaxing with the guidance of physicians. The test result shows that the model can assess patients' physical condition well and provides a reliable basis for making follow training plan. In future, more data will be collected to improve predictive model.

References

[1] M. L. Rao, China Guideline for Cerebrovascular Disease Prevention and Treatment. Beijing[M] *People's Medical Publishing House*, ch.1, (2007)

[2] Feigin, V.L, Forouzanfar, M.H, Krishnamurthi, etc. Global and regional burden of stroke during 1990–2010: Findings from the Global Burden of Disease Study 2010, *The Lancet.* 383, 245–255. (2014)

[3] Naghavi. M., Wang. H, Lozano. R, et al. Global, regional, and national age-sex specific all-cause and cause-specific mortality for 240 causes of death, 1990–2013: A systematic analysis for the Global Burden of Disease Study 2013.*The Lancet*, 385, 117–171(2015).

[4] L. Liu, D. Wang, K. L. Wong, and Y. Wang, Stroke and stroke care in china huge burden, significant workload, and a national priority, *Stroke*, vol. 42, no. 12, pp. 3651-3654, (2011).

[5] Langan J, DeLave K, Phillips L, et al. Home-Based Telerehabilitation Shows Improved Upper Limb Function in Adults with Chronic Stroke: A Pilot Study

[J]. *Journal of Rehabilitation Medicine*, 45(2): 217-220, (2013).

[6] Chen J, Jin, W, Zhang X.X, et al. Telerehabilitation Approaches for Stroke Patients: Systematic Review and Meta-analysis of Randomized Controlled Trials. [J]. *Stroke Cerebrovascular Disease*. 24, 2660–2668 ,(2015)

[7] Nurdiana Nordin,Sheng Quan Xie and Burkhard Wünsche Assessment of movement quality in robot- assisted upper limb rehabilitation after stroke: a review, Journal of *NeuroEngineering and Rehabilitation* , 11:137(2014)

[8] Rachele Bertani, Corrado Melegari, Maria C. De Cola.etc. Effects of robot-assisted upper limb rehabilitation in stroke patients: a systematic review with meta-analysis, *Neurological Sciences*, pp:1-9 May(2017)

[9] E.V. Olesh, S. Yakovenko, V. Gritsenko, Automated assessment of upper extremity movement impairment due to stroke [J]. *PLOS ONE* 9 (2014).

[10] Yu L, Wang Jp, Fang Q, et al. Brunnstrom stage automatic evaluation for stroke patients using extreme learning machine[C]. *proceedings of the IEEE Biomedical Circuits and Systems Conference Proceedings*, Hsinchu, Taiwan: 380-383, November (2012)

[11] S. Patel, R. Hughes, T. Hester, et al, A novel approach to monitor rehabilitation outcomes in stroke survivors using wearable technology, Proceedings of the IEEE, vol. 98, no. 3, pp. 450-461, (2010).

[12] D.F. Specht, A general regression neural network [J]. IEEE Transactions on Neural Net

[13] works, :568 - 576 ,Nov (1991)

3D Object Recognition Based on ADAPTIVE-SCALE and SPCA-ALM in Cluttered Scenes

Dan XU, Xu-Zhi WANG, Wang-Gen WAN, Xiang-Jie LI

School of Communication & Information Engineering, Institute of Smart City, Shanghai University, Shanghai, China
1172039852@qq.com,wanwg@staff.shu.edu.cn,wangxzw@shu.edu.cn,1364616657@qq.com

Abstract—In this paper a novel 3D object recognition method which can improve the recognition accuracy of object recognition in the cluttered scenes was proposed. The proposed method use the adaptive-scale to detect the keypoint (ASDK) of 3D object in the cluttered scenes, it use the algorithm of Sparse Principal Component Analysis Augmented Lagrangian Method (SPCA- ALM) to extract the feature of object, the algorithm of SPCA-ALM has a good performance in the high dimensional due to the Spares PCA, and the ALM can raise the speed of the SPCA. The experiment shows that the proposed method can decrease the time of 3D object recognition and improve the recognition accuracy.

1 .Introduction

3D object recognition has been a widely used in the computer vision during the past several decades. Many significances works have been done, such as automatic navigation, remote sensing, mobile manipulation, intelligent surveillance, automatic assembly, robotics, biometric analysis and so on. In the past years, 2D Image recognition has been extensively investigated. But with the development of technology people are more interested in 3D scenes, 3D scenes have several advantages for object recognition due to its range images. For example, (i) Features extracted from range images are commonly not affected by scale, rotation and illumination. (ii) Compare to 2D images, it has more geometrical information from range images. Nowadays, Kinect can catch the range images, and it have the potential to overcome many difficulties which faced by 2D images in the context of object recognition. Existing 3D object recognition approaches can be divided into two main categories: the point cloud data [18]and rgb-d data. Lai K, Bo L, Ren X, et a proposed a large-scale hierarchical multi-view rgb-d object dataset [10]. Filliat D, Battesti E, Bazeille S, et al use RGBD object recognition and visual texture classification for indoor semantic mapping [16]. In literature [1], the method of 3D object recognition in cluttered scenes with local surface features was proposed. However, those methods didn't solve the problem that the accuracy of object recognition is relatively low in the cluttered scenes.

In this article, we proposed a novel method which can solve above problem. The proposed method firstly use the point cloud data to recognition the object in the cluttered scenes, and using adaptive-scale to detection keypiont, then using ASDK SPCA-ALM to select informative object features, third, we descript the feature and match the feature, finally, we make hypothesis generation and hypothesis verification.

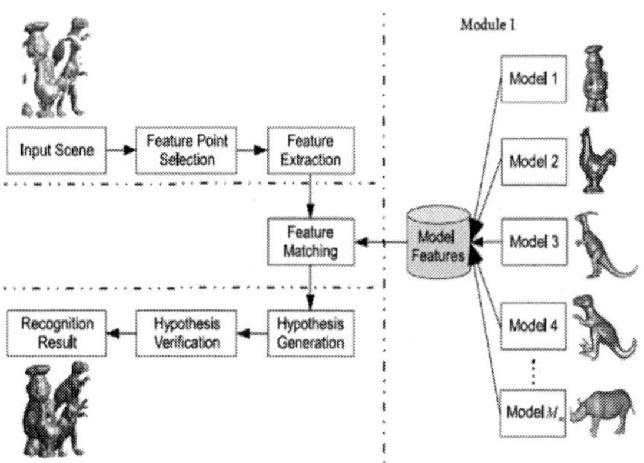

Figure 1.The flow chart of Object Recognition

2. Object Recognition

This part is made by four steps as follows: Firstly, in Section A we should use adaptive-scale detection to get the keypoint; Then in Section B we mainly study about the informative feature selection; in Section C introduces the feature description and feature Match, Finally, in Section D we describes Hypothesis Generation and Hypothesis Verification. Figure.1 shows the flow chart of Object Recognition [17].

2.1. Adaptive-scale Keypoint Detection ASDK

3D object recognition have several steps, Keypoint detection is the first step and is also the most important step. Keypoint detection included surface mesh decimation and sparse sampling. Though several keypoint detection methods were proposed, the keypoint detected can't meet the demand of experimental. Because when detecting the keypoint, they do not or seldom consider the difference of information points. Hence, we should according to their distinctiveness to detect keypoints. Keypoint detection methods can be broadly divided into two categories based on whether the scale is predetermined or adaptively detected: the one is fixed-scale keypoint detection methods and the other is adaptive-scale keypoint detection methods. As shown in Figure.2 is the adaptive-scale keypoint detection method, (a) is 3D Viewer and (b) is Range Image. Fixed-scale keypoint detection is detected the keypiont in a space which has a fixed scale. Adaptive-scale keypoint detection is to build a scale-space, after the scale-space was built in the range image, select extreme specificity measures for points in space and scale communities as keypoints. According to the information of the keypoint to change the scale-space. Then, the location and scale of the keypoints can be detected.

2.2. ASDK SPCA-ALM

Feature extraction is the second step of 3D object Recognition, in this paper we use the ASDK SPCA-ALM to extract the feature, firstly, detecting keypoint and then extracting the feature around it.

PCA method which can decompose the data matrix A's empirical covariance matrix eigenvalue to compute the PCs, in general, the entries of the corresponding PVs of PCA are dense and nonzero. But in some conditions, the PV needs to be obtained which can use a combination of several nonzero variables to describe the maximum variance and it can increase the interpretability of these data. Sparse principal component analysis can determine the hidden information in the targeted data, which involving the physical interpretation of the coordinate axis. Thus, we computed an empirical covariance matrix for every object category of the database to recognize the visual words by Sparse PCA.

In the past decades, Sparse PCA has become a very popular research topic. Most widely used methods including SPCA, SCoTLASS and SLRA, these methods intended to find modified PVs with sparse entries. Nevertheless, all the above method need to solve nonconvex objective functions. In order to overcome the drawback. In this paper we use ASDK to detect the keypoint and use Augmented Lagrangian Method (ALM) to improve the speed of SPCA, ASDK SPCA-ALM was rapid convergent and speed in ℓ -minimization. And it can solve the semidefinite relaxation form of Sparse PCA using ALM.

Figure 2. Adaptive-scale keypoint detection

This part we introduce the SPCA-ALM with ASDP. Matrix $\Sigma \in S^n$ is a positive semidefinite that represents the empirical data covariance, we use SPCA to process the objective following:

$$\max_{\|x\|_2 \le 1} x^T \Sigma x - \rho\|x\|_0 \qquad (1)$$

The $\rho > 0$ can follow the `1-norm relaxation and lift procedure for semidefinite relaxation to control the sparsity in x., it is a scalar parameter, and a nonconvex rank constraints can be dropped, (1) can be written as:

$$\max_X Tr(\Sigma X) - \rho\|X\|_1 : Tr(X) = 1, X \ge 0 \qquad (2)$$

DOI: 10.1051/itmconf/20171201022

The matrix variable X $\quad X = xx^T$. We rewrite this problem as:

$$\min_{U \in S^n} \lambda_{\max}\left(\Sigma + U\right) : -\rho \le U_{ij} \le \rho \quad (3)$$

The maximum eigenvalue function $\lambda_{\max}(\cdot)$ can be approached by a smooth, once Σ is fixed and given. uniform objective:

$$f_{\mu}(U) = \mu \log\left(Tr \exp\left(\frac{\Sigma + U}{\mu} \right) \right) \quad (4)$$

$$\nabla f_{\mu}(U) = \exp\left(\frac{\Sigma + U}{\mu} \right) \Big/ Tr \exp\left(\frac{\Sigma + U}{\mu} \right) \quad (5)$$

The $\mu = \epsilon / 2\log(n)$ produces an $\epsilon -$ approximate solution. The formula (3) can be rewritten as:

$$\min_{U} f_{\mu}(U) : -\rho \le U_{ij} \le \rho \quad (6)$$

Based on the formulation above established, then we use ALM to increase the speed of the ASDK SPCA. ALM is to eliminate constraints and add a penalty term to the cost function that describe a high cost to impossible points. We can rewrite an unconstrained form for the box-constraint convexity problem of (6):

$$F(U, Y) = \min_{U} \left\{ f_{\mu}(U) + \sum_{1 \le i, j \le n} P\left(U_{ij}, Y_{ij}, c\right) \right\} \quad (7)$$

The $Y_{ij}, 1 \le i, j \le n$ is Lagrange variable, and c is the variable which represent penalty severity.

$$P(\mu, y, c) = \begin{cases} -\dfrac{y^2}{2c} & \textit{otherwise,} \\ y(\mu - \rho) + \dfrac{c}{2}(\mu - \rho)^2 \; \textit{if} \; \rho - \dfrac{y}{c} \le \mu, \\ y(\mu + \rho) + \dfrac{c}{2}(\mu + \rho)^2 \; \textit{if} \; -\rho - \dfrac{y}{c} \le \mu. \end{cases} \quad (8)$$

It is worth to notice that we should solve the unconstrained minimization problem in (7) when we iteration of the outer loop of the algorithm, and this method has no closed-form solution. Thus, the first order gradient technique is used to obtain the best value. After getting the minimized of augmented Lagrange function, we use the rule to update the Lagrange multipliers Y:

$$Y_{ij}^{k+1} = \begin{cases} Y_{ij}^k + c^k\left(U_{ij}^k - \rho\right) & \textit{if} \; Y_{ij}^k + c^k\left(U_{ij}^k - \rho\right) > 0 \\ Y_{ij}^k + c^k\left(U_{ij}^k + \rho\right) & \textit{if} \; Y_{ij}^k + c^k\left(U_{ij}^k + \rho\right) < 0 \\ 0 & \textit{otherwise.} \end{cases} \quad (9)$$

We can get the primal variable by the gradient in (5), once the algorithm is convergent, *i.e.*, $X^k = \nabla f_{\mu}\left(U^k\right)$. As the leading eigenvector of X^k the sparse principal component can be recovered.

2.3. Feature Description and Match

The geometric information of the local surface can be extracted after detecting the keypoint, and it can be encoded into a feature descriptor. Recently the proposed methods can be classified into three categories: signature based, histogram based, and transform based methods. The core issue of the local feature description [16] are invariance and robust. When descriptor feature, we need to consider the invariance of perspective, scale, and rotation in shape recognition and object retrieval. And we also need to consider the invariant of shape of feature descriptor.

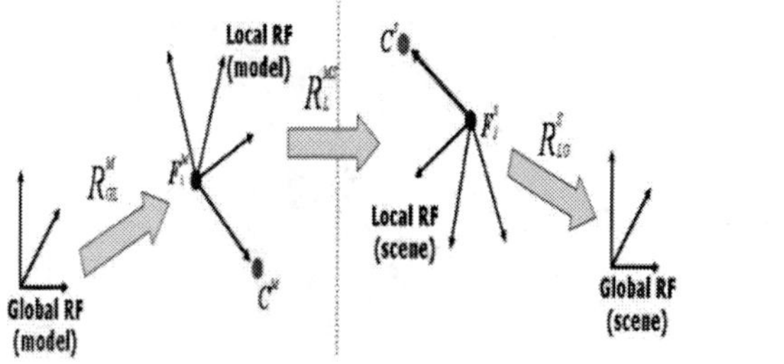

Figure 3. feature match in the local RF, (left) the model feature. (right) the scene feature

How to choose an appropriate matching strategy when searching the model feature library, the efficiency is an important issue. The simplest approach is to use a brute-force search, which matches a scene feature with all model features. The computational complexity of this approach is O(Nf), the Nf is the number of model features. A faster alternative is to adopt an appropriate data structure or indexing method. Hough transform is one of the basic methods of image processing which is widely used in the geometry image recognition, there are many improvements proposed. The most basic Hough transform is detected from the black and white images straight line. As shown below: We make a Hof elections for the scene and the model in global coordinate, and then converted to a local coordinate, if the parameters get from the Hough election in the local coordinate are equal, that means election hypothesis is correct, otherwise the Hof elections is wrong. In the Fig.3 $V_{i,G}^{M}$ is the Hough variables of the model under the global

 DOI: 10.1051/itmconf/20171201022

coordinates , $V_{i,L}^{M}$ is the Hough variables of model under the local coordinates , F_i^M is the Feature points in the model library, F_j^S is the Feature points in the scene, C^M is the reference point, R_{GL}^{M} is the conversion between Local coordinate and global coordinate , $V_{i,L}^{S}$ is the Hough variables of scene Under the local coordinates, $V_{i,G}^{S}$ is the Hough variables of scene Under the global coordinates. In Figure 4 shows the result of feature match, the chairs from scene match to the model library chair, the yellow chairs represent objects in the scene.

$$V_{i,G}^{M} = C^{M} - F_{i}^{M} \qquad (10)$$

$$V_{i,L}^{M} = V_{i,L}^{S} \qquad (11)$$

$$V_{i,L}^{M} = R_{GL}^{M} \cdot V_{i,G}^{M} \qquad (12)$$

$$V_{i,G}^{S} = R_{LG}^{S} \cdot V_{i,L}^{S} + F_{j}^{S} \qquad (13)$$

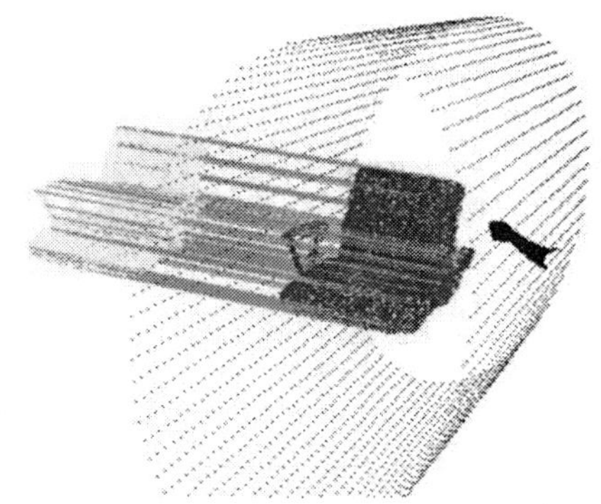

Figure 4. The chairs from scene match to the model library chair. The yellow chairs represent objects in the scene

2.4. Hypothesis Generation and Verification

Hypothesis generation have two tasks: get potential candidate models in the scene and generate hypotheses for each candidate model conversion. Feature matching sometimes wrong, the point in the scene [9] and model to match the other point, which appears outliers, as shown in Fig 5, where C is the reference point, a point on the model left and right for the scene the point where the green dot on the spot did not match the model, became the outliers, the green dotted line represents a successful match, a red dotted line represents the match fails.

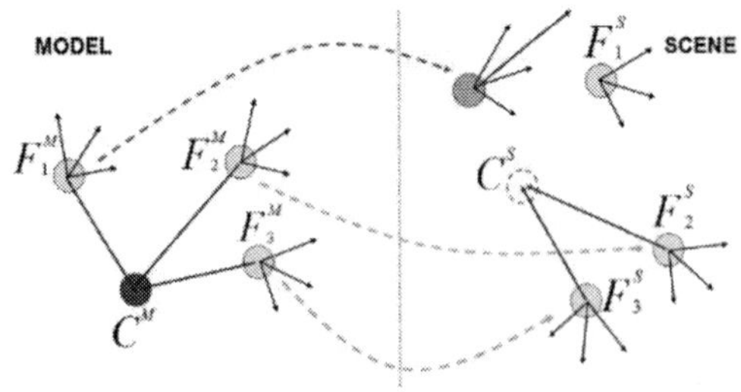

Figure 5. generate hypotheses for each candidate model conversion.(left) the keypoint from model. (Right) the keypoint from scene.

The purpose of Hypothesis verification is to find the correct hypothesis from the false assumption that inside the existing authentication methods into separate authentication methods and global validation methods[11], hypothesis testing is independent of the assumptions used method of converting the objects in the scene aligned with the candidate models. Global hypothesis testing methods are as follows: 1. All the assumptions xi as a binary set x; 2. Geometrical Cues (goodness of fit, Multiple Assignment, randomness) Construction cost function, 3. optimization of the cost function (Simulated Annealing)

3. Experimental Results

In this paper, we use a laser scanner to get the point cloud data, then we use ASDK SPCA-ALM to extract feature among the keypiont, at the same time SPCA-ALM use to extract the feature from the same object and compare the two methods. Figure 6(a) shows that the estimation error increased with the dimension, when the dimension attach 300 the Error of the two methods are equal, then ASDK SPCA-ALM will have a smaller error rate compared with SPCA-ALM. while Figure 6(b) compares the speed of two methods , the chart shows that with the increased sharply ASDK SPCA-ALM spend less time. And in Figure 7 is the final recognition result of the chair from the model.

Conclusion

In order to get a better recognition rate of the object in the cluttered scenes, this paper presents a novel method which use Adaptive-scale Detection to get keypoint and use Sparse PCA to extract feature, then use Augmented Lagrangian Method to get the best value of recognition time and a better recognition accuracy. The experiment shows that the proposed method can decrease the time of 3D object recognition and improve the recognition accuracy. In the future, we will consider the combination of convolutional neural network and recurrent neural network to identify

DOI: 10.1051/itmconf/20171201022

object, currently machine learning is a hot research field. If we consider the machine learning method, I believe that it will get a better recognition performance.

Acknowledgement

This research was partially supported by the National Nature Science Foundation of China (No.61373084) and the Innovation Program of Shanghai Municipal Education Commission (No.14YZ011).

References

[1] Guo Y, Bennamoun M, Sohel F, et al. 3D Object Recognition in Cluttered Scenes with Local Surface Features:A Survey[J]. IEEE, 2014.
[2] Lai K, Bo L, Ren X, et al. Detection-based object labeling in 3D scenes[C]//Robotics and Automation (ICRA), 2012 IEEE International Conference on. IEEE, 2012: 1330-1337.
[3] Bo L, Ren X, Fox D. Depth kernel descriptors for object recognition[C]//Intelligent Robots and Systems (IROS), 2011 IEEE/RSJ International Conference on. IEEE, 2011: 821-826.
[4] A. d'Aspremont, L. El Ghaoui, M. Jordan, and G. Lanckriet. A direct formulation for Sparse PCA using semidefinite programming. SIAM Rev., 2007.
[5] Lai K, Bo L, Fox D. Unsupervised feature learning for 3d scene labeling[C]//Robotics and Automation (ICRA), 2014 IEEE International Conference on. IEEE, 2014: 3050-3057.
[6] Guo Y, Sohel F, Bennamoun M, et al. A novel local surface feature for 3D object recognition under clutter and occlusion[J]. Information Sciences, 2015, 293: 196-213.
[7] An Y, Li Z, Shao C. Feature Extraction from 3D Point Cloud Data Based on Discrete Curves[J]. Mathematical Problems in Engineering, 2013.
[8] Lai K, Bo L, Ren X, et al. Sparse distance learning for object recognition combining rgb and depth information [C]//Robotics and Automation (ICRA), 2011 IEEE International Conference on. IEEE, 2011: 4007-4013.
[9] Othman A, El Ghoul O. A novel approach for 3D head segmentation and facial feature points extraction [C]//Electrical Engineering and Software Applications (ICEESA), 2013 International Conference on. IEEE, 2013: 1-6.
[10] Lai K, Bo L, Ren X, et al. A large-scale hierarchical multi-view rgb-d object dataset[C]//Robotics and Automation (ICRA), 2011 IEEE International Conference on. IEEE, 2011: 1817-1824.
[11] Gomes R B, da Silva B M F, de Medeiros Rocha L K, et al. Efficient 3D object recognition using foveated point clouds[J]. Computers & Graphics, 2013, 37(5): 496-508.
[12] Bariya P, Nishino K. Scale-Hierarchical 3D Object Recognition in Cluttered Scenes[J]. 2010, 119(5):1657-1664.
[13] Blum M, Springenberg J T, Wulfing J, et al. A learned feature descriptor for object recognition in rgb-d data[C]//Robotics and Automation (ICRA), 2012 IEEE International Conference on. IEEE, 2012: 1298-1303.
[14] Lai K, Bo L, Ren X, et al. RGB-D object recognition: Features, algorithms, and a large scale benchmark [M]//Consumer Depth Cameras for Computer Vision. Springer London, 2013: 167-192.
[15] Silberman N, Hoiem D, Kohli P, et al. Indoor segmentation and support inference from RGBD images[M]//Computer Vision–ECCV 2012. Springer Berlin Heidelberg, 2012: 746-760.
[16] Filliat D, Battesti E, Bazeille S, et al. RGBD object recognition and visual texture classification for indoor semantic mapping[C]//Technologies for Practical Robot Applications (TePRA), 2012 IEEE International Conference on. IEEE, 2012: 127-132.
[17] Naikal N, Yang A Y, Sastry S S. Informative feature selection for object recognition via sparse PCA[C]//2011 International Conference on Computer Vision. IEEE, 2011: 818-825.
[18] Guan P, Huang J, Anvar A, et al. Multi-view 3D object recognition from a point cloud and change detection: U.S. Patent 9,619,691[P]. 2017-4-11.

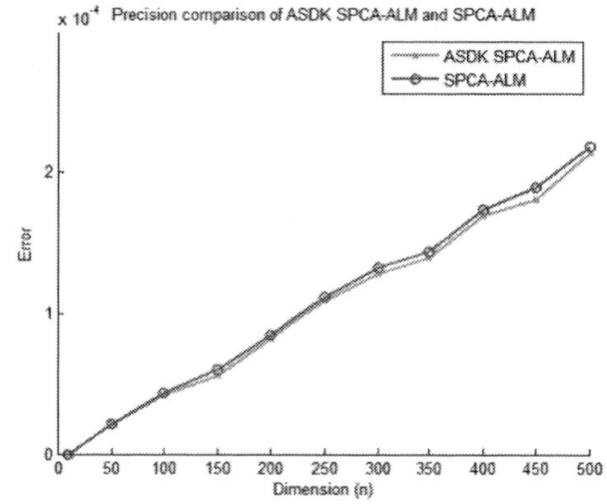

(a) Recognition Error with Dimension

DOI: 10.1051/itmconf/20171201022

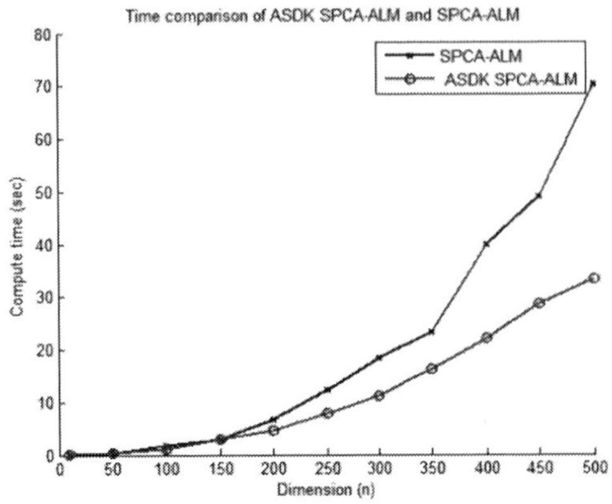

(b) Recognition Speed with Dimension

Figure 6. A result of ASDK SPCA-ALM and SPCA-ALM

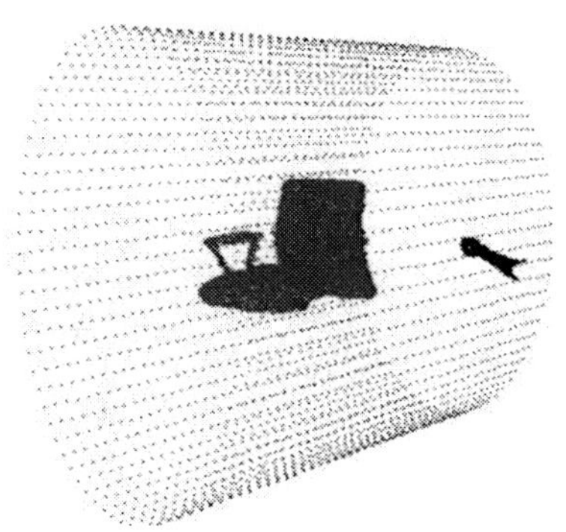

Figure 7. Final recognition out of the chair from the model

ITM Web of Conferences 12, 01023 (2017) DOI: 10.1051/itmconf/20171201023
ITA 2017

Ros Based Remote Robot Task Monitoring and Control System

Yao-Yao CHENG, Dian-Xi SHI

National Laboratory for Parallel and Distributed Processing National University of Defense Technology,Changsha,China
905199669@qq.com, dxshi@nudt.edu.cn

Abstract—This paper defines a novel robot task based on ROS. Meanwhile, a ROS based remote robot task monitoring and control system is implemented, through which operators can remotely operate robots to achieve tasks as defined above. In addition, operators can use the system to monitor each task's running status and each task's running node process information so that the work load of remote robots can be known.

1 Introduction

George Devol of America designed the first electronic procedure programmable industrial robot in 1954. And, Unimation's first robot Unimate was put into use in General Motors in 1962, marking the birth of the first generation of robots[1]. Since then, the robot began to slowly penetrate into human life. With the strengthening of technology and communication capabilities, the infiltration speed faster and faster. In decades of years, the human has created the robot, has realized from static ones to movable ones, and make them learn to crawl and walk. Today, robots even can also use artificial intelligence to challenge human, such as the chess competition between Lee Se-dol and AlphaGo. At present, robots mostly serve the human as the service robot helping to do cleaning and repeat boring industrial work. At the same time, they can be also used to explore the deep sea and outer space, which makes an indelible contribution to mankind and in turn promotes the robot technology. It has developed into a cross discipline of many fields--robotics, including mechanics, electronics, biology, cybernetics, computer science, bionics, artificial intelligence, systems engineering and so on[2].

With the rapid development of robotics and more kinds of sensor data is acquired[3], more and more robots are being applied to our life, how to effectively control the robot has become a problem which is worth being studied. Moreover, the extensive use of robots makes the work environment of robots more extreme, more complex and more high-risky[4], such as disaster relief environment, high voltage and high radiation area. Considering mankind's both safety and capability of operating robots, researchers turn to how to remotely control a robot, which is called tele-robotics.

In terms of recent research on tele-robotics, there are a lot of related work. In the research and implementation of robots' virtual simulation and remote control system, a virtual reality environment[5] was constructed by using OpenGL, which was used for safety testing before sending remote control commands. The C/S mode remote communication method, based on WinSock mechanism, was used for robots' communication. The modular design concept was applied into the establishment of the system. Wang et al. put forward a novel control framework for internet based tele-robotics[6], which can guarantee the non-distortion-transfer of control information and can reduce the difference of action time between the local simulated virtual robot and the remote real robot, solving the inherent network time delay problem in the remote control. By the way, the remote tracking control of a mobile robot subject to a bilateral time-delay was addressed and a proposed delay compensation strategy was demonstrated by means of experiments[7]. The event-based remote control strategy was adopted to overcome the problem of network time delay and the algorithm to control robots' formation was proposed using "leader-follower" approach to realize the simulation result of robots' formation, which enables robots to have high self-organizing ability[8].Based on the robot operating system, a human-computer interaction system for space robot was designed to control the remote mechanical arm using human body posture and voice of the operator, and receive the state of the arm and its surrounding virtual reality environment using sensors[9].The work[10] focused on providing the control and software architecture that bridges the tele operator, the sensorial data from the task circumstance and the robot's locomotion system as well as the end-effectors. And two key components was added to promote the system: a video display of predicted operator intentions and a haptic-based controller for automated

DOI: 10.1051/itmconf/20171201023

grasping. The work refers that mostly remote control only controls robots to pick and place, in other words, some simple discrete action commands. What the remote control system proposed in this paper was very different from previous research. A Multi-level Fusion Architecture (MUFA) for controlling the navigation of a tele-commanded Autonomous Guided Vehicle was designed[11].By combining the client station's instructions and the ability to move autonomously according to information around, an intelligent navigation system was achieved[11].And the paper[12] introduces a formal framework of muti-agent system, so do I will design a control framework for robots' running tasks.

It's found that the tele-robotics research often combines local simulation and remote control to strengthen the control performance of the remote robot. On the other hand, there are much work on network latency when remote control information is transferred. Numerous surveys have indicated that that most tele-robotics systems select socket mechanism for communication. One reason is that socket can be used to build long-term links, not like HTTP turned off once the request has received[13]. The other is that command messages can be easily handled as short byte streams, which is suitable for socket to transfer, rather than large files, which call for HTTP.

When operating robots carrying out tasks remotely, the simulation system can only show the surface layer of the robots' working state, but the workload is not visible to operators. So a system able to monitor task execution status and how much a task occupies system resources remotely is anticipated. This paper, first of all, defines a novel task. Next, the design framework of the remote robot task monitoring and control system is presented. The forth section, three kinds important technology, such as multi-thread socket communication mechanism, the algorithm of parsing tasks' nodes and the access to information of running nodes, is illustrated one by one. The fifth section, the functions of the realized system are displayed. Conduction lies in the last section.

2 Task definition

The task, in daily life, is the work which to be taken, duty and responsibility need to pay attention to. In the field of computer, it refers to a process or a series of transaction, completed by the computer, as well as the professional term of the basic work unit. In the paper, we define the novel task by instantiation. First of all, a few professional terms are introduced as follows.

ROS node: A node is an executable file, which can run in the ROS environment. It can communicate with other nodes by ROS Master. It is also a separate process. Nodes mentioned later in this paper refers to the ROS node.

Launch file: ROS uses the tool ---"roslaunch" to start the file. A full launch file, written in the form of XML, includes basic node list. The launch file executes, which can start the tool---"roscore" and one-time start the batch multiple nodes defined in the launch file.

Package: Package, is the most basic unit organization of ROS code. Each Package includes library files, executable files, scripts, and other files. When a node is to be started, the node is searched by the package where it lies.

In the ROS environment, we used to define the executable file of a node in a package, where there can exist multiple executable files. Then, batch multiple nodes run after starting the launch file where the node list is defined through the tool---"roslaunch". Here, the task remotely operated is defined as the transaction the multiple nodes completed. So, a launch file defines a task for the robot to complete. Starting a launch file means starting a task. Each package, of course, there can be multiple launch files so that different tasks, made up of different nodes, can execute. As a result of the batch starting of nodes, operations of the robot is simplified. So it is reasonable that writing the node list into launch files and defining a launch file as a task.

3 System design framework

3.1 Function structure

In general, the function structure of the remote robot task monitoring and control system includes the server-side console, intermediate socket communication mechanism and the remote robot client, as shown in Figure 1. The sever-side console is consist of the task control and monitoring module, the command encapsulation and sending module and the task status update module. On the other hand, the remote robot client's functions are split into the robot registration module, the command reception, parse and execution module, the task node parsing module, and running information acquisition module. The detailed descriptions of each module function and the connections between them will be discussed in subsequent sections.

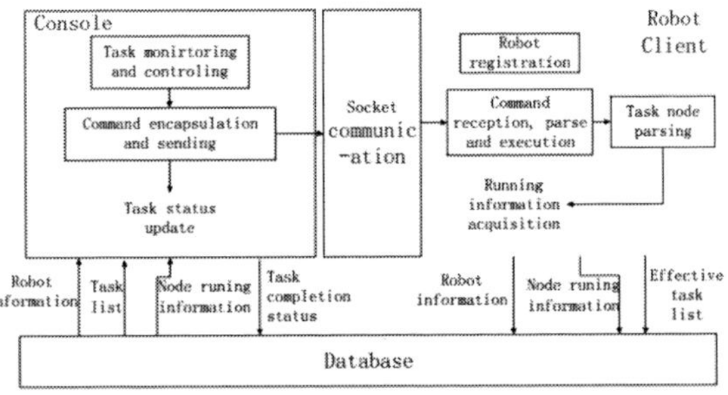

Figure 1. Function structure diagram

3.1.1 *The robot client*

Robot registration module: A robot will store information, including robot IP and name, into the database by registering when the client on the robot starts, so that the server-side console can directionally manage and control the robot identified by the unique IP, in other word, directionally send commands and obtain the robot's task running information. Moreover, effective task list of the robot will be also registered to the database, in order that the console visually starts effective tasks on the robot.

Command reception, parse and execution module: The robot client receives commands to operate tasks from the console through the socket communication mechanism. Because commands is transferred in the form of byte streams, they need to be parsed into the executable command after reception, then execute in the ROS environment to operate the robot.

Task node parsing module: Each launch file defines a task indirectly, and each task contains at least one node, so extracting the node list from the launch file is achievable. Using DOM parse method the task list is gained easily.

Running information acquisition module: In the ROS environment, each node is a process, so the access to the node information is the process information acquisition. The name of a node is known and unique, and we have access to the node's progress ID from the ROS Master by submitting the node name to the ROS Master, which is realized by a tool rewritten from the ROS tool---"rosnode". Finally, the process ID is used to acquire the node process running information.

3.1.2 The Server-client console

Task monitoring and control module:It includes the control of tasks and the monitoring of task statuses. Control of the task refers to a task start, pause and end. Task control, must get a robot list and effective task list from the database to send commands directionally. Task status monitoring shows us each robot's running task information and task completion progress and real-timely updates.

Command encapsulation and sending module: A command includes command type and related parameters, such as the name of the task which the command operates. Multiple fields are encapsulated into a byte stream and then are sent to the robot client through the socket communication mechanism.

Task status update module: Task statuses --- non-started, running, finished, among which the task status changes. These changes can be stored into status tables in the database rea-timely.

3.2 Running flow

The remote control and monitoring system flow chart introduces how the whole system work and is operated, as shown in Figure 2.

First, the robot client registers IP and local effective task list to the database, followed by the console directionally sending task operation commands to the robot. The command to start a task or finish a task sent to the robot client will be parsed to commands working on the nodes of the task. Running task's node list and the running information of all nodes of the task obtained in the local will register into the database real-timely. Sequentially, the console will query all the task's nodes information from the database and display on the console. The console changes the task status by operating the task, and the change will update to the database, so that the console can real-timely query the task completion progress. What aforementioned is the control process of the remote control and monitoring system, including real-time remote operations on the task , the console's remote monitoring the task completion progress and running information. The running information reflects how much the system resource the task has occupied. The system function complete and effective, will not cause the heavy load to the local robot.

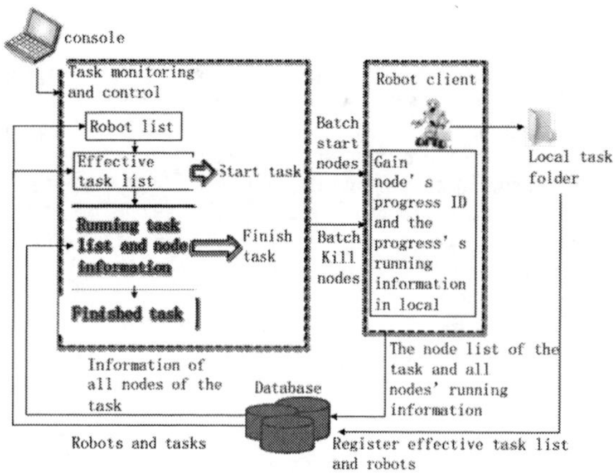

Figure 2. Function structure diagram

4 Core technology

4.1 Socket muti-thread communication mechanism

The robot client as the socket communication server, uses multiple threads to monitor and handle the command sent from the console. The console as the socket communication client, can continuously send commands to the robot client. Two kinds of commands work. One is to operate the task, the other is the request to refresh the running task information.

There is the socket server running a permanently monitoring procedure so as to receive requests from the console continuously and provide appropriate services. In order to realize the function that the server can respond to the continuous request, the multi-threaded parallel processing mechanism[14] needs to be adopted. That is, the server listeners on the specified port to monitor whether the client request comes, and once the request heard, the server will start a special service thread to respond to the client request but keep listening in aim to wait for the arrival of the next request.

What the socket communication has to deal with is command encapsulation and command sending.

DOI: 10.1051/itmconf/20171201023

First of all, command encapsulation is to pack information to be transferred into a byte stream. The content of the command message contains the machine number, the command type, the name of the task to execute. The three fields of the command are spliced into a byte stream in a fixed format.

Next, command messages transfer from the client to the server through the socket. Each time a command request is sent, the socket connection is reopened, so each message transfer is independent. The procedure stated above, is called command sending.

4.2 Task node parsing

XML(Extensible markup language) is a standard language W3C (World Wide Web Con2 association) defined for data transfer and exchange[15]. It is independent of any language and architecture, providing a loose tree structure to represent a semi-structured data suitably. With the advantages of strict definition, clear structure and flexibility, it can be used to describe all kinds of complex information, becoming one of the most widely used formats for data exchange and storage in computer system[16].

Launch files are written in XML described above, and the node list is extracted by retrieval of elements whose tag is <node>. Because of the fact that each element has the name attribute, through which we can obtain the names of all the nodes. The list of all nodes of each task will register into the database and under the task as node list. For understanding more easily, the following example is given. TABLE I is an example of a launch file.

TABLE I. LAUNCH FILE EXAMPLE

```
<launch>
  <node name="listener-1" pkg="rospy_tutorials"
            type="listener" launch-prefix="xterm -e"/>
  <node name="listener-2" pkg="rospy_tutorials"
        type="listener" launch-prefix="xterm -e"/>
  <node name="listener-3" pkg="rospy_tutorials"
        type="listener" launch-prefix="xterm -e"/>
  <node name="talker" pkg="rospy_tutorials
       type="talker" respawn="true" />
  <node pkg="gmapping " type="slam_gmapping"
name=" slam_gmapping ">
      <remap from="scan" to="base_scan"/>
  </node>
    <node pkg="rviz" type="rviz" name="rviz"
respawn="true" />
</launch>
```

After parsing the launch file through the method above, then the parsed node list is: listener-1, listener-2, listener-3, talker, slam_gmapping and rviz and will be stored into the database. When viewing the task's detail running information, the nodes of the node list will be visited one by one and be displayed to operators.

4.3 Node information acquisition

When the task starts, the task information registers into the running status table, including the node list. And then retrieve the node list gaining the name of each node. There exists no same node name in the same ROS network, that is, the name of a node in the same robot is unique. In view of the fact that each node is a process, the node's progress ID is gotten from the ROS Master by submitting the node name to the ROS Master, which is realized by a tool rewritten from the ROS tool---"rosnode". Performed by the shell process, the running information is obtained through the process ID and is stored into the node running information table. The console visit the database to get the running information of all nodes of the running task. In addition, the console makes the robot client update the latest node information into the database through the refresh request, so the console will refresh the running information of the nodes from the database. The node running information acquisition flow chart is as shown in Figure 3.

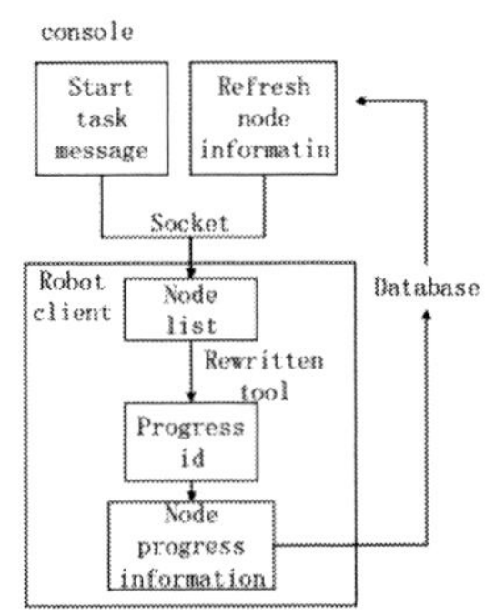

Figure 3. Node information acquisition chart

5 Experimental result

5.1 Experimental Condition Description

Two computers is needed to test the system performance. One acts as the host machine of the console, the other provides ROS to simulate executing robot task. In this section, RVIZ is used to detect the system's performance by the robot's dynamically mapping through path exploration, which is considered as a task. The gmaping package provided by ROS is used to generate the map, and it is a implementation of the famous open source OpenSlam package in the ROS framework. This package provides the Slam for the laser device, and according to the input and attitude data of the laser device builds a grid based 2D map. Due to hardware limitation, we will replay the data collected already to simulate the robot input, and the data will be exported to the SLAM for mapping, finally the map will be displayed in the RVIZ. The following TABLE II is the remote launch file launched.

TABLE II. LAUNCH FILE OF THE TASK FOR TEST

```
<launch>
<node name="listener" pkg="rospy_tutorials"
type="listener" launch-prefix="xterm -e"/>
<node name="talker" pkg="rospy_tutorials"
type="talker" launch-prefix="xterm -e"/>
<node pkg="gmapping " type="slam_gmapping"
name=" slam_gmapping ">
<remap from="scan" to="base_scan"/>
</node>
  <node pkg="rviz" type="rviz" name="rviz"
```

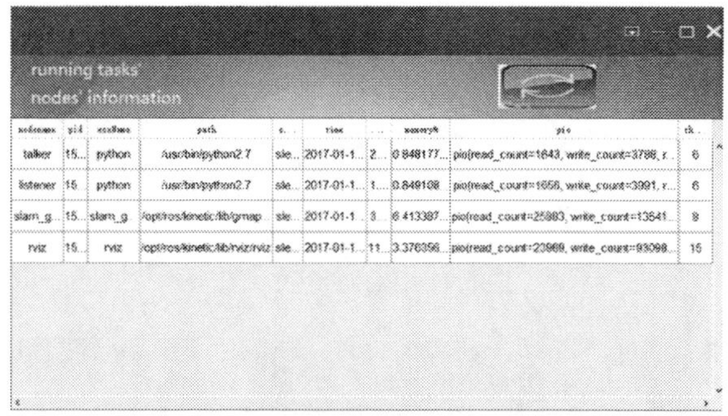

Figure 5. Running node information

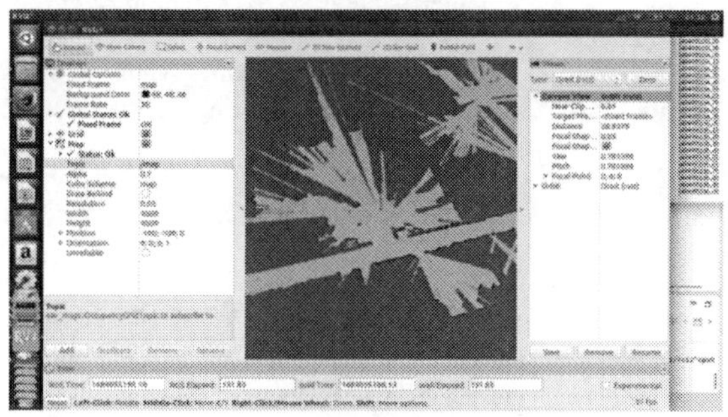

Figure 6. the process of building a 2D map

5.2 Experimental Demonstration

5.2.1 Console

Install the console program on the master control computer, and run the program. The main function window is shown as Figure 4. The functions includes starting tasks, stopping tasks, viewing task running information and task completion status.

Viewing the task running information is as shown in Figure 5. The running information of all the nodes of a special task is viewed, namely monitoring the occupation of system resources. It can be seen from Figure 5 that the list of the nodes running under the task called “testpy” we launched remotely contains talker, listener, slam_gmapping and rviz. Each node’s process ID, program name, execution file directory, process status, running duration, memory occupation rate, etc. are presented.

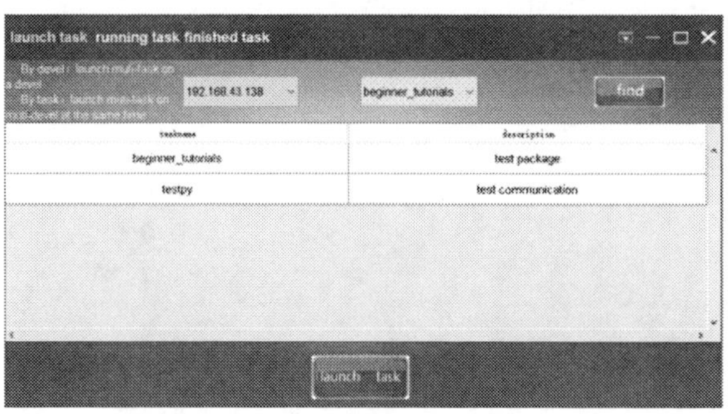

Figure 4. Main function window figure caption

5.2.2 Robot client

After the task is remotely started, the robot client will start listener, talker, slam_gmapping and rviz. These nodes are defined in the same task, so they will start at the same time. Figure 5.3 is the process of building a 2D map.

5.3 System Performance

As is stated above, the experiment has launched two tasks, which are proved to work very well.

The system performance analysis is carried out in terms of the timeliness of the communication and the work load the system has brought to the host computer.

It has been tested and concluded that the socket communication has guaranteed adequate reliability and timeliness. Meanwhile, the map exploring task, which typically occupies much system resources, tells us that the system causes relative work load, but it is within the range of the computer.

Discussion

In this paper, we propose a new definition of the task, which is the combination of the transactions done by multiple nodes in a launch file. We also implement an artificial interaction system for managing tasks and monitoring tasks. The previous study focuses on simple commands controlling remotely the surface behaviors of mobile robots. When controlled and monitored, tasks are materialized to specific nodes, which is of basic need to remotely operating robots to perform complex tasks. These two contributions are of great significance for tele-robotics and robots’ better serving for human.

The running information of each task, such as occupied memory, CPU and other system resources, has not been strictly counted, so the next step work can go around monitoring the running information of a task but not a task's nodes. As a result, something about the remote robot's resource load is clearer.

References

[1] Cai Zixing. Robotics[M]. Beijing: Tsinghua University Press, 2000.

[2] Jing, Zhu. Robotics and control technology [M]. Zhejiang University press, 1991 (in Chinese)

[3] Peng S L, Li S S, Chen L, et al. Scalable base-station model-based multicast in wireless sensor networks[J]. Journal of computer science and technology, 2008, 23(5): 780-791.

[4] Tang Yusong, Liu Jingtai, Lu Guizhang. Analysis of [J]. robot based on robot remote operating system remote network technology, 2000, 22(1): 67-72, 80.

[5] LI Lianzhong, ZHAI Jingmei, HE Haiyang. Research and implementation of robots' virtual simulation and remote control system 2015 [J].

[6] Yong-ming W, Nan-feng X, Hong-li Y I N, et al. A novel control framework for internet based tele-robotics[J]. Journal of Harbin Institute of Technology: English edition, 2008, 15 (5): 602-607

[7] Alvarezaguirre A, Nijmeijer H, Oguchi T, et al. REMOTE CONTROL OF A MOBILE ROBOT SUBJECT TO A COMMUNICATION DELAY[C]. international conference on informatics in control, automation and robotics, 2016: 55-62.

[8] LONG Xiao-Lin, JIANG Jing-Ping. Web- based remote control of multi-robot [J]. Engineering Journal of Wuhan University, 2005, 38(3): 122-125.

[9] Zuo XuanChen, Han Liangliang, Zhuang Jie, et al. Design of space robot human machine interaction system based on ROS.Computer engineering and design, 2015, 36 (12): 3370-3374.

[10] Belzunce A, Li M, Handroos H. Control system design of a teleoperated omnidirectional mobile robot using ROS[C]//Industrial Electronics and Applications (ICIEA), 2016 IEEE 11th Conference on. IEEE, 2016: 1283-1287.

[11] Aude E P L, Carneiro G, Serdeira H, et al. CONTROLAB MUFA: A multi-level fusion architecture for intelligent navigation of a telerobot[C]//Robotics and Automation, 1999. Proceedings. 1999 IEEE International Conference on. IEEE, 1999, 1: 465-472.

[12] Wang H, Wu Q. A formal framework of multi-agent systems with requirement/service cooperative style[J]. Journal of Computer Science and Technology, 2000, 15(2): 106-115.

[13] Chen Hao, Zhang Wei. Based on java socket network TCP/IP programming [J]. CD-ROM software and applications, 2013 (2): 35-37.

[14] Sun Xiaomeng, Wang Zhibin. Multi thread Socket communication based on [J]. TCP Journal of Eastern Liaoning University: Natural Science Edition, 2013, 20 (): 178-182.

[15] Extensible Markup Language(XML)1. 1(Second Edition)[EB/ OL] . [2007207226] .http://www. w3. org/TR/ 2006/REC2xml11220060816/.

[16] Beeri C , Milo T. Schemas for Integration and Translation ofSt ructured and Semi2St ructured Data [M] // Lecture Notes in Computer Science,1999.

DOI: 10.1051/itmconf/20171201024

Accelerating Relevance Vector Machine for Large-Scale Data on Spark

Fang LIU[1*], Hao ZHONG[2], Si-Han LI[2]

[1] *National Engineering Laboratory for Fiber Optic Sensing Technology,Wuhan University of Technology, Wuhan 430070, China*
[2] *School of Computer Science and Technology,Wuhan University of Technology, Wuhan 430070, China*
fangliu@whut.edu.cn, klordy@163.com, lsh751874894@163.com

Abstract: Relevance vector machine (RVM) is a machine learning algorithm based on a sparse Bayesian framework, which performs well when running classification and regression tasks on small-scale datasets. However, RVM also has certain drawbacks which restricts its practical applications such as (1) slow training process, (2) poor performance on training large-scale datasets. In order to solve these problem, we propose Discrete AdaBoost RVM (DAB-RVM) which incorporate ensemble learning in RVM at first. This method performs well with large-scale low-dimensional datasets. However, as the number of features increases, the training time of DAB-RVM increases as well. To avoid this phenomenon, we utilize the sufficient training samples of large-scale datasets and propose all features boosting RVM (AFB-RVM), which modifies the way of obtaining weak classifiers. In our experiments we study the differences between various boosting techniques with RVM, demonstrating the performance of the proposed approaches on Spark. As a result of this paper, two proposed approaches on Spark for different types of large-scale datasets are available.

1 Introduction

With the rapid development of the Internet, data based on Internet statistics and analysis have mostly become large-scale or even massive datasets. Organizing and classifying such large-scale and fast-growing data efficiently and precisely is a difficult problem. When using traditional platforms for data analysis, the majority of classification algorithms run serially. Moreover, operating platforms are largely limited by computer performance, when the amount of data increases, the performance of serial algorithms is sharply reduced.

The Relevance Vector Machine (RVM) [1] is a new supervised learning method. Unlike Support Vector Machine (SVM) [2], RVM is a Bayesian-based probabilistic sparse model. By means of Gaussian prior probabilities affected by hyperparameters, a machine learning task is performed with the Bayesian frame, and autocorrelation determination (ARD) is used to remove uncorrelated points and obtain a sparse model. Because the posterior distribution of most parameters tends toward zero during iterative learning, the training samples corresponding to non-zero parameters are not related to the decision domain samples and represent only the prototype samples in the training data. Such samples are called relevance vector, which embody the core features of the data. The biggest advantage of RVM is that they greatly reduce the computation of kernel functions, and the choice of kernel function is no longer limited by Mercer's condition. Based on the above advantages, RVM has obtained good performance in fields such as image recognition [3] and speech recognition [4].

The time complexity of RVM algorithm is $O(n^3)$ and its space complexity is $O(n^2)$. Therefore, when the number of samples that must be processed increases, the time and resources required for RVM training increase dramatically, resulting in a serious decrease in the algorithm's efficiency. In order to solve this problem, Tipping and Faul [5] proposed a fast marginal likelihood maximization method that refreshes one coefficient at a time. However, this method can get stuck in a suboptimal solution. Seeger and Ribeiro [6] applied RVM to large-scale text sets using ensemble, boosting and incremental methods, which integrates ensemble learning with RVM. This strategy performs well in accelerating the training procedure. Yang et al. [7] proposed recursive Cholesky decomposition for RVM on GPUs. This strategy was proved to be much faster, but still could not run on large-scale datasets. DIMITRIS and ARISTIDIS [8] proposed a modified RVM algorithm based on expectation maximization for image recognition. This method effectively improved the time efficiency of RVM for large-scale image recognition. However, this method only considers the time efficiency of RVM for large amounts of data, and did not solve the problem of resource consumption. Chao Dong and Lianfang Tian [9] used the idea proposed by Seeger and Ribeiro to apply RVM to a large amount of data in the Beowulf Cluster, which allows the algorithm to successfully handle large image recognition datasets in a cluster environment; however, the algorithm is difficult to implement and the efficiency of the cluster when running such tasks was poor.

In recent years, distributed technology has been developing rapidly, and many distributed frameworks have emerged. The most widely used distributed frameworks include Storm, Hadoop and Spark. Using these distributed frameworks, the efficiency of algorithms can be improved effectively. For processing iterative computing, traditional MapReduce has the advantages of automatic fault tolerance, balanced load and scalability; its acyclic data flow model, however, causes a large number of disk IO operations, which greatly limits its performance. Compared with MapReduce, Spark runs iterative calculation tasks based on memory. It loads the data in memory using Resilient Distributed Dataset [10], making them easy to reuse and accelerating iterative computation dramatically. Considering the performance of Spark in memory iteration, we choose to implement the algorithm on the Spark platform.

The content of this paper revolves around the fundamental principles of RVM and ensemble learning [11]. We incorporate the Discrete AdaBoost and the modified AdaBoost in RVM and obtain two algorithms for large-scale datasets. Next section briefly reviews the basic process of RVM to lay the foundations of the proposed approaches. Section III introduces the basic concept of the AdaBoost algorithm, as well as the modification and combination of the AdaBoost algorithm with RVM algorithm on the Spark platform. Section IV mainly describes the detailed implementation of the experiments on the Spark platform and the analysis of relevant experimental results.

2 Relevance Vector Machine

RVM is a machine learning algorithm based on Bayesian theory. It uses a maximum likelihood function to obtain hyperparameters, and then assigns zero to the weights according to the hyperparameters to guarantee the sparsity of the algorithm. Given a sample set $(x_{i1},...,x_{iM},y_i), i=1,2,...,N$, where $X=(x_{i1},...,x_{iM})$ is the feature vector of the sample and $y_i \in Y=\{-1,+1\}$ is the class label of each sample, the model of RVM can be represented as follows:

$$y(x)=\sum_{n=1}^{N} w_n K(x,x_n)+w_0 \tag{1}$$

where $K(\cdot,\cdot)$ is the kernel function and w_n represents the weight of all the samples. Additionally, RVM uses a Bernoulli distribution to construct the probability density function as:

$$p(t_i \mid x)=N(t_i \mid y(x_i;w),\sigma^2) \tag{2}$$

where the expected value is $y(x_i;w)$ and variance is σ^2.

In order to avoid over-fitting, RVM defines a Gauss prior probability distribution as below:

$$p(w \mid \alpha)=\prod_{i=0}^{N} N(w_i \mid 0,\alpha_i^{-1}) \tag{3}$$

where α is a ($N+1$)-dimensional hyperparameter used to constrain the parameter. After many iterations, most of the hyperparameters tend toward infinity, leading the corresponding weights to zero which ensures the sparsity of the final model.

When executing a classification task, the posterior probability of the weights can not be calculated. However, Laplacian theory can be used to approximate the calculation: for the current fixed α, find the maximum possible weight w_{MP}. Use the second-order Newton method in (4) to get w_{MP}.

$$\log\{p(t \mid w)p(w \mid \alpha)\}=\sum_{n=1}^{N}[t_n \log y_n+(1-t_n)\log(1-y_n)]-\frac{1}{2}w^T Aw \tag{4}$$

where $y_n=\sigma\{y(x_n;w)\}$ and $A=diag(\alpha_0,\alpha_1,...,\alpha_N)$.

Using the Laplacian method, the log posterior probability is quadratically approximated. Then, taking two derivatives on (4) results in the following:

$$\nabla_w \nabla_w \log p(w \mid t,\alpha)\mid_{w_{MP}}=-(\Phi^T / B\Phi+A) \tag{5}$$

where $\Phi=[\varphi(x_1),\varphi(x_2),..., \varphi(x_N)]^T$ and $B=diag(\beta_1,\beta_2,...,\beta_n)$. Use (5) to obtain the covariance matrix Σ. Next, update the hyperparameter α through Σ and w_{MP}. The updated hyperparameter can thus be represented as:

$$\alpha^{new}=\gamma_i / w_{MP}^2 \tag{6}$$

where $\gamma_i=1-\alpha_i\Sigma_{ii}$ and Σ_{ii} is the i-th diagonal element of the matrix represented in (7).

$$\Sigma=(\Phi^T B\Phi+A)^{-1} \tag{7}$$

The model function defined by the relevance vector is a high-dimensional hyperplane, which can approximate the test samples on both sides of the plane. Thus, the classification results are obtained according to the different planes..

3 Rvm Expansion Methods On Spark

3.1 Spark platform

Spark is an open-source parallel computing framework developed by the UC Berkeley AMP Lab based on MapReduce [12]. Fig. 1 shows the general Spark work-flow used in this paper. This framework proposes an abstract flexible distributed dataset called RDD (Resilient

Distributed Dataset). The researchers manipulate the data by calling RDD's Transformation and Action operations. These operations are performed on the data based on the partition established when the RDD was defined. Spark shows extraordinary effectiveness for machine learning tasks on large-scale data. Fig. 2 shows the basic running logic diagram of an RDD in Spark. The whole procedure is a directed acyclic graph. Spark divides the process into stages according to the different dependencies between RDDs. Each stage contains a series of function operations, the entire process is triggered by the RDD Action function.

3.2 Basic Principles of the AdaBoost RVM

Adaboost is an ensemble learning algorithm based on probably approximately correct(PAC) [13] learning theory.

Common AdaBoost algorithms include Discret AdaBoost, Real AdaBoost and Gentle AdaBoost. All of these algorithms have achieved great performance in fields including face detection [14] and network security [15].

The core idea of the algorithm is to train different (weak) classifiers on the training set, and then combine these weak classifiers to form a strong final classifier. The algorithm obtains the confidence of each classifier and revises the weight of each sample according to the classification of each sample and the accuracy of the overall classification. Then, the revised weights are used for the next classifier for testing. In the end, the resulting weak classifiers are merged into the final decision classifier.

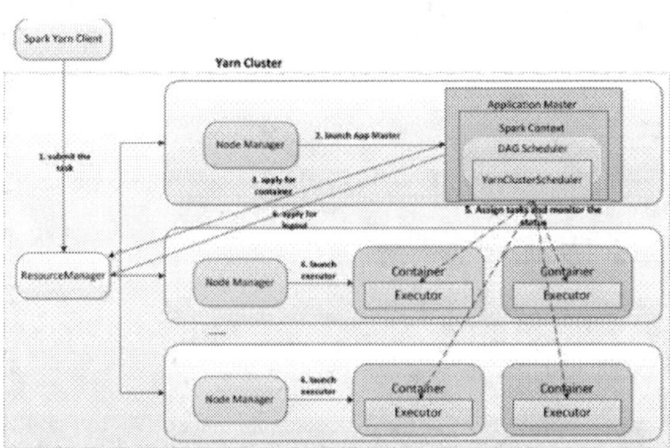

Fig. 1. Flowchart of Spark on Yarn

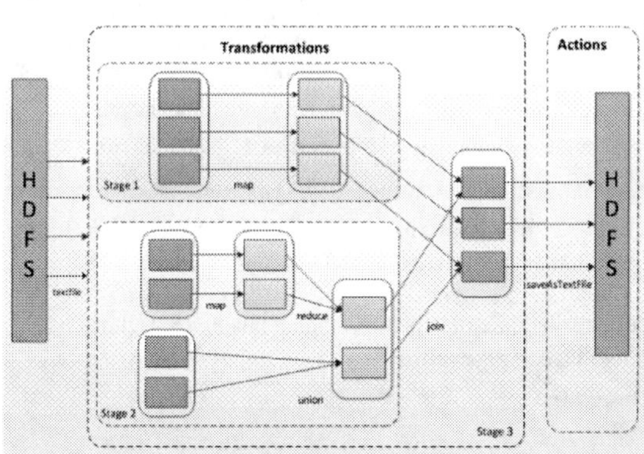

Fig. 2. Running logic of RDD

In this study, algorithms are implemented on Spark. Whereas samples are randomly distributed on Spark, which may lead to a partial data imbalance in some blocks, on this occasion, the final classifier may also be influenced. To overcome this problem, the training samples in each block are judged before training. If the threshold is exceeded, the training data of this block are regarded as an imbalance dataset. For imbalanced dataset, the training data are modified by creating synthetic examples from the minority class using the SMOTE [16] algorithm.

Giving the training dataset $(x_{i1},...,x_{iM},y_i), i=1,2,...,N$, where $y_i \in Y=\{-1,+1\}$ represents the class label of each sample, and the weight of each sample is initialized as $D_1(x_i)=1/N, i=1,2,...,N$. For $t=1,2,...,T$, where T represents the number of weak classifiers, a weak classifier and the corresponding weighted error ε_t are obtained. Then, calculate the confidence coefficient α_t using ε_t. Meanwhile, the weight $D_{t+1}(x_i)$ of each sample is updated for the next iteration at last.

Finally, through combining all the weak classifiers and the related confidence coefficients, the final classifier is :

$$H_{final}(x) = sign(\sum_{t=1}^{T}\alpha_t h_t(x)) \tag{8}$$

In the above process, different AdaBoost algorithms are obtained by combining different weak classifier acquisition and sample weight update methods in each iteration process. This paper integrates RVM with the AdaBoost algorithm and modified AdaBoost algorithm, and then takes full advantage of the Spark platform to implement these algorithms. Under these circumstances, the algorithms perform well on large-scale datasets. Fig. 3 shows the basic process of the algorithm.

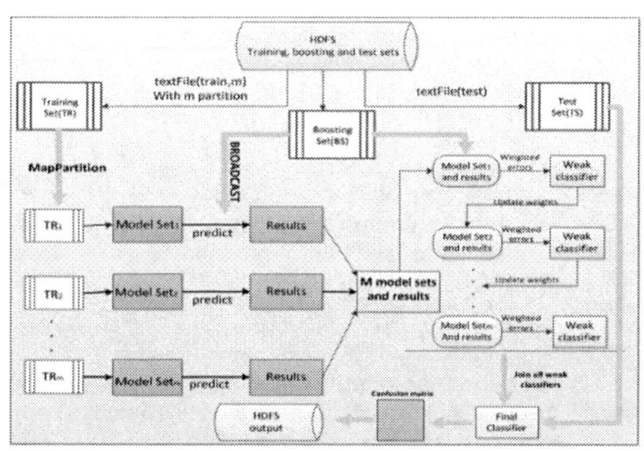

Fig. 3. Flowchart of the proposed DAB-RVM

3.3Discrete AdaBoost RVM

This section describes the combination of the Discrete AdaBoost and RVM algorithms on Spark. First, the whole dataset are divided into three parts as training, boosting and test sets. Afterward, the training set are divided into blocks and operate using RDD. RangePartitioner(#iter).

Meanwhile, the boosting set are shared with all the slaves by broadcast for boosting. In addition, modify the imbalanced dataset in each slave through the SMOTE algorithm before training weak classifiers. Then, train a weak classifier for each feature based on the data from each block and obtain the classification result of the boosting set for each weak classifier. Next, the weight of each sample is initialized and, for all weak classifiers obtained from the same block, calculate the weighted error as (9) and select the weak classifier with the smallest weighted error.

$$err_s = \sum_{k:H_c(x_k)\neq y_k} w_i(k) \tag{9}$$

Afterwards, calculate the confidence coefficient of each classifier based on the weighted error as (10) and update the weight as (11).

$$\alpha_s = \frac{1}{2}\log(\frac{1-err_s}{err_s}) \tag{10}$$

$$w_{s+1}(i) = w_s(i)\exp(-\alpha_s y_i H_s(x_i)) \tag{11}$$

Finally, the final classifier can be represented as (12).

$$G_{final}(x) = sign(\sum_{s=0}^{T-1}\alpha_s H_s(x)) \tag{12}$$

3.4All Features Boosting RVM

The proposed algorithm described above splits the data into different blocks and distributes it into different datanodes; then, for each block in a datanode, trains a weak classifier on each feature of the samples on the block. This process needs to train $m \times n$ models (m represents the number of features of each sample and n represents the number of blocks that training set has been split into). So, when dealing with a high-dimensional large-scale dataset, the training process may take too much time.

As the number of the blocks which the training data is split into becomes large, and RVM belongs to a not so weak classifier, the weak classifier can be trained using all the features of the samples, which means that each block gets a single weak classifier. After training, divide all the classifiers into T groups and iterate over all groups. At each iteration, do a weighted regression based on least-squares and obtain a classifier in each group with the smallest weighted error. Finally, T classifiers are integrated into the final classifier, shown as (12).

In addition, as the output of Discrete AdaBoost can only be +1 or -1, which may be slightly rough. Thus, we adopt the principle of Gentle AdaBoost to select the weak classifiers. As for the Gentle AdaBoost, the output of the weak classifier are:

$$H(x) = P_w(y=1\,|\,x) - P_w(y=-1\,|\,x) \tag{13}$$

Meanwhile, the calculation of weighted error and weighted updating are also changed as shown in (14) and (15).

$$\varepsilon_s = \sum_{i=1}^{N}\omega_i[H_s(x_i) - y_i]^2 \tag{14}$$

$$\omega_{s+1}(i) = w_s(i)\exp(-y_i H_s(x_i)) \tag{15}$$

AFB-RVM, as shown in Algorithm 1, reduces the number of weak classifiers that need to train, especially on high-dimensional large-scale datasets. Thus, the time efficiency of this method increases significantly.

Algorithm 1. AFB-RVM

Input:

1: Total N samples: $<(x_{11},...,x_{1m},y_1),...,(x_{N1},...,x_{Nm},y_N)>$, where $y_i \in \{-1,+1\}$.
2: Split the N training examples into TR, BS and TS.
3: Split the training data TR into several blocks and distribute to different slaves.
4: Modify the data of each block with K synthetic examples from the minority class using SMOTE algorithm.
5: Train a single weak RVM classifier based on all the features of each block.
6: Integer T specifying the number of required weak RVM classifiers and BS as the boosting examples.
7: Divide all the weak classifiers into T groups.
8: Initialize $w_1^i = 1/D_{Boost}$, where D_{Boost} represent the size of D_2.
9: **for** c=0,2,…,T-1 **do**
10: Fit the regression function $H_c(x)$ by weighted least-squares of y_i to x_i with w_i
11: Update $G_{final}(x) \leftarrow G_{final}(x) + H_c(x)$
12: Update the weight based on (15) and renormalize.
13: **end for**
14: **Output**: the final hypothesis as (12)

4 Experimental Results And Analysis

To verify the feasibility of the proposed algorithms, this section compares the performance of the above algorithms and the serial RVM algorithm on the UCI dataset (Image Segmentation) and artificial datasets. Image Segmentation (IS) is an image segmentation dataset with 2310 samples divided into seven categories (GRASS, PATH, WINDOW, CLEAR, FOLIAGE, SKY, and BRICKFACE). Each sample has 19 attribute values and one class label.

Because the time complexity of RVM is $O(n^3)$ and the space complexity is $O(n^2)$, when the number of samples is too large, the efficiency of RVM drops sharply. Therefore, RVM is executed on Image Segmentation and the smaller simulated datasets to compare with the three algorithms described above. For large-scale datasets, the other three algorithms in this paper are executed for comparative analysis.

 DOI: 10.1051/itmconf/20171201024

4.1 Experimental Environment

All experiments are executed on a cluster composed of four nodes: the master node (namenode) and four computing nodes (datanode).All the nodes are dual-core with 4G memory.

The specific details of the softwares used and their configurations are below:

· Distributed platform: Hadoop 2.5.2 and Spark 1.5.1

· Development language: Scala 2.10.4 and JDK 1.7.0_51

· Operating System: Cent OS 6.5

4.2 Performance Measures

To evaluate a binary decision task, a contingency matrix representing the possible classification results, as shown in Table 1, is defined.

Metrics defined on Table 2 are generated from this contingency matrix. These metrics on Table 2 are the main methods to evaluate a classification model. Precision reflects the proportion of true positive samples in the positive cases determined by the classifier, and recall reflects the proportion of positive cases that are correctly determined. The ideal situation is that both precision and recall are close to 1. However, in real applications, precision and recall are mutually influential and contradictory. Therefore, to evaluate the model, F1 and Accuracy are chosen to evaluate the model instead of precision or recall.

Table 1. contingency matrix for classification.

	Positive class	Negative class
Assigned Positive	TP	FP
Assigned Negative	FN	TN

TABLE 2. PARAMETERS from the contingency matrix

Measure	Formula
Accuracy	$\frac{TP+TN}{TP+FP+TN+FN}$
Precision (P)	$\frac{TP}{TP+FP}$
Recall (R)	$\frac{TP}{TP+FN}$
F1-measure (F1)	$\frac{2\times P\times R}{P+R}$

4.3 Result on Image Segmentation

In this section, three algorithms are analyzed by comparing the performance of RVM, DAB-RVM, and AFB-RVM on IS. The experimental data is split in the ratio 6:1:3 corresponding to the training, boosting and test datasets, respectively.

For the proposed algorithms, accounting for the randomness of each partition, the average F1 and Accuracy of ten experiments are selected for evaluation. Table 3 shows the average F1 and Accuracy of these algorithms on IS. Additionally, Fig. 4 shows the quotient of training time between RVM and the proposed algorithms on Image Segmentation (r represents the proportion of training samples extracted from IS).

TABLE 3. F1 for DAB-RVM and AFB-RVM on is

	F1			Accuracy		
	DAB-RVM	**AFB-RVM**	**RVM**	**DAB-RVM**	**AFB-RVM**	**RVM**
GRASS	97.0%	92.2%	95.0%	94.5%	94.2%	96.4%
PATH	92.3%	91.4%	92.9%	94.9%	93.0%	94.1%
WINDOW	79.2%	77.9%	82.3%	81.0%	81.0%	85.9%
CEMENT	69.6%	77.1%	78.8%	81.0%	81.2%	86.9%
FOLIAGE	68.8%	64.9%	79.9%	86.5%	86.1%	90.2%
SKY	92.3%	95.8%	96.8%	87.8%	87.5%	96.5%
BRICKFACE	90.2%	96.3%	97.5%	91.9%	92.3%	98.7%
Average	84.2%	85.1%	89.0%	88.2%	87.9%	92.7%

Table 3 show that F1 value of RVM is 3-4% higher than that of DAB-RVM and AFB-RVM, and its classification accuracy is higher by 2-4%. However, Fig. 4 shows that AFB-RVM has a remarkable improvement in time efficiency.

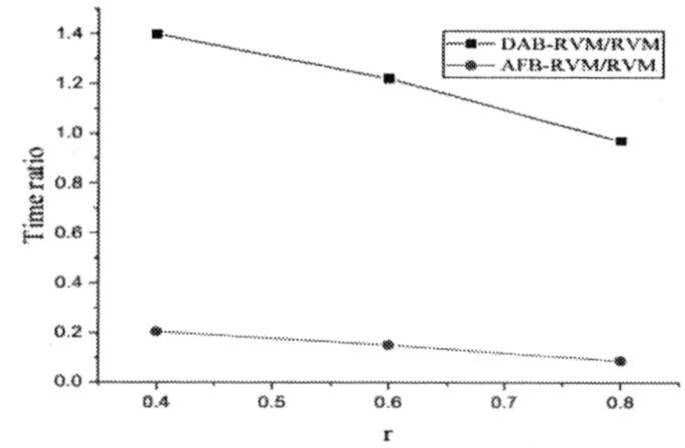

Fig.4 Quotient of training time between GAB-RVM, AFB-RVM and RVM

4.4 Result on Simulated Datasets

To test the performance of the proposed algorithms for different numbers of samples, we choose different scales of simulation data. The two selected simulation datasets contain 10,000 and 1,000,000 samples (referred to as SSD and SLD).

1) *Experiment using SSD*

The overall performance of RVM, DAB-RVM and AFB-RVM on these simulated datasets is further tested with SSD (ratio 6:1:3 for training, boosting and testing). Table 4 shows the minimum, maximum and mean values of F1 and Accuracy for ten experimental results of the RVM, DAB-RVM and AFB-RVM algorithms with SSD1.

TABLE 4. F1 values for baseline RVM, DAB-RVM and AFB-RVM with SSD during ten experiments

	F1			ACCURACY		
	DAB-RVM	AFB-RVM	RVM	DAB-RVM	AFB-RVM	RVM
Min	84.86 %	89.39 %	90.80 %	86.32 %	87.42 %	90.72 %
Max	91.42 %	90.72 %	92.33 %	92.14 %	93.10 %	94.30 %
Average	88.89 %	90.08 %	91.46 %	89.07 %	90.16 %	91.69 %

It can be concluded from Table 4 that when the number of samples reaches 10,000, the disparity between DAB-RVM, AFB-RVM and baseline RVM is much smaller than on IS.

2) Experiment on SLD

The performance of these algorithms has been verified through experiments on SSD. Moreover, to determine the types of datasets to which these algorithms apply. Several copies of SLD in different dimensions are generated and used to verify the related algorithms. Additionally, these training sets revolved are all too large for RVM, so only DAB-RVM and AFB-RVM are involved in this experiment.

First, obtain a ten-dimensional SLD with class labels of +1 and -1. Table 5 shows the average F1 and Accuracy values of the DAB-RVM, and AFB-RVM results obtained by selecting different ratios of data as training data under this dataset.

TABLE 5. Average values of F1 on ten-dimensional SLD of different ratios

Percentage of training data	DAB-RVM	AFB-RVM	DAB-RVM	AFB-RVM
20%	82.21%	83.15%	84.52%	86.01%
40%	86.91%	88.34%	87.11%	89.44%
60%	87.21%	90.15%	89.12%	90.18%
80%	89.05%	91.72%	89.94%	91.05%

Because DAB-RVM and AFB-RVM obtain their weak classifiers in different ways, The data of different dimensions are used to verify the time performance of the algorithms. Fig. 5 shows the ratios of training time of DAB-RVM to AFB-RVM.

4.5 Results Analysis

From the results in Table 3, it can be concluded that the Accuracy and F1 values of RVM are 2-4% and 3-4% higher than those of DAB-RVM and AFB-RVM. However, the data in Fig. 4 show that AFB-RVM have reduced the training time greatly. Taking all this into consideration, when dealing with small datasets, it is still better to use RVM.

Moreover, from the results in Table 4, when the training data becomes larger, the Accuracy and F1 values of RVM are only 1-2% and 1.5-2.5% higher, respectively, than those of DAB-RVM and AFB-RVM. Compared with the results of Image Segmentation, the disparity with RVM gets smaller. Finally, analyzing the results in Table 5, we find that DAB-RVM and AFB-RVM perform very well with large-scale datasets, especially when the percentage of training data reaches 60%. Furthermore, from the data in Fig. 5, it is easy to find that, when the dimension of the sample is higher, the running efficiency of AFB-RVM is more obvious.

From the analyses above, it can be concluded that DAB-RVM is more suitable for large-scale datasets with few features, while AFB-RVM is more suitable for large-scale datasets with many features.

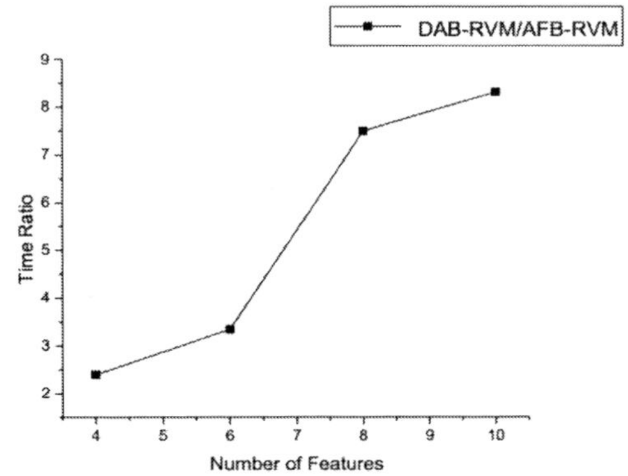

Fig. 5. Training time ratios of DAB-RVM to AFB-RVM

5 Conclusion And Future Work

In this paper, we combine Discrete AdaBoost and Gentle AdaBoost with RVM to classify large-scale datasets on a distributed platform. Then, to reduce the training time for high-dimensional large-scale datasets, we propose the AFB-RVM, which alters the method of Gentle AdaBoost for obtaining weak classifiers and incorporates it into RVM. Experimental results on Spark for image segmentation and simulated datasets demonstrated that the proposed algorithms perform well when dealing with large-scale dataset and have achieved great improvements in time efficiency. Future improvements could be carried on by extending the algorithms to multiclass classification and optimizing the output of the weak classifiers.

Acknowledgment

This work was supported by the National Natural Science Foundation of China (No. 61402345) and the Fundamental Research Funds for the Central Universities (WUT: 2017 IVB072).

References

[1]. Tipping, Michael E. "Sparse bayesian learning and the relevance vector machine." Journal of Machine Learning Research 1.3(2001):211-244.
[2]. Vapnik, Vladimir N. The Nature of Statistical Learning Theory. The nature of statistical learning theory /. Springer, 2000:1564-1564.

[3]. Gupta, Rishabh, K. U. R. Laghari, and T. H. Falk. "Relevance vector classifier decision fusion and EEG graph-theoretic features for automatic affective state characterization." Neurocomputing 174(2015):875-884.

[4]. Zhou, Yan, et al. "Deception detecting from speech signal using relevance vector machine and non-linear dynamics features."Neurocomputing 151(2015):1042-1052.

[5]. Tipping, Michael E, and A. C. Faul. "Fast Marginal Likelihood Maximisation for Sparse Bayesian Models." International Workshop on Artificial Intelligence and Statistics 2003.

[6]. Silva, C, and B. Ribeiro. "Towards expanding relevance vector machines to large scale datasets. " International Journal of Neural Systems18.1(2008):45-58.

[7]. Yang, Depeng, et al. "High Performance Relevance Vector Machine on GPUs." Symposium on Application Accelerators in High PERFORMANCE Computing 2010.

[8]. DIMITRIS TZIKAS, ARISTIDIS LIKAS, and NIKOLAS GALATSANOS. "LARGE SCALE MULTIKERNEL RELEVANCE VECTOR MACHINE FOR OBJECT DETECTION." International Journal of Artificial Intelligence Tools 16.6(2011):967-979.

[9]. Dong, et al. "Accelerating Relevance-Vector-Machine-Based Classification of Hyperspectral Image with Parallel Computing."Mathematical Problems in Engineering 2012.1024-123X(2012):865-883.

[10]. Zaharia, Matei, et al. "Spark: Cluster Computing with Working Sets." (2010):10-10.

[11]. Friedman, Jerome, T. Hastie, and R. Tibshirani. "Additive logistic regression: a statistical view of boosting." Annals of Statistics 28.2(2000):págs. 374-376.

[12]. Dean, Jeffrey, and S. Ghemawat. "MapReduce: Simplified Data Processing on Large Clusters. " Conference on Symposium on Opearting Systems Design & Implementation 2004:107-113.

[13]. Valiant, L. G. "A theory of the learnable." Communications of the Acm27.11(1984):1134-1142.

[14]. P. Ithaya Rani, and K. Muneeswaran. "Facial Emotion Recognition Based on Eye and Mouth Regions." International Journal of Pattern Recognition & Artificial Intelligence 30.07(2016).

[15]. Zhuang, Weiwei, Q. Jiang, and T. Xiong. "An Intelligent Anti-phishing Strategy Model for Phishing Website Detection." International Conference on Distributed Computing Systems Workshops IEEE Computer Society, 2012:51-56.

[16]. Chawla, Nitesh V., et al. "SMOTE: synthetic minority over-sampling technique." Journal of Artificial Intelligence Research 16.1(2002):321-357.

Design and Implementation of Behavior Recognition System Based on Convolutional Neural Network

Bo YU

School of Software Engineering, Beijing University of Technology, Beijing, China
e-mail: yuubbo@126.com

Abstract—We build a set of human behavior recognition system based on the convolution neural network constructed for the specific human behavior in public places. Firstly, video of human behavior data set will be segmented into images, then we process the images by the method of background subtraction to extract moving foreground characters of body. Secondly, the training data sets are trained into the designed convolution neural network, and the depth learning network is constructed by stochastic gradient descent. Finally, the various behaviors of samples are classified and identified with the obtained network model, and the recognition results are compared with the current mainstream methods. The result show that the convolution neural network can study human behavior model automatically and identify human's behaviors without any manually annotated trainings.

1 Introduction

In recent years, with the rapid development of electronic information science and technology and video signal collection technology, human behavior recognition based on computer vision [1] has attracted more and more attention based on. Behavior recognition in computer vision to achieve detection, tracking, analysis and recognition of human actions [2] in video image based on is the key technology in the field of intelligent control and pattern recognition. Intelligent monitoring is aimed at using the computer outside image information into a digital signal, and then through a series of calculation instead of the human brain processing and understanding of visual information, so as to realize the intelligent analysis and automatic recognition of monitoring picture.

At present, researchers at home and abroad for the analysis and recognition of human behavior in video surveillance has done a lot of work. The identification methods can be divided into two categories: Based on behavior recognition method based on model matching and behavior recognition method of state space. Behavior recognition method based on model matching (Template Matching [3,4]) refers to the first to establish a good image template sequence to represent the static target behavior of the human body, then it will match the target template video image sequence detection in the template and, if the match succeeds the behavior is the behavior characteristics, identification or template it is determined, this kind of behavior is not. Recognition method based on state space (State Space Approaches) [5,6] defines specific posture state, then the state is connected by the way of probability. The action sequence of test set can be seen as the traversal process of current static posture, and then through the joint probability calculation during operation in order to achieve the action of the action scores. Deep learning is a research direction in recent years very popular, convolutional neural network(CNN)[7] as the representative of deep learning network improves the traditional neural network recognition effect. And the convolutional network implements a recognition method of end to end, it does not need to manually design features, images can be directly used as the input data network, avoid data reconstruction and feature extraction of the complex process in the traditional recognition algorithm.

Deep learning has attracted many researchers to study it, and have in some fields of computer vision has been successful. Especially in recent years, deep learning algorithms have been successfully applied in various fields such as speech recognition, image recognition, and gradually extended to research on behavior recognition with time series. In this paper, a method based on convolution neural network is proposed. The unsupervised learning of the network is realized through the human behavior data set, and the deep learning network model is established. The experimental results show that the network can identify various behavior effectively, compared with other recognition rate has improved.

2 The Framework of Behavior Recognition System

Human behavior recognition is mainly divided into two processes: the identification and understanding of human behavior feature extraction and motion, as shown below. Feature extraction is to extract the key features of this information in the data in the video data or image data, the feature information is the key task of recognition, feature extraction in fact directly affects the final recognition result.

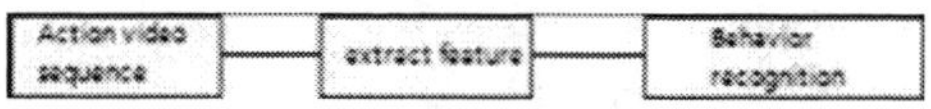

Figure 1 the main work of human behavior recognition

This algorithm is mainly composed of three parts, respectively, for video pretreatment, model training and behavior recognition part. In the video preprocessing part, firstly the original behavior of video preprocessing, using block updating background subtraction method to achieve target detection, two value image motion information is extracted, then the image input channel convolutional neural network, through the iterative training parameters of the network, to construct a model for convolution Behavior Recognition finally, you can use this network to identify human behavior, the flow chart of the system is shown in figure 2.

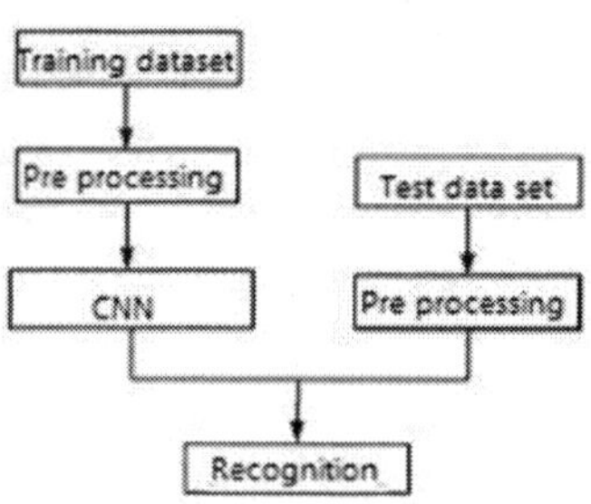

Fig. 2 flow chart of behavior recognition system

3 Behavioral Target Detection

Behavior of target detection is appropriate to process the image information of the human body contains behavior, remove the static background, detect the target motion information and behavior to carry, reliable data is provided for the subsequent recognition stage of the visual system. The behavior of target detection principle is as far as possible to retain the characteristic information of this behavior, while eliminating the redundancy information of the target, in the foundation of many application background detection is a very important step. This paper uses the Gauss mixture model based background subtraction in the background of the moving target detection. The principle is very simple, the basic process shown in figure 3.

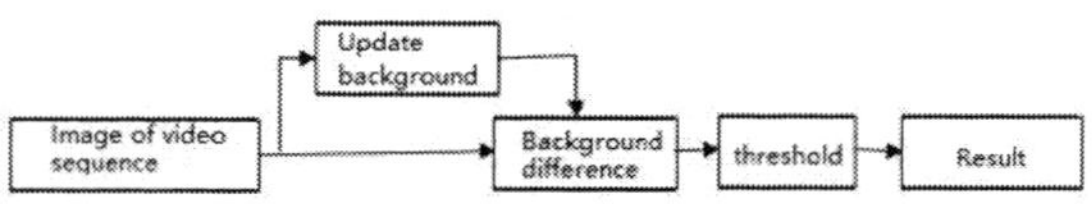

Figure 3 behavior target detection process

First, using the formula (2-1) f_{bk} image background image f_k and calculate the current frame difference, then the difference image D_k filtering processing, can extract moving objects.

$$D_k(x,y) = |f_k(x,y) - f_{bk}(x,y)| \qquad (2\text{-}1)$$

Among them, $f_k(x,y)$ for the current frame image, $f_{bk}(x,y)$ as the background image, $D_k(x,y)$ for the difference image.

$$R_k(x,y) = \begin{cases} 1 \; D_k(x,y) > T \\ 0 \; D_k(x,y) \le T \end{cases} \qquad (2\text{-}2)$$

Among them, the threshold value of the image two is set to T, and the target area in the image is set to 255. The background subtraction method to the current frame and background image subtraction, the accuracy of motion target extraction is accurate or not will directly affect the final results. So if there is no background model update, it will lead to large error detection, such as light change accumulated to a certain time will be beyond the range of motion detection, the background part may be mistakenly classified as foreground moving objects.

When the background initialization is complete, need to adaptively update the parameters of the background image, to obtain an updated background estimation image for the $B_t = [\mu_t, \sigma_t^2]$ the use of sigma, type (2-3) update parameters.

$$\begin{cases} \mu_t = (1-\alpha)\mu_{t-1} + \alpha \times f_t \\ \alpha_t^2 = (1-\alpha)\sigma_{t-1}^2 + \alpha(f_t - \mu_t) \\ \alpha = K\frac{1}{\sqrt{2\pi\delta}}e^{-\frac{(\mu_{t-1}-f_t)^2}{2}} \end{cases} \qquad (2\text{-}3)$$

Alpha is the learning rate, indicating the background update rate, between 0 and 1. The following figure shows the KTH data set by the algorithm in different scenarios under the behavior of foreground extraction results.

Fig. 4 foreground extraction

DOI: 10.1051/itmconf/20171201025

4 Convolutional Neural Network

For deep learning, suppose we have a training sample set (x^i, y^i), then the neural network can provide a kind of complex nonlinear model of $h_{W,b}(x)$, it has the parameters W, b as the weight parameters of the neural network, so as to fit the data in the dataset. The neural network consists of neurons, as shown in figure 5.

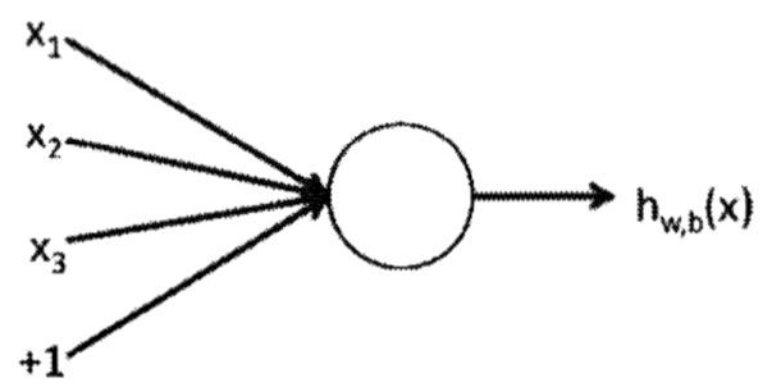

Fig. 5 neurons in neural networks

This neuron is a $\{x_1, x_2, x_3\}$ and intercept operation unit B as the input value, the output is

$$h_{W,b}(x) = f(W^T x) = f(\sum_{i=1}^{3} W_i x_i + b) \quad (3\text{-}1)$$

Among them, the function f is called the activation function. In this paper, we use the ReLU function as the activation function.

The neural network is many neurons together before a neuron output layer is after a neuron's input, as shown in figure 6.

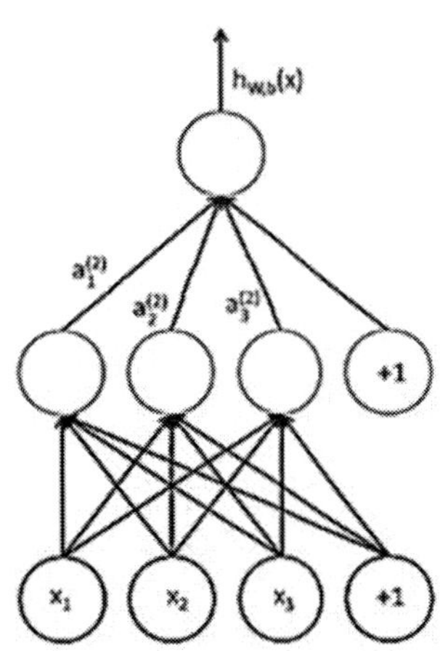

Fig. 6 neural network

The use of the circle to represent the nodes of the network, labeled "+1" node called the bias node. The left side of the neural network is the input layer, the right side of the output layer, the middle layer is called the hidden layer. It can be seen that there are 3 input units, 3 hidden units and 1 output units.

4.1convolution layer

The process of convolution layer processing is a layer of the image and the convolution kernel convolution, convolution processing is a basic operation of image processing. Related formulas are as follows:

$$y_{mn} = f\left(\sum_{j=0}^{J-1}\sum_{i=0}^{I-1} x_{m+i,n+j} w_{ij} + b\right),$$

$$(0 \le m < M, 0 \le n < N) \quad (3\text{-}2)$$

Among them, X is a layer of two-dimensional data of the input image, w convolution kernel, B is a layer of bias, Y output, ReLU activation function. In the high dimensional input processing like images, each neuron is only partial region and input data connection, and use parameters in roll layer sharing is to control the amount of parameters.

4.2 sampling layer

The feature map sampling layer will be a layer of the sampling operation, reduce space dimension data layer, reduce the number of network parameters, making the computing resources cost less, and can effectively prevent over fitting. In this paper, the maximum sampling is used:

$$y_{mn} = \frac{1}{S_1 S_2}\left(\sum_{i=0}^{S_1-1}\sum_{j=0}^{S_2-1} x_{m*S_1+i,n*S_2+j}\right)$$

(3-3)

The sample size (S_1, S_2) is two-dimensional vector, x means input, y means output.

4.3 activation function

The input of each activation function is a number, and then a fixed mathematical operation is performed. The activation function used in the ReLU function in this paper, the function formula is f (x) =max (0, x), as shown in figure 7.

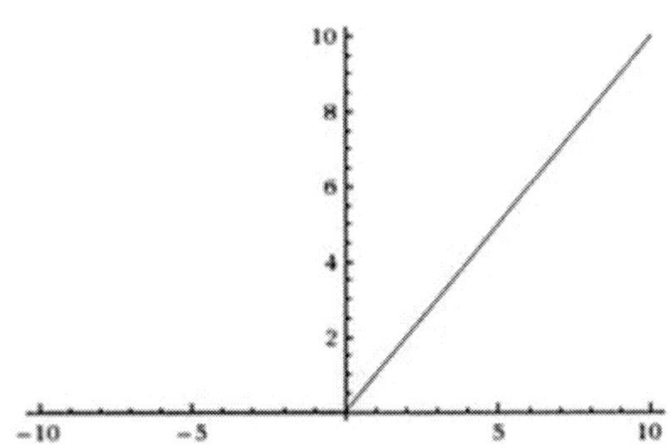

Fig.7 ReLU activation function

5 Experimental Process and Result Analysis

The selection of training samples from the KTH database, the database provides 6 kinds of behavior video, including normal walking, jogging, running, boxing, waving, clapping hands waving, each class has 25 people to complete the action, and each divided into four scenes, respectively in indoor and outdoor.

Convolutional network structure in this paper, a total of seven layers, including five volumes of sediments from three sampling layer, a connecting layer and an output layer. First, the input video data in accordance with the method of section second of the processed image, then a convolution of adjacent four successive images, the second layer is the largest under sampling layer, layer convolution kernel after deconvolution on a layer of feature map through the 3 volume layer finally fully connected layer processing using softmax regression model classification. Structure as shown in figure 8.

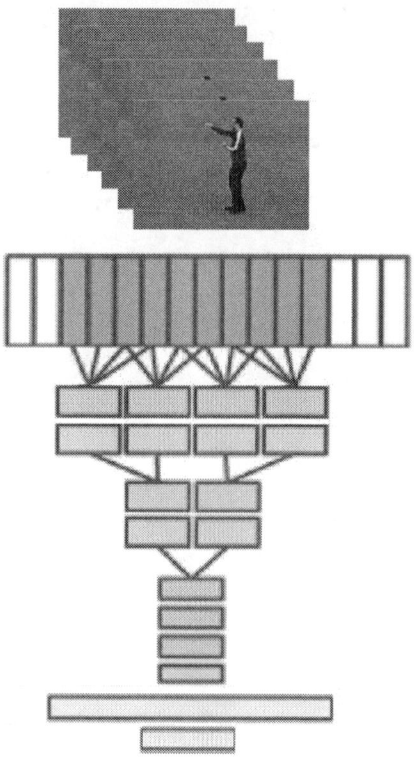

Fig. 8 convolution neural network structure

The video is divided into training set and test set for each video, video of the people will continue to repeat, the training set is used to construct the network, and then classify the test set. As can be seen from the following figure, in all kinds of behavior, the fist and applause in the test of the most confusing. At the same time, because between walking and running and jogging only in the video frequency and motion amplitude difference, so improve the recognition difficulty, for this system, the recognition rate is still relatively good.

(%)	boxxing	clapping	waving hand	jogging	running	walking
boxxing	83	17				
clapping	8	92				
waving hand	11		89			
jogging				94	3	3
running				3	96	1
walking						100

Fig.9 the recognition rate of the algorithm on the kth dataset

6 Copyright Forms and Reprint Orders

You must submit the IEEE Electronic Copyright Form (ECF) per Step 7 of the AT author kit's web page. THIS FORM MUST BE SUBMITTED IN ORDER TO PUBLISH YOUR PAPER.

Acknowledgment

This paper proposes a behavior recognition method based on convolutional neural network, learning the characteristics of human behavior through convolution unsupervised neural networks, then experiments are carried out by the neural network model of KTH human data set, experimental results show that the structure can do better on the human body for classification.

References

[1] Wang H, Klaser A, Schmid C, Liu C L. Action recognition by dense trajectories. Proceedings of the 2011 IEEE Conference on Computer Vision and Pattern Recognition (CVPR). Providence, RI: IEEE, 2011. 3169¡3176

[2] Soomro K, Zamir A. Action recognition in realistic sports videos. Computer Vision in Sports. 2014.

[3] Niu F, Adbel-Mottaleb M, HMM-based Segmentation and Recognition of Human Activities from Video Sequences[C], IEEE International Conference on Multimedia and Expo, Amsterdam, Netherlands, 2005

[4] Zhou Hanning, Kimber D.Unusual Event Detection Via Multi-Camera Video Mining[C]. 18th International Conference on Pattern Recognition, Hong Kong, China, 2006

[5] Brand M, Oliver N and Pentland A. Coupled hidden Markov models for complex action recognition. In: Proc IEEE Conference Computer Vision and Pattern Recognition, Puerto Rico, 1997, 994-999.

[6] Chen Yufeng, Liang Guoyuan, Lee K. Abnormal Behavior Detection by Multi-SVM based Beyesian Betwork[C].International Conference on Information Acquistion. Guangzhou, China, 2010.
[7] Le Cun Y, Bottou L, Bengio Y, et al. Gradient-based learning applied to document recognition[J]. Proceedings of the IEEE, 1998, 86(11): 2278-2324
[8] Wang H, Schmid C. Dense trajectories and motion boundary descriptors for action recognition[J]. International Journal of Computer Vision, 2013, 103(1): 60-79
[9] Zhang Fan, Gao li, Lu Haixian. Star Skeleton for Human Behavior Recognition[C].IEEE International Conference on Audio, Language and Image Processing, Shanghai, China, 2012.
[10] H. Wang and C. Schmid,Action recognition with improved trajectories, in ICCV, 2013.
[11] H. Kuehne, H. Jhuang, E. Garrote, T. Poggio, and T. Serre, HMDB:a large video database for human motion recognition, in ICCV, 2011.
[12] I. S. Jacobs and C. P. Bean, "Fine particles, thin films and exchange anisotropy," in Magnetism, vol. III, G. T. Rado and H. Suhl, Eds. New York: Academic, 1963, pp. 271–350.
[13] M. Baccouche, F. Mamalet, C.Wolf, C. Garcia, and A. Baskurt, Action classification in soccer videos with long short-term memory. recurrent neural networks, in International Conference on Artificial Neural Networks (ICANN), 2010.
[14] A. Farhadi, M. Hejrati, M. Sadeghi, P. Young, C. Rashtchian, J. Hockenmaier, and D. Forsyth, Every picture tells a story: Generating sentences from images, in ECCV, 2010.
[15] G. Kulkarni, V. Premraj, S. Dhar, S. Li, Y. Choi, A. C. Berg, and T. L.Berg, Baby talk: Understanding and generating simple image descriptions, in CVPR, 2011.
[16] Y. Yang, C. L. Teo, H. Daum´e III, and Y. Aloimonos,Corpusguided sentence generation of natural images, in EMNLP, 2011.
[17] M. Mitchell, X. Han, J. Dodge, A. Mensch, A. Goyal, A. Berg,K. Yamaguchi, T. Berg, K. Stratos, and H. Daum´e III, Midge: Generating image descriptions from computer vision detections, 2012

Requirement Analysis for the Collaborative Supply and Logistics Management of Fresh Agricultural Products

Jun LI, Yu-Chuan LIU, Hong-Mei GAO*

Department of Economic Management,Tianjin Agricultural University,Tianjin, China
Department of Economic Management, Tianjin Agricultural University, Tianjin, China
e-mail: ycliu_icloud@me.com, t00258@mail.tut.edu.tw, Corresponding author: gaohongmei@126.com*

Abstract—Issues and concerns for food safety, agro-processing, and the environmental and ecological impact of food production have been attracted many research interests. Traceability and logistics management of fresh agricultural products is faced with the technological challenges including food product label and identification, activity/process characterization, information systems for the supply chain, i.e., from farm to table. Application of information technologies for food processing and logistics industry in the fields of smart packaging and materials, automation and control technology, standards and their application scenarios, and production management principles were wildly studied. A collaborative research project for the supply and logistics of fresh agricultural products in Tianjin was performed. System analysis for the logistics management information system is studied. The model-driven business transformation, an approach uses formal models to explicitly define the structure and behavior of a business, is applied for the review and analysis process. Requirements for the logistic management solutions are proposed. Development of this research is crucial for the solution integration of supply and logistic management information system for fresh agricultural products.

1 Introduction

The heightened awareness of food-related safety issues among food consumers drives the demand for more information about the vertical food supply chain about the origin and handling of the basic commodities and food products generated and consumed throughout the world. Developments of agro-food industries are facing global challenges that can only be supported by information technologies. The major IT development lines, the support potential of their integration, organizational requirements for the utilization, and possible consequences for the future organization of the agro-food sector were reviewed [1]. Traceability is an essential subsystem of quality management, and must be managed by setting up a traceability system, which keeps the data tracking of product routes and of selected attributes. A traceability system can consist two elements, the routes of the product, path along which products can be identified throughout the manufacturing, distribution and retail procedures, and the extent of traceability wanted [2]. Food traceability requires that all stakeholders within the food supply chain, including agriculture and feed producers, food manufacturers, retailers, etc., must be able to identify the source of all raw materials and ingredients to whom the products have been sold. The food companies must apply identification systems and data handling procedures and these must be integrated into their quality management system. The sector encompassing information technology (IT) centers ought to find a reasonable compromise between the simple, step by step passing of traceable unit IDs for the neighboring actors, and the accumulated enormously huge databases of the actors. The traceability system is to provide services for the supply chain actors on cooperative basis of the mutual interests [3]. In addition, the IT centers must support the supply chain and value chain management, as well as the work of the authorities, that are responsible for the human health. Opara [4] reviewed the concepts of supply chain management and traceability in agriculture and highlighted the technological challenges, including food product label and identification, activity/process characterization, information systems for data capture, analysis, storage and communication, and the integration of the overall traceable supply chain in implementing traceable agricultural supply chains. Wang et al. [5] addressed that the values on traceability can be integrated with the supply chain management processes to manage the business process and improve its performance. Bosona and Gebresenbet [6] summarized the literature review on the food traceability issues. It was pointed out that the development of full chain food traceability system is quite complex in nature, and a deeper understanding of real processes from different perspectives such as economic, legal, technological, and social issues are essential. Consequently, studies on the integration of traceability activities with food logistics activities, the linkage between traceability system and food manufacturer, standardization of data capturing and communication protocol for different drivers, and performance evaluation frameworks for food traceability system need to be focused.

A new model and prototype of a new Farm Information Management System, which meets the changing requirements for advising managers with formal instructions, recommended guidelines and documentation requirements for various decision making processes, was developed [7]. As achieving end-to-end traceability across the supply chain is quite a challenge from a technical, a co-ordination and a cost perspective, Kelepouris et al. [8] suggested a radio frequency identification (RFID) technology and outlined both information data model and system architecture that made traceability feasible and easily deployable across a supply chain. Based on an integration of alphanumerical codes and RFID technology, the traceability system for Parmigiano Reggiano (the famous Italian cheese) was developed [9]. Manthou et al. [10] provided empirical insights regarding the use of Internet-based applications in the agri-food supply chain by focusing on the Greek fruit canning sector. The companies' perceptions regarding perceived benefits, constrained factors and motivation factors towards the use of Internet-based applications were studied. A PDA-based Record-keeping and Decision-support System for traceability in cucumber production was developed on Windows Mobile platform invoking a Geographic Information System (GIS) control [11]. Two agricultural production enterprises were chosen as case study to evaluate the system and the results show that the efficiency of production record-keeping and decision-support is improved by the simple and friendly system. The state-of-the-art review in the recent advancements of food processing and packaging industry in the fields of smart packaging and materials, automation and control technology, standards, and their application scenarios, and production management principles and their improvements was proposed [12].

The logistics and information flow play an important role in the fresh agricultural products supply chain. The purpose of this research is to further provide a complete study on the

issues and solutions for the logistics and information management of fresh agricultural products. A full life-cycle business-to-technology method, model-driven business transformation MDBT [13], is both a modeling methodology and a set of innovative technologies that allow business strategies to be realized by choreographing workflow tools and human activities. MDBT uses formal models to explicitly define the structure and behavior of a business component. Kumaran et al [14] presented a new approach to IT service workflow automation and a new generation of service-delivery management systems based on the model-driven transformational approach and service-oriented architecture. The MDBT approach is applied to propose an integrated solution. Development of this research is crucial for the solution integration of information and logistics management in fresh agricultural products supply chain business.

2 Model-Driven Business Transformation Approach

Model-driven business transformation, MDBT developed by IBM research, uses formal models to explicitly define the structure and behavior of a business component. These models can be employed to monitor, analyze, and improve its performance, and leverages these models in the construction of its IT systems. The framework is made up of four layers: business strategy, business operations, solution composition, and IT implementation. Each layer constitutes a different level of abstraction, performs a well-defined function, and has a different audience. The strategy layer defines the goals and objectives of the business system. The operation layer describes the operations performed by the business system to achieve the goals. The composition layer is an abstraction of the computational elements that are needed to execute the business operations. The implementation layer specifies how the computational elements are implemented on IT platform. Figure 1 shows the MDBT framework, including the separation of concerns, connections between model layers, and the closed-loop architecture using the business process modeling component.

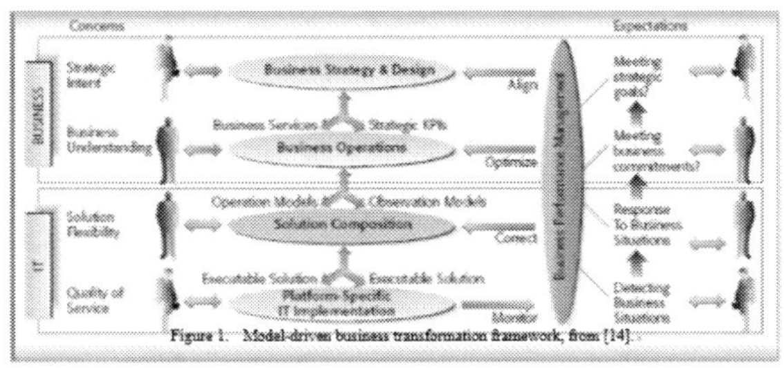

Figure 1. Model-driven business transformation framework, from [14].

In the MDBT approach, the transformation process begins with the identification of the strategic goals and objectives of the business component. This leads to a set of initiatives that support these goals. These initiatives determine the definition, analysis, optimization, and implementation of the business operations of the organization such that the strategic goals can be achieved. Formal definition of the business operations and the operational KPIs (key performance indicators) is the next step of transformation process which was referred as the business operation model. A business operation model is different from the more familiar workflow models. A business operation model, on the other hand, defines the key business artifacts and the operations performed on these artifacts. The third step of solution composition in MDBT is the judicious use of technology to support the execution of business operations. This involves the generation of a platform-independent solution composition model and the realization of this model on a specific software platform. The final step in MDBT is to create an implementation of the IT solution on a specific IT platform. Once the solution is deployed, business owners can monitor and analyze business performance using KPIs and continuously improve the models, both at the business and IT levels, based on this performance analysis.

3 Solution Requirements Analysis by MDBT

The infrastructure of the fresh agricultural products logistics management can be summarized as shown in Fig. 2. The solid lines stand for the logistic flow of the products, and the dashed lines are the required information flow to assure the food safety. As indicated in Fig. 2, the traceability information is required during the farming process of the agricultural products. The process and ingredient information is necessary if the products are sent to the food industry for more process. The logistics information during the transportation and storage for all the supply chain stages to Ensure the completeness of the traceability management. By applying MDBT approach, the definition of goals and objectives should firstly analyzed in strategy layer. As the project team reviewed the current fresh agricultural products supply chain in Tianjin, the first two issues are the product loss during the logistics procedure and cost (and/or effectiveness) of the cold chain logistics. The objectives are consequently to improve the effectiveness and efficiency for fresh agricultural products logistics management. The KPIs for hardware protection can be fresh agricultural products loss during transportation, handling, and storage procedures. The KPIs for the software management can be the easy and complete access of the traceability data through the whole supply chain process, i.e., the farming data, process and ingredient information, the transportation and storage environment condition histories.

The second step of business operation analysis for MDBT is to perform the business operation. Considering the supply chain process shown in Fig. 2, some observations can be made:

- End customers can receive the fresh agricultural products via an O2O scenario directly from the e-commerce provided by the agricultural corporations. The transportation procedures can be minimized so that the product loss caused can also be reduced.
- The O2O scenario also provides an optimized product combinations both for the customer and supplier. The products delivered can be optimized according to the farming production condition and the customers' order requirement. The balance of the supply and demand can be optimized and the effectiveness of farming production can be improved.
- The HMR, home meal replacement, is more and more popular as the necessity of ready-to-eat convenience increased significantly. The traceability information of the farming and food process is an important issue for HMR brand marketing.

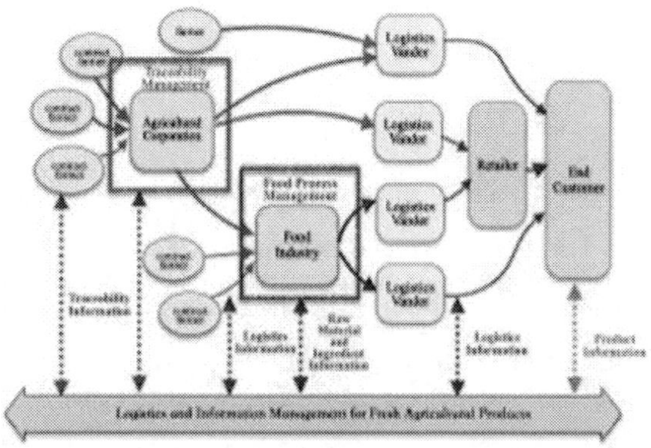

Figure 2. Infrastructure of the fresh agricultural products logistics management.

Detail solution requirements are further studied through the supply chain processes. Figure 2 shows that the logistics information flow between the supply chain enterprises can be shared and integrated for further enhancement of the supply chain management efficiency. The information system must be designed to cope with the intricate farming data, food processing information, and the rigmarole product transportation and storage information. The platform independent solution requirements are proposed in this paper. The information system should cover the farming, food processing, and logistics of the supply chain process. The specific functional requirements from configuration management analysis include:

3.1 Farming data information management

Food traceability can be found mostly by attaching a 2-dimensional label, QR (quick response) code is the usual case, on the package of the food or agro-products. A mobile farming information system to collect the farming data and directly transmitted to the traceability system by cell phone and two dimensional codes was proposed in [15]. The basic traceability information is consisted of the farmer, cropland, and crop planted. All the farming activities are performed on the cropland. The farming activities can be divided into three categories:

- Farming operations for all kind of crops like seeding and pruning without the need of further attribute records.
- Fertilizing operations which the fertilizer and amount used need to be recorded.
- Disease prevention operations with the use and records of pesticides.

All the required operations are encoded into QR codes. Different fertilizers and pesticides are all encoded into distinct QR code. By scanning the proper QR code, the farmer can easily upload the operation messages into the data collection system. As the usage of pesticide is critical for the pesticide residual can be harmful to human, the relationship of allowable pesticide for crop is constructed to guarantee that safety of pesticide usage. The main information entities and their relationships of the traceability information system are shown in Fig. 3. The basic traceability information is consisted of the farmer, cropland, and crop planted. All the farming activities are performed on the cropland. The farming activities can be divided into three categories: the farming operations for all kind of crops like seeding and pruning without the need of further attribute records; the fertilizing operations which the fertilizer and amount used need to be recorded; and the disease prevention operations with the use and records of pesticides. All the required operations are encoded into QR codes and every farming operation is transformed into distinct QR code label. Different fertilizers and pesticides are all encoded into distinct QR code. By scanning the proper QR code, the farmer can easily upload the operation messages into the data collection system. As the usage of pesticide is critical for the pesticide residual can be harmful to human, the relationship of allowable pesticide for crop is constructed to guarantee that safety of pesticide usage.

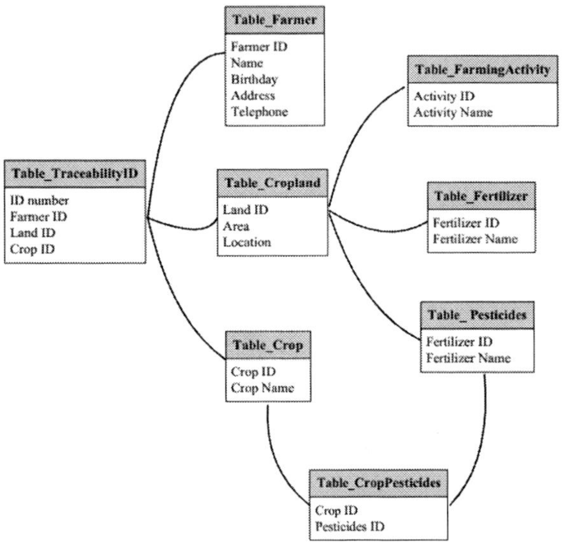

Figure 3. Main database entities for the mobile traceability data collection system, from [15]

3.2 Food processing information management

As the rapid development and change of industrial society, modern families tend to buy prepared food as home meal replacement (HMR), like the famous Chinese Beijing ducks, instead of cooking in kitchens. For food industries to collect and keep all the food safety related processing data, it is necessary to inolement the computer integrated manufacturing (CIM) system. The CIM system integrating the engineering, production control, and manufacturing by information technologies, plays as an important strategy to improve the performance of a manufacturing firm. The highly automated production processes of 300 mm wafer fabrication in semiconductor business is one of the most complicated CIM systems. Different types of automated material handling systems (AMHS) including, overhead shuttle vehicle (OHV), overhead hoist transporter (OHT), automatic guided vehicle (AGV), rail-guided vehicle (RGV), are employed for the inter-bay and/or intra-bay material transportation of work-in- process (WIP) to be properly processed at specified production equipments. The process equipments and AMHS are all planned, monitored, and controlled by the information systems of manufacturing execution system (MES) and material control system (MCS). The key requirements for the design and implementation of the similar CIM system in food industry can be summarized as followed.

- Design and analysis of the AMHS system for mixed production with different types of agricultral products should be analyzed in.food industry.
- Proper production planning with the considerations of the constraints of production machines and the scheduling and dispatching rules to plan the proper daily work orders and WIPs control.
- Detail analysis for the requirements of MES and MCS systems for the new automated process flow is necessary to assure the software systems can achieve properly the control and management purpose.
- Developments of the new production equipments and the MES and MCS control software must be proposed. The customized information systems for production control and management must be designed and developed according to the system requirement analysis.
- Effective project management is indispensable for the system implementation of CIM project consists of design, analysis, simulation, and verification of equipments, AMHSs, and information systems.

3.3 Logistics information management

Venders in the fresh agricultral products supply chain are usually located far away from food industries, retailer, and customers. Transportation of fresh agricultral products can be summarized in two manners. The first type is transported directly by the food industries (or agricultural corporations). The other is to be delivered by the third-party services such as DHL. The quality of transportation and fresh agricultral products must be controlled and guaranteed during transportation. The cold chain logistics is hence become inevitable. As to provide and integrate the logistics information, the cold chain logistics vehicle need to be upgraded with information accession and transmission. Some suggestions are listed:

- To instantly record the products receiving information at farmer site, a handhold device to input the information and transmit wirelessly to the server of the system is required.
- The transportation management functions include: products receiving and recording, warehouse entrance check and record, and report for transportation management.
- The storage management functions are similar to the warehouse management functions and include: warehouse receiving, automatic storage location assignment, load to storage location, unload from storage location, lot split, storage location change, inventory check, and production releasing.

4 Summary and Conclusion

The fresh agricultural products supply chain is reviewed and the logistics and information management requirement are studied based on the project experience in Tianjin. Because of the importance food safety and the complex business characteristics through the food supply chain, the requirements for fresh agricultural products logistics and the related information management is proposed in this paper. The requirements are summarized by the MDBT approach to provide a service-oriented-architecture solution. Three major functions for the information management system, including the farming data, food processing, and logistics, are suggested. With the proposed functional requirements, the results of this paper can be fruitful for the further design of the fresh agricultural products logistics information management systems.

Acknowledgment

This work was financially supported by the National Training Program of Innovation and Entrepreneurship for Undergraduates 2015 of the Ministry of Education of PRC (project no. 201510061019) and Tianjin Administration of Foreign Affairs (project no. 20171200248).

References

[1] G. Schiefer, "New technologies and their impact on the agri-food sector: an economists view," Comput. and Electron. in Agr., Vol. 43, no. 2, pp. 163-172, 2004.

[2] T. Moe, "Perspectives on traceability in food manufacture," Trends in Food Science & Technology, Vol. 9, pp. 211-214, 1998.

[3] M. Varga and B. Csukas, "On the way toward the sector spanning agrifood process traceability," Agricultural Informatics, vol. 1, no. 1, pp. 8-18, 2010.

[4] L. U. Opara, "Traceability in agriculture and food supply chain: a review of basic concepts, technological implications, and future prospects," J. of Food Agric. Environ., vol. 1, no. 1, pp.101-106, 2003.

[5] X. Wang, D. Li, and L. Li, "Adding value of food traceability to the business: a supply chain management approach," Int. J. of Serv. Oper. and Informat., vol. 4, no. 3, pp. 232-257, 2009.

[6] T. Bosona and G. Gebresenbet, "Food traceability as an integral part of logistics management in food and agricultural supply chain," Food Control, vol. 33, pp. 32-48, 2013.

[7] C. G. Sørensena, S. Fountasb, E. Nashf, L. Pesonend, D. Bochtisa, S. M. Pedersene, B. Bassoc, S. B. Blackmoreg, "Conceptual model of a future farm management information system," Comput. and Electron. in Agr., vol. 72, no. 1, pp. 37-47, 2010.

[8] T. Kelepouris, K. Pramatari, and G. Doukidis, "RFID-enabled traceability in the food supply chain," Ind. Mana. Data Syst., vol., 107, no. 2, pp. 183-200, 2007.

[9] A. Regattieri, M. Gamberi, and R. Manzini, "Traceability of food products: General framework and experimental evidence," J. of Food Eng., vol. 81, no. 2, pp. 347-356, 2007.

[10] V. Manthou, A. Matopoulos, and M., "Vlachopoulou, Internet-based applications in the agri-food supply chain: a survey on the Greek canning sector," J. of Food Eng., vol. 70, no. 3, pp. 447-454, 2005.

[11] M. Li, J. P. Qian, X. T. Yang, C. H. Sun, and Z. T. Ji, "A PDA-based record-keeping and decision-support system for traceability in cucumber production," Comput. and Electron. in Agr., vol. 70, no. 1, pp.69-77, 2010.

[12] N. P. Mahalik and A. N. Nambiar, "Trends in food packaging and manufacturing systems and technology," Trends Food Sci. Tech., vol. 21, no. 3, pp. 117-128, 2010.

[13] S. Kumaran, "Model Driven Enterprise," Proceedings of the Global Enterprise Application Integration Summit, pp. 166–180, Banf, Canada, 2004.

[14] S. Kumaran, P. Bishop, T. Chao, P. Dhoolia, P. Jain, R. Jaluka, H. Ludwig, A. Moyer, and A. Nigam, "Using a Model-Driven Transformational Approach and Service-Oriented Architecture for Service Delivery Management", IBM System Journal, vol. 46, no. 3, pp. 513-529, July 2007.

[15] Y. C. Liu and H. M. Gao, "Development and Applications of Mobile Farming Information System for Food Traceability in Health Management," in Applied Computing in Medicine and Health, edited by D. Al-Jumeily, A. Hussain, C. Mallucci, and C.Oliver, Elsevier, Aug. 2015, pp. 244-268.

Chinese Word Sense Disambiguation Using a LSTM

Xue-Ren SUN, Shao-He LV, Xiao-Dong WANG, Dong WANG

National Key Lab of Parallel and Distributed Computing,National University of Defense Technology,Changsha, China
snowman1003@qq.com,shaohelv@nudt.edu.cn, xdwang@nudt.edu.cn, dongwang@nudt.edu.cn

Abstract—Word sense disambiguation (WSD) is a challenging natural language processing (NLP) problem. We propose a new strategy for WSD, which at first replaces the interesting word in a sentence by the different synonyms corresponding to the different meanings, and then justify whether the transformed sentence is "legal". A legal sentence is still legal after one or more word are replaced by other ones with the same meaning. A long short-term memory (LSTM) network-based model is proposed to perform the sentence/text classification. Furthermore, we build a Chinese WSD dataset based on HIT-CIR Tongyici Cilin (Extended) dataset. The model is evaluated on the new dataset and achieves better performance than the state-of-the-art.

1 Introduction

Word sense disambiguation is a challenging problem in natural language processing. It's a basic problem in semantics and a supportive technology for many semantic problem, such as sentiment analysis, semantic analysis and so on.

It is known that, a word may have multiple meanings, no matter in Chinese or English. For example, a Chinese word "zu" have two common meanings, which are "si wang" and "shi bing". In English, "death" and "soldier" are the meanings. However, in a specific context, the meaning of a word should be doubtless. For instance, there is a Chinese sentence:

Zhu Geliang sheng yu 181 nian, zu yu 234 nian.

In this context, the Chinese word "zu" has no ambiguity, it definitely means "death". The word sense disambiguation problem aims to find the proper meaning of a word in a specific context automatically. Specific to this example, we should find the meaning "death" automatically based on the context.

In this paper, we use a new strategy to convert the word sense disambiguation problem into a text classification problem. The strategy replaces a word in a context with its different synonyms corresponding to its different meaning. For example, the word "zu" in the sentence above can be replaced with "si wang" and "shibing" respectively. As a result, the sentence above are converted into two sentences. We consider the sentence replaced with "si wang" correct, and the other one wrong. Using this rule, we can convert sentences with words being disambiguated into two sets: the positive set and the negative set. What we should do now is to train a model to have the ability to distinguish whether a sentence is correct or wrong.

To this end, we propose a novel classifier model based on long short term memory(LSTM) network [1]. The model consists of a LSTM and a multilayer perceptron(MLP). We adopt an LSTM network to model the long-range semantics of a sentence and an MLP to perform the classification.

As a supervised machine learning model, training is an essential step. And the training step needs large data to complete the work. So far, there has not been a Chinese WSD dataset large enough. To satisfy the need of the training, we build a Chinese WSD dataset based on HIT-CIR Tongyici Cilin (Extended) [2] dataset.

The HIT-CIR Tongyici Cilin (Extended) dataset encodes 77343 words with a perfect rule based on synonyms. Moreover, a corpus from People's Daily is also labeled by the same rule. The corpus contains 11331 sentences, about 350 thousand words. We extract sentences containing polysemes from the corpus to build our Chinese WSD dataset. We evaluate our model on the corpus and achieved good results.

The rest of this paper is structured as follows. In Section II, we introduce some related work about the WSD problem. Then in Section III, the strategy and the model are explained in detail. Afterwards, the experiments and results are presented in Section IV. We conclude the research in Section V.

2 Related Work

Recently, many works have been done on word sense disambiguation problem. One approach [3] presents an unsupervised vector-space model using global context and local context to represent different meaning of a word as different vectors. This work uses k-means clustering algorithm, and the results are not so ideal.

Another work [4] uses synonyms to replace original words in context to fake context. Then a naïve bayesian model is put forward to predict the meaning of a word. But the model isn't universal. Such a model can only classify one word's meanings. If a new word comes, new corpus should be gathered and a new model should be trained.

Most recently, there is another work [5] based on Bi-directional LSTM (Bi-LSTM). This model has the same disadvantage as the work above, i.e., lack of universality. Therefore, it is still open to design a framework for the universal WSD task.

3 Method

3.1 Problem Statement of WSD

Up to now, many strategies have been proposed on this problem. Some of them use context semantic information [3], and others take advantage of the additional information, such as a semantic dictionary [5]. However, none of them considered synonym as a resource to solve the problem.

A single word may have different synonyms corresponding to its different meaning. As in the example shown before, the word "zu" has many synonyms, among which "si wang" corresponds to "death" and "shi bing" corresponds to "solider". Therefore, if we replace the original word "zu" with its difference synonyms, the original sentence is converted into different sentences. Among these generated sentences, only one sentence is "legal", i.e., correct in semantic, because only one synonym is suitable in the sentence. For example, there is a Chinese sentence below:

Zhu Geliang sheng yu 181 nian, zu yu 234 nian.

If we replace the word "zu" with its different synonyms, we could get two generated sentences:

Zhu Geliang sheng yu 181 nian, si wang yu 234 nian.(1)

Zhu Geliang sheng yu 181 nian, shi bing yu 234 nian.(2)

One can observe that, sentence (1) is correct in semantics, because the word "si wang" is suitable in this sentence. Also, sentence (1) didn't change the meaning of the original sentence. In comparison, sentence (2) is not semantic "legal". Firstly, the word "shi bing" is not appropriate in this sentence. The sentence is not clear and coherent at all. Secondly, it misses the original meaning "death" in the original sentence. In a word, sentence (2) is a wrong sentence.

Assume that there is a corpus containing many sentences, each of which has a word to disambiguate. We call these sentences as "sentences to disambiguate". For any sentence to disambiguate, one can generate many sentences using the synonyms of the word being disambiguated. The count of the sentences depends on the number of meanings the word to be disambiguated has. Among the sentences generated, one is correct and the others are wrong.

As a result, we transform the WSD problem to a sentence classification task. That is, we need to justify whether the new sentence is legal or not after the interesting word in the sentence is replaced by other of similar meaning.

3.2 Sentence Classification Based on LSTM

Using the strategy we introduce above, we get a corpus with positive examples and negative examples, and the amount of them are the same. From another point of view, the positive and negative examples can be treated as two different kinds of data. If we can train a model having the ability to classify sentences into these two categories, the WSD problem is changed into a text classification problem.

In this paper, we propose a text classification model based on LSTM and MLP, which references the model in [5]. However, there are several problems in their model. Firstly, the model is not universal. Once the model is trained, it only has the ability to disambiguate one word. If another word come, it will be necessary to collect corpus related to the word and train the model anew. Moreover, the model is based on Bi-LSTM [6], which considers the characteristic of English, where there exists parenthesis and subordinate clause. So the preceding part or the following part of the text alone has complete semantic information. But considering the characteristic of Chinese and the strategy's difference to their work, we use LSTM to model a sentence to get the complete semantic information of it.

The model's structure is shown as figure 1. The first layer of the model is an embedding layer. In this layer, a word is modified into a vector which can be used to calculate in computer. In this paper, we use a state-of-the-art tool word2vec [7] to complete the work.

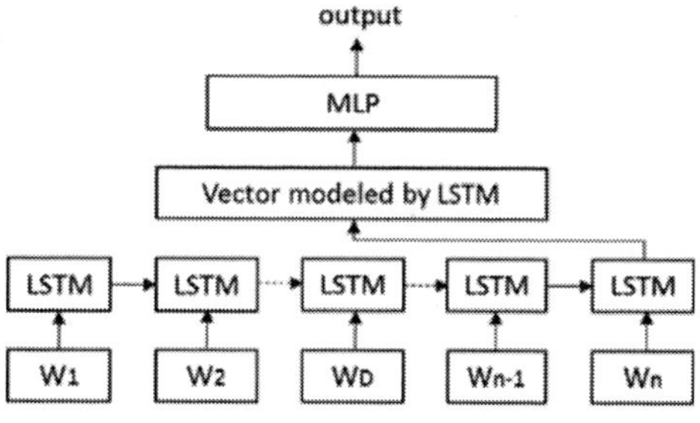

Figure 1. Model structure based on LSTM to classify texts.

DOI: 10.1051/itmconf/20171201027

The core idea of word2vec is that words similar in semantic have similar context. This tool has two training models. One is CBOW(Continuous Bag-of-Words) model and another is skip-gram model. The difference between these two models is that the training method are different. The skip-gram uses current word to predict the context, while the CBOW model uses the context to predict current word. It could be observed in its loss function. For the quality of the two models are close, so we just choose CBOW model as our training model. The corpus we used to train the model is Wikipedia Chinese corpus [8].

The second layer of our model is a standard LSTM layer. LSTM was used in various natural language processing tasks to model a text. It solve the gradient explosion and long-term dependence problem of general recurrent neural networks (RNN) [9] model. Consider the characteristic of Chinese and the need of complete semantic information of a sentence in our classification strategy, we didn't choose Bi-LSTM to model the preceding part and the following part of the text separately. As a result, we were only concerned about the output in last time step of a sentence.

The third layer is a MLP layer, which undertakes the task of classification. As we says above, the output of the second layer is a vector. And to perform a classification task, we need a sorter. The most common and effective method is a MLP sorter. We use one full connection hidden layer with 64 neurons and one output layer with one neuron in the MLP. The activation function is sigmoid and the output a classification result, which is the probability of the sentence to be legal. In another word, higher probability means the synonyms we replaced with the original word is more likely to be proper in the context.

For the training part, the loss function we use is binary cross-entropy [10] instead of the quadratic cost function. Because the traditional quadratic cost function has many disadvantages. For example, while using the back propagation algorithm to train the model, the larger the initial loss is, the slower the training proceeds. The binary cross-entropy loss function is as follows:

$$Loss = -\frac{1}{n}\sum_{x}[y\log a - (1 \quad y)\log(1 \quad a)]$$

In the function, a is the probability the model predicted, y is the real label of a sentence, x means all the sentences in the corpus.

Further, to overcome the problem of overfitting, we use the dropout technology [11] during the training process. The dropout means to ignore some weights randomly in the hidden layer while training. It prevents some situation in which weights are updated only under other specific characteristics and situations.

4 Experiment

4.1 New Dataset

There have been some datasets related to WSD task. The most popular datasets are the senseval [12] datasets. The senseval datasets includes Chinese WSD task dataset, in which the sentences are encoded by Hownet [13], a Chinese semantic dictionary. However, this dataset two disadvantages. Firstly, there are only hundreds sentences in the dataset. The amount is too small to process neural network training. Secondly, the encoding resource, Hownet, is based on morpheme instead of paraphrase or synonym. Considering this, we don't evaluate this model on this dataset.

Instead, we extract and build a new Chinese WSD dataset from HIT-CIR Tongyici Cilin (Extended) Corpus [2]. The dictionary has many rows of words. Words in the same row may have the same or close meaning. Especially, if there is only one word in a row, it's a monoseme. The dictionary uses different symbols to distinguish the difference. Table I shows the difference symbols of different senses. The symbol "=" in the end of a code means words in this row have exactly the same meaning, "@" means monoseme, and "#" means words in this row has similar meanings.

TABLE I. different symbols in HIT-CIR Tongyici Cilin (Extended)

Different symbols in codes	Example words
Ba01A02=	wuzhi zhi su
Ba01A03@	wan wu
Ba01B10#	daoti bandaoti chaodaoti

We only consider the words in rows with "=" as synonyms. As shown in the example above, words in rows with symbol "#" don't have the same meaning. The words "ban dao ti" and "chao dao ti" are not the same as "dao ti". So, we can't consider them as synonyms. We call the words row with "=" as "synonyms row".

If one word appears in different synonyms rows, we regard it as a polyseme. Further, in the corpus encoded in Cilin, if a sentence contains a polysemy we found by the rule above, it is necessary to disambiguate the polysemy word. In the end, we find 9799 sentences. For each sentence, we gather all the correct sentences generated based on the sentence in the corpus as the "is case set". In the same way, we gather all the wrong sentences as the "counter case set". To balance these two set, we only choose one wrong sentence corresponding to one original sentence in the corpus. As a result, these two sets constitute the word sense disambiguation corpus.

Finally, we build a Chinese word sense disambiguation corpus which contained 19598 sentences. Half of these sentences are correct and the other half are wrong.

4.2 Parameters Setting

The model we build have several parameters to set. The typical parameters are the size of word embedding, the rate of the dropout and the batch size during training. What's more, we also evaluate different RNN models, such as GRU(Gated Recurrent Network) [14] and simple RNN.

In the training step, we randomly pick 80% of the dataset as training set and the remaining 20% as the test set. In all the experiments below, the ratio remains the same. And for the record, all the results are obtained on the test set.

The experiments are all processed on a personal computer using Ubuntu 14.04 as operation system, Keras as code framework and having an 8GB internal memory, Intel i5 CPU and Nvidia Geforce 840m GPU. Moreover, we use the GPU to accelerate the training speed. The training time is measured on this situation.

4.3 Results and Discussion

Firstly we set the parameters as follows: embedding size is 256, batch size is 100, model is LSTM and dropout is 0.5. The training accuracy changes with the increase of the epoch. The result is as figure II.

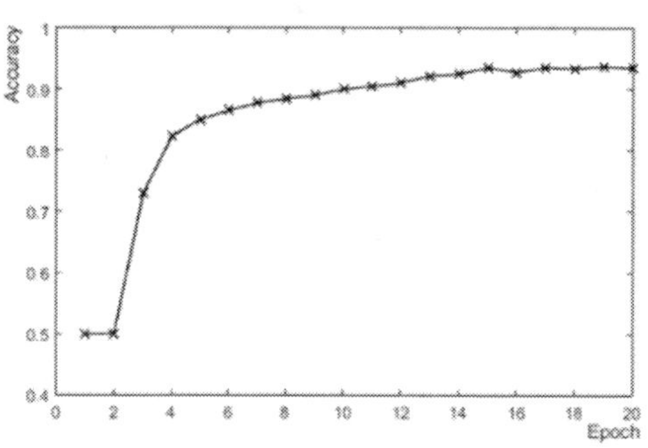

Figure 2. Training accuracy changes with the increse of epoch.

The result shows that the model has been trained well after 15 epochs. Afterward, the accuracy doesn't increase obviously. So in the experiment below, we set the epoch of the training as 15. It also shows that the strategy and the model we build is effective in the WSD task.

Secondly we evaluate different RNN models in order to prove the superiority of LSTM. The results are shown in Table II. Other parameters are also presented in the table.

Results on different RNN models

Mo del	Embeddin g size	Batch size	Dropou t	Predicting accuracy
RN N	256	100	0.5	0.64
GR U	256	100	0.5	0.50
LST M	256	100	0.5	**0.78**

As we can see, the LSTM model achieved the best result in the task, which proves the superiority successfully. In the experiments below, the LSTM model won't be changed.

Thirdly we evaluate the influence of the embedding size to the accuracy. We choose different embedding size as 64, 128 and 256. The results are shown in table III.

Results on different embedding size

Model	Embeddin g size	Batch size	Dropout	Predicting accuracy
LSTM	128	100	0.5	0.75
LSTM	256	100	0.5	**0.78**
LSTM	512	100	0.5	0.65

The result shows that the accuracy doesn't increase obviously with the growth of embedding size. It even decreases when the embedding size is large. The increase of calculation brings no profit. In the end, we choose 256 as our embedding size next.

Afterward, we change the batch size to find its influence on the accuracy. We use 50, 100, 150 as the value to evaluate. The result is concluded as table IV.

Results on different batch size

Model	Embedd ing size	Batc h size	Drop out	Predictin g accuracy	Training time
LSTM	256	50	0.5	0.49	1.5h
LSTM	256	100	0.5	**0.78**	10min
LSTM	256	150	0.5	**0.78**	8min

The result shows that it's important to use a batch size that is large enough, or the training time will be too long to endure. And if the batch size is too small, the predicting accuracy will also be bad. As a result we choose 100 as our batching size.

At last, we change the dropout rate to find a proper one that could complete the task best. We choose 0, 0.3, 0.5, 0.8 as candidates. Table V shows the results.

DOI: 10.1051/itmconf/20171201027

Results on different dropout rate

Model	Embed ding size	Batch size	Dropout	Predicting accuracy
LSTM	256	100	0	0.74
LSTM	256	100	0.3	0.75
LSTM	256	100	0.5	**0.78**
LSTM	256	100	0.8	0.73

One can see that if we set the dropout rate properly, it helps to increase the predicting accuracy. If we don't use this technology at all, the result may not become the optimal one.

In summary, the proposed model achieves better performance than the new state-of-the-arts. Also, an optimal parameter setting is provided after extensive experiments.

Conclusion

In this paper, we discuss a new method to solve the word sense disambiguation problem after transforming the original problem into sentence classification. An LSTM-based framework is proposed to perform the sentence classification. We also build a Chinese WSD dataset based on HIT-CIR Tongyici Cilin (Extended). Promising results is achieved in the dataset for the proposed method.

In future, we plan to 1) integrate the model with a multiple-class classifiers, so the meaning of a word can be output directly and 2) test the model for the English WSD task.

References

[1] Hochreiter, Sepp, and Jürgen Schmidhuber. "Long short-term memory." Neural computation 9.8 (1997): 1735-1780.

[2] Che, Wanxiang, Zhenghua Li, and Ting Liu. "Ltp: A chinese language technology platform." Proceedings of the 23rd International Conference on Computational Linguistics: Demonstrations. Association for Computational Linguistics, 2010.

[3] Huang, Eric H., et al. "Improving word representations via global context and multiple word prototypes." Proceedings of the 50th Annual Meeting of the Association for Computational Linguistics: Long Papers-Volume 1. Association for Computational Linguistics, 2012.

[4] Yang, Zhizhuo, and Heyan Huang. "Chinese Word Sense Disambiguation based on Context Expansion." COLING (Posters). 2012.

[5] Kågebäck, Mikael, and Hans Salomonsson. "Word Sense Disambiguation using a Bidirectional LSTM." arXiv preprint arXiv:1606.03568 (2016).

[6] Schuster, Mike, and Kuldip K. Paliwal. "Bidirectional recurrent neural networks." IEEE Transactions on Signal Processing 45.11 (1997): 2673-2681.

[7] Mikolov, Tomas, et al. "Distributed representations of words and phrases and their compositionality." Advances in neural information processing systems. 2013.

[8] Denoyer, Ludovic, and Patrick Gallinari. "The wikipedia xml corpus." International Workshop of the Initiative for the Evaluation of XML Retrieval. Springer Berlin Heidelberg, 2006.

[9] Williams, Ronald J., and David Zipser. "A learning algorithm for continually running fully recurrent neural networks." Neural computation 1.2 (1989): 270-280.

[10] Shore, John, and Rodney Johnson. "Axiomatic derivation of the principle of maximum entropy and the principle of minimum cross-entropy." IEEE Transactions on information theory 26.1 (1980): 26-37.

[11] Srivastava, Nitish, et al. "Dropout: a simple way to prevent neural networks from overfitting." Journal of Machine Learning Research 15.1 (2014): 1929-1958.

[12] Mihalcea, Rada, Timothy Anatolievich Chklovski, and Adam Kilgarriff. "The Senseval-3 English lexical sample task." Association for Computational Linguistics, 2004.

[13] Dong, Zhendong, and Qiang Dong. "HowNet-a hybrid language and knowledge resource." Natural Language Processing and Knowledge Engineering, 2003. Proceedings. 2003 International Conference on. IEEE, 2003.

[14] Cho, Kyunghyun, et al. "Learning phrase representations using RNN encoder-decoder for statistical machine translation." arXiv preprint arXiv:1406.1078 (2014).

The C programming Micro lecture designing mode study in mobile learning circumstance

Qing-Ting ZHU, Min ZHU*

Computer Center, East China Normal University, Shanghai, china
qtzhu@cc.ecnu.edu.cn,mzhu@cc.ecnu.edu.cn

Abstract—With the exuberant developing of mobile communication tech and education resources, the mobile, non-formal, fragmented, personal learning concepts started to threaten the traditional college education. This article explored the function that the Micro lecture applying in the personal study of students in the C program course education based on mobile learning circumstance; discussed the role Micro lecture can play in c program course education. And, according to the cognitive ability of students, the constitute elements and the general structure of the Micro lecture supporting platform are divided by program design, which eventually offer the applying model of c program teaching based on Micro lecture in the perspective of mobile learning.

1 Introduction

Mobile learning belongs to the next generation. In recent years, the fraction of college students own the smart phone generally over 90%. A big portion of them hope to utilize the time to study effectively during daily life, and also hope to use the mobile learning to connect the interval between two learnings, to achieve high-effective learning (Wei Wang, etc., 2009) [1]. The mobile learning regarded as an extension of e-learning allows the learners to use the mobile terminals to study whenever and wherever, with the supporting of mobile communication tech(ZhiXin Hou, 2014) [2]. At the same time, the Micro lecture is the novel course form suits the small capacity teaching designed specifically for certain teaching theme, normally no more than 10 m, like modern fast pace, mobile learning, ubiquitous learning, fraction learning (MingZhuo Liu, 2013) [3].

The micro lecture focused MOOCs, especially the ally constitutes with Coursera, edX, Udacity, etc., crushed higher education in different countries seriously. To implement the Education information construction development plan for the next ten years (2011-2020), the education department national college teaching network training center hold the first national college micro lecture contest in 2013, and also initialed the explore that applying micro lecture into education in China. The new generation teaching model as Micro lecture will subvert of support the college lecture education has been popularly concerned by the teachers in universities.

Most of the support system of program design courses build their course center based on network, which provides PPT for lecture, experiment materials, assignments delivering, online task, testing, BBS, etc. The students can connect the the course website from computer, and get the relevant course support through. In the meanwhile, the advantage of mobile learning is to convenient the students to learning fractionally whenever and wherever; support the personality of learning and the real time interaction. The author believe Micro Lecture can be used as the kernel learning resource of mobile learning. It is the beneficial extension and supplement of course education.

As a result, the article aimed to analyze the role micro lecture can play in the C program course education and its existence form; proposed the divide method and general structure design of micro lecture based on c program course; proffered the reasonable teach applying solution; facilitated the students to learn c program design course in mobile circumstance with the idea of micro lecture.

2 The Concept Of Micro Lecture

2.1the Concept of Micro Lecture

There were plenty of experts explained and settled the concept of micro lecture from different angles. XiaoJun

DOI: 10.1051/itmconf/20171201028

Zhen regards micro lecture as the learning method supporting flipped, blended, mobile, fractional and other learning methods from the angle of learning resource. It conveys the ideas through the terse but forceful micro teaching videos; developed a scenario, interesting and visualized digitalized learning resource that specifically aiming at the knowledge from certain subject or the teaching process [4].

A micro lecture can be a video, flash, audio or text. It's convenient for the transmission. Normally, the learning duration will be between 5 to 10 minutes, so in another word, to some extent, it is micro content.

2.2 the Constitution and Category of Micro Lecture

The constitute elements of micro lecture can be differed from the different comprehension of micro lecture. TieSheng Hu started from " The whole process of teaching activities, the applying circumstance of the resources and the growth and development of the resource constitution" of micro lecture, proposed seven micro lecture resource constitute elements includes "micro teaching video, micro teaching plan, micro courseware, micro exercise, micro rumination, micro review, micro feedback". (XiaoBin Su, etc. [5])

According to teaching category, that of micro lecture normally contains teaching, answering, inspiring, discussing, presenting, experiment, performing, learning, cooperate learning, explore learning, etc.

According to the major step of class teaching, micro lecture can be divided into reviewing before class, new subject lead-in, knowledge perceiving, exercise testing, summary expanding.

2.3 the Position of Micro Lecture in Teaching

The author believes that micro lecture can't replace the current traditional class education completely, like the internet based college education can't replace the formal record based college education. At present, micro lecture will spark more with the real college education.

Micro lecture should root into the realistic courses. As kernel teaching resource, micro video can play different parts in daily lecture, like course introducing, kernel concept presenting, explore process presenting, post exercises, etc. (LeMing Liang, etc. , 2013 [6]).

3 The Design Of C Program Designing Micro Lecture Structure

C language program design is a practical, skill-oriented course. As a programming design introduction course, the content of the course includes c language grammar and being familiar with IDE (integrated development environment), algorisms and the designing of program structure. Study by cases or questions is the generally used teaching method. The difficult of applying this method in the class is control the schedule of the course for reaction speed of students are differed. Micro Lecture can extend the class teaching into pre-class and post-class perfectly, implement a personal learning chance for students with separated pace, and enable the teachers to take care students in all levels.

3.1 the Modular Design of Lecture

In the C language teaching, the logical though ability, problem analyzing and solving ability should be considered as priority. The language knowledge should be introduced gradually during the process of training student's ability, so does the language applying ability (LianJun Chen, 2011) [7]. According to the conceive principle of students, we take the program design of different data as principal line, take the present, calculate, input, output, classic algorism and the transmission of data in functions as clue, take language knowledge to assist, start from applying, distribute difficulties and key points, reconstitute the detailed teaching content into three parts by advanced teaching as Fig 1 presented.

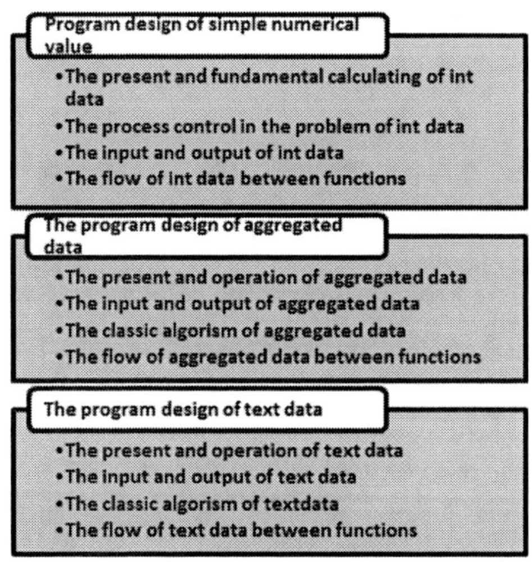

Fig 1.The modular design of the main content of micro lecture

The functions, pointers and files are all difficulties in C language teaching. According to traditional division of knowledge structure, all sorts of data processing will be present disordered, so the difficulties will accumulate. We design the content and divide the method from the solution of problems, focus on solving certain data type, how to present this kind of data, what are the conventional calculating and operations, what are the classic algorisms, how the data flow in the functions while organize multi-function grogram structure.

The knowledge of function, pointer and file scattered in the circumstance that they are applied typically. For the teaching of function and pointer, the definition and using of function are learned in the simple program designing phase,

Micro Lecture Type	Media Material	Applying Form
Study requirements	Micro text	APP submit
Introducing tasks	Micro screen video	Download online, study offline
Knowledge explanation	Micro video or PPT	Download online, study offline
Post-class exercise	Micro test	APP submit
Debug operation presenting	Micro screen video	Download online, study offline
Classic Algorism	Flash or micro video	Download online, study offline
Expanded knowledge	Video or PDF files	Download online, study offline
Feedback and comment	Micro text	APP submit

TABLE 1 .LIST OF CONSTITUTE ELEMENTS OF C PROGRAM DESIGNING MICRO LECTURE

so does the flowing of Int data in main function and subfunctions. In the text program designing phase, the flowing of text data in main function and subfunctions will be taught. On one hand the modular designing thought will be taught through the whole process of teaching, on the other hand the difficulties of function and pointer are scattered, so the student can command function and pointer after times of training.

3.2 the Designing of Micro Lecture Constitute Element of C Program Design

The demand of teaching mode should be considered while designing the constitute elements of micro lecture. We reconstituted the teaching process of C program design course. As fig 2 presented, the right of the fig is the learning process of students, and the left side is the teaching process of teachers. The middle one is the resource supporting system of micro lecture group.

During the teaching, program design is the principal line go through modules. With the method of gradually introduction, key grammar knowledge was picked. Practical and interesting program examples are serving as the introducing tasks. The class being lectured by examples, from the proposal, analyze, algorism design till the terminal code testing of questions, so the students can learn the whole process of program developing. Teachers introduce the knowledge while analyzing and explaining the cases, and then explain grammar.

To solve the problem that students are lacking necessary sensible perception of the knowledge, we take "experienced learning", let students "acting from learning and learning from acting" by introducing tasks, and then teacher offer a separate task that familiar with the example, let the students lead the process, solve their own problems, so the learned principles can be tested and applied in the experiment. The students can understand the learning tasks and targets sensibly, and their ability of using knowledge can be trained comprehensively.

Micro lecture constitutes with micro content like learning requirements, knowledge explaining, operation presenting exercise, classic algorism explaining, feedback comment, expanded reading, so a supporting resource system formed. Different types of micro lecture took different media ingredient for the creating, like table 1 presented. There are two ways for the student to acquire micro lecture: passive App, as the learning requirements and feedback comments can utilize short message or App message; the studying resources can be downloaded as knowledge and classic algorism explaining by students, who can get offline learning whenever they want.

In addition, micro lecture acted as the supplement of class education, to be exquisite instead of comprehensive. The kind of micro lecture as classic algorism and expanded knowledge can be gradually accumulated through teaching. The proper micro lecture picking is the difficulty, kernel, focus and fallible point of the program learning.

3.3 The General Design of Micro Lecture Supporting System Based on Mobile Learning

The learning mode in the mobile circumstance can be divided into the studying mode based on offline resource, short message service and link browsing (ShengQuan Yu, 2005) [8]. In light of these three learning models, supporting system based on mobile learning can be constitute by three related models, supporting different types of micro lecture resource, as Fig 3 described.

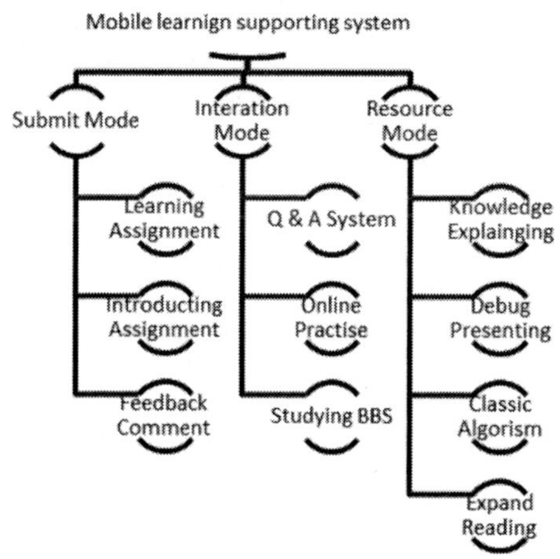

Fig 3 .The supporting system based on micro lecture in mobile learning

Submit Mode support the study mode based on short message service, send the study assignments, introducing assignments and feedback comments to the devices of students through APP. The online practice of interaction modes support the study based on linking browse, and enable the device link the server as PC to study remotely, get into course website, finish online practice and discuss the assignments with teachers and classmates in BBS. The resource mode supports study based on offline resource, meanwhile offers search function, select the explanation of required knowledge, classic algorisms, etc. The micro lecture resources can be downloaded to the cell phone for the users to study offline.

4 The Micro Lecture Supported C Program Design Teaching Application Model

The micro lecture teaching application owns two features. The first one is ordinarily the studying of micro lecture suits independent learning more, during the class or not. The second one is that the studying of micro lecture will be more effective before and after the class. Considering the limitation of time during the class, micro lecture are fewer arranged (XiaoBin Su, 2014) [9]. As a result, the principal application model of supporting system of micro lecture should be the differentiated teaching during the class and post-class tutoring after the class. In addition, during the class, teachers can have more time to solve the question, organize study group. The teaching application model presented as Fig 4.

The learning process of students started from submitting the study tasks and introduce tasks, and then definite the study tasks; finish the tasks; forming perceptual realization to the content about to learn; summarize the introduce tasks with teacher in the class; listen to the explanation teacher offered for the relevant knowledge; think about the questions teacher asked positively; discuss the new questions with the cooperation of classmates; watching micro lecture material like knowledge explanation, operation present exercise, classic algorisms based on the requirement of the post-class assignments and their own understanding of the lecture after the class; execute independent tasks and online exercises; discuss with teachers and classmates through BBS, so their understanding of the courses and the practical ability can be promoted continuously.

Conclusion

What is micro lecture and how to apply micro lecture to college education is the focus of current college educators. The author holds that micro lecture can't replace formal class, but it can act as the extension of class teaching, support personal study and differentiated teaching served around students. The article discussed the C programming Micro lecture designing mode study in mobile learning circumstance, and proposed a doable solution.

References

[1] Wang wei, Zhong Shaochun, &LV Senlin (2009). Empirical Research on Mobile Learning Of Colleague Students [J]. Open Education Research 15(2), 81-86.
(Wei Wand, ShaoChun Zhong, CenLin Lv (2009).College students mobile learning example research [J]. Developing education research, 14(4):81 86
[2] ZhiXin Hou, YiZhi Wang (2014) .The personal study system research based on mobile learning [J].China education Informationalize. 2014(11)68-71
[3] MinZhuo Liu, ZhiTing Zhu (2013). The design analyze and mode construction of micro lecture [J].China Educational Technology,(12)127-131
[4] XiaoJun Zhen (2014). My definition of Micro Lecture [EB/OL]. http://blog.sina.com.cn/s/blog_4711a0210102e6ge.html, 2014-04-21.
[5] XiaoBin SU, YuQi Guan, DongMing Qian, TingZhi Zhu (2014) Micro Lecture concept analyze and its teaching application research [J]. China Educational Technology.(7):94-99
[6] Su Xiaobing, Guan Jueqi, Qian Dongming&Zhu Zhiting(2014) Research on the Concept and Instructional Application of Micro-Lesson.
[7] LeMing Liang, QiaoQiao Cao (2013). Micro Lecture design mode research – comparison research analyze of micro lecture based on China and abroad [J].Open Education Research. (1):67-75.
[8] LianJun Chen, QingTing Zhu (2011). C language program design teaching research serving for ability foster [J].Computer Education (14): 102-105
[9] ShenQuan Yu, Fang Mao. Informal learning – E Learning research and applying new field [J]. China Educational Technology, 2005(10): 18-23.
[10] Mi Wang. The content design research of fragmental-oriented learning micro video courses [D]. Shanghai: East China Normal University. 2013

 DOI: 10.1051/itmconf/20171201028

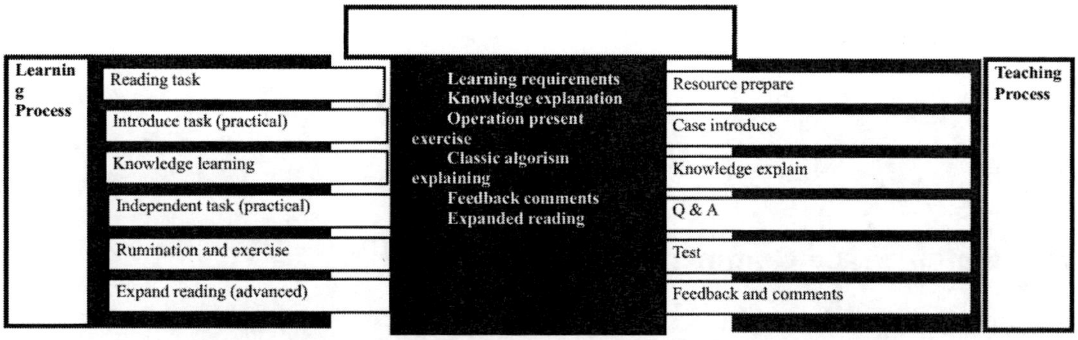

Fig 2.The teaching mode reconstitution with the support of micro lecture

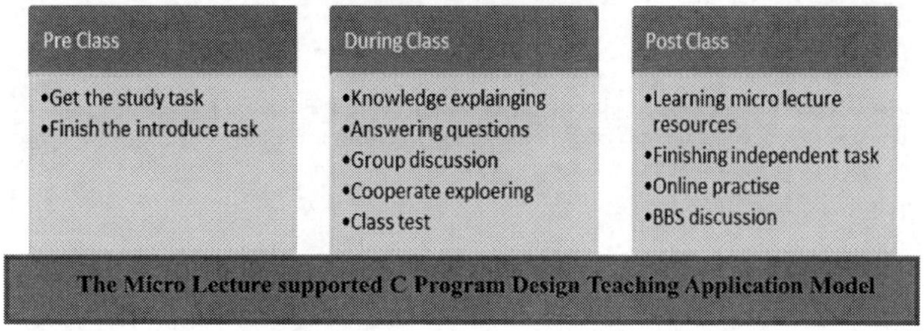

Fig 4.The micro lecture supported C program design teaching application model

DOI: 10.1051/itmconf/20171201029

How to Optimize the Commission Allocation

Lan YI, Wan-Ling LI

Economics and Management School of Wuhan University, Wuhan 430072, China
China Resources Vanguard. Co., Ltd, Shenzhen 518020, China
lanyi66@aliyun.com,liwanling1@crvanguard.com.cn

Abstract—in this paper, the commission allocation mechanism between the mobile application store and the mobile application developer is studied under the game theory. Firstly, based on the non-cooperative game theory, the paper researches the equilibrium solution of the inter-firm game under the conditions of different sales scale, and then extend the study to the circumstance of infinite game. In addition, the paper analyzes the Pareto improvement achieved by choosing cooperative strategy of strategic alliance from different parts. Finally, problem of the commission allocation problem is resolved.

1Introduction

Apple Corporation announced part of its Apple Store sales data in Sept, 2016, it showed that over 0.7 billion iPhone, iPad and iPod's global user had downloaded totally 140 billion applications through the Apple Store. The Apple user paid more than 1.1 billion US$ in S1 of 2016 and the Apple store had created 1.9 million jobs in USA, 1.2 million jobs in Europe and 1.4 million jobs in China .

The application store not only provided tens of thousands of software to the mobile phone's user, it also created a highly effective marketing channel to application exploiter to reached the end-user directly. Through reviewing various mobile phone's application stores and the application developer's payment allocation model, it is discovered that most application store seek a fix percentage of commission from the developer's application sales. For instance, Apple's App Store, is gaining approximately 20% to 30% of its total sales from the application store. Base on the current fix commission basis, is this sufficient to motivate application developer to provide high quality application? Does the commission vary between higher qualities versus normal qualities application developers? How does the total income change if both parties formed strategic alliance cooperation? How does the commission allocated reasonably between both parties? This article will analyze and provide answer to these questions.

2 Literature Review

Jeuland and Shugan(1983), Monahan(1984), Moorthy (1987), Cachon and Lariviere(2005) and other scholars suggested various methods to coordinates both parties through the studies of cooperation model between the marketing channel and upstream supplier. One of the methods that they suggested is to allocate a certain percentage of the sales income between upstream and downstream corporation.

The contract among supply chain members that focuses on income mechanism has continuously being studied extensively by scholars. Tsay and Lovejoy (1999), Anupindi and Bassok (1999) and other scholars referenced the cooperation model between the marketing channel and supplier, and the overall supply chain as a foundation for model establishment. Based on the foundation, types of foundation model have been discussed, including the price adjustment, the returns of income, quantity elasticity and other utilization of the rewards and penalty mechanism.

Li, Wang and Zhao (2009) have applied the game theory on departmental store and specialist retailers as a breakthrough point. The studies suggest fluctuation commission cooperation model depending on the sales volume adjustment of the upstream and downstream manufacturer's income distribution. The studies also pointed out the suitable range of sales volume for the model.

Based on the income sharing mechanism, Chen and Gao (2006) suggest the general model for multi-stages supply chain coordinates which analyzes the win-win condition for the members that involves in the supply chain. Lin and Zhu

(2004) considered introduce the penalty mechanism to improve game theory for income sharing mechanism. Graham (1999), Landeros (1995) and other scholars continued to expand the studies regarding the above literature review that discussed issues on cooperation model between the marketing channel and supplier. They emphasized that the importance of promise and effectiveness in optimizing relations.

Landerous(1995) et al. summarized various factors that restrict win-win outcome of the alliance between the upstream and downstream manufacturer. Furthermore, Coughlan (2001) pointed out that both parties will have great difficulties to perform a full cooperation if upstream supplier and downstream retailer both position themselves in a rational supposition that only pursues own benefit maximization. Under this circumstances, it would be a challenge to optimize the returns of the overall supply chain.

In the recent research, scholars started studying the cooperation organization structure within the channel. The studies tend to focus on "partnership" and "alliance" cooperation, it is believe that this kind of cooperation mechanism will be helpful in enhancing the confidence level as well as reduces the transaction cost. As a whole, presently the academia research outcome provided various valuable theories for the cooperation model between the application store and exploiters. However, the current theory is incapably to explain the choice of cooperate model under some specific market environment (for example, the internet market environment). Moreover, within the academia there is lack of analysis regarding key factors that influences the cooperation model, such as, sales volume.

In addition, most studies focuses on the rational supposition that only pursues own benefit maximization of the upstream and downstream manufacturer, there are lack of studies that concentrate on cooperation game theory perspective based on the collective rationality to analyze bilateral game theory relations. Therefore, this article attempts to have the different view on these two new perspectives.

3 Non-Cooperate Perspective Game Theory Model

Firstly in this section, we will established the non-cooperate perspective game theory model, by identifying the basic game theory environment between the application store and the application exploiter under the scope of internet market background.

Secondly, we will discuss the dynamic influence between the bilateral game theory and sales volume balances under the game theory in a static situation.

Finally, we will expand the game theory from single phase to multiple phases, in order to analyze the changes in strategic selection and other condition of the bilateral long-term cooperative game.

3.1 Basic assumptions and definitions

We make assumptions for bilateral game conditions based on the characteristics of the internet market, bilateral game and mobile phones application products:

Assumption 1: Market characteristics

Internet is a perfect channel to access complete information and the cost of the information flow is extremely low; assuming that all mobile phone application product is at a very low price and the price maintain at the same level; application store does not have the right and unable to restrict the exploiter to develop application sales channel through internet; internet search engine will be able to provide excellent promotion service for the developer's website.

Assumption 2: bilateral game

Application store and developers are completely rational, both parties receives fully symmetrical information. The application store has two strategic choices to adopt fixed commission or variable commission basis as a source of return; developer has also two strategic choices to create or not create its own sales channel through website.

Assume that the research and development cost for mobile phone application equals to "D", marginal cost for the production and sales of the application equals to zero. Investment of developer's sales channel in the website equals to "I", developer's website can implement its advertisement promotion through internet search engine or individual website, the advertisement expenses has direct relation with "click quantity", and therefore, it is correlated to sales volume, assume that "r" equals to internet promotion expense per selling unit. Under the circumstances when future sales are unfavorable and the visit quantity of the application store cannot be guaranteed, developers will choose to sell its application in the application store as their first priority.

3.2 Game model based on fixed commission cooperative basis

Based on the assumptions above, the profit function of developer's application sales in the application stores equals to:

$$\pi_s = PQ(1-K) - D \quad (1)$$

If developer create another sales channel and adopted internet as its advertisement promotion then the profit functions equals to:

$$\pi_o = Q(P-r) - I - D \quad (2)$$

π in function (1) and (2) equals to corporate profit, "P" equals to selling price of the application, "Q" equals to selling quantity, "K" equals to sales commission returns of the application store (this section refers to fixed commission, therefore, "K" equals to a constant value), "r" equals to coefficient of internet promotion expense, "*I*" equals to developer's cost of self-developed internet sales channel, "*D*" equals to application research and development cost.

Sales channel developed by application developers will cause decrease in sales of the relevant applications in the application store. Assume that the total social demand stays constant, dependent variable "λ" equals to the proportion of application sales volume of the total sales volume, after the developers created its own internet sales channel.

Therefore, after the developers created another channel, two sources of sales returns will be recognize which includes:

$$\pi_{ss} = \lambda PQ(1-K) - D \quad (3)$$

$$\pi_{so} = (1-\lambda)Q(P-r) - I - D \quad (4)$$

The condition for the developers to create its own internet sales channel is the total sales returns of both channel is larger than the return of application that only distribute in the application store, then, $(1) \le (3)+(4)$.

As a result, inequality of function (5) is the condition for the developers to create its own internet sales channel:

$$(PK-r)Q \ge \frac{I}{1-\lambda} \quad (5)$$

As P is a constant value, therefore, when $PK \le r$, it suggests that the promotion expense will be higher if developer creates its own internet sales channel, furthermore, the proportion of the sales return is lower in the application store. As a result, it is not economical for the developers to create its own internet sales channel, therefore, function(5)does not establish.

When $PK \ge r$, it suggests that the advertising expense will be lower if developer creates its own internet sales channel, conversely, the proportion of the sales return is higher in the application store. Developers can choose to create its own internet sales channel, but the condition is that the sales volume does not satisfy function (6):

$$Q \ge \frac{I}{(1-\lambda)(PK-r)} \quad (6)$$

If fixed commission is constantly used while the sales volume of the application is in a very high level, then the developers would probably shift their selling distribution to other marketing channel. Although it results in extra cost for developer to create another channel, it reduces developer's commission expense for the application store. In such circumstances, developer's basic trade-off is the cost of the marketing channel and commission, and the main factor that influences trade-off is the sales volume.

Proposition 1: When the developer creates its own internet sales channel advertising expense is lower, application store's proportion of sales return is higher, the relationships satisfy $PK \ge r$, and the sales volume satisfy $Q \ge \frac{I}{(1-\lambda)(PK-r)}$, then developer will choose to create internet sales channel other than the application store.

4 Game Model Based on Variable Commission Cooperative Basis

When application sales volume satisfies function (6), then developer will create extra internet sales channel, this strategy not only increase its return, it also reduce the return of the application store. Under such circumstances, application store will consider adopting variable commission strategy which will decrease commission proportion from the higher sales application developers; ultimately it will reduce the motive of the developers to distribute its application in other internet sales channel.

Variable commission strategy is defined as the proportion return of the application store will vary according to the sales fluctuation of the developers. This economic significance is that the application stores provide rent return to developers as a reward through transferring partial income to developers which will reduce the motive of the developers to distribute in other channel.

Meanwhile, application store faces the basic trade-off, which is to shift the return losses and return brings from developers that not distribute in other channel. The core factor that influences this trade-off is the demand of the application. Therefore, application store should only provide proportion of the variable commission that satisfies the conditions below: (1) from the developer's perspective, the effectiveness is indifferent whether it creates or not creates distribution in other channel; (2) under the condition where return of application store is larger than the proportion of fixed commission, the developer favor the return from the application store rather than the return in internet channel.

When the market demand satisfies function (6) and (1) = (3) + (4), resulting the function of application store's variable commission present as shown below:

$$K_m = \frac{I+(1-\lambda)Qr}{PQ(1-\lambda)} = \frac{I}{PQ(1-\lambda)} + \frac{r}{P} \quad (7)$$

From function (7) it is found that, when developer's cost of self-developed internet sales channel "*I*" and internet promotion expense per selling unit "*r*" is higher, then the proportion of variable commission "K_m" can be set in a higher level. Under such circumstances, it is sufficient for the application store to transfer minimal payment to prevent developers to distribute in other channel.

When the sales volume divergence of the application developers influence by the developers distributing in other channel are relatively low and "λ"is larger, then proportion of K_m will be higher.

It is because, meanwhile consumer are more willing to purchase application in the application store (which makes application store higher selling share). As a result, the application store has stronger bargaining power than developers during the game.

Similarly, it is sufficient for the application store to transfer minimal payment to prevent developers to distribute in other channel, which will guaranteed the return of the application stores.

When the market response of the developer product is favorable (when sales volume "Q" is larger), the bargaining power of developers will be stronger, then application store will need to reduce the cost of developer.

Proposition 2: When application store adopt a variable commission basis, then the value can be express as $K_m = \frac{I}{PQ(1-\lambda)} + \frac{r}{P}$, the commission proportion will be positively relation to "I","r", "λ"; and negatively relation to sales volume "Q", therefore, the developer's return is indifferent regardless it creates or not creates distribution in other channel.

Expression (7) can reference by the application store to design the proportion of variable commission, the better practical value for "I","r", "λ"and "Q" can be obtain through market research.

Thus, the application store fixed commission model may not be the golden rule, an application store should recognize the scope of various cooperative model, should alter the cooperative model that best suits the market and internal characteristics.

4.1 Game model based on non cooperative perspective

1) Static game model

In static game model, application store has two strategies which involves fixed and variable commission basis. Developer has also two strategies which are create or not create its own internet selling channel. These strategies can be express as the diagram below:

TABLE I. TABLE 1 EXPRESSION OF GAME STRATEGIES FOR BOTH PARTIES

		Application developers	
		Create internet sales channel	Not create internet sales channel
Application store	Fix commission basis	$PQ(1-\lambda K)-rQ(1-\lambda)-D-I$ (8) $PQ\lambda K - C$ (9)	$PQ(1-K)-D$ $PQK-C$ (10)
	Variable commission basis	$Q(P-r)-D+\frac{I}{\lambda-1}$ $\frac{\lambda I}{1-\lambda}+Q\lambda r-C$	$Q(P-r)-D+\frac{I}{\lambda-1}$ $\frac{I}{1-\lambda}+Qr-C$ (11)

When $Q \geq \frac{I}{(1-\lambda)(PK-r)}$ is within the selling scope, and if, application store choose fixed commission basis, then creating an internet sales channel is a dominant strategy for developer.

If application store choose to adopt variable commission basis, then the developer's return is indifferent whether it creates or not creates distribution in other channel. Therefore, regardless of any strategy that the application store adopts, when the sales volume reaches $Q \geq \frac{I}{(1-\lambda)(PK-r)}$ then creating an internet sales channel is a dominant strategy for developer.

Under such circumstances, application store will adopt fixed commission basis, because developer is unable to alter its internet sales channel strategy under variable commission basis, therefore, combination strategy of fixed commission basis and creating internet sales channel as the Nash equilibrium solution for this game model.

Proposition 3:When sales volume of the application satisfies $Q \geq \frac{I}{(1-\lambda)(PK-r)}$, application store would select a strategy of fixed commission basis and creating internet sales channel as the Nash equilibrium solution for this game model.

When sales volume of the application satisfies $\frac{I}{(1-\lambda)(PK-r)} \leq Q \leq \frac{I}{(1-\lambda)(P\lambda K-r)}$, the return is greater when selecting "variable commission basis and not create its own internet selling channel" strategy in comparison to "fixed commission basis and creating internet sales channel" strategy; which can be express as $\frac{I}{1-\lambda}+Qr-C \geq PQ\lambda K - C$.

If application store choose a variable commission basis $K_m = \frac{I}{PQ(1-\lambda)} + \frac{r}{P}$ causing the return of the applications developer to be equal, then developers will choose not to create its own internet selling channel.

Proposition 4:When sales volume of the application satisfy:

$$\frac{I}{(1-\lambda)(PK-r)} \leq Q \leq \frac{I}{(1-\lambda)(P\lambda K-r)},$$

then the choice of the application store can be express as $K_m = \frac{I}{PQ(1-\lambda)} + \frac{r}{P}$, a variable commission basis. If developer choose not to create its own internet selling channel in such condition, then (variable commission, not create internet channel) it will become Pareto Improvement payment combination.

However, Pareto Improvement in proposition 4 cannot be achieving in a sustainable manner when the game is in a static situation. It is because the equilibrium condition does not satisfy the rational supposition under the condition of non-cooperative game theory.

Once rational developer anticipated that the strategy of not to create an internet channel, then developer will choose fix commission strategy under the principle of self-interest maximization which will earn a return from divergence agreement.

It does not make any sense for application store and developer to negotiate in the early stage of the cooperation, simply because, this Pareto Improvement payment combination does not form an equilibrium solution; both parties will not proactively compliance with commitments. In summary, under the condition where sales volume of the application is moderate, then both parties will face a Prisoner's Dilemma, an equilibrium solution will be fixed commission basis and creating internet sales channel strategy.

When the sales volume of the application continues to growth $Q \geq \frac{I}{(1-\lambda)(P\lambda K-r)}$, then the return would be smaller if variable commission has been selected over fixed commission basis, can be express as $\frac{I}{1-\lambda}+Qr-C \leq$ $PQ\lambda K-C$.

Variable commission of the application store can be expressed as $K_m=\frac{I}{PQ(1-\lambda)}+\frac{r}{P}$ and $\frac{dK_m}{dQ}<0$, when the sales reaches certain extent, the expense of shifting a source of income is greater than the losses in return from the fix commission basis. Therefore, sales volume within certain range, application store will insist a fix commission basis and developer will also create an internet sales channel strategy.

Proposition 5: When sales volume of the application reaches $Q \geq \frac{I}{(1-\lambda)(P\lambda K-r)}$, then equilibrium solution for application store and developer will be: application store select a fixed commission basis and developer create its own internet selling channel.

Based on above proposition, it can be seen that game balance between the application store and developer is determined by the sales changes of the application.

4.2 Repeated game model

In this section, we discussed the changes of the long-term cooperation model between the application store and developer. It is also to expand static game model, which has been discussed in last section, into multiple period repeated game model.

4.2.1 Finitely repeated game

When production volume satisfy $\frac{I}{(1-\lambda)(PK-r)} \leq Q \leq \frac{I}{(1-\lambda)(P\lambda K-r)}$ condition, and the game period between the application store and developer are limited, then the subgame perfect Nash equilibrium can be determine via backward induction which is fixed commission basis and creating internet sales channel strategy. This prisoner dilemma will never ever reaches Pareto Improvement (variable commission basis and developer not to create its own internet selling channel)

4.2.2 Infinitely repeated game model

Assume that game has repeated infinitely, we considered that both parties will adopt a trigger strategy as equilibrium game. Application developer's trigger strategy is initially insisted not create its own internet selling channel until a period when application store chosen a fixed commission strategy; developer will continue to create its own internet selling channel as a retaliation.

From the application store's perspective, when it selected variable commission basis, both strategies that the developer selected will make no different. Therefore, it will not be concern if application store's adopt a trigger strategy when developer departure from the contract. Assume that δ as stochastic discount factor of application store.

If application store departure from the contract and selected a fixed commission basis at any stage of the game, then return of the relevant period will be $PQK-C$; and the additional return compared to the previous contract can be express as $Q(PK-r)-\frac{I}{1-\lambda}$.

However, opportunistic behavior of the application store will trigger developer to create its own internet selling channel forever as a punishment. At this stage, return of the application store will reduce $PQ\lambda K-C$ in each period.

Therefore, if conditions below are satisfied, then application store will not departure from the contract to choose a fixed commission strategy in any given period:

$$\left[Q(PK-r)-\frac{I}{1-\lambda}\right]+\delta[PQ\lambda K-C]+\delta^2[PQ\lambda K-C]+\cdots\cdots \leq$$

$$(\frac{I}{1-\lambda}+Qr-C)+\delta(\frac{I}{1-\lambda}+Qr-C)+\delta^2(\frac{I}{1-\lambda}+Qr-C)+\cdots\cdots$$

Conditions above can be solved as:

$$\delta^* \geq \frac{C + PQK - 2Qr - \frac{2I}{1-\lambda}}{C + PKQ - PQ\lambda K - Qr - \frac{I}{1-\lambda}} \quad (12)$$

δ^* means the level of important of the future return to application store. When present discounted value in the future satisfies condition (12), then application store will never choose to exploit developer at any point of time.

Therefore, both parties trigger strategy is in sub game perfect Nash equilibrium, Pareto improvement (variable commission basis and not to create its own internet selling channel) will be an equilibrium solution in each period. Under such condition, application store and developer resolve the finitely game dilemma.

The reason behind this is, if game repeated infinitely and each participant has enough patience, then the return of any short-term opportunistic behavior is minimal. If the return of application store's present discounted value does not satisfy condition (12), then Pareto improvement (variable commission basis and not to create its own internet selling channel) will not achieve. Proposition 6 has been obtained as a result of above analysis.

Proposition 6:If the game between the application store and developer repeated finitely, (fix commission basis, create internet channel) is the equilibrium solution of each period. Only the game repeat infinitely and the app store's present discounted value ratio satisfy condition (12), the strategy (variable commission basis and not to create its own internet selling channel) will be sub game perfect Nash equilibrium then Pareto improvement achieve.

All in sum, if the partners want to obtain higher return, they should abandon the short-sighted current cooperation idea and develop a long-term and steady cooperation relationship. The longer they cooperate, the higher the return will be.

In the analysis of this section, although the solution to Pareto improvement of two parties came upon, we can get a greater discounted value solely assuming the two parties' long-term gamble and app store. And can the two sides cooperate without the assumptions? If so, how the two parties distribute the cooperating surplus? Next we make a penetrating analysis of the problem based on cooperating game theory.

5. The Theory Model on Cooperative Game Perspective

On the basic of the above, a deep issue is the conflict between individual and collective rationality. To more definitely, application store and developer are based on optimal self-utility, only to find losses of the common interests. Supposing that the two sides form the strategic alliance to make more profit rather than trade for the market, we can approach that how the two parties sign the binding cooperative agreement and improve Pareto according to cooperative game theory.

With cooperative game, cooperative parties pay attention to individual rationality instead of collective rationality. In the model, although there is a conflict between individual rationality and collective rationality, the two-party-paying-term raises efficiency and gets the Pareto improvement when cooperating. The core is, the two sides in strategic alliance design a binding mechanism in order to come to equilibrium fairly and effectively. In other words, they get variable commission and do not develop a news channel. What's more, they get surplus by distributing in reason so as to establish a stable cooperative relationship.

For there is no a definite solution to explain 'fair', there is no Nash equilibrium in cooperative game theory in the same way. Even so, with the development of cooperative game theory, a lot of effective solutions have been introduced, in which there is the significant and generally acceptable Shapley Value. With Shapley Value, we elaborate cooperative mechanism between app store and developer.

For app store and develop in strategic alliance, surplus coming from cooperation is $Q(P-r)-D+\frac{I}{\lambda-1}+\frac{I}{1-\lambda}+Qr-C=PQ-D-C$. If wanting to reach a binding agreement and get the common income, they need to use Shapley Value to calculate how many they should get from the surplus.

Strictly for developer, the Shapley value is

$$\frac{0!\quad(1!\ )}{2!}[PQ(1-\lambda K)-rQ(1-\lambda)-D-I-0]+\frac{1!(0!)}{2!}[PQ-D-C-(PQ\lambda K-C)]$$

$$=PQ(1-\lambda \mathrm{K})-\mathrm{D}-\frac{1}{2}(\mathrm{Q}-\lambda \mathrm{Q}+\mathrm{I}) \quad (13)$$

Proposition 7::In the relationship of strategic cooperate game, the software store should share the final benefit from

$$PQ(1-\lambda \mathrm{K})-\mathrm{D}-\frac{1}{2}(\mathrm{Q}-\lambda \mathrm{Q}+\mathrm{I})\cdot$$

Likewise, for app store, the Shapley Value is

$$\frac{0!\quad(1!\ )}{2!}[PQ\lambda K-C-0]+\frac{1!(0!)}{2!}[PQ-D-C-(PQ(1-\lambda K)-rQ(1-\lambda)-D-I)]$$

$$=PQ\lambda K-C+\frac{1}{2}(Q-\lambda Q+I)$$

Proposition 8:In the relationship of strategic cooperate game, the software store should share the final benefit from

$$PQ\lambda K-C+\frac{1}{2}(Q-\lambda Q+I) \quad (14)$$

The difference benefit of developer got from cooperative and non-cooperative is: $(1-\lambda)(r+\frac{1}{2})Q+\frac{I}{2}$: (13-8). The positive value means that cooperative model of developer would get much more than non-cooperative. App store would get $\frac{Q}{2}(1-\lambda)+I$ in the same way. Above all, the two equations prove cooperative model is better than non-cooperative in this situation. Shapley Value indicates the value of cooperative working. The conclusion has been proved by economy authorities on the fair and effective of this model. Therefore, the model is a powerful evidence of cooperate and distribute the surplus between application store and developer.

6 Conclusion and Discussion

Studying the cooperative model between mobile application stores and developers, the paper extends and analyses dynamic and static non-cooperative and cooperative model, based on cooperative and non-cooperative game theory. It tries to analyze the selections and their influential factors of various business competitive and cooperative relative enterprises. Proposition 5 under the dynamic game theory of complete information indicates that sales of products determines competitive pattern. More importantly, we find that the fixed division proportion system prevailing in current market is not the most scientific or effective. So when designing cooperation model of application store, every main operator and phone manufacturer in our country is supposed to create a new cooperative mechanism according to its local conditions instead of entirely aping the business model of the application store. It is proved by proposition 6 of repeated game model that a balanced cooperative model is decided by cooperative agreement in the case of a long-term cooperation between both sides. In other words, the longer the expected mutual cooperation, the bigger possibilities of Pareto improvement. Thus we can draw a conclusion that the following ways determine sharing and personal profit between application stores and developers. Firstly, under the background of Internet sales model, application stores and developers should identify the market demand and product characteristics, having a good understanding on and realistic expectation about them. Secondly, either party has to establish steady and long-term relationship. For instance, they use cooperative ways of strategic alliance, cross shareholding and joint venture especially mergers and acquisitions, which change one-off deal into long-term relationship.

In addition, with the cooperative game theory, the allocation of the sharing benefits on cooperative parties is analyzed. Specifically, the paper, under proposition 7 and 8 of cooperative game theory model, shows how to fairly and effectively distribute the surplus, improved by cooperation and Pareto between both sides, who aim at collective rationality. Therefore, according to the observation, application stores and developers can sign a binding contract so as to guarantee the cooperation and maximum profits between the two parties.

References

[1] Jeuland,Abel P., Steven M.Shugan. Managing Channel Profits. Marketing Science, 1983, 2(3):239-272.
[2] J.Monahan.A Quantity Discount Pricing Model to Increase Vendor Profits . Management Science ,1984(30):720-726
[3] K.S.Moorthy, Managing channel profits:Comments, Marketing Science 6, 1987:375~379.
[4] Cachon, Gérard P., Martin A. Lariviere.Supply Chain Coordination with Revenue-Sharing Contracts: Strengths and Limitations.Management Science, 2005, 51(1):30-44.
[5] TsayA.,Lovejoy.W. Quantity flexibility contracts and supply chainperformance. Manufacturing and Service Operations Management,1,1999:89~111
[6] AnupindiR.and Bassok .Y. Centralization of stocks: Retailers vs.Manufacturer .Management Science,45,1999:178~191
[7] Coughlan Anne T, Erin Anderson, Louis W. marketing channels. Sixth Edition,Printice Hall, 2001
[8] Graham T S,Daugherty P J,Dudley W N. The Long-term Strategic Impact of Purchasing Partnership. InternationalJournal of Purchasing and Materials Management,1994,30(4):
[9] 13-18
[10] Landeros R,Reck Ret al. Maintaining Buyer-supplier Partnerships. InternationalJournal of Purchasing and Materials Management,1995,31(3):3-11
[11] Guillermo Owen, Game Theory. Second Edition, Academic Press,1982
[12] Lin,Xudong,Shunquan Zhu.Study on Game Model of Profit Distribution in Supply Chain Corporation.Value Engineering,2004,23(5): 29-31.
[13] Li,Hao, Gao Wang, Ping Zhao.Employing float commission rate to optimize the revenue-sharing mechanism.Journal of systems engineering, 2011,26(3): 352-359
[14] Chen, Fuhua, ChengxiuGao. Multi-Stage Supply Chain Coordination by Revenue Sharing Contracts. Journal Of Wuhan University(Natural Science Edition), 2006, 52(3): 291-295.
[15] Chen, Yuanzhi, Jianming, xia.Establishment and Operation of the Model of Supply Chain Management Strategy.Journal of Finance and Economics,2004,30(3): 75-84.
[16] Sun, Penggui.Supply Chain Mangement and Enterprises's Relation Strategy[J].Journal of Finance and Economics,2002,28(4):58-63.
[17] Zhang, Weiying, Game Theory and Information Economics,ShangHaiSanlian Press

Design of Slag Thickness Fuzzy Control System for Slag Adding Robot

Yuan GUO, Xiao-Hui ZHAN, Xin-Yuan* CHEN, Jiang-Hong DENG

College of Machinery and Automation, Wuhan University of Science and Technology, Wuhan, China
323111116@qq.com,598258094@qq.com, 13627293882@163.com,Dengjianghong325@163.com

Abstract: According to the defect of artificial slag adding and open-loop slag adding in continuous casting mold, a slag adding robot with real-time slag thickness detection and feedback control is developed. That is, the laser ranging sensor is applied on the basis of the open-loop slag adding robot. Then the real-time information of in-mold slag thickness can be obtained. And the coupling relation of three factors: real-time slag thickness, mold work slagging speed and robot slagging rate are taken into comprehensive consideration. Therefore fuzzy controller is built to realize the fuzzy PID control of the slagging robot feeding electro-mechanical system and achieve the intelligent control of slag thickness in the mold. The simulation and application results show that the slag adding robot based on fuzzy PID control has good effect and quick response. The slag can be pressed according to the requirement, which is beneficial to energy saving and consumption reduction, and improves the quality of the billet.

1Introduction

In the process of continuous casting of steel, the thickness of the mold powder seriously affects the quality of billet [1-5]. Too great thickness of the mold fluxes would lead surface crack of billet to be increased and slag powder to be loosen. However, oxidation of molten steel, fast cooling and the wear of the mold will happen if the thickness is too small. Therefore, it is necessary to precisely control the thickness of the slag [6-9]. At present artificial slag adding is adopted in most enterprises without accuracy. A few enterprises use slag machine to replace artificial slag adding to achieve automation.But in this open-loop way the amount of slag added can't be real-time adaptively controlled with the change of the parameters. In this paper adding slag process of the mold fluxes is taken into account. By associating with the actual slag requirements a slag adding robot is developed. Through the laser distance measuring sensor, the thickness of the mold fluxes is real-time scanned and measured, and feedback control can be realized to adjust the amount of slag dropping accurately so as to realize the accurate control of the thickness of the mold fluxes in the mold[10-13].

2. System of slag thickness adaptive slag adding robot

2.1 Open-loop System of Slag Machine

The slag adding robot of continuous casting mold developed by our research group, which consists of electronic control system ①, movement system②, adding slag system ③, and Lifting system ④.The adding slag system is made up of hopper 1, gear reducer 2 and 4, transporting motor 3, swinging-rod motor 5, transporting pipe 6, guiding device 7, transporting spiral 8,discharging port 9 and so on. The structure of the slag adding robot is shown in Fig.1.

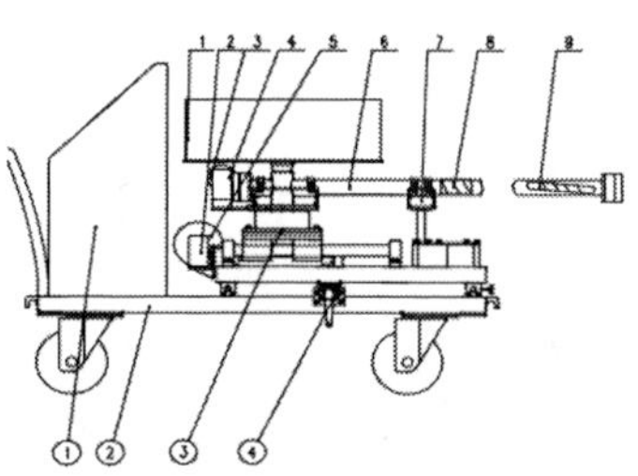

Fig.1 The structure of the slag adding robot

The mold fluxes is fed from the hopper into the feed pipe, and the feed motor drives the feed screw to deliver the slag to the discharge port, then the mold fluxes falls into the mold. The swing bar motor drives the feed pipe to swing slag in the slag adding area of the mold. Fig. 2 is a diagram of open-loop slag adding. The single tube distribution range is 1300mm * 250mm, the single pipe slag flow range is from 0.15L/min to 1.5L/min and the feeding cycle is from 6s to 60s.

DOI: 10.1051/itmconf/20171201030

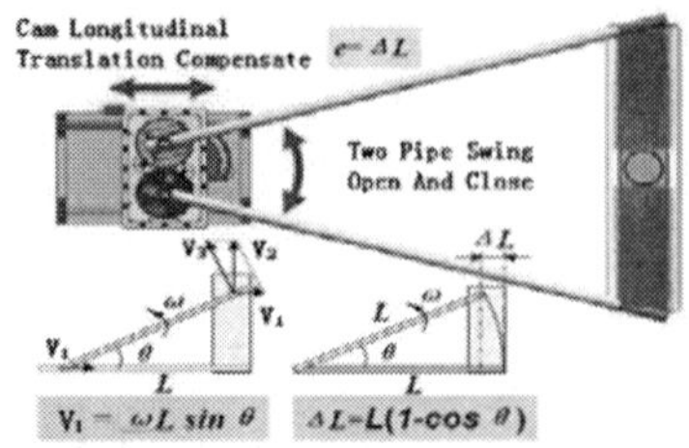

Fig. 2 The diagram of slag adding for the open-loop slag adding robot

2.2 System of Closed-loop Slag Adding Robot

Based on the developed open-loop slag adding robot, the laser distance measuring sensor (as shown in Fig. 3) is added to the discharge port of the feed pipe to measure the thickness of mold fluxes[14-18]. In order to avoid the influence of the color of molten steel on the measurement results, a green laser with different wavelength range was selected. By using the real-time slag thickness measured through the laser distance measuring sensor as a feedback signal, the closed-loop control of slag adding robot is realized.

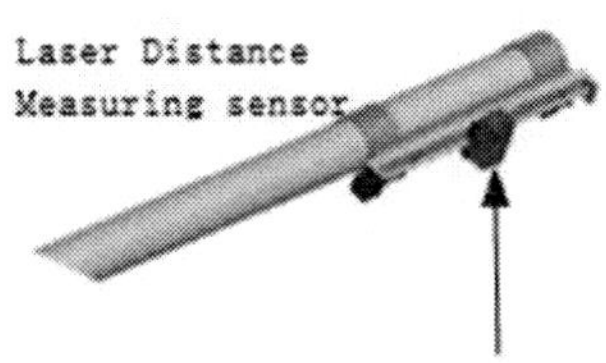

Fig. 3 Laser scanning device for slag thickness

2.3 Control Model of the Slag Adding

In the process of adding slag, the instructions are transferred from the computer to the inverter firstly, and then the inverter transfers the received signal to the feeding motor, a feeding screw driven by the feeding motor drives the mold fluxes to the discharge port so as to add the mold fluxes into the crystallizer. The components of the slag adding process are connected in series, and the transfer function of each link is calculated. The inverter can be simplified into an inertial link [19-20] in the process of adding slag, that is, the transfer function of the converter is:

$$G_1(S)=\frac{K_1}{1+T_1S} \tag{1}$$

The coefficient of proportionality K_1 of the inverter is 5, and T_1 is the time constant of the inertial link, it usually tens to hundreds of ms, and the value of T_1 is 0.3. In the process of adding slag, the feeding motor can be simplified as an inertial link, that is, the transfer function of the feeding motor is:

$$G_2(S)=\frac{K_2}{1+T_2S} \tag{2}$$

In the formula, *K2* is the transmission coefficient of the feeding motor, and T_2 is the electromechanical time constant of the dragging system for the feeding motor, and K_2 is 0.2124; T_2 is 0.075 according to the selected feeding motor.

The reducer and feed screw can be equivalent to a proportional link in the process of slag adding, the coefficient of proportionality is K_3, and the value is 0.133. The open-loop transfer function of the slag adding robot is:

$$G(S)=\frac{K_1K_2K_3}{(1+T_1S)(1+T_2S)} \tag{3}$$

The open-loop transfer function of the slag adding robot can be calculated by substituting the specific value in formula (3):

$$G(S)=\frac{0.1416}{(1+0.075S)(1+0.3S)} \tag{4}$$

The thickness of adding slag fed back from the laser distance measuring sensor is fed to the computer, and the closed-loop control of slag adding capacity of the slag adding robot can be realized. The closed-loop control flow of the slag adding robot is shown in fig. 4.

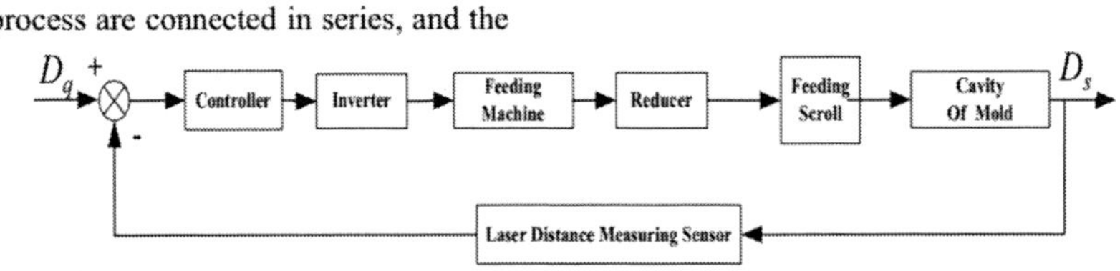

Fig. 4 Closed- loop control flow chart of adding slag robot

The slag is added to the mold as needed, and the amount of slag added is expected to be as follows:

$$D_q=h-D_c+D_x \tag{5}$$

In the formula, D_q is the expected thickness of the adding slag, h is the best thickness of mold fluxes and its range is 35mm~50mm, D_c is the thickness of the slag measured by the laser distance measuring sensor, and D_x is the thickness consumed by the mold in unit time. And the expected amount of the adding slag is:

$$Q=\frac{D_q lx}{t} \tag{6}$$

In the formula, *l* is the width of the mold, *x* is the length the mold, and *t* is the unit time.

3. Design of the controller

In the thickness control system of the adding slag robot, the controller is the core of the system. During the crystallization period, the thickness of the mold fluxes should be 35mm-50mm, the conventional PID controller often has poor parameter setting and poor adaptive ability [8-9], so the adaptive fuzzy PID control is adopted.

The structure of the fuzzy PID controller is shown in Fig.5, and the parameters of the PID are adjusted by fuzzy control. Set the deviation *e* and deviation change rate *ec* as input signal of the fuzzy controller, the fuzzy *E* and *EC* were obtained through fuzzy inference, self-tuning parameters such as Δk_p、Δk_i and Δk_d of the fuzzy PID can be obtained by the fuzzy inference, *yd* is the expected amount of the adding slag, *Ds*(*t*) is the actual thickness of the adding slag. The adjustment process of fuzzy PID parameters is to obtain the self-tuning values of three parameters of PID by fuzzy inference and constantly check and correct in the process of adding slag. The adjustment of the fuzzy PID parameters is as follows:

$$\begin{cases} k_p = k_p^{'} + \Delta k_p \\ k_i = k_i^{'} + \Delta k_i \\ k_d = k_d^{'} + \Delta k_d \end{cases} \tag{7}$$

In the formula, the initial parameters of the PID controller are k'_p、k'_I and k'_d

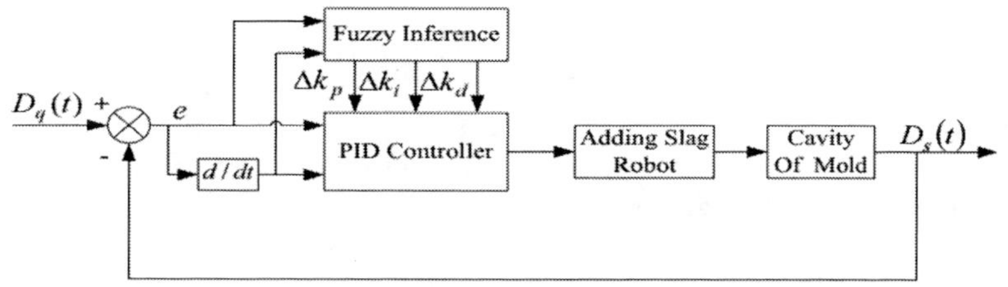

Fig. 5 Structure diagram of fuzzy controller

Determination of initial parameters of PID: Z-N method is used to obtain initial parameters of PID controller. In the control process, the Z-N frequency domain tuning method is based on the stability analysis of the frequency domain response PID tuning method. The main idea of the method is: setting for the transfer function of the control system of the slag thickness, which the root locus can be obtained. The point through the jω axis, the corresponding gain is Km, the corresponding values for ω is ωm [20-25]. The formula is as follows:

$$k_p = 0.6k_m \tag{8}$$

$$k_d = \frac{k_p \pi}{4\omega_m} \tag{9}$$

$$k_i = \frac{k_p \omega_m}{\pi} \tag{10}$$

In the formula, km is the gain value of the K when the system starts oscillation, and the ωm is the oscillation frequency.

Between the actual output quantity and the desired output quantity of the crystallization slag thickness protector control system, the deviation e and the deviation change rate ec are the input quantity, and the three change value of the parameters (Δkp、Δki and Δkd)of fuzzy PID are the output quantity. The mold fluxes thickness of the crystallizer is in the range of 35mm~50mm, the domain of the basic theory of the deviation e is [-7.5,7.5], the basic domain error rate is [-5,5], the three basic domain of the PID are Δkp∈[-0.3,0.3]、Δki∈[-0.06,0.06] and Δkd ∈[-6,6].

In the selection of the membership function, generally the Gauss type and the triangle type are used, the Gauss type is used for the boundary part of the deviation *e* and the deviation change rate *ec*, while the triangle type is used for the PID three tuning parameters and the other parts except the deviation *e* and deviation change rate *ec* because the calculation of the triangle type is simple. The slag quantity deviation *e*, the deviation change rate *ec*, the PID self-tuning parameter Δk_p、Δk_i and Δk_d are all set as {*NB, MN, NS, ZO, PS, PM, PB*}. They respectively represent the negative big, negative middle, negative small, zero, positive small, positive middle and positive large. The fuzzy control rule table is shown in table 1.

Table 1 Fuzzy control rules tables of the Δk_p、Δk_i and Δk_d

Δk_p、Δk_i、Δk_d		EC						
		NB	NM	NS	ZO	PS	PM	PB
E	NB	PB/NB/PS	PB/NB/NS	PM/NM/NB	PM/NM/NB	PS/NS/NB	ZO/ZO/NM	ZO/ZO/PS
	NM	PB/NB/PS	PB/NB/NS	PM/NM/NB	PS/NS/NM	PS/NS/NM	ZO/ZO/NS	NS/ZO/ZO
	NS	PM/NB/ZO	PM/NM/NS	PM/NS/NM	PS/NS/NM	ZO/ZO/NS	NS/PS/NS	NS/PS/ZO
	ZO	PM/NM/ZO	PM/NM/NS	PS/NS/NS	ZO/ZO/NS	NS/PS/NS	NM/PM/NS	NM/PM/ZO
	PS	PS/NM/ZO	PS/NS/ZO	ZO/ZO/ZO	NS/PS/ZO	NS/PS/ZO	NM/PM/ZO	NM/PB/ZO
	PM	PS/ZO/PB	ZO/ZO/NS	NS/PS/PS	NM/PS/PS	NM/PM/PS	NM/PB/PS	NB/PB/PB
	PB	ZO/ZO/PB	ZO/ZO/PM	NM/PS/PM	NM/PM/PM	NM/PM/PS	NB/PB/PS	NB/PB/PB

The method of solving fuzzy rules in this paper is the gravity method, the formula is as follows:

$$u_0 = \frac{\int_v u\mu(u)\mathrm{d}u}{\int_v \mu(u)\mathrm{d}u} \tag{11}$$

In the formula: u is the element of output domain, u_0 is the result of defuzzification, and $\mu(u)$ is the membership function.

In the course of adjustment of PID fuzzy parameters, when the thickness of the slag in the mold gets smaller, we should increase the amount of slag added to the system, increase the value of k_p, and take the larger k_p. However, in order to avoid differential supersaturation we should take smaller k_d and take k_i=0 in order to avoid over retrieval. When the slag thickness is moderate, the effect of kd on the system is great, so the value of k_d should be adjusted reasonably.

4. Fuzzy PID Control And Simulation

Fuzzy PID control model was built by the Matlab/Simulink toolbox, and simulation analysis is carried out as well. The three initial parameters of the PID controller are: kp=114, ki=1.6, kd=74, step signals and slag adding are respectively used as the input signals for the simulation analysis. The simulation results are shown in Fig. 6 and Fig. 7. The horizontal axis in Fig. 6 is time, and Fig. 7 is a fuzzy PID control diagram for controlling the side of a mold during a slag adding cycle.

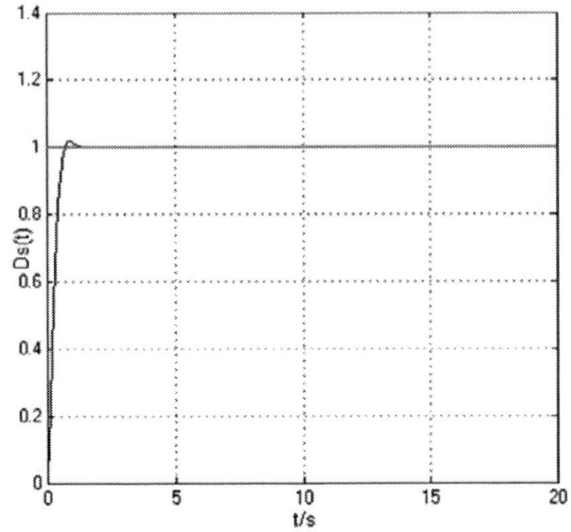

Fig. 6 Response of step signal

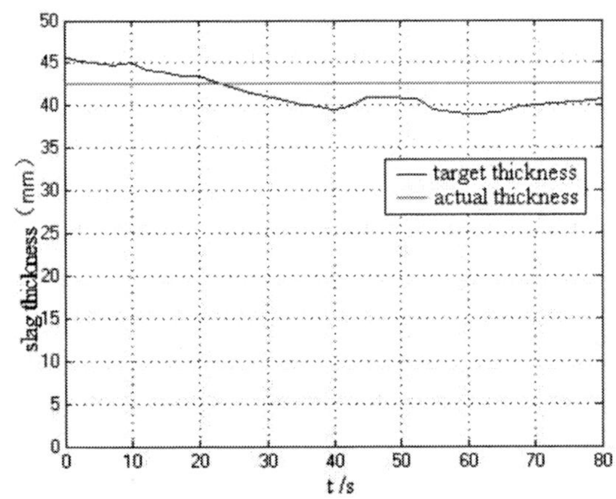

Fig. 7 Fuzzy PID control effect diagram

It can be seen in Fig. 6 that the system has fast response speed and high control precision. Fig. 7 showed that the mold fluxes thickness of the PID fuzzy control system of the crystallizer focus between the 35mm-50mm, which meets the control requirements, and the control effect of the system is good.

5. Field Service

The equipment developed by the research group has been used online for about 2 years in the 4th steel mill of Wuhan Iron and Steel (Group) Corp. The result shows that the equipment can reduce the slag consumption efficiently and is conducive to the quality and stability of the products. The thickness of the slag ranges from 35mm to 49mm.The picture of the field service is shown in fig.8.

Fig.8 Online application scheme of fuzzy control slag adding robot in the 4th steel mill ofWuhan Iron and Steel (Group) Corp.

Conclusion

In this paper, the laser distance measuring sensor is used as feedback device in order to meet the requirement of slag adding process. The fuzzy controller has been developed by adopting adaptive fuzzy PID algorithm. And the slag adding robot with closed- loop system could achieve real-time adjustment as required. So the slag adding robot can adapt to the change of continuous casting crystallization process parameters and realize slag adding on demands. The field application shows that the control system of this equipment has good effect on stability and control accuracy.

Acknowledgement

Fund project: Supported by Hubei science and technology support plan project（2015BAA023）
Project supported by key technological research project of Wuhan (2016010101010011)

References

[1]Effect of casting powder on casting blank Quality and Continuous Casting Process [J] LYS Science-Technology & Management, 2009, 06:61.

[2] Man-tang DING. Research of Fluoride-free Protective Slag Used in low C Steel. Advanced Materials Research Vol 803, 2013: 312-316

[3] Continuous Casting Technology question-answering [M]. First edition. Beijing: Chemical Industry Press, 2013:273-300.

[4]Zhong Yuntao, Liqiang. Application of Mold Power in Continuous casting machine. [J] Continuous Casting, 2013 04:9-13.

[5]Memon I, Chen L, Majid A, et al. Travel Recommendation Using Geo-tagged Photos in Social Media for Tourist [J]. Wireless Personal Communications, 2015, 80(4): 1347-62.

[6]Memon I. Authentication user's privacy: An integrating location privacy protection algorithm for secure moving objects in location based services[J]. Wireless Personal Communications, 2015, 82(3): 1585-1600.

[7]Arain Q A, Memon H, Memon I, et al. Intelligent travel information platform based on location base services to predict user travel behavior from user-generated GPS traces[J]. International Journal of Computers and Applications, 2017: 1-14.

[8]Memon I, Arain Q A. Dynamic path privacy protection framework for continuous query service over road networks[J]. World Wide Web, 2017, 20(4): 639-672.

[9]Arain Q A, Memon I, Deng Z, et al. Location monitoring approach: multiple mix-zones with location privacy protection based on traffic flow over road networks[J]. Multimedia Tools and Applications, 2017: 1-45.

[10]Memon I. A secure and efficient communication scheme with authenticated key establishment protocol for road networks[J]. Wireless Personal Communications, 2015, 85(3): 1167-1191.

[11]Arain Q A, Zhongliang D, Memon I, et al. Privacy Preserving Dynamic Pseudonym-Based Multiple Mix-Zones Authentication Protocol over Road Networks[J]. Wireless Personal Communications, 1-17.

[12]Arain Q A, Uqaili M A, Deng Z, et al. Clustering Based Energy Efficient and Communication Protocol for Multiple Mix-Zones Over Road Networks[J]. Wireless Personal Communications, 1-18.

[13]Memon I, Arain Q A. Optimal placement of mix zones in road networks[J]. arXiv preprint arXiv:1705.11104, 2017.

[14]Memon I, Arain Q A, Memon M H, et al. Search me if you can: Multiple mix zones with location privacy protection for mapping services[J]. International Journal of Communication Systems, 2017.

[15]Mangi F A, Xiao S, Jamro D A, et al. Manipulating Electromagnetic Wave Linear-to-Circular Polarization Conversion Transmitter Based on Periodic Strips Array[C]//Information Science and Control Engineering (ICISCE), 2016 3rd International Conference on. IEEE, 2016: 1342-1345.

[16]Memon M H, Li J P, Memon I, et al. Efficient object identification and multiple regions of interest using CBIR based on relative locations and matching regions[C]//Wavelet Active Media Technology and Information Processing (ICCWAMTIP), 2015 12th International Computer Conference on. IEEE, 2015: 247-250.

[17]Memon M H, Khan A, Li J P, et al. Content based image retrieval based on geo-location driven image tagging on the social web[C]//Wavelet Active Media Technology and Information Processing (ICCWAMTIP), 2014 11th International Computer

Conference on. IEEE, 2014: 280-283.

[18]Memon I, Mangi F A, Jamro D A. Collision avoidance of intelligent service robot for industrial security system[J]. IJCSI International Journal of Computer Science Issues, 2013, 10(3).

[19]Kamenyi D M, Wang Y, Zhang F, et al. Authenticated privacy preserving for continuous query in location based services[J]. Journal of Computational Information Systems, 2013, 9(24): 9857-9864.

[20]SuZhiwei, ChenXinyuan, DengJianghong, Zhan Xiaohui. Design of casting power adding area rectangular compensation mechanism for casting power feeder of continuous casting crystallizer. [J] Chinese Journal of Engineering Design, 2015 05:420-424.

[21]Chen Xinyuan, SuZhiwei, Zhan Xiaohui. A kind of wide slab mold with double pipe automatic slag machine. [P].CN201510174589.1，2015 05 15.

[22]PengAnhong, Transmitting Function of Inverter Induction Motor[J]， Anshan Institute of I & S.technology，2000 06 447-449.

[23]AL—GHAMDI A S.Performance Analysis of Automated Control System for Condenser Water Treatment Unit [J]. Engineering , 2012, 4(1):35-39

[24]Chen Lifu, Pan Gongyu, Zhang Qingqing. Self-adaptive Fuzzy—PID controller of pneumatic active suspension [J]. Machinery Design&Manufacture. 2010 (08).

[25]Liu Jinkun. Advanced PID Control and MATLAB Simulation. [M] Beijing: Electronic Industry Press. 2010:77-87.

Adaptation of intelligent control systems to technological processes of oil-and-gas production enterprises

Iakov Korovin[1,a]

[1]*Southern Federal University, Rostov-on-Don, Russia*

Abstract. The paper is dedicated to research, supported by the Russian Scientific Foundation that is targeted on the development of novel technology of oil enhancement recovery, based on the hybrid application of various artificial intelligence techniques. An approach of dynamic control of electric submersible oil pump is suggested. The key idea is a real time technological management, applying artificial neural network tool. Research evaluation results are presented.

1 Adaptation of Intelligent Control Systems To Technological Processes Of Oil-And-Gas Production Enterprises

At present reduction of production cost of hydrocarbon feed by means of complex intellectualization of control processes of technological objects for oil-and-gas production industry is a pressing scientific problem. In modern conditions, when the majority of oilfields are hard-to-extract ones, when costs of products are relatively low, and competition between world oil-and-gas production companies is relentless, optimization of technological processes of oil-and-gas production become a key problem. The most promising approach to solution of the specified problem is adaptation of facilities for generation of actual and effective recommendations on accepted control decisions concerning functional and strategic horizons of scheduling. It can be achieved by means of implementation of modern, complex approaches to data processing which cover all stages of hydrocarbon feed production [1].

Problems of development and adaptation of control of oil production enterprises had been actively solved since the middle of the 50-s. However, these problems were solved slowly and without any sufficient effect because of a number of reasons. The main reasons which restrained development of control were the following. Not all processes and objects were controlled. Automation implemented not a complex, which is why not relieve the operational staff, management structure of the enterprise was not perfect, economic effectiveness was not provided. Control facilities were adjusted to existing equipment, outdated, unreliable, and unsuitable for control in some cases. Control facilities and controlled equipment were not a single whole. Vendors produced equipment and control facilities separately. Equipment which was used for oil production was installed without obligatory control tools. Facilities and systems of control and remote control were designed for large number of flowcharts of field gathering and oil-and-gas treatment. In some cases these flowcharts were not optimal for control. As a result, a large number of types and designs of control and remote control was created, and it complicated organization of serial production and increased costs, though quality of such devices was low.

At present Russian specialists and scientific teams carry out ambitious works, concerning creation of control systems for oilfield production, but they do not take into account transition of quantitative modifications of parameters into qualitatively new condition of the system. Such transition is not always evident for traditional mathematical formalization of the process [2].

Owing to adaptation of an adequate model of an oil production complex, it will be possible to organize timely preventive actions for reduction of idle-time of equipment. At the same time, analysis of data of technological processes will provide the personnel of the oil-and-gas enterprise with tools of effective scheduling of the used methods of reservoir stimulation for long-time increasing indices of reservoir recovery rate. At present, these problems are the most needed for organization of control of oil production processes during the whole life of the oilfield.

It is possible to achieve a higher level of control of technological objects, including approaches to analysis and prediction of equipment failures, time per fault on workshop (manufactory) tier by means of implementation of modern methods of deep data analysis with use of neural networks [3].

Owing to use of intelligent approaches to estimation of real-time changes and logs, it is possible to form in an automatic mode (if it is necessary) regulatory and control actions for technological equipment of control objects of pump stations, providing constant control of operability

[a] Corresponding author: korovin_yakov@mail.ru

of the main and auxiliary equipment of technological control objects of pump stations.

Adaptation of these facilities will provide not only safe functioning of the main and auxiliary equipment of control objects of a pump station in all operation conditions, but also anticipatory actions to increase effectiveness of functioning of controlled equipment. Automatic diagnostics of condition and adaptive control of technical facilities also contribute to reduction of the number of stoppage and failures of technological equipment. As a result, idle time of equipment drops down and its loading become optimal.

In general, the main tendencies of development of automatic control systems are as follows:

• Growth of the performance of automatic control systems;

• Increasing of the number of interfaces for connection with external oil-well data sources (various sensors);

• Capability of storing and processing of large data arrays;

• Increasing of quantity and complexity of control algorithms.

Further development of the tendencies, described above, will unavoidably lead to development of a complex of so-called "digital well". Evidently, a high-performance reliable controller CS ESP will play the main role in this complex.

To provide more effective adaptation of intelligent control systems, we have decided to use frequency converters (FC) [4]. At the moment they are the only devices which provide regulation of rotary speed of an asynchronous motor.

Use of frequency converters has a number of main advantages, such as:

• Smooth start of both the motor and the pump equipment. At the start moment the spinup of the pump impeller is gradual and smooth until the set-up operating parameters are achieved. Just owing to this fact it is possible to achieve a considerable reduction of mechanical loads to the pump, and also reduce starter current. As a result, risk of hydraulic impacts is also considerably reduced.

• Besides, owing to this, the resource of the pump equipment is consumed more efficiently, and hence, its life of operation grows. Also, we should pay attention to the well, which can experience hydraulic impacts;

• If water supply is performed by a well pump without use of a special, accumulator bottle (hydraulic accumulator) of diafragm (i.e. directly), and the water draw-off does not exceed the pump delivery, then use of frequency converter in this case will regulate both the pump power and the water draw-off owing to reduction of the rotation rate of the pump impeller. In turn, the less the power, the better saving of electric energy.

So, use of frequency converters provides more effective adaptation owing to smooth control of pump equipment.

Summing up everything that was said above, we can conclude, that the worldwide tendency of "intellectualization" of oil production control systems is to transfer more and more number of functions directly to the controlled mechanism, and is the necessary condition which provides a considerable growth of production rate, and above all to increase the equipment life.

2 The Experimental Results And Benefits

For the analysis of offered method of sharing of a set of neural networks efficiency, the following experiment was conducted [5][6][7][8][9][10][11][12][13][14]. Nine test samples, with quantity of various classes from 1 to 256 were prepared. Further each test sample was classified with use application from 1 to 256 neural networks, in each case the quantity of neural networks didn't exceed the quantity of classes in the sample. In tab. 1 the bottom triangular matrix, describing the results of classification of each test sample (lines) at various number of neural networks (columns) is represented.

Table 1. The table of dependence of classification quality on various test sample classes and neural networks number.

classes \ nets	1	2	4	8	16	32	64	128	256
1	0.99	X	X	X	X	X	X	X	X
2	0.96	0.97	X	X	X	X	X	X	X
4	0.86	0.89	0.92	X	X	X	X	X	X
8	0.81	0.82	0.87	0.91	X	X	X	X	X
16	0.78	0.81	0.83	0.85	0.9	X	X	X	X
32	0.72	0.76	0.79	0.82	0.86	0.89	X	X	X
64	0.66	0.71	0.74	0.8	0.82	0.85	0.87	X	X
128	0.6	0.65	0.69	0.74	0.75	0.79	0.82	0.84	X
256	0.59	0.61	0.67	0.7	0.71	0.73	0.76	0.8	0.82

From the table it can be seen that the best quality of classification is reached when the number of neural networks is equal to the maximum number of possible classes. The graph of classification quality dependence of initial test set, handled by one neural network (dotted line) is shown at Fig.1 so as the graph of recognition quality dependence of initial test set, handled by a set of the neural networks corresponding to each set classes quantity (continuous line).

Thus, the hypothesis of efficiency of application of "its private" neural network for each class handling [7] is experimentally proved.

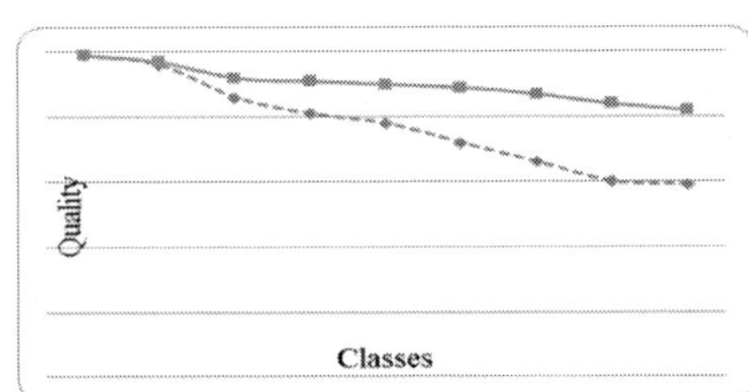

Figure 1. Classification quality dependence of initial test set, handled by one neural network and by a set of the neural networks.

Acknowledgement

This paper is published due the financial support of the Russian Science Foundation (RSF) via the grant No 15-19- 00196.

References

1. A.D. Brents, *Automatic control systems in oil-and-gas industry*. – Moscow: Nedra, (1982). 27 p.
2. Y.A. Balakirov, L.V. Kapushchak, E.A. Slepyan, *Optimal control of oil production processes*. -Kiyev: TECHNICS, (1987). 119 p.
3. S.A. Alyokhin, S.G. Kipnis, V.A. Orudzhev, A.K. Ostrovskaya, *Automatization of intermittent functioning well*. - M.:Nedra. (1980). 32 p.
4. Frequency converters for a well pump [On-line resource]. Access: http://moikolodets.ru/chastotnyj-preobrazovatel-dlya-skvazhinnogo-nasosa-518
5. S.V. Kononov, S.Ya. Korovin, Neftyanoe khozyaystvo – Oil Industry, 2006, no. 10, pp 10 -14
6. G.A. Galuev, Ya.S. Korovin, S.Ya. Korovin, S.N. Matveev, *Radiotechnika*, (2006), no. 3, pp. 42-49.
7. Ya.S. Korovin, Neftyanoe khozyaystvo – Oil Industry, (2007), no. 1, pp 80- 85.
8. D.P. Wasserman, *Neural computing: theory and practice*, Van Nostrand Reinhold, (1989), 220 p.
9. W.A.S. Clearning, H.G. Zimmermann, R. Neuneier, *Neural networks in financial engineering*. Proceedings of the Third International Conference on Neural Networks, (1996).
10. *Neural networks*. STATISTICA Neural Networks, Moscow: Goryachaya liniya-Telecom Publ., (2000), 182 p.
11. R. Feraud, F. Clerot, J.L. Simon, D. Pallou, C. Labbe, S. Martin, *Kalman and neural network approaches for the control of a vp bandwidth in an atm network*. Lecture Notes in Computer Science. Springer-Verlag Gmb. (2000). Vol. **1815**, p. 0655.
12. Ju.A. Perez-Ortiz, Ju. Schmidhuber, F.A. Gers, D. Eck, *Improving long-term online prediction with decoupled extended kalman filters*. Lecture Notes in Computer Science. Springer-Verlag Gmb. (2002). Vol. **2415**, p. 1055.
13. Ju.R. Rabunal, Ju. Dorado, A. Pazos, D. Rivero, *Rules and generalization capacity extraction from ann with gp*, Lecture Notes in Computer Science, Springer-Verlag Gmb, (2003). Vol. **2686**, pp. 606-613.
14. E. Cantu-Paz, *Pruning neural networks with distribution estimation algorithms*, Lecture Notes in Computer Science, Springer-Verlag Gmb, (2003). Vol. **2723**, pp.790-800.
15. I.S. Korovin, M.V. Khisamutdinov, A.I. Kaliaev, *The Application of Evolutionary Algorithms in the Artificial Neural Network Training Process for the Oilfield Equipment Malfunctions' Forecasting*, 2nd International Symposium on Computer, Communication, Control and Automation (3CA 2013), Proccedings, pp. 253-257.

Anonymous Social Network Ecological Status and Governance Strategies

Zhi-Ye LIN, Yong-Jing WANG

Department of Creative and Design,Fuzhou University ZhiCheng College,Fuzhou, China
zylin91@163.com,yunkim.wang@hotmail.com

Abstract—Anonymous social network has attracted ever-increasing attention from research community in recent years, however, it also brings some complications to ours daily life. We want to clarify the status of anonymous social network and put forward some governance strategies. In this paper we focus our attention on analyzing shortcomings of current regulatory strategies by comparing and analyzing the data from anonymous social network application Secret and social network application Sina Weibo. Combining with the characteristics of information dissemination in anonymous social network, we mainly put forward an governance strategy based on geographical location.

1 Introduction

Anonymous social network is attracting more and more people's attention and use, Secret and Whisper have become popular applications in young people. But the current laws and managements are based on real-name system[1], how to monitor and guide the negative information effectively in anonymous social network has become an urgent problem.

2 Ecological Status

To clarify the status of anonymous social network, we crawled data of the anonymous social application Secret from October 25, 2015 to January 24, 2016, including 1179 hottest-messages and 1200 ordinary messages. And we obtained the Sina data through the official APIs from May 3, 2014 to May 11, 2014, including 500 hottest-microblogs and 84168 ordinary-microblogs. We use the constructed emotional dictionary[2] to analyze text emotional tendencies and text themes of the anonymous networks by comparing and analyzing the data from anonymous social network application Secret and social network application Sina Weibo, and the result as shown in table I.

TABLE I. TEXTUAL EMOTIONAL TENDENCY AND THEMES IN SECRET AND SINA WEIBO

LIWC Dictionary	Secret (%)	Sina Weibo (%)	Example Words
Positive emotion	10.2	29.6	hope, love
Negative emotion	39.8	16.8	anger, hate
Sadness	19.6	9.0	sad, cry, grief
Anger	16.4	4.0	why, kill, anger
Sexual	16.3	0.7	love, incest

From table I, we can figure out that the textual emotional tendency and themes of messages are much different in anonymous social network and real-name social network, i.e., social network. Especially in pornographic, nearly 16.3% of text is related to sexual in Secret, in contrast, only 0.7% in Sina Weibo, over staggering 20 times, and other negative emotions are not optimistic too. What interesting is, the proportion of the positive emotion and negative emotion is opposite in domestic and foreign applications. The information characteristics of foreign anonymous social application Whisper and social application Twitter are shown as table II[3], the ecological status is much better.

TABLE II. TEXTUAL EMOTIONAL tendency AND THEMES IN WHISPER AND TWITTER

LIWC Dictionary	Whisper (%)	Twitter (%)	Example Words
Positive emotion	42.1	33.9	love, nice, sweet
Negative emotion	28.8	16.1	hurt, ugly
Sadness	6.5	3.3	grief, sad
Anger	14.1	8.7	anger, kill
Sexual	19.8	9.1	love, incest

From table II, we can figure out that the foreign anonymous social application (Whisper), 42.1% text have positive emotions, only 28.8% of the emotions are negative. The overall ecology tends to be positive, which is totally different in Secret. We can not deny the existence of cultural differences, but we believe that the main reason is resulted from the anonymous social application platform itself. A lack of correct guides will lead to more people to generate negative information, which exacerbate the negative environment of the network. And we will conduct a experiment to confirm the opinion in our further research. The Secret is caught in such a whirlpool, which is a basic characteristic of the current domestic anonymous social application.

3 Regulatory Incompatibility

In social networks, the identity of the network and the reality are eventually unified. However, the anonymous social networks broke the unity of identity. In anonymous social networks, people have a virtual identity which has noting to do with reality. Therefore, the information regulatory strategies of the real-name system appear incompatible, and we concluded several reasons.

3.1The absence of identity

The society have established a better legal system for the possible problems under the real-name network, e.g., people who forward defamation messages 500 times will be judged. But the premise of the law is that we can identify everyone which is just missing in anonymous social networks. What we should know is that the law restricts people's identity not people themselves actually.

3.2The lack of opinion leader

We can intervene or guide the information dissemination through critical nodes such as opinion leaders under social networks, because these critical nodes have huge node entry levels[4], which means numbers of people will accept the critical node's message. In anonymous social networks, however, the relationship between users tends to be more equal, there is no critical nodes to guide the information dissemination. In other words, the network topology in social networks is different with anonymous social networks.

3.3Misguidance of anonymous social platforms

The anonymous social networks are at the stage of development, so that they have lowered its user access requirements to acquire continued expansion of user volume and influence. Also, anonymous social network, i.e., Secret, is not strict in messages audit, there is still a large amount of negative information in the information that is reviewed, as shown in table I.

4 The Characteristics of Information Dissemination in Anonymous Social Networks

4.1User access threshold is at low level

The anonymous social networks are at the stage of development have lowered its user access requirements to acquire continued expansion of user volume and influence. Anonymous social application, Secret can successfully register and publish information on the platform without having to import any valid information. Another anonymous application WuMi, which requires users to import contacts to establish initial relationships, but whether the contacts are imported does not affect the normal use.

4.2Users tend to be equal

Anonymous social networks have blurred the identities of users, so that users tend to be equal to each other, and there is no opinion leaders in anonymous social networks. Users connect to each other by locations, interests, etc., there is no significant difference between out-degree and in-degree. Anonymous social network topology is more like a classical network model.

4.3The information audit is not strict

Anonymous social network applications such as Secret audits information by filtering through sensitive words. However, the current information review is clearly not rigorous enough. There is still a lot of illegal information in the anonymous platform, such as pornography and insulting words.

5 Governance Strategy Based on Location

The audit mechanism of anonymous social network information are keyword filtering and semantic recognition. And the library of sensitive words is usually a default

DOI: 10.1051/itmconf/20171201032

keyword library. But the question is, the sensitive words in different region are different and changing over time. Therefor, we should select the corresponding sensitive keyword library based on location.

5.1Sensitive word library selection based on location

Establish a sensitive word library based on geographical location: Although the cyberspace of anonymous social network is completely separated from the real world, location is the only parameter that can reflect user characteristics. There are two types of geography, one is the specific function place, i.e., hospital, bar etc. The other is the location of region, i.e., city, block etc.

For geographical location L, its sensitive word library can be expressed as a set,

$$L = \{k_1, k_2, ..., k_n\} \quad (1)$$

k_n is the sensitive word, but these sensitive words do not appear on average, different keywords have different word frequency.

2) Select the sensitive word library: We have set up corresponding sensitive word libraries for all geographical locations and functional places. So how to select the corresponding sensitive library is the key of information audit. Typically users have a limited range of daily activities actually, for user U , the set of his daily geographical locations can be expressed as S ,

$$S = \{L_1, L_2, ..., L_U\} \quad (2)$$

When user U is posting an anonymous message, the relationship between the user and the sensitive word library is T ,

$$T = \frac{m_1}{l} + m_2 c \quad (3)$$

m_1 , m_2 are non-zero coefficient, and l indicates the distance between the posting position and the center of sensitive word library, c means the frequency of the sensitive word. The process of selecting the sensitive word library is actually the process of maximizing of T , i.e.,

$$G = \max(T_1, T_2, ..., T_U) \quad (4)$$

The relationship between user and sensitive word library is shown in Fig. 1.

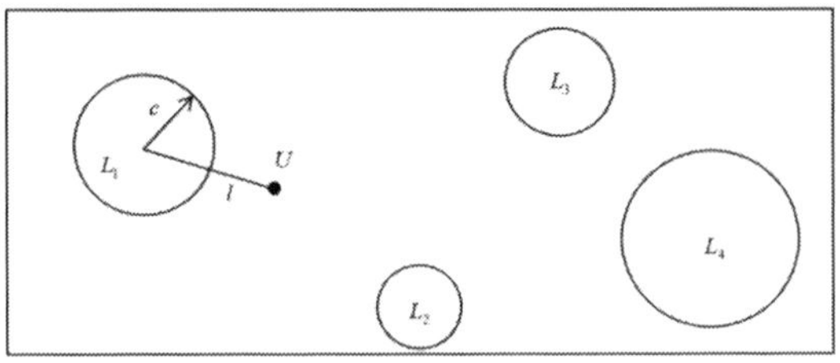

Figure 1. The relationship between user and library

5.2Information dissemination scope control

Negative information, such as rumors, pornographic, etc., we hope to control the scope of transmission and reduce the effect to other users. For positive information, we hope to increase the spread of scope to effect more users, so that we can guide the overall network environment. The information dissemination scope should be related to the following factors: the quality of the information, the attention of information and the poster's characteristics.

1) *The quality of the information:* Information quality refers to the text emotional tendencies, keywords and themes. As judging the credibility of the information[5], we also need to refine the keywords. For message M , we refine the keywords and get set K_M ,

$$K_M = \{km_1, km_2, ..., km_i\} \quad (5)$$

km_i is the keyword for message M , similarly, we can refine the emotion collection E_M . Therefore, the quality of information can be expressed as Q_M ,

$$Q_M = q_1 \sum K_M + q_2 \sum E_M \quad (6)$$

q_1 , q_2 are non-zero coefficient.

2) *The attention of the information:* The attention means that users are interested in the information, the more people interested, the more attention the information draws. The information's attention attenuates at a certain rate over time and spread distance.

The attention of information M can be expressed as H_M ,

$$H_M = h_1 x - h_2 t - h_3 d \quad (7)$$

h_1 , h_2 , h_3 are non-zero coefficient, x is the number of people who are interested, t is the time since the information posted, d is the degree of information spreads. We set threshold δ to judge whether people still interested in the information.

If $H_M \geq \delta$, means the information M still has the value of spreading, it should be kept in transmission queen. Otherwise, it means that the information has no value of dissemination and should be removed from the transmission queen.

3) *The user's characteristics:* User characteristics can be easily represented by user accounts[6]. The main factors include the quality of posts, the number of posts and the number of responses. So we can assign an initial value to each new user and adjust the value based on the user's usual usage. The users' posts and responses can be statistically calculated, and the more user posts and responses, the higher the value of the user. So we can represent the user's value by V_U.

Above all, the information dissemination scope can be expressed as

$$D_M = k_1 Q_M + k_2 H_M + k_3 V_U + D_0 \quad (8)$$

k_1, k_2, k_3 are non-zero coefficient, D_0 indicates the initial scope of information dissemination. The scope of information varies with the information quality, the attention of information and user characteristics.

6 Other Strategies

As the network environment manager, the anonymous social network platform has the responsibility and obligation to purify the network ecology. Here are some strategies.

- Anonymous platform should promote the propagation of moral and clarify the freedoms and responsibilities of users.
- Through new user entrance examination, making user understand the moral restricts.
- Using keywords filtering combined with artificial audit mechanism.
- Establishing a reward and punishment mechanism.
- Setting up emotional guides.

Conclusion

In this paper, we conducted three conclusions. First, the ecological status of social network and anonymous social network are much different in some cases, especially in negative information. Second, although we have established a better legal system for the possible problems under the real-name network, but anonymous social network lacks the basic features of real names, which makes current governance strategies show incompatibility. Third, we have conducted a comprehensive study to explore and derive the formula of the dissemination of information scope in anonymous social network. We believe the results are helpful for future researchers and related network holders. And we will do some experiment to verify our conclusions in further research.

References

[1] P. Hangyu, "Real-name system: dealing with irresponsible microblogs," Public Communication of Science & Technology, 2012(13): 176-185.
[2] Wang D L, "User character mining and analysis based on Chinese microblogging," Beijing University Of Posts And Telecommunications, 2015: 36-41.
[3] Qazvinian, et al, "Rumor has it:Identifying misinformation in microblogs," Proceedings of the 2011 Conference on Empirical Methods in Natural Language Processing. 2011: 1589-1599.
[4] W. Xindong, et al, "Analysis on the influence of online social network," Chinese Journal of Computers, 2014(04): 735-752.
[5] Castillo C, et al, "Information credibility on Twitter," roceedings of the 20th International Conference on World Wide Web. New York: ACL, 2011: 675－684.
[6] Wang G, et al, "Whispers in the dark: analysis of an anonymous social network," Proceedings of the 2014 Conference on Internet Measurement Conference. ACM,2014: 137-150.

A Watermarking Algorithm Based on DCT and JPEG Quantization Table

Yun-Ping ZHENG[1, a], Zi-Lun XI[1, b]

[1]*School of Computer Science and Engineering, South China University of Technology, 510006, Guangzhou, China*

Abstract. In this paper, we propose a scheme of watermark embedding and extracting based on DCT transform and JPEG quantization table. Firstly, the image is divided into non-overlapping 8 × 8 blocks, and each block is transformed by DCT. Then, a pair of points with the same quantization value is selected by the JPEG quantization table in order to embed one watermark bit, and the adjustment coefficients are adaptively selected by using the visual masking property of HVS. The experimental results presented in this paper showed that our proposed algorithm is robust to JPEG compression under different quality factors.

1 Introduction

With the rapid development of science and technology, information transmission has become more and more convenient, but the protection of information in the transmission process has also become the primary issue. Digital watermarking technology is an effective way to solve this problem, and it is able to protect information security, achieve security traceability and copyright protection [1-4]. Some identification information (digital watermarking) is directly or indirectly embedded into the digital carrier, and does not only affect the value of the original carrier, but is also uneasy to be detected or modified. And it can be easily recognized and identified by the manufacturer. According to the hidden information we extracted, we can achieve the purpose of confirming the content creators and buyers, sending secret information and judging whether the carrier has been tampered with.

With the increasing of the image quality and size, the burden of the transmission is increased when the watermarked image needs to be transmitted to the receiver. In order to reduce the load of the channel and increase the speed of information transmission, image compression becomes an essential part of image transmission. In the existing compression technology, JPEG compression is widely used in the field of image and video processing because of its good compression performance and good reconstruction quality. Therefore, if the image is compressed by JPEG, whether the embedded watermark information can be effectively extracted becomes a problem that should be considered in the watermarking algorithm [5-7].

In order to improve the quality of the extracted watermark from the watermarked image after JPEG compression, this paper proposes a watermarking scheme based on JPEG quantization table. Considering the security of the watermark, the watermark image is firstly scrambled with K times Arnold transform [8,9]. Moreover, in order to improve the robustness of the algorithm, the image is divided into non-overlapping 8 × 8 blocks, and each block is transformed by DCT [10-12]. And then, we select the intermediate frequency coefficients of each block to embed one watermark bit using the adjustment coefficients which are calculated by the visual masking property of HVS [13,14]. The experimental results show that, comparing with the watermarking algorithm which does not use the JPEG quantization table [15], the algorithm we proposed in this paper has better quality of the extracted watermark under different quality factors of JPEG compression, and the quality of the watermarked image is also not weaker than the other algorithms'.

The rest of this paper is as follows: Section 2 introduces the related technologies used in this paper. Section 3 introduces the watermark embedding and extracting algorithm. Section 4 is the experimental result, and the last Section 5 concludes the full paper.

2 Related technologies

In this paper, the watermark image is firstly scrambled by K times Arnold transform, and the K is used as the key to the receiver of the image, so that the watermark cannot be restored to the original image even if the watermark is extracted. Then, the image is divided into non-overlapping 8 × 8 blocks, and each block is transformed by DCT. After that we select the appropriate watermark embedding position and using the JPEG quantization

[a] Corresponding author: zhengyp@scut.edu.cn
[b] Zilun Xi: 418151189@qq.com

table. After the watermark bit is embedded, the adjustment coefficients calculated by the HVS's visual masking property are used to adjust the embedding points to ensure the robustness and transparency of the image.

2.1 Arnold transform

Arnold transform which is also called Cat transform, is a kind of transformation which is proposed by Arnold in ergodic theory. Cat mapping can substitute each pixel position in the image to achieved the encryption, and is widely used in digital image scrambling. And Arnold transform is periodic, when the iteration is integer times of the cycle, the image can be restored to the original image. Therefore, if we use an iterative time K as a key, the image can only be restored with the key value. So that it greatly improves the security of image.

For an $N \times N$ digital image, the two-dimensional Arnold transform is defined by:

$$\begin{pmatrix} x' \\ y' \end{pmatrix} = \begin{pmatrix} 1 & 1 \\ 1 & 2 \end{pmatrix} \begin{pmatrix} x \\ y \end{pmatrix} (\mathrm{mod}\ N) \quad (1)$$

where, $x, y \in \{0,1,2,\cdots,N-1\}$ is the pixel position before the transform, (x',y') is the position after the transform, and mod is for modular arithmetic.

2.2 Discrete cosine transform

Discrete Cosine Transform (DCT) is the best orthogonal transformation obtained in the minimum mean square error conditions. It utilizes the character of the Fourier transform, use image edge fold to transform the image into even function form. And then transform the image by the two-dimensional Fourier. After transformation the image contains only cosine terms, so called the process discrete cosine transform.

The two-dimensional DCT transform is defined by:

$$F(u,v) = \frac{2}{\sqrt{MN}} c(u)c(v) \sum_{x=0}^{M-1} \sum_{y=0}^{N-1} f(x,y) \cos\frac{(2x+1)u\pi}{2M} \cos\frac{(2y+1)v\pi}{2N}$$

$$c(u), c(v) = \begin{cases} \frac{1}{\sqrt{2}}, & u, v = 0 \\ 1, & ohterwise \end{cases} \quad (2)$$

The corresponding inverse 2D DCT transform is given by:

$$f(x,y) = \frac{2}{\sqrt{MN}} \sum_{u=0}^{M-1} \sum_{v=0}^{N-1} F(u,v)c(u)c(v) \cos\frac{(2x+1)u\pi}{2M} \cos\frac{(2y+1)v\pi}{2N} \quad (3)$$

2.3 JPEG quantization table

JPEG quantization table is used in the quantization process of JPEG compression, which is divided into luminance quantization table (Table 1) and color quantization table (Table 2). Because the grey image is processed in this paper, only the luminance quantization table is considered.

The algorithm proposed in this paper considers the JPEG luminance quantization table in the watermark embedding process. For each 8 × 8 block after DCT transform, we select a pair of coefficients which has the same value in the quantization table as the watermark embedded bits, so that the embedded watermark has good robustness to JPEG compression.

Table 1. JPEG Luminance Quantization Table.

16	11	10	16	24	40	51	61
12	12	14	19	26	58	60	55
14	13	16	24	40	57	69	56
14	17	22	29	51	87	80	62
18	22	37	56	68	109	103	77
24	35	55	64	81	104	113	92
49	64	78	87	103	121	120	101
72	92	95	98	112	100	103	99

Table 2. JPEG Color Quantization Table.

17	18	24	47	99	99	99	99
18	21	26	66	99	99	99	99
24	26	56	99	99	99	99	99
47	66	99	99	99	99	99	99
99	99	99	99	99	99	99	99
99	99	99	99	99	99	99	99
99	99	99	99	99	99	99	99
99	99	99	99	99	99	99	99

2.4 Visual masking property of HVS

In the process of watermark embedding, it is important to select the watermark adjustment coefficient. The greater the value is, the higher robustness of the watermark has, but the transparency of the watermark image will be relatively poor, and vice versa.

Usually in the digital watermarking technology, the following characteristics of the human visual system are used:

Firstly, the human visual sensitivity to the different brightness regions is different, usually on the middle grey was the most sensitive. In the wide range of medium scale, Weber Ratio is a constant 0.02, and decreases to the low and the high grey area. We suppose the maximum contrast sensitivity is β, the current block is $B(x,y)$, and the luminance average is $Ave(x,y)$, so that the masking factor of the different brightness to noise $w(x,y)$ is defined by:

$$w(x,y) = \begin{cases} \frac{[(\beta-0.02)(Ave(x,y)-I_1)^2]}{I_2^2} + 0.02, if\ Ave(x,y) < I_1 \\ 0.02, if\ I_1 \le Ave(x,y) < I_2 \\ \frac{[(\beta-0.02)(Ave(x,y)-I_2)^2]}{(255-I_2)^2} + 0.02, if\ Ave(x,y) \ge I_2 \end{cases} \quad (4)$$

where, I_1 and I_2 are the pre-set thresholds, which are 80 and 160 in this paper.

Secondly, the human eye is more sensitive to the smooth area than the texture region. Experimental results show that the smooth region entropy is smaller, while the

DOI: 10.1051/itmconf/20171201033

texture region has larger entropy. Therefore, the entropy of each block is used to represent the texture masking factor. We suppose $Entropy(x,y)$ is the entropy of the block $B(x,y)$, and normalized it into $[a,b]$, so that the texture masking factor $e(x,y)$ can be calculated by:

$$e(x,y)=\frac{[(b-a)(Entropy(x,y)-min(E))]}{[max(E)-min(E)]}+a \quad (5)$$

where, a and b are the pre-set thresholds, which can affect the robustness and transparency, usually $a,b\in[1,8]$.

Integrated the analysis from (4) and (5), each block's noise masking factor (the adjustment coefficient used in this paper) of the image can be expressed by:

$$K(x,y)=w(x,y)e(x,y) \quad (6)$$

3 Embedding and extracting

3.1 Watermark embedding

The embedding process is depicted as follows:

Step 1. Watermark information pre-treatment: Use *K* as the key, and the watermark image is scrambled by *K* times Arnold transform.

Step 2. Image segmentation: Divide the carrier image into non-overlapping 8 × 8 blocks.

Step 3. Adaptive adjustment coefficient acquisition: Use (6) to calculate the adaptive adjustment coefficient $k(i)$ of each block, and then normalize $k(i)$ to $[c,d]$.

Step 4. DCT: Use DCT to transform each block.

Step 5. Watermark embedding: Select a pair of coeffic-ients $C1(x_1,y_1)$ and $C2(x_2,y_2)$ which has the same value in the quantization table, and use the following algorithm to embed one watermark bit.

```
if watermark bit == 0
  if C1 < C2
    C1 ↔ C2
  end
else if watermark bit == 1
  if C1 ≥ C2
    C1 ↔ C2
  end
end
```

And using the following algorithm to adjust the embedded bit.

```
if C1 > C2
  if C1 − C2 > k(i)
    C1 = C1 + k(i)/2;
    C2 = C2 − k(i)/2;
  end
else
  if C2 − C1 < k(i)
    C1 = C1 − k(i)/2;
    C2 = C2 + k(i)/2;
  end
end
```

Step 6. IDCT: Use IDCT to transform each embedded block to get the watermarked image.

3.2 Watermark extracting

The extracting process is depicted as follow:

Step 1. Image segmentation: Divide the watermarked image into non-overlapping 8 × 8 blocks.

Step 2. DCT: Use DCT to transform each block.

Step 3. Watermark extracting: According to the coeffi-cients we used in the embedding process $C1(x_1,y_1)$ and $C2(x_2,y_2)$, use the following algorithm to extract one watermark bit.

```
if C1 > C2
  watermark bit == 0
else if C1 ≤ C2
  watermark bit == 1
end
```

4 Experimental results

In this Section, we use the 512 × 512 grey-scale images of Lena as the carrier image *I*, and the 64 × 64 binary image of "Watermark Information" in Chinese as the watermark *W*. And c and d are 10 and 20 respectively.

The peak signal to noise ratio (*PSNR*) and the normalized correlation (*NC*) are computed in order to evaluate the performance of watermarking scheme. The *PSNR* is used to estimate the visual perception between the watermarked image and the original image. And the *NC* is used to estimate the quality of the watermark extracted from the image under JPEG compression with the original watermark. *PSNR* and *NC* are defined equation (7) and (9).

$$PSNR=10log_{10}\frac{255^2}{MSE} \quad (7)$$

where

$$MSE=\frac{1}{MN}\sum_{i=0}^{M}\sum_{j=0}^{N}[I(i,j)-I'(i,j)]^2 \quad (8)$$

$$NC=\frac{\sum_{i=0}^{m}\sum_{j=0}^{n}W(i,j)W\prime(i,j)}{\sqrt{\sum_{i=0}^{m}\sum_{j=0}^{n}W(i,j)^2}\sqrt{\sum_{i=0}^{m}\sum_{j=0}^{n}W\prime(i,j)^2}} \quad (9)$$

The original image and the watermarked image are shown in Fig. 1 and Fig. 2 respectively, and Fig. 3 and Fig. 4 show the original watermark and the watermark extracted from the watermarked image respectively. Their *PSNR* and *NC* are provided in Table 3.

Figure 1. Original Lena image

Figure 2. Watermarked Lena image

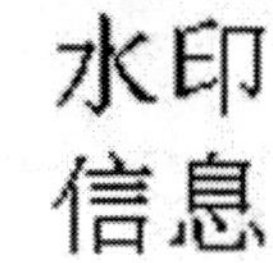

Figure 3. Original watermark

Figure 4. Extracted watermark

Table 3. *PSNR* and *NC* without attacking.

PSNR(dB)	*NC*
42.053	0.998

From the image and the data above, the proposed algorithm can guarantee the transparency of the watermarked image and extract the watermark with good quality.

Experimental evaluation of the robustness of the proposed algorithm compared with Xiong et al. [15], Gu et al. [16], Zhao et al. [17], AR et al. [18] under different quality factor of JPEG compression, are shown in Table 4. In the table below, before the '/' is the value of *PSNR*, and after '/' is that of *NC*. The variable *Ave* stands for average of *PSNR* and *NC* respectively.

Table 4. Values of *PSNR* and *NC* under different quality factor of JPEG compression.

Algorithm	*QF*						*Ave*
	95	85	75	65	55	45	
Proposed	39.8170 / 0.9983	37.5452 / 0.9983	36.2988 / 0.9967	35.6141 / 0.9403	35.2483 / 0.8137	34.8292 / 0.7482	37.3921 / 0.9159
Xiong et al. [15]	39.3803 / 0.9983	37.1121 / 0.9983	36.2582 / 0.9602	35.7421 / 0.8552	35.5119 / 0.7492	35.1225 / 0.7211	36.5212 / 0.8804
Gu et al. [16]	37.0602 / 0.8879	35.7189 / 0.8879	34.9779 / 0.8879	34.3944 / 0.8792	33.7231 / 0.8307	35.1950 / 0.8149	35.1783 / 0.8648
Zhao et al. [17]	43.0676 / 0.9223	39.1604 / 0.9107	37.5442 / 0.8618	36.7038 / 0.7907	35.9818 / 0.7264	35.3930 / 0.6345	37.9751 / 0.8077
AR et al. [18]	38.6172 / 0.9983	36.5456 / 0.9983	34.7289 / 0.8781	35.8504 / 0.6848	35.7025 / 0.6293	35.3176 / 0.5943	36.1270 / 0.7972

From the Table 4, with the decrease of the quality factor of JPEG compression, there is a decreasing trend to the five algorithms' *PSNR* and *NC* in some extent. Although Zhao et al. [17] has a little better the value of *PSNR*, the algorithm we proposed shows a lot better in extracted-watermark image's *NC*. The algorithm we proposed has a better *PSNR* and *NC*, so that we can say the proposed algorithm has a good robustness to JPEG compression than the others.

5 Conclusions

In this paper, a scheme of watermark embedding and extracting based on DCT transform and JPEG quantization table is proposed. The embedding process is in the DCT domain of the image, and use *K* as a key to encrypt the watermark before embedding. And the adjustment coefficients are adaptively selected by using the visual masking property of HVS. The experimental results show that the proposed algorithm can generate a high quality watermarked image, and can also extract a high quality watermark from the watermarked image.

At the same time, the proposed algorithm has a good robustness to JPEG compression, and can extract relatively good watermark under the different quality factors of JPEG compression.

Acknowledgment

This work is supported by the National Natural Science Foundation of China under Grant No. 61300134, the Research Fund for the Doctoral Program of Higher Education of China under Grant No. 20120172120036, the Natural Science Foundation of Guangdong Province of China under Grant No. S2011040005815, No. S2013010012515, and No. 2015A030313206, the Fundamental Research Funds for the Central Universities of China under Grant No. 2015ZM133, and Chinese National Scholarship Fund under Grant No. 201406155015, and the National Training Program of Innovation and Entrepreneurship for Undergraduates under Grant No. 201610561130.

References

1. Li B Z, Guo Y. Blind image watermarking method based on linear canonical wavelet transform and QR decomposition. IET image processing, 2016, 10(10):773-786.
2. WANG, Shen, SONG, et al. Quantum Cosine Transform Based Watermarking Scheme for Quantum Images. Chinese Journal of Electronics, 2015, 24(2):321-325.
3. Zong T, Xiang Y, Guo S, et al. Rank-Based Image Watermarking Method With High Embedding Capacity and Robustness. IEEE Access, 2016, 4:1689-1699.
4. Bhowmik D, Oakes M, Abhayaratne C. Visual Attention-based Image Watermarking. IEEE Access, 2016, PP(99):8002-8018.
5. El'Arbi M, Ben Amar C. Image authentication algorithm with recovery capabilities based on neural networks in the DCT domain. IET Image Processing, 2014, 8(11):619-626.
6. Korus P, Bialas J, Dziech A. Towards Practical Self-Embedding for JPEG-Compressed Digital Images. IEEE Transactions on Multimedia, 2015, 17(2):157-170.
7. Preda R O, Vizireanu D N. Watermarking-based image authentication robust to JPEG compression. Electronics Letters, 2015, 51(23):1873-1875.
8. Nidaa Hasan Abbas, Sharifah Mumtazah Syed Ahmad, Abd. Rahman Bin Ramli, et al. A multi-purpose watermarking scheme based on hybrid of lifting wavelet transform and Arnold transform. 2016 Al-Sadeq International Conference on Multidisciplinary in IT and Communication Science and Applications (AIC-MITCSA). 2016.
9. Khalili M, Asatryan D. Colour spaces effects on improved discrete wavelet transform-based digital image watermarking using Arnold transform map. IET Signal Processing, 2013, 7(3):177-187.
10. Yang Y, Lei M, Liu X, et al. Novel Zero-Watermarking Scheme Based on DWT-DCT. China Communications, 2016, 13(7):122-126.
11. Dong H, He M, Qiu M. Optimized Gray-Scale Image Watermarking Algorithm Based on DWT-DCT-SVD and Chaotic Firefly Algorithm. International Conference on Cyber-Enabled Distributed Computing and Knowledge Discovery. IEEE Computer Society, 2015:310-313.
12. Moosazadeh M, Ekbatanifard G. Robust Image Watermarking Algorithm Using DCT Coefficients Relation in YCoCg-R Color Space. Eighth International Conference on Information and Knowledge Technology. 2016.
13. Provenzi E. Rudiments of Human Visual System (HVS) Features. Computational Color Science. John Wiley & Sons, Inc. 2017:1-11.
14. Makbol N M, Khoo B E, Rassem T H. Block-based discrete wavelet transform-singular value decomposition image watermarking scheme using human visual system characteristics. IET Image Processing, 2016, 10(1):34-52.
15. Xiong XG, Wang DL. Color image watermarking scheme based on HVS and relationship in DCT domain. Computer Engineering & Science, 2014, 36(2): 311-316.
16. Bocheng GU, Jianzhen WU. DCT-based Medical Image Watermarking Algorithm. Guide of Science & Education, 2015(1): 137-138.
17. Zhao CY, Shi HW, Ke-Xin HU, et al. Blind watermarking algorithm for color image based on DCT transform. Computer Engineering & Design, 2015(3):597-602.
18. Yuliani AR, Rosiyadi D. A watermarking scheme based on DCT using HVS characteristic. IEEE International Conference on Computer, Control, Informatics and ITS Applications, 2015:165-168.

Modeling and Analysis of 3d Printing Ws-Bpel Business Processes Based on Servicenet

Cheng-Lei ZHANG[1,2], Bu-Yun SHENG[1#], Fei-Yu ZHAO[1], Xi-Yan YIN[1], Jing-Jing CAO[1]

[1] *School of Mechanical and Electronic Engineering, Wuhan University of Technology, Wuhan 430070, China;*
[2] *School of Mechanical & Vehicle Engineering, Liyin University, Liyin 276005, China*
E-mail: shengby@whut.edu.cn

Abstract—To solve the problem that whether the described Web service by business process execution language were interactive compatible, a method of WS-BPEL(Web Services Business Process Execution Language) parsing and execution was proposed. The service compatibility checking algorithm based on the Mediation model, which can provide multi-level service checking compatibility, and realize the goal of Service Cooperation or the demand of Value-Added Services. Based on BPMN specification, a task modeling and management tool was proposed to support the service components for assembly component. It supports both Web service automatic retrieval and service content analysis based on QoS information, and the task execution model between the BPMN specification task descriptions was transformed into the BPEL specification task description model. Finally, a model transformation strategy based on meta-model mapping was put forward. The algorithm was designed and examples were given to demonstrate the efficiency of 3D Printing WS-BPEL.

1 Introduction

In recent decades, many experts and scholars, as well as enterprises themselves from all over the world, have been devoted to exploring and studying how to solve the problem of a lack of capital, technology, personnel and equipment, so as to improve their business management model [1]. In order to improve the intangible assets and comprehensive competitiveness of enterprises, we propose an idea that transforms a vertical department management based on the principle of "division of labor" and "institutionalized management theory" into business process management based on cloud manufacturing (CMfg) in this paper [2]. For the changes in the external business environment and continuous improvement in the internal conditions, enterprises have led to a large number of new business processes [3].

Meanwhile, with the continuous development of key technologies of business management logic engine and CMfg service task management tool, CMfg service composition modeling arose at a timely moment. CMfg is defined by Li Bohu [4] as service-oriented, efficient, low consumption and knowledge-based networks for new manufacturing patterns and technology. Ye Yanming [5] came up with a social business process management and process recommendation method. The method was mainly used for mining process execution meta-paths that had high matching degree with the building process framework, which was conducive to the procedure convergence of social process modeling. Lu Jianfeng [6] put forward an integration framework based on Business Process Management (BPM). This framework was designed to provide unified modeling , executing and monitoring environment for various business processes within and cross enterprises. Business Process Execution Language for Web Services (BPEL4WS or BPEL) was used to define business service collaboration mode. Piero Fraternali [7] gave a model-Driven Approach to Social BPM Applications; this chapter has discussed the levels of adoptions of social features inside organizations and business process models, and examined the requirements that Social BPM poses to process specification languages.

This paper focuses on the Business Management Logic Engine. This engine is running in the cloud environment, which will do in response to the transaction with the increasingly wide range of manufacturing resources and manufacturing capacity. In order to deploy the manufacturing service business process file, the execution processing service business process processor realizes the interpretation and implementation of manufacturing service process will replace the concurrent processing in the event-based concurrent processing mode to executes the expression framework and finally monitoring and scheduled business process. Taking the project requirements into consideration, a new business management logic engine of service resource network for intelligent manufacturing is applied to achieve the CMfg operation mode with multiple enterprises.

2The Business Management Logic Engine

This paper focuses on the key technologies of business management logic engine and the architecture, such as dynamic service collaboration, task running supervision, transaction processing and so on.

2.1the key technologies of business management logic engine

The specific research is as follows:

1) Mediation-Based Dynamic service collaboration adaptation

The main problem of service collaboration is how to ensure the consistency and correctness of the service cooperation, to realize the goal of service or the demand of value added services. The introduction of conversational services has brought new effects to the service coordination. For this, this paper firstly proposes that services participate in collaboration must satisfy the whole service collaborative requirement by using input/ output modules, and also need to meet the needs of the whole in the interactive protocol service level[8]. That is, the services invocation temporal relationships and the interaction between services and services must meet the requirements of accuracy and consistency (protocol compatibility).

According to the problems above, this paper proposes a top-down approach to achieve the service collaboration. This is as shown below:

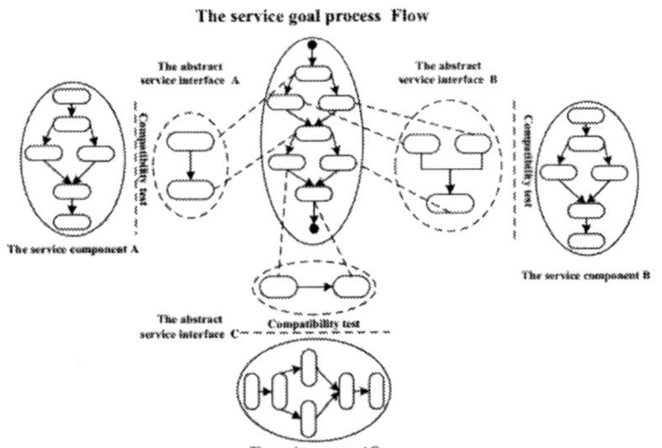

Figure 1. The Role-Based Distributed Compatibility Checking Method

Firstly, the global coordinated service process is strictly described as a contractual relationship of collaboration and public News between services. The formula of the message expression is shown as:

Choreography = (M, R, PCHOR)

,and the contract relation is shown as:

P = a→P | μX·F(X) | P□Q | PΠQ |P ; Q | P|Q | SKIP | STOP

Finally, the characteristics of the interactive adapter are analyzed by Asynchronous communication method of abstraction task flow and service interface, so this paper will automatically generate an algorithm of automatic generation when fit under the premise of adaptive[9]. This system achieves to cooperation target through the distributed interaction of the adapter, and ensures to the correctness of cooperation by the interaction of adapters and service component. This method is as shown below:

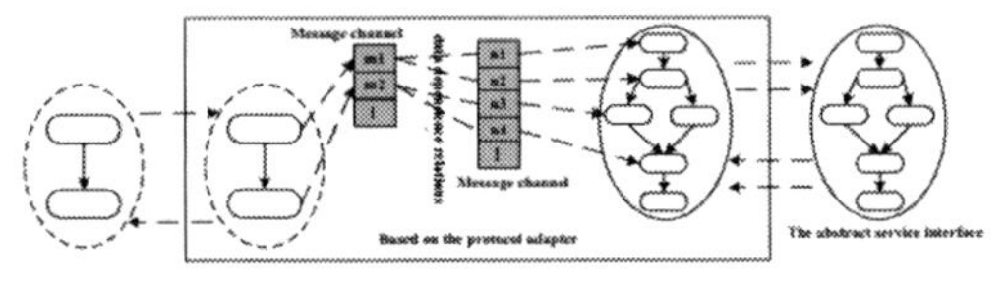

Figure 2. Adapter automatically generated model based on data dependence

The workflow of adapter automatically generated model based on data dependence is as shown:

First of all, this paper establishes a message channel that is supported data exchange under Bilateral agreement:

Pipe_mr= [(|| i<nleft?msi) → synth → right!mr → SKIP] [close→ SKIP]

Then, establishes an asynchronous communication protocol between POA and PSI according to the corresponding mapping relationship of message M in the coordination model.

(||i<nPipe_mi) //[POA_AC||PSI_AC]

Finally, the adapter construction tool can be obtained by (||i<nPipe_mi)//[POA ∪ AC||PSI ∪ AC].

2) Reliability Assurance Mechanism of service cooperation based on transaction

Transaction is a key technology of distributed system reliability. The characteristics of Transaction are long time operation characteristics of service coordination, Cross-domain coordination, strict autonomy and heterogeneity of the Web service. The traditional transaction technology is difficult to be directly applied to reliability guarantee of service coordination. From the perspective of adaptative Services Cooperative transaction model, we study the key technology of relaxed atomic security, failure recovery and concurrency control of transactional services.

First of all, proposes a Transactional Service Coordination Model (TSCM) based on hierarchical. The model is described as the static composition of Transactional Service Coordination, including structure, attributes, and constraints and so on. The attributes of TSCM are divided into two groups: retrievable attributes and compensable attributes. According to retrievable and compensable attributes of TSCM, these attributes are divided the web services of different transaction behaviors into four classes, pivot, compensable, retrievable and trivial. And TSM are characterized by the status transfer diagrams.

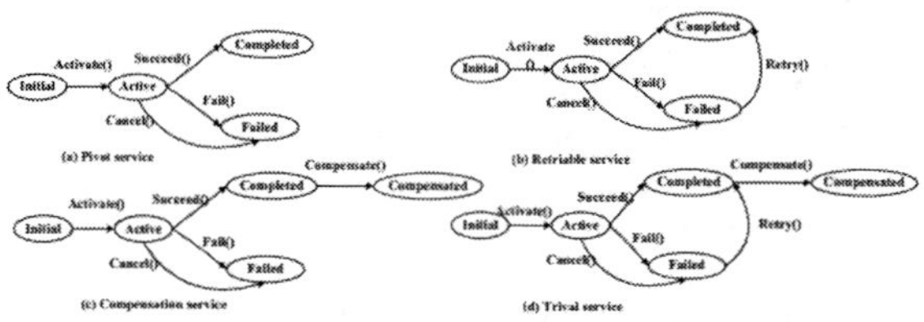

Figure 3. The state transition diagram of different types of services

Secondly, on the basis of TSCM model, we take advantage of the semantic information contained in the user-defined relaxed atomicity requirement and put forward a TSCM-FR. The TSCM-FR is a service cooperative failure recovery algorithm based on relaxation atomic driven. There is an exception handling mechanism based on TSCM-FR to capture the possible failures that allow the fault to be handled flexibly at different levels. This is as shown in the following figure [10]. When making atomic drive failure recovery, Multi-level exception handling system is based on the concept that the optimal configuration is a series of selection rules, and the service cooperation is finished by the automatic retrying and compensation.

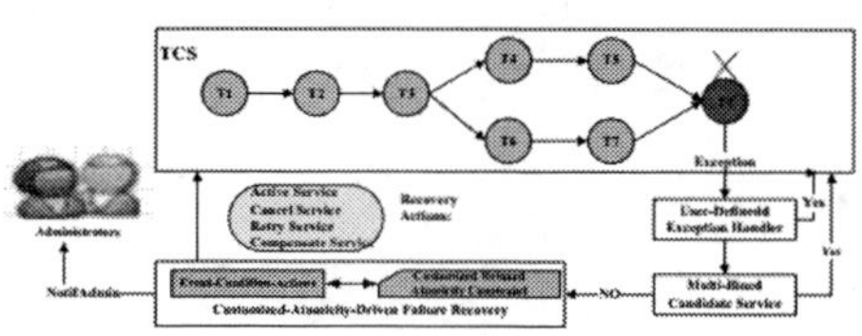

Figure 4. Multi-level exception handling system diagram

Thirdly, as a transactional service collaboration model, the back-end relaxes isolation among services, and the finished intermediate results are visible to the outside world. This relaxation makes the collaboration inconsistency for multiple transactional services in the execution of concurrent, and increases the difficulty of development. In order to solve this problem, we put forward a distributed concurrency control protocol based on transaction service collaboration model (TSCM-CC). In TSCM-CC, the service provider maintains a local dependency graph, which is synchronized with the service call. If the service call does not rely on any executed service, the direct execution is allowed; If the service call depends on the executed service, it needs to judge whether to establish a corresponding dependency relation, and then enter the execution again.

Finally, based on the above, we extend the syntax and deployment descriptor specification for the most popular service collaboration description language. This language is also called WS-BPEL [11-13]. This extension increases the transaction characteristics of the language, and the concept of Candidate Sphere is introduced to support of transaction and atomicity. On this basis, this paper realizes a transactional service collaborative support framework based on the AOP mechanism. This framework is as shown below

.

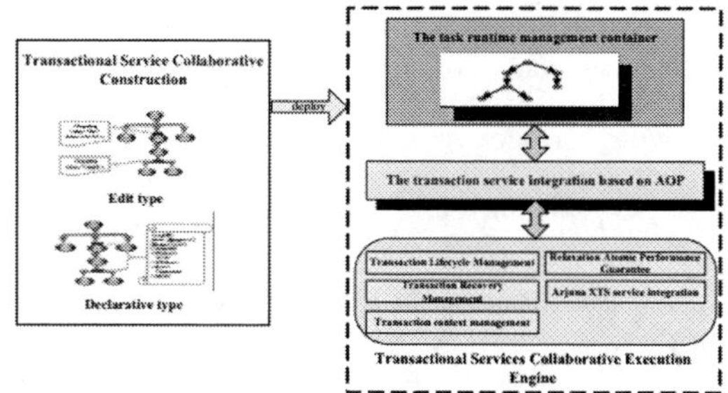

Figure 5. The transactional services collaborative support framework

3) *Situational-oriented monitoring and adaptive recovery mechanisms for service collaboration*

Because of the dynamic nature of service computing environment, it is possible to deviate from the execution of services collaboration and business objectives when the service collaboration is performed. The traditional design methods for analysis and verification cannot guarantee the correctness of the operating system. The service collaboration needs to be monitored of monitoring services at runtime, collects all kinds of situation information. Based on the pre-defined strategy, the dynamic adjustment of the collaborative structure is realized [13]. Based on this, the software system is correctly maintained and supported to the adaptive evolution of service coordination. Situation is a characterization of internal and external factors. The external factors include user needs and business environment changes. The internal factors include services coordination runtime under unexpected circumstances. The situation-oriented services collaboration includes the functional and non-functional aspects of service collaboration.

The definitions of Monitoring event definitions is:

e ::= start | end | msg (link.input/output = message)

The Collaborative Task Instance Monitoring Requirements Description Language is:

b ::= e | Yb | Ob | Hb | b S b |! b | b Logop b|n Relop n | true | false

n ::= Count (b) | Time (b) | b? n : n | n Numop n | 0 | 1 | ...

The Description Language of Collaborative Task Class Monitoring Requirements is:

B ::= And(b) | Y B | O B | H B | B S B | N Relop N | ! B | B Logop B | true| false

N ::= Count(b)| Sum(n) | Avg(n) | N Numop N | 0 | 1 ⋯

In view of services coordination, we put forward a kind of service collaborative monitoring method based on dynamic AOP technology, it is as shown in the figure below.

In the monitoring of functional aspects, the service collaborative monitoring method based on dynamic AOP technology is supported on the expression of complex

DOI: 10.1051/itmconf/20171201034

events, and through the event tree to organize the hierarchical relationship between behavior constraint automaton and composite event automaton to correctly identify events, so as to effectively monitor the collaborative behavior, check whether the predefined constraint violation. In the monitoring of non-functional aspects, the service collaborative monitoring method based on dynamic AOP technology is collect all kinds of situation information, including the statistical service called time, service execution reliability, etc [14].

2.2the architecture of business management logic engine

The business management logic engine is an independent work engine that can be deployed on any Java/J2EE application server. The business management logic engine is supports in the form of WS-BPEL1.1, and its architecture is shown in figure:

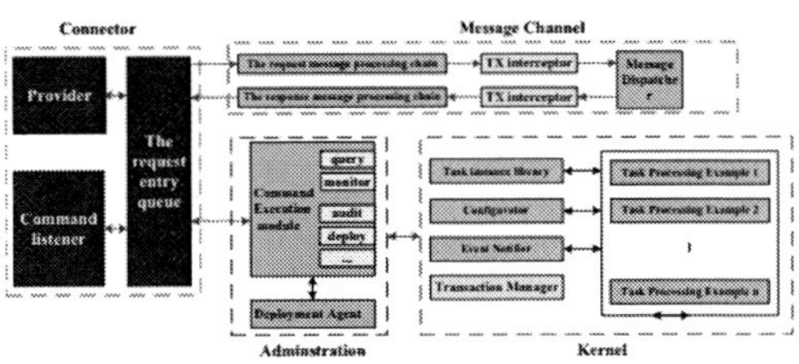

Figure 6. The Business logic engine management architecture diagram

The Business logic engine management mainly includes the following functional modules:

- Connector module: The message Provider module is responsible for receiving and sending SOAP messages.
- Message Channel module: The request message and response message processing chain module which support messages request and response before and after the customization of processing needs.
- Administration module: This module is the command execution module to achieve the deployment of the task, monitoring, query and other operations, and deployment agent module is responsible for parsing and deploy operating of tasks.
- Kernel module: The event notification module has an event notification mechanism based on Pub/Sub mode.

3 New chaos optimal algorithm for BPMN

Business Process Modeling and Notation, is called BPMN. It includes these entities are combined into a business flow chart. The Business Process Management Initiative has developed a set of standard that is also called BPMN. It defines a Business Process Diagram(BPD), which is based on a flowcharting that is designed to create a graphical model of business process operations. By the BPMN business process design specification, this paper has developed a platform task management tool based on model-driven[15]. It is a task modeling and management tool which supports the integrated component of service components. It provides a unified task modeling visualization development tool that allows users to use a graphical drag and drop so that easily, intuitively and effectively design, modification and maintenance of CMfg task flow, and WYSIWYG, which greatly improves the usability of the tool.

In this paper, we mainly focus on the key technologies of the composite choice of multi-service QoS constraints, service portfolio model conversion and others. It is as follows:

3.1 The composite choice of multi-service QoS constraints

The problem of composite choice of multi-service QoS constraints is real a difficult NP problem. The major difficulty is that the solution space is too large to completed in polynomial time. At present, many studies are optimizing the search algorithm, but the effect is not ideal. Although some studies have improve the speed of discovery, the accuracy of service discovery will not meet the needs of the users. In response to this problem, we firstly propose to a method of personalized modeling. It can track and learn the user's interests and behaviors, and can accept the user's various constraints.

Definition: The user's preference value of service x is the average of attributes of service w_i, the formula is as follows:

$$Pref(x) = \frac{1}{M(x)} \sum_{w_i \in x} Pref(w_i) \tag{1}$$

Definition: The user's preference value of service w_i, the formula is as follows:

$$Pref(w_i) = I(X(w_i); V) = log \frac{P(X(w_i) \mid V)}{P(X(w_i))} \tag{2}$$

Where w_i is the attributes of service x, $Pref(x)$ is the user's preference value of service x.

Based on the above-proposed formula, a personalized model is as follow:

$$Pref(x) = \frac{1}{M(x)} \sum_{w_i \in x} log \frac{P(X(w_i) \mid V)}{P(X(w_i))} \tag{3}$$

On this basis, we propose a constraint model based on user personalization model and service association model. On the one hand, the constraint model is one of the most effective ways to reduce the search space and improve the service choices' efficiency, on the other hand the constraint model reflects the users' characteristics and preferences, it can find a more effective combination of service satisfaction.

Based on constrained model, we propose an efficient heuristic selection algorithm for composite services. Unlike the previous work, it isn't focus on the optimization of the discovery algorithm. On the user's point of view, it is efficiency to obtain service discovery when mining users' information.

3.2 The transformation of service composition model

Task Description Model(TDM) is geared to serving the needs of business people or domain exporters. In order to facilitate mutual understanding between business people , it is to describe the tasks that uses the standard graphic elements defined by the BPMN specification. Task Execution Model(TEM) is geared to serving the needs of technical staffs. There are great differences between the BPMN model and BPEL model in terms of structural features, expression forms and expression ability. Therefore, it is feasible to realize the automatic transformation from BPMN model to BPEL model [16]. A feasible way is to find a way of abstract expression that can shield the details of the model. Keep a model level transformation when abstract model is transformed. Then, based on semantic equivalence, the model transformation strategy is carried out mapping transformation on the basis of semantic equivalence. The model transformation diagram is as follows:

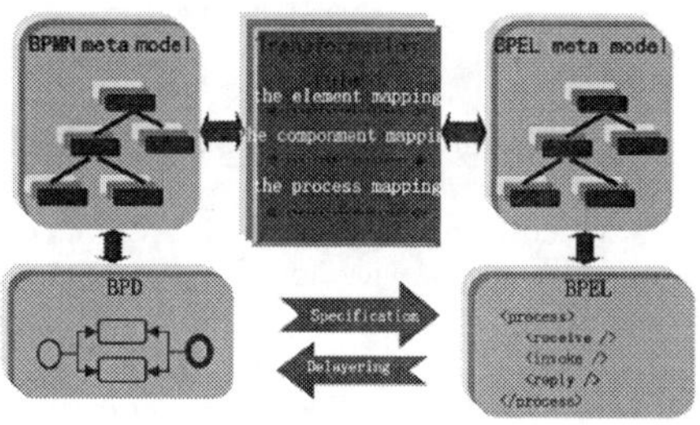

Figure 7. The model transformation diagram

In this paper, it is the mapping of metal model between the three levels of elements, components and processes. The mapping is as follows:

3.3 the element mapping

Element is the basic component elements of model. Since the semantics of BPMN is stronger than the semantic representation of BPEL, and therefore, in order to get the completed element matching in elements mapping ((i.e. for each element, an element can be found in the other model with the matching) , we take the cutting strategy to get a set of core BPMN elements. Here, we have discussed this topic that the BPMN-based task model is the task model based on BPMN core elements [17].

3.4 the component mapping

According to the characteristics of the different componential structure, the paper makes several common mapping strategies. The component mapping is as follows:

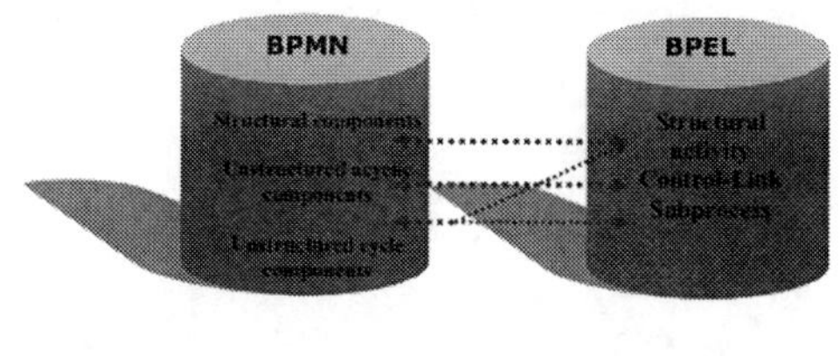

Figure 8. The component mapping diagram

For structural components, it can be directly mapped to the structure activities of semantic BPEL. As follows: Sequence、Switch、While、Pick、Flow.

3.5 the process mapping

The process mapping is on the basis of the component mapping and component specification. In short, component specification is a process by which components can be replaced by a simple task activity [18]. Through an iterative process of component specifications, process can be unceasing reduction, and ultimately the process mapping simplify it into a simple component . Finally, the whole process mapping is realized by component mapping.

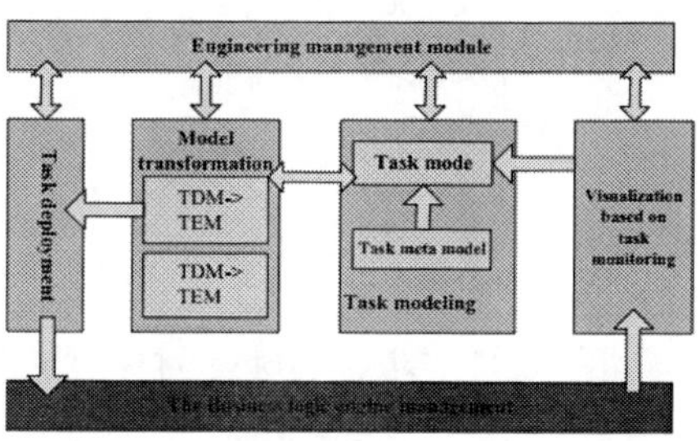

Figure 9. The architecture of platform task management tool

4 Case study

In order to verify the reliability and universality of the Business Process Management, and assess the performance and effect of this engine, we took a verification application in the 3D cloud printing creative and innovation product development. The service resources of the above-mentioned case may be released in our 3D Printing Colosseum manufacturing business process engine; moreover, the corresponding order/task workflows may be summarized in view of requirements of our case; and the following solution is given in view of the actual situations on how to carry out our research. The WS-BPEL snippet is as follow:

```
<sequence>
<receive1>···</receive1>
<flow>
<sequence>
<invoke1>···</invoke1>
<invoke2>
...
<tarfetlink1>···</tarfetlink1>
</invoke2>
<receive2>···</receive2>
</sequence>
<invoke3>
...
<sourcelink1>...</sourcelink1>
</invoke3>
<receive3>
...
<sourcelink2>···</sourcelink2>
</receive3>
</sequence>
<sequence>
<invoke4>···</invoke4>
<invoke5>
...
<targetlink2>···</targetlink2>
</invoke5>
</sequence>
</flow>
<reply>···</reply>
</sequence>
```

Figure 10. The WS-BPEL snippet

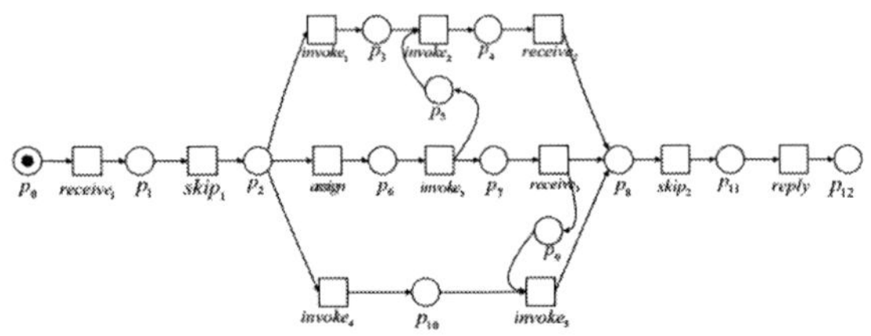

Figure 11. The logic representation

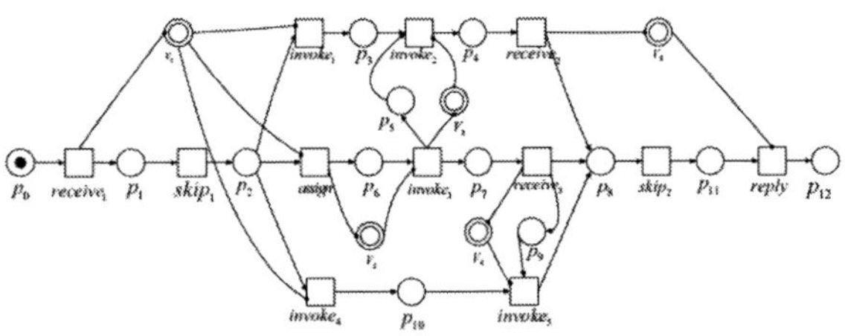

Figure 12. The semantic representation

In what follows, we have carried out several experiments to evaluate the impact of the heuristics for reducing the Web Services Business Process Execution Language and to prove the effectiveness of our approach in the 3D Printing Colosseum manufacturing business process[19]. We have also generated a WS-BPEL process composed by 12 activities, a set of 30 potential users, a role hierarchy of 6 roles, 3 separation of duty and 4 binding of duty and context constraints. Such 3D Printing Colosseum manufacturing business process has a MaxRoles value equal to 6. We have considered four test cases that are summarized in Table 1. It is in the following cases:

a) we varied the number of potential user from 30 to 70 and kept the number of separation of duty and binding of duty and context constraints equal to 4, and the value of MaxRoles is 6.

b) we varied the number of potential user to 30 and kept the number of separation of duty and binding of duty and context constraints equal to 4, and the value of MaxRoles is [3,5].

c) we varied the number of binding of duty constraints defined for the process from 0 to 5 and we set the number of separation of duty and context constraints to 4, the value of MaxRoles to 6 and the number of potential users to 30.

d) we varied the number of binding of duty and context constraints from 0 and set the number of separation of duty constraints defined for the process from 3 to 5, MaxRoles value to 6 and the number of potential users to 30.

TABLE I. TEST CASES PARAMETERS

Test case	Business process	Num of BoD	Num of SoD	MaxRoles	Num of Users
1	12 activities	4	4	6	30-70
2	12 activities	4	4	[3,5]	30
3	12 activities	[0,5]	4	6	30
4	12 activities	0	[3,5]	6	30

Conclusions

In this paper, we first analyzed the applications of CMfg service composition modeling, concluded the key technologies of business management logic engine, new chaos optimal algorithm for BPMN, and proposed the model transformation diagram. Based on these works, a service compatibility checking algorithm based on adaptation mechanism with the service interface and source service component of Business Management Logic Engine was proposed to guide the multi-level service compatibility checking [21]. A Business Process Diagram (BPD) is also designed for graphical model of business process operations.

Acknowledgments

This work is partially supported by the National Key Technology Research and Development Program of China and Nature Science Foundation of Hubei Province, China (No. 2016YFB1101700) and (No. 2015CFA115).

References

[1] B. Q. Huang, C. H. Li, C. Yin, X. P. Zhao, Cloud Manufacturing Service Platform for Small and Medium-sized Enterprises, Int J Adv Manuf Techno, vol. 65, No. 12, 2013, pp. 1261-1272.

[2] T. X. Song, C. L. Zhang, B. Q. Huang, A cloud manufacturing service platform for small and medium enterprises, Computer Integrated Manufacturing Systems, vol. 5, No. 5, 2013, pp. 47-52,.

[3] Turetken, A. Elgammal, W. van den Heuvel, and M. Papazoglou, Capturing compliance requirements: A pattern-based approach. IEEE Software, special issue on Software Engineering for Compliance, vol. 29, No. 3, 2012, pp. 28–36.

[4] F. Tao, Y. J. Laili, L. Zhang, Z. H. Zhang, A.Y. C. Nee, QMAEA: a quantum multi-agent evolutionary algorithm for multi-objective combinatorial optimization, SIMULATION, vol. 90 , No. 2 , 2014 , pp. 182–204.

[5] Y. Ye, Y. Xu, J. Yin, et al, Social business process management and process recommendation method, Computer Integrated Manufacturing Systems, vol. 22 , No. 2 , 2016 , pp.413-421.

[6] X. W. Liu, Y. Yang, X. D. Xu, C. C. Li, et al, Research on profit mechanism of 3d printing cloud platform based on customized products, Applied Mechanics & Materials, vol. 703 , 2014 , pp. 318-322.

[7] C. M. Wei, C. L. Zhang, T. X. Song, et al, A Cloud Manufacturing Service Management Model and Its Implementation, International Conference on Service Science, ICSS) , vol. 5 , No. 5 , 2013 , pp. 60-63.

[8] M. E. Rangiha, B. Karakostas, Process recommendation and role assignment in social business process management, Science and Information Conference. IEEE, 2014 , pp.810-818.

[9] S. Usuki, H. Kanaka, K. T. Miura, Generation and control of 3D standing wave illumination for wide-field high-resolution 3D microscopic measurement, International Journal of Precision Engineering and Manufacturing, vol. 14, No. 1,2013, pp.55-60.

[10] S. Moser, A. Martens, K. Gorlach, et al, Advanced Verification of Distributed WS-BPEL Business Processes Incorporating CSSA-based Data Flow Analysis, International Journal of Business Process Integration & Management, vol. 4, No. 4,2007, pp.47-59.

[11] T. S. Heinze, W. Amme, S. Moser, A Restructuring Method for WS-BPEL Business Processes Based on Extended Workflow Graphs, Business Process Management. Springer Berlin Heidelberg, vol. 2009, pp.211-228.

[12] Hildebrandt T. A Standard-driven Implementaion of WS-BPEL 2.0[J]. Grass & Forage Science, 2017, 40(40):183-192.

[13] G. Hayashi, E. Chiappetta, Analysis of the Change in Farmer Service Requirement and Farmers' Collaboration Foundation Under the Agricultural Industrialization in Northwest Region-the Explanation of Traditional Cooperation Decline and Cooperation Difficult, Journal of Northwest A & F University, vol. 71, No. 9, 2013, pp.100–101.

[14] C. L. Zhang, A Cloud Manufacturing Service Platform for Small and Medium Enterprises, MNaster dissertation, Dept of Mechanical Eng, Hubei University of Technology, Wuhan city, Mass, 2013.

[15] Q. Yin, C. H. Li, Modeling for personalized Web service selection with QOS constraints based on GA and fuzzy control, Computer Engineering & Applications, vol. 43, No. 27,2007, pp.226-229.

[16] D. Margaris, C. Vassilakis, P. Georgiadis, Improving QoS delivered by WS-BPEL scenario adaptation through service execution parallelization, The, ACM Symposium. ACM, vol. 2016, 2016, pp.1590-1596.

[17] A. Barnawi, A. Awad, A. Elgammal, et al, An Anti-Pattern-based Runtime Business Process Compliance Monitoring Framework, International Journal of Advanced Computer Science & Applications, vol. 7, No. 2, 2016, pp.1-22.

[18] R. Thullner, S. Rozsnyai, J. Schiefer, H. Obweger, M. Suntinger, Proactive business process compliance monitoring with event-based systems. In Enterprise Distributed Object Computing Conference Workshops (EDOCW), 15th IEEE International, vol. 2011, pp.429–437.

[19] B. T. Nguyen, D. H. Nguyen, T. T. Nguyen, Translation from BPMN to BPEL, current techniques and limitations Symposium on Information and Communication Technology. ACM, vol. 2014, pp.21-30.

[20] H. Dun, W. Zhao, Y. Huang, et al. Modeling and Analysis of WS-BPEL Business Processes Based on ServiceNet. 2008 15th Asia-Pacific Software Engineering Conference, vol. 2008, pp.265-272.

[21] Parimala N, Kohar R. A quality metric for BPEL process under evolution[C]// Eleventh International Conference on Digital Information Management. IEEE, 2017.

A New Model-CELBF for Medical Image Segmentation Based on Image Entropy

Chao Zhang[1], Yu-Cui Guo[2], Feng-Shan Liu[3]

[1]*Department of Mathematical Sciences Delaware State University, Dover, DE, USA*
[2]*School of Science Beijing University of Posts and Telecommunications, Beijing, China*
[3]*Department of Mathematical Sciences Delaware State University, Dover, DE, USA*
[1]*czhang11@students.desu.edu*, [2]*ycguo@bupt.edu.cn*, [3]*fliu@desu.edu*

Abstract: A new model (named CELBF) for medical image segmentation based on LBF and image entropy is proposed in this paper. We introduced image entropy to deal with the inhomogeneity of image gray level. Some real medical images are processed by using this new model and finite difference algorithm. The results show that new model improves the speed of segmentation and increases noise robustness. Compared with LBF model, the new model can segment inhomogeneity medical image more quickly and more accurately. Meanwhile the CELBF model has more strong robustness with noise.

1. Introduction

Medical image is widely used in medical diagnosis. At present, the image segmentation methods are mostly used to locate the lesion boundary. The earlier image segmentation methods were based on low-level image knowledge, such as image gray, edge, and so on. Typical segmentation methods include threshold method, region growing method, edge detection method, etc. With the increasing of image types and higher quality demand, more and more high-level techniques are used for image segmentation, and therefore some classic methods were developed to solve the problems of complex image segmentation based on clustering, partial differential equations, and graph theory, etc. Among the classic methods, the image segmentation method based on partial differential equation (PDE) is one of the most popular methods in the field of image segmentation. A lot of good results have been developed based on image segmentation method and the image segmentation method is still widely used [1-5]. Partial differential equation (PDE) image segmentation is a nonlinear image segmentation method which was developed in 1980s. Its basic idea is to make the continuous mathematical model of the image to follow with a partial differential equation, and the corresponding segmentation result is obtained when the stable solution of the equation is obtained. The most important advantage of this technique is that the curve is continuous and smooth in the process of evolution. The classical model of image segmentation based on partial differential equation (PDE) is the active contour model which is based on the deformable model. The basic principle of the deformable model is that the curve moves and changes under the action of the driving forces including the internal and the external forces, in which the internal force is based on the geometric characteristics of the curve and keeps the smoothness of the curve; external force drives curve approximation to the boundary of the object through prior information of the target and the image information. Under the action of the internal force and the external force, the curve moves to the boundary of the target under the smoothness condition. The active contour model makes deformation of the curve through minimizing the energy. In the active contour model, an energy function of the curve is defined firstly, and then the given energy function is minimized to make the curve evolving to the boundary of the target.

In this paper, a new algorithm (named CELBF) for medical image segmentation based on information entropy is proposed. We combined the CV and the LBF models and used the concept of information entropy. The numerical results with MATLAB are satisfactory.

2. Mathematical Basis of the Model

Mathematics plays an important role in the development of image segmentation and penetrates into the various branches of image segmentation. PDE, as an applied mathematics, has become a hot topic in the field. Meanwhile, because the partial differential equation method is suitable for many kinds of images, it has very important theory and application value. The ideas of partial differential equations being applied to image processing can be traced back to the work of Gabor [6] in 1965 and Jain [7] in 1977. But a substantial progress thanks to Koenderink [8] and Witkin [9], for they put forward an idea of that signals and different scales of the convolution of Gauss function is equivalent to the heat diffusion equation with initial value of signal in 1984 and 1985 respectively, which was based on the theory of multi-scale analysis. Koenderink and Witkin also solved image denoising problems using the thermal diffusion equation. In 1993, an axiomatic system was formed by L. Alvarez [10] et al through the ingenious processing for the derivation of the Affine Morphological Scale Space equation, which marks that the formal formation of the discipline of image processing based on the partial differential equations.

During the last few decades, the image segmentation method based on differential equations has made great progress. Many kinds of typical active contour models based on geometric region have been proposed. Here we mainly introduce the CV model and the LBF model, because our new model in this paper is obtained mainly by introducing the image entropy method and by combining the CV model and the LBF model.

2.1 Chan-Vese (CV) Model

The CV model is a classical geometric active contour model based on region, which was proposed by Chan and Vese [3] in 2001. The CV model can be defined as that the image set I defined in Ω is divided into two parts by the active contour C, and the two parts were recorded as $inside\ (C)$ and $outside(C)$. We use c_1 and c_2 to represent the average value of the internal gray level of the curve and the average value of the external gray level of the curve respectively. The fitting energy functional is defined as follows:

$$E_{CV}(C,c_1,c_2)=\lambda_1\iint_{inside(C)}|I(x,y)-c_1|^2dxdy+\lambda_2\iint_{outside(C)}|I(x,y)-c_2|^2dxdy+uLength(C)+vArea(inside(C))$$

where $Length(C)$ is the length of the contour curve which plays a role of regularization, $Area(inside\ (C))$ is the internal area of the contour curve, $u,v\geq 0$ are two parameters; λ_1,λ_2 are two weight coefficients, and $\lambda_1,\lambda_2>0$. The first two terms on the right hand side of the formula are called the "fitting" terms which are mainly used to control the fitting error for the contour curve fit edge. The other two terms are called the "smooth" terms for getting a smooth curve in the process of evolution. The final position of the contour curve can be obtained by minimizing the energy functional.

Let the level set function ϕ be represented by the following formula:

$$\begin{cases}\phi(x,y)=0\,, & (x,y)\in C\\ \phi(x,y)>0\,, & (x,y)\in inside(C)\\ \phi(x,y)<0\,, & (x,y)\in outside(C).\end{cases}$$

In order to apply the level set method, the Heaviside function is introduced

$$H(x)=\begin{cases}1, & x\geq 0\\ 0, & x<0.\end{cases}$$

And the Dirac function is as

$$\delta(x)=\frac{d}{dx}H(x).$$

In this method, the Heaviside function is used to divide the region of evolution, and the Dirac function is used to define the value of evolution around the zero level set function. Here,

$$Length(C)=\int_0^{L(C)}ds=\iint_\Omega\delta(\phi)|\nabla\phi|dxdy,$$

$$Area(inside(C))=\iint_\Omega H(\phi)dxdy,$$

$$\iint_{inside(c)}|I(x,y)-c_1|^2dxdy=\iint_\Omega|I(x,y)-c_1|^2H(\phi)dxdy,$$

$$\iint_{outside(c)}|I(x,y)-c_2|^2dxdy=\iint_\Omega|I(x,y)-c_2|^2(1-H(\phi))dxdy.$$

Thus, the energy functional of the level set function is obtained as

$$E_{CV}(\phi,c_1,c_2)=\lambda_1\iint_\Omega|I(x,y)-c_1|^2H(\phi)dxdy+\lambda_2\iint_\Omega|I(x,y)-c_2|^2(1-H(\phi))dxdy+u\iint_\Omega\delta(\phi)|\nabla\phi|dxdy+v\iint_\Omega H(\phi)dxdy.$$

At this point, the level set of the image $I(x,y)$ is:

$$I(x,y)=c_1H(\phi)+C_2(1-H(\phi)).$$

Fixing ϕ and minimizing the energy functional $E_{CV}(\phi,c_1,c_2)$, we have

$$c_1 = \frac{\iint_\Omega I(x,y)H(\phi)dxdy}{\iint_\Omega H(\phi)dxdy},$$

$$c_2 = \frac{\iint_\Omega I(x,y)(1-H(\phi))dxdy}{\iint_\Omega (1-H(\phi))dxdy}.$$

In the CV model, usually we set $v = 0$. The energy functional $E_{CV}(\phi, c_1, c_2)$, is minimized using the variation method and gradient descent flow technique and Euler-Lagrange equation is obtained as

$$\frac{\partial E}{\partial \phi} = -\delta(\phi)\left(u \cdot div\left(\frac{\nabla\phi}{|\nabla\phi|}\right) - \lambda_1(I-c_1)^2 + \lambda_2(I-c_2)^2\right) = 0.$$

The regularized Heaviside function is often used in the numerical calculation as

$$H_\varepsilon(x) = \frac{1}{2}\left[1 + \frac{1}{\pi}\arctan\left(\frac{x}{\varepsilon}\right)\right]$$

and the corresponding Dirac function is

$$\delta(x) = \frac{1}{\pi}\frac{\varepsilon}{\varepsilon^2 + x^2}.$$

Our goal is to expand the capture range and to prevent the occurrence of singular cases. For the CV model, due to the fact that both c_1 and c_2 represent the average gray values of the internal and external of the contour curve and therefore are global variables, CV model is a segmentation model based on global information. Although it has advantages with respect to noise robustness, calculation simplicity, etc., it cannot be used for non-uniform gray image segmentation.

2.2 Local Binary Fitting (LBF) Model[3,4,11]

Let x be a point in the image area and C be the contour curve, and the fitting energy function at the point x is defined as

$$E_x^{Fit} = \lambda_1 \int_{inside(C)} K_\sigma(x-y)|I(y) - f_1(x)|^2 dy + \lambda_2 \int_{outide(C)} K_\sigma(x-y)|I(y) - f_2(x)|^2 dy$$

where $f_1(x)$ and $f_2(x)$ are gray fitting values of the image at the point of x, K_σ is the Gauss kernel function with a standard deviation of σ, and

$$K_\sigma = \frac{1}{\sqrt{2\pi}\sigma}e^{-\frac{|x|^2}{2\sigma^2}}.$$

Let ϕ be the level set function of contour curve C. Using the level set method, we have

$$E_x^{Fit} = \lambda_1 \int_{inside(C)} K_\sigma(x-y)|I(y) - f_1(x)|^2 H(\phi)dy + \lambda_2 \int_{outide(C)} K_\sigma(x-y)|I(y) - f_2(x)|^2(1-H(\phi))dy.$$

The total fitting energy function is

$$E^{Fit} = \int_\Omega E_x^{Fit}\,dx.$$

Adding the set regularization $\int_\Omega \frac{1}{2}(|\nabla\phi| - 1)^2 d\sigma$ term, the total energy functional of LBF model is

$$E^{LBF} = E^{Fit} + \int_\Omega \frac{1}{2}(|\nabla\phi| - 1)^2 d\sigma + v|C|.$$

Firstly fixing ϕ in above formula, after minimizing the energy functional E^{LBF} with respect to $f_1(x)$ and $f_2(x)$, we have

$$f_1(x) = \frac{\int_\Omega K_\sigma(x-y)I(y)H(\phi(y))dy}{\int_\Omega K_\sigma(x-y)H(\phi(y))dy}$$

$$f_2(x) = \frac{\int_\Omega K_\sigma(x-y)I(y)\left(1 - H(\phi(y))\right)dy}{\int_\Omega K_\sigma(x-y)\left(1 - H(\phi(y))\right)dy}.$$

Then fixing the fitting factors $f_1(x)$ and $f_2(x)$, after minimizing the energy functional E^{LBF} with respect to ϕ, the evolution equation of the energy functional E^{LBF} is obtained using a gradient descent flow:

$$\frac{\partial\phi}{\partial t} = -\delta_\varepsilon(\phi)(\lambda_1 e_1 - \lambda_2 e_2) + u\left[\Delta\phi - div\left(\frac{\nabla\phi}{|\nabla\phi|}\right)\right] + v\delta_\varepsilon(\phi)div\left(\frac{\nabla\phi}{|\nabla\phi|}\right) \qquad (2.1)$$

where

$$e_1 = \int_\Omega K_\sigma(x-y)|I(x) - f_1(y)|^2 dy,$$

$$e_2 = \int_\Omega K_\sigma(x-y)|I(x) - f_1(y)|^2 dy.$$

In the LBF model, $f_1(x)$ and $f_2(x)$ are the fitting energy of the image at the point x which are local energy related variance. Therefore, the LBF model is based on the local image information. Meanwhile, due to the introduction of the local energy, the LBF model has good segmentation effect for inhomogeneity image. Its disadvantages are that it is sensitive for contour initialization and poor noise robustness, etc.

3. A New Model Celbf Based On Information Entropy

Considering the advantages and the disadvantages of the CV model and the LBF model [12], we created a new local fitting energy functional to replace the ones in the CV and the LBF models. The new energy functional is defined as:

$$E^{NLGF} = \omega E^{GIF} + (1-\omega)E^{NLIF} + \nu L(\phi) + \mu P(\phi) \quad (3.1)$$

Where

$$E^{GIF} = \lambda_1 \iint_{inside(C)} |I(x,y) - c_1|^2 dxdy + \lambda_2 \iint_{outside(C)} |I(x,y) - c_2|^2 dxdy$$

is a global fitting factor,

$$E^{NLIF} = \sum_{i=1}^{2} \int_\Omega \lambda_i |I(x,y) - f_i(x)|^2 M_i(\phi) dx$$

is a new local fitting energy functional level set, and

$$f_1(x) = \frac{K(x) * (I(x)H(\phi))}{K(x) * H(\phi)},$$

$$f_2(x) = \frac{K(x) * \left(I(x)(1 - H(\phi))\right)}{K(x) * (1 - H(\phi))}.$$

Use gradient descent to solve the equation (3.1), we have the final curve evolution equation:

$$\frac{\partial \phi}{\partial t} = -\delta_\varepsilon(\phi)(F_1 + F_2) + u\left[\Delta\phi - div\left(\frac{\nabla\phi}{|\nabla\phi|}\right)\right] + \nu\delta_\varepsilon(\phi) div\left(\frac{\nabla\phi}{|\nabla\phi|}\right) \quad (3.2)$$

Where $F_1 = \omega(\lambda_1(I(x) - c_1)^2 - \lambda_2(I(x) - c_2)^2)$

$$F_2 = (1-\omega)\left(\lambda_1 \int_\Omega K_\sigma(y - x)|I(x) - f_1(y)|^2 dy - \lambda_2 \int_\Omega K_\sigma(y - x)|I(x) - f_2(y)|^2 dy\right).$$

We call F_1 and F_2 the global intensity fitting (GIF) force and the local intensity fitting (LIF) force, respectively.

In order to deal with the gray inhomogeneity of images, we introduce the concept of image entropy in our model. The image entropy was introduced for the first time to image segmentation in 1972 by Freden [13]. From then, the concept of entropy has played an important role. At present, image entropy is commonly used in image segmentation.

Let p_i be a distribution of a given image I_i. Based on Shannon's information theory, the image entropy is

$$E_I = -\sum_{i=1}^{n} p_i \log p_i$$

Where the distribution function of the image p_i can be given by a variety of ways depending on the segmentation method.

In this paper, let $I: \Omega \subset R^2 \to R$ be an image and $\Omega_x \subset \Omega$ be a neighborhood of x with a radius of r. Then the local entropy for point x is defined as

$$E(x, \Omega_x) = -\frac{1}{\log|\Omega_x|} \int_{\Omega_x} p(y, \Omega_x) \log p(y, \Omega_x)\, dy$$

Where $p(y, \Omega_x)$ is the distribution function of gray level [10,14] which is shown as

$$p(y, \Omega_x) = \frac{I(y)}{\int_{\Omega_x} I(z)dz}, y \in \Omega_x.$$

The reason for the LBF model being sensitive to noise is that the gray level variation of image is not considered when the local fitting energy E^{LBF} is defined. In this paper, we consider the gray variation information and also modify the energy in (2.1). Then we propose a weighted LBF model that is based on image entropy to improve robustness to the noise. We define this model as CELBF model. We define a new fitting energy functional at contour curve C of LBF model as

$$E(C, f_1, f_2) = \int_\Omega E_r(x) E_x(C, f_1(x), f_2(x)) dx$$

Where $E_r(x) = E(x, B(x,r))$ is the local entropy for point x.

By minimizing the energy functional, we obtain the level set differential equation of our model

$$\frac{\partial \phi}{\partial t} = -\delta_\varepsilon(\phi)(F_1 + F_2) + u\left[\Delta\phi - div\left(\frac{\nabla\phi}{|\nabla\phi|}\right)\right] + \nu\delta_\varepsilon(\phi) div\left(\frac{\nabla\phi}{|\nabla\phi|}\right)$$

Where $F_1 = \omega(\lambda_1(I(x) - c_1)^2 - \lambda_2(I(x) - c_2)^2)$

$$F_2 = (1-\omega)\left(\lambda_1 \int_\Omega E_r(x) K_\sigma(y - x)|I(x) - f_1(y)|^2 dy - \lambda_2 \int_\Omega E_r(x) K_\sigma(y - x)|I(x) - f_2(y)|^2 dy\right).$$

With this model, several groups of images were segmented by using finite difference method and MATLAB. Comparing with the results of LBF model, our results are satisfactory.

4. Result and analysis

Using our new CELBF model, we obtained better results than the CV model and the LBF model.

4.1 Segmentation Time

Figure 4.1 shows the segmentation results of two typical gray inhomogeneous images, which both are taken from the literature [13]. One is a true T-type image (127*90), and the other is the X-ray blood vessel image (111*110). The segmentation results of the two images are obtained from the CELBF model and the LBF model respectively using the same parameters of $\lambda_1 = \lambda_2 = 1, \mu = 1, \Delta t = 0.1, h = 1, \sigma = 3$, $and\ \omega = 0.01$ and 0.065 for CELBF model. It is not difficult to see that the CELBF model achieves almost the same segmentation results as the LBF model from the figures. However, the CELBF model used fewer iterations and faster segmentation speed. The speed of the CELBF model is approximately 1/2 of the LBF model. It is show that the CELBF model has greatly improved the speed of segmentation while ensuring the accuracy

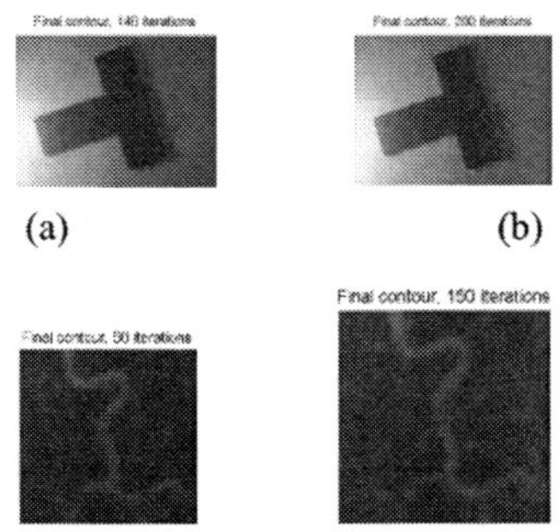

(a) (b)

(c) (d)

Figure 4.1

4.2 Segmentation for Magnetic Resonance Imaging (MRI)

Segmentation methods are widely used for dealing with MRI images. Figure 4.2 (a) (189 * 164 * 3) and 4.2 (e) (157 * 141) are two real human brain Magnetic Resonance Imaging. The segmentation results of the two images are obtained from the CELBF model and the LBF model with the same parameters of $\lambda_1 = \lambda_2 = 1, \mu = 1, \Delta t = 0.1, h = 1, \sigma = 3$, and $\omega = 0.35$ in our CELBF model. Figure 4.2 (b, c, d) and Figure 4.2 (f, g, h) are segmentation results obtained by using the LBF model with 60, 200 and 500 iterations respectively. The segmentation results show that our CELBF model has better segmentation ability for complex brain MRI images. Our model ensures the accuracy of segmentation and improves segmentation speed. LBF model cannot get accurate segmentation results on complex images, and therefore it shows that the CELBF model works well with variance of grayscale level of the image to a certain extent.

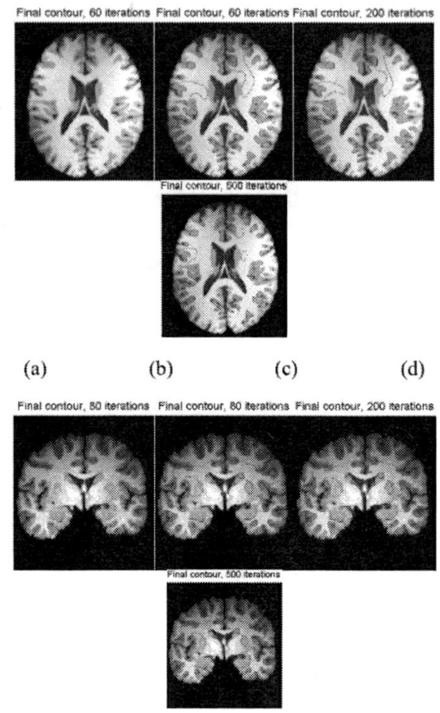

(a) (b) (c) (d)

(d) (e) (f) (g)

Figure 4.2

4.3 Noise Sensitivity Degree

Figure 4.3 (a) and 4.3 (c) are the segmentation results of human brain Magnetic Resonance Imaging (MRI) (119*78)using the CELBF model and the LBF model under the same parameters. It is easy to see that the results are same under both models without noise; furthermore the CELBF model is faster than LBF. Figure 4.3(b) and Figure 4.3(d) are segmentation results with Poisson noise using the two models. We can see from the results that noise has some effect for both models, but it has more effect for the LBF model.

(a) (b)

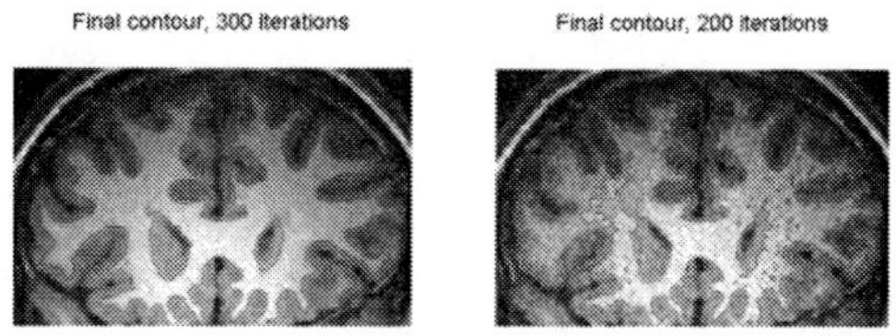

(c) (d)

Figure 4.3

Figure 4.4 (b) and Figure 4.4(c) are segmentation results for a simple synthetic image (64*61) using the two models. This image is relatively simple for segmentation because of the target and the background has obvious contrast. Therefore, both two models achieve good results. But CELBF model is faster than the LBF model. Figure 4.4(b) and 4.4(d) are segmentation results for the image with noise. Even though we have segmented some part of the target. It is obvious that CELBF model can obtained less unnecessary segment. It means that CELBF greatly reduces the sensitivity to noise.

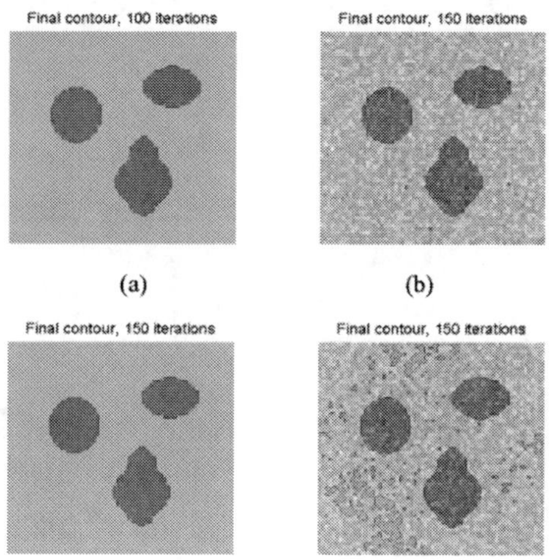

(c) (d)

Figure 4.4

Figure 4.5 (a) shows the segmentation results of a human brain MRI (189 * 163 * 3) for the CELBF model. Figure 4.5 (b) and 4.5 (c) are the results with Gaussian noise with standard deviations of 0.01 and 0.02, respectively. All of these three images have been accurately segmented. It can be seen from the experimental results that the noise has a certain impact on our model, but the impact is minimal.

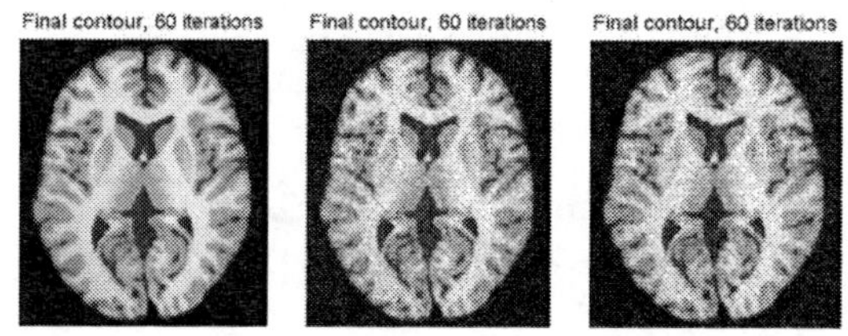

(a) (b) (c)

Figure 4.5

The experimental results illustrate further that the CELBF model has more advantages on medical images with gray inhomogeneity, weak edge images and complex background images. CELBF has strong robustness to noise, and so on.

5. Conclusion

Image segmentation methods based on partial differential equation is widely used. However, the existing models are generally sensitive to noise, and lack of robustness and evolution speed. In this paper, we propose an improved LBF model based on image entropy (defined as CELBF). Using this model and MATLAB, several groups of medical images segmentation are simulated. The segmentation results show that our CELBF model improves the robustness of the LBF model and the segmentation speed at the same time. Therefore, the CELBF model can better deal with medical images with gray inhomogeneity. Our model has advantages with respect to segmentation speed, accuracy and noise robustness.

References

[1] M. Kass, A. Witriw, and D. Terzopoilos, "Snakes: active contour models," International Journal of Computer Vision, 1988, 1:321-369

[2] V. Caselles, F. Catte, T. Coll, and F. Dibos, "A geometric model for active contours in image processing," Numerische Mathmatik., 1993,66:1-31.

[3] T. Chan, and L. Vese, "Active contours without edge," IEEE Transactions on Image Processing, 2001,10(2):266-277..

[4] C. Li, C. Kao, C. Gore, and Z. Ding, "Implicit active contours driven by local binary fitting energy," IEEE Computer Vision and Pattern Recognition,2007,6:17-22.

[5] C. Li, C. Xu, C. Gui, and M. D. Fox, "Level set evolution without re-initialization; a new variational formulation," IEEE Computer Society Conference on Computer Vision and Pattern Recognition, 2005, 1:430-436

[6] D. Gabor, "Information theory in electron microscopy," Laboratory Investigation, 1965, 14:801-807.

DOI: 10.1051/itmconf/20171202001

[7] A. K. Jain, "Partial differential equations and finite-difference methods in image processing, part 1: Image representation," Optimization Theory and Applications, 1997, 23: 65-91.

[8] J. J. koenderink, "The structure of images," Biological Cybernetics, 1984, 50:363-370.

[9] A. P. Witkin, "Scale-space filtering," Proceedings of the 8th International Joint Conference Artificial Intelligence (IJCAI), Karlsruhe Germany, 1983, 2:1019-1021.

[10] L. Alvarez, F. Guichard, P. L. Lions, and J. M. Morel, et.al. "Axioms and fundamental euations of image processing," Archive for Rational Mechanics and Analysis, 1993, 16(9):200-257.

[11] C. Li, C. Kao, J. C. Gore, and Z. Ding, "Minimization of region-scalable fitting energy for image segmentation," IEEE Transactions on Image Processing, 2008, 17(10):1940-1949.

[12] L. Wang, C. Li, Q. Sun, D. Xia, and C. Kao, "Active contours driven by local and global intensity fitting energy with application to brain MR image segmentation," Computerized Medical Imaging and Graphics, 2009, 33:520-531.

[13] B. R. Frieden, "Restoring with maximum likelihood and maximum entropy," Journal of the Optical Society of America, 1982, 62(4):511-518.

[14] M. Sezgin, and B. Sankur, "Survey over image thresholding techniques and quantitative performance evaluation," Journal of Electronic Imaging, 2004, 13(1):146-165.

DOI: 10.1051/itmconf/20171202002

A Comparison Study to Identify Birds Species Based on Bird Song Signals

Xin Guo[1], Qing-Zhong Liu[2]

[1]*Department of Computer Science, Sam Houston State University, Huntsville, TX 77382, USA*
[2]*Department of Computer Science, Sam Houston State University, Huntsville, TX 77382, USA*
[1] *xxg004@shsu.edu*, [2]*liu@shsu.edu*

Abstract: this paper presents a comparison study in automatically identifying bird species based on bird acoustic signals, using audio files from XENO-CANTO online database. The features including Mel-Frequency Cepstral Coefficients (MFCC), geo-related meta-features, and the integration are compared. The learning classifiers Linear Discriminant Analysis (LDA), Support Vector Machine (SVM), k-Nearest Neighbor (kNN), and Ensemble Learning are examined. Our experimental results show that in the comparison study, ensemble learning using discriminant learner with the integration of MFCC features and geo meta-features obtains the best detection performance.

1. Introduction

Birds live worldwide and rank as the class of tetrapod with the most living species, at approximately ten thousands, in which more than half identified species being passerines, known as perching birds or songbirds. Bird vocalizations are traditionally divided into bird calls and bird songs. The distinction between songs and calls is based on complexity, length, and context and has a lot of exceptions. Songs are longer and more complex, mainly produced by males and associated with courtship and mating during the breeding season, while calls tend to be shorter, simpler and produced by both sexes throughout the year; serve such functions as alarms or keeping members of a flock in contact [1].

Bird watching is a traditional and popular activity focused on observation of birds. Due to fact that many birds are more easily heard than photographed, it is promising to rely on their sounds as a convenient and reliable method for species identification. With the rapid development of digital technology, portable devices such as mobile phones are equipped with outdoor recording functionality, adequate storage capacity, and computational power to do onsite recording analysis. It is easier than ever for bird watcher to record bird sounds during bird watching. On the other hand, professionals like ornithologist, ecologists, traditionally take advantage of long-term semi-automatic acoustical monitoring without human presence at recording site for scientific research or ecosystem evaluation purpose [2].

The motivation of bird species identification goes beyond bird watching. Bird is a good indicator of the state of their surrounding ecosystem; since they are widely distributed and react quickly to changes in environmental conditions such as habitat loss, declining biodiversity, and climate change. Acoustical monitoring for tracking bird migration and for estimating populations of bird species provides information to understand and evaluate the changes in environment. Recognition by bird sounds also would be a powerful tool for automatic identifying bird in cases such as in areas near airports to prevent collisions with aircraft [2].

Automatic bird species identification based on birdsongs is a recent application of machine learning, essentially of pattern recognition and classification. The challenge can be broken down into two main stages. First, each of the bird sounds recording should be analyzed, normally by signal processing tools, to produce a discriminative feature set that represent the original bird audio signal regarding its species. Techniques widely used in feature extraction include temporal and spectral measurements, Linear Predictive Coding, Mel Frequency Cepstral Coefficients (MFCC). Then these feature sets serve as input to a classification system. Several algorithms have been employed, including probabilistic and instance based classifier, neural networks and support vector machines [3].

Linear prediction coding (LPC) is a tool used mostly in audio signal processing and speech processing for representing the spectral envelope of a digital signal, using the information of a linear predictive model [4]. It is one of the most powerful speech analysis techniques. The basic idea behind this model is that a speech sample can be approximated with a linear combination of previous speech samples. LPC analysis tries to determine the coefficients of a forward linear predictor by minimizing the prediction error in the least squares sense.

The cepstral coefficients are the results of taking the inverse Fourier transform representation of the logarithmic magnitude spectrum of a signal. LPC derived cepstral coefficients (LPCCs), is a very effective representation for speech coding, analysis, synthesis, and recognition. A significant property of the LPC spectral modeling is that the LPC spectrum matches the signal spectrum closely near the spectral peaks. So the linear prediction cepstral coefficients (LPCCs) are more robust and reliable features for speech recognition and have been proven to be more relevant than LPCs [5, 8].

MFCC is a frame-level feature. It is computed by transforming the spectrum of a frame into the Mel scale, which approximates the human auditory system's response more closely than the linear frequency. The steps that are applied in the traditional method to get the coefficients are started with reemphasizing the sampled signal and then applying the framing and windowing on it, then taking the Fast Fourier Transform (FFT) for each windowed frame, the signal now is a power spectrum, this signal enters to a Mel filter bank and the length of the output is equal to the number of filters created, after taking a discrete cosine transform to the log of the filter bank's output, an array of features that describe the spectral shape of the signal [6,7,18].

The earlier works for birdsongs identification focused on template matching usually used in conjunction with dynamic time warping (DTW). First one manually obtains a collection of templates including intervals with no bird sound, and then slides them across a target spectrogram. DTW algorithm is used to stretches either the template or the target spectrogram to calculate some measure of similarity. This can be viewed as simultaneous segmentation and classification [9].

Lopes et al. [3] presented a comparison of the performance of 3 feature sets originally implemented for music analysis combined with a series of machine learning algorithms applied to the bird species identification problem. Experiments were conducted in order to evaluate various combinations of feature sets and classifiers in a database composed by 101 audio records from 3 bird species. Somervuo et al. [10] found that MFCC outperforms sinusoidal features and a collection of spectral features such as spectral centroid, bandwidth, roll-off, flux, etc. Lee etc. designed image shape features to identify bird species based on the recognition of fixed-duration birdsong segments where their corresponding spectrograms are viewed as gray-level images [11]. Chou and Liu [12] applied a wavelet transformation to transform sections of the bird songs. Then the first five order MFCCs are computed, and same order MFCC are aligned. Neal et al. [13] proposed a supervised time-frequency audio segmentation method using a Random Forest classifier. Springer [14] addressed the issue when multiple species of birds sing concurrently in the same recording. Zhao et al [15] designed acoustic environment signatures that can be used for background noise recognition.

In this paper, we make a comparison study by comparing MFCC features and geo-metadata features with the use of several machine learning classifiers.

2. Methodology

2.1 Data Set

XENO-CANTO is a collaborative database containing more than 192k audio records that cover 9120 bird species observed all around the world by more than 2000 contributors at the time of writing and these numbers keep growing during each day. Recordings in the dataset are not consisting only bird song. A substantial part of the elements contain background noise such as sounds from other animals, wind and machine noise, or electric hum, which is near to the real world applications. Contributors also provide the metadata of each audio file including geographical information, date and /or time of the day and/or presence of background species.

The lifeclef2014 Bird Identification Task is based on a subset of XENO-CANTO database. It contains 14027 audio recordings belonging to the 501 bird species in the area of South American centered on Brazil [16]. Additional information includes the audio file associated metadata in XML format.

2.2 Feature Extraction

The dataset is sourced from a large online collection of user-submitted recordings, and therefore suffers from inconsistent audio quality. The recordings have varying audio quality due to atmospheric conditions like wind and rain, interfering bird and insects calls, quality of the recording equipment, and varying professionalism of the recordist. In order to avoid bias in the evaluation related to recording devices, the organizers preprocessed the whole audio data to normalize frequency sample to 44.1.kHz wav format. A temporal signal is first transformed into a serie of frames where each frame consists in 16 mfcc (Mel-filter cepstral coefficients), including energy (first coefficient). Each frame represents a duration of 11.6 ms (e.g 512 temporal bins of a signal sampled at 44 100 Hz). Two successive frames overlap of 33% i.e. 3.9 ms.

The mel scale is a means of mapping the physical frequency to the perceptual representation. The mapping between the physical frequency scale (Hz) and perceptual frequency scale (mel) is approximately linear below 1000 Hz and logarithmic at higher frequencies. The relation between the physical frequency scale and the mel frequency scale can be described as:

The mel scale maps the physical frequency to the perceptual representation. The mapping between the physphysicalquency scale (Hz) and perceptual frequency scale (mel) is approximately linear below 1000 Hz and logarithmic at higher frequencies. The mapping between mel frequency scale and physical frequency scale can be described as:

$$mel = 2595\log\left(1+\frac{f}{700}\right) \quad (1)$$

Where f is the spectral frequency of the input bioacoustics signal using short-time Fourier transform.

In the process of MFCCs feature extraction, the Fourier spectrum is filtered by a set of mel-scale filters. The MFCCs are computed by performing DCT on the logarithmic energy output by every bandpass filter

$$c_m = \sum_{k=0}^{K-1}\log(E_k)\cos\left(m\frac{\pi}{K}(k+0.5)\right) \quad (2)$$

$$0 \le m \le L-1.$$

Where K is the number of bandpass filters, L is the desired length of MFCCs, and Ek is the energy of the output of the k-th bandpass filter. L is set to 16 according to the study in the reference [17].

Let take a particular MFCC features, denoted by the matrix C= $\{c_{m,t}\}$ (m=0, 1, ..15; t=1,2,...n) wherein n is the number of frames. The Following 16 MFCC features are extraction based on equation (3),

$$\bar{c}_m = \frac{\sum_{t=1}^{n}\left|c_{m,t}\right|}{n} \quad (3)$$

Additionally, we retrieve the following 16 MFCC features regarding the first derivative based on equation (4),

$$\bar{c}_m^1 = \frac{\sum_{t=1}^{n-1}\left|c_{m,t+1}-c_{m,t}\right|}{n-1} \quad (4)$$

And the following 16 MFCC features are designed based equation (5)

$$\bar{c}_m^2 = \frac{\sum_{t=1}^{n-2}\left|c_{m,t+2}+c_{m,t}-2*c_{m,t+1}\right|}{n-2} \quad (5)$$

Based on equations (3), (4) and (5), a total of 48 MFCC features are extracted.

Additionally, the three geo-meta features Latitude, Longitude and Elevation were extracted from XML file.

3. Experiments

We select the learning classifiers including Linear Discriminant Analysis (LDA), Support Vector Machine (SVM) with linear kernel, and quadratic kernel, k-Nearest Neighbor (kNN), and Ensemble Learning [19] using discriminant analysis and kNN learners respectively for our comparison study. The following section discusses results obtained using the subset of 2014 BirdCLEF dataset when trying to find which classifier is scalable as bird species number increases, all results are obtained using 5-fold cross validation.

Table 1 lists the detection accuracy by applying the six classifiers to the three feature sets, 48-dimensional MFCC, 3-dimensional META, and the integration of MFCC and META on four different numbers of bird species 5, 10, 50 and 100 bird species (with 275, 494, 1892, or 3263 instances respectively). The ROC curves and confusion matrix are provided in Figures 1 to 5 by using the ensemble learning with the subspace discriminant classifier.

The accuracies of all 6 classifiers decrease dramatically as number of bird species increase from 5, 10, 50, to 100. SVM and Ensemble learning with Discriminant learner for random subspace have comparable highest accuracy but in our experiments the training time of SVM is much longer than ensemble learning. The integration of MFCC with geo-meta features obtains the best detection accuracy.

The experimental results show that ensemble learning with discriminant has the best performance. To compare the detection performance under different parameter of subspace dimensionalities, we adjust the subspace parameter from the default value 26 to 30, 40, and 50, respectively. Table 2 shows the detection accuracy under different subspace parameters with discriminant ensemble learning. Figure 6 shows the ROC curve in detecting all 501 species birds by using MFCC and geo-meta features together.

4. Conclusions

In this study, we conducted a comparison study identifying bird species based on bird songs. Our study shows that the integration of MFCC features and geo-meta features obtains the best detection accuracy with the use of discriminant ensemble learning in our comparison study.

Our future study includes develop more reasonable features and adopt deep learning techniques to identify the performance under different input parameters. The optimization of the parameters will be explored too.

Table 1. Validation Accuracy (%) On Different Species With Different Learning Classifiers

	MFCC Features				Geo-Meta Features				MFCC+Geo-Meta Features			
Number of species	*5*	*10*	*50*	*100*	*5*	*10*	*50*	*100*	*5*	*10*	*50*	*100*
Linear Discriminant	46.2	31.8	15.3	10.5	34.2	22.3	6.2	3.6	44.4	33.6	16.8	11.9
Linear SVM	52.4	39.7	18.8	13.3	43.6	25.5	8.6	4.7	56	43.1	22.1	15.2
Quadratic SVM	44.4	39.9	19.5	14	45.1	28.7	9.7	7	52.4	42.5	21.9	15.7
Medium kNN	42.5	30.4	11.2	8.7	44.7	27.9	10	7.3	41.8	28.7	12.4	8.9
Ensemble: Subspace Discriminant	56.7	43.1	23.3	16.4	33.5	21.1	6	3.6	59.6	46.2	26.3	18.8
Ensemble: Subspace kNN	42.9	35	15.5	12	36.4	25.5	10.6	7.4	52.7	36.2	18	14.6

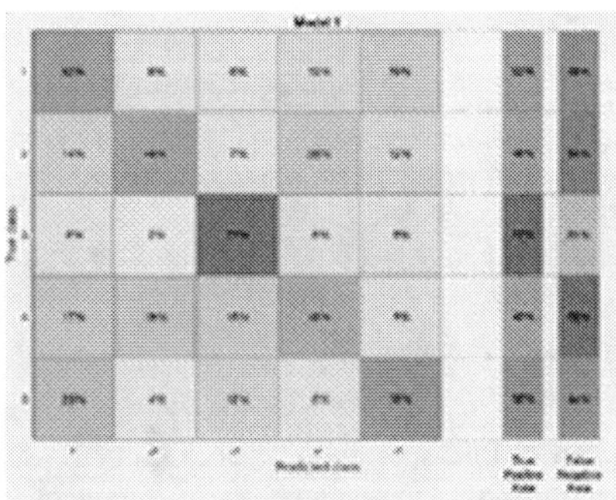

(a)

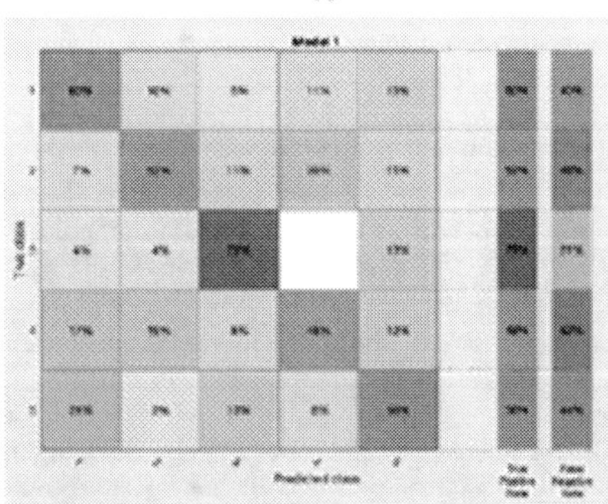

(b)

Figure 1: Confusion matrix of 5 species subsets with Ensemble: Subspace Discriminant classifiers using MFCC features only (a) and using MFCC and META features (b)

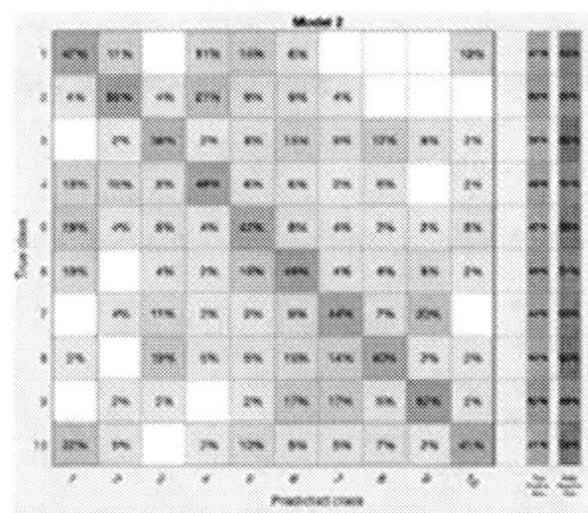

(a)

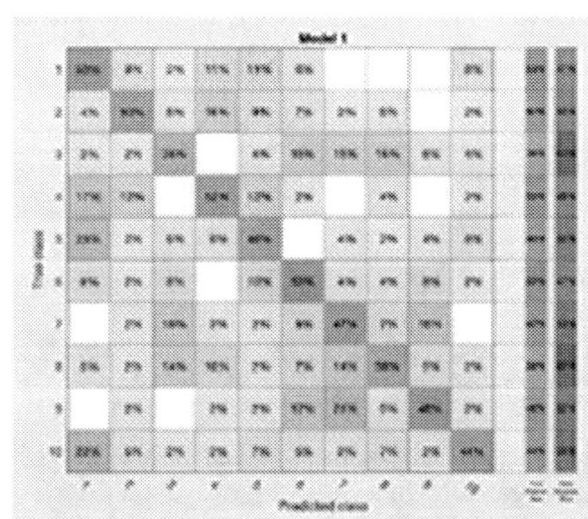

(b)

Figure 2: Confusion matrix of 10 species subsets with Ensemble: Subspace Discriminant classifiers using MFCC features only (a) and using MFCC and META features (b)

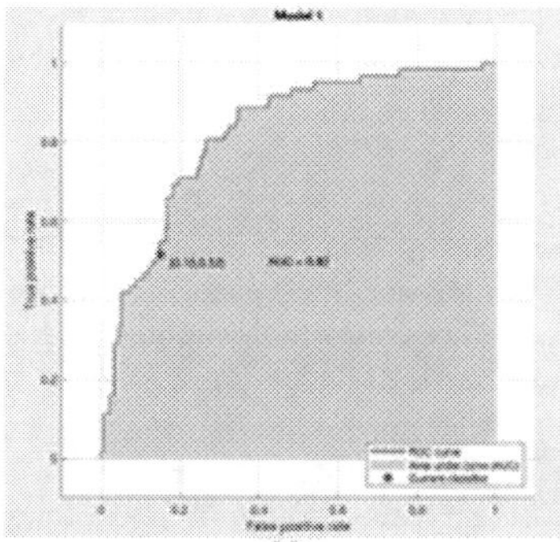

(a)

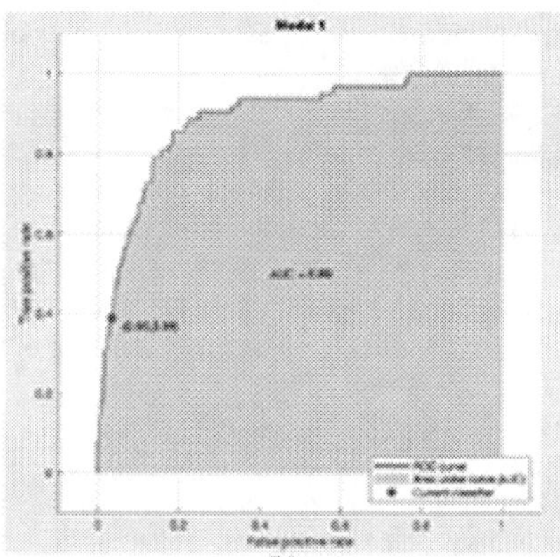

(b)

Figure 3: ROC curve of 5 species subsets with Ensemble: Subspace Discriminant classifiers using MFCC features only (a) and using MFCC and META features (b)

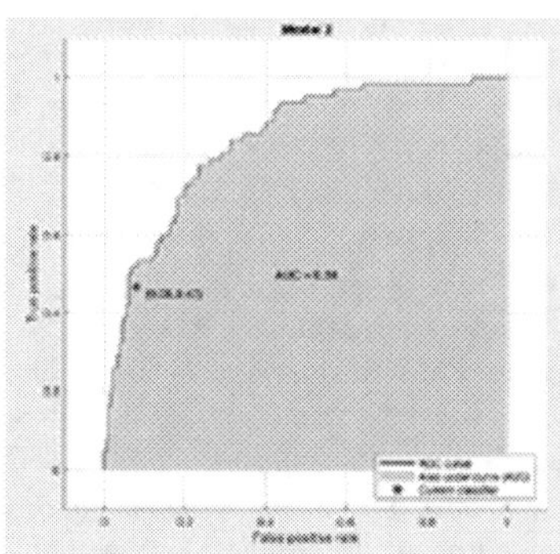

(a)

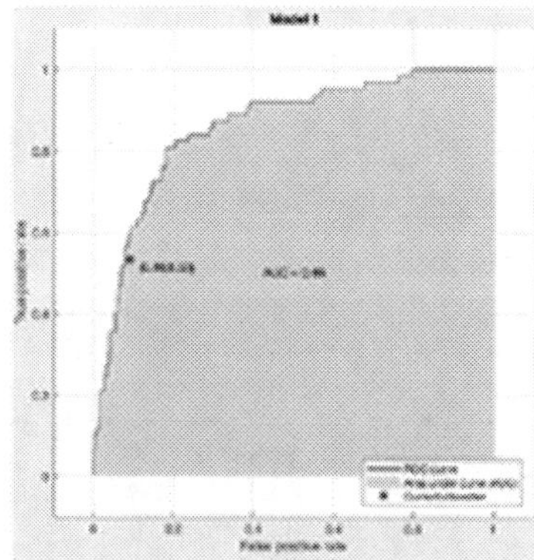

(b)

Figure 4: ROC curve of 10 species subsets with Ensemble: Subspace Discriminant classifiers using MFCC features only (a) and using MFCC and META features (b)

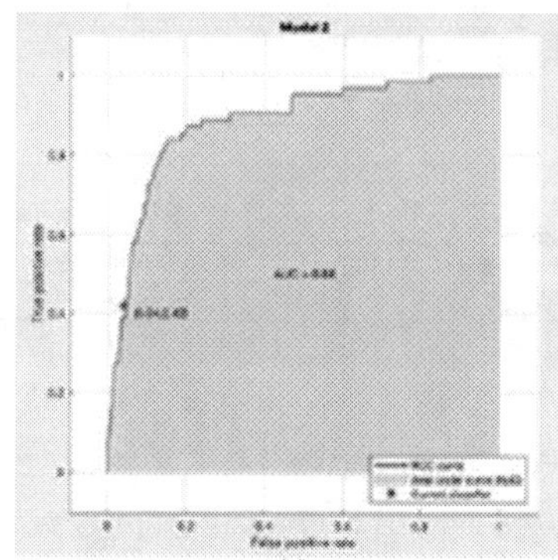

(a)

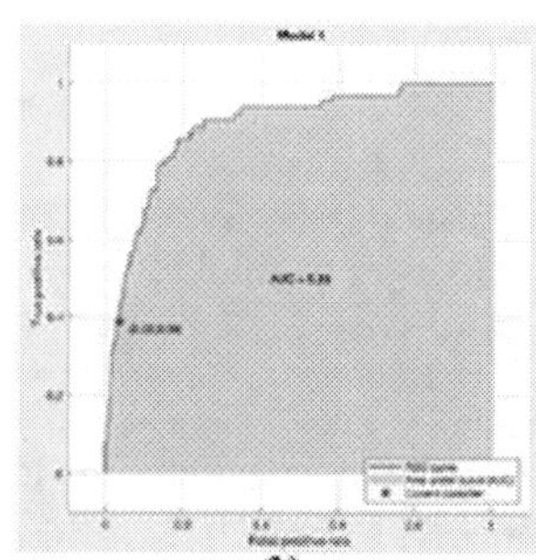

(b)

Figure 5: ROC curve of 50 species subsets with Ensemble: Subspace Discriminant classifiers using MFCC features only (a) and using MFCC and META features (b)

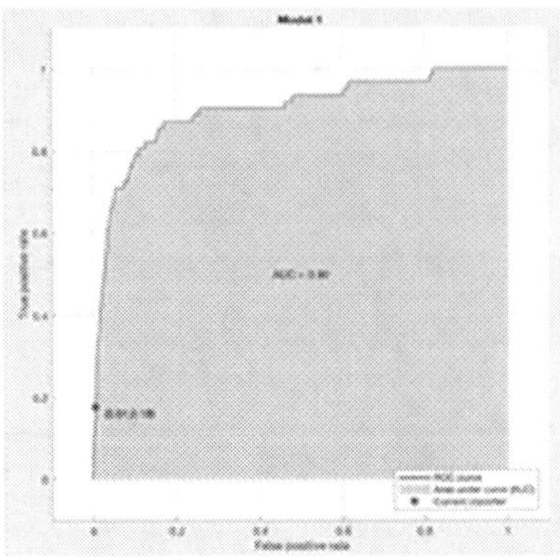

Figure 6: ROC curve of 501 species subsets by applying Ensemble: Subspace Discriminant classifier to MFCC and META

Table 2. Validation Accuracy (%) On Different Species By Discriminant Ensemble

Subspace dimension	Number of species			
	5	10	50	100
26	58.9	42.7	24.8	19.4
30	60	43.7	26.4	20.0
40	61.1	44.3	27.0	21.4
50	60.7	44.1	27.3	21.8

Acknowledgements

The support for this study from the college of science and engineering technology of the sam houston state university (shsu), and from the shsu computer science department is highly appreciated.

References

[1] http://web.stanford.edu/group/stanfordbirds/SUFRAME.html, accessed on April 25, 2017.

[2] M. Lopes, L. Gioppo, T. Higushi, C. Kaestner, C. Silla, A. Koerich, "Automatic bird species identification for large number of species," 2011 IEEE International Symposium on Multimedia (ISM), pp.117-122, 5-7 Dec. 2011.

[3] M. Lopes, A. Lameiras Koerich, C. Nascimento Silla, C. Alves Kaestner, "Feature set comparison for automatic bird species identification," in 2011 IEEE International Conference on Systems, Man, and Cybernetics (SMC), pp.965-970, 9-12 Oct. 2011

[4] L. Deng and D. O'Shaughnessy. Speech processing: a dynamic and optimization-oriented approach. Marcel Dekker. pp. 41–48. ISBN 0-8247-4040-8, 2003.

[5] Speech Technology: A Practical Introduction. Topic: Spectrogram, Cepstrum and Mel-Frequency Analysis, http://www.speech.cs.cmu.edu/15-492/slides/03_mfcc.pdf

[6] C. Chou and H. Ko, "Automatic Birdsong Recognition with MFCC Based Syllable Feature Extraction". In: Hsu CH., Yang L.T., Ma J., Zhu C. (eds) Ubiquitous Intelligence and Computing. UIC 2011. Lecture Notes in Computer Science, vol 6905. Springer, Berlin, Heidelberg.

[7] Practical Introduction to Frequency-Domain Analysis. MathWorks Online Documentation of Signal Processing Toolbox. Online Web Resources.

[8] C. Lee, Y. Lee, and R. Huang. "Automatic recognition of bird songs using cepstral coefficients." Journal of Information Technology and Applications 1,1, 17-23, 2006.

[9] S. E. Anderson, A. S. Dave, and D. Margoliash. Template-based automatic recognition of birdsong syllables from continuous recordings. J. Acoust. Soc. Am., 100(2):1209–1219, 1996. ISSN 0001-4966.

[10] P. Somervuo, A. Harma, S. Fagerlund. "Parametric representations of bird sounds for automatic species recognition", IEEE Transactions on Audio, Speech, and Language Processing 14,6: 2252-2263, 2006.

[11] C. Lee, S. Hsu, J. Shih and C. Chou, "Continuous birdsong recognition using Gaussian mixture modeling of image shape features." IEEE Transactions on Multimedia,15, 2: 454-464, 2013.

[12] C-H. Chou and P-H. Liu, "Bird Species Recognition by Wavelet Transformation of a Section of Birdsong", Symp. and Workshop Ubiq., Auton. Trusted Comput., Brisbane, Australia, pp.189–193, July 2009.

[13] L. Neal, F. Briggs, R. Raich and X. Fern. "Time-frequency segmentation of bird song in noisy acoustic environments. " 2011 IEEE International Conference on. Acoustics, Speech and Signal Processing (ICASSP), 2011. DOI: 10.1109/ICASSP.2011.5946906

[14] J. Springer, Z. Duan, and B. Pardo. "Approaches to multiple concurrent species bird song recognition." The 2nd International Workshop on Machine Listening in Multisource Environments, 2013. http://www.ece.rochester.edu/~zduan/resource/SpringerEtal_BirdSongRecognition_ChiME13.pdf

[15] H. Zhao, and H. Malik. "Audio recording location identification using acoustic environment signature." IEEE Transactions on Information Forensics and Security 8, 11 (2013): 1746-1759.

[16] H. Goeau, H. Glotin, W. Vellinga, R. Planque, A. Rauber and A. Joly. LifeCLEF Bird Identification Task 2014. https://hal.inria.fr/hal-01088829/file/CLEF2014wn-Life-GoeauEt2014a.pdf

DOI: 10.1051/itmconf/20171202002

[17] O. Dufour, T. Artieres, H. Glotin and P. Giraudet (2014). "Clusterized mel filter cepstral coefficients and support vector machines for bird song identification", In . Proc. 1st International Workshop on Machine Learning for Bioacoustics, joint to The 30th International Conference on Machine Learning (ICML 2013) Atlanta, USA, June, 2013, pages 89-93.

[18] D. P. W. Ellis. PLP and RASTA (and MFCC, and inversion) in Matlab, 2005. Online web resource.

[19] R. Polikar, "Ensemble learning." Ensemble machine learning. Springer US, 2012. 1-34.

DOI: 10.1051/itmconf/20171202003

Evaluation of Above Ground Biomass Estimation Accuracy for Alpine Meadow Based on MODIS Vegetation Indices

Bao-Ping MENG, Tian-Gang LIANG*, Jing GE, Jin-Long GAO, Jian-Peng YIN

State Key Laboratory of Grassland Agro-ecosystems, College of Pastoral Agriculture Science and Technology, lanzhou University, Lanzhou 730020, China
mengbp09@lzu.edu.cn, Correspondence: tgliang@lzu.edu.cn, gej12@lzu.edu.cn, gaojl16@lzu.edu.cn, yinjp2013@lzu.edu.cn

Abstract—Animal husbandry is the main agricultural type over the Tibetan Plateau, above ground biomass (AGB) is very important to monitor the productivity for administration of grassland resources and grazing balance. The MODIS vegetation indices have been successfully used in numerous studies on grassland AGB estimation in the Tibetan Plateau area. However, there are considerable differences of AGB estimation models both in the form of the models and the accuracy of estimation. In this study, field measurements of AGB data at Sangke Town, Gansu Province, China in four years (2013–2016) and MODIS indices (NDVI and EVI) are combined to construct AGB estimation models of alpine meadow grassland. The field measured AGB are also used to evaluate feasibility of models developed for large scale in applying to small area. The results show that (1) the differences in biomass were relatively large among the 5 sample areas of alpine meadow grassland in the study area during 2013–2016, with the maximum and minimum biomass values of 3,963 kg DW/ha and 745.5 kg DW/ha, respectively, and mean value of 1,907.7 kg DW/ha; the mean of EVI value range (0.42-0.60) are slightly smaller than the NDVI's (0.59-0.75); (2) the optimum estimation model of grassland AGB in the study area is the exponential model based on MODIS EVI, with root mean square error of 656.6 kg DW/ha and relative estimation errors (REE) of 36.3%; (3) the estimation errors of grassland AGB models previously constructed at different spatial scales (the Tibetan Plateau, the Gannan Prefecture, and Xiahe County) are higher than those directly constructed based on the small area of this study by 9.5%–31.7%, with the increase of the modeling study area scales, the REE increasing as well. This study presents an improved monitoring algorithm of alpine natural grassland AGB estimation and provides a clear direction for future improvement of the grassland AGB estimation and grassland productivity from remote sensing technology.

1 Introduction

Grassland biome is supported by the basic principles of primary productivity, especially for various animals of the grassland [1]. The above-ground biomass (AGB) of grassland provides the basis for estimating the net primary productivity of grassland [2]. Therefore, it is very important to monitor the productivity for administration of grassland resources and grazing balance, i.e. the number of livestock units that grassland can feed for specific length of time, and the quality and quantity of AGB [3]. In particular, as the main grazing area, the AGB estimation is more prominent in the Tibet plateau of China [4-5].

Numerous studies about grassland AGB have indicated that there is an increasing prominent role for grassland ecosystems [1]. However, grasslands in Tibetan Plateau (TP) are facing soil erosion, salinization, desertification and degradation caused by human activities and climate change. Accurate measurements of grassland biomass and its temporal and spatial variation are important for the utilization and protection of grassland resources. Grassland AGB can be estimated by using both traditional (or ground based) and remote sensing methods. With the development of science and technology, monitoring using remote sensing data has gradually replaced the traditional methods, for its large scale, frequency, low cost, and massive information [6]. The MODIS vegetation indices have been successfully used in numerous studies on grassland AGB in the TP. However, there are considerable differences of AGB estimation models both in the form of the models and accuracy of estimation. Previous studies stated a relatively large uncertainty in the evaluation of AGB and a lack of quantitative accuracy analysis on relatively large spatial scales. For alpine meadow grassland, the most suitable type of remote sensing estimation model is currently unknown and the applicability of these models still needs to be proved.

In this study, considering the factors discussed above, a region of alpine meadow grassland in the TP area is used to

DOI: 10.1051/itmconf/20171202003

conduct the following investigations: (1) to construct and analyze the AGB estimation models and their accuracies based on the MODIS NDVI and EVI in study area; (2) the data from the sample plots observed inside the study area are used to validate the applicability of previous grassland models based on MODIS data and to investigate the reasons for errors from different models, and (3) based on the above research results, we propose a method to improve the accuracy of grassland AGB estimation.

2 Data And Methods

2.1 Study Area

The study area (102°23'-102°26'E, 35°5'-35°7'N) is located in the Yangji Community of Sangke Town in Xiahe County, Gansu Province, with the size of approximately 3.86 km (N-S) × 2.77 km (E-W) and a mean elevation of 3,050 m. The natural grassland type in the study area is alpine meadow. The study area is cold and wet throughout the year, and it belongs to the continental monsoon climate of the temperate plateau. The annual average temperature is 2.1 °C; the annual average rainfall is 580 mm.

The study area consists of five fenced experimental sample areas (A–E) of natural alpine meadow grassland (Fig. 1), with a total area of 161.36 ha. Specifically, area A (19.38 ha) is used to conduct natural grassland reseeding tests, area B (16.06 ha) is used for grazing utilization experiments; area C (7.52 ha) acts as a non-treatment testing control area; area D (19.30 ha) is an experimental area for grassland enclosure; and area E (99.10 ha, accounting for 61.55% of the total experimental area) was used for artificial fertilization experiments. The grassland growth in these five experimental areas differed because of the above different usages.

2.2 Sampling Strategy And Data Collection

A total of 13 sample plots of 30 m×30 m are set up inside the 5 experimental sample areas. In each sample plot, five quadrats (1.5 m×1.5 m each) are set up as shown in figure 1, the central point and the four corner points are used to represent the entire plot. To reduce artificial sampling error of biomass measurements, a strategy of 9 sub-quadrats are also used for avoiding repeat sampling in each year， The sub-quadrat identification number (1 to 9) is the order that we used to sample grass each time, e.g., sub-quadrat 1 was used in the first time of any year, 2 was used in the second time of the same year, etc. (Fig 1). The locations of the 13 sample plots are selected based on the following factors: 1) the growth status of the grassland is relatively uniform and is spatially representative, and 2) each sample area, in order to corresponding MODIS pixel, the distance between adjacent plots is more than 250m. During the grassland growth seasons from 2013–2016, observations were performed approximately once a month and total of 9 field investigations were conducted over the four years.

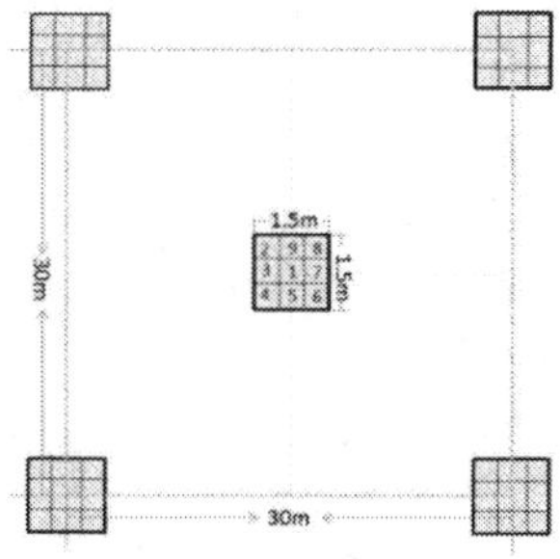

Fig. 1. Distributions of plot

2.3 Previously Established Biomass Inversion Models Based on the MODIS Vegetation Index Over the Tibetan Plateau

In this study, in order to validate the applicability of previous grassland models, we select five previous constructed AGB inversion models based on MODIS data in Tibetan plateau (table 1). The model I is an exponential function model, with coefficient of determination (R^2)of 0.75 and overall estimation accuracy up to 80%, which was based on the 10-d maximum composite MODIS NDVI (with a 1 km resolution) and field measurement data from the end of July to the end of September in 2007 in the TP area [1]. Model II is an exponential function model, with R^2 of 0.49, and RMSE of 671.8 kg DW/ha, which was constructed by measurement data from the TP during July–August of 2005 and 2006 with the monthly maximum composition 1 km resolution MODIS NDVI [5]. Model III and IV are power function models, with the R^2 values of 0.63 and 0.62, calculated by the MODIS EVI at 500 m and 1 km resolution in the Gannan prefecture [7- 8]. Model V is a power function model, with R^2 values of 0.63, which constructed by 250m resolution MODIS EVI in Xiahe County [9].

Table 1 The existing AGB estimation models for alpine grassland in the Tibetan Plateau region

Model	MODIS	Formula	R^2	Literature
I	NDVI	$y=225.42\times e^{4.4368x}$	0.75	Xu et al, 2007
II	NDVI	$y=268.810\times e^{2.398x}$	0.49	Feng et al, 2011
III	EVI	$y=3738.073x^{1.553}$	0.63	Cui et al, 2012
IV	EVI	$y=5320.7x^{1.977 6}$	0.62	Wang et al,2010
V	EVI	$y=1719.1x^{2.2588}$	0.63	Bao et al, 2010

2.4 Preprocessing of MODIS Vegetation Index Data

The MODIS vegetation index data are selected from the MODIS 16-d maximum composite NDVI vegetation index product (MOD13Q1) of the United States National Aeronautics and Space Administration. In total, 9 images spanning the years 2013–2016 are selected with a spatial resolution of 250 m from orbit number h26v05 (table2). During the period of field sampling (2013-2016), the NDVI and EVI are used to construct the grassland AGB models and performance of the models using the field measurements assessment.

Table 2 Date between MODIS images and field measurements in the study area

Date of MODIS	Measurement time
2013.07.29-08.13	2013.08.06-09
2014.06.27-07.12	2014.06.28-29
2014.07.13-28	2014.07.27-31
2014.08.14-29	2014.08.14-15
2014.09.15-30	2014.09.26-28
2015.07.13-28	2015.07.11-17
2015.08.14-29	2015.08.10-11
2015.08.30-09.14	2015.09.14-18
2016.07.29-08.13	2016.07.29-30

2.5 Construction of Grassland Biomass Monitoring Model And Accuracy Evaluation

The average dry weight of AGB in all the sub-quadrats of each plot is estimated as the biomass for that sample plot. The grassland biomass of different sample plots are taken as the dependent variable and NDVI, EVI as the independent variables. The Leave-One-Out Cross Validation (LOOCV) method, RMSE(Equation 1), and relative estimate error (REE) (Equation 2) are used to evaluate the accuracy and estimation errors of the linear, exponential, logarithmic, and power regression models for the 2 vegetation indices.

$$RMSE = \sqrt{\frac{\sum_{i=1}^{n}(y_i - y_i')^2}{n}} \quad (1)$$

$$REE = \sqrt{\frac{\sum_{i=1}^{n}[(y_i - y_i')/y_i']^2}{N}} \quad (2)$$

where y_i represents the ground-measured value, y_i' is the estimated value, i represents for a sampling plot, n stands for the number of sample plots.

In addition, in order to study the relative estimation error of the alpine meadow grassland AGB monitoring model on the regional scale (e.g., the experimental area of this study; the Xiahe County; the Gannan prefecture; and the whole Tibetan Plateau), the REE are used to assess the performance of each previous model.

3 Results And Analysis

3.1 Statistical Analysis of Ground Observation Agb And the Corresponding MODIS NDVI

Table 3 shows the statistical results of AGB in the surveyed sample plots and the NDVI, EVI calculated using the corresponding remote sensing data from 2013–2016. There are considerable differences in the biomass during the grass growing season in the 5 sample area of study area. The average values range from 1,480.3–2,097.8 kg DW/ha over the past four years, while the coefficient of variation range from 0.40–0.64. The largest biomass from the 5 sample areas is 3,963 kg DW/ha, and the minimum is 745.5 kg DW/ha. The magnitude of the variation in the EVI values and dispersion degree are larger than NDVI (standard deviation and coefficient of variation range from 0.07–0.11 and 0.09–0.17), with standard deviation and coefficient of variation range of 0.05–0.12 and 0.15–0.24, respectively. In contrast to the mean of EVI value range are slightly smaller than the NDVIs (0.59-0.75) with mean value range of 0.42-0.60.

Table 3. Descriptive statistics of grassland above ground biomass (AGB) and corresponding MODIS indices during July-September of 2013-2015 in the study area, Xiahe County.

Index	Statistics	Sample area					
		A	B	C	D	E	all
Biomass (kg DW/ha)	Max	3963.0	2415.5	3348.9	3669.3	3788.0	3963.0
	Min	745.5	928.1	954.6	944.1	786.5	745.5
	Ave	2097.8	1480.3	1775.3	2182.6	2002.4	1907.7
	Std	1336.3	586.3	877.5	924.5	810.2	916.6
	CV	0.64	0.40	0.49	0.42	0.40	0.48
NDVI	Max	0.79	0.71	0.75	0.84	0.84	0.84
	Min	0.49	0.53	0.50	0.66	0.60	0.49
	Ave	0.65	0.59	0.64	0.75	0.74	0.67
	Std	0.11	0.07	0.10	0.07	0.07	0.09
	CV	0.17	0.12	0.16	0.09	0.09	0.14
EVI	Max	0.52	0.44	0.75	0.62	0.61	0.75
	Min	0.26	0.30	0.46	0.37	0.32	0.26
	Ave	0.42	0.36	0.60	0.50	0.51	0.48
	Std	0.10	0.05	0.12	0.08	0.08	0.09
	CV	0.24	0.15	0.20	0.15	0.16	0.15

3.2 Grassland Biomass Monitoring Model in the Study Area And Evaluation of Its Accuracy

The results of the accuracy evaluation validated by LOOCV for the grassland biomass models constructed on MODIS

DOI: 10.1051/itmconf/20171202003

NDVI and EVI are listed in table 4. It is found that in the four types of grassland AGB estimation models (linear, logarithmic, power, and exponential), the exponential model performs the best, with the smallest RMSE and REE, while the power model performs the second. Among the two vegetation indices, the exponential model based on EVI is the best, with the smallest RMSE of 656.6 kg DW/ha and REE of 36.3%, and the highest estimation accuracy of the AGB (Fig. 3). Table 5 shows parameters of the best fit model for MODIS EVI. As shown, the model passes the T test and F test at a significance level of 0.01.

Table 4 The validation results by Leave-One-Out Cross Validation for the grassland biomass models based on MODIS NDVI and EVI

Vegetation index	Model	Accuracy evaluation	
		RMSE(kg/ha)	REE (%)
NDVI	Linear	686.8	40.0
	Exponential	676.3	36.5
	Logarithm	720.7	61.5
	Power	680.1	36.8
EVI	Linear	686.9	38.0
	Exponential	656.6	36.3
	Logarithm	715.8	58.6
	Power	662.8	36.4

Table 5 The results of model fits with the optimum inversion models based on MDOIS EVI

Vegetation index	Parameter estimation and T test			Regression significance test	
	Parameter	Estimated value	T	R^2	F
EVI	b	3.862	9.235 **	0.55	85.291**
	a	286.599	4.963 **		

Note: **represents P<0.01; a and b represent the constant and exponential term of the model, respectively; T and F are the significant values according to T and F tests.

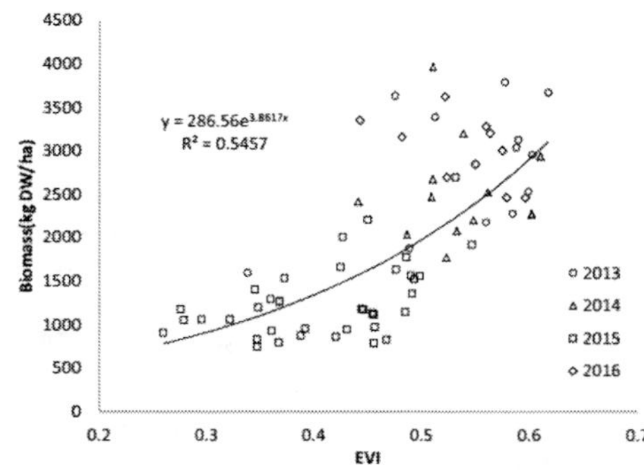

Fig. 3. The best fit models constructed based on MODIS EVI

3.3 Assessment of Previously Established Biomass Inversion Models Based on the MODIS Vegetation Index Over the Tibetan Plateau

Table 6 shows the statistical analysis using the biomass data measured on the ground surface during 2013–2016 in our study area to examine the REE of the aforementioned five models. As shown, the model V error is the smallest (45.8%), followed by IV, III, II, and I. Among the five models, the models I and II based on the entire Tibetan Plateau perform the worse. Although model I achieves the lowest error in the Tibetan Plateau (Table 8), its estimation error of grassland AGB in the study area is highest (68.0%). Models III, V, and IV are built on the regional area (Xiahe and Gannan) of the Tibetan Plateau, their estimation errors are much smaller (45.8%-48.9%).

Compared with this study, the estimation error of grassland AGB is the smallest in the study area scale (namely, the study area of Xiahe County), with REE of 36.3%. Although the previous inversion Models I–V can reflect the overall variation trend of grassland biomass, their estimation errors are higher when applied to our study area.

Table 6 The estimation error for the grassland AGB based on existing inversion models

Model	Study area	REE (%)	Literature
I	Tibetan Plateau	68.0	Xu et al., 2007
II	Tibetan Plateau	55.8	Feng et al, 2011
III	The northeast of Tibetan Plateau（Gannan Prefecture）	48.9	Cui et al., 2012
IV	The northeast of Tibetan Plateau（Gannan Prefecture）	46.5	Wang et al,2010
V	The northwest of Gannan Prefecture（Xiahe County)	45.8	Bao et al., 2010

4 Conclusions

Feasibility study on previous models developed at broad scales based on MODIS indices applied to our small study area suggests that the REE of these models is higher than that of the model constructed in this study by 9.5%–31.7%. Models V, IV, and III based on Xiahe County and Gannan Prefecture do not show considerably differences on the estimation error of AGB, ranging from 45.8%–48.9%, however, the models I and II based on the Tibetan Plateau scale show much larger estimation error, up to 68.0% and 55.8%, respectively.

Discussions

In this study, although the optimum models for the remote sensing monitoring of grassland biomass in the study area are determined, due to the limitations of factors such as the duration of sampling on the ground (only the growing seasons of the grassland from 2013–2016 were sampled), there is still some error and uncertainty for these inversion models. Compared with MSS, TM, HJ-CCD and SPOT, MODIS has relatively low spatial resolution and large estimation error of grassland AGB. Nevertheless, it is still particularly suitable for monitoring grassland AGB of widely distributed scale, due to its high temporal resolution (daily) and large spatial coverage (2,330 km). The result of this study shows that with the increase of the modeling study area, the REE of estimation model are increased gradually. The reason is that in large areas (the Tibetan Plateau area or an entire prefecture or county), the types of natural grassland pasture are complicated, and the geographical distribution is wide, the spatial heterogeneity is strong, and the vegetation index value is subjected to influence from many features and factors (e.g., the ecological environment of the grassland). Therefore, the models built based on large scale, when applied to small local areas (such as this experimental area), would result large errors and low accuracy, poor stability, and large spatial variations. This conclusion is similar to other studies in other areas [10-12].

Therefore, it is important to explore new research approaches to grassland AGB monitoring based on MODIS data to improve the accuracy of grassland remote sensing inversion over large regions in the future. These approaches mainly involve the following aspects: (1) enhance the spatial representativeness of ground sampling sites, for example, by increasing their number and area and improving the range observed by the ground sampling site and the corresponding spatial matching problem given the size of satellite image pixels; (2) improve the temporal matching between ground sampling sites and remote sensing data, for example, by better scheduling the times of field investigations to reduce the time differences between ground surveys and satellite image acquisitions; (3) incorporate new remote sensing observation techniques (e.g., a hyperspectral imagery and the UAV remote sensing technique) and strengthen research on the spectral characteristics of the grassland vegetation community and the applications of the narrow band remote sensing vegetation index in monitoring grassland AGB [11, 13]; and 4) construct multi-factor grassland AGB estimation models based on statistical analysis and machine learning techniques. These multi factors include climatic factors (e.g., sunlight, temperature, and rainfall), soil factors (e.g., soil nutrients, soil structure and fertility), biological factors (e.g., grassland type, species richness, and distribution of malignant weeds), and management factors (e.g., pasture, fencing enclosures, and rotational grazing) [14-16].

Acknowledgments

This study was supported by the National Natural Science Foundation of China (31672484, 31372367, 41101337 and 41401472), the Project of the Ministry of Agriculture (201203006)

References

[1] Xu B.; Yang X.; Tao W.; Qin Z.H.; Liu H.Q.; Miao J.M. Remote sensing monitoring upon the grass production in China. Acta Ecologica Sinica, 2007, 27(2):405-413, DOI:10.1016/S1872-2032(07) 60012-2.

[2] Lauenroth W.K.; Hunt H.W.; Swift D.M.; Singh J.S. Estimating aboveground net primary production in grasslands- a simulation approach. Ecological Modelling,1986,33:297–314,DOI: 10.1016/0304-3800(86)90045-1.

[3] Ali I, Cawkwell F, Green S, et al. Application of statistical and machine learning models for grassland yield estimation based on a hypertemporal satellite remote sensing time series. Geoscience and Remote Sensing Symposium. IEEE, 2014, 5060-5063, DOI: 10.1109/IGARSS.2014.6947634

[4] Ma W.H.; Fang J.Y.; Yang Y.H.; Mohammat A. Biomass carbon stocks and their changes in northern China's grasslands during 1982-2006. Science China Life sciences, 2010, 53(7): 841-50,DOI: 10.1007/s11427-010-4020-6.

[5] Feng Q.S.; Gao X.H.; Huang X.D.; Yu H.; Liang T.G. Remote sensing dynamic monitoring of grass growth in Qinghai-Tibet plateau from 2001 to 2010. Journal of Lanzhou University, 2011, 47(4):75-74.

[6] Ali I.; Cawkwell F.; Dwyer E.; Barrett B.; Green S. Satellite remote sensing of grasslands: from observation to management—a review. Journal of Plant Ecology, 2016, DOI: 10.1093/jpe/rtw005.

[7] Cui X.; Guo Z.G.; Liang T.G.;Shen Y.Y.; Liu X.Y.; Liu y. Classification management for grassland using MODIS data: a case study in the Gannan region, China. International Journal of Remote Sensing, 2012,

33(10):3156-3175,DOI:10.1080/01431161.2011.634861.

[8] Wang Y, Xia W T, Liang T G, Wang C. Spatial and temporal dynamic changes of net primary product based on MODIS vegetation index in Gannan grassland. Acta Prataculturae Sinica, 2010, 19(1): 201-210.

[9] Bao H M. Dynamic Monitoring and Prediction of Aboveground Biomass of Natural Grassland—A case study in Xiahe County of Gansu Province. master thesis, Gansu agricultural university, Lanzhou, 2010.

[10] Ullah S.; Si Y.; Schlerf M.; Skidmore A.K.; Shafique M.; Iqbal I A. Estimation of grassland biomass and nitrogen using MERIS data. International Journal of Applied Earth Observation and Geoinformation, 2012, 19: 196–204, DOI: 10.1016/j.jag.2012.05.008.

[11] Gao T.; Yang X.Y.; Jin Y.X.; Ma H.L.; Li J.Y.; Yu Q.Y.; Zheng X. Spatio-Temporal Variation in Vegetation Biomass and Its Relationships with Climate Factors in the Xilingol Grasslands, Northern China. Plos One, 2013,8(12):e83824-e83824,DOI:10.1080/01431161.2013.823000.

[12] Ahamed T.; Tian L.; Zhang Y.; Ting K.C. A review of remote sensing methods for biomass feedstock production. Biomass and Bioenergy, 2011, 35:2455-2469, DOI: 10.1016/j.biombioe.2011.02.028.

[13] Liu M.; Liu G.H.; Gong L.; Wang D.B.; Sun J. Relationships of biomass with environmental factors in the grassland area of Hulunbuir, China. Plos One, 2014, 9(9):e102344-e102344, DOI: 10.1371/journal.pone.0102344.

[14] Li F.; Jiang L.; Wang X.F.; Zhang X.Q.; Zheng J.J.; Zhao Q.J. Estimating grassland aboveground biomass using multitemporal MODIS data in the West Songnen Plain, China. Journal of Applied Remote Sensing, 2013, 7(1):124-131, DOI: 10.1117/1.JRS.7.073546.

[15] Liang T.G.; Yang S.X.; Feng Q.S.; Liu B.K.; Zhang R.P.; Huang X.D.; Xie H.J. Multi-factor modeling of above-ground biomass in alpine grassland: A case study in the Three-River Headwaters Region, China. Remote Sensing of Environment, 2016, 186:164-172, DOI: 10.1016/j.rse.2016.08.014.

[16] Diouf A.A.; Hiernaux P.; Brandt M.; Faye G.; Djaby B.; Diop M.B.; Ndione J.A.; Tvchon B. Do Agrometeorological Data Improve Optical Satellite-Based Estimations of the Herbaceous Yield in Sahelian Semi-Arid Ecosystems?. 2016, 8(8). DOI: 10.3390/rs8080668

DOI: 10.1051/itmconf/20171202004

Pattern Identification of Subthalamic Local Field Potentials in Parkinson's Disease

Kun Zhang [1,2], Bin Feng [1,2], Yun-Peng Zhang [1], Yong-Zhi Huang [2,3] and Shou-Yan Wang [1,4,*]

[1]*Suzhou Institute of Biomedical Engineering and Technology, Chinese Academy of Sciences, Suzhou, Jiangsu, China*
[2]*School of Communication and Information Engineering, Shanghai University, Shanghai, China*
[3]*The Functional Neurosurgery Group, Department of Surgery, John Radcliffe Hospital, Oxford, UK*
[4]*Institute of Science and Technology for Brain-Inspired Intellgenc, Fudan University, Shanghai, China*
**Shouyan WANG: shouyan@fudan.edu.cn*

Abstract. The local field potentials (LFP) in Parkinson's disease (PD), which contain abundant information related to disease and symptoms, are important for clinical treatment. The amplitudes of oscillations in LFP and the balance between them were found to be involved in brain functional state of PD patients. The LFP recorded from subthalamic nucleus before and after medication treatment were selected in this study. The power spectral ratio between frequencies and the percentage of energy corresponding to the wavelet packet nodes in the overall signal energy based on wavelet packet analysis related to symptoms were extracted as features. The brain states related to medication treatment in patients were classified using machine learning. The Naive Bayesian classifier and support vector machine (SVM) classifier were used to classify the states of off and on medication conditions. The results showed that the Naive Bayesian classifier was better than SVM classifier with higher accuracy. The specificity of Naive Bayesian classifier reached to 82.4%. The method proposed in this paper can accurately identify the brain functional state of PD patients.

1. Introduction

Parkinson's disease (PD) is a common degenerative disease of the central nervous system.At present the PD is estimated to affect around 180 out of 1,00,000 people.
The accurate identification of PD is of great significance to clinical diagnosis and treatment.At the present stage, machine learning method has been widely used in clinical medical science research.The use of machine learning to diagnose PD had achieved a good diagnostic effect [1]. PD patients with wearable sensor gait data and patients voice signals data also were used to diagnose PD[2].

The subthalamic nucleus (STN) is closely related to symptoms of PD patients [3].The local field potential (LFP) signals were recorded by implanted electrode into the patients STN which contains abundant information related to disease and symptoms[4,5].Therefore, this paper used the machine learning procedure to study the patients LFP before and after medication treatment, achieved the identification and judgment of brain function in PD patients.

In this paper, the amplitudes and dynamic regularity of oscillations in STN LFP as PD features were analysed.The balance in LFP different frequency bands and the power spectral ratio between frequencies and the percentage of energy corresponding to the wavelet packet nodes in the overall signal energy based on wavelet packet analysis related to symptoms were extracted as features. In this paper, established the model of brain function judgment in PD patients and provided a method that identified brain functional state of PD patients in order to achieve intelligent,adaptive and closed-loop deep brain stimulation (DBS).

2. Methods

2.1 LFP Recording and Preprocessing

17 patients participated in this study as they were undergoing surgical DBS treatment at John Radcliffe Hospital (JRH), Oxford, UK. Postoperative magenitic resonance imaging confirmed the successful implantation of DBS electrode within the STN. The bipolar electrode recordings were made 3-5 days post-operatively from adjacent pairs of the externalized electrode. DBS electrode is 3389(Medtronic, Minneapolis, MN,USA),it has four ring Pt-Ir cylinder surface contact. The distance between every contacts is 0.5 mm, the diameter of contact is 1.27 mm, length is 1.5 mm. The four contacts defined as 0-1-2-3, using the adjacent contact differential record when recording. The LFP signals were then amplified using isolated CED 1902 amplifier (Cambridge Electronic Design, UK),magnification of 10000 times,

digitized using CED1401 II and acquired using Spike2.The signals LFP sampling frequency is 2000 Hz.

17 patients underwent bilateral implantation of quadripolar DBS electrodes in STN. Five sides recording LFP signals had problems, so a total of 29 sides data. The recordings took place after 1.5 h of taking the usual pre-surgery dose of medication for the on medication condition. The recordings took place after withdrawal of medication 24h and medication efficacy had diminished for the off medication condition. Patients were instructed to relax for the recordings, which lasted around 5 min. Interception of stable and non-tremor 25 s data length for analysis. LFP were low-pass filtered (<90Hz, Chebyshev I). Interference around 50Hz is removed by an adaptive filter based on the signal in 40-60Hz band. Then LFP were high-pass filtered (>3Hz, Chebyshev I)[6]。

2.2 Classification Model Flow of Brain Function State

Firstly, the model is used to analyze the PD patients LFP before and after medication treatment, and then extracts features that are closely related to the PD. So as to we can classify the PD patients LFP before and after medication treatment, and accurately identify the brain functional state of PD patients. The brain functional state of PD patients identification model flow chart is shown in Figure 1:

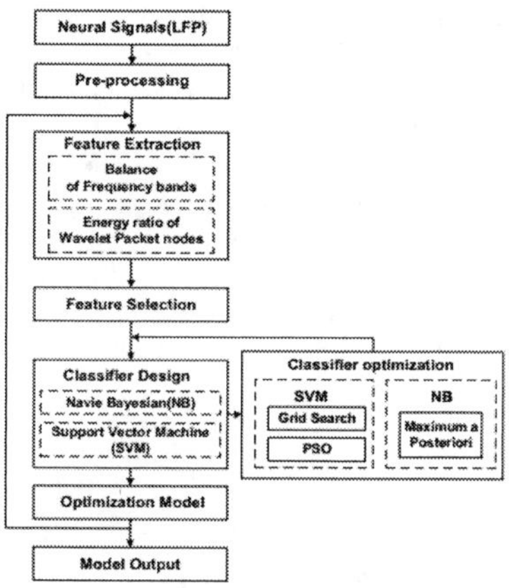

Figure 1. Flow chart of identify the brain functional state identification

3. Feature Extraction and Classifier Design

3.1 Balance Feature

Medication have different effects on the different frequency bands of LFP oscillations .In this paper, we used the power spectrum to analyze the data of 17 PD patients with a total of 29 sides. Quantify the degree of synchronization of the different frequency bands of patients LFP before and after medication treatment (Figure.3).From the Figure 3,we can see that the power spectral density(PSD) amplitudes of LFP oscillations increase in theta bands (4-8 Hz),and high beta bands (20-30 Hz),and decrease in the range of low beta bangs(12-18 Hz).And only in the low beta bands Dopamine drugs can significantly suppress the STN oscillations of the band (P <0.05, t-test, Figure.3).We can also find that the balance of PSD between different frequency bands in LFP before and after the medication are also different.

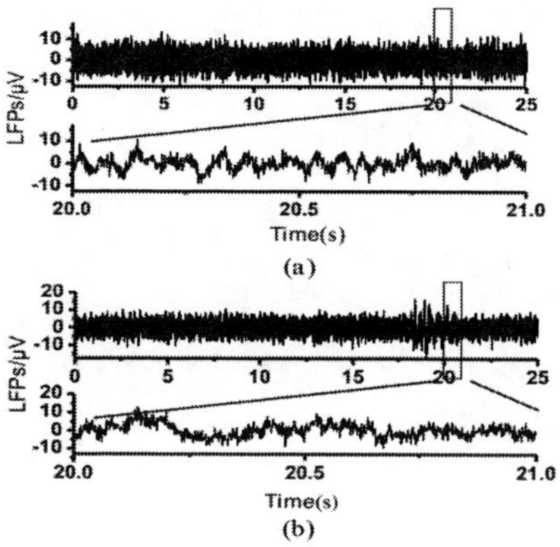

Figure 2. Local field potentials recorded off (a) and on (b) medication

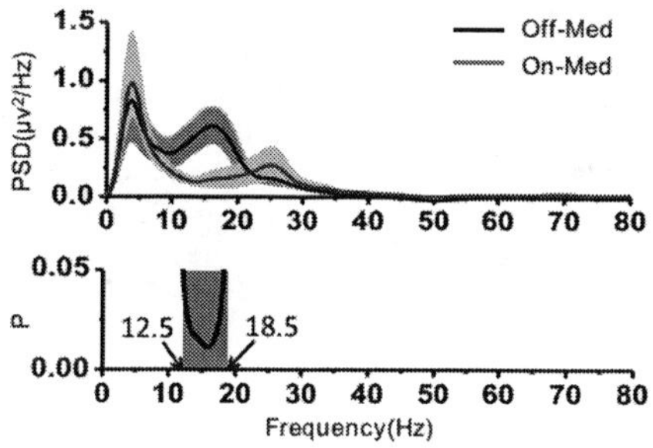

Figure 3.Power spectral density of LFP and the t-test significant of on and off medication

In this paper, the low frequency compoments of LFP signals were divided into four bands: theta (4-8 Hz), alpha (8-12 Hz), low beta (12-18 Hz) and high beta (20-30 Hz).Respectively calculated the power spectral ratio between each frequency band, used paired sample t-test analysis of STN LFP before and after medication to extract characteristics of different frequency bands energy ratio closely related to PD, for quantitying balance between different frequency bands.

Table 1 shows the balance between the low frequency different compoments of LFP signals for PD patients

Before and after medication treatment .The energy ratio between the different bands is calculated by the ratio of the parameters in the longitudinal direction of the table to the parameters in the transverse direction. As can be seen in Table 1 that the ratio of 20-30 Hz to 12-18 Hz inpatients STN LFP significantly increase after medication treatment(t-tset, P <0.01),while the ratio of 12-18 Hz and 8-12 Hz, 12-18 Hz and 4-8 Hz ,8-12 Hz and 4-8 Hz, the significantly decrease after medication treatment (t-tset,P<0.05).Therefore, this paper selected these four parameters as the characteristic biomarkers for PD patients LFP, and was used to accurately identify the STN brain functional state of PD patients.

Table 1. The balance of different LFP frequency bands on and off medication

Balance	Theta	Alpha	L-beta	H-beta
Theta	1			
Alpha	1.39±1.19 0.55±0.26 **	1		
L-beta	5.89±9.39 0.73±0.89 *	2.81±2.79 1.12±0.85 **	1	
H-beta	3.29±5.54 1.43±2.27	2.06±2.54 2.12±2.51	1.04±0.85 1.78±1.31 **	1

Note :Theta:(4-8 Hz), Alpha:(8-12 Hz), L-beta:(12-18 Hz), H-beta:(20-30 Hz). * represent P<0.05, ** is P<0.01, t-test.

3.2 Wavelet Packet Feature

3.2.1 Wavelet Packet Transform

Wavelet packet transformation (WPT) is widely used in signal analysis,it has excellent time-frequency local characteristics and can describe the characteristics of a non-stationary signal within a local time range. WPT provides a more accurate method than others to divide the frequency bands and can make further decomposition in the high frequency bands [7]. The i level p point node (i,p)can be calculated using fast algorithm for orthogonal WPT:

$$\psi_{i+1}^{2p}(k)=\sum_{n=-\infty}^{\infty} l[n]\ \psi_i^{p}\left(k-2^{i}n\right)$$
$$\psi_{i+1}^{2p+1}(k)=\sum_{n=-\infty}^{\infty} h[n]\ \psi_i^{p}\left(k-2^{i}n\right) \tag{1}$$

where l[n] is a low pass wavelet filter and h[n] is a high pass wavelet filter. Wavelet Packet Decomposition is a kind of high and low pass filtering using a pair of conjugated high-pass and low-pass filter to iterate the signals. Different wavelet basis correspond to different wavelet filters, we used Meyer wavelet basis analyzing LFP signals[8].The coefficients of decomposition of the i th layer can be calculated according to the coefficients of i-1, by this way all other coefficients can be obtained. The frequency range of each node can also be calculated through:$[0,f_s/2^{i+1}],[f_s/2^{i+1},2f_s/2^{i+1}],[2f_s/2^{i+1},3f_s/2^{i+1}],\ldots,[(2^{i-1}-1)f_s/2^{i+1},f_s/2]$. f_s is the sampling frequency.

3.2.2 Energy of LFP Wavelet Packet node

WPT of PD patients STN LFP before and after medication can decompose accurately. LFP signals In this paper, sampling frequency of the LFP signals down to 384 Hz and the down-sampling LFP signals was decomposed by 6-layers WPT. The decomposition results are showed in the Table 2.Then we reconstructed each wavelet packet node and calculated the percentage of energy of wavelet packet nodes reconstructed signals and total energy of signals to achieve features wavelet packet nodes. Assuming that (i,j) is the j th node of the i th layer.The energy ratio of reconstructed signals is:

$$p_{i,j}=\frac{E_{i,j}}{\sum_{j=0}^{2^N-1} E_{i,j}} \tag{2}$$

$p_{i,j}$ is the energy ratio of energy of reconstructed signals and total energy of signals and N is the layer number of decomposition.

Table 2 shows Wavelet Packet nodes of PD patients before and after medication and their energy ratio. As seen from Table 2, we can find that there are some differences between energy ratio before and after medication. The energy ratio of the Wavelet Packet nodes [6.2], [6.6] and [6.7] reconstruct signals significantly decrease after the medication. while energy ratio of nodes [6.0] and [6.1] significantly increase. Then we calculate every node using Fisher feature extraction method, then choose the subset of features that have the greatest distinguishing feature and obvious features that has the bigger Fisher score. Fisher score of nodes in Table 2 can be arranged from large to small as [6.7]、[6.6]、[6.1]、[6.2] and [6.0].We choose the first three nodes [6.7]、[6.6] and [6.1] to analysis(Figure.4). From Figure.4 we find that these Wavelet Packet feature nodes can distinguish PD patients before and after taking medicine accurately.

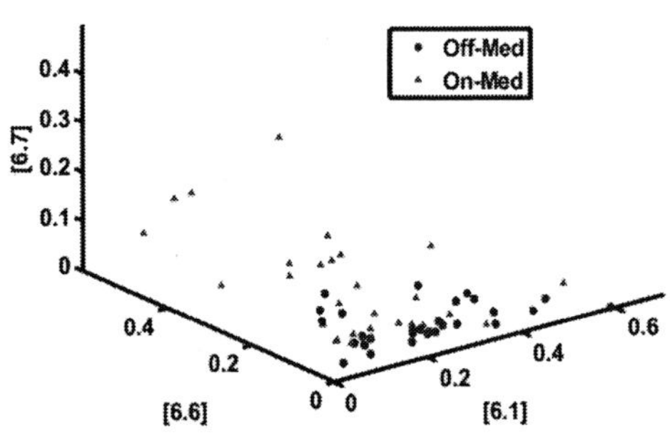

Figure 4. Scatter diagram of feature distribution.Energy ratio of Wavelet Packet nodes[6.1],[6.6]and [6.7] on and off medication

Table 2. Wavelet Packet nodes and energy ratio of Wavelet Packet nodes on and off medication

Wavelet Packet nodes	[6.0]	[6.1]	[6.3]	[6.2]	[6.6]	[6.7]
Frequency band/Hz	0-3	3-6	6-9	9-12	12-15	15-18
Off-Med energy ratio	0.037± 0.040	0.14± 0.12	0.095± 0.065	0.088± 0.053	0.13± 0.13	0.11± 0.097
On-Med energy ratio	0.065± 0.081	0.23± 0.14	0.12± 0.072	0.062± 0.027	0.048± 0.024	0.045± 0.031
P(t-test)	0.02*	0.0008**	0.1432	0.0171*	0.0016**	0.0009**
Fisher	0.10	0.2	0.04	0.19	0.372	0.457

Note: * represent p<0.05, ** is p<0.01, t-test

3.3 Brain Functional State Classification

3.3.1 Navie Bayesian Classifier

Navie Bayesian(NB) Classifier can flexibly process and classify data, it has quite fast calculation rate of classification. Navie Bayesian Classifier is a kind of inverse probability derivation method that infers the probability of the unknown according to probability of something happened[9].In this paper,firstly, we analyzed the nerve oscillation characteristics of PD patients in known states, calculated the probability distribution of its characteristics and probability of occurrence of LFP signals nerve oscillation of unknown state patients. Finally,we infered the state of brain function of unknown state patients using Maximum a Posteriori(MAP) Navie Bayesian Classifier.After all, we can build a detection and identification model of PD patients brain function state to achieve fast patients brain function state determination.

$$P(\omega_i|X) = P(\omega_i)\prod_{k=1}^{n} P(X_k|\omega_i) \quad (3)$$

The sample is defined as $X=(X_1, X_2, X_3, \ldots, X_k)$. Where X_k means the kth characteristic. $P(\omega_i)$ is prior probability of category ω_i.

3.3.2 Support Vector Machine Classifier

Support Vector Machine(SVM) Classifier is based on Structural Risk Minimization and statistics theory to deal with classification problem and is widely used in Biomedical field[10,11]. SVM classifier is a maximum interval function classifier containing hard interval

$$\min \mathrm{P} = \frac{1}{2}\|w\|^2 + C\sum_{i=1}^{n}\xi_i \quad (4)$$

support vector machine and soft margin support vector machine. SVM classifier aims to:

C is regularization parameter that penalizes the errors made by the model and $_i$ is slack vector.

Bring the results of the calculation to the original function and simplify it to get function dual form:

$$\max_a = \sum_{i=1}^{n} a_i - \frac{1}{2}\sum_{i=1}^{n}\sum_{j=1}^{n} a_i a_j y_i y_j \langle \phi(X_i), \phi(X_j) \rangle \quad (5)$$

The constraint : $0 \le a_i \le C, i = 1,\ldots,n$, $\sum_{i=1}^{n} a_i y_i = 0$.

When proceeding PD patients brain function state detection, we used LibSVM software package developed by team of professor Zhiren Lin of Taiwan University to analyze patients LFP.We analysed following four steps:Firstly, normalize PD patients characteristic LFP signals. Then used Radial basis function to transform signals dimension. And then used cross validation to train data and used Particle Swarm Optimization(PSO) algorithm to choose SVM Classifier optimal parameters, regularization parameter *C* and gamma in Kernel Function. Finally, implement an overall training to form a SVM classier having stronger generalization ability and more precision as well as to establish the brain functional state of PD patients identification model.

4. Experimental Results

The balance of energy ratio between 4 bands in the low frequency compoments of PD patients STN LFP and the percentage of energy corresponding to the wavelet packet nodes [6.7], [6.6] and [6.1] in the overall signal energy based on wavelet packet, that can effectively reflect the brain functional state of PD patients.In this paper,we selected these seven parameters as the features of the classification of brain function state of PD patients,used the naive Bayesian classifier and SVM classifier for classification and used 5-fold cross validation, the results shown in Table 3.

Table 3. Classifier comparison

Algorithm	NB	SVM
Accuracy(%)	71.90±2.31	68.10±2.19
Sensitivity(%)	61.03±4.00	59.31±3.91
Specificity(%)	82.41±3.79	77.93±5.91

As shown in Table 3, the Naive Bayesian classifier is more accurate classification than the SVM classifier in PD *patients*, and naive Bayesian classifier classification detection the highest specificity is 82.7±13.79% for the PD and SVM classification the highest specificity is only 77.93±5.91. For the detection sensitivity is also naive Bayesian classification accuracy higher than SVM classifier.

5. Discussion

In the diagnosis of PD, the behavioral characteristics of the patients were diagnosed in the past and were not analyzed from the intrinsic patterning characteristics of the patient.With the continuous development of DBS at present, it has been more important to analyze the patterning characteristics of LFP signals that contains a wealth of physiological information.In this paper,specific nerve oscillations were closely related to the pathogenesis of PD: the energy balance between the low frequency bands and the energy ratio of each nodes to reconstruct the signals after wavelet packet transformation.The detection model was established using the maximum a posteriori Naive Bayesian and SVM classifier to achieve the classification of the brain functional state of PD patients.The results show that the accuracy, specificity and sensitivity of Naive Bayesian classifier identification algorithm are higher than SVM classifier.In addition, the specificity of the identification algorithm is high, but the sensitivity still has room for improvement. Less sample data, prone to over-fitting, is one of the reasons for the lower accuracy of classification, so to increase the experimental sample of PD will be the focus of the next step.The study of the characteristics of PD patientd LFP can improve the accuracy of detection classification in the further, which will be the important direction of the next step.

References

1. S Patel, K Lorincz, R Hughes, IEEE T INF TECHNOL B, 13, 864 (2009)
2. MA Little, PE Mcsharry, EJ Hunter, IEEE Trans Biomed Eng, 56, 1015 (2009)
3. JS Brittain, P Brown, Neuroimage, 85, 637, (2014)
4. G Foffani, A Priori , M Egidi, Brain, 126, 2153 (2003)
5. N Jenkinson, P Brown, TRENDS NEUROSCI, 34, 611 (2011)
6. YN Wang, XY Geng, YZ Huang, J Biomedical Eng, 33, 49 (2016)
7. MA Li, JY Ma, JF Yang, Chin J Sci Instru, 33, 1721 (2012)
8. KA Mamun, M Mace, ME Lutman, J NEURAL ENG, 12, 056011 (2015)
9. M Peker, B Sen, D Delen, J HEALTHC ENG, 6, 281 (2015)
10. E Byvatov, U Fechner, J Sadowski, J Chem Inf Comput Sci, 43, 1882 (2003)
11. S Pan, S Iplikci, K Warwick, EXPERT SYST APPL, 39, 10764 (2012)

Computing Optimal Mixed Strategies for Terrorist Plot Detection Games with the Consideration of Information Leakage

MingChu Li[1a], Zekun Yang[2b], Kun Lu*[3c], Cheng Guo*[4d]

[1]School of Software Technology, Dalian University of Technology, Dalian, China
[2]School of Software Technology, Dalian University of Technology, Dalian, China
[3]School of Software Technology, Dalian University of Technology, Dalian, China
[4] School of Software Technology, Dalian University of Technology, Dalian, China
[a]mingchul@dlut.edu.cn, [b]zekunnyang@gmail.com, [c]lukun@dlut.edu.cn, [d]guocheng@dlut.edu.cn

Abstract: The terrorist's coordinated attack is becoming an increasing threat to western countries. By monitoring potential terrorists, security agencies are able to detect and destroy terrorist plots at their planning stage. Therefore, an optimal monitoring strategy for the domestic security agency becomes necessary. However, previous study about monitoring strategy generation fails to consider the information leakage, due to hackers and insider threat. Such leakage events may lead to failure of watching potential terrorists and destroying the plot, and cause a huge risk to public security. This paper makes two major contributions. Firstly, we develop a new Stackelberg game model for the security agency to generate optimal monitoring strategy with the consideration of information leakage. Secondly, we provide a double-oracle framework DO-TPDIL for calculation effectively. The experimental result shows that our approach can obtain robust strategies against information leakage with high feasibility and efficiency.

1. Introduction

In the past few years, an increasing threat is originated from the terrorist organization, which is continually training and directing their supporters to launch coordinated attacks in their home countries, especially in European countries. To detect and thwart such attacks, domestic security agencies need to allocate security resources to monitor potential terrorists. Among all of the important factors, confidentiality is a basic requirement for security stuff during executing the monitoring task. A spotted security stuff cannot collect information from alerted terrorists, he will be even cheated by intentional terrorists with wrong information. Hence, the security agency fails to monitor the plot, which results in a huge risk to public security. Unfortunately, the security agency probably leak their information unconsciously. For example, Snowden[1] whose disclosure revealed several classified program of NSA. Consequently, the defender strategies become fragile and easy to attack. To sum up, designing robust strategy against the leakage becomes crucial to security agencies.

Recent years, security game theory has been widely used to protect large scale critical infrastructure and targets such as airport [2], transportation network [3], coast ports [4], etc. Coordinated attack is a rising hotspot for academic research, there are already some literature about this problem. There has been some research [5, 6] on security game mechanism against coordinated attack. For example, Wang et al. [5] proposed a Terrorist Plot Detect(TPD) game model for security agencies to monitor the potential terrorists. Guo et al.[6] introduced a coalitional security game (CSG) to address the issue that attackers can form coalitions that can dramatically increase their ability to achieve malicious goals. Most of the models of Stackelberg security games assume the attacker is not able to observe the defender's real-time pure strategy, so the attacker makes decision only based on his knowledge about the defender's mixed strategy. However this assumption cannot explain the leakage we mentioned above. The information leakage effect was ignored in most of the literature about coordinated attacks. Xu et al. [7] first introduced the concept of "information leakage"(IL) in security game domain, they also discussed the model and the computation of the leakage in the simplest defender-attacker security game. However, the effect of the information leakage in other security game setting are missing in the present study, and the efficient algorithms to handle it in the specify case still needs to be investigated.

This paper develops the optimal defender strategy in Terrorist Plot Detect game taking the information leakage into account. In the presented model, the information leaks as the attacker can discover specific terrorists' monitoring information. For the sake of simplicity, we assume that at the same time there is only one terrorist's monitoring information that can be leaked, but all terrorists in the network have the probability to discover its monitoring status.

The rest of the paper is organized as follows. In section 2 we give a brief introduction to the TPD models, then we propose our TPDIL (Terrorist Plot Detect game considering Information Leakage) model. In section 3, a DO-TPDIL (Double Oracle algorithm for TPD games considering Information Leakage) framework is proposed based on double-oracle framework to solve the problem efficiently. Our experiments in section 4 show that the model can decrease the loss of defender's utility, which verify the feasible of our approach.

2. Model

In this section, firstly, we will introduce the Terrorist Plot Detect(TPD) game model proposed by Wang et al.[5]. Then we will give the Terrorist Plot Detect game with the consideration of Information Leakage (TPDIL) model and LP formulation to calculate the optimal strategy for defender given the probability of IL.

2.1 TPD Game Model

As introduced by Wang et al. [5], a Terrorist Plot Detect(TPD) game is a Stackelberg game between a leader (security agency, defender) and a follower (terrorist plot planner, attacker). The defender first allocates R resources to monitor the attacker's social network $G=(V,E)$, where V is the set of vertices(potential terrorists) and E is the set of edges(relations between terrorists). Then the attacker chooses a connected subgraph to launch a coordinated attack based on his knowledge of the defender schedule. The defender's pure strategy $S=\langle S_v \rangle$ is a $|V|$ -dimensional 0-1 vector of R monitoring resources, and defender will monitor terrorist i if $S_i = 1$ an $\mathring{a}_{\hat{\imath} V} S_i = R$. The defender's mixed strategy is a probability distribution over pure strategies, $x=\langle x_S \rangle$, x_S is the probability that pure strategy S is played, and $\mathring{a}\ x_S = 1$. The attackers pure strategy is a connected subgraph $V' \hat{I}\ V$ denoted by a 0-1 vector $A=\langle A_i \rangle$, $A_i = 1$ means terrorist $i \hat{I}\ V$ will attend the plot, 0 otherwise. The attacker's mixed strategy is denoted by a probability distribution $y=\langle y_A \rangle$, and y_A is the probability of playing attacker pure strategy A .

The utility of TPD game is defined as follows: TPD game is a zero-sum game, the attacker gains exactly the defender loses. Given a defender allocation S and an attacker subgraph A , if there is no intersection between S and A , i.e., $S ?\ A \quad ?$, which means the defender fails to detect the plot, the attacker will win $P(A)$. $P(A)$ is a subgraph utility function and the definition can be found in [5], the defender's cost is $-\ P(A)$. Otherwise the defender wins and the reward of destroying the plot is 0, attacker's utility is also 0.

Without information leakage, given the attacker's strategy space A and the defender's strategy space S , the defender's optimal mixed strategy can be calculated by the following linear programming(LP) (1) formulation.

$$
\begin{aligned}
&\max \quad U \\
&s.j. \quad U\ ?\ U_d(x,A) \qquad A\ ?\ \mathrm{A} \\
&\qquad \mathring{a}_{s\hat{\imath}\,\mathrm{S}}\ x_S = 1 \\
&\qquad x_S\ ?\ 0 \qquad\qquad S\ ?\ \mathrm{S}
\end{aligned} \tag{1}
$$

2.2 Model of Information Leakage

Xu et al. [7] introduced the two related IL model: PRobabilistic Information Ieakage (PRIL) model and ADversarial Information Leakage (ADIL) model. Let $p_i(p_i\ ^3\ 0)$ denote the probability that vertex i's "monitoring status" is being leaked, in other words, attacker is aware of whether terrorist i is being watched or not. With probability $p_0 = 1 -\ \mathring{a}_{\hat{\imath} V}\, p_i$, no vertices leak information. In PRIL model, every single vertex has probability to leak its information, thus we have a $(n+1)$ -dimensional probability vector $\overset{r}{p}=(p_0, p_1,..., p_n)$ where $n=|V|$. $\overset{r}{p}$ is usually given by domain experts and may be determined by the nature or capability of terrorists. ADIL is a special case that only one chosen vertex 's status is being leaked, let i be the vertex, then $p_i > 0$, for any v 构$i, v \quad 0$, $p_v = 0$, and $p_0 = 1 -\ p_i$. This model captures the fact that few attacker own counter-reconnaissance or surveillance ability. With certain probability, they succeed in observing a specific high-value vertex's status, like the ringleader of the plot or someone who has been arrested before.

In a simplest TPD game, let $t_{iu}(\textit{Ø}t_{iv})$ denote the status that terrorist i is being monitored (not being monitored). The defender's utility of PRIL model is defined as Eq.(2) :

$$
DefU = p_0 u_0 + \mathring{a}_{i=1}^{n}\ p_i(u_i + v_i) \tag{2}
$$

where $u_0 = \min_{A_k} U_d(x, A_j)$ is the defender's utility when there is no information leakage. The defender's utility when terrorist i leaks out its monitoring status as t_i ("being watched") is defined as Eq.(3):

$$
u_i = \min_{A_k}[U_d(x_{iu}, A_k) Pr(x_{iu}\,|\,t_{iu})] \tag{3}
$$

DOI: 10.1051/itmconf/20171203001

And the defender's expected utility when target i leaks as status $\O t_i$ (i.e., not being monitored) is defined as Eq.(4) :

$$v_i = \min_{A_k} [U_d(x_{iv}, A_k) Pr(x_{iv} \mid t_{iv})] \quad (4)$$

Which means that defender choose the minimax strategy to minimize attacker's best response.

Given a defender mixed strategy x and a attacker's pure strategy A, let $U_d(x, A)$ denote defender's payoff. According to the definition, $U_d(x, A) = \sum x_S U_d(S, A)$, and $U_d(S, A) = P(A)$ if the vertices in S fails to overlap the nodes in A, otherwise $U_d(S, A) = 0$. Given a defender mixed strategy $x = \langle x_S \rangle$, let $x_u(x_v)$ denote the defender's mixed strategy probability distribution after observing t_{i*} (* = u or v)., the new distribution can be calculated as follows.

$$x_{*S} = \frac{x_S \Pr(x_S \mid t_{i*})}{\sum x_S \Pr(x_S \mid t_{i*})} \quad (5)$$

Notice that comparing to the simplest security game discussed in [7], the leakage message(only one node's status) in TPDIL is the same. However, instead of considering the number of targets, the defender now have to take a much more complex attacker strategy space, which grows up in an exponential way, into consideration. A direct challenge is that we can't use the origin compact matrix representation in [7], because the marginal coverage probability is helpless to describe the relationship between both player's pure strategy in our model. The ADIL model is defined in a similar way. Let terrorist i denote the special terrorist whose monitoring status is being leaked, $DefU = p_0 u_0 + (1 - p_0)(u_i + v_i)$, where u_i and v_i is defined as above.

2.3 Equilibrium

Under zero-sum condition, the Stackelberg equilibrium (SSE) is equivalent to maximin equilibrium and minimax equilibrium, thus the optimal defender mixed strategy x in TPDIL game can be calculated by solving the following LP(6).

$$\begin{aligned}
\max \quad & p_0 u_0 + \sum_{i=1}^{n} p_i (u_i + v_i) \\
s.j. \quad & u_0 \le U_d(x, A) && \forall A \in \mathcal{A} \\
& u_i \le \min_A (U_d(x_{iu}, A) \Pr(x_{iu} \mid t_{iu})) && \forall A \in \mathcal{A} \\
& v_i \le \min_A (U_d(x_{iv}, A) \Pr(x_{iv} \mid t_{iv})) && \forall A \in \mathcal{A} \\
& \textstyle\sum_{S \in \mathcal{S}} x_S = 1 \\
& x_S \ge 0 && \forall S \in \mathcal{S}
\end{aligned}$$
(6)

However, the LP(6) contains $(2|L|+1) \times |X| \times |Y|$ restrains, where $|L|$ is the number of information leakage cases, in our model, is the network size $|V|$. The $|X|$ stands for the defender strategy space S , which grows exponentially with the number of resources R , and $|Y|$ is the attacker strategy space, which grows exponentially with $|V|$. As a result, it is impractical to directly to solve this LP.

3. Approach

As we discussed above, both player's strategy space grows in the exponentially way, which make solving the problem in a large scale network become impractical. The double oracle framework is a normal form for solving zero-sum games with large strategy space. To solve the TPD game in a real-world scale network, Wang et al. [5] presented an algorithm DO-TPD(an Double Oracle algorithm for TPDs) to obtain solution for both players. DO-TPD initials with solving the equilibrium with a small and limited game, then both player compute the improving strategies and add them to the strategy space iteratively, and finally the solution meets the global equilibrium when no improving strategies can be found. However, the solutions obtained from DO-TPD don't consider the information leakage. We extend DO-TPD to DO-TPDIL(an Double Oracle algorithm for TPD games considering Information Leakage) in a novel way. Next, we start with an overview of DO-TPDIL, and then present its components.

3.1 DO-TPDIL Overview

Our DO-TPDIL algorithm is sketched in Algorithm 1. DO-TPDIL also initials the small strategy space $\langle S', A' \rangle$ by solving the linear program LWA-LP presented by Wang et al.[5], where the attacker is restricted to use "lone-wolf" attack represented as a single vertex. In the initialization procedure, the game degenerates to the simplest form of security game because the attacker ignores the network structure. The defender strategy can be represented by marginal coverage probability of each vertex, and the mixed strategy can be efficiently sampled with Comb Sampling algorithm[8].

 DOI: 10.1051/itmconf/20171203001

Algorithm 1 DO-TPDIL overview

Initialize S' , and all $A_i \subset A_\cup'$ using *LWA*-LP
repeat
    $(x, y_\cup) \leftarrow CoreLP(S', A_\cup)$
    for leak case i, $x_i \subset x$, $y_i \in y_\cup$ do
        $S^+ \leftarrow betterOD(x_i, y_i)$
        if $S^+ = \emptyset$ then
            $S^+ \leftarrow bestOD(x_i, y_i)$
        $S' \leftarrow S' \cup S^+$
        $A_i^+ = attackerOracle(x_i, y_i)$
        $A_i = A_i \cup A_i^+$
        $A_\cup = A_\cup \cup A_i^+$
until $S^+ = \emptyset$ and $A_i^+ = \emptyset$ for all leak case i
return $(x, y_\cup)$

Here we regard t_{iu} and t_{iv} as two separated cases, thus there are totally $2|V|+1$ possible cases. Let A_i denotes the attacker's best response in each case i, then we have $A_{\cup} = A_0 \cup A_1 \cup \cdots \cup A_{2n}$, where A_0 is the attacker's response with no leakage, i.e., the origin attacker's solution in TPD. Then DO-TPDIL solves CoreLP with the above restricted strategy space. The attacker's strategy space $A_{È}$ ' has only $|V|$ strategies first, so the restricted CoreLP can be solved efficiently. Obviously, the "restricted version" solution is not enough to form the origin TPDIL's SSE solution. To improve both player's utilities, DO-TPDIL calls the subsequent oracles to find improving strategies. The process repeats until no improving strategies can be found in all case, and the obtained solution is a minimax equilibrium solution [9], and is equivalent to SSE and NE strategies in zero-sum game [10].

3.2 CoreLP

The CoreLP in TPDIL is computed as follows. Firstly, the defender computes its mixed strategy x against $A_{È}$ ' by solving LP(1) with S = $S¢$ and A = $A_{È}$. Then the attacker updates all the A_i Î $A_{È¢}$ respectively. Specifically, let case j denote the case t_{iu} (t_{iv}), i.e., the terrorist i leaks as being monitored (not being monitored). The attacker first incurs the defender strategy space S_j which only contains the defender pure strategy that can be used in case j. S_j can be calculated by Eq.(5). Then he can obtain his optimal mixed strategy y_i in this case by solving LP(1) with S = S_j and A = A_i . $y_{È}$ is the collection of the attacker's mixed strategy probability distribution in each case.

3.3 Defender Oracle

The goal of the defender oracle is to find pure strategy that can improve the player's utility, however finding the improving strategy is different between TPD game and TPDIL game. One problem is that the solution generated by the defender oracle in DO-TPD may be pointless in a specific leakage case. For example, if the attacker observes the case t_{iu} , then a defender pure strategy that doesn't contain the leak point i will be meaningless. We need to add particular restrains in defender oracle to discard these invalid solution. Given a specific leakage case j and the related attacker's strategy space A_j , the best defender oracle in DO-TPDIL(denoted as bestOD) will solve the defender best oracle in DO-TPD[5] (denoted as TPD-*bestOD*) as the MILP (7).

The variables in this MILP have the same meaning with the TPD-bestOD, and the idea is that defender chooses an allocation which can overlap the attacker's subgraphs as much as possible. I is an 0-1 indicator, $I = 1$ when case j is terrorist i leaks as being monitored(i.e., t_{iu} case), and this ensures that the strategy can be used in case j to against the specific attacker A_j , and $I = 0$ is on the contrary(i.e., t_{iv} case). If there is no leakage, the defender will call LP(7) by removing the last restrain, and setting $A_j = A_0$.

$$
\begin{aligned}
\max \quad & -\sum\nolimits_{A \in A_j} (1 - Z_A) y_A P(A) & \\
s.j. \quad & z_A \le \sum_{u \in V} A_u S_u & \forall A \in A_j \\
& \sum_{u \in V} A_u S_u \le R & \\
& S_u \in \{0,1\}, z_A \in [0,1] & \\
& S_i = I & \qquad (7)
\end{aligned}
$$

Unfortunately, the bestOD problem is still NP-hard, because the process still has to search the whole network to find the best response, including or excluding the leak point has a negligible effect on network scale. To speed up the oracle process, we propose a fast oracle called betterOD. The idea is finding some sub-optimal("better") solutions to meet the criterion $U_d(S,y) > U_d(x,y)$ in each leakage case, while it can be solved within much less time than bestOD process. The bestOD process only needs to be called when betterOD fails to find an answer.

3.4 Better OD

In our betterOD algorithm, we need to use the algorithm TPD-betterOD presented by Wang et al. [5]. The TPD-betterOD algorithm provides us an approach to find defender's sub-optimal strategy given attacker's mixed strategy y. Notice that, the defender searches the whole network to find pure strategy depends on attacker's mixed strategy y in TPD-*betterOD*. We add C as the candidate nodes range instead of the whole network to prevent pointless strategies which break the leakage precondition.

Our betterOD is shown in Algorithm 3. Firstly, the betterOD algorithm sets the candidate nodes, if the node leaks as case t_{iv} , then betterOD will restrict the candidate nodes as $C = V \setminus \{i\}$ to prevent meaningless strategies in lines 2~3. Secondly, betterOD calls TPD-betterOD to search strategy by selecting vertices that bring the maximum marginal utility in a greedy way. Finally, in t_{iu} case, if the strategies obtained from line 4 don't contain the leak point i , betterOD will discard these strategy and return the rest part.

Algorithm 3 *betterOD* (x, y, i)

1. $S_{better} = \emptyset, C = V$
2. if *i is leaked as* t_{iv} then
3. $C = C \setminus \{i\}$
4. S_{better} = TPD-*betterOD*(x, y, C)
5. if i *is leaked as* t_{iu} then
6. for all $S \in S_{better}$ do
7. if *S doesn't contains leak point i* then
8. $S_{better} = S_{better} \setminus \{S\}$
9. return S_{better}

3.5 Attacker Oracle(AO)

The attacker oracle algorithm for TPDIL works in the same way with DO-TPD. In each leakage case i , the attacker only considers the defender's probability distribution x_i after observing t_{iu} or t_{iv} . Then he will call the attacker better oracle to find improving strategies, if fail, he will turn to the attacker best oracle. The algorithm detail we refers to [5].

4. Experimental Evaluation

We evaluate the performance of our approach through extensive evaluations. All LP and MILP computations are solved by CPLEX 12.60.

All computations are run on a machine with 2.2 GHZ Intel qual core CPU and 8 GB memory. The parameters keep the same with [5]. All the experiments are run with the ADIL model. The leak point is random chosen from the network, and the $p_i = 0.5$ unless otherwise stated. All the results are sampled over 20 times.

Our experiments use the following three types of network: (i) Random trees (RT), where each new node is connected to a random picked existing node. (ii) Erdős-Rényi random graphs(ER(V, M)) [11], where M links are randomly assigned between all possible vertices pairs, we use the networks with $M = V$ labelled as ER(1). (iii) Barabási-Albert scale-free network(BA(k))[12], where each new node is connected to k existing nodes with the proportional to the edges the existing node already has, we use BA scale-free network with parameters $k = 1$ labeld as BA(1). By default, the capability of each vertex t_v is randomly chosen in [1, 5], and the network externality measure $d = 0.1$.

4.1 Scale-Up Analysis

In Figure. 2, we test our algorithm in different network. Results show that our algorithm can help to reduce the complexity of solving the problem. The naive FullLP's runtime increases in an exponentially way, and it runs out of memory when the network size is about 20. Our approach can help the player to solve the problem with the network size of 40.

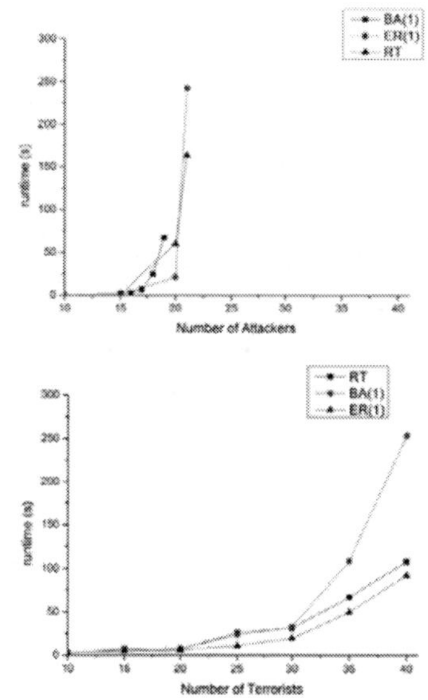

Figure 1. Runtime in different networks: (a)FullLP (b) DO-TPDIL approach.

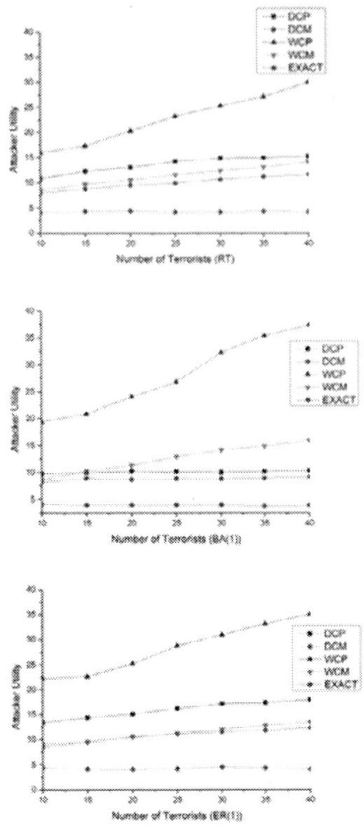

Figure 2. Attacker utility against different defenders (a) RT network, (b) BA(1) network, (c) ER network

4.2 Solution Quality Analysis

We use the following centrality measure based heuristic baselines proposed by [5] to evaluate the solution quality of our approach: (i) DCP: defender only monitors the vertices with top R degree values. (ii) DCM: a defender mixed strategy where the vertex marginal coverage probability is normalized degree centrality; (iii) WCP: defender only monitors vertices with top R node capability values. (iv) WCM: a defender mixed strategy where the vertex marginal coverage probability is normalized weight centrality. All the mixed strategies are sampled by Comb Sampling algorithm[8]. The result by our approach is denoted by line EXACT.

In Figure 2. , we compare the solution quality obtained from our approach and other 4 heuristic baselines. Results show that the solution obtained from the heuristic baselines performs badly in information leakage model, the performance becomes worse with the network size growing up. The defender utility from our approach can remain stable as the network grows, and the value indicates our approach's effectiveness. In all the three network, the mixed strategy (DCM, WCM) always performs better than the corresponding pure strategy.

This shows the necessary of using randomized mixed strategy in TPD game even with the consideration of information leakage.

5. Conclusion

In this study, we considered partial information leakage in Terrorist Plot Detect games. We focused on the modeling and the computation of the new game to help defender decreasing the loss caused by leakage. We proposed an efficient double oracle framework to speed up finding efficient strategy, instead of searching strategy from the whole strategy space. The experimental results show the feasibility and efficiency of our approach.

Acknowledgment

This paper is supported by NSFC under grant numbers: 61272173, 61572095. Corresponding authors: Cheng Guo: guocheng@dlut.edu.cn, Kun Lu: lukun@dlut.edu.cn.

References

[1] Edward Snowden: Leaks that exposed US spy programme. http://www.bbc.com/news/world-us-canada-23123964

[2] J. Pita, M. Jain, J. Marecki, F. Ordóñez, C. Portway, M. Tambe, et al., "Deployed ARMOR protection: the application of a game theoretic model for security at the Los Angeles International Airport," in Proceedings of the 7th international joint conference on Autonomous agents and multiagent systems: industrial track, 2008, pp. 125-132.

[3] J. Tsai, C. Kiekintveld, F. Ordonez, M. Tambe, and S. Rathi, "IRIS-a tool for strategic security allocation in transportation networks," in AAMAS, 2009, pp. 37-44.

[4] B. An, F. Ordóñez, M. Tambe, E. Shieh, R. Yang, C. Baldwin, et al., "A deployed quantal response-based patrol planning system for the US Coast Guard," Interfaces, vol. 43, pp. 400-420, 2013.

[5] Z. Wang, Y. Yin, and B. An, "Computing Optimal Monitoring Strategy for Detecting Terrorist Plots," in AAAI, 2016, pp. 637-643.

[6] Q. Guo, B. An, Y. Vorobeychik, L. Tran-Thanh, J. Gan, and C. Miao, "Coalitional security games," in Proceedings of the 2016 International Conference on Autonomous Agents & Multiagent Systems, 2016, pp. 159-167.

[7] H. Xu, A. X. Jiang, A. Sinha, Z. Rabinovich, S. Dughmi, and M. Tambe, "Security games with information leakage: modeling and computation," presented at the Proceedings of the 24th International Conference on Artificial Intelligence, Buenos Aires, Argentina, 2015.

[8] J. Tsai, Z. Yin, J.-y. Kwak, D. Kempe, C.

Kiekintveld, and M. Tambe, "Urban security: Game-theoretic resource allocation in networked physical domains," in National Conference on Artificial Intelligence (AAAI), 2010.

[9] H. B. McMahan, G. J. Gordon, and A. Blum, "Planning in the presence of cost functions controlled by an adversary," in ICML, 2003, pp. 536-543.

[10] Z. Yin, D. Korzhyk, C. Kiekintveld, V. Conitzer, and M. Tambe, "Stackelberg vs. Nash in security games: Interchangeability, equivalence, and uniqueness," in Proceedings of the 9th International Conference on Autonomous Agents and Multiagent Systems: volume 1-Volume 1, 2010, pp. 1139-1146.

[11] P. Erdös and A. Rényi, "On random graphs, I," Publicationes Mathematicae (Debrecen), vol. 6, pp. 290-297, 1959.

[12] A. L. Barabási and R. Albert, "Emergence of scaling in random networks," science, vol. 286, pp. 509-512, 1999.

Set-Valued Stochastic Equation with Set-Valued Square Integrable Martingale

Jun-Gang Li [1] , Shi-Qing Zheng [2]

[1]*Department of Statistics North China University of Technology, Beijing 100144, China.*
[2]*Department of Statistics North China University of Technology, Beijing 100144, China.*
[1]*jgli@ncut.edu.cn,* [2] *1416922582 @qq.com*

Abstract: In this paper, we shall introduce the stochastic integral of a stochastic process with respect to set-valued square integrable martingale. Then we shall give the Aumann integral measurable theorem, and give the set-valued stochastic Lebesgue integral and set-valued square integrable martingale integral equation. The existence and uniqueness of solution to set-valued stochastic integral equation are proved. The discussion will be useful in optimal control and mathematical finance in psychological factors.

1. Introduction

Set-valued theory is used in optimal control(cf.[1]), mathematical finance(cf. [2]), fixed point theory(cf. [3]). Set-valued and fuzzy set-valued theory can be used to account for psychological factors(cf.[4,5]).In [6], stochastic control problems are discussed by stochastic integral with respect to set-valued square integral martingales. M. Malinowski *et al.* discussed the set-valued stochastic integral driven by semi-martingale and the set-valued stochastic differential equations driven by semi-martingale in [7]. J. Li *et al.* discussed set-valued stochastic Lebesgue integral and set-valued stochastic differential equaton in [8,9,10]. Puri and Ralescu defined fuzzy set-valued martingales and proved convergence theorems of fuzzy set-valued martingales in [11]. J. Li *et al.* discussed the space of fuzzy set-valued square integrable martingales in [12] and fuzzy set-valued stochastic Lebesgue integral in [13].

In this paper, we shall give the set-valued stochastic integral equation :

$$F(t)=F(0)+(L)\int_0^t b(s,F(s))ds+(M)\int_0^t \sigma(s,F(s))dG(s)$$

the first integral is set-valued stochastic Lebesgue integral (see [9,10]), the second integral is set-valued square integrable martingale integral (see [6]). Aumann integral measurable theorem of the second integral shall be given. The existence and uniqueness of the solution to the equation shall be proved.

We organize our paper as follows: in Section 2, we shall introduce some necessary notations, definitions, and results about set-valued stochastic variables and martingales.

Furthermore, we shall give the Aumann integral measurable theorem. In Section 3, we shall give the set-valued stochastic integral equation with respect to set-valued square integrable martingale, and prove the existence and uniqueness of the solution to the set-valued stochastic integral equation.

2. Preliminary on Set-Valued Random Variables and Martingales

Throughout this paper, assume that $(\Omega, \mathcal{A}, \mu)$ is a complete probability space, the σ-field filtration $\{\mathcal{A}_t: t\in I\}$ satisfies the usual conditions (i.e. Containing all nullsets, non-decreasing and right continuous), $I=[0,T]$ with $T>0$, R is the set of all real numbers, N is the set of all natural numbers, R^d is the d-dimensional Euclidean space with usual norm $\|\times\|$, $\mathfrak{B}(E)$ is the Borel field of the space E. Let $K(R^d)$ be the family of all nonempty, closed subsets of R^d. Let $K_c(R^d)$ (resp. $K_k(R^d)$, $K_{kc}(R^d)$) be the family of all nonempty closed convex (resp. compact, compact convex) subsets of R^d. For any $x\hat{\text{I}}\ R^d$, A,B are nonempty subsets of R^d, define the distance between x and A,

$$d(x,A)=\inf_{y\in A}\|x-y\|,$$

$$A+B=\{a+b:a\in A,b\in B\},$$

$$A\ominus B=\{x\in R^d:x+B\subset A\}.$$

The *Hausdorff metric* on $K(R^d)$ is defined as

$$d_H(A,B) = \max\{\sup_{a \in A} d(a,B), \sup_{b \in B} d(b,A)\}$$

for $A, B \in K(R^d)$. For $B \in K(R^d)$, define

$$\| B \|_K = d_H(0,B) = \sup_{a \in B} \| a \|.$$

If $F : (\Omega, \mathcal{A}) \to K(R^d)$ satisfies that for any open set $O \subset R^d$, $F^{-1}(O) = \{\omega \in \Omega : F(\omega) \cap O \neq \Phi\} \in \mathcal{A}$, then F is called $\mathcal{A}$-measurable (or a set-valued random variable, random set, multivalued function.).

Let $f = \{f(t), \mathcal{A}_t, t \in I\}$ be a R^d-valued adapted stochastic process. Let $L^p[\Omega, \mathcal{A}_t, \mu, R^d]$ be the set of R^d-valued $\mathcal{A}_t$-measurable random variable x with $E[\| x \|^p] < \infty$ $(1 \le p < \infty)$, write $\| x \|_p = [E[\| x \|^p]]^{1/p}$.

Let $S_F^p(\mathcal{A}) = \{f \in L^p[\Omega, \mathcal{A}, \mu : R^d] : f(\omega) \in F(\omega), a.e.\ \omega \in \Omega\}$

For short, denoted by S_F^p. A set-valued random variable $F : \Omega \to K(R^d)$ is called *integrable* if S_F^1 is non-empty. F is L^p-bounded if and only if the real-valued random variable $\| F \|_K \in L^p[\Omega; R]$ If F is L^1-bounded, then F is also called *integrably bounded*. Let $L^p[\Omega, \mathcal{F}, \mu, K(R^d)]$ be the family of all $K(R^d)$-valued L^p-bounded $\mathcal{F}$-measurable random variables. Similarly, we have notations $L^p[\Omega, \mathcal{F}, \mu, K_c(R^d)]$, $L^p[\Omega, \mathcal{F}, \mu, K_{kc}(R^d)]$, $L^p[\Omega, K(R^d)]$ and so on. A set-valued stochastic process $F = \{F(t), \mathcal{A}_t, t \in I\}$ is called a set-valued martingale if

(i) $F = \{F(t), \mathcal{A}_t, t \in I\}$ is adapted and for any $t \in I$, $F(t)$ is L^1-bounded;

(ii) for any $t \ge s$, $t \in I$, $E[F(t) | \mathcal{A}_s] = F(s)$, a.e. (μ).

A set-valued martingale $F = \{F(t), \mathcal{A}_t, t \in I\}$ is call-ed square integrable, if $\sup_{t \in I} E[\| F(t) \|_K^2] < \infty$.

Denote $CMS(F)$ as the set of R^d-valued continuous martingale selections of set-valued square integrable martingale F.

Concerning more notations, definitions and more results of set-valued random variable, set-valued martingales, readers could refer to [6,14].

Definition (cf.[6]) Assume $F = \{F(t), \mathcal{A}_t, t \in I\}$ is a separable square integrable set-valued martingale and for any fixed $\omega \in \Omega$, $F(\omega, t)$ is lower semicontinuous with $F(0) = 0$ a.e., g is a predictable bounded stochastic process. For any $\omega \in \Omega$, $t \in I$, define

$$(A)\int_0^t g(s,w)dF(s,w)$$
$$= \{\int_0^t g(s,w)df(s,w) : f \in CMS(F)\},$$

then $(A)\int_0^t g(s,w)dF(s,w)$ is said to be the *Aumann type stochastic integral* of g with respect to the set-valued square integrable martingale F.

By Therom 4.4 and Therom 4.7 in [6], we have the following Aumann integral measurable theorem:

Theorem 1 Assume that $F = \{F(t), \mathcal{A}_t, t \in I\}$ is a separable square integrable set-valued martingale and for any fixed $\omega \in \Omega$, $F(w,t)$ is lower semicontinuous with $F(0) = 0$ a.e., g is a predictable bounded stochastic process. For any $\omega \in \Omega$, $t \in I$, we have that

$$cl\{(A)\int_0^t g(s,w)dF(s,w)\}$$
$$= cl\{\int_0^t g(s,w)df(s,w) : f \in CMS(F)\}$$

is a set-valued random variable.

The above theorem is useful to discuss the theory of Aumann integral, etc.

3. Set-Valued Stochastic Integral Equation

We consider the following set-valued stochastic integral equation

$$F(t) = F(0) + (L)\int_0^t b(s, F(s))ds + (M)\int_0^t \sigma(s, F(s))dG(s), \quad (1)$$

Where for any $t \in I$, $F \in L^2(K(R^d))$ with initial condition $F(0)$ being an L^2-bounded set-valued random variable, $b : I \times K(R^d) \to K(R^d)$ is measurable, $\sigma : I \times K(R^d) \to R^d \otimes R^m$ is bounded predictable measurable, $G(s)$ is a set-valued square integral martingale. $(L)\int_0^t b(s, F(s))ds$ is set-valued stochastic Lebesgue integral (see [9]), $(M)\int_0^t \sigma(s, F(s))dG(s)$ is stochastic integral with respect to set-valued square integral martingale (see Definition 4.5 in [6]).

Theorem 2 Assume that $b(t,F), \sigma(t,F)$ satisfy the following conditions:

(1) Linear bound condition:

$$\| b(t,F)\|^2 + \| \sigma(t,F)\|^2 \leq \alpha^2(1+\| F\|_K^2);$$

(2) Lipschitz continuous condition:

$$\|b(t,F_1(t)) - b(t,F_2(t))\| + \|\sigma(t,F_1(t)) - \sigma(t,F_2(t))\| \leq \alpha\, d_H(F_1(t),F_2(t))$$

where $\alpha > 0$ is a constant;

(3) Set-valued integral inequality:

$$Ed_H^2\left(\int_0^t \sigma(s,F_1(s))dG_s, \int_0^t \sigma(s,F_2(s))dG_s\right) \leq E\int_0^t d_H^2(F_1(s),F_2(s))ds$$

Then for any $F(0) \in L^2(K(R^d))$, there exists a unique solution to equation (1).

Proof: First, it is obviously the existence of b,σ which satisfies (1),(2),(3).

If $F(t) \in L^2(K(R^d))$, for $\forall t \in I$, then

$$E\| b(t,F(t))\|_K^2 + E\| \sigma(t,F(t))\|^2 \leq \alpha^2(1+E\| F\|_K^2).$$

Without loss of generality, assume that $b \in L^2(K(R^d))$, $\sigma \in L^2(R^d \times R^m)$.

Step 1. $F_0(t) = F(0)$,

$$F_{n+1}(t) = F(0) + \int_0^t b(s,F_n(s))ds + \int_0^t \sigma(s,F_n(s))dG_s, n \geq 0$$

We shall prove that for any $n \geq 0$, F_n satisfies:

(a) $\quad F_n \in L^2(K(R^d))$, for $\forall t \in I$

(b) $\quad \lim_{s \to t} Ed_H^2(F_n(t),F_n(s)) = 0.$

For $n=0$, it is obviously right. Suppose that F_n has properties $(a),(b)$ for any fixed n, we shall prove so does F_{n+1}.

Let $Y(t) := \int_0^t b(s_1,F_n(s_1))ds_1$ by Theorem 3.6 in [9], (a) holds to $Y(t)$.

$$Ed_H^2(Y(t),Y(s))$$
$$= Ed_H^2\left(cl(Y(s)+\int_s^t b(s_1,F_n(s_1))ds_1), Y(s)\right)$$
$$\leq Ed_H^2\left(\int_s^t b(s_1,F_n(s_1))ds_1, 0\right)$$
$$= E\left\| \int_s^t b(s_1,F_n(s_1))ds_1 \right\|_K^2$$

By the Linear bound condition (1) and norm property of set-valued Lebesgue integral, it satisfies (β)

Let $Z(t) := \int_0^t \sigma(s_1,F_n(s_1))dG_{s_1}$ It is obviously that (a) holds.

$$Ed_H^2(Z(t),Z(s))$$
$$= Ed_H^2\left(\int_0^t \sigma(s_1,F_n(s_1))dG_{s_1}, \int_0^s \sigma(s_1,F_n(s_1))dG_{s_1}\right)$$
$$= Ed_H^2\left(\int_0^s \sigma(s_1,F_n(s_1))ds_1 + \left(\int_0^t \sigma(s_1,F_n(s_1))dG_{s_1} \ominus \int_0^s \sigma(s_1,F_n(s_1))dG_{s_1}\right), \int_0^s \sigma(s_1,F_n(s_1))dG_{s_1}\right)$$
$$\leq Ed_H^2\left(\int_0^t \sigma(s_1,F_n(s_1))dG_{s_1} \ominus \int_0^s \sigma(s_1,F_n(s_1))dG_{s_1}, 0\right)$$
$$\leq Ed_H^2\left(\int_s^t \sigma(s_1,F_n(s_1))dG_{s_1}, 0\right)$$

By Theorem 1 and Theorem 4.7 in [6], the set-valued integral $\int_s^t \sigma(s_1,F_n(s_1))dG_{s_1}$ is represented by Aumann integral.

Therefore,

$$\lim_{s \to t} \int_s^t \sigma(s_1,F_n(s_1))dG_{s_1} = \{0\}, \text{ a. e..}$$

Thus, we have $\lim_{s \to t} Ed_H^2(Z(t),Z(s)) = 0.$

Step 2. Now we shall prove that F_n convergences to F.

Let

$$F_0(t) = F(0),$$
$$F_{n+1}(t) = F(t_0) + \int_0^t b(s,F_n(s))ds + \int_0^t \sigma(s,F_n(s))dG_s, n \geq 0$$

We have

$$d_H(F_1(t),F_0(t))$$
$$= d_H\left(F_0(t) + \int_0^t b(s,F_0(s))ds + \int_0^t \sigma(s,F_0(s))dG_s, F_0(t)\right)$$
$$\leq d_H\left(\int_0^t b(s,F_0(s))ds, 0\right) + d_H\left(\int_0^t \sigma(s,F_0(s))dG_s, 0\right)$$
$$= \left\| \int_0^t b(s,F_0(s))ds \right\|_K + \left\| \int_0^t \sigma(s,F_0(s))dG_s \right\|_K$$

For the first part, we have

$$E\left\| \int_0^t b(s,F_0(s))ds \right\|_K^2 \leq E\left(\int_0^t \| f(s,F_0(s)) \|_K ds\right)^2$$
$$\leq tE\left(\int_0^t \| b(s,F_0(s)) \|_K^2 ds\right)$$
$$= t\int_0^t E\| b(s,F_0(s)) \|_K^2 ds$$
$$\leq t\alpha^2 \int_0^t (1+E\| F_0(s) \|_K^2)ds$$
$$\leq A^2 t,$$

For the second part, by inequality (3), we have

$$E\|\int_0^t \sigma(s,F_0(s))dG_s\|_K^2$$
$$= Ed_H^2(\int_0^t \sigma(s,F_0(s))dG_s,0)$$
$$\leq E\int_0^t d_H^2(F_0(s),0)ds$$
$$= tE\|F(0)\|_K^2$$

Let $B^2 = E\|F(0)\|_K^2$,

$$Ed_H^2(F_1(0),F_0(t))$$
$$\leq 2E\|\int_0^t b(s,F_0(s))ds\|_K^2 + 2E\|\int_0^t \sigma(s,F_0(s))dG_s\|_K^2$$
$$\leq 2(A+B)^2 t.$$

By the same way, we have

$$Ed_H^2(F_{n+1}(t),F_n(t))$$
$$= E(d_H(F(0)+\int_0^t b(s,F_n(s))ds+\int_0^t \sigma(s,F_n(s))dG_s,F(0)$$
$$+\int_0^t b(s,F_{n-1}(s))ds+\int_0^t \sigma(s,F_{n-1}(s))dG_s$$
$$\leq Ed_H(F(0),F(0))+Ed_H(\int_0^t b(s,F_n(s))ds,\int_0^t b(s,F_{n-1}(s))ds)$$
$$+Ed_H(\int_0^t \sigma(s,F_n(s))dG_s,\int_0^t \sigma(s,F_{n-1}(s))dG_s)$$
$$\leq 2Ed_H^2(\int_0^t b(s,F_n(s))ds,\int_0^t b(s,F_{n-1}(s))ds)$$
$$+2Ed_H^2(\int_0^t \sigma(s,F_n(s))dG_s,\int_0^t \sigma(s,F_{n-1}(s))dG_s)$$
$$\leq 2tE\int_0^t d_H^2(b(s,F_n(s)),b(s,F_{n-1}(s)))ds$$
$$+2E\int_0^t d_H^2(F_n(s),F_{n-1}(s))ds$$
$$\leq 2ta^2E\int_0^t d_H^2(F_n(s),F_{n-1}(s))ds$$
$$+2E\int_0^t d_H^2(F_n(s),F_{n-1}(s))ds$$
$$= 2(ta^2+1)E\int_0^t d_H^2(F_n(s),F_{n-1}(s))ds$$

Iterating the above process, we get

$$Ed_H^2(F_{n+1}(t),F_n(t)) \leq 2^{n+1}(ta^2+1)^{2n}(A+B)^2\frac{t^{n+1}}{(n+1)!}$$

i.e.

$$\Delta_n(t) = E\sup_{s\in[0,t]} d_H^2(F_{n+1}(s),F_n(s))$$
$$\leq 2^{n+1}(ta^2+1)^{2n}(A+B)^2\frac{t^{n+1}}{(n+1)!}$$

Thus,

$$\Delta_n(T) \leq 2^{n+1}(Ta^2+1)^{2n}(A+B)^2\frac{T^{n+1}}{(n+1)!}.$$

Therefore, we have

$$\sum_{n=1}^{\infty}\Delta_n(T) < \infty.$$

This ensures the existence of the strong solution.

Step 3. Let F, G be two solutions to equation (1). The uniqueness of the solution is the same to the proof of the existence.

Remark 3 Furthermore, fuzzy set-valued martingale integral, fuzzy set-valued stochastic Lebesgue integral [13], and fuzzy set-valued stochastic integral would be useful in the area.

Acknowledgment

The authors would like to thank reviewers for their valuable comments. This work was supported by youqing NCUT-XN132.

References

[1] M. Kisielewicz, Differential Inclusions and Optimal Control, Kluwer Academic Publishers, 1991.

[2] I. Karatzas, Lectures on the Mathematics of Finance, American Mathematical Society, Providence, RI, 1997.

[3] A. Fryszkowski, Fixed Point Theory for Decomposable Sets, Kluwer Academic Publishers, 2004.

[4] S. Li and L. Guan, "Fuzzy set-valued Gaussian process and Brownian motion, " Information Sciences, vol.177, pp. 3251–3259, August 2007.

[5] J. Li and J. Wang, "On a fluid queue with a fuzzy set-valued Gaussian process input, " unpublished.

[6] S. Li, J. Li and X. Li, "Stochastic integral w.r.t. set -valued square integrable martingale, " Journal of Mathematical Analysis and Applications vol.370, pp. 659-671, October 2010.

[7] M. Malinowski, "On a new set-valued stochastic integral with respect to semimartingales and its applications," Journal of Mathematical Analysis and Applications vol.408, pp.669-680, Decembe 2013.

[8] J. Li S. Li and Y. Ogura, "Strong solution of Ito type set-valued stochastic differential equation, " Acta Mathematica Sinica, English Series, vol.26, pp. 1739-1748, September 2010.

[9] J. Li and S. Li, "Set-valued stochastic Lebesgue integral and representation theorems, International Journal of Computational Intelligence Systems, " vol.1, pp. 177-187, May 2008.

[10] J. Li and S. Li, "Ito type set-valued stochastic differential equation, " Journal of Uncertain Systems, vol.3, pp.52-63, February 2009.

[11] M. L. Puri and D. A. Ralescu, "Convergence theorem for fuzzy martingales," Journal of Mathematical Analysis and Applications vol.160, pp.107-122, September 1991.

[12] J. Li, S. Li and Y. Xue, "The Space of Fuzzy Set-Valued Square Integrable Martingales, " IEEE

DOI: 10.1051/itmconf/20171203002

International Conference on Fuzzy Systems, pp. 872-876, August 2009.

[13] J. Li and J. Wang, "Fuzzy set-valued stochastic Lebesgue integral," Fuzzy Sets and Systems, vol.200, pp.48-64, August 2012.

[14] S. Li, Y. Ogura and V. Kreinovich, Limit Theorems and Applications of Set-Valued and Fuzzy Set-Valued Random Variables, Kluwer Academic Publishers, 2002.

Low Cost and High Concurrency ID Maker in Distributed Environment

Kan Yao [1], Hu-Xuan Ni [2], Yuan Wang [3], Jing Tuo [4], Yun-Feng Li[5], Jun-Jie Ding[6]

[1]*State Grid Hubei Electric Power Research Institute, Wuhan, China*
[2]*State Grid Hubei Electric Power Research Institute, Wuhan, China*
[3]*State Grid Hubei Electric Power Research Institute, Wuhan, China*
[4]*State Grid Hubei Electric Power Research Institute, Wuhan, China*
[5]*State Grid Hubei Electric Power Research Institute, Wuhan, China*
[6]*State Grid Hubei Electric Power Research Institute, Wuhan, China*
[1] *351784661@qq.com*, [2]*312929323@qq.com*, [3]*365054779@qq.com*, [4]*77191928@qq.com*, [5]*460651211@qq.com*, [6] *10390449@qq.com*

Abstract: In many practical computer engineering projects, will use the ID as a unique identifier. Many methods to generate ID, but it is not easy to choose a cost-effective solution. Through the improved ID method to generate common defects, ID manufacturing is to build a high performance and low cost, for rapid generation of distributed only under the environment of ID.

1. Introduction

Architecture of a web system, the system is the only ID is often encountered problems, in order to adapt to the needs of different scenarios and performance requirements, the common method of generating ID has the following:

1.1 Relational Self Growth Field Generation ID

This is the way, the most common use of the database, the database only. The code is relatively simple, each increment to lock field, expensive. ID digital natural sorting, paging and sorting of the results is very helpful. But the drawbacks in the performance is not up to the requirements of the situation, it is difficult to expand in a single data or read and write separate or more from a major case, only one main library can be generated, the risk of a single point of failure.

1.2 UUID

The use of machine information and time stamp, a theory on the generation of the only global ID. by numberandletter, string length generally in about 32. Has the advantages of rapid, simple. But the disadvantages are obvious: no ranking, cannot guarantee the increasing trend. With UUID as the primary storage, query efficiency low. The storage space is relatively large, if it is a massive database, you need to consider the problem of storage. The amount of data transmission is also great, UUID and reading is not intuitive.

1.3 REDIS

REDIS is a memory database, ID increment operation more quickly, when the traditional relational database since the increased pressure becomes larger, sometimes will take REDIS to generate ID. but when there is no REDIS system, also need the introduction of new components, increasing the complexity of the system. To encoding and the workload is relatively. But there is a single point of failure and the cost of network communication, redis is usually used in the form of a list in the data cache, landing the advantage is not obvious, the need for additional open disk synchronous refresh function, in order to guarantee the redis after the restart of ID only.

1.4 U Se Zookeeper To Generate Unique ID

Zookeeper mainly through the znode data version to generate a serial number, can generate 32 bit and 64 bit data version number, the client can use the version number as a unique serial number. This method is mainly rely on the zookeeper to generate a unique ID, and multistep call API, if the competition is high, need to consider the use of.Zookeeper distributed lock in a production environment requires at least three machines, in order to ensure that a process can be down. And each ID needs network communication, each request time at the MS level.

In summary, the common method of manufacturing ID will frequently produce expensive network communications, network cost. Relational database and redis are single point failure problem obviously. While the use of zookeeper cluster, in order to ensure the high availability of cluster server, you need at least three or more expensive machines, in order to solve the above problems., reduce network communication, improve the clustering performance, then defines a new ID machine, the following named id_maker.

2. System Architecture

Wherever In order to reduce the network communication as much as possible, we can get a batch of ID after the cache to the corresponding machine, so as to avoid the distribution of ID to store ID machine request. Then when the ID is fast enough, then get ahead of another batch of ID, added to the original cache architecture as shown Are in figure1below

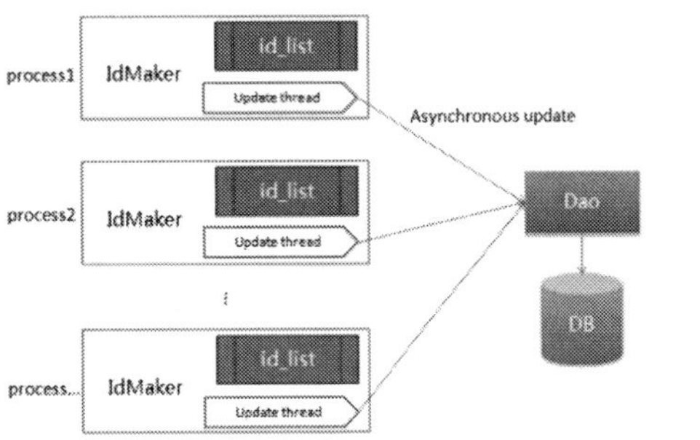

Figure1. nnotation Dao: Data Access Object DB: Database.

I id_list is used to store the list of Id blocks obtained from Dao, most of which are discontinuous between blocks and blocks

There is a unified update thread behind each use process, if the number of id_list in ID is less than 10% of each allocation depth of the configuration, the new block will be filled

E Dao is used to assign each type of manufacturer from the DB global unique ID list block, mainly responsible for the implementation of SQL (UPDATE Fid=Fid Falloc_size WHERE Fsect=xxx;)It's features like Michi Ko, each of the types used have a pool, each ID will be filled with a large piece of water level, when the water level is insufficient to update the water level

3. Unified Configuration

As shown in figure 2:

Type: used to distinguish between different business needs

Used id: inform current usage of Id

Block size: each time the size of the block, the configuration determines the height of the water level of each fill. The smaller the value of the business can be configured smaller, equivalent to the appropriate increase in the value of the configuration can be large

Initial size: there will be an initial water level item at the time of the first increase in configuration. When used for initial data entry, do not repeat the existing data

4. Interface Definition and Realization

4.1 Interface Definition Code Is As Follows

Public abstract class IdMaker {public abstract long createId() throws IdException; public int createIdIntSafe() throws IdException;}

Public class IdMakerFactory { public IdMaker getIdMaker(int type);}

4.2 Realization

Pull the ID from the local buffer ID, if the number of the buffer pool is found to be 1/10 of the original, then start the update, fill. If there is no buffer in itself, then directly from the DB (as shown in figure 3):

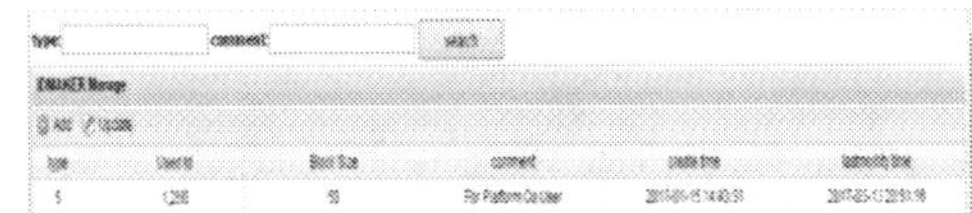

Figure2. configuration

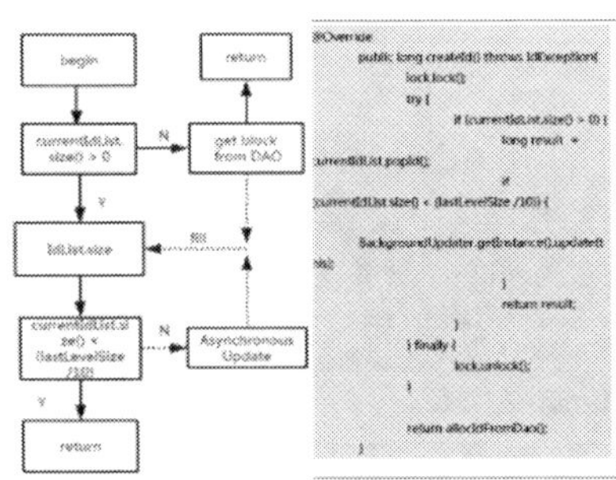

Figure3.

4.3 Database Table Design:

Field name	Field type	Meaning
Fsect	INT	the type of business
Fid	BIGINT	current depth
Falloc_size	INT	each allocation size
Fdesc	VARCHAR(128)	business description
Fcreate_timestamp	INT	create time
Flastmodify_timestamp	INT	last modified time

CREATE TABLE tallocid_bysect (Fsect INT UNSIGNED NOT NULL, // the type of business
Fid BIGINT UNSIGNED NOT NULL DEFAULT 1000// current depth
Falloc_size INT UNSIGNED NOT NULL DEFAULT 500 //each allocation size
Fdesc VARCHAR (128) NOT NULL DEFAULT '', //

business description
Fcreate_timestamp INT NOT NULL DEFAULT 0 // create time
Flastmodify_timestamp INT NOT NULL DEFAULT 0//last modified time
PRIMARY KEY (Fsect)

5. Conclusions

Easy to use, only need to configure different types, can support the needs of a variety of different types of online ID generated.

High availability in MySQL crash case, each machine can be configured with large enough buffer pool. Combined with the rapid MySQL downtime monitoring system, operation and maintenance can be involved in.

Less input resources, only a single MySQL can be carried on the theory of infinite number of types of business infinite number of distribution (depending on the frequency of CPU)

Production speed, no network communication pressure. Every time to get ID is an integer of 1 operation, time-consuming basic for 0

References

[1] [1]Distributed Systems: An Algorithmic Approach, Second Edition (Chapman & Hall/CRC Computer and Information Science Series)

[2] [2]Big Data: A Revolution That Will Transform How We Live, Work, and Think2013-03

[3] [3] Java programming ideas (fourth edition) paperback - June 1, 2007 Shi Er (author), Chen Haopeng (translator)

The Evaluation Method for Operation Efficiency of Equipment System Based on Data Farming and Mining

Zheng Wang

College of Information System and Management, National University of Defense Technology, Changsha, Hunan
joshuakai900901@163.com

Abstract: Through process data and results data resulted from operation efficiency simulation of equipment system, based on information measure criteria, data farming and mining method is used. Final simulation results are provided against specific models and verification is carried out on the internal relationships of equipment system and the effectiveness of equipment tactics capability. In addition, its focus is made on utilizing high-performance calculations, running it in the whole parameter space of models, obtaining a number of effective sample space data, and further analyzing it to find implicit laws and results by Big Data Mining technology and Data Visualization technology, in order to facilitate the problem-oriented system efficiency simulation.

1.Introduction

Evaluation method research for operation efficiency of equipment system is an important part of equipment system demonstration. Due to the complexity of operation efficiency of equipment system, a new challenge is put forward to conventional operation simulation. Data Farming is used to study and analyze new technology of complex system. Data Farming technology provides new technical support for the operation efficiency evaluation of equipment system. On account of evaluation difficulties and features for operation efficiency of equipment system, it presents a new evaluation method for operation efficiency of equipment system based on the combination of Data Farming and Data Mining.

2.Evaluation Difficulties and Features for Operation Efficiency of Equipment System

Coordination operation efficiency evaluation under the joint operation conditions is required to analyze and assess the extent to achieve the target by all kinds of weapons or weapon system during joint operations and various operations [1]. Under the premise of joint operations becoming main operation type increasingly, the research on coordination operation efficiency evaluation has a great significance in the development of military construction and national defense industry, and can be used to overall optimize the use of existing equipment, assist in making military operations plans and decisions and provide a support to make new weapon system requirements and development programs [2] [3]. Besides, it can also support industrial department to do the trade-off research on weapon system improvement and modification [4], analyze the general design parameters of new models, review the system integrated scheme and so on.

The modeling simulation method and standardization research for coordination operation efficiency evaluation of equipment system centers on realistic needs of equipment information reform is also an innovation research platform of military theory to explore new concept and technology of information system operation. Meanwhile, the research is made on efficiency evaluation method of system-to-system confrontation operation requirements adaptive to information conditions, which is the representative core support technology of military complex system [5][6].

Currently, the modeling simulation method and standardization research for coordination operation efficiency evaluation of equipment system mainly consists of two parts: the modeling and simulation research is a more thorough study, but the modeling and simulation for coordination operation efficiency evaluation is a significant and challenging subject, which is a comparative weak part of research. Different from operation mode of a single conventional equipment or equipment system, the presence of operation efficiency of equipment system provides higher requirements for system coordination, mainly including: 1) Information is highly shared. Information share is to maximize the value of entity itself and use information to create new value. 2) Every mission is integrated. Although most time these missions belong to different entities in the system, in essence they are closely related. System is required to fully integrate all missions, in order to perform missions coordinately and smoothly. Just the coupling on the missions makes these entities form a coordination system. 3) All kinds of resources are deployed and optimized. As long as the system implements information share and mission integration, all kinds of resources in the system can break through various barriers and obstacles, in order to achieve a common target under unified management and coordination.

Multiple combat units perform combat missions jointly, which constitute a typical coordination system. Subject to the influence of various uncertainty factors of battlefield environment and the complexity of fleet size, the coordination operation process of multiple combat units is a complicated control problem, whose complexity mainly reflects the following aspects: the modeling complexity caused by the diversity of combat units and combat environment; the combination complexity caused by the amount growth of equipment and targets; the distribution complexity of combat units and the human complexity in multiple combat units. Relative to conventional operation simulation, operation efficiency evaluation of equipment system is more complicated and difficult. In addition, during the operation efficiency evaluation of equipment system, measurement is made qualitatively on the coordination between combat units, the emotive factors between command and control staff, etc.

However, in the conventional operation simulation, generation of cases is relatively difficult, the amount of available sample space is limited, it is helpful to verify the capacity of equipment system, but there is a big gap in the whole efficiency comprehensiveness of equipment system.

Therefore, there is a difficulty for the conventional operation simulation in the operation efficiency evaluation adaptive to equipment system. In recent years, constantly maturing data farming technology can generate a number of reliable sample data by farming data, while data mining technology is used to mine potential information in the database [7]. The combination of data farming technology and data mining technology can copy with the complexity in the operation efficiency evaluation of equipment system to some extent.

3.Generation of System Simulation Sample Space Based on Data Farming Technology

In 1996, Doctor Alfred G. Brandstein and Doctor Gary E. Horne proposed the data farming technology. It is a new problem-based technology that can provide effective solutions against problems of interest to user. The development of data farming technology is based on the following technical conditions:

a) The development and improvement based on agent model provides the possibility to master key elements during operations;

b) With the enhancement of computer capability, lots of analytical data can be produced;

c) The data organization, analysis and visualization capability is improved.

After Doctor Alfred G. Brandstein and Doctor Gary E. Horne developed the data farming technology, it was further complemented and improved by many scholars. It is now generally believed that the data farming technology mainly contains Fertilizing, Cultivating, Planting, Harvesting, Regenerating, etc.

a) Fertilizing: Through mainly communicating with military researchers and associated experts, analysis is made on how to grasp some key elements during operations, but these elements used to be ignored, such as morale, command capability, intuition, etc.

b) Cultivating: Military experts put forward many views on key elements under specific battlefield environment and these views need to be analyzed and applied;

c) Planting: Expertise is used in the establishment of models, meanwhile the models are run, and the elements of interest are investigated and analyzed in a wide variable space;

d) Harvesting: Data generated by running models are collected, meanwhile some new technologies are developed and used to analyze these data;

e) Regenerating: On the basis of explaining and analyzing the farming results, next data farming is done under the guide of analysis results.

Above steps influence each other and have reference to each other, which form a whole data farming process, as shown in Figure 1.

Core concept of data farming is that through repeated calculation and constant feedback loop, a wide operation variable analysis space is obtained, in which user can excavate for answers to concerned problems. Moreover, in the variable analysis space, data farming especially attaches importance to the processing of outlier, and emphasizes the exploration of some key problems by the analysis of outlier. Above features are main differences between data farming technology and general operation simulation technology.

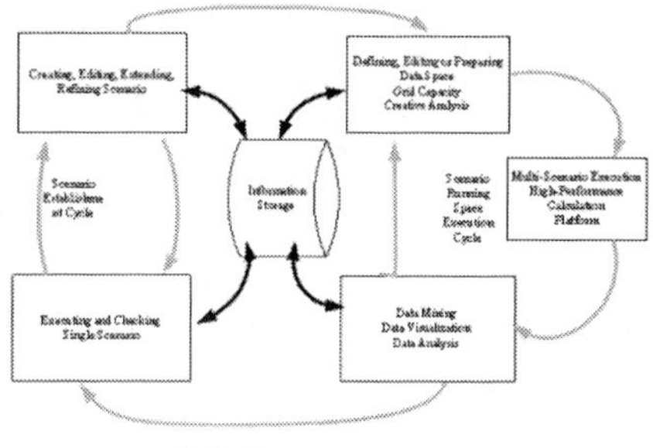

Fig. 1: Data Farming Process

Data farming is a reproductive method based on the problem analysis, i.e. the problem-based repeated train and data acquisition and analysis. This method can generate a lot of acceptable approximate values that are effective to answer studied problems. Data farming is not to use a specific model to give final answers, but to study the possibility space of answers to problems from a holistic perspective, and to transform conventional analysis methods and research ideas. In essence, it is to use high-performance calculations, run it in the whole parameter space of models, and gain hidden clues that cannot be obtained directly. The basic idea is to generate as much information as possible in the area of concern, use visualization, data mining and other methods to analyze data in specific sample space, obtain answers to problems of concern and its development trend, and guide the next farming. For problems of interest, users begin to generate data based on high-performance, including Fertilizing, Cultivating, Planting; Harvested data is analyzed by means of mining, visualizing and so on; finally, obtained results are stored to guide the next farming, i.e. implementing the

DOI: 10.1051/itmconf/20171203004

regenerating process of farming. Through the cycle repetition, answers to problems of concern by user are gained. For example, for the simulation model of a fighter fleet based on Analytic Hierarchy Process (AHP), data farming is used to obtain data (normalization processed), as shown in table 1. Also, data farming process is a closed loop with analysis and verification, thus the reliability of obtained sample data based on data farming is guaranteed.

Table 1: Farming and Harvesting the Performance Index Of The Fighter Fleet

Normalized Index	1	2	3	4	5	6	7
Situation cognition quality	0.843	0.848	0.862	0.873	0.892	0.910	0.917
Decision-making time	0.672	0.663	0.691	0.682	0.695	0.624	0.683
Information acquisition capability	0.878	0.862	0.891	0.885	0.902	0.856	0.883
Information distribution capability	0.786	0.842	0.792	0.845	0.746	0.867	0.891
Information protection capability	0.787	0.702	0.702	0.690	0.791	0.675	0.658
Coordination reliability	0.823	0.832	0.834	0.823	0.845	0.817	0.825
Coordination credibility	0.889	0.901	0.875	0.886	0.903	0.872	0.863
Target detection probability	0.740	0.772	0.709	0.700	0.724	0.673	0.712
Target acquisition probability	0.532	0.459	0.527	0.541	0.519	0.473	0.509
Probability of kill	0.583	0.571	0.585	0.498	0.519	0.536	0.572

4.Application of Big Data Mining In Simulation-Based Efficiency Evaluation Of Equipment System

Data farming technology resolves the sample space covering insufficiency problem in the operation efficiency evaluation simulation of equipment system. As performance or index of complex equipment system is numerous, by virtue of an evaluation model usually only using part of equipment data, or facing a type of evaluation targets, it is difficult to establish a unified evaluation model to describe the equipment comprehensively. When evaluating the equipment system, more and more elements need to be considered. For example, there are many indices of missile defense platform, performances vary in different territory, weather and application conditions, and many factors need to be considered to evaluate its operation performance. These element data describe the equipment system and its environment subtly, but the system evaluation model or algorithm is also required to make full use of these data, in order to generate more accurate results.

The grasp of comprehensive data is essential to provide accurate evaluation results of equipment system. With the development of information technology, there are more and more types of equipment represented by the information equipment, and system structure are more and more complicated, thus it is gradually difficult for conventional system evaluation method to process the equipment system with huge data. Big data mining technology can deal with huge data in the operation efficiency evaluation process of equipment system. Data mining is also called knowledge discovery in database, is a complex process that credible, novel, valuable modes or laws and other knowledge are extracted from huge data, and is one of means to analyze data farming results. It is simply explained to use software tools and database technologies to preprocess data and seek for useful hidden information and clues from lots of existing data. It is a integrated information processing technology that applies the machine learning into large database. The data mining process is shown as Figure 2. This process can use six basic steps to define, as follows:

a) Defining problems
b) Preparing data
c) Browsing data
d) Generating model
e) Browsing and verifying model
f) Deploying and updating model

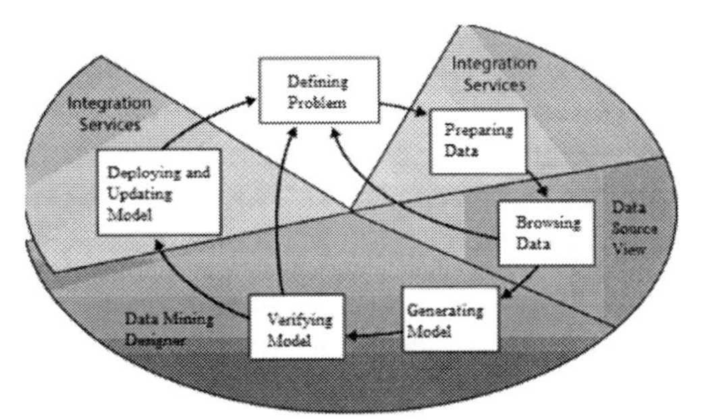

Figure. 2: General data mining process

For a specific complex military problem research, data farming method can be used to run lots of military models to obtain huge data. The database-based analysis on these huge data is the application of data mining technology. In accordance with interestingness of user, data is searched, merged and focused; Data miner is used to characterize, associate, classify and cluster data; the whole data mining process is a repeated iterative cycle that every technology is used to detect the small differences of data and different technologies and methods are used to constantly make the cycle analysis to get better or different results.

For example, in allusion to BMS simulation system in section 2, data is obtained by data farming. Data mining technology can be used to excavate BMS system

 DOI: 10.1051/itmconf/20171203004

characteristics hidden in data. According to different efficiency evaluation needs, different data mining algorithms are used respectively, such as characterization, association, classification, cluster, etc. For instance, we can use the association algorithm of data mining, such as Apriori algorithm, to find the association relationship between data。

5.Case Study

Data farming and data mining are used to implement the operation efficiency evaluation of equipment system, as shown in Figure 3.

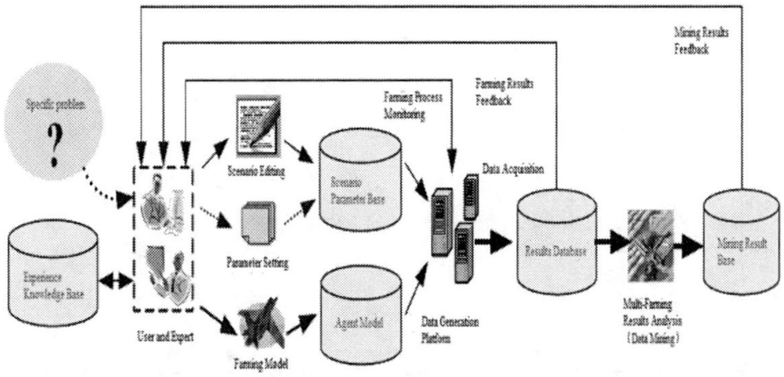

Figure. 3: Operation efficiency evaluation process of equipment system based on Data farming and data mining

The efficiency evaluation for coordination operation system of fighter fleet is still taken as an example. In section 2, data farming can be used on the coordination operation system of fighter fleet to obtain data, as shown in Table 1. Based on data farming, Apriori algorithm can be used to obtain the association relationship between every column of data in Table 1, as shown in Table 2. Table 2 shows that decision-making time is associated with information acquisition capability, information protection capability is associated with coordination reliability, etc.

These conclusions can help us to adjust the model of BMS simulation system to better make the efficiency evaluation of BMS system. For the same reason, other different data mining algorithms, such as neural networks, support vector machine etc., are used to excavate all kinds of information hidden in data mining results database, and provide the simulation for users and experts, to further adjust the simulation model.

6.Conclusion

This paper presents an evaluation method for operation efficiency of equipment system based on data farming and mining. Compared with conventional operation simulation method, its focus is on utilizing the data farming technology, running it in the whole parameter space of models, obtaining a number of effective sample space data, and further analyzing it to find implicit laws and results by Big Data Mining technology and Data Visualization technology, in order to facilitate the problem-oriented system efficiency simulation. This method has a certain reference value for the accurate evaluation on operation efficiency of equipment system by the use of small sample experiment data.

References

[1] Y. Liu, Research on the Passive Radar Guidance Technique and its Efficacy Evaluation Method under Confrontation Condition. *Doctoral dissertation*. National University of Defense Technology, 2010.

[2] J. Wang, Y. Liu, B. Deng, S. Geng, Analysis of Jamming Effectiveness against Early Warning Aircraft Tracking System. *Journal of Naval University of Engineering*, 2012.

[3] Chevalier, Tomas R., and Ove K. Steinvall. "Laser radar modeling for simulation and performance evaluation." *SPIE Europe Security+ Defence*. International Society for Optics and Photonics, 2009.

[4] Ewing, T., & Tentner, A, Using a scalable modeling and simulation framework to evaluate the benefits of intelligent transportation systems (No. ANL/TD/CP-101364). Argonne National Laboratory, Argonne, IL (US), 2000.

[5] Patenaude, A., Study on the Effectiveness of Modeling and Simulation in the Weapon System Acquisition Process. OFFICE OF THE SECRETARY OF DEFENSE WASHINGTON DC, 1996.

[6] Ender, T., Leurck, R. F., Weaver, B., Miceli, P., Blair, W. D., West, P., & Mavris, D. Systems-of-systems analysis of ballistic missile defense architecture effectiveness through surrogate modeling and simulation. *IEEE Systems Journal*, 4(2), 156-166, 2010.

[7] R. Ju, The research on the system evaluation method based on data farming and data mining. *Doctoral dissertation*. National University of Defense Technology, 2006.

A New Algorithm of Shape Boundaries Based on Chain Coding

Xin Zhao[1], Jun Zheng[2], Yan Liu[*3]

[1]*Shanghai Zhongqiao College, Shanghai, China*
[2]*School of Computer Science and Software, Engineering, East China Normal University, Shanghai, China*
[3]*School of Computer Science and Software, Engineering, East China Normal University, Shanghai, China*
[1] *zhaoxin203@126.com*, [3*]*yliu@cc.ecnu.edu.cn*

Abstract; A new method to obtain connected component in binary images is presented. The method uses DFA automaton to obtain chain code and label the component boundary. It is theoretically proved that the algorithm improves the image encoding efficiency closer to the lowest time consumption.

Keywords-*image shape; boundary tracing; chain code; automaton; boundary processing*

1. Introduction

Connected component obtaining in a binary image is one of the most fundamental operations in pattern recognition and image analysis. The purpose of labeling is to treat the individual connected components of a digitized image as separate objects.

Rosenfeld presented tracing idea in 1978[1]. The subsequent work[2,3] are effective, but have less efficiency then Rosenfeld .The well-known TP algorithm is proposed in [4], but some errors including losing inner contours, connectivity and traversing some of the boundary pixels more than one time can be found.

Several algorithms based on label equivalences have been proposed. Chang et al. [5] outperforms other methods using label equivalences and ordinary computers and thus is picked out to represent existing methods based on label equivalences with more than two passes.

The report of Seong-Dae Kim et al. described a two-step run-length algorithm [6]. The method computes chain code from run-length coding representation. It preserves the connectivity information between runs and never loses the inner or outer contours.

A fast algorithm is proposed inn this paper. It uses DFA automaton to obtain chain code and label the component boundary specifically for binary image. The algorithm makes full utilization of the automaton in the labelling method to avoid tracing contours more than once. Our algorithm improves the current binary image encoding efficiency regarding algorithmic complexity and memory usage.

2. Proposed Algorithm

Freeman introduced chain code to represent digital curves [7] first. Ernesto Bribiesca used a derivative of the Freeman chain code for shape representation and defined vertex chain code (VCC) [8] in 1999. Then Bribiesca presented a new measure of tortuosity for 2D curves which based on geometric structure of Slope Chain Code (SCC)[9].

It has been proved that chain code provide a compact representation and preserve all the information of the image [10, 11]. Bribiesca also proved that chain coding data has higher ratio of lossless compression [12].

The deterministic finite automaton (DFA) is suitable for modelling the collaboration entities in a collaboration session. A finite automaton is a five-tuple notation $A = (Q, \Sigma, \delta, S, F)$ 。

A is the name of the automaton. Q is the finite set of states of the automaton. Σ is the finite set of input symbols. $\delta : Q \times \Sigma \rightarrow Q$ is the transition function, which takes as parameters as state from Q and a symbol(from Σ ,and returns a state in Q for deterministic Finite Automata(DFA). $S \in Q$ is the start state. $F \in Q$ is the finite set of final or accepting states, which is a subset of Q .

 DOI: 10.1051/itmconf/20171203005

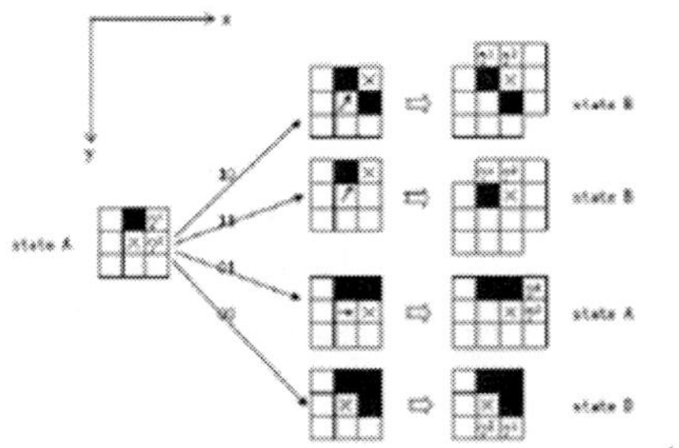

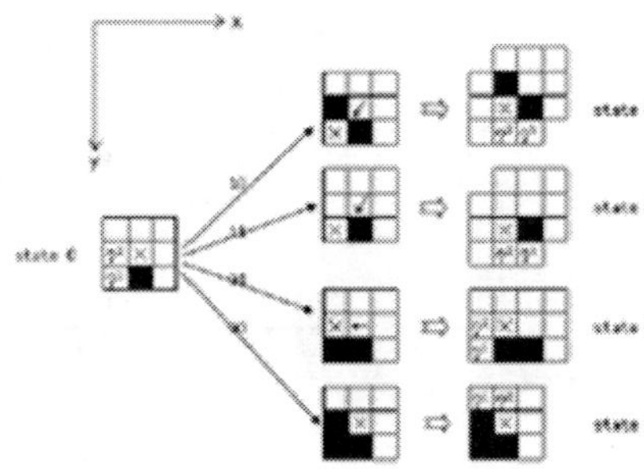

In DFA, for each $Q \times \Sigma$ of state and input there is a unique next state giver by the transition function.

For the usage of automaton, pixels on image contour are divided into 4 states. All states can transform to related states under given condition. However, the automaton traverses on the outside boundary of the image.

2.1 The 8-Connected Automaton

The new examining sequence is proposed and pitched as in Fig.1. Assuming position with arrow is the current position of tracer, which is a white pixel on the outside boundary. The points labeled by 'a', 'b' should be examined in turn until the automaton gets the next state. That is, the automaton only uses four points - the black point, the point with arrow, and the points with 'a' and 'b'. Point with 'a' must be examined first. And only under special condition, point with 'b' will be examined later.

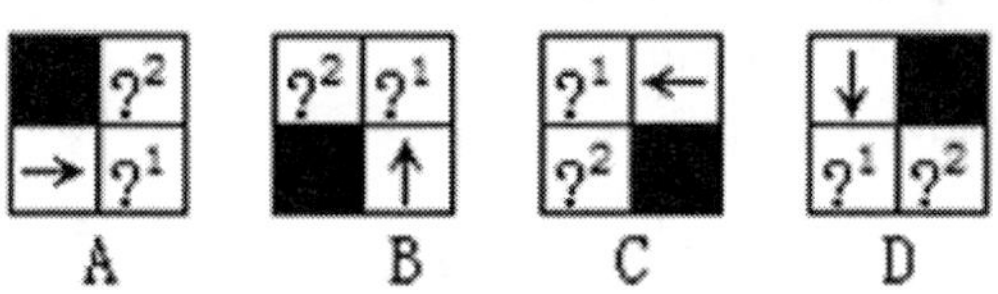

Figure1. The four states of 8-connected automaton.

So value of points 'a' and point 'b' are input of DFA. The input can be '0x', '10' or '11' according to the following definition:

0x: a=0(a is black, b is not examined)
10: a=1, b=0(a is white , b is black)
11: a=1, b=1 (a is white , b is white)

The transition of state A is given in fig.2 (a). Because of the space symmetry of the internal state of the automaton, the state transition graph of State B, C and D can be obtained by rotate the state transition graph of State A by $90^\circ, 180^\circ$, and 270° as shown in (b),(c),(d) of fig.2.

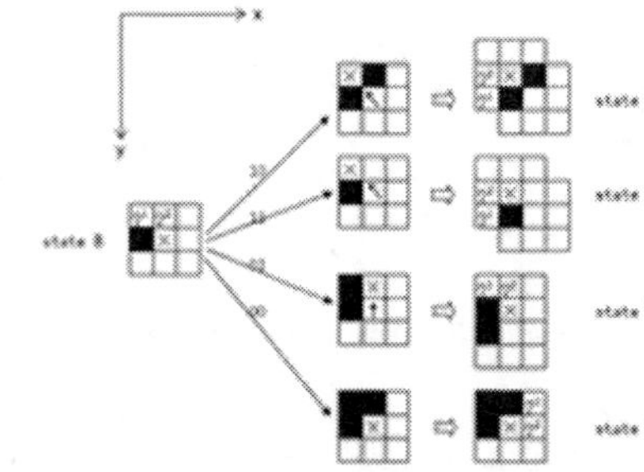

(a)Transition of state A (8-connected) (b) Transition from state B (8-connected)

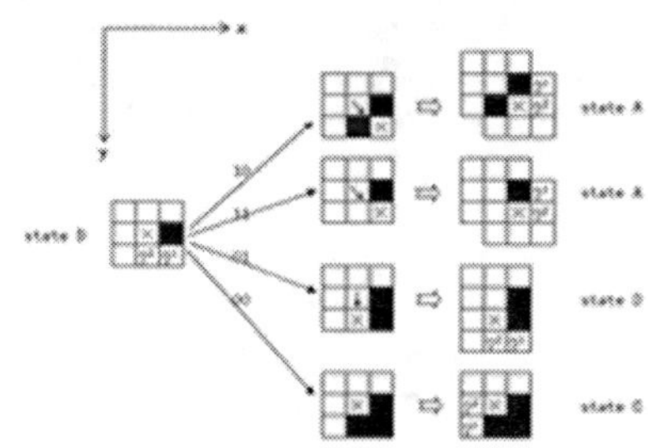

(c)transition from state C (8-connected) (d)transition from state D (8-connected)

Figure2. Automaton transition of 4 states.

Procedure of transition of state A in 8-connected image:

When current state is state A, the automaton first examines the point with 'a' (pixel at coordinates (x+1, y)).If it is black, change current state to state D.

If it is white, examine the point with 'b'. If pixel where 'b' located is black, state is still state A. And automaton goes forward to coordinates (x+1, y). If pixel with 'b' is white, change state A to state B, and automaton goes forward to coordinates (x+1, y-1).

According to the transition image, the automaton is given in fig 3.

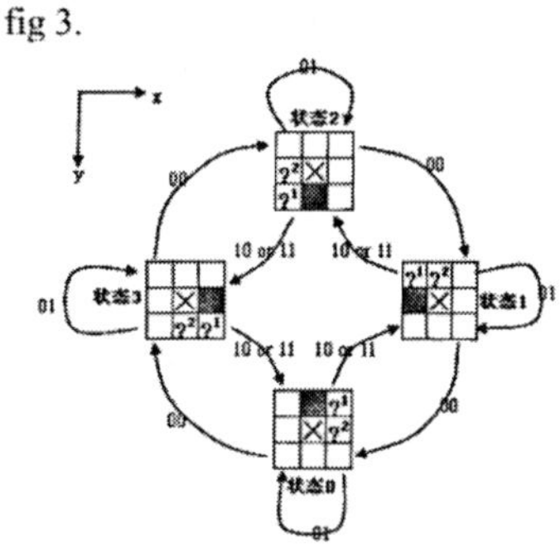

DOI: 10.1051/itmconf/20171203005

Figure3. DFA of 8-connected image tracer.

In addition, chain code can be obtained the same time. Freeman 8-direction code is Output according to tab.1.

Table1. Output of Freeman 8-direction code

	State A	State B	State C	State D
State A	0	1	-	-
State B	-	2	3	-
State C	-	-	4	5
State D	7	-	-	6

2.2 How to Find a New Contour

To find a new contour and start the automaton needs to examine whether current situation complies with state A — upper pixel is black and lower pixel is white. Starting procedure of automaton with 8-connected image is shown in fig.7.

To terminate the automata is simple, it only needs to analyze whether the automata have returned to the starting point. If automata traces back to the starting position again, it will terminate and begin to find a new contour - the next position with state A.

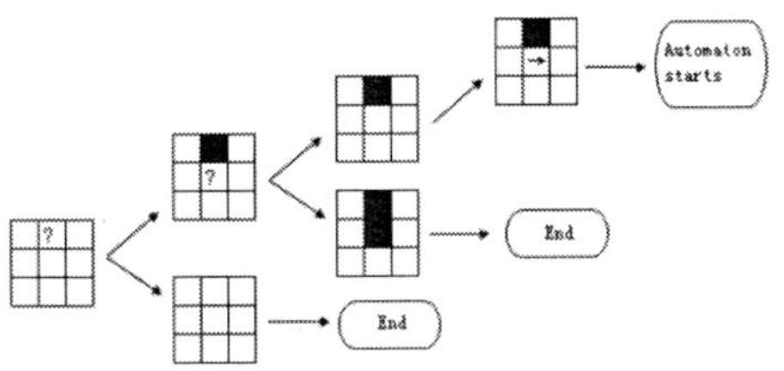

Figure4. Starting procedure of automaton.

3. Performances Comparison

The performances of algorithms are shown in tab 3. (AK stands for Kim algorithm; AFC stands for Fuchang method; AA_e stands for algorithm using automaton) In these figures, the size of the test image (M pixels) is plotted along the horizontal axis, while the average processing time (ms) of each method is plotted along the vertical axis.

Table2. Performances of compared methods

Document type	Image size(M pixels)	Algorithms		
		AA-e	*AFC*	*AK*
		Average processing time(ms)		
Halftone picture	0.16	7.1	9.54	10.23
	0.64	20.8	26.3	31.4
	2.56	85.2	115.85	128.7
Headlines	0.16	8.03	11.2	12.01
	0.64	19.89	28.1	32.63
	2.56	66.5	91.7.	103.3
Legacy document	0.16	6.4	9.2	10.8
	0.64	20.7	27.42	33.4
	2.56	67.6	90.1	107.1
Newspaper	0.16	7.5	10.9	12.01
	0.64	22.8	28.64	36.05
	2.56	70.8	92.37	115.2

4. Conclusion

This paper presents a new method to obtain connected component in binary images. The time consumption in this method is, in expense of additional work memory, this method is closer to the lowest time consumption.

The algorithm makes full utilization of the automaton in the labeling method to avoid tracing contours more than once. The connectivity information is fully preserved and the inner and outer contours can be distinguished. The new algorithm only labels west side of the outer contour and east side of the inner contour and it is capable of generating all types of chain code after tracing the contours.

It is theoretically proved that our algorithm improves the current binary image encoding efficiency regarding algorithmic complexity and memory usage. In experiments on six types of images of various sizes, we compare our method with other algorithm. The results show that our algorithm outperforms that in all six types of binary image in terms of computational speed especially for complex image.

References

[1] Rosenfeld A. Algorithms for image/vector conversion [J]. Computer Graphics, 1978(12): 135-139.

[2] Hermilo S C, Bribiesca E, Ramon M R D. Efficiency of chain codes to represent binary objects [J]. Pattern Recognition, 2007, 40: 1660-1674.

[3] Merrill R D. Representation of contours and regions for efficient computer search [J]. Comm ACM, 1973, 16 (2): 69-82.

DOI: 10.1051/itmconf/20171203005

[4] Pavlidis T, Algorithms for Graphics and Image Processing [M]. Rockville: Computer Science Press, 1982.

[5] F. Chang, C.J. Chen, C.J. Lu, A linear-time component-labeling algorithm using contour tracing technique, Comput. Vis. Image Und. 93 (2004) 206–220.

[6] Kim S D, Lee J H, Kim J K, A new chain-coding algorithm for binary images using run-length codes [J]. CVGIP, 1988, 41: 114-128.

[7] H. Freeman, Computer processing of line drawing images, Computational Surveys 6 (1974) 57-97.

[8] Bribiesca E, A new chain code [J]. Pattern Recognition, 1999, 32: 235-2

[9] Bribiesca E, A measure of tortuosity based on chain coding, Pattern Recognition ,Volume 46, Issue 3, March 2013, Pages 716–724

[10] Liu Y K, Wei W, Wang P J. Compressed vertex chain codes [J]. Pattern Recognition, 2007, 40: 2908–2913.

[11] Hermilo S C, Bribiesca E, Ramon M R D. Efficiency of chain codes to represent binary objects [J]. Pattern Recognition, 2007, 40: 1660-1674.

[12] Hermilo S C, Bribiesca E, Ramon M R D. Efficiency of chain codes to represent binary objects [J]. Pattern Recognition, 2007, 40: 1660-1674.

[13] Gu G Q,Chen K, Region-Labeling-Automata for Images in Square, Triangular and Hexagonal Lattice, Advances in Computer and Information Technology, The Journal of Three Dimensional Images, 17 (2003)161-165.

Enhanced Microblog Network Representation with User-Generated Content

Yue Hu[1], Shu-Qiang Yang[1], Bin Zhou[1]

[1]College of Computer, National University of Defense Technology, Changsha, China
[1]huyue15a@nudt.edu.cn

Abstract: The real-world networks are so sparse that only utilizing the limited edges cannot capture valuable user feature fully. However, the existing network embedding methods usually took the network structure into consideration merely. Therefore, inspired by the assumption that there exist latent relationships between those who generate similar text information, we proposed to enhance the original network structures by incorporating the latent relationships extracted from user-generated content into the raw network topology and furthermore to learn the representation for the revised network. Eventually, we evaluate our proposed method in two inference tasks and the experiment results demonstrate that the network representation generated by our enhanced network embedding method has a better performance than the baseline method on dataset provided by Sina Microblog.

1. Introduction

With the widespread popularity of social network services such as Sina Microblog, networks are ubiquitous in our daily life and play an increasingly important role in the study for our society. However, the diversity and complexity of network information is not propitious for capturing more valuable user features. Moreover, it is difficult to perform these subsequent applications such as interest recommendation, user profile and so on. A straightforward idea is to learn user representation with these available network information. As is known to all, a large-scale network constitutes a high-dimension space so that network representation seeks to embed the networks into a low-dimensional space. In recent year, network representation learning has drawn extensive attention.

1.1 Related Work

Network representation is essentially network embedding in low-dimension space. Many outstanding research effort has been proposed in network embedding. Earlier manifold learning [1] can be considered the originator, such as Isomap, Laplacian Eigenmaps (LE) and Locally Linear Embedding. Inspired by the word embedding [2], DeepWalk [3] exploited Random Walk [4] to generate vertex sequence as sentence in corpus and then introduced Skip-Gram [5] into network representation learning firstly in binary network. Because DeepWalk did not establish a unified objective function, what's worse, the vertex sequences generated randomly are effected by a lot of noise. Hence, a recent work from Tang et al. [6] proposed to model the first-order and second-order proximity respectively and then presented a simple method to incorporate these two representation vector. Furthermore, GraRep [7] proposed by Cao et al. took the N-order network structure into consideration, where $N > 2$. In order to address the randomness of vertex sequence in DeepWalk, nore2vec [8] added flexibility in exploring neighborhoods to learn richer network representations. As described above, these methods learned network representations only based on the structure information. Certainly, the available network information is not only the network topology but also other information. Thus, Yang et al. presented TADW [9] to model the text feature and network structure simultaneously with inductive matrix completion algorithm to learn better vertex representation. GENE [10] proposed by Chen et al. incorporated the group information into network embedding. Besides, Li et al. [11] proposed multi-faceted representation jointly with diverse information like user-generated contents, user attributes and user-user network graphs.

However, in real world, networks are usually sparse, that is, there are a small quantity of edges between vertex pair. Therefore, only utilizing the limited structure information is difficult to learn the network representation and to have a good performance in the following tasks. As we know, social networks produce not only the user-user network topology, but also other diverse information from each user like text information, image information, video information and emoji information. Assumed that those with similar user-generated text tend to have common interests and concerns, which indicates there exists latent relationship between them.

Hence, motivated by the sparseness problem and inspired by the aforementioned assumption, a feasible method is to enhance the original network structure with rich user-generated content. Our work proposes how to incorporate the latent relationship extracted from text information into the original network structure and then learn the network representation with the revised network topology based on the classic network embedding model LINE [6]. Finally, we conduct several experiments to evaluate the performance of representation vector with our proposed method in gender and age inference tasks compared with the baseline method.

Generally speaking, the major contribution is that we extract the latent relationship from user-generated text to integrate into the raw network structure information and then learn the network representation with LINE [6], which addresses the sparseness problem of real-world networks.

2. Method

In this section, firstly, we give the definition of the problem. Then we describe the latent relationships extracted from user-generated content and the relationships which integrate the first-order proximity and the second-order proximity for the given network structure. Finally, we introduce how the initial network was revised on the basis of these relationships as above.

1.2 Definition

The vertex corresponding to a user in microblog network usually has rich text information which is published until now.

A network with rich text information is denoted as $G = (V, E, T)$, where $V = \{v_i\}$ is user vertex set and $E = \{(v_i, v_j)\}$ is the edges associated with a weight $w \in \{0,1\}$. $T = \{t_i\}$ is user-generated blogs set where each entity t_i corresponds to a text paragraph of user v_i.

Therefore, our study aims to capture the latent information from user-generated content and to learn the low-dimensional representation $y_i \in \mathbb{R}_k$ from the revised network G'' for each vertex, where k is expected to be much smaller than $|V|$.

1.3 Latent Relationships from User-generated Content

Considering that users who publish similar blogs usually have several common interests, that is to say, they are likely to be friends or they have the potential to become friends. Thus, the relationship extracted from user-generated contents is named latent relationship.

The extraction of latent relationships can be essentially attributed to a matter of text similarity problem. However, each blog text is not more than 140 words, so it is necessary to integrate all the history blogs generated by each user into a text paragraph. Because the colloquial expression style of blog text makes text analysis vulnerable to noise data, text preprocessing is crucial for the accuracy of subsequent tasks and some targeted measures must be taken such as the stop words filtering, abnormal words replacement, and words segmentation. Here some specific preprocessing measures for user-published blogs are shown as follows,

Some texts separated by symbol "#" in microblog which are named the topic of this blog represents some interests of users, as a result, these topic phrases should be extracted directly used as the keywords for the corresponding user-generated texts.

Contents after symbol "@" usually represent user name and do not need to be cut further.

Filter the useless noise data in raw texts such as punctuation and special symbols.

Replace all abnormal words in contrast to the abnormal vocabulary. Abnormal words are some popular networks-parlances which have been widely recognized. For example, if you want say "thanks", you can use "3Q" or "3q". Also, in order to avoid some special expression, you can separate one Chinese character into two or more parts.

Replace the original complex form of simplified Chinese character in contrast to the simple word list.

Remove the stop words.

Calculate TF-IDF for corpus and filter out the low-frequency words according to the pre-set threshold.

HanLP is used to cut the remaining texts which have been preprocessed by above-mentioned measures.

Then we adopt the Latent Dirichlet Allocation (LDA) [2] model which identifies the latent topic information in a large corpus to extract the feature vector, at last, the cosine similarity between any two vectors indicates the weight of latent edge between the corresponding two users.

LDA is a generative probabilistic model covering document, topic and word layers, which is based on the idea that documents are represented as random mixtures over K latent topics where each topic is characterized by a multinomial distribution over words and each document subjects to a multinomial distribution over k latent topics. Hence, the generation process for each document w in a corpus $\mathbb{D}$ consisting of M documents is described as follows,

For each document M_i, choose $\theta \sim \mathrm{Dir}(\alpha)$, where $\mathrm{Dir}(\alpha)$ is the Dirichlet distribution for parameter α and parameter θ is a topic vector, each column of which represents the probability that each topic appears in this document.

For w_{ij} which is the jth word in the ith document, where $j \in \{1,2,\cdots,N_i\}$ and $i \in \{1,2,\cdots,M\}$, then choose a latent topic z_i from the topic vector θ according to the conditional probability distribution $p(z_i|\theta)$ and generate a word w_j according to the conditional probability distribution $p(w_j|z_i,\beta)$.

Given the parameters α and β, the joint distribution of the model is defined as follows,

$$p(\theta, \mathbf{z}, \mathbf{w}|\alpha, \beta) = p(\theta|\alpha) \prod_{i=1}^{N} p(z_i|\theta)\ p(w_j|z_i, \beta).$$

Here ware regarded as the observed variable while θ and z are as the hidden variables, then we use the Expectation Maximization Algorithm (EM) to learn parameters α and β.

Supposed that the top T topics are retained, then each text paragraph is embedded into a feature vector $t_{v_i} = \{w_1, w_2, \cdots, w_T\}$, where w_i is the weight value corresponding to the ith topic and the weight denotes the likelihood that the texts generated by user $v_i$belongs to the jth topic.

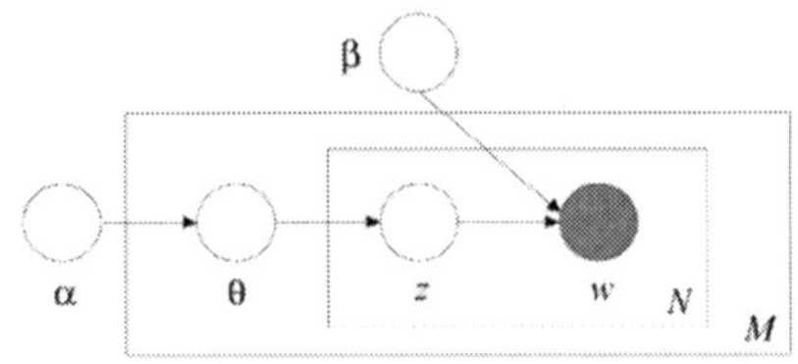

Figure 1. Graphical model representation of LDA which is composed of three layers. α and β are sampled only once during the generation process. The outer plate represents documents and parameter θ is sampled for each document, and therefore the probability that each document generates topic z is different. The inner plate represents the repeated choice of topics and words within a document and the word w is generated by z and β.

Afterwards, each feature vector describes the topics associated with each user-generated contents, in other words, the concerns or interests can be obtained from user-published blogs. Thus we extract the latent relationships from these representation vectors with cosine similarity. Certainly, other similarity measures such as Pearson Correlation Coefficient, Jaccard Coefficient and so on can also be used to calculate the similarity between individuals. Given two representation vector t_{v_i} and t_{v_j} , then w'_{ij} indicates the latent relationship between user v_i and user v_j, and it is defined as follows,

$$w'_{ij} = \frac{\overrightarrow{t_{v_i}} \cdot \overrightarrow{t_{v_j}}}{\left\|t_{v_i}\right\| \cdot \left\|t_{v_j}\right\|}.$$

Accordingly, the latent adjacency matrix extracted from user-generated blogs can be described as matrix $W' \in \mathbb{R}^{|V|\times|V|}$, where each entry $w'_{ij} \in [0,1]$.

1.4 Integrated Relationships from Network Structure

As we all know, real-world social network is usually sparse because there exists a small amount of edges which denotes the friendship between users. Moreover, the direct friendship is voluntarily established by users according to their own preferences so that it plays a significant role in network embedding problem only considered the network structures. However, the direct friendship is not enough to describe the network structure, what's more, it is possible that those who are not friends have something in common. As a matter of fact, there exists a fact that users who share similar friends tend to have common interests or similar characteristics in the social media.

Therefore, LINE [6] took the above facts into consideration and firstly introduced first-order and second-order proximity to characterize the local and global structure information as fully as possible.

First-order Proximity: Given the edge setE, for each pair of vertices in E, the weight on the corresponding edge indicates the first-order proximity. Let w^1_{ij} be an entry of the first-order proximity matrix W^1, and then w^1_{ij} is shown as follows,

$$w^1_{ij} = \begin{cases} 1, & if(v_i, v_j) \in E \\ 0, & otherwise \end{cases}.$$

Second-order Proximity: The number of common neighbors for any pair of vertices is used to define the second-order proximity, which describes the similarity of these two users' neighborhood structure in social network. Given the neighbor vertices set of user v_i and user v_j as $\mathcal{N}_{v_i}$ and $\mathcal{N}_{v_j}$ respectively, then the number of common neighbor vertex is calculated and the second-order proximity between user v_i and v_j is defined as follows,

$$w^2_{ij} = \frac{2 \times \left|\mathcal{N}_{v_i} \cap \mathcal{N}_{v_j}\right|}{\left|\mathcal{N}_{v_i}\right| + \left|\mathcal{N}_{v_j}\right|}.$$

Now, we exploit the first-order and second-order proximity jointly into the adjacency matrix extracted from the network structure. Accordingly, we introduce W to donate the integrated adjacency matrix where each entry w_{ij} is composed of the two corresponding proximities and is shown as follows,

$$w_{ij} = \lambda \cdot w^1_{ij} + \mu \cdot w^2_{ij},$$

Where λ and μ are the normalized coefficient and their value is adjusted iteratively until the result reaches optimal.

1.5 Revised Network with Latent Relationships

In this section, we firstly describe how to revise the network structure with the latent relationships extracted from user-generated contents and then use LINE [6] to learn the embedding representation for the extended network topology. Besides, the original network G have two changes as a result of the revise for the original adjacency matrix: firstly, there exists latent friendship between users who are not friends originally. From the perspective of graph theory, that is, the weight w_{ij} on the edge of pair of vertex (v_i, v_j) changes from 0 to w(w $\in$ [0,1]). Secondly, the relationship between users becomes stronger, and thus the weights of some edges increase.

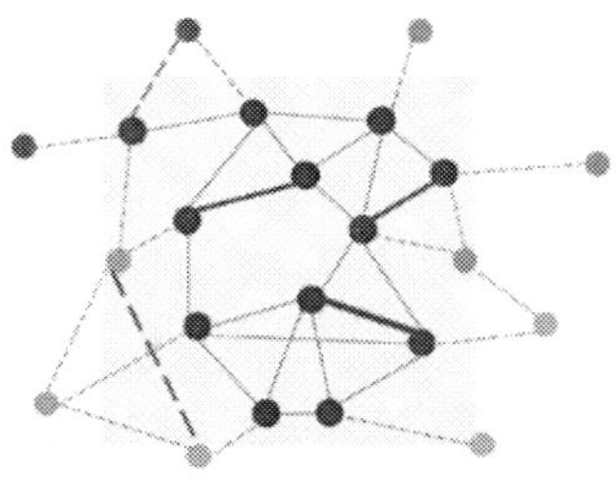

Figure 2. Schematic of enhanced network topology. The sub-graph of gray nodes is the original topology and other color nodes isolated at first. After revised, these edges indicated by dotted line are newly generated, notably, the thickness of line represents the different weight value.

Let W'' be the adjacency matrix of the revised network where each entry w''_{ij} is defined as follows,

$$w''_{ij} = \frac{w_{ij}+w'_{ij}}{\max_{i,j}\{w_{ij},w'_{ij}\}}.$$

However, some entries in the revised adjacency matrix are too small to make much sense and it is more reasonable to remove them. Therefore, we take the final revised adjacency matrix as the input data of LINE [6] to calculate the low-dimension representation. LINE [6] firstly introduced the first-order and second-order proximity and learned the corresponding representation vector for each vertex on the basis of first-order and second-order proximity separately, and then described how to incorporate these two representation vectors into the final vertex representation.

Essentially, the first-order proximity is the weight of edge between the vertices in the network. In order to model the first-order proximity, LINE [6] utilized the direct weight to build the empirical probability and then used the joint probability built by the representation vector to establish the object function. Suppose that $\vec{v}_{i1}$ and $\vec{v}_{i2}$ are the vector representation of vertex v_i and v_j separately, the joint probability between v_i and v_j was defined as follows,

$$p_1(v_{i1}, v_{j1}) = \frac{1}{1+\exp(-\vec{v}_{i1}\cdot\vec{v}_{j1})}.$$

Meanwhile, the empirical probability was defined as follows,

$$\widehat{p_1}(v_{i1}, v_{j1}) = \frac{w''_{ij}}{\sum_{(v_i,\ v_j \in E)} w''_{ij}}.$$

Consequently, LINE [6] adopted Kullback-Leible (K-L) divergence to establish the object function, and then LINE learned network representation by minimizing the object function which was shown as follows,

$$\min \mathcal{L}_1 = \min D_{KL}(\widehat{p_1}(v_{i1}, v_{j1}) || p_1(v_{i1}, v_{j1})),$$

Where measured the difference between the two probability distributions $\hat{p}$ and p was defined as follows,

$$D_{KL}(\hat{p}||p) = \sum_{i=1}^{n} \hat{p}(x) \cdot log\frac{\hat{p}(x)}{p(x)}.$$

In order to establish the second-order proximity model, LINE [6] assumed that each vertex play two roles which are the object vertex and the context of other vertices. Hence, $\vec{v}_{i2}$ denotes the representation when v_i is the object vertex while $\vec{v}'_{i2}$ denotes the representation vector when v_i is as the content of other vertices. Similarly, LINE [6] defined the conditional probability of "context" vertex v_j generated by "object" vertex v_i as follows,

$$p_2(v_j|v_i) = \frac{\exp(\vec{v}'^{\,T}_{j2} \cdot \vec{v}_{i2})}{\sum_{k=1}^{|V|} \exp(\vec{v}'^{\,T}_{k2} \cdot \vec{v}_{k2})}.$$

Also, the empirical probability was defined as follows,

$$\widehat{p_2}(v_j|v_i) = \frac{w''_{ij}}{d_i},$$

where d_i is the out-degree of vertex v_i. Therefore, LINE [6] established the object function for the second-order proximity by minimizing the K-L divergence to obtain the corresponding network representation. Afterwards, these two representation vectors optimized by Negative Sampling Algorithm(NEG) [13] are put together to denote the final representation $\vec{v}_i$ for each vertex v_i in LINE model, where $\vec{v}_i = \vec{v}_{i1} + \vec{v}_{i2}$.

2. Experiments

In this section, we conduct several experiments for the proposed methods and introduce the experimental results on a real dataset. Moreover, we use some inference tasks to evaluate the quality of the vector representation and compare our method with the baseline method.

2.1 Datasets

We conduct the experiments on dataset extracted from Sina Microblog provided by SMP CUP 2016. The dataset involves about 2.5 million users and covers 550 million friendships, and there are 4, 4000 users with microblogs texts and 3000 users with label among them. For the inference tasks, the dataset are divided into two subsets. One is used for training and the other is for testing. Besides, there are four kinds of data including user information, labels, relationships and user-published contents.

2.2 Baseline Methods

Since our proposed methods exploits the rich text information of each vertex to extend the original network structure, it is necessary to demonstrate the improvements over network embedding only considering the network topology information. However, the real-world social network structure is a binary network, that is, the weight value of each edge is either 0 or 1. Thus, we compare our methods with DeepWalk [3] and LINE only based on the network structures to validate the performance. Inspired by Word2Vec [2], DeepWalk [3] treated the vertex sequence as the sentence in the corpus. Random walk was used to generate the standard input sequence and then Skip-gram model trained the above sequences to learn the latent representation for each vertex in the network.

2.3 Experiment Settings

For our proposed methods, the number of vertex $|V|$ in the dataset is 1560. The number of topic in LDA topic generation model is set as 60, in other words, the dimension of user-generated text vector is 60. For DeepWalk [3], the number of available vertex is 1155. We used the default parameters, for instance, windows size is 5, walk length is 40, number of random walks to start at each node is set as 10 and the number of latent dimensions to learn for each node is set as 64. For the negative sampling in LINE model, the number of negative samples is set as 5.

2.4 Experiment Results and Analysis

The representation vector extracted from user-generated contents according to LDA indicates the latent relationships. Here, the text representation corresponding user v_i is described as follows,

$$\vec{t}_{v_i} = \{topic_1: w_1, topic_2: w_2, \cdots, topic_T: w_T\}$$

In order to visualize the performance of the representation vector, we choose the top three topics for each user-generated blogs and then calculate the corresponding coordinate values in the three axes by adding the weight value to the topic number value. Figure 3 shows the distribution of user-generated texts representation.

At the same time, we visualize the network structure to compare the changes of the network topology before and after revised as shown in Figure 4 and Figure 5.

For the dataset, only five percentage of users are statistically friends each other. Obviously, it can be found from Fig 6 that the second-order proximity is more than the first-order proximity, which is the same as our above-mentioned views for the real-world network.

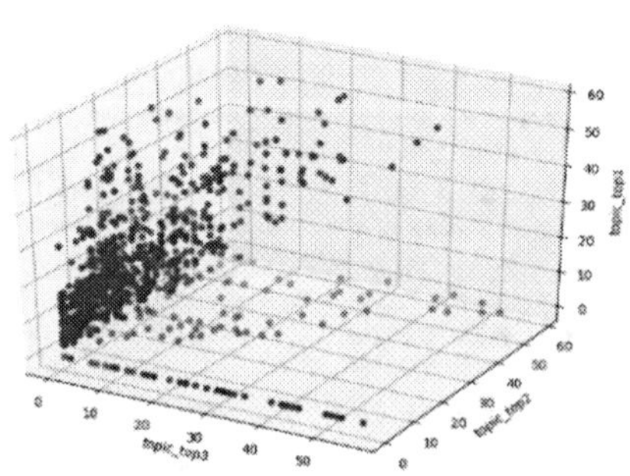

Figure 3. The distribution of user-generated texts representation. The clustering phenomenon of the representation vector indicates the similarity of the user-generated text.

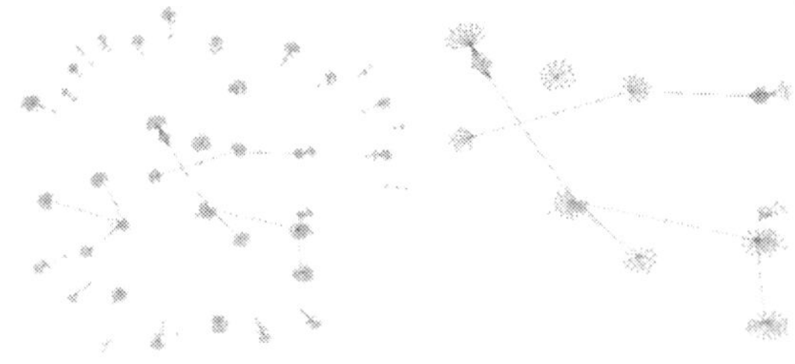

(a). the whole network (b). the sub-network

Figure 4. Visualization of the latent network topology with user-generated text.

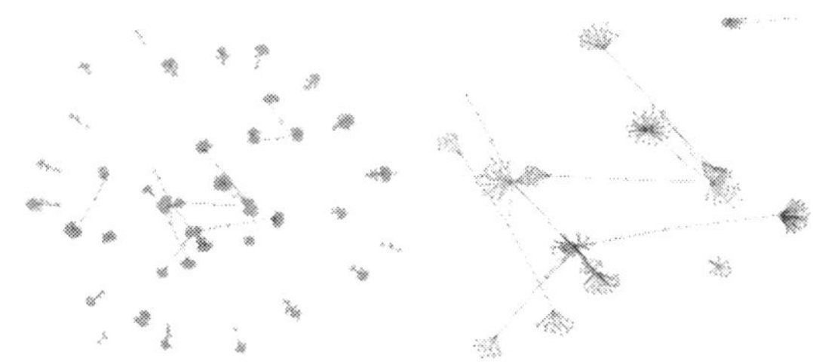

(a). the whole network (b). the sub-network

Figure 5. Visualization of the final network topology after revised by the user-generated text.Compare with Fig 4, the number of edge increase and the thicker lines indicates that the relationship gets stronger.

2.4.1 Gender Inference

In the real-world network, the task of gender inference is a supervised binary classification problem based on the representation vector generated by our proposed methods.

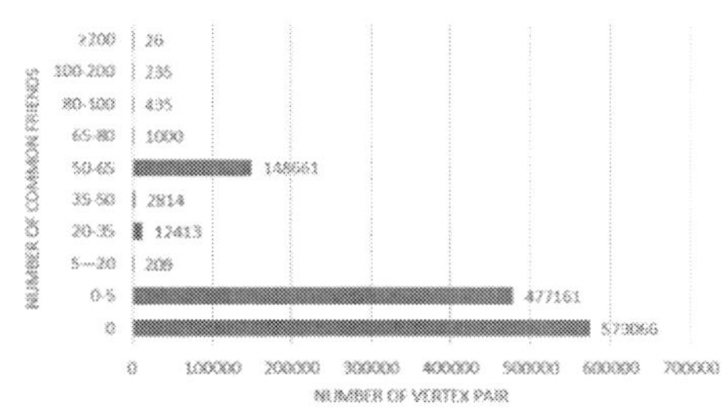

Figure 6. The number of common friends for each vertex pair. The quantity of common friends between user is different, especially, several of which is up to more than 200. Although the half of vertex pairs have no common friends, the second-order proximity plays an significant role in network topology.

Thus, we used linear kernel for SVM model and took the final representation vector as the extracted feature to train the gender classifier. Similarly, we used accuracy, precision, recall and F1-measure to analyses the classification results and evaluate the performance. Accuracy is a metric to measure the number of samples that are classified correctly in the test samples. For classification tasks, precision is referred to as positive predictive value while recall is referred to as the true positive rate or sensitivity. And F1-measure is the harmonic mean of precision and recall.

Table I. Results of Gender Inference Task on Baseline Method

Percentage	Accuracy	Precision	Recall	F-1
13.40%	67.10%	0.6710	1.0	0.8030
22.07%	71.00%	0.7100	1.0	0.8300
30.74%	73.20%	0.7340	0.996	0.8450
39.39%	72.30%	0.7230	1.0	0.8390
48.05%	72.80%	0.7420	0.9730	0.8420
Average	71.38%	0.7160	0.9938	0.8318

Table II. Results of Gender Inference Task on Our Method

Percentage	Accuracy	Precision	Recall	F-1
3.85%	75.00%	0.7500	1.0	0.8570
10.26%	73.40%	0.7340	1.0	0.8466
16.67%	73.10%	0.7320	0.9580	0.8300
23.08%	73.10%	0.7400	0.9730	0.8410
29.49%	72.40%	0.7430	0.9620	0.8380
35.90%	73.20%	0.7510	0.9620	0.8430
42.31%	72.30%	0.7540	0.9380	0.8360
48.72%	72.60%	0.7510	0.9470	0.8380
55.13%	72.70%	0.7520	0.9470	0.8380
Average	**72.88%**	**0.7414**	**0.9652**	**0.8408**

Table I shows the classification performance based on the DeepWalk model only considering the network structure information. And Table II shows the evaluation results on our proposed methods. From these tables, we can obviously find that the accuracy and precision has been significantly improved, in particular, the average precision increases by 3% based on our enhanced representation method. Moreover, the first column indicates the proportion of the test samples to the whole data set. As the proportion increases, the accuracy rate decreases slightly. As is known to all, the small the percentage, the more training samples, which means that the classifier trained by SVM is more accurate.

2.4.2 Age Inference

For the age inference task, if not considering the false age, the age range of users is extremely wide which vary from children to the older. And the most noteworthy is the majority is the teenager aged between 18 and 30 years old. In order to infer the ages of the test samples more accurately, we divided the age into four levels. Similarly, the inference task is also a supervised classification problem but a multi-labels classification. Therefore, we exploit SVM which is firstly a classic binary classification algorithm to deal this problem. Intuitively, there exits two ways to extend SVM classifier. One is one-to-one and the other is one-to-rest. So we used these two extended SVM algorithms [14] to accomplish the age inference task respectively and used accuracy metric to evaluate the performance of our proposed method compared with the baseline method.

Table III. Results of Age Inference Task on Baseline Method

Percentage	13.04%	21.74%	30.43%	39.13%	47.83%
Accuracy	69.03%	72.54%	70.70%	70.76%	71.53%
	65.82%	70.20%	71.55%	71.65%	70.63%

Table IV. Results of Age Inference Task on Our Method

Percentage	10.26%	23.08%	29.49%	42.31%	48.72%
Accuracy	76.25%	74.72%	75.43%	74.82%	73.95%
	77.50%	75.28%	73.70%	75.18%	73.16%

As is shown in both two tables, the accuracy in the first row is calculated by extended SVM classifier with one-to-one while the accuracy in the second row is with one-to-rest method. Compared the accuracy in Table III to those in Table IV, the result with our proposed method corresponding similar percentage has been greatly improved. For example, when the test sample accounts for about 10 percent of the sample overall, with the SVM algorithm extended by one-to-one method, the accuracy of inferring the age of test samples increased from 69.03% to 76.25%. Furthermore, we compared the results from age inference as described in Figure 7. As can be seen, the user representation extracted by the proposed method achieves better results than the baseline only considering network structure.

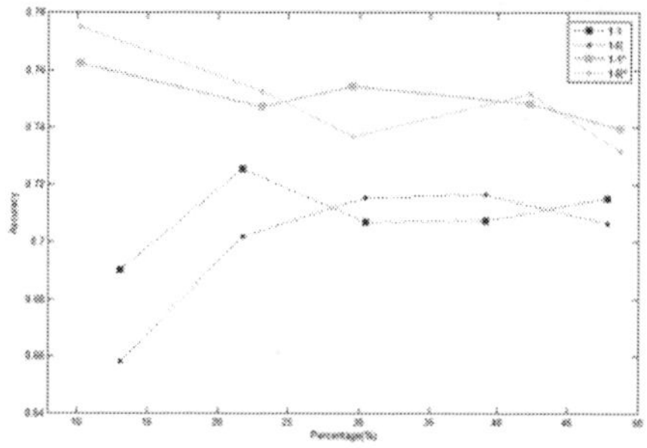

Figure 7. Comparison of age inference results. The gray is accuracy with baseline method while the pink is accuracy with our proposed methods.

3. Conclusion

In this paper, considering the sparseness of network structure in the real world, we study how to exploit other network information to extend the structure information and present a more explicit description for each user. We assume that the user-generated content shows his interests and the similar user-generated texts represent some latent relationships between user pairs. Hence, we propose an enhanced network representation method by integrating the latent relationships extracted from rich texts into the original network structure. Experimental results demonstrate that the representation learned by our proposed method achieves improvement in accuracy metric of user gender and age inference tasks in comparison with the baseline method. For future work, we intend to incorporate multi-faceted network information into the user model and use the feature vector to address other further applications such as hierarchical community detection based on node feature representation and so on.

Acknowledgment

The authors want to thank the relevant outstanding effort and the collaboration from my workmates in our research group. This work was supported by Virtual Community Discovery and Evolution (No 2013CB329606), the National Basic Research Program of China (973 Program No.2013CB329600) and the National Natural Science Foundation of China (NSFC No.61502517).

References

[1] H. Zhou, W. U. Wei, Q. Z. Teng, X. M. Yang, L. I. Min, and D. Y.Tao, "Research of manifold learning algorithm," *Application Research of Computers*, vol. 24, no. 7, pp. 214–217, 2007.

[2] R. Collobert and J. Weston, "A unified architecture for natural language processing:deep neural networks with multitask learning," in *International Conference*, 2008, pp. 160–167.

[3] B. Perozzi, R. Al-Rfou, and S. Skiena, "DeepWalk: online learning of social representations," pp. 701–710, 2014.

[4] R. Metzler and J. Klafter, "The random walk's guide to anomalous diffusion: a fractional dynamics approach," *Physics Reports*, vol. 339, no. 1, pp. 1–77, 2000.

[5] J. R. Shewchuk, "An introduction to the conjugate gradient method without the agonizing pain," Ph.D. dissertation, Carnegie Mellon University,1994.

[6] J. Tang, M. Qu, M. Wang, M. Zhang, J. Yan, and Q. Mei, "Line: Largescale information network embedding," in *International Conference on World Wide Web*, 2015, pp. 1067–1077.

[7] S. Cao, W. Lu, and Q. Xu, "Grarep:learning graph representations with global structural information," 2015, pp. 891–900.

[8] A. Grover and J. Leskovec, "node2vec: Scalable feature learning for networks," 2016, p. 855.

[9] C. Yang, Z. Liu, D. Zhao, M. Sun, and E. Y. Chang, "Network representation learning with rich text information," in *International Conference on Artificial Intelligence*, 2015, pp. 2111–2117.

[10] J. Chen, Q. Zhang, and X. Huang, "Incorporate group information to enhance network embedding," in ACM International on Conference on Information and Knowledge Management, 2016, pp. 1901–1904.

[11] J. Li, A. Ritter, and J. Dan, "Learning multi-faceted representations of individuals from heterogeneous evidence using neural networks," *Computer Science*, 2015.

[12] D. M. Blei, A. Y. Ng, and M. I. Jordan, "Latent dirichlet allocation," *Journal of Machine Learning Research,* vol. 3, pp. 993–1022, 2003.

[13] Q. V. Le and T. Mikolov, "Distributed representations of sentences and documents," *Computer Science*, vol. 4, pp. 1188–1196, 2014.

[14] C. W. Hsu and C. J. Lin, "A comparison of methods for multiclass support vector machines," in *IEEE TRANS. NEURAL NETWORKS,* 2002, pp. 415–425.

Retrieval of Cloud Water Variables by 1D-Var Algorithm

Qun-Bo Huang[1*], Wei-Min Zhang[2], Bai-Nian Liu[3], De Xing[4], Xiang Xing[5], Teng-Ling Luo [6], Wei-Feng Wang[7], Xiao-Gang Zhang[8]

[1*]Academy of Ocean Science and Engineering National University of Defense Technology, Changsha, China
[1*]College of Computer, National University of Defense Technology, Changsha, China
[1*]Weather Center of PLA Air Force, PLA Air Force, Beijing, China
[2]Academy of Ocean Science and Engineering National University of Defense Technology, Changsha, China
[3]Academy of Ocean Science and Engineering National University of Defense Technology, Changsha, China
[3]College of Computer, National University of Defense Technology, Changsha, China
[4]Academy of Ocean Science and Engineering National University of Defense Technology, Changsha, China
[4]College of Computer, National University of Defense Technology, Changsha, China
[5]Academy of Ocean Science and Engineering National University of Defense Technology, Changsha, China
[5]College of Computer, National University of Defense Technology, Changsha, China
[6]Academy of Ocean Science and Engineering National University of Defense Technology, Changsha, China
[6]College of Computer, National University of Defense Technology, Changsha, China
[7]Weather Center of PLA Air Force, PLA Air Force, Beijing, China
[8] Meteorological Observatory, Fourteen Suboffice of Jiuquan, No. 435, Jiuquan, China
[1*]hqb09@163.com, [8] 13830140531@163.com

Abstract: Data assimilation of satellite observations in cloud and rain regions is a worldwide problem. In the paper, we designed the background field and their error covariance of three cloud water variables (cloud cover, cloud liquid water and cloud ice water) at first. The experiment results demonstrate that 1D-Var (One-dimensional variational data assimilation) can retrieve the three variables efficiently. The cloud liquid water and cloud ice water can be obviously improved by 1D-Var. However, the retrieved effect of low cloud cover is still to be improved. It has the positive potential to assimilate the satellite observations in cloud and rain regions.

1. Introduction

Clouds and precipitation are produced under certain weather conditions, which are related to the majority of the important weather phenomena (such as thunderstorms, hail, tornadoes, heavy rain and so on). The assimilation of satellite data in cloud and rain regions will improve the accuracy of numerical weather forecast, and which is currently a hotspot problem in the world.

Chevallier and Bauer simulated satellite observations under cloud and rain condition by RTTOV, and then compared with Special Sensor Microwave/Imager (SSM/I) observations [1]. Ma et al. analyzed the error of simulated brightness temperature and the sensitivity to cloud parameters (cloud cover and cloud height) of the infrared instrument channels on NOAA14 [2]. Ding et al. used the RTTOV8.7 to test the simulated effect of the brightness temperature of HIRS/3 in the cloudy regions existing a typhoon [3].

1D-Var is typically used as a retrieval and pre-processing method due to its algorithmic simplicity and easy to control [4]. Huang studied the basic principles of the 1D+4D-Var two-step method and designed a 1D+4D-Var system process which is employed to assimilate the cloud and rain affected SSM/I data [5].

Based on the 1D-Var software developed by ECMWF, This paper presents a method of retrieving the cloud water variables by satellite observations. We firstly investigate the fundamental problems of cloud and rain data assimilation. Section II describes the algorithm process of 1D-Var. Section III designs the background field and the error covariance matrix of cloud water variables. Section IV shows and analyzes the numerical experiment results. Finally, conclusions and plans for future work are provided in section V.

2. 1D-Var algorithm

According to the Bayesian and variational theory, the cost function in 1D-Var can be expressed as:

$$J(\mathbf{x})=\frac{1}{2}(\mathbf{x}-\mathbf{x}_b)^T\mathbf{B}^{-1}(\mathbf{x}-\mathbf{x}_b)+\frac{1}{2}\left[\mathbf{y}^0-H(\mathbf{x})\right]^T\mathbf{R}^{-1}\left[\mathbf{y}^0-H(\mathbf{x})\right] \quad (1)$$

Where the background error is assumed to not dependent on the observation error, and which are Gaussian distribution. x is background profile, B and R are the background error covariance matrix and the observation error covariance matrix, y is satellite observation. H(x) represents the radiance which is simulated by the forward model of RTTOV, where x is the input parameter of RTTOV.

By minimizing the cost function (1), the optimal state variables (i.e. analysis field) can be obtained.

$$\mathbf{x}_a = \arg\min_{\mathbf{x}}(J(\mathbf{x}_b)) \quad (2)$$

Minimization algorithms are generally the conjugate gradient method or quasi-Newton iteration method [6].

3. Background Field And Matrix B

The process of minimization calculation is controlled by the background and the observation error covariance matrix. The background error covariance matrix B is an essential parameter for variational analysis, which is utilized to control the vertical distribution and transmission of observation information. The vertical correlation conceals in the matrix B (the row of which is usually called as a structural function) is then transmitted to the analysis field. If background error can't clear in the retrieved/analysis field, it will lead to completely distorted analysis information, and may even have a bigger error than that of the background state.

The real matrix B is too difficult to learn, so we usually get it by statistical method. However, if the statistical sample is not sufficient, the theoretical calculation becomes an alternative tool, and this is the idea of the paper.

Assuming that background field consists of three variables (t, q and o_3) which are not related to each other. The covariance matrix can be expressed as a block diagonal matrix B which consists of three sub-matrices $\mathbf{B}_t$, $\mathbf{B}_q$ and $\mathbf{B}_{o3}$:

$$\mathbf{B} = \begin{bmatrix} \mathbf{B}_t & \mathbf{O} & \mathbf{O} \\ \mathbf{O} & \mathbf{B}_q & \mathbf{O} \\ \mathbf{O} & \mathbf{O} & \mathbf{B}_{o3} \end{bmatrix} \quad (3)$$

where the three sub-matrices represent the vertical correlation among the three variables, and should be banded because of the large correlation between the adjacent atmospheric pressure levels.

For cloud and rain affected satellite observations, we mainly consider the liquid and ice water content in clouds in the atmosphere which are determined by three variables: cloud cover, cloud liquid water content and cloud ice water content.

For cloud cover, the background field is:

$$\mathbf{x}_{cc}(k) = \begin{cases} 1.0\times10^{-4} & ;k>itrop \\ 0 & ;k<itrop \end{cases} \quad (4)$$

Where k is the atmospheric pressure levels, $itrop$ is the level number of the tropopause where the lowest temperature level locates between the 35hPa and 500hPa. If the pressure level is less than $itrop$, which is above the tropopause; If the pressure level is bigger than $itrop$, which is below the tropopause.

For cloud liquid water content, the background field is:

$$\mathbf{x}_{clw}(k) = \begin{cases} 2.0\times10^{-6} & ;k>itrop \text{ and temperture>260K} \\ 0 & ;k<itrop \text{ and temperature} \le 260\text{K} \end{cases}$$

(5)

For cloud ice water content, the background field is:

$$\mathbf{x}_{ciw}(k) = \begin{cases} 2.0\times10^{-6} & ;k>itrop \text{ and temperture>274K} \\ 0 & ;k<itrop \text{ and temperature} \le 274\text{K} \end{cases}$$

(6)

The design of background error covariance B needs to consider the correlation between the vertical pressure levels, and meeting the conditions as follows: (1) the levels below the tropopause and above the tropopause are independent of each other, (2) the levels above the tropopause are independent of each other, (3) the levels below the tropopause are only related to the pressure difference between the pressure levels. If the correlation is less than 0.01, it should be set to zero. On this basis, the spatial correlation matrix can be derived:

$$SC_{ij} = \begin{cases} 0 & ;\ i,j<itrop,\ \text{and}\ i\neq j \\ 1 & ;\ i,j<itrop,\ \text{and}\ i=j \\ 0 & ;\ i<itrop\ \&\ j>itrop;\ \text{or}\ i>itrop\ \&\ j<itrop \\ \exp(-((p_i-p_j)/100)^2) & ;\ i,j>itrop \end{cases}$$

(7)

We further assume that there is no correlation among different variables, and the spatial correlation of different variables is determined by the spatial correlation matrix, the final background error covariance matrix B is:

$$\mathbf{B} = \begin{bmatrix} s_{cc}^2 SC & \mathbf{O} & \mathbf{O} \\ \mathbf{O} & s_{lw}^2 SC & \mathbf{O} \\ \mathbf{O} & \mathbf{O} & s_{iw}^2 SC \end{bmatrix} \quad (8)$$

where s_{cc}, s_{lw} and s_{iw} are the standard deviation of cloud cover, cloud liquid water and cloud ice water content.

4. Experiment Results

In this paper, we judge the cloud type by the height (pressure level) of clouds. The height of low clouds are usually lower than 2000 meters (about 800hPa), the high

DOI: 10.1051/itmconf/20171203007

clouds are located in the height above 6000 meters (about 500hPa), and the middle clouds are located in about 500hPa~800hPa. We select the brightness temperature of HIR and AMSU-A channels to form a joint observation data set, and meanwhile choose several typical cloud and rain affected atmospheric profiles to analyze.

In Table 1, for profile 1, the cloud covers of three types are not large. The low-middle cloud amount is more than high cloud in profile 2. The low-middle cloud cover and high cloud cover have not been much difference in profile 3. The high cloud amount of profile 4 is significantly more than low cloud cover.

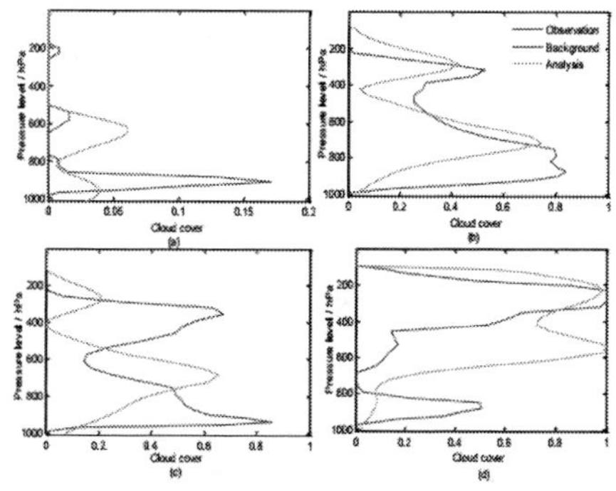

Figure 1. The vertical distribution of cloud amount of different cloud types in profile 1 (a), profile 2 (b), profile 3 (c) and profile 4 (d). Observational cloud cover (red line), background cloud cover (blue line), 1D-Var analysis cloud cover (green line).

The vertical distribution of observational cloud amount (red) of different cloud types in each profile can be seen from Fig. 1. The figure can reflect the vertical distribution of cloud more intuitionistic.

Table1. The cloud cover in each profile

Profile number	Cloud cover and cloud height					
	Low cloud cover	*Low cloud height (hPa)*	*Middle cloud cover*	*Middle cloud height (hPa)*	*High cloud cover*	*High cloud height (hPa)*
1	0.1719	933.1	0.0156	539.7	0.0078	202.2
2	0.8438	875.1	0.8047	788.7	0.5312	318.4
3	0.8594	943	0.4922	791.7	0.6719	352.2
4	0.5078	882.9	0.1719	538	1	228.8

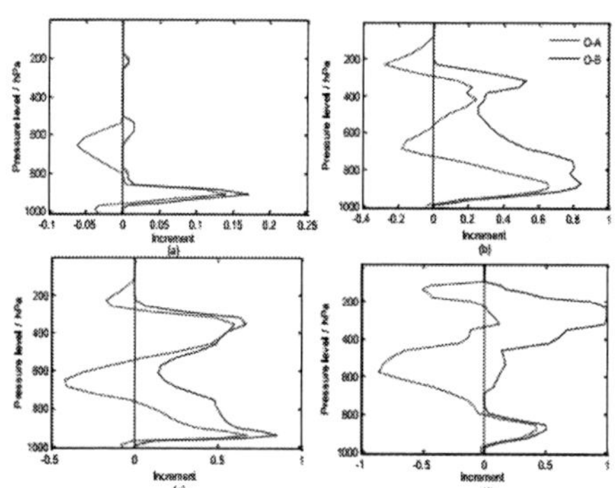

Figure 2. The vertical distribution of cloud amount of different cloud types in profile 1 (a), profile 2 (b), profile 3 (c) and profile 4 (d). Analysis increment (observation minus analysis, red line), background increment (observation minus background, blue line).

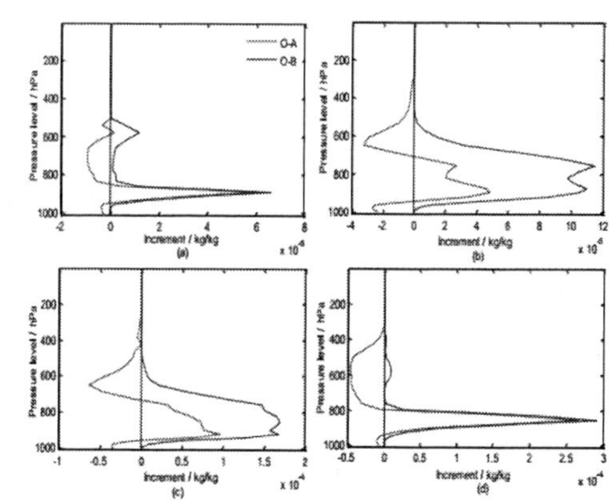

Figure 3. The vertical distribution of increment of cloud liquid water amount in profile 1 (a), profile 2 (b), profile 3 (c) and profile 4 (d). Analysis increment (observation minus analysis, red line), background increment (observation minus background, blue line).

Compared to the coarsely initial background estimation of cloud cover, 1D-Var analysis can be closer to the observation, especially when the cloud base is

DOI: 10.1051/itmconf/20171203007

relatively high and the cloud amount is relatively small (Fig. 1(d)). However, if the cloud base is too low and the cloud cover is too large (Fig. 1b, 1c), false bias field may be produced, for instance, the low cloud leads to the total cloud cover field to be distorted though the cloud covers are all not large in Fig. 1(a). From the analysis incremental (observation minus analysis, red line) in Fig. 2, It can also be seen that the 1D-Var retrieved effect is better where the high cloud exists.

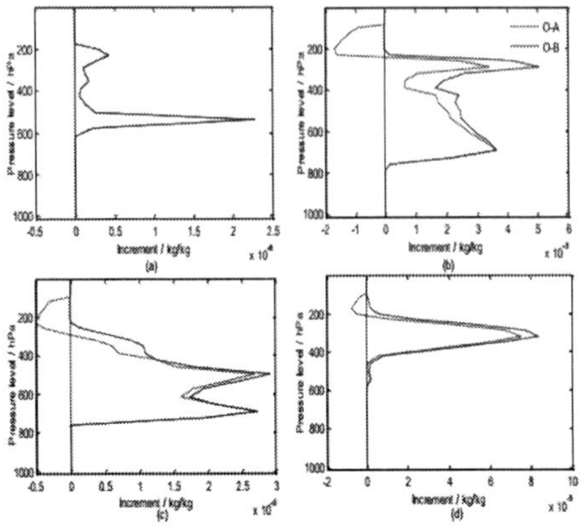

Figure 4. The vertical distribution of the increment of cloud ice water amount in profile 1 (a), profile 2 (b), profile 3 (c), profile 4 (d). Analysis increment (observation minus analysis, red line), background increment (observation minus background, blue line).

Fig. 3 and Fig. 4 show the vertical distribution of incremental cloud liquid water and cloud ice water, respectively. The height of cloud water is generally lower than 600hpa, the analysis and background increment have no much difference different when the cloud amount is small (Fig. 3(a)). However, 1D-Var can significantly improve the quality of cloud liquid water when the low cloud cover becomes big (Fig. 3(b), 3(c)). For ice cloud, the increments are close in the lower atmosphere because ice cloud usually distributes high in the atmosphere. It is clear that they separate from each other above 400hPa, the main reason may be that the water vapor reduces and scattering effect increases along with the altitude becomes higher.

5. Conclusions

Built on the 1D-Var algorithm, we investigated the retrieved effect of three cloud water variables (cloud cover, cloud liquid water and cloud ice water) in atmospheric field. The results of the experiment show that the performance of 1D-Var system works well and can obtain good estimation of cloud cover when the cloud amount is small, however, the retrieved cloud amount is not too ideal when the cloud cover is large or the cloud height is too low. 1D-Var has an overall reformative effect on cloud liquid water and cloud ice water. But due to the strongly physical nonlinearity in cloud and rain, the observed operator may not be able to describe the physical process accurately. Next, we will estimate more precise background and its error covariance of cloud water variables to obtain a better inversion effect.

Acknowledgment

The work was supported by the Natural Science Foundation of China (Grant No. 41375113).

References

[1] F. Chevallier and P. Bauer, "Model Rain and Clouds over Oceans: Comparison with SSM/I Observations," Monthly Weather Review, vol. 131, 2003, pp. 1240-1255.

[2] G. Ma, Z. Y. Fang and F. Y. Zhang, "The Impact of Cloud Parameters on the Simulated Errors in RTTOV5," Quaterly Journal of Applied Meteorology, vol. 12, 2001, pp. 385-392.

[3] W. Y. Ding, Q. L. Wan, Z. T. Chen, Y. Y. Huang and C. Z. Zhang, "Assimilation of HIRS/3 Brightness Temperature in Cloud Condition and Its Impact to CHANCHU Typhoon", Acta Meteorologica Sinica, vol. 68, 2010, pp. 70-78.

[4] Y. L. Liu, "Application Research of 1D-Var Retrieval Technology in Cloud- and Precipitation effected Satellite Microwave Observation Data Assimilation", Changsha: National University of Defense Technology, 2013.

[5] Q. B. Huang, "A Variational Data Assimilation Technology of the Cloud and Rain Affected Satellite Microwave Data", Changsha: National University of Defense Technology, 2011.

[6] Q. B. Huang, X.. Q. Cao, M. B. Zhu, W. M. Zhang and B. N. Liu, "New data assimilation system DNDAS for high-dimensional models", Chin. Phys. B, vol. 25, 2016, pp. 50502-050502.

A Time Series Forecasting Method

Zhao-Yu Wang[1], Yu-Chun Lin[2], Shie-Jue Lee[3], Chih-Chin Lai[4]

[1]*Department of Electrical Engineering, National Sun Yat-sen University, Kaohsiung, Taiwan*
[2]*Department of Electrical Engineering, National Sun Yat-sen University, Kaohsiung, Taiwan*
[3]*Department of Electrical Engineering, National Sun Yat-sen University, Kaohsiung, Taiwan*
[4]*Department of Electrical Engineering, National University of Kaohsiung, Kaohsiung, Taiwan*
1zywang@water.ee.nsysu.edu.tw, 2yuchun@water.ee.nsysu.edu.tw, 3leesj@mail.ee.nsysu.edu.tw, 4 cclai@nuk.edu.tw

Abstract: This paper proposes a novel time series forecasting method based on a weighted self-constructing clustering technique. The weighted self-constructing clustering processes all the data patterns incrementally. If a data pattern is not similar enough to an existing cluster, it forms a new cluster of its own. However, if a data pattern is similar enough to an existing cluster, it is removed from the cluster it currently belongs to and added to the most similar cluster. During the clustering process, weights are learned for each cluster. Given a series of time-stamped data up to time t, we divide it into a set of training patterns. By using the weighted self-constructing clustering, the training patterns are grouped into a set of clusters. To estimate the value at time t + 1, we find the k nearest neighbors of the input pattern and use these k neighbors to decide the estimation. Experimental results are shown to demonstrate the effectiveness of the proposed approach.

1. Introduction

Clustering is an unsupervised classification technology, with a purpose of forming meaningful clusters for the objects under consideration. Usually, similar objects are grouped in the same cluster, and different objects are grouped in different clusters. Clustering techniques play a very important role in the field ofartificial intelligence [1] [2] [3] [4]. In particular, they are widely applied in times series data analysis in a variety of areas, such as bioengineering [5],environmental monitoring [6], economic applications, and so on. In the process of clustering time series data, using the same weight for each dimension may cause bad effects. To deal with this difficulty, Huang et al. proposed TSKmeans [7], which is K-means with weights, to assign different weights to different dimensions of the data. A similarity measure based on the weighted Euclidean distance was adopted. Through quadratic programming, smooth subspace in time stamps can be produced. It was shown that TSKmeans can result in better clusters than the original K-means for time series data.

This paper proposes another weight-based clustering method for time series forecasting. Instead of using K-means, an iterative self-constructing clustering method is adopted. The method performs several rounds of clustering until convergence is reached. In each round, all the data points are processed incrementally. If a data point is not similar enough to an existing cluster, it forms a new cluster of its own. However, if a data point is similar enough to an existing cluster, it is removed from the cluster it currently belongs to and added to the most similar cluster. In each iteration of clustering, weights are learned for each cluster. When convergence is reached, the clustering process stops with a desired number of clusters.

The weight-based self-constructing clustering technique is then applied to time series forecasting. Given a series of time-stamped data up to time t, we divide it into a set of training patterns. By using the weight-based clustering, the training patterns are grouped into a set of clusters. To estimate the value at time t + 1, we find the k nearest neighbors of the input pattern and use the weighted sum of the centers of these k neighbors to be the estimate. Experimental results are shown to demonstrate the effectiveness of the proposed approach.

The rest of this paper is organized as follows. The weight-based self-constructing clustering technique is described in Section 2. Our proposed time series prediction method is presented in Section 3. Experimental results are shown in Section 4. Section 5 gives a conclusion.

2. Weight Self-Constructing Clustering

We describe the weighted self-constructing clustering algorithm in detail. Also, we improve the method by incorporating weights in the calculation of similarity, just as TKmeans does to K-means. First of all, we briefly introduce TSKmeans [7]. TSKmeans is a K-means incorporated with weights. It tries to make the distance between the data points contained in a cluster and the center of the cluster small through the use of weights of time stamps. Given X = $\{X_1, X_2, \ldots, X_n\}$ is a set of n time series patterns. Each pattern Xi = $\{X_{i1}, X_{i2} \ldots, X_{im}\}$ is the ith pattern characterized by m values, i.e., m time stamps. The membership matrix U is a n×k binary matrix, k is the total number of clusters, with $u_{ip} = 1$ indicating that Xi belongs to cluster p and u_{ij}, j ≠ p, is 0. The centers and weights of clusters are represented by two sets of k vectors Z = $\{Z_1, Z_2, \ldots, Z_k\}$ and W = $\{W_1, W_2, \ldots, W_k\}$, with j$W_{pj}$ being the weight of the jth time stamp for the pth cluster. The purpose of TSKmeans is to minimize the following objective function:

$$P(U,Z,W) = \sum_{p=1}^{k} \sum_{i=1}^{n} \sum_{j=1}^{m} u_{ip} w_{pj} (x_{ij} - z_{pj})^2 + \frac{1}{2}\alpha \sum_{p=1}^{k} \sum_{j=1}^{m-1} (w_{pj} - w_{p,j+1})^2 \quad (1)$$

Subject to

$$\begin{cases} \sum_{p=1}^{k} u_{ip} = 1, \ u_{ip} \in \{0,1\} \\ \sum_{j=1}^{m} w_{pj} = 1, 0 \le w_{pj} \le 1 \end{cases} \quad (2)$$

by the application of quadratic programming. Using these weights in each iteration of Kmeans until convergence is reached.

At the beginning, TSKmeans generates randomly the centers of clusters and sets initial values for the weights of clusters. Then the following three steps are done iteratively:

◎Step 1. For each pattern Xi, compute the distance D_{pi} between it and cluster p by

$$D_{pi} = \sum_{j=1}^{m} w_{pj} (x_{ij} - z_{pj})^2 \quad (3)$$

for 1 ⩽ p ⩽ k, 1 ⩽ i ⩽ n. A pattern is assigned to the cluster with the smallest distance. If pattern i is assigned to cluster p, then u_{ip} is set to 1 and u_{ij} is set to 0, j ≠ 0.

◎Step 2. Update the centers of all clusters by

$$Z_p = \frac{\sum_{x_i \in \, cluster\, p} x_i}{total\ number\ of\ patterns\ in\ cluster\ p} \quad (4)$$

for 1 ⩽ p ⩽ k.

◎Step 3. Use known U and Z to update W by applying quadratic programming to Eq.(1) with

$$\alpha = \sum_{i=1}^{n} ||X_i - \frac{\sum_{j=1}^{n} X_j}{n}||^2 \quad (5)$$

If clusters have changed in the current iteration, then go back and Steps 1–3 are performed again. Otherwise, TSKmeans stops.

We perform several rounds of clustering until convergence is reached. In each round, one full training cycle on the training set of N patterns $(X^{(1)}, Y^{(1)})$, $(X^{(2)}, Y^{(2)})$, . . . , $(X^{(N)}, Y^{(N)})$, is done. Two parts are involved in a pattern. The first part is the input vector and the second part is the corresponding output. Note that the dimensionality of the input vector is m. Let K be the number of existing clusters. Each cluster C_p, 1 ≤ p ≤ K is characterized by its center $Z_p = \{Z_{p1}, Z_{p2}, \ldots, Z_{pm}\}$, deviation $V_p = \{V_{p1}, V_{p2}, \ldots, V_{pm}\}$, height H_p, size S_p, and weight $W_p = \{W_{p1}, W_{p2}, \ldots, W_{pm}\}$. Initially, K is 0. Suppose we are in the rth round, r ≥ 1. For pattern i, $(X^{(i)}, Y^{(i)})$ 1 ≤ i ≤ N, where $X^{(i)} = \{x_1^{(i)}, x_2^{(i)}, \ldots, x_m^{(i)}\}$, we calculate the similarity between $(X^{(i)}, Y^{(i)})$ and each existing cluster by

$$\mu_p(X^{(i)}) = \prod_{j=1}^{m} \exp[-w_{pj} (\frac{x_j^{(i)} - z_{pj}}{v_{pj}})^2] \quad (6)$$

$$L_p(Y^{(i)}) = |H_p - Y^{(i)}| \quad (7)$$

for 1 ≤ p ≤ K. Two cases are considered:

Case 1. If

$$\mu_p(X^{(i)}) < \epsilon \ \text{or} \ L_p(Y^{(i)}) > \psi \quad (8)$$

for 1 ⩽ p ⩽ K, we do the following:

1. If $(X^{(i)}, Y^{(i)})$ currently does not belong to any cluster, it forms a new cluster C_{K+1} of its own. And we have K = K + 1, $Z_K = X^{(i)}$, $V_K = \{v_0, v_0, \ldots, v_0\}$, $L_K = Y^{(i)}$, $S_K = 1$, and W_K containing m randomly generated numbers.

2. If $(X^{(i)}, Y^{(i)})$ currently belongs to cluster Ca, we remove $(X^{(i)}, Y^{(i)})$ from C_a and update the characteristics of Ca. And a new cluster C_{K+1} containing only $(X^{(i)}, Y^{(i)})$ is created as previously

Case 2. If

$$\mu_p(X^{(i)}) \ge \epsilon \ \text{or} \ L_p \le \psi \quad (9)$$

for some existing clusters, we do the following:

1. If $(X^{(i)}, Y^{(i)})$ currently does not belong to any cluster, we add it to the most similar cluster, say Ct, and update the characteristics of Ct.
2. If $(X^{(i)}, Y^{(i)})$ currently belongs to cluster Ca, we remove $(X^{(i)}, Y^{(i)})$ from Ca, updating the characteristics of Ca, and we add $(X^{(i)}, Y^{(i)})$ to the most similar cluster Ct as before.

After all the patterns are considered, if none of the cluster assignments has changed, we stop with K clusters. If the cluster assignments of some patterns have changed, we update the weights W by minimizing the objective function of Eq.(1). Then we proceed with the next round of clustering.

3. Time Series Prediction

Suppose we are given a time series A that is indexed by the natural numbers as

A1,A2,....At (10)

where Ai denotes the value taken at time i. We'd like to estimate the value at time t + 1 based on these t values.

Firstly, we take each window of continuous q values and the value following the window as a training pattern. As a result, we have n = t−q training patterns. Each training pattern looks like (X, Y). For example, the first training pattern is (X_1, Y_1) where $X_1 = \{A_1, A_2, \ldots, A_q)$ and $Y_1 = A_{q+1}$, the second training pattern is (X_2, Y_2) where $X_2 = \{A_2, A_3, \ldots, A_{q+1})$ and $Y_2 = A_{q+2}, \ldots$, and the last training pattern is (X_2, Y_2) where $X_{t-q} = \{A_{t-q}, A_{t-q+1}, \ldots, A_{t-1})$ AND $Y_{t-q} = A_t$.

Secondly, we use the weight-based clustering method of the previous section to cluster these n training patterns into J clusters $C_1, C_2, \ldots, C_J$. Each cluster C_i, $1 \le i \le J$ has its center $Z_i = \{z_{i1}, z_{i2}, \ldots, z_{im}\}$, deviation $V_i = \{v_{i1}, v_{i2}, \ldots, v_{im}\}$, height H_i, size S_i, and weight $W_i = \{w_{i1}, w_{i2}, \ldots, w_{im}\}$.

Thirdly, we take $X = \{x_1, x_2, \ldots, x_q\} = \{A_{t-q+1}, A_{t-q+2}, \ldots, A_t)$ and compute

$$\mu_p(X) = \prod_{j=1}^{m} \exp[-w_{pj}(\frac{x_j - z_{pj}}{v_{pj}})^2] \quad (11)$$

for Cp, $1 \le p \le K$. Then we find k clusters with the largest k μ's. Let these clusters be $C_{p1}, C_{p2}, \ldots, C_{pk}$.

Finally, we estimate the value at time t + 1 as

$$\hat{A}_{t+1} = \frac{\mu_{p1}(X)H_{p1} + \mu_{p2}(X)H_{p2} + .. + \mu_{pk}(X)H_{pk}}{\mu_{p1}(X) + \mu_{p2}(X) + .. + \mu_{pk}(X)} \quad (12)$$

and we are done.

4. Experimental Results

In this section, we present and compare the experimental results of several clustering methods on the Poland dataset [8]. There are 1,500 instances in the dataset. The first 1,000 instances are taken for training and the remaining instances are taken for testing. The methods to be compared with include ANFIS [9], NN-MAT [10], ARMA [11], and Sorjamaa [12]. the original K-means, TSKmeans, and SCC. For convenience, our proposed method is called SCC with weights, abbreviated as SCC-W. To evaluate the effectiveness of these methods, the following performance measures are adopted [13]:

Maximum absolute error (MAE). It is defined as

$$MAE = \max |y_i - \hat{y}_i| \quad (13)$$

where yi is the desired value and $\hat{y}_i$ is the predicted value. MAE takes the maximum difference magnitude among all the testing instances.

Root-mean-square error (RMSE). It is defined as

$$RMSE = \sqrt{\frac{\sum_{i=1}^{N_t}(y_i - \hat{y}_i)^2}{N_t}} \quad (14)$$

where yi is the desired value and $\hat{y}_i$ is the predicted value, and Nt is the number of testing instances.

These measures have a common property: a lower value indicates a better prediction performance. We have found that SCC-W provides the best performance in terms of both MAE and RMSE. The window size = 5 and k = 2 are used for BCC-W. However, From this table, different window sizes may affect the performance of SCC-W, as shown in Table 1. As can be seen, the performance of SCC-W slightly varies as window size varies. The forecasted values are very close to the target values. We can conclude that SCC-W has a good prediction capability.

Table1. effect of different window sizes(WS)

	MAE	RMSE
WS = 3	0.0415	0.0614
WS = 5	**0.0355**	**0.0556**
WS = 6	0.0394	0.0613
WS = 7	0.0380	0.0614
WS = 9	0.0399	0.0620

5. Conclusion

We have presented a weight-based self-constructing clustering method and applied it to time series forecasting. Given a series of time-stamped data up to time t, we divide it into a set of training patterns. By using the weight-based clustering, the training patterns are grouped into a set of clusters. To estimate the value at time t + 1, we find the k nearest neighbors of the input pattern and use the weighted sum of the centers of these k neighbors to be the estimate. Experimental results have shown that the proposed approach is effective and promising for time series forecasting.

References

1. S. Haykin. 1999. *Neural Networks – A Comprehensive Foundation*. Upper Saddle River, NJ, USA: Prentice-Hall.
2. D. L. Olson and Y. Shi. 2007. *Introduction to Business Data Mining*, vol. 10. McGraw-Hill/Irwin Englewood Cliffs.
3. C.-S. Ouyang, W.-J. Lee, and S.-J. Lee. 2005 .A TSK-type neurofuzzy network approach to system modeling problems. *IEEE Transactions on Systems, Man, and Cybernetics, Part B (Cybernetics)*, 35(4):751-767.
4. S.-J. Lee, C.-S. Ouyang, and S.-H. Du. 2003. A neuro-fuzzy approach for segmentation of human objects in image sequences. *IEEE Transactions on Systems, Man, and Cybernetics, Part B (Cybernetics)*, 33(3):420-437.

5. T.-Y. Chiu , T.-C. Hsu , C.-C. Yen , J.-S. Wang. 2015. Interpolation based consensus clustering for gene expression time series. *BMC bioinformatics*, 16(1):117.
6. B. DeVries , J. Verbesselt , L. Kooistra , M. Herold. 2015. Robust monitoring of small-scale forest disturbances in a tropicalmontane forest using landsat time series. *Remote Sensing of Environment*, 161:107-121.
7. X. Huang , Y. Ye , L. Xiong , R.Y. Lau. , N. Jiang , S. Wang. 2016 . Time series k-means: A new k-means type smooth subspace clustering for time series data. *Information Sciences*, 367:1-13.
8. Y. Chen, E. Keogh, B. Hu, N. Begum, A. Bagnall, A. Mueen, G. Batista. 2015. The UCR time series classification archive.
9. J.-S. R. Jang. 1993. ANFIS: Adaptive-network based fuzzy inference systems. IEEE Transactions on Systems, Man, and Cybernetics, 23(3):665-685.
10. M. T. Hagan, H. B. Demuth, and M. H. Beale. 1995. Neural Network Design. PWS Pub. Co..
11. G. E. P. Box, G. M. Jenkins, and G. C. Reinsel. 2008 .Time Series Analysis: Forecasting And Control. WILEY.
12. A. Sorjamaa, J. Hao, N. Reyhani, Y. Ji, and A. Lendasse. 2007. Methodology for long-term prediction of time series. Neurocomputing, 70(16-18):2861-2869.
13 . X. Huang , Y. Ye , H. Guo , Y. Cai , H. Zhang , Y. Li. 2014. DSKmeans: a new kmeans-type approach to discriminative subspace clustering. Knowledge-Based Systems, 70:293-300.

Construction of Index System Based on Advanced Persistent Threat

Jia Lin[1], Rong Jiang[2], Yu-Lu Qi[3], Shu-Qiang Yang[4], Ai-Ping Li[5]

[1]*School of Computer National University of Defense Technology, Changsha, China*
[2]*School of Computer National University of Defense Technology, Changsha, China*
[3]*School of Computer National University of Defense Technology, Changsha, China*
[4]*School of Computer National University of Defense Technology, Changsha, China*
[5]*School of Computer National University of Defense Technology, Changsha, China*
1e-mail: linjia15@nudt.edu.cn

Abstract: With the proliferation of advanced persistent threat (APT), APT attack effect evaluation is playing an increasingly important role in cyberspace. As one of the hot issues of network security, the evaluation to its attack effect can quantify the harm caused by APT. Then according to the evaluation results, we can derive specific measures to the network attack. At present, a lot of work has done in the network attack effect evaluation index system. However, a significant barrier to the development of APT attack effect evaluation is that the existing index system is either from the point of view of the network security situation, or for a single attack weapons to customize. In this paper, an evaluation index system is proposed through analysing the features of APT. Through this index system, we can not only quantify APT attack effect, but also visually observe the APT ability from various angles. Then, we use the analytic hierarchy process (AHP) to model the evaluation process and calculate the weight of each indicator. Finally, the Ukrainian Power Outages is taken as an example to validate the proposed index system. The experimental results verify the effectiveness of the index system.

1. Introduction

With the rapid development of computer technology, the role of computer networks is more and more important. However, with the expansion of network size and the development of related technologies, the forms and means of cyber security threats are constantly changing. Network security has become a bottleneck restricting the development of social informatization.

Advanced Persistent Threat (APT) is one of the hot topics in the field of network security. APT means using of advanced means of attack on specific targets for long-term continuous attack on the form of network attacks. Almost all means of the network attacks can be applied to APT, so the defense of APT is still a difficult problem in the field of network security.

The assessment of the effectiveness of network attacks can be achieved on the quantification of network attacks, and giving reasonable recommendations according to the results. So as to achieve the purpose of active defense. Therefore, we establish an APT evaluation index system, and model the assessment based on the index system.

The remainder of this paper is organized as follows. In section 2, we briefly review relate works. In section 3, we propose an APT attack evaluation system and model it based on AHP. Then, in section 4 we take the Ukrainian Power Outages as an example to validated the validity of the model. Finally, we draw our conclusion in section 5.

2. Related Works

The construction of the evaluation index system of network attack is one of the hotspots of safety research at home and abroad. A lot of work has been done in index system at home and abroad.

Wang Juan et al. put forward 25 indicators from the perspective of the network situation [1]; Duan Bin et al. put forward a hierarchical worm hazard assessment index system from the perspective of the features of worms [2]. Wang Zhiping constructs a multi-level and multi-dimensional network security index system from 4 perspectives: basic operation dimension, fragile dimension, threat dimension and risk dimension [3]. Han Lansheng et al. proposed a set of three-level hazard evaluation index system for all computer virus [4]. Ai Peng puts forward a set of three-level network evaluation index system for all types of network attacks from the perspective of whether the systems, networks and services are normal or not [5].

The above research work, either from the perspective of the network situation, or only consider a single means of attack. Therefore, we propose an evaluation index system of APT from the perspective of composite attack.

DOI: 10.1051/itmconf/20171203009

3. Construction of Index System

In this section, we introduce APT and present the index system based on its features firstly. Then, we introduce the process of data normalization and index weight calculation.

3.1 About APT

For the definition of APT, there is no uniform standard. Generally, APT refers to the use of advanced means of attack on specific targets for long-term continuous attack on the from of network attacks. Its essence is a specific target for the precise attack. The term APT was originally originated in the 2005-2006, where network security engineers working with the Air Force described some of the security incidents. Some scholars believe that only those involving foreign organizations, directed against specific targets for long-term and deliberate attack is called APT. After the exposure of Google's Aurora operations in 2009, APT gradually spred in the media. Since then, all the delicate and persistent attacks are called APT. In recent years, security incidents related to APT are increasing. Fig. 1[6] shows the number of APT in recent years.

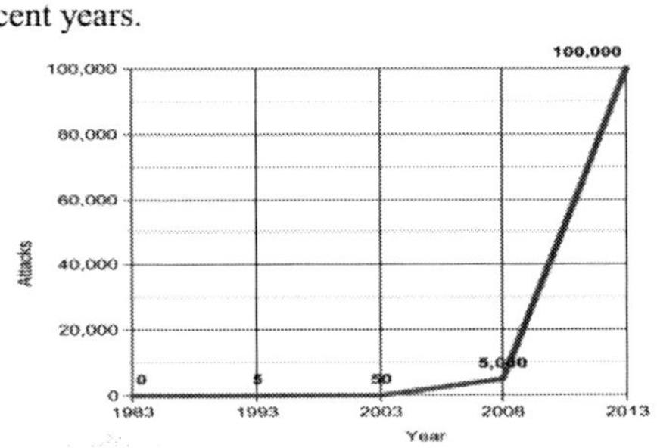

Figure 1. Number of APT

The concept of APT has 3 meanings:

Advanced: Attackers have the ability to evade detection, gain and maintain access to well-pretected networks and sensitive information systems. They usually have sufficient resources to attack.

Persistent: It is difficult to completely curbed APT and clear from the network system.

Threat: APT has both the ability and the intention to attack.

3.2 Evaluation Index System of APT

According to the definition of APT and its inherent features, we propose a complete index system, as shown in table I

Table1. Evaluation Index System of APT

U000 Attack Effect Evaluation of APT	U100 Persistent	U110 Attack Duration	/
		U120 Attack Frequency	/
	U200 Hiding Ability	U210 Static Hiding Ability	/
		U220 Dynamic Hiding Ability	U221 Load Hiding Ability
			U222 Run Hiding Ability
		U230 Communication Hiding Ability	U231 Communiction Mode Hiding Ability
			U232 Communication Content Hiding Ability
	U300 Diffusibility	U310 Scale of Diffusion	U311 Number of Affected Machines
			U312 Highest Authority of the Affected Machines
		U320 Diffusion Ability	U321 Number of Infected Platforms
			U322 Dependency on User Behavior
			U323 Camouflage
			U324 Exploit Ability
	U400 Intractable	U410 Copy Ability	U411 Number of Static Copies
			U412 Number of Dynamic Copies
		U420 Recover Ability	U421 Static Recovery Capability
			U422 Dynamic Recovery Capability
		U430 Update Ability	/
	U500 Harmfulness	U510 Cause Paralysis Class	U511 Ability of Destruction
			U512 Duration of Destruction
		U520 Information Theft Class	U521 Value of Stealing Information

Description:

Persistent: Including not only the total duration of the attack, but also the attack frequency.

Hiding Ability: The probability of being detected and the clearance of the activity traces is complete or not.

Diffusibility: Including horizontal diffusion (scope of influence), vertical diffusion(rights) and methods of dissemination.

Intractable: Backup, complexity of clean and so on.

Harmfulness: Most of APT can be divided into paralysis class and information theft class by attack effect.

All indicators can be divided into consumption indicators and gain-type indicators. For gain-type indicators, the greater the index value is, the greater the valuation is; consumption indicators are the opposite. So set the consumption indicator value negative.

3.3 Calculation

In the evaluation of attack effectiveness, the calculation mainly includes data normalization and index weight calculation.

3.31 Data Normalization

Normalization, also known as quantification. Raw data often have different dimensions. Therefore, the raw data need to be normalized to eliminate the difference in dimensions. We divide the index into quantitative indicators and qualitative indicators. The normalization methods of qualitative indicators and quantitative indicators are not the same. Since data normalization is not the main work of this study, we briefly introduce the normalization of these two types of data.

3.32 Normalization of Quantitative Indicators

Quantitative indicators are assessment indicators that can be accurate quantitative definition, accurate measurement. Quantitative indicators are usually integer or floating-point values.

For the normalization of quantitative indicators, we use a linear normalization method. The normalized formula is:

$$X_{norm} = \frac{X-X_{min}}{X_{max}-X_{min}}. \quad (1)$$

In this formula, X is the value of the current indicator. X_{norm} is the value after normalization. X_{max} and X_{min} are respectively the maximum and minimum values of a certain range.

3.33 Normalization of Qualitative Indicators

Qualitative indicators refer to indicators that can not be directly analyzed and evaluated directly through data, and the objective of the evaluation is analyzed and analyzed to reflect the evaluation results.

In general, qualitative indicators can be classified into Boolean types and level types. For Boolean types, we can convert "True" to 1 and "False" to 0. For level types, the normalization is shown in table II.

Table2. Normalization of Qualitative Indicators

Disappointing	Acceptable	Moderate	Good	Outstanding
0.1	0.3	0.5	0.7	0.9

3.34 Weight Calculation

We use AHP to calculate the index weight. AHP is a systematic analysis method proposed by A.L. Saaty[7], an American operational scientist. There are already a lot of work done using AHP for weight calculation. Due to space constraints, we don't elaborate on AHP. Only describes the calculation of the weights of the indicators under U400.

The scale of the judgment matrix is shown in table III.

Table3. Scale of Judgment Matrix

Scaling	Meaning
1	Representing two factors compared to the same importance
3	Indicating that one factor is slightly more important than the other
5	Indicating that one factor is obviously more important than the other
7	Indicating that one factor is strongly more important than the other
9	Indicating that one factor is extremely more important than the other
2,4,6,8	The median of the two adjacent judgments
Reciprocal	Indicator i and j compared to determine a_{ij}, then j and i compared to determine $a_{ij} = {}^{1}/_{a_{ij}}$

According to table III, we construct the judgment matrix A as follows:

$$A = \begin{bmatrix} 1 & 1/3 & 5 \\ 3 & 1 & 9 \\ 1/5 & 1/9 & 1 \end{bmatrix}. \quad (2)$$

The eigenvalue of A is 3.0291 and the eigenvector is $[0.3662,\ 0.9265,\ 0.0868]^T$.

The average random consistency indicators are shown in table 4.

Table4.Average Random Comsistency Index

n	1	2	3	4	5	6
RI	0	0	0.52	0.89	1.12	1.24

Consistency index of A:

$$CI = \frac{\lambda_{max}-n}{n-1} = 0.01455 \quad (3)$$

Consistency ratio of A:

$$CR = \frac{CI}{RI} = 0.02798. \quad (4)$$

Since CR < 0.1, it is acceptable to judge the consistency of the matrix.

The index weight of U410, U420, U430 is:

$$0.265 : 0.672 : 0.063. \quad (5)$$

The weights of other indicators are calculated by similar methods. The final indicator weights are shown in table 5

Table5. Index Weight

Index	U100	U200	U300	U400	U500	U110
Weight	0.225	0.135	0.21	0.175	0.255	0.5
Index	U120	U210	U220	U230	U221	U222
Weight	0.5	0.231	0.692	0.077	0.5	0.5
Index	U231	U232	U310	U320	U311	U312
Weight	0.7	0.3	0.7	0.3	0.4	0.6
Index	U321	U322	U323	U324	U410	U420
Weight	0.192	0.258	0.233	0.317	0.265	0.672
Index	U430	U411	U412	U421	U422	U510
Weight	0.063	0.5	0.5	0.5	0.5	1
Index	U520	U511	U512	U521		
Weight	0	0.6	0.4	1		

4 Experiment

In order to verify the validity of the proposed index system, we take the Ukrainian Power Outages as an example to experiment it.

December 23, 2015, the Ukrainian electricity sector suffered malicious code attacks. At least 3 zones were attacked and led to hours of power outages around 15 p.m. local time.

According to the Antiy's analysis report about Ukrainian Power Outages[8], we can see that this attack was initiated by the SandWorm, caused a large area of power outages, lasted 3 to 6 hours. It mainly uses BlackEnergy and KillDisk to achieve the purpose of attack.

Firstly, BlackEnergy encrypts itself and its installation package is named the same as the system process. So BlackEnergy's static hidden ability is strong. Secondly, BlackEnergy runtime injects the process into Svchost.exe to hide itself. Finally, BlackEnergy's update ability is weak.

For KillDisk, its features include:

1. Overwrite MBR and partial sectors.
2. Clean up the system log.
3. Process traversal and clean up the process.
4. File erase.
5. End process.
6. Shutdown operation.

Through its function, KillDisk is very destructive, but the difficulty of removal is low.

Due to the high concealment of APT itself, some data cannot be obtained, such as the Attack Duration and the Number of Affected Machines. As the Ukrainian Power Outages is a paralysis attack, the total duration of the attack is less than the average APT event. Other unknown data are also available.

In summary, the index values of the Ukrainian Power Outages are shown in table 6

Tablr6 Index Value of the Ukrainian Power Outages

Index	U110	U120	U210	U221	U222	U231
Value	0.3	0.1	0.9	0.9	0.9	0.1
Index	U232	U311	U312	U321	U322	U323
Value	0.1	0.5	0.7	0.3	-0.7	0.9
Index	U324	U411	U412	U421	U422	U430
Value	0.1	0.1	0.1	0.1	0.1	0.3
Index	U511	U512	U521			
Value	0.9	0.7	X			

Therefore, the evaluation of the Ukrainian Power Outages is:

Persistent:

$$U100 = 0.5 \cdot 0.3 + 0.5 \cdot 0.1 = 0.2. \quad (6)$$

Hiding Ability:

$$U200 = 0.231 \cdot 0.9 + 0.692 \cdot (0.5 \cdot 0.9 + 0.5 \cdot 0.9) + 0.077 \cdot (0.7 \cdot 0.1 + 0.3 \cdot 0.1) = 0.8384. \quad (7)$$

Diffusibility:

$$U300 = 0.7 \cdot (0.4 \cdot 0.5 + 0.6 \cdot 0.7) + 0.3 \cdot (0.192 \cdot 0.3 - 0.258 \cdot 0.7 + 0.233 \cdot 0.9 + 0.317 \cdot 0.1) = 0.4695. \quad (8)$$

Intractable:

$$U400 = 0.265 \cdot (0.5 \cdot 0.1 + 0.5 \cdot 0.1) + 0.672 \cdot (0.5 \cdot 0.1 + 0.5 \cdot 0.1) + 0.063 \cdot 0.3 = 0.1126. \quad (9)$$

Harmfulness:

$$U500 = 1 \cdot (0.4 \cdot 0.9 + 0.6 \cdot 0.7) + 0 \cdot 1 \cdot X = 0.78. \quad (10)$$

Attack Effect Assessment of APT:

$$U000 = 0.225 \cdot 0.2 + 0.135 \cdot 0.8384 + 0.21 \cdot 0.4695 + 0.175 \cdot 0.1126 + 0.255 \cdot 0.78 = 0.4677. (11)$$

The evaluation results are shown in Fig. 2.

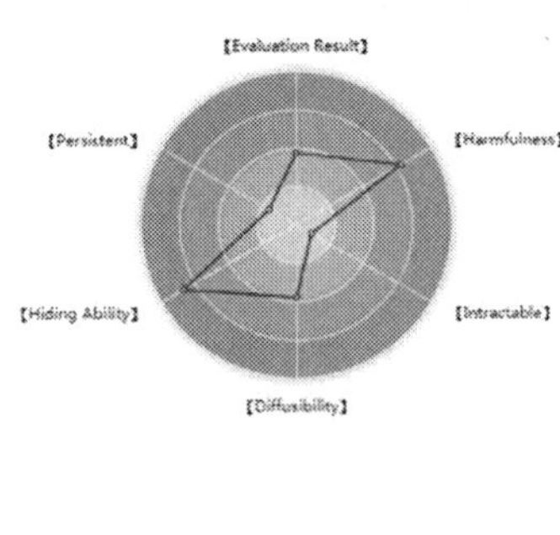

Figure 2. Evaluation Result of the Ukrainian Power Outages

Through the analysis of the Ukrainian Power Outages, we can see that there was no warning before the attack occurred. During the attack, the new 0day vulnerability was not used and the attack time was short. After the attack occurred, MBR and some sectors are overwritten, the system log is cleared and the controlled host cannot boot. Attack deals one-time damage to a controlled host, but the intransigence of malicious code is poor.

The above analysis and calculation results are basically the same, the Ukrainian Power Outages has a high degree of concealment and harm. But the continuity and intractability are poor. Its diffusion is moderate. Its comprehensive attack effect is moderate.

5 Conclusion

In this paper, a set of APT evaluation index system is proposed by analyzing the features of APT. And then use AHP to calculate the weight of this index system. Finally, the validity of the index system is verified by experiments. The experiment results show that it cannot only calculate the quantitative results of APT, but also see the ability of APT in five dimensions.

Acknowledgment

This work is supported by National Key Research and Development Program (No.2016YFB0800804).

References

[1] W. Juan, Z. Fengli, F. Chong and C. Lisha, "Study on index system in network situation awareness," Computer Applications, vol. 27, no. 8, pp. 1907–1909, 2007

[2] D. Bin, H. Weihong, and L. Aiping, "Research on quantitative assessment model for internet worm threat," Netinfo Security, no. 6, pp. 41–47, 2016.

[3] W. Zhiping, "Research of Network Security Situation Evaluation Based On Index System," National University of Science Technology, 2010.

[4] H. Lansheng, Z. Cong, Z. Mengsong and L. Qiwen, "Fuzzy Evaluation Model fro Harms of Computer Virus," Journal of Chinese Mini-Micro Computer System, vol. 31, no. 7, pp. 1297–1301, 2010.

[5] A. Peng, "Research and Implementation of Evaluation Technology of Network Attack Effect," National University of Science Technology, 2015.

[6] https://baike.baidu.com/pic/APT%E6%94%BB%E5%87%BB/5030382/0/dc54564e9258d10979684498d258ccbf6c814d15?fr=lemma&ct=single#aid=0&pic=dc54564e9258d10979684498d258ccbf6c814d15.

[7] T. L. Saaty, "how to make a decision: The analytic hierarchy process," European Journal of Operational Research, vol. 48, no. 1, pp. 9–26, 1990.

[8] "A Comprehensive Analysis Report on Ukraine Power Grid Outage," http://www.antiy.com/response/A Comprehensive Analysis Report on Ukraine Power Grid Outage/A Comprehensive Analysis Report on Ukraine Power Grid Outage.html, 2016.

DOI: 10.1051/itmconf/20171203010

A Survey of MAC Protocols on Wireless Body Area Network

Khushbu Khalid[1], Guo-Hui Li[2]

[1]*School of computer science and Technology, Huazhong University of Science and Technology, Wuhan, China*
[2]*School of Computer Science and Technology, Huazhong University of Science and Technology, Wuhan, China*
[1]*khushbukhalid@yahoo.com*, [2]*guohuili@hust.edu.cn*

Abstract: Wireless sensor networks have traditionally been used for military purposes but now its usage has widened in different areas of life including medical terms which are called wireless body area network (WBAN). WBAN is playing a vital role in every aspect of medical science for monitoring the continuous health of patients' body without hindering the normal physiological activities in human body. All physiological data like a heartbeat, blood pressure and body temperature can be collected and then transferred to the data servers for further monitoring through WBAN. In this paper we will discuss about WBAN and some MAC protocols that has been designed to improve energy efficiency in WBAN

1. Introduction

Wireless sensor network is an ad hoc network in which a big amount of sensor nodes are connected to collect and deliver data. In the past, the researchers of wireless sensor network observed that this is not suitable for WBAN because WSN has a lot of sensors and all sensors are not working at the same time. It may cause data loss, more energy conservation and may deliver non-reliable data which does not give the accurate result. WSN depends on Bluetooth and 802.11 technologies, has been designed for the big data but for WBAN a small data delivery technology is needed because the radius of the human body is small and for big data delivery there may have a chance to lose the data. Therefore, it cannot deliver the emergency data and this cannot observe the heat of the human body. WAN is not directly attached to a network neither with a router nor with any other device, but the nodes helps to transmit the data. WSN is widely used in some areas like the channel of crowd and containers can be sorted, determine the impurities in ecology, examine the structure, recruit the surroundings, and control the traffic on roads and in health observations. As the health industry is progressing rapidly. Healthcare machines are establishing to monitor the health of human body and to improve the quality of life that's why researchers are more focused on health care devices to make them more reliable. WBAN is an application of WSN and it is designed for communication and to focus the physical parameters around the body like blood pressure, ECG, sugar level and heart rate etc. Generally, it is based on two devices sensors and actuators. The function of sensors is to observe the vital signs of the human body and the function of actuators is to take actions based on the data they receive from sensors. Basically, the sensors are attached to the internal or external body and continuously monitor health without disturbing the daily life and patients do not need to stay at the hospital. In WBAN, IEEE 804.15.4 protocol is designed in which data cannot be lost and emergency data can be delivered efficiently so that it can give more accurate results about human body temperature. As it is about the health of a human body so it is very sensitive if it may lose any of data. Therefore, we cannot compromise on this issue and more reliable health care devices are used. The major problems are the life of the battery which is installed in a body. Moreover, the battery is non-rechargeable and cannot even replaceable which are the drawbacks in WBAN. Previously, many protocols had been designed in WSNs but that protocols are unable to fulfil the requirements of WBANs because it might work in the different environment and also the design is quite different. Generally, redundancy occurs in WSN because a big amount of sensor nodes are densely attached to gather the data and sends it to all the nodes and all nodes cannot work at the same time but in WBAN only 256 nodes are attached to the human body. Data is sensitive in WBAN as all nodes are active and data is more reliable to transfer as compared to WSN. It is the cause of energy consumption because all the nodes are working at the same time so in health measuring process of the human body so there is a need for protocols and techniques that may consume less energy in order to observe the health continuously. The whole communication system of WBAN can be categorized in three tiers. In tier1 the sensors which are installed inside the human body communicate to each other and this communication can be termed as intra-body communication. In tier2 the sensors which are implemented on the human body communicate with the personal device. This communication can be termed as extra-body communication. Tier3 is also an extra-body communication where personal devices transfer the collected data to the server.

2. Mac Protocol Design and Challenges

Lifetime of a network is the main objective of WSN. In this portion. we have explained about the energy efficient MAC protocols with some sources of energy wastes which tells the occurrence of energy wastes in the network and basic properties of a stable network

2.1 Attributes of a Good Protocol

Some of the attributes that are required to design a good MAC protocol are discussed below.

Energy Efficiency: Energy efficiency is an important attribute in the protocols. It is better to change the sensor node than to recharge the battery because the energy is being used either to send the data or it is kept on for a long time. MAC is proposed to monitor the energy while it is working or not working. It should help to stop the energy wastes. It has to sleep or turn off mode when nothing is transferring. Sometimes WBAN has to monitor the patients for a long time so MAC protocol should have to work efficiently and look after all the usage of energy in the network in order to save energy like from retransmission or collision. MAC protocol should help sensor node to turn off or go to sleep mode to decrease the waste of energy and can operate at low power.

Latency: It is required to observe the events in all nodes and sends the information to the base station (sink) and it can take the actions immediately to avoid all the collisions in the future. It may also relate to the delivery of packets because it's the time or the duration in which the packets are reaching the destination. In some applications there is a chance to the occurrence of short latency and short latency can be fatal in case of WBAN. The packets should be delivered on time even if the medium is not reachable it can use intermediate nodes to send packets to reach on time and to avoid worst scenarios.

Throughput: It is data transfer from node to the destination per unit time. It can be used in different applications in different ways. Some of the reasons like packets collisions, retransmission and latency, can be responsible for effecting the throughput. It also depends on patient's parameter because some patients need to be monitored regularly and some monitored irregularly.

Mobility: One of the most likeable attributes is mobility because if the patient needs to be monitored continuously at the hospital he can feel uncomfortable. No one is happy to stay at the hospital for a long time. Patient is allowed to go anywhere and no need to stay at the hospital and the health of the patient can be measured without disturbing the daily life.

Fairness: It is compulsory for the sensor networks that the packets receiving by the nodes are reaching properly to the sink. Although it depends on the energy efficiently and throughput, so energy efficiently increased by energy wastes. One node may have more data send with others so it needs to cooperate with all and reach on time to the destination.

2.2 Major Sources of Energy Wastes

Collision: During the process of transfer of data, some of the packets are being corrupted because of the interference and the nodes try to send the data again due to which it consumes a lot of energy. It is obvious that receiver has to choose any of the packets and drop the packet if they reach at the same time. As a result, it requires more energy in order to receive other packets that are delayed.

Overhearing: During the heavy traffic, overhearing is not good because it can causes major issues like if the packets are supposed to reach the given destination but they reach to another place.

Control packet overhead: When a small byte of data is transferred to the node it usually consumes more energy that is unacceptable for the network to use an energy that is responsible just for sending a small size data which decrease the capacity of the channel. To control this process it requires a fine approach that handles the situation.

Over emitting: It may happen in some cases that the receiver is not ready to receive the packets. Sometimes the traffic is so busy that receiver cannot able to handle all the packets at the same time and because of this error, there is greater chance to lose the packets.

Idle listening: Most of the time the sensor nodes are in idle state because if no data is transferring it may also listen to the network which is one of the big causes of energy wastes

3. Energy Reduction Methods In Mac Protocols for Wban

As the energy of the battery cannot be used for a lifetime as sometimes the patients need monitoring without any interruption. To save the battery usage it can be required in three places, sensing the data, data processing and communication. During the communication, a big amount of energy is used because idle listening, over emitting and traffic consumes the battery. To stop this consumption duty cycling is applied, it can increase the network life because it controls the idle listening. Sleep and active mode increase the performance of the network and saves its energy. There are three methods to save energy, low power listening LPL, schedule contention and TDMA.

3.1 Low Power Listening

In this technique sleep and wake up mode is determined all nodes are sleeping and just one node is awake to see the channel if packets are coming or not. It is also known as channel pooling. Because of this sleep and wake-up technique, most of the energy is saved. The nodes can only wake up at the time of receiving packets. LPL works well among networks because it has fixed data rate and it's very sensitive to the data variation. Its performance is tainted in the state of highly changing data traffic rates. However, it increases efficiently for already known periodic traffic rates. Wise-MAC is an LPL based MAC protocol. This

DOI: 10.1051/itmconf/20171203010

protocol reduces idle listening by employing non-persistent CSMA and preamble sampling techniqu

3.2 Schedule Contention

For WBANs contention based MAC protocol is not good because it is very sensitive to lose the data. Schedule based MAC, all the contenders (sensor nodes) contend for the channel before transmitting data. This mechanism is not acceptable for health issues because it has a chance to the collision of data packets and loss of packets. To stop and avoid collision both scheduled and contention based MAC are used together. Nodes are allowed to follow a specific schedule for communication of data. It is also a cause of extra energy because of different clusters. It can schedule differently. As MAC is a multi-hop network in WSN. By default, the duty cycle is applied to all nodes which are the basic function of this technique. Some of the MAC protocols based on scheduling are, TDMA, CDMA and FDMA. High computational overhead and limitation of sensor nodes, CDMA and FDMA are not recommended to use in WBANs. The nodes are only active while sending data otherwise keep sleeping. When data packets and synch reach simultaneously the node is dividing in two parts. The frame is the complete cycle of listening and sleep and cycle starts from the wake-up mode. If the node is sleeping it wait until it wakes up.

3.3 TDMA

In this mechanism, a base station gives time slots to all nodes. TDMA based MAC protocols performance basis on the traffic amount of the network. TDMA based Macs are efficient in the scenarios when networks have more traffic because the channel is efficiently used. If network traffic isn't enough and sensor node doesn't have data to send or receive then all other nodes need to wait for their slots and it causes wastage of the bandwidth. TDMA is the best mechanism because it increases power efficiency, just because it wakes up only at the time of transmission otherwise it sleeps all the time and it's also best for the synchronization of devices.

4. Energy Efficient MAC Protocol

WSN is growing so fast and the sensor nodes consume a lot of energy. In order to save the energy researchers have designed some electronic devices that consume less energy. By using these devices some protocols of energy efficiency have been designed. (MAC) medium access control is the technique that basically used to avoid the collisions from interfering nodes. The function of protocols is to define a mechanism that communicates each other in such a way that able to control the traffic and gives the reliability so the packets reach the destination. It also helps to organize nodes and sequence of the network in such a way that the sender and receiver communicate each other without collision. There are two types of channel Contention based channel and Contention free channel .Before the transmission of data, it does not allocate the channel to sensor nodes. Every node is struggling for the channel is contention based. If the nodes sends the data and at the same time the channel is busy then the node will wait until the channel is free and then sends the data to the channel and the state of sensing channel is called clear channel assessment (CSA) and in contention free mechanism which is TDMA, every node has given a specific time slots in which it has to send the data and the frame is organized by base station which is also called central node (sink) and the node has to follow the organization blindly. Similarly the sensor nodes never transfer the data to the node to the node which is not allocated to it.

4.1 Body Mac

To reduce energy TDMA based MAC protocol was proposed. In this protocol uplink and down link were defined and nods will be in sleeping unless they have no data. It is also good in low duty cycle. Burst bandwidth procedure, periodic bandwidth procedure and adjust bandwidth procedure are three types of bandwidth procedures. The bandwidths that have periods and reduces bandwidth to the half is burst bandwidth, in periodic bandwidth each part of frames in MAC and stored and every part has the special access to the channel. Total bandwidth that needs to increase or to decrease from periodic bandwidth is adjusting bandwidth. Some of the drawbacks are that the node can sense the data and transfer it even if it is in sleep mode, so in an emergency it is highly useful protocol to send the data. The first one is a beacon which is responsible for synchronization of data. The second part is downlink which is used to manage the process of transferring the data from the coordinator. The last one is uplink which is further divided into two parts contention access period (CAP) and contention free period (CFP).in CAP nodes fight to send the packets and responsible for sending small packets. CFP is basically used to increase the communication effecting energy

4.2 Med Mac

To improve the channel access mechanism Med Mac was designed. It is also used for reduction of energy. To communicate the data the slots they have given are the usually different size and different lengths. This protocol is used to initialize the network or for traffic emergency. Sometimes it is used for communication of low data rates, time stamp scavenging with adaptive guard band algorithm (AGBA) used in med Mac.

Generally, a guard time is used between two consecutive time slots using AGBA, this guard time can be adjusted and depends upon clock drifts. Drift adjustment factor (DAF) is used to guard band and helps to stop the extra guard bands. With a comparison with IEEE 802.15.4, it is used for low data rates like temperature, respiration and pulse etc. and medium data rates like ECG. For WBAN it is not suitable for high data rates and Med Mac can be used only for low and medium data rates.

4.3 Energy Efficient Low Duty Cycle

This is a new protocol with a static nature. This protocol is used for a large amount of data; the static nature of this protocol increased the life of the network. The master node (MN) is used to gather data from nodes and transmits by

DOI: 10.1051/itmconf/20171203010

the monitoring station. MS is used to observe the receive data which is also responsible for synchronization. This protocol has the static nature with fixed data rate generation. It is not suitable for the dynamic type of network. It is TDMA base protocol. Guard time (Tg) is used between each time slots. This Tg helps to avoid collisions between time slots .this is the protocol that decreases the idle listening. It is widely used in the medical area. For example, to monitor patients no need for the assistant. Minimum power is used. To monitor ECG it can be used which is very important in the field of medicine

5. D. IEEE.802.15.4

It builds a connection among all the devices and it can consume less power, low cost and data rates are also low.IEEE.802.15.4 consists of three parts that are used in super frames. ADAPTED CSMA/CA, ALGORITHM and GUARANTEED TIME SLOTS. Contention access period (CAP) and contention free period (CFP) are used for these schemes. Generally, IEEE.802.15.4 has two protocols that are random and scheduled. Traffic latency is very low is CSMA /CA. Star topology is used in WBAN and TDMA mechanism is being required in MAC protocols in WBAN. If it is compared IEEE.802.15.4 protocol it has used the concept of master/slave communication.IEEE.802.15.4 is not suitable for BANs platform because it has low data rate, low flexibility and power consumption. Some of the protocols are defined below to examine the energy consumption. IEEE 802.15.4 has the ZigBee technology and has two types of devices.

FFD (full function device): It is usually the router the router or gateway or coordinator of the network which helps with other networks.

RFD(reduced function device): It has low power consumption and low complexity.

IEEE.802.15.4 is divided into three bands of frequency 868 MHz, 915 MHz and 2.4 GHz and they are divided into 27 sub channels. 2.4 GHz has 16 sub channels, 915 MHz has 9 sub channels, and 868 MHz has 1 sub channel. It consists of two operational modes. Beacon enabled mode and non-beacon enabled mode. Beacon enables wises a super frame that has active and inactive parts. Active period has three parts which are contention access period, beacon and contention-free period.To support critical data end node are assigned seven guaranteed time slots but because of this kind of transmission this is not suitable for WBAN and CSMA/CA is used in non-beacon mode.

5.1 E. Enhanced MAC Protocol

The concept of IEEE 802.15.4 has been extended by CHEOLLYO LEE at el and it is clear that this protocol is not suitable for all types of applications. It is useful only for the devices that are used for health care. To measure human body a WBAN does not need many more devices but it needs a connection to some hops. IEEE 802.15.4 is not supportive to send the emergency data because in medicine there are some moments in which data needs to send in an emergency. Contention based medium is also known as CSMA/CA and guarantee time slots GTS both methods are used by the frame of the IEEE.802.15.4. This protocol cannot fulfil the requirements of WBAN because for WBAN critical time is the basic requirement and data needs to send emergency. This protocol is required to send the data quickly. Beacon is responsible for the periodic synchronization among BAN coordinator and other nodes. Super frame consists of primary beacon (PB), polling period (PB), emergency slot (ES), secondary beacon (SB), contention access protocol (CAP) and contention fee period (CFP). At the end of super frame an active period can be added .polling period and emergency time slot can be used for the extension of the function of the super frame with CAP and CFP. The devices that have installed inside or outside the body used only two-hop communication. Moreover, the division of slot interval is big and proficiency is low.

5.2F.Extended Enhanced MAC Protocol

It has been extended by this algorithm which is based on IEEE.802.15.4 concepts. Super frame of IEEE.802.15.4 is given below. Contention based (contention access period) and contention free access mechanism (guaranteed slot time) both techniques has been supported by this algorithm

It supports both, the contention based (contention access period) and contention free access mechanism (guaranteed time slot).It does not provide any solution for the emergency data and for guarantee delivery of date. On emergency data, sensor nodes need to send the data. It cannot wait for the time slot. Therefore, to transfer the data fast emergency slot (ES) has been used with the contention access period (CAP), contention free period (CFP), polling period (PP), primary beacon (PB) and secondary beacon (SB).

In the super frame structure of Enhanced MAC protocol. Along with ES, Contention Access Period (CAP), Contention Free Period (CFP), Polling Period (PP), Primary Beacon (PB) and Secondary Beacon (SB) have also been used.

Primary beacon (PB) is responsible for the BAN coordinator and the devices to synchronize. The basic purpose of PB is to be with super frame information e.g. beacon order, super frame order and slot insights excluding the CFP specifications. In PP the node that waits for polling request is basically responsible for the extraction of data. ES is used for transmission of emergency data. ES has also very short interval because the emergency event occurs rarely. IEEE 802.15.4 and Enhanced MAC protocol generally support one or two hops communication. As the nodes are implanted on both sides of the body the back side as well as the front side and because of the shadow of the body there is a chance of losing the packet. BAN coordinator is responsible for sending the data in Enhanced MAC protocol but all the nodes unable to get the information due to its two-hop connectivity. For the enlarge delivery of packets ratio EEM (Extended Enhanced protocol MAC) proposed a tree-based hierarchy which helps to keep remain the connection up to multiple hops. In EEM, the primary beacon has been send to all nodes by BAN coordinator. First hop and BAN coordinator participate in primary period. The emergency slot has been used for the emergency data and the CSMA/CA technique has been used which is started by the nodes at first hop and BAN coordinator in order to deliver the packets from nodes. Then secondary beacon has been sent by the personal server to all nodes. In CFP contention free period, the nodes are multi-hops and they require to send packets from fixed slots because of no direct connection with P.S, the nodes can transmit packets at first level of hierarchy but failed on other levels, so Tree Based Hierarchy has their super frame which allows other nodes to work as coordinator at multi-hop nodes in guaranteed time slot (GTS).

6. Conclusions

In this paper we discuss about the WSN and its charactristics along with different energy efficient MAC protocols. In BSN, Body sensor networks reliability of long life of the battery is the necessity that can be supported on the patient's body. The concept of developing energy efficient MAC protocol has become popular and exciting and it has been a good area of research over last decade. Reliability and energy efficiency are the fundamental issues that should take care of.

We also explained the extended enhanced MAC protocol in which tree-based hierarchy has been used which is not limited to only two-hop communications and I observe that it increases the reliability as compared to other previous protocols. .

More work can be done for the improvisation of average and maximum delay of extended enhanced MAC protocol in the future.

References

[1] Giuseppe Anastasi, Marco Conti, Mario Di Francesso, et al. Energy conservation in wireless sensor network: A survey, Adhoc Networks, 2008, 20(7):537-568.

[2] S.R. Gandham, M. Dawande, R. Prakash, et al. Energy efficient schemes for wireless sensor networks with multiple mobile base stations, in: Proc. IEEE Globecom 2003, San Francisco, CA December 1–5, vol. 1, 2003, pp. 377–381.

[3] V. Raghunathan, C. Schurghers, S. Park, M. et al. Energy-aware wireless microsensor networks, IEEE Signal Processing Magazine (2002) 40–50.

[4] G. Anastasi, M. Conti, M. Di Francesco, et al. How to prolong the lifetime of wireless sensor networks: 2004, pp.234-236.

[5] M.C. Vuran, O.B. Akan, I.F. Akyildiz, Spatio-temporal correlation: theory and applications for wireless sensor networks, Computer NetworksJournal 45 (3) (2004) 245–261.

[6] E. Fasolo, M. Rossi, J. Widmer, et al. In-network aggregation techniques for wireless sensor networks: a survey, IEEE Wireless Communications 14 (2) (2007).

[7] S. Ullah, P. Khan, N. Ullah, S. Saleem, et al. Areview of wireless body area networks for medical applications, vol. abs/1001.0831, 2010.

[8] D. Smith, D. Miniutti, T. A. Lamahewa, and L. Hanlen, Propagationmodels for body area networks: A survey, IEEE Antennas and Propagation Mag., Dec. 2013.

[9] J. Y. Khan, M. R. Yuce, G. Bulger, and B. Harding, Wireless bodyarea network (WBAN) design techniques and performance evaluation,J. of medical systems, 2012, vol. 36, no. 3, pp. 1441–1457.

[10] A. Zhang, D. Smith, D. Miniutti, et al.Performance of Pico-net co-existence schemes in wireless body areanetworks,IEEE Wireless Commun. andNetw. Conf. (WCNC), April 2010. pp. 1–6.

[11] R. Shah and M. Yarvis, Characteristics of on-body 802.15.4 networks,2nd IEEE Workshop on Wireless Mesh Networks (WiMesh), Sept. 2006,pp. 138 –139.

[12] E. Reusens, W. Joseph, B. Latre, et al. Characterization of onbody communication channel and energy efficient topology designfor wireless body area networks,IEEE Trans. Inf. Technol. Biomed.,Nov. 2009, vol. 13, pp. 933 –945.

[13] Polastre J, Hill J, Culler D, Versatile low power media access for wireless sensor networks. Proceedings of International Conference on Embedded Networked Sensor Systems; NewYork, NY, USA. 2004, pp. 95–107.

[14] Wei Y, Heidemann J, Estrin D, An energy-efficient MAC protocol for wireless sensor networks, Proceedings of IEEE Infocom 2002; New York, pp. 1567–1576.

[15] Van Dam T, Langendoen K, An adaptive energy efficient MAC protocol for WSNs. Proceedings of ACM Conf on Embedded Networked Sensor Systems, SenSys 2003, pp. 171–180.

[16] Zhen B, Li HB, Kohno R, IEEE body area networks for medical applications. Proceedings of IEEE International Symposium on Wireless Communication Systems 2007.

[17] Cheolhyo Lee, Hyung-Soo Lee, et al. An enhanced MAC protocol of IEEE 802.15.4 for Wireless Body Area Networks, Dec 2010, pp. 916-919.

[18] A. Milenkovic, C. Otto, et al. Wireless sensor networks forpersonal health monitoring: Issues and an implementation,ComputerCommunications, 2006 vol. 29, pp. 2521–2533.

[19] C. Otto, A. Milenkovic, et al. System architecture of a wireless body area sensor network for ubiquitous healthmonitoring,J. Mob. Multimed, Jan. 2005, vol. 1, pp. 307–326.

[20] D. Smith and L. Hanlen, Wireless body area networks: Towards awearable intranet, ISCIT Tutorial, Sept. 2012.

[21] M. Chen, S. Gonzalez, et al. Bodyarea networks: A survey, Mobile Networks and Applications, 2011, vol. 16,pp. 171–193.

[22] S. Ullah, B. Shen, et al.A study of medium access control protocols for wireless body areanetworks,arXiv preprint arXiv:1004.3890, 2010.

[23] H. Kwon and S. Lee, Energy-efficient multi-hop transmission in bodyarea networks,20th IEEE Int. Symp. on Personal, Indoor andMobile Radio Comm. (PIMRC), Sept. 2009, pp. 2142 –2146.

[24] B. Latr´e, B. Braem, et al. Asurvey on wireless body area networks,Wirless Network, Jan. 2011, vol. 17,pp. 1–18.

[25] I.F. Akyildiz, W.Su,et al. Wireless sensor networks: A survey, Computer Networks 38(4)(2002)

ITM Web of Conferences 12, 03011 (2017) DOI: 10.1051/itmconf/20171203011
ITA 2017

Failure Analysis and Evaluation of Reinforced Computer Equipment

Hua Wang, Xian-Yu Li and Jian-Qun Zheng

Beijing Shi QingHe DaLou Zi Jiu, 100085 Beijing, China
Email: 919wh_cn@sina.com

Abstract. Based upon the synopsis of failure analysis and fault tree analysis, this paper puts up the component framework of reinforced computer equipment and typical fault tree, carries out practical analysis and systematic application of failure analysis and fault tree analysis, and implements mechanism analysis, correction measures and probability evaluation. This will benefit capability improvement of reinforced computer equipment and related information system.

1 Introduction

Failure analysis is to carry out technology and management activities of estimating product failure modes, searching product failure mechanism and causes, and advancing countermeasures so as to prevent further similar failure. It is of practical importance to reliability engineering, safety engineering and maintenance engineering [1-2].

Fault tree analysis is generally to search for diversified causes, and ascertain potential design bugs of hardware and software by means of deductive method, so as to take corrective measures. It can also be used to compare various design projects as viewed from safety, and provide standards for the establishment of use, testing and servicing procedures.

Reinforced computer equipment is developed to perform business data processing and information transfer. It has found wide application in various information systems, and taken an important role in system operation. Failure analysis and fault tree analysis are undoubtedly meaningful to the performance and quality of reinforced computer.

2 Resume

Reinforced computer mainly carries out data processing and information transfer, and plays a more and more important role in routine operation of related information system. During the scheme, primary, normal and customization phases of equipment development, failure analysis technology is emphasized to ensure equipment availability and effectiveness; moreover fault tree analysis finds finer application in equipment failure analysis process [3-5].

Fault tree analysis comprises qualitative analysis and quantitative analysis. Qualitative analysis is to look for causes and related combinations that conduce to top event, and identify all fault modes, namely all the minimal cutsets, so as to distinguish latent faults, and improve equipment design. Quantitative analysis is to compute generant probability of top event based on generant probabilities of bottom event and logic relation of fault tree. The generant probability of top event is usually described in (1) and (2).

$$P(T) = P\left(\bigcup K_j(t)\right) = \sum_{j=1}^{N_K} P[K_j(t)] - \sum_{i<j}^{N_K} P[K_i(t)K_j(t)] + (-1)^{N_K-1} P[K_1(t)K_2(t)\cdots K_{N_K}(t)] \quad (1)$$

$$K_j(t) = \prod_{i\in K_j} F_i(t) \quad (2)$$

And wherein

P(t) — generant probability of top event;

K_j — the jth minimal cutset;

N_k — mumberof minimal cutset;

$P[K_j(t)]$ — generant probability of the jth minimal cutset during time t;

$F_i(t)$ — generant probability of the ith component of the jth minimal cutset during time t.

The construction steps of fault tree analysis consist of system investigation and fault analysis, top event choice, fault tree depiction and fault tree simplification. The emphases are as follows:

- Boundary condition should be explicit;
- Fault events should be strictly defined;
- Fault tree should be constructed step by step and from top to bottom;
- Gate shouldn't be directly connected to another gate;
- Events should be concretely described.

3 Equipment structure

The Reinforced computer is composed of power supply module, computation module and connection module. Power supply module includes connector plug, filter, backboard and AC-DC electrical source; computation module includes mainboard, hard disk and mainboard backboard; and connection module includes 20pin connection lines that provide computation module with 12V, 5V and3.3V currents for power supply module. Its connection structure is described in Fig. 1.

4 Problem description

The reinforced computer equipment (JJ3) ran into fault during system customized experimentation. When it turned on for a period of time, electrical source indicator was lit, and schedule bar of operating system were read orderly; however, it rebooted automatically while schedule reading was not finished, and repeated over and over. Related function and deductive analysis was accordingly implemented with respect to the computer fault, and equipment fault tree is established as Fig. 2.

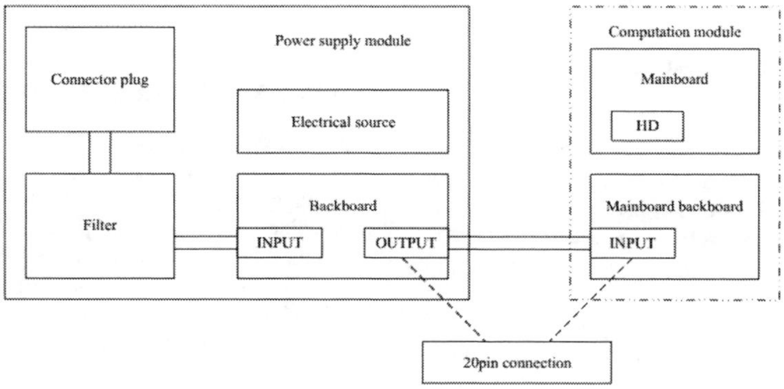

Figure 1. Equipment component connection structure.

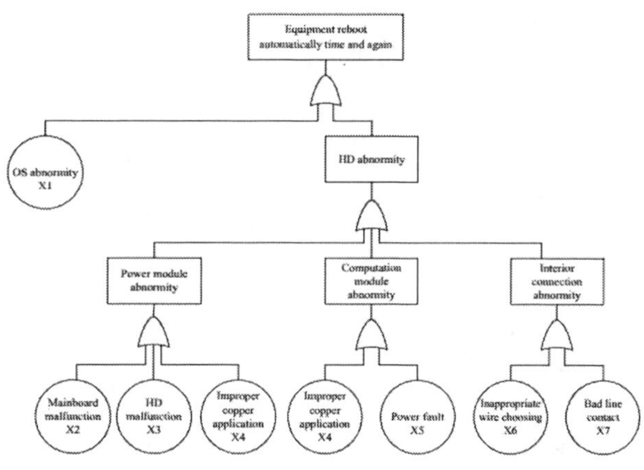

Figure 2. Equipment fault tree of reinforced computer equipment.

And we adopt the following labels:

X1 — OS abnormity;

X2 — mainboard malfunction;

X3 — hard disk malfunction;

X4 — copper application of backboard PCB falling short of routing requirement;

X5 — electrical source malfunction;

X6 — 20pin connection lines being inappropriately chosen;

X7 — bad contact of 20pin connection lines.

5 Problem investigation

To examine whether improper connection of electrical wires with backboards of electrical source or mainboard result in equipment malfunction, we can renewedly interpose and pull the electrical wires of doubtable equipment with linker of backboards of electrical source and mainboard.

We interpose and pull out the 20pin connection lines and linker of backboards of electrical source and mainboard, restart the equipment, and then operation system is normal; continuously perform restarting experiment for six hours, although the fault phenomenon does not appear. Moreover, we replace the former 20pin connection lines with spare 20pin connection lines, and continuously test the equipment for thirty hours, yet there is no abnormity.

DOI: 10.1051/itmconf/20171203011

We take out 20pin stretch feet from the troubled equipment, and make clear that stretch feet aren't injured by means of observation, so we can eliminate factors of manufacture technics. Thus press and joint technics of cable stretch feet has no problem. And we make experiment on new 20pin stretch feet connection for five times, and find nothing wrong with stretch feet, so we can deduce that equipment malfunction does not result from linker use. Thus cable stretch feet are abnormal during the general use process of the linker.

Above all, we can remove fault source X1~X6, and X7 need further analysis and testing [6-7].

6 Fault Mechanism Analysis

Equipment mainboard and power supply is composed of units which are shown in Fig. 3. P17C9X is the translation chip of PCIE to PCI that provides PCI expansion function; P17C9X is charged by 12V power supply, and when there is something wrong with 12V power supply, system will fail to realize PCI expansion function. Equipment mainboard make use of serial interface function of SuperIO that is charged by 3.3V power supply, and when there is something wrong with 3.3V power supply, system will fail to realize serial interface function. CPU of mainboard, PCH, memory and chips are charged by 5V power supply, and when there is something wrong with 5V power supply, equipment mainboard will fail to function and system have contact drop and shut off. And consequently it most probably is the abnormity of 5V electricity of linker that result in the equipment fault.

While electrical connection is joined to backboard linker, contact point produces contact resistance and heat energy with current on. The number of heat produced lies on the size of not only current but also contact resistance; and the littler contact area is, the more contact resistance, then the number of heat produced is greater while the same size of current. Wire is such material of positive temperature that resistance increases while temperature rises. The load of 5V power supply will continually enlarge after a period of operation time, and when the max current of stretch line interface is achieved, the excess heat generated will certainly consume essential task energy; thus 5V power of mainboard charged fall short of normal demand of power supply, and moreover, system automatically shut down.

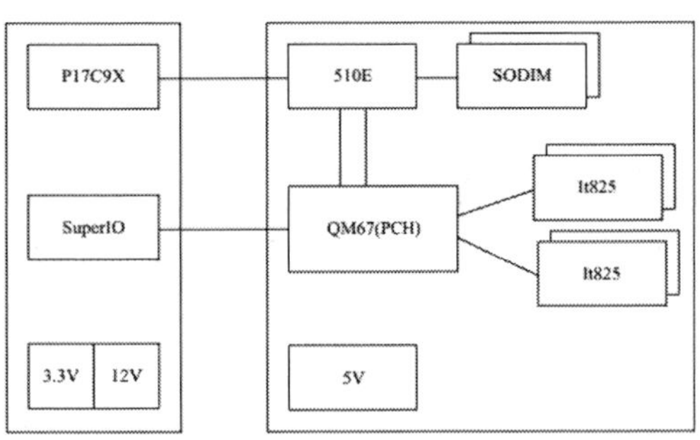

Figure 3. Equipment mainboard and power supply structure.

Equipment mainboard adopts AT task mode, and system AC-DC power will generates output when AC220V power has not been shut off after equipment fault; and mainboard automatically reboots as soon as it inspects electrical input, although 5V power of mainboard can't attain normal demand of power supply, and thus system schedule bar will display equipment status of automatic shutdown and reboot time after time.

To sum up, we can deduce that connection of 5V electricity of linker went down to loose from the above analysis.

7 Validation and Evaluation

We fix 20pin connection of fault equipment into spare equipment, and manually touch the related connection pins, hence the fault phenomenon shows again; and then we replace the faulted 20pin connection with new one, and carry through testing for 30 hours, and there isn't question with the equipment. We take out and fix the faulted 20pin connection into the linker, glue the linker ends, so as to ensure cable connector plugs well contact with electrical outlets of mainboard and electrical backboards. We continuously carry through testing for 30 hours during which the equipment has been rebooted ever and again, and the equipment works properly.

Technics is supplemented to glue the linker ends, and ensure cable connector plugs well contact with electrical outlets of mainboard and electrical backboards.

We completely identify the products that comprise 20pin connection of electrical source, and implement linker ends gluing with respect to similar products; moreover, we add the requirements for joint position gluing in product design files and carry out related gluing procedure alteration.

According to equipment operation circs and related indexes shown in Table 1, the probability of equipment reboot automatically time and again can be evaluated [1, 8]. And we shall pay more attention to improper wire contact, mainboard malfunction and electrical source malfunction in equipment development works.

$$P(T)=\sum_{j=1}^{7}P[K_j(t)]=\sum_{j=1}^{7}F_j(t)=0.0059$$

DOI: 10.1051/itmconf/20171203011

Table 1. The probability of minimal cutsets.

Minimal Cutset	K1	K2	K3	K4	K5	K6	K7
Related Event	X1	X2	X3	X4	X5	X6	X7
Probability	0.0005	0.0011	0.0006	0.0009	0.0008	0.0007	0.0013

8 Conclusions

Aiming at the fault took place during the experimentation of reinforced computer equipment, fault tree is set up, and detail analysis is presented; moreover, the fault is exactly located with its mechanism clear. Further, the equipment is effectively rectified, and technics is meliorated while similar products are fully corrected. Failure analysis and fault tree analysis are practically useful to the capability and stability of reinforced computer and information system, and it is necessary to continually investigate equipment faults, ascertain hidden mechanism and improve related system performance.

Acknowledgment

We are grateful to the specialists and secretaries for their insight and guidance, understanding and patience, and they are a constant source of support and encouragement.

References

1. Rui Kang, Qingchi Tu, *Fandamentals of RMS Engineering* (National Defence Industry Press, 2012)
2. Shengkui Zeng, *Reliability Design and Analysis* (National Defence Industry Press, 2012)
3. Bo Guo, *System Reliability Analysis* (National Defence University Press, 2005)
4. Weidong Liu, Yingjiang Xu, Xiyao Gao, Mechanical design and manufacturing, **6**, 118 (2007)
5. Guoyin Liu, Shaofen Lin, etc, Ocean Engineering, **37**, 70 (2008)
6. Qi Zhang, Jie Liao, Jianjun Wu, etc, Ordnance Transaction, **2**, (2008)
7. Yong Liu, Boqing Hu, Naval University of Engineering, **1**, (2002)
8. Pecht M, Das D, Ramarkrishnan A, Microelectronics Reliability, 42, 1259 (2002)

Design and Achievement of User Interface Automation Testing of Linux Based on Element Tree of DogTail

Wen-Chao Yuan [1,a], Hong-Mei Zhu[2] and Zi-Qian Sun [3]

[1]College of Computer Science and Technology, Shan Dong Agricultural University, Tan'an 271000;
[2]Red Hat Software(Beijing)Co., R&D Branch, Beijing 100190
[a] Corresponding author:yuanwenchao1@163.com

Abstract. As Linux gets more popular around the world, the advantage of the open source on software makes people do automated UI test by unified testing framework. UI software testing can guarantee the rationality of User Interface of Linux and accuracy of the UI's widgets. In order to set free from fuzzy and repeated manual testing, and improve efficiency, this paper achieves automation testing of UI under Linux, and proposes a method to identify and test UI widgets under Linux, which is according to element tree of DogTail automaton testing framework. It achieves automation test of UI under Linux. According to this method, Aiming at the product of Red Hat Subscription Manager under Red Hat Enterprise Linux, it designs the automation test plan of this series of product's dialogs. After many tests, it is indicated that this plan can identify UI widgets accurately and rationally, describe the structure of software clearly, avoid software errors and improve efficiency of the software. Simultaneously, it also can be used in the internationalization testing for checking translation during software internationalization.

1 Introduction

With the development of the science technology and wide-spreading of the computer application software. Linux operating system gets more and more concerning and approving. It has the advantages of security, freedom and open source, which appeals more and more users. User Interface provides user information as carrier. And the user's experience relies on its design and development. Owing to the open source of software, Linux users can debug and upload the new version software at any time. During this process, it is necessary to implement UI testing.

UI testing is the test for user interface, which can ensure the qualification of the user interface. Recent years, many researchers are working on studying and improving the method of UI testing. He Hao [1] proposes a effective and common UI testing method that is based on Silk and XML, but this method has limit of operating system. Memon [2] proposes a method that it creates test cases by AI classification technology. However, the maneuverability of this method is not good during testing. Wu Hengshan [3] proposes a method that is based FSM testing model of Graphical User Interface state finiteness by analysing problems of GUI automation testing, which gives method of building model and testing. His method can produce GUI testing path and testing input data automatically. Wang Zhao [4] proposes that building model can utilize colored Petri net for user interface object and designs methods that are based on different testing coverage criteria. Lu Yongzhong [5] creates a GUI automation testing system which is based on event flow chart. The system implements reverse engineering for GUI of tested criteria to get event flow and expected results of it. Then the method produces test case by daily smoking testing based on Ant Colony Optimization and Depth Regression Testing based on width-first search algorithm. Finally, it tests the GUI by implementing these produced test cases. However, these testing methods are not specific for the testing framework. And it is restrained by testing bench. Zheng Yaoming [6] proposes a method of function testing system of Linux GUI which are based on LDTP testing framework. It produces test script by keyword driven technology. But this method does not involve multilingual and multi-version testing. It is difficult to implement.

Red Hat Subscription Manager is the product of Red Hat Enterprise Linux, which is the product about system subscriptions. International software requires multilingual and multi-version internalization testing and localization testing. Each kind of testing will test again and again.

This paper analyses several common testing tools firstly. Then it creates a widget identification method of element tree of DogTail based on applications of Linux [7]. It designs the automation testing plan for the product of Red Hat Subscription Manager under Red Hat Enterprise Linux. The method records UI widget information in the form of element tree and produces automation testing script [8].It is an efficient testing method in Linux operating system environment. Simultaneously, this plan can describe UI each widget's structure and connection. It shortens more time of identifying widget, reduces the redundancy of testing script and improves efficiency of testing.

2 Related Work

In more and more violent market competition, in order to improve software testing efficiency, automation testing plays an more and more important role [9]. It makes tester set free from repeated testing [10].Automation testing can finish fussy and repeated parts of the testing accurately and efficiently. It can shorten testing]time[11], improve testing coverage area and save labor source.[12] UI's automation testing relies on testing script, which can trigger UI widget automatically and check the validity of widget to ensure the qualification of the user interface. For any kind of testing such as function testing or internationalization testing, UI automation is very popular and important. There are some automation framework ideas like: testing script modularization [13], test libraries, data driven[13,14,15]and keyword driven [16]. These will be used repeatedly at many times, which is important for the repetition and function test of same system. Most important of all, it is more effective in multi-version test [17].

There are many kinds of automation testing tools at home. For example, Rational Robot testing tool is created by IBM Rational company, WinRunner is supplied by Mercury, and QTP [18] is produced by Hewlett-Packard Development Company. These automation testing tools are quick to develop script, efficient to manage script and accurate to check script.

Whereas, these tools are limited by operating system. They are almost utilized at environment of Windows operating system instead of Linux. Linux operating system differs from Windows [19].It has universal and unified [20] desktop such as GNOME or KDE. DogTail is a kind of automation testing framework for open source. Relying on the advantage of open source, more and more testers are using and updating it. It is a framework for UI programmed by python. Although it does not have test case for the application, it provides a convenient and practical framework to produce their own testing scripts. Generally, most UI testing tools achieve automation by capturing the information of visual interface at a specific application. However, DogTail sets up a memory model of UI element by utilizing metadata connected with Accessibility.

3 Method of UI Testing Based on DogTail Element Tree

3.1 DogTail Automation Testing Introduction

DogTail framework provides two kinds of Application Programming Interface (API) for testing script. One is procedural API, the other is object-oriented API. Procedural API is used for function test of desktop application. As for simple user, it can help them to write script to finish some simple operations for UI object. And it is contained in the module named procedural of DogTail. If user needs to finish some meticulous operations, the object-oriented API can achieve it successfully. This kind of API can drive the application easily to reach a specific state to finish testing and revising errors. This API is contained in the module named tree of DogTail.

3.2 DogTail Automation Testing Workflow

In the specific automation testing of UI, it needs to select a specific application. The main work is identifying information and triggering action for the widget by searching and locating dialog and widgets of window. User Interface widget consist of element of dialog. Firstly, DogTail can capture information of the dialog, which is generated by function of it. Then it will locate widgets including button, label, sub-menu, sub-dialog one by one to identify information such as attribute, word, and formation and so on. These information is on basis of writing automation testing scripts for UI. Finally, DogTail will show the feedback after executing the testing scripts. In addition, testers will get the results after analysing the feedbacks. Generally, there are several kinds of errors like UI widgets truncation, shortcut key repetition and not availability, information unlocalization and UI widgets loss and not availability.

3.3 Element Tree of DogTail Theory

In Linux operating system, its desktop applications are in the form of tree. DogTail automation testing framework is the set of many modules of scripts written by python language. For example, Tree module and procedural module can finish operations of UI. Internationalization module can achieve internationalization and localization. Different modules will finish the automation testing by cooperating each other. In the tree module which can operate with GUI elements meticulously, it contains many classes. Each class defines implementations methods. The most important class of tree modules is node class. Here is the process of the design:

Firstly, it needs to design a element tree. The root of the tree is application named ROOT. ROOT application has the higher authority. It defines another desktop applications, high-level windows and dialogs generated by ROOT application as its offsprings. And it continues to define the widgets like button, labels and textboxes of the offsprings as the next generation of it Node is the element that includes ROOT application, applications, windows and widgets. It can be instantiated in the element tree. In a summary, node class is the mixed interface to the accessible elements and accessible user interface.

Then, in the element tree, next work is to search a node and locate it for automation testing. Module named Predicate of DogTail framework can finish searching. It can search nodes with the criteria. DogTail automation testing framework applies a kind of high-level searching mode. It will search one node or some nodes which are satisfied with criteria formulated by tester with the method of 'backoff and retry' algorithm.

Finally, after searching and locating a specific node successfully, it will define this node as a variable for programming. The variable will achieve operations by invoking functions in the class named action. In the action class, it defines and achieves functions for the node. These functions are exports made by the specific node on the accessible layer. For example, it has actions like click, write.

3.4 Element Tree of DogTail Development

Linux operating system's UI automation testing is on the basis of the searching node and matching it with rules. What is different from Windows operating system is that it does not have specific testing tools except testing framework. However, because of its unity, it is convenient for every tester to test UI, which makes UI's automation testing more efficient and universal. This paper proposes the method of element tree of DogTail for UI automation testing. Here are steps of developing:

3.4.1 Preparations:

It is necessary for tester to install an Unix-like operating system such as Red Hat Enterprise Linux. And it requires to install DogTail automation framework and GUI. It still needs to install Python language support.

2. Testing Script Programming

This paper proposes establishing the model of element tree of DogTail, and coding for node on searching, locating, identifying and operating at the testing script. There are three-level identification for nodes. The first-level identification is identifying ROOT application. The second-level identification is identifying desktop applications and high-level windows and dialogs. The third-level identification is identifying widgets of windows. DogTail automation testing framework can identify node information by information of string name. After identification, it will set the node as the variable. By invoking functions and methods, the variable can make operations and language testing.
Here are the specific steps:

(1)Configure environment and import modules. DogTail need import functional modules to the testing script so that it can finish related operations. In fact, It is made of many python language scripts that can achieve sub-module functions. The definition is below:

```
#! /usr/bin/python
from dogtail import tree
from dogtail.utils import tree
from time import run
from os import environ, path, remove
```

(2)Invoke functions to start or shutdown the dialog. It will invoke the 'run' function from the module named Util. The function can start the desktop applications and windows to be tested.

(3)If it is successful to search the node, the node will be set the value to get the authority. By coding, it can finish dominating the widgets of the main dialog. If the main dialog can generate the sub-dialog, it need set value for the node of sub-dialog after matching the string name of sub-dialog. Then the sub-dialog node will continue to execute its widgets for testing.

(4)Execute methods of Action class for operation. String name is the key to be identified. DogTail can obtains the string name of dialogs and widgets of UI automatically, then matches it with them in testing script. If successful, the node can succeed to achieve operations like Click (),and Close().The definition is below:

```
#Get a handle to subscription-manager-gui's menu
Systemmenu=subscription_manager_gui.menu('Sys
tem')
Systemmenu.click()
Systemmenu.grabFocus()
Systemmenu.menuItem('Register').click()
#Get a handle to subscription_manager_gui System
Registration Dialog
Register_Dia =
subscription_manager_gui.dialog('System Registration')
Register_Dia.child(roleName = 'text').text = 'xxx
xxx xxx'
Register_Dia.button('Next').click()
```

(5)Import internationalization modules. This module can achieve testing of language translations. International software has the feature of the multilingual and multi-version. Thus as for translation testing, it needs to import related modules and language support to be tested to complete internationalization testing . It usually cooperate with gettext modules. The definition is below:

```
Def translateAllStrings(appName):
"""
Test of the translation functions.
Take all user-visible strings in an app that's running
in the default localeand try translating them all into
locale that this script is running in.
"""for string in
root.application(appName).getUserVisibleStrings():
print(("User-visible string:%s" %string))
print(("Translation
is :%s"%dogtail.i18n.translate(string)))
print(("Packagedependencies:%sdogtail.distro.pack
ageDb.getDependencies('subscription-manager-gui')))
```

DOI: 10.1051/itmconf/20171203012

```
#print
dogtail.i18n.getMoFilesForPackage('subscription-manager-gui',True)
print (("Translation domains:%s"%dogtail.i18n.getTranslationDomainsForPackage('subscription-manager-gui',True)))
```

(6)According to above method, it need to go through all the nodes of the element tree of the tested application to identify and check the information and function of the UI's widgets.

4 Analysis of the Testing Result

4.1Automation Testing Result Analysis

For the basic and weakly logical operation on the Linux user interface like function testing and stress testing, DogTail framework can achieve the goal clearly. By writing simple Python language testing script, it can finish numerous repeated operations. In addition, there are convenient feedbacks to be reference for testers to conclude testing results. It saves more manpower and resources. For the strongly logical operations, testing script will often need to import more modules to cooperate to complete testing.

As for the testing result, it is based of feedbacks after executing testing scripts. This paper will compare it from the aspect of logicality and time index with traditional manual testing, which can show the advantage of DogTail testing framework. Here is the specific analysis:

4.2 Feedbacks Analysis of Testing Script

After locating a specific node, DogTail can invoke the node's main dialog and test it by the method of this paper. The testing script should defines and quote information from the main dialog and widgets of the dialog including its string name, location and invalid area. Besides information, another definition in the scripts is actions to be executed of the widget. Figure1 shows the tested dialog.Figure2 shows the feedbacks of the testing.

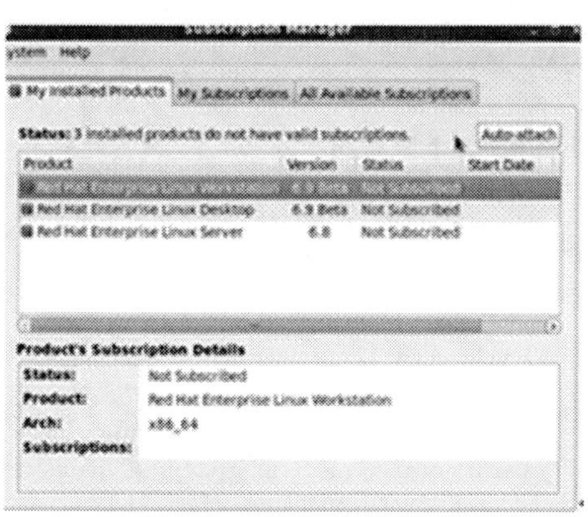

Figure1. The dialog of tested software

Figure2. the dialog of tested software

In the tested main dialog of Subscription Manager, the menu of 'System' is a widget. Its string name is 'System' and its attribute is menu. It also can generate other submenu. After defining the actions, such as click(),it will return coordinate. For example. (34,63),(125,86). If the string name of the UI' widget is not correct, after 20-time searching, it will report specific error of no matched widget. The feedback can help us to revise and check the information of widget.

4.3Testing Performance Analysis

By contrast with traditional manual UI testing, there is the advantages of the element tree of DogTail of UI automation testing:

(1)The method element tree of DogTail of UI automation testing shortens the time of identifying UI's widgets and reduce repetition errors comparing with traditional methods. The method also is suitable for another UI testing of Linux, which is more universal and efficient. As for fussy and repeated test case, it can make better use of resource and finish the testing accurately.

(2)Information of the node is different in international product such as string name of the dialog and UI information. Because they are in different language. For manual testing, tester need master many kinds of language. However, obviously, it is impossible. Therefore, it usually requires tester from different country in testing language to cooperate to finish testing. The method that is proposed by this paper will invoke target language vocabulary list to solve the problem. Target language vocabulary list is translation list from the source language to target language to identify UI elements. It can help drive tested software, which can solve the problem of cross language.

(3)The other feature of the method is clearly describing software structure. The elements of the tested software are distributing in the element tree in the form of node. The producing connection of each generation and attribute is obvious. It avoids the problems that complex connection of each widget leads to a testing mess. However, manual testing only tries to click each widget again and again. It is easy to test the same widget many times or miss the widget.

(4)The feedback of testing is timely and accurate. After executing the test scripts, it will show the correct or fault information of the testing automatically, which can be the reference to the testing results.

In summary, the method of element tree of DogTail automation testing framework tests the software accurately and efficiently. This plan is not only suitable for another application in Linux ,but also suitable for language translation testing. It can guarantee the accuracy and rationality of UI testing and improve the testing efficiency.

5 Conclusion

The advantage of the Linux operating system's UI testing is open source and uniformity. Linux in any version can implement automatic testing by using DogTail testing framework. When testing different desktop project, tester only installs different desktop support. International software is not only open source but also multilingual and multi-version. This paper proposes the method of element tree of DogTail testing framework to search, identify and trigger actions. It can not only describe the UI structure clearly and but also implement internationalization testing. The method guarantees the rationality of UI's widgets and avoids the lack testing and repetition testing according to the element tree, which makes the automation testing more logical. Simultaneously, the method also ensures the quality of the tested product and provides the reference for extra UI testing. How to handle the feedbacks of UI automation testing and automatically produce bugs is the next concern for the research.

Acknowledgements

The research work was supported by Shandong Internat ional Science and Technology Cooperation Project "Co llaborative research on methods and technologies of lar ge scale ontology modularization".

References

1. He Hao,Cheng Chunling,Zheng Zhengyu,Zheng Dengji. effective and common UI testing method based on Silk and XML [J].Journal of Computer Applications,2013,(01):258-261.
2. MEMON A M. Automatically repairing event sequence-based GUI test suites for regression testing [J]. ACM Transaction on Software Engineering and Methodology, 2001, 27(2): 144 - 155
3. Wu Hengshan,Wang Jinhong. Automation Testing Model of GUI Based on Effectiveness of Interface [J].Journal of HuazhongUniversity of Science and Technology(Natural Science version),2004,(12):34-36.
4. Wang Zhao , Bai Xiaoying, Dai Guilan.GUI Test Case automatically Producing Technology of Colored Petri Net Model [J].Journal of Tsinghua University (Science and Technology),2008,(04):600-603.
5. Lu Yongzhong,Yu Xinghua, Nie Songlin, Pei Xiaobing,Wang Chun. GUI Automation Testing System 's Development Based Event-flow Chart [J].Computer Engineering and Science,2008,(05):142-146.
6. Zheng Yaoming. Design and Development based on LDTP on function testing automatic script producing system of Linux GUI[D].Beijing Jiaotong University,2010.
7. Yuan Bing. Software Testing Methods and Technology 's Research on Linux Desktop System [D].Hunan University,2005.
8. Jiang Wei, Wang Houxiang, Automation Testing of GUI[J].Ship Electronic Engineering ,2004. 24(3):50-52
9. Ron Patton, Software Testing, Second Edition, Same Publishing, July, 2005.
10. Abt. Achieving the Full Potential of Software Test Automation. Logigear, 2004(5), 26-29
11. Kanglin Li, Mengqi Wu. Effective GUI Test Automation Developing an Automated GUI Testing Tool[M].Sybex,2004
12. You Zeqing. Automation testing framework of GUI software's research and development[D].Southwest University,2012.
13. Sun Y, Jones E L. Specification-Driven Automated Testing. Proceeding of the 42nd Annual Southeast Regional Conference,2004
14. Li Feng, Sheng Zhuang.Action-Driven automation test framework for Graphical User face (GUI) software testing[C]. Autotestcon, 2007.IEEE 17-20, 2007:22-27
15. Jian Ping Zhao,Xiao Yang Liu,Hong Ming Xi,Li Ya Xu,Jian Hui Zhao,Huan Ming Liu. A Lightweight-Leveled Software Automated Test Framework[J]. Advanced Materials Research,2014,2817(834
16. Liu Sheng, Software Automation Testing Framework's Design and Practice Beijing: Posts & Telecom Press, 2009
17. Bu Qianqian. Automation Testing Framework of GUI software 's research and application [D].University of Electronic Science and Technology of China,2010.
18. Zhang Qianqian. Automation Testing Tools based on Widget Identification of GUI 's Research and Development [D].Southeast University,2015.
19. Xi Haitao,Wang Fang. GUI and Related Technology of Linux Operating System's Discussion[J]. Heilongjiang Science and Technology Information,2013,(14):142.
20. Liu Shubin, He Yuzhu, Liu Jinkun. Universal Automation Testing Software Platform of Linux's design and development [J]. Electronic Measurement Technology,2009,(01):70-72+81.

On Construction of Good Quaternary Additive Codes

Luo-Bin Guo, Yang Liu, Liang-Dong Lu and Rui-Hu Li

School of Science, Air Force Engineering University, Xi'an, shaanxi 710051, China

Abstract. In this paper we present construction of some additive codes with very good parameters over the four elements finite field, each of these quaternary additive codes has double code words than its corresponding optimal linear code of the same length and minimum distance.

1. Introduction

Additive codes are generalizations of linear codes over finite fields, they have close relations with quantum error-correcting codes, for a general introduction of additive codes and a theory of quantum codes, please see [1] and [2]. In [3-7], some authors discussed the parameters of optimal additive codes and explicit construction of short length additive codes with length $n \le 15$ and leaves several cases unsolved. The results of [3-5] shows that, for length $n \le 15$, there are quaternary additive codes have double codewords than their corresponding optimal linear code of the same length and minimum distance. As for larger length additive codes, little are known on their parameters, let alone on construction of additive codes with good parameters and compare them with their counterpart linear codes. Thus, it is an interesting topic to discuss construction of additive codes with good parameters.

Here we concentrate on the construction of good quaternary additive codes. Before give our discussion, let us introduce some basic knowledge on quaternary field, quaternary additive codes and make some notations.

Let $F_4 = \{0,1,\omega,\overline{\omega}\}$ be the Galois field with four elements such that $\overline{\omega} = 1+\omega = \omega^2$, $\omega^3 = 1$, and the conjugation is defined by $\overline{x} = x^2$. An additive subgroup C of F_4 is called an additive code over F_4. If C contains 2^m vectors, C is called an $(n,2^m)$ additive code. A matrix whose rows form a base of C over F_2 is called an additive generator matrix of C. Especially, if C is a k-dimensional subspace of F_4^n over F_4, C is called a linear code over F_4 and is denoted as $[n,k]_4$. It is easy to see that an $[n,k]_4$ code is an additive $(n,2^m) = [n,2^{2k}]$ code. However, generally, an $[n,2^{2k}]$ additive code is not a linear code, for details please see [1].

An $[n,k,d]_4$ linear code is called an optimal linear code if there is no $[n,k,d+1]_4$ code, neither $[n,k+1,\ge d]_4$ code. For details on parameters of optimal linear code over F_4, please see [8].

Notation: In the following of this paper, we use $G = (a_{ij})_{m\times n}$ to denote an additive generator matrix of an additive $(n,2^m)$ code C, in order to present the matrices in compact form, we use '2' to denote ω and use '3' to denote $\overline{\omega}$ in the remain of this paper.

2. Construction of Additive Code

In this subsection, we construct generator matrices of some additive codes by combinational method, our discussion is presented in two cases.

Case I: construction of $(n,2^5,d)$ additive codes.

To save space, we need some special matrices as follows.

Let

$$0_3 = (0,0,0), 1_3 = (1,1,1), 2_3 = (2,2,2),$$

$$0_4 = (0,0,0,0), 1_4 = (1,1,1,1),$$

$$2_4 = (2,2,2,2), 3_4 = (3,3,3,3),$$

$$X = (0,1,2,3), Y = (1,3,2,0),$$

$$G_{5,31}=\begin{pmatrix} 0_4 & 1_4 & 1_4 & 1_4 & 1_4 & 1_4 & 1_4 & 0_3 \\ 1_4 & 0_4 & 1_4 & 2_4 & 2_4 & 2_4 & 2_4 & 0_3 \\ 3_4 & 2_4 & 3_4 & 0_4 & 1_4 & 2_4 & 3_4 & 0_3 \\ X & X & X & X & X & X & X & 1_3 \\ Y & Y & Y & Y & Y & Y & Y & 2_3 \end{pmatrix}.$$

It is not difficult to check that $G_{5,31}$ generates an additive code $C_{5,31}$ with parameters $(31,2^5,24)$, and the weight polynomial of this code is $1+31z^{24}$.

Puncturing $C_{5,31}$ on coordinate 1, 2, 3, 4, 29, one can obtain an additive code $C_{5,26}$ with parameters $(26,2^5,20)$, and the weight polynomial of this code is $1+30z^{20}+z^{24}$.

CaseII: construction of $(n,2^7,d)$ additive codes.

In this case, we use combinational and inductive methods to construct additive codes. Firstly, define

$$A_1=\begin{pmatrix} 1&1&1&1&1&1&1\\ 2&2&2&2&2&2&2\\ 0&0&0&0&0&0&0\\ 0&0&0&0&0&0&0\\ 2&3&1&1&3&2&0\\ 3&1&2&1&2&0&3\\ 3&2&1&3&0&1&2 \end{pmatrix}$$

$$A_2=\begin{pmatrix} 1&1&1&1&1&1&1\\ 2&2&2&2&2&2&2\\ 1&1&1&1&1&1&1\\ 2&2&2&2&2&2&2\\ 2&3&1&1&3&2&0\\ 3&1&2&1&2&0&3\\ 3&2&1&3&0&1&2 \end{pmatrix}$$

$$A_3=\begin{pmatrix} 1&1&1&1&1&1&1\\ 2&2&2&2&2&2&2\\ 2&2&2&2&2&2&2\\ 3&3&3&3&3&3&3\\ 2&3&1&1&3&2&0\\ 3&1&2&1&2&0&3\\ 3&2&1&3&0&1&2 \end{pmatrix}$$

$$A_4=\begin{pmatrix} 1&1&1&1&1&1&1\\ 2&2&2&2&2&2&2\\ 3&3&3&3&3&3&3\\ 1&1&1&1&1&1&1\\ 2&3&1&1&3&2&0\\ 3&1&2&1&2&0&3\\ 3&2&1&3&0&1&2 \end{pmatrix}$$

$$A_5=\begin{pmatrix} 0&0&0&0&0&0&0\\ 0&0&0&0&0&0&0\\ 1&1&1&1&1&1&1\\ 2&2&2&2&2&2&2\\ 2&3&1&1&3&2&0\\ 3&1&2&1&2&0&3\\ 3&2&1&3&0&1&2 \end{pmatrix}$$

$$B_1=\begin{pmatrix} 1&1&1&1&1&1&1&1\\ 2&2&2&2&2&2&2&2\\ 0&0&0&0&0&0&0&0\\ 0&0&0&0&0&0&0&0\\ 2&3&1&1&3&2&0&0\\ 3&1&2&1&2&0&3&0\\ 3&2&1&3&0&1&2&0 \end{pmatrix}$$

$$B_2=\begin{pmatrix} 1&1&1&1&1&1&1&1\\ 2&2&2&2&2&2&2&2\\ 1&1&1&1&1&1&1&1\\ 2&2&2&2&2&2&2&2\\ 2&3&1&1&3&2&0&0\\ 3&1&2&1&2&0&3&0\\ 3&2&1&3&0&1&2&0 \end{pmatrix}$$

$$B_3=\begin{pmatrix} 1&1&1&1&1&1&1&1\\ 2&2&2&2&2&2&2&2\\ 2&2&2&2&2&2&2&2\\ 3&3&3&3&3&3&3&3\\ 2&3&1&1&3&2&0&0\\ 3&1&2&1&2&0&3&0\\ 3&2&1&3&0&1&2&0 \end{pmatrix}$$

$$B_4 = \begin{pmatrix} 1 & 1 & 1 & 1 & 1 & 1 & 1 & 1 \\ 2 & 2 & 2 & 2 & 2 & 2 & 2 & 2 \\ 3 & 3 & 3 & 3 & 3 & 3 & 3 & 3 \\ 1 & 1 & 1 & 1 & 1 & 1 & 1 & 1 \\ 2 & 3 & 1 & 1 & 3 & 2 & 0 & 0 \\ 3 & 1 & 2 & 1 & 2 & 0 & 3 & 0 \\ 3 & 2 & 1 & 3 & 0 & 1 & 2 & 0 \end{pmatrix}$$

$$B_5 = \begin{pmatrix} 0 & 0 & 0 & 0 & 0 & 0 & 0 & 0 \\ 0 & 0 & 0 & 0 & 0 & 0 & 0 & 0 \\ 1 & 1 & 1 & 1 & 1 & 1 & 1 & 1 \\ 2 & 2 & 2 & 2 & 2 & 2 & 2 & 2 \\ 2 & 3 & 1 & 1 & 3 & 2 & 0 & 0 \\ 3 & 1 & 2 & 1 & 2 & 0 & 3 & 0 \\ 3 & 2 & 1 & 3 & 0 & 1 & 2 & 0 \end{pmatrix}$$

$$G_{7,31} = \begin{pmatrix} 0_{31} \\ 0_{31} \\ G_{5,31} \end{pmatrix}$$

Using the above matrices as blocks, we can construction four matrices as follows:

$$G_{7,35} = (A_1, A_2, A_3, A_4, A_5)$$

$$G_{7,72} = (B_1, B_2, B_2, B_3, B_3, B_4, B_4, B_4, B_5)$$

$$G_{7,96} = (B_1, B_1, G_{7,72}, B_5)$$

$$G_{7,127} = (B_1, B_1, B_1, \cdots \quad B_4, G_{7,31})$$

It is not difficult to check that $G_{7,35}$ generates an additive code $C_{7,35}$ with parameters $(35,2^7,26)$, and the weight polynomial of this code is $1+105z^{26}+15z^{28}+7z^{30}$. Puncturing $C_{7,35}$ on any one coordinate of $G_{7,35}$, one can obtain an additive code $C_{7,34}$ with parameters $(34,2^7,25)$, and it is not difficult to calculate the weight polynomial of this code $C_{7,34}$ is $1+78z^{25}+27z^{26}+12z^{27}+3z^{28}+6z^{29}+z^{30}$.

Similarly, we can check that $G_{7,72}$ generates an additive code $C_{7,72}$ with parameters $(72,2^7,54)$, and the weight polynomial of this code $C_{7,72}$ is $1+112z^{54}+12z^{56}+3z^{64}$.

Puncturing $C_{7,72}$ on the first coordinate, one can obtain an additive code $C_{7,71}$ with parameters $(71,2^7,53)$, and the weight polynomial of this code is $1+84z^{53}+28z^{54}+12z^{55}+3z^{64}$. Puncturing $C_{7,72}$ on the ninth coordinate, one can obtain another additive code $C'_{7,71}$ with parameters $(71,2^7,53)$, and the weight polynomial of this new code is $1+84z^{53}+28z^{54}+9z^{55}+3z^{56}+3z^{64}$. Hence, we know there are at least two non equivalent additive codes with parameters $(71,2^7,53)$.

The matrix $G_{7,96}$ generates an additive code $C_{7,96}$ with parameters $(96,2^7,72)$, and the weight polynomial of this code is $1+118z^{72}+9z^{80}$.

Puncturing $C_{7,96}$ on the first coordinate, one can obtain an additive code $C_{7,95}$ with parameters $(95,2^7,71)$, and the weight polynomial of this code is $1+87z^{71}+31z^{72}+9z^{79}$. Puncturing $C_{7,96}$ on the twenty-fifth coordinate, one can obtain another additive code $C'_{7,95}$ with parameters $(95,2^7,71)$, and the weight polynomial of this new code is $1+90z^{71}+38z^{72}+6z^{79}+3z^{80}$. Hence, we know there are at least two non equivalent additive codes with parameters $(95,2^7,71)$.

The matrix $G_{7,127}$ generates an additive code $C_{7,127}$ with parameters $(127,2^7,96)$, and the weight polynomial of this code is $1+127z^{96}$.

3. Discussion and Conclusion

According to Ref.[8], for n=34,35,72,71,96,95,127 and k=3,4, optimal $[n,k,d]_4$ linear code has parameters as follows:

$$[35,3,26]_4, [35,3,25]_4;$$

$$[35,4,24]_4, [34,4,24]_4;$$

$$[72,3,54]_4, [71,3,53]_4;$$

$$[72,4,53]_4, [71,4,52]_4;$$

$$[96,3,72]_4, [95,3,71]_4;$$

$$[96,4,71]_4, [95,4,70]_4;$$

$$[127,3,96]_4, [127,4,95]_4.$$

Comparing the above linear codes with our additive codes given in last section, we can obtain the following fact hold:

(1) The additive code $(35,2^7,26)$ has double codewords than the optimal linear $[35,3,26]_4 = (35, 2^6,26)$ code; the additive code $(34,2^7,25)$ has double codewords than the optimal linear $[34,3,25]_4 = (34, 2^6,25)$ code.

(2) The additive code $(72,2^7,54)$ has double codewords than the optimal linear $[72,3,54]_4 = (72, 2^6,54)$ code; the additive code $(71,2^7,53)$ has double codewords than the optimal linear $[71,3,53]_4 = (71, 2^6,53)$ code.

(3) The additive code $(96,2^7,72)$ has double codewords than the optimal linear $[96,3,72]_4 = (96, 2^6,72)$ code; the additive code $(95,2^7,71)$ has double codewords than the optimal linear $[95,3,71]_4 = (95, 2^6,71)$ code.

(4) The additive code $(127,2^7,96)$ has double codewords than the optimal linear $[127,3,96]_4 = (127, 2^6,96)$ code.

From [9]-[12], we know that additive codes have many new applications, we wish that using our method one can construct much more additive codes for other usage.

Whether one can further construct new good additive codes from the above $(n,2^7,d)$ codes given in Cases II, by puncturing on several coordinates? This need further study in the future.

Acknowledgement

This work is supported by National Natural Science Foundation of China under Grant No.11471011 and Natural Science Foundation of Shaanxi under Grant No. 2017JQ1032.

References

1. A.R. Calderbank, E.M. Rains, P.W. Shor and N.J.A. Sloane, IEEE. T. Inform. Theory, 44, 1369-1387(1998).
2. V.Tonchev, Discrete Math., 257, 549-557(2002).
3. A.Blokhuis, A.E. Brouwer, Eur. J. Combin. 25, 161-167(2004).
4. J.Bierbrauer, G.Faina, S.Marcugini, F. Pambianco, Proc. 10th Int. Workshop Algebraic Combin. Coding Theory, Zvenigorod, Russia, 15- 18 (2006).
5. J. Bierbrauer, Y. Edel, G. Faina, S. Marcugini, F. Pambianco, IEEE. T. Inf. Theory, 55, 952-954(2009).
6. J. Bierbrauer, D. Bartoli, G. Faina, S. Marcugini F. Pambianco, Finite Fields Th. App., 26, 29-40(2015).
7. J. Bierbrauer, Introduction to Coding Theory (Chapman \& Hall/CRC Press, London, 2004).
8. M. Grassl., http://www.codetables.de.
9. P. Gaborit, W. C. Huffman, J. L. Kim, V. Pless, DIMACS Ser. Discrete Math. Theor. Comput. Sci., Amer. Math. Soc., Providence, 56, 135-149 (2001)
10. T. A. Gulliver, J. L. Kim, IEEE. T. Inf. Theory, 50, 359-366 (2004),.
11. G. Hohn, Math. Ann., 327, 227-255 (2003).
12. W. C. Huffman, V. S. Pless, Fundamentals of Error-correcting Codes, (Cambridge University Press, Cambridge, 2003).

Research on Quality Grade Classification Method of Daily-use Porcelain Based on Multi-agent Technology

Yong-Hong ZHU, Liang-Ying LI, Jun-Xiang WANG, Dong WANG

School of Mechanical and Electronic Engineering, Jingdezhen Ceramic Institute
Jingdezhen, China,zyh_patrick@163.com,Liangyingli@163.com,wjx851113851113@163.com,79973351@qq.com

Abstract:Due to the influence of factors such as environment, materials and so on in the ceramic production process, different levels and different kinds of defects such as crack, fall slag, deformation, roast flower sticky glaze and so on appeared on ceramic products. In this case, the artificial discerning and classification efficiency is very low. In order to improve ceramic products quality classification efficiency and intelligent level, a kind of method of applying multi-agent technology to ceramic products quality grade classification is presented, and the ceramic classification system structure and function implementation scheme based on multi-agent technology are also given in the paper. At the same time, Kalman filtering algorithm and C4.5 classification algorithm is effectively fused to process data by the multi-agent. In the end, an application example is given. Through applying the method proposed to the sampling daily-use porcelain classification, the result shows that the method proposed is effective and feasible in the daily-use porcelain classification. This will provide a new approach and new idea for the application of multi-agent technology to the ceramics field.

1Introduction

In ceramic production process, uncertain factors such as raw materials preparation, temperature control and so on can lead to various defects of eventually fired ceramics, including crack, deformation, fall slag, roast flower sticky glaze, crack glaze, brown eye (pinhole, pore), spots, dirty marks, dirty Al2O3, glaze peels edge peeling , excess glaze, orange glaze, glaze bubble, glazed, ripple, smoked, off color, melt hole, body powder (sludge, glaze slag), concave and convex, and so on[1]. After ceramic products out of ceramic kiln cool, all products need be classified. Unqualified products are usually removed, some products with no very serious defects are screened, and defective products which can be normally used are sold at a low price. At present, ceramic products mainly rely on manual screening, and qualified or unqualified products rely on artificial experience judgment. Hence, this kind of classification method greatly affects the production efficiency. Under the great environment of today's highly developed science and technology and acceleration of society pace, enterprises will have to keep up with the rhythm and shorten the production cycle in order to survive.

Multi-agent system is a hot research content of artificial intelligence field, starting from the mid-1980-s. In recent years, multi-agent technology research has entered the stage of relative prosperity and also slowly began to be applied in various industry fields. In complex control system, L. L. Li, etc. proposed a kind of control method of city commercial user pricing system based on multi-agent technology, and constructed corresponding agent by simulating government, users, companies, monitoring, interactive personnel and so on respectively, then used agent interactive to simulate price fluctuations led to by city gas network demand and operational changes[2] . X. M. Luo, etc. applied the multi-agent technology to missile combat system, and puts forward the anti-radiation missile operational effectiveness assessment model based on Bayesian network[3]. In image processing, W. N. Xie, etc. put forward to detect and analyze the synthetic aperture radar images by using multi-agent two-dimensional Otsu method, and used multi-agent genetic algorithm to determine the maximum threshold of the distance measurement function between variable and constant in order to obtain detection results[4]. However, the application of multi-agent technology to daily-use porcelain quality grade classification has not yet been reported. So far, daily-use porcelain has still be classified by manual operation. Hence, labor intensity of workers is great and production efficiency is low. Based on the above research results, the application of multi-agent technology to ceramics quality grade classification will be conducive to greatly reduce labor intensity and to improve production efficiency, and is with the vital significance.

Ceramic products quality classification in ceramic industry production is a relatively complicated process. In

DOI: 10.1051/itmconf/20171203014

this paper, multi-agent alliance network structure was used to analyze data, a small multi-agent alliance network used for detection and classification is rebuilt on the basis of the fully multi-agent network structure of ceramic production process control system[5-8]. When the multi-agent alliance network detects and classifies ceramic products, an agent begins to interact with other agents. After the completion of interaction, through using pre-defined criteria, the interaction with the agents which generate positive impact is enhanced and the interaction with the agents which generate negative impact is abated so as to improve the automation level, to bring more profits for enterprises and to promote the development of ceramic industry.

2 Multi-agent Technology

Agent is a small branch of artificial intelligence. It is generally regarded that the agent concept came from the Dartmouth conference launched together by the father of artificial intelligence, a computer scientist Marvin Ming and the founder of framework theory, J. McCarthy in 1956. With the development of science and technology, the agent is given more and more new features and is generally with three basic features shown in Figure1[9]. Autonomy means that it is without persons or other devices' direct interference and with the ability to control their own behavior; Groups means that it can work with other agents together to achieve shared goals; Self-adaption means that it is with the ability to change their behavior by learning. An agent system includes four dimensional connotations such as agent, environment, interaction and organization shown in Figure2 [9]. The agent means the internal inference. The environment means that perception and action of agents in the environment. The interaction means the interaction of an agent with other agents. The organization means the structuralization and management of relationship among agents.

Figure 1. Three characteristics

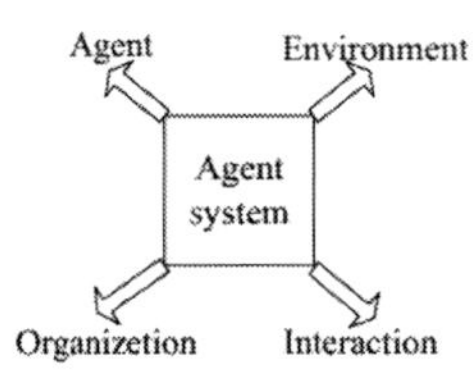

Figure 2. Four connotations

The multi-agent network structure given in the article includes complete network structure and alliance network structure shown in Figure 3 and Figure 4 respectively. Alliance network system structure-based the multi-agent system is with three-tier multi-level structure such as low layer agent, middle layer agent and high layer agent. High layer agent understands the structures of all middle layer agents and low layer agents, often interacts with the other high layer agents and manage middle layer agents at various places. Middle-layer agent manages several low layer agents, and only belongs to a high layer agent. Low layer agent is reactive agent and generally with several special functions, and only belongs a middle layer agent. Its basic components is shown in Figure 5.

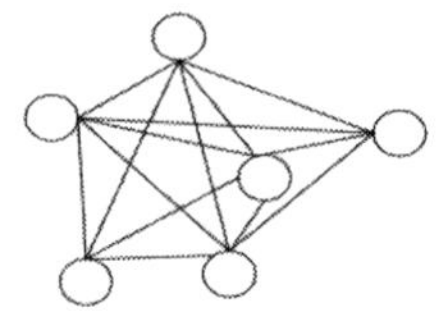

Figure. 3 Complete network Structure

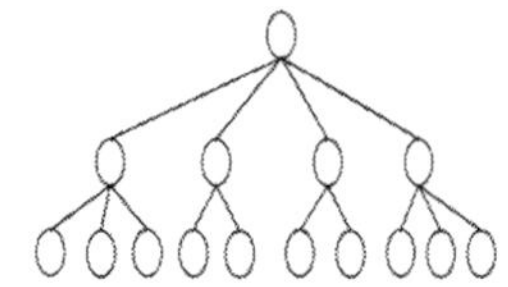

Figure. 4 Alliance network structure

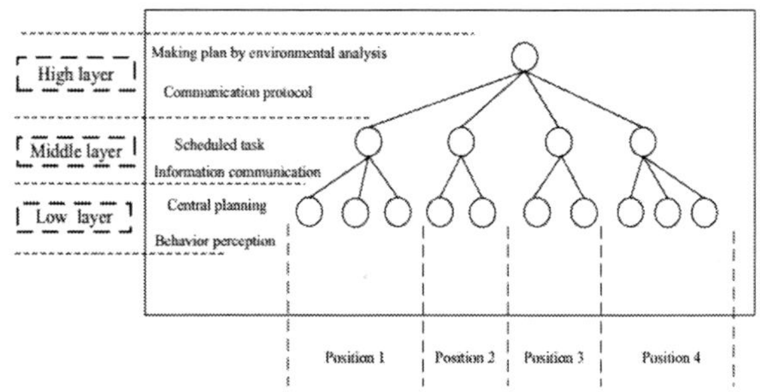

Figure 5. Composition relationship of multi-agent platform

3 The Structural Composition and Function Modules of Daily-use Porcelains Classification System

3.1 Multi-agent Species of the Classification System

The multi-agent of the classification system is mainly composed of interactive agent, task agent, management agent, resource agent and execution agent. The relationship among them is shown in Figure. 6.

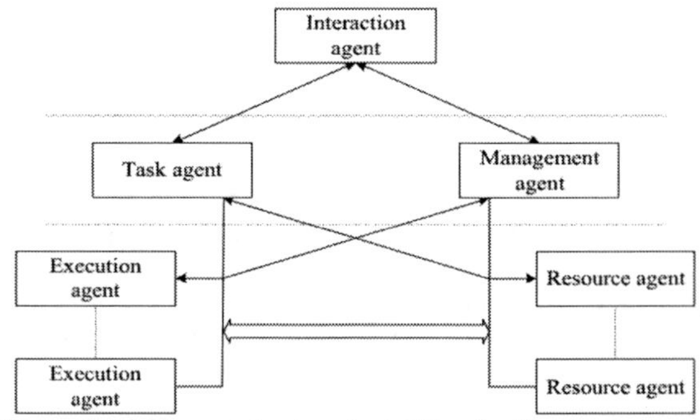

Figure 6. Multi-agent structure chart of the classification system

DOI: 10.1051/itmconf/20171203014

3.2 The Classification System Architecture

Multi-agent-based daily-use porcelain quality classification system architecture is shown in Figure 7.Man-machine interface agent transforms instruction information into the system task. Then, each agent in the system completes the data analysis, data diagnosis and implementation respectively. At last, these agents feedback the results to the terminal network server and the terminal function server. The two terminal servers are data accessing terminals, but their functions is not the same in the system. In fact, there is a standby database in the system, and the information in the database can not be lost. A major role of the database is that the safe and detailed database can be used to invoke in the system if the information agent fails. Man-machine interface agent converts the final task results to man-machine interface output format, and reports the overall solution situation so as to complete final task. Finally, the users can observe the work situation of the system via the man-machine interface.

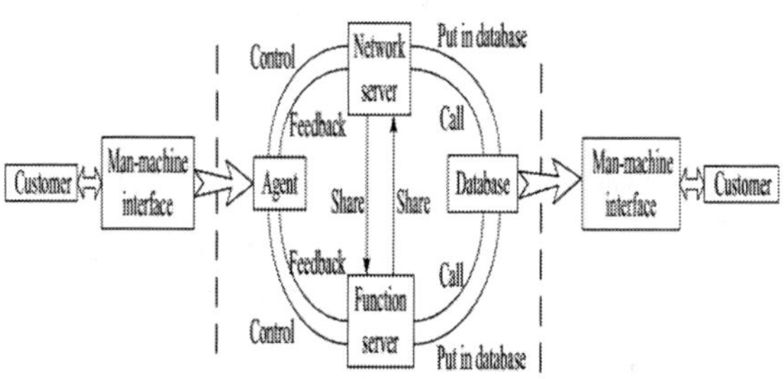

Figure 7. Multi-agent-based daily-use porcelain quality classification system architecture

3.3 Detection and Classification System Flow

After the completion of the whole system task allocation, the executive agent starts detection, and the resource agent starts information collection and data analysis. If the corresponding defect types and quality levels can be determined via the analysis, each agent interacts and saves useful information in order to accumulate. If there exists any abnormal, then the system further inquires and diagnoses the abnormal until the system extracts useful information and stores it in the information agent in order to invoke it at any time. The users can query the final results, including new abnormal data, defect types, the products number corresponding to quality grade, scrap percentage and so on. The detection and classification system flow chart is shown in Figure 8.

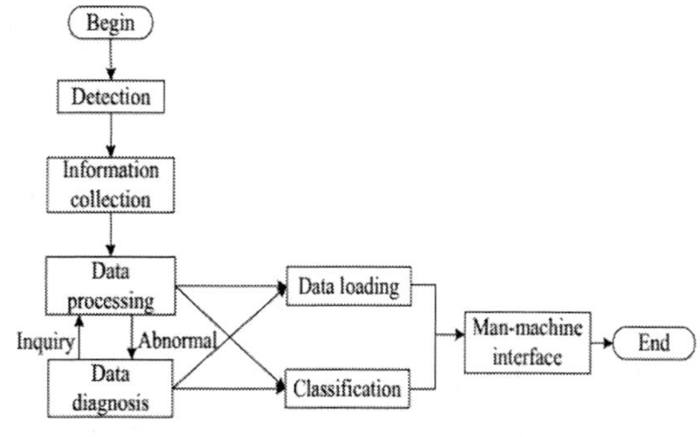

Figure 8. Detection and classification system flow chart

3.4 The System Function Module Design

The system is mainly used to collect and to process the information related to daily-use porcelain quality. If there are abnormal circumstances in the process, the system can give the hints and saves processed results into the database in order to query them. The system generally includes the following four modules.

User Interface Module. The module is mainly used to upload relevant detection and classification information files to the operator, and to provide the interface of querying results for the users.

Information Collection Module. The module is mainly used to collect data information related to daily-use porcelain quality, including useful information and various kinds of interference information which can not be avoided.

Information Processing Module. This module is mainly used to process the received information related to ceramic quality in accordance with the criterion defined based on multi-agent algorithms, and makes decision.

Data Access Module. The module is used to provide the relevant database access manner, so that the actuator executes tasks quickly and the users easily query the system

3.5 Database Design

By understanding whole production environment of daily-use porcelain, the database of the detection and classification system includes surrounding environment information, archives information of ceramic varieties, system detection and classification tools information, national standard information of daily-use porcelain detection, detection and classification results information and so on. For instance, China standard of daily-use porcelain includes GB / T 3532-2009, GB 3300-91, GB-T 3295-1996, GBT 3300-2008, GBT 3301-1999, GB-T 4742-1984, GB-T 4966- 1985, GB-T 15614-1995, QBT 1503-1992 and so on.

 DOI: 10.1051/itmconf/20171203014

4 Functions Implementation of Multi-agent System

4.1 Agent Functions Implementation

Interactive Agent. Interactive agent, otherwise known as man-machine interaction agent, receives instructions from users through the man-machine interface such as defect types, defect standards and classification commands, and helps users complete the required query information in the whole production At the same time, the agent gives advice on users for the next query, and reduces the omission or repetition of the users' information query so as to improve the production efficiency.

Task Agent. Task agent receives the task instructions about ceramic defect detection and quality grade classification given by previous users. Then, it gives an overall layout of the task., and decomposes the task after the layout. At last, it assigns each agent an appropriate task through agents communication.

Management Agent. Management agent is mainly used to plan as a whole system. It monitors and feedbacks the work state of each agent by analyzing users instruction information, and coordinates each agent work by calling the knowledge base of the whole system reasonably so that they can carry out their duties and finish the operation of the whole system quickly and accurately.

Resource Agent. In this system, resource agent is connected to the terminal sensors, CCD cameras, etc. After processing the collected information, it passes processed information to the task agent and the management agent so that the management agent can arrange other agents to carry their duties reasonably and processes the data into the same space and time data understood by all agents so as to complete the data matching among agents .

Executive Agent. Executive Agent is responsible for the terminal data process and inference in the whole detection and classification system, that is, data association, state estimation, attribute estimation after detection, and controls machine classification.

Other Agents. The other agents in the system mainly refers to communication agent and information agent which play a supplementary role. When each agent communicates each other, information agent is mainly used to collect the useful information for the system so as to make the agents communicate more fluently in future. Communication agent is responsible for communicating with the other agents in the whole ceramic kiln control system and linking the union type agent information database with other agents together to share information so as to complete the whole control.

4.2 The Implementation of Communication Among Agents

In the production system of daily-use porcelain, the industrial equipment of the whole system is relatively fixed and control terminals are also relatively fixed. Hence, According to the above characteristics, the communication among multi agents can be realized based on Switched Ethernet. Not only Switch Ethernet switches will be isolated from the conflict in each port and avoid the spread of the conflict, but also the full bandwidth can be used for each node of access switch.

4.3 The Implementation of Information Collection and Decision-making Process

Man-machine interface agent translates the received instruction information into the task of the system. Task agent decomposes the task into several sub-tasks that are easy to accomplish. Management agent sends a task description information to both execution agent and resource agent and calls for tenders for each sub-task. The relevant execution agents bid for the task and the management agent determines the agent which has winned bid. The management agent sends the information to the winning bidder to confirm that it will perform the task. At the same time, it sends the information to the task agent so as to make each sub-task assigned to each successful bidder. The execution agent analyzes the task and calls the information agent and communication agent in order to get enough information for operation and reasoning, hence, each sub-task has been completed. Task agent summarizes the task results of each execution agent, and get the results of the total task after comprehensive analysis. Man-machine interface agent converts the final task to the output format of man-machine interface, and reports the overall situation, hence, the task has been completed eventually. Information processing and decision-making process is shown in Figure 9.

5 Daily-use Porcelain Classification Algorithm

5.1 Discrete Kalman Filtering Algorithm

Although the C4.5 algorithm is with pruning function, it is very necessary for the signal data to filter in order to obtain more accurate data at the time of data processing[10]. The noise caused by light or electronic equipment can not be avoided in industrial production, At this time, not only there exists small error data, but also there exists small part of large error data. These error data had adverse effect on the detection and self-adaption of agents. These large errors which affect results are called the field value. In order to obtain the accurate and reasonable preprocessing data results, it is necessary to remove the outliers from the signal data. In this paper, the Kalman filtering algorithm is used to remove the outliers.

 DOI: 10.1051/itmconf/20171203014

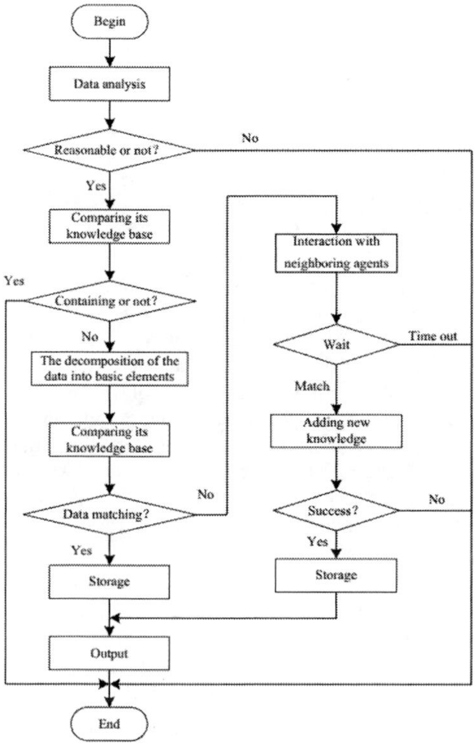

Figure 9. Information processing and decision-making process flow chart

Discrete Kalman filtering system equations.
State equation

$$X\left(k+1\right)=\Phi\left(k+1\right)X\left(k\right)+G(k)w(k) \quad (1)$$

Measurement equation

$$Z(k)=H(k)X(k)+v(k) \quad (2)$$

Where, X(k+1) is the state estimation vector at $t=(k+1)T$, $\Phi(k+1)$ is the state transfer matrix, $G(k)$ is the state noise weighting matrix, $w(k)$ is the noise vector, $Z(k)$ is the measurement vector at $t=kT$, $H(k)$ is the measurement transfer matrix, $v(k)$ is the measurement noise vector. $w(k)$ and $v(k)$ are uncorrelated zero mean Gaussian white noise sequence and satisfy the following equations.

$$\begin{cases} E[w(k)w^T(i)]=Q(k)\delta_{ki} \\ E[v(k)v^T(i)]=R(k)\delta_{ki} \\ E[w(k)v^T(i)]=0 \end{cases} \quad (3)$$

Where, $Q(k)$ and $R(k)$ are the state noise matrix and measurement noise matrix respectively, δ_{ki} is Kronecker function with $\delta_{ki}\neq 0(k=i)$, $\delta_{ki}=0(k\neq i)$.

Discrete Kalman Filtering Algorithm.
Filtering gain updating equation:

$$K(k)=P(k\,|\,k-1)H^T(k)\times[H(k)\times P(k\,|\,k-1)H^T(k)+R(k)]^{-1} \quad (4)$$

State updating equation:

$$\hat{X}(k+1\,|\,k+1)=\hat{X}(k+1\,|\,k)+K(k+1)\times$$

$$[Z(k+1)-H(k+1)\hat{X}(k+1\,|\,k)] \quad (5)$$

One step prediction equation of state:

$$\hat{X}(k\,|\,k-1)=\Phi(k\,|\,k-1)\hat{X}(k-1\,|\,k-1) \quad (6)$$

One step prediction equation of covariance:

$$P(k+1\,|\,k)=\Phi(k+1\,|\,k)P(k\,|\,k)\Phi^T(k+1\,|\,k)+$$

$$G(k)Q(k)G^T(k) \quad (7)$$

Covariance updating equation:

$$P(k+1\,|\,k+1)=[I-K(k+1)\times H(k+1)]P(k+1\,|\,k) \quad (8)$$

Through Kalman filtering algorithm, the measured value is compared with the known feature vector and weighted correction of the state estimates is made. This algorithm can be summed up as data prediction and the cycle recursive process of measurement data correction.

5.2 C4.5 Decision Tree Classification Algorithm

Assume that the measured data is the set A. $(c_1,c_2,c_3,\cdots$ denotes m categories in A, $(c_1,c_2,c_3,\cdots$ denotes n the values of attribute C in A, $(A_1,A_2,A_3,\cdots$ denotes n subsets of A divided by n values of attribute C, $|A_i|$ denotes the sample number at

$C = C_i$, $|B_j| = freq(B_j, A)$ denotes the sample number of B_j, $|B_{jc}|$ denotes the sample number of B_j at $C = C_i$. C4.5 decision tree algorithm is as follows.

Category probability. $P(B_j) = |B_j| / |A|$ (9)

Attribute probability. $P(c_j) = |A_j| / |A|$ (10)

Conditional probability of belonging to the category B_j at $C = C_i$.

$$P(B_j|C_i) = |B_{jc}| / |A_i| \quad (11)$$

Class information entropy.

$$H(B) = -\sum_j p(B_j)\log_2 p(B_j) = Info(A) \quad (12)$$

Conditions information.

$$H(B/C) = -\sum_j p(B_j/C_i)\log_2 p(B_j/C_i) = -\sum_{i=1}^{n} \frac{|A_i|}{|A|} Info(A_i) = Info_c(A) \quad (13)$$

Information gain.

$$I(B,C) = H(B) - H(B/C) = Info(A) - Info_c(A) = gain(c) \quad (14)$$

Splitting information.

$$H(C) = -\sum_i p(C_i)\log_2 p(C_i) = -\sum_{i=1}^{n} \frac{|A_i|}{|A|} \log_2 \frac{|A_i|}{|A|} = split\_Info(C) \quad (15)$$

Information gain ratio.

$$gain\_ratio(c) = I(B,C)/H(C) = gain(C)/split\_Info(C) \quad (16)$$

6 Classification Example

The test data is the test results of small size bowls in a ceramics factory. The deformation caliber size error of a bowl is obtained by image processing technique. The crack and fall slag belong to the internal characteristics of bowls. These internal defects are extracted to get the defect data through the contrast increasement of linear gray value tensile. However, the harmonics and vibration of electronic devices lead to fuzzy image feature extraction so as to cause some great errors. These great errors are called outliers. In this paper, Kalman filtering algorithm is used to estimate test data tracks so as to eliminate abnormal data. Then, C4.5 decision tree algorithm is used to process the generalized data so as to get the entire test data tree. If the product test data meet the optimum conditions of the whole tree, the product is high quality product. If the product test data does not meet all optimal sub-tree layer conditions but at least meet the trunk tree conditions, then the product is qualified. If the product test data does not meet the above condition, the product is unqualified. The data processing flow chart is shown in Figure 10.

At first, taking deformation caliber size for example, raw data results of a batch of sample bowl deformation caliber sizes are shown in Table 1.

According to Chinese national standard, daily-use porcelain products within ± 1.5mm caliber error are qualified. The standard caliber size of this kind of tested bowl is 60mm. The bowl caliber size errors are generally less than 3mm. However, from the table 1, we noticed that some data deviation is too large and can not appear in the actual production process. These data belong to abnormal data. Through using Kalman filtering algorithm, these abnormal data were filtered to get the data within error range which would be smoothed. Then, C4.5 decision tree was used to classify the bowl according to filtered data.

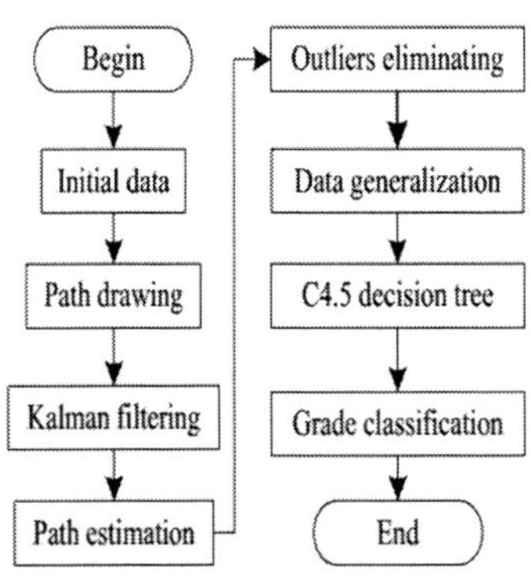

Figure 10. Data processing flow chart

DOI: 10.1051/itmconf/20171203014

TABLE 1. SAMPLE INITIAL DATA

Batch	Sample initial data				
1	60.4	60.3	61.2	61	60.1
2	60	59.6	60.7	70	60.8
3	59.3	61	62.1	67	60.6
4	61.1	61.1	61.2	61.3	60.5
5	59.8	69	60.8	60.9	60.2

Secondly, these crack and fall flag defects are extracted to get the defect data through the contrast increasement of linear gray value tensile and utilization of Laplace point detection operator. In addition, through using image processing technique the boundary and image characteristics of roast flower sticky glaze are extracted and filtered to get test data sample error of relevant attributes. Table 2 is some defects test data error generalization table of some sample bowls. Due to the limited space , data acquisition process of Table 2 is omitted.

The application of C4.5 decision tree classification algorithm is as follows.

(1) Computing classification information about whether the product can pass the check of this class attribute, we can get the following results.

There are seven positive examples y and seven counterexamples n about whether the product can pass the check.

$$P(y)=\frac{1}{2},P(n)=\frac{1}{2},$$

$$H(B)=-\frac{1}{2}\log_2\frac{1}{2}-\frac{1}{2}\log_2\frac{1}{2}=1$$

TABLE 2. TEST DATA SAMPLE ERROR GENERALIZATION TABLE

Sample	Deformation (Caliber mm)	Fall slag (Diameter mm)	Crack (Length mm)	Roast flower sticky glaze (Area mm²)	Pase checik
1	(0, 1.0)	(0.5,1.5)	(0, 3)	≥5	Yse
2	(1, 1.5)	≥1.5	≥6	(0, 1)	No
3	(0, 1.0)	(0,0.5)	(0, 3)	(1, 5)	Yse
4	(0, 1.0)	(0.5,1.5)	(3,6)	≥5	No
5	(1, 1.5)	(0,0.5)	(0, 3)	≥5	Yse
6	(1, 1.5)	(0.5,1.5)	(3,6)	(0, 1)	Yse
7	≥1.5	(0.5,1.5)	(3,6)	(0, 1)	No
8	(0, 1.0)	(0,0.5)	(0, 3)	(1, 5)	No
9	(1, 1.5)	(0,0.5)	(0, 3)	(1, 5)	Yse
10	(0, 1.0)	(0.5,1.5)	(3,6)	(1, 5)	Yse
11	(1, 1.5)	≥1.5	(0, 3)	(0, 1)	Yse
12	≥1.5	≥1.5	(3,6)	(0, 1)	No
13	(0, 1.0)	(0.5,1.5)	≥6	(0, 1)	No
14	≥1.5	(0,0.5)	≥6	(1, 5)	No

(2) Taking "deformation attribute" as an example, there are different kind of caliber bowls which are with (0,1.0), (1,1.5) and ≥1.5 grade in Table 2. The number of bowls with (0,1.0)mm , (1,1.5) and ≥1.5 grade is 6,5 and 3 respectively. When the bowl caliber size error is in (0.1.0) mm, $y=3$, $n=3$; When the bowl caliber size error is in (1,1.5)mm, $y=4$, $n=1$; When the bowl caliber size error is greater than or equal to 1.5, $y=0,n=3$. According to equations (12)-(16), we get

$$H(B/C)=-\frac{6}{14}(\frac{1}{2}\log_2\frac{1}{2}+\frac{1}{2}\log_2\frac{1}{2})-\frac{5}{14}(\frac{4}{5}\log_2\frac{4}{5}+\frac{1}{5}\log_2\frac{1}{5})-\frac{3}{14}(0\log_2 0+1\log_2 1)=0.69$$

$$H(C)=-(\frac{6}{14}\log_2\frac{6}{14}+\frac{5}{14}\log_2\frac{5}{14}+\frac{3}{14}\log_2\frac{3}{14})=1.52$$

$$gain\_ratio(c)=I(B,C)/H(C)=\frac{1-0.69}{1.52}=0.20$$

(3) Similarly, information gain rate of "fall flag", "crack", and " roast flower sticky glaze " is as following respectively.

Fall slag $gain\_ratio(c)=I(B,C)/H(C)=\frac{1-0.97}{1.1}=0.03$

Crack $gain\_ratio(c)=I(B,C)/H(C)=\frac{1-0.63}{1.1}=0.34$

Roast flower sticky glaze

$$gain\_ratio(c)=I(B,C)/H(C)=\frac{1-0.97}{1.43}=0.05$$

Through comparing the gain rate of each attribute, it is known that the information gain of crack is the largest in this example. Hence, the crack is selected as the root node test attribute. The root node of the defect attribute is shown in Figure 11.

Comparing the condition information entropy of each attribute by calculating, the sub-trees are established successively as shown in Figure 12.and Figure 13.

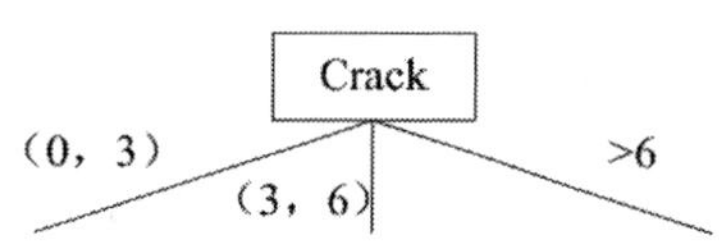

Figure 11. The decision tree step 1

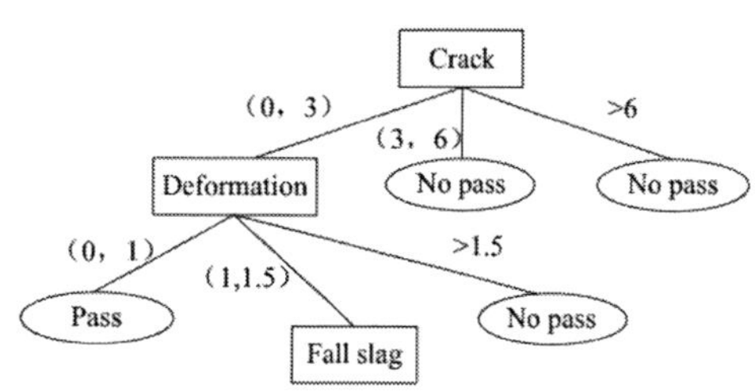

Figure 12. The decision tree step 2

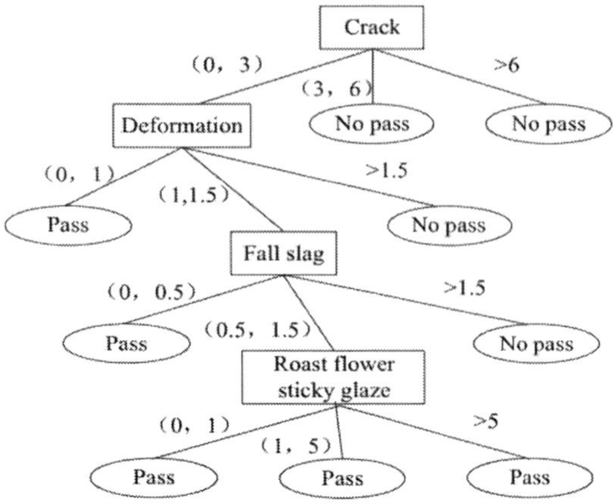

Figure 13. The decision tree step 3

For example, the part of the classification rules is as follows.

(1) If crack length is less than 3mm and deformation caliber size error is less than 1mm, then the check is passed.

(2) If crack length is less than 3mm and deformation caliber size error is within (1,1.5)mm and fall slag diameter is less than 0.5mm, then the check is passed.

(3) If crack length is Is greater than 3mm, then the check is not passed.

(4) If crack length is less than 3mm and deformation caliber error is greater than 1.5mm, then the check is not passed.

(5) If crack length is less than 3mm and deformation caliber error is within (1,1.5)mm and fall slag diameter is greater than 0.5mm, then the check is not passed.

By comparing the gain rate of each attribute, we can know that the crack is chosen as the test attribute. Then, a decision tree is established to obtain the next level of test attributes until all attributes are tested through using recursive method. At last, according to "If ...and ...and..., then..." rule, the test results are determined and the porcelain quality grade classification work has be finished.

Summary

In the paper, multi-agent technology-based daily-use porcelain detection and quality grade classification method had been studied. A small alliance type multi-agent network was established to detect and to classify daily-use porcelain products based on the complete multi-agent network structure of the whole ceramic production process control system. Based on discrete Kalman filtering algorithm and C4.5 decision tree classification algorithm, the classification algorithm used for daily-use porcelain product is proposed. Multi-agent-based detection and classification system structure of daily-use porcelain quality and the implementation of various functions are presented. Finally, an application example is given and demonstrates the feasibility and effectiveness of the method proposed. This will provide a new idea and new method for the detection and classification of daily-use porcelain quality and expand the application fields of multi-agent technology. Hence, the method proposed in the paper is with important application value. In the future, this method will be further optimized so as to be able to be applied in the practical engineering.

Acknowledgement

This work was financially supported by the National Natural Science Foundation of China (No. 61563022 and No. 61402209) and Jiangxi Province Natural Science Foundation of China (No. 20152ACB20009).

References

[1] G. Q. Zhong, G. L. Hu, and Z. X. Zhang, "Defect analysis for sanitary ceramics," China Ceramic Industry(In Chinese),. Vol.15, pp.35-37 2008.

[2] L.L. Li, C.Z. Gong, and K.J. Zhu, "Multi-agent simulation on natural gas time-of-use pricing in urban industrial and commercial users, " Systems Engineering Theory & Practice(In Chinese),vol. 34, pp. 392-398.,2014

[3] X.M. Luo, "Research on the combat efficiency evaluation modeling of anti-radiation missile based on multi-agent technique," Journal of the Academy of Equipment Command&Technology(In Chinese). vol. 21, pp. 111-115, 2010.

[4] W.N. Xie, P.A. Qiao, and X.Y. Pan, "Change detection in SAR images using multi-agent genetic and two-dimensional Otsu algorithm," Computer Engineering and Design(In Chinese), vol. 35, pp. 3532- 3537, 2014.

[5] J. H. Lin, Z. Liu, and Y.F. Chen, "An emotion decision-making model in multi-agent environment," PR&AI (In Chinese), vol. 28, pp. 369-376, 2015.

[6] W.K.Liu, "Study on cooperative control and optimization of complex multi-agent networks[D]," Wuhan: Huazhong University of Science &Technology (In Chinese), pp. 6-19, 2011.

[7] Y.H. Guo, G. Goncalves, and T. Hsu, "Multi-agent Based Self-adaptive Genetic Algorithm for the Long-term Car Pooling Problem, " Journal of Mathematical Modelling and Algorithms in Operations Research, vol. 20, pp. 45-66 , 2013.

[8] G.Y. Sato, H.J.S.D. Azevedo, and J.P.A. Barthès, "Agent and multi-agent applications to support distributed communities of practice: a short review," Autonomous Agents and Multi-Agent Systems. Vol. 25, pp. 87-129, 2012.

[9] A. Birukou, E. Blanzieri, and P. Giorgini, "Implicit: a multi-agent recommendation system for web search,"

Autonomous Agents and Multi-Agent Systems, vol. 24, pp. 141-174, 2012
[10] F.M.A. Klingert, and M. Meyer, "Effectively combining experimental economics and multi-agent simulation: suggestions for a procedural integration with an example from prediction markets research, " Computational & Mathematical Organization Theory, vol. 18, pp. 63-90, 2012.

Mining Telecommunication Circles via the Call Record and Short Messages

Shuai ZOU, Ping-Jian ZhANG

School of Software Engineering, South China University of Technology, Guangzhou, China
767186977@qq.com,pjzhang@scut.edu.cn

Abstract—Telecommunication circles are groups of similar customers in telecommunication networks. Mining such circles provides with telecommunication operators great value in developing prospective customers while retaining old ones. However, most of the existing community detecting algorithms utilize mainly the structure of the complex network and ignore the strength of relationship. This paper improves the classic CPM (Clique Percolation Method) algorithm by taking into account both the call record and short messages, and proposes a new algorithms called SR_CPM (Strengthened Relationship CPM). The new algorithm is applied to telecommunication networks and demonstrates superior effectiveness over CPM.

1 Introduction

Telecommunication users constitute a huge, but relatively sparse social network. Community discovery has become a very hot research topic of data mining for many years. Telecommunication circles are groups of similar customers in telecommunication networks. Finding out these circles is of great value for operators, helping them make more attractive pricing package politics, obtain prospective customers while retaining old ones. However, current community discovery algorithms in the literature mainly focuse on the people's personal behaviors as well as population attributes. This paper will employ information such as call record and short messages, and present an improved CPM algorithm called SR_CPM (Strengthened Relationship CPM). A group of experiments are designed and results show that the new algorithm is effective and efficient.

In this paper, part two introduce the related work, part three introduce an improved CPM algorithm and part four introduce the application of SR_CPM in telecommunication data set.

2 Related work

The complex networks have the characteristics of "small world", "scale-free", and community structure. Many social networks in real life can be abstracted as complex networks, and telecommunication networks are the typical ones. Farrahi[2] et al. have studied the location driven daily behavior patterns using classification method. Kim[10] et al. set up a logistic regression model to handle the Korea Telecom Data. Especially, community discovery technology is well suited to find out the community structure in complex networks. Early community discovery algorithms are derived from graph theory like the spectral bisection community discovery[3], or derived from the hierarchical clustering algorithm, ,which introduces a measure Q[4], to reflect the degree of modularity of community division. Based on this concept, Girvan and Newman proposed the GN algorithm[1] by deleting the edge of the network in the largest number of edges to the community Division. In addition to the non-overlapping community detection algorithm mentioned above, research workers also put forward a series of overlapping community discovery algorithms that employee the idea of clique filtering[5] , seed expansion[6] , hybrid probability model[7] and edge detection[8] , etc.

3 An improved CPM algorithm

3.1 Existing Problems of Community Discovery Algorithm

Although many community detection algorithms has been proposed, it is still a challenging work to find out community structure from the complex network. There are still a lot of problems need to be solved.

1. Most of the current algorithms are based on static networks.

2. The effect and performance of the community discovery algorithms have been a problem. It is a great

challenge to design highly effective algorithms with low time complexity.

3. Most of the existing community discovery algorithms only consider the connections between nodes while ignore the strength of the connection and the inherent attributes of the nodes.

3.2 Improved Clique Fitering Community Discovery Algorithm

The main contribution of this paper is to improve the CPM algorithm, called SR_CPM, which is more suitable for the community discovery in the telecom user call network.

3.2.1 *Algorithm idea*

There are mainly two kinds of methods to expand the CPM to weighted network.

a) Set a global threshold w, remove edges with weights less than w and then use the traditional CPM algorithm to partition the network to communities.

b) Farkas[9] et al. proposed a clique intensity function for CPM in the clique algorithm. For a k-clique containing k* (k-1) /2 edge, its clique intensity is defined as:

$$I(C)=\left(\prod_{\substack{i<j\\ i,j\in C}} w_{ij}\right)^{2/k(k-1)} \quad (1)$$

And cliques whose intensity is less than some prescribed value are ignored.

The first method is simple but the choice of threshold w is difficult and greatly influences the quality of community partition. The second method is generally more effective but suffers from huge computations. Moreover, the intensity function is an absolute index hence and it is not easy to set the threshold either. This paper will introduce a simple and relative measurement.

3.2.2 *Definitions*

Definition 1:Coefficient of Variation

The coefficient of variation is the ratio of the standard deviation to the mean.

$$c.v=\frac{\sigma}{\mu} \quad (2)$$

The advantage of coefficient of variation over other statistical indices is that it is relative and easy to calculate.

Definition 2:Weighted k-clique based on the coefficient of variation (k-clique-w_c.v).

Let G=(V,E,W) be a weighted network, W represents edge weights. A k-nodes complete subgraph $G' = (V', E', W')$ has a total of $\frac{k(k-1)}{2}$ edges. If the coefficient of variation of the $\frac{k(k-1)}{2}$ edges is less than some prescribed threshold $C.V^*$, we call the k nodes a weighted k-clique based on the coefficient of variation. Similarity, weighted k-clique based on deviation is denoted by k-clique-w_σ.

3.2.3 *Algorithm Procedure*

There are three steps in the process of SR_CPM algorithm:

Firstly, find out all the cliques which are not included in other cliques.

a) Calculate the degree of each node in the network and record the largest value g-1 and then turn to b.

b) Set C to be the collection of all nodes in the network and then turn to c.

c) Construct $C^* = \{v_i | v_i \in C \text{且} d(v_i) \geq m-1\}$ and then take a node v_i from C^* randomly. For v_i, we define two collections A and B. A is a collection of all the nodes which connects each other and contains node v_i during the exection of the algorithm, and B is a collection of nodes that are connected to each node in A. Then, turn to d.

d) Iterate recursively to find all the cliques that include v_i and whose size is g. Let **|X|** stands for the number of elements in the collection X.

1) Initialize the collection A = {v_i}, B={the neighbors of v_i}.

2) Each time we move a node from the set B to the set A and adjust the set B by deleting the node that is no longer connected to all the nodes in set A.

3) If |A|< g and B =Φ, or A∪B is a subset of some clique or |A|+|B|<g, stop calculation and return to the previous step in recurrsion.

If |A| = g and B =Φ and the weight of nodes in set A satisfies definition 2, a new clique is obtained. Record the new clique and return to the previous step in recurrsion and continue to find new cliques.

If |A| = g and B =Φ and the weight of nodes in set A does not satisfies definition 2, return to the previous step in recurrsion and continue to find new cliques.

If|A|< g and B≠ Φ, execte the (2) recursively.

All the cliques which have the size of g and start from v_i are obtained in the end.

e) Delete v_i from C^*, delete v_i and all the edges connected to it in the network.

f) If $C^* \neq \Phi$, get the next node from the C^* and repeat procedure d ~ e. If $C^* = \Phi$, set g = g-1 ,repeat the procedure b ~ e until g=2.

Secondly, constructing the clique-clique overlap matrix C according to all the weighted cliques found in the previous step.

Thirdly, constructing clique connection matrix and find the k-cliques according to the input k and the matrix C.

3.3 Analysis of the experimental results of the improved algorithm

3.3.1Experimental data

The data set is the classical complex network data set Les Miserables. This data set is a character relationship network constructed according to the relationships among the characters in the Miserable world. The node in the network stands for a character in the novel. If two characters appeared in the same chapter, there will be an edge between two nodes. The weight of the edge stand for the number of times when the two characters appeared in the same chapter. There are 77 nodes and 253 edges in the data set.

3.3.2 Evaluation function

Evaluation function use community partition quality evaluation function—the extension of modular Q which is an evaluation function for overlapping community organizations EQ:

$$EQ=\frac{1}{2M}\sum_{ij}\frac{1}{O_iO_j}\left(W_{ij}-\frac{W_{i.}W_{j.}}{2M}\right)\delta\left(c_i,c_j\right) \quad (3)$$

O_i and O_j represent the number of communities that node i and node j belong to respectively.

3.3.3 Result analysis

The SR_CPM_c.v stands for the SR_CPM algorithm using k-clique-w_c.v and the SR_CPM_σ stands for the SR_CPM algorithm using k-clique-w_σ. For k = 3 and k=4, the results are shown in figure 1.

Under different cv*, the EQ value of the SR_CPM_c.v algorithm for k = 3 is generally larger than the corresponding EQ value for k = 4. This shows the nature that the network is roughly a 3-clique community to some extent. The EQ value increases first and then decreases along with the increase of the variation coefficient threshold cv*, which has a small fluctuation in the middle. The difference of the coefficient of variation cv* shows that the algorithm requires different levels of the degree of dispersion of the edge weights in the clique, that is to say, the degree of familiarity between the users is required. The smaller the cv* is, the smaller the degree of dispersion of

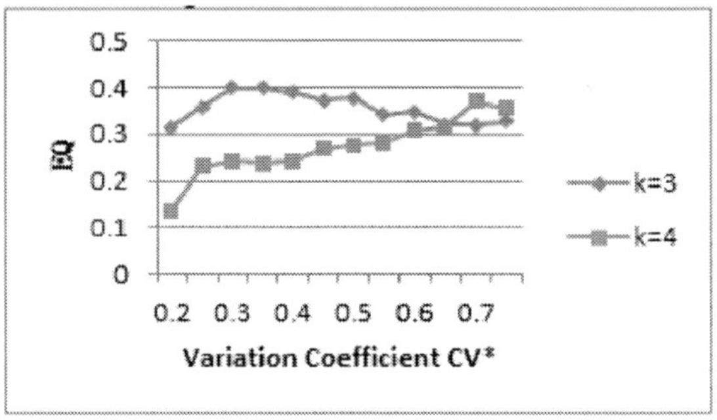

Figure 1. SR_CPM_c.v Change of EQ value under different parameters

the weights will be in the clique and the more severe the conditions for the formation of cliques will be. The larger the value of cv* is, the discrete degree of edge weights requirement in the clique is more broadly. When cv* is too small, some real community structures may not be considered cliques. Although the connections inside the community are very close, the edges among communities is not sparse and then the EQ value is still low. With the

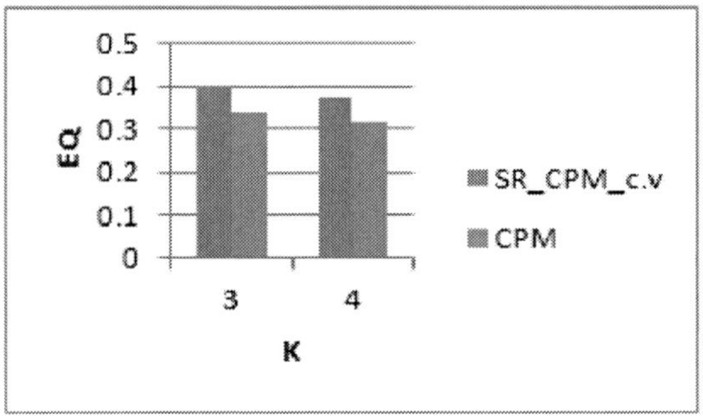

Figure 2.The comparision between SR_CPM_c.v and CPM

increase of the cv* value, the formation condition of the cliques is gradually broad and the EQ value increases gradually as more reasonable nodes join the community. When the cv* is too large, the restrictive condition of constructing a clique in weight is becoming weaker and weaker. Thus, some complete subgraphs with different edge weights are also considered cliques and the EQ value decreases gradually. The algorithm is close to CPM algorithm to some degree without considering the intensity information of the node.

The coefficient of variation of C.V and standard deviation to measure the degree of dispersion are introduced into the definition of cliques. The experimental results show that the SR_CPM is more reasonable in the division of community structure compared to CPM.

DOI: 10.1051/itmconf/20171203015

4 Application of SR_CPM Algorithm in Telecommunication data Set

4.1 Experimental data

The data set used in the experiment is coming from a telecommunications company data record. There are 3 files including the user information, the call log records and the SMS records. The dataset has been transformed to protect the privacy of the users. The original data contains 382779 users, 76907842 call records and 20947956 SMS records. After preprocessing, the two data set Call_mess_table and User_info are shown below.

Table 1. CALL_MESS_TABLE

Serial number	Attribute name	Type	Meaning
1	user_a_nbr	varchar(8)	phone number of user a
2	user_b_nbr	varchar(8)	phone number of user b
3	all_raw_dur_ab	int	length of the call between a and b
4	call_times	int	times of the call between a and b
5	mess_num_ab	int	short messages between a and b

Table 2. USER_INFO

Serial number	Attribute name	Type	Meaning
1	acc_nbr	varchar(8)	Phone number of the user
2	gender_n	int	Is gender unknown
3	gender_f	int	Is sex female
4	gender_m	int	Is sex male
5	urban_id_0	int	Is it the city
6	urban_id_1	int	Is it the county
7	urban_id_2	int	Is it rural
8	urban_id_3	int	Whether the urban and rural identity is unknown
9	certi_latn_551	int	Is the identity card attributable to 551
10	prob_level_100	int	Whether the amount of consumption in the 0 to 100
11	prob_level_200	int	Whether the amount of consumption in the 100 to 200
12	prob_level_300	int	Whether the amount of consumption in the 200 to 300
13	prob_level_800	int	Whether the amount of consumption in the 300 to 800
14	cust_level	numeric(10,2)	User level

The SR_CPM and CPM algorithm are used to partition the community in the two data sets respectively.

4.2 Experimental Content

Two data sets are extracted in this experiment: data set 1 is user call network 1 which has 623 nodes and 3391 edges consisting of a record of 27913 calls from the 623 users and 5624 SMS records. Data set 2 is user call network 2 which has 2403 nodes and 14094 edges consisting of a record of 98152 calls from the 2403 users and 14094 SMS records.

Community discovery is an unsupervised learning process. The structure of the network is not known in advance, so the final results of the community need to be evaluated. There is no authoritative evaluation index of community partition which can be applied to any kind of network at present. The research on the quality evaluation function of the community partition with the weighted network is very little compared with the non-weighted network. It is not easy to evaluate the quality of weighted complex networks. There are a variety of defects in the weighted network when the community evaluation index of many kinds of unauthorized network is applied to the weighted network. Due to the lack of effective social evaluation index of doubt and the weighted complex network classification information, it makes the objective evaluation of the weighted network community discovery algorithm results become extremely difficult. The commonly used evaluation indexes include clustering

 DOI: 10.1051/itmconf/20171203015

coefficient, strong and weak associations and modularity. This paper is still using EQ evaluation function.

4.3 Result Analysis

The SR_CPM algorithm divides the data set into 33 societies (overlapping community structure), and the CPM algorithm divides the data set into 61 societies (with overlapping community structure) with the parameters k = 4 and m = 2.The relationship between community size ranking and community size is shown in figure 3 and 4.

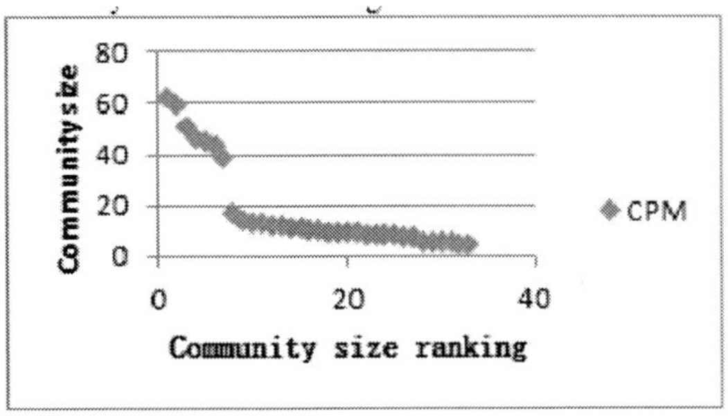

Figure 3 .The distribution of Community size ranking of CPM

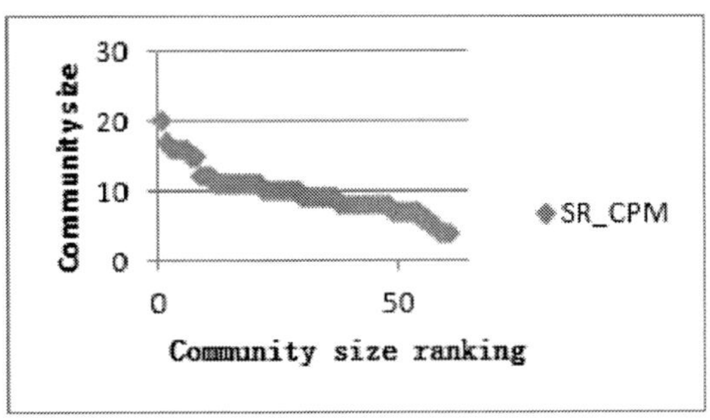

Figure 4.The distribution of Community size ranking of SR_CPM

The SR_CPM algorithm proposed in this paper is better than the CPM algorithm in the case of reasonable parameter settings, and it can find the reasonable community structure in the weighted network. However, if the parameters are set so that the formation conditions are too harsh, the quality of community partition may be inferior to the corresponding parameters of the CPM algorithm. In addition, the division of the SR_CPM algorithm to get the community is different according to the input of different parameters. Telecom operators can adjust them to meet the needs of practical applications.

Acknowledgment

This work is supported by the Guangzhou Science Technology and Innovation Commission (Grant No. 201604010099).

References

[1] Girvan M,Newman M E J. Community structure in social and biological networks[J]. ProcNatlAcadSci USA,2002,99(12):7821-7826
[2] Farrahi K,Gatica D. Discovering daily routines from large—scale mobile data[J]. Proceeding of the 16th ACM international conference on Multimedia,2008:849-852.
[3] Pothen A,Simon H,Liou K-P.Partitioning sparse matrices with eigenvectors of graphs[J].SIAMJ Matrix Anal Appl,1990,11(3):430—452.
[4] Newman M E J,Girvan M. Finding and evaluating community structure in networks[J]. Phys Rev E,2004,69(2):026113.
[5] Palla G,Dernyi I,Farkas I,et al. Uncovering the overlapping community structure of complex networks in nature and society[J]. Nature,2005,435(7043):814-818.
[6] Lancichinetti A,Fortunato S,Kertesz J. Detecting the Overlapping and Hierarchical Community Structure in Complex Networks[J].New Journal of Physics,2009,11:033015
[7] Newman ME, Leicht EA. Mixture Models and Exploratory Analysis in Networks[J]. Proc Natl Acad Sci USA,2007,104(23): 9564-9569
[8] Evans T,Lambiotte R. Line Graphs, Link Partitions, and Overlapping Communities[J]. Physical Review E,2009, 80(1):16105.
[9] Farkas I, Palla G, Vicsek T. Weighted network modules[J]. New Journal of Physic, 2007, 9(6):180-198.
[10] Kim H S,Yoon C H. Determinants of subscriber chum and customer loyalty in the Korean mobile telephony market[J].Telecommunications Policy,2004,28(9):75 1-765

DOI: 10.1051/itmconf/20171203016

Research on the Method of Building Dem by Contours

Ji-Wen ZHU, Jin-Ling YANG, Jiang LIU , Dan-Dan LIU, He ZHANG

School of Surveying and Mapping Engineering,Heilongjiang Institute of Technology ,Harbin, P. R. China
1060968268@qq.com,21714200@qq.com,121281531@qq.com, 1802363325@qq.com, 411489974@qq.com

Abstract—Digital elevation model (DEM), as an important product of digital photogrammetry and digital surveying and mapping, it plays an increasingly important role in the field of surveying and mapping and geographic information system. In this paper, it introduces the current generation methods of DEM by contour, and analyzes those interpolation methods that commonly are used to build DEM, and then describes the advantages and disadvantages of different building DEM methods systematically. Focusing on the DEM that represented by Grid and TIN, it compares the optimization methods of interpolation contour data systematically, and makes the contour interpolating DEM reflect the surface condition of the real nature more effectively.

1 Introduction

As a kind of basic data, the digital elevation model, DEM, plays an important role in Geomatics (mainly in Geographic Information System). The application of digital elevation model requires the high-quality DEM, and the contour map is an important and inexpensive source to generate DEM, which has an important research value and significance. The DEM data mainly be obtained through digitizing the paper topographic map, processing the aerial remote sensing image and surveying and mapping. At present, digitizing the paper topographic map is the more convenient and effective method to build the DEM. The contour map is an important carrier which employs two-dimensional plane to represent three-dimensional terrain. That can greatly reduce the personnel cost and effectively guarantee the DEM precision using the digital contour map to generate practically the DEM.

Once the DEM build by the contour map can meet the required geometric accuracy, the terrain contour will be the most important data source to construct the DEM. Although building DEM by contour has been already be studied, most of the literatures did not pay enough attention to the changes of some terrain. In various geological applications, the accuracy of the DEM is the most remarkable question, because its quality affects the precision of the subsequent application results. Therefore, it is important to research the high-quality DEM based on contour and provide high-quality data sources for the subsequent application [1]. In this paper, the commonly methods of generating the DEM by contours, namely Grid DEM and Triangulated Irregular Network (TIN) DEM, are analyzed and compared. Based on contour map generating the high-quality DEM, this paper studies the contour discretization, data interpolation, the process of generating the DEM, and finally presents the generating process of the DEM through the experiment.

2 Technical Proposals

The main technology of this paper includes the TIN construction, the contour discretization, the conversion the TIN to grid, the DEM interpolation, and so on. The specific technology process is shown in Figure 1.

2.1 Construction of TIN DEM by contours

TIN usually has its own unique advantages to be used to describe the surface of the terrain using the different resolution. The TIN can be constructed by the following three steps:

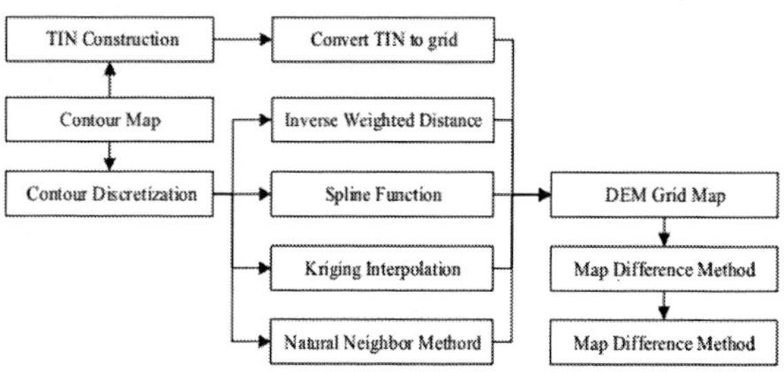

Figure 1. The flow chart of making DEM technology

1) Divide the original data into blocks

In order to quickly retrieve the adjacent points of the processed triangle without having to retrieve the desired data, the original data should be divided into blocks.

2) Determine the first triangle

Firstly, a point A is selected from data points arbitrarily. Secondly, the nearest point of point A is obtained as point B. Then points near point A and B are regarded as $C_i(i=1,2,...,n)$, and point C_i A, and B to form a triangle. Finally the cosine the angle of each triangle vertex is calculated following formula 1.

$$\cos\angle C_i = \frac{a_i^2 + b_i^2 - c_i^2}{2a_i b_i} \quad (1)$$

Where, $a_i = BC_i$, $b_i = AC_i$, $c_i = AB$.

If the condition $\angle C_j = \max\{C_i\}$ is satisfied, C_i is referred to as the third vertex of this triangle. In general TIN has many forms, and the Figure 2 shows two forms of the TIN.

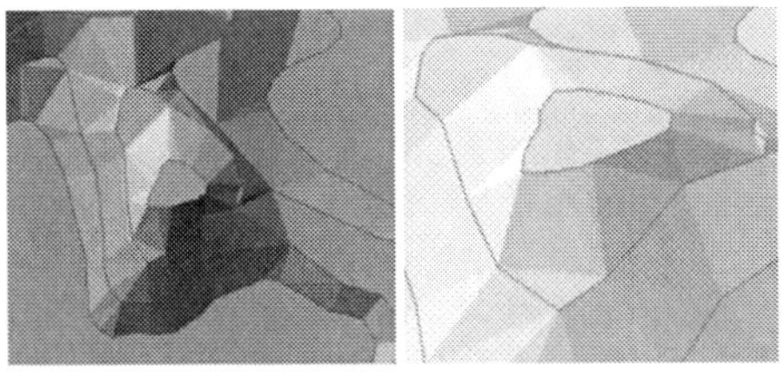

Figure 2. Irregular triangle network expressions

2.2Contour established the Grid DEM

Digital elevation model can be extracted from different digital terrain model(DTM), such as GRID DEM, contour and irregular triangle network DEM. The generation of GRID from contours is simply considered to process the line and convert discrete points. Because the size of the grid is fixed, the DEM can be stored in a two-dimensional array in the computer. We can regard the stored elevation value as the elevation of the center point of the grid or the average value of the grid points, so we can obtain the elevation value of each point by interpolation method from these grids. The Gird DEM is shown in Figure 3.

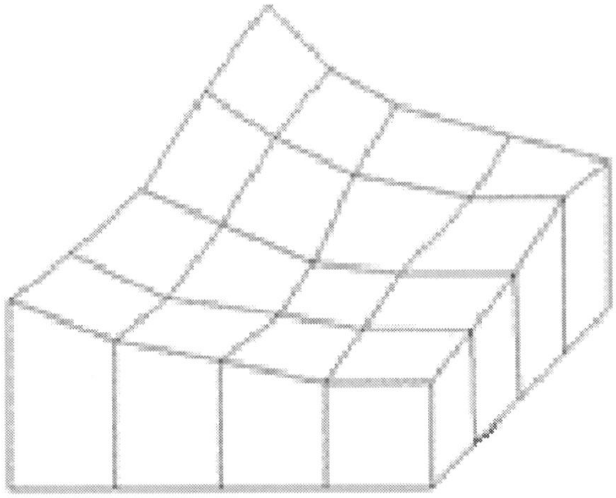

Figure 3. Digital elevation surface model of GRID

2.3Discretization of contour

Discretization of the contour is regard as the procedure that the contour data is converted to discrete points, and then discrete data is interpolated to get the grid elevation value [2]. In the process of building digital elevation model, the interpolation is the necessary relevant processing after the discretization of the contour. Through the interpolation we can realize the transition of the points state from disordered ordered state [3]. In this paper, the multiple methods are adopted to generate DEM and visibility analysis is carried out to the results.

2.4Interpolation algorithm of the DEM

Interpolation is the method of extrapolating the unknown data based on the given data [4]. In general, interpolation is divided into three stages: data sampling, data processing and data recording. This paper's research methods mainly involve: Inverse Distance Weighted method, spline interpolation method, Kriging Interpolation method and Natural Neighbor interpolation method.

1) Inverse Distance Weighted, IDW

The inverse distance weighted interpolation is that in order to obtain the unknown value of the point the weighted calculation is carried out through the value of the other points which is adjacent to the point of unknown value, when the weighting value depends on the distance between the points[5]. The algorithm formula is as bellow:

$$z(x,y) = \sum_{i=1}^{n}(d_i)^{-p} z_i \Big/ \sum_{i=1}^{n}(d_i)^{-p} \quad (2)$$

Where, $z(x,y)$ is estimate of the interpolation point at the location (x,y); n is the number of measured samples; d_i is the distance between point i and interpolation points; z_i is the numerical of i th known point; P is power of distance, and it has great influence on the interpolation results, whose selection criterion is the minimum of the mean absolute error. In this paper, $p=2$ is selected in the experiment.

2) Spline Function Interpolation

Spline function interpolation method is one of the accurate interpolations, where all sampling points occupy the interpolation surface and range of the value of the sample points did not completely limit estimation value of interpolation points [6]. In this paper, the tension spline interpolation method is adopted [7].

3) Kriging Interpolation

This method also fully uses the spatial correlation of points, which automatically identify the spatial distribution of points and as far as possible to eliminate the error caused by the nonuniform distribution of sampling points. Its formula is as follow:

$$z(x,y)=\sum_{i=1}^{n}\lambda_i z(x_i,y_i) \qquad (3)$$

Where, $z(x,y)$ is the estimate of the interpolation point at the location (x,y);, λ_i is the weighted value of the i sampling points.

4) Natural Neighbor Interpolation, NNI

It is the new method of gridding. The basic principle of the method is that a group of primeval Thiessen polygons are modified to generate new Thiessen polygons when the data set is added a new point, where the interpolation weights is determined by the average value of the neighbor points weights and proportional to the Thiessen polygons.

3 Related Experiment and Analysis

3.1Experiment data

In this paper, we select the map of Hegang, Heilongjiang Province to test the satellite image map as shown in Figure 4. The projection coordinate system is GCS_Beijing_1954, the projection type is Gauss Kruger.

Figure 4. satellite image map of Hegang

3.2Discretization of contour map

First of all, the file format needs to be converted. The page window of the file conversion function is as shown in Figure 5(a). The line file is not assigned, so the contour assignment should be firstly carried out. It is assigned the starting elevation of the line, which is 440 meters. The contour interval is 10 for the contour. Because of the selection method of the paper is from high to low, the increment of height should be -10 meters. The assigned contour is shown in Figure 5 (b).

(a) Contour conversion function page (b) Contour assignment

Figure 5. The process of contour generation

The second step is data preprocessing. Because there is no elevation value in attribute table when the elevation value of points in attribute table of MAPGIS 6.7 is shown as "label" type in ArcGIS 10, we need data preprocessing. The process includes: we click the "Preview" button and modify preview mode to table; in the pop-up menu, we choose "add fields" tab and will name the field as "ELEV", whose type is selected as double precision, and accuracy and scale is the same to the "label"; we open ArcMap to modify the point data, and then open the data attribute table; click the editor and start to edit attribute table.

3.3Generate DEM by Interpolation method

The DEM is generated based on the aforementioned principle of the interpolation and Grid, where we employ four interpolation to build DEM seen as Figure 6.

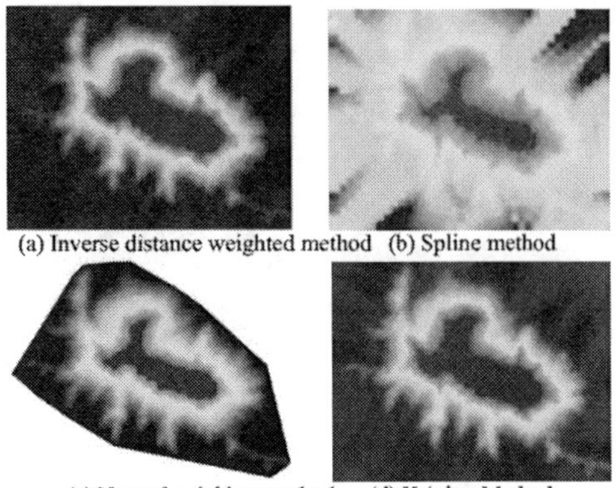

(a) Inverse distance weighted method (b) Spline method

(c) Natural neighbor method (d) Kriging Method

Figure 6. Four results of interpolation methods based on Grid

For TIN, the basic idea of constructing DEM is firstly to generate TIN by contour and then transfer TIN to GRID. In order to analyze the elevation difference of different interpolation algorithms, the error map is directly used to reflect the error of different interpolation algorithms. Results are shown as Figure 7.

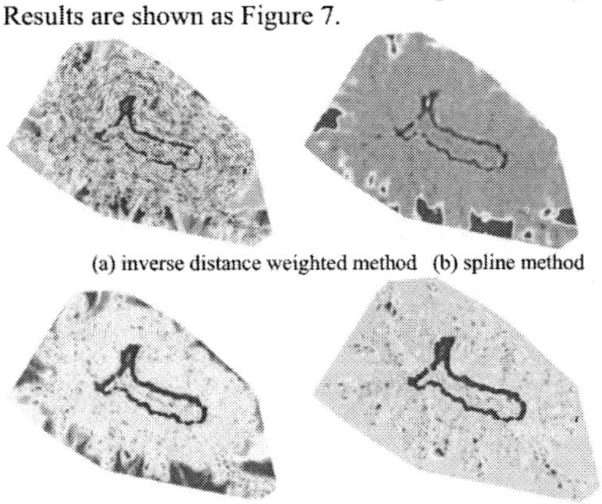

(a) inverse distance weighted method (b) spline method

(c) Kriging method (d) natural neighbor method

Figure 7. The results of TIN method for constructing DEM

3.4Result Analysis

According to the spatial distribution maps it can be seen that the main elevation difference of the area is to be reflected around the terrain structure lines; the main elevation difference among different Grid DEMs is appeared on the flat top of the mountain and the flat area, which are constructed by the conversion of TIN to Gird, spline function, NNI and IDW method. The value of the elevation constructed by the conversion of TIN to Gird is often larger than value of the elevation constructed the spline function; the main elevation difference between NNI and the conversion of TIN to Gird lies in the ridge, valleys, r and flat areas, which has larger area and no contour; the value of the elevation constructed by the conversion of TIN to Gird is close to by NNI method; the value of the elevation constructed by IWD method is close to by Kriging method.

Conclusion

In this paper, the theory and method of the DEM generation from contour map has been described, and the interpolation algorithm of the DEM generation from contour map is analyzed systematically through experiments, where four algorithms are employed in these experiments such as spline function, Kriging, NNI and IDW method. According to the distribution map of spatial error, we analyze the results of different method. The experiment results show that different approaches should apply to different practical applications, especially building DEM from the flat area and the change area of the terrain structure. Based on these experiments, we can build high-quality DEM taking requirements into account. It should be noted that the contour map is small experiments, and in the future the bigger and more complex map will be employed for further study.

Acknowledgment

This work was financially supported by Natural Science Foundation Programs of Heilongjiang province(D201413).

References

[1] Hoppe H. "Smooth view-dependent level-of-detail control and its application to terrain rendering,"Visualization'98. Proceedings, IEEE. pp.35-42,1999.

[2] Zhang Kaixuan, etc. "Research on DEM generation method based on contour," Engineering of Surveying and Mapping.vol.16(3),pp. 15-18,2007.

[3] M.J.Gooch,J.H.Chandler. "Failure prediction in auto matically generated digital elevation models,"Computer & Geosciences.vol. 27,pp.159-176,2001.

[4] Feng Gui, Lin Zongjian. "High Accuracy Interpola-tion Algorithm and Realization of DEM," Remote Sensing Information. Vol.4,pp.132-133,2000.

[5] Han Fujiang, etc.. "Research on Simi lar between DEM Interpolation Method and Visualization Analysis Results,"Geography and Geographic Information Science.vol. 23(1),pp.242-245,2007.

[6] Luan Xiaoyan."TIN Generation Algorithm and its 3D Display [J]. Ocean Surveying and Mapping," vol.24(5) ,pp.9-41,2004..

[7] Cronin T. "Classifying hills and valleys in digitized terrain," Photogrammetric Engineering & Remote Sensing. Vol.66(9),pp.1129-1137,2000.

Prediction Based Energy Balancing Forwarding in Cellular Networks

Jian-Jun YANG, Ju SHEN

Department of Computer Science and Information Systems, University of North Georgia, Oakwood, GA, USA
Department of Computer Science, University of Dayton, Dayton, OH, USA
e-mail: jianjun.yang@ung.edu, jshen1@udayton.edu

Abstract— In the recent cellular network technologies, relay stations extend cell coverage and enhance signal strength for mobile users. However, busy traffic makes the relay stations in hot area run out of energy quickly. Energy is a very important factor in the forwarding of cellular network since mobile users(cell phones) in hot cells often suffer from low throughput due to energy lack problems. In many situations, the energy lack problems take place because the energy loading is not balanced. In this paper, we present a prediction based forwarding algorithm to let a mobile node dynamically select the next relay station with highest potential energy capacity to resume communication. Key to this strategy is that a relay station only maintains three past status, and then it is able to predict the potential energy capacity. Then, the node selects the next hop with potential maximal energy. Moreover, a location based algorithm is developed to let the mobile node figure out the target region in order to avoid flooding. Simulations demonstrate that our approach significantly increase the aggregate throughput and decrease the delay in cellular network environment.

1 Introduction

The new technology of Cellular Networks are able to make a lot of mobile users(cell phones) connect a relay station near to them and then they connect to a base station. This technology enhances the service of a single relay station. However, the energy costs of relay stations go up very fast. Hence, the efficiency of energy utilization in Cellular Networks has attracted great interest in academic research and industrial applications, such as 3GPP and ITU[1]. Consequently, a new area called green cellular networks appeared. The European Commission is working on many new projects to taking care of the energy issue of Cellular Network systems. There systems cover many research topics, such as energy aware radios, energy efficient network design, cognitive radio for power saving, cooperative schemes[2]. The study of Energy in Cellular Network is in all layers of the protocols and a wide variety of system architectures.

The busy traffic near a relay station often makes the energy of the relay station go down very quickly. However, other relay stations with low traffic are idle with high energy. Many cell phones are connected in a hot relay station because by a kind of forwarding algorithm, such as shortest path forwarding, a large number of cell phones are connected to the same relay station. But, it is important to find the best tradeoff between energy efficiency and the performance [3]. In order to balance the energy utilization among different cells, it is needed to transfer the over-loaded traffic from hot cells to neighboring cooler ones. The challenge is how to balance the energy utilization of the relay stations in order to get the best tradeoff among all the relay stations in a cellular network.

Scholars have come up with many research topics in terms of energy efficiency with network performance[1][4], such as balancing deployment cost and throughput, balancing achievable rate, balancing the bandwidth utilized, and balancing average end-to-end service delay. In this paper, we propose a prediction based algorithm for a mobile node(cell phone) to find one of its neighboring relay stations with possibly maximal energy in the next time, and then its chooses that relay station instead of using the fixed relay station to forward data. A relay station only saves its last three energy status, and then it predicts the potential energy in the next time. We further devise an algorithm to let the mobile node narrow the region on finding its neighboring relay stations in order to avoid opposite forwarding.

The rest of the paper is organized as follows. Section II discusses the related research on this topic. Section III proposes a novel method that select the best relay station. We evaluate the proposed schemes by simulations and describe the performance results in Section IV. Section V concludes the paper.

 DOI: 10.1051/itmconf/20171203017

2 Related Work

Scholars have developed many approaches to solve energy utilization questions in Cellular Networks. The approaches are classified into several categories. The first one is based on dynamic channel allocation, meaning channel borrowing from cooler cell[5][9]. The second one is based on Base Station selection [6]. The third type contains strategies based on power control and cell breathing [6][7]. The last category consists of strategies on relay-assisted traffic transfer [8].

The research of multi-hop wireless network is basic yet very important in wireless networks. Many scholars also work on energy efficiency topics with the infrastructure of multi-hop wireless networks, meaning multi-hop cellular network[15][16]. In this kind of structure, relay stations are network components that are used to store and forward data received from base stations to mobile users(cell phones), and vice versa. Deploying relay stations can extend the coverage and enhance the signal strength, which help improve the performance for mobile users near the edge of the cell. In addition, the appearance of multi-hop cellular network transfers over-loaded traffic from hot cells to cooler cells by relay stations. The relay-based load balancing schemes are flexible and introduce less interference.

A scheme to separate the networks to two parts were designed in[10], which divided the channels into two parts, one for the ad-hoc overlay network, the other for the cellular network. In[9][11], the authors proposed dynamic load balancing schemes in the integrated cellular and ad-hoc relaying systems. The ad-hoc relaying stations include an overlay ad-hoc network, which helps relay traffic among different cells. A dynamic traffic-aware base station switching mode was designed in [12], where the base station can change its operating modes between standard base station operations and switching to relay station mode, the so called BS-RS Switching model. Moreover, the propagation distance was shortened in this approach [10].

3 Problem Formulation

3.1The basic idea

In cellular networks, each base station covers a number of cell phones in a hexagonal cell. We consider a cellular network containing a set of base stations(BS), relay stations(RS) and mobile users(cell phones)(MU), denoted by {A1 , A2 , A3... }, {S1,S2, S3... }, and {c1,c2, c3... ,}. Each BS is located at the center of the cell. Each RS is located at a boundary of cells. The traditional communication between two mobile users ci to cj is that ci communicates to its base station Ai, then Ai communicates to Aj which covers cj , and then Aj communicates to cj. In new generation cellular network, the relay stations are used to assist communications between cell phone to cell phone or cell phone to base station. Fig. 1 shows an instance with several base stations, relay stations and cell phones, where the lower right cell is a hot cell with a large number of cell phones and busy data traffic and the other cells are cooler cells with less cell phones. Note that the cell phones in all figures of this paper represent active cell phones.

Data transmission takes place when a cell phone(initiator) intends to talk to another cellphone(receiver). The scenario is simple if the two are in the same cell[15]. We study the circumstance that the receiver is in another cell. In Fig. 1, the communication between c_1 and c_2 is such an instance, in which data is relayed from c_1 to S_1, then from S_1 to A_1, and continues until

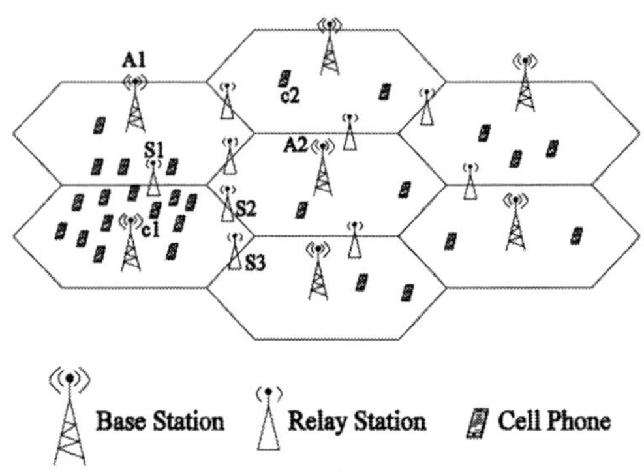

Figure 1. Topology of a Cellular Network

it reaches c_2. In the scenario, S_1 is hot with a lot of cell phones nearby. Hence, its energy is going down very quickly. However, S_2 covers less cell phones and its energy is going down slowly. Therefore, our focus in this paper is to design an approach to help c_1 find S_2 or even S_3 as the next relay station to forward the message, and to bypass the hot relay station S_1 as well.

Since a mobile cell phone is able to select a relay station and hand over to it[15], we develop an approach to let each mobile node find the RS with highest potential energy and hand over to it. We start our basic idea by a simplified case as Fig. 2. Suppose c1 intends to talk to c2. If c1 selects S1 to conduct relay, it may not be a good choice because S1 is busy and may run out of energy shortly. Our goal is to let c1 select the relay station that will have the highest potential energy. In our approach, each RS can predict its future energy right after this time slot based on its historical and current energy, which is defined as potential energy of the RS in this paper. In this example, our strategy will make c1 choose S2.

3.2Computation of Potential Energy

The mobile initiator needs to know which relay station is the one that has the potential highest energy. The energy varying trend is essential to determine an RS's potential energy. Suppose the current time is k. A relay station Si saves its Energy changes of the last three times t0, t1,and t2. By Computational Method, we define a factor $L_{i,k}$ as follows:

$$L_{i,k}=\prod_{\substack{i=0\\ i\neq k}}^{m}\frac{(t-t_i)}{(t_k-t_i)}E_{i,m} \quad (1)$$

Where $E_{i,m}$ is the energy of RS_i at time m.
The for a near future time p, the energy of RS_i can be calculated as:

$$E_{i,p}=\sum_{k=0}^{p} L_{i,k} \quad (2)$$

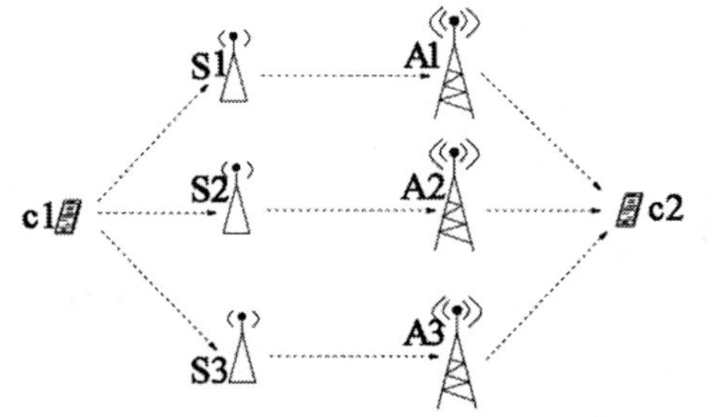

Figure 2. The communication initiator making a chocie of a relay station

Each RS Si keeps its energy status of the last three times. When a mobile user ci intends to send packages to another mobile user cj, ci sends a call for energy message to its neighbor relay stations. Then it figures out the RS with highest energy, and then selects the RS as relay station. Obvious, ci will not find an RS in the opposite direction of cicj as the relay station. In cellular networks, each device is equipped with GPS and hence it knows its location. We assume the initiator knows the target's location. It is very common in geographic routing [13][14]. When ci intends to set up a talk with cj, cicj is virtually connected, then cicj is used as the internal bisector to make an angle of 120 degrees. Then ci finds its relay station within this angle.

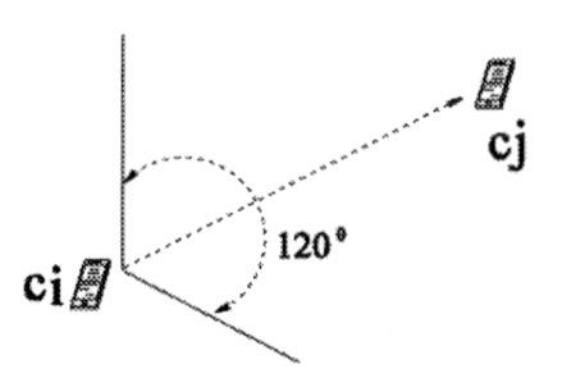

Figure 3. The communication initiator figureing out the region of next relay station

4 Algorithm

Algorithm 1 Energy data request

1. A mobile user c_i figures out the 120 degree area.
2. C_i send energy data request message to its neighboring relay station within the 120 degree area.

In algorithm 1, when a mobile node ci intends to set up a talk with another mobile node cj, ci figures out the 120 degree area with its location and the location of cj. Then ci sends an energy data request message to its neighbor relay station within the area.

Algorithm 2 Prediction for future energy

1. A relay station S_i keeps its energy of the last three times.
2. S_i calculates $L_{i,k}$ with equation (1).
3. Upon receiving energy-requesting message, calculates $E_{i,p}$, the energy of next time p with the equation (2).
4. Reply $E_{i,p}$ to the message sender.

In algorithm 2, a relay station, say Si, saves its energy status of the last three times. It also periodically updates and saves its energy data of the last three times. When Si receives an energy-requesting message, it calculates $E_{i,p}$, the energy of next time p per the equation (2), and then replies $E_{i,p}$ to the message sender.

Algorithm 3 Find next relay station

1. Insert received energy data to a priority queue.
2. Perform pull() from the priority queue.
3. Use the result of step 2 to figure out the relay station as its next relay station.

In algorithm 3, When a mobile node receives the returned energy data message, its use a priority queue to find the relay with the possible highest energy, and then set the relay station as its next RS to relay the communication.

5 Performance Evaluation

We performed the evaluations with a simulated noiseless radio network environment using MATLAB. We create a topology that consists of 20 hexagonal cells. A base station is located in the center of each cell and a relay station is located at each edge. We randomly distribute a number of mobile users to the cells. We performed a sequence of experiments in which the number of mobile users is changed from 200 to 800 with increment of 50. For each number of mobile users, we measure the aggregate throughput 10 times and present the average. We also measure the average total delay of communications for a large number of pairs of communications.

Our approach considers energy balance with prediction. We compare our approach prediction for energy

DOI: 10.1051/itmconf/20171203017

balance("Prediction EB") with an approach without considering energy balance("No EB").

Figure 4 shows that our approach("Prediction EB") results in the less delay. It is because our approach selects the relay station with potential maximum energy as the next RS for communication. Fig. 5 shows our evaluation of aggregate throughput. Of the two approaches, the scheme without energy balance("No EB") has the lower throughput. If one RS runs out of energy and turns down, there will be a hole[13] and the whole throughput will be decreased dramatically. This indicates that energy balance can improve aggregate throughput because the traffic are allocated more reasonable to the relay stations. The throughput of our method is higher.

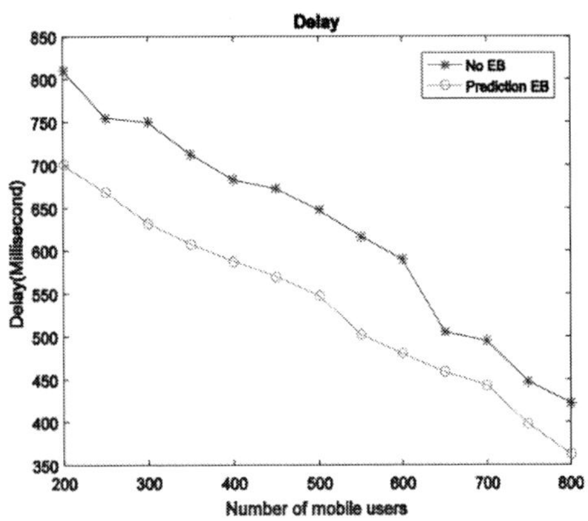

Figure 4. The delay of two approaches

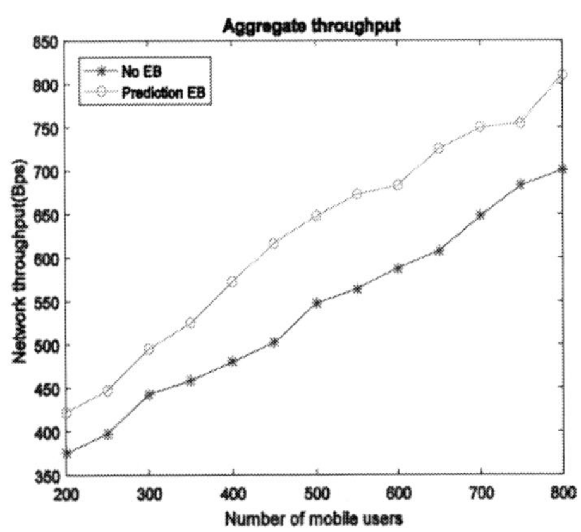

Figure 5. The aggregate thrughtput of two approaches

Conclusion

In this paper, we present a prediction based mechanism to balance energy utilization in cellular network. In the approach, each relay station only needs to remain the last three status of its energy changes, and then it is able to predict its future energy. The message initiator selects the relay station with potential highest energy to relay data transmission. Simulations demonstrate that our approach results in higher throughput in the network and lower delay over related approaches.

References

[1] H. Ziaul, H. Boostanimehr and V.K. Bhargava, "Green cellular networks: A survey, some research issues and challenges," Communications Surveys & Tutorials, IEEE 13.4 (2011): 524-540.J. Clerk Maxwell, A Treatise on Electricity and Magnetism, 3rd ed., vol. 2. Oxford: Clarendon, 1892, pp.68–73.

[2] M. Gruber, et al., "EARTH: energy aware radio and network technologies,"Personal, Indoor and Mobile Radio Communications, 2009 IEEE 20th International Symposium on. IEEE, 2009.K. Elissa,

[3] Y. Chen, et al., "Fundamental trade-offs on green wireless net-works,"Communications Magazine, IEEE 49.6 (2011): 30-37.

[4] J. Yang, B. Payne, M. Hitz, Z. Fei, L. Li and T. Wei, "Location Aided Energy Balancing Strategy in Green Cellular Networks," 23th IEEE International Conference on Computer Communication Networks(ICCCN), Workshop on Wireless Mesh and Ad-hoc Networking (WiMAN 2014), Shanghai, China, 2014.

[5] S. Patra, et al., "Improved genetic algorithm for channel allocation with channel borrowing in mobile computing," Mobile Computing, IEEE Transactions on 5.7 (2006): 884-892.

[6] S. Hanly, "An algorithm for combined cell-site selection and power control to maximize cellular spread spectrum capacity," Selected Areas in Communications, IEEE Journal on 13.7 (1995): 1332-1340.

[7] M. Soleimanipour, W. Zhuang and G.H. Freeman, "Optimal resource management in wireless multimedia wideband CDMA systems," SMobile Computing, IEEE Transactions on 1.2 (2002): 143-160.

[8] E. Yanmaz, and O. Tonguz, "Dynamic load balancing and sharing performance of integrated wireless networks," Selected Areas in Communications, IEEE Journal on 22.5 (2004): 862-872.

[9] J. Yang and Z. Fei, "Bipartite Graph Based Dynamic Spectrum Allocation for Wireless Mesh Networks," Distributed Computing Systems Workshops, 2008. ICDCS'08. 28th International Conference on (pp. 96-101). IEEE, Beijing, 2008.

[10] X. wang, et al., "A survey of green mobile networks: Opportunities and challenges," Mobile Networks and Applications 17.1 (2012): 4-20.

[11] M. Etoh, T. Ohya and Y. Nakayama, "Energy consumption issues on mobile network systems,"

DOI: 10.1051/itmconf/20171203017

Applications and the Internet, 2008. SAINT 2008. International Symposium on. IEEE, 2008.
[12] S. Alam, et al., "Energy efficient relay-assisted cellular network model using base station Switching," Globecom Workshops (GC Wkshps), 2012 IEEE. IEEE, 2012.
[13] J. Yang, and Z. Fei, "ITGR: Intermediate Target Based Geographic Routing," Computer Communications and Networks (ICCCN), 2010 Pro-ceedings of 19th International Conference on (pp. 1-6). IEEE, Zurich, Switzerland, August 2010.
[14] J. Yang and Z. Fei, "HDAR: Hole detection and adaptive geographic routing for ad hoc networks," Computer Communications and Networks (ICCCN), Proceedings of 19th International Conference. IEEE, 2010.
[15] G. Josh, "On Relay-assisted Cellular Networks," thesis, Department of Electrical Engineering, Indian Institute of Technology-Mombay, June, 2010
[16] J. Yang and Z. Fei, "Broadcasting with Prediction and Selective Forward-ing in Vehicular Networks," International Journal of Distributed Sensor Networks, 2013 (2013).

A New Depth Saliency Method Based on Selective Difference

Qiu-Xia CHEN, Li-Hua FU, Can-Can LI, Hao-Gang DING

Beijing University of Technology,Beijing, China
yuxiu_15@163.com,fulh@bjut.edu.cn,can1669103125@163.com,dinghaogang26@163.com

Abstract—Stereopsis plays an important role in the human visual system. In this paper, we propose a novel regional contrast based saliency method, which works on depth images based on selective difference. In this work, we measure the saliency of a region based on regional contrast and take depth difference in horizontal direction into consideration. Besides, center prior is used here to refine the initial saliency map. The proposed method can better reflect the influence of depth information on saliency detection, and the results are more in line with human vision.

1 Introduction

Human visual system can quickly obtain the information of interest regions from complex scenes [1]. Saliency analysis simulate the selective mechanism of human vision, which is widely used in the field of computer vision, including object detection and recognition, image retrieval, compression and retargeting. Saliency detection method can be divided into two parts: bottom-up(data-driven) and top-down(task-driven)[2]. In this paper, we focus on the bottom-up saliency detection model.

The purpose of saliency detection is to simulate the human visual perception, and locate the most salient object rapidly and accurately. Saliency detection mainly depends on the collection of visual information and the extraction of features, previously, most of the saliency detection methods use color images as input, calculate the saliency value based on visual features such as color, shape, orientation, texture, etc[3-9]. When the salient object has at least one distinctive visual feature, the salient object can be detected as salient, on the contrary, lack of 3D spatial information, the detection result is not valid, as shown in Fig. 1(e) and 1(f).

Stereopsis provides a very useful cue for saliency detection[10], which can be used to identify salient objects with similar visual features. Recently, depth images has been used as the fourth channel combined with the existing 2D model to improve the saliency map [11-13,15]. Alternatively,

Fig. 1 Saliency maps generated by different methods This example shows that the saliency method based on depth information supplies a powerful cue for saliency detection.

the depth image is also used to construct the 3D layout[14]. To fully exploit the characteristics of depth information, Niu et al.[16] proposed a saliency detection model based on global disparity contrast and stereo photography domain knowledge, Ran et al.[17,18] proposed a depth-aware saliency method using anisotropic center-surround difference. In addition, a variety of priors[12,17] are used to refine the initial saliency map. Ran and Niu are both based on the basic hypothesis and characteristics of depth images: salient regions have a strong contrast with the background regions, therefore, it's easier to detect the most salient object based on depth images. This assumption ignores the large background area at the bottom of the depth image, which are always mistakenly detected as salient.

In this paper, we propose a novel depth saliency method to solve the problems mentioned above. Experiments show that the model can obtain the complete salient objects, at the same time, effectively weaken the saliency of background regions.

2 Depth-aware Saliency Detection based on Selective Difference

In this paper, we propose a depth contrast based saliency detection model. Firstly, we obtain the depth images and segment the color image into multiple image sub-regions. Then we measure the saliency of a region based on global contrast and consider the depth difference in horizontal direction. Besides, center prior is used to refine the initial saliency map. Finally, we obtain a binary image as the final saliency map.

2.1 Pretreatment

There are many devices used to obtain depth images, such as ToF(Time of Flight), Laser Rangefinders, Structured light scanner and so on. The optical flow method proposed by Sun et al.[19] is used here for easy access. As shown in Fig. 2(a) and 2(b) are respectively corresponding to the left and right eyes at the image, (c) corresponding to the depth map, obviously, the farther away the camera is, the brighter the pixel is, and vice versa.

In this work, we get the sub-regions of color images using SLIC(Simple Linear Iterative Clustering)[20] algorithm. Besides, Gaussian template is used to smooth the depth images for better accuracy.

2.2 Saliency Detection based on Regional Contrast

It is easier to attract people's attention in the area of the image, which have a larger contrast with the surrounding objects. Meanwhile, the spatial distance also plays a very important role, and the high contrast of the adjacent area makes it easier for a region to cause visual attention[3]. Cheng et al.[3] proposed a saliency method based on spatial relations and regional contrast. In this work, the RC(Region Contrast) method is improved here to calculate the saliency value based on depth information, which is calculated as follows:

$$S_G(R_i) = \sum_{R_k \in C_L(R_i)} d(c_i, c_k) w(c_i, c_k) \tag{1}$$

$S_G(R_i)$ represents the global selective difference of region R_i. In this work, we set L as the neighborhood radius of R_i, $C_L(R_i)$ represents all the regions in the neighborhood radius of R_i. Considering the continuity of depth information, we take c_i (the centroid of region R_i) to represent region R_i.

$$d(p,q) = \begin{cases} d_q - d_p, d_q - d_p > 0 \\ 0, \quad d_q - d_p \le 0 \end{cases} \tag{2}$$

$d(p,q)$ represents depth contrast between pixels p and q, and d_p, d_q respectively corresponding to the depth value of pixel p and q.

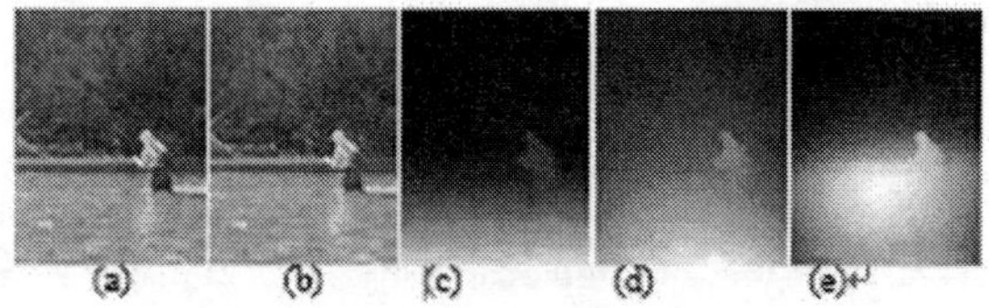

Fig. 2 Saliency map based on regional contrast. (a) Left image, (b) Right image, (c) Depth image, (d) L is set to the image diagonal, (e) L is set to three-third of the image diagonal.

$$w(p,q) = e^{-D_s(p,q)/\sigma^2} \tag{3}$$

Particularly, considering the influence of spatial distance between two pixels, we set $w(p,q)$ as the weight of the distance. $D_s(p,q)$ is the spatial distance between pixels p and q, and σ^2 is assigned to control the spatial distance.

Fig. 2 shows the results of the saliency detection based on regional contrast. As shown in Fig. 2(e), the saliency map is more in line with the expectations and now L is set to three-third of the image diagonal.

2.3 Saliency Detection in horizontal direction

Salient objects are usually surrounded by the background regions, which is extended to the whole range of the depth image, thus some background regions are mistakenly detected as salient. For example, as shown in Fig. 2(e), the water at the bottom of the image detected as salient areas, has a high contrast with respect to the other regions, thus it is detected as salient.

We observe that depth difference between pixels of each line is smooth in some background regions, such as the ground at the bottom of the image. To describe it in more detail, the depth difference of horizontal direction in the background regions is smooth, conversely, the depth difference is abrupt in areas with salient objects. Similar views are presented in [16], and the difference is that we take the selective difference, not the absolute difference, as the comparison result. According to this characteristic, a new detection method in horizontal direction is proposed to suppress the saliency of background regions and highlight the saliency of salient objects. In this work, we define the saliency as follows:

$$S_L(R_i) = \frac{\sum_{p \in R_i} d(p,B)}{n_i} \quad (4)$$

$S_L(R_i)$ represents the local selective difference of region R_i. n_i is the number of pixels of region R_i. p is a pixel of region R_i.

$$d(p,B) = \begin{cases} d_r^B - d_p, d_r^B - d_p > 0 \\ 0, \quad d_r^B - d_p \le 0 \end{cases} \quad (5)$$

$d(p,B)$ represents the contrast between the depth value d_p of pixel p and the mean value d_r^B (also known as the mean depth value of the sampling pixels in line r).

$$d_r^B = \frac{\sum_{q \in r_\alpha} d_q}{cols * \alpha} \quad (6)$$

cols is the column of the image, also known as the number of pixels of each row. α is the factor of the sampling point for each row. r_α is the sampling pixels in line r.

As shown in Fig. 3(d), only the upper half of the object is detected as salient for the first example, in which d_r^B is set to the mean depth of all the pixels in line r; in Fig. 3(f), d_r^B is set to the mean depth of 1% pixels with lower depth in line r, as we can see, almost the whole object is detected as salient for the first example, meanwhile, the salient regions mistakenly detected in the second example can be removed by thresholding segmentation.

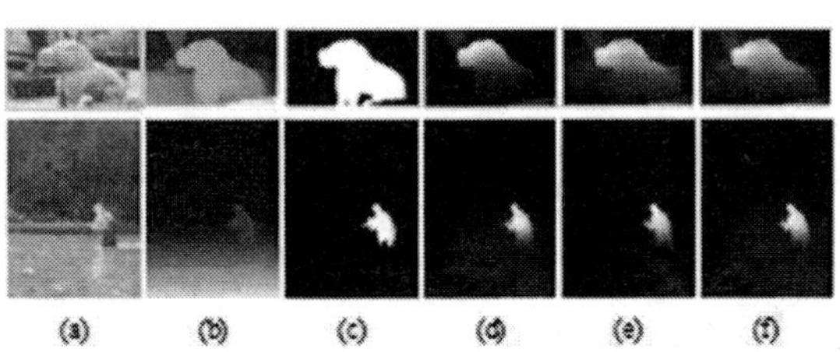

Fig. 3 Saliency detection in horizontal direction. (a) Color images, (b) Depth images, (c) Ground Truth, (d) $\alpha = 1$, (e) $\alpha = 0.1$, (f) $\alpha = 0.01$.

2.4 Final saliency map

The saliency value of region R_i is the product of global and local selective difference, as shown in equation (7), which is then normalized to [0,255] and assigned to each pixel in region R_i. We can obtain the initial saliency map after completing all the sub-regions in a depth image.

$$S_{sd}(R_i) = S_G(R_i) S_L(R_i) \quad (7)$$

Finally, center prior is used to refine the initial saliency map, which refers to the characteristic that salient objects tend to live in the center of the image. A two-dimensional Gaussian weighted filter is presented here to obtain the final saliency map.

3 Experiments

In this paper, we have evaluated the results of our approach on the publicly available data set NJUDS2000 provided by Ran et al.[17], as well as we known, the data set is the largest of this kind, and has ground truth in the form of accurate human-marked labels for salient regions.

We employ the precision-recall curve to evaluate the performance of our method, which is widely used in saliency map comparison. Specifically, we obtain a binary image from each saliency map using a gradually increasing threshold from 0 to 255, and then compare with the ground truth salient object mask to get the precision and recall. We compare the proposed saliency method with 2 advanced 2D saliency detection methods: RC[3], PCA[21]; And 2 authoritative detection methods based on depth information, including ACSD[17,18] and SS[16]. The algorithm we proposed is implemented by C++ programming, the results of other methods are compiled by the author's source code, except SS. Besides, Cheng's evaluation code [3] is used here to get the precision-recall curves of different methods.

3.1 Experimental Setup

The number of super-pixels in image segmentation is taken as the length of the image diagonal. The radius σ of Gaussian template is set to 7. In saliency detection based on regional contrast, the neighborhood radius L is set to one-third of the length of image diagonal, and the weight of spatial distance σ^2 is set to 0.4. In saliency detection in horizontal direction, the factor of the sampling point α is set to 0.01. To optimize the initial saliency map, the two-dimensional Gaussian weighted filter $G(x, y, \sigma_x, \sigma_y)$ is used to optimize the initial saliency map, in which σ_x, σ_y are respectively corresponding to the half-height and half-width of images.

3.2 Results and Discussion

We show the saliency comparison in Fig. 5-7(at the end of this paper), and the precision-recall curves are given in Fig. 4. As shown in Fig. 5, almost all the depth-aware saliency methods perform better than the 2D saliency methods. An exception is SS in Fig. 6, which is based on depth

DOI: 10.1051/itmconf/20171203018

information. The background regions mistakenly detected as salient due to it's absolute value in the local contrast. Our method succeeded in surpressing the saliency of the ground area in Fig. 5 and Fig. 6. As shown in Fig. 5 and Fig. 6, ACSD performs the most close to our method as it takes center and depth priors into consideration, but it fails to distinguish the salient objects and the background when there are background regions at the bottom of the image. The precision of SS not exceed 0.6, while ACSD and our method both with priors reaches a precision far more than 0.8. An explanation is that the data set for comparison containing too much images like this in Fig. 6. As we can see, the precision of ACSD without priors almost drop to 0.7, in contrast, our method without center prior remains high in precision value. This suggests that priors do make a difference. In 2D saliency methods, RC nearly reaches 0.8. The limitation of our method is that the lower half of salient objects might be lost, which can be seen in Fig. 6.

We implement our method in *C++* and *MATLAB* R2010b, and test a machine with a 3.30GHz *Intel Core i5-4590 CPU* and 8GB memory. The running time is 0.431s for a 499*372 image.

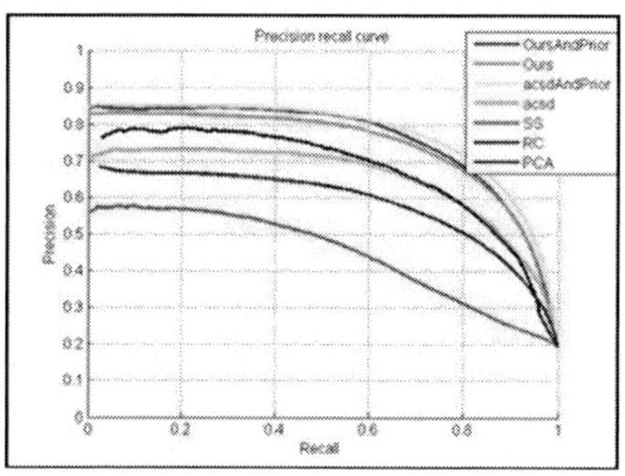

Fig. 4 Precision-recall curves of different methods.

Conclusion

In this paper, we present a new depth-aware saliency method based on selective difference. We measure the saliency of a region based on regional contrast and consider the depth difference in horizontal direction, and the validity of depth information is proved in saliency detection. However, as shown in Fig. 7, it's difficult to detect salient objects for all the 3D methods, due to the poor quality of depth images. Interestingly, the 2D saliency method get better results in Fig. 7. The problem is hoped to be solved with the improvement of depth acquisition technology, or we can try to solve the problem by combining the existing 2D saliency methods. We believe the proposed saliency methods can supply a powerful prediction in efficient object detection, reliable image recognition and classification, leading to improved image retrieval.

References

[1] L. Itti. Visual salience. Scholarpedi., 2007, 2(9):3327.

[2] Y. Fang, Z. Wang, W. Lin, and Z. Fang. Video saliency incorporating spatiotemporal cues and uncertainly weighting. IEEE Trans. Image Process., 2014, 23(9): 3910-3921.

[3] M. M. Cheng, G.-X. Zhang, N. J. Mitra, X. Huang, and S.-M.Hu. Global contrast based salient region detection. in Prol. IEEE Conf. Comput. Vis. Pattern Recog (CVPR)., 2011, pp. 409-416.

[4] L. Itti, C. Koch, and E. Niebur. A model for saliency-based visual attention for rapid scene analysis. IEEE Trans. Pattern Anal. Mach. Tntell., 1998, 20(11): 1254-1259.

[5] L. Zhou, Z. Yang, Q. Yuan, Z. Zhou, and D. Hu. Salient region detection via integrating diffusion-based compactness and local contrast. IEEE Trans. Image Process., 2015, 24(11): 3308-3320.

[6] M. M. Cheng, N. J. Mitra, X. Huang, P. H. S. Torr, and S. M. Hu. Global contrast based salient region detection. IEEE Trans. Pattern Anal. Mach. Intell., 2015, 37(3): 569-582.

[7] J. Sun, H. Lu, and X. Liu. Saliency region detection based on Markov absorption probabilities. IEEE Trans. Image Process. Lett., 2015, 24(5): 1639-1649.

[8] X. Wei, Z. Tao, C. Zhang, and X. Cao. Structured saliency fusion based on Dempster-Shafer theory. IEEE Signal Process. Lett., 2015,22(9): 1345-1349.

[9] C. Yang, L. Zhang, H. Lu, X. Ruan, and M. H.Yang. Saliency detection via graph-based manifold ranking. in Proc. IEEE Conf. Comput. Vis. Pattern Recog . (CVPR), 2013, pp. 3166-3173.

[10] Y. Fang, J. Wang, M. Narwaria, P. Le Callet, and W. Lin. Saliency detection for stereoscopic images. IEEE Trans. Image Process., 2014, 23(6): 2625-2636.

[11] C. Lang, T. V. Nguyen, H. Katti, K. Yadati, M. Kankanhalli, and S. Yan. Depth Matters: Influence of Depth Cues on Visual Saliency. In ECCV, 2012.

[12] J. Ren, X. Gong, L. Yu, W. Zhou, and M. Yang. Exploiting global priors for RGB-D Saliency detection. In CVPRW, 2015, pp. 25-32.

[13] H. Peng, B .Li, W. Xiong, W. Hu, and R. Ji. RGBD Salient Object Detection: A Benchmark and Algorithms. In ECCV, 2014.

[14] A. Ciptadi, T. Hermans, and J. M. Rehg. An In Depth View of Saliency. In BMVC, 2013.

[15] K. Desingh, K. M. Krishna, D. Rajan, and C. V. Jawahar. Depth Really Matters: Improving Visual Salient Region Detection with Depth. In BMVC, 2013.

[16] Yuzhen Niu, Yujie Geng, Xueqing Li, and Feng Liu. Leveraging stereopsis for saliency analysis. in IEEE Conference on Computer Vision and Pattern Recognition. IEEE, 2012, pp. 454-461.

[17] R. Ju, L. Ge, W. Geng, T. Ren, and G. Wu. Depth saliency based on anisotropic center-surround difference. ICIP, 2014.

[18] R. Ju, Y. Liu, T. Ren, L. Ge, and G. Wu. Depth-aware salient object detection using anisotropic center-surround difference. Signal Process. Image Commun., 2015, 38(10): 115-126.
[19] Deqing Sun, Stefan Roth, and Michael J Black. Secrects of optical flow estimation and their principles. in IEEE Conference on Computer Vision and Pattern Recognition. IEEE, 2010, pp. 2432-2439.
[20] Radhakrishna Achanta, Appu Shaji, Kevin Smith, Aurelien Lucchi, Pascal Fua, and Sabine Susstrunk. Slic superpixels compared to state-of-the-art superpixel methods. IEEE Transactions on Pattern Analysis and Machine Intelligence., 2012, 34(10):2274-2282.
[21] R. Margolin, A. Tal, L. Zelnik-Manor, What makes a patch distinct? IEEE Conference on Computer Vision and Pattern Recognition, 2013, pp. 1139-1146.

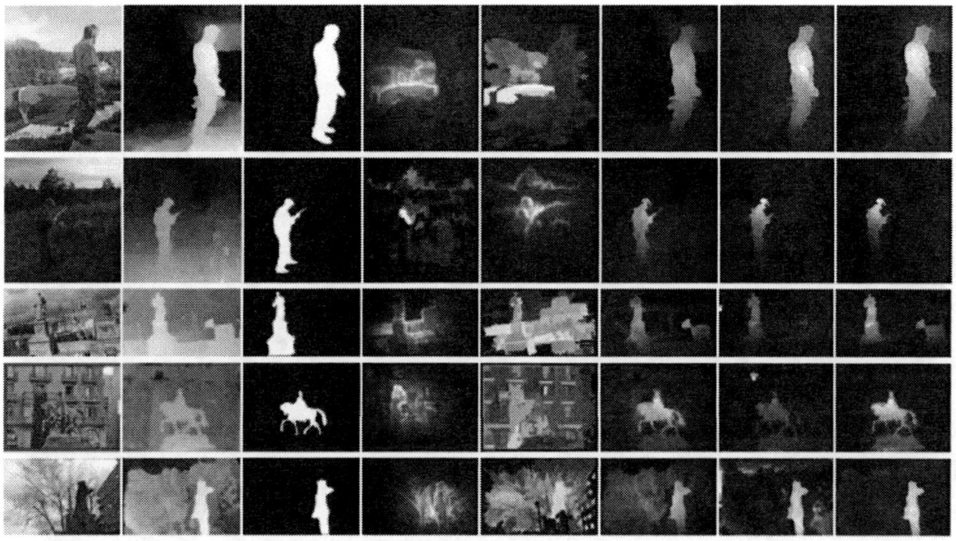

Fig. 5 Saliency comparison of different methods

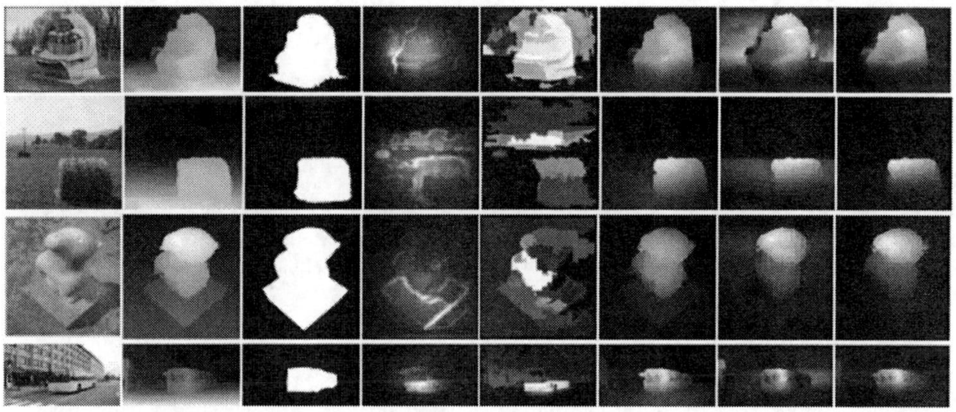

Fig. 6 Saliency comparison of different methods

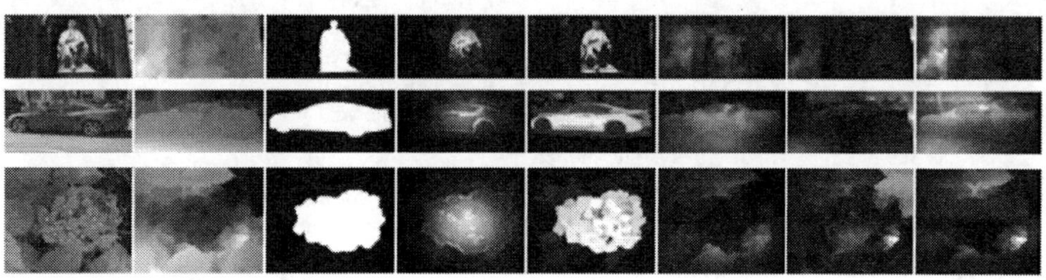

Fig. 7 Failure cases of depth based saliency detection.

Modeling Dynamics of Wikipedia: An Empirical Analysis Using a Vector Error Correction Model

Feng-Jun LIU[1,a], * Jiang-Nan QIU[1,b] and Na ZHAO[2,c]

[1]Faculty of Management and Economics, Dalian University of Technology, 116024 Dalian, Liaoning, China
[2]School of Management Science and Engineering, Shandong Technology and Business University, 264005 Yantai, Shandong, China

[a]liufengjunmail@163.com, [b]qiujn@dlut.edu.cn, [c]zhaonawfxy@163.com

*Corresponding author: Feng-Jun LIU

Abstract. In this paper, we constructed a system dynamic model of Wikipedia based on the co-evolution theory, and investigated the interrelationships among topic popularity, group size, collaborative conflict, coordination mechanism, and information quality by using the vector error correction model (VECM). This study provides a useful framework for analyzing the dynamics of Wikipedia and presents a formal exposition of the VECM methodology in the information system research.

1 Introduction

Wikipedia has become one of the most striking emblems of mass collaboration. Its unprecedented success has posed challenges to traditional theories of public goods and collective-action, which has inspired many scholars from various fields to study it [1, 2]. Existing research highlights many factors that are crucial to the success of Wikipedia, including topic popularity, group size, collaborative conflict, coordination mechanism, and information quality, etc [3]. However, most of these studies examine the relationships among factors from a static perspective without considering the dynamic evolution of Wikipedia. Although some scholars have already explored the statistical properties in many aspects of Wikipedia by statistical methods and revealed the dynamic relations among factors by visual analysis tools [4-7]. there are lack of rigorous empirical studies. So far, the dynamic mechanism of Wikipedia is not completely known.

As an attempt complementary to the previous studies, this study constructs the PSCCQ model, a system model consisting of five microcosmic factors (i.e., topic popularity, group size, collaborative conflict, coordination mechanism, and information quality), with which we explore the fundamental dynamic mechanism behind Wikipedia.

Our study makes several key contributions. First, we build the PSCCQ conceptual model from a systemic perspective, and provide strong empirical evidence to support the validity and usefulness of this model. Second, the VECM methodology provides a statistically rigorous yet atheoretical approach for analyzing the dynamics of temporal relationships among variables without strong theoretical restrictions. In summary, this paper promotes the importance of taking a systematic view of the dynamics of Wikipedia by utilizing the VECM approach in concert with the PSCCQ model.

2 Research model

The process of collaborative knowledge building in Wikipedia demonstrates complex self-cleaning, self-regulating, and self-developing dynamics of the mass of participants that are akin to a kind of evolution [8]. The co-evolution theory provides an effective theoretical lens for analyzing the dynamics of Wikipedia. Based on the co-evolution theory, A few scholars have attempted to analyze the dynamic interactions among factors, modules, and subsystems of the Wikipedia system. For example, Cress and Kimmerle built a theoretical model for describing the co-evolution between the Wiki's social system and the individuals' cognitive systems [9]. Kimmerle et al. used the social network analysis to graphically visualize co-evolutionary processes of individual knowledge learning and collective knowledge building [7].

Based on the co-evolution theory, we build the PSCCQ model as a theoretical framework to analyze the dynamic interactions among topic popularity, group size, collaborative

DOI: 10.1051/itmconf/20171203019

conflict, coordination mechanism, and information quality, and reveal the dynamics of Wikipedia (cf. Fig. 1).

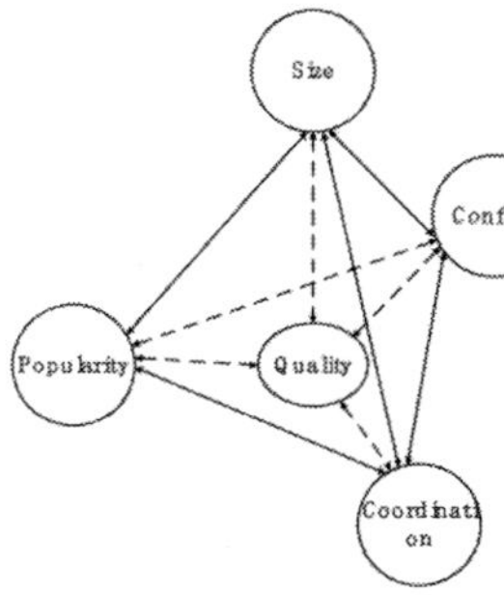

Figure 1. The PSCCQ model.

3 Research setting

3.1 Research context

We select a specific Wikipedia article—global warming as research object for several reasons. Firstly, global warming belongs to a featured article, which means that it is identified as one of the best articles. Secondly, it is also one of the most frequently viewed articles in Wikipedia. It has around 50 million page views, ranking 152 in English Wikipedia article traffic. Thirdly, global warming has always been one of the most intensely controversial topics in Wikipedia. In summary, this case represents one of the most typical, highly concerned and intensely controversial articles in Wikipedia, so it is ideal for deeply examining the dynamics of Wikipedia.

3.2 Data collection

Following Ransbotham, Kane, and Lurie [10], we use the relative search frequency in Google to reflect the topic popularity of global warming. We determine the number of times that users of Google search for keywords from the article title each month from Google Trends. The number of unique editors contributed to an article in Wikipedia is widely used to measure group size in previous studies [11], so we adopt it to measure group size during the monthly observation period. Rollback has been frequently used to model conflicts and identify edit wars in Wikipedia [12]. Therefore, we measure collaborative conflict by calculating the monthly number of rollbacks in the article. The most important coordination mechanism in Wikipedia is communication [13]. We operationalize coordination mechanism as the monthly accumulated number of discussions recorded in the article talk page during the study period. The number of edits provides a good indicator of a "high level of quality" for Wikipedia articles [3]. We quantify information quality as the number of edits in the given month.

Using monthly counts of each variable, we obtain five time series. With the data from February 2004 to November 2015, we have a total of 142 monthly observations in the form of time series, as shown in Fig 2.

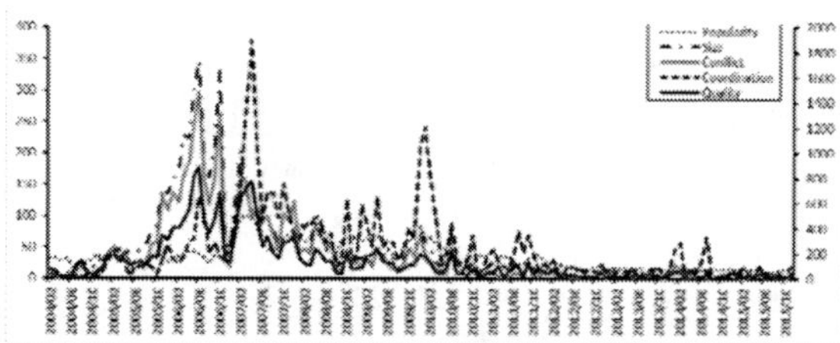

Figure 2. Time series plot.

4 Model specification and estimation

Selection of a VECM involves three basic decisions: (1) Unit root test, (2) lag length selection, and (3) co-integration test. Non-stationary data generally lead to spurious regression due to non-constant mean and variance [14]. Therefore, we first test the stability of variables. The results indicate that all variables are stationary at first differences implying that all variables are integrated of order one. Before co-integration test, we need to select an optimal lag length to ensure that the model is not mispecified [15]. The results show that the optimal lag length is identified to be lag 4. Finally, the Johansen co-integration test results show that there are co-integration relationships among the variables.

The estimates of VECM regression coefficients typically are not as informative as analyzing relationships among variables because of the complicated dynamics inherent in VECM models [15, 16]. Therefore, we report the general estimation results in Table 1 and then provide a detailed analysis using Granger causality tests, impulse response functions, and forecast error variance decomposition in the next section.

5 Empirical analysis

5.1 Granger causality tests

Granger causality tests help to determine whether the lagged values of one variable help to predict values of another variable [17]. Table 2 presents the results of Granger causality tests based on the VECM. Fig 3 provides a reduced form model of PSCCQ, as uncovered by the Granger causality tests.

DOI: 10.1051/itmconf/20171203019

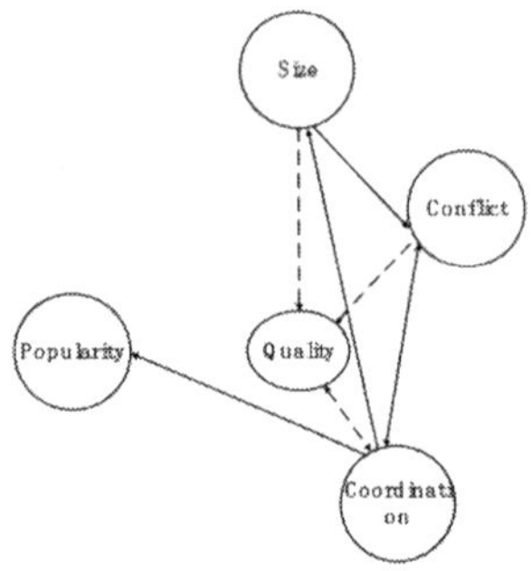

Figure 3. Reduced form model of the PSCCQ.

5.2 Impulse response functions

Impulse response functions (IRFs) plot the response of current and future values of the endogenous variables to a one-unit increase in the current value of a random disturbance term [18], which provide a more intuitive description of the dynamics of temporal relationships among variables. Fig 4 provides twenty possible impulse response functions for the estimated VECM.

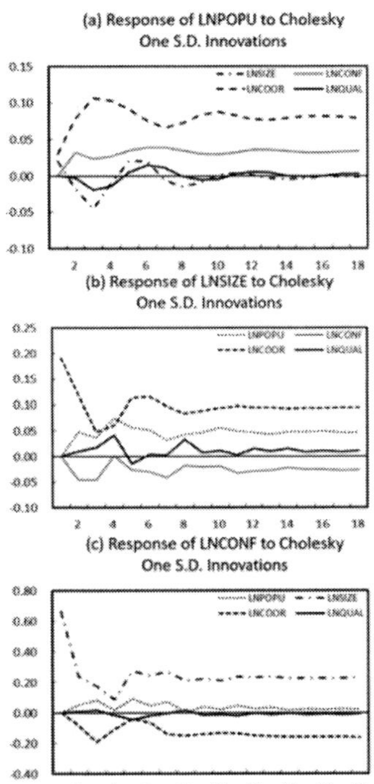

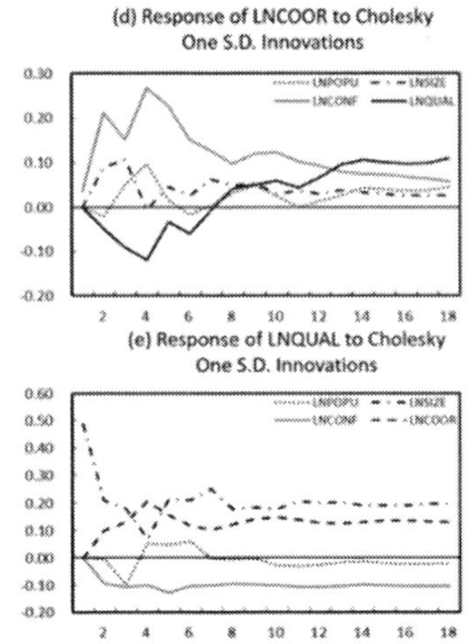

Figure 4. Impulse responses (Impulse→Response).

The results of the IRFs analysis basically corroborate the results of the Granger causality tests. Specifically, the feedback relationship between *LNCONF* and LNCOOR identified previously holds, which can be found in the significantly negative response of *LNCONF* at forecast horizons 3 and 8-18 in Fig 4c and in the significantly positive response of LNCOOR at forecast horizons 2-11 in Fig 4d. Similarly, we can also confirm the feedback relationship between *LNCOOR* and *LNQUAL*. Additionally, the unidirectional relationships among the variables identified previously also hold. The response of *LNPOPU* to a one standard deviation shock in *LNCOOR* has a maximum value of 0.107 at the 3th period, as shown in Fig 4a. Turning now to the response of *LNSIZE* to *LNCOOR*, we find that *LNSIZE* initially reaches the maximum value of about 0.2, then gradually decreases, and achieves stability until the 10th period (cf. Fig 4b). The significantly positive response of *LNSIZE* to *LNCONF* can be seen during the whole period, (cf. Fig 4c). Fig 4e reveals the *LNQUAL* responses to a shock in each variable. The response of *LNQUAL* to *LNSIZE* reflects a discernible decline, which declines from 0.48 to 0.19. In parallel, the magnitude of the effect of *LNCONF* on *LNQUAL* is about -0.1 which persists over the entire forecast period.

5.3 Forecast error variance decomposition

Forecast error variance decomposition (FEVD) analysis provides the relative importance of the variance of the error made in forecasting a variable because of specific shocks of all variables in the system at a specified time horizon [18]. Fig 5 provides a graphical representation of the FEVD, where each graph depicts the proportions of forecast error variance, up to 12 periods (one year) ahead, accounted for by shocks in each variable.

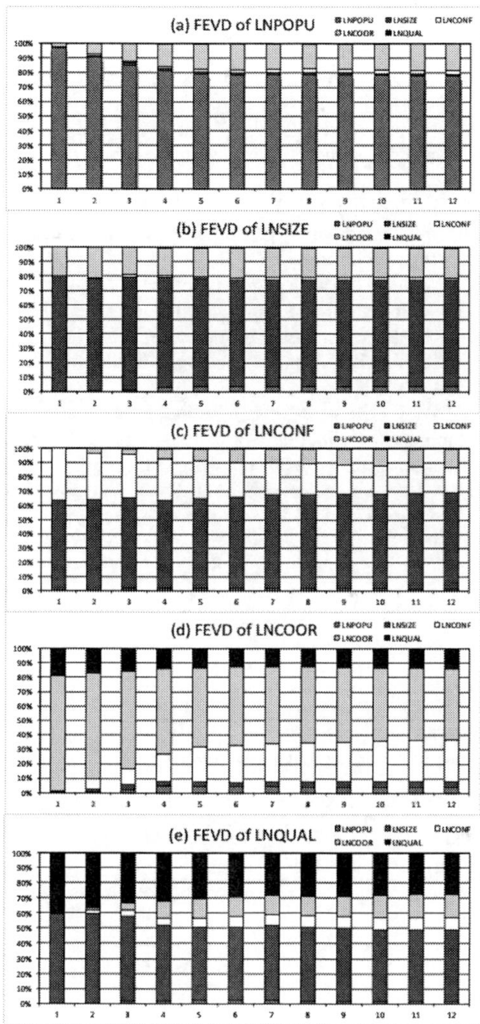

Figure 5. Forecast error variance decompositions.

As would be expected, the results of the FEVD further corroborate the results of the Granger causality tests and IRFs. Specifically, approximately 20% of the *LNPOPU* (or *LNSIZE*) error variance is accounted for by a shock in *LNCOOR* (cf. Fig 5a and Fig 5b). The *LNSIZE* accounts for the large majority of the *LNCONF* error variance, reaching nearly 67.73% at the end of the forecast period, while the explanation ability of *LNCOOR* is relatively low, only about 13% (cf. Fig 5c). Moreover, Fig 5d shows that *LNCONF* and *LNQUAL* together account for approximately 43% of the error variance in *LNCOOR*, about 29% and 14% respectively. With respect to the FEVD of *LNQUAL*, the result indicates that the *LNSIZE* has the greatest impact on *LNQUAL*, followed by *LNCOOR*, *LNCONF* and *LNPOPU* (cf. Fig 5e).

Discussion

We have systematically investigated the dynamic interrelationships among topic popularity, group size, collaborative conflict, coordination mechanism, and information quality in Wikipedia through a detailed empirical analysis. What's more, our study demonstrates the usefulness of the PSCCQ framework and VECM methodology can be applied to formally and practically analyze the dynamics of Wikipedia. Our first finding shows that the critical importance of coordination mechanism in effectively harnessing the "wisdom of the crowd" in the online collaborative environment. Our second finding shows that too many contributors involved in a particular project may be detrimental to group performance. Wikipedia managers should not necessarily pursue a more-is-better strategy towards the number of contributors.

This paper also has some limitations. First, a potential limitation of our study relates to sample data. A potential extension of the research is to apply panel vector autoregression (PVAR) to further explore the dynamics of Wikipedia with large sample. Second, we overlook the network characteristics of Wikipedia community. Future research should combine the network dynamics with the knowledge dynamics to give a fuller picture of the dynamics of Wikipedia.

Acknowledgment

This work was supported by the National Natural Science Foundation of China (No. 71573030) and the Doctoral Scientific Research Foundation of Shandong Technology and Business University (No. B5201705). The authors would like to thank Ye Zhang for excellent technical support and Professor Na Zhao for critically reviewing the manuscript.

References

[1] T. Yasseri and J. Kertész, "Value production in a collaborative environment," J Stat Phys, vol. **151**, pp. 414-439, (2013).

[2] M. Mesgari, C Okoli, M Mehdi, F. Arup Nielsen, and A. Lanamaki, "'The sum of all human knowledge': a systematic review of scholarly research on the content of Wikipedia," J Assoc Inf Sci Tech, vol. **66**, PP. 219-245, (2014).

[3] Y. Ren, J. Chen, and J Riedl, "The impact and evolution of group diversity in online open collaboration," Manage Sci, vol. **62**, pp. 1668-1686, (2015).

[4] J. Yun, S. H. Lee, and H. Jeong, "Intellectual interchanges in the history of the massive online open-editing encyclopedia, Wikipedia," Phys Rev E, vol. **93**, pp. 012307, (2016).

[5] T. Yasseri, R. Sumi, A. Rung, K. András, and K. János, "Dynamics of conflicts in Wikipedia," PloS One, vol. **7**, pp. e38869, (2012).

[6] F. Flöck, D. Laniado, F. Stadthaus, and A. Maribel, "Towards better visual tools for exploring Wikipedia article development–the use case of "gamergate controversy," ICWSM. pp. 1-8, (2015).
[7] J. Kimmerle, J. Moskaliuk, A. Harrer, and U. Cress, "Visualizing co-evolution of individual and collective knowledge," Inform Comm Soc, vol. **13**, pp. 1099-1121, (2010).
[8] U. Cress, I. Feinkohl, J. Jirschitzka, and J. Kimmerle, Mass Collaboration and Education, vol. **16**, Switzerland: Springer, pp. 85-104, (2016).
[9] U. Cress and J. Kimmerle, "A systemic and cognitive view on collaborative knowledge building with Wikis," Int J Comp.-Support Collab Learn, vol.**3**, (2008).
[10] S. Ransbotham, G. C. Kane, and N. H. Lurie, "Network characteristics and the value of collaborative user-generated content." Mark Sci, vol. **31**, pp. 387-405, (2012).
[11] G. C. Kane and S. Ransbotham, "Research note—content and collaboration: an affiliation network approach to information quality in online peer production communities," Inf Syst Res, vol. **27**, pp. 424-439, (2016).
[12] M. Jankowski-Lorek, S. Jaroszewicz, L. Ostrowski, and A. Wierzbicki, "Verifying social network models of Wikipedia knowledge community," Inf Sci, vol. **339**, pp. 158-174, (2016).
[13] A. Kittur and R. E. Kraut, "Beyond Wikipedia: coordination and conflict in online production groups," CSCW, pp. 215-224, (2010).
[14] R. F. Engle and C. W. J. Granger, "Co-integration and error correction: representation, estimation, and testing," Econometrica, vol. **55**, pp. 251-276, (1987).
[15] W. Enders, Applied Econometric Time-Series, New York: John Wiley & Sons Limited, 1995, pp. 127-134.
[16] H. Lütkepohl, New Introduction to Multiple Time Series Analysis, Berlin: Springer Heidelberg, pp. 269-324, (2005).
[17] C. W. J. Granger, "Investigating causal relationships by econometric models and cross-spectral methods," Econometrica, vol. **37**, pp. 424-438, (1969).
[18] J. H. Stock and M. W. Watson, "Vector autoregressions," J Econ Perspect, vol. **15**, pp. 101-115, (2001).

Table 1. General VECM estimation results

	D(LNQUAL)	*D(LNPOPU)*	*D(LNSIZE)*	*D(LNCONF)*	*D(LNCOOR)*
R-squared	0.417172	0.288289	0.30871	0.437351	0.363726
Adj. R-squared	0.333911	0.186617	0.209954	0.356973	0.27283
Mean dependent	-0.00396	-0.005373	-0.000913	-0.008516	0.015874
S.D. dependent	0.773045	0.219413	0.482391	1.037013	0.955626
F-statistic	5.010411	2.83546	3.125993	5.441155	4.001551

Table 2. Granger causality tests based on the VECM.

Variables	*D(LNQUAL)*	*D(LNPOPU)*	*D(LNSIZE)*	*D(LNCONF)*	*D(LNCOOR)*
D(LNQUAL)		2.5455	5.0556*	7.8581**	6.8042**
D(LNPOPU)	1.0086		2.2433	4.5436	8.4576**
D(LNSIZE)	4.3569	1.5993		1.1003	7.9319**
D(LNCONF)	0.8781	1.5987	7.0872**		7.5498**
D(LNCOOR)	6.5173*	4.8347	2.9189	8.6165**	

Note: *, ** and *** indicate significance at 10%, 5% and 1% level, respectively.

An Automatic Parkinson 's Disease Recognition System Based on Multi - Feature Selection of Motion Signals

Tian-Yu Shen[1,2], Ji-Ping Wang[2], Jing Chen[2], Da-Xi Xiong[2], and Li-Quan Guo[2,a]

[1]*School of communication and information engineering, Shanghai University, 200444 Shanghai, China*
[2]*Suzhou Institute of Biomedical Engineering, Chinese Academy of Sciences, 215163 Suzhou, China*
[a] *Corresponding author: guolq@sibet.ac.cn*

Abstract. Parkinson's disease (PD) seriously affects human health so it has wide application value for its automatic diagnosis. In this study, 5 wearable inertial sensors were used in acquiring the acceleration and angular velocity signals under 4 paradigm actions. Total of 27 features were extracted from the signals, including amplitude, frequency, fatigue degree, self similarity, cross correlation and approximate entropy of an action. Genetic algorithm and BP neural network was used for feature selection and data classification. The experiment data were acquired from 10 PD patients and 10 healthy subjects. The results showed that the classification efficiency was improved after feature selection, and the average sensitivity, specificity and accuracy of the classification were 87%, 100% and 93% respectively. It may have certain application value in computer aided diagnosis of Parkinson's disease.

1. Introduction

Parkinson's disease (PD) is a neurological degenerative disease whose main clinical symptoms include motor symptoms such as tremor, muscle rigidity, dyskinesia, postural balance disorders, and non-motor symptoms such as loss of mood, sleep disorders and depression[1-2].The prevalence rate of people over 65 years old in China is 1700 per 10 million, and increases with age. So It is of great significance to quickly and accurately diagnose Parkinson's disease [3]. Currently, the diagnosis of PD is mainly based on clinical scales such as UPDRS, which contains medical history, clinical symptoms and anti-PD drug response [4]. Clinical diagnosis has high sensitivity, but the specificity is less than 75%. Identification of subclinical or early stage of Parkinson's disease provides the possibility of early neuroprotective therapy, delaying the development of the disease [5].

Quantitative assessment of Parkinson's disease based on motion signals is an objective assessment method that can improve the accuracy of PD diagnosis, improve the diagnostic criteria for PD, and establish a large-scale data analysis of PD. It uses wearable inertial sensors on the body to collect acceleration, angular velocity and other motion signals to be analyzed to obtain quantitative parameters to assess the motor function of patients[6][7]. Körver R J P et al. [8] used the asymmetry parameters to evaluate the shoulder motion function; Yoneyama M et al. [9] used periodic, cross-correlation and other parameters for gait analysis of PD patients. But most of the current studys only focus on a single symptom or one body part, and an automatic identification model of Parkinson's disease with high accuracy is needed.

Therefore, five wearable inertial sensors were used in our study to obtain the three-axis acceleration and angular velocity signals of the patients when doing the paradigm motion tasks. Twenty-seven quantitative parameters describing the motor function of different body parts were extracted. Finally feature selection algorithm and BP Neural network was used to establish a Parkinson 's disease automatic identification model.

2. Materials and Methods

2.1 Wearable Sensors

A total of five sensor nodes were used in this study, which can collect three axis acceleration, angular velocity and magnetic signals at the same time. The size of each node is 39×33×16mm, the average weight is 18g, and the sampling rate is 100HZ. The hardware circuit of the sensor node mainly includes the sensor module, the power module and the control module. MPU9250 chip is used as the motion sensor module, CC3200 chip is used as the control module, and lithium battery is used for power supply. When working each node acquires and transfers the motion data to the host computer wirelessly through the wifi communication network. The physical map of the sensor node and the positions to wear in body are shown in Figure 1:

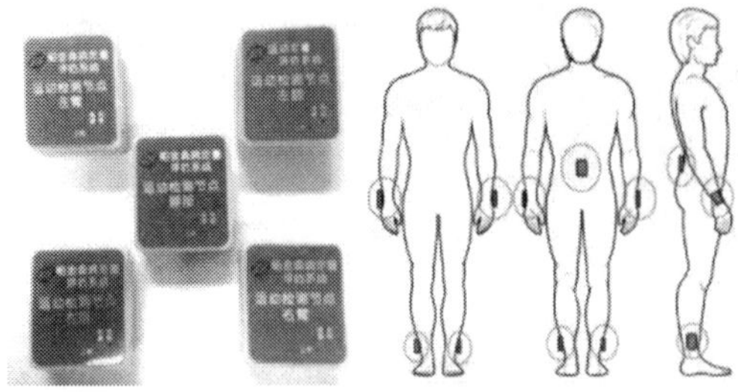

Figure 1. Wearable sensor nodes and the wearing positions.

2.2 Experiment & Data Acquisition

The PD group in the experiment included 10 patients with mild to moderate Parkinson's disease, age 58.7±8.5 years, height 165.8 ± 7.8 cm, weight 69.8 ± 11.5 kg, Hoehn-Yahr stage I-III. The control group included 10 young healthy subjects without any motion related disease, age 25.2 ± 2.2 years, height 168.1 ± 7.1cm, weight 62.8 ± 10.4kg. The 4 paradigm action tasks included 10m time up and go, hand rotation, leg raising and standing still, time duration of each action was 20s, and between every two tasks there was a 1~2min rest. The 5 wearable inertial sensors were worn on the left hand, right hand, left leg, right leg and waist of the subject's body using an elastic bandage. When completing the action tasks, the sensor nodes send the motion signals to the host computer to be displayed and saved. The experiment was conducted at the Second Affiliated Hospital of Soochow University and the informed consent of the subjects and their families was obtained.

2.3 Data Preprocessing

The x, y, z triaxial acceleration and angular velocity signals were filtered using a median filter of 5 points to remove isolated noise points. In order to eliminate the baseline offset, all the signals were detrended. For 10m time up and go, hand rotation and leg raising task, the angular velocity with maximum signal to noise ratio from the corresponding three-axis signals were selected through the calculation of variance to do further analysis. For standing still task, the x, y two-axis acceleration signals from the waist node were used. Due to abnormal shaking during standing, there were some abnormal signals. So the standard deviation σ x(i) of the data from a 100-point sliding window and the standard deviation σ x of the residual data were calculated for comparison. If σ x(i) ≥ 2 σ x, the outliers x(i) from the window were removed.

2.4 Motion Function Features Extraction

For the 10m time up and go, hand rotation and leg raising task, angular velocity signal v(t) after preprocessed was used. Mean value E(v(t)) and the standard deviation σ (v(t)) of the signal were calculated, and the judgment threshold value T0 was obtained according to the formula (1). Figure 2 shows the triaxial angular velocity signals of left hand rotation and the judgment threshold T0 in the selected signal.

$$T_0 = E(v(t)) + \sqrt{2} * \sigma(v(t))/2 \quad (1)$$

The value of v(t) was compared with the threshold value T0 each time to obtain the number and frequency of accomplished actions. Then the angle signal A(t) was obtained by integrating the velocity signal v(t), and the amplitude information of the action was calculated. Due to the turning action in walking, the time required for the angle signal A(t) of the waist node to change from 40° to 140° was defined as the turning time. In addition, the fatigue level was defined as the ratio of action frequency for the first five actions and the last five actions. For the acceleration signal of the waist node when standing still, the root mean square RMSA was calculated, and then the velocity signal v(t) was obtained by integrating the acceleration signal to get the average velocity MV.

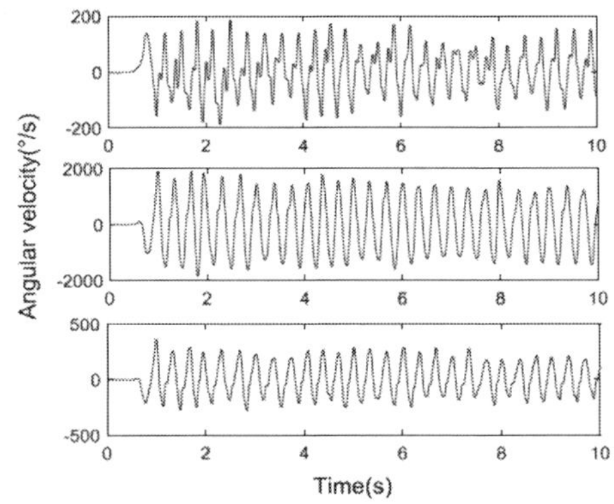

(a)

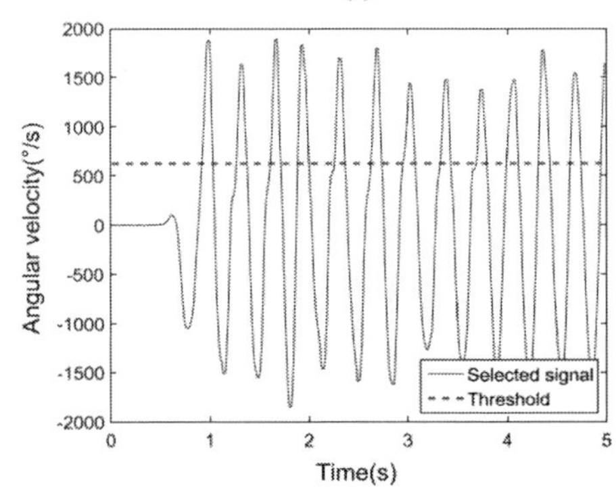

(b)

Figure 2. (a) The triaxial angular velocity signals of left hand rotation. (b) The judgment threshold T0 in the selected signal.

The parameters above were the results of intuitive analysis of the signal. In order to obtain the randomness characteristic, the approximate entropy (ApEn) was calculated. First, the acceleration or angular velocity signal X(i) was processed according to the formula (2) in order to reconstruct the m-dimensional phase space, in which $1 \le i \le N-m+1$.

$$\mathbf{X}(i)=\left[x(i),x(i+1),\cdots \quad n-1)\right] \tag{2}$$

The distance between vectors **X(i)** and **X(j)** was calculated using formula (3), in which $0\le k\le m-1$, $1\le i,j\le N-m+1$.

$$d_{ij}=\max\left|x(i+k)-x(j+k)\right| \tag{3}$$

The similarity tolerance $r>0$ was selected , for each **X(i)**, the number of $d_{ij}\le r$ were counted, and the ratio of the number to the total number of vectors $C_i^m(r)$ was calculated:

$$C_i^m(r)=\frac{1}{N-m+1}\{number\ d_{ij}\le r\} \tag{4}$$

Then take the logarithm of the ratio $C_i^m(r)$ and find the mean value $\Phi^m(r)$:

$$\Phi^m(r)=\frac{1}{N-m+1}\sum_{i=1}^{N-m+1}\ln C_i^m(r) \tag{5}$$

Finally increase the dimension m by 1, repeat the above steps to obtain $C_i^m(r)$ and $\Phi^{m+1}(r)$. Then the approximate entropy (ApEn) was calculated:

$$ApEn(m,r,N)=\Phi^m(r)-\Phi^{m+1}(r) \tag{6}$$

In order to obtain more features of the gait, the angular velocity signals of the left leg and the right leg were used to do the detrend fluctuation analysis (DFA) to obtain their self-similar parameters, and the detrend cross correlation analysis (DCCA) was used to obtain the cross-correlation parameters. First, the mean value $E(x)$ for the signal was calculated, i = 1, 2 ... N, and the cumulative sequence $y(k)$ was obtained by the formula (7):

$$y(k)=\sum_{i=i}^{k}(X_i-E(x)) \tag{7}$$

The sequence $y(k)$ was divided into $[N/n]$ intervals of length n, and the fitting function $yn(k)$ of each interval was obtained by linear least squares method. Then, the fluctuation mean square $F(n)$ of $y(k)$ was calculated :

$$F(n)=\sqrt{\frac{1}{N}\sum_{k=1}^{N}[y(k)-y_n(k)]^2} \tag{8}$$

By repeating the above operations on all time scales, the relation curves of $F(n)$ and fragment size can be obtained. The slope determine scaling exponent alpha of the *log* $(F(n))$ to *log* (n) was calculated as self similar parameter. The cross-correlation parameters were obtained from the two time series covariates in the same way.

According to the methods mentioned above, a total of 27 features related to motor function were extracted, as shown in Table 1:

Table 1. Features extracted from motion signals.

Paradigm action tasks	Body parts	Quantitative parameters
10m time up and go	bilateral lower limbs waist	amplitude(°), frequency(count/min), ApEn, DFA, DCCA turning time(s)
hand rotation	bilateral upper limbs	amplitude(°), frequency(count/s), fatigue, ApEn
leg raising	bilateral lower limbs	frequency(count/s), fatigue, ApEn
standing still	waist	*RMSA*(m/s^2), *MV*(m/s), ApEn

2.5 Feature selection & Classification

The 27 extracted features were normalized to construct a feature vector as input to the network, 14 from the 20 subjects were randomly selected as the training set and 6 were used as the test set to do the BP neural network classification. Since the feature vector dimension was too large, the feature selection algorithm based on genetic algorithm was used to optimize the BP neural network. The chromosome length was set to 27, the population size was set to 20, and the maximum evolutionary algebra was set to 100. The fitness function was chosen as the reciprocal of the square sum of the classify error, as shown in formula (9), where Tp was the predicted value and T was the true value.

$$f(X)=\frac{1}{SE}=\frac{1}{sse(T_p-T)} \tag{9}$$

A total of five times classifications were carried out to improve the reliability of the results. The classification efficiency was compared before and after using the genetic algorithm each time. Accuracy, sensitivity, specificity and modeling time were used as indicators to evaluate the classification efficiency.

3. Results and Discussion

The results of the five times classifications were shown in Table 2 and Figure 3, where BP represented the BP neural network classification result and GA represented the result after genetic algorithm feature selection. It can be seen that the sensitivity, specificity and accuracy of the classification after feature selection were improved. Finally, the overall classification sensitivity, specificity and accuracy rate reached 87%, 100% and 93% respectively. The feature vector dimension required for each modeling after the feature selection was reduced to about half of the original dimension, which also shortened the time required for modeling. These results showed that the classification efficiency of the BP neural network was improved after the feature selection algorithm.

 DOI: 10.1051/itmconf/20171203020

Table 2. The classification results of each time.

Num		Sen	Spc	Acc	Modeling time(s)
1	BP	0.50	1.00	0.67	0.16
	GA	1.00	1.00	1.00	0.12
2	BP	0.50	1.00	0.83	0.14
	GA	1.00	1.00	1.00	0.06
3	BP	0.50	1.00	0.67	0.06
	GA	0.75	1.00	0.83	0.06
4	BP	1.00	0.75	0.83	0.14
	GA	0.50	1.00	0.83	0.06
5	BP	1.00	0.33	0.67	0.09
	GA	1.00	1.00	1.00	0.06
Mean	BP	0.67	0.80	0.73	0.12
	GA	0.87	1.00	0.93	0.07

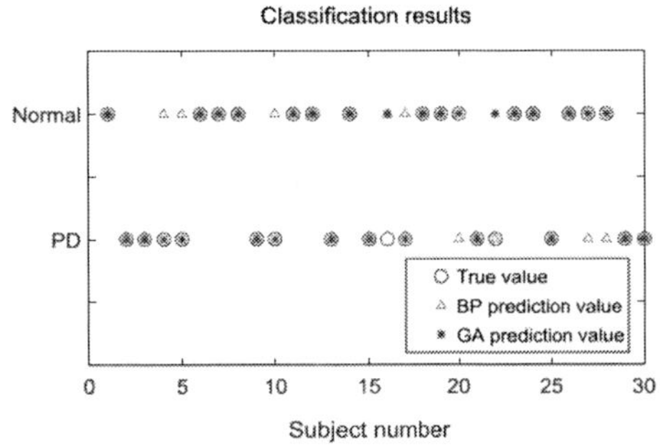

Figure 3. The overall classification results.

The evolution curve of the fitness function of the genetic algorithm was shown in Figure 4. It can be seen that as the evolutionary algebra increased to 100, the average fitness and the optimal fitness rised and eventually stabilize. Due to the number of experimental subjects was limited, the classification performance of this method need further verification, and the future work can also study the influence of frequency domain features on classification results.

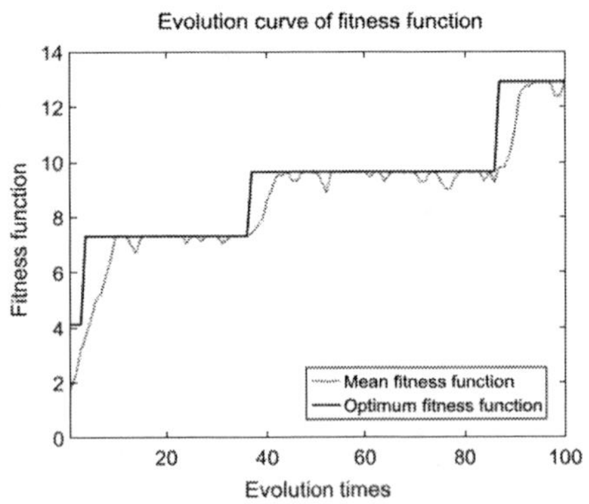

Figure 4. The evolution curve of fitness function.

4. Conclusion

In order to quickly diagnose Parkinson's disease, this paper proposed a classification algorithm based on multi-feature of motion signals. 5 wearable inertial sensors were used to obtain the acceleration and angular velocity signals of motion, multi-scale motor function parameters of different body parts were extracted from the signals, and genetic algorithm was used to select the parameters to participate in the BP neural network classification. The results showed that the classification sensitivity, specificity and accuracy of the method were 87%, 100% and 93% respectively. This may have certain application value in the early diagnosis and computer-aided diagnosis of Parkinson's disease.

References

1. Jankovic, J. Parkinson's disease: clinical features and diagnosis. Journal of Neurology Neurosurgery & Psychiatry ,79.4(2008)
2. Moustafa A A, Chakravarthy S, Phillips J R, et al. Motor symptoms in Parkinson's disease: A unified framework. Neuroscience & Biobehavioral Reviews, 68(2016)
3. Zhang ZX RG, Hong Z, et al. Parkinson's disease in China: prevalence in Beijing,Xian, and Shanghai. Lancet ,365.3(2005)
4. Goetz, C. G. The Unified Parkinson's Disease Rating Scale (UPDRS): Status and recommendations. Movement Disorders, 18.7(2003)
5. Postuma, Ronald B, et al. MDS clinical diagnostic criteria for Parkinson's disease. Movement Disorders Official Journal of the Movement Disorder Society ,30.12(2015)
6. Yang, K., et al. Objective and quantitative assessment of motor function in Parkinson's disease-from the perspective of practical applications. Annals of Translational Medicine ,4.5(2016)
7. Dai H, Lin H, Lueth T C. Quantitative assessment of parkinsonian bradykinesia based on an inertial measurement unit. BioMedical Engineering OnLine, 14.1(2015)
8. Körver R J P, Heyligers I C, Samijo S K, et al. Inertia based functional scoring of the shoulder in clinical practice[J]. Physiological measurement, 35.2(2014)
9. Yoneyama, M, et al. Accelerometry-based gait analysis and its application to Parkinson's disease assessment--part 1: detection of stride event. IEEE Trans Neural Syst Rehabil Eng, 22.3(2014)

High Precision Infrared Temperature Measurement System Based on Distance Compensation

Jing Chen[1], Ji-Ping Wang[1], Tian-Yu Shen[1,2], Da-Xi Xiong[1], and Li-Quan Guo[1,a]

[1]*Suzhou Institute of Biomedical Engineering, Chinese Academy of Sciences, 215163 Suzhou, China*
[2]*School of communication and information engineering, Shanghai University, 200444 Shanghai, China*
[a] *Corresponding author: guolq@sibet.ac.cn*

Abstract. To meet the need of real-time remote monitoring of human body surface temperature for optical rehabilitation therapy, a non-contact high-precision real-time temperature measurement method based on distance compensation was proposed, and the system design was carried out. The microcontroller controls the infrared temperature measurement module and the laser range module to collect temperature and distance data. The compensation formula of temperature with distance wass fitted according to the least square method. Testing had been performed on different individuals to verify the accuracy of the system. The results indicate that the designed non-contact infrared temperature measurement system has a residual error of less than 0.2℃ and the response time isless than 0.1s in the range of 0 to 60cm. This provides a reference for developing long-distance temperature measurement equipment in optical rehabilitation therapy.

1. Introduction

Optical rehabilitation therapy as a noninvasive physical therapy, it and has no side effects, by using different wavelengths of light to irradiate to tissue, to cause the organization of cytochrome, mitochondria and other molecular a series of biological effects to achieve the purpose of therapy [1]. These biological effects have the effect of promoting tissue wound healing, anti-inflammatory analgesic, relieving muscle tissue fatigue and promoting tissue repair and so on. Therefore, optical rehabilitation therapy is widely used in the treatment of dermatology, surgery, rehabilitation and other diseases. The thermal effect of optical rehabilitation therapy can cause angiectasis, faster blood flow, and can improve microcirculation as well as immunity, but at the same time the tissue warming caused by thermal effect will cause the patient's irradiated site burns if not well controlled. Therefore, real-time monitoring of the patient's irradiated site temperature can effectively prevent burns when physiotherapy occurs.

Real-time monitoring of the temperature of the irradiated part of the patient can be used by measuring the temperature of the human body infrared radiation. Environmental factors, distance coefficient, emissivity some other factors will affect the infrared temperature accuracy [2]. According to the law of The Total Radiation of the Stewart-Boltzmann, the radiation intensity of any object is always proportional to the actual emissivity of the object. The body's skin emissivity will have some differences according to skin's state, the race, but its range is around 0.95. The infrared temperature measurement error caused by emissivity can be ignored [3]. In view of the influence of distance factors on infrared temperature measurement, there are many research results. There is a relatively fixed relationship between the temperature error of the infrared thermometer and the distance [4]. At present, the typical solution is to use ultrasonic distance compensation to improve the accuracy of infrared temperature measurement, but the measurement distance is limited within 10cm.

For optical rehabilitation therapy's 0-60cm long distance non-contact temperature measurement needs, a non-contact high-precision real-time infrared temperature measurement system based on distance compensation is designed. The system uses the laser distance measuring module to collect the distance numerical in real time to compensate the temperature and eliminate the influence of the distance factor on the infrared temperature measurement result. Laser ranging is not susceptible to ambient light, temperature and other factors, thus making the distance measurement system and the final temperature monitoring very stable.

2. System Design

The basic principle of the non-contact temperature measurement system based on distance compensation is to measure the surface temperature by the high-precision infrared temperature measurement module and measure the distance between the detection terminal and the human body in real time. The distance compensation is compensated by the distance compensation formula to meet the needs of long-range non-contact temperature measurement [5].

The system block diagram shown in Figure 1. mainly includes micro-controller, high-precision infrared temperature measurement module, laser distance measuring module and display modules and other parts. Microcontroller is the high-performance ARM chip STM32F103ZET6. The main controller collects the high-precision infrared temperature measurement module MLX90614's temperature data through the SMbus in real time and synchronously acquires laser distance measurement module VL53L0X's distance data through the IIC bus. And then it analyzes and processes the data and uploads the processed temperature value to the PC for display and storage through the USB to RS232 Bridge.

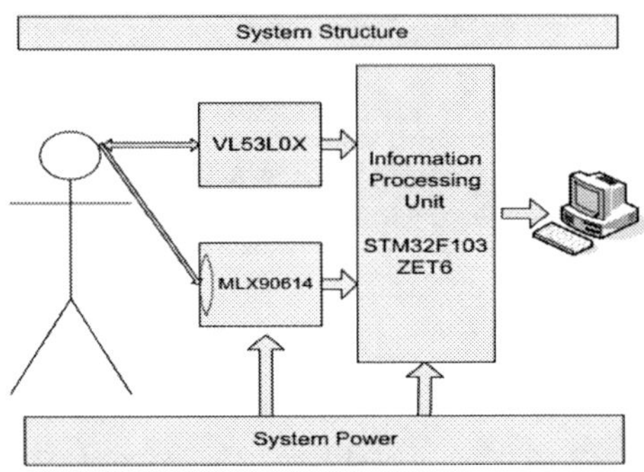

Figure 1. System Block Diagram.

The high precision infrared temperature measurement module MLX90614 internal integrates infrared thermopile sensor MLX81101 and signal processing dedicated integrated chip MLX90302. The MLX90302 is designed to handle the output signals of infrared sensor. MLX90302 measures the object and ambient temperature by the internal state machine, and then calculates and outputs the calculation results through the SMbus. In the range of 0-120℃, MLX90614 measurement accuracy can reach 0.5℃, for the body temperature measurement of about 37℃, the measurement accuracy can be up to about 0.1℃.

The MLX90614 module also integrates filters to block visible and near-infrared radiation, and the wavelength passband of the filter is 5500nm to 14000nm. The radiation wavelength of the human body is near 9000nm,and the optical therapy exposure wavelength range is 200nm to 1400nm. So the filter can effectively filter out the impact of ambient light and light of physical therapy.

The optical lens and the outer package determine the infrared field measuring range and the distance coefficient. Above the infrared sensor there is an eyepiece which can guarantee that a sphere with the diameter of 20cm can fully-fill the entire perspective in the range of 0-60cm. The angle of the surrounding environment on the lens is very small, so the impact of direct thermal radiation in the environment can be ignored.

The laser distance measuring module consists of VL53L0X laser temperature sensor. The VL53L0X based on FlightSense™ technology is the world's smallest ToF (Time-of-Flight) module, it integrates light sources, SPAD photon detectors and advanced microcontrollers (managing the entire ranging function). The laser ranging module VL53L0X connects with STM32F103ZET6 through the IIC bus to read and write data.

3. Experiment and Data Processing

3.1 Experiment and Data Collection

In order to verify the performance of the system and the accuracy of temperature measurement, experiments and tests were carried out on 4 healthy adult yellow skin men(A, B, C, D)from the laboratory.

To measure the actual temperature of the irradiated area of the patient, Microlife's contact infrared temperature sensor, Model: FR1DM1, measurement accuracy 0.1℃, was used to test the temperature of the forehead (regarded as a spherical heating element with the diameter of 20cm) as the reference value of the actual temperature of the irradiated area.

The temperature of four subjects was measured using a non-compensated infrared temperature measurement system and Microlife FR1DM1 at room temperature. The distance between 0 and 60cm was divided into 6 parts. Temperature was measured three times at each point and was averaged to reduce the chance of accidental errors.

Arbitrarily selected one of the subjects' data to use the compensation algorithm to compensate for the fitting formula, and combine it to the infrared temperature measurement system. After the distance compensation, a test was carried out under the same condition to test the temperature of the four subjects to verify the distance compensation effect.

To verify the effect of different colors had on temperature measurement of the infrared temperature measuring system with distance compensation, a black and white skin temperature experiments under the same experimental conditions was carried out.

3.2 Data Processing

As could be seen from 4 sets of data measured by non-compensated infrared temperature measurement system, data were in line with the following trends: In the range of 0 to 20cm, the error was kept within 0.2℃. But when the distance was greater than 20cm, the measurement error increased rapidly as the distance increases. When the distance was 60cm, the error reached 2℃. Figure 2 was the relationship between the measured values T(O), T(A) of the randomly selected subjects C and the measured distance.

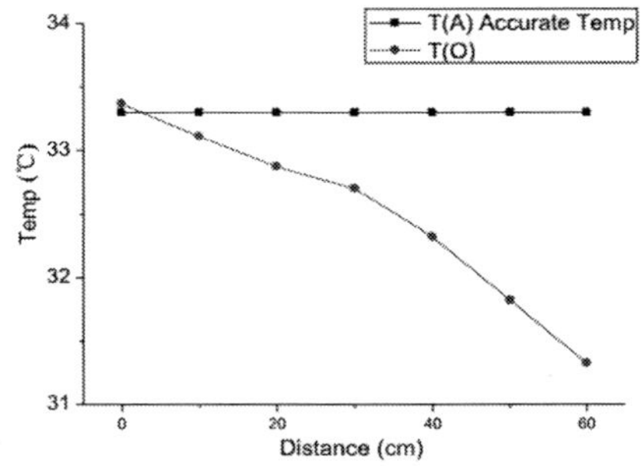

Figure 2. T(O), T(A) of subject C

As the distance increased, the error between the measured value T(O) measured by the infrared temperature measurement system and the actual temperature reference value T(A) measured by Microlife FR1DM1 became larger. In order to filter the effect of the actual temperature had on the fitting results, the ratio of the value measured by non-compensated infrared temperature measurement system to the actual temperature measured by Micro life FR1DM1 was used as the measuring factor Y to discuss the effect of the distance x had on temperature. The system used the least squares method to obtain the ratio of T (O) to T (A), that is, the relationship between the measured factor Y and the distance x. The relationship between the measurement factor Y and the distance x between 0-60cm could be characterized by a quadratic function, regarded the quadratic function (1):

$$Y = \hat{a}_0 + \hat{a}_1 x + \hat{a}_2 x^2 \quad (1)$$

as the approximate fitting curve, the mean square error was as following:

$$Q(a_0, a_1, a_2) = \sum_{i=1}^{n} (a_0 + a_1 x_i + a_2 x_i^2 - y_i)^2 \quad (2)$$

Let the mean square error (2) be the smallest, and the equation (3) was obtained by the method of finding the extreme value.

$$\begin{pmatrix} n & \sum_{i=1}^{n} x_i & \sum_{i=1}^{n} x_i^2 \\ \sum_{i=1}^{n} x_i & \sum_{i=1}^{n} x_i^2 & \sum_{i=1}^{n} x_i^3 \\ \sum_{i=1}^{n} x_i^2 & \sum_{i=1}^{n} x_i^3 & \sum_{i=1}^{n} x_i^4 \end{pmatrix} \begin{pmatrix} a_0 \\ a_1 \\ a_2 \end{pmatrix} = \begin{pmatrix} \sum_{i=1}^{n} y_i \\ \sum_{i=1}^{n} x_i y_i \\ \sum_{i=1}^{n} x_i^2 y_i \end{pmatrix} \quad (3)$$

Solve $\hat{a}_0, \hat{a}_1, \hat{a}_2$ to get the fit formula. From the definition of the measurement factor Y, it could be seen that the temperature after compensation T(C) is T (O)/Y. Fit the above experimental data to get the distance compensation formula:

$$Y = 1.00168 + 0.0000486382x - 0.0000208635x^2 \quad (4)$$

x was the distance, Y was the measurement factor, and the correlation coefficient R2 of the equation (4) was 0.9998.

Take the fitting formula into the system for distance compensation and test the subject C's forehead temperature T(C) in the same external environment. As could be seen from Table 1, the maximum error of the system with distance compensation reduced from 2℃ to 0.2℃ under the same test conditions.

Table 1. Forehead temperature T(C) of subject C.

Distance (cm)	T(A) ℃	T(O) ℃	T(C) ℃
0	33.3	33.37	33.43
10	33.3	33.11	33.33
20	33.3	32.87	33.40
30	33.3	32.70	33.24
40	33.3	32.32	33.34
50	33.3	31.82	33.44
60	33.3	31.32	33.32

In order to test the effect of the fitting algorithm had on different individuals, the remaining three subjects were subjected to a temperature test with infrared temperature measurement system with distance compensation and the results were compared with Micro life FR1DM1 under the same conditions. The temperature comparison curves of the actual temperature T(A) measured by Micro life FR1DM1 and the forehead temperature T(C) measured by the infrared temperature measurement system with distance compensation were shown in Figure 3.

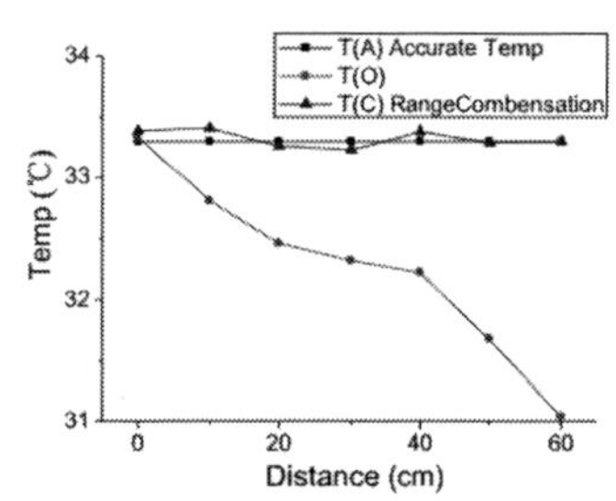

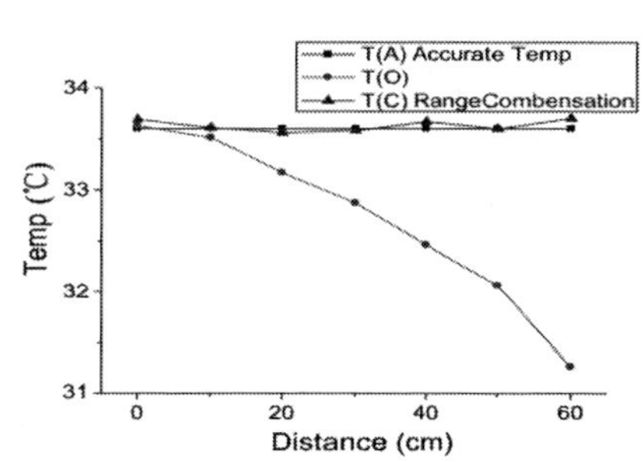

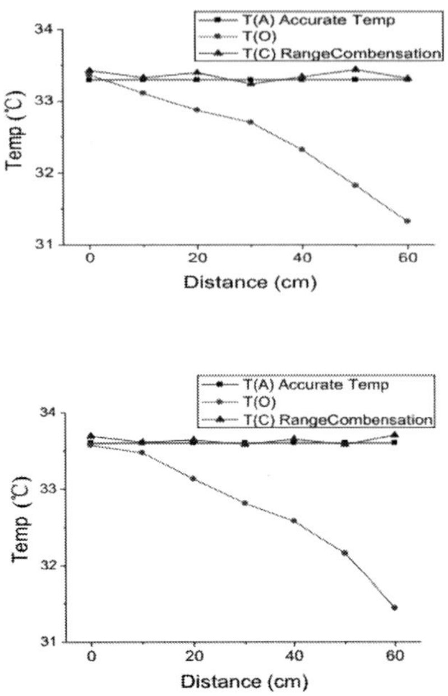

Figure 3. T (O), T (A) ,T(C) of four subjects

As the fitting algorithm used the data from the 6 points from 0 to 60cm, in order to ensure the reliability of the system in the full range of 0 to 60cm, randomly selected subject A to measure temperature at random distances from 0 to 60cm, and the recorded results were shown in Figure 4.

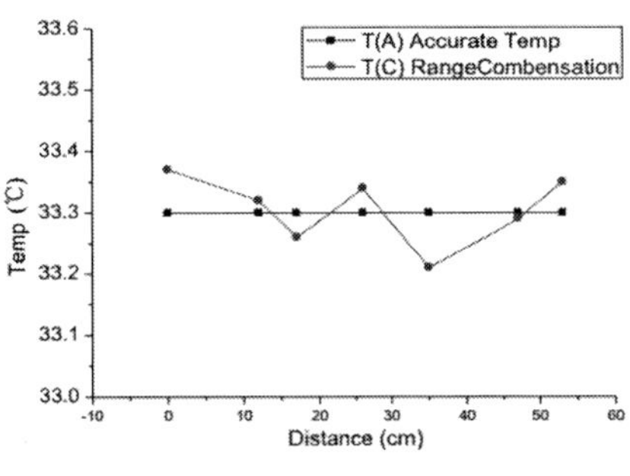

Figure 4. T(C), T (A) of subject A

In order to further explore the effect of skin color had on the accuracy of the system temperature measurement, two subjects were randomly coated with black and white edible pigments on the forehead to simulate the black and white complexion. The results of the two sets of tests measured by the infrared temperature measurement system with distance compensation in the range of 0-60cm were compared with the actual temperature values measured by Microlife FR1DM1, and the maximum error was no more than 0.2℃. Figure 5 was the result of black skin and white skin. It could be seen that the skin color had no effect on the system measurement accuracy.

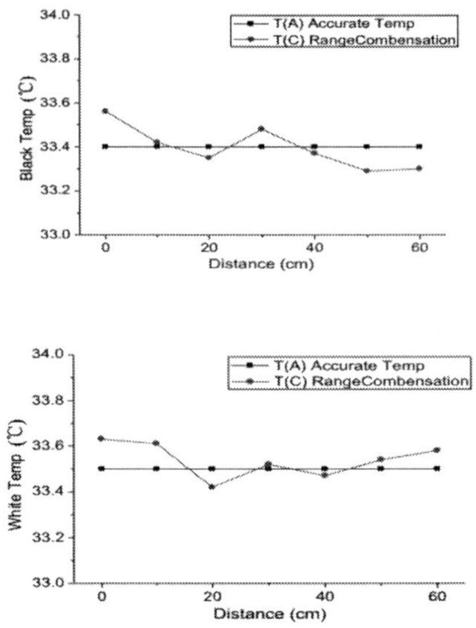

Figure 5. T(C), T (A) of black and white skin

4. Results and Discussion

The errors of the infrared temperature measurement system, based on distance compensation of four yellow skins, a simulated black skin, and a simulated white skin have been shown in table 2, where D(cm) is the distance between the temperature measurement system and the irradiated part of the subject, ε is the error between the forehead temperature T(C) measured by the infrared temperature measurement system based on distance compensation and the actual temperature value T(A) measured by Microlife FR1DM1, ε_{MAX}(℃) is the maximum error between T(C) and T(A). It could be seen that the temperature measurement accuracy of the infrared temperature measurement system based on distance compensation has been improved, and the maximum measurement error in the range of 0-60cm is kept within 0.2℃ and the measurement result has not affected by the skin color.

Table 2. Error of forehead temperature

NO. / D(cm)	A	B	C	D	BLACK	WHITE
	ε=T(C)-T(A) ℃					
0	0.09	0.09	0.13	0.09	0.16	0.13
10	0.11	0.01	0.03	0.01	0.02	0.11
20	-0.04	-0.04	0.1	0.04	-0.05	-0.08
30	-0.07	-0.02	-0.06	-0.02	0.08	0.02
40	0.08	0.07	0.04	0.05	-0.03	-0.03
50	-0.01	0	0.14	-0.02	-0.11	0.04
60	0	0.1	0.02	0.1	-0.1	0.08
ε_{MAX} (℃)	0.11	0.1	0.14	0.1	0.16	0.13

During the test, 20 sets of real time data have been collectedper second and the system response is very sensitive and the response time of the system is less than 0.1s.

It could be seen from the above results, the infrared temperature measurement system based on distance compensation, in the range of 0-60cm , the temperature measurement accuracy was 0.2℃, the system response time was less than 0.1s. The system could meet the need of the optical rehabilitation therapy and other long-range non-contact measurement. However, due to the limited sample of the experiment, the fitting formula used in this system needs further verification. The follow-up work is to collect more diversified data and find a more precise temperature compensation formula.

5. Conclusion

To meet the need of real-time remote monitoring human body surface temperature for optical rehabilitation therapy, a non-contact high-precision real-time temperature measurement method based on distance compensation has been proposed, and the system design is carried out. In order to verify the accuracy of the system, six different subjects were tested. The results show that the designed non-contact infrared temperature measurement system has a residual error of less than 0.2℃ and a response time of less than 0.1s in the range of 0-60cm. This provides a reference for developing long-distance temperature measurement equipments in optical therapy.

References

1. Zhen Yang,Shi Cheng Zhang,Li Yang. Altering Spectrum Method in Temperature Measurement Using Infrared Imager in Complex Background Environment[J]. Advanced Materials Research (2012)
2. Wiezorrek R,Bialasiewicz A A,Engelmann K,Grasedyck K,Richard G. [Necrotizing keratitis in chronic polyarthritis. Combined immunosuppressive and surgical therapy].[J]. Der Ophthalmologe : Zeitschrift der Deutschen Ophthalmologischen Gesellschaft, **95**, 9 (1998)
3. Westermann Simone,Buchner Heinz H F,Schramel Johannes P,Tichy Alexander,Stanek Christian. Effects of infrared camera angle and distance on measurement and reproducibility of thermographically determined temperatures of the distolateral aspects of the forelimbs in horses.[J]. American Veterinary Medical Association. Journal(2013)
4. Zhang Y, Wang X S, Ming H E. Influence of Distance on Temperature Measurement Accuracy of Infrared Thermal Imager and Error Correction[J]. Infrared (2011)
5. Zhang Y C, Chen Y M, Fu X B, et al. A method for reducing the influence of measuring distance on infrared thermal imager temperature measurement accuracy [J]. Applied Thermal Engineering (2016)

DEFINE: A Service-Oriented Dynamically Enabling Function Model

Wei-Yi Tan [1,a], Zhi-Gang Sun [1], Wei Quan [1]

[1] *National University of Defense Technology, Changsha, China*
[a] *tanweiyi15@163.com*

Abstract. With the rapid expansion of network scale and the continuous evolution of network applications, the Internet becomes much more open and uncontrollable, and inevitably faces a variety of security threats. In order to satisfy the requirements of the current Internet security and transmission performance, the general solution is increasing specific devices (e.g., firewalls, network monitors) to detect and defend against attacks. However, these devices typically use a dedicated hardware-based or software-based architecture which is closed, leading to limited scalability, management complexity. And deploying a new application needs to develop new equipment, which take a long development cycle and costs a lot.

In this paper, we introduce an innovative Dynamically Enable Function In Network Equipment (DEFINE) to allow tenant get the network service quickly. First, DEFINE decouples an application into different functional components, and connects these function components in a reconfigurable method. Second, DEFINE provides a programmable interface to the third party, who can develop their own processing modules according to their own needs. To verify the effectiveness of this model, we set up an evaluating network with a FPGA-based OpenFlow switch prototype, and deployed several applications on it. Our results show that DEFINE has excellent flexibility and performance.

1 Introduction

With the rapid expansion of network scale and the emergence of new network technologies, network traffic and the number of users growing exponentially, the Internet faces much more challenges on security, scalability, robustness, and mobility [3]. In order to overcome these difficulties, more and more specific middleboxes [7] (e.g., firewall, network monitor, DPI detector) have been added in the network to guarantee the performance and resist the external attacks.

While these specific network devices guarantee high performance, they also bring some problems, such as limited flexibility caused by a closed architecture, and complicated to manage due to the differences in device standards between the vendors. Furthermore, it is hard to exchange information (e.g., switch states) between devices from distinct vectors, leading to difficulties in deploying network services from a network-wide vision. A typical solution is deploying additional equipment in the network to meet new needs, which costs a lot. For example, an enterprise usually installs various devices to meet network service (e.g., QoS) or security needs from different departments, which is not only complicated to configuration and management, but also expensive to deploy so many devices. This limitation becomes much more serious in a cloud network, as a cloud has much more virtual networks requiring a logic-dependent set of devices for each virtual network.

From the recent trend of network technology, the future network will be much more flexible, scalable, and easy to manage [2]. An ideal network will be that network functions/services can be deployed on any device and removed at any time without deploying or designing new hardware/software-based devices [1], which greatly reduces the cost of network operation and maintenance, and improve the flexibility of the network at the same time.

DEFINE has two important features. The first one is service-oriented, that is, a service-oriented network device is considered as a "services/functions pool", i.e., it integrates many services/functions the user wanted. And, only a simple instruction from a high-level controller can start any one service on this device, which greatly reduces the time to deploy new services/ functions, such as firewall, QoS, load balance (LB) etc.

Another feature is dynamic assignment. Dynamic assignment means that the remote controller can dynamically load new functions transferred from a center code library, a bit like the app store, or terminates any running functions according to the change of the user's demand or exception, such as memory overflow. Therefore, DEFINE not only enables the device perform

DOI: 10.1051/itmconf/20171203022

any functions pre-stored on network device (service pool), but also any other specific functions (such as deep packet detection, TCP handshake agent) developed by third part by a remote transferring function.

Furthermore, DEFINE also provides the controller interface to read/write state in corresponding modules in data-path pipeline. DEFINE offloads some common packet processing functions on the hardware data path to accelerate network functions.

In summary, the contributions of this paper are:

We present a dynamic assignment model, which decouples the application into several functional components, and provides API to third party, which can create and load new functions on device directly.

We proposal a dynamic management algorithm on processes, which automatically adjust the resource threshold of each process related to the number of processes running on device currently. When the resource occupancy of one function exceeds its threshold, one optimal process will be chosen and terminated by taking into count the function dependent relationship and the importance of high-level application.

We implemented DEFIEN on an open source platform (FAST), and evaluated the feasibility and performance of DEFINE by loading a DDoS detection application.

The rest of the paper is organized as follows: Section 2 introduces the motivation and challenges of our work. Define is proposed in section 3, and process resource management strategy on DEFINE is shown in section 4. Section 5 provides the experimentation and evaluation of DEFINE on FAST. Finally, section 6 draws conclusions from the results.

2 Motivation and Challenge

2.1 Motivation of Creating Service in Network

In recent years, cloud computing has gained great success by sharing computing resources. Enterprises and tenants can rent computing resources in cloud to reduce their costs and management investment in infrastructure. Inspired by this, network service provider can also learn from the idea of cloud services, exchange business model from only providing users with interconnection services to providing a variety of specific network internal services defined by users, such as firewall, load balance, DPI. Nowadays, the typical network internal service needs from the following aspects:

User-defined routing: users want differentiated routing capabilities, such as low-latency routing, low-cost links, routing without passing through some specific areas. The current inter-domain routing protocol (BGP) obviously cannot meet this need.

Cloud computing environment: cloud computing has been explosive growth in recent years, while the cloud only gives users the access to cloud server without configuring their own network services on the cloud devices, such as switches and routers.

Games and video live service: users of this type of service are scattered around, but applications require shorter application access latency, such as video transcoding, aggregation of game updates. Implementing these services within the network can reduce processing latency and improve the user satisfaction.

Network detection: many applications need to detect real-time network conditions (such as accessibility, congestion, link delay, etc.) to check the fault or path selection. However, due to the distributed nature of the Internet, these detection servers must be distributed around the world, and if detected within the network, will be more accurate and complete network state information than detecting at the network edge.

There are also some technologies presented to overcome these difficulties, e.g., network function virtualization [5], to build separate virtual networks for different users on the physical network, including virtual node resources and link resources. Users can deploy a variety of services on their virtual networks. This approach is similar to IaaS (Infrastructure as a service) in cloud computing, but this has the obvious drawback that users still need to manage virtual networks like physical networks. And through the support DEFINE network equipment deployed to the network, you can provide users with a variety of services.

2.2 Challenges

At present, the deployment of new network services in the network faces some problems. Developing a new network service is a long process, especially when the equipment vendor needs to add a third-party technology to the device. Since vendors take into consideration the property and security of the devices, these devices systems and hardware architecture are usually closed. While third parties can gain access to the code base through a number of commercial means, this process requires a lot of money and time overhead, which is obviously not allowed for deploying a new technology/service.

The problem is exactly what DEFINE is trying to solve. DEFINE, by decoupling the application into different functional components and reinterpreting the interaction between components with a common perspective, provides a simple application deployment model, as well as a set of platform interaction interfaces that ensure fast application development and deploy. In addition, in order to allow third-party applications to coexist peacefully, DEFINE proposed a process management algorithm. Finally, DEFINE has also proposed a viable path for collaborative applications for different applications.

2.3 Related Work

Network Function Virtualization (NFV) [5] is used to solve the existing limitation number and inflexibility of current network equipment. NFV uses a standard virtualization technology, which removes the traditional functions on the specific devices to a union and high-performance server. NFV runs on a standard server, and the network function can be performed on this server without redesign a new network device.

However, the DEFINE presented in this paper is quite different from the NFV. First, the inter-operability

DOI: 10.1051/itmconf/20171203022

between NFV systems is weak. In an actual network, the resources between distinct heterogeneous systems cannot be shared to satisfy the need of collaborative services. In addition, the interaction and switching process between systems is complex, and cannot meet some real-time requirements of service (e.g., computer games). Second, the performance of NFV cannot be guaranteed. Since NFV is based on software, which has additional cost to send packets from the network card to CPU, and this I/O cost can become a bottleneck. However, DEFINE is a cooperation method based on hardware and software, i.e., the general packet processing part is offloaded to the hardware-based data path, and software data path is used to deal with the complex part, e.g., state processing. In this way, the performance has been greatly improved. Finally, different form NFV which has both a specific physical part and virtualization resources that requires complicated management, Define is based on the existing network architecture, which can load different application functions to the device with simple configuration. That is, DEFINE does not involve any complex network management, which greatly reduces difficulties of operation and maintenance.

3. Define Architecture

3.1 Design Idea

As the control logic and forwarding logic of traditional network devices are tightly coupled, the control plane expansion and customization is so complicated that deploying new application on existing network directly is difficult. DEFINE inherits the idea of separation and separation from SDN, decoupling the application into different functional components, and the components running in the controller are responsible for deploying the policy. The components in the network device are forwarded under this policy. Reduce the complex functions of network equipment bearer, and improve the flexibility of network function loading and deployment. However, in SDN, most control operations and decision are processed in the control plane, which causes the controller to respond frequently to the data plane that greatly increases the load of the southbound interface to become a system bottleneck. Therefore, DEFINE offloads some of general functions of the control plane into the data plane and gives sufficient computation resources to allow the application to customize its own data plane functionality so that it can perform operations that can only be handled in the controller before.

DEFINE overall structure is shown in Figure 1. DEFINE design a set of communication instructions to achieve that data plane application can get specific packets from hardware-based data path (match some pre-defined rules) by registering a callback function, and sends back the processed packets to the hardware-based data path. For example, in Figure 1, there are functions A, B, and C represent the message processing logic for applications A, B, and C, respectively. They can receive the destination packets from the forwarding pipeline through the API provided by DEDINE. Some special applications, e.g., firewalls that implement interception, may drop their packets after they are viewed, protecting the target network or the terminal from malicious traffic attacks.

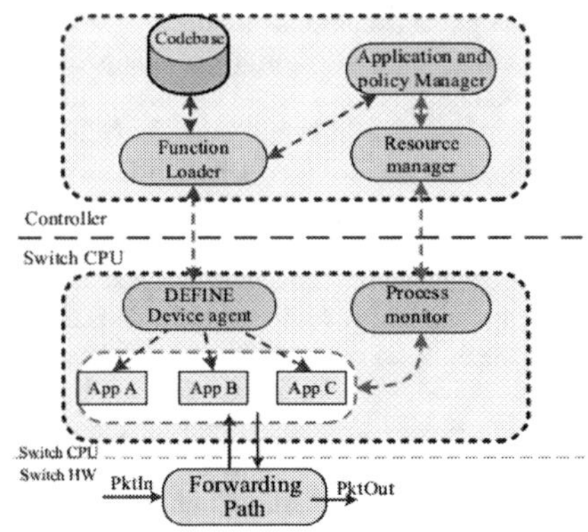

Figure 1: Architecture of DEFINE Framework

3.2 Key Modules in DEFINE

DEFINE defines a complete process from third-party application development, application registration to user application loading.

In DEFINE, controller consists of a code library, application and policy management module, function load module, resource manager. In the software-based data plane, DEFINE has designed a DEFINE agent to receive functions from the controller to load instructions and application code and recompile and run locally on the device.

Furthermore, we design a process detector in the data plane that polls the resource occupancy rate of each application process at regular intervals, passes the passive or proactive way to the resource manager in the controller. The resource manager then makes scheduling decisions according to the consideration of function priority and dependent relationship.

Application and policy manager: It is charge of two main functions. First, it receive the function code from a network administrators, and it store that code into codebase and information of the function into a function table in DEFINE for further usage. Second, this module also receives service requests from each network tenant, and it translates them into service policies and stores the policies into a policy table.

Function loader: This module is mainly responsible for receiving and analyzing command from the application and policy management module, and obtain code file from the code-base. Then, send the Function_ Loading message to the DEFINE device agent, which contain a {Function ID, Function Type, Path},

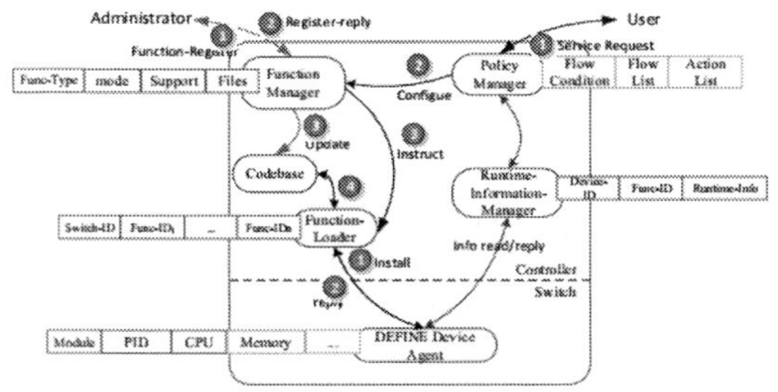

Figure 2: DEFINE workflow

Where Function ID and Path are both used to load a function code in codebase

Table 1. Parameters in the 3-tuple

Parameter(s)	Explanation
Function ID	The unique identifier of the function
Function Type	Indicating the function types.
Path	The path of code file

Resource Manager: The resource manager in the controller is primarily responsible for the unified management of the functions that are running on the device. Through the process management algorithm, dynamically calculate the threshold of the resource occupancy rate of each process. Once an application resource occupancy rate exceeds the limit value, the function limit message will be sent to the device agent, then the agent will limit the rate that the process receives packets.

DEFINE Device Agent: It is a daemon on the data plane. It proxies the connection between the switch's data plane and the controller, which allows it to intercept messages between them. In addition, it is responsible for loading the application, managing the forwarding table of the device, and forwarding the data packets sent from the forwarding path to the specific application processing component.

Process Monitor: Collects the resource occupancy rate of all application processes on the device, including CPU usage and memory usage, and sends the information to the resource manager in either active or passive manner.

3.3 Define

A typical operation of DEFINE works as follows. A network administrator registers network service to DEFINE. After registration, tenants need to create their service requests and submit them into DEFINE. Then, DEFINE parses the submitted service requests to understand the intention of tenants and writes the corresponding service policies to policy table. Next, DEFINE inform Function Loader that 3-tuple mentioned above and the latter obtain function code from codebase. When the DEFINE device agent receives a message from the Function Loader that instructs it to load a function, it:

- Writes the function's code to a local temporary file.

Registers the function information in a local table so that it gets called whenever the agent receives a message from controller with the funcion's ID in its type field.

Compiles the function's code, and dynamically links it to the DEFINE data path agent.

Starting function.

Table 2: The API of DEFINE

API	Description
Message2Switch (Message SwitchID)	The interface that application's controller component use to sends the message to the switch component
Message2Controller (Message)	The interface that application's switch component use to sends the message to the controller component
AddCaptureRule (MatchCondition, Module ID)	Register a packet handler to receive packet that match this condition
AddCopyRule (MatchCondition)	Register a packet handler to receive a copy of the packet that matches this condition.
DeleteRule (RuleID)	According to the rule ID, delete the corresponding flow table rules
GetFlowStatics (MatchCondition)	application can obtain statistics for a specific stream with this interface.
FunctionDestroy (Module Id)	When the service is stopped, the controller deletes the corresponding information in the tables and the rule table entries assigned to it.

DEFINE opens up some API for the application, summarized in Table 2. The application's components can use these interfaces to interact with each other and select packets that it want to receive. The details of each interface are as follows:

Message2Switch (Message, SwitchID): This interface allows an application to send messages from controller component (application code running in the controller) to the switch component (application code running in the switch). Where Message is the message content for the internal communication, and Switchld is the switch ID that identifies the destination device.

Message2 controller (Message): The device agent sends a message to the controller through this interface, and Message is the internal communication content of the application.

AddCaptureRule（MatchCondition, Module ID）: With this interface, the function can register its paceket handler to receive specific packet when it through the data plane. The characteristics of the data stream are specified by the MatchCondition , which is Generally the five tuple of packet's header. ModuleId is the function id that device agent allocate, the forwarding path uses it to decide which module to forward the packet to. AddCaptureFlowRule can convert the application's custom packet match condition to a Rule Table Entry and write it to the Rule Table and then get the returned Rule ID. The Rule Table contains a set of flow rule entry, which the data plane can use to select specific data flow to send to a functional module. In DEFINE, before the packet pass through data plane, it will first match rules in Rule Table, and then match the Standard forwarding table to decide the next destination in the network where the packet should forward to.

Add Copy Rule (Match Condition): This interface will copy the packet that match the conditions, and then forwarded this copy to the packet handler, and then the original packet will enter to the standard forwarding flow table.

Get Flow Statics (Match Condition): The device agent can send a request message to the data plane through this interface, and can obtain the relevant flow statistics including the total number of bytes, the sending rate and so on. And then the relevant information to obtain the message and then delivered to the application.

Delete Rule (Rule ID): When the application no longer needs to receive the specified packet, call this function to delete the corresponding rule.

4 Process Management

4.1 Lightweight Process Managerment Algorithm

In this section, we present a lightweight process management algorithm is utilized in Resource Manager of DEFINE to manager the application process running on the device. Network equipment deployed in the network must ensure reliability and robustness. Due to the limited computing resources and storage resources of the network equipment, the resources of each process must be allocated reasonably so as to ensure that the resources are not occupied excessively by the individual processes, which will impact other processes, and then damage to the overall performance of the device.

This algorithm mainly consider two factors, the end time and value of the process. The process with shorter running time, or the process is more important, will get more resources. The algorithm is shown in Formula (1):

$$r_i = \frac{v_i + \frac{1}{P_i} \times k}{\sum_{n=1}^{m} v_n + \frac{1}{P_n} \times k} \qquad (1)$$

The formula (1) detail is as follows:

r_i: The maximum percentage of equipment resources that the process can occupy;

v_i: The value of process;

k: Scale factor;

P: The estimated running time of the process;

This algorithm takes full account of the value of the process and the time factor. The value of the process is the primary consideration of the allocation of resources, applications process can be allocated to the more resources if it is more important than the others. For example, firewalls, intrusion detection systems, etc. should give them high priority to ensure their normal operation. When the value of the process is almost the same, we add time factors as a secondary consideration, if a process's estimated run time is relatively short, it will be allocated more resources. Because they can release the resources in a shorter time.

4.2 A Method to Deal with Process Dependencies

With the process management algorithm mentioned above, we can calculate each process's threshold of resource. In general, when the resource occupancy rate of a process exceeds the threshold, the Resource Manager sends the message to the DEDINE device agent to limit the rate that the process receive packet.

However, in some cases, there may be dependency between the applications. As shown in Figure 3, each node in the diagram represents a process, and a parent node has a child node, indicating that the application represented by this child node depends on the application represented by this parent node.

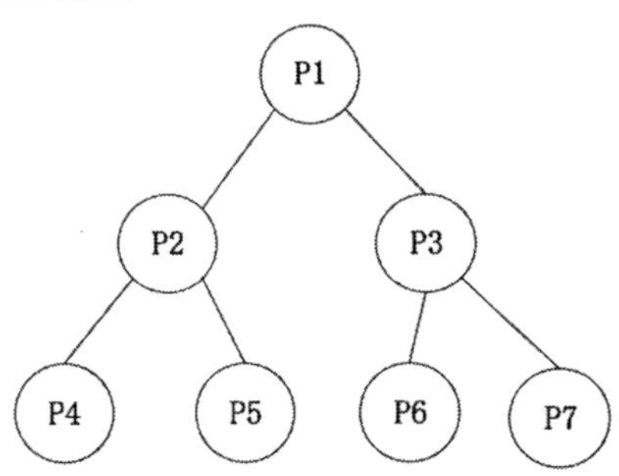

Figure 3: Diagram of process dependency

For example, we assume there is a quite simple Scenario that only after the packet pass through the intrusion detection system detection (P2), and then can be sent to the web application (P4). When the resource occupancy rate of P2 exceeds the threshold, if we choose to turn it off, it will cause all processes that depend on it not working properly. In this case, DEFINE prefers to close the application that depends on it, P4 or P5. It needs to traverse the left and right sub-trees of P2, find all of its leaf nodes, and compare the value of the leaf nodes. Finally, DEFINE limit the resource of the process that has the least value. This mechanism minimizes the impact of the process to be limited on other applications on the device, ensuring system performance.

5. Performent Evalueation

In this section, to verify the feasibility and evaluate the efficiency of DEFINE, we set up an evaluating network. To demonstrate the Rapid and simple development of our framework , we also implement a DDoS attack detection application that can capture the key features of DDoS attack traffics on the data plane by polling the values of counters in OpenFlow switches.

5.1 Evaluation Environment

We create a testbed presented in figure 4. It consists of a FPGA-based OpenFlow switch prototype [] with eight Gigabit ports, a 1.99GHz Intel Celeron J1900 CPU and a 2GB memory that runs Ubuntu 14.04 , a control platform, a quad-core Intel i5 CPU with 8GB of RAM.

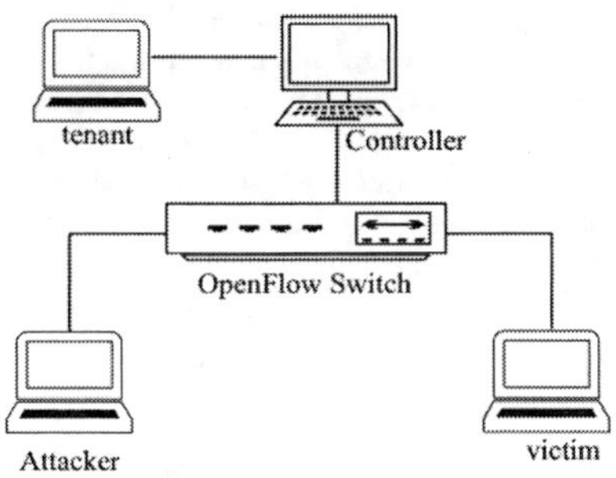

Figure 4 : Diagram of our testbed network.

5.2 Startup Time and Network Cost Measurement

We measure two metrics to estimate the performance overhead of DEFINE. First,we measure the startup time of the DDoS attack detection application. It is an important feature to estimate the performance of DEFINE, because it determines how long the tenants can get the service. Second, we estimate the network cost that represents total cost of delivering and parsing a message between a tenant and an OpenFlow switch.

Fig. 5 presents the test results of the starting the application in the Open Flow switch time (Represented by red) and the network cost (Represented by green).

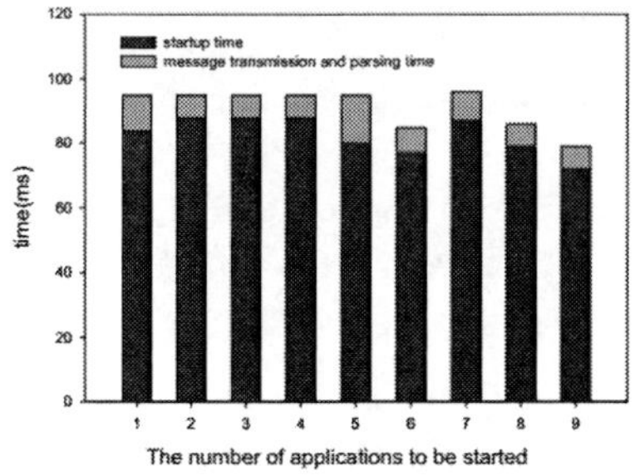

Figure 5 : The number of time takes to transmit message and start different applications.

In this case, we started nine different types of applications to understand the overhead more clearly. In the case of the starting application time, starting an application probably takes about 100ms, which is an expected result from the real network environment case. Another important thing

From the result is that the time for DEFINE to transmit and parse message is less than 10ms, which means that the framework of is quite efficient.

6. Conclusion

Current approaches to create services on IP network is a lengthy process. Because the network equipment customarily have been closed. The DEFINE framework provides a better approach that overcomes these challenges. It allows applications to improve performance by extending devices with custom functionality. We implement a DDOS attack detection application and run it on an OpenFlow switch, to demonstrate the deployment of DEFINE. We have evaluated DEFINE in real networks. With promising results, we believe that DEFINE is a meaningful step towards creating services on IP network.

References

[1] James Kelly, Wladimir Araujo Kallol Banerjee. Rapid Service Creation using the JUNOS SDK. PRESTO'09, August 21, 2009, Barcelona, Spain.

[2] Eric Keller, Jennifer Rexford. The "Platform as a Service" Model for Networking.

[3] D. Taylor and J. Turner, "Diversifying the Internet," in IEEE GLOBECOM, November 2005.

[4] Chen Li, Xiaodong Duan, Wei Chen, Weijiang Cheng [D]. Thinking and Practice of SDN and NFV.

[5] M.B.Anwer, M.Motiwala, M. b. Tariq, and N. Feamster, "SwitchBlade: A Platform for Rapid Deployment of Network Protocols on Programmable Hardware," in Proc. ACM SIGCOMM, 2010

[6] Seugwon Shin, Phillip Porras, Vinod Yegneswaran, Martin Fong, Guofei Gu, FRESCO: Modular Composable Security Services for Software-Defined Networks.

[7] Aaron Gember, Robert Grandl, Junaid Khalid, and Aditya Akella. Design and implementation of a framework for software-defined middlebox networking. In ACM SIGCOMM Computer Communication Review, volume 43, pages 467–468. ACM, 2013.

Based On Intrinsic Mode Function Energy Tracking Method of Circuit Breaker Vibration Signal Feature Extraction Studies

Yi-Hang Sun [1]

[1] *Beijing Institute of Mechanical Equipment, Beijing, China 100854*

Abstract In order to detect a mechanical type of structural failure of the circuit breaker, the characteristics of the circuit breaker mechanical vibration signal is analyzed in this paper. A combination of medium voltage circuit breaker based on empirical mode decomposition (EMD) amount of energy and support vector machine (SVM) theory vibration signal feature vector extraction and analysis of fault classification method is proposed. First, the vibration signal of the circuit breaker is decomposed by EMD, then intrinsic mode function (IMF) is obtain. The major fault feature information intrinsic mode functions the amount of energy of the component is obtained by discrete sampling points and the amount of energy. Using the amount of energy of IMF component as a feature vector, the failure of the test sample signal as input feature vector into trained "BT-SVM" support vector machine classification mechanism for fault classification. The differences and fault type of vibration signals can be identified by this method through the experimental analysis.

1. Introduction

A circuit breaker is very critical distribution systems important equipment. With the distribution network automation and reliability requirements increase, the circuit breaker itself is also increasing reliability requirements [1-3].

In the operation process of the circuit breaker contains a lot of important status information when a fault message appears fault signal when the feature vector extraction is critical fault signal analysis in the current analysis method is only suitable for the fast Fourier transform analysis of stationary signals, while the mechanical vibration signal is non-stationary nature, must be found suitable for the analysis of non-stationary signal processing method. Wavelet analysis, short-time Fourier transform methods have their limitations, it can not be good for non-stationary signal analysis, so this article will EMD method is applied to the circuit breaker vibration signal feature vector extraction field, it is a new suitable for analyzing non-stationary signal analysis methods. EMD is a Chinese-American NordenE .Huang et al proposed [4-7], it is suitable to handle nonlinear and non-stationary signals, it has a high signal to noise ratio, can decompose complex signals, resulting in finite IMF component, IMF component contains the original signal at different time scales local characteristic signal. By analyzing the local signal characteristics including IMF to accurately extract the important features of the original signal, each IMF frequency components contained in the signal sampling frequency is not correlated with the signal itself, it is adaptive [8-9].

2. Vibration Signal EMD

If there are any complex signals are composed of a plurality of different IMF, each IMF can be linear or non-stationary, non-linear, each intrinsic mode function must meet the following two conditions: First, the entire data segment, the number of extreme points and the number of zero crossings must be equal or differ at most no more than one; secondly, at any time, by the formation of the local maxima and the envelope formed by the local minimum point the average value of the lower envelope is zero, i.e., the lower envelope locally symmetric with respect to the time axis.

(1) determine the signal all the local extreme points, and then use the left and right cubic spline local maxima joined together to form the upper envelope.

(2) a cubic spline in all the local minimum points are connected to form the lower envelope, the upper and lower envelope should envelop all the data points.

(3) the average envelope denoted $m_1(t)$, is given by:

$$x(t) - m_1(t) = h_1(t) \tag{1}$$

(4) If $h_1(t)$ is not the IMF conditions, as the original data to, repeating steps (1) to (3), to obtain the envelope of the average $m_{11}(t)$ of the judgment meets the IMF conditions: $h_{11}(t) = h_1(t) - m_{11}(t)$, if not met, then the loop

times k , to obtain $h_{1(k-1)}(t)-m_{1k}(t)=h_{1k}(t)$, so as to satisfy IMF conditions: $h_{1k}(t)$ .Mind $c_1(t)=h_{1k}(t)$, $c_1(t)$ for the first signal component to meet IMF conditions of $x(t)$.(5) $c_1(t)$ separated from $x(t)$ the obtained:

$$r_1(t)=x(t)-c_1(t) \tag{2}$$

As $r_1(t)$ raw data repeating steps (1) to (4), to obtain a second component c_2 of $x(t)$ which satisfy the conditions of IMF. Repeat the cycle times n to obtain the signal component of $x(t)$ which satisfy the conditions of IMF. "Screening" process by limiting the stopping criterion S_d processing result of two successive magnitude of the difference between the standard to achieve the decomposition is stopped when less than 0.3.

$$S_d=\sum_{t=0}^{T}\frac{|(h_{(k-1)}(t)-h_k(t))|^2}{h_k^2(t)} \tag{3}$$

3. "Binary tree" Support Vector Machine

In this paper, two-dimensional space can be divided into two kinds of support vector machines briefing formation process. Figure (1) shows, rectangular and elliptical dot points represent two types of data samples, H is classified lines, H0 and H1 intermediate samples were classified by a sample line and parallel to the nearest classification line, the spacing between them Be the classification interval. For linearly separable problems, there always exists a hyper plane $\omega\cdot x+b=0$ two types of training samples can be completely separated, H0 and H1 is the sample points on the support vector [21].

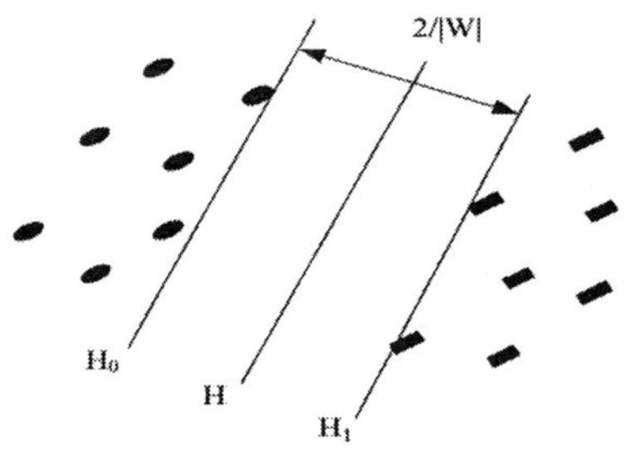

Fig1 Classification line based on 2-D linear separability

But the reality is that the majority of non-linear, and for the case of non-linear, SVM generally taken to introduce slack variables ξ_i and punishment factor C form hyperplane constraints:

$$y_i[(\omega\cdot x+b)]\geq 1-\xi_i \tag{4}$$

Where ω is the surface normal vector classification for classification threshold. In the generalized optimal hyper plane problem by introducing Lagrange multipliers, build generalized optimal hyper plane problem can be converted to solve the dual quadratic programming problems. According to functional theory, as long as the kernel function of $K(x,y)$ satisfies Mercer condition, you can achieve linear transformation, the formation of classification function is:

$$f(x)=\mathrm{sgn}\{(\sum_{i=1}^{n}a_i^* y_i K(x_i,x)+b^*)\} \tag{5}$$

Where a_i^* is the Lagrange multiplier for classification, b^* is the kernel function for classification threshold. Commonly used kernel $K(x_i,x)$ functions are polynomial kernel function, radial basis function, Sigmoid kernel function. Select a different kernel functions to get different support vector machine classifier. This choice by comparing polynomial kernel function belongs to the global kernel function, has global feature that allows data points that are far apart can affect the value of the kernel function, can meet the requirements. Polynomial kernel function:

$$K(x_i,x)=[(x_i.x)+1]^q \tag{6}$$

Wherein x_i is the input feature vector, q is the order. Support vector machine classification algorithm is divided into: "binary" Support Vector Machine (BT-SVM), it Can be seen that the traditional method of binary tree method avoids the situation can not be separated, and only construct k-1 个 SVM classifier, the test does not necessarily need to calculate all of the classifier discriminant function, which can save test time, while improving the training and test speed.

4. The Amount of Energy Law

Testing according to the signal $x(t)$ and known theoretical knowledge, without considering the actual dimensions of the case $x^2(t)$,the vibration signal is the time integral of the square of the known signal energy,

$$Q(i)=\int_{-\infty}^{+\infty}|x(t)|^2\,dt \tag{7}$$

When the signal $x(t)$ is discrete signals, the signal energy interval signal value added and,

$$Q(i)=\sum_{t=0}^{n}|x^2(t)|\Delta t \tag{8}$$

Where Δt is the sampling interval, sampling interval in this article 0.1ms, for the entire range of the total energy of the signal on the segment is $Q(i)$.

For example, the fault signal by EMD decomposition obtained after a series of key information $c_1(t),c_2(t)\ldots c_n(t)$ that contains the failed IMF components, the IMF component from high frequency components contained in the end, the circuit breaker failure occurs division closing different mechanical vibration signal generated by the energy value of IMF there are obvious differences.

5. Empirical Mode Decomposition Energy of Mo Extraction And Classification Process

The signal will be collected first EMD decomposition, the IMF components and extracts the feature vector fault signal input learn good in SVM classification.

(1) The raw vibration signal with EMD, take the main fault information including the first n IMF components, the paper take the first six IMF components.

(2)Calculated for each IMF (discrete signal) component of total energy $Q(i)$:

$$Q(i)=\sum_{t=0}^{n}c_i^2(t)dt \quad (n=5000) \qquad (9)$$

(3)The IMF component of the total energy of the normalization process:

$$E_i=\frac{Q(i)}{E} \qquad (10)$$

Where the total energy of the IMF components, the total energy of the original vibration signal.

(4) IMF component to the total energy of structural elements feature vector T:

$$T=[E_1,E_2,...,E_n] \qquad (11)$$

(5)Using the "binary" Support vector machine as classifier, using training samples of fault feature vector training SVM, determine the parameters of SVM classifier.

(6)The failure of the test sample input trained SVM feature vectors in order to determine the output of SVM classifier breaker vibration signal failure type.

6. Analysis of Experimental Results

6.1breaker Vibration Signal EMD Decomposition and Feature Extraction

In this paper, KL HVB type 12KV vacuum circuit breaker to do the test, using the Shanghai casting Swiss company YD-1 type acceleration sensor, acceleration reaction force change, range 0-1000m/s2, sensor installed in the circuit breaker operating mechanism outside the vertical direction. Extraction vacuum circuit breaker in case of no-load condition and two normal fault condition vibration signal. Namely: normal (a1, a2), closing solenoid jam (b1, b2) and the spindle jam fault (c1, c2) signal,This can expect the three vibration signal waveform has a different energy transmission capacity, whereby when the signal is decomposed into different time scales, different characteristics can be obtained.

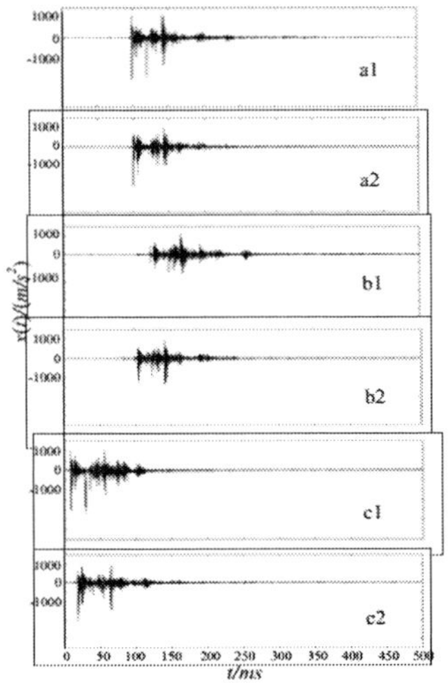

Fig.2 Normal and Fault signals

Using formula (11) were calculated in the normal state, the switch magnet and the spindle jam fault energy value decomposition of IMF, as the main energy vibration signal and the amount of information generated in the IMF components are the first few components of through experiments and data processing can be drawn, the signal energy is concentrated on the first six IMF components, viz. Here, as shown in Table 1, wherein, E1-E6 is calculated from the information contained signal IMF1-IMF6 principal eigenvectors as a test of SVM input signal, the process is the tracking signal generated by the energy distribution a process.

6.2 SVM Fault Status Classification

In this paper, "binary" Support vector machine classification algorithm, set to a normal state, the closing magnet jam fault is 2, the spindle jam fault is 3. By analyzing the feature vectors, taking into account the experience. This classification kernel function using polynomial kernel, the order q Take 2, penalty coefficient C take 100 to 10 sets of data for each sample the amount of energy range calculation.

Classification process conducted by Equation 5 to 10 have done each sample set of training data, for example, constitute a three sample classification. The first category is the second positive type, the first and third types is negative class training to obtain SVM1. Then the first category as being Class III negative class training to get SVM2. Kernel function of the inner product of a matrix composed of 30 groups of data. The classification process is counted twice Lagrange multipliers and are shown in Table 1, to obtain two kinds of support vector machines SVM1 and SVM2, thus SVM training is complete

Tab.1 Experiment results

	E_1	E_2	E_3	E_4	E_5	E_6	Classification results
Normal signal Ⅰ (1)	0.4039	0.322 8	0.1244	0.082 0	0.024 2	0.02 27	1
Normal signal Ⅰ (2)	0.4498	0.265 7	0.1344	0.088 7	0.025 5	0.02 40	1
Normal signal Ⅰ (3)	0.4283	0.303 4	0.1195	0.090 5	0.022 8	0.02 23	1
Fault signal Ⅱ(1)	0.6057	0.244 6	0.0715	0.027 8	0.020 2	0.01 63	2
Fault signal Ⅱ(2)	0.6467	0.217 4	0.0918	0.016 5	0.012 9	0.00 58	2
Fault signal Ⅱ(3)	0.6317	0.233 1	0.0834	0.018 0	0.015 6	0.01 15	2
Fault signal Ⅲ(1)	0.5658	0.246 3	0.0867	0.054 3	0.021 0	0.01 65	3
Fault signal Ⅲ(2)	0.5384	0.271 5	0.0843	0.050 9	0.025 3	0.01 95	3
Fault signal Ⅲ(3)	0.5500	0.255 8	0.0857	0.053 1	0.023 9	0.01 73	3

7. Conclusion

In this paper, empirical mode decomposition method breaker vibration signal decomposition, the total energy use of IMF as a feature vector representation breaker failure, and as the input vector of SVM, the use of "one to one multi-category" Support Vector Machine classification mechanism for training, classification results obtained. The experimental results show that this method can effectively extract the circuit breaker fault vibration signal feature vector and can correct for state recognition and fault classification.

References

[1] Wu Jianwen,Lian Shijun. A kind of fault isolation and lockout features microprocessor-based protection boundary switch [C].2007 Anual Conference on Relay Protection and Automation in China.2007.

[2]Sun Yihang,Wu Jianwen.Design on Intelligent Integrated Controller of Circuit Breaker Based on Dual-core CPU.2011 1st International Conference on Electric Power Equipment-Switching Technology[C],2011,315-318

[3] Wu Jianwen,Sun Yihang Zhang Luming,et al. A range of failure is isolated circuit breaker controller [P].201110104084.X.

[4]Huang N E,et a1..The empirical mode decomposition and the Hilbert spectrum for nonlinearand non--stationary time serie analysis[J] Proc.R.Soc.Lond.A 1998 45(4):903-995.

[5] Li Tianyun, Zhao Yan, Ji Xiaohui. Application of hht method for analysis of fault signal in electric power system [J]. Transactions of China Electrotechnical Society, 2005, 20(6): 87-91(in Chinese).

[6] Yang Y, Yu D J, Cheng J S. A roller bearing fault diagnosis methodbased on EMD energy entropy and ANN [J]. Journal of Sound andVibration, 2006(294): 269-277.

[7] Cheng J S, Yu D J, Tang J S, et al. Application of frequency family separation method based upon EMD and local Hilbert energy spectrum method to gear fault diagnosis [J]. Mechanism and Machine Theory, 2008(43): 712-723.

[8]Loh CH, et a1.Application of the empirical mode decomposition-Hilbert spectrum method to identify near-fault ground-motioncharacteristics and structural nssdonses[J].Bulletin of theseism gical society of america 2001(91):1339-1357

[9] Cheng Junsheng.. Studying and Application of Hilbert-Huang Transform in the Fault Diagnosis of Rotating Machinery [D],Hu nan Univ ersity.,2005.

An Improved Algorithm Research on the PrefixSpan Based on the Server Session Constraint

Hong-Guo CAI [1, a], Chang-An YUAN [2, b,*]

[1]*Department of Mathematics and Computer Science, the Guangxi College of Education, Nanning, 530023, China*
[2]*computer and information engineering college, the Guangxi Teachers Education University, Nanning, 530023, China*
[a]*webminning@163.com*, [b]*yca@gxtc.edu.cn*
**Corresponding author: yca@gxtc.edu.cn*

Abstract: When we mine long sequential pattern and discover knowledge by the PrefixSpan algorithm in Web Usage Mining (WUM).The elements and the suffix sequences are much more may cause the problem of the calculation, such as the space explosion. To further solve the problem a more effective way is that. Firstly, a server session-based server log file format is proposed. Then the improved algorithm on the PrefixSpan based on server session constraint is discussed for mining frequent Sequential patterns on the website. Finally, the validity and superiority of the method are presented by the experiment in the paper.

1 Introduction

Sequential pattern mining is one of the important areas of data mining which would discover frequent ordered events and sub sequences. There have three sequential pattern mining algorithms are mostly discussed [1]. Among them, the GSP (sequence Patten General) algorithm and the SPADE (Sequential Patten Discovery usage Equivalent classes) algorithm are directly or indirectly by the way of the Apriori method to mine Frequent Sequential pattern .The PrefixSpan (prefix projection mode) algorithm is different from the GSP algorithm and the SPADE algorithm that need to generate all the candidate frequent patterns. The pattern growth method of the PrefixSpan algorithm is by the way for separately constructing prefix and suffix sequence conditions. Some analysis of the three algorithms had shown that the PrefixSpan algorithm has the best overall performance [2][3]. More and more improved algorithms are studied on the basis of these [4][5]. Because sequential pattern mining is mainly a computational challenge, the sequential pattern mining algorithms that based some constraint are particularly efficient and become the focus of research.

The Web Usage Mining (WUM) is an important branch of the Web mining [6-8]. The sequential pattern mining of the WUM can service such as the intelligent website etc. The data source of WUM is mainly access records that the users had browsed Web server. The Web services technology has also become more and more perfect with the rapid development of dynamic web site. The traditional technology to record server log could not keep up with the technological innovation. In this paper, a server log record format based on session server is studied. This log format can better record users' access behaviors under the traditional Web technology and The Web services technology. That can greatly improve the efficiency of sequence pattern discovery and the log data preprocessing comparing with traditional login WUM. In general, the data preprocessing in WUM accounted for 70% of the entire work by traditional logs. In order to mine frequent sequential patterns based new server logs format, the concept of server session constraint was defined. Then the improved algorithm on the PrefixSpan based on the server session constraint (ss-PrefixSpan) is discussed. Finally, the validity and superiority of the ss-PrefixSpan algorithm are presented by the two experiments.

2 Web Server Logs Based on the Server Session

There are five commonly used formats for logging user's access logs on a Web server: the W3C extended log file format, the Microsoft IIS format, the NCSA common log file format, the Intensive binary log format, the ODBC log format. In order to further analyze the log records and ensure the consistency of terms in log format. W3C WCA (Web Characterization Activity) had issued a draft of the Web terminology standardization associated with the WUM. The draft provided a series of definitions of the data abstraction by WCA W3C and included users, page view, click-stream, user session, server session and episode. These definitions could be looked up in the W3C website [9].

With the development of the technology of the web2.0 and web services the commonly used formats for logs record had been unable to meet the need of Web services in cloud computing. In this paper, the standardized log file format based on server session had been defined. It has the following advantages:□The server sessions would be saved in the hard disk rather than in the memory that used to discard.□Each user is uniquely identified through the cookies login or IP/ proxy / path etc. Each user's click stream is split into different session and the unique session ID marks the click stream.□The efficiency of the standardized log file is better than traditional log file for the identification and session in WUM.

Definition1 the server session entity: When a session begins, a session number that uniquely identifies the session is assigned by the server. In order to analyze user behavior, the server session entity makes up of the session identification and a series of operation entities.

Definition2 the session identification entity:[beginning | end] – session ID - user ID - time stamp. Each session has a beginning and end tag. The user ID can be the anyway to identify a user. The time stamp would record the time from the beginning to the end of the session.

Definition3 the operation entity: Session ID - Service - operation - time stamp. The Service is that the server' page had been requested (or application program called).The operation is the server' page had responded [10, 11].

Definition4 the server session constraint: the click-stream can be seen as the selection of the template nodes. A server session had been equal to the different themes of the division of the website can be seen as a different navigation template. The node is a meaningful sub sequence of the server session. There is a corresponding the server session constraint and the given node of the navigation template. is a choice for the node. The operation entity is a choice for the node [10].

For example, a server session of the purchase type would be presented. It needn't be in accordance with the order of the attraction, the resident, the purchase and the leave that is distributed in the server session sequence. What's more, the operation entity may also repeat. They can be expression by BNF (Backus-Naur Form) :< the session identification entity for begin><the pages for the purchase >< the session identification entity for end>|(< the session identification entity for begin > { < the pages for the attraction > | < the pages for the resident > | < the pages for the purchase > } < the session identification entity for end >).

3 The Ss-PrefixSpan Algorithm

The sequential pattern growth which does not need to generate candidate is one type of the frequent pattern mining methods. The PrefixSpan algorithm had first put forward the theory of the Prefix Projection sequential pattern growth. The algorithm is that. Firstly, find out the frequent items. Then, generate set of projection database .Each projection database would be related to a frequent item and be mined single-handed. Lastly, the Prefix pattern and the Suffix pattern are constantly constructed by iterated method. The definitions of Item, Prefix, Suffix and Projection had been presented in literature [9].

For example, the table1 is the input of the initial sequence and the table2 is the sequence patterns mined by the PrefixSpan algorithm.

Table 1 . the input of the initial sequence

<(b d) c b (a c)>
<(b f) (c e) b (f g)>
<(a h) (b f) a b f>
<(b e) (c e) d>
<a (b d) b c b (a d e)>

Table 2. the projected databases and sequential patterns mined by PrefixSpan

Prefix	Projected (postfix) database	Sequential patterns
<a>	<(_c)> <(bf)abf> <(bd)bcb(ade)>	<a>, <aa>, <ab>, <aba>, <abb>
<b>	<(_d)cb(ac)> <(_f)(ce)bf> <(_f)abf> <(_e)(ce)d> <(_d)bcb(ade)>	<b>, <ba>, <bb>, <bba>, <bbc>, <bbf>, <bc>, <bca>, <bcb>, <bcba>, <bcd>, <b(ce)>, <bd>, <(bd)>, <(bd)a>, <(bd)b>, <(bd)ba>, <(bd)bc>, <(bd)c>, <(bd)ca>, <(bd)cb>, <(bd)cba>, <be>, <bf>, <(bf)>, <(bf)b>, <(bf)bf>, <(bf)f>
<c>	<b(ac)> <(_e)bf> <(_e)d> <b(ade)>	<c>, <ca>, <cb>, <cd>, <(ce)>, <cba>
<d>	<cb(ac)> <bcb(ade)>	<d>, <da>, <db>, <dc>, <dba>, <dbc>, <dca>, <dcb>
<e>	<bf> <d>	<e>
<f>	<(ce)bf> <abf>	<f>, <fb>, <ff>, <fbf>

There are many sequence patterns that have been accessed by users in WUM. In that way, so many projection databases would be constructed which can cause a significant overhead. Then the initial sequence patterns and the size of candidate item sets can be reduced by the server session constraint method. The dimensions of the suffix databases that would be scanned are exponentially reduced [11-15].

Based on the above reasoning, we have the algorithm of ss-PrefixSpan as follows.

Algorithm (ss-PrefixSpan: the improved PrefixSpan algorithm based on the server session constraint)

Input: A sequence database, and the minimum support threshold *min_sup*

Output: The complete set of sequential patterns

Parameters: a: a sequential pattern; SD |a the a-projected database, if a≠<>, otherwise, the sequence database SD; ss: selection sequence by the specified constraint type.

Method:

1. Scan SD once, if meeting up ss, restructured SD'.
2. Scan SD' |a, find the set of frequent items b +such that **b** can be assembled to the last element of a to form a sequential pattern <b> can be appended to a to form a sequential pattern.
3. For each frequent item b, append it to a to form a

sequential pattern a', and output a'.

4. For each a', restructured a -projected database SD' |a'.
5. The loop executes to the step 2.

Analysis (constraint space efficiency): if *N: the length of the candidate sequences; A': the average candidate length; s: the size of the SD; s': the size of the SD'.* **Then,** the space size of the PrefixSpan : $\sum = \int(N\ A's)$, the space size of the ss-PrefixSpan : $\sum' = \int(N\ A's')$.Then the main factor of the space efficiency is $\frac{s'}{s}$. So the scale of the constraint size becomes obvious .The space efficiency is better and better.

4 Experimental Results and Performance Study

In this section, we report our experimental results on the performance of the ss-PrefixSpan algorithm. The data in experiment 1 was drawn from the Off-line Training manage Web that is developed by ourselves in our College and the programming of the log record based server session had been designed. The 600 thousand sequences had been caught. Figure 1shows the scalability of the ss-PrefixSpan algorithm with respect to the number of sequences when the support threshold is set to 0.1% and 0.2%. The experimental results show that the Sequential pattern mining based on the server session can successfully mine sequence patterns.

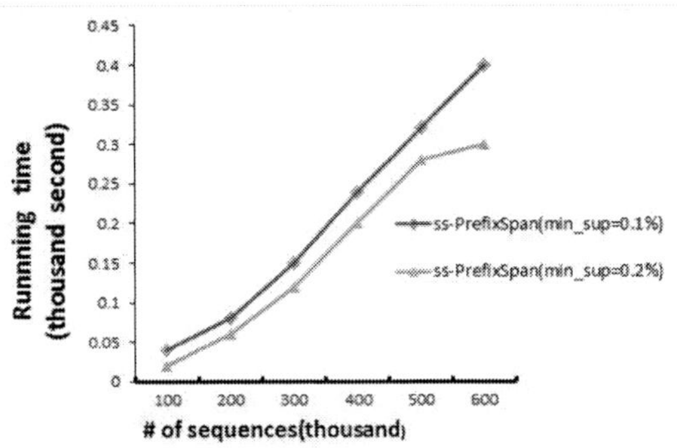

Figure 1. Scalability of ss-PrefixSpan

The experiment 2 is based on the e-commerce website mentioned in section 2.The sequence patterns of the purchase type would be mined based the server session from the simulation data. The service operations are represented by three bit integers which are not more than 4 at the highest level. The highest level of the integer represented the type of the operation entity. The For example, the number of 32 belongs to the type of the purchase. The number of 45 belongs to the type of the leave. The number of 123 belongs to the type of the attraction. The number of 2 belongs to the type of the resident. There had generated 100 thousands session identification entities and 80 thousands operation entities. The experiment had selected the execution time as the main means to compare the performance of the ss-PrefixSpan algorithm, the PrefixSpan algorithm, the GSP algorithm and the SPADE algorithm. The experimental results show the superiority of the ss-PrefixSpan algorithm.

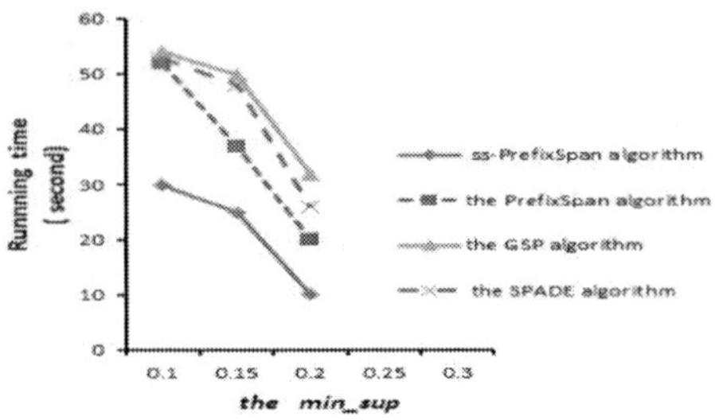

Figure 2. The execution time at the different support

Summary

In this paper, we have developed a novel, scalable and efficient record log in a renovation of web technologies that changed rapidly. This log format can better record users' access behaviors under the traditional Web technology and The Web services technology. Then the ss-PrefixSpan algorithm is discussed for the logs based on the server session. Finally, the validity and superiority of the ss-PrefixSpan algorithm are presented by the two experiments which provide a reliable basis.

Acknowledgements

This work is supported by the National Science Foundation of China Grant #61562008 and the scientific research project of the Guangxi Education Department Grant #ZD2014083 and #KY2015LX588. YUAN Chang-an is the corresponding author (e-mail: yca@gxtc.edu.cn).

References

1. Yin J,ZhengZ,CaoL.Uspan:an efficient algorithm for mining high utility sequential patterns. Proceedings of the 18th ACM SIGKDD .2012.
2. J.Yin,Z.Zheng,L.Cao,Y.Song,W.Wei. Efficiently mining Top-k high utility sequential patterns.2013 IEEE 13th International Conference on Data Mining (ICDM 2013) .2013.
3. Wang Le, Wang shui, Liu Sheng-lan, Wang Hui-bing. An algorithm of Mining Sequential pattern with wildcards based on Index-Tree[J]. Chinese Journal of Computers.2016.11, 39(178).
4. Wu Xindong, XieFei, Huang Yongming, Hu Xuegang, Gao Jun. Mining sequential patterns with wildcards and One-Off conditions[J]. Journal OfSoftware.2013, 24(8).
5. CHENG Si-Yuan, MA Chao, LI Cong-Cong. High Utility Sequential Pattern Mining Algorithm Based on MapReduce .Computer Systems & Applications.2015, 24(12).
6. Zaki M J . SPADE: an efficient algorithm for

mining frequent sequences[J] . Machine Learning,2001, 42 (1/ 2) : 31-60.

7. CeddiaJ ,Sheard J , Tibbey G. WAT :a tool for classifying learning activities from a log file[C]/ / Proceedings of the 9thAustralasian Conference on Computing Education . Darling Hurst: Australian Computer Society, 2007.
8. Liang Q A, Miller S, Chung J . Service mining for Web service composition[C]/ / IEEE International Conference on In Formation Reuse and Integration. Las Vegas,Nevada, 2005.
9. Han J W, Kamber M. Data Mining: Concept s and Techniques [M]. The 2nd editor.San Francisco: Morgan Kaufmann Publishers, 2006.
10. Asbagh M J,Abolhassani H. Web service usage mining: mining for executable sequences [C]/ / Proceedings of the 7th WSEAS International Conference on Applied Computer Science .Wisconsin : World Scientific and Engineering Academy and Society ,2007.
11. Lin M Y ,Hsueh S C , Chang C W. Fast discovery of sequential patterns in large databases using effective time-indexing[J] . Information Sciences , 2008 ,178 (22) :4228-4245.
12. SilvestriC, Orlando S. Approximate mining off frequent patterns on streams [J]. Intelligent Data Analysis, 2007 ,11 (1).
13. Mulvenna M D ,Anand S S ,Büchner A G. Personalization on the net using Web mining [J]. Communications of ACM, 2000, 43 (8):1222-1251.
14. CAI Hong-guo, YUAN Chang-an, etc. Server Session Constraint-based Serial Pattern Growth Mining Research .The journey of Zhengzhou University.2010, 42(1).
15. J Pei,J Han,B Mortazavi-Asl,H Pinto,Q Chen. PrefixSpan: Mining Sequential Patterns Efficiently by Prefix-Projected Pattern Growth. International Conference on Data Engineering , 2001:215-224.

 DOI: 10.1051/itmconf/20171203025

A Survey of Search Strategies in the Dynamic Symbolic Execution

Yu LIU[*], Xu ZHOU[a] and Wei-Wei GONG[b]

National University of Defense Technology, Changsha, China
[a]zhouxu@nudt.edu.cn, [b]IssacGong@outlook.com
**Corresponding author: liuyunudt@gmail.com*

Abstract: Dynamic symbolic execution (DSE) is an important way to discover software vulnerabilities. One key challenge in DSE is to find proper paths in the huge program execution space to generate effective inputs. Currently, the main search strategies used for DSE include classical search strategy, heuristic search strategy, and pruning redundance strategy. This paper reviews and compares the main search strategies of DSE in recent years, including the Generational strategy, CarFast, Control-Flow Directed Search, Fitness-Guided Search strategy, Context-Guided Search strategy, RWset technique and Veritesting.

1 Introduction

Recent years have witnessed a widespread concern over the dynamic symbolic execution for software vulnerability analysis. The key idea behind dynamic symbolic execution was put forward by King, James C [1] 40 years ago. Dynamic testing tools [2,4,12,13,14,16,17,18,19] based on it have been coming out with the remarkable development of constraint solving technology [6]. Meanwhile, DSE has become a key approach to discover the program vulnerabilities.

As an approach of software testing, DSE is supposed to explore as many program nodes and paths as possible, which contributes to the discovery of more bugs in a given time budget. DSE starts with the user-given or random input, through which an execution path can be discovered; by calculating the constraints on this path, it is able to gain new inputs covering more different paths. Every change of path condition makes more optional branches available to DSE. With the expanding of the test case set, DSE will gain a large exploration space, which will bring challenge for selecting the best path [10].

Even a simple program may have a huge exploration space (e.g. the program in Fig. 1). In a given time budget, selecting an appropriate path directly affects the efficiency of DSE. Classical path selection approaches include BFS, DFS and Random Search, since each path has the same importance, it is difficult to avoid the path explosion problem. In order to address that, heuristic search approaches such as the Generational strategy [14], CarFast [5], Control-Flow Directed Search [23] and Fitness-guided Search Strategy [21] are applied to DSE to enhance its efficiency. Heuristic approaches make good use of program execution context but fail to take full advantage of DSE's high semantic insight which can be used to prune redundant paths and find the effective execution path for DSE.

```
example(char* input,int num)
{
        int counter = 0,value = 0;
        if(num == 200)
                exit();
        if(num >= 100){
                for(int i = 0;i < 100;i++){
                        if(input[i] == 'S')
                        {
                                counter ++;
                                value += 2;
                        }
                }
                if(counter == 50)
                        bug();
        }
        if(num < 50){
                value = 10;
        }
        else{
                value = 20;
        }
        counter = value + 10;
        return counter;
}
```

Figure 1. An example program under test

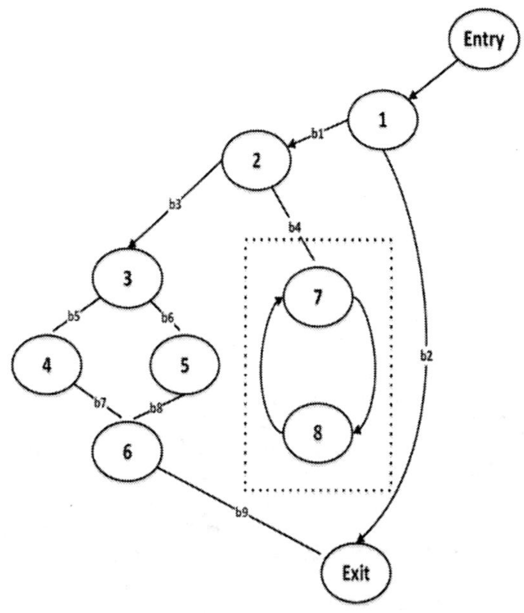

Figure 2. The topology of the example program

The remainder of the paper is organized as follows. Section 2 introduces the dynamic symbolic execution. We explain path search strategy in the dynamic symbolization execution in Section 3. Section 4 makes a comparison of theses search strategies. We conclude in Section 5.

2 Overview of Dynamic Symbolic Execution

2.1 Symbolic Execution

The main idea of symbolic execution is to represent variable values in the program with symbolic values. The symbolic execution maintains a symbolic state consistent with the program execution state. The symbolic state consists of a symbolic path constraint *PC* and a symbolic memory state σ. In classical symbol execution, σ is initialized to empty and *PC* is initialized to true. σ and *PC* are being updated during symbol execution. For example, for an input variable v, the symbol value s_0 is introduced into the mapping $\{v \longmapsto s_0\}$; at each assignment statement, σ is updated, representing variables in the program as symbolic expressions over the symbolic values. In the statement if (e) S1 else S2, the condition *e* is evaluated under the current symbolic memory state as σ (e), and *PC* is updated to $PC \wedge \sigma(e)$, generating a new path constraint *PC'* with the initial value being $PC \wedge \neg \sigma(e)$. When the symbolic execution of a path comes to an end, the concrete input values generated by *PC* using a constraint solver will be executed, steering the execution of the program towards the path of *PC*, and the same execution result is obtained.

2.2 Dynamic Symbolic Execution

DSE is based on classical symbolic execution [1,26], and combines concrete execution with symbolic execution to make the latter faster and more accurate. DSE includes three main strategies.

The first one is concolic symbolic execution adopted in DART [4] and CUTE [18]. Dynamic symbol execution maintains two states, one is the concrete state and the other is the symbolic state. The concrete state maps all variables to their concrete values, while a symbolic state maps only variables without concrete values to their symbolic values. Concolic execution starts from a specific input and collects symbolic constraints at the conditional statements along the execution path. When the program execution reaches a conditional branch, concolic execution fork two new states where it generates two corresponding inputs respectively by solving constraints and then explore both branches independently. In theory, concolic execution can cover all program paths, while in practice it usually stops when a user defined coverage criteria are met, or the time budget expires.

The second one is called Execution-Generated Testing. The EGT [27] approach which is used by EXE and KLEE is a technique of generating testcases by solving the constraints on concrete values of program. EGT starts with a symbolic input rather than a concrete one. When program read external variables, EGT replaces it with a symbolic variables. All the variables depending on these symbolic variables will be operate symbolically. If the operation based on concrete values, it should be executed with concrete values. In the process of symbolic execution, the EGT adds constraints to the symbolic variables. When the symbol execution of a path comes to an end, we can generate input by solving these constraints on this path.

The last one is symbolic guided fuzzing, which is used by SAGE [14] and Driller [2]. As a combination of symbolic execution techniques and fuzzing techniques [2,8,14,15,20], symbolic-guided fuzzing utilizes the rapid test generating of fuzzing techniques and the good semantic insight into the program of symbolic execution. Symbolic-guided fuzzing use the dynamic symbol execution to guide how to mutate inputs [20], or just generate input to supplemental fuzzing[2]. The testcases generated by the Symbolic-guided fuzzing can trigger previously-unexplored code, which is not reachable by the fuzzing approach. Besides. Symbolic-guided fuzzing has better execution efficiency than pure dynamic symbolic execution.

2.3 The Importance of Search Strategy

In reality, it is not feasible to traverse all execution paths under a fixed time budget. This is referred to as the path explosion [10]. Therefore, each dynamic symbol execution is inevitable to face an important problem of how to choose a proper path in the huge path space. Some search strategies are adopted to the dynamic symbol execution to solve this problem. These strategies improve the coverage of symbolic execution,

DOI: 10.1051/itmconf/20171203025

which enables dynamic symbol execution to detect bugs in a more efficient way.

3 Search Strategies in the Dynamic Symbolization Execution

The search strategies used in the implementation of DSE can be divided into three categories: classical search strategy, heuristic search strategy, and pruning redundance strategy.

3.1 Classical Search Strategy

The classical search strategy uses the typical tree traversal algorithms which are independent of any prior knowledge of the execution tree. Typical tree traversal algorithms include DFS, BFS and Random Search.

DFS. Applied in symbolic execution tools such as DART[4] and CUTE[18] in the early days, DFS is the earliest search algorithm that used in dynamic symbolic execution. DFS has a good memory model that applies to dynamic symbolic execution: it first explores a path until the end, which provides an incremental path constraints. The previously used symbol constraint states are stored in memory for reuse by the solver. However, DFS may get trapped in loops and iterations that rely on symbolic input for conditional evaluation in the program. In addition, as the execution path becomes longer, the constraints will become larger, which will make the constraint solving more difficult.

BFS. BFS algorithms are rarely used in dynamic symbolic execution because it tends to choose a new path execution every time, which will make the dynamic symbol execution to continually switch the program states and the symbol states, resulting in a very poor memory utilization. What is worse, BFS algorithm will rapidly increase the exploration space of the program, making the path explosion problem more obvious.

Random Search. The random search algorithm executes from the root node of the program execution tree, and it will randomly select a path to continue the execution when a conditional branch appears. This selection method may provide a quick access to the deep of the program execution tree, however, it is of little stability and hard to guarantee a reliable path coverage. Hybrid concolic testing[11] interleaves random testing with concolic execution and utilizes random testing to rapidly increase path coverage. When the random testing saturate, it switches to the symbolic mode and uses the concolic execution to reach deeper uncovered nodes. Hybrid concolic testing shows a better coverage than DFS and pure random search.

3.2 Heuristic Search Strategy

Heuristic search strategy uses DSE to obtain the context information, select metrics (e.g., high statement coverage, node coverage, path coverage), and calculate the weight for the candidate path. Different heuristic algorithms focus on the different criteria, which makes a great difference of the results.

The Generational Strategy. The Generational strategy was introduced by SAGE [14], which is a whole-program white-box file fuzzing tool for x86 Windows applications. The generational search starts with an input seed and maintains a worklist. Each time generational search fetches an input from the *workList* for symbolic execution at a time. The generational search fetches an input from the *workList*, then starts the symbolic execution. After a single execution, *ExpandExecution* function based on path constraints is applied to generate new input. These *childInputs* are symbolically executed respectively, and scored according to the incremental block coverage. Then the *childInputs* will be inserted into the *workList* according to the score. Each new input limits the backtracking through the *bound* parameter. This search method can maximize the number of new test cases generated per symbolic execution, at the same time avoid any redundant search. Heuristics enables the generational search to maximize code coverage in a short time.

CarFast. CarFast [5] algorithm is a kind of heuristic algorithm which is based on the information of CFG graph. The main idea is that the number of program states contained in each branch in the program is different. In order to cover more states, branches containing more states should take the priority in dynamic symbolic execution. For the purpose of calculating the state information contained in the branches, CarFast algorithm needs to analyze the CFG graph of the program and sort the branches. CarFast algorithm works by analyzing the program CFG, which may result in a low efficiency of DSE when the program scale becomes large.

Control-Flow Directed Search. Control-Flow Directed(CFD) Search [7,23] uses the static structure of the program to direct the dynamic symbolic execution to explore path space of the program. Firstly, Control-Flow Directed Search generates the control flow graph of the program, then assigns values to each edge. The two branch edges of the conditional jump have a weight of 1, the remaining edges (including the function calls) have a weight of 0. For undiscovered program nodes, the total weight of the reachable path is computed. The path of the least weight is selected for exploration. Control-Flow Directed Search always selects the path with the fewest constraint, which reduces pressure of the solver.

Fitness-Guided Search Strategy. Fitness functions were originally used in search-based software [22], and introduced by Pex [24] as Fitnex strategy, a guide strategy of the dynamic symbolic execution. Fitness-Guided Search (FGS) Strategy flips a branch according to the fitness value of each branching node. Fitness value for the branch b is calculated by the formula (F (p) - FGain (b)). F (p) is the fitness function of path p. Fitness functions are derived from the boolean binary predicates [28]. The fitness function calculates the distance from a path to a target, which can be expressed as a fitness value. For example, for the if (counter == 50) in Fig.1 line 14, the fitness function is "if (|50 – x| == 0) then 0 else |50 – x|". FGain (b) is the fitness gain of the branch *b*, which indicates the increase (or the decrease) of the path's fitness value when the branch is flipped. For example, when we flip the branching node code for the false branch of Fig.1 line 8 (input[i] == 'S') to the true branch, the fitness gain is 1.For each branch node, composite fitness value is (F(p) - FGain(b)). The Fitness-Guided Search Strategy always selects the branch with the smallest composite fitness value for the execution, which makes each symbolic execution closer to the target. At the same time, in order to achieve better results, Fitness-Guided Search Strategy also integrates other simple search strategies.

Context-Guided Search Strategy. Context-Guided Search(CGS) Strategy selects the branch with new context for the dynamic symbolic execution based on the context information of the executed program, so as to obtain better branch coverage. Context-Guided Search Strategy uses *k-context* to represent context information and determine whether to execute a new branch through the comparison of *k-contexts*. *k-context* is calculated from the information of preceding branches and dominator and defined as a sequence of k preceding branches in an execution path. For example in Fig.2, *2-context* of b5 is (b3,b5). Under *∞-context*, CGS becomes BFS. In the CGS strategy, k incrementally increases. While computing the *k-context*, CGS needs to take the dominator information into account. In CFG, node d dominates node n, written as d dom n, if every path from the entry node to node n must go through node d[8]. It can be applied to edges (e.g. In Fig.2, b1 dominates b5 since all the execution paths heading for b5 must go through b1). In the calculation of *k-context*, CGS considers non-dominating branches only in the context information. For example in Fig.2, *2-context* of b5 is (b1,b5) instead of (b1,b3,b5), since b3 is the dominator of b5.When the dynamic symbolic execution encounters branch selection, the CGS algorithm compares the *k-context* of the current branch with those in the context cache. If the *k-context* did not appear before, the branch is selected for the next input. CGS algorithm makes good use of the context information, and has a very good efficiency.

3.3 Pruning Redundance Strategy

Strictly speaking, the strategy of pruning redundance strategy is not a search strategy. However, by reducing the search space, this method can effectively control the path explosion problem, and select the path suitable for DSE.

RWset. The main idea of the RWset [25] technique is that when the dynamic symbolic execution reaches a branch that has the same state as some previous execution, the branch can be pruned. At the same time, if two states that only differ in program values that are not subsequently read can be seen as identical, which can also be combined into a state. RWset truncates a path as soon as possibl e, thereby enhancing the efficiency of the dynamic symbolic execution, and reducing the path explosion.

Veritesting. Veritesting [9] is a combination of DSE and SSE, and has been integrated into the angr [29] platform as an effective selecting method to avoid path explosion. Veritesting starts with DSE, when the program encounters a branch and needs to fork new executions, it switches to an SSE-style approach. In SSE mode, Veritesting uses SSE to analyze a dynamically recovered CFG, removes some unexecutable paths from CFG, and unrolls loops. Finally, it merges the states obtained by SSE with the previous DSE states, and then continues the dynamic symbolic execution. This method solves the DSE path explosion overhead with SSE solution overhead, which gains better node coverage and path coverage in most cases.

Table 1. The comparison of Search strategies

	Main Cost	Criteria	Usage of Semantic Insight	Tools
DFS/BFS	--	--	--	DART CUTE
Random Search	--	--	--	DART
Generational Search	ExpandExecution	Code coverage	The hierarchy of the program topology diagram	SAGE
CarFast	Analysis of CFG	Statement coverage	The state information of the CFG	CarFast
CFD	Calculating the weight of edge	Shortest path	Topological structure of CFG graph	CREST
FGS	Solving fitness function	Closer to the target	Fitness value of conditional branch	Pex
CGS	Comparing k-context	Path coverage Node coverage	The context dependency of the program path	--
RWset	Pruning statement	Merge Statements	Program status using DSE	RWset
Veritesting	SSE	Reduce invalid paths	DSE status and SSE status	Angr MergePoint

4 The Comparison of Search Strategies

No matter what search strategy it is, its main purpose is to choose the best path for the dynamic symbol execution within a limited time and help it achieve a better performance. The comparison of these strategies is in Table 1.

In theory, DFS and BFS enable a full traversal of the execution tree. However, this approach is not feasible because of the huge search space. The heuristic search algorithm abandons completeness, selects specific metrics, and uses the program context, CFG and other information to prioritize the paths of the dynamic symbolic execution, in order to achieve the optimal performance with the limited time cost. The method of pruning redundant paths reduces the state space of DSE, so as to improve the efficiency of DSE.

5 Conclusion

DSE is an effective means of finding software vulnerabilities. Search strategies play a major role in the improvement of DSE. In this paper, we discuss and compare the main search strategies of DSE, divide them into three categories: classical search strategy, heuristic search strategy, and pruning redundance strategy. In the future, the research on the combination of pruning redundant paths with a heuristic search approach could possibly enhance the execution efficiency of DSE.

Acknowledgement

This work is partially supported by National High-tech R\&D Program of China (863 Program) under Grants 2015AA01A301, by program for New Century Excellent Talents in University, by National Science Foundation (NSF) China 61272142, 61402492, 61402486, 61379146, 61272483, by the laboratory pre-research fund (9140C810106150C81001)

References

1. King, James C. "Symbolic execution and program testing." *Communications of the ACM* 19.7 (1976): 385-394.
2. Stephens, Nick, et al. "Driller: Augmenting Fuzzing Through Selective Symbolic Execution." *Proceedings of the Network and Distributed System Security Symposium*. 2016.
3. Seo, Hyunmin, and Sunghun Kim. "How we get there: a context-guided search strategy in concolic testing." *Proceedings of the 22nd ACM SIGSOFT International Symposium on Foundations of Software Engineering*. ACM, 2014.
4. Godefroid, Patrice, Nils Klarlund, and Koushik Sen. "DART: directed automated random testing." *ACM Sigplan Notices*. Vol. 40. No. 6. ACM, 2005.
5. Park, Sangmin, et al. "CarFast: achieving higher statement coverage faster." *Proceedings of the ACM SIGSOFT 20th International Symposium on the Foundations of Software Engineering*. ACM, 2012.
6. De Moura, Leonardo, and Nikolaj Bjørner. "Satisfiability modulo theories: introduction and applications." *Communications of the ACM* 54.9 (2011): 69-77.
7. CREST. Automatic test generation tool for C. https://code.google.com/p/crest/.
8. A. V. Aho, M. S. Lam, R. Sethi, and J. D. Ullman. Compilers: Principles, Techniques, and Tools. Addison Wesley, 2nd edition, Sept. 2006.
9. Avgerinos, Thanassis, et al. "Enhancing symbolic execution with veritesting." *Proceedings of the 36th International Conference on Software Engineering*. ACM, 2014.
10. Cadar, Cristian, and Koushik Sen. "Symbolic execution for software testing: three decades later." *Communications of the ACM* 56.2 (2013): 82-90.
11. Majumdar, Rupak, and Koushik Sen. "Hybrid concolic testing." *29th International Conference on Software Engineering (ICSE'07)*. IEEE, 2007.
12. Chipounov, Vitaly, Volodymyr Kuznetsov, and George Candea. "S2E: a platform for in-vivo multi-path analysis of software systems." *ACM SIGPLAN Notices* 46.3 (2011): 265-278.
13. Ciortea, Liviu, et al. "Cloud9: a software testing service." *ACM SIGOPS Operating Systems Review* 43.4 (2010): 5-10.
14. Godefroid, Patrice, Michael Y. Levin, and David A. Molnar. "Automated Whitebox Fuzz Testing." *NDSS*. Vol. 8. 2008.
15. Caselden, Dan, et al. *Transformation-aware exploit generation using a HI-CFG*. No. UCB/EECS-2013-85. CALIFORNIA UNIV BERKELEY DEPT OF ELECTRICAL ENGINEERING AND COMPUTER SCIENCE, 2013.
16. Babic, Domagoj, and Alan Hu. "Calysto." *2008 ACM/IEEE 30th International Conference on Software Engineering*. IEEE, 2008.
17. Cadar, Cristian, Daniel Dunbar, and Dawson R. Engler. "KLEE: Unassisted and Automatic Generation of High-Coverage Tests for Complex Systems Programs." *OSDI*. Vol. 8. 2008.
18. Sen, Koushik, Darko Marinov, and Gul Agha. "CUTE: a concolic unit testing engine for C." *ACM SIGSOFT Software Engineering Notes*. Vol. 30. No. 5. ACM, 2005.
19. Cadar, Cristian, et al. "EXE: automatically generating inputs of death." *ACM Transactions on Information and System Security (TISSEC)* 12.2 (2008): 10.
20. Cha, Sang Kil, Maverick Woo, and David Brumley. "Program-adaptive mutational fuzzing." *2015 IEEE Symposium on Security and Privacy*. IEEE, 2015.
21. Xie, Tao, et al. "Fitness-guided path exploration in dynamic symbolic execution." *2009 IEEE/IFIP International Conference on Dependable Systems & Networks*. IEEE, 2009.

22. McMinn, Phil. "Search-based software test data generation: A survey." *Software Testing Verification and Reliability* 14.2 (2004): 105-156.
23. Burnim, Jacob, and Koushik Sen. "Heuristics for scalable dynamic test generation." *Proceedings of the 2008 23rd IEEE/ACM international conference on automated software engineering*. IEEE Computer Society, 2008.
24. Tillmann, Nikolai, and Jonathan De Halleux. "Pex–white box test generation for. net." *International conference on tests and proofs*. Springer Berlin Heidelberg, 2008.
25. Boonstoppel, Peter, Cristian Cadar, and Dawson Engler. "RWset: Attacking path explosion in constraint-based test generation." *International Conference on Tools and Algorithms for the Construction and Analysis of Systems*. Springer Berlin Heidelberg, 2008.
26. Clarke, Lori A. "A program testing system." *Proceedings of the 1976 annual conference*. ACM, 1976.
27. Cadar, Cristian, and Dawson Engler. "Execution generated test cases: How to make systems code crash itself." *International SPIN Workshop on Model Checking of Software*. Springer Berlin Heidelberg, 2005.
28. Tracey, Nigel, John Clark, and Keith Mander. "Automated program flaw finding using simulated annealing." *ACM SIGSOFT Software Engineering Notes*. Vol. 23. No. 2. ACM, 1998.
29. Shoshitaishvili, Yan, et al. "SOK:(State of) The Art of War: Offensive Techniques in Binary Analysis." *Security and Privacy (SP), 2016 IEEE Symposium on*. IEEE, 2016.

Air Operators' Safety Assurance System

Zhi-Hui XIE*

Civil Aviation Management Institute of China, Beijing, China
**Corresponding author: xiezhihui@camic.cn*

Abstract: Construction of air operators' safety assurance system is important for national civil aviation authority to perform the safety oversight work systematically and efficiently on the air operators. The system is a combination of management process, tools, information platform, which utilize system configuration model and data collection tools to accomplish the air operator system design evaluation and performance evaluation, and output the advice for national civil aviation authority inspectors to take action to improve the air operators' safety design and performance according to the regulation. Process has been designed to realize design and performance evaluation, and strengthen the safety assurance function during the air operator certification and surveillance phases. Based on the system configuration model, risk indicators, data collection tools and other tools, the system could perform configuration setting, planning, task assignment, data collection, analysis and action during the certification and surveillance. The application of the safety assurance system to different operators has been considered.

1 Necessity for the Regulator to Construct its Safety Assurance System

As international civil aviation organization promotes the safety management system (SMS) globally, each member state should develop the State Safety Program (SSP) to promote its safety management on civil aviation industry. The regulatory authorities of member states, apart from formulating regulations to require air operators to set up SMS, should also construct their own mechanisms of risk management and safety assurance for their oversight[1]. Air operators' safety assurance system (SAS) is the specific embodiment of the regulatory authorities' safety assurance work on air operators' oversight.

As the target of the aviation safety oversight, air operators vary in their business models and operational scope. Some air operators operate commercial transport with jumbo aircraft and some with small aircraft. Some are civil aircraft maintenance companies. The former two types of companies undertake commercial air transport activities necessary for the economic and social development, and the latter provides maintenance support services for the former two. The overall configuration framework of the regulatory elements applicable to different operators can be developed through the construction of operators' SAS. The oversight may be much more systematic and standardized if we formulate inspection plans for different operators by choosing applicable elements under this framework.

A large proportion of air operators engage in commercial air transport operations, featuring cross regional activities. Air operators have several sub-bases and a number of stations besides their main operational base where aircraft fly to and from the bases and stations as the nodes of their network. Regarding such operational feature, the Chinese regulators, especially CAAC regional administrations and their agencies, execute corresponding oversight responsibilities by the region[2], which makes it very complicated to coordinate among the certificate administration where a certain air operator's main base resides, the local administrations where the operator's bases reside and the local administrations of the stations where the operator flies in terms of oversight task allocation, oversight information collection, information analysis and assessment[3]. On the other hand, the air operator's SAS is to formulate monitoring programs and collect monitoring information centered on certification management office. The development of such system will be conducive to realize the centralized allocation and management of monitoring tasks as well as centralized analysis and decision-making of monitoring information.

The national civil aviation authority's traditional way of oversight on air operators is to verify the compliance of their system design and actual operation against the regulations by implementing certification and supervision. This focuses on the inspection of the air operators' compliance with the regulatory procedures, but the traditional oversight seldom collects the information such as the air operator' s control and measurement of its own implementation of the procedures, and the implementation of the procedure-related authorities and responsibilities. In terms of system safety management, the national civil aviation authority also needs to expand the collection of such data[4]

2 Concept and Characteristics of Air Operators' Safety Assurance System

Concept of air operators' SAS: air operators' safety assurance system is a safety assurance system that adopts the systematic safety concepts such as system configuration and safety properties to design data collection tools, collect and analyze the information needed to carry out air operators' safety oversight, update the oversight program, formulate correction requirements and track the operators' corrective activities. The system, supported by the certification team or the certification management office of the national civil aviation authority, assesses the operator's safety management status in terms of design and operational performance. The system, via IT platform, realizes the collection and analysis of cross-region and cross-department safety monitoring information on the operator, as well as the centralized allocation and control of monitoring tasks, and centralized and scientific decision-making on operators' oversight.

3 Framework Design of Air Operators' Safety Assurance System

3.1 Function of Air Operators' Safety Assurance System

Through air operators' safety assurance system, the national civil aviation authority may conduct functions of initial certification as well as supervision and inspection on air operators. The national civil aviation authority, on the basis of civil aviation safety regulations, conducts certification and monitoring on air operators, and facilitates them to implement their own safety responsibilities accordingly. The basic oversight process is as follows: at the start of the air operator, the regulator will conduct certification to the operator according to the corresponding civil aviation regulations in five steps, i.e. advance application, formal application, documents review, demonstration and verification, and certificate issuance. The operation certificate and operation specifications will be issued upon acceptance. After the establishment of the operator, the inspectors will, by supervision and inspection, confirm the air operator's actual operation constantly meets the safety standards for certification. If the operator has substantial changes in its operational scope and operation features, the operator needs to go through the regulator's supplementary certification so as to ensure that the operator's operational system meet the regulatory requirements after the changes, and the operation specifications should be revised accordingly and accepted by the regulator during the supplementary certification.

3.2 Framework of Air Operators' Safety Assurance System

To better support the operational certification as well supervision and monitoring, air operators' safety assurance system set up two closed-loop processes including design assessment process and performance assessment. Within each closed loop, there are five work modules, i.e. system configuration, program management, task management, data collection, analysis and assessment, and action[5]. The five work modules complete the closed-loop management of operational certification and supervision. In addition, after each closed-loop cycle, based on the analysis and assessment.

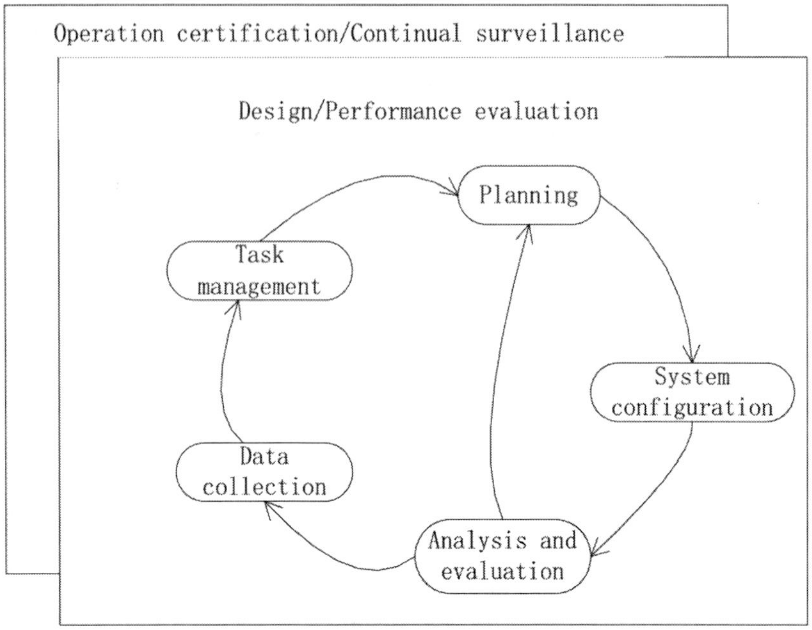

Figure 1. Major flow chart of air operators' safety assurance system

1) System configuration. The operators' safety assurance system uses system configuration function to review the monitoring scope and elements of each operator. The system, targeted at typical air operators, designs the system configuration model of air operators, which divides the operators' major internal systems into six systems, and each system is subdivided into a subsystem and elements. The allocation of the systems, subsystems and elements determines the scope and weight of the oversight data collection. The inspectors may, if necessary, adjust the certification monitoring fields by adjusting and setting certain operators' system configuration. Scenarios that need to set or adjust the operators' configuration include: at the operator's initial certification; when the operator's operational model undergoes a substantial change; in addition, when the government regulator considers it necessary to do so due to other reasons. For air operators with different operational features, based on the above systems/subsystems framework, we may set specific elements of the subsystems. For example: taking a large-aircraft public air operator as an example, its operation control system can be divided into three subsystems of training and qualification, flight operations and maintenance engineering management, flight planning and monitoring, and within each subsystem, specific elements are also set. In addition, at configuration design, for specific subsystems, we can divide elements into three weight categories of high, medium and low criticality according to their significance on operation safety, which will affect the priorities of the design and performance assessment of these systems in the future.

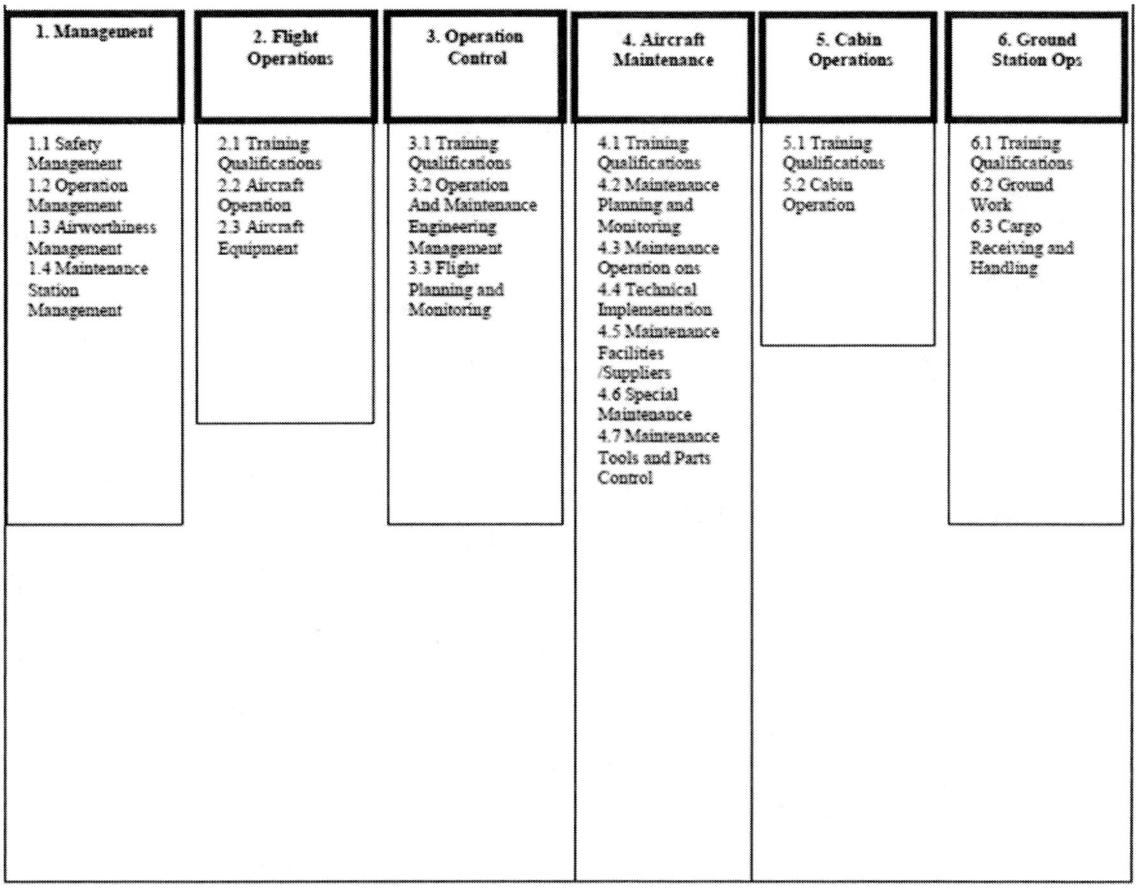

Figure 2. Configuration: Breakdown of operators' major systems and subsystems

2) **Planning management.** The core of planning management is to determine the priority of the monitoring tasks, to confirm the monitoring areas of special attention by identifying major hazards at the air operator's system level and operational environment level. The system designs 25 risk indicators to assess major hazards at the air operator's system level and operational environment level. The 25 risk indicators are correlated to the systems, subsystems and elements, which enables risk indicators to correlate with the specific monitoring programs broken down from the systems, subsystems and elements. Inspectors may, by setting specific levels of risk indicators, achieve the overall configuration of the program priorities. In terms of both internal and external perspectives, risk indicators can be classified into two categories: system stability risk indicators and operational risk indicators. The system stability risk indicators are classified into two categories: operational stability indicators and air operators' dynamic indicators. The operational risk indicators are divided into two categories: performance historical indicators and environmental risk indicators.

Table 1. Risk indicators classification

Level 1 Indicators	**System stability risks**		**Operational risk indicator**	
Level 2 Indicators	**Operational stability risk indicator**	**Operator' s dynamic indicator**	**Performance historical indicator**	**Environmental risk indicator**
Description	Organizational and environmental factors that operators cannot directly control but may improve the system stability and safety by effective management of such factors.	Organizational and environmental factors that operators can directly control and use to improve the system stability and safety.	Air operators' operational performance measured in a certain time period.	Operational environment that may lead to or directly trigger air operators' system failure.

 DOI: 10.1051/itmconf/20171203026

Example	e.g. operators' financial situation and personnel mobility, etc.	e.g. cooperation with the government, effectiveness of SMS	e.g. statistics of incidents/occurrences, safety monitoring performance, etc.	e.g. fleet age, complexity of aircraft types, etc.

3) **Task management.** After the certification team or the supervisor of the certification management office completes the overall design of the monitoring program via the planning function, they may assign specific certification or monitoring tasks to inspectors in various professions and regions. The time needed for an inspector to complete the corresponding monitoring task can be rationally assessed via the system, which will match the monitoring task arrangements with the inspector's available work time. At the same time, through the task management function, we may review the inspector's profession and training status, and better integrate the assigned monitoring tasks with the inspector's professional qualification, and finally form a detailed task monitoring plan.

4) **Data collection.** The monitoring tasks, finalized through task allocation function, are carried out by inspectors of specific professionals. An important task of the monitoring is to collect the data of the operator's safety status by monitoring activities. The system provides the inspectors with systematic data tools, among which the most important one is: the element design checklist and the element performance monitoring checklist. As for the element design checklist and the element performance monitoring checklist, the inspectors collect data for design and assessment by using the questions designed in the checklist for safety attributes monitoring. On the one hand, the government inspectors use them when they conduct design assessment at the time of certification; on the other hand, the government inspectors also use them when they conduct assessment of the operator's systematic design at the time of supervision. At the same time, the operator, as the applicant at initial certification, can also use the checklist for safety attributes monitoring to review their own safety management design in order to have better compliance with the regulations. In the design of checklist for safety attributes monitoring, the system has designed six safety attributes for each monitoring element so as to assess the systematic design related to the air operator. The six safety attributes include: procedure attribute, control attribute, process measurement attribute, interface attribute, responsibility attribute and authorization attribute. Please see the following table for meaning of the six safety attributes. Each element in the air operator configuration corresponds to one of the operational processes of the air operator. The following figure shows that the six safety attributes can be used to carry out the process design and performance assessment corresponding to the elements.

Table 2. Description of safety attributes

Safety attributes	Description
Procedure	The approach to complete a process and documentation of this approach
Control	Inspection and restrictions designed to ensure that the desired results, and making them become part of the process
Process metrics	Used to verify the problems or potential problems occurred in the inspection process so as to promptly correct
Interface	The inter relationships among the processes must be managed to ensure the desired results
Responsibility	A designated person should be responsible for the quality of the process, who is qualified with sufficient knowledge
Authorization	A designated person should have the authority to set and change the process, who should be clearly identified and have the qualifications and sufficient knowledge

 DOI: 10.1051/itmconf/20171203026

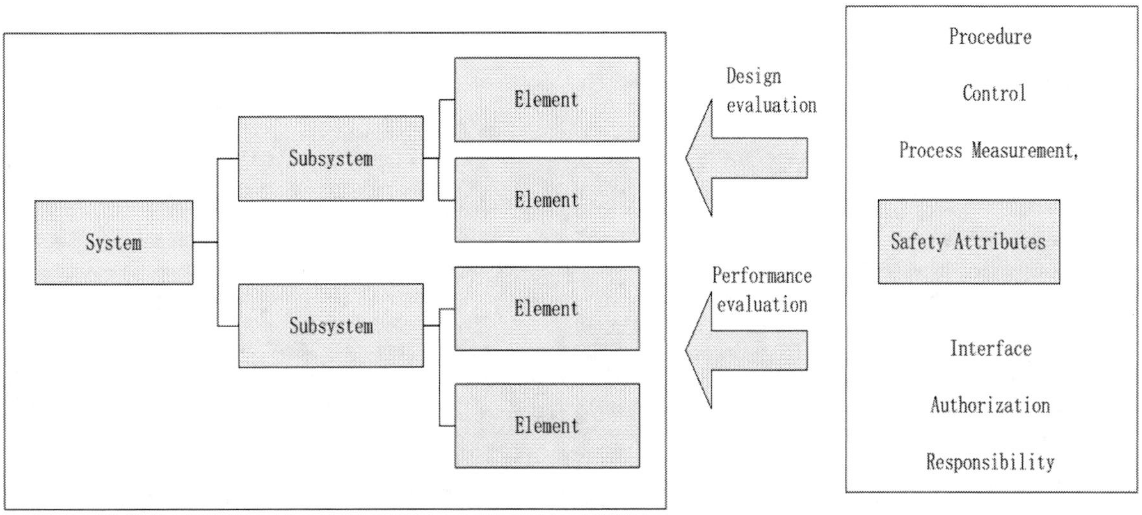

Figure 3. Relationship of system configuration and data collection tool

5) **Analysis assessment and action.** Based on the operator's data collected via the data collection function, the operator's safety assurance system will be analyzed and assessed in areas of analysis and assessment module and action module: assess the design and the performance, and take necessary measures accordingly. Based on the risks of the problem and the severance for the government regulators to take action, the results of the design or performance assessment may be divided into the following four scenarios can.

4 Application Prospect of the Air Operator's Safety Assurance System

The safety assurance system of air operators not only decides whether the operator's operational system meets the regulatory requirements in terms of design and performance assessment, but also identifies major hazards or risks uncontrolled in the existing regulations, which provides an important basis for the revision of the regulations and adjustment of safety oversight policies in the future.

The existing safety oversight model reflects the concept of adopting approaches of design assessment and performance assessment to ensure the operators' operational safety level: at the time of the airline's establishment, the regulator uses operation certification to ensure the carrier complies with the civil aviation regulations' in system design; After the carrier starts operation, the regulator, by supervision and inspection, ensures the carrier's operational safety level meets the standards at the time of the operation certificate issuance; After the certification, the regulator uses supplementary certification to assess the operator's changes to the system. The establishment of the air operator's safety assurance system will enable the regulator to use the design assessment function on the operators more systematically at the time of certification or supplementary certification, and conduct updated assessment on a periodic or non-periodic basis to check whether the system design complies with the regulations and the safety attributes; in addition, when the regulator conducts demonstration and verification as well as the follow-up supervision and inspection of the operation certification, the system's performance assessment function may be used for the assessment of the operational effectiveness. The combination of design assessment and performance assessment embodies the idea of system safety. The system may especially be useful for fairly comprehensive design assessment and performance assessment on air operators that do not update operational systems for years and may, for a long time, focus more on the performance assessment rather than receiving fairly comprehensive design assessment.

The application of the system may be further conducive to air operators' cross-regional regulation. The existing organizational structure of the government's oversight on carriers classifies the oversight responsibilities by geographic regions whereas the operational scope of the air carriers breaks through such segmentation of administrative areas as air carriers operate cross regionally. Thus, supervision or supplementary certification on a single carrier often requires the coordination of several regional civil aviation regulators. Safety assurance system can be adopted to realize the centralized oversight planning, cross-regional and separate implementation of the oversight tasks, standardized collection and analysis of the oversight data, and air operators' real-time safety status so as to take prompt oversight action.

References

1. 2009 ICAO. Safety Management Manual(SMM),2009
2. Li Xiang, Huang Jian—hui, Chen Ke Jia, Comparison of aviation safety management between China and USA [J]. Journal of Safety Science and Technology,2012,(12)
3. CAAC, Flight Standards Oversight System Inspector Manual, 2012
4. Zhang Yuping, Study on development of safety oversight system of air transportation in the United States [J]. Journal of Safety Science and Technology, 2012,(10)
5. FAA.8900.1.Flight Standards Information Management System,2014
6. CAAC, AC-121 /135-FS-2008-26 Requirements on Safety Management System of Air Operator Requirements on Safety Management System of Air Operator, CAAC AC-121 /135-FS-2008-26 Requirements on SafetyManagement System of Air Operator, 2008
7. Sun Ruishan, Liu Lu, Comparative analysis on accident trend of civil aviation between China and America [J]. Journal of Safety Science and Technology, 2012,(9)
8. LI Jing, HE Pei, Study on acceptable level of safety in civil aviation industry of China [J]. Journal of Safety Science and Technology,2010,(10)

Personalized and Accurate QoS Prediction Approach Based on Online Learning Matrix Factorization for Web Services

Jian-Long XU[1,2*], Chang-Sheng ZHU[1]

[1]*Shantou University, Shantou, P.R.China*
[2]*Guangdong Key Laboratory of Big Data Analysis and Processing, Guangzhou 510006, P.R. China*
cszhu@ stu.edu.cn
* *Corresponding author: xujianlong@stu.edu.cn*

Abstract: Quality of Service (QoS) prediction has played an important role in service computing. However, in the real-world scenario of Web service, many user-observed QoS values are unknown and vary over time. In order to provide high accurate and efficient QoS prediction performance for Web services, we propose a personalized and accurate QoS prediction approach namely PAOMF. Our prediction model is built by employing matrix factorization and online stochastic gradient descent algorithm. Extensive experiments are conducted on real world public datasets, which demonstrate the effectiveness and efficiency of our proposed approach.

1 Introduction

Quality of Service (QoS) of Web services has been widely concerned and researched [1-2] in recent years. QoS is widely used evaluation to select suitable service from many services with similar or equivalent functionality [3]. Users (applications that invoke the services) can select optimal service by ranking the QoS of services. Many QoS-based approaches have been proposed for Web service composition [4], Web service selection [5], fault-tolerant Web services [6], etc. Accurate QoS values of Web services are desired to work well for these approaches. However, in many cases, QoS properties (e.g., response time, invocation failure rate) observed by different user (e.g., located in different geographical location) are usually different. Additionally, it is expensive and too time-consuming for users to directly invoke all of Web services. QoS values of most services are unknown and unfixed. There are not sufficient personalized user-observed QoS for users to select optimal Web services. Moreover, the QoS properties may vary when users invoke the same Web service over time. The users need new and optimal Web services to replace low quality Web services with better ones. Therefore, it is an urgent task to predict the unknown QoS based on known QoS, which can be able to guarantee the accuracy performance.

To address the problems above, this paper presents a personalized real-time QoS prediction approach based on online learning matrix factorization for Web services, named PAOMF. In this approach, we build a QoS prediction model by employing matrix factorization and online stochastic gradient descent algorithm. We conduct extensive experiments in real world public datasets and compare with other well-known methods.

The paper is organized as follows. Section 2 presents related work. Section 3 describes our approach. We demonstrate the experimental results in Section 4. Finally, we conclude the whole paper in Section 5.

2 Related Work

Personalized QoS prediction methods for Web service have caused much attention recent years. In most of the existing reports, many researchers explore to obtain high accurate prediction result, and the popular method is collaborative filtering (CF). CF can be divided into neighborhood-based CF and model-based CF. Typical neighborhood-based CF are UPCC (User-based Pearson Correlation Coefficient), IPCC (Item-based Pearson Correlation Coefficient) and UIPCC (IPCC+UPCC) [7]. Considerable research has been conducted based on these methods. Zheng et al. [8] proposed a hybrid collaborative filtering algorithm which combines UPCC and IPCC. Ma et al. [9] presented a highly accurate prediction algorithm (HAPA) to predict unknown QoS values by keeping the original linear relationship. However, neighborhood-based CF method predicts QoS by employing the values of similar users or similar items. When the QoS data are very sparse, the prediction accuracy is not good.

Matrix factorization (MF) is a typical model-based CF approach. MF-based QoS value prediction method is to train a model according to the available QoS data in the user-service matrix. MF-based method has been widely applied in Web service QoS value prediction. Tang et al. [10] proposed a network-aware web service QoS prediction approach by integrating MF with the network map. Su et al. [11] proposed neighbor information combined non-negative matrix factorization algorithm by utilizing the information of the observed data. He et al. [12] proposed a location-based hierarchical matrix factorization (HMF) method to perform personalized QoS prediction by using the global QoS matrix and local QoS matrices. In our previous work [13], we presented reputation-based Matrix factorization (RMF) method which integrated MF with reputation to achieve accurate unknown QoS values prediction results. Memory-based methods are easy to implement and understand. Relative to neighborhood-based CF, MF can achieve better performance. In this paper, we focus on MF to construct the QoS prediction model.

In recent years, online learning has received emerging attention. Existing method [10, 11, 12, 13] above are based on batch learning techniques which generate the predictor by learning on the entire training data set at once. When the data come sequentially, batch learning method cannot update the prediction model in time. The online learning method is an effective way to handle large scale data, especially streaming data. It can quickly adjust the model to reflect the change of the data timely and improve the online prediction accuracy [14]. Many researchers focus on integrating online learning with collaborative filtering. Abernethy et al. [15] present an algorithm for learning a rank-k matrix factorization online for collaborative filtering tasks. Qiao et al. [16] present an online nonparametric max-margin matrix factorization for flexible recommendation. Lin et al. [17] present First Order Sparse Collaborative Filtering (SOCFI) and Second Order Sparse Online Collaborative Filtering (SOCFII) to deal with the user-item ratings for online collaborative filtering. In this paper, we study online learning algorithms to solve the issues facing batch-trained MF algorithms and integrate online learning with MF for QoS values prediction in Web services.

3 Personalized and Accurate QoS Prediction Approach Based on Online Learning Matrix Factorization

To provide high performance prediction service, we design a personalized and accurate QoS prediction framework which is based on online learning matrix factorization (PAOMF). Figure 1 shows the system architecture of our framework.

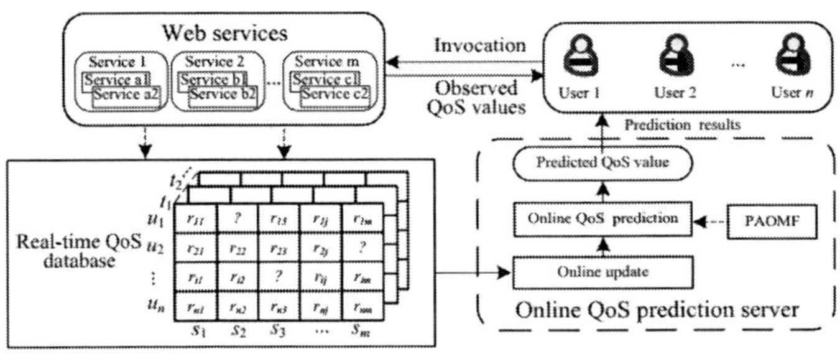

Figure 1. Framework of QoS prediction

The framework works as follows: 1) The online QoS prediction server collects the user-observed QoS data in real-time and save them to database. These data are transformed to normalized QoS data. 2) The PAOMF model performs update if new data come. 3) Online QoS prediction server prediction the unknown QoS value and returns prediction results to the target users who can use these QoS values to invoke the optimal Web services. Our goal of QoS prediction is to employ the observed QoS data to estimate the unknown values at each time slice. Because a user may invoke a few servers (not all the servers) and the quantity of QoS value obtained is limited, so many entries in the user-service-time invocation matrix are unknown. Thus, our main task is to fulfill unknown values in the matrix. However, since the QoS values may vary over time, the prediction model must adapt this condition and work effectively.

Let $U=\{u_1, u_2,\ldots, u_m\}$ be the set of m users, $S=\{s_1, s_2,\ldots, s_n\}$ be the set of n services, R be a $m\times n$ user-service sparse matrix $R\in\mathbb{R}$, r_{ij} ($i\leq m, j\leq n$) represent the value of a certain QoS property (e.g., response time, throughput) at a certain time slice. We can decompose QoS value matrix to multiplication of two low dimensional matrices with the following equation:

$$R \approx \tilde{R} = U^T S \quad (1)$$

where $U\in\mathbb{R}$ denotes the feature matrice of user U, and $S\in\mathbb{R}$ represents service latent feature matrices, the factor l is called dimensionality [7]. $\tilde{R}=\left\{U_i^T S_j\right\}_{n\times m}=\left\{\tilde{r}_{ij}\right\}_{n\times m} (1\le i\le n,\ 1\le j\le m)$ is the approximate matrix of R. U_i and S_i denote the $i^{th}$and j^{th} column of U and S, respectively. In the real-time condition, we suppose the new coming QoS value is $(i, j, r_{ij}, t_{ij})\in R_t$, where t denotes each time slice, R_t is the QoS value matrix at t slice. The objective function of MF for personalized QoS prediction can be represented as:

$$\min_{U,S} \mathcal{L} = \frac{1}{2}\sum_{i=1}^{m}\sum_{j=1}^{n} E_{ij}\left(r_{ij} - U_i^T S_j\right)^2 + \frac{\lambda_u}{2}\|U\|_F^2 + \frac{\lambda_s}{2}\|S\|_F^2 \quad (2)$$

where E_{ij} is a indictor function, whose value is 1 if r_{ij} is known or otherwise. $\|\cdot\|_F$ represents Frobenius norm which is employed to avoid the over-fitting issue during the learning process. λ_u, λ_s are both small positive decimals. In Eq.2, the first term presents the squared error between the observation and predicted value, and the last two terms are the corresponding regularizations. In order to get a local minimum of Eq.(2), we employ online algorithm named stochastic gradient descent algorithm and obtain the following update equations:

$$U_i \leftarrow U_i - \alpha(I_{ij}(U_i^T S_j - r_{ij})(U_i^T S_j)' S_j + \lambda_u U_i), \quad (3)$$

$$S_j \leftarrow S_j - \alpha(I_{ij}(U_i^T S_j - r_{ij})(U_i^T S_j)' U_i + \lambda_s S_j), \quad (4)$$

where α is the learning rate. The main idea of personalized and accurate QoS prediction based on online learning matrix factorization (PAOMF) algorithm can be simply described as follow: at each time slice, when a new data sample (i, j, r_{ij}, t_{ij}) comes, PAOMF performs online updating on its corresponding factors U_i and S_j using Eq. (3) and Eq. (4).

4 Experiments

As illustration in section 3, our main task is to employ the observed QoS data to estimate the unknown values at each time slice. In this section, we conduct the experiments and compare the prediction accuracy of our approach with other methods. We also discuss the key parameters which impact the prediction model.

In this paper, the real world Web service QoS datasets released by Zheng et al. [18] are used to conduct all experiments. These released datasets are obtained based on PlanLab [18]. The datasets contain 142 users and 4,500 Web services for 64 consecutive time slices, at an interval of 15 minutes, and their corresponding QoS values are response time and throughput. In our experiments, we use the throughput datasets to verify our approach. This datasets can be expressed as a $142 \times 4{,}500 \times 64$ matrix.

In the experiments, the evaluation metrics of prediction accuracy are MRE (Median Relative Error) and 90% NPRE (Ninety Percentile Relative Error) which are defined as follows:

$$MRE = \underset{I_{ij}=0}{median}(\left|\tilde{r}_{ij} - r_{ij}\right| / r_{ij}) \quad (5)$$

$$NPRE = 90\% \times \left|\tilde{r}_{ij} - r_{ij}\right| / r_{ij} \quad (6)$$

We conduct compare our method with UIPCC [7] and probabilistic matrix factorization PMF [19] which employ batch learning to update the prediction model. We use different matrix density whose densities are 10% to 50% at a step increase of 10%. The dimensionality is set to 10. λ_u and λ_s are set to 30 and 0.001 with PMF and PAOMF, respectively. The learning rate is set to 0.01. Figure 2 shows the MRE and NPRE results of different methods with different density.

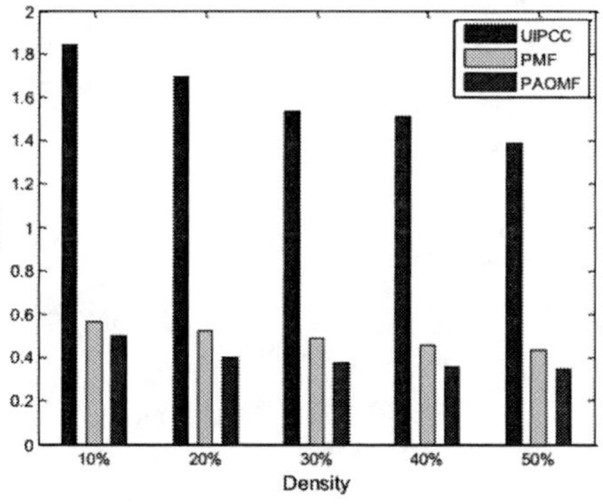

(a) MRE for throughput

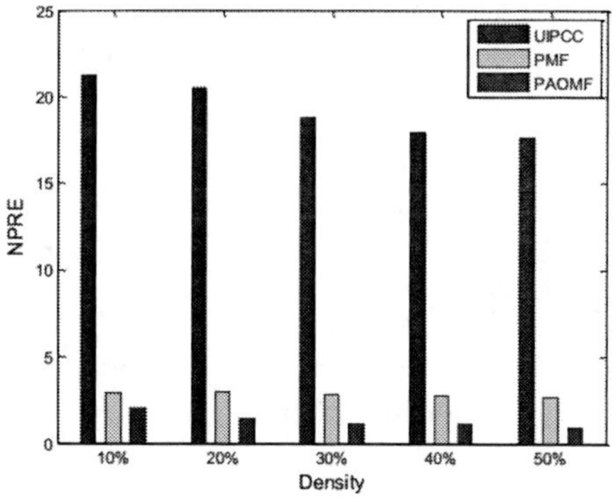

(b) NPRE for throughput

Figure 2. Accuracy comparison

The experimental results show that that no matter what the matrix density is, our PAOMF approach has smaller MRE and NPRE values relative to PMF for throughput with different matrix densities. In average sense, PAOMF can achieve 53.2% improvement in MRE and 63.5% improvement in NPRE than PMF model, which indicates further higher accuracy and effectiveness of our approach. Due to the sparsity of data, UIPCC has the lowest accuracy. As opposed to PAOMF with dynamically adapting to new patterns, PMF has a declining accuracy of the predictions after each factorization since its static nature.

To study the impact of dimensionality, we assess how many potential dimensionalities in the model learning is enough to character user and service latent features. We conduct experiments using different number of latent feature in the model by varying the value of dimensionality from 2 to 30.

DOI: 10.1051/itmconf/20171203027

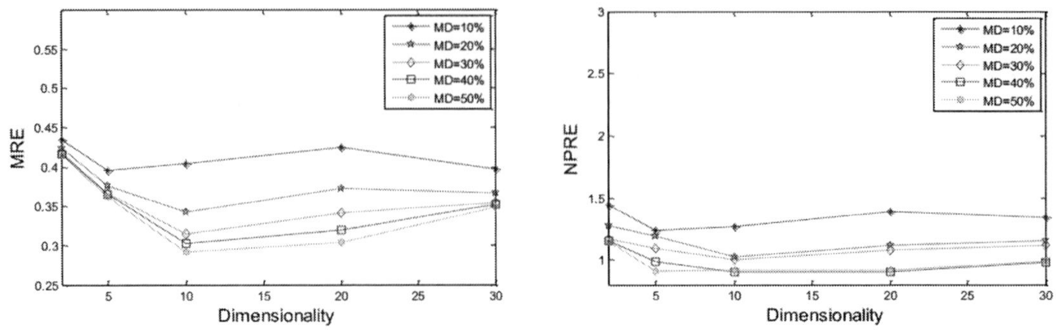

(a) MRE for throughput

(b) NPRE for throughput

Figure 3. Impact of dimensionality

Figure 3 (a) and (b) shows the impact of dimensionality on MRE and NPRE, respectively. Generally, a higher dimensionality means the more latent features are used to characterize users and services for training the prediction model, which may enhance the prediction performance. However, we notice that: 1) MRE and NPRE drop quickly when the dimensionality increases from 2 to 10. 2) When the dimensionality is larger than 10, MRE and NPRE increase slowly with the increasing of dimensionality. This is due to the fact that too many latent features might cause the over-fitting problem which will do harm to the performance. Furthermore, the higher value of dimensionality means the more time of learning these features. Therefore, too small or large dimensionality value will affect the prediction accuracy and efficiency. It seems that the best value of dimensionality is about 10 in this experiment. In other experiments, we set dimensionality =10.

To study the impact of λ_u and λ_s, we also conduct some experiments. Similar to dimensionality, λ_u and λ_s are used to avoid over-fitting through controlling the proportion of the two regularization terms which are used to in Eq. (2). In this experiment, we assume $\lambda_u = \lambda_s$, and set λ_u and λ_s from 0.0001 to 0.01, vary the density from 10% to 50% with a step value of 10% for each matrix corresponding each time slices. Figure 4 shows that the experimental results.

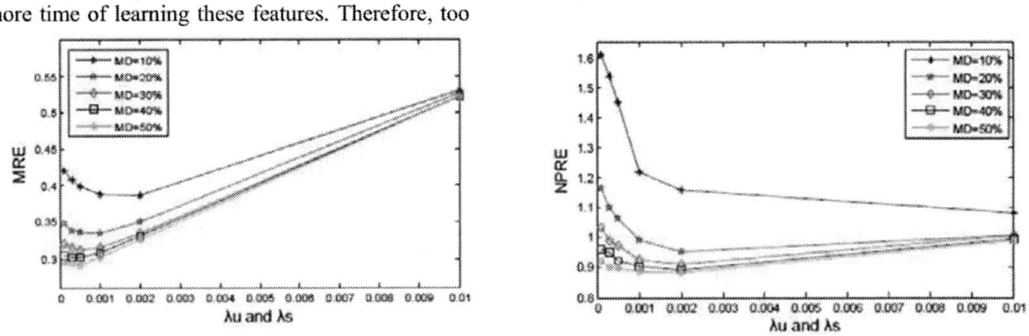

(a) MRE for throughput

(b) NPRE for throughput

Figure 4. Impact of λ_u and λ_s

From Figure 4, we can observe that: 1) When the matrix density increases, performances of MRE and NPRE all improve. 2) With the increasing of λ_u and λs, the overall accuracy of prediction result first increases, then drops after reaching an optimal value. 3) If λ_u and λs are large (e.g., $\lambda_u = \lambda_s$=0.01) or too small (e.g., $\lambda_u = \lambda_s$=0.0001), the prediction accuracy is unsatisfactory. 4) The optimal value seems to be about 0.0005 for MRE and 0.002 for NPRE. Therefore, the optimal value of λ_u and λ_s can be set in accordance with the matrix density and the evaluation metrics.

5 Conclusion and Future Work

In order to provide high performance QoS prediction result for Web services in real-time condition, we design a personalized and accurate QoS prediction approach based on online learning matrix factorization (PAOMF). In this approach, we build a prediction model based on matrix factorization and online stochastic gradient descent algorithm. Sufficient experiments based on real-world datasets show that our model can achieve 53.2% improvement in MRE and 63.5% improvement in

NPRE than PMF model, which indicates the outstanding performance our approach. In future, we plan to employ some techniques to further improve the prediction performance, such as clustering techniques, taking cold start into consideration, and so on.

Acknowledgment

This research was financially supported by the Guangdong High-Level University Project "Green Technologies for Marine Industries", Guangdong Common Colleges Young Innovative Talents Project (No. 2016KQNCX056), and Shantou University National Fund breeding project (No.NFC16001).

References

1. Mousa A, Bentahar J, An Efficient QoS-aware Web Services Selection Using Social Spider Algorithm, Procedia Computer Science. 94 (2016) 176-182.
2. Christi J C R, Premkumar K, Survey on recommendation and visualization techniques for QOS-aware web services, IEEE International Conference on Information Communication and Embedded Systems, 2015, pp.1-6.
3. Yu T, Zhang Y, Lin K J, Efficient algorithms for Web services selection with end-to-end QoS constraints, Acm Transactions on the Web, 1 (2007), Article 6.
4. Karimi, Mohammad Bagher, A. Isazadeh, and A. M. Rahmani, QoS-aware service composition in cloud computing using data mining techniques and genetic algorithm, Journal of Supercomputing (2016) 1-29.
5. Wang S, Hsu C H, Liang Z, et al. Multi-user web service selection based on multi-QoS prediction[J]. Information Systems Frontiers, 16 (2014) 143-152.
6. Zhu X, Qin X, Qiu M. QoS-Aware Fault-Tolerant Scheduling for Real-Time Tasks on Heterogeneous Clusters, IEEE Transactions on Computers, 60 (2011) 800-812.
7. Zibin Zheng, and M.R. Lyu, Personalized Reliability Prediction of Web Services, ACM Transactions on Software Engineering and Methodology (TOSEM), 22 (2013) 12:1-12:25
8. Z. Zheng, M. Lyu, and I. King, "Wsrec: A collaborative filtering based web service recommender system," in Proceedings of the 2009 IEEE international Conference on Web Services, 2009, pp. 437–444.
9. Ma, Y., Wang, S., Hung, P. C. K., Hsu, C. H., Sun, Q., & Yang, F. A highly accurate prediction algorithm for unknown web service qos values. IEEE Transactions on Services Computing, 9 (2015) 511-523.
10. Tang M, Zheng Z, Kang G, et al. Collaborative Web Service Quality Prediction via Exploiting Matrix Factorization and Network Map. IEEE Transactions on Network & Service Management, 13 (2016) 126-137.
11. Su K, Ma L L, Sun Y F, et al. Non-negative matrix factorization model for Web service QoS prediction, Journal of Zhejiang University (Engineering Science Edition, 49 (2015) 1358-1366.
12. Pinjia He, Jieming Zhu, Zibin Zheng, Jianlong Xu, and Michael R. Lyu, Location-based Hierarchical Matrix Factorization for Web Service Recommendation, International Conference on Web Services, Alaska, 2014, pp.297-304.
13. Jianlong Xu, Zibin Zheng, and Michael R. Lyu, Web Service Personalized QoS Prediction via Reputation-based Matrix Factorization, IEEE Transactions on Reliability, 65 (2016) 28-37
14. Shalev-Shwartz S: Online Learning and Online Convex Optimization. Foundations and Trends in Machine Learning, l4 (2011) 107-194.
15. Abernethy J, Canini K, Langford J, and Simma A, Online Collaborative Filtering Di.ens.fr, 2011, pp. 271-280.
16. Zhi Qiao, Peng Zhang, Wenjia Niu, Chuan Zhou, Peng Wang, Li Guo, Online Nonparametric Max-Margin Matrix Factorization for Collaborative Prediction, 2014 IEEE International Conference on Data Mining (ICDM), Shenzhen, 2014, pp.520-529
17. Lin F, Zhou X, Zeng W. Sparse Online Learning for Collaborative Filtering. International Journal of Computers Communications & Control, 2016, 11(2):248.
18. Yilei Zhang, Zibin Zheng, Michael R. Lyu: WSPred: A Time-Aware Personalized QoS Prediction Framework for Web Services. In: the 22th IEEE Symposium on Software Reliability Engineering (ISSRE), Los Alamitos, California, 2011, pp. 210-219.
19. R. Salakhutdinov and A. Mnih. Probabilistic Matrix Factorization. Advances in Neural Information Processing Systems, 2007, pp. 1257-1264.

Adaptive Load Balancing Strategy Based on LVS

Chen FU[1,*], Li-Jun ZHANG[2]

[1]*roomF217, new main building, Beihang University, No.37, xueyuanroad, HaiDian District, BeiJing, China*
[2]*roomG807, new main building, Beihang University, No.37, xueyuanroad, HaiDian District, BeiJing, China*
ljzhang@buaa.edu.cn
**Corresponding author: fuchen319@163.com*

Abstract: Linux Virtual Server (LVS) is a load balancing server that deployed on a cluster of real servers and the load balancer running on the Linux operating system. In the scheduling module, we designed an adaptive load balancing strategy. Firstly, we introduce the traffic state prediction. The algorithm we choose is Radial Basis Function (RBF) neural network. Secondly, we update weights according to the real-time usage of CPU, memory and hard disk. Then we conduct a series of experiments and the adaptive strategies have a better performance on load balancing.

1 Introduction

With the continuous development of network technology, the Page View of users and the load of servers are increasing exponentially. How to provide high quality and uninterrupted network services to users becomes a difficult problem for the Internet Service Provider(ISP) to solve. The use of a single server architecture is difficult to meet this demand, so the model of server farm[1] makes the problem solved. Server clustering techniques is a group of independent, high-speed Internet through a computer interconnected into a whole, and through a single system model to be managed. When the users interact with the cluster, the cluster is just like a separate server. As a kind of Server clustering techniques, the Linux LVS has been widely concerned and applied. It is a highly scalable and available server that deployed on a cluster[2] of real servers and the load balancer running on the Linux operating system. The architecture of the real servers is transparent to internet users, and the internet users interact as if it was a single high-performance server. The LVS can be used to build highly scalable and highly available network services as an advanced load balancing solution.

This paper includes three sections: first, we introduce the LVS model that how to guarantee the scalability and availability[3] with a cluster of real servers. Second, we introduce the new adaptive load balancing strategy. We designed a new scheduling algorithms base on the traffic state prediction and the changing weights of each real servers. We used RBF neural network[4] to predict the future network traffic. The weights is calculated according to the real-time usage of CPU, memory and hard disk at a certain time interval. Finally, we conduct a series of experiments. That compare the performance of the new adaptive load balancing strategy with other simple strategies and give a comprehensive evaluation. Then we discuss the future work that how to improve the performance.

2 Server Load Balance and LVS

2.1 Server Load Balance and LVS Introduction

Virtual server is a scalable and available server built on a cluster of loosely coupled independent real servers[5]. The architecture of the cluster is fully transparent to request clients outside the cluster. Clients interact with the cluster as if it was a single high-performance and highly available web server. The request clients are not affected by the interaction with that cluster and not need modification[6]. The architecture of a virtual server is showed in Fig.1.

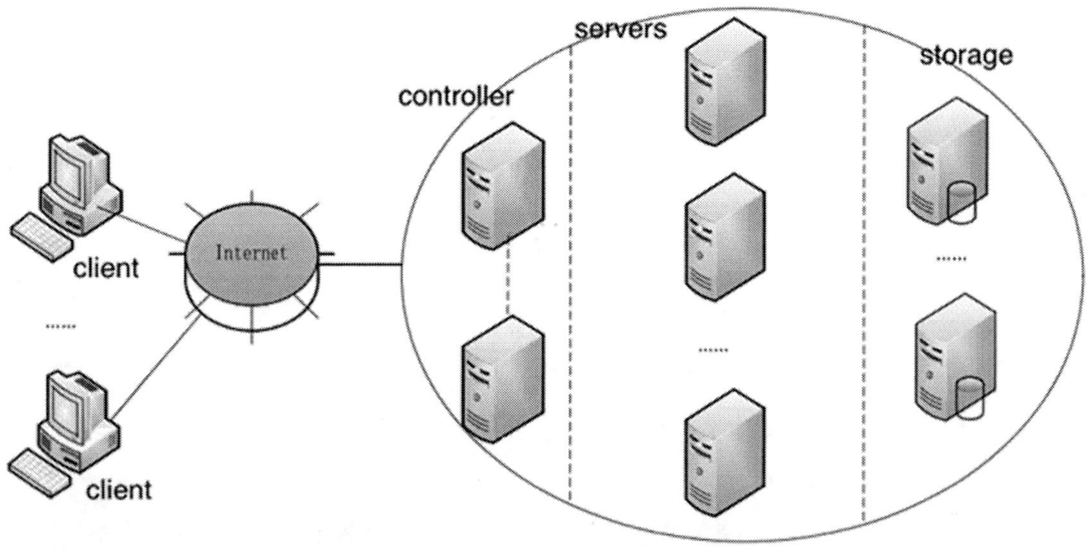

Figure 1. The architecture of a virtual server

The real servers are interconnected by the high-speed LAN or by the geographically dispersed WAN. The load balancer is the front-end of the real servers. It schedules requests packets to the real servers and make parallel services[7] of the cluster to appear as a virtual service on a virtual IP address. Scalability is achieved by transparently adding or removing a real server in the cluster. High availability is provided by detecting node and reconfiguring the cluster appropriately.

2.2 Load Balance Based on LVS

The traditional network service providers always use sever farm and load balancer to improve the availability and scalability of network service[8]. That always has two situations for traditional load balance on servers, one is using the same functional servers to provide the unified service; the other one is using different type servers to provide different services. For the first type, every internet user can obtain the service from any one real server just as the system only has one real server. While in the second one, each server provide same or different type of service, then we must distribute the requests data packets to different servers according to the packets content. In this paper, we only focus on the first one.

Round-robin scheduling algorithm, just as its word meaning, directs the request packets to the real servers in a round-robin manner. It treats all real servers as equals regardless of number of connections or response time.

The weighted round-robin scheduling can treat the real servers of different processing capacities. Each server will be assigned an integer that indicates the processing capacity. The default number is 1[9]. However, it may lead to dynamic load imbalance if the load of requests vary highly. In this paper, we calculate the weight according to the real-time usage of CPU, memory and hard disk at a certain time interval.

3 Traffic State Prediction with RBF and Load Balance Process

In this paper, we present a new internet load balancing scheduling algorithm that using the past number of data packets to predict the future number in a certain time, then we count the probability of each real server with the predicted number. With the data collecting module of LVS, we read the collected data at regular intervals and compute the future data packets number, then send the number to the RBF Scheduling algorithm module to distribute the data packets. The prediction algorithms used here is designed base on the RBF neural network.

3.1 The RBF Neural Network

The structure of RBF is showed as Fig.2. It is three layers artificial neural network, which are input layer, hidden layer and output layer.

DOI: 10.1051/itmconf/20171203028

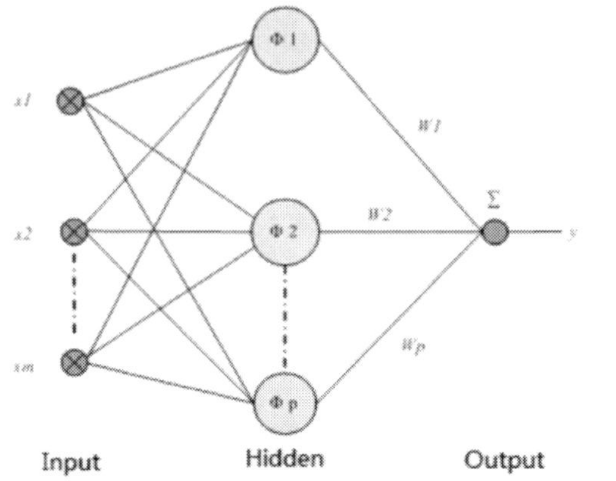

Figure 2. The RBF neural network

$x(k) = [x_1, x_2, x_3, \dots, x_m]$ is the input layer and m is the number of input units. $\Phi = [\phi_1, \phi_2, \dots, \phi_p]$ is the hidden layer and p is the number of hidden layer units. The ouput layer is Y. The following Eq.1 shows the output if RBF.

$$\mathrm{F(x)} = \sum_p^P W_p \Phi_p \|X - X_p\| \quad (1)$$

We used Gaussian function as the RBF function in the hidden layer, which is showed by the following Eq.2.

$$r_j = exp\left[-\frac{\|x-c_j\|^2}{2\delta_j^2}\right].\ j = 1,2, \dots, p \quad (2)$$

The output layer is the sum of the hidden layer, $Y = F(x)$.

We use the gradient descent method[10] to solve RBF, which can simplify the solving process. The first step is training all the parameters of the network with supervised learning algorithm. The parameters include the center of radial basis function c_j, variance δ and the weight between hidden layer and output layer. The center c_j can be computed by k-means clustering function from the input samples. And in order to avoid the radial basis function too sharp or too flat, the variance δ is counted by Eq.3. d_{max} is the max distance between centers and M is the number of centers.

$$\delta = \frac{d_{max}}{\sqrt{2M}} \quad (3)$$

Secondly, we use the gradient descent method to train the RBF neural network. The deviation from real output to desired output is the cost function, just as Eq.4 shows.

$$\mathrm{E} = \frac{1}{2}(y(x) - d)^2 \quad (4)$$

In every training, the parameters are decreased in gradient-decent by the speed as Eq.5.

$$\Delta w_j = -\eta \frac{\partial \mathrm{E}}{\partial w_j} = \eta \sum_{i=1}^P e_j G(||X_i - c_j||) \quad (5)$$

The training process is doing until the value of the cost function meets the accuracy we need. So the algorithm can predict the traffic arrived in the next interval with RBF network and computes the probability of each real server. The next time, an internet load report packet arrived, the RBF will be training again.

3.2 The Process of Server Load Balance Based on LVS

The whole process of the server load balance presented in this paper is:

1 When the host send packets to the virtual IP, the load balancer will reveive the packets. The data statistics module will count the number of packets, and then send the packets to the scheduling module one by one. Different distribute algorithm can be selected for scheduling module, such as round-robin and weighted round-robin. We designed random, past load pressure and status predication scheduling algorithm in this module.

2 For the predication scheduling algorithm, a calculation script is executed at regular intervals. It will read the statistics of the data statistics module, and count the future traffic by the past data statistics. Finally, it will update the prediction data for the status predication scheduling algorithm.

3 A weight getting script is also executed at regular intervals. It send request information to every real server. The weight calculating scripts on real server will read the usage of CPU, memory and hard disk, then calculate the weight of the current state and send the result back. Finally, the script on the load balancer will update the weights of real servers.

4 The real server receive the request packets distributed by the load balancer. After complete the processing of the request, it send the result to the request host directly.

DOI: 10.1051/itmconf/20171203028

4 Experiments and Results

The experiments conducted here are under LVS load balancing architecture. The hosts and servers is created under the Vmware Workstation. We focus on the load pressure of servers, and also test the link delay and packet loss rate between the host and the real server. Iperf is the test tool to send data packets, and we created 200 virtual machines as hosts and 8 real machine as servers here. The server IP is 192.168.50.160. The 200 hosts send the packets to the IP at a random interval. The average link delay, packets lost rate and the square deviation of the data packets number will be counted as the key test object.

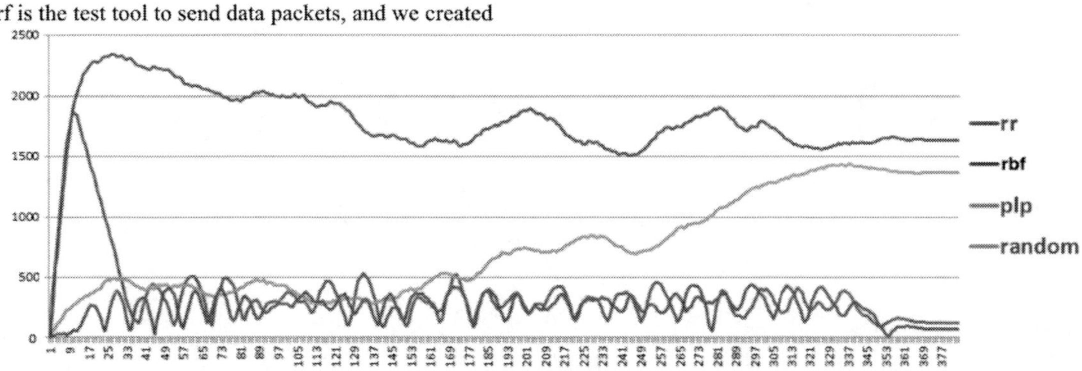

Figure 3. The square deviation of packets

The square deviation of data packets number accepted by all the real servers is showing as Fig.3. We can clearly see that the prediction method based on RBF and the simple past load pressure performed much better than the random and round-robin and RBF curve is more gentle, so its performance is the best stability.

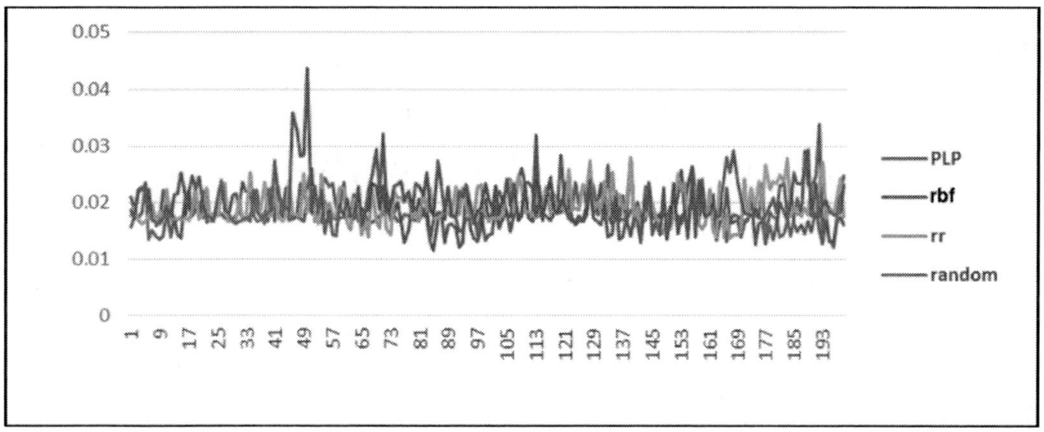

Figure 4. The link delay of packets

DOI: 10.1051/itmconf/20171203028

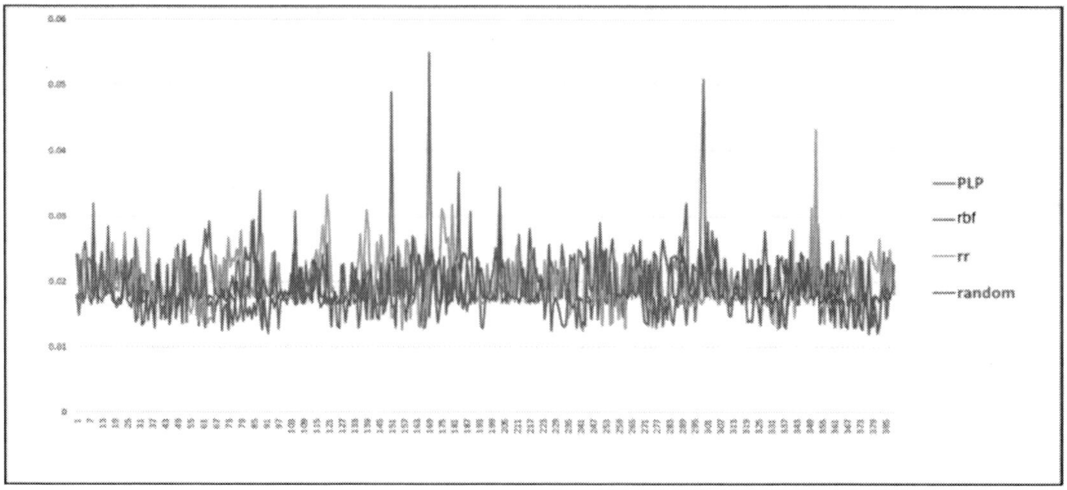

Figure 5. The loss of packets

The link delay between host and the real server is showing as Fig.4. We can see that all the load balancing methods have the similar performance and the average of link delay is below 0.02ms. The packet loss rate between hosts and real servers is showing as Fig.5. It's obvious that all the load balancing methods also have the similar performance and the highest rate of loss is below 1%. Above that, we can conclude that the prediction strategy has a better performance on internet load balancing.

Summary

In this paper, we discuss the load balance on LVS and design an adaptive load balancing strategy. We implement the model with virtual machines for service request hosts and real machines for service reply servers. We created a new strategy that predicts the future traffic state and get the real status of each server in a certain time. The load server distribute the load depend on the future traffic and the weights of severs. The experiments results show that the new adaptive load balancing strategy has a better performance in load balance and has similar cost with other simple strategies. In the future, we will optimize the RBF's solving process and optimize the server weight coefficient. This work is supported by SKLSDE-2015ZX-07 project by State Key Laboratory of Software Development Environment of Beihang University and YCSJ-02-2015-05 project by Graduate Innovative Practice Fund of Beihang University.

References

1. Chen, Mike Y. & Brewer, Eric. 2002. Active connection management in internet services. In Network Operations and Management Symposium, 2002. NOMS 2002. 2002 IEEE/IFIP :265–280. IEEE.
2. Eunmi Choi, Yoojin Lim, and Dugki Min. Performace Comparison of Various Web Cluster Architectures [J]. Lecture Notes in Computer Science, May 2005, vol. 3398:617-624.
3. Ahmad I., Ghafoor A. and Mehrotra K. Performance Prediction of Distributed Load Balancing on Multicomputer Systems [J].ACM, 1991: 830-839.
4. Jain P. and Gupta D. An Algorithm for Dynamic Load Balancing in Distributed Systems with Multiple Supporting Nodes by Exploiting the Interrupt Service [J]. Academy Publisher, 2009:232-236.
5. Information on http://www.linux-mag.com/2003-11/clusters_01.html
6. Hamdi M. and Lin C.K. Dynamic Load Balancing of Data Parallel Applications on a Distributed Network. In 9th International Conference on Supercomputing, ACM, 1995: 170-179.
7. Information on http://www.linux-vs.org/
8. Canini, Marco. Kuznetsov, Petr. Levin, Dan. & Schmid, Stefan. 2013. Software transactional networking: Concurrent and consistent policy composition. In Proceedings of the second ACM SIGCOMM workshop on Hot topics in software defined networking :1–6.ACM.
9. Mitchell, T.M. 2003. Machine learning. Beijing: China Machine Press.
10. Shi W, MacGregor M H, Gburzynski P. Load balancing for parallel forwarding. IEEE/ACM Transactions on Networking (TON), 2005, 13(4): 790-801

SemDiff: Finding Semtic Differences in Binary Programs based on Angr

Shi-Chao WANG[1,*], Chu-Lei LIU[2,a], Yao LI[3,b], and Wei-Yang XU[4,c]

[1]*National University of Defense Technology, China*
[2]*Haerbin Engineering University, China*
[3]*National University of Defense Technology, China*
[4]*National University of Defense Technology, China*
[a]*634390770@qq.com,* [b]*Faith_ly@yeah.net,* [c]*286406726@qq.com*
**Corresponding author: wshchao@163.com*

Abstract: We introduce SemDiff, a novel technology for finding semantic differences between two binary files. Now, the vendor will release the information to patch the previous version which has vulnerability. Then, we can compare the differences and similarities between the two versions to get the unpublished details of the 1day vulnerabilities. Tools, such as BinDiff, BinHunt and iBinHunt ,have worked on this project before, however , there are some weaknesses on them. Just like BinDiff, a comparison method based on structure, can not be effective for judging the semantic differences. Though the other two tools(BindHunt and iBinHunt) can recognize the differences we focus on, they can not effectively verify the functional inlining and spend a pretty long time to finish the process because the use of graph-based isomorphism algorithm. In the paper, we first propose SemDiff, which uses the existing tool(angr) to generate the intermediate language(VEX). Then, because of the nature of program, the data read from and written to the memories, we record these information to implement the comparison. Last, an improved BinDiff algorithm is used to match the basic blocks. In this paper, we take some real vulnerabilities as examples, such as CVE-2010-3974-Microsoft Windows to test our tool, reaching a good goal, matching more blocks than BinDiff and taking less time than BinHunt and iBinHunt.

1 Introduction

Now, for the purpose to protect the source code, many software vendors make the source code of their programs unavailable and when the vulnerabilities occurs, the patch is released in binary mode, rather than the source code. As Microsoft and other companies, when they publish a patch, no details are showed [1]. This situation increases the difficulty in analyzing the potential vulnerabilities to protect us from those threats, which may hijack our data, steal our privacy and so on. So, it is significant for us to understand the differences between the two versions. And, finding out the 1day vulnerabilities is one of the roles of the SemDiff.

However, because of instruction obfuscation, mutation optimization technology and other practical problems, the binary comparison is difficult. Modifying the software process call graph, using the Proxy point, changing the function symbols, sharing basic blocks, adding entry points, re-allocating registers, instruction sequence replacement, all increase the difficulties.

In addition, there are may prior works for solving these problems. Almost four types of methods have been developed for automatically comparing the structural similarities of executables, the class of BinDiff[2-4], Fingerprint and String Hashing[1,11,12], Bipartite Graph matching such as GED[1,13] and other graph methods[6,7]. The detailed introduction is showed as follows.

In this paper, we propose a new method called SemDiff to find the semantic differences between the two programs. Our method, compared with previous methods, such as BinDiff and BinHunt, provides a kind of rapid and accurate matching. For BinDiff, it only relies on structural information, which leads to many unmatched functions that should be matched. Our method is based on the control flow on basic blocks, symbolic execution[8] and the theorem prover. We first construct the intermediate representation of the program(we used the VEX there), then generate the control flow graph of the basic blocks. After that, we record the data written to and read from memories and registers, and then we put them into theorem prover to judge the similarity. Last, we use these information and the SemDiff to match the blocks.

Our approach is an interprocedural analysis rather than an intraprocedural analysis. Intraprocedural analysis limit to the scope of the current function, however, interprocedural analysis has the ability to enter sub-functions [9]. Needless to say, in-process analysis is much simpler than the process. However , sometimes we want to follow the path to find what we want, they may occur in different functions.

Our aritcles is organized as follows: Section 2 introduces the whole framework and an overview of each part of the SemDiff, the next Section 3 shows the SemDiff algorithm which is improved from BinDiff, then we present the experiment and the analysis of them in Section 4. The limitation and future work are summarized in Section 5.

2 System Architecture

Fig.1 shows the whole system architecture. Firstly, the two binary files are loaded into angr platform, and angr runs its own disassembler, converting the execution files to assembly code. Then, they become the intermediate representation blocks through the IR convertor, which is then loaded into the CFG constructor to generate intermediate language representations control flow graph. After that, using the symbol execution to record the data which are judging by theorem proving. Last put the data into the SemDiff to get the matched set.

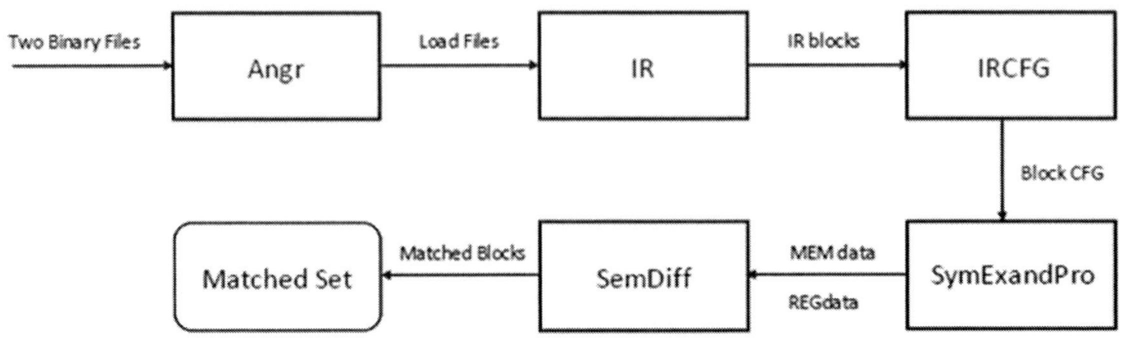

Figure 1. System architecture of the SemDiff

2.1 Angr

The writer of angr wants to create a user-friendly binary analysis suite, allowing a user to simply start up iPython and easily perform intensive binary analyses with a couple of commands. That being said, binary analysis is complex, which makes angr complex. The more details can be seen in [10].

2.2 Intermediate Representation

In VEX, the code is broken down into smaller blocks which is called IRSBs. IRSB is a single entry and multiple exit, which contains three elements:1.a type environment; 2.a list of statement; 3.a jump that exits form the end of the IRSB.

2.3 Symbolic Execution and Theorem Proving

Symbolic execution is a well known technique for representing scalar program analysis with symbolized values. We can perform symbolic execution to get the results of each step, and record the contents which are written to each memory and register. Because the core of executing the program is the data which are read from or written to the memory and register. So we use them to represent the semantic performance of a basic block. To determine the two basic blocks are functionally identical, we define a rule as follows:

definition1: (pair basic blocks equivalence formulas of data) Given two list of data that are recorded in the memories and registers: $X = [x_0, x_1, \ldots, x_m]$*, and* $Y = [y_0, y_1, \ldots, y_n]$*. For every* x_i *in X, there is a bijection, that,* $y_j = f(x_i)$ *is existed, then, we call the data is same. The formula is described as follows:*

$$\forall x_i, \exists y_j = f(x_i), f(x) \text{ is a bijection}$$

3 SemDiff Algorithm

Now, we propose our SemDiff as three parts(WholeMatch, MatchPro, SemDiff).As with the previous algorithms, at the beginning of the initially matching process, we find the blocks which are uniquely matched, what is said that, we find some basic blocks that have the same symbol expressions in each addresses. Because there may some different blocks with the same data. This is also well explained in practice. In different functions, there are some similar blocks, for different functions may call the same part of the function.

Algorithm 1: Whole Match

function wholeMatch(S_A, S_B):
$M \leftarrow \emptyset$
foreach $a_i \in S_A$ and $b_j \in S_B$ **do:**
  if $\exists f(a_i) = b_j$ **then:**
$M \leftarrow M \cup (a_i, b_j)$
$S_A \leftarrow S_A \backslash a_i$
$S_B \leftarrow S_B \backslash b_j$
break
return (M, S_A, S_B)

Figure 2. Algorithm 1

Algorithm 2: Match propagation

```
1 function MatchPro(M, S_A, S_B):
2 foreach(a_i, b_j) ∈ M do:
3 M' = M
4 SubS_A = FindPaAndCh(a_i)
5 SubS_b = FindPaAndCh(b_j)
6 SubM', S_A, S_B = wholeMatch(SubS_A, SubS_B)
7 M' = M' ∪ SubM'
8 M = M'
9 return (M, S_A, S_B)
```

Figure 3. Algorithm 2

For the first part of the algorithm(Fig.2), S_A and S_B are the basic block sequences of the two programs partly. At the beginning, we assign the empty set to the Match set, because we do not perform the matching process. Then, the third line, we check if each a_i in Sa has the only match b_j in Sb, and whether a_i is the only match to b_j. If there is a bijection existing, add the pair (a_i, b_j) into the match set and delete the elements a_i, b_j from the S_A, S_B respectively.

Then, it is the second part (Fig.3). We call it the match propagation, because it is applied in the propagation progress. The input of the second part is the match set which is got from the first step and the remaining unmatched basic block sequence (S_A, S_B). Then we match each block from a small set, which is the line 4 and line 5 shown. $SubS_A$ is the set of the parent nodes and children nodes to the matched block a_i, also $SubS_B$ is the set of block b_j. After we get the subset, we use them into the wholeMatch to get the matched blocks. The reason why we use this way is the remaining blocks after the step one are the blocks with the different data or more than two blocks have the same symbol expressions. Then, we reduce the scope of the block lists to find more matching blocks through the context of the matched blocks.

Algorithm 3: SemDiff

```
1 function SemDiff(Path_A, Path_B):
2 S_A ← Path_A
3 S_B ← Path_B
4 M' ← ∅
5 (M, S_A, S_B) = wholeMatch(S_A, S_B)
6 while M' ≠ M:
7 M' = M
8 M, S_A, S_B = MatchPro(M, S_A, S_B)
9 M, S_A, S_B = wholeMatch(S_A, S_B)
10 return (M, S_A, S_B)
```

Figure 4. Algorithm 3

The last part is a loop (Fig.4), which is the whole process of our SemDiff algorithm. The main core of the SemDiff is the line 8 and line 9. After the line 8, we may get two remaining lists which may have the unique blocks with the same symbol expressions but they are not the parent node or the child node of the matched blocks. If we do not execute the line 9, we may miss some of them.

4 Experiment

Our experiment is carried out in the system Ubuntu 14.04, running in an angr virtual environment. The language which we use is Python. We first run a sample program. The sample's input is the same two paths. Our purpose is to illustrate our SemDiff's efficiency. Then we run two real program with vulnerability. The inputs are the paths of unpatched and patched program respectively.

4.1 The sample

We test a simple sample named fauxware, and finally find all the blocks matched with score 1 experienced 4 times during 45.301483 Seconds.

4.2 CVE-2010-3974

We first run the unpatch version and patch version, and change them into IR blocks, like Fig.5.

```
0x400774:  lea rax, qword ptr [rbp - 0x20]
0x400778:  mov    edx, 8
0x40077d:  mov    rsi, rax
0x400780:  mov    edi, 0
...
0x400785:  call 0x400530
```

```
00 | ------ IMark(0x400774, 4, 0) ------
01 | t4 = GET:I64(bp)
02 | t3 = Add64(t4,0xffffffffffffffe0)
03 | PUT(rax) = t3
...
16 | t10 = Sub64(t8,0x0000000000000080)
PUT(rip) = 0x0000000000400530; Ijk_Call
```

Figure 5. Assembly instruction and IR instruction

DOI: 10.1051/itmconf/20171203029

Then, we preprocess the data by ignoring the address of memory and register like Fig.6.

```
<BV640x100000e>
<BV640#56(mem_8+(7*reg_10_64[7:0]))>
<BV64reg_38_64+0xffffffffffffffe0>
<BV64__add__(reg_38_64,0x8,0x8)>
```

Figure 6. Final Data

We then run the basic block comparison. We finally find some matched blocks with score between 0.8 and 0.9. We then check the content. According to the knowledge, we find the vulnerability point existing in these blocks. One of the blocks in patched version is illustrated as Fig.7.

```
lea    ecx,ss:[ebp+var_1C]
push ecx
push ss:[ebp+arg_0]
...
jz loc_100C1DD
```

Figure 7. Blocks with score 0.8-0.9

We then trace these blocks path and finally find out the vulnerability in the unpatch version.

Summary

In this paper, we introduce a novel technique named SemDiff. It is based on the angr platform. The main technique we use is the symbol execution, Theorem Proving and the updated the comparison algorithm. Though SemDiff has worked well on some files, it depends on the angr platform seriously. So sometimes it can not well support the PE file. And the way to find the vulnerability is still manual operations. We will develop our tools to find the vulnerability automatically in the future.

Acknowledgement

We would like to thank Thomas Dullien for his fascinating seminar on BinDiffthat inspired this study.

References

1. Martial Bourquin, Andy King, Edward Robbins,BinSlayer :Accurate Comparison of Binary Executables(2013).
2. T. Dullien and R. Rolles. Graph-based comparison of executable objects. In Symposium sur la Se´curite´ des Technologies de l'Information et des Communications (2005).
3. Halvar Flake. More fun with graphs. Black Hat Federal (2003).
4. Halvar Flake. Structural comparison of executable objects. In Proceedings of the IEEE Conference on Detection of Intrusions and Mal- ware & Vulnerability Assessment - DIMVA, 2004,pp 161–173.
5. S. Bardin, P. Herrmann, and F. Ve´drine. Refinement-Based CFG Reconstruction from Unstructured Programs. In VMCAI, volume 6538 of LNCS, 2011, pp 54–69.
6. D. Gao, M.K. Reiter, and D. Song. Binhunt: Automatically finding semantic differences in binary programs. In Poceedings of the 10th International Conference on Information and Communications Security (ICICS 2008), 2008.
7. Jiang Ming, Meng Pan, and Debin Gao ,iBinHunt: Binary Hunting with Inter-Procedural Control Flow,Springer Berlin Heidelberg, 2013, 7839:92-109.
8. King, J.: Symbolic execution and program testing. Communications of the ACM 19(7) (1976).
9. Josselin Feist, Laurent Mounier and Marie-Laure Potet,Statically detecting use after free on binary code, Journal of Computer Virology and Hacking Techniques (2014).
10. S Yan, C Kruegel, G Vigna, R Wang(State of) The Art of War: Offensive Techniques in Binary Analysis, IEEE Symposium on Security and Privacy,(2016).
11. J. Oh. Fight against 1-day exploits: Diffing Binaries vs Antidiffing Binaries. In Black Hat USA, 2009. http: //www.blackhat.com/presentations/bh-usa-09/OH/ BHUSA09-Oh-DiffingBinaries-PAPER.pdf.
12. J. Oh. ExploitSpotting: Locating Vulnerabilities Out Of Vendor Patches Automatically. In Black Hat USA, 2010. http://www. darungrim.org/Presentations.
13. K. Riesen, M. Neuhaus, and H. Bunke. Bipartite graph matching for computing the edit distance of graphs. In Graph-Based Representa- tions in Pattern Recognition, volume 4538 of Lecture Notes in Computer Science, pp 1–12. Springer, 2007.

DOI: 10.1051/itmconf/20171203030

DLTAP: A Network-efficient Scheduling Method for Distributed Deep Learning Workload in Containerized Cluster Environment

Wei QIAO[1,a], Ying LI[2,b] and Zhong-Hai WU[3,*]

[1]*School of Software and Microelectronics, Peking University, Beijing, China*
[2]*School of Software and Microelectronics, Peking University, Beijing, China*
[3]*School of Software and Microelectronics, Peking University, Beijing, China*
[a]*qiaowei@pku.edu.cn,* [b]*li.ying@pku.edu.cn*
**Corresponding author: wuzh@ss.pku.edu.cn*

Abstract: Deep neural networks (DNNs) have recently yielded strong results on a range of applications. Training these DNNs using a cluster of commodity machines is a promising approach since training is time consuming and compute-intensive. Furthermore, putting DNN tasks into containers of clusters would enable broader and easier deployment of DNN-based algorithms. Toward this end, this paper addresses the problem of scheduling DNN tasks in the containerized cluster environment. Efficiently scheduling data-parallel computation jobs like DNN over containerized clusters is critical for job performance, system throughput, and resource utilization. It becomes even more challenging with the complex workloads. We propose a scheduling method called Deep Learning Task Allocation Priority (DLTAP) which performs scheduling decisions in a distributed manner, and each of scheduling decisions takes aggregation degree of parameter sever task and worker task into account, in particularly, to reduce cross-node network transmission traffic and, correspondingly, decrease the DNN training time. We evaluate the DLTAP scheduling method using a state-of-the-art distributed DNN training framework on 3 benchmarks. The results show that the proposed method can averagely reduce 12% cross-node network traffic, and decrease the DNN training time even with the cluster of low-end servers.

1 Introduction

Large-scale deep learning, for instance, Deep Neutral Network (DNN), has driven advances with higher accuracy than traditional techniques in many different fields especially at image classification [1, 2], speech recognition [3] and text processing [4]. To train DNNs on a large-scale, researchers have exploited distributed deep learning systems [1, 5, 6, 7], such as DistBelief [1] and Tensorflow [7]. Compared to DistBelief, Tensorflow is more flexible, faster and easy to use. It introduces a new distributed programming paradigm that a DNN job is divided into a number of parameter server tasks (ps tasks) and worker tasks, which can be flexibly allocated in the cluster. It is different from previous parameter server concept [5] that there is no need for a centralized global parameter server to store all the parameters of a job. This flexible training approach brings some benefits, but on the other hand introduces new challenges: (a) how to provision resources for tasks in a timely and elastic way; and (b) how to schedule ps and worker tasks on the distributed environment to improve job performance.

With the cloud computing revolution brought by Docker [8], the advantages of containers in improving resource utilization and production efficiency have attracted much attention. The development of containerization technology has greatly accelerated the popularization and application of deep learning. To put deep learning task into container and make the container as the unit of management can enable broader and easier deployment of deep learning algorithms for building cloud-based distributed deep learning platform [9]. In addition, it enables higher levels of utilization and can transition from training to serving smoothly. However, container isolation brings a certain degree of performance loss, mainly due to the cost of network communication when updating the gradient between the ps task and the worker task.

In this paper, the issue of non-optimal network transmission for distributed deep learning workload in containerized cluster environment is put forward and solved by our network-efficient scheduling method called DLTAP. The main objective is to take aggregation degree of ps task and worker task into consideration, and the comparison demonstrates that it can greatly reduce the cross-node network transmission traffic caused by ps task and worker task. More importantly, in this way, we can also accelerate the training speed of DNNs.

The remainder of this paper is organized as follows. Section 2 describes the related works on container scheduler. Section 3 presents in detail the statement of problem and the proposed method. Section 4 presents the experimental results. Concluding remarks are covered in the last section.

2 Related Works

Container schedulers are aimed at scheduling a container to a most appropriate node. Docker Swarm [10] is simple to use due to the same usage with original Docker API engine, but it does not provide features to handle node failures which makes it not recommendable in a production environment. Mesos [11] is a kind of two-level scheduler [12] which uses a single active resource manager to offer compute resources to multiple parallel "scheduler frameworks". Choosing Mesos with Marathon [13] is an excellent combination if you already have a Mesos cluster. Kubernetes [14] is the third container-management system for automating deployment, scaling, and management of containerized applications influenced by Borg [9]. It aims to provide better ways of managing related, distributed components across varied infrastructure, while still benefiting from the improved utilization containers enable. Aurora [15] is a Borg-like scheduler that runs on top of Mesos, but it works for long running services. Tupperware [16] is a Borg-like system and it increases efficiency by reducing time spent on getting app to run in production. But only a few details have been disclosed.

However, all these schedulers treat each container as a "black box" and do not take into account characteristics of task running in the container that results in performance loss. In this paper, we differentiate containers by their running DNN tasks, i.e., ps task and worker task, and considering their network transmission traffic during scheduling.

3 Proposed Method

Problem Statement. We assume a relatively uncomplicated case, the cluster consists of four physical machines, including one as the master, remaining three are slaves, respectively recorded as s1, s2 and s3. We use a DNN based on standard data set MNIST [17]. The network structure is a modified version of LeNet5 [18] with 3 million parameters. In the case, the job is divided into two ps tasks, recorded as ps1, ps2, and three worker tasks, recorded as wk1, wk2, wk3. All parameters of our model are evenly distributed among ps tasks. Each worker task will send the appropriate gradient updates to the corresponding ps1 and ps2 after each mini-batch of input data trained, and receive the latest parameters they send back.

Considering two different scheduling scenarios. We assume that each host is load balanced due to other workloads. The first is that wk1 and wk3 are on s1, ps1 and ps2 are on s2, wk2 is on s3, as is shown in Fig. 1(a). In this scenario, a total of 6 cross-node network transmissions occur after each mini-batch of input data trained. The second scenario is that wk1, wk3 and ps1 are on s1, ps2 is on s2, wk2 is on s3, as is shown in Fig. 1(b). So a total of 4 cross-node and 2 inner-node network transmissions are generated after each mini-batch of input data trained. A significant difference is that the first scenario is 2 more times than the second scenario of cross-node network transmission after each mini-batch of input data trained. After massive experimental tests, we find that the network throughput decreased 12% and the training time reduced 15% in the second scenario compared with those in the first scenario. In Section 4 there will be a detailed comparative analysis. Here we call the first scheduling situation "the non-ideal" scheduling scenario, and the second scheduling situation the "ideal" scheduling scenario.

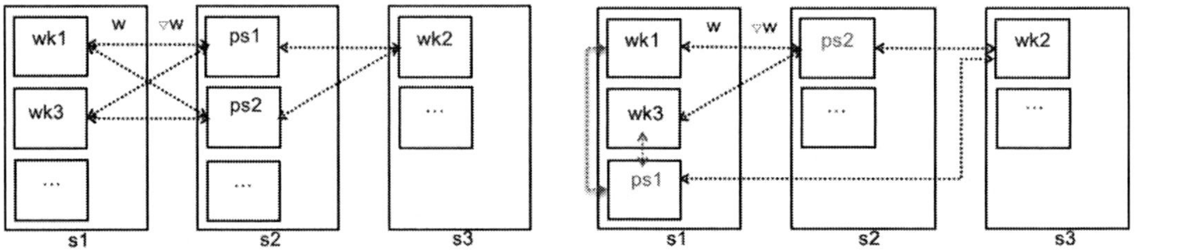

(a) A non-ideal scheduling scenario (b) An ideal scheduling scenario

Figure 1. The two scheduling scenarios.

Proposed Method. The default Kubernetes scheduling method includes two steps. The first step is to filter out the nodes that do not meet certain requirements and the second step is ranking the remaining nodes to find a best fit for the pod. A pod is a group of one or more containers in Kubernetes. In our design, a pod has only one Docker container, and each ps task or worker task is put into a pod. In the ranking process, different priority methods take different dimensions into account. Each priority method is weighted by a positive number and the final score of each node is calculated by adding up all the weighted scores.

Despite the fact that there is a certain probability to produce non-ideal scheduling scenario by using the default scheduling method, we want to minimize this probability. To this end, we propose a new scheduling method DLTAP. The core idea is to improve the aggregation degree of ps tasks and worker tasks in one node. The DLTAP scheduling method is shown in Fig. 2.

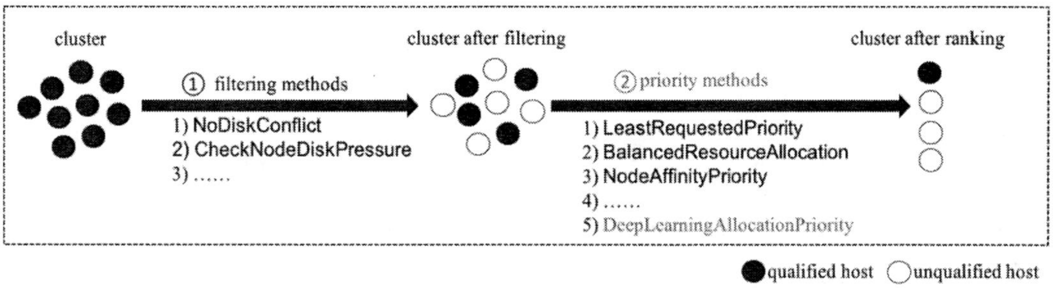

Figure 2. The DLTAP scheduling method.

Our method belongs to the ranking process and is divided into two steps. It is assumed that our training job consists of several ps tasks and worker tasks. Firstly, distribute each worker task according to the initial hybrid scoring model by Eq. 1. Secondly, distribute each ps task according to the new hybrid scoring model by Eq. 2. In the second step, the method calculates the current ps task aggregation degree for each remaining node by Eq. 3, and then, the result is added to the initial hybrid scoring model. Algorithm 1. outlines the ps task distributing process of DLTAP scheduling method.

$$finalScoreNodeA = \sum_{i=1}^{N}(weight_i \times defaultPriorityMethodScore_i). \quad (1)$$

$$finalScoreNodeA' = finalScoreNodeA + weightOfDLTAP \times priorityScoreOfDLTAP. \quad (2)$$

$$priorityScoreOfDLTAP = \frac{count(current\ job's\ worker\ tasks\ in\ current\ node)}{total\ number\ of\ current\ job's\ worker\ tasks)}. \quad (3)$$

After the scores of all nodes are calculated, the node with highest score is chosen as the host of the ps task. If there are more than one nodes with equal highest scores, a random one among them is chosen. The ps task distributing process completes until all of them are scheduled to the appropriate node.

Algorithm 1. The ps task distributing process of DLTAP.

Definition: *container* indicates the container waiting to be scheduled and there is a ps task in it.
nodes indicate all normal working hosts.
nodeNameToInfo indicates node level aggregated information.
hostPriorityList indicates the priority of scheduling to a particular host, higher priority is better.
hostPriorityList = *{host$_1$: score$_1$, host$_2$: score$_2$, ..., host$_n$, score$_n$}*.
weightOfDLTAP indicates the weight of our method in the new hybrid scoring model.
Input: *container*, *nodes, nodeNameToInfo*
Output: *hostPriorityList*
1. Initialize *hostPriorityList*.
2. Get current running job id from *container*.
3. for node in *nodes*:
4. currentNodeWorkerTaskNumbers = 0
5. for innerContainer in *nodeNameToInfo*[node.Name].getContainers():
6. if innerContainer belongs to current job and innerContainer is a worker task:
7. currentNodeWorkerTaskNumbers++.
8. score = currentNodeWorkerTaskNumbers / the total number of job's worker tasks.
9. *hostPriorityList*.add(node, score * *weightOfDLTAP*)
10. Return *hostPriorityList*.

4 Experiments Evaluation

To measure the DLTAP's performance, we have built a deep learning prototype platform based on open-sourced Tensorflow and Kubernetes, which has one master and 3 slaves with 2 GB of memory, 2 cores and 60 GB of storage. A common gigabit Ethernet switch connects each node. All slave nodes in the cluster are load balanced.

We performed our evaluations with three different models, including fully connected neural networks (FCNs) [19], convolutional neural networks (CNNs) [2] and recurrent neural networks (RNNs) [20] with Long Short-Term Memory (LSTM) [21]. For FCNs, a 4-layer, a 6-layer, and an 8-layer neural network (FCN-4, FCN-6, FCN-8) are constructed. For CNNs, we choose the classical LeNet5 and make some changes. A small size of LeNet5 (LeNet5-SS) with 0.3 million parameters and a big size of LeNet5 (LeNet5-BS) with 3 million parameters are constructed. For RNNs, we select 2 model with different size, with input length of 16 (LSTM-16) and 32 (LSTM-32) respectively. The detailed neural networks configuration can be found in Table 1.

Table 1. The experimental setup of neural networks.

Model	Network	Layer	Parameters [million]
FCN	FCN-4	4	0.03
	FCN-6	6	0.3
	FCN-8	8	3
CNN	LeNet5-SS	6	0.3
	LeNet5-BS	6	3
RNN	LSTM-16	2	0.3
	LSTM-32	2	3

Performance on network throughput. Firstly, we use a FCN-8 job divided into a ps task and a worker task to test. We compare network throughput in the cross-node situation which is that ps task and worker task are in different node, and the inner-node situation which is that ps task and worker task are in same node. We can see from Fig. 3(a) that network throughput of the cross-node is less than the inner-node since inner-node transmission need not to pass the actual physical NIC.

Secondly, we train a FCN-8 job in the ideal scheduling scenario (defined above), we calculate the cross-node network throughput of outgoing traffic for each node associated with current job training. Then the value of each node are added up respectively. This job runs many times, and we take the average of multiple results as the cluster network throughput generated by the job in this scenario. The same experiments are also tested in the scenario of non-ideal scenario (defined above). The results are shown in Fig. 3(b). The results show that the cluster network throughput under the ideal scheduling scenario is less than that under the non-ideal scheduling scenario. Because our method reduces the network transmission of the parameters across the nodes.

Finally, we use FCN-4, FCN-6, FCN-8 to run same tests respectively under two different scheduling scenarios. The results are shown in Fig. 3(c). We observe that the larger the model the more obvious the saving cluster network throughput. The method leads to a 12.11%, 14.39% and 18.89% decrease in cluster saving network traffic for FCN-4, FCN-6 and FCN-8 respectively.

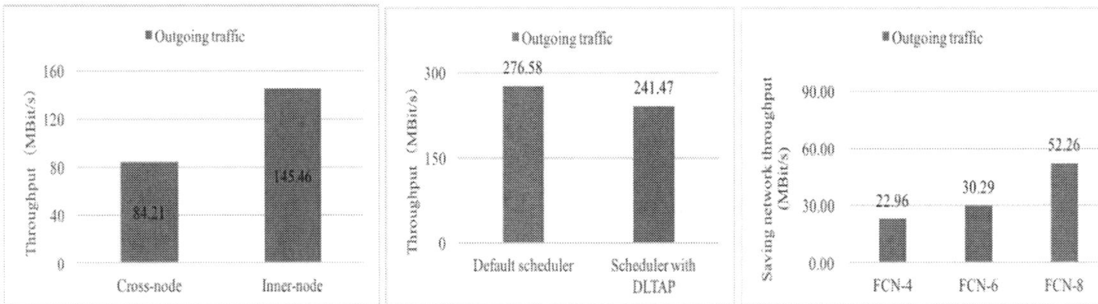

(a) Cross-node and inner-node network throughput comparison. (b) Cluster cross-node network throughput comparison. (c) Saving network throughput comparison.

Figure 3. Network throughput comparison.

Performance on training time. We use FCN-4, FCN-6, FCN-8 respectively to run multiple times in each of two scheduling scenarios. Fig. 4(a) illustrates the training time of different job instances when training steps vary from 0 to 10,000 with an increment of 2000. The results prove that the improved scheduler reduces the training time of the job. The reason is that worker tasks can update the gradients and get new parameters faster after each mini-batch of input data trained.

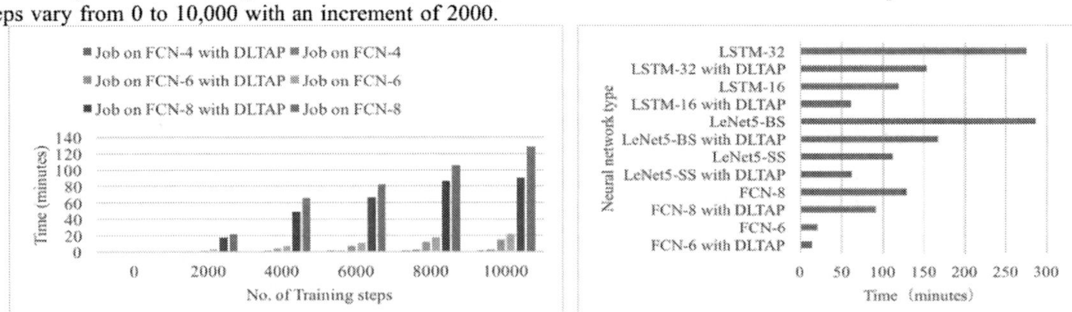

(a) Training time comparison on FCN-4,6,8. (b) Training time comparison on different models.

Figure 4. Training time comparison.

DOI: 10.1051/itmconf/20171203030

Performance on different network model type. We use FCN-4, FCN-6, LeNet5-SS, LeNet5-BS, LSTM-16 and LSTM-32 respectively to test the sensitivity of different types of models to the DLTAP. Fig. 4(b) shows that, in the same training steps, the reduction percentage in training time of LSTM-32, LeNet5-BS and FCN-8 is nearly the same. But the training time of LSTM-32 and LeNet5-BS are far greater than the FCN-8's because their worker tasks need more computation to converge.

Summary

Our work points out a network transmission issue for deep learning workload in the containerized cluster environment. We propose DLTAP to alleviate this issue, in particularly, to decrease cross-node network transmission about parameters by improving the degree of aggregation for ps task and worker task, and confirm its effectiveness and performance by massive experiments. The main contribution is that we consider the types of task running in the container as a crucial scheduling factor. Experiments using a state-of-the-art distributed DNN framework demonstrate that our method can averagely reduce 12% cross-node network traffic, and decrease the DNN training time even on a cluster of 4 low-end servers. Moreover, we find that the larger the model the more significantly it effects. In light of these results, we believe that DLTAP can be used as a significant part of scheduling methods for distributed deep learning workload in containerized cluster environment.

In the future, as worker tasks are inherent compute-intensive, we will investigate and further improve the performance of scheduler by considering the factor of GPUs when perform scheduling decisions.

References

1. J. Dean, G. Corrado, R. Monga, K. Chen, M. Devin, M. Mao, A. Senior, P. Tucker, K. Yang, Q. V. Le, et al. Large scale distributed deep networks. In NIPS, 2012.
2. A. Krizhevsky, I. Sutskever, and G. E. Hinton. ImageNet classification with deep convolutional neural networks. In NIPS, 2012.
3. G. E. Dahl, D. Yu, L. Deng, and A. Acero. Context-dependent pre-trained deep neural networks for large-vocabulary speech recognition. IEEE Transactions on Audio, Speech, and Language Processing, 20(1), 2012.
4. R. Collobert, J. Weston, L. Bottou, M. Karlen, K. Kavukcuoglu, and P. Kuksa. Natural language processing (almost) from scratch. The Journal of Machine Learning Research, 12:2493–2537, Nov. 2011.
5. Li M, Zhou L, Yang Z, et al. Parameter server for distributed machine learning[C]//Big Learning NIPS Workshop. 2013, 6: 2.
6. Chilimbi T, Suzue Y, Apacible J, et al. Project adam: Building an efficient and scalable deep learning training system[C]//11th USENIX Symposium on Operating Systems Design and Implementation (OSDI 14). 2014: 571-582.
7. Abadi M, Agarwal A, Barham P, et al. TensorFlow: Large-scale machine learning on heterogeneous systems, 2015[J]. Software available from tensorflow. org, 2015, 1.
8. Docker Project on https://www.docker.io/, 2014.
9. Verma A, Pedrosa L, Korupolu M, et al. Large-scale cluster management at Google with Borg[C]//Proceedings of the Tenth European Conference on Computer Systems. ACM, 2015: 18.
10. Docker Inc. Docker Swarm. 2015. url: https://github.com/docker/swarm (visited on 01/15/2016).
11. Hindman B, Konwinski A, Zaharia M, et al. Mesos: A Platform for Fine-Grained Resource Sharing in the Data Center[C]//NSDI. 2011, 11: 22-22.
12. Schwarzkopf M, Konwinski A, Abd-El-Malek M, et al. Omega: flexible, scalable schedulers for large compute clusters[C]//Proceedings of the 8th ACM European Conference on Computer Systems. ACM, 2013: 351-364.
13. Marathon on https://mesosphere.github.io/marathon/
14. Kubernetes on http://kubernetes.io, Aug. 2014.
15. Apache Aurora on http://aurora.incubator.apache.org/, 2014.
16. A. Narayanan. Tupperware: containerized deployment at Facebook. http://www.slideshare.net/dotCloud/tupperware-containerized-deployment-at-facebook, June 2014.
17. MNIST on http://yann.lecun.com/exdb/mnist/
18. LeCun, Y., Bottou, L., Bengio, Y., and Haffner, P. 1998. Gradient-based learning applied to document recognition. In Proceedings of the IEEE, 86(11):2278–2324, (Nov. 1998).
19. Y. LeCun, B. Boser, J. S. Denker, D. Henderson, R. E. Howard, W. Hubbard, and L. D. Jackel, "Backpropagation applied to hand- written zip code recognition," Neural computation, vol. 1, no. 4, pp. 541–551, 1989.
20. W. Zaremba, I. Sutskever, and O. Vinyals, "Recurrent neural network regularization," arXiv preprint arXiv:1409.2329, 2014.
21. S.HochreiterandJ. Schmidhuber, "Long short-term memory," Neural computation, vol. 9, no. 8, pp. 1735–1780, 1997.

Co-integration Analysis of Rural Labor Non-agricultural Activities and Household Income

Fan SHI [1,a] Xue-Hui ZHANG [2], and Shu-Wei CHEN [3,b]

[1]*Economics and Management School, Wuhan University, Wuhan, China 43007*
[2]*Dongguan Securities Research Institute, Shenzhen, China 518000*
[3]*School of Public Administration, Henan University of Finance and Economics, Zhengzhou, China 450046*
[a]*afanti525@hotmail.com*, [b]*shuweichen@126.com*

Abstract: The role of non-agricultural activities of rural labors in their household income is a noteworthy topic. This paper focuses on the long-term and stable equilibrium relationship between the two. Based on 1985 - 2012 Statistical Yearbook data, this study conducted corresponding calculation reasoning and co-integration test of the non-agricultural activities of rural labors and their household income, with the results showing: Long-term equilibrium relationship exists between the two, witnessing short-term fluctuations and a trend of short-term fluctuations to long-run equilibrium.

1 Introduction

Labor migration is an important way of rural residents to improve living standards, obtain fair opportunities to compete and transfer from low income to high income. [1]With the migration of rural labors to urban non-agricultural sectors increasingly frequently and regularly, rapid growth of their wages and consequent constant growth of their household income, the rural household income inequality appears. Relationship between the migration of rural labors to urban non-agricultural sectors and their household income and its impact on their household income inequality become noteworthy.

Multiple scholars have made academic researches on the impact of labor migration on the income inequality. Some believe labor migration helps reduce or mitigate income inequality. For example, Li Shi (in 1999)[2] proposed that labor migration could improve their household income, and contribute to inhibiting their income inequality. Cai Fang and Wang Meiyan (in 2009)[3] suggested that the increasing labor migration and growing income inequality structured a paradox due to ignorance or underestimation of the income "resident migrants", namely migratory groups, resulting in underestimation of rural income and exaggeration of urban income. Others believed labor migration might expand rural household income inequality. For example, Yan Haokun and Xu Minghui (in 2008)[4] stated that against the household registration system, namely an "access threshold", in other words, institutional constraints, labor migration expanded instead of reduced income inequality. Zhu Changcun and Ma Jingzhi (in 2009)[5] commented that rural human capital characterized by inner overflow only made competitive human capital workforce obtain high income, making labor migration expand income inequality to certain extent. However, some scholars argued that it was improper to simply conclude labor migration would expand or narrow the income inequality, which should be viewed separately depending on the circumstances. For instance, Liao Xianlang (in 2012)[6] analyzed the reason for synchronous expansion of labor migration and income inequality and suggested labor migration narrowed the income inequality without reflecting its effect against labor migration restrictions and unbalanced regional economic development. Cai Wu and Cheng Xiaojun (in 2012)[7] thought that labor migration and income inequality witnessed benign interaction and simultaneous reduction of relative income of disadvantaged groups, exacerbating the predicament of impoverished poor and low-income groups.

This paper conducts an overall analysis of the relationship between labor migration and income instead of any value judgment. It starts with labor migration, analyzes the relationship between labor migration income effects and household income and the role in rural household income with the co-integration method.

2 Variable Selection, Data Description and Research Methods

2.1 Variable Selection and Data Description

This paper takes rural household annual per capita net

income (RHAPCNI) as the dependent variable, the number of non-agricultural employed rural labors (NNENNERL) and rural household per capita wage income (RHPCWI) as the independent variable. It takes the time series data of 28 year (1985 to 2012) as the sample observations. Based on the data continuity and integrity, it has the data from previous *China Statistical Yearbooks* and takes 1985 as the base year, smoothing out the price fluctuation and eliminating the influence of the price factors.

It is necessary to explain **the measurement of the number of non-agricultural employed rural labors**. In terms of the definition of the number of non-agricultural employed rural labors, the total amount of migrant workers, out-of-town migrant workers and local migrant workers has been announced since 2007, lacking systematic statistics before 2007, sufficient samples, continuity and measurement analysis, and therefore it is necessary to find alternative data. China Statistical Yearbooks indicate the number of employed rural residents and the primary industry employees. The number of urban labors engaged in the primary industry is extremely limited, even negligible. Therefore, this paper takes the difference between the number of employed rural residents and the number of the primary industry employees as the alternative measurement standard for urban labors engaged in non-agricultural secondary and tertiary industries. **In terms of measurement income variables of migrant workers,** based on the consistency with per capita household income variable, this paper takes per capita income of rural household as an alternative, and consequently per capita wage income of rural households as an alternative to the income of migrant workers.

In addition, logarithm taken by the dependent variable and the independent variable can eliminate time-series heteroscedasticity. At the same time, logarithmic transformation of data does not change the original co-integration relationship, achieving a linear trend. In data processing, this paper takes the natural logarithm of the independent variable and the dependent variable respectively: logarithm of rural household per capita wage income (LRHAPCNI), logarithm of the number of non-agricultural employed rural labors (LNNERL) and logarithm of rural household per capita wage income (LRHPCWI), as shown in Table 1:

Table 1. RHAPCNI, NNERL, RHPCWI and natural logarithm of China's rural residents from 1985 to 2012

Year	RHAPCNI	NNERL	RHPCWI	LRHAPCNI	LNNERL	LRHPCWI
1985	397.6	5935	72.2	5.985	8.689	4.279
1986	399.4	6735	76.9	5.990	8.815	4.343
1987	410.4	7337	84.7	6.017	8.901	4.439
1988	411.6	7818	89.0	6.020	8.964	4.489
1989	380.9	7714	86.4	5.943	8.951	4.459
1990	415.7	8794	84.1	6.030	9.082	4.432
1991	419.5	8928	89.9	6.039	9.097	4.499
1992	443.4	9592	104.3	6.094	9.169	4.647
1993	458.5	10866	96.8	6.128	9.293	4.573
1994	492.3	12174	106.0	6.199	9.407	4.663
1995	541.4	13495	121.4	6.294	9.510	4.799
1996	612.6	14208	143.4	6.418	9.562	4.966
1997	648.5	14199	159.7	6.475	9.561	5.073
1998	677.5	13844	179.7	6.518	9.536	5.191
1999	703.3	13214	200.5	6.556	9.489	5.301
2000	717.6	12892	223.7	6.576	9.464	5.410
2001	747.7	12276	243.9	6.617	9.415	5.497
2002	785.4	11481	266.6	6.666	9.348	5.586
2003	818.9	11302	286.8	6.708	9.333	5.659
2004	875.0	12141	297.5	6.774	9.404	5.695
2005	949.0	12816	342.4	6.855	9.458	5.836
2006	1030.5	13407	394.9	6.938	9.504	5.979
2007	1128.5	13637	435.1	7.029	9.521	6.076
2008	1218.5	13538	474.5	7.105	9.513	6.162
2009	1323.0	13616	529.2	7.188	9.519	6.271
2010	1466.9	13487	602.5	7.291	9.509	6.401
2011	1634.4	13912	694.2	7.399	9.541	6.543
2012	1809.1	13829	787.8	7.501	9.535	6.669

Source: Calculated according to China Statistical Yearbooks

2.2 Research Methods

This paper analyzes the relationship between income of non-agricultural employment of rural labors, migrant income and rural household income. According to analysis needs, the following regression model is created:

$$RHAPCNI_t = \beta_0 + \beta_1 NNERL_t + \beta_2 RHPCWI + \mu_t \quad (1)$$

In Formula (1), RHAPCNI represents rural household per capita income, NNERL represents the number of non-agricultural employed rural labors, RHPCWI represents migrant income replaced by per capita wage income, μ represents random error to contain variables the formula does not take into account or unobservable

 DOI: 10.1051/itmconf/20171203031

factors. In order to eliminate lead variance which may exist to conduct quantitative logarithmic conversion at both sides of Formula (1) without altering original time series co-integration relationship, expressed as follow:

$$LRHAPCNI_t = C + \beta_1 LNNERL_t + \beta_2 LRHPCWI_t + \varepsilon_t \quad (2)$$

In Formula (2), C is a constant term.

Specific analysis ideas are as follows:

Firstly, stability test, namely, unit root test of variables, was conducted. This study mainly adopted ADF test.

Secondly, based on the stability test, co-integration test was conducted for long-term and stable equilibrium between variables.

Thirdly, co-integration test is a long-term, balanced and stable relationship test, flawed to short-term equilibrium relationship. Error correction model (ECM) provides a way to examine the co-integrated short-term behavior so as to integrate the long-term relationship and short-term relationship between the variables. Thus, it is necessary to repeat the error correction model analysis.

In the end, Granger causality test was conducted, which is the final variable regression verification.

3 Empirical Test and Result Analysis

Co-integration theory is a quantitative analysis method developed on the basis of time series vector auto-regression analysis outweighing traditional linear regression in terms of statistical stringency and scientificity.

3.1 Variable Stability Test (ADF Test)

In case of time series quantitative analysis, if two or more data are not stable, the regression may be spurious. Normally, spurious regression may be caused by unstable time series, making the regression results distorted[8]. Thus, in case of regression analysis of the time series model, it is necessary to conduct the variable stability test. EViews7.2 was used to conduct ADF test of the original series and first difference analysis. Specific test results are shown in Table 2

Table 2. Stability (ADF) test results

Series	ADF test			
	Inspection type (C, T, L)	ADF statistics	Threshold	Conclusion
LRHAPCNI	(C,T,1)	-1.3951	-3.2335*	Unstable
LNNERL	(C,0,1)	-2.0300	-2.6299*	Unstable
LRHPCWI	(C,T,1)	-1.5639	-3.2292*	Unstable
ΔLRHAPCNI	(C,0,1)	-4.2924	-2.9810**	Stable
ΔLNNERL	(0,0,1)	-2.0809	-1.9550**	Stable
ΔLRHPCWI	(C,0,1)	-3.714	-3.7115***	Stable

Note: Δ represents first order difference; In (C, T, L), C, T, L represents respectively intercept term, trend term and lag order; ADF test lag order is determined by AIC rule, ***, **, * respectively represent significant drop against 1%, 5% and 10%.

The test results shown in Table 2 indicate the original series LRHAPCNI, LNNERL and LRHPCWI surpass the threshold 10% significance level, that is, series value presents unstable characteristics. However, after first order difference, they have their series converted to ΔLRHAPCNI, ΔLNNERL and ΔLRHPCWI. Their ADF test results show that their statistics are less than 5%, 5% and 1% significance threshold, ADF test after difference is stable, namely first order integration, meeting the co-integration test prerequisite.

3.2 Co-integration Test

Although the difference method can eliminate the series instability trend, the converted series often limits the economic issues discussed, even loses its economic significance. To eliminate the above effects, Engle & Granger (in 1987) suggested that the series itself was instable, but its linear combination might be a stable series. The co-integration equation could explain the long-term stable equilibrium relationship between series.

In terms of co-integration equation long-term and stable equilibrium relationship, it is proper to analyze based on 2 test objects: one is co-integration test based on regression coefficients, and this study adopted OLS for regression estimation. The other is co-integration test based on regression residuals, and this study adopted ADF test. As it relates to 3 variables, it is necessary to conduct the co-integration test with the 2 independent variables and the dependent variable respectively. If both are successful, the co-integration equation witnesses a stable equilibrium relationship. The specific test is as follows:

Firstly, co-integration test between variables LRHAPCNI and LNNERL:

The first step, use OLS to estimate co-integration equation of the 2 variables:

$$\mathrm{LRHAPCNI} = -6.2742 + 1.3751\mathrm{LNNERL} \quad (3)$$
$$(-2.7670) \quad (5.6569)$$
$$R^2 = 0.8517 \quad DW = 0.0712 \quad F = 32.0001$$

Formula (3) shows that the t value of various coefficients and equation overall F value are greater than the critical value at 5% level, the single regression coefficient and overall regression equation in the model are both significant. But DW value is only 0.0712. It is necessary to test if LRHAPCNI and LNNERL have long-term co-integration relationship, that is, to have the residual term stability test. If successful, there should be a long-term stable equilibrium relationship between the two series.

The second step, use ADF test to have residuals unit root test, results are shown in Table2

Table 3. Residuals (E_t) stability (ADF) test results

Series	ADF test			
	Test type (C, T, L)	ADF statistics	Threshold	Conclusion
ΔE_t	(0,0,0)	-3.714	-4.8280	Stable

Note: Δ represents first order difference; In (C, T, L), C, T, L, respectively represent intercept term, trend term and lag order; ADF test lag order is determined by AIC rule

Table3 shows, the ADF test statistics of E_t is less than the threshold of significance level 1%, rejecting the null hypothesis, indicating that at 1% significance level there is no unit root, and the residuals are stable, so between variables LRHAPCNI and LNNERL exists long-term stable equilibrium relationship, namely co-integration relationship.

Secondly, Co-integration test between variables LRHAPCNI and LRHPCWI

The same as above, the first step, use OLS to estimate the co-integration equation of the 2 variables:

$$\mathrm{LRHAPCNI} = 3.2188 + 0.6302\mathrm{LRHPCWI} \quad (4)$$
$$(46.5121) \quad (48.5821)$$
$$R^2 = 0.98 \quad DW = 0.5467 \quad F = 2360.223$$

Formula (4) shows that that the t value of various coefficients and equation overall F value are greater than the critical value at 1% level, the single regression coefficient and overall regression equation in the model are both significant. But DW value is only 0.5467. It is necessary to test if LRHAPCNI and LRHPCWI have long-term co-integration relationship, that is, to have the residual term stability test. If successful, there should be a long-term stable equilibrium relationship between the two series.

The second step, use the ADF test to have residuals unit root test, results are shown in Table 4:

Table 4. Residuals (E_t) Stability (ADF) Test Results

Series	ADF test			
	Test type (C, T, L)	ADF statistics	Threshold	Conclusion
E_t	(0,0,0)	-2.7175	-2.6649	Stable steady

Note: Δ represents the first order difference; In (C, T, L), C, T, L, respectively represent intercept term, trend term and the lag order; ADF test lag order is determined by AIC rule.

Table 4 shows, the ADF test statistics of E_t is less than the threshold of significance level 1%, rejecting the null hypothesis, indicating that at 1% significance level there is no unit root, and the residuals are stable, so between variables LRHAPCNI and LNNERL exists long-term stable equilibrium relationship, namely co-integration relationship.

Based on the above analysis, long-term co-integration relationship exists between variables LRHAPCNI, LNNERL and LRHPCWI. Therefore, long-term co-integration relationship exists in the equation established by the 3 variables.

(3) Error correction model (ECM)

The above regression analysis shows that long-term stable equilibrium relationship exists between RHAPCNI, NNERL and RHPCWI, but this relationship is subject to certain short-term imbalance. In order to solve this imbalance, it is necessary to establish ECM containing error correction term[9]。

According to the theory of error correction, it is

proper to establish the appropriate error correction model:

$$\Delta LRHAPCNI_t = \beta_0 - \lambda ECM_{t-1} + \beta_1 \Delta LNNERL_t + \beta_2 \Delta LRHPCWI_t + \varepsilon_t \quad (5)$$

In Formula (5), ECM_{t-1} indicates the error correction term, λ indicates error correction coefficient, β_1 and β_2 represent respectively the independent variable ΔLNNERL , ΔLRHPCWI coefficients, ε_t indicates random disturbance term. This distribution lag model introducing balance error to the first order difference uses OLS to have regression:

$$\Delta LRHAPCNI_t = 0.161 - 0.332ECM_{t-1} + 0.357\Delta LNNERL_t + 0.366\Delta LRHPCWI_t \quad (6)$$

(1.8188) (2.9613) (2.8938)

$$R^2 = 0.5199 \quad D.W. = 2.0178 \quad F = 7.9401$$

Formula (6) shows in terms of the short-term fluctuation rule of LRHAPCNI impacted by LNNERL and LRHPCWI, the fitted value of the model is OK, the regression coefficient t value meets ECM_{t-1} 10% level significance, and the other two variables are 1% level significance. D.W. value is equal to 2.02, indicating absence of self-correlation. Error correction coefficient is negative, in line with the reverse correction mechanism. The model suggests that in the long run, some long-term stable equilibrium relationship exists between NNERL, RHPCWI and RHAPCNI. When short-term fluctuation deviates from the long-term stable equilibrium, equilibrium state will be recovered at the speed 0.332.

(4) Granger Causality Test

The above analysis shows long-term stable equilibrium relationship exists between the per capita net income of rural households and the number of non-agricultural employed rural labors and rural households per capita wage income, but does this balance have any causal relationship? It is to be verified yet. This section intends to take Granger causality test to test whether there is any causal relationship between these variables. The results are as follows:

Table 5. Granger Causality Test Results

The null hypothesis	Lag period	F- statistics	Prob.	Conclusion
LNNERL is not LRHAPCNI Granger causality	2	3.5614	0.0466	Refused
LRHAPCNI is not LNNERL Granger causality	2	1.295	0.2955	Accepted
LRHPCWI is not LRHAPCNI Granger causality	4	2.8105	0.0635	Refused
LRHAPCNI is not LRHPCWI Granger causality	4	5.1459	0.0082	Refused

Table 5 shows in case of Lag Period 2, LNNERL is LRHAPCNI Granger causality, LRHAPCNI is not LNNERL Granger causality, which shows the impact of non-agricultural employed rural labors on per capita net income of rural households is larger, but in turn the impact of the per capita income of rural households on employment of rural labors is not significant. In case of Lag Period 4, LRHAPCNI and LRHPCWI witness two-way Granger causality, showing the per capita net income of rural households and rural household per capita wage income have two-way effect relationship.

4 Summary and Implications

Based on related data of China Statistical Yearbook from 1985 to 2012, adopting the co-integration theory, this paper makes an empirical analysis of the long-term balance and equilibrium relationship between the per capita net income of rural households, the number of non-agricultural employed rural labors and rural household per capita wage income and their mutual influences. The results show:

The long-term equilibrium relationship exists between rural household per capita net income, non-agricultural employed rural labors and per capita wage income of rural households, but witnessing the short term fluctuations which are adjusted to long-run equilibrium. The relationship between per capita rural household income and non-agricultural employed rural labors is: The impact of non-agricultural employed rural labors on rural household per capita income is significant while the impact of rural household per capita income on non-agricultural employed rural labors is not obvious. A two-way Granger causality exists between per capita household income of rural labors and rural household per capita wage income, and the impact at 10% level is significant.

It can give us the following policy implications: First, it is necessary to accelerate non-agricultural employment of rural labors, and improve the income of rural households. Constant and rapid income increase of rural households is bound to have an important positive impact on income of rural households, which requires further elimination of institutional barriers to non-agricultural employment of rural labors, facilitating non-agricultural employment of rural labors. Second, it is necessary to enhance wage income proportion in rural household income, increase investment in human capital in rural

DOI: 10.1051/itmconf/20171203031

areas, reduce non-agricultural employment cost, guarantee wages of migrant workers and improve the income of rural labors comprehensively.

Summary

The role of non-agricultural activities of rural labors in their household income is a noteworthy topic. This paper focuses on the long-term and stable equilibrium relationship between the two. Based on 1985 - 2012 Statistical Yearbook data, this study conducted corresponding calculation reasoning and co-integration test of the non-agricultural activities of rural labors and their household income, with the results showing: Long-term equilibrium relationship exists between the two, witnessing short-term fluctuations and a trend of short-term fluctuations to long-run equilibrium.

References

1. Sun Sanbai, Huang Wei, Hong Junjie: Why free labor migration is so important? - Based on the perspective of intergenerational income mobility [J] Economic Research, 2012 (5): 147 - 159
2. Li Shi, Chinese rural labor migration and income growth and distribution [J] Chinese Social Sciences, 1999 (2): 16 - 33
3. Cai Fang and Wang Meiyan, Why does labor migration fail to reduce urban and rural inequality [J] Economic Perspectives, 2009 (8): 4 - 10
4. Yan Haokun and Xu Minghui. Rural labor migration and regional economic inequality [J]. Agricultural Economy, 2008 (6)
5. Zhu Changcun and Ma Jingzhi, Generalized spillover of urban rural human capital and economic inequality [J]. China Rural Survey, 2009 (4)
6. Liao Xianlang, Research on rural labors migration and urban-rural income inequality [J] population and economy, 2012 (6): 16 - 52
7. Cai Wu and Cheng Xiaojun, Urban and rural labor migration, urban employment and income disparities - Theoretical and Empirical Study [J]. Economics and Management, 2012 (12)
8. Chen Shuwei and Zhang Heping. Empirical Analysis of the Relationship between Urban and Rural Residents Consumption, Government Consumption and Economic Growth in Qinghai Province, 2013 (6): 137 – 133
9. Xu Hangzhou and Guo Yuyan, Co-integration Analysis of Rural Non-agricultural Income and Rural Land Circulation [J]. Population of China. Resources and Environment, 2011 (6): 61-66

Optimization Method of Fusing Model Tree into Partial Least Squares

Fang YU[a], Jian-Qiang DU[*], Bin NIE[b], Jing XIONG, Zhi-Peng ZHU, and Lei LIU

School of Computer, Jiangxi University of Traditional Chinese Medicine, Nanchang, 330004, China
[a]eshter_yuu1992@163.com, [b]460092757@qq.com
** Corresponding author: jianqiang_du@163.com*

Abstract: Partial Least Square (PLS) can't adapt to the characteristics of the data of many fields due to its own features multiple independent variables, multi-dependent variables and non-linear. However, Model Tree (MT) has a good adaptability to nonlinear function, which is made up of many multiple linear segments. Based on this, a new method combining PLS and MT to analysis and predict the data is proposed, which build MT through the main ingredient and the explanatory variables(the dependent variable) extracted from PLS, and extract residual information constantly to build Model Tree until well-pleased accuracy condition is satisfied. Using the data of the maxingshigan decoction of the monarch drug to treat the asthma or cough and two sample sets in the UCI Machine Learning Repository, the experimental results show that, the ability of explanation and predicting get improved in the new method.

1 Introduction

In real life, some actual processes are complex nonlinear processes, the nonlinear relationship reflects not only between independent variable and the independent variables, but also between independent variable and dependent variable[1]. Since the experiment and some objective or non-objective factors, it usually results in small data sample set, and some sample data size is even less than the sample dimension. PLS[2] was first proposed by Herman Wold, including principal component analysis (PCA),Canonical Correlation Analysis(CCA) and Multiple Linear Regression(MLR). It has a good explanatory power for the data with multiple independent variables[3], multiple dependent variables and a small sample size, however the nature of linear regression in PLS can not completely reflect the characteristic of the traditional Chinese medicine data.

In 1996, Qin S.J. [4] proposed a RBF neural network combined with PLS, which can establish a good nonlinear prediction model, while it's hard to explain the characteristic for its linear approximation to continuous function. Paper [5] proposed an algorithm with fuzzy neural network model embedded into the iterative PLS, and achieved good nonlinear mapping effect, but the results of the model is vulnerable to membership function. In 2013, paper[6] proposed a Kernel Partial Least Squares Method, which mapped the nonlinear data to high dimension linear space with the help of kernel function, to extract the relationship between dependent variables and independent variables as much as possible, the method can well reflect the nonlinear structure contained in sample data, however, choosing a good kernel function is extremely difficult.

Model Tree[7] is an algorithm proposed by Quinlan, which the leaf node adopt multiply linear function instead of the average processing method in traditional regression tree, it is constructed by several multiply linear pieces, and has a piecewise linear approximation to any unknown variable distribution trend, not only is the model structure simple, but also easy to explain the nonlinear data, with high efficiency and good robustness. Based on this, to make up the defect of the linear nature in PLS method within the model, it uses MT as the internal model in PLS to interpret the nonlinear characteristics in TCM data.

2 Partial Least Square(PLS)

Partial Least Square algorithm can not only build regression model for data with multi-independent variables, dependent variables, but also adapts to the situation when sample sizes are less than variables numbers[8].

The introduction of PLS is as follows:

To make the explanation easy, assume there are independent variables set $X=(x_1,x_2,\cdots,x_i,\cdots,x_p)$ and dependent variables set $Y=(y_1,y_2,\cdots,y_j,\cdots,y_q)$. t, u are the linear weight combination of independent variables and dependent variables, and they must satisfy the two conditions below: ①try to carry variance information of independent variables and dependent variables respectively as soon as possible; ②the correlation coefficient between the two is largest.

Extracted first principle component information from

X, Y as t_1, u_1, then make the t_1, u_1 do multiply linear regression, judge the residual information ,if satisfy the requirements, then terminate the process, else continue to extract principle component information from the residual information, the above procedure continues until satisfactory accuracy is achieved.

3 Model Tree(MT)

Model Tree(MT)[9] adopt multiply linear regression rather than the average processing method in leaf node like traditional classification and regression tree(CART). It divides the sample data into several discrete areas according to certain rules and choose a suitable model to construct a regression model for the areas. the model includes: tree building, searching for splitting attributes, handling internal nodes, pruning, smoothing, and prediction. The detailed introduction about how to build Model Tree browse paper[10-11].

4 MTree-PLS

4.1 The Algorithm Flow for MTree-PLS

MTree-PLS is formed by two modular: one is PLS, to extract principle component and to eliminate multiple variable correlation, the other is MTree, to establish the relationship between independent variables and dependent variables and to make the model nonlinear. MTree-PLS is built over the traditional partial Least Square(PLS), the external model still adopt the original method to extract principle component t, the internal model build Model Tree with the extracted principle components and dependent variables, then do multiply linear regression in leaf nodes of Model Tree, and get the predicted value, if the residual information satisfy the pre-defined condition, stop to build tree, else ,continue to build Model Tree by the residual information till satisfied accuracy obtained.

The process of the MTree-PLS algorithm is as follows.

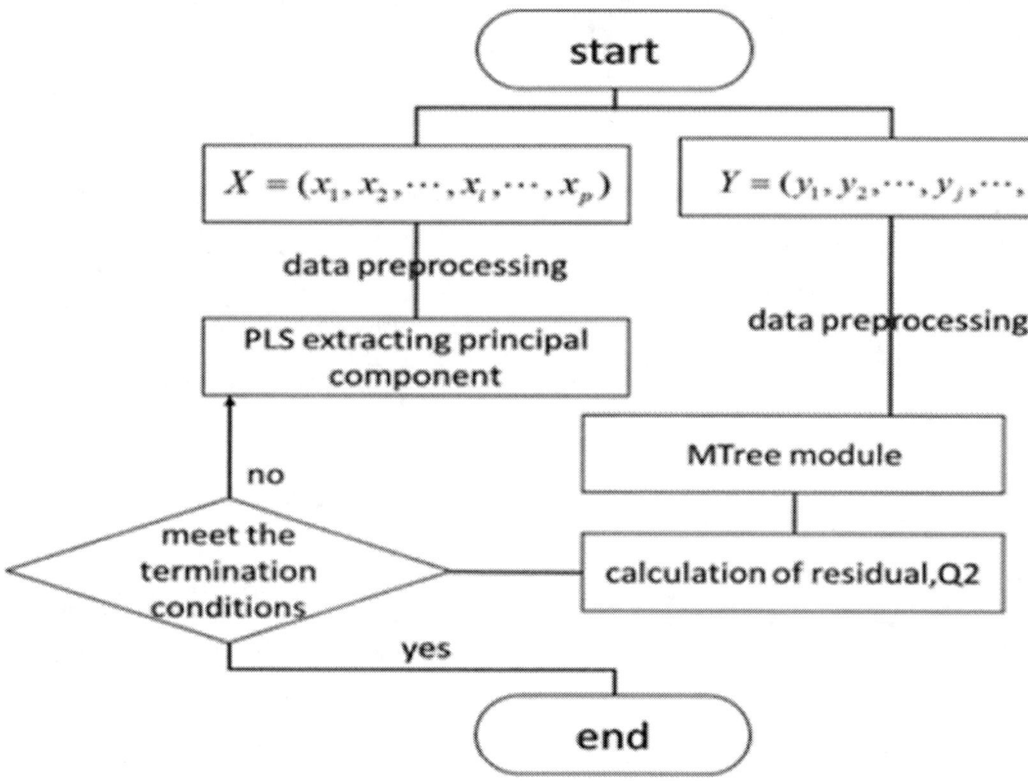

Figure 1. the process of the MTree-PLS algorithm

4.2 An Algorithm for Constructing Model Tree of Principal Components

The method for using Principal Components to construct Model Tree is to build Model Tree through Principal Components t_1 extracted from independent variable by PLS and the original dependent variable Y. Due to the t_1's linear characteristics, it can find the best split point by calculating the error of multiply linear regression between t_1 and Y, then split the t_1 into two subset according to the best split node, continue to split the subset in the manner above till the number of leaf nodes is less than the threshold predefined or the error fluctuation is not that obvious. The algorithm for using Principal Components to construct Model Tree shows in algorithm 1.

Algorithm 1: using Principal Components to build Model Tree

Input: principal component t, the attributeListY
Output: the built Model Tree RT
Step01 construct the basic regression tree RT.
Step02 Search for splitting attributes.
search the splitting attribute of the subtree to internal nodes in RT, then make them form a set, which is called regression attributes.
Step03 Handles the internal nodes
select the current node data samples and part or all of its regression attributes to regression, traverse the current regression model, choose the regression model with the least error of the current sample data, as a regression model of the current node.
Step04 pruning
Traversing from bottom to top for RT, record all the leaf nodes
Build linear fitting regression equation f_{parent}, f_{leaf} respectively for each parent node and leaf node.
if $f_{parent}RMSE < f_{leaf}RMSE < f_{leaf}RMSE$
Pruning for the subtree
else preserve the leaf node
In particular, if the subtree 's parent node is the root, no pruning operation.
end
Step05 Smoothing
Traversing from bottom to up for the RT
Combine the fitting function of the child nodes and parent nodes into a new linear function,

$$f_{new} = \frac{n \cdot f_{child} + k \ f_{parent}}{n+k} \quad (1)$$

if $f_{new}RMSE - f_{child}RESE < Q$., (Q is the fixed threshold)
$f_{child} \to f_{new}$.
else no smoothing is performed
end
Step06 return RT
End of the algorithm

Introduction: RMSE is the Root Mean Square Error, expressed as follows

$$RMSE = \sqrt{\frac{\sum_{i=1}^{n}(f_{obj,i} - T_{model,i})^2}{n}} \quad (2)$$

In the formula (1), n is the number of sample data of current father node, k[12] is a smoothing constant(defaults k=15), f_{child} and f_{parent} are a fitting function of current leaf nodes and current parent nodes respectively, f_{new} is a fitting function under smoothing.

4.3 Fusing Model Tree into Partial Least Squares

MTree-PLS get the principal components t_1 by using PLS, then adopt t_1 to do multiply linear regression with X, and meanwhile build MT with Y and t_1, it still employs the original PLS to get residual information of X, and the residual information of Y is the disparity between Y and the predicted $\hat{Y}$ which is the regression values by the leaf nodes of Model Tree. If not meet the accuracy requirements, then continue to extract the main component by using residual information and use the principal component and the residual information of Y to continue to build trees. Repeat the above procedure, terminating the algorithm until a nonlinear model with satisfactory precision is constructed.

The detailed steps are as follows:

(1) Data preprocessing
normalizing X,Y, to obtain E_0 and F_0;

(2) Extracting principal component
t_1 is the first principal component extracted from E_0, existing $t_1 = E_0 w_1$., $u_1 = F_0 v_1$., w_1, v_1 is respectively the weight of E_0 and F_0, and $\|w_1\|=1$, $\|v_1\|=1$., make:

$$\begin{aligned} &\mathrm{var}(t_1) \to \max \\ &\mathrm{var}(u_1) \to \max \\ &r(t_1,u_1) \to \max \end{aligned} \quad (3)$$

According to the $\mathrm{cov}(t_1,u_1) = r(t_1,u_1)\sqrt{\mathrm{var}(t_1)\mathrm{var}(u_1)}$ $\Rightarrow \mathrm{cov}(t_1,u_1) \to \max$.,

and $\mathrm{cov}(t_1,u_1) = \frac{1}{n} < t_1, u_1 >$., plug $t_1 = E_0 w_1$., $u_1 = F_0 v_1$. in this, then:

$$\max < E_0 w_1, F_0 v_1 > = (E_0 w_1)^T (F_0 v_1) \quad \max \quad (4)$$

According to the principle of Lagrange multiplier, respectively calculated w_1、v_1 are the eigenvectors corresponding to the largest eigenvalue of $X^T Y Y^T X$ and $Y^T X X^T Y$. Thus, it is easy to calculate the corresponding t_1.

(3) Regression of the principal component model tree
Extracted principal components t_1 from E_0 ,implements the linear regression about E_0 to t_1, $E_0 = t_1 p_1' + E_1$, whereby $p_1 = E_0^T t_0 / \|t_1\|^2$. Due to t_1 carry the information of dependent and independent variables, and will make t_1 and $F_0(j)$, (j=1, 2, 3, . . . q) build model tree $tree(1j)$ separately, and calculates the corresponding prediction coefficient $predict(t_{1j})$ of the model and residual information matrix $E_1 = E_0 - t_1 p_1'$, $F_1 = F_0 - \sum_{j=1}^{q} t_1 * predict(t_{1j})$.

(4) Judge the condition, stop the cycle operation
It can be judged whether the model satisfied the precision requirement according to the explanation of the model(R^2) or the Sum of Residual Squares of training set (SSETrain). if satisfy the condition, stop counting, if not,

then using residual messages E_1、F_1,follow the steps(2), until meet the conditions.

(5) Integrating the equation of MTree-PLS

$$F=\sum_{j=1}^{q} t_1.predict(t_{1j})+\sum_{j=1}^{q} t_2.predict(t_{2j})+L+\sum_{j=1}^{q} t_m.predict(t_{mj}) \quad (5)$$

The standardized for coefficients and reduction multiple regression equation of Y to X.

The algorithm of Fusing Model Tree into Partial Least Squares as follows:

Algorithm 2: the algorithm of Fusing Model Tree into Partial Least Squares

Input: The original sample data(Dataset(D)), the property list of independent variable: attributeList X_{n*p}, dimension: p, the property list of dependent variable: attributeList Y_{n*q}, dimension: p.

Output: equation of MTree-PLS

Step01: Extracting the attributeListX, attributeListY as (X,Y) from the original data, and Standardized the (X,Y) as (E_0,F_0)

Step02: partial least squares regression(PLSR)

$i=1$

while judge the number i of the principal component satisfying the requirements or not

Based on the Lagrange principle to get weight coefficient w_i, v_i

Calculate the maximum eigenvector w_i、v_i corresponding to the maximum eigenvalue of matrix $F_{i-1}^{'}E_{i-1}E_{i-1}^{'}F_{i-1}$ and $F_{i-1}^{'}E_{i-1}E_{i-1}^{'}F_{i-1}$

Calculate the score vector $t_i=E_{i-1}w_i$ and build tree $tree$(i)

Get the corresponding predicting coefficient $predict(t_{ij}),(j=1,2L\ q)$

Regression equation $E_{i-1}=t_ip_i^T+E_i$ and $F_{i-1}=F_i+\sum_{j=1}^{q} t_i.predict(t_{i,j})$

Load vector $p_i=X_{i-1}^Tt_i/\|t_i\|^2$

Get the residual information matrix E_i and F_i

i=i+1

end

Step03

Integration the equation of MTree-PLS

$$F=\sum_{j=1}^{q} t_1.predict(t_{1j})+\sum_{j=1}^{q} t_2.predict(t_{2j})+L+\sum_{j=1}^{q} t_m.predict(t_{mj}) \quad (6)$$

Anti-standardized to the coefficient of the equation, and get the equation of the Y and X.

Step04 end

5 Experimental Analysis

The experimental data is from the key laboratory of Modern Preparation of TCM, Ministry of Education in Jiangxi University of Traditional Chinese medicine, which supports us with the precious data of maxingshigan decoction of the monarch drug to treat the asthma or cough, the paper still choose another two sample sets in the UCI Machine Learning Repository, namely yacht_hydrodynamics[13] and CCPP_Folds5x2_pp[14] to testify the improved algorithm.

5.1 The Explaining about the Experimental Data

The part of data about maxingshigan decoction of the monarch drug to treat the asthma(mxsgpc) showed in Table 1, has a total of 46 samples. it is about the impact of pharmacological indicators about the blood medicine composition in rats under 10 distinct dosage of herbal ephedra respectively. There are five compositions about the blood medicine composition in rats, There are two pharmacological indicators namely, incubation period (Unit: s) and cough duration (Unit: min). The first five compositions is the independent variable, the rest two is dependent variable.

Table 1. the data of maxingshigan decoction of the monarch drug to treat the asthma

ephedrine	pseudoephedrine	methylephedrine	wild black cherry glycosides	licorice glycosides	incubation period(s)	cough duration (min)
0.93	0.52	0.14	0.00	0.51	79	8
0.97	0.48	0.16	0.34	0.53	51	18
0.95	0.53	0.17	1.67	0.48	44	22
0.92	0.59	0.39	0.00	0.57	66	9
1.09	0.43	0.41	0.00	0.42	71	19
…	…		…	…	…	…

The part of data about maxingshigan decoction of the monarch drug to treat the cough(mxsgzk) showed in Table 2, has a total of 62 samples. it is about the impact of pharmacological indicators about the blood medicine composition in rats under 10 distinct dosage of almond respectively. There are five compositions about the blood medicine composition in rats There are one pharmacological indicators namely, cough times. The first five compositions is the independent variable, the rest one is dependent variable.

 DOI: 10.1051/itmconf/20171203032

Table 2. the data of maxingshigan decoction of the monarch drug to treat the cough

ephedrine	pseudoephed rine	methyl ephedrine	amygdalin	wild black cherry glycosides	cough times
402.00	369.93	48.46	0.79	1.87	25
491.00	385.79	47.32	0.00	0.00	50
412.00	314.74	41.28	0.00	0.00	35
519.00	316.81	39.50	0.61	1.42	37
387.09	290.05	15.29	0.81	3.17	40
...	...	...	...	...	...

The description of yacht_of hydrodynamics(yacht) and CCPP_Folds5x2_pp(CCPP) shows in http://archive.ics.uci.edu/ml/.

5.2 Analysis of the Procedure and Result of the Experimental

To validate the effect of the new model, it adopt the traditional PLS and Random Forests Regression (RFR) as a contrast. Based on this, it divides the original data randomly in the proportion of 7:3, 70% of them are training set and the rest are test set and adopts the experimental data of maxingshigan decoction of the monarch drug to treat the asthma or cough and two sample sets in the UCI Machine Learning Repository to compare.

Table 3. Description of the experimental data

data name	sample number	independent variables number	dependent variables number	train sample number	test sample number
maxingshigan decoction cure asthma	46	5	2	32	14
maxingshigan decoction cure cough	62	5	1	43	19
yacht_hydrodynamics	308	7	1	216	92
CCPP_Folds5x2_pp	9568	4	1	6700	2868

Table 4. The result among PLS、RFR and MPTree – PLS

	PLS		MPTree-PLS		RFR	
	SSETrain	SSETest	SSETrain	SSETest	SSETrain	SSETest
maxingshigan decoction cure asthma	20580.6507	30434.7553	7485.3271	14618.4831	2184.2919	21114.3382
maxingshigan decoction cure cough	3841.8357	1761.1864	1568.5878	1653.9989	3558.0025	1777.0677
yacht_hydrodynamics	15990.5122	8151.6082	455.5790	1400.0808	8706.8571	4900.1754
CCPP_Folds5x2_pp	161316.0535	70113.7642	128136.5498	59418.3421	145551.7916	64731.8109

Review the Sum of Squares for Error of Training Set(SSETrain), Sum of Squares for Error of Testing Set(SSETest) separately. The result is as follow. It can be seen clearly in the figure below:

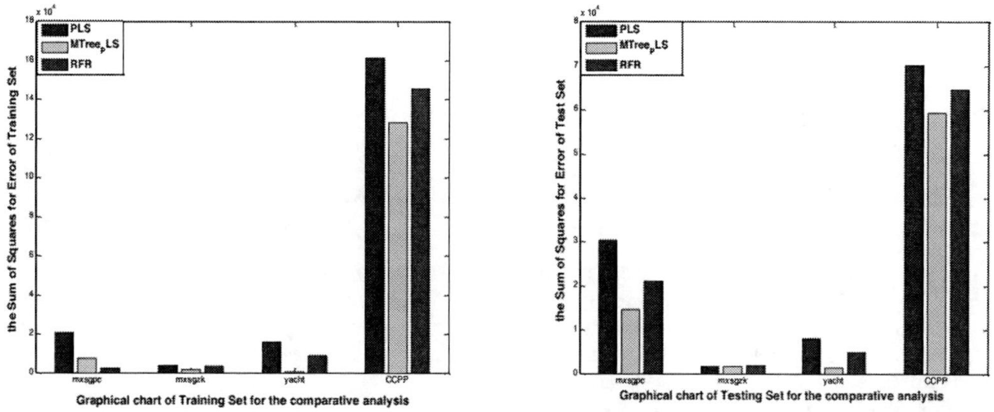

Figure 2. Graphical chart for the comparative analysis

From Table 4 and Fig 2, we can see the four points below:

Firstly, PLS has a poor ability of explanation and prediction to nonlinear data and shows obvious inadaptability than the improved PLS.

Secondly, No matter SSETrain or SSETest in the data of maxingshigan decoction cure asthma or cough, yacht_hydrodynamics and CCPP_Folds5x2_pp, compared with PLS and RFR algorithm, the improved PLS has different level of good effect.

Thirdly, although the SSETrain of the improved algorithm is not so well than the RFR', but the prediction ability of RFR is poor in evidence.

Last, the improved PLS method not only has good adapt ability to TCM data, but also has good adapt ability to UCI'S nonlinear data with middle or huge level sample.

In summary, the Model Tree shows a strong analytical and predictive effect for multidimensional nonlinear data. whether it is for small or large sample data, in the degree of interpretation of the model, or the analysis and prediction of data, The improved algorithm is superior to the PLS and the RFR.

5.3 The analysis of the Algorithm's Time Complexity

For the PLS, the time complexity is mainly expressed in the principal component extraction. Since the eigenvalues and eigenvectors can be solved by the singular value matrix, only the covariance matrix exists in the time complexity, and the time complexity is $O(n^2)$. For the model tree, the time complexity is mainly reflected in the part of the tree built, as $O(n^2)$. For the improved algorithm, it is assumed that the number of the principal components extracted is m, and each time a tree is built when extracting a principal component, so the time complexity of the improved algorithm is $O(mn^2)$.

Summary

To deal with Partial Least Squares can't well explain nonlinear data, the thesis put forward Fusing Model Tree into Partial Least Squares. The Partial Least Square make full use of the nonlinear characteristic that the regression model constructed by model tree is formed by many multiple linear segments and after a series of experiments, the conclusion shows the improved algorithm can well explain the level of the model and have more accurate prediction ability. However, the number of leaf node directly decide the calculate result of model. Thus, what we should study further is to choose appropriate leaf node.

Acknowledgement

This work is supported by the Key Laboratory of modern preparation of Traditional Chinese Medicine (TCM), Ministry of Education and two National Natural Science Foundations (61363042 & 61562045). This research also is supported by a major project of Jiangxi Natural Science Foundation (20152ACB20007) and the Postgraduate innovation fund of Jiangxi University of Traditional Chinese Medicine(JZYC16S05).

References

1. Zhang Boli, Wang Yongyan. Components compatibility theory and practice of development of modern Chinese medicine prescriptions, the key scientific issues of basic research [M]. Shenyang: liaoning science and technology press, 2010.
2. Wold H. Nonlinear estimate by iterative least squares procedures. Research Papers in Statistics, 1966, Wiley, New York.
3. Abdi H, Williams L. Partial Least Squares Methods: Partial Least Squares Correlation and Partial Least Square Regression [M]. Reisfeld B, Mayeno A N, Humana Press, 2013: 930, 549-579.
4. Qin S J, McAoy T J. Nonlinear FIR modeling via a neural net PLS approach. Computer & Chemical Engineering, 1996, 20(2):147-159.
5. Zhou Lin. Feature extraction method based on nonlinear PLS research [D]. Nanjing university of

science and technology, 2011.
6. Liu Yu. The modeling and simulation of the response surface based on local kernel PLS method [D]. Tsinghua university, 2013.
7. Quinlan J R. Learning with continuous classes[C]. Proceedings of the 5th Australian joint Conference on Artificial Intelligence. Singapore, 1992.
8. Abdi H, Williams L.Partial Least Squares Methods:Partial Least Squares Correlation and Partial Least Square Regression[M].Reisfeld B,Mayeno A N, Humana Press,2013: 930, 549-579.
9. Gu Yayun, Hu Linxian. The application of M5 model tree in thermal power plant load optimization [J]. Energy saving technology. 2013, 31(5): 426-429.
10. Frank E, Wang Y, Inglis S, et al. Using Model Trees for Classification[J]. Machine Learning, 1998, 32(1):63-76.
11. Wang Y, Witten I H. Induction of model trees for predicting continuous classes. Working paper 96/23[C] 1997.
12. Malerba D, Appice A, Bellino A et al. Stepwise Induction of Model Trees.[C] Congress of the Italian Association for Artificial Intelligence on Advances in Artificial Intelligence. Springer-Verlag, 2001:20-32.
13. UCI Machine Learning Repository[Z],[2013-01-03]. http://archive.ics.uci.edu/ml/datasets/Yacht+Hydrodynamics.
14. UCI Machine Learning Repository[Z],[2014-03-26]. http://archive.ics.uci.edu/ml/datasets/Combined+Cycle+Power+Plant.

ITM Web of Conferences 12, 03033 (2017) DOI: 10.1051/itmconf/20171203033
ITA 2017

An Interactive Modeling Method of 3D Model Based on National Cultural Resource Database

Chuan-Ming SUN[a], Song-Yin ZHENG[b,*], Guo-Xin TAN[c], and Wen-Yuan ZHANG[d]

National Research Center of Cultural Industries, Central China Normal University, Wuhan 430079, China
[a]cms@mail.ccnu.edu.cn, [b]zhengsongyin@126.com [c]gxtan@mail.ccnu.edu.cn, [d]wenyuanzhang@126.com
**Corresponding author: zhengsongyin@126.com*

Abstract: Aiming at solving the problems of low efficiency and complicated operation of 3D modeling in the process of virtual product development of national culture, this paper discusses a synthesis approach of surface geometry model based on data-driven. Firstly, a shape-based matching algorithm is used to retrieve the corresponding components in the database. Secondly, a new model will be generated through segmenting and assembling these components. Finally, this approach is applied to construct 3D model of scenes and characters in ancient Badong town. The application shows that this approach can generate the geometric model of characters and scenes efficiently and economically in cultural activities.

1 Introduction

Virtual 3D reconstructions of destroyed or disappeared cultural heritage can display the cultural activities to viewers effectively. For example, Selma Rizvić present their work on interactive virtual cultural heritage applications with storytelling and show how users appreciate this presentation form, considering it as breathing life into 3D geometry[1].Athanasios Voulodimos presents a system designed and developed for the 3D reconstruction of cultural heritage assets based on photogrammetry and clustering[2]. But these approaches also either need a large amount of time to construct the database or have more complicated steps.

This paper discusses a modeling method of data-driven geometry model by reassembling the components of existing 3D models in the resource database to create new models. First of all, a component matching algorithms in database is designed. Second, an optimization algorithm for surface model alignment is used. Third, an intelligent grid cutting algorithm is discussed. Finally, based on the 3D model data of the cultural resource database, this approach is applied to construct the 3D model of scenes and characters in ancient Badong town which was existed in Song dynasty.

2 Modeling Method of 3D Model Based on Resource Database

In the modeling of virtual cultural products, the most important problem is the construction of realistic virtual scene and role model. In this paper, the 3D modeling method is divided into three categories, for example, primitive construction method, model reconstruction method and sample interpolation synthesis method[3]. The method of primitive construction mainly adopts the traditional modeling software (Maya, 3Ds Max, etc.) for interactive editing of 3D model, which requires creators to have higher creativity and use software expertly. As the result, the efficiency is not high; Model reconstruction methods focus on a certain information based on a particular human body or scene for geometric reconstruction, information sources include photos, video, 3D scanning, which requires higher information of shape information. The sample interpolation synthesis method needs to construct the sample database before, and then realize parameterized feature of the reconstructed 3D model. Finally, the 3D model can be generated by mapping the characteristic parameters to the model geometry. This method has high modeling efficiency, but the structure of the sample database is complicated. By the geographical, historical and cultural factors, there is a big difference in modeling of characters and activity scenes in different cultural activities. In order to realize the rapid and efficient modeling of the virtual product model of the national culture, a 3D model modeling method is designed based on the national cultural resource database, which integrates the 3D model geometric representation and modeling method.

DOI: 10.1051/itmconf/20171203033

2.1 Component Retrieval

The retrieval methods of 3D model can be divided into text-based retrieval and content-based retrieval. Text-based retrieval has matured, but the text is difficult to fully describe the complex 3D model. Content-based retrieval is automatic retrieval based on the actual content (geometry, topology, etc.) of a 3D model. The core is to extract a set of features to represent the 3D model, and then to retrieve the model by comparing its eigenvalues[4]. The existing algorithms of this method can be divided into three categories:(1)shape-based retrieval techniques, such as the shape distribution algorithm proposed by Osada[5]; (2) topological structure-based retrieval techniques, such as Hilaga's Reeb graph topology matching method; (3) Based on the comparison of image retrieval technology, such as 2D contour comparison method based on 3D model proposed by Funkhouser[6] .

The 3D models of national culture need higher shape fidelity, Osada's shape distribution method is used in this section. That is, by calculating the probability distribution of the model data, a description of the shape distribution of the models which are obtained. Since the shape distribution method is based on a large number of statistical data, it can satisfy the scaling invariant, rotation invariant, translation invariant and symmetric invariant, and is robust to noise, resampling and simplification. Using a large number of samples, the Euclidean distance of any two points on the surface of the 3D model is calculated (as shown in Fig.1 for a cross-sectional distance of a column model). Using these data, the model features can be described by the shape distribution data.

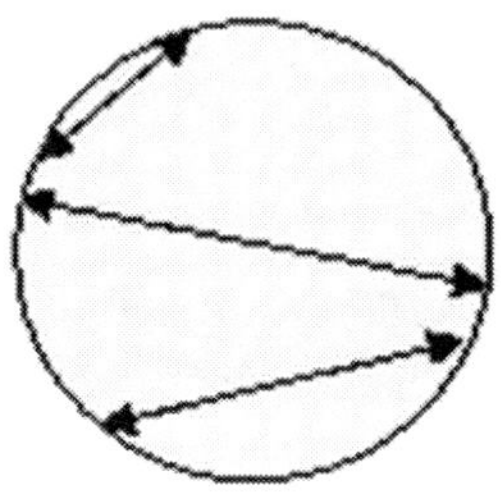

Figure 1. D2 distance of column cross-section

In this section, f and g are used to express the probability distributions of the two models respectively, $\hat{f}$ and $\hat{g}$ are used to express the distribution functions of the two models, $\hat{f}(x)=\int_{-\infty}^{x} f$, $\hat{g}(x)=\int_{-\infty}^{x} g$. Then the Minkowski L N distance of the probability distribution of the two models is $D(f,g)=(\int|f-g|^{N})^{1/N}, N=0,1,\infty$; The Minkowski LN distance of the distribution function is $D(f,g)=(\int|\hat{f}-\hat{g}|^{N})^{1/N}, N=0,1,\infty$ and similar model matching is performed by comparing the distance.

2.2 Component Segmentation

The components are sub-blocks of 3D models. There are many different method to display 3D models, and grid have become an important representations of 3D models [7]. At present, there are some 3D grid segmentation algorithms include watershed algorithm, grid representation based on entity representation, grid segmentation based on topology information and hierarchical decomposition based on fuzzy clustering. The interactive segmentation method can adjust the model segmentation in real time and improve the success rate of component acquisition. The existing 3D model interactive segmentation methods include: segmentation of 3D models using commercial modeling tools. By selecting the sequence vertices on the model surface grid and segmenting the model along the shortest path between them.

a The model to be split

b Mark line

c Segmentation component

d Target component

Figure 2. Segmentation of 3D Model

According to the interactive segmentation method based on minimum cut in image domain, a simple and efficient interactive segmentation method is proposed by Zhao Mingxi[8]. First of all, the user only need to enter two groups or one group of mark lines on the screen which represent the background or objects, the system imposed some constraints. Then, a minimal cut algorithm with hard constraints is used to obtain the initial segmentation result on the simplified grid. Finally, the results are mapped back to the original grid, using the global optimal minimum cut algorithm to smooth the split results. It contains three steps which are shown in Fig.2:

(1)Grid simplification: This step is only used for the grid which has millinons of triangles. The first step is to simplify the grid. Because the quadratic grid simplification algorithm have features of good algorithm complexity and feature preserving, this algorithm is used to simplify the grid with large amount of data.

(2) Segmentation from the simplified grid: Using a screen-based interactive interface, users can easily specify a representative triangle on a simplified grid. Using these representative triangles as hard constraints, using this algorithm to find the best segmentation. For the results of the segmentation, the user can continue to adjust the results by adding triangles.

(3) Smooth cutting: the cutting edge is usually very rough when mapping cutting results from the simplified grid back to the original grid. On this basis, the traditional minimum cut algorithm will be used to smooth the cutting results.

2.3 Component Assembly

After getting the model component, how to automatically assemble into a new model is also an urgent problem to be solved. This paper has developed an interactive tool that allows the user to select and fix components which can be assembled to the new model, and then process the interface cracks of the assembled model surface. There are two difficult problems to be solved: components replacement and components seamless bonding.

The first problem is how to replace components which are existed in model. For example, using the component model which are retrieved form the resource database can replace the corresponding component of an existing model. It is necessary to provide an automatic command to fix the two corresponding components in the same coordinate system. This procedure is to achieve the invariant of the translation, the zoom, the rotation and the symmetry, and to achieve the minimum square sum of the distance between the each point of component surface and the nearest point of the other component. In this paper, by moving the centroid of the components to make it coincide with the centroid of the target component, the best translation can be achieved. The optimal scaling is achieved by changing the size ratio of the source components so that the mean variance (square sum of distances from each point to the centroid) is equal to the mean variance of the target component. Optimized rotation requires the use of Horn's method to establish point-to-point correspondence. ICP algorithm is a commonly method to calibrate two models, which converges a local optimal solution to minimize the sum of the squared-distance of the two models.

When assembling components into the model, it is difficult to create a seamless, smooth surface between the interface. This paper provides a simple method which was proposed by Kanai to connect these components seamlessly. This method is shown as follows: When connecting the two components, the user should select an open contour C1, C2 in each 3D grid model boundary (Fig.3(a)). When the "join" command is executed, the heuristic algorithm is used to automatically chamfer and mix, and achieve the vertex correspondence. That is, firstly, finding a pair of closest vertices V1 and V2 on C1, C2, as shown in Fig.3(b). And then, for C2, determining the positioning of C1 by checking the vector dot product from V1 to V1', the same method to define the vector from V2 to V2'. If the dot product is negative, then the positioning of C1 need be changed. Then, through the greedy algorithm iterations increment the current vertex on C1 or C2, picking a point where the Euclidean distance is the smallest in the current two vertices, and the corresponding vertex will be established. Finally, according to the corresponding vertex, the chamfer boundary is constructed (Fig.3(c)). In addition, the join command can smooth these nodes within the user-specified chamfer distance and the number of iterations by averaging the positions of the vertices and other neighbors. And then, a combined model (Fig.3(d)) with no traces is assembled.

DOI: 10.1051/itmconf/20171203033

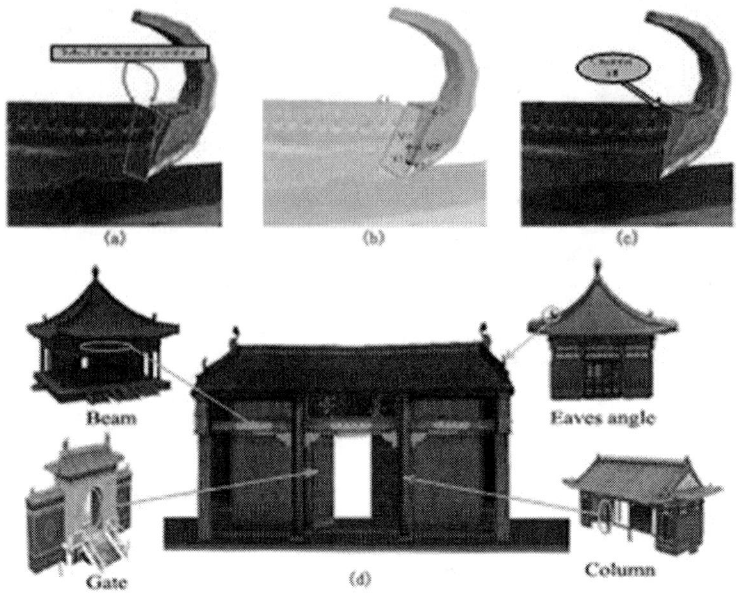

Figure 3. Assembly of 3D Model

3 Experiment

The three gorges dam is a huge project and the biggest hydropower station in china. When this dam project finished, many areas inclulde ancient cultural relic were submerged under water. As one of the key projects in the Three Gorges area, Archaeologists found the relics of old Badong town which was existed in Northern Song Dynasty, inluding official district, warehouse area, residential area, business district and so on,. Based on the national culture resource database, the models can be retrieved for intelligent segmentation to access the target components. These components can be combined into a variety of architectural and role models that can be displayed in a virtual environment. Finally, though the application of 3D geographic information system and VR technology, a experimental system, virtual Badong, is developed to rebuild these historic Badong town in the computer and display it from internet which is shown in Fig.4.

As Badong town is the ancient distribution center of immigrants, it also has very rich cultural. "Sayerhe" folk dance is an ancient funeral dance in this area. Through the deep research of the cultural activities and clothing in ancient Badong town, we bind the dance motion to the corresponding role model, and use motion data to drive the role model for cultural activities. In the virtual Badong, "sayerhe" folk dance is rebuilt and displayed online which is shown in Fig.5.

Figure 4. Government of Badong town

Figure 5. "sayerhe" folk dance

Summary

To sum up, a modeling method for 3D model based on resource database is proposed to rebuild the 3D scene and role modeling conveniently. Based on the analysis of the geometric representation and modeling method of the 3D model, the modeling method is used to generate the virtual scene and the role model in the cultural activities quickly and efficiently. Finally, based on archaeological data and the national cultural resource database, the 3D scene model and related characters are reconstructed, and the digital "sayerhe" folk dance also is displayed in this system. The application of "virtual Badong" prove that this method can be used for the representation of historical geography scenes and the protection of intangible cultural heritage.

Acknowledgement

This research was supported by the Research Funds for the Central Universities "Research on Knowledge visualization of traditional folk dance" and project of Scientific and Technical Supporting Programs of Hubei(NO. 2014BAA156).

References

1. Selma Rizvić, How to Breathe Life into Cultural Heritage 3D Reconstructions, European Review, 25(1) February 2017, pp. 39-50.
2. AthanasiosVoulodimos; Nikolaos Doulamis, et al. Four-dimensional reconstruction of cultural heritage sites based on photogrammetry and clustering, Journal of Electronic Imaging, 26(1), 011013 (Nov, 2016).
3. Xu Aiguo. Research on 3D Garment Simulation Technology in Virtual Human Animation[D]. Zhejiang Hangzhou: Zhejiang University, 2006.
4. YANG Yu-bin, LIN Hui, ZHU Qing.Research on Retrieval of Content-based 3D Model[J]. Journal of Computer Science, 2004,27(10): 1297-1310.
5. OSADA R, FUNKHOUSER T,et al.Shape distribution[J].ACM
6. Transactions on Graphics, 2002,21(4):807-832.
7. Funkhouser T, Min P, Kazhdan M et al. A search engine for 3d models, ACM Transactions on Graphics, 2003, 22(1):83-105.
8. RICHARD J. A survey of free-form object representation and recognition techniques[J]. Computer Vision and Image Understanding, 2001, 81: 166-210.
9. ZHAO Ming-xi.Study on Grid Processing Algorithm Based on Perception Feature [J].Shanghai Jiaotong University,2006.10.

Magnetite (Fe_3O_4) Nanoparticles Alleviate Growth Inhibition and Oxidative Stress Caused by Heavy Metals in Young Seedlings of Cucumber (*Cucumis Sativus L*)

Alexandre KONATE[1,a], Xiao HE[2,b], Yu-Kui RUI[1,c*], Zhi-Yong ZHANG[2,d*]

[1]College of Resources and Environmental Sciences, China Agricultural University, Beijing 100093, China.
[2]Key Laboratory for Biomedical Effects of Nanomaterials and Nanosafety, Key Laboratory of Nuclear Radiation and Nuclear Energy Technology, Institute of High Energy Physics, Chinese Academy of Sciences, Beijing 100049, China.
[a]alexandrekonate28@gmail.com, [b]hexiao@ihep.ac.cn, [c]ruiyukui@163.com, [d]zhangzhy@ihep.ac.cn, *ruiyukui@163.com
*Corresponding author: ruiyukui@163.com

Abstract: Accumulation of heavy metals in the ecosystem and their toxic effects through food chain can cause serious ecological and health problems. In the present study, experiments were performed to understand how the addition of magnetite (Fe_3O_4) nanoparticles reduces the toxicity caused by Cd, Pb, Cu, and Zn in cucumber plants. Plant growth parameters, lipid peroxidation, and antioxidant enzymes were measured in seedling samples treated with either metals or metals supplemented with Fe_3O_4 to demonstrate the reduction in metal-induced oxidative stress conferred by Fe_3O_4. Results showed that the toxic effect of metals on seedling growth parameters can be arranged in the rank order of inhibition as follows: Cu > Cd > Zn > Pb. Exposure to metals significantly decreased the seedlings growth, the activities of superoxide dismutase (SOD) and peroxidases (POD), while the malondialdehyde (MDA) content significantly increased in cucumber seedlings. The reducing activity of nano-Fe_3O_4 against heavy metals stresses was confirmed in this study by the decrease in MDA content. The correlation between the decrease of MDA concentration and the increase in SOD and POD activities in the presence of nano-Fe_3O_4 suggest that the MDA reduction in the tested seedlings can result from the increased enzyme activity.

1 Introduction

Accumulation of heavy metals (e.g Cd, Cu, Zn and Pb) in the ecosystem and its toxic effects through food chain can cause serious ecological and health problems. At higher concentrations, all heavy metals are toxic to living organisms including plants. The excess accumulation of these metals in plant tissues may disturb various physiological processes such as inhibition of root growth and damage to plasma membrane permeability [8]. Previous studies [23] have demonstrated that heavy metals can enhance lipid peroxidation (MDA) and cause oxidative stress in plants by generating reactive oxygen species (ROS), superoxide anion radicals (O^{-2}), hydroxyl radicals (•OH) and hydrogen peroxide (H_2O_2). To remove ROS and reduce the toxic effect of heavy metals, plants have evolved a series of antioxidant enzymatic mechanisms including superoxide dismutase (SOD) and peroxidase (POD). Due to their potential application in the remediation of polluted soils and water as well as biomedicine, magnetic (Fe_3O_4) nanoparticles are gaining more interest in research [17]. Many studies have shown that iron compounds have a high ability for heavy metal adsorption. According to Hu et al.[7], magnetite nanoparticles could be potential adsorbents to reduce heavy metals concentration in the natural environment (contaminated water or soil). The key drivers in the adsorption of heavy metals by iron oxide nanoparticles are their surface properties. Innovative approaches are desirable in order to prevent or reduce the toxic effects of heavy metals on plants. The knowledge about the use of nanoparticles such as nano-Fe_3O_4 to reduce the root growth inhibition and oxidative stress induced by heavy metals in terrestrial plants is very limited [29, 12]. Limited beneficial effects of nano-Fe_3O_4 on the Cd-induced growth have been observed in wheat and cucumber plants [29]. However, several biological roles of nano-Fe_3O_4 on heavy metals stress in plants are needed to be studied. According to Shen et al.[21], nano-Fe_3O_4 can be used to adsorb metal ions. Investigation into how nano-Fe_3O_4 can be used as an intervention strategy to respond to oxidative stress caused by heavy metals could be essential to protect the environment and public health. We hypothesized that the inhibitory effects of the selected metals may be reduced by nano-Fe_3O_4 and the reducing effect would vary depending on the type of the metal. Root elongation, accumulation of metals, SOD and POD activities, and MDA content were investigated in this study to test these hypotheses. The aim of the present study was to determine the effects of selected heavy metals (Pb, Zn, Cd and Cu) on cucumber seedlings and subsequently to determine the effects of reducing metal toxicity in plants by magnetite (Fe_3O_4) nanoparticles.

2 Materials and Methods

2.1 Nano-Fe3O4, Heavy Metals, and Plant

We synthesized magnetite (Fe_3O_4) nanoparticles with a size of about 6nm following the procedures from Xiao et al.[27]. The four heavy metals ($PbCl_2$, $ZnSO_4.H_2O$, $CdCl_2$ and $CuCl_2.2H_2O$) were purchased from Xilong Chemical Co., Ltd., China. The analytical grade chemicals were purchased from Beijing Chemical Works. Seeds of Cucumber (*Cucumis sativus* L. var.zhongnong No.16) were obtained from Chinese Academy of Agricultural Sciences. A sample of the

DOI: 10.1051/itmconf/20171203034

seeds was tested in a preliminary experiment to determine the germination rate (greater than 95%). The seeds were refrigerated at 4 °C before use. Dynamic Light Scattering (DLS) equipment (ZETA SIZER 90, Nano series, Malvern, UK) and Tecnai G2 20 S-Twin transmission electron microscope 119 (FEI Co., Japan) operating at 200 KV were used to evaluate the agglomeration of nano-Fe_3O_4 in water

2.2 Preparation of Nano-Fe3O4 Suspensions and Metal Solutions

The growth of seedlings was investigated at 1mM, 10 mM (Pb, Zn, Cd, and Cu), and 2000mg/L (nano-Fe_3O_4) using water as solvent and control. We chose 2000 mg/L concentration as the upper limit in this study because, according to the US EPA [26] guidelines, this level could be regarded as the phytotoxicity level on tested plant species if there is no negative effect on root growth under such a high concentration. The accumulation of metals and the oxidative stress were investigated only at 1 mM of the selected metals with or without nano-Fe_3O_4 (2000mg/L). Thus, nano-Fe_3O_4 particles were suspended directly in deionized water or the metal (1 mM) solution, and then an ultrasonic vibration was applied for 40 min to obtain properly dispersed and stable nano-Fe_3O_4 suspensions of each selected metal concentration.

2.3 Seedling Exposure

Cucumber seeds were immersed in 10% sodium hypochlorite solution for 10 min and then rinsed four times with DI-water to ensure surface sterility (USEPA.[26]. One piece of wet filter paper was put into each 100 mm × 15 mm Petri dish. The seeds were transferred onto the filter paper in groups of 50 in the Petri dishes. Finally, distilled water was added into the Petri dishes. The seeds were left on the wet filter paper in the covered Petri dishes to produce radicles within 24h in a dark growth chamber at 25 °C with 75% relative humidity. Once approximately 95% of the cucumber seeds had produced radicles, the seedlings were exposed to the test solutions as described below.

2.3.1 Effects of nano-Fe3O4 and heavy metals on seedling growth.

Seeds with radicles (at 1 d) were transferred onto another filter paper (10 seedlings) in a Petri dish at about 1 cm apart from each other [13]. 5 mL of nanoparticles suspension or metal solution was subsequently added. Only distilled water was added to the Petri dishes of the control group. All the Petri dishes were covered, sealed with parafilm, and placed in the dark in a growth chamber at 25 °C with 75% relative humidity. After 5 days, the seedlings were removed from the growth chamber and the seedling root and shoot lengths were measured by a millimeter ruler. Tolerance index, seedling viability, seedling growth and the inhibitory effects of nanoparticles and metals were also determined. A completely randomized design with four replicates per treatment was used for all experiments.

2.3.2 Effects of nano-Fe3O4 particles on metal toxicity and their accumulation in seedling

In order to investigate the effects of nano-Fe3O4 on heavy metal-induced root growth inhibition and their accumulation in the seedlings, the first experiment was repeated. 5 mL of a test medium (metal solution or metal solution+ nano-Fe3O4) was added. In each case, metal solution (1mM) was used as a solvent and control. The seedling root length was measured by a millimeter ruler after 5 d. The roots and shoots were then separated and dried at 60 °C. The dry samples were used to determine the total Fe, Pb, Zn, Cd and Cu contents in the tissues of cucumber seedlings grown in the metal solutions with or without nano-Fe3O4 by Inductively Coupled Plasma Mass Spectrometry (ICP-MS, Thermo X7, USA) following the methods previously described by Le et al.,[11]. All the experiments used a completely randomized design with four replicates per treatment.

2.3.3 Effects of nano-Fe3O4 on the oxidative stress induced by heavy metals in the seedlings

To examine the oxidative stress induced by heavy metals and investigate the effects of nano-Fe3O4 on the reduction of metal stress in the seedlings, we repeated the second experiment with the same concentrations: metal (1mM) and nano-Fe3O4 (2000 mg/L). Firstly, the effects of each metal and nanoparticles were compared to those of water. Secondly, the alleviation effects of nano-Fe3O4 on the oxidative stress induced by metals to the cucumber seedlings were examined. Thus, seedlings of cucumber treated with metals solution or metal+ nano-Fe3O4 for 5 d were used to determine the antioxidant activities (SOD and POD) and MDA concentration as described by Le et al.,[11]. All experiments used a completely randomized design with four replicates per treatment.

2.4 Statistical Analysis

Each treatment was conducted with four replicates and the results were expressed as mean ± SD (standard deviation). One-way ANOVA followed by Tukey's HSD (equal group size) or Bonferroni (unequal group size) test was employed to determine the statistical differences. $P < 0.05$ was considered to be a significant difference. All statistical analyses were performed using Statistical Packages for the Social Sciences (SPSS) Version 20.0 and OriginPro 8. Other relevant calculations on the exposure of the selected metals were made based on Ahmad et al.[1] and Shaikh et al.[19]. The length of shoot and root were determined using a centimeter scale.

$$T.I. = \frac{\textbf{Mean root length in metal solution}}{\textit{Mean root length in distilled water}} \times 100 \quad (1)$$

$$\textbf{Inhibitory rate (\%)of Shoot} = \frac{\textit{Shoot length of control} - \textit{shoot length of treatment}}{\textit{Shoot length of control}} \times 100 \quad (2)$$

$$\textbf{Inhibitory rate (\%)of Root} = \frac{\textit{Root length of control} - \textit{Root length of treatment}}{\textit{Root length of control}} \times 100 \quad (3)$$

3 Results and Discussion

3.1. Characterization of Nano-Fe3O4

The Fig. 1 shows the TEM image and the particle size distribution histograms for nano-Fe3O4 (Fig. 1A-a). The TEM image showed that the nano-Fe3O4 on average had a diameter size of 6.78 ± 1.68 nm. The hydrodynamic size and zeta potential of 50 mg/L nano-Fe3O4 in deionized water were measured by dynamic light scattering (DLS) equipment. The hydrodynamic size was 251±7.87 nm and the NPs were well dispersed with a negative zeta-potential (-13.9±0.26). The hydrodynamic diameters and their corresponding TEM image sizes were different due to the agglomeration in water and dry state of the sample particles, respectively.

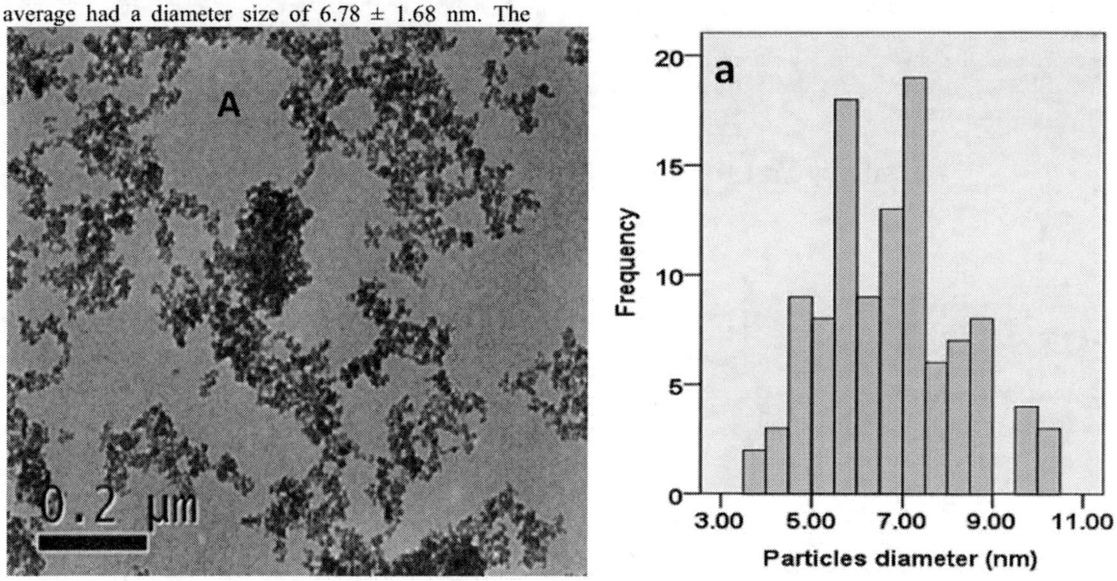

Figure 1. TEM image and particle size distribution histogram of nano-Fe_3O_4.

3.2 Effects of Nano-Fe3O4 and Heavy Metals on Seedling Growth

Table 1, showed the effects of nano-Fe3O4 and metals (Pb, Zn, Cd and Cu) on the growth of cucumber seedlings. The results showed that the synthesized nanoparticles did not have an effect on the growth of cucumber seedlings when compared to control (Table 1)

Table 1. Effect of nano-Fe_3O_4 or metals on cucumber seedling growth

NPs or Heavy metals	Concentration	Root length(Cm)	Inhibitory rate (%)	Shoot length(cm)	Inhibitory rate (%)
H_20	0	5.57±1.86	0	6.71± 1.49	0
NPs	2000mg/L	5.71±1.74	-2.47	6.97±1.50	-3.99
Pb		1.86±0.66*	66.55	4.69±1.11*	30.09
Zn		1.64±0.89*	70.48	3.55±1.27*	46.96
Cd	1mM	0.45±0.06*	91.80	2.52±0.92*	62.34
Cu		0.31±0.22*	94.48	1.68±0.46*	74.97

The values were expressed as mean ± SD (standard deviation) of four replicated samples with 10 seeds for each replication. * indicated significant difference from the control (P< 0.05).

The effect of nanoparticles on plant growth is thus dependent on various factors such as the particle size and the tested concentration of nano-Fe3O4 or the plant species under study [17]. In the present study, the most important response of plants to heavy metals toxicity is the inhibition of seedling growth and the induction of oxidative stress in cucumber seedlings. There were great morphological differences between the metal-treated and control seedlings. An important difference was also found between the treatments of the four tested metals (Cd, Cu, Pb and Zn). Growth inhibition is one of the most common agriculture indices of heavy metal tolerance but also a response to heavy metal stress [14]. Growth inhibition by the heavy metals (1mM concentration) was in the order: Cu > Cd > Zn > Pb (Table 1). These results were in agreement with those of Fargašová[3], who reported that trace elements had toxic inhibitory effects of on the mustard seedling in a descending order of Cu > Se > Cd > Zn > Pb. Unlike our experiment the later authors, included Se in their study. It has been demonstrated that Cd can interfere with the uptake, transport and the use of some nutrients elements (e.g., ca, P, K, etc.) and water by plants [2]. Cadmium can also reduce plant cellular activities due to the generation of oxidative stress and the inhibition of the enzyme activity [29]. In plants, heavy metals can be transported across membranes nutrients transporters. During the transportation phase of heavy metals within the plant form roots to the shoots, the most important site of toxic action might be the root [25]. The inhibition rank order of root and shoot elongation was similar. However, inhibition of growth by the four metals was greater in roots than shoot (Table 1). This could be attributed to the high accumulation of the metals in roots than in the shoots. Our results showed that the shoot and root length decreased significantly under the treatments of Cd and Cu as compared with Zn and Pb. Zinc and Pb are not generally considered as an essential element for plant growth. Their effects on seedlings can change according plants species, organs and metabolic process [20].

3.3 Effects of Nano-Fe3O4 on Metal-induced Root Growth Inhibition

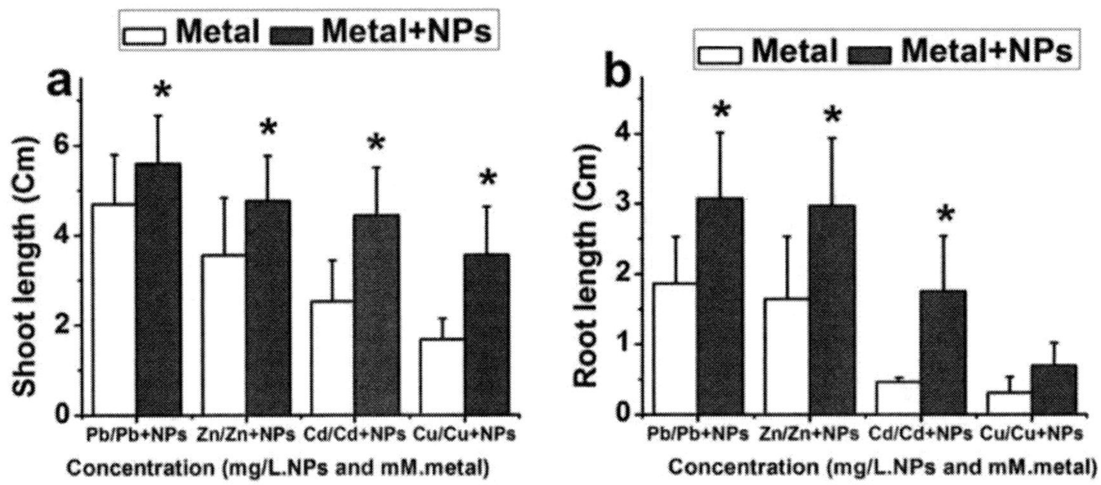

Figure 2. Shoot length (a) and root length (b) of cucumber seedlings after their exposure for 5 days to 1mM of four different metals (Pb, Zn, Cd, or Cu) solutions or 2000mg/L of nano-Fe3O4 (6 nm) prepared with solution (1mM) of these four different metals (Pb, Zn, Cd, or Cu) as solvents. The values were expressed as mean ± SD (standard deviation) of four replicated samples with 10 seedlings for each replication. Significant differences from control (1mM) were marked with "asterisk" ($P<0.05$)

The utilization of metal oxides nanoparticles in decontaminating the polluted media have been reported in different studies [21]. The types of nonmaterial have been proposed as sorbents due to their large surface area but also because they are easy to synthesize. The electronic properties and the unique structure of magnetic (Fe3O4) nanoparticles make them the powerful adsorbents in decontaminating process of polluted soils and water. In order to understand more on the effect of nanoparticles, each heavy metal (1mM) with or without nano-Fe3O4 (2000mg/L) was compared (Fig 2). Root and shoot growth were positively affected by the presence of nano-Fe3O4 when compared with metal solutions (1mM) without nano-Fe3O4, except for roots of seedlings exposed to Cu solution where no significant effect of nano-Fe3O4 was noted (Fig. 2b). The presence of nano-Fe3O4 significantly reduced inhibition on root growth induced by the selected heavy metals (Pb, Zn, Cd and Cu) by 39.32%, 44.50%, 73.95%, 37% in the root, and 16.17%, 25.30% 43% and 52.79% in the shoot, respectively (Fig. 2a-b). In agreement to our results, Wang et al.[28] observed that, among the oxide nanoparticles used in their study, Fe3O4 was not different from the control (DI-water). However, the addition of Cd solution showed positive effects. The seedling root growths of the tested species were promoted at the concentration (2000mg/L Fe3O4) as seen in the present study. In general, the increase in seedling growth in our study, clearly demonstrates that presence of nano-Fe3O4 affected the uptake of heavy metals and reduced their toxicity in cucumber seedlings.

 DOI: 10.1051/itmconf/20171203034

3.4 Tolerance Index and Seedling Viability

Fig. 3 shows the effects of nano-Fe3O4 and the tested metals (Pb, Zn, Cd and Cu) on seedling viability (Fig. 3a) and the tolerance index (Fig. 3b). The results showed a 100% viability in both control and nano-Fe3O4 treated seedlings. The inhibitory rates of seedling viability by the metal treatments decreased in the order, Cu > Cd > Zn > Pb.

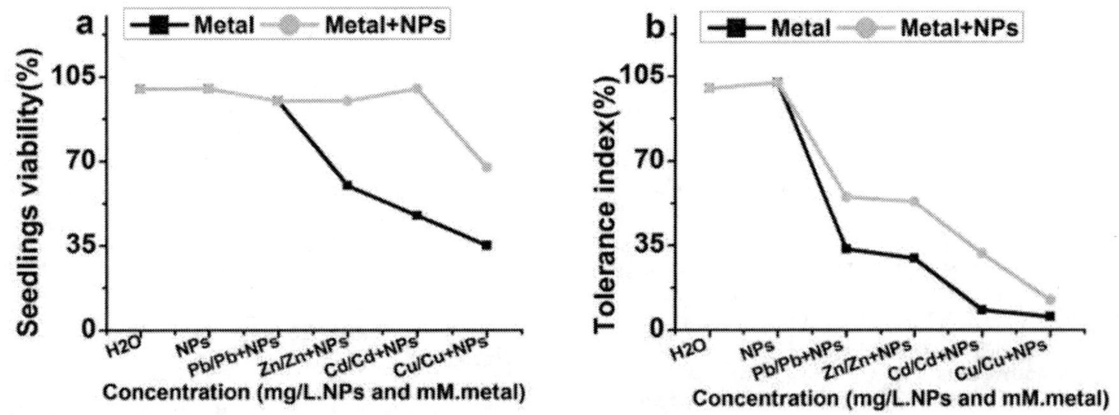

Figure 3. Viability and tolerance index (%) of cucumber seedlings after their exposure to nano-Fe3O4, metals (Pb, Zn, Cd and Cu) and metal+nano-Fe3O4 for 5 days

The seedling viabilities were: 47.5%, 35%, 67% and 60% at 1mM for Cd, Cu, Pb and Zn, respectively. Interestingly, the viability of cucumber seedlings increased with the addition of nano-Fe3O4 in the metal solutions by 95%, 95%, 100 and 67.5% for Pb, Zn, Cd and Cu respectively. The comparison with metal solutions alone showed that the addition of nano-Fe3O4 significantly increased seedling viability which was inhibited by the selected metals (Pb, Zn, Cd and Cu), and the inhibitory rates of seedling viability from the metal+nano-Fe3O4 treatments were in the order, Cu > Zn = Pb > Cd. The tolerance index of seedlings increased in the presence of nano-Fe3O4 compared with metals solutions (1mM) without nano-Fe3O4, except in the case of Cu+nano-Fe3O4 (Fig. 3b). Nano-Fe3O4 suspension had no effect on the tolerance index of seedlings grown in Cu solution. Plant tolerance systems to heavy metals need the coordination of different physiological and biological processes. Different plant species have different mechanisms to tolerate heavy metals.

Table. 2 Effects of nano-Fe3O4 on heavy metals uptake by cucumber seedlings

Heavy metals and NPs	Heavy metal concentrations ($mg.kg^{-1}$) in seedlings					
	Shoot			Root		
	Metals-NPs	Metals+NPs	Reduction in metal uptake (%)	Metals-NPs	Metals+NPs	Reduction in metal uptake (%)
Pb	32.59±11.58	4.37±1.22	86.59	1141.30±72.75	196.83±50.30	82.75
Fe	85± 19.46	119.18±26.11		162.87±20.49	3020.89±280.52	
Zn	64.54±10.07	37.37±12.03	42.09	424.62±18.21	174.96±27.83	58.79
Fe	71.29±22.46	121.97±27.63		184.61±18.39	2987.69±287.79	
Cd	59.20±14.87	6.06±1.09	89.76	563.36±75.52	88.08±18.79	84.36
Fe	60.08±17.45	127.11±12.16		174.92±15.88	3140.59±265.56	
Cu	8.58±2.06	4.45±0.37	48.13	186.78±28.84	54.13±10.75	71.01
Fe	67.06±13.62	116.39±31.26		198.56±23.40	3315.07±308.87	

The values were considered as mean ± SD (standard deviation) of four replicated samples with 10 seedlings for each replication. Significant differences from control (1mM of metal) were marked with "asterisk" ($P<0.05$)

Table 2 shows the effects of nano-Fe3O4 on heavy metal accumulation and their effect on cucumber seedlings. Seedlings received the tested metal solutions (1mM) with or without nano-Fe3O4 (2000 mg/L). All the heavy metals (Pb, Zn, Cd and Cu) were taken up by shoot and root of the cucumber seedlings (Table 2).

Most of the tested metals had higher accumulation in the roots compared with the shoots. Previous studies found similar results in Allium sativum [34], wheat seedlings [28, 29], native plants [32] and water hyacinths [14]. When cucumber seedlings were exposed to 1mM concentration of tested metal solutions without nano-Fe3O4, accumulation of metals in plants were in the order of Pb > Cd > Zn > Cu and Zn > Cd > Pb > Cu for root and shoot samples, respectively. The highest concentration in the root and shoot were of Pb and Zn treatments, respectively. The accumulation of Pb in plants could be depending on the tested concentration in the growth medium [14]. Some plants considered as stable to heavy metals can transport higher concentration of heavy metals from root to leaf [18]. The results were supported by the report of Yilmaz et al. [31] for Pb accumulation in roots and those of Jadia and Fulekar[10] and Wang et al.[28] for Zn accumulation in shoots. In this study, accumulation heavy metals were significantly reduced in cucumber seedlings with the addition of nano-Fe3O4 (Table 2). The addition of nano-Fe3O4 reduced metal concentrations and changed the accumulation order in the cucumber seedlings as follows: Pb > Zn > Cd > Cu and Zn > Cd > Cu > Pb for root and shoot samples, respectively. The reduction rate of metal concentrations in seedling varied according to the type of heavy metals as follows, Cd > Pb > Cu > Zn (Table 2). The order of metals decreasing in the root was similar with that found in shoot. In detail, the addition of nano-Fe3O4 (2000mg/L) significantly ($P < 0.05$) decreased the metal (Pb, Zn, Cd and Cu) uptake by cucumber seedlings by 82.75%, 58.79%, 84.36% and 71.01%, in the roots and 86.59%, 42.09% 89.76% and 48.13% in the shoot, respectively at 1mM concentration (Table 2). Our results show the role of nano-Fe3O4 in reducing the uptake of heavy metals by the seedlings of cucumber. In the present study, nanoparticles were visually observed on root surface after 5d, suggesting that their adsorption capacity could inhibit the uptake of heavy metals and thus protect root seedlings. The zeta potential results show that the synthesized nano-Fe3O4 (6nm) used in this study was negatively charged, which could increase their adsorption capacity. It has been reported that the adsorption capacity of Fe3O4 nanoparticles depends on of various parameters including the different electrostatic attraction between heavy metal cations and negatively charged adsorption sites [4]. The use of magnetite nanoparticles as adsorbents provides a convenient approach to reduce the uptake of heavy metals and mitigate their toxicity in plants. The particle sizes play an important role in nano-Fe3O4 application because their properties such as surface area greatly depend upon the dimension of the particles. Magnetite nanoparticles with small size (less than 30 nm) have a large surface area. These properties of nano-Fe3O4 can be strongly useful in the adsorption process. The above-mentioned observations from our study showed that the reduction in the uptake of the tested heavy metals, and the decrease in their toxicity in the cucumber seedlings could be associated with the sizes and surface area of nano-Fe3O4, but also their adsorption capacity.

3.5 Antioxidant Enzyme Activities and Lipid Peroxidation Assays

3.5.1 Effect of nano-Fe3O4 and heavy metals on antioxidative enzyme activity and MDA content

As seen in the Fig. 4, SOD and POD activities as well as MDA content were not significantly different ($P < 0.05$) between seedlings treated with nano-Fe3O4 at 2000mg/L only and control (DI-water). However, the SOD activity decreased significantly in the roots and shoots of cucumber seedlings under the stress of Cd and Cu (Fig. 4a-b). When seedlings were exposed to Pb and Zn solutions, SOD activity increased significantly in roots but did not change in shoot as compared to control (DI-water). Among the tested metals, only Cd treatment reduced the POD activity in root and shoot of cucumber seedlings followed by Cu which only decreased the POD activity in roots (Fig.4c-d). Heavy metals are a risk factor in plants and can induce disturbance in their life cycle and consequently, decrease its growth [18]. The decline in SOD activity under Cd and Cu stress indicated that oxygen scavenging function of SOD was impaired [22]. These observations are similar with the results from Allium sativum [34] and Jatropha curcas L [22]. In the roots, an increase in the activity of SOD was noted under Pb and Zn stress (Fig. 4b), which could be due to the metal tolerance ability in the cucumber plants.

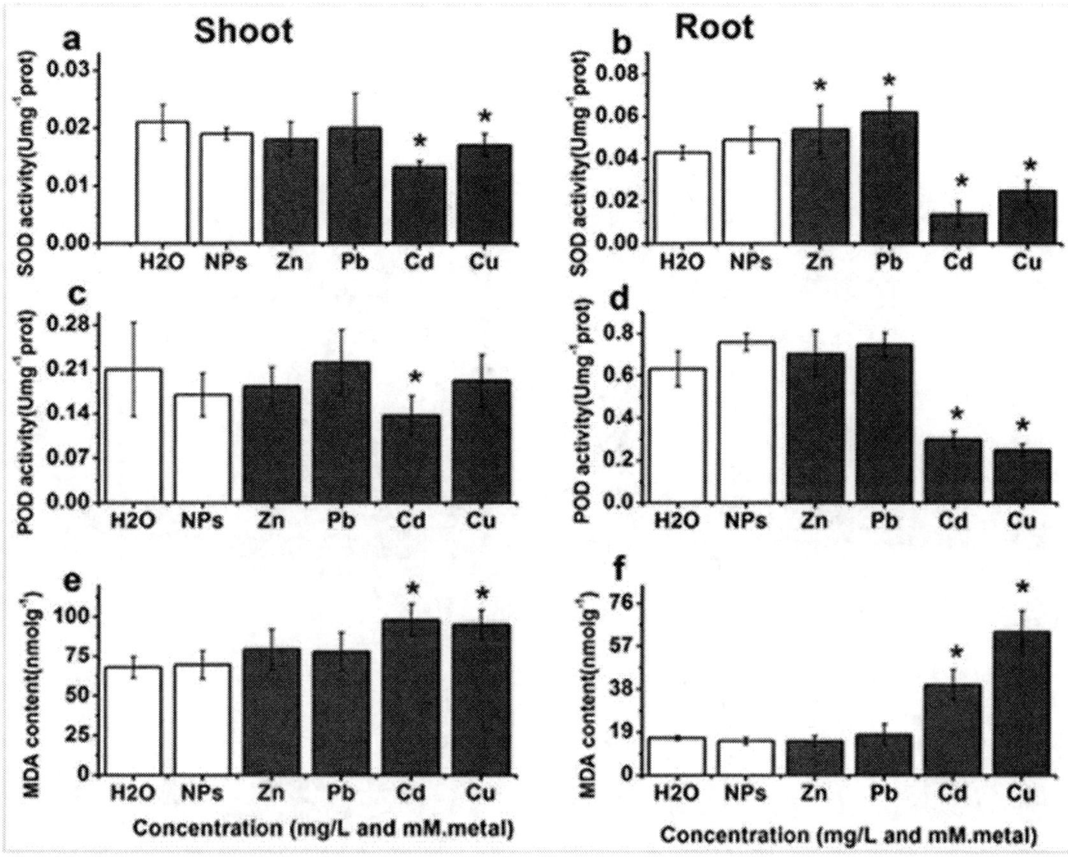

Figure 4. SOD and POD activities and MDA content in the root and shoot of cucumber seedlings treated with H2O, nano-Fe3O4 (2000mg/L) and four heavy metals (Pb, Zn, Cd and Cu) at 1mM concentration. SOD in shoot (a) and root (b); POD in shoot (c) and root (d), MDA content in shoots (e) and roots (f). The values were expressed as mean ± SD (standard deviation) of four replications. The asterisk "*' indicated the significant differences versus controls at ($P < 0.05$).

MDA concentration is usually used as a biomarker of lipid peroxidation resulting from oxidative stress [24]. In the present study, MDA concentration increased significantly in roots and shoots of cucumber seedlings when exposed to Cd and Cu treatments (Fig. 4e-f). On the other hand, Pb and Zn treatments had no effect on MDA concentration in roots and shoots of cucumber seedlings when compared to control (DI-water). The increase in MDA content suggested that Cd and Cu indirectly lead to production of superoxide radicals, which resulted in increased lipid peroxidation products and caused oxidative stress in the tested seedlings [12]. Our results were supported by the reports on cucumber plants [24] and strawberry [16]. Certain plants can tolerate, uptake and translocate high concentrations of some heavy metals even if they are toxic to other organisms [15]. The treatments of Zn and Pb did not affect the MDA content suggesting that cucumber seedlings have efficient mechanism to tolerate the stress induced by Zn and Pb under the experimental condition noted in the present study[22]

3.5.2 Alleviation of oxidative stress induced by heavy metals in cucumber seedlings by nano-Fe3O4

In this experiment, results of metal+nano-Fe3O4 were compared to their corresponding metal solutions (Fig. 5). As seen in the Fig. 5a-b and 5c-d, the addition of nano-Fe3O4 and Pb or Zn had no obvious effect on SOD and POD activities in cucumber seedlings. The SOD activity significantly increased by 43.02% and 33% in the shoots, and by 76.06% and 53.55% in roots, with the addition of nano-Fe3O4 to the solution (1mM) of Cd and Cu, respectively (Fig. 5a-b). The POD activity also, significantly increased by 49.21% and 30.53% in the shoots, and by 69.23% and 65.04% in roots, with the addition of nano-Fe3O4 to the solution (1mM) of Cd and Cu, respectively (Fig.5c-d).

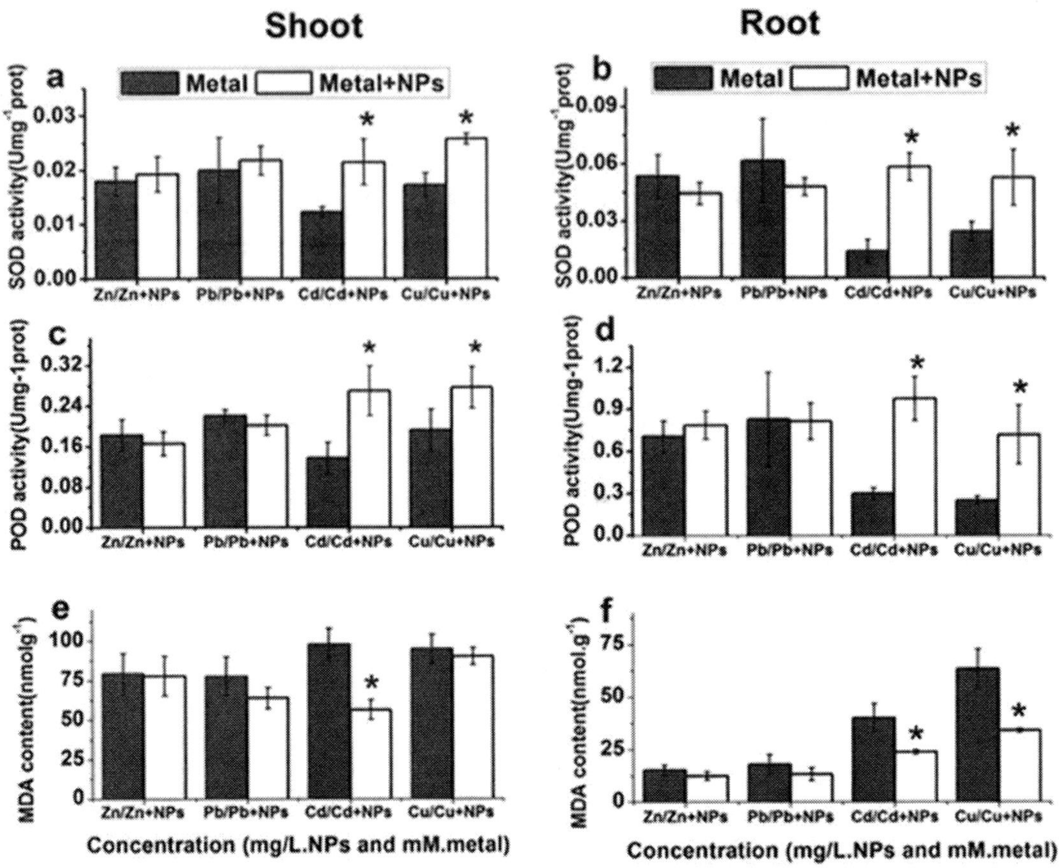

Figure 5. SOD and POD activities and MDA content in the root and shoot of cucumber seedlings treated with 1mM of four heavy metals (Pb, Zn, Cd and Cu) with or without nano-Fe3O4 (2000mg/L). SOD in shoot (a) and root (b); POD in shoot (c) and root (d), MDA content in shoots (e) and roots (f). The values were expressed as mean ± SD (standard deviation) of four replications. The asterisk "*' indicated the significant differences versus controls (Corresponding metal solution without nano-Fe3O4) at (P< 0.05).

The Cd and Cu treatments without nano-Fe_3O_4 caused decrease in the SOD and POD activities in shoot and root of cucumber seedlings (Fig. 4a-b and 4c-d). The addition of nano-Fe_3O_4 significantly up-regulated the decrease in the activities of SOD and POD under Cu and Cd stresses, suggesting that nano-Fe_3O_4 particles played a protective role by increasing the seedlings ability to scavenge the O_2- radicals and H_2O_2, and prevent the oxidative stress to cells [33, 14]. Heavy metals (e.g., Pb, Cd and Cu) initially induce a severe oxidative stress in living organisms, which in turn causes lipid peroxidation and H_2O_2 accumulation [6]. Here, we performed an experiment to test whether external nano-Fe_3O_4 could be used as a regulator or be capable of initiating antioxidant intervention in response to oxidative stress brought about by heavy metals. The MDA concentration was used as one of the main indicator to evaluate the effects of nano-Fe_3O_4 on the oxidative stress induced by metals. The MDA concentration significantly decreased ($P < 0.05$) in the roots by 40.39% and 46.21%, on addition of nano-Fe_3O_4 to the Cd and Cu solutions, respectively, (Fig. 5f). In the shoot, only the addition of nano-Fe_3O_4 and Cd showed a positive effect with decrease in MDA content by 42.31% (Fig. 5e). The MDA concentration in the cucumber seedlings did not change significantly with the presence of nano-Fe_3O_4 in the solutions of Pb and Zn. The reduction role of nano-Fe_3O_4 against heavy metals stress was confirmed in this study by the decrease in MDA content on the addition of nano-Fe_3O_4. We observed in our study a correlation between the decrease in MDA concentration and the increase in SOD and POD activities in the presence of nano-Fe_3O_4, suggesting that the decline in MDA content under Cd and Cu could be due to the increase in antioxidative enzyme activities in the presence of nano-Fe_3O_4, which reduced H_2O_2 levels, increased the ability of cucumber to scavenge the radicals and reduced membrane damage. Previous studies found similar results in the seedlings of *Kandelia candel* [33]. It has been reported that the oxidative damage induced by Cd toxicity could be alleviated by enzymatic and non-enzymatic antioxidants in plants [30]. Guo et al.[5] found that the presence of salicylic acid (SA) significantly increased the activities of SOD and POD which had been negatively affected by Cd stress, but also decreased significantly the MDA concentration in roots of rice (*Oryza sativa*) when compared with the Cd treatment alone. The reducing effects of SA on Cd toxicity were attributed to the increased level in the activities of antioxidant enzymes.

6 Conclusions

In this study, exposure of heavy metals (Pb, Zn, Cd and Cu) inhibited cucumber seedling growth and seedling viability. Copper (Cu) and cadmium (Cd) had the strongest unfavorable effect on the growth of young cucumber seedlings, respectively. Although most of the heavy metals accumulated in roots, lower levels of the same were translocated into and accumulated in the shoots. The total activity of SOD and POD decreased significantly in the roots and shoots of cucumber seedlings under Cd and Cu stress. When exposed to Pb and Zn solutions, SOD activity increased significantly in roots but did not change in shoot as compared to control (DI-water). On the other hand, MDA concentrations increased significantly in roots and shoots of cucumber seedlings when exposed to Cd and Cu treatments. The addition of nano-Fe_3O_4 significantly decreased root growth inhibition, reduced and alleviated oxidative stress induced by the heavy metals tested in the cucumber seedlings. Our study showed that nano-Fe_3O_4 (6nm) could mitigate metal-induced oxidative stress, growth inhibition and enhancing metal tolerance in the seedlings of cucumber.

Acknowledgement

The work was supported by National Natural Science Foundation of China (No. 41371471) and NSFC-Guangdong Joint Fund (U1401234). The Ministry of Science and Technology of China (no. 2011CB933400, 2012CB932504 and 2013CB932703), and National Natural Science Foundation of China (no. 11275215, 11275218, and 11375009).

References

1. Ahmad, M.J. Akhtar, Z.A. Zahir, A. Jamil, Effect of cadmium on seed germination and seedling growth of four wheat (*Triticum aestivum L.*) cultivars. *Pak. J. Bot* **2012,***44* (5), 1569-1574.
2. P. Das, S. Samantaray, G.R. Rout, Studies on cadmium toxicity in plants: a review. Environmental Pollution **1997**, **98**(1): 29-36.
3. A. Fargašová, Toxicity comparison of some possible toxic metals (Cd, Cu, Pb, Se, Zn) on young seedlings of Sinapis alba. *L. Plant Soil Environ* **2004,** *50* (1), 33-38.
4. L. Giraldo, A. Erto, J.C. Moreno-Piraján, Magnetite nanoparticles for removal of heavy metals from aqueous solutions: synthesis and characterization. *Adsorption* **2013,***19* (2-4), 465-474.
5. B. Guo, Y. Liang, Y. Zhu, F. Zhao, Role of salicylic acid in alleviating oxidative damage in rice roots (Oryza sativa) subjected to cadmium stress. *Environmental Pollution* **2007,***147* (3), 743-749.
6. H. Guo, C. Hong, X. Chen, Y. Xu, Y. Liu, D. Jiang, B. Zheng, Different Growth and Physiological Responses to Cadmium (Cd) of the Three Miscanthus Species. *PloS one* **2016,** *11* (4), e0153475.
7. J. Hu, I. Lo, G. Chen, Removal of Cr (VI) by magnetite. Water Science and Technology **2004**, **50**(12): 139-146.
8. K. Hussain, K. Sahadevan, N. Salim, Bio-accumulation and release of mercury in Vigna mungo (L.) hepper seedlings. *Journal of stress physiology & Biochemistry* **2010,** *6* (3).
9. C. D. Jadia, M. H. Fulekar, Phytoremediation: the application of vermicompost to remove zinc, cadmium, copper, nickel and lead by sunflower plant. *Environmental engineering and management journal* **2008,** 7 (5), 547-558.
10. V.N. Le, Y. Rui, X. Gui, X. Li, S. Liu, Y. Han, Uptake, transport, distribution and Bio-effects of SiO2 nanoparticles in Bt-transgenic cotton. *Journal of nanobiotechnology* **2014,***12* (1), 50.
11. L. Lin, W. Zhou, H. Dai, F. Cao, G. F. Zhang, Selenium reduces cadmium uptake and mitigates cadmium toxicity in rice. *Journal of hazardous materials* **2012,** *235*, 343-351.
12. Y. Ma, X. He, P. Zhang, Z. Zhang, Z. Guo, R. Tai, Z. Xu, L. Zhang, Y. Ding, Y. Zhao, Phytotoxicity and biotransformation of La_2O_3 nanoparticles in a terrestrial plant cucumber (Cucumis sativus). *Nanotoxicology* **2011,** *5* (4), 743-753.
13. S. Malar, S. S. Vikram, P. J. Favas, V. Perumal, Lead heavy metal toxicity induced changes on growth and antioxidative enzymes level in water hyacinths [Eichhornia crassipes (Mart.)]. *Botanical Studies* **2014,** *57* (1), 1.
14. R.B. Meagher and A. C. Heaton, "Strategies for the engineered phytoremediation of toxic element pollution: mercury and arsenic." Journal of Industrial Microbiology and Biotechnology 2005, **32**(11-12): 502-513.
15. *F. Muradoglu, M. Gundogdu,* S. Ercisli, T. Encu, F. Balta, H. Z. Jaafar, M. Zia-Ul-Haq, Cadmium toxicity affects chlorophyll a and b content, antioxidant enzyme activities and mineral nutrient accumulation in strawberry. *Biological research* **2015,** *48* (1), 1.
16. N. Pariona, A. I. Martinez, H. Hdz-García, L. A. Cruz, A. Hernandez-Valdes, Hernandez-Valdes, A., Effects of hematite and ferrihydrite nanoparticles on germination and growth of maize seedlings. *Saudi Journal of Biological Sciences* **2016**.
17. M. Saberi, F. Tarnian, A. Davari, A. Ebrahimzadeh, Comparing cadmium and copper sulfate effects on seed germination and seedling initial growth properties in two range Species. International Journal of Agriculture and Crop Sciences **2013**, **5**(9): 997.
18. I. R. Shaikh, P. R. Shaikh, R. A. Shaikh, A. A. Shaikh, Phytotoxic effects of heavy metals (Cr, Cd,

Mn and Zn) on wheat (Triticum aestivum L.) seed germination and seedlings growth in black cotton soil of Nanded, India. *Research Journal of Chemical Sciences* **2013,** *3* (6), 14-23.
19. P. Sharma and R. S. Dubey, "Lead toxicity in plants" Brazilian Journal of Plant_Physiology **2005**, **17**(1): 35-52.
20. Y. Shen, J. Tang, Z. Nie, Y. Wang, Y. Ren, L. Zuo, Preparation and application of magnetic Fe_3O_4 nanoparticles for wastewater purification. *Separation and Purification Technology* **2009,** *68* (3), 312-319.
21. X. Shu, L. Yin, Q. Zhang, W. Wang, Effect of Pb toxicity on leaf growth, antioxidant enzyme activities, and photosynthesis in cuttings and seedlings of Jatropha curcas L. *Environmental Science and Pollution Research* **2012,** *19* (3), 893-902.
22. S. J. Stohs, D. Bagchi, E. Hassoun, M. Bagchi, Oxidative mechanisms in the toxicity of chromium and cadmium ions. *Journal of Environmental Pathology, Toxicology and Oncology* **2001,** *20* (2).
23. S. Sun, M. Li, J. Zuo, W. Jiang, D. Liu, Cadmium effects on mineral accumulation, antioxidant defence system and gas exchange in cucumber. *Zemdirbyste-Agriculture* **2015,** *102* (2), 193-200.
24. N. Suzuki, "Alleviation by calcium of cadmium-induced root growth inhibition in Arabidopsis seedlings." Plant Biotechnology **2015, 22**(1): 19-25.
25. US EPA. **1996**: U.S. Environmental Protection Agency (US EPA. **1996**). Ecological effects guidelines. OPPTS 85O.4150, Terrestrial Plant Toxicity, EPA 712-C-96-163. Public.
26. L. Xiao, J. Li, D. F. Brougham, E. K. Fox, N. Feliu, A. Bushmelev, A. Schmidt, N. Mertens, F. Kiessling, M. Valldor, Water-soluble superparamagnetic magnetite nanoparticles with biocompatible coating for enhanced magnetic resonance imaging. *Acs Nano* **2011,***5* (8), 6315-6324.
27. H. Wang, G. Zhong, G. Shi, F. Pan, In *toxicity of Cu, Pb, and Zn on seed germination and young seedlings of wheat (Triticum aestivum L.)*, International Conference on Computer and Computing Technologies in Agriculture, Springer: **2010**; pp 231-240.
28. M. Wang, L. Chen, S. Chen, Y. Ma, Alleviation of cadmium-induced root growth inhibition in crop seedlings by nanoparticles. *Ecotoxicology and environmental safety* **2012,** *79*, 48-54.
29. J. Wu, J. Guo, Y. Hu, Gong, H, Distinct physiological responses of tomato and cucumber plants in silicon-mediated alleviation of cadmium stress. *Frontiers in plant science* **2015,** *6*.
30. K. Yilmaz, I. E. Akinci, S. Akinci, Effect of lead accumulation on growth and mineral composition of eggplant seedlings (Solarium melongena). *New Zealand Journal of Crop and Horticultural Science* **2009,** *37* (3), 189-199.
31. J. Yoon, X. Cao, Q. Zhou, L. Q. Ma, Accumulation of Pb, Cu, and Zn in native plants growing on a contaminated Florida site. *Science of the total environment* **2006,** *368* (2), 456-464.
32. F. Q. Zhang, Y. S. Wang, Z. P. Lou, J-D, Dong, Effect of heavy metal stress on antioxidative enzymes and lipid peroxidation in leaves and roots of two mangrove plant seedlings (Kandelia candel and Bruguiera gymnorrhiza). *Chemosphere* **2007,** *67* (1), 44-50.
33. H. Zhang, Y. Jiang, Z. He, M. Ma, accumulation of cadmium and oxidative burst in garlic (Allium sativum). *Journal of Plant Physiology* **2005,** *162* (9), 977-984.

DOI: 10.1051/itmconf/20171203035

The Experiment Research of the MoS_2 Using As the Solid Lubricant

Shi-Rong ZHANG [1,a], Jiang-Le LI [1,2,b], and She-Liang WANG [1,c]

[1]*Xi'an University of Architecture and Technology ,Xi'an 710055,China;*
[2]*Henan University of Urban Construction ,pingdingshan 467036,China*
[a]*122822169@qq.com,* [b]*35563470@qq.com,* [c]*1659128979@qq.com*

Abstract: This paper investigated the theory of the friction sliding isolation structure, The MoS_2 solid lubricant was adopted as isolation bearing friction materials, A new sliding isolation bearing was designed and made. The formula of the friction factor and the compression stress was proposed.

1 Introduction

Isolation solution is a kind of safe and economic damping technology .The friction sliding isolation system adopt a special isolation system which can separate the whole structure into three part: the upper one ,the isolation one and the lower one. It permit the upper part of the structure have a whole horizontal movement towards the foundation or the lower part. Then the transmit of the earthquake power is limited, Meanwhile it can dissipate the earthquake energy through the friction when the structure is sliding .so it can isolate the earthquake. This technology has many advantages, such as easy to carry on, low cost ,avoiding the sympathetic vibration ,extending the structure's natural vibration period and good for considering the random of the earthquake excitation. So the friction sliding system have a wonderful future as a useful isolation technology [1-6].

2 Design of Isolation Bearing and the Friction Factor Experiment

MoS2 is a solid powder with grey metallic luster, Its molecular structure is hexagonal crystal with forms of S-Mo-S connected together as show in Fig .1.S-Mo is connected with strong polar bond which is hard to break ,but S-S is connected with weak molecular link .This link is so weak that it is easy to break down and result in sliding when a small shear stress comes. This kind of sliding plane excite in every couple of sandwich layer ,So MoS2 has more lubricating properties.[7,8]

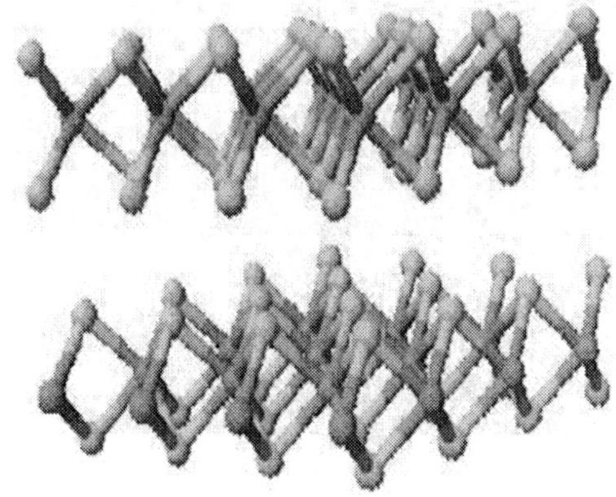

Figure 1. The molecular structure of MoS_2

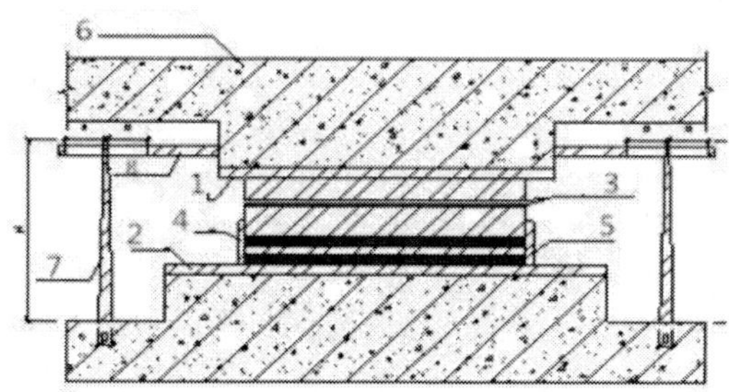

(1.upper plate 2.lower plate3.MoS_2 layer4 box
5. rubber 6.the bottom foundation beam
7.displacement restrictor 8.director plate)

Figure 2. The new friction sliding isolation bearing

As a good solid lubricating powder, MoS_2 have more advantages of standing high pressure and high temperature, having low friction and wide suitability of speed. For this reason, the new friction sliding isolation bearing was invented as show in Fig .2.

2.1 Experiment Device and Test System

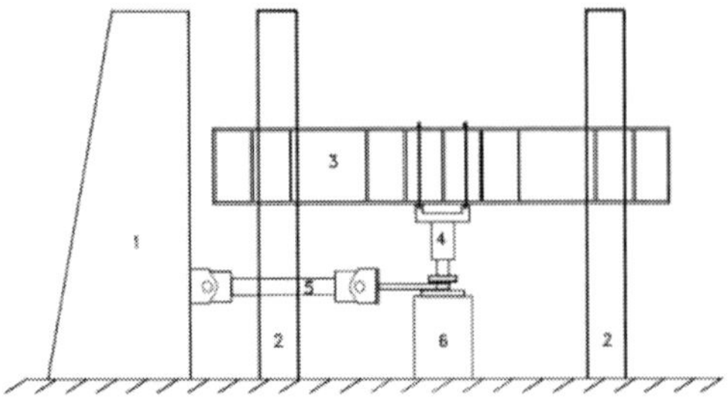

(1.reaction wall 2 reaction frame 3reaction beam 4 hydraulic jack 5 servo actuator 6 pier base)

Figure 3. Experiment device system

Figure 4. Experiment load device

This experiment only test the friction efficient between the steel pate with MoS2 sprayed on for simplicity .The lower cover plate of the friction sliding isolation bearing was fixed at the pier base. The middle slider was connected with the hydraulic jack .The displacement meter were respectively fixed at the upper cover plate ,the lower cover plate and the slider . The pressure was provided by the vertical hydraulic jack. When the applied load reach to the load condition, the pressure was kept unchanged ,then the load was applied by the horizontal hydraulic jack and the value of the horizontal hydraulic jack was recorded .When the middle slider start to slide ,the slider was kept in uniform motion. Then the pressure stopped to apply when the curve of the horizontal force and the displacement occurred horizontal stable stage(the value of the displacement meter is about 6 mm).The servo actuator was unloaded . The system was reloaded and the experiment data was recorded again .The experiment device system was shown in Fig.3. The experiment device was shown in Fig.4.

2.2 Experiment Condition

To test the feasibility and the friction behavior of the designed friction sliding bearing which used MoS2 as the slip material ,The sample' upper cover plate ,lower cover plate and slider were all spayed by MoS2.The vertical pressure were 35t,45t,55t,65t,75t.Every experiment condition was loaded twice. The experiment condition was shown in table .1.

Table 1. The experiment conditions of the friction sliding bearing

Condition	sample	Material	load(t)
1	The sample slider (first, second group)	MoS_2	35
2			45
3			55
4			65
5			75
1	The sample slider (third group)	Carbon fiber cloth	35
2			/
3			55
4			/
5			75

2.3 The Results and Analysis of the Experiment

The curve of the horizontal pulling and the appropriate displacement was shown in Fig.5. The fist part of the chart is the first loading and the second part is the second loading. It shows the curve has a horizontal line at first for the space between the slider and the fixing device. As the horizontal force is increasing, the curve rise vertically. At the initial stage of the sliding ,the slider can't turn behaviors from static to motion state quickly. It is because that there is a initial touching stage at the surface of the upper cover plate ,the lower plate and the slider. At this period the horizontal force and the displacement increase at the same time ,so the curve shows an upward sloping curve. When the slider is sliding totally ,the horizontal force is unchanged but the displacement has a constant increase. The curve reach a horizontal stable stage . At the second time the curve shows more simple ,it has no touching stage just the vertical rise stage and the horizontal stable stage is there as shown.

It indicate that the friction efficient is not large with the first group and the second group. The friction curve are smooth when the bearing at the total sliding stage. The frictional behavior are stable and the material MoS_2 is a good friction material. It can be used in the isolation system. But the third group is not suitable ,The friction

DOI: 10.1051/itmconf/20171203035

efficient of the third group is obviously larger .Replacing MoS_2 with the carbon fiber cloth on

the bearing makes the friction efficient unstable, and the friction behavior is not as stable as the material MoS_2.So the carbon fiber cloth is not a suitable friction material.

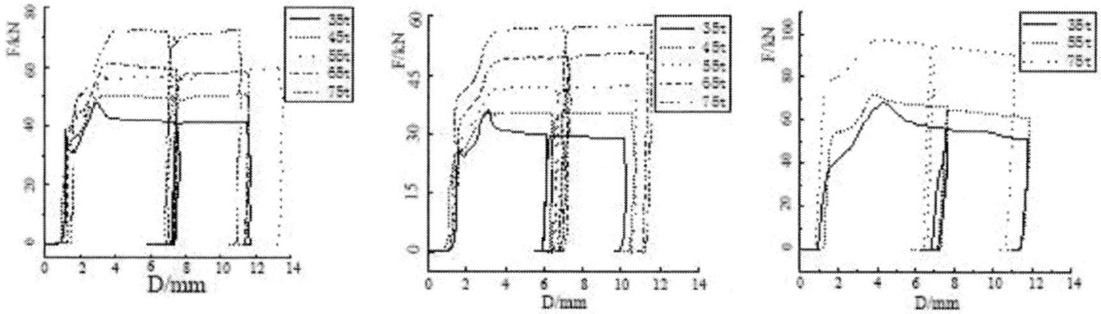

(a) the first group (b) the second group (c)the third group

Figure 5. the horizontal force and the displacement curve

The first two group of samples had a slim abrasion on the surface of the friction plane as shown in Fig .6.The friction material and the slider were in good conditions. But the third group had a terrible tearing as shown in Fig.7.

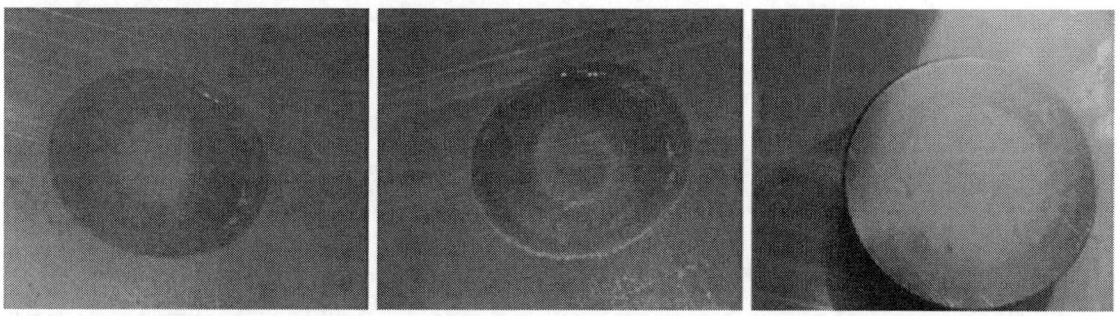

Figure 6. The upper cover plate, the lower cover plate and the slider after the experiment

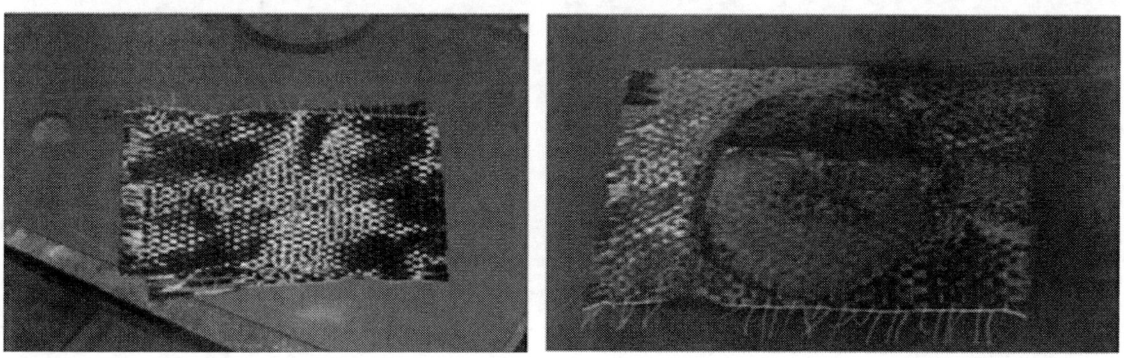

Figure 7. the carbon fiber cloth before the experiment and after the experiment

The friction efficient of the MoS2 material can be tested from the respective restoring force curve as shown in Fig.8.

 DOI: 10.1051/itmconf/20171203035

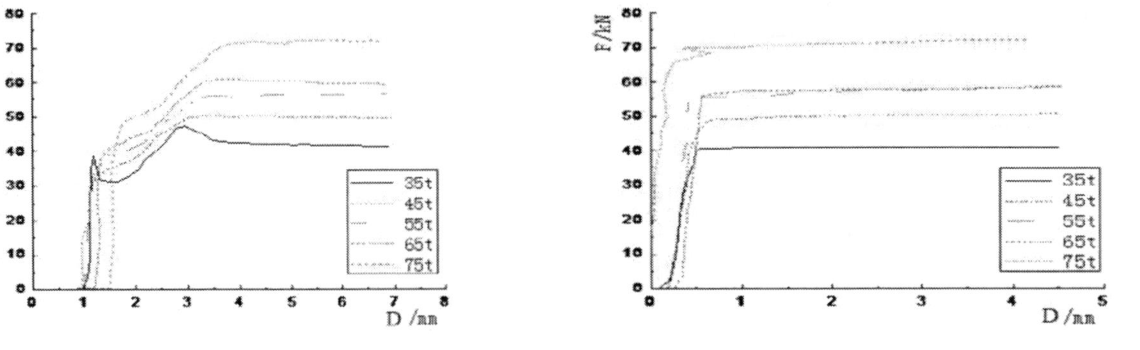

(a)the first loading

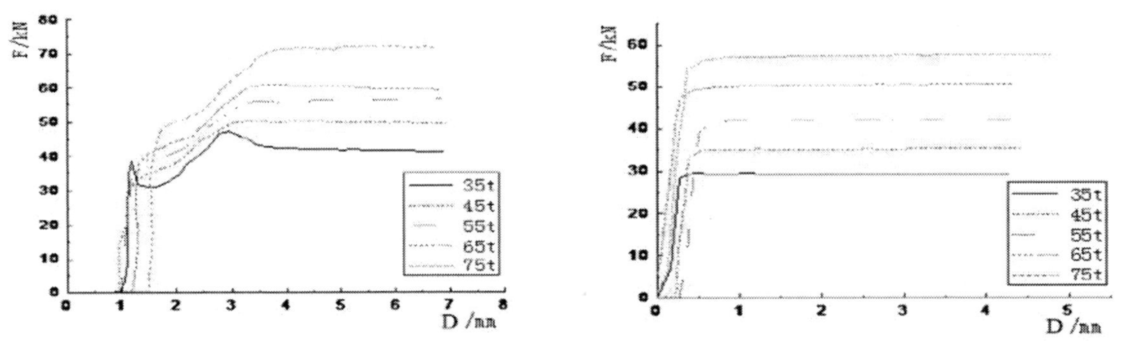

(b) the second loading

Figure 8. The restoring force model experiments

It shows that this restoring force model accords with the coulomb friction model. So it indicates that the design of the new friction sliding isolation bearing using MoS_2 as isolation bearing friction materials is reasonable .

The friction efficient can be calculated by the restoring force model. Then the curve of the vertical pressure and the friction factor is shown in Fig.9.

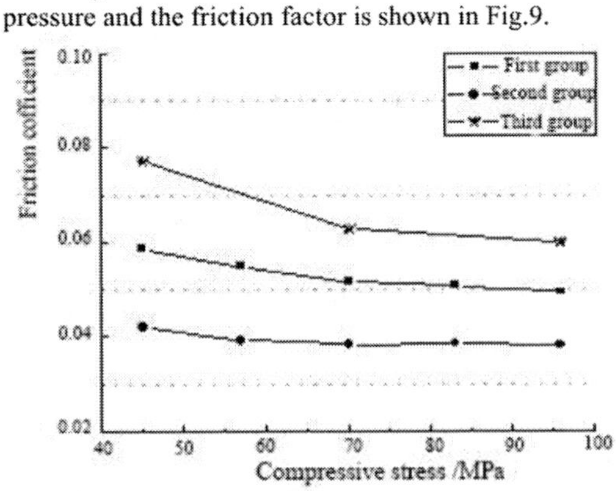

Figure 9. The friction factor under the different pressure

It shows the friction efficient is smaller and smaller as the vertical pressure is increasing. The friction efficient of the second group is smaller than the first group. It indicates that the friction factor is related to the loading times. It is changed to be smaller after many times loading .This phenomenon may be related to the rough degree of the surface, after many times loading the surface become more and more smoother than before.

Averaging the friction efficient of the two group,the curve of the friction efficient and the compress stress was shown in Fig.10.It shows the friction factor is a stable value about 0.04~0.05.As the compression stress increases from 44.58 MPa to 70.06 MPa ,the friction efficient of the isolation bearing decreases from 0.0505 to 0.0455.The decrease rate is about 10.0%.As the compression stress increase from 70.06MPa to 95.54MPa ,the friction efficient decrease from 0.0455 to 0.0438.The decrease rate is about 3.7%.The decrease bring down gradually as long as the compression stress is increasing .With the friction efficient under different compression stress be fitted with the exponential form, the formula of the friction efficient and the compression stress was shown in formula (1).

$$\mu = 0.04358 + 0.08883 e^{-\frac{\sigma}{17.44575}} \quad (1)$$

It can deduce that the friction efficient under different compression stress compared with the experiment data as the table shown in table.2,this formula is very correct .It is a good formula which can be used to choose the approximate friction efficient for the new friction sliding isolation bearing.

Table.2 The contrast of the friction factor's fitting value and the experiment value

Vertical force(t)	Fitting value	Experiment value	The error(%)
35	0.0505	0.0505	0
45	0.0469	0.0474	1.1
55	0.0452	0.0455	0.7
65	0.0444	0.0447	0.7
75	0.0440	0.0438	0.5

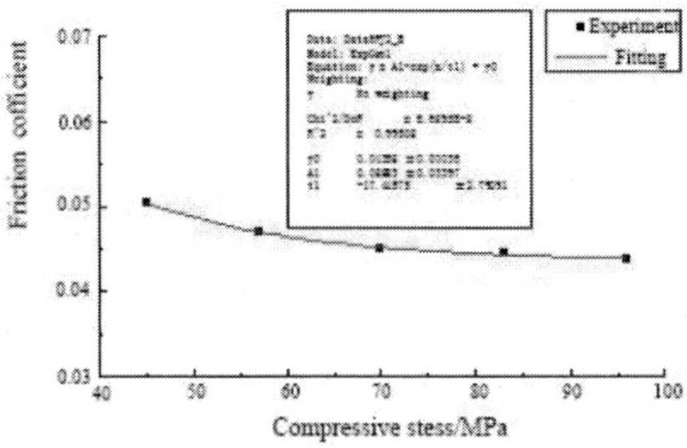

Figure 10. the curve of the friction factor and the compress stress

3 Conclusion

The MoS_2 material have a stable frictional behavior. The friction factor is about 0.04~0.05, It can be used as the friction material in the isolation system of building. The isolation layer's restoring force model accords with the coulomb friction model, it indicates that the design of the new friction sliding isolation bearing is reasonable .through the exponential fitting form, the formula of the friction factor and the compression stress is proposed. Compared with the experiment value ,the biggest error of this formula is 1.1%, so it can be used to choose the approximate friction factor of the new friction sliding isolation bearing.

References

1. Takeda junichi, JIXiaoHui.the isolation and vibration control of the structure[M].Beijing: China Architecture & Building Press, 1997.
2. Calantarients,J.A.Improvements in and connected with building and other works and appurtenances to resist the action of earthquakes and the like[R]. Paper No.325371, Engineering Library, Stanford University. Stanford, California, 1909.
3. Lee,D.M.and Medland.I.C. Base isolation ---An historical development and the influence of high mode responses[J]. Bulletin of the New Zealand national Society for Earthquake Engineering. 1978,11(4):219-233.
4. Lee,D.M.and Medland.I.C.Estimation of base isolated structure responses[J].Bulletin of the New Zealand national Society for Earthquake Engineering, 1978,11:234-244.
5. R.I.Skinner W H Robinson et al,XIELili.Introduction to engineering isolation [M].BEIJING: Seismological Press,,1996.
6. Jolivet,J and Richli,M.H. Aseimic foundation system for nuclear power stations [C]Proceedings 4th International Conference on Structural Mechanics in Reactor Technology San Francisco, California, Paper K.9/2,1977.
7. Helmut Krawinkler ,Dynamic Modeling of Concrete Structure, Harry G. Harris Editor ACI Publication,1982.
8. Dimitar Jurukovski, Experimental Testing of Materials, Elements and Components of Structures. University "Kiril and Metodij",Skopje,1982.

DOI: 10.1051/itmconf/20171203036

Acoustic Measurement of the Length of Air-plasma Filament Induced by an Intense Femtosecond Laser Pulse

Si-Qing WU[1,*], Bing DAI[2], Gang XIONG[1],and Wu-Xiong XU[1]

[1]*School of Electronic and Information Engineering, Hubei University of Science and technology, Xianning, 437100, China.*
[2]*Wuhan National Laboratory for Optoelectronics, Huazhong University of Science and technology, Wuhan 430074, China*
**Corresponding author: wusiqingccnu@163.com*

Abstract: The paper studies acoustic emission from air-plasma filament induced by a strong femtosecond laser pulse. Acoustic signal is detected with a sensitive directional microphone. Acoustic measurement provides a new method to determine the length of a filament. Compared with other methods, acoustic measurement is simpler, more sensitive, and with higher spatial resolution. Information of filament length is experimentally acquired through measuring acoustic pressure at different position of filament. On the basis of the relationship between acoustic signal and free-electron density in filament, profile of free-electron density is demonstrated

1 Introduction

Since the advent of ultra-short laser pulses, plasma filament as a result of intense femtosecond pulse lasers propagating in air becomes a hot research field in ultra-fast spectroscopy. The intriguing potential perspectives for some physics events, such as atmospheric remote sensing[1,2], terahertz wave generation[3], lidar (light detection and ranging)[4] and lightning discharge control[5,6], attract strong interest of researchers. Experimental results reported by Brodeur[7], Nibbering[8] et al, have shown that such plasma filaments can propagate tens of meters and up to several kilometers in atmosphere, beyond Rayleigh range of laser beam[9]. The underlying physical mechanism for the optical process is considered as laser Kerr nonlinear self-focusing effect. When an intense femtosecond laser pulse propagates in air, air acts as a Kerr nonlinear medium to focus beam. In focal region, peak optical intensity increases and photoionization is induced, resulting in the generation of plasma. When dynamic equilibrium emerges between self-focusing and defocusing, a narrow and long plasma column is produced [10-12].

Because optical intensity in plasma exceeds 6×10^{13} W/cm^2 [13], and electron density exceeds 10^{18} cm^{-3} [14], plasma filament induced by strong femtosecond laser is not directly measured using suitable instrument. Therefore, measure for plasma column is only indirectly implemented based on filament manifest phenomenon. Based on acoustic radiation from plasma induced by strong femtosecond laser pulses [15,16], acoustic measuring method is employed to examine the plasma filament, depending on our laboratory existing femtosecond laser system. Length of filament is examined through detecting acoustic pressure at different position of filament.

2 Experimental Details and Results

In our experiment, a strong femtosecond laser pulse amplification system (Spectra-Physics) is employed to ionize air into gas plasma, which radiates photo- acoustic pulse signal in ambient. This system utilizes a mode locked Mai Tai Seed laser oscillator to generate initial pulse, and Ti: Sapphire Regenerative Amplifier is necessary to strengthen pulse energy to peak value of 5mJ. Output Gaussian-pulse is centered at 800nm and repetition rate is set at 1 kHz. Full-width-half- magnitude (FWHM) of pulse is around 50 fs and beam diameter is roughly 8mm. Laser pulse is focused into air to create plasma filament by an achromatic plano-convex spherical lens (GCL-010157B). Diameter of lens is 25.4mm, and its focal-length is 1000mm. Plasma filament is brightly visible to naked eyes in a range of about several cm around lens focal region.

Acoustic emission from plasma is detected by a directional microphone (HT-280) placed at a distance d of 2 mm, and microphone is vertical with laser guiding direction from beginning to end. Diameter of microphone is 9 mm, restricting the directly measured filament to a length of 14mm. Frequency-range of the microphone is 20Hz-20kHz and sensitivity is -38±2dB. Acoustic signal are transformed by microphone to an electronic signal which is then delivered to a digital phosphor oscilloscope (Tektronix DPO4032), for measurement of acoustic pulse waveform. Oscilloscope has 350MHz bandwidth and 1MΩ input impedance. Experimental setup is presented schematically in Fig.1.

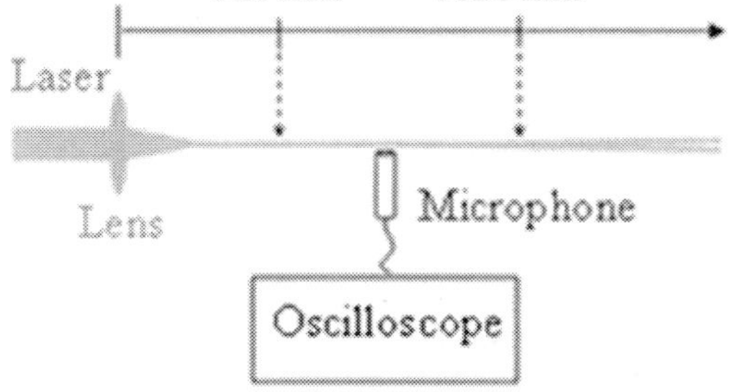

Figure1. Experimental schematic of photo acoustic emission from laser-induced air plasma filament.

By measuring amplitude of acoustic signal as a function of distance from center of lens, the dependence of the signal on propagating distance can be determined. Fig.2 shows the results for the case of 3mJ laser-pulse focused by a 1000mm focal-length lens. Acoustic signal is firstly detected at the position of 920mm away from center of lens. Then, the translational stage mounting directional microphone is moved along laser transporting direction with a step of 2mm, keeping the distance between microphone and filament unchanging, until the place standoff lens center of 1020mm. For reducing the influence of direction errors from microphone position, measurements in Fig. 2 are average results of several measures.

From Fig.2, one can find out that peak amplitude of acoustic signal significantly becomes stronger at the position of 928mm (arrow ①) away from center of lens, and obviously becomes smaller at the place (arrow ②) standoff lens center of 1000mm. In the experiment, we also develop a thin glass piece to roughly inspect plasma filament. We find out, at about 928mm location from center of lens, there is an obvious bright spot and a small pit on the thin glass piece; however, at more than 1000mm position, filament cannot be examined. The experiment examining result is consistent with the changing trend of acoustic signal in Fig.2. Therefore, we can come to a conclusion that, the length of air filament induced by the focused intense femtosecond laser pulses is at least 72mm, from the location of 928 mm to the position of 1000mm away from lens center. Note that, at the range of 54mm from 934mm (arrow ③) to 988mm (arrow ④) away from lens center, acoustic signals are relatively stronger, and we can catch sight of a bright plasma filament with naked eyes. In addition, we notice that plasma filament firstly emerges before geometrical focus of lens. The reason for this situation is mainly due to the fact that, Kerr nonlinear self-focusing effect results in laser pulses to focus ahead of time, which leads to air plasma filament forming in front of geometrical focus of lens [15,17]. Note that, since laser is operating at kHz repetition rate, measurements are thus cumulative the average of several filaments and does not primarily mimic true measurement of filament generated by single pulse.

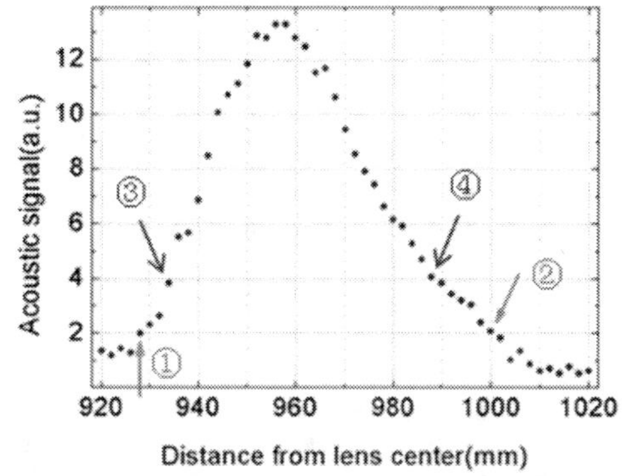

Figure.2 Peak amplitude of acoustic signal at different position.

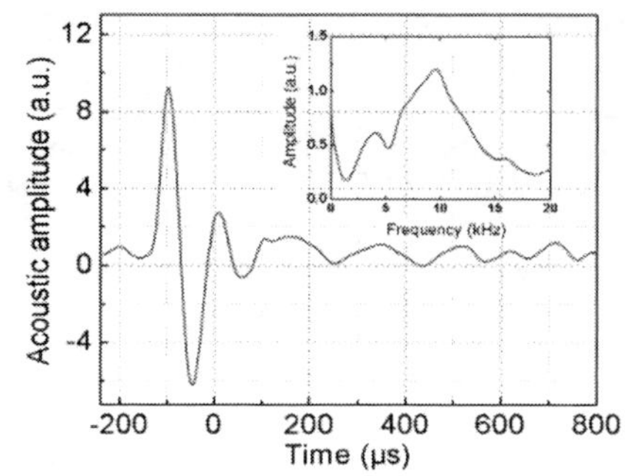

Figure.3. An acoustic signal collected by oscilloscope. Inset is corresponding spectrum.

Fig.3 shows a waveform of acoustic pulse emitted from plasma filament. The acoustic signal is recorded by directional microphone fixed at a location of 950mm away from lens center, and temporally resolved using an oscilloscope with a sampling frequency of 50 kHz. This waveform is composed of 1~2 main oscillatory pulses followed by a series of small ripples, and pulse duration is around 125μs. By taking Fourier transformation, acoustic spectrum can be obtained, as showed in inset of Fig. 3. From spectrum graph, one can understand that the spectrum covers total frequency component in microphone responding range. At the same time, we are aware of peak amplitude of acoustic pulse emerging at central frequency of microphone responding range, i.e. 10 kHz. The dips in spectrum are a result of microphone response, and they are not related to acoustic emission. In the experiment, before and after plasma filament, we can still detect a pulsed acoustic signal, which is background acoustic noise. Background noise is measured at several mv in out laboratory, and noise level is 2 orders of magnitude under the maximal acoustic signal detected at the center of filament. However, background noise does not interference the measurement of acoustic signal that is drawn in Fig. 2, because noise is removed from the measured acoustic pulse.

3 Discussion

Under illumination of intense femtosecond laser pulses, multiphoton-ionization (MPI) of air molecules takes place in subpicoseond time scale through releasing free electrons, forming air plasma filament. Optical field enhances free electron temperature, Te, to the order of 10^4-10^5 K, while the temperature of neighboring molecules or ions, Tm, is much lower [18]. Within the following 10^{-9}-10^{-8} s, Tm rapidly ascents through energy transfer due to elastic and inelastic collision between hot electrons and the surrounding air molecules (nitrogen and oxygen), until thermal equilibrium appears[19,20]. This sudden increase of localized gas temperature gives rise to a shock wave that persists for a short distance, then relaxing into acoustic wave [21,22].

As to the physical processes of energy transfer between free electrons and heavy particles (ions and air molecules) in a femtosecond pulse-induced plasma, F. Vidal et al.[23] have given detailed theoretical analysis. The time of the energy transfer from electrons to heavy particles should been in the range of 10^{-9}–10^{-8} s. The final thermal equilibrium is achieved in 10^{-6}-10^{-5} s after the exciting laser pulse[23], and equilibrium temperature in air filament is approximately 0.1 eV (corresponding to a temperature of 1200 K).

The relevance between acoustic pulse from air-plasma filament and initial free-electron density in air plasma was been deeply studied by some researchers. For instance, it was been verified that the maximum amplitude of acoustic signal is scaled with exciting-laser energy absorbed by the gas[24], when acoustic method was employed to survey multiphoton absorption by polyatomic molecules. In turn, the absorbed optical-energy is scaled with initial free-electron density yielded through MPI, when gas and exciting-laser wavelength are appropriate. Consequently, the detected microphone signal that is displayed in Fig.3 provides a direct consequence for the free-electron density contour in plasma filament.

Summary

Long plasma filament can emerge as a result of strong femtosecond laser pulse focused by a large focal-length lens to propagate in air, and acoustic-pulse signal can be emitted in the ambient. Experiments show that, at different location of plasma filament, intensities of acoustic signal are discriminate, and acoustic intensities are dependent on the distance from lens center in the form of the normal distribution along laser transmission direction. Length of air plasma filament can be indirectly measured through examining acoustic signal eradiated from plasma. Being a fast, real-time and non-destructive measurement, and only easy measuring device provided, acoustic measurement is a good method for examining long plasma filament in atmosphere, in spite of some deviation arising at the position of the beginning and ending of plasma filament. Simultaneously, free-electron density profile is acquired, based on the relevance between acoustic signal and free-electron density in filament.

Acknowledgement

The authors gratefully acknowledge support from Ph.D. Foundation-Launched Project (No. BK1523) of Hubei University of Science & Technology.

References

1. G. Mejean, J. Kasparian and E. Salmon Appl. Phys. B 77 357 (2003).
2. F. Theberge, W. Liu and S. A. Hosseini Appl. Phys. B 81 131 (2005).
3. B. Sun and J. Q. Yao Chinese J. Lasers 33 1350 (2006).
4. J. Kasparian and J. P. Wolf Opt. Commun. 152 355 (1998).
5. X. M. Zhao, J. C. Diels and C. Y. Wang IEEE J. QE. 31 599 (1995).
6. H. Pépin, D. Comtois and F. Vidal Phys. Plasm. 8 2532 (2001).
7. E. T. J Nibbering, P. F. Curley and G. Grillon Opt. Lett. 21 62 (1996).
8. Brodeur, C. Y. Chien and F. A. Ilkov Opt. Lett. 22 304 (1997).
9. L. Wöste, C. Wedekind and H. Wille Las Optoelektron 29 51 (1997).
10. S. Eisenmann, A. Pukhov and A. Zigler Phys. Rev. Lett. 98 155002 (2007).
11. F. Vidal, D. Comtois and C. Y. Chien IEEE Trans. Plasma Sci. 28 418 (2000).
12. W. Liu, J. Bernhardt and F. Thberge J. Appl. Phys. 102 033111 (2007).
13. J. Kasparian, R. Sauerbrey and S. L. Chin. Appl. Phys. B 71 877 (2000).
14. H. Yang, J. Zhang and Y. T. Li. Phys. Rev. E 66 016406 (2002).
15. Z. Q. Hao, J. Yu and J. Zhang Chin. Phys. Lett. 22 636 (2005).
16. J. Yu, D. Mondelain and J. Kasparian Appl. Opt. 42 7117 (2003).
17. S. Petit, A. Talebpour, A. Proulx and S. L. Chin Opt. Comm. 175 323 (2000).
18. G. N. Gibson, R. R. Freeman and T. J. McIlrath Phys. Rev. Lett. 67 1230 (1991).
19. J. Yu, D. Mondelain, J. Kasparian, E. Salmon, S. Geffroy, C. Favre, et al. Appl. Opt. 42 7117 (2003).
20. Filin, R. Compton, D. A. Romanov and R. J. Levis Phys. Rev. Lett. 102 155004 (2009).
21. X. W. Ni, B. Zou, J. P. Chen, B. M. Bian, Z. H. Shen and J. Lu Acta Phys. Sin. 7 143 (1998).
22. H. Sobral, M. Villagran-Muniz, R. Navarro-Gonzalez and A. C. Raga Appl. Phys. Lett. 77 3158 (2000).
23. F. Vidal, D. Comtois, C. Y. Chien, A. Desparois, B. La Fontaine, T W Johnston, et al. IEEE Trans. Plasma Sci. 28 418 (2000).
24. S. L. Chin, D. K. Evans, R. D. McAlpine and W. N. Selander Appl. Phys. 21 658 (1982).
25. [24]S. L. Chin, D. K. Evans, R. D. McAlpine and W. N. Selander Appl. Phys. 21 658 (1982)

Study on Interval Optimal Control Method for Ramp's Merging Areas in Urban Expressway

Jiang-Hong JIN[a], Wei LI [b], Jin-Yan HU[c], and Dan-Dan LI[d]

Institute of Operational Research and Cybernetic, Hangzhou Dianzi University, Hangzhou, China
[a]jin8023hong@126.com, [b]weilihz@126.com, [c]hjybbloveyou@163.com, [d]lidandan9203@163.com

Abstract: How to solve the problem of urban expressway traffic congestion is an urgent problem for the government and the transportation department. Ramp's merging areas, as the interaction link between internal and external traffic of expressway system, is the main research object of this paper. Taking Hangzhou Qiushi expressway on the road section of the entrance ramp as the target section , the interval optimal control model considering vehicle speed, time occupancy and vehicle spacing as interval variables is proposed, and the single dynamic adjustment algorithm of on-ramp is given.

1. Introduction

In recent years, urban traffic congestion has become one of the troubled problems plaguing the government and traffic department. Urban expressway system, as the main road of urban traffic, plays a very important role in urban residents travel. However, due to the high volume of traffic, urban expressway traffic congestion has become increasingly serious.

Taking the traffic system of Hangzhou, Zhejiang as the research object, we find that it is impossible to solve the increasing traffic demand by building more roads and enlarging the scale of the traffic network. Hangzhou has long planned the "four vertical and five horizontal" traffic trunk and gradually completed. However, the problem of traffic congestion has not been improved. In fact, it is the lag of management technology research. Therefore, the management and optimization of urban traffic should arouse people's attention.

Urban transportation system is a very complicated system. At present, it is impossible to establish a unified interval optimization model for the whole system. However, according to the study we found that traffic jam phenomenon in the large, heavily intertwined ramp is significant. On account of the characteristics of traffic flow, Chen put forward the ramp control method based on time occupancy and velocity as control variables [1]. Actually, the traffic volume, speed and time occupancy of the same road section are interval numbers. Therefore, we propose the interval optimal control model of ramp based on reference [1], and use a single dynamic adjustment algorithm of on-ramp to give the control scheme.

Throughout the paper, we follow the notations given in [2-5].

An interval number is defined as

$$a^I = [\underline{a}, \overline{a}] = \{a \in R | \underline{a} \le a \le \overline{a}\}.$$

The set of all intervals is denoted by IR. If $\underline{a} = \overline{a} = a$, then a^I is the real number a.

Operations over closed real intervals are defined by the general rule

$$a^I * b^I = [\underline{a}, \overline{a}] * [\underline{b}, \overline{b}] = \{a * b \mid \underline{a} \le a \le \overline{a}, \underline{b} \le b \le \overline{b}\},$$

where $* \in \{+, -, \times, \div\}$ and division is defined only if $0 \notin b^I = [\underline{b}, \overline{b}]$.

A unit of time, the number of vehicles through a certain point, a section or a lane of the road is known as traffic flow. Generally traffic flow is notated by q^I.

$$q^I = \{q \mid \underline{q} \le q \le \overline{q}\}.$$

Calculation formula of q is defined as

$$q = \frac{N}{T},$$

where T is length of time , N is the number of vehicles in period T.

Generally, the degree of compactness between vehicles on the road is called intensity, and it is represented by time occupancy or density. Generally time occupancy is notated by o^I, formula of o is defined as

$$o = \frac{\sum_{i=1}^{N} \Delta t_i}{T},$$

where Δt_i is time for vehicle i crossing the section.

2. Model Establishment

The basic goal of expressway ramp control is that main traffic flow of the expressway is in a steady state and safety of the vehicle is ensured. Based on the analysis for vehicle interaction characteristics and traffic flow stability mechanism of ramp's merging areas in urban expressway[6,7], we propose a guided real-time dynamic coordinated control strategy to limit the amount of traffic entering the expressway, so that the actual traffic volume of the expressway does not exceed its maximum capacity.

Change of time occupancy on the main line can achieve the control of the on-ramp adjustment rate. As much as possible to play the main line capacity, while we guarantee that time occupancy of the main line swing in the vicinity of the desired time share.

Time occupancy control model is given below,

$$f_k^{\mathrm{I}} = q_{k-1}^{\mathrm{I}} + \varphi_1 \cdot [o_c - o_{k-1}^{\mathrm{I}}],$$

where q_{k-1}^{I} is range of flow for the on-ramp during the-1 period, φ is regulating coefficient (obtained by a large number of tests), k is critical value of occupancy on the main road upstream, it is obtained by parameter calibration, o_{k-1}^{I} is time occupancy on the main road upstream during the k-1 period.

Vehicle speed model is given below,

$$g_k^{\mathrm{I}} = q_{k-1}^{\mathrm{I}} + \varphi_2 \cdot [v_{k-1}^{\mathrm{I}} / v_c - 1],$$

where v_{k-1}^{I} is average speed on the main road upstream in the k-1 period, v_c is critical value of speed on the main road upstream.

In order to reduce the jamming degree of on-ramp traffic to the main traffic flow, we establish the control model considering lane-change safe distance.

$$m_k^{\mathrm{I}} = q_{k-1}^{\mathrm{I}} + \varphi_3 \cdot [S_{k-1}^{\mathrm{I}} / S_c - 1],$$

where S_{k-1}^{I} is vehicle spacing of kerb lane in the k-1 period, S_c is lane-change safe distance.

For traffic flow under different conditions, different weights are given to the above models to determine the actual on-ramp regulation rate. Finally, the interval optimal control model of ramp is obtained.

$$r_k^{\mathrm{I}} = \mu_1 f_k^{\mathrm{I}} + \mu_2 g_k^{\mathrm{I}} + \mu_3 m_k^{\mathrm{I}},$$

where $\mu_1 + \mu_2 + \mu_3 = 1$.

Remark. If r_k^{I} is too small,the vehicle is prohibited from entering the ramp. This is likely to cause the ramp to close in a long time; while r_k^{I} is too large to lead traffic congestion on the expressway downstream. Therefore, the minimum ramp rate $r_{\min}^{\mathrm{I}}$ and the maximum regulation rate $r_{\max}^{\mathrm{I}}$ are provided for the expressway ramp. The actual value is determined by comprehensive data analysis.

3. Algorithm

In fact, the interval optimization problem is usually transformed into an optimization problem based on real variables. Through r_k^{I} we easily obtain that

$$\overline{r_k} = \mu_1 \overline{f_k} + \mu_2 \overline{g_k} + \mu_3 \overline{m_k},$$
$$\underline{r_k} = \mu_1 \underline{f_k} + \mu_2 \underline{g_k} + \mu_3 \underline{m_k}.$$

In view of the complexity of the Hangzhou traffic problem, we take the lower bound $\underline{r_k}$ of the on-ramp rate of the target road as an example to realize dynamic adjustment algorithm of on-ramp control.

The control strategy of the on-ramp traffic flow is mainly guided real-time dynamic coordinated control method. First of all, we set the detectors in the main lane and ramp to test traffic flow, speed, time share of each lane and vehicle spacing of the outer lane in a certain period of time; then transmit to the control terminal simultaneously and calculate the on-ramp adjustment rate; finally, we output the control scheme.

We use the signal machine to export control program. The amount of traffic allowed to import the main line is defined as

$$n = \frac{C \cdot \underline{r_k}}{3600},$$

where $\underline{r_k}$ is the lower bound of the on-ramp rate, C is sampling period of export in the ramp's merging areas.

Based on the signal timing method in the unified way, we can determine the corresponding display time of light color.

The lane-change safe distance of the lane is determined by the combination of the speed and acceleration of the target lane. Assume $\underline{r_k}$ is relatively small, that is, traffic flow of the main line is relatively large, at this point we consider whether to generate safe lane spacing.

To sum up, dynamic adjustment algorithm of ramp control has the following steps.

1) The relevant data of the target road section is detected by detectors in the sampling period. Actually , period is generally 20 seconds.

2) Compute

$$\underline{r_k} = \mu_1 \underline{f_k} + \mu_2 \underline{g_k} + \mu_3 \underline{m_k}.$$

3) If $\underline{r_k} < \underline{r_{min}}$, then set $\underline{r_k} := \underline{r_{min}}$. Consider whether to generate lane-change safe distance. If not, then the on-ramp is normally open; otherwise, go to step 5.

4) If $\underline{r_k} > \underline{r_{max}}$, then the on-ramp is open all the time.

5) Output corresponding display time of light color, then go to step 1.

4. Model Evaluation and Analysis

We collected the vehicle speed and vehicle spacing of the target road in the period, vehicle spacing and other data. Using *Vissim* simulation software, we analyzed the above model by traffic simulation, and verified the accuracy and practicability of the interval optimal control model. The model has the following advantages.

a) Although the single-point ramp regulation can not achieve the optimal target of the system, the single-point ramp control is much lower than the multi-ramp coordination control in terms of technical complexity and investment cost.

b) In most cases, local problems are often more serious than the system, only in the local problem is resolved under the premise, in order to better alleviate the system problems.

But our model's shortcomings are given below.

a) The urban expressway ramp control for accidental factors caused by traffic congestion problems difficult to be adjusted in time, flexibility and adaptive performance is relatively poor, the lack of special circumstances for traffic management and control methods of research.

b) $\underline{r_k}$ should be adjusted with the other ramp to get an optimal solution on the entrance rate at the same time, perhaps we can maximize the protection of the main road traffic efficiency.

5. Conclusion

Ramp's merging areas are the key nodes of the cross correlation between expressway mainline and urban road network, the traffic operating conditions of which play a direct impact on the effective expressway system functions. We propose interval optimal control model of ramp based on three interval variables (vehicle speed, time occupancy and vehicle spacing), and use the single dynamic adjustment algorithm of on-ramp to give control scheme. Traffic system is a complicated system composed of people, vehicles, roads and environment. To establish a unified interval optimization model which can describe and explain the complex behavior of various traffic flow is far-reaching.

Acknowledgment

This research was financially supported by the NNSF of China (Grant Nos. 61673145) and NSF of Zhejiang Province (Xinmiao2016R407079).

References

1. X. Chen, D. Wang, S. Jin, and C. Wang, "On-ramp metering control strategy of urban expressway," Journal of Jilin University Engineering and Technology Edition. S1 (2008) 45-50. (in Chinese)
2. R.E. Moore, Interval Analysis, Prentice-Hall, Englewood Cliffs, NJ, 1966, pp. 21-22.
3. M. Fiedler, J. Nedoma, J. Ramik, J. Rohn, and K. Zimmermann, Linear optimization problems with inexact data, Springer-Verlag, New York, 2006.
4. F. Wang, W. Wei, H. Qi, and D .Wang, "Research on Discontinuous Flow Speed-density Relation Model," Journal of Highway & Transportation Research & Development. 31 (7) (2014) 108-114.
5. X. Luo, Y. Chen, and Y. Huo, "Study on the relationship of flow-speed-density of mixed traffic flows," Journal of Southwest Jiaotong University.33 (2) (1998).
6. M. Papageorgiou, S.H. Hadj, and J.M. Blosseville, "ALINEA: a local ramp feedback control law for on-ramp metering," Transportation Research Record. 1320 (1991) 58-64.
7. Y. Wang, M. Papageorgiou, J. Gaffney, and I. Papamichail, "Local ramp metering in the presence of random-location bottlenecks downstream of a metered on-ramp," International IEEE Conference on Intelligent Transportation Systems. 2178 (2010) 1462-1467.

Application of Privacy-aware Role-based Access Control Model in IHE-XDS

Daniya Dauletbek[a], Shi-Zhong YUAN[b]

School of Computer Engineering and Science, Shanghai University, Shanghai, China
[a]daniya.dauletbek@gmail.com, [b]szyuan@shu.edu.cn

Abstract: Integrating the Healthcare Enterprise (IHE)'s Cross-Enterprise Document Sharing (XDS) profile is an open standards-based architecture specification for EHR systems. In EHR systems, it is necessary to provide a mechanism for access control to protect security and privacy of patient data. On the basis of related studies, this paper addresses the issue of access control and privacy protection of privacy data in XDS-based EHR systems, aiming to identify a suitable, privacy-aware role-based access control model based on specific access requirements for IHE-XDS. Privacy-aware role-based access control model is an extension model of RBAC model. It not just has the benefits of RBAC, but additionally adds restrictions on the permission assignment for the roles by using the purpose enforcement and privacy-aware access control enforcement. The proposed model could further protect privacy data, while decreasing the complexity of the role assignment.

1. Introduction

The XDS (Cross-enterprise Document Sharing) integration specification proposed by the IHE (Integrating Healthcare Enterprise) is used to solve the problem of cross-system information sharing. Medical information on IHE-XDS systems is sensitive and should be protected from unauthorized access. So for IHE-XDS systems it is important to guarantee the confidentiality and integrity of information and the privacy of patients. In order to meet these needs a generally utilized approach such as Role-Based Access Control (RBAC) model, which is a fundamental security obstruction for securing information in healthcare information system is used. The RBAC model is an alternative to the traditional access control models and it is an extensible and flexible access control model. The basic idea of RBAC is to introduce the concept of roles between users and access, connecting the users and roles to control the user's access to system resources by authorizing the role. Although the main consideration of the RBAC model is the protecting security of the system, but it is not intended to enhance the privacy policy because of the lack of three important elements of the privacy policy that described in the OECD (Organization for Economic Co-operation and Development) Guidelines, such as purpose binding, conditions and obligations. The types and possibilities of inconsistencies between policies also will increase, so the models applicable to describe the privacy protection such as Privacy-Aware RBAC (P-RBAC) by Q Ni et al. [9] and Purpose-Based Access Control model by JW Byun et al. [11] have been proposed. In these two models Purpose-Based Access Control model [11] is a comprehensive approach for privacy preserving access control based on the notion of purpose, which describes the reason(s) for data collection and processing and organized in a tree structure. The motivations for adopting purpose based approach are the fundamental policies for private information concern with which data object is used for what purposes. Purposes in this approach are divided into two categories: intended purpose and access purpose. Intended purposes tell how data should be used and access purpose tells how data will be used. One of the important improvements of the Privacy-Aware RBAC model [9] that has mentioned above is that it changes the description of permissions and introduces elements such as purpose, condition, and obligation. This model is extended model of the well-known RBAC model in order to provide full support for expressing highly complex privacy-related policies. Consistent with the classic RBAC model and according to the different model functions Privacy-Aware RBAC model contains a series of conceptual models such as Core P-RBAC, Hierarchical P-RBAC, Conditional P-RBAC and Universal P-RBAC. Compare to the traditional models, the two last mentioned models are more able to meet the requirements of IHE-XDS. In additional to meet the security and privacy requirement that mentioned in IHE profiles [21, 22] Basel Katt et al. [4] have already designed security architecture and proposed a Prototypical Implementation model. Although the model proposed by Basel Katt et al. can satisfy the requirements of IHE-XDS, but due to lack of component of privacy-aware access control policies enforcement, cannot ensure the purpose and condition of access. Because this component is in charge of enforcing security and privacy access control policies on personal data, and these policies takes into account of preferences such as purposes for accessing data, entities the data may/may not be disclosed to, etc. Therefore, the model designed in this paper is the comprehensive model that based on the advantages of the two last models that mentioned above and it not only has the features of the role hierarchy of general RBAC, but also can provide the conditions, purposes and other fine-grained modules that required by privacy protection. So compared to the model proposed by Basel Katt et al. and the latest access control models, the model proposed in this paper can further enhance the security control and privacy protection of the privacy information of patient's. The model extends access control with the help of the notion of purpose, and takes the authorization management based on "purpose management". Through the purpose binding for the role and developing a common policy; In accordance with the different emphasis on patient's privacy, sets the purpose property for privacy data and formulates a personal policy. Under the premise of the unchanged general policy of the system, the patients can be adjusted personal policies with personal requirements of privacy. This paper elaborated on the idea of designing a Privacy-Aware RBAC model in IHE-XDS, presenting important elements of the model, such as conditions and purposes, and XACML policy execution.

2. Privacy-aware RBAC Model

The model designed in this paper is based on several features that belong to the RBAC and PRBAC model proposed by Yang et al.[13] and the P-RBAC model that proposed by Zhang et al.[7] This model is the model that comprehensively enforcing the security control and privacy protection by using the advantages of the components of Purposes, Conditions. The model includes the privacy protection logic and the access control policy of RBAC, in which the authorization assignment is needed in the privacy protection. Mainly combining the good aspects of the RBAC model and Purpose-Based RBAC model and create the comprehensive Privacy-Aware RBAC model that can be applied to IHE-XDS. Because the more complete and newer models are: Purpose-Based RBAC model and Privacy-Aware RBAC model. The model proposed in this paper is shown in the Figure1 below.

In the Figure1 User represents the user, indicates the subject. Role represents a kind of authority or title that has certain power and responsibility. Object represents the privacy information set that user requested. Action is an executable operation. Purpose indicates the purpose of the user accessing the privacy information that is collection of all purposes. Condition indicates the condition for the user to access the privacy information. In this model, the principle of role-based authorization, and assignment of permission, and the user obtains the permission to access the privacy information by being granted the appropriate role, and also the features of the condition is the same to the core P-RBAC model proposed by Q Ni et al. [9]. But the difference is that in this model further analyze in detail the Intended Purpose. The Intended Purpose consists of two parts, AIP (Allowed Intended Purpose), PIP (Prohibited Intended Purpose). Respectively indicates data can be accessed and prohibited for a particular access purpose. In this model, "Purpose" also possible to perform the responsibilities of access purpose. Because the privacy information can be only be accessed if the AC (Access Purpose) matches the IP (Intended Purpose). Because of this principle, Intended Purpose is associated to the component of "Purpose" in this model.

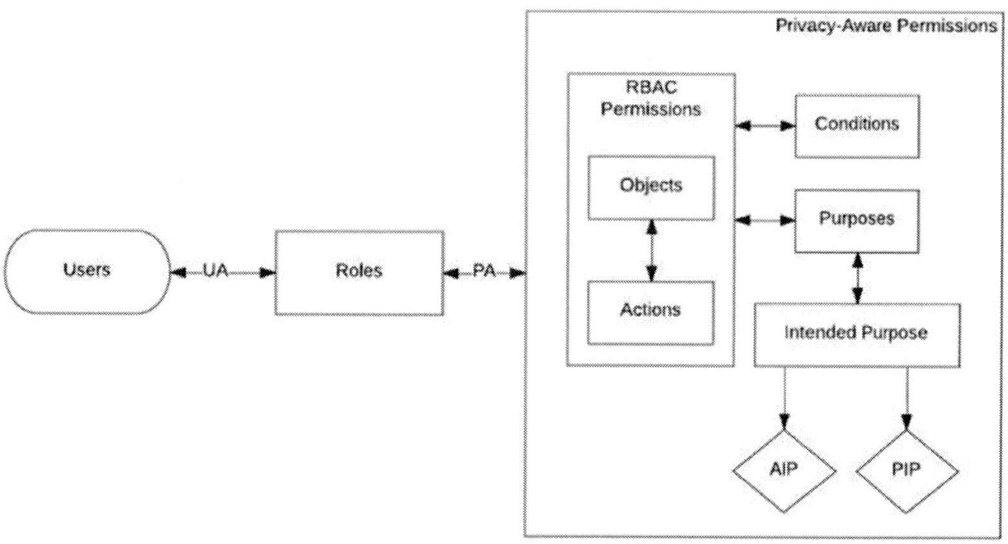

Figure 1. Privacy-Aware RBAC model in IHE-XDS

AP (Purpose) indicates Access Purpose, IP indicates the Intended Purpose, the allowed purpose of the Intended Purpose is AIP, prohibited purpose of the Intended Purpose is PIP. Thus, an Intended Purpose IP can be expressed as <AIP, PIP>. AIP and PIP are purpose sets. Where IP=<AIP, PIP> is an intended purpose, then IP^*=AIP↓-PIP↕,

IP_P=PIP↕. The meaning of IP^* is that, although the information provider gives the allowed intended purpose and prohibited intended purpose to indicate their willingness to use the information, but AIP and PIP will unavoidably occur conflict. Therefore, the principle of "prohibition of priority" is adopted here, that is, when occur conflicts between allowed purpose and prohibited purpose, determined as prohibited purpose. IP_P indicated a collection of information that cannot be accessed. If the PT is assumed to be the purpose tree, there is an intended purpose IP=<AIP, PIP> and an access purpose P on the PT, respectively. If $P \in IP^*$, then it is called P and IP matches, shows that under P, the information visitor can fully access the information.

Here:

- UA refers to (User Assignment): UA:$\subseteq$ User × Role
- PA refers to (Permission Assignment): PA$\subseteq$ Role × PP, refers to the many-to-many mapping between the role set and the permission set of access purpose.
- assigned_user: Role → 2User , represents that a role is mapped to a collection of user, indicates a user who granted a specific role. Its function is expressed as: assigned_user (r) = {u ∈ User | <u, r> ∈ UA}
- assigned_role: User → 2Role , represents that a user is mapped to a collection of role that represents the role that granted a specific user. Its function is expressed as: assigned_role (u) = {R ∈ Role | <u, r> ∈ UA}
- assigned_access_permission: Role → 2PP ,indicates that a role is mapped to a set of access that represents to grant access permission to the specific role. Its function is expressed as:
- assigned_access_permission (r) = {pp ∈ PP | <r, pp> ∈ PA}
- RBAC permissions: RBAC_Perm $\subseteq$ O × A.
- P-RBAC permissions: P $\subseteq$ O × A × C × Pu.

In the Privacy-Aware access control model, it is necessary to use a streamlined language form to express the conditional requirements in the privacy policy. That language uses a context variable (CV) to characterize, in the variables recorded privacy-related information that needs to be considered while executing the permissions. Although the conditional language LC_0 has only limited ability of expression, but for the privacy authority, LC_0 can characterize the conditional expression requirements in most of the permissions.

Conditional description language LC_0 Define CV as a set of context variables, for each variable $x \in CV$, there is a finite range of values defined as D_x, the range is represented by the relational operator equal sign (=) and the inequality (≠). In the various types of conditions, the definition of constant conditions for the use of logical operators false (F) and true (T) that expressed condition. The definition of the Meta conditions (ac, atomic condition) is the information expressed using the following expression: (x op_r v), where $x \in CV$, $v \in D_x$, $op_r \in \{=, \neq\}$. The condition LC_0 is defined as:

- Constant condition is a component of LC_0 condition set.
- Meta-condition ac is LC_0 condition.
- If c_i, c_j are the two conditions in LC_0, then c_i, c_j and the relationship of $c_i \wedge c_j$ belongs to LC_0.

In order to show the ability of the model to be truly defined in the customization policy, according to the privacy needs of patient, proposed a graphic algorithm that uses in this access control model as shown in the Figure2.

3. Implementation Scheme of Privacy-Aware RBAC model for IHE-XDS

The research done by Basel Katt et al. [4] is a solution to solve the Access control and privacy issues in the system of distributed EHR system that utilizes IHE profiles. They put forward the security architecture and prototyping implementation in the context of the health @ net project. The Health @ net project is a core component of the development of an eHealth system according to IHE integration profile. They used the XACML as a policy language in the security architecture. The same language is used in the model designed in this paper. At the first let us approximately analyze the XACML before giving explanation to the model.

XACML policy execution consists of three main components:

- Policy
- Policy enforcement point (PEP)
- Policy decision point (PDP)

Figure 2. Graphic algorithm of authorization process of privacy enforcement

The XACML policy enforcement point (PEP) is the gateway that determines whether an operation is allowed or not. PEP accepts access requests, which are specially formatted XML documents that define a set of data values.

PEP forwards request to policy decision point (PDP).

The features of the components used in the Figure:

- Policy Administration Point (PAP) - This is the point at which the policy is managed.
- Policy Decision Point (PDP) - the point at which the authorization decision is evaluated and issued.
- Policy Enforcement Point (PEP) - A point that blocks user access requests for resources and enforces PDP decisions.
- Contextual Handler: Context information is associated with an access request, such as the purpose of accessing the data, the role of the requester, and so on.

Central Administration is the core of the security architecture that proposed by Basel Katt et al. [4], that is to say that all the privacy information exists in this part. In this architecture, the researchers have added PEP to the Registry, Consumer and Repository. In this research, in order to enhance the protection and security of privacy data, we would like to make some changes in the Central Administration of the model that proposed by Basel Katt et al. [4], and design a specific model. The main change made by this research is to connect the Central Administration directly to the PEP. And then establish a privacy-aware access control enhanced component between the information visitor and the information provider to enhance the security control and privacy protection of the privacy data. So, why do this research wants add PEP to the policy administration point and policy decision point? Because the benefits of PEP include:

- PEP is a single point of access.
- Policy is decoupled from applications/services.
- Policy can be managed independently of applications and services, so they can focus on providing business values.
- Auditing in PDP and PEP is simpler than auditing in many different applications/services.
- Implementation of change is simplified. Policies can be managed and deployed to explicit architectural functions (i.e. PAP and PDP).

Since unauthorized requests never get to the application / service (because it is blocked by PEP), it is not very easy to compromise the application. This is not the case if PEP and PDP are basically implemented in the applied security model. The PEP, PDP, PAP and PIP can be implemented using hardened, approved components.

Context awareness computing is becoming more and more important. Context-based authorizations will be simplified through isolated policy management and enforcement.

In general, the policy is essential to ensure that logical results are achieved. The purpose of policy management is to adapt the dynamic adaptability of the behavior of support in the process by changing the policy. This kind of system has two main management agents: 1) Policy decision point (PDP). 2) Policy enforcement point (PEP).

In the process of implementing Privacy-Aware RBAC model that can be applied for IHE-XDS, this paper has used some features of the XACML architecture. As shown in the Figure3.

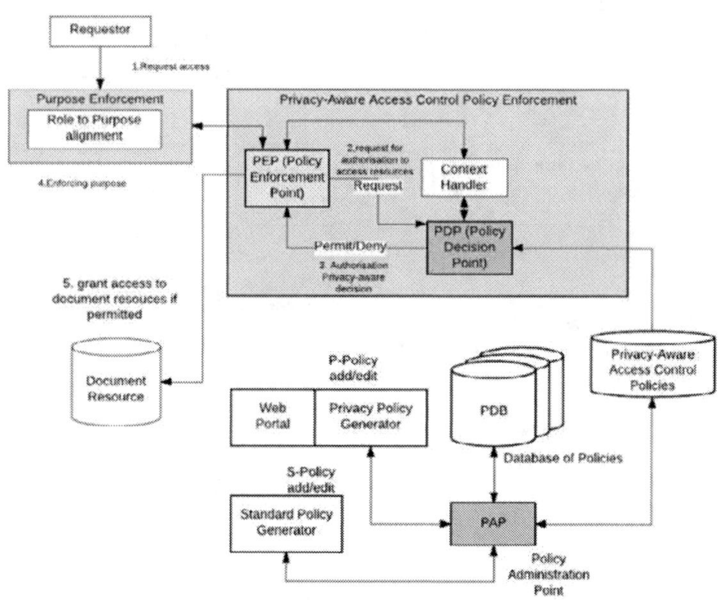

Figure 3. Implementation scheme of Privacy-Aware RBAC model for IHE-XDS

 DOI: 10.1051/itmconf/20171203038

First of all, the PAP (Policy Administration Point) is connected to the PDB (Policy Library - DataBase of Policies), and the PAP (Policy Administration Point) enters the privacy access control policy to the Policy Library (PDB). After that the requestor sends an access request to the PEP (Policy Enforcement Point); the PEP will send the request to the Context Handler after the request is obtained. The Context Handler will translate the request into a standard format and send the request to the PDP, let it make the judgment of policy through DataBase of Policies. After the PDP obtains the judgment request, first, through the policy administration point will search the policy from the DataBase of Policies, and get the appropriate authorization policy, then, according to the privacy authorization policy, the PDP will send the result of decision to the Context Handler, after the Context Handler obtains the decision result, it will convert the result to the local format of the PEP (Policy Enforcement Point), and returns it to the PEP (Policy Enforcement Point). At last, PEP determines whether the authorization decision is made correct or incorrect, and if there is no error, it will it will execute the authorization decision and return the result to the requester through the execution part. The task of PAP is to manage the policies and policy sets, and make them available for PDP. These policies and policy sets refer to specific goals and complete policy. PEP is a component that receives a request when the access requestor wishes to take certain actions on the information (resource) and make a request. PEP will send the request to the Context Handler.

The Context Handler maps the request and attributes to the XACML request context and sends request to the PDP. When evaluating a request, the PDP requires some attributes and sends the attribute to the context handler through the query. At the same time, Purpose Enforcement part will be connected to the PEP (Policy Enforcement Point) and will strengthen the purpose of access through the PEP, requester can access to the Document Resource only if the role and the purpose are relatively accurate. A simple example of an access control policy using all of the above concepts is shown below. Using XML-based symbols to represent it, it is for illustrative purposes only.

```
Access Purpose
<policy>
  <name>policy-ID1</name>
  <target>ALL-ATTRIBUTES</target>
  <trigger>
    <expression>
      <and>
<condition>Request.Obj.Location=="PII.DB"</conditi
on>
          <condition>Context.Request.Purpose contained
in Context.PrivacyPreferences.Purpose</condition>
      </and>
    </expression>
  </trigger>
  <rules>
    <rule>
      <expression>
        <or>
<condition>Request.Role=="Admin"</condition>
          <and>
<condition>Request.Purpose=="surgicaldepartment"</c
ondition>
    <condition>Request.Role=="surgeon"</condition>
          </and>
          <and>
    <condition>Request.Purpose=="Research"</conditi
on>
<condition>Request.Role=="programmer"</condition>
          </and>
        </or>
      </expression>
      <action>
<decision>yes</decision>/action&gt;</action>
    </rule>
  </rules>
</policy>
```

In addition, proposed a graphic algorithm of PDP evaluating request as shown in Figure4.

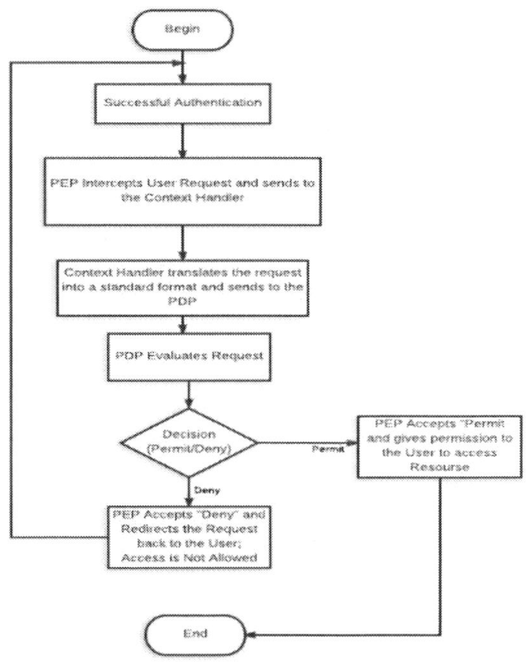

Figure 4. Graphic algorithm of PDP evaluating request

4. Discussion and Conclusion

This paper has discussed Privacy-Aware RBAC policies with conditions and purposes and also has presented the comprehensive model based on the advantages of RBAC model, notion of purpose and privacy-awareness that aims at enhancing the privacy policies in IHE-XDS. The work in this paper has extended previous work that has been proposed by scholars significantly in several aspects. First , it utilizes role describing the function and privacy requirement, and after that permission assignments obtain the privacy authorization through playing roles and interact with other components such as purposes and conditions through receiving and sending data specified by roles. Second, it introduces privacy-aware access control policy enforcement, sets the enforcement point in the privacy policy, enforcement point just can obtain the privacy data if decision point has permitted the request, in this way the security of privacy data is enforced. But this paper is far from complete. Many details are bypassed, such as does not consider the time property of privacy data, detailed obligation mechanism and further validation, etc. Our future work is enriching and completing this model, to extend our model to deal with other elements of privacy such as obligations and complex conditions. Despite the fact that these elements are not easy to deal with, but they are essential parts of privacy protection.

References

1. Ferraiolo D., Kuhn R.. Role Based Access control [A]. In 15th NIST-NCSC National Computer Security Conference [C]. 1992:554-563
2. Health Information Technology for Economic and Clinical Health Act: Public Law 111-5.
3. IHE IT Infrastructure Technical Framework, Supplement 2012: Basic Patient Privacy Consents Integration Profile, IHE ITI Technical Committee, Revision 9.0 – Final Text, August 31, 2012.
4. Basel Katt, Ruth Breu, Michael Hafner, Thomas Schabetsberger, Richard Mair, Florian Wozak. Privacy and Access Control for IHE-Based Systems. Springer Berlin Heidelberg. 2009: pp 145-153
5. Lisa M. Kern, Rainu Kaushal. Health information technology and health information exchange in New York State: New initiatives in implementation and evaluation[J]. In: Journal of Biomedical Informatics 40(2007) S17-S20.
6. K.Irwin, T. Yu, abd W.H.Winsborough. On the modeling and analysis of obligations. In CSS'06, NewYork, NY, USA, 2006:134-143.
7. Zhang Y Q, Sun B, Liu J, et al. Study on fine-grained RBAC model based on AOP[J]. Electronic Design Engineering, 2011.
8. R.S.Sandhu, R.J.Coyne, H.L.Fwinstein, C.E.Youman. Role-Based Access Control Model. IEEE Computer Volume 29(2) ,Feb 1996: 38-47,.
9. Q Ni, D Lin, E Bertino, J Lobo. Conditional Privacy-Aware Role Based Access Control. Springer Berlin Heidelberg, 2007, 4734(4):72-89
10. Agrawal R, Kiernan J, Srikant R, Xu Y, Hippocratic databases.VLDB, HongKong, 200227.
11. JW Byun, N Li. Purpose based access control for privacy protection in relational database systems[J]. Vldb Journal International on Very Large Data Bases, 2008, 17(4):603-619
12. YANG N, BARRINGER H, ZHANG N. A purpose-based access control model[A]. Proc of the 3rd International Symposium on Information Assurance and Security (IAS)[C]. IEEE, 2007. 143-148.
13. Yang C Y, Liu C T, Tseng T W. Design and Implementation of a Privacy Aware Framework for Sharing Electronic Health Records[C]// International Conference on Healthcare Informatics. 2015:504-508.
14. Elisa Bertino, Carolyn Brodie, Seraphin Calo. Analysis of Privacy and Security Polices [J].IBM Journal of Research and Development, 2009:1-31.
15. Colombo Pietro, Ferrari Elena. Enforcement of Purpose Based Access Control within Relational Database Management Systems[A]. IEEE Transactions on Knowledge and Data Engineering, March 2014
16. Lampson B W. Protection of Information System. Proc 5thPrinceton Conference on Information Sciences and Systems, Princeton. 1971:437-44
17. Kabir M E, Wang H. Conditional purpose based access control model for privacy protection[C]// Twentieth Australasian Conference on Australasian Database. Australian Computer Society, Inc. 2009:135-142.
18. Organization for Economic Co-operation and Development. OECD guidelines on the protection of privacy and transborder flows of personal data of 1980. Available at http://www.oecd.org
19. Yoonjeong Kim et al. Privacy-aware Role Based Access Control Model: Revisited for Multi-Policy Conflict Detection [C]. Acm Research in Applied Computation Symposium, 2012:344-34720.
20. Ravi Sandhu, David Ferraiolo and Richard Kuhn. The NIST model for role-basedaccess control: towards a unified standard. Proceedings of the fifth ACM workshop on Role-based access control. Berlin, Germany, July 26-28 2000:47-63.
21. IHE Integrating the Healthcare Enterprise. IHE IT infrastructure white paper-hie security and privacy rhrough IHE. Technical report, 2007.
22. IHE Integrating the Healthcare Enterprise. IT infrastructure technical framework-basic patient privacy consents (BPPC). Technical report, 2007.

An Authenticated Key Agreement Scheme Based on Cyclic Automorphism Subgroups of Random Orders

Jun YANG[a], Jian-Hua ZHANG[b]

School of Computer Science and Technology, Southwest Univ. for Nationalities, Chengdu, P.R.C.
[a]junyang898@163.com, [b]jianhuazhang@SWUN.edu.cn

Abstract: Group-based cryptography is viewed as a modern cryptographic candidate solution to blocking quantum computer attacks, and key exchange protocols on the Internet are one of the primitives to ensure the security of communication. In 2016 Habeeb et al proposed a "textbook" key exchange protocol based on the semidirect product of two groups, which is insecure for use in real-world applications. In this paper, after discarding the unnecessary disguising notion of semidirect product in the protocol, we establish a simplified yet enhanced authenticated key agreement scheme based on cyclic automorphism subgroups of random orders by making hybrid use of certificates and symmetric-key encryption as challenge-and-responses in the public-key setting. Its passive security is formally analyzed, which is relative to the cryptographic hardness assumption of a computational number-theoretic problem. Cryptanalysis of this scheme shows that it is secure against the intruder-in-the-middle attack even in the worst case of compromising the signatures, and provides explicit key confirmation to both parties.

1 Introduction

Cryptographic techniques are an essential tool to guarantee the security of communication in modern society. Today, the security of nearly all of the cryptographic schemes used in practice is based on number theoretic problems [1,2,3]. However, schemes like these will become insecure as soon as large enough quantum computers arrive. The reason for this is Shor's algorithm [4], which solves number theoretic problems like integer factorization and discrete logarithms in polynomial time on a quantum computer. Therefore, one needs alternatives to those classical public key schemes which are based on mathematical problems not affected by quantum computer attacks. Group-based cryptography is one of the main candidates for this [3,5,6].

In 2016, using semidirect product of two groups, Habeeb et al [7] proposed a key exchange protocol (the HKKS protocol) based on the work of [8, 9]. Unlike all the operating principles of the existing Diffie-Hellman-like protocols, its basic passive security is based on a stronger computational group-theoretic assumption than the current assumptions of hardness of discrete logarithm problems.

However, the HKKS protocol is still a "textbook" key exchange protocol which is actually not suitable for use in real-world applications due to its lack of any oracle interaction among users (public key owners) and an attacker [10]. In this paper, having discarded the unnecessary disguising notion of semidirect product in the HKKS protocol, we will establish a simplified yet enhanced authenticated key agreement scheme (denoted by the HYZ scheme) based on cyclic automorphism subgroups of random orders, which includes mutual identification of Alice and Bob. Our contributions are:

1) The passive security of the HYZ scheme, which is relative to the cryptographic hardness assumption of a computational number-theoretic problem, is analyzed in terms of formal security terminology. Additionally, selection of protocol parameters for passive security is analyzed.

2) To guarantee its active security, we utilize the "encryption-then-signature" mode to protect twofold for the protocol messages. We show that the HYZ scheme is secure against the intruder-in-the-middle attack even in the worst case of compromising the signatures, and obtains the highest level of assurance regarding key agreement, i.e., explicit key confirmation to both parties [11]: A is assured that B has computed the shared symmetric key K , and no one other than B can compute K .

The organization of the paper is as follows. In Section 2, the HYZ scheme is proposed. In Section 3, the shared key formula is proven and its passive and active security properties are discussed. Conclusions are given in Section 4.

DOI: 10.1051/itmconf/20171203039

2 The Proposed Scheme

In this section, we describe the HYZ scheme utilizing a kind of public-key infrastructure (PKI) [11,12]. Our strategy is to make hybrid use of certificates which are signed by a TA (Trusted Authority) and symmetric-key encryption as challenge-and-responses in the public-key setting. Each user U has a digital signature function sig_{U} with verification algorithm ver_{U}. The TA also has a signature scheme with a public verification algorithm ver_{TA}. The verification algorithms are compiled and made public by the TA, who certifies that ver_{U} is actually the verification algorithm for U and not for any malicious attacker Mallory. Each user U has a certificate

$$\mathrm{Cert}(\mathrm{U}) = \left(\mathrm{ID}(\mathrm{U}),\ ver_{\mathrm{U}},\ sig_{\mathrm{TA}}\left(\mathrm{ID}(\mathrm{U}),\ ver_{\mathrm{U}}\right)\right),$$

where ID(U) is certain identification information for U.

The public domain parameters consist of a group $(G,\cdot)$, a given element $g \in G$ with order $r > 1$ and a given element $\phi \in \mathrm{Aut}(\mathrm{G})$ with order s. Denote $\phi^0 = \mathrm{Id}_{\mathrm{Aut}(\mathrm{G})}$. Suppose that Alice and Bob want to establish a symmetric key K to use in an encryption function E_K. $x \in_U S$ means [10] sampling element x is taken uniformly random in set S.

1) Alice chooses a random number $m \in_U \{0, 1, 2, \ldots, s-1\}$. Then she computes and sends the following to Bob:

$$a \leftarrow \prod_{i=0}^{m-1} \phi^i(g)$$

$$\mathrm{A} \rightarrow \mathrm{B}:\ \left(\mathrm{Cert}(\mathrm{A}),\ a\right)$$

2) Bob chooses a random number $n \in_U \{0, 1, 2, \ldots, s-1\}$. Then he computes and sends the following to Alice:

$$b \leftarrow \prod_{j=0}^{n-1} \phi^j(g)$$

$$K_{\mathrm{B}} \leftarrow \phi^n(a)\cdot b$$

$$C_{\mathrm{B}} \leftarrow E_{K_{\mathrm{B}}}\left(sig_{\mathrm{B}}\left(\mathrm{ID}(\mathrm{A}) \parallel b \parallel a\right)\right)$$

$$\mathrm{B} \rightarrow \mathrm{A}:\ \left(\mathrm{Cert}(\mathrm{B}),\ b,\ C_{\mathrm{B}}\right)$$

3) Alice computes:

$$K_{\mathrm{A}} \leftarrow \phi^m(b)\cdot a$$

4) Using K_{A} Alice decrypts C_{B} to obtain $sig_{\mathrm{B}}\left(\mathrm{ID}(\mathrm{A}) \parallel b \parallel a\right)$.

5) Submitting $\mathrm{Cert}(\mathrm{B})$ to TA, Alice asks TA to verify that ver_{B} is Bob's verification algorithm.

6) Alice uses ver_{B} to verify Bob's signature in Step 4). If the signature is not valid, then she "rejects" and quits. Otherwise, she "accepts", computes and sends the following to Bob:

$$C_{\mathrm{A}} \leftarrow E_{K_{\mathrm{A}}}\left(sig_{\mathrm{A}}\left(\mathrm{ID}(\mathrm{B}) \parallel a \parallel b\right)\right)$$

$$\mathrm{A} \rightarrow \mathrm{B}:\ C_{\mathrm{A}}$$

7) Using K_{B} Bob decrypts C_{A} to obtain $sig_{\mathrm{A}}\left(\mathrm{ID}(\mathrm{B}) \parallel a \parallel b\right)$.

8) Submitting $\mathrm{Cert}(\mathrm{A})$ to TA, Bob asks TA to verify that ver_{A} is Alice's verification algorithm. Finally, Bob uses ver_{A} to verify Alice's signature in Step 7). If the signature is not valid, then he "rejects" and quits. Otherwise, he "accepts".

3 Proof of the Shared Key and Security Analysis

3.1 Proof of the Shared Key

Theorem 1 : Alice and Bob share the same symmetric key K, i.e.,

$$K_{\mathrm{A}} = K_{\mathrm{B}} = K = \prod_{i=0}^{m+n-1} \phi^i(g).$$

Proof: Since $\phi \in \mathrm{Aut}(\mathrm{G})$, by the definition in [13], one has

$$\phi^m(b) = \phi^m\left(\prod_{j=0}^{n-1} \phi^j(g)\right) = \prod_{j=0}^{n-1} \phi^m\left(\phi^j(g)\right) = \prod_{j=0}^{n-1} \phi^{m+j}(g) = \prod_{j=m}^{m+n\ 1} \phi^j(g).$$

Hence, $K_{\mathrm{A}} = \phi^m(b)\cdot a$

$$= \prod_{j=m}^{m+n-1} \phi^j(g)\cdot\prod_{i=0}^{m-1+\ -} \phi^j(g) = \prod_{i=0}^{m\ n\ 1} \phi^i(g).$$

Similarly, $K_{\mathrm{B}} = \phi^n(a)\cdot b$

$$= \prod_{i=n}^{n+m-1} \phi^i(g)\cdot\prod_{j=0}^{n-1+\ -} \phi^j(g) = \prod_{i=0}^{m\ n\ 1} \phi^i(g)$$

Therefore, $K_{\mathrm{A}} = K_{\mathrm{B}} = K$. This completes the proof.

3.2 The Passive Security Properties of the HYZ Scheme

Taking $\phi = \mathrm{Id}_{\mathrm{Aut}(\mathrm{G})}$, we see that the standard Diffie-Hellman protocol is a special case of the HYZ scheme, and so it provides a heuristic evidence of the basic security of the HYZ scheme.

From the random numbers $m,\ n \in \{0, 1, 2, \ldots, s-1\}$ chosen by Alice and Bob, and their shared key

$K = \prod_{i=0}^{m+n-1} \phi^i(g)$, one of the necessary conditions for passive security of the HYZ scheme is that the order s should be chosen large enough to thwart exhaustive key search.

The two cyclic automorphism subgroups of $\mathrm{Aut}(G)$ of random orders involved in the HYZ scheme are $\langle\phi\rangle_m = \{\phi^0, \phi^1, \phi^2, \ldots, \phi^{m-1}\}$ and $\langle\phi\rangle_n = \{\phi^0, \phi^1, \phi^2, \ldots, \phi^{n-1}\}$, both of which act on g. The period of ϕ with respect to g is defined to the smallest positive integer t such that $\phi^t(g) = e_G$ (the identity element of group G). Another necessary condition for passive security of the HYZ scheme is that the period t should be chosen large enough; otherwise, whenever $i \geq t$, we have $\phi^i(g) = \phi^{i-t}(\phi^t(g)) = \phi^{i-t}(e_G) = e_G$, which shows that large private exponents m and n would be wasted in the final result $K = \prod_{i=0}^{m+n-1} \phi^i(g)$, and thus the key space size

$$\left\{K = \prod_{i=0}^{m+n-1} \phi^i(g) : m, n \in_U \{0, 1, 2, \ldots, s-1\}\right\}$$

would be limited (we call this phenomenon "falsely big data").

The basic security of the HYZ scheme is based on the cryptographic hardness assumption of the following computational number-theoretic problem: Given ϕ, g and $a \left(= \prod_{i=0}^{m-1} \phi^i(g)\right)$, it is computationally infeasible to compute m. More specifically, consider the following experiment for a pair of group-generation algorithms $(\mathcal{G}_1, \mathcal{G}_2)$, algorithm $\mathcal{A}$, and the security parameter n (1^n denotes the string comprised of n ones) :

The cyclic automorphism subgroup factoring experiment $\mathrm{CASF}_{\mathcal{A},\mathcal{G}}(n)$:

1. Run $\mathcal{G}_1(1^n)$ to obtain (G, g), where g is an element with order $r > 1$ in group G.
2. Run $\mathcal{G}_2(1^n)$ to obtain $(\mathrm{Aut}(G), \phi)$, where ϕ is an element with order s in the automorphism group $\mathrm{Aut}(G)$.
3. Choose a uniform $a \in G$.
4. $\mathcal{A}$ is given ϕ, g and a, and outputs $x \in \{0, 1, 2, \ldots, s-1\}$.
5. The output of the experiment is defined to be 1 if $a = \prod_{i=0}^{x-1} \phi^i(g)$, and 0 otherwise.

Definition: We say that the CASF problem is hard relative to polynomial-time algorithms $(\mathcal{G}_1, \mathcal{G}_2)$ if for all probabilistic polynomial-time algorithms $\mathcal{A}$ there exists a negligible function negl such that

$$\Pr\left[\mathrm{CASF}_{\mathcal{A},\mathcal{G}}(n) = 1\right] \leq \mathrm{negl}(n).$$

The CASF assumption is that there exists a pair of $(\mathcal{G}_1, \mathcal{G}_2)$ for which the CASF problem is hard.

If the adversary is passive, then the session in the HYZ scheme will terminate with both parties "accepting" (provided they behave honestly). That is, A and B successfully identify themselves to each other, and they both compute the key K. The adversary cannot compute any information about the key K, assuming the intractability of the CASF problem.

3.3 The Active Security Properties of the HYZ Scheme

We first shall show how the HYZ scheme is secure against the intruder-in-the-middle attack even in the worst case that the ciphertexts C_A and C_B are decrypted by the intruder, or the signatures of the legitimate communication parties are obliviously leaked to an outsider, as shown in Figure 1.

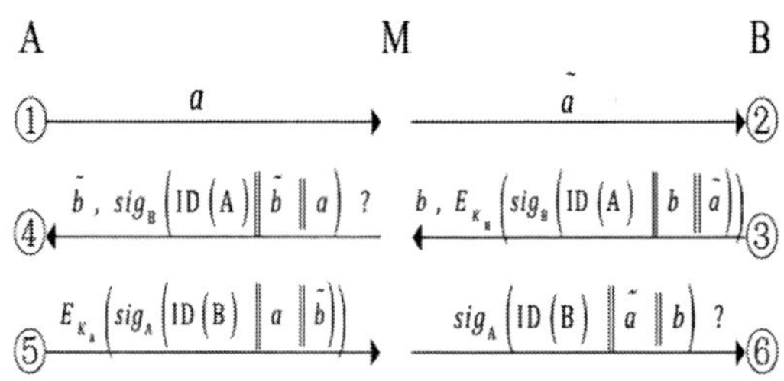

Figure 1. Thwarted intruder-in-the-middle attack on the HYZ scheme

Suppose that Mallory intercepts a in pass ① and replaces it with $\tilde{a}$ in pass ②. M then receives $\left(\mathrm{Cert}(B), b, E_{K_B}\left(sig_B\left(\mathrm{ID}(A) \parallel b \parallel a\right)\right)\right)$ from Bob in pass ③. He would like to replace $(b, \tilde{a})$ with $(\tilde{b}, a)$. However, this means that he must also replace the signature by $sig_B\left(\mathrm{ID}(A) \parallel \tilde{b} \parallel a\right)$ in pass ④. Unfortunately for M, he cannot compute B's signature on the string $\mathrm{ID}(A) \parallel \tilde{b} \parallel a$ because he doesn't know B's signing algorithm sig_B. Similarly, M is unable to replace $sig_A\left(\mathrm{ID}(B) \parallel a \parallel \tilde{b}\right)$ in pass ⑤ by $sig_A\left(\mathrm{ID}(B) \parallel \tilde{a} \parallel b\right)$ in pass ⑥ because he does not know A's signing algorithm sig_A.

This situation is illustrated in Figure 1, in which the question marks indicate signatures that the adversary is unable to compute. It is the use of signatures that provides for mutual identification of A and B. This in turn thwarts the intruder-in-the-middle attack.

Next, we shall show that the HYZ scheme provides explicit key confirmation [11].

The HYZ scheme is established involving mutual identification in the public-key setting. So, if an adversary is active, he will be detected by the honest participants in the session.

Using the properties discussed above, let us see what we can infer about the HYZ scheme if A or B "accepts." Suppose that A "accepts."Let us analyze why A should believe that B has computed K .The reason for this belief is that in step 4), A uses her symmetric key K_A to decrypt C_B which has been encrypted by B using K_B in step 2), which is identical to K_A by Theorem 1, and has obtained B's signature $sig_B\left(\mathrm{ID}\left(\mathrm{A}\right) \,\|\, b \,\|\, a\right)$.Now, assuming that B executed the scheme according to its specifications, and the signature is valid in step 6), A can infer that B has computed the value of $K_B = \phi^n\left(a\right)\cdot b$.

The analysis from the point of view of B is similar.

Summarizing the discussion above, we have established the following theorem.

Theorem 2: The HYZ scheme is an authenticated key agreement scheme that provides explicit key confirmation to both parties, assuming that the CASF problem is intractable.

4 Conclusion

Based on the HKKS protocol and cyclic automorphism subgroups of random orders, we proposed the HYZ scheme and proved its shared key formula. Two necessary conditions for its passive security are analyzed: the order s of automorphism $\phi\in\mathrm{Aut}\left(\mathrm{G}\right)$ and the period of ϕ with respect to g should be chosen large enough to thwart exhaustive key search and avoid the phenomenonof "falsely big data", respectively. Furthermore, we conducted the $\mathrm{CASF}_{\mathcal{A},g}\left(n\right)$ experiment, defined the CASF problem and depicted the CASF assumption in terms of formal security terminology. To guarantee its active security, we utilized twofold protections for the protocol messages. It was showed that the HYZ scheme is secure against the intruder-in-the-middle attack even in the worst case of compromising the signatures, and is an authenticated key agreement scheme that provides explicit key confirmation to both parties, assuming that the CASF problem is intractable.

Compared with the HKKS protocol, the security of the HYZ scheme has been improved in a number of aspects. Future work includes cryptanalysis of the HYZ scheme resistance to the “linear algebra attack” mounted by Romank'ov [14].

Acknowledgement

The Research of both authors was supported by the Fundamental Research Funds for the Central Universities–Southwest University for Nationalities (2014NYB04) and Sichuan Provincial Project of Science and Technology(2012JY0096).

References

1. J. Hoffstein, J. Pipher, and J. H. Silverman, An Introduction to Mathematical Cryptography, New York: Springer Science + Business Media, LLC, 2008, pp. 59–62.
2. J. Katz and Y. Lindell, Introduction to Modern Cryptography, 2nd ed., Boca Raton: CRC Press, 2015, pp. 285–286, p. 320.
3. A. Petzoidt, J. Ding, and L.Wang, "Eliminating decryption failures from the simple matrix encryption scheme". http://eprint.iacr.org/2016/010.
4. P. Shor, "Polynomial-time algorithms for prime factorization and discrete logarithms on a quantum computer". SIAM Journal on Computing, 1997, 26 (5) : pp. 1484–1509.
5. A. G. Myasnikov, V. Shilprain, and A. Ushakov, Group-based cryptography, Basel-Boston-Berlin: Birkhauser Verlag, 2008, pp. 77–78.
6. E. Alkim, L. Ducas, T. Poppelmann, et al, "Post-quantum key exchange - a new hope". http://eprint. iacr.org/2015/1092.
7. M. Habeeb, D. Kahrobaei, C. Koupparis, et al, "Using semidirect product of (semi)groups in public key cryptography", A. Beckmann et al (Eds): CiE 2016, LNCS, Springer International Publishing Switzerland, 2016: pp. 132–141.
8. M. Habeeb, D. Kahrobaei, and V. Shilprain, "Public key exchange using semidirect product of (semi)groups", M. Jacobson et al (Eds). Applied Cryptography and Network Security. Springer Berlin Heidelberg, 2013: pp.475–486.
9. D. Kahrobaei, C. Koupparis, and V. Shilprain, "Public group-based cryptography using matrices over group rings", Groups, Complexity, Cryptology , 5 (2013) : pp. 97–115.
10. W. Mao, Modern Cryptography: Theory and Practice, Upper Saddle River: Prentice Hall PTR, 2004, pp. 358–362.
11. D. R. Stinson, Cryptography: Theory and Practice, 3rd ed., Boca Raton: Chapman & Hall/CRC, 2006, pp. 367–368, pp. 429–436 .
12. W. Trappe and L. C. Washington, Introduction to Cryptography with Coding Theory, 2nd ed. , Upper Saddle River: Pearson Prentice Hall, 2006, pp. 256–259.
13. S. Lang, Algebra, Revised 3rd ed., New York: Springer-Verlag New York, Inc., 2002, p. 10, p. 54.
14. V. Romank'ov, "Linear decomposition attack on public key exchange protocols using semidirect products of (semi)groups", Computer Science, 2015 (August): pp. 1–7.

 DOI: 10.1051/itmconf/20171203040

Optimizing Performance of Hadoop with Parameter Tuning

Xiang CHEN[1,a], Yi LIANG[1,b], Guang-Rui LI[2,c], Cheng CHEN[1,d], and Si-Yu LIU[1,e]

[1]*Faculty of Information Technology, Beijing University of Technology, Beijing, China*
[2]*NO.10 Building, Suzhou Software Park, No.78, China Mobile Software Technology Co., Ltd, Suzhou, China*
[a]*chenxiang1@emails.bjut.edu.cn*, [b]*yliang@bjut.edu.cn*, [c]*liguangrui@cmss.chinamobile.com*, [d]*ccheng@emails.bjut.edu.cn*, [e]*liusifen@emails.bjut.edu.cn*

Abstract: Optimizing Hadoop with the parameter tuning is an effective way to greatly improve the performance, but it usually costs too much time to identify the optimal parameters configuration because there are many parameters. Users are always blindly adjust too many parameters and are sometimes confused about which one could be changed at a higher-priority. To make optimization easier, classifying the parameter based on different applications will be helpful. In this paper, we will introduce a method that can classify these parameters in order that users can optimize performance more quickly and effectively for different applications.

1 Introduction

With the rapid development of the Internet, the era of big data has arrived as the amount of data on the web has been expanding dramatically. MapReduce was firstly proposed by Google in 2004 and has been a popular parallel computing model for big data processing [1]. The core ideal of MapReduce platform is to store and compute mass data based on distributed computational nodes, and to realize localization process of data through task scheduling so as to improve the efficiency of data process. The most popular implementation of the MapReduce model is the Hadoop framework [2]. Hadoop is an open source software platform managed by the Apache Software Foundation and has proven to be very helpful in storing and managing vast amounts of data cheaply and efficiently. Users can develop and run applications easily on systems with thousands of nodes by Hadoop. Now Hadoop is widely used in industry and commerce for many big data related tasks.

As Hadoop is widely used to process big data offline [2][3], improving the Hadoop's performance is meaningful and important both in academic area and industry. The excellent performance means effectiveness and hign throughput of the Hadoop.

The performance of the application is closely related to its configuration on Hadoop. There is a large number of parameters in the configuration and they need the user to set them. A bad configuration of the inappropriate parameters' values will seriously affect the performance. It will take much time for users to change the parameter's value to achieve a better performance. What's more, users always tune these parameters with lack of guidance and may result in the poor performance. To execute a different application, they may need to repeat this procedure.

From the above, in this paper we propose a solution for this problem. We introduce a method that can classify these parameters into three categories, the parameters in the same group can significantly impact on one category of application. User can tune these parameters firstly to reduce the main bottleneck of the application. It can be much more effective and save much time.

2 Significance Parameters

Parameter Name	Brief Description	Range of Value
mapred.map.tasks	Number of map tasks	[6,24]
mapred.reduce.tasks	Number of reduce tasks	[6,24]
mapred.compress.map.output	Compress the maps' outputs or not	[true,false]
mapred.child.java.opts	Java opts for task tracker child processes	[256MB,2048MB]
io.sort.factor	Number of sorted streams to merge during sorting	[10,50]
io.sort.mb	Buffer memory to use while sorting files	[128MB,1024MB]
dfs.block.size	Data size processed per mapper task	[32MB,256MB]
dfs.replication	Block replication number	[1,3]

Hadoop parameters control various aspects of job behavior during execution. About 200 parameters can be set by users, but not all the parameters have great impact on the Hadoop, and some of them even have no impact on the performance. As a conservative estimate, the settings of more than 25 of these Hadoop parameters can have significant impact on application performance [4]. To reduce the difficulty of our experiments, we chose some of them as examples and show them in Table 1.

The parameter with appropriate value will bring high performance for Hadoop. We set the range of each parameter because too large or too small of the parmeter values will obviously affect the perforamnce. User can optimizing performance of Hadoop with parameter tuning in the range. But user still should select the useful paramters for different application to improve the performance, the guidance for parameter selection could be valuable.

In the following of this paper, we will describe the classification method in detail, then we evaluate the impact of our method by experiments.

3 Classification Method

In this section we will describe our classification method. To make our method suitable for most case, with different application, we have different conclusions of optimization. For a given application, we usually can divide it into three categories by its bottleneck, that is IO-bound, CPU-bound and hybrid [5]. Every category of application has a corresponding parameters class for optimizing. Based on it, these parameters are generally divided into four categories: IO-tuning, CPU-tuning, both-tuning and none. It is obvious that IO-tuning parameters are used for IO-bound application, CPU-tuning parameters are used for CPU-bound application and both of them are used for hybrid application.

We can run a typical application to help us evaluate the impact of the parameter. In our experiment, we focused on the metrics of execution time and it can reflect the performance. Then our classification method shows the following: First of all, we chose a typical IO-bound application, such as Sort. To evaluate a parameter, we changed the parameter's value in the range while the other parameters kept unchanged. Then we executed the same application several times with different value of this parameter and got some experimental data. To cut errors, we can repeat this experiment more than once and take the average value for further analysis. We defined a new metrics δ to denote the importance of this parameter on the application, it is calculated by this formula:

$$\delta = \sqrt{\frac{\sum_{i=1}^{N} (T_i - T)^2}{N}} \quad (1)$$

T is the average execution time of the experiment, Ti represents that the *ith* Execution time for this parameter, N is the times of experiments. We can set a threshold value for the δ, if the δ greater than the threshold, we think this parameter have a great impact on this application, it is worth optimizing this category of application by this parameter. The application is IO-bound, and so this parameter will be classified to IO-tuning parameters.

The threshold value is set by user, with different decision of threshold value may result in the difference of the classification result of parameters. The inappropriate values of threshold may affect the optimization effect. More experimental result will increase the accurate of threshold selection.

In this way, we can classify all the parameters into four categories.

4 Experiment and Evaluation

4.1 Environment

For simplicity, we ran experiments with Hadoop cluster configurations of one master and one slave. The experiments were performed under Hadoop 1.2.1, the new Hadoop version was not used in the experiment because the resource management framework YARN in Hadoop 2 provided a unified resource management and scheduling for the application. The configuration space compared to the 1.2.1 version is less, Using the lower version Hadoop to facilitate the show the optimization of effect.

Each machine has two 6-core 2.4 GHz Intel Xeon E5645 processors and 16GB of memory. They all ran Ubuntu 14.04.3 LTS with kernel 14.04 operating system and ext4 file system. For the experiments in this paper, to make the application runtime short, the input data of all experiments was about 16GB.

We ran our experiment with typical IO-bound Sort benchmark and CPU-bound Kmeans benchmark to help us classify these predefined parameters. Then we tried to optimize the CPU-bound Wordcount benchmark by the classification. All the workload is generate by the BigDatabench [6].

4.2 Classify These Parameters

Table 2~4 shows the experimental data of running Sort benchmark while changing the value of specified parameters and keep the others unchanged. Due to limited space, we didn't list the experimental result of all the parameters and have only shown the typical parameter which is easy to estimate.

Table 2. Execution time of change the value of mapred.map.tasks and keep the others unchanged

mapred.map.tasks	4	6	8	10	12
execution time (s)	1346.43	1312.16	1444.8	1277.86	1294.43

Table 3. Execution time of change the value of io.sort.mb and keep the others unchanged

io.sort.mb (MB)	128	256	512	1024	2048
execution time (s)	1223.9	1242.0	1294.2	1261.2	1100.8

Table 4. Execution time of change the value of dfs.block.size and keep the others unchanged

dfs.block.size (MB)	32	64	128	256	512
execution time (s)	1196.1	1095.6	1057.3	1145.9	1230.5

We changed the parameter's value in the range while the other parameters kept unchanged. Then the execution time of Sort benchmark is changed by this parameter tuing and the shorten time means the performance gains of our optimization work. The Sort benchmark is IO-bound, the performance bottleneck of Sort is the imited bandwidth of disk. The parameter which can improve the disk bandwidth or the processing effeciency of Hadoop will significant improve the performance of this type of application.

In this way, with the experimental result, the δ of these parameters can be obtained. The δ of these parameters respectively is 59.36188, 66.05308 and 63.32071. The difference between them is not large and threshold value is set to 30, all of these parameters are large than the threshold value and they all be regarded as IO-tuning parameters.

Table 5~7 shows the experimental data of running Kmeans while changing the value of specified parameters and keep the others constant.

Table 5. Execution time of change the value of mapred.map.tasks and keep the others unchanged

mapred.map.tasks	8	10	12	14	16
execution time (s)	658.31	634.28	633.54	627.46	653.38

Table 6. Execution time of change the value of io.sort.mb and keep the others unchanged

io.sort.mb (MB)	128	256	512	1024	2048
execution time (s)	622.36	613.27	606.85	614.89	610.91

Table 7. Execution time of change the value of dfs.block.size and keep the others unchanged

dfs.block.size (MB)	32	64	128	256	512
execution time (s)	884.59	614.89	685.08	476.24	454.16

The Kmeans benchmark is CPU-bound and the performance bottleneck of Sort is the low efficiency of processing data. Only the parameter which can improve the processing effeciency of Hadoop can significant improve the performance of this type of application. And this can guide the decision of CPU-tuning parameter.

From experimental results, we can obtain the δ of these parameters. The δ of these parameters respectively is 12.13479, 5.12432 and 156.45732. Because Kmeans is CPU-bound, it is easy to conclude that mapred.map.tasks and io.sort.mb is not CPU-tuning parameter, and dfs.block.size is not CPU-tuning parameter.

In summary, mapred.map.tasks and io.sort.mb are CPU-tuning parameters, dfs.block.size is both-tuning parameter. With the experiments, all the parameters can be classified to corresponding categories.

4.3 Evaluation

We tried to optimize Naïve Bayes benchmark by the classification result, and the experimental results shown as Figure 1. In the X-axle, the number means tuning one paramter in the range while the others constant. The distance between height of point A and height of point B is the execution time reducing by tuning this parameter, so the downtrend means the optimization effect of the parameter.

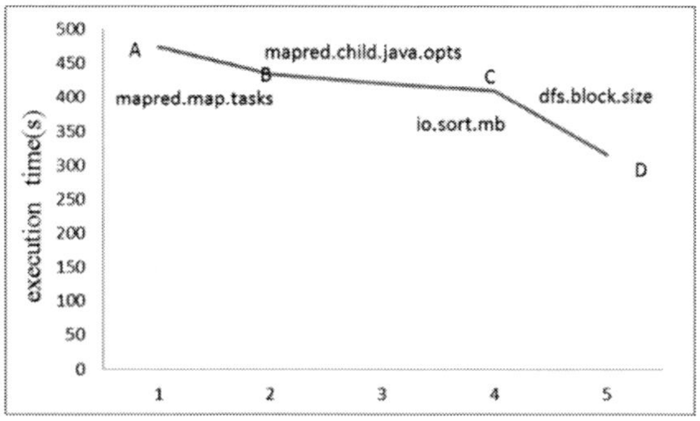

Figure 1. impact of paramters on Naïve bayes

In Figure 1, for the CPU-bound application, the useful parameters should be the CPU-tuning or both-tuning parameters, such as dfs.block.size. The downtrend betwent C and D is the execution time reducing by the dfs.block.size tuning. It is about 23.2% shorted than before and it is the maximum value in our optimization work. It means optimizing Hadoop with dfs.block.size tuning can be a most effective way to improve application's performance, it demonstrates the helpful of our classification method. The classification result provides the optimization guidance for users.

Summary

In this paper, we focuses on the performance of Hadoop big data processing platform and introduce a classification method for different types of applications. It can help user optimize Hadoop application with the parameter tuning in a quickly and effective way.

Acknowledgment

I would like to express my gratitude and appreciation to Professor Yi Liang for great efforts she had put into this paper. Her enlightening advice and continued support have made this research work a valuable experience for me.

References

1. Dean J, Ghemawat S. MapReduce: simplified data processing on large clusters[C]// Conference on Symposium on Opearting Systems Design & Implementation. USENIX Association, 2004:10-10.
2. Apache Hadoop [P/OL]. Available: http://hadoop.apache.org/.
3. White T, Cutting D. Hadoop : the definitive guide[J]. O'reilly Media Inc Gravenstein Highway North, 2009, 215(11):1 - 4.
4. Babu S. Towards automatic optimization of MapReduce programs[C]// Proceedings of the 1st ACM Symposium on Cloud Computing, SoCC 2010, Indianapolis, Indiana, USA, June 10-11, 2010. 2010:137-142.
5. Wang L, Zhan J, Jia Z, et al. Characterization and Architectural Implications of Big Data Workloads[J]. 2015:145-146.\bibitem{RefJ}
6. Wang L, Zhang S, Zheng C, et al. BigDataBench: A big data benchmark suite from internet services[C]. International Symposium on High PERFORMANCE Computer Architecture, 2014:488-499.

Research on the Numerical Simulation of Sleeper in the Pipeline Global Buckling Controlling Practice

Wen-Bin LIU[a], Ai-Min LIU[b]

CCCC Tianjin Port Engineering Institute Co., Ltd. Tianjin, China
[a]liuwenbin3943@163.com, [b]liuaimin1987@163.com

Abstract: This paper analyzed the lateral buckling of pipelines located in Western Africa with ABAQUS software. The application of sleepers in practice is explored to guide the pipeline buckling controlling design.

1 Introduction

High temperature and pressure are applied on the submarine pipeline to ensure the fluency of oil. The high temperature and pressure load causes large stress in the cross-section of pipeline, and leading to large lateral global displacement of deep-sea pipeline. Uncontrolled lateral global buckling causes large deformation of pipeline, threatening the safety of pipeline systems.

In engineering practice, there are two kinds of method to deal with this uncontrolled global buckling: preventing method and triggering method. The preventing method usually includes: (1) pre-cooling the oil to reduce the additional stress; (2) using pipe-in-pipe or increasing the number of tube to enhance the flexural rigidity; (3) installing traction device to introduce pre-tension into the pipelines. The triggering method is mainly implemented by: (1) placing sleepers in design location; (2) snaked-laying pipelines; (3) adding distributed buoyance devices on the pipelines. Comparing to the preventing method, the triggering method reduce the cost a lot, but requiring more delicate design. In addition, with the increasing operation water depth, the triggering method becomes more feasible for implementing in practice. The triggering method becomes an advanced research hotspot.

This paper analyzed the lateral buckling of pipelines located in Western Africa with ABAQUS software. The application of sleepers in practice is explored to guide the pipeline buckling controlling design.

2 The engineering Case

The case locates in the Western Africa, and the working water depth is 1150 - 1500 m. The specific data about the pipeline system is shown in Table 1.

The properties of surface soil determine the post-buckling pipeline's deformation. The property of surface soil is usually unstable, and to obtain certain strength of surface soil is difficult. In order to ensure the accurate of calculating results, the upper-limit value, lower-limit value and the mid-value are considered in analysis. The relative parameters of surface soil are shown in Table 2.

Table 1. Pipeline system's design parameters

Outer diameters	Wall thickness	Modulus of elasticity	Steel's density	Thermal expansion coefficient	Poisson's ratio	Soil resistance coefficient	Steel's yield strength
D/mm	t/mm	E/GPa	ρ_S/kg·m^{-3}	α/°C^{-1}	υ	φ	σ_s/MPa
323.9	19.1	206	7850	1.1×10^{-5}	0.3	0.4	520

Table 2 Strength of surface soil

Depth /m	Lower-limit value *Su* (kPa)	Mid-value *Su* (kPa)	Upper-limit value *Su* (kPa)
0	0.5	0.75	1
0.15	1	2	3
0.7	8	11	15
0.9	8	11	15

The sleepers are placed under the pipelines in several preset location in this case to trigger the lateral buckling. The sleeper is a large diameter (1 m) solid tube, showing in the Figure 1.

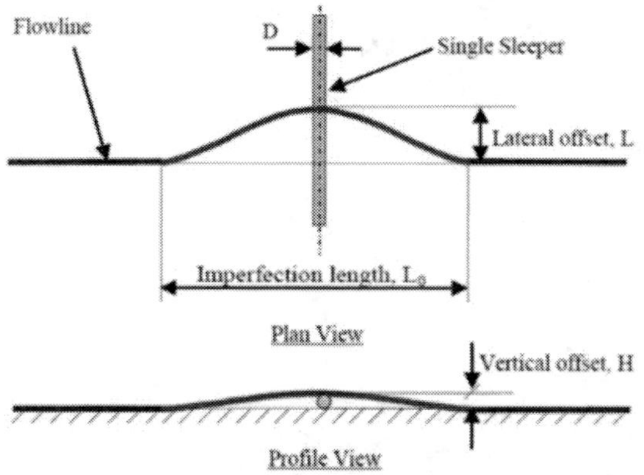

Figure 1. Sketch of a pipeline laying on a sleeper

The symbol H is the vertical height of the sleeper. The symbol L represents the lateral offset of pipeline, and L0 represents the length for the pipeline segment un-touching the seabed.

3 Numerical Simulation

For analyzing the excepted effect of the sleeper, the pipeline is simulated in the software ABAQUS. The pipeline is modeled with the S4R element. The element in the pipeline segment within 200 m of the sleeper is 0.5 long, and the element in other segment is 5 m long. The total length of pipeline is 7400 m, including 2 sleepers located at 2 different places. A part of finite element analysis model is shown in Figure 2.

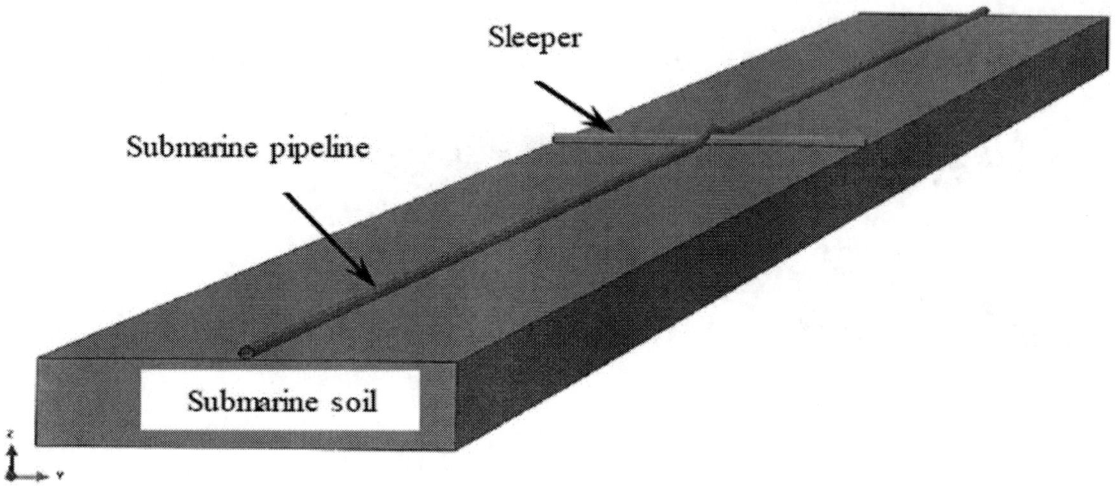

Figure 2. A part of finite element analysis model

The entry endpoint of the pipeline can move freely in axial direction. The exit endpoint of the pipeline can expand freely, but the shrinking movement of the exit endpoint is restricted by an anchor chain. The restriction of the anchor chain is simulated as a spring. The relationship between restricting force and displacement is displayed in Figure 3. The maximum tension of the anchor chain is 1 MN, and the corresponding extension length is 0.12 m.

The lateral friction coefficient between pipeline and soil is 0.9 when the lateral displacement is no more than 25 mm. The lateral friction coefficient is 0.7 when the lateral displacement is larger than 25 mm. This dynamical soil resistance is simulated using a subroutine VFRIC. The calculating result is displayed in Figure 4.

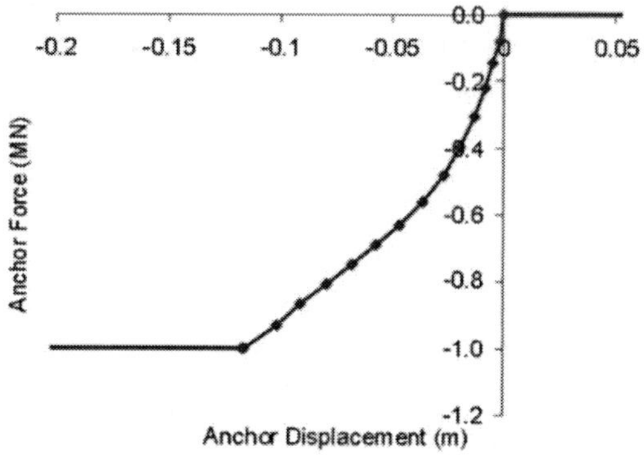

Figure 3 The relationship between anchor force and displacemen

(a) The lateral buckling of the pipeline with a sleeper

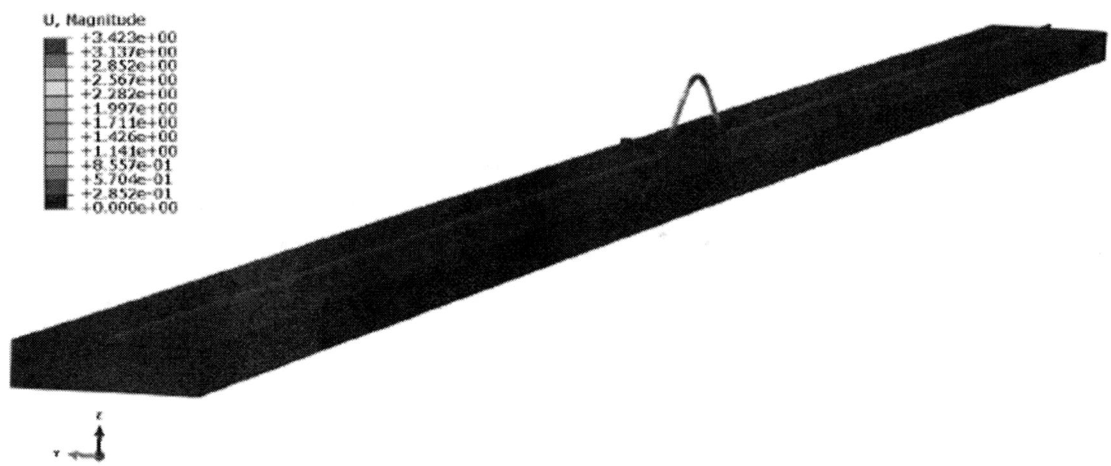

(b) The vertical buckling of the pipeline with a sleeper

Figure 4. Simulation results

From the Figure 4 (a), we can see that the critical lateral buckling force is less than the critical vertical buckling force. This is because the vertical buckling needs to overcome the self-weight of the pipeline. The pipeline laid on the even seabed is easier to experience lateral buckling. But with the lightening of pipeline's self-weight, vertical buckling can happen on the light segment laid on the sleepers. The post-buckling pipeline which suffers vertical buckling rises up, separating with the seabed in operation. After the pipeline shut down, and this rising segment of pipeline drops down, touching the seabed and the sleeper again. This rising and dropping reciprocating movement causes pipeline vibration, influencing the safety of pipelines.

4 Conclusion

The pipeline laid on sleepers is easier to suffer lateral buckling rather than vertical buckling. While with the lightening of pipeline's self-weight, the vertical buckling becomes possible. The light pipeline will suffer vertical buckling first, and then experience lateral buckling.

Acknowledgment

The authors are grateful for the support provided by the Natural Science Foundation of Tianjin (16JCQNJC07200), Key Laboratory of Port Geotechnical Engineering of

Tianjin and Key Laboratory of Port Geotechnical Engineering, Ministry of Communications, PRC.

References

1. Bruton D, Carr M, Crawford M, et al. (2005) "The safe design of hot on-bottom pipelines with lateral buckling using the design guideline developed by the safebuck joint industry project" Proceedings of the Deep Offshore Technology Conference, Vitoria, Espirito Santo, Brazil.
2. Bruton D, Carr M, White D, et al. (2007) "The influence of Pipe-Soil interaction on Lateral Buckling and walking of pipelines- The SAFEBUCK JIP" Proc. International Offshore Investigation and Geotechnics (OSIG) Conference.
3. Bruton D, Bolton M, Carr M, et al. (2008) "Pipe-soil interaction with flowlines during lateral buckling and pipeline walking - The SAFEBUCK JIP" Offshore Technology Conference.
4. Chee K Y and Walker A. (2011). "Assessment of Numerical Modelling of Pipeline Lateral Buckling." Proc., Int. Symp. on Lateral Buckling, Australia.
5. Hong ZH, Liu R, Liu WB, Yan SW. (2015a) "A lateral global buckling failure envelope for a high temperature and high pressure (HT/HP) submarine pipeline." Applied Ocean Research, 51:117-128.
6. Hong ZH, Liu R, Liu WB, Yan SW. (2015b) "Study on lateral buckling characteristics of a submarine pipeline with a single arch symmetric initial imperfection" Ocean engineering, 108: 21-32.
7. Junior E P, da Rocha R S, da Costa Á M, et al. (2004) "Experimental Tests and Numerical Simulation in a Reduced Model in a Pipeline With ZIG-ZAG Geometry: A Parametric Study" International Pipeline Conference. American Society of Mechanical Engineers, 399-407.
8. Konuk I, Yu S. Continuum (2007) "FE modeling of lateral buckling: study of soil effects" 26th International Conference on Offshore Mechanics and Arctic Engineering. American Society of Mechanical Engineers, 347-354.
9. Liu R, Liu W, Wu X, et al. (2014) "Global lateral buckling analysis of idealized subsea pipelines" Journal of Central South University, 21: 416-427.

Automatic Human Facial Expression Recognition Based on Integrated Classifier From Monocular Video with Uncalibrated Camera

Tao YU[1,2,3], Jian-Hua ZOU[1,2], and Qin-Bao SONG[3]

[1]*Systems Engineering Institute, School of Electronic & Information Engineering, Xi'an JiaoTong University, 28 Xian-Ning West Road, Xi'an city, Shaanxi Province, 710049, PR China*
[2]*State Key Laboratory for Systems Engineering, Xi'an Jiaotong University, 28 Xian-Ning West Road, Xi'an city, Shaanxi Province, 710049, PR China*
[3]*Research Institute of Computer Software & Theory, Department of Computer Science & Technology, School of Electronics & Information Engineering, Xi'an Jiaotong University, 28 Xian-Ning West Road, Xi'an city, Shaanxi Province, 710049, PR China*

Abstract: An automatic recognition framework for human facial expressions from a monocular video with an uncalibrated camera is proposed. The expression characteristics are first acquired from a kind of deformable template, similar to a facial muscle distribution. After associated regularization, the time sequences from the trait changes in space-time under complete expressional production are then arranged line by line in a matrix. Next, the matrix dimensionality is reduced by a method of manifold learning of neighborhood-preserving embedding. Finally, the refined matrix containing the expression trait information is recognized by a classifier that integrates the hidden conditional random field (HCRF) and support vector machine (SVM). In an experiment using the Cohn–Kanade database, the proposed method showed a comparatively higher recognition rate than the individual HCRF or SVM methods in direct recognition from two-dimensional human face traits. Moreover, the proposed method was shown to be more robust than the typical Kotsia method because the former contains more structural characteristics of the data to be classified in space-time

1 Introduction

Human facial expression recognition is valuable in many areas, such as medical diagnosis,[1-3] teaching,[4, 5] and human–computer interaction (HCI),[6-8] and it has been actively studied for many years. The recognized facial expressions are typically categorized in two types: two-dimensional (2D) expressions[7, 9, 10] and three-dimensional (3D) expressions.[11-13] The former usually recognizes the processed traits that are directly acquired from 2D facial images. The latter often utilizes the 3D traits acquired from multi-view-angle facial images obtained by several cameras, from special 3D expression databases, or via special sensors. Other methods combine 2D with 3D traits to recognize facial expressions.[14-16] These methods of acquiring and processing traits typically integrate the two above types.

Currently, facial expression recognition methods mainly include neural networks,[17] support vector machines (SVMs),[16, 18] Markov chains,[13, 19] and others. It is apparent that different learning machines are suited for different kinds of datasets. When these learning machines are independently utilized, they often cannot independently overcome limitations. Alternatively, a real dataset often must be significantly changed at the cost of considerable useful trait information. Thus, recognition accuracy will be affected.

To retain trait information as much as possible, we therefore consider integrating learning machines with a special architecture to improve the overall performance. Moreover, in typical situations, 2D facial expression images are most often obtained. Thus, we attempt to acquire and utilize reflected 3D information from 2D images to directly realize approximated 3D recognition.

In this paper, we propose an automatic recognition framework for human facial expressions from a monocular video with an uncalibrated camera. From a deformable template, similar to a facial muscle distribution, the associated expression traits are extracted, regularized, and normalized. They are then arranged line by line in a matrix in accordance with the changing of the traits in space-time with complete expressional production. Next, the dimensionality of the trait matrix is reduced by a method of manifold-learning neighborhood preserving embedding (NPE). Finally, with the refined matrix as input, a classifier that integrates the hidden conditional random field (HCRF) with SVM is used to recognize the expression.

The remainder of this paper is arranged as follows. Section 2 describes the principle of facial expression recognition and outlines the proposed method. Section 3 describes our experiment to verify the proposed method, and the results are analyzed. Our conclusions are presented in Sec. 4

2 Facial Expression Recognition Principle

Figure 1 illustrates the presented facial expression recognition framework. The 2D dynamic expression sequence from monocular vision is used as the input expression to be trained or tested. Here, the centroids of the different facial-area gray values in the expression image are employed as traits. A gray level has various attributes—brightness, contrast, and saturation— that change with differing depths. Therefore, the gray values include some depth information, especially relative changing values. These traits are characterized by movement in space-time as each facial expression is produced.

The same types of expression traits typically move in space-time with the same styles and have the same periodicities. Here, for each type of expression, only one facial expression cycle is needed in the recognition framework. With the production of this one cycle, that is to say, under a complete expressional production, the associated traits change in space-time, thereby forming time sequences. All the time-sequences are arrayed in a matrix. Thus, the problem of recognition is transformed into the problem of handling all the time-sequence data. Key details are described in the subsections below.

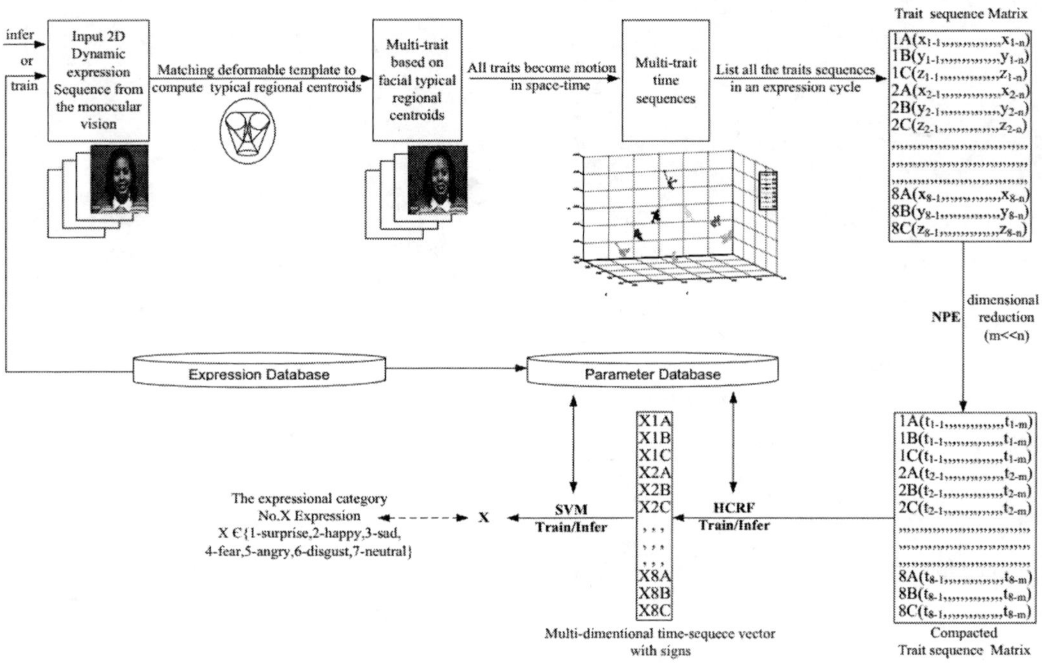

Figure 1. Principle of facial expression recognition.

2.1 Extracting and Processing Traits

Figure 2. Principle of deformable template matching. a) Distribution of facial muscles. b) Deformable expression template. c) Examples of real face matching with the deformable template.

Figure 2 depicts the principle of the deformable template that is used for detecting traits of human facial expressions. First, the human face is detected with a face detector. If the detection is successful, then the eyes, nose, and mouth are respectively detected with related detectors in the facial region. (If the detection of one of these sense organs fails, we determine the organ's possible area in the facial region according to certain proportions. These proportions are based on general prior anatomy knowledge of the normal, common human face. If facial detection is not successful, we search other regions in the image with the face detector.) Then, all above detected areas are drawn with a corresponding circle, triangle, and ellipse. Next, we connect the different positions on the sides of the detected areas with lines, thus comprising the deformable template.

This strategy effectively reduces processing time. Meanwhile, all detectors are designed as in Ref. [20]. All detection of the areas noted above is automatically performed; manual assistance is not required. By combining Figs. 2(a) and (b), it is evident that the template traits proposed herein are highly consistent with the usual distribution of human facial muscles. This approach is thus convenient for analyzing expressions in terms of the human anatomical structure. Figure 3 provides an example of the template for detecting common human expressions, which is realized with the Microsoft Visual C++ 6.0 platform environment.

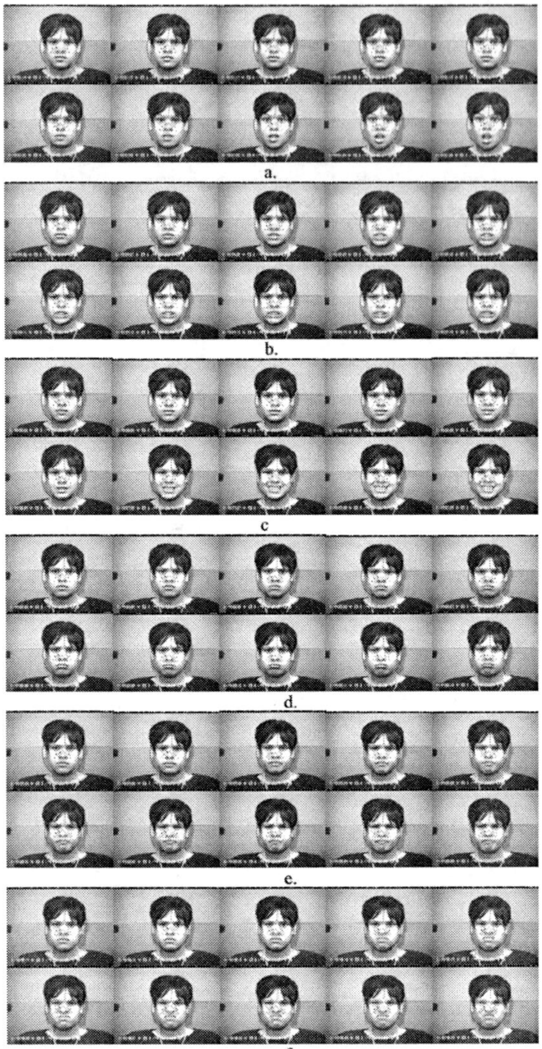

Figure. 3 Examples of the deformable template matching with a real face of different expressions. a) Surprise. b) Fear. c) Happiness. d) Sadness. e) Anger. f) Disgust.

As shown in Fig. 2, based on the anatomy of human facial muscle configurations and dynamics,[21, 22] the facial expression is divided into eight areas. In each area, we employ an associated centroid to describe all the regional pixel global changes in space-time as different expressions are produced. Each centroid is computed by Eq. (1), where, at time t, n_i is the number of pixels in region i, and x_m, y_m and z_m are the corresponding horizontal coordinates, vertical coordinates, and gray values of each pixel. As a person forms a facial expression, all pixels in the facial image are in motion in space-time. At the given moment, all the above centroids are in motion as well. These centroids moving in space-time form time sequences.

$$centroid_i^t = \left(\frac{\sum_{m=1}^{n_i} x_m^t}{n_i}, \frac{\sum_{m=1}^{n_i} y_m^t}{n_i}, \frac{\sum_{m=1}^{n_i} z_m^t}{n_i} \right)_i, \quad i \in I = \{1,2,,,,8\} \qquad (1)$$

Figure 4 depicts the time sequences of the motioning centroids in the MATLAB tool with the above expressions gradually being produced, starting from the neutral expression of one person. It is apparent that the distributions and shapes of the time sequences differ from the different kinds of expressions. Thus, they can be used as the basis for distinguishing between each other.

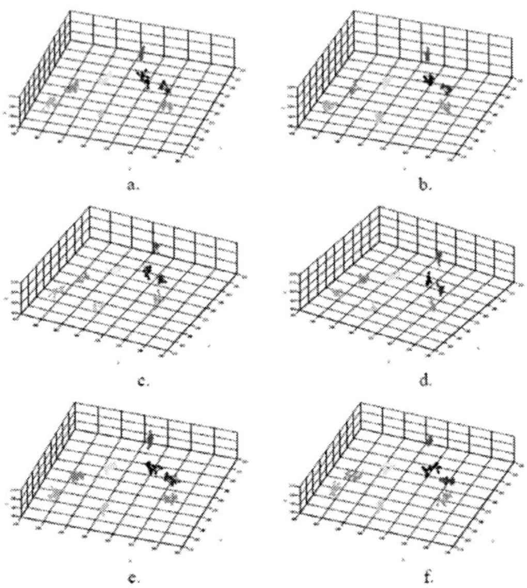

Figure 4. Time-sequences of motioning centroids on different expressions changed from neutral expression of one person. a) Surprise. b) Fear. c) Happiness. d) Sadness. e) Anger. f) Disgust.

Equation (2) describes the principle of preprocessing for the time sequences above. This includes extracting relative changing values, normalizing, and scattering.

$$centroid\_verified_i^t = \arg\min_{j \in J} \left\{ \left| \frac{centroid_i^t - \underset{t \in T}{Min}\{centroid_i^t\}}{\underset{t \in T}{Max}\{centroid_i^t\} - \underset{t \in T}{Min}\{centroid_i^t\}} \times 10 - j \right| \right\} \qquad (2)$$
$$j \in J = \{1,2,,,,10\}$$

2.2 Facial Expression Recognition

In general, here, the mechanism we adopted is similar with that in Ref. [23] where we studied gait recognition, because they are all the problems of multi-sequence classification although in different application fields. Of course, some associated definitions and settings are also different. Next, combing with Ref.[23], we elaborate our method as below.

1) NPE for reducing time-sequence dimensionality

NPE is detailed in Ref. [24], and its main principle is expressed in Eqs. (3) to (5). Before applying NPE,[24] we note that each time-sequence i (i = 1, . . . , 8 × 3 = 24) produced by the associated curve is regarded as data point x_i. To preserve the correlation property among curves, the means of constructing an adjacency graph is the k-nearest neighbor (KNN), and k is set to 24. That is, each time-sequence is reconstructed by 23 other adjacent time-sequences in the facial expression. It is hence reasonable to assume that each local neighborhood is linear, although these data points may reside on a nonlinear sub-manifold.

Then, we use Eq. (3) to compute weight matrix W of the structural relation existing in the data points. We employ Eq. (4) to compute the projections on reducing dimensionality, and Eq. (5) is applied to realize, in turn, the final transformation of reducing dimensionality for each data point, x_i.

$$\begin{cases} \min \sum_i \left\| x_i - \sum_j W_{ij} x_j \right\|^2 \quad \textit{with} \ \text{constraints:} \ \sum_j W_{ij} = 1, j = 1, 2, \ldots, k & (3) \\ X(I-W)^T(I-W)X^T a = \lambda X X^T a \quad \textit{where} \ X = (x_1, \ldots, x_k), \ I = diag(1, \ldots, 1) & (4) \\ y_i = A^T x_i = (a_0, a_1, \ldots, a_{m-1})^T x_i \quad \textit{where} \ y_i \ \textit{is a} \ m-\text{dimensional vector.} & (5) \end{cases}$$

Initially, each of the motion curves in a facial expression for one expression cycle has 50 space samples. By using NPE, the corresponding time-sequence dimensionality is reduced from 50 dimensions of one facial expression cycle to 24 dimensions. The local manifold structure is preserved in low-dimensional space with optimal embedding.

2) Integrating SVM with HCRF for classifying multiple time-sequences

a)HCRF for marking all time-sequences with signs

According to Fig. 1, we assuming the expression type for subject No. X (X = 1, 2, . . .7). This is because different centroids in the human facial expression correspond to different motion time-sequences. All time-sequences of expression type No. X are marked with X1A, X1B, X1C, X2A, X2B, X2C, . . ., X8A, X8B, and X8C, respectively.

The mapping between the sequences and corresponding labels is conducted by HCRF's training or inferring. Here, the HCRF method, as in Ref. [25], is principally similar to that in Ref. [26]. The associated formulas are Eqs. (6) and (7).

Equation (6) describes the principle of inferring label y from the HCRF model given observation x, the HCRF models parameters $\theta^{□}$ and window parameter w which is used to incorporate long-range dependencies. Equation (7) describes the estimation for the HCRF model parameters θ

In combination with instructions in Ref. [25], the typical method of the conjugate gradient in Ref. [27] is used to estimate parameters $\theta^{□}$. In both equations above, all the terms' interpretations and all the parameters' meanings are same as that in Ref.[23].

In this paper, the number of hidden states is set to ten, and window size w is set to 0,1,2 fator testing. In training, each type of time-sequence in each human face sub-area for all facial expressions of all persons, and its corresponding label, are learned with a separate HCRF model. In inferring, the tested sequence is run with the HCRF model to produce the same time-sequence type. The class label with the highest probability corresponds to the label of the test sequence.

$$\begin{aligned} \arg\max_{y \in Y}\left(P(y \mid x, \theta^*, w)\right) &= \arg\max_{y \in Y}\left(\sum_h P(y, h \mid x, \theta^*, w) a\right) \\ &= \arg\max_{y \in Y}\left(\frac{\sum_h e^{\Psi(y,h,x;\theta^*,w)}}{\sum_{y' \in Y, h \in H^m} e^{\Psi(y',h,x;\theta^*,w)}}\right); \quad (6) \\ \textit{among}: \ \Psi(y, h, x; \theta^*, w) &= \sum_{j=1}^{n} \varphi(x, j, w) \cdot \theta_h^*[h_j] + \sum_{j=1}^{n} \theta_y^*[y, h_j] + \sum_{(j,k) \in E} \theta_e^*[y, h_j, h_k]; \\ \theta^* = \arg\max_\theta\left(L(\theta)\right) &= \arg\max_\theta\left(\sum_{i=1}^{n} \log P(y_i \mid x_i, \theta, w) - \frac{1}{2\sigma^2}\|\theta\|^2\right); \quad (7) \end{aligned}$$

b) SVM for classifying all multi-sequence signs

Here, SVM is used as the final classifying means to recognize the facial expression by employing the marked features associated with the facial expression as input.

Now, we address the problem of multiclass classification. On multiclass SVM, we apply the one-against-one approach[28, 29] that is suitable for practical use, as in Ref. [30]. In this method: if the amount of training categories in the database is K, then $K(K-1)/2$ binary SVM classifiers are needed; each classifier adopts the C-support vector classification (CSVC) model with the radial basis function kernel, in which two parameters are considered: C and γ; the two parameters are selected by using typical cross validation via a parallel grid search, and all $K(K-1)/2$ decision functions finally share the same (C, γ).

For training data from the ith and jth classes, Eq. (8) displays the binary classification problem to be solved. In Eq. (8), each term's interpretation and each parameter's meaning are same as that in Ref. [23]. In addition, during final classifying, the voting strategy suggested in Ref. [29] is used to predict that x is in the class with the largest vote. In this strategy, if $\text{sign}(((w^{ij})^T\Phi(x_t)) + b^{ij})$ infers that x is in the ith class, then the vote for the ith class is increased by one; otherwise, the jth class is increased by one. For the case in which two classes have an identical vote, the one with the smaller index is selected.

$$\begin{cases} \min_{w^{ij}, b^{ij}, \xi^{ij}} \left(\frac{1}{2}(w^{ij})^T w^{ij} + C\left(\sum_t (\xi^{ij})_t\right)\right) \quad \textit{where} \ \xi_t^{ij} \geq 0 \ ; & (8) \\ \textit{subject to} \ \left((w^{ij})^T \phi(x_t)\right) + b^{ij} \geq 1 - \xi_t^{ij}, \quad \text{if } x_t \text{ in the ith class;} \\ \qquad \left((w^{ij})^T \phi(x_t)\right) + b^{ij} \leq -1 + \xi_t^{ij}, \quad \text{if } x_t \text{ in the jth class.} \end{cases}$$

3 Experiment

3.1 Testing Environment

To validate the performance of the proposed method application in a basic environment, all experiments were conducted in an environment of Microsoft Visual C++ 6.0 as the platform on a Pentium 1.73-GHz personal computer.

The proposed facial expression recognition framework was tested with the Cohn–Kanade AU-Coded

Facial Expression (CKACFE) database,[31] which includes 486 sequences digitized into 640 by 480 or 490 pixel arrays with 8-bit precision for gray-scale values from 97 posers. Each sequence began with a neutral expression and proceeded to a peak expression. The peak expression for each sequence was coded using the Facial Action Coding System (FACS) [32] and then assigned an emotion label. Each poser had at most seven kinds of emotions: neutrality, surprise, sadness, disgust, anger, fear, and happiness.

In our experiment, we adopted the leave-one-out cross validation to train/infer the facial expression. We first employed subject No. 1 to obtain all expressions for recognition; the expressions of the remaining subjects were used for training. Then, we used all expressions of subject No. 2 for testing; the expressions of all others were used for training. Next, we again changed the order and repeated the training/inferring experiment until all subject expressions could be inferred. At last, we computed the rate of successful recognitions for each type of expression and regarded it as the final result.

The associated computation is shown as Eq. (9), where function_infer can be regarded as the whole function corresponding to the relative recognizing system of HCRF+SVM when the *i*th expression is testing emotion x_i ($x_i > 0$). Only when the function's result equals input x_i is the result correct at this point:

$$\begin{cases} R_{\text{recognition rate}} = \frac{1}{N}\sum_{i=1}^{N}\delta\left(x_i - \text{function\_infer}_i^{hcrf/svm}(x_i)\right) \quad (9) \\ where: \ \delta \text{ is the unit pulse function: } \delta(m)=1 \text{ if } m=0, \text{ and zero otherwise.} \end{cases}$$

Combining the methods in Section 2, in training for HCRF, the conjugate gradient method presented in Ref. [27] is used to estimate the associated parameters. In training for SVM, the method of cross validation via a parallel grid search, as in Ref. [30], is used to estimate the associated parameters. According to Section 2, since there are 97 subjects, each subject has seven kinds of expressions. Each expression corresponds to eight 3D time-sequences. Thus, there are $8 \times 3 = 24$ HCRF models and $7 \times (7 - 1) / 2 = 21$ SVM classifiers in total. When training for all the expressions in the CKACFE database is finished, all the trained parameters for the associated HCRF models and SVM classifiers are saved to another database.

In addition, just after reducing the dimensionality of the associated time-sequences, we use these temporal associated data as input, with HCRF and SVM respectively used as independent classifiers to recognize the facial expression. In this case, one HCRF model corresponds to one type of expression; that is, there are seven HCRF models, and the number of SVM classifiers is the same as in the previous case. Of course, another database on associated trained parameters is produced from the CKACFE database after training. At last, at the same window parameter w, we conduct the comparisons of the recognition rates above with the results of the proposed recognition framework and the typical Kotsia method.[16]

3.2 Testing Results and Analysis

Figure 5 illustrates the distribution of the different expression time-sequences of all individuals in the CKACFE Database. It is evident that the different kinds of expressions correspond to different types of time-sequence distributions, thereby providing considerable convenience for recognizing expressions with these time-sequences.

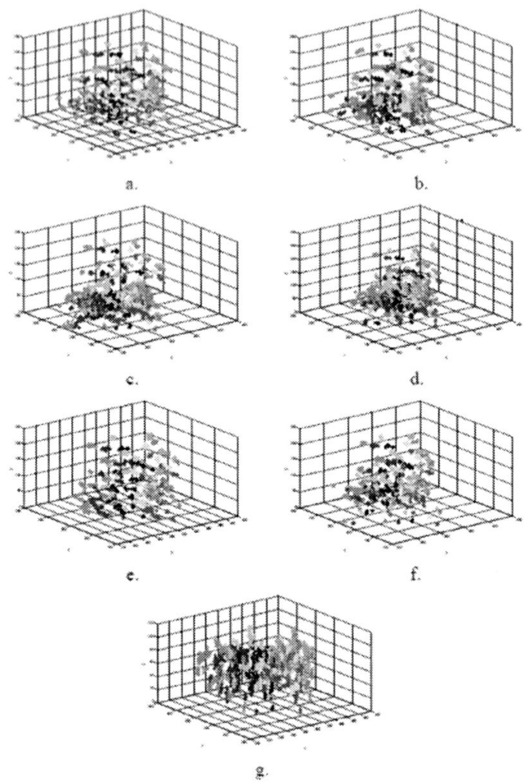

Figure 5. Distribution of different expression time-sequences of all individuals in the Cohn–Kanade AU-Coded Facial Expression Database. a) Surprise. b) Fear. c) Happiness. d) Sadness. e) Anger. f) Disgust. g) Neutrality.

Table 1 and Fig. 6 present the results of comparisons of the proposed integrated classifier, the HCRF+SVM method, with the typical Kotsia method[16] and independent HCRF and SVM classifiers for facial expression recognition. It is evident that the recognition rate of the proposed method is more stable than that of the Kotsia method; the Kotsia method is higher than ours in very few cases. The HCRF+SVM recognition rate is higher than those of independent HCRF and SVM.

According to the principle in Sec. 2, when the NPE method reduces the dimension of the time-sequences, the local neighborhood structure on the data manifold is preserved. When HCRF trains or infers the signs of the time-sequences, the sequences where the underlying graphical model captures temporal dependencies across frames is modeled and long-range dependencies are incorporated. Meanwhile, when SVM trains or infers the final expression of the relative signs, the separating margins of decision boundaries on classification are maximized as the data are mapped into high-dimensional space. Thus, compared with HCRF or SVM, the combined HCRF+SVM method obtains more structural traits of the data to be classified when handling the data, thereby making the recognition more efficient.

Table 1 Associated comparisons of the HCRF+SVM integrated classifier with a typical method and independent classifiers, HCRF and SVM, for facial expression recognition at different window parameters *w*.

Method / recognition rate(%) / expression	kotsia	hcrf+svm $w=0$	hcrf+svm $w=1$	hcrf+svm $w=2$	hcrf $w=1$	svm
neutrality	99.6	95.8	97.1	96.5	82.3	75.8
surprise	95.3	96.3	98.3	96.1	82.7	78.1
sadness	94.1	96.9	98.4	97.4	83.5	78.3
disgust	82.5	98.6	96.9	98.6	85.8	79.3
fear	99.5	96.8	98.3	97.1	84.2	77.1
angry	92.3	98.4	97.8	98.3	85.1	78.9
happiness	98.2	97.1	98.2	97.3	84.2	78.2

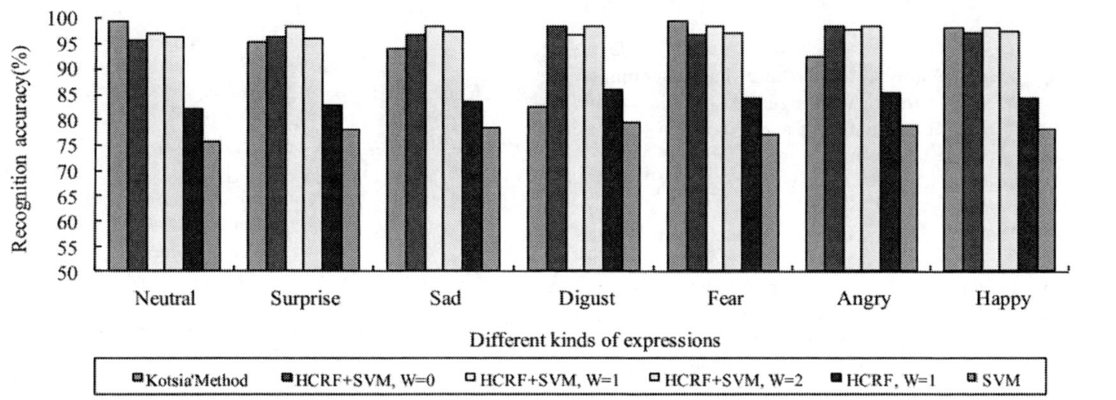

Figure 6. Associated comparisons of the integrated classifiers HCRF+SVM with the typical method and single classifier HCRF/SVM for facial expression recognition at different window parameters, *w*.

In addition, it is evident that the recognition rate differs from different window sizes, *w*. Furthermore, when *w* equals one, the recognition rates are universally higher than at other window sizes. From the whole effect, the results of the proposed recognition framework are satisfactory.

In the phase immediately after reducing the dimensionality of the associated time-sequences, the independent HCRF recognition rate is slightly higher than that of the independent SVM because HCRF is more fitting for classifying time-sequences than SVM. Meanwhile, SVM takes the correlated sequences as independent parameters, which is unreasonable to some extent. In addition, in terms of the respective HCRF or SVM, the changing trends of the recognition rates at different expressions are consistent with those of the integrated HCRF+SVM classifier.

3 Conclusion

In this paper, we proposed a framework based on the HCRF+SVM integrated classifier for human facial expression recognition. According to universal human-facial muscle distributions, the method employs the centroids of different areas of the facial image as traits. This approach is convenient for analyzing expressions in terms of the human anatomical structure. With any production of an expression, these centroids move in space-time, forming multiple time-sequences. After applying NPE for reducing the dimensionality of trait time-sequences, the local neighborhood structure on the data manifold is preserved. The proposed integrated classifier HCRF+SVM obtains more structural characteristics of the data in space-time during inferring. Consequently, the experimental testing produced higher recognition rates than the respective HCRF or SVM directly from trait sequences. Moreover, the proposed method was shown to be more robust than the typical Kotsia method.

In future work, we intend to improve the proposed method's robustness to different illuminations and occlusions. In addition to the datasets used in the present study, we will evaluate in other situations whether the adopted integrated classification can handle other kinds of datasets. Moreover, in the strategy of the two-stage classification herein proposed, the first stage identification error will affect the next stage's recognition accuracy. That is, errors can easily occur. We will therefore consider using only one mathematical model to directly perform the classification of multi-sequences, thereby further improving the recognition rate.

References

1. H. C. Breiter, et al., Response and habituation of the human amygdala during visual processing of facial expression. Neuron. 17(5): p. 875-887(1996).
2. D.L. Roter, et al., The expression of emotion through nonverbal behavior in medical visits. Journal of General Internal Medicine. 21(S1): p. S28-S34(2006).
3. H.S. Friedman, Nonverbal communication between patients and medical practitioners. Journal of Social Issues. 35(1): p. 82-99(1979).
4. P.W. Garner, Emotional competence and its influences on teaching and learning. Educational Psychology Review. 22(3): p. 297-321(2010).
5. H.A. Smith, Nonverbal communication in teaching. Review of Educational Research. 49(4): p. 631-672(1979).
6. C.L. Lisetti and D.J. Schiano, Automatic facial expression interpretation: Where human-computer interaction, artificial intelligence and cognitive science intersect. Pragmatics and Cognition (Special Issue on Facial Information Processing: A Multidisciplinary Perspective). 8(1): p. 185-235(2000).
7. M.S. Bartlett, et al., Real Time Face Detection and Facial Expression Recognition: Development and Applications to Human Computer Interaction, in IEEE Conference on Computer Vision and Pattern Recognition Workshop, CVPRW'03 p. 53-53(2003).
8. R. Cowie, et al., Emotion recognition in human-computer interaction. Signal Processing Magazine. 18(1): p. 32-80(2001).
9. K.-Y. Chang, T.-L. Liu, and S.-H. Lai, Learning partially-observed hidden conditional random fields for facial expression recognition, in IEEE confference on Computer Vision and Pattern Recognition, CVPR. p. 533-540(2009).
10. Z. Zhang, et al., Comparison between geometry-based and Gabor-wavelets-based facial expression recognition using multi-layer perceptron, in proceedings. third IEEE international conference on Automatic face and gesture recognition. p. 454-459(1998).
11. I. Mpiperis, S. Malassiotis, and M.G. Strintzis, Bilinear models for 3-D face and facial expression recognition. IEEE TRANSACTIONS ON INFORMATION FORENSICS AND SECURITY. 3(3): p. 498-511(2008).
12. Y.V. Venkatesh, A.A. Kassim, and O.V.R. Murthy, A novel approach to classification of facial expressions from 3D-mesh datasets using modified PCA. Pattern Recognition Letters. 30(12): p. 1128-1137(2009).
13. Y. Sun, et al., Tracking vertex flow and model adaptation for three-dimensional spatiotemporal face analysis. IEEE TRANSACTIONS ON SYSTEMS, MAN, AND CYBERNETICS—PART A: SYSTEMS AND HUMANS. 40(3): p. 461-474(2010).
14. J. Sung and D. Kim, Pose-Robust Facial Expression Recognition Using View-Based 2D+3D AAM. IEEE TRANSACTIONS ON SYSTEMS, MAN, AND CYBERNETICS—PART A: SYSTEMS AND HUMANS,. 38(4): p. 852-866(2008).
15. F. Tsalakanidou and S. Malassiotis, Real-time 2D+ 3D facial action and expression recognition. Pattern Recognition. 43(5): p. 1763-1775(2010).
16. I. Kotsia and I. Pitas, Facial expression recognition in image sequences using geometric deformation features and support vector machines. IEEE TRANSACTIONS ON IMAGE PROCESSING. 16(1): p. 172-187(2007).
17. [17]. H. Soyel and H. Demirel, 3D facial expression recognition with geometrically localized facial features, in International Symposium on Computer and Information Sciences. p. 1-4(2008).
18. H. Tang and T.S. Huang, 3D facial expression recognition based on properties of line segments connecting facial feature points. IEEE International Conference on Automatic Face & Gesture Recognition: p. 1-6(2008).
19. Y. Sun and L. Yin, Facial Expression Recognition Based on 3D Dynamic Range Model Sequences. European Conference on Computer Vision, ECCV, Marseille, France, October 12-18, : p. 58-71(2008).
20. F. Adolf, How-to build a cascade of boosted classifiers based on Haar-like features, in Book OpenCV's Rapid Object Detection(2003).
21. A.M. Burrows and J.F. Cohn, Anatomy of Face: Springer US. 16-23(2009).
22. M.Z. Siemionow and E. Sonmez, Face as an Organ: The Functional Anatomy of the Face: The Know-How of Face Transplantation Springer London. 70:1227(2011).
23. Yu, T. and J.H. Zou, Automatic Human Gait Imitation and Recognition in 3D from Monocular Video with an Uncalibrated Camera. Mathematical Problems in Engineering. 2012. 2012, Article ID 563864,doi:10.1155/2012/563864: p. 1-35.
24. X. He, et al., Neighborhood preserving embedding. Tenth IEEE International Conference on Computer Vision, ICCV. 2: p. 1208-1213(2005).
25. L. Morency A. Quattoni, C. Christoudias, and S. Wang, Hidden-state Conditional random Field Library. User guide MIT CSAIL: p. 1-17(2007).
26. S.B. Wang, A. Quattoni, L. P,Morency, D.Demirdjian, , and T. Darrell, Hidden conditional random fields for gesture recognition. IEEE Computer Society Conference on Computer Vision and Pattern Recognition. 2: p. 1521-1527(2006).
27. W.W. Hager and H. Zhang, A new conjugate gradient method with guaranteed descent and an efficient line search. SIAM Journal on Optimization. 16(1): p. 170-192(2005).
28. U.H.G. KreBel, Pairwise classification and support vector machines, in Advances in kernel methods, MIT Press: Cambridge, MA. p. 255-268(1999).
29. J. Friedman, Another approach to polychotomous classifcation, Technical report, Department of Statistics, Stanford University(1996).

30. C.C. Chang and C.J. Lin, LIBSVM: a library for support vector machines. ACM Transactions on Intelligent Systems and Technology (TIST). 2(3): p. 27(2011).
31. T. Kanade, J.F. Cohn, and Y. Tian, Comprehensive database for facial expression analysis. Proceedings. Fourth IEEE International Conference on Automatic Face and Gesture Recognition, : p. 46-53(2000).
32. P. Ekmanand and W.V. Friesen, Facial action coding system(FACS). Agriculture(2002).

Assisted Diagnosis Research Based on Improved Deep Autoencoder

Zhang-Han KE[a], Yu-Kai DUAN[b], Yu TIAN[c], and Hao LIU[d]

Software College, Northeastern University, Shenyang, China
[a]petrus@stumail.neu.edu.cn, [b]duanduan@stumail.neu.edu.cn, [c]20134838@stu.neu.edu.cn, [d]20134832@stu.neu.edu.cn

Abstract: Deep Autoencoder has the powerful ability to learn features from large number of unlabeled samples and a small number of labeled samples. In this work, we have improved the network structure of the general deep autoencoder and applied it to the disease auxiliary diagnosis. We have achieved a network by entering the specific indicators and predicting whether suffering from liver disease, the network using real physical examination data for training and verification. Compared with the traditional semi-supervised machine learning algorithm, deep autoencoder will get higher accuracy.

1 Introduction

How to use medical data and extract the useful knowledge from the complex data effectively in the context of the intermittent observation of the condition, the complexity of various medical examinations, and the large amount of medical literature has become a more and more interesting problem for people. Disease auxiliary diagnosis is one of the directions, which is hoping to predict the possible illness of the subject by analyzing the information such as physical examination. Disease auxiliary diagnosis will use the most common customer's physical examination report as the original materials. From these materials we can collect the relevant data and mine the hidden information to assist in the diagnosis. It will not only help out-patient physicians in small and medium-sized hospitals to make more accurate judgments without other complex operations and testing, but also provide follow-up recommendations to help find the cause quickly in the scenario of failing to detect the disease.

With the development of machine learning, there are many studies and algorithms in the field of disease auxiliary diagnosis, but many algorithms cannot replace manual diagnosis because of the request of high accuracy of the prediction in the medical field. However, with the rapid develop in computer performance in recent years, making the deep learning rises again. At present, the deep learning in the image, voice and other aspects has been significantly beyond the previous methods, which makes the use of artificial intelligence in the field of high precision requirements possible. Therefore, the use of deep learning to achieve the diagnosis of the disease is of practical significance.

A mass of medical data does not have final conclusions, and the general recommendation cannot be identified as the disease of the subject in most cases, it means that most of the data are unlabeled. Such as the hospital experts mark their analysis on the label one by one, which not only does not play the role of assistant physician, but also increase the workload of the physician. Thanks to the implementation of unsupervised and semi-supervised learning on neural networks, we can also use deep learning to train unlabeled data. The supervised learning is a process that the learning machine guides the learning by label, which could establish a model for predicting unlabeled samples. The unsupervised learning focuses only on unlabeled samples, its task is only to describe the way data are organized or clustered. Combining with the above two approaches, the implementation of semi-supervised learning is a process based on labeled training samples and utilized by unlabeled samples themselves. Deep autoencoder is a network which can be applied for semi-supervised classification, in the case of sufficient unlabeled data, it only requires a small amount of labeled data to complete the classification task.

2 Related Work

Autoencoders have been relatively long history and have matured. Rumelhart proposed the concept of autoencoder and applied it to high dimensional complex data processing in 1986. That promotes the development of neural networks. The simplest autocoder includes an encoder and a decoder that implements the mapping of data to itself. Of course, the ability of the single layer of autoencoders is limited to expressing data. The stack autoencoder is subsequently presented. The structure trains an autoencoder every time, then it removes the decoding layer and the encoded results will train the new encoder as input, so on we will eventually get a chain encoder. The advantage is that it contains a number of encoders, each layer is an abstract representation of the

DOI: 10.1051/itmconf/20171203043

different characteristics of the data, so its ability to express data is greatly enhanced. But this structure also has the characteristics of training difficulties. On the one hand the structure will take a lot of time to carry out a complete training of each layer of encoder, on the other hand, In the case of a certain amount of data, each layer uses the same data for repeated training, it will easy to appear network fitting problem. Then Hinton improved the structure of the prototype autoencoder, which in turn produced the DAE. This structure can be a one-time training in the network of encoders which can greatly improve the speed and reduce the risk of fitting.

In order to solve the problem of autoencoder is difficult to train and make it have better application in a particular scene. A series of related work has emerged. Benjio proposed the concept of coefficient autoencoders that further deepening the DAE research in 2007[1]. Vincent proposed the noise reduction autoencoder, it adds corrupt vector into the input data to prevent over-fitting phenomenon and that achieved good results in 2008[2]. Benjio summarized the existing depth structure and expounded the general method of constructing deep learning neural network by stacking autoencoder in 2009[3]. Salah limited the process of raising and reducing dimension and proposed a shrink autoencoder in 2010[4]. Telmo studied the performance of DAE trained with different cost functions, pointing out the direction for the development of cost function optimization strategies in 2013[5]. Taylor explored the relationship between DAE and unsupervised feature learning and detailed how to construct different types of depth structures using autoencoders in 2012[6].

In recent years, the study of neural networks has proposed many effective schemes including ReLU and BatchNormalization. The ReLU activation function simulates the activation model of neurons accepting signals from the biological point of view. It obtains sparse activation by unilateral suppression. The sparsity makes the key factors in the data be preserved and strengthened and the secondary factors (noise) discarded. It causes the robustness of the data can be enhanced. Many practices prove that ReLU compared to Sigmoid function is a better choice. In the case of Loss large network convergence speed is faster than Sigmoid. Batch Normalization solves the Internal Covariate shift problem by normalized processing of the output of the network layer, so that the data transmitted in the network is in a relatively stable distribution. Because the network does n't have to adapt to the distribution of large input data, it can accelerate the training of the network. Batch normalization also can make the network use a greater learning rate. This results in a fairly good convergence of the general network weights initialization situation.

3 Our Work

As mentioned above, the deep autoencoder can effectively learn the distribution and characteristics from the untagged data set, which is of great significance in semi-supervisory training. We can use the untagged data training network model to modify the network structure and add the classifier, then training classifier with a small amount of tagged data alone, in order to achieve the effect of classification. Because the number of diseases is large and there is a clear distinction between the boundaries of one disease and between different indicators, we first focus on a class of diseases for analysis and research. We can easily extend this model to apply to other disease prediction. We choose liver disease as our first network prediction category. We select six categories of common liver disease I as the predictor, and select gender, age, and 12 indexes which have a strong correlation with the disease and 6 indexes which have a weak correlation, as input: X = {x_1, x_2, ..., x_20} (Table 1). The network will use these indicators to predict the final possible outcome diseases.

3.1 Data Processing

We have fetched the data from one hospital and the origin data is in a mess, so the collected data needs to be preprocessed. Firstly, we should extract indexes related to liver diseases, and discard observations with too many NAs. The remaining NA data is done by randomly generated in the normal range. Secondly, the distribution of the examination indicators are all positive and the difference between the indicators is large, which will not be conducive to network training, leading to slow convergence or even no convergence. Here, we use the simplified Batch Normalization, in order to make the mean of all data to 0 and the variance to 1. For each input data X = (X1, X2, X3 ... Xk), we normalize each dimension in the following way:

$$x_k' = \frac{x_k - E[x_k]}{\sqrt{v[x_k]}} \tag{1}$$

For the untagged pre-training data and the tagged fine-tuning data, the above processing is required to obtain the data that can be used.

3.2 Improving the Network

Similar to the traditional Deep Auto encoders used for classification, the network will be divided into the pre-training part and the fine-tuning part. Table 2 shows our pre-training network structure. First, the data is passed through a series of encoders to compress the data into a low-dimensional representation, which will then be restored to data with the same dimension as the input through a series of decoders. Finally, the output with the original input are passed into squared error layer to calculate the deviation and propagates backwards, optimize the parameters of the network:

$$x_k' = \varphi_\lambda\left(\phi_\lambda\left(x_k\right)\right) \tag{2}$$

$$\Gamma_{loss} = \frac{1}{2n}\sum\nolimits_1^n \left\| x_k' \quad x_k \right\|^2 \tag{3}$$

The training of the traditional deep autoencoder is relatively difficult, and the initialization of the network parameters also has a high demand. With the emergence of some new techniques, deep neural network training has become relatively easier. So we consider the following ways to improve the traditional depth of the automatic encoder:

1) Some of the indicators used for prediction are independent with a particular disease, but the sigmoid function assumes that all active outputs are valid, and the ReLU function selectively discards the value of the active output less than 0. So we can think that ReLU activated in the optimization process will discard independent indicators with the disease, and enhance the sparseness of the network. So we use the ReLU activation function instead of the Sigmoid activation in the traditional deep encoders.

2) With the increase of network depth, the stability of the network will decline, and the initialization of the parameters is particularly important. However, the emergence of BN makes the network initialization easier, so we add the BN layers in the network except the last encoding-decoding step, This specification adjusts the distribution of the encoded data to ensure that the next encoder can learn the characteristics of the raw data without problems with the input data. The addition of BN makes the Deep Autoencoder converge faster and easier to train.

In the above process, the depth automatic encoder learns and optimizes the non-label data. It obtains a network that can express itself finally. In order to have the network classification function, the network decoder need to be partially removed and the encoder need to be at the end of a classifier. Then we use the tagged data {x, Labal} to train the classifier individually. the classifier outputs optimize the classifier by Softmax layers and calculating deviations from the data labels. Because the fine-tuning network only needs to optimize the classification layer parameters, only a small amount of label data can be made to have a classification effect. The classifier and error calculation are as follows:

$$z_k = h(\phi_\lambda(x_k)) \tag{4}$$

$$\sigma_i(z) = \frac{e^{z_i}}{\sum_{j=1}^{n} e^{z_j}} \tag{5}$$

$$\Gamma_{loss} = \log \sigma_i(z) \tag{6}$$

3.3 Network Structure

The final Pre-train network contains four encoders and decoders and the input data is a 20-dimensional vector. The first layer encoder will enhance the representation of the data. The output vector expands to 24-dimensional and compresses it. The three-tier decoder compresses the data to 18,14 and 8 dimensional. Then there are four decoders corresponding to the four encoders, and finally reduce the data to 20-dimensional vectors. At the meanwhile, calculate the square error layer together with the input data and update reversely by BP algorithm. Then there are four decoders corresponding to the four encoders, and finally reduce the data to 20-dimensional vectors. At the meanwhile, calculate the square error layer together with the input data and update reversely by BP algorithm. Table 1 is the PRE-TRAIN network structure.

In the Fine-tune stage, all decoders are removed, and after the fourth-level encoder, a full-link classifier is added. At this stage, the dimension of the output data is the same as the final class. At the last, the loss is calculated by the Softmax layer with the data tag. Table 2 is the fine-tune network structure.

Table 1. Pre-Train Network

Pre-Train Network
encoder1 + bn + relu
encoder2 + bn + relu
encoder3 + bn + relu
encoder4
decoder4 + bn + relu
decoder3 + bn + relu
decoder2 + bn + relu
decoder1
square loss

Table 2. Fine-Tune Network

Fine-Tune Network
encoder1+ bn + relu
encoder1+ bn + relu
encoder1+ bn + relu
encoder1
classifier
softmax + loss

4 Experiments

It is natural that optimize our network by using the stochastic gradient descent with minibatch (based on BP with momentum). Minibatch size is 128 in pre-train stage while 64 in fine tune stage. Since the amount of disease-free data is many times than diseased data, in order to prevent the overfitting of disease-free data, each minibatch in the fine tune phase used 16 positive samples (disease) and 48 negative samples (disease-free) as input. We also use weight decay normalization to prevent the overfitting problem (L2 factor is 10^{-4}), base learning rate is 10^{-3}. During pre-train phase, learning rate will be adjusted several times with factor 0.1.We final get a high accuracy of test task(93%), compare our improved deep autoencoder with common deep autoencoder (use sigmoid and without batch normalization), the convergence rate of

DOI: 10.1051/itmconf/20171203043

the network has been acceleration, and the accuracy of network have a little improvement. Comparisons with other semi-supervised learning methods still require more experiments, and we will continue to do experiments in the next work.

5 Conclusion

We tried to use the network-optimized deep autoencoder for liver disease prediction and have gotten good results. It could demonstrate that we can accomplish the actual classification tasks in the condition of less labeled data. In addition, due to the uniformity of the physical indicators of the physical examination, when we put all the indicators as input, the deep autoencoder can predict more class of disease effects by fine tuning a trained network.

References

1. Bengio Y, Lamblin P, Popovici D, et al. Greedy layer-wise training of deep networks[C]. Proc, of the 20th Annual Conference on Neural Information Processing System. 2006:153-160.
2. Vincent p, Larochelle H, Bengio Y, Extracting and coin-posing robust features with denoising auto-encoders[C].Proc. of the 25th International Conference on Machine Learning. 2008:1096-1103.
3. Bengio Y. Learning deep architectures for Al[J]. Foundations and Trends in Machine Leaning, 2009,2(1):1-127.
4. Salah R, Vincent P, Muller X, et al. Contractive autp-encoders: Explicit invariance during feature extraction[C]. Proc. of the 28th International Conference on Machine Learning.2011:833-840.J. Clerk Maxwell, A Treatise on Electricity and Magnetism, 3rd ed., vol. 2. Oxford: Clarendon, 1892, pp.68–73.
5. Amaral T, Silva L M, Alexande L A, et al. Using different cost functions to train stacked auto_encoders[C]. Proc. of the 12th Mexican International Conference on Artificial Intelligence. 2013:114-120.
6. Guyon I, Dror G, Leaire V, et al. Auto-encoders unsupervised learning and deep architectures[C]. Proc. of the 28th International Conference on Machine Learning.2012:37-50

An Energy-efficient MAC Protocol for Wireless Body Area Networks

Chong-Qing ZHANG[1,a], Yong-Quan LIANG[1,b], Li-Na NI[1,c] Ying-Long WANG[2,d], and Ming-Lei SHU[2,e]

[1] *College of Information Science and Engineering, Shandong University of Science and Technology, Qingdao 266590, China*
[2] *Shandong Provincial Key Laboratory of Computer Networks, Shandong Computer Science Center (National Supercomputer Center in Jinan)*
[a]*zhangchongqing@sdust.edu.cn*, [b]*lyq@sdust.edu.cn*, [c]*nln2004@163.com*, [d]*wangyl@sdas.org*, [e]*shuml@sdas.org*

Abstract: A WBAN node may be working in two monitoring modes, all-transmit mode and few-transmit mode. Every mode has its own usage scenarios. To effectively prolong its lifetime, a node should be working in few-transmit mode as much as possible. An adaptive medium access control (MAC) protocol is specially designed to serve the nodes working in few-transmit mode. Experimental results show the proposed MAC protocol can improve the energy efficiency and satisfy the data delivery delay demands simultaneously.

1 Introduction

The resultant force from the advances of microelectronics, wireless communications, intelligent sensors and battery has given rise to the birth of wireless body area networks (WBANs). With many prominent advantages, WBANs are hopeful to launch a wave of medical, entertainment, gaming, sports and fitness applications [1].

A WBAN generally takes on a star structure which is comprised of one coordinator and some sensor nodes. A sensor node may be working in two monitoring modes. A node working in this first mode senses the physiological phenomenon with a certain frequency and reports all the measurements to the coordinator. In contrast, a node working in the second monitoring mode still needs to sense the target with a certain frequency, but the measurements are only conveyed to the coordinator on some occasions. In this paper, we name this two monitoring modes *all-transmit* mode and *few-transmit* mode.

Two monitoring modes have their own usages. The all-transmit mode can collect vast quantities of detailed information about one patient's body in a long period of time so that the medical staff can master the change-rules through analyzing these information. Compared to the all-transmit mode, the few-transmit mode only delivers data to the coordinator when some abnormal conditions are detected. As a result, it cannot provide enough detailed information for the medical staff to detailedly trace the patient's health in a long run, but it still can afford proactive wellness management, including early detection and prevention of diseases.

The traffic patterns generated by two monitoring modes are different. Generally speaking, nodes working in all-transmit monitoring mode produce busy periodic traffic which consumes a mass of communication resource. Transporting these vast quantities of data from the nodes to the coordinator means high cost of energy because communication dominates the energy consumption in such case [1]. In consequence, the lifetime of a node adopting this monitoring mode will be severely shortened. Compared to the all-transmit mode, the traffic generated by the few-transmit mode is rather sporadic and low. Hence, the prominent advantage of the few-transmit mode lies in the greatly reduced communication energy, which means much longer service time.

The few-transmit mode is particularly suitable for the healthcare of people with rather good or passable health conditions, e.g., the elderly and chronically ill people. For these people, it is unnecessary to adopt the all-transmit mode to closely monitor these people's health conditions. With the potential of saving more energy, the few-transmit mode is more appropriate for these applications. However, the normal operation and higher energy efficiency still cannot be obtained without the help of suitable MAC protocols [2, 3]. For a sensor node, radio is generally the part which consumes most energy. In order to extend the lifetime of a node from days to years, the only way is duty cycling the radio, that is, turning on its radio only when necessary and keeping it turned off otherwise, and this is just one task of the Medium Access Control (MAC) layer which drives the radio hardware [4].

In this paper, an adaptive medium access control (MAC) protocol is specially designed to serve the few-transmit nodes (thus it is called FT-MAC). With elaborate design, the superframe structure can support a WBAN in which the few-transmit nodes and the all-transmit nodes coexist. The rarity of traffic in the few-transmit mode is taken into account to improve the energy efficiency. Long superframe structure is adopted to cut down the overhead of transmitting and receiving beacon frames. Most of the superframe is assigned to be inactive period to reduce the duty cycle. Short insertion time slots are embedded into the inactive part of the superframe to meet the communication demands of the few-transmit nodes. Special mechanisms are designed to handle the transmissions of big frames and possible collisions caused by multiple nodes. Experimental results demonstrate the proposed MAC protocol can improve the energy efficiency and satisfy the data delivery delay demands simultaneously.

Section 2 introduces the superframe structure of the proposed MAC protocol. The performance of the proposed protocol is evaluated in Section 3. Finally, conclusions are drawn in Section 4.

2 Superframe of FT-MAC

Figure 1 (a) shows FT-MAC's basic superframe structure, which is used when all nodes are working in the few-transmit mode. The beginning of the superframe is a beacon frame which contains information such as timestamp, beacon interval, time slot length, time slots assignments, etc. Following the beacon frame, there may exist an optional broadcast period and a contention free period (CFP) which contains some guaranteed time slots (GTS). The optional broadcast period is used by the coordinator to broadcast long messages to all the nodes. One GTS slot in the optional CFP period can be used by the coordinator to transmit a long frame to one node, or can be used by one node to transmit a long frame to the coordinator.

Following the CFP period is a long inactive period which occupies most of the superframe. Because the traffic is very low when all nodes are working in the few-transmit mode, a long inactive period can help the coordinator and nodes to save energy. Short active insertion slots are inserted into the inactive period to deliver data. An insertion slot can be shared by all nodes to transmit data or network commands to the coordinator directly. Slotted Aloha is used by all nodes to share an insertion slot.

At the end of a superframe is an optional contention access period (CAP) which is used by all nodes with data to transmit the data using carrier sense multiple access with collision avoidance mechanism (CSMA/CA). The existence of this CAP period depends on if there are collisions happen or not during current superframe. If there are frames collided in one insertion slot, such a CAP period will be activated to retransmit these frames.

The superframe structure displayed in Figure 1 (a) cannot satisfy the demands of a WBAN in which there are nodes working in the all-transmit mode. The superframe structure shown in Figure 1 (b) is designed for such occasions. In Figure 1 (b), loop periods replace the place of the inactive period in Figure1 (a). One loop period begins with an active period that is used for the nodes working in the all-transmit mode to transmit their data. The active period can adopt complex structure to accommodate the nodes working in the all-transmit mode.

From Figure 1, it can be observed that one insertion slot can be composed of one DATA section and one ACK section. Multiple DATA sections can be included in an insertion slots to convey data for the coordinator and nodes working in the few-transmit mode. If the traffic in the WBAN is low, then only one DATA section is configured in one insertion slot. If one DATA section is not enough, then more DATA sections are used. For a WBAN of dozens of nodes, this mechanism can divide the nodes into several groups to alleviate collisions. To support communications of two directions, two types of insertion slots are designed. One is used for the coordinator to transmit data packets or commands to nodes, and the other one is used for nodes to transmit data packets or commands to the coordinator. We call the first type of insertion slots "download" insertion slots and the second type of insertion slots "upload" insertion slots.

DOI: 10.1051/itmconf/20171203044

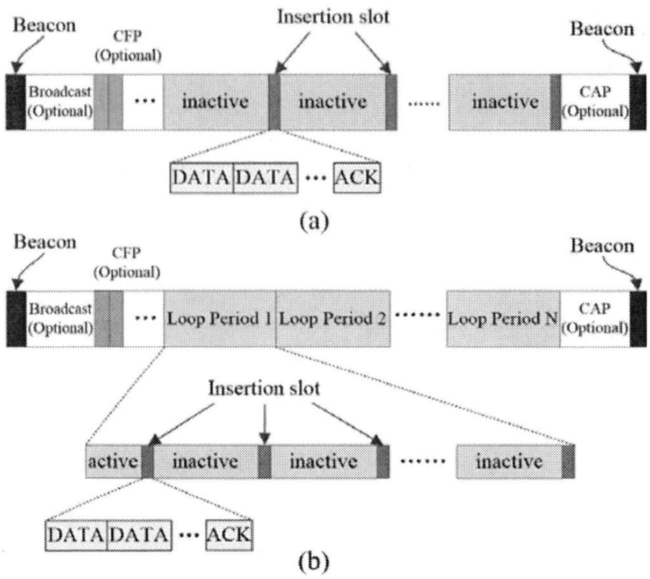

Figure 1. The superframe structure of FT-MAC

Because there is only one ACK section in one insertion slot, one download insertion slot only has one DATA section. This means the coordinator can only send data to one node and be acknowledged by that node. For an insertion slot, there can be multiple DATA sections, which are acknowledged by the coordinator using the same ACK section. Only unicasts are acknowledged, and broadcasts are not acknowledged.

The ACK section can also be used by the coordinator to send special "BREAK", "CAP", "SYNC" commands to all the nodes. The coordinator can also use download insertion slot to send these commands. A "BREAK" command means the current superframe will be broken, and a new superframe will start. If a node receives such a command, it waits for the end of ACK section and prepares to receive a new beacon. A "CAP" command signifies an additional CAP period. If a node receives such a command, it waits for the end of the ACK section, and then enters a CAP period. After the CAP period, all nodes prepare to receive a new beacon frame and start a new superframe. "SYNC" commands are adopted to transmit time synchronization information to all nodes. If a node receives such a command, it retrieves the synchronization data and uses it to synchronize its clock.

3 Performance Evaluation

Two star WBANs are used in the experiments. One WBAN has 5 nodes and another has 20 nodes. OMNeT++ [5] is adopted as the simulation tool. The parameters of the radio parts of all nodes and the coordinators are based on CC2520 [6]. The energy efficiency and data delivery delay of three MAC protocols, 802.15.4 [7], AB-MAC [8] and FT-MAC are compared. The beacon lengths of 802.15.4 and FT-MAC are assumed to be 30 and 34 bytes. The ACK frame length of 802.15.4 is 5 bytes. The DATA frame and ACK frame of FT-MAC are 10 bytes and 6 bytes. For FT-MAC, the number of insertion slots in a superframe is 4. For AB-MAC, the number of standby slots in a superframe is also set to be 4. The settings of 802.15.4 and AB-MAC are from [8] and [9].

We fix the beacon/standby/insertion intervals all to be 0.5s and examine the performance of three MAC protocols under different traffic. Both the WBAN of 5 nodes and the WBAN of 20 nodes are used here. For the WBAN of 20 nodes, two FT-MAC schemes are used. The first scheme sets only one DATA section in an insertion slot and the second sets two DATA sections in an insertion slot. 20 nodes are divided to 2 groups, and each group uses one DATA section. All nodes are configured to have a same data occurrence interval. 90% of the data are small data, and 10% of the data are big data. The average data interval changes from 1 to 10000 seconds.

Figure 2 and Figure 3 display how the average power consumed by a node change with the traffic. As the figures show, AB-MAC and FT-MAC cost less energy when the traffic is low. However, as the traffic becomes high, the energy consumptions of AB-MAC and FT-MAC increase more rapidly than 802.15.4. Beyond one point, the average power of AB-MAC and FT-MAC exceed 802.15.4. The speed of AB-MAC grows the fastest because the adaptive beacons grow fast and AB-MAC communicates twice to deliver a frame. FT-MAC only communicates once to deliver a small data, and it only has to communicate twice for a big data. By using two DATA sections, FT-MAC GN = 2 can reduce the collisions so that it can gain higher energy efficiency.

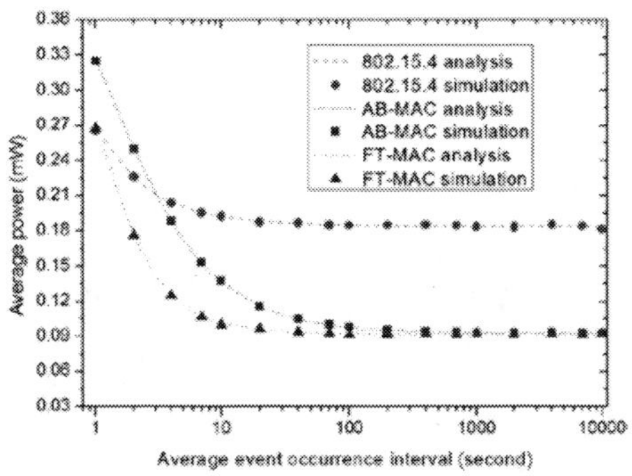

Figure 2. The effect of the average event occurrence interval on node average power (5 nodes)

Figure 4 and Figure 5 shows the effect of the average data occurrence interval on the average power consumed by the coordinator. As the traffic grows, the coordinator needs to increase its duty cycle to convey more traffic. Therefore, the average powers of all protocols increases with the traffic become high. As the traffic is low, both AB-MAC and FT-MAC cost less energy than 802.15.4. The average power of AB-MAC grows the fastest as the traffic becomes dense. The reason lies in the beacon frames and access slots brought by the increasing traffic. FT-MAC and FT-MAC GN = 2 grow slower than AB-MAC, yet they both grown faster than 802.15.4. The reason to explain this lies in the CAP periods and beacon frames caused by collisions. FT-MAC GN = 2 spends less energy than FT-MAC because it can alleviate collisions effectively.

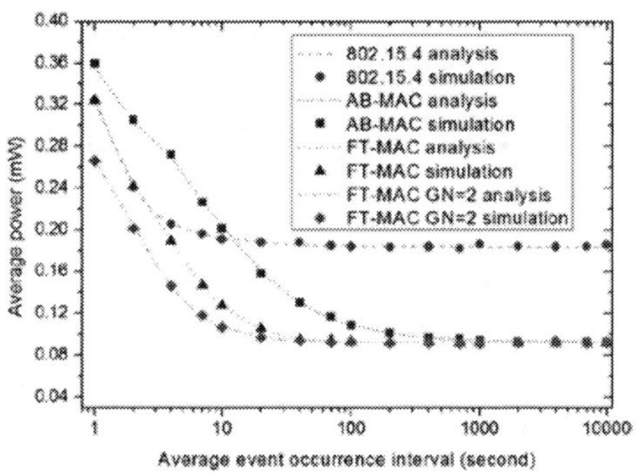

Figure 3. The effect of the average event occurrence interval on node average power (20 nodes)

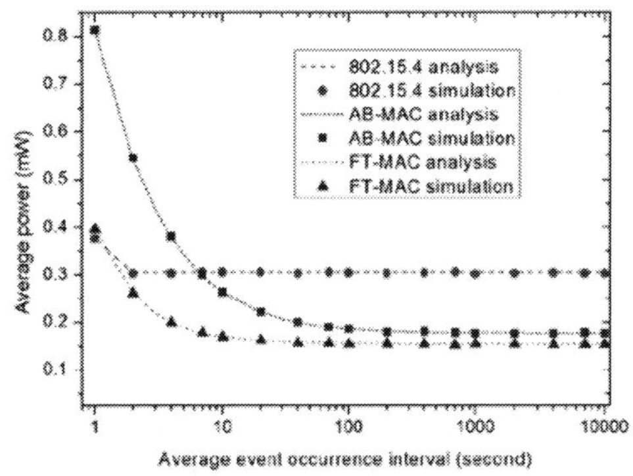

Figure 4. The effect of the average event occurrence interval on coordinator average power (5 nodes)

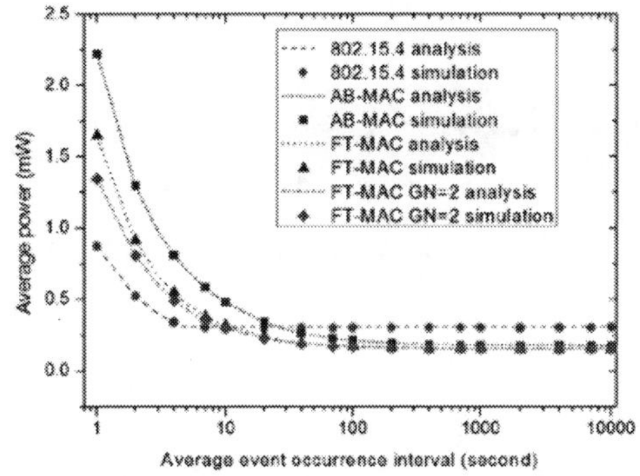

Figure 5. The effect of the average event occurrence interval on coordinator average power (20 nodes)

Finally we examine how the average frame delay changes with traffic. The average frame delays of three MAC protocols are shown by Figure 6 and Figure 7. For 802.15.4, the average frame delay remains almost constant for the WBAN of 5 nodes, and the average frame delay only increases a little as the traffic grows high for the WBAN of 20 nodes. The delays of AB-MAC and FT-MAC are a little higher than 802.15.4 because the frames have to wait longer time, and their delays exhibit obvious rise as the traffic becomes busy. This can also be explained by the beacon frames and other periods introduced by busy traffic.

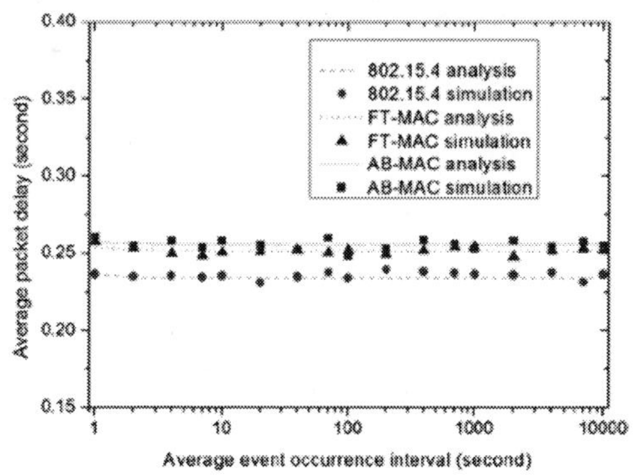

Figure 6. The effect of the average event occurrence interval on average frame delay (5 nodes)

DOI: 10.1051/itmconf/20171203044

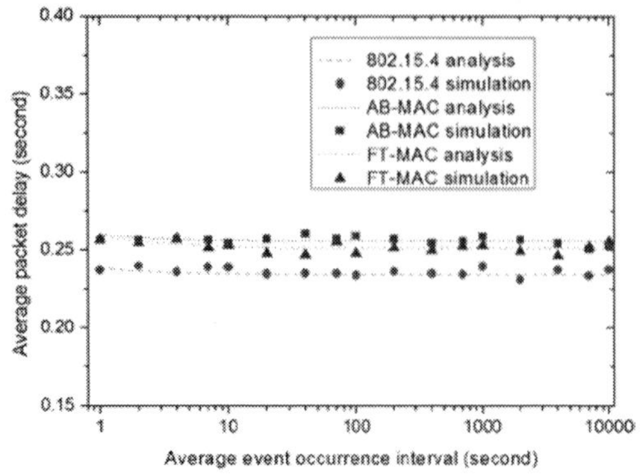

Figure 7. The effect of the average event occurrence interval on average frame delay (20 nodes)

5 Conclusion

In this paper, we analyze the tasks and two working modes of WBAN nodes. To extend the lifetime, a node should try to work in few-transmit mode as much as possible. Focusing on the requirements of the nodes working in few-transmit mode, a beacon-enabled adaptive MAC protocol (FT-MAC) is proposed. FT-MAC adopts long superframes to reduce the overhead of beacon frames to save energy. Short insertion time slots embedded in the inactive period are used to provide opportunities for few-transmit nodes to transmit their data. Insertion time slots can be viewed as a combination of the beacon frames and CAP periods used in traditional MAC protocols. Different transmission mechanisms are designed for small data and big data. By adopting a flexible structure, FT-MAC can support a WBAN in which few-transmit nodes and all-transmit nodes coexist. For a WBAN of dozens of nodes, multiple DATA sections can be used as a makeshift to alleviate the collisions if the traffic is not busy. However, as the traffic become busy, beacon frames and other periods caused by frequent collisions result in severe performance degradation. As a result, FT-MAC is not applicable for WBAN applications with high traffic.

Acknowledgment

This research was financially supported by Shandong Provincial Science and Technology Project under Grant No. 2014GSF118107, Open Research Fund from Shandong provincial Key Laboratory of Computer Network under Grand No. SDKLCN-2014-04, Postdoctoral Innovation Special Fund of Shandong Province, Project of Shandong Province Higher Educational Science and Technology Program under Grant J13LN18, J15LN19, Open Project of Tongji University Embedded System and Service Computing of Ministry of Education of China under Grant ESSCKF 2015-02, Qingdao Postdoctoral Researchers Applied Research Projects fund (Cloud computing in mine geology data storage and analysis application).

References

1. Movassaghi S., Abolhasan M., Lipman J., Smith D. and Jamalipour A., "Wireless Body Area Networks: A Survey", IEEE Commun. Surv. Tutor, 2014, 16, (3), 1658-1686.
2. Otal B., Alonso L. and Verikoukis C., "Highly reliable energy saving MAC for wireless body sensor networks in health-care systems", IEEE J. Sel. Area. Comm, 2009, 27, (4), 553-565.
3. Marinkovic S., Popovici E. , Spagnol C., Faul S. and Marnane W., "Energy-efficient low duty cycle MAC protocol for wireless body area network", IEEE T. Inf. Technol. B, 2009, 13, (6), 915-925.
4. Bachir A., Dohler M., Watteyne T. and Leung K., "MAC Essentials for Wireless Sensor Networks", IEEE Commun. Surv. Tutor, 2010, 12, (2), 222-248.
5. OMNeT++ Discrete Event Simulator. Available online: http://www.omnetpp.org/.
6. CC2520 Datasheet-2.4GHz IEEE 802.15.4/ZigBee® RF Transceiver. Available: http://www.ti.com/ lit/ds/ symlink/cc2520.pdf
7. IEEE Standard for Information Technology Part 15.4: Wireless Medium Access Control (MAC) and Physical Layer (PHY) Specifications for Low-Rate Wireless Personal Area Networks (LR-WPANs). IEEE Standard 802.15.4 Working Group Standard, 2006. Available online: http://standards.ieee.org/ findstds/standard/802.15.4-2006.html
8. Kim S., Lee J. H., Eom D. S., "An adaptive beaconing MAC protocol providing energy-efficient healthcare service", Wireless Personal Communications, 2014, 75, (4), 1915-1936.
9. Timmons N. and Scanlon W., "Analysis of the performance of IEEE 802.15.4 for medical sensor body area networking". Proc. Int. Conf. Sensor and Ad Hoc Communications and Networks, Santa Clara, California, USA, October, 2004, pp. 16-24.

An Evolutionary Game Model of Multi-Topics Diffusion in Social Network

Jia-Hao SU[a], Ming FANG[b], Jiang JIANG[c], and Ying-Wu CHEN[d]

College of Information System and Management, National University of Defense Technology, Changsha, China
[a]sujiahao15@nudt.edu.cn, [b]mingxfz@gmail.com, [c]jiangjiangnudt@163.com, [d]ywchen@nudt.edu.cn

Abstract: One major function of social networks is the dissemination of information such as news, comments, and rumors. The information passing from a sender to a receiver intrinsically involves both of them by considering their memory, reputation, and preference, which further determine their decisions of whether or not to diffuse the topic. To understand such human aspects of the topics dissemination, we propose a game theoretical model of the multi-topics diffusion mechanisms in a social network. Each individual in the network is considered as both sender and receiver, who transmits different topics taking into account their payoffs and personalities (including memories, reputation and preferences). Several cases were analyzed, and the results suggest that multi-topics dissemination is strongly affected by self-perceived, gregarious and information gain.

1 Introduction

A social network is an ensemble of communicating personalities based on the concept of social proximity [1]. The participants in a social network can form communities [2], influence other participants [3]. One major function of social networks (in particular, massive online social networks) is the dissemination of information such as news, comments, and rumors [4-7]. As an important form of social organization, Information can shape public opinion, inform public behavior [5], further, rumors can spread astoundingly fast through social networks [8].

Due to its significance, information diffusion has been one of the focuses in social network research. In precious work, epidemic models [9] have been widely adopted by researchers for information diffusion due to the analogy between epidemics and the spread of information. Reference [10] investigate the adoption of the classic Susceptible-Infected-Removed (SIR) model for information dissemination. Yang and Leskovec [11] developed a linear influence model to focus on influence of individual node on the rate of dissemination through the implicit network. These studies have a macroscopically eye on the description of information diffusion through social networks.

In recent years, researchers gradually observe that game behaviors between individuals in social network, game-theoretic models, as a new perspective of interpreting social diffusion, are increasingly adopted by computer scientists for analyzing network behaviors. For example, Kostka et al. [8] carried out examinations on the dissemination of competing rumors in social network, using concepts of game theory and location theory, modelling the selection of starting nodes for the rumors as a strategy game. Zinoviev et al. [12, 13] adopted game theoretic models to understand human aspects of information dissemination in which personalities of individuals are considered. Qiu et al. [14] come to a result that information dissemination can be divided into several stages, and the speed of spreading is influenced by characteristic of individuals in the network. Wu et al. [15] focused on the influence of trust in the spreading of information.

However, these researches focus on one topic in the network, several topics will be diffused at the same time in the real network. Sun and Yao [16] discuss the multi-topics, but they aimed at studying the process of competitive information diffusion. In this paper, we focus on more general topics, not only the competitive ones. We introduce a framework taking into consideration that people may care about several aspects. In particular, a utility function is defined to capture what factors shape individuals' choice in social networks.

Our model of multi-topics diffusion and influence as processes taking place on social networks, node is either sender or receiver. We focus on factors that characterize human behaviors, analyze how these factors affect information propagation based on the assumption that individuals aim at maximizing their utilities by picking optimal strategy, and show several laws.

The remainder of this paper is organized as follows. Section II presents the overview of the model and Section III analyses simulation results.

2 Evolutionary Game Model

2.1 Model Setting

Social network is a set of nodes transmit the information from one to another [17]. Nodes represent individuals or organizations, edges stand for social relationships. The information spreading in social network, affects the network in several aspects, such as node's properties, appearance and disappearance of edges. Getting down to fundamentals, it's individuals' various behaviors that lead to the diffusion of information.

As some topics are acknowledged by one node, it will choose someone to disseminate to its neighbor or not, which is decided by several factors, such as its preference, and the information's popularity.

Let us introduce a topic diffusion model in social network. Specifically, every two nodes' interaction is described as a two-player game, in simple terms, different players choose the optimal strategy to achieve best payoffs according to the opponent's strategy.

It is assumed that there is a network consisting of M nodes which represents M participants, $\mathbf{P}=\{p_1, p_2, ..., p_M\}$, and there are N topics, $\mathbf{T}=\{t_1, t_2, ..., t_N\}$, transmitted in this network. As a real person, we can only recognize and remember the finite topics. Thus, we assume that every participant can remember K ($K \leqslant N$) topics, which is denoted as $\boldsymbol{x}_i=\{x_{i1}, x_{i2}, ..., x_{iK}\}$ and these K topics will be updated after each game. And, for p_i, it has $K+1$ pure strategies, $\boldsymbol{s}_i=\{s_{i0}, s_{i1}, s_{i2}, ..., s_{iK}\}$, where s_{i0} represents that p_i does not transmit any topic and s_{ik} represents p_i transmits topic x_{ik}, $k=1,2,...,K$.

In order to construct a precise model to explain the real situation, two factors are introduced into this model. One is reputation, each participant is influenced by its neighbor according to the neighbor's reputation. We define $\mathbf{R}$ to describe the influence, where

$$\mathbf{R}=\begin{bmatrix} r_{11} & r_{12} & \cdots & r_{1M} \\ r_{21} & r_{22} & \cdots & r_{2M} \\ \vdots & \vdots & \ddots & \vdots \\ r_{M1} & r_{M2} & \cdots & r_{MM} \end{bmatrix} \quad (1)$$

$$\sum_{\substack{1\leq i'\leq m, \\ i'\neq i}} r_{ii'}=1,\ 0\leq r_{ii'}\leq 1,\ r_{ii}=\ self_i,\ i,i'=1,2,\ldots,M.$$

$r_{ii'}$ represents the degree that $p_{i'}$ influence p_i. Specially, when $i'=i$, $r_{ii'}$ represent its self-perceived, which is defined by parameter $self_i$, $0 \leqslant self_i \leqslant 1$. Another is preference, every participant has their unique preference on these topics, which is denoted by $\mathbf{U^0}$, where

$$\mathbf{U^0}=\begin{bmatrix} u^0_{11} & u^0_{12} & \cdots & u^0_{1N} \\ u^0_{21} & u^0_{21} & \cdots & u^0_{2N} \\ \vdots & \vdots & \ddots & \vdots \\ u^0_{M1} & u^0_{M1} & \cdots & u^0_{MN} \end{bmatrix} \quad (2)$$

$$u^0_{ij}\in R,\ i=1,2,\ldots M,\ j=1,2,\ldots,N.$$

If $u^0_{ij}>0$, it represents how p_i likes t_j, if $u^0_{ij}<0$, it represents how p_i hates t_j; and if $u^0_{ij}=0$, it represents p_i does not care about t_j.

2.2 Utility Function

Now, we take a simple game as example to discuss the problem. Assuming that the two players are p_i and $p_{i'}$, $i\neq i'$, there is a directed edge from p_i to $p_{i'}$, and they both have $K+1$ respective strategies. We assumed that p_i and $p_{i'}$ take σ_i and $\sigma_{i'}$ as their strategy. And during this game, three conditions (as Fig. 1) will happen: (a) such as p_1 and p_4 in Fig. 1, $\sigma_i=t_j$, and $\sigma_{i'}=t_j$, p_i will gain a gregarious profit and pay the cost of diffusion, denoted as (3); (b) such as p_1 and p_3, $\sigma_i=t_j$, $\sigma_{i'}=t_{j'}$, $t_j\neq t_{j'}$ and $t_{j'}\notin \boldsymbol{x}_i$, p_i will get an information gain, denoted as (4); (c) such as p_1 and p_2, $\sigma_i=t_j$, $\sigma_{i'}=t_{j'}$, $t_j\neq t_{j'}$, but $t_j\in \boldsymbol{x}_i$, p_i will have no profit, and its payoff is denoted as (5).

$$u_{ii'}=\alpha * u^0_{ij}-c_j \quad (3)$$

$$u_{ii'}=1/n*\beta*u^0_{ij'}-c_j \quad (4)$$

$$u_{ii'}=-c_j. \quad (5)$$

Where parameters α and c_j represent the gregarious profit and the cost of diffusing t_j respectively. And, β and n represent the information gain and the number of neighbors of p_i. Specially, when $\sigma_i=s_{i0}$, there will be no gregarious profit and no cost of diffusion.

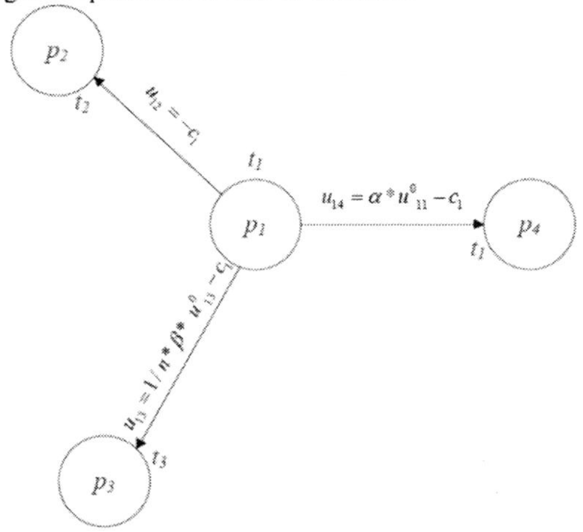

Figure 1. The example of utility function on three conditions, where $t_1\neq t_2\neq t_3$, and $t_3\notin \boldsymbol{x}_1$, $t_2\in \boldsymbol{x}_1$.

For each game on the network, the whole payoff of p_i is denoted as u_i, where,

$$u_i=\sum_{i'=1}^{M} e_{ii'} * u_{ii'},\quad i'\neq i \quad (6)$$

$$e_{ii'}=\begin{cases} 1 & r_{ij}>0 \\ 0 & r_{ij}=0 \end{cases}. \quad (7)$$

$e_{ii'}$ denotes whether the edge from i to i' exists or not in the network.

2.3 Situation Update

During the process of information propagation, p_i's memory, strategy, and the neighbors' influence will be updated.

2.3.1 Memory update:

As is known that personal memory is limited and it will be changed by surroundings. Based on the illustration of limit, the update will be demonstrated here. After each game, p_i will send one topic and receive several topics from neighbors. Obviously, the more spreaders transmit the topic and the deeper the influence of spreader is, the higher probability of the topic will be remembered by p_i. So, the influence degree of each topic can be calculated according to the influence matrix **R**. That is to say,

$$w_{ij} = r_{ij} * \sigma_{i'j} \tag{8}$$

$$\sigma_{i'j} = \begin{cases} 1 & \sigma_{i'} = t_j \\ 0 & \sigma_{i'} \neq t_j \end{cases}. \tag{9}$$

Where w_{ij} means the influence of t_j on p_i, and $\sigma_{i'j}$ means whether strategy of $p_{i'}$ is choosing t_j to diffuse or not. Then, the topics are ranked by its influence, and the top K will be taken into $\boldsymbol{x}_i$. Meanwhile, if the number of $w_{ij}>0$ is less than K, the topics in last memory will be selected into $\boldsymbol{x}_i$ according to its order.

2.3.2 Influence update:

Game Theory assumes that the players are rational person and want to gain the most profit. Therefore, each player will seek the players who could bring positive profit and abandon the players who might bring negative profit. In order to imitate such process, the influence of p_i's neighbor need to be updated as

$$r_{ii'} = \begin{cases} e_{ii'} * (r_{ii'} + \sum_{j=1}^{M} \sigma_{i'j} * u^0_{ij}) & i' \neq i \\ self_i & i' = i \end{cases} \tag{10}$$

That is to say, if one of p_i's neighbor transmits a topic which p_i likes, its influence will raise; but if it transmits a topic p_i hates, its influence will descend. Noting that $r_{ii'}$ may become a minus with the game going on. To deal with such situation, a trick is made here. Once $r_{ii'} \leqslant 0$, we find a new participant $p_{i''}$ and let $r_{ii'} = 0$ and $r_{ii''} > 0$, which imitates the process mentioned above. The neighbors who need to be abandoned is simple to determine, but the new neighbors who needed to be selected is not obvious. In this paper, the p_i's new neighbor is recommended by p_i's present neighbors as follows.

a) Neighbor Selection: The present neighbor of p_i is selected according to $\pi_{ii'}$, where

$$\pi_{ii'} = \frac{r_{ii'}}{\sum_{\substack{1 \le i' \le M \\ i' \neq i}} r_{ii'}} \tag{11}$$

b) Neighbor Recommendation: The present neighbor will select its neighbour $p_{i''}$ randomly and recommend $p_{i''}$ to p_i. And if $r_{ii''}>0$, step *a)* and *b)* should be repeated until $r_{ii''}=0$.

c) Influence Establishment: We give $r_{ii''}$ a rand positive number which is less than 1 as $p_{i''}$'s initial influence on p_i.

Finally, **R** needs to be normalization as (12), so that it can satisfied the assumption in *A*.

$$r_{ii'} = \frac{r_{ii'}}{\sum_{\substack{1 \le i' \le M \\ i' \neq i}} r_{ii'}} \tag{12}$$

2.3.3 Strategy update:

With the memory update of p_i, the new strategy will emerge. We choose the topic x_{i1} which p_i pays most attention on, and calculate its payoff denoted by $u_{i'}$ based on the present situation. Then the probability of changing strategy is $1/\{1+exp[(u_i-u_{i'})/q]\}$, where q is a noise coefficient which represents the bounded rationality of p_i.

3 Case Study

In order to derive the topic dissemination process, we conducted several experiments in a simulation directed network, consisting of M individuals. And whether the edge from p_i to $p_{i'}$ exists obeys the binomial distribution. Where $M=50$ and the probability of link is 0.5.

After the network constructed, the game is initialed as Section □. Here, we initial the variable as follows: $r_{ii}\sim U(0,1)$, $u_{ij}\sim N(0.05)$ and $r_{ii'}$ is normalized as (12). In addition, we set $N=100$ and $K=10$ in this case.

We start our analysis with how topics dissemination differs according to the parameters α, β, and $self_i$ that affect utility function. Before carrying out the contrast experiment, entropy is introduced in to assess the topics distribution.

3.1 Evaluator

During each game, every participant will have a strategy of transmitting some topic or not. Therefore, the proportion of each topic t_j in the step τ will be calculated easily, which is denoted as

$$\delta_j^\tau = \frac{\sum_{i=1}^{M} \sigma_{ij}}{M} \tag{13}$$

Where σ^τ_{ij} means whether p_i disseminate t_j in the step τ. Then the topics' entropy in the step τ is denoted as

$$E^\tau = -\sum_{j=1}^{N} \delta_j^\tau * \log_2 \delta_j^\tau \tag{14}$$

DOI: 10.1051/itmconf/20171203045

Analogy with the information theory, the smaller the entropy is, the less disorder the information is. In this paper, the smaller the entropy is, the more concentrated the topics are.

3.2 Constract Experiment

3.2.1 Profit parameter

In this paper, we fix $self_i$=0.2, and compare the parameters α, β.

Fig. 2 and Fig. 3 shows the influence of gregarious and information gain on the multi-topics diffusion respectively.

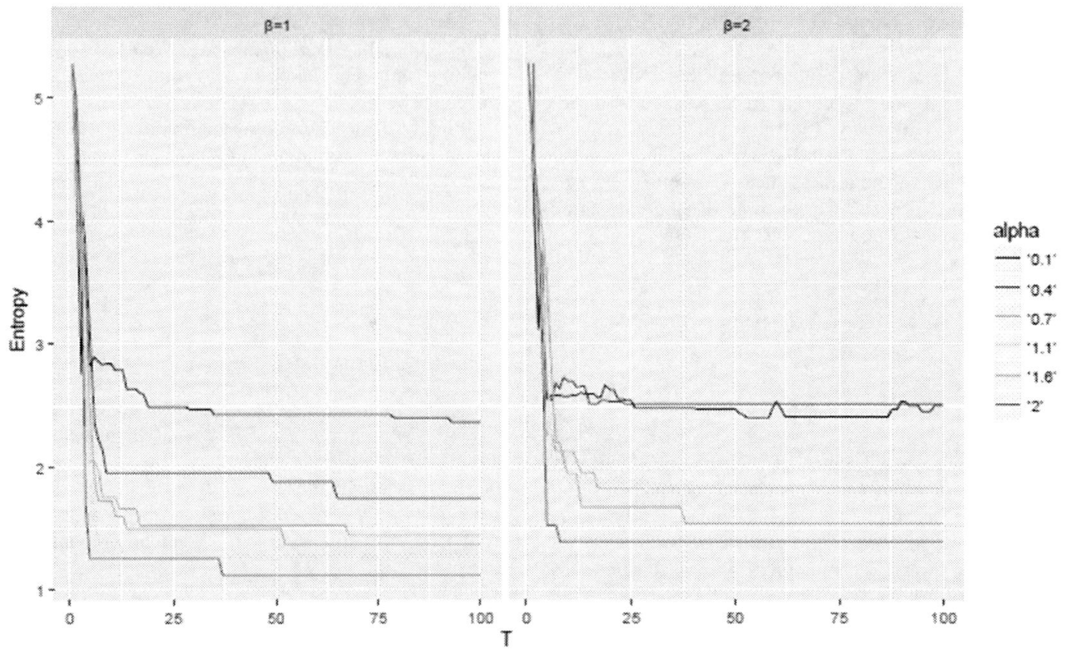

Figure 2. The relation between the changing of α and that of entropy during the game process when $self_i$=0.2, β=*1 or 2*.

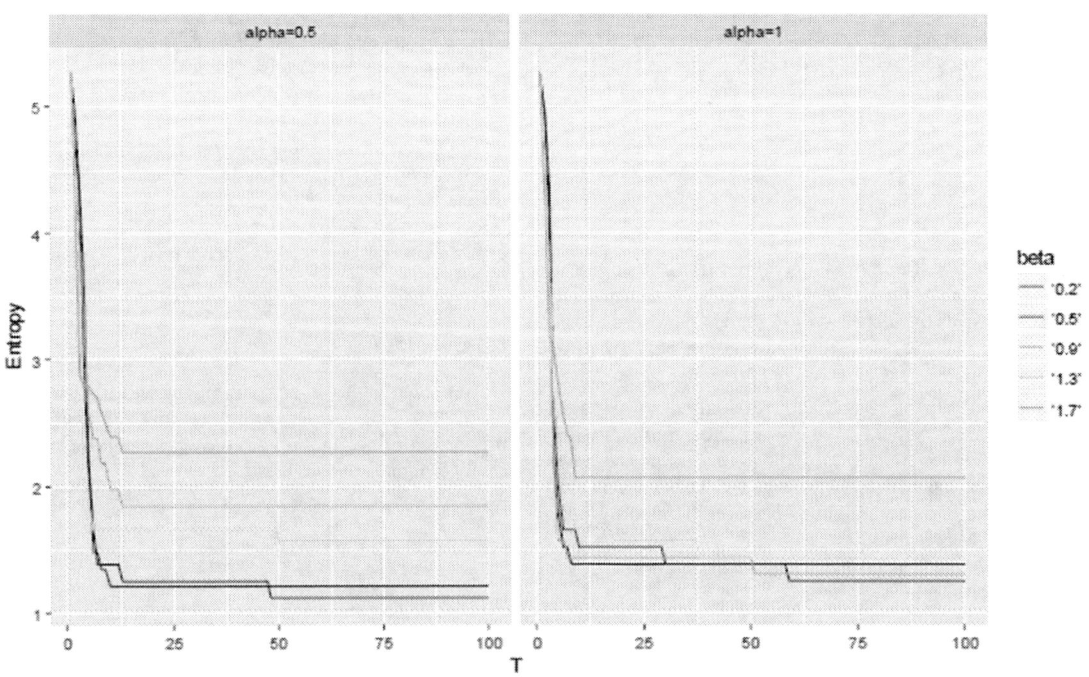

Figure 3. The relation between the changing of β and that of entropy during the game process when selfi=0.2, α=0.5 or 1.

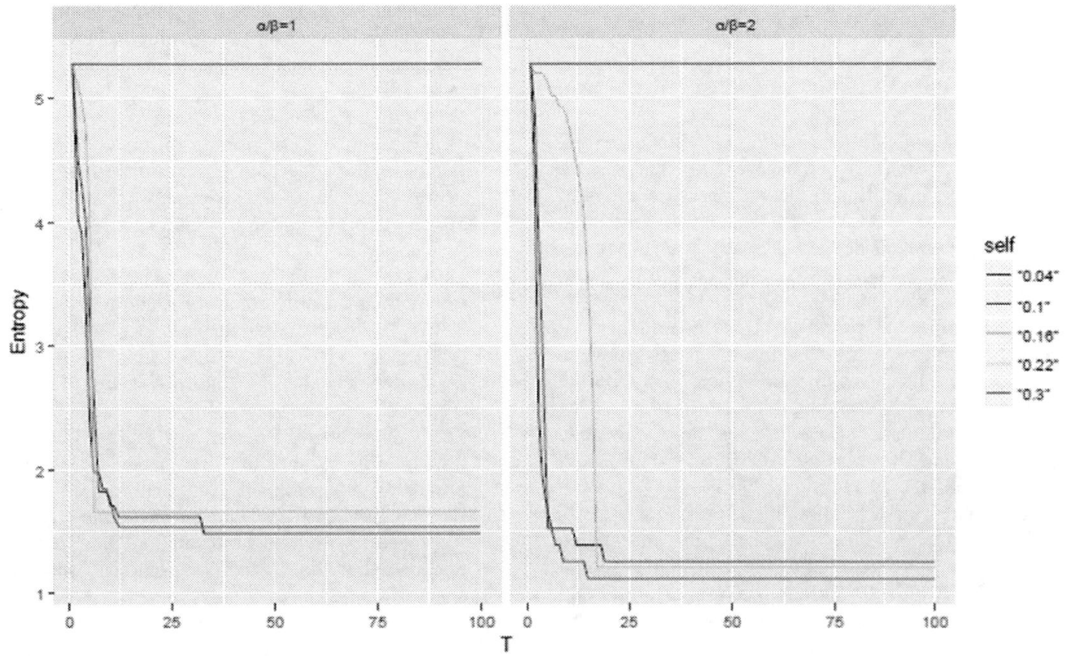

Figure 4. The relation between the changing of α and that of entropy during the game process when $self_i$=0.2, β=*1 or 2*.

The X-axis represents the steps of game and the Y-axis means the entropy of the topics propagated in the network in a particular step. Fig. 2 reveals that the smaller α is, the higher the entropy is. And the smaller α is, the later the entropy converges. Even when $\alpha=1$, the topics cannot be convergent. And this property is authentic no matter what β is. Similarly, Fig. 3 reveals that the larger β is, the entropy is. And the larger β is, the earlier the entropy converges.

3.2.2 self-perceived parameter

Subsequently, we compare the parameter $self_i$. As shown in Fig. 4, $self_i$ is inversely proportional to entropy, and the smaller $self_i$ is, the later the entropy converged. Even when $self_i \geq 0.22$, each individual will insist on their initial topics. This property occurs no matter what the parameters α, β are.

4 Conclusion and Future Directions

In this paper, a multi-topics diffusion model in social network based on evolutionary game theory is presented. Social network consists of nodes with personality, thus utility function and interact rules are proposed as close to reality as possible, considering memory, reputation and preference in social networks. Afterwards, a simulation experiment is carried out.

Our analysis reveals interesting insights into the nature of multi-topics diffusion. Multi-topics diffusion is strongly related with gregarious and information gain. If the participants prefer gregarious gain, the topics will be converged. But if the participants prefer information gain, the topics will be diversified. In addition, self-perceived will lead the topics diffusion significantly.

It is our hope that this paper will provide some new insights into the research of multi-topics diffusion in social network. To improve our model, several directions are proposed:

- Considering the initial network, variable network densities and structures can be studied. And the topology of network can be discussed, for example, the node's degree, clustering coefficient, assortative, communities and etc.
- The parameters α, β and $self_i$ is not a fixed value, each participant has its unique parameters. Then the different proportion of parameters value must lead to different topics diffusion, which is interesting to discuss.
- Government can be introduced in the game as a special participant, who has a different utility function.
- Considering the alterable topics makes the model more reality. In another word, the topics will not be fixed, the new topics will be produced and those who have little concentration will fade away.

Acknowledgment

This work was supported by the National Natural Science Foundation of China (Nos. 71331008, 71671186, 71522014)

References

1. S. Liu, "Information Diffusion in Online Social Network", Ph.D., University of Illinois at Chicago, USA, Oct. 2015.
2. E. Spertus, M. Sahami, and O. Buyukkokten, "Evaluating Similarity Measures: A Large-scale Study in the Orkut Social Network", Proceedings of the Eleventh ACM SIGKDD International Conference on Knowledge Discovery in Data Mining, ACM Press, Aug. 2005, pp. 678-684, doi: 10.1145/1081870.1081956.
3. D. Crandall, D. Cosley, D. Huttenlocher, J. Kleinberg and S. Suri, "Feedback Effects Between Similarity and Social Influence in Online Communities", Proceedings of the 14th ACM SIGKDD International Conference on Knowledge Discovery and Data Mining, ACM Press, Aug. 2008, pp. 160-168, doi: 10.1145/1401890.1401914.
4. L. Cliff and J. Erik, "Follow the (Slash) Dot: Effects of Feedback on New Members in an Online Community", Proceedings of the 2005 International ACM SIGGROUP Conference on Supporting Group Work, ACM Press, Nov. 2005, pp. 11-20, doi: 10.1145/1099203.1099206.
5. M. Nekovee, Y. Moreno, G. Bianconi and M. Marsili, "Theory of rumour spreading in complex social networks", Physica A: Statistical Mechanics and its Applications, vol. 374, Jan. 2007, pp. 457-470, doi: 10.1016/j.physa.2006.07.017.
6. D. Zanette, "Dynamics of rumor propagation on small-world networks", Physical review. E, vol.65, Apr. 2002, pp. 041908, doi: 10.1103/PhysRevE.65.041908.
7. D. Watts, P. Dodds and M. Newman, "Identity and search in social networks", Science, vol. 296, May 2002, pp. 1302-1305, doi: 10.1126/science.1070120.
8. J. Kostka, Y. Oswald, and R. Wattenhofer, "Word of Mouth: Rumor Dissemination in Social Networks", Structural Information and Communication Complexity: 15th International Colloquium, Springer Press, Jun. 2008, pp. 185-196, doi: 10.1007/978-3-540-69355-0_16.
9. L. Liu, F. Feng, L. Wang, "Information propagation and collective consensus in blogosphere: a game-theoretical approach", Physics, vol.91, Jan. 2007, pp. 1946-1974.
10. D. Gruhl, R. Guha, D. Liben and A. Tomkins, "Information Diffusion Through Blogspace", Proceedings of the 13th International Conference on World Wide Web, ACM Press, May 2004, pp. 491-501, doi: 10.1145/988672.988739.
11. J. Yang and J. Leskovc, "Modeling Information Diffusion in Implicit Networks", 2010 10th IEEE International Conference on Data Mining (ICDM 2010), IEEE Computer Society, Dec. 2010, pp. 599-608, doi: 10.1109/ICDM.2010.22.
12. D. Zinoviev and V. Duong, "A Game Theoretical Approach to Broadcast Information Diffusion in Social Networks", Proceedings of the 44th Annual Simulation Symposium, Society for Computer Simulation International, Apr. 2011, pp. 47-52.
13. D. Zinoviev and V. Duong, "A Game Theoretical Approach to Modeling Information Dissemination in Social Networks", arXiv preprint, Jun. 2010, arXiv:1006.5493.
14. W. Qiu, Y. Wang and J. Yu, "A game theoretical model of information dissemination in social network", 2012 IEEE International Conference on Complex Systems (ICCS), IEEE Press, Nov.2012, pp.1-6, doi: 10.1109/ICoCS.2012.6458551.
15. H. Wu, A. Arenas and S. Gómez, "Influence of trust in the spreading of information", Physical review. E, vol. 95, Jan. 2017, pp. 012301, doi: 10.1103/PhysRevE.95.012301.
16. Q. Sun and Z. Yao, "Evolutionary game analysis of competitive information dissemination on social networks: An agent-based computational approach", Mathematical Problems in Engineering, Vol. 2015, Jun. 2015, pp. 12, doi: 10.1155/2015/679726.
17. Y. Reddy, "Role of Game Models in Social Networks", 2009 International Conference on Computational Science and Engineering (CSE), IEEE Computer Society, Aug. 2009, pp. 1131-1136, doi: 10.1109/CSE.2009.147

GPU-Accelerated Apriori Algorithm

Hao JIANG[a], Chen-Wei XU[b], Zhi-Yong LIU[c], and Li-Yan YU[d]

School of Computer Science and Engineering, Southeast University, Nanjing, China
[a]hjiang@seu.edu.cn, [b]wei1517@126.com, [c]zyliu278@163.com, [d]756250742@qq.com

Abstract: This paper propose a parallel Apriori algorithm based on GPU (GPUApriori) for frequent itemsets mining, and designs a storage structure using bit table (BIT) matrix to replace the traditional storage mode. In addition, parallel computing scheme on GPU is discussed. The experimental results show that GPUApriori algorithm can effectively improve the efficiency of frequent itemsets mining.

1 Introduction

The overhead of association rule mining mainly comes from the generation and processing of frequent itemsets. In order to get frequent itemsets, a large amount of computation and enough storage is needed. Therefore, the improvement of association rule mining algorithm should focuse on how to improve the processing speed and reduce the storage space. This paper combines Apriori algorithm with GPU Technology, and introduces the algorithm of GPUApriori. On the one hand, a compressed storage scheme is designed to simplify the connection operation and reducing the storage usage of the algorithm. On the other hand, in order to fit the parallel computing architecture of GPU [4], parallelization of the Apriori algorithm is proposed.

2 Improvement of Storage Structure

2.1 Apriori Algorithm

The Apriori are based on the property that subset of a frequent itemsets must be frequent, it uses an iterative procedure with the data subsets, and utilizes large frequent itemsets generated in the preceding stage to produce frequent itemsets in the next stage[7]. In Apriori algorithm, there are two parts: Firstly, generated all 1-item candidates, and counted their number of occurrences to achieve 1-item frequencies. Secondly, joined the k-item frequencies to generate (k+1)-item candidates, tested their amount and quality (fit the above property) to generate (k+1)-item frequencies. The algorithm iterates the process until the number of the (k+1)-item candidates is 0.

2.2 Maintaining the Integrity of the Specifications

Apriori algorithm mainly uses horizontal and vertical storage structure. This paper introduces another mode (the bit table (BIT) matrix). This way can be well applied to the multi-core concurrency of GPU, and has the ability to replace the complex joined operation of Apriori with the operation "&" between two matrices. Therefore, BIT matrix Storage Structure can improve algorithm efficiency. Figure 1 shows the difference between the BIT matrix storage structure and the traditional one.

Horizontal Storage Structure

Trans IDs	Items IDs
1	ABCD
2	ABD
3	ACD
4	BCD

Vertiacl Storage Structure

Items IDs	Trans IDs
ABD	1,2
ACD	1,3
BCD	1,4

BIT Matrixl Storage Structure

Item IDs / Trans IDs	A	B	C	D
1	1	1	1	1
2	1	1	0	1
3	1	0	1	1
4	0	1	1	1

Figure 1. BIT Matrix and Traditional Storage Structure

The BIT matrix can be well applied to the multi-core concurrency of GPU. In these matrices, one column uses one bit to represent, and every column (item) information for each row (transaction) is stored by some "unsigned integer". The number of "unsigned integer" depends on the how many the column in the dataset. Figure 2 shows the state of the BIT matrix in memory.

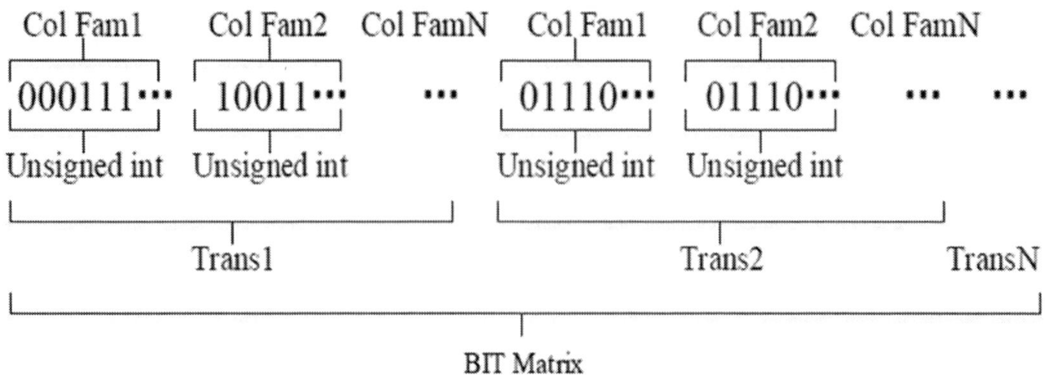

Figure 2. Storage Form of BIT Matrix in Memory

This structure is different from the general sense of the array, so that a new kind of read and write operation logic need to be fulfill. Read and Write operations are made using a tag variable ("unsigned integer"), which value is "0x80000000". Through the shift manipulation of the tag variable and the operation "&" between the shifted tag variable and the corresponding variables in the BIT matrix, the reading operation can be achieved. Using the relevant variables table in the matrix and shifted tag variable to finish the operations of "|=" and "-=", then the value of "0" or "1" can be write in the BIT matrix.

The Apriori algorithm based on the BIT matrix storage structure also needs to complete the operation of converting the traditional storage structure into the BIT form. Firstly, in the conversion process, the array of BIT matrix is initialized, and set the value of all elements to "0". Then, needed to traverse every transaction in the database, and wrote "1" to the corresponding positions in the BIT when reading the items in each transaction, the operation of updating the number of per items can be performed simultaneously. Finally, 1-item candidates can be built when this procedure is over.

3 Gpuapriori Algorithm Based on BIT Matrix

3.1 Candidate Itemsets Generation

The candidate itemsets generation based on BIT is equivalent to the join step in Apriori algorithm. It uses the operation "&" between the k-item frequent BIT (FBIT) and the 1-item FBIT to generate (k+1)-item candidate BIT (CBIT), and completes the support count of (k+1)-item CBIT. Figure 3 describes the process of candidate itemsets generation based on BIT matrix in every tread.

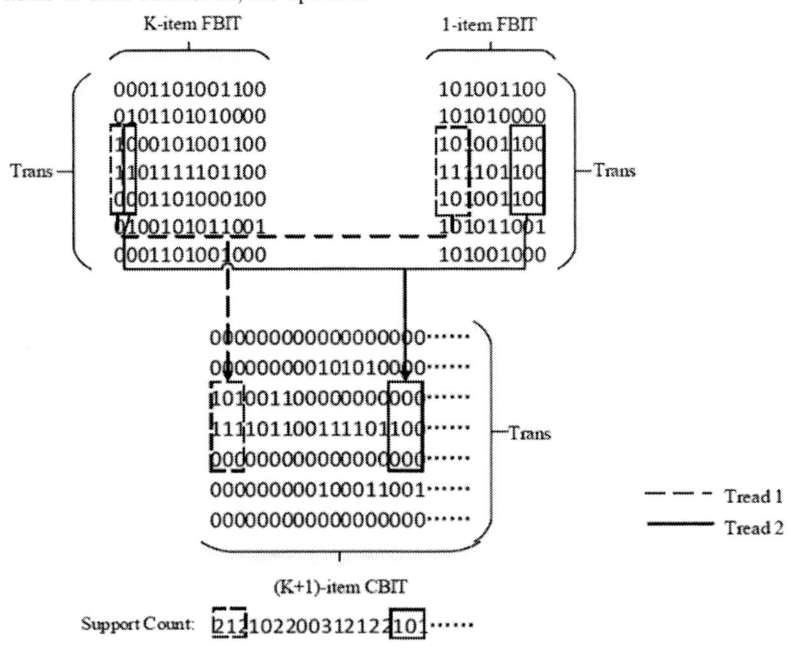

Figure 3. The Process of (k+1)-item CIT generation

BIT matrix is suitable for Gird-Block-Thread structure of GPU, multiple threads can be parallel processing of each part of the table. Algorithm 3-1 shows a single GPU thread executes the operation of candidate itemsets generation based on BIT matrix.

Algorithm 1: Join Step of GPUApriori
Input: k-item FBIT and 1-item FBIT Output: (k+1)-item CBIT, Support Count of (K+1)-item CBIT: S1 1. 1-item FBIT is divided into several small F1 matrixes according to the size of 32*100, k-item FBIT divided into several FK columns. 2. Every GPU thread parallel processes a F1 matrix and a FK columns and achieves a CK+1 matrix (part of (k+1)-item CBIT) and its support count (refer to Figure 4). 3. GPU thread get the matrix CK+1 and set it to the corresponding position of (k+1)-item CBIT (Atomic operation). 4. Returned to 2 until all F1 matrix and FK column are processed completely.

3.2 Frequent Itemsets Generation

This section focuses on the pruning step of GPUApriori algorithm. The core of the pruning step is to sort out a Range table, which records all the indexes of the (K+1)-item FBIT, and then filters the (K+1)-item CBIT according to the index set.

Algorithm 3-2 describes an algorithm for filter the (K+1)-item CBIT to achieve the (K+1)-item FBIT.

Algorithm 3-2: Pruning Step of GPUApriori
Input: (K+1)-item CBIT, Support Count of (K+1)-item CBIT: S1, Minimum support: T Output: (K+1)-item FBIT, Support Count of (K+1)-item FBIT: S2 1. Parallel set (K+1)-item CBIT's badsets to 0 in S1, Initialize the index table Range //badsets includes many items that do not accord with ascending order or contain duplicate, such as "121", "aba", "111". 2. Parallel sorting the items in S1 and Range according to the S1. 3. Searching for the first S1[i] greater than or equal to T. The index of the (K+1)-item FBIT can be achieved in the Table Range (Range[i~n]). 4. Parallel reset the (K+1)-item CBIT according to the Range[i~n], (K+1)-item FBIT and S2 can be obtained.

3.3 The Whole Process of Gpuapriori

The algorithm needs the cooperation between CPU and GPU. It includes four steps: reading the data and generate the 1-item CBIT, building the 1-item FBIT, joining operation between two FBIT and pruning steps of the CBIT, The flow chart of the GPUApriori is shown in the Figure 4.

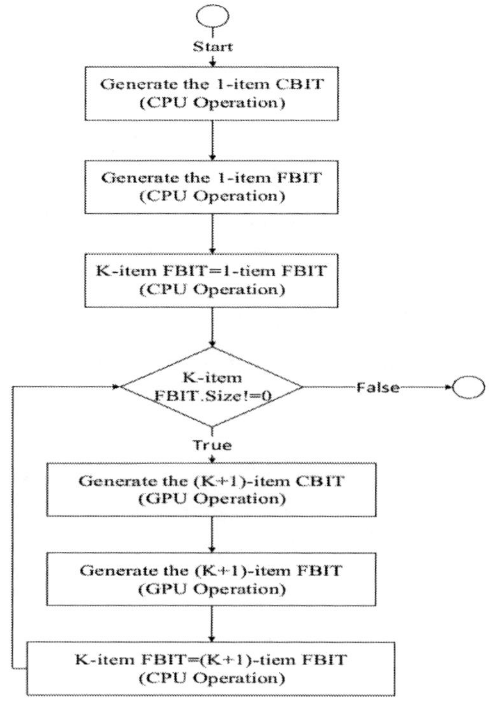

Figure 4. The Flow Chart of the GPUApriori

4 Experimental Result

4.1 Experimental Environment

The experiment of this paper is based on the GPU platform. The detailed information of this platform is listed in TABLE I.

Table 1. Table Type Styles

Hardware Platform	CPU: Intel® CoreTM i7-4790K Processor GPU: NVIDIA Quadro K600 Memory: 8GB(2*4GB Kingston 1600MHz) Disk: ST1000DM003-1CH162-931.51GB
Software Platform	OS: Windows 7 Pro CUDA: CUDA Toolkit 7.5 Visual Studio 2013

4.2 Experimental Method

This experiment tests the performance of two algorithms, 1) Traditional Apriori algorithm based on CPU, named CPUApriori; 2) Apriori algorithm based GPU and named GPUApriori. Experimental measure the performance of the algorithms with different support count from the same data set.

Our benchmark datasets are from the Frequent Itemset Mining Repository. Selected Retail, Mushroom, Chess, TI0I4D100K experimental datasets, and those datasets are presented in TABLE 2.

Table 2. Experimental Datasets

Database	Type	#Items	#Trans
Retail	Sparse	16,470	88,162
T40I10D100K	Sparse	1,000	100000
Chess	Dense	75	3196
Mushroom	Dense	119	8,124

4.3 Experimental Result

The experimental results are shown in Figure 5, Figure 6, Figure 7 and Figure 8.

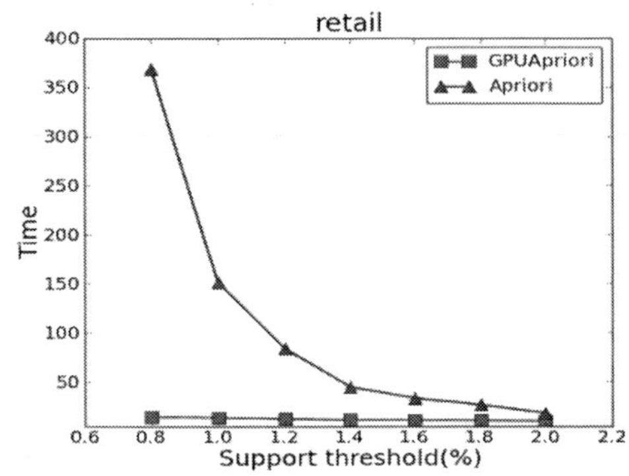

Figure 5

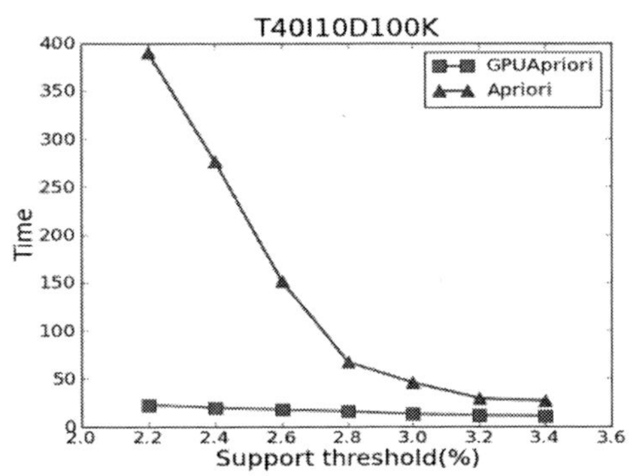

Figure 6

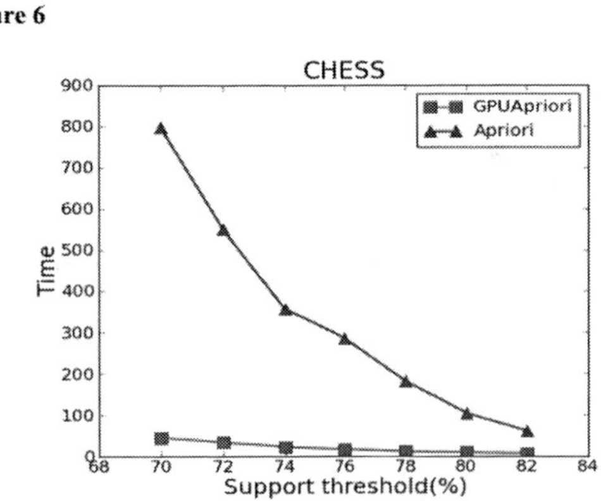

Figure 7

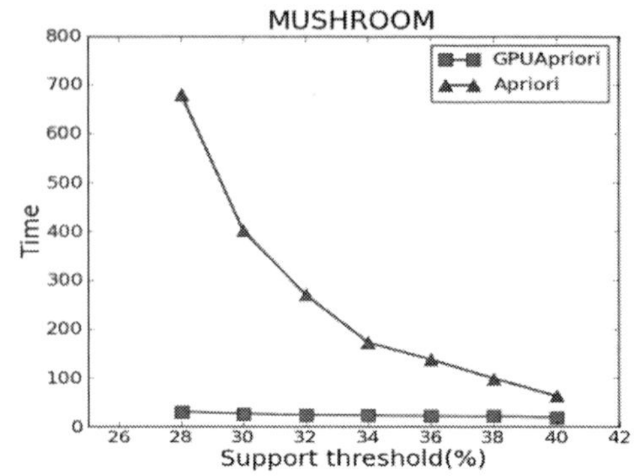

Figure 8

Figure 5, Figure 6 shows the running time of the two algorithms in the Retail and T40I10D100K experimental datasets with different support levels. Found from the comparison in contrast with the GPUAriori algorithm and the algorithm on the CPU, GPUAriori has a greater advantage. Moreover, when the minimum support is smaller, the speedup of GPApriori is higher than that of the another. Simultaneous. Figure 7 and Figure 8 show that the GPApriori algorithm has a much more efficient acceleration in a dense data set.

The Experimental shows that the GPUApriori algorithm performs well in performance testing, In addition, When the Apriori algorithm is calculating the larger and more dense dataset, GPU compared with the CPU algorithm will have a faster acceleration.

5 Discussion

In this paper, the association rules mining algorithm in data mining is studied, and presented the parallel processing of joining step and pruning step in GPUApriori based on BIT matrix. The parallel GPUApriori algorithm is implemented in the experiment, and the results show that the GPUApriori algorithm has better running efficiency, which reflects the parallel acceleration effect of GPU. In future, research should focus on the other algorithms of frequent itemsets mining, in order to develop other parallel algorithms based on GPU.

References

1. JIAWEI HAN. Data mining concepts and techniques [M]. Morgan Kaufmann Publishers, 2011-07-25.J. Clerk Maxwell, A Treatise on Electricity and Magnetism, 3rd ed., vol. 2. Oxford: Clarendon, 1892, pp.68–73.
2. Agrawal R, Strikant R. Fast algorithms for mining association rules. 20[J]. Proc. int. conf. very Large Database Vldb, 1994,23(3):21-30.K. Elissa, "Title of paper if known," unpublished.
3. Han j, Kamber M, Pei J. Data mining, southeast Asia edition: Concepts and techniques [M]. Morgan kaufmann, 2006.

4. Owens J D, Houston M, Luebke D, et al. GPU computing.
5. Nvidia B. NVIDIA CUDA Programming Guide [J]. 2012.
6. Bell, Jason. Apache Spark [M] Machine Learning: Hands-On for Developers and Technical Professionals. John Wiley & Sons, Inc, 2015:273-314.
7. Zaharia M, Chowdhury M, Das T, et al. Resilient distributed datasets: a fault-tolerant abstraction for in-memory cluster computing[C] Proceedings of the 9th USENIX conference on Networked Systems Design and Implementation. USENIX Association, 2012:141-146.
8. J. Guo and Y.-g. Ren, Research on Improved A Priori Algorithm Based on Coding and MapReduce," in Web Infromation System and Application Conference (WISA), 2013, pp.294-299.
9. Sacasere A, Omiecinski E, Navathe S B. An Efficient Algorithm for Mining Association Rules in Large Databases [J]. Vidb Journal. 1995:432-444.
10. Park J S, Chen M S, Yu P S/ Efficient parallel data mining for association rules[C] International Conference on Information and Knowledge Management.ACM, 1995:31-36.
11. Qiu H, Gu R, Yuan C, et al. YAFIM: A Parallel Frequent Itemset Minging Algorithm with Spark[C] Parallel & Distributed Processing Symposium Workshops.IEEE, 2014:1664-1671.

Energy Efficiency Optimizing Based on Characteristics of Machine Learning in Cloud Computing

Xiao-Bo CAI[1,a], Yuan-Xia JI[2,b], and Ke HAN[3,*]

[1]School of basic and Information Engineering, Yunnan Agricultural University, Kunming, China
[2]Yunnan Agricultural University library, Kunming, China
[3]School of Electrical Engineering, Kunming Metallurgy College, Kunming, China
[a] xbcai918@qq.com, [b]253667802@qq.com
* Corresponding author: hanke81@qq.com

Abstract: Energy efficiency is one of the most important issues for large-scale server systems in current cloud computing. the main method about the power-performance tradeoff by fixing one factor and minimizing the other, from the perspective of optimal load distribution. However, there still exist several main challenges about Energy efficiency due to the complexities of real cloud computing application scene. The paper adopts machine learning theory to save energy consumption by decrease redundant computation for high energy-efficiency cloud computing environment. give the typical k-means and Page Rank applications, the Experiments show that the presented algorithm can save power consumption apparently. The research combines the machine learning theory and distributed technology, and presents a creative way to challenged problems in energy-efficiency cloud.

1 Introduction

With the rapid increase in the scale and the number of the data centers, the data center energy consumption is growing rapidly. The US Environmental Protection Agency reported that in 2011, the world's data center consumed 18.8 billion kwh of electricity in 2010, about 1.1% ~ 1.5% of the global total power generation [1]. The green data center has become one of the hot spots. Currently, the data center energy management mainly uses DVS / DVFS or sleep / wake technology, which make the idle nodes with the low energy consumption state [2-4]. The energy saving for data center is mainly on Map Reduce computing tasks. Although these algorithms can reduce the energy consumption on certain extent, but these algorithms are subject to certain restrictions which did not take account of the typical application (machine learning task) running in the data center.

Firstly, we analyze the typical machine learning algorithms to saving the energy consumption of the data center. the machine learning tasks are computationally intensive applications, the energy consumption is mainly in the data analysis and calculation[6-8] .However, these algorithms need to continually classify and analyze the data in the process of machine learning, where there is a lot of redundancy in the process, which leads to unnecessary energy consumption[9-12]. Based on above, we have designed and implemented an energy-saving mechanism for machine learning, the method achieve energy-saving by matching the input data.

The MapReduce Computing Framework is a widely used as a programming model in the data center; there is a lot of work to focus on the study energy consumption and specific control methods of MapReduce model. MapReduce framework is generally divided into two parts: one is distributed storage, the other is distributed computing. The storage node is divided into two parts: one is the hot spot and the other is the non-hot spot which in a low-power state [13]. The different types of data stored in different areas. The effects of different configuration parameters on energy consumption in MapReduce are studied and they also provided enterprise-based benchmarks for MapReduce's energy consumption [14]. running a computational task should use all of the compute nodes and turn off all the compute nodes while the task is completed, which is better energy savings compared to only use one part of the compute nodes[15]. Reducing energy consumption by adjusting or controlling the physical location of virtual machine[16]. The data compression method is given to reduce the system's energy consumption [17]. Using DVFS technology to save energy for computing-intensive applications [18-19]. Different scheduling mechanisms for heterogeneous cluster are proposed, which can enable low power consumption without seriously affecting system throughput [20-21].

This paper Section I describes the related work. Section II analyzes the data center characteristics of energy consumption and the machine learning algorithm. Section III introduces the proposed energy saving algorithm. Section IV shows experimental data and correlation analysis.

DOI: 10.1051/itmconf/20171203047

2 The Core Idea

The accurate calculation results are not needed usually in the distributed computing by machine learning-oriented algorithm. Such as clustering algorithm, the recommended algorithms and relevance of different users of different commodities, and the last ranking of each point in PageRank, which do not require accurate calculation results. The user allows these calculations have errors within a range. the random initialization make the different results with the same data set. In fact, some programs cannot guarantee the error range of calculation process as k-means, PageRank and proposed algorithm. Usually users tend to specify a convergence value, when the value is smaller than the set value, the calculation is judged to be convergent. The machine learning for the user on the results have a lot of fault tolerance.

This paper proposes a policy to achieve the purpose of removing redundant calculations and saving energy consumption by compare the calculated data to determine whether the previous calculation results can be reused. At the same time, the mean error of the calculation results is controlled to a certain extent. In this paper, the the key to the question is to judge the calculation may be redundant calculation. We proposed input data matching degree, input / output correlation and other basic concept concepts.

2.1 Match Degree

In this paper, the twice input data match degree is the similarity degree between two data input and output results . If the two calculations are exactly the same, then the two input exactly match.

2.2 The Correlation between Input and Output

We use correlation to describe the effect of input data changes on the calculated output. Machine learning in the input data can be divided into multiple independent input, their correlation with the calculation results can be individually.

2.3 The Input Matching Module

The module is mainly used to calculate the data matching degree between the input of this task and the before task. This module save d the previous calculation results, the corresponding input value and the the correlation vector.In order to determine whether this calculation is redundant, the system needs to call the Match function to compare the similarity between the calculation and the previous calculation. When the Match function returns true, it means that the calculation can be considered redundant. And the current First, system constructs the difference vector by calling the user-defined Diff function which calculates the difference of the input vector. Then, calculate the vector inner product by the difference degree vector and relevance vector. Finally, the matching degree is compared with the threshold set by the user. If the matching degree is less than the threshold, the matching is successful. TaskTracker sent the output data address directly to the JobTracker, and notify the energy consumption module matching success.

When the TaskTracker receives the calculated input data, it passes the input data to the input matching module first. If a matching input is found, the stored calculation result is output and the node is set to a low power state. If no match the input, then call the calculation module for Map or Reduce calculation. The following describes the specific design and implementation of each module.

3 Matching Algorithm Design

3.1 System Design and Implementation

We use the correlation to describe the influence of the change of the input data to calculate the output and assign the task According to the situation of energy consumption of the current node. Task Tracker contains the input matching module, the energy consumption module and computing module.

3.2 Task Input

All input data that requires input matching must be abstracted as an input vector, such as most of the machine learning algorithms are based matrices, and each row of the matrix is seen as a dimension of the vector. In this system, we provide a higher level of abstract (InputObj) interface to each input vector type for the user. The users can complete the interface as needed. Such as in k-means, the data in the local data block will not change, we only store and compare the cluster center point coordinates in the process of input matching. Therefore, the input vector should be center Point of all the cluster collection, and clustering center point need to complete the InputObj interface. For the application which have large amount of data or multiple input changes, the user should extract characteristic value or calculation of hash of the input data to a reasonable abstraction to reduce the amount of data storage cache and input matching the amount of calculation.

3.3 Save the Results

It is necessary to the previous calculation results are cached locally is necessary to remove the redundancy calculation. We need to consider the MapTask calculation results 'cache problem in Hadoop, the Reduce Task data stored in the distributed file system by TaskTracker .TaskTracker store the MapTask calculation results in the local directory. When the calculation task of MapTask is completed, the MapTask calculation result will be deleted immediately. But in our system, TaskTracker save the calculation result' output path of input path, When the input matches a stored input, the TaskTracker sends the corresponding calculation result path to the JobTracker. The user can also clear the cached intermediate calculation results manually. The basic algorithm of input matching is as flowing.

DOI: 10.1051/itmconf/20171203047

```
bool Match(vector<ObjInput> v1,vector
<ObjInput>v2,vector<double>rel)
Vector<double>diff=rel.clone()
For i in 1,...,n
diff[i]=Diff(v1[i],v2[i])
double d=Σdiff[i]*rel[i]
return(d<threhold)
```

4 Experiments and Analysis

We use the power socket to test the configuration of the Intel i7-4770 processor, 32GB memory and 2TB hard drive single-node state of the energy consumption. Then we randomly select n computing points as the end of the connection. We use the custom data generation program to generate 400K data points (205MB), where the average number of connections per point is 20 and the maximum number of iterations is set to 10. First, we conducted an evaluation test on the application of energy consumption.

Energy Efficiency Evaluation

This section describes the energy consumption evaluation results. the input difference threshold is set 0.05 for k-means and PageRank applications.

Currently, the system is for the isomorphic data center, so the power of all nodes can be considered similar, the energy of all nodes of the MapTask Get the power consumed by the Map phase, and then use the power outlet to obtain the real-time power of the ReduceTask node, that is, the power consumed by the Reduce stage, and then the total power consumption of the single iteration is obtained by accumulating. Similarity, the total energy consumption of the whole calculation can be multiplied by the number of iterations by the energy consumed by a single iteration. For the optimized power calculation, we consider two kinds of processing methods respectively.

Free energy-saving method Mode is simply to free the Map Task node that processes the redundant data blocks, the original MapTask used to calculate the time will become idle time, the power calculation can be calculated by the original time Power is replaced by the power of a single node in the idle state. Considering that the data to be processed at the Shuffle stage is the same, its power and the power consumption can be considered the same. Here is the use of alternative methods to estimate the savings of electricity, through the same method of calculation the total energy consumption of the application;

The other is to use the dormant way to deal with the original Map Task calculation time, that is, by dormant way to deal with redundant computing, through Reduce the data request of the Reduce Task or the job assignment request of the Job Tracker to wake up the node, which we call the dormant energy-saving party

In this case, the power of the node is further reduced, but the corresponding hardware support is needed, and the total power is calculated in the same way as the former similarly, the power consumption can be estimated by replacing the original calculated time power with the power in the dormant state.

Finally, by calculating the power consumption of all MapTask and the power consumption of ReduceTask for each iteration, we can get each iteration Figure 1 show the comparison of the power before and after the optimization of k-means and PageRank, and it can be seen that in the k-means application, we also use a simple method based on idle energy saving can achieve 10% of the energy savings, and through the sleep-based energy-saving methods, the original program in 25% of the consumption of electricity can be saved;

Figure 2 shows the case where the k-means applies 20 iterations of total power consumption. Figure 20 shows the case where PageRank applies 10 iterations of total power consumption, where the free energy saving method can save around 5% for k-means applications Power consumption, and through the hibernation-based energy-saving method, nearly 23% of the total k-means application can be saved; for PageRank applications, based on the idle energy-saving method can save 5% of the total power consumption, Energy-saving methods, nearly 20% of the total energy consumption in the entire PageRank application can be saved.

In this paper, we use machine learning algorithm to save the energy consumption of data center .the algorithm eliminate the unnecessary redundancy calculation by matching input and calculation result. This paper analyzes the energy consumption and accuracy. The experimental results show that Error control in a certain range of the remise, the system effectively saves the energy consumption of the system. The next step we will work focus on the system in the heterogeneous environment of the work.

Acknowledgment

This research was supported by with the nature and Science Fund fromYunnan province ministry of education of China (No. 2016ZZX241); the nature and science Fund from Yunnan Kunming Metallurgy College (No.2015XJQN004); The nature and science Fund from Yunnan Agricultural University (No.2016ZR17)

References

1. Beloglazov A, Buyya R. Optimal online deterministic algorithms and adaptive heuristics for energy and performance efficient dynamic consolidation of virtual machines in cloud data centers[J]. Concurrency and Computation: Practice and Experience, 2012, 24(13): 1397-1420.
2. Wang XR, Wang YF. Coordinating power control and performance management for virtualized server clusters. IEEE Trans. on
3. Parallel and Distributed Systems, 2011,22(2):245–259. [doi: 10.1109/TPDS.2010.91]
4. Tam D. Facebook processes more than 500 TB of data daily. 2012.
5. http://www.cnet.com/news/facebook-processes-more-than-500-tb-of-data-daily/
6. Low Y, Gonzalez J, Kyrola A, Bickson D, Guestrin C, Hellerstein JM. Graphlab: A new framework for parallel machine learning.
7. arXiv preprint arXiv:1006.4990. 2010.

8. Wang YF, Wang XR, Chen M, Zhu XY. Partic: Power-Aware response time control for virtualized web servers. IEEE Trans. on
9. Parallel and Distributed Systems, 2011,22(2):323−336. [doi: 10.1109/TPDS.2010.79]
10. Qian ZP, Chen XW, Kang NX, Chen MC, Yu Y, Moscibroda T, Zhang Z. MadLINQ: Large-Scale distributed matrix computation
11. for the cloud. In: Proc. of the 7th ACM European Conf. on Computer Systems. ACM Press, 2012. 197−210. [doi: 10.1145/2168836.
12. Williams C. What is a green data center. 2011. http://www.mnn.com/green-tech/computers/stories/what-is-a-green-data-center
13. Kliazovich D, Bouvry P, Khan SU. DENS: Data center energy-efficient network-aware scheduling. Cluster Computing, 2013,16(1):
14. 65−75. [doi: 10.1007/s10586-011-0177-4]
15. Koomey J. Growth in data center electricity use 2005 to 2010. 2011. http://www.analyticspress.com/datacenters.html
16. Zhou L, Li J, Li F, et al. Energy consumption model and energy efficiency of machine tools: a comprehensive literature review[J]. Journal of Cleaner Production, 2016, 112:3721–3734.
17. Yuan L, Zhan JF, Sang B, Wang L, Wang HN. PowerTracer: Tracing requests in multi-tier services to save cluster power
18. consumption. Technical Report, Institute of Computing Technoly, Chinese Academy of Sciences, 2010.
19. Chase JS, Anderson DC, Thackar PN, Vahdat AM, Doyle RP. Managing energy and server resources in hosting centers. In: Proc. of
20. the 18th Symp. on Operating Systems Principles. 2001. [doi: 10.1145/502034.502045]
21. Chen G, He WB, Liu J, Nath S, Rigas L, Xiao L, Zhao F. Energy-Aware server provisioning and load dispatching for
22. connectionintensive Internet services. In: Proc. of the NSDI. 2008. 337−350. http://dl.acm.org/citation.cfm?id=1387613
23. Chen Y H, Krishna T, Emer J S, et al. Eyeriss: An Energy-Efficient Reconfigurable Accelerator for Deep Convolutional Neural Networks[J]. IEEE Journal of Solid-State Circuits, 2017, 52(1):1-12.
24. Demaine E D, Lynch J, Mirano G J, et al. Energy-Efficient Algorithms[J]. 2016:321-332.
25. Lu T, Chen MH, Andrew LL. Simple and effective dynamic provisioning for power-proportional data centers. IEEE Trans. On Parallel and Distributed Systems, 2013,24(6):1161−1171. [doi: 10.1109/TPDS.2012.241]
26. Chen YP, Ganapathi AS, Fox A, Katz RH, Patterson DA. Statistical workloads for energy efficient mapreduce. Technical Report,
27. No. UCB/EECS-2010-6, University of California at Berkeley, 2010.
28. Lang W, Patel JM. Energy management for mapreduce clusters. Proc. of the VLDB Endowment, 2010,3(1-2):129−139.
29. Yao Y, Huang L, Sharma A, et al. Data centers power reduction: A two time scale approach for delay tolerant workloads[C]//INFOCOM, 2012 Proceedings IEEE. IEEE, 2012: 1431-1439.
30. Ye K, Huang D, Jiang X, et al. Virtual machine based energy-efficient data center architecture for cloud computing: a performance perspective[C]//Proceedings of the 2010 IEEE/ACM Int'l Conference on Green Computing and Communications & Int'l Conference on Cyber, Physical and Social Computing. IEEE Computer Society, 2010: 171-178.
31. Pedram M. Energy-efficient datacenters[J]. Computer-Aided Design of Integrated Circuits and Systems, IEEE Transactions on, 2012, 31(10): 1465-1484.
32. Gao P X, Curtis A R, Wong B, et al. It's not easy being green[J]. ACM SIGCOMM Computer Communication Review, 2012, 42(4): 211-222.

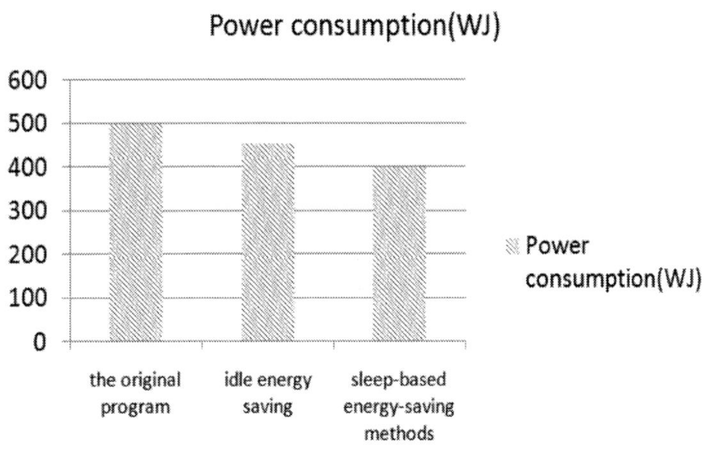

Figure 1. Total energy consumption of k-means

DOI: 10.1051/itmconf/20171203047

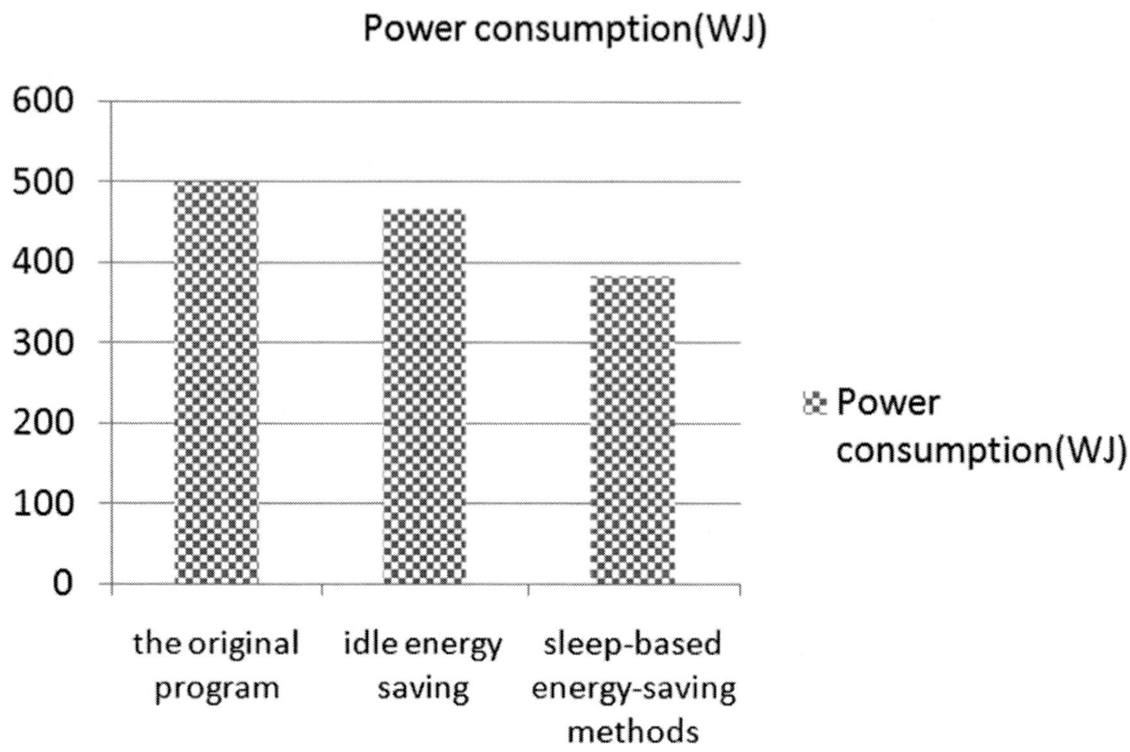

Figure 2. Total energy consumption of PageRank

DOI: 10.1051/itmconf/20171203048

Parallelization of K-Means Clustering Algorithm for Data Mining

Hao JIANG[a], Liyan YU[b]

College of Computer Science and Engineering, Southeast University, Nanjing, China
[a]hjiang@seu.edu.cn, [b]yly.sunshine@qq.com

Abstract: In this paper, we studied the parallelization of K-Means clustering algorithm, proposed a parallel scheme, designed a corresponding algorithm, and implemented the algorithm in GPU environment. The experimental result shows that the GPU-based parallelization algorithm has a good acceleration effect compared with the CPU-based serialization algorithm.

1 Introduction

Cluster analysis is an important research topic in the field of data mining.[1] Clustering is the process of classifying a set of physical or abstract objects into similar object classes. The objects in the same cluster have high similarity, and the differences in the different clusters are large. The automatic clustering is able to identify dense and sparse regions in the object space, and then find interesting correlations between the global distribution pattern and the data attributes. [2] In the context of the application of large data and increasing mass data, the data size has reached TB or even PB level, which puts forward a higher requirement of the cluster. Massive data and huge processing tasks can not be completed by the general computer within the specified time. In order to improve the ability to deal with massive data and enhance the real-time data processing, parallelization of the clustering algorithm become an attractive choice. Today's widely used methods are distributed computing systems, such as Hadoop[3] and Spark[4], which combine multiple computers into a unified distributed system, and each computer processes user data to improves processing efficiency. In order to fully tap the computing power of a single computer, you can transplant the appropriate parallel computing algorithm to GPU platform, and with the GPU's powerful parallel computer capability the computer's data computing capabilities will be improved. Similarly to the CPU, you can easily add a number of GPU to the same computer, to further improve the efficiency of a single computer data processing. It is not difficult to imagine that if a multi-GPU computer with powerful computing power is organized into a distributed cluster, it will greatly improve the data processing capacity compare to the same level of computer clusters. Therefore, the parallelization of GPU-based K-Means algorithm has a wide range of practical application value.

2 Overview of K-Means Algorithm

The K-Means[5] algorithm is one of the most famous and most commonly used clustering algorithms proposed by MacQueen. The algorithm is simple, fast and easy to implement. The K-Means algorithm uses K as the input parameter to divide the N sets of objects into K clusters, which makes the similarity in the same cluster high, and the similarity between different clusters is low. The similarity of clusters is about the mean measure of the objects in the cluster, and can be regarded as the centroid or center of gravity of each cluster. The K-Means algorithm can be described as follows: Given a sample set $D=\{x\_1,x\_2,\cdots, x\_N\}$, and $x_i \in \chi \subseteq R^n$ is the eigenvector of the instance, the K-Means algorithm is designed to map N samples to $k(k \leq N)$ clustering centers $C=\{c\_1,c\_2,\cdots, c\_k\}$, and make sure that the square sum of the distance between each sample and its nearest clustering center is minimized, and square sum of that distance is called The Square Error Function, marked as E, as shown in equation (1).

$$E = \sum_{i=1}^{k} \sum_{x_i \in C_i} \| x_i - C_i \|^2 \qquad (1)$$

The processing flow of the K-Means algorithm:

Input: Data set $D=\{x_1, x_2, \cdots, x_N\}$, and $x_i \in \chi \subseteq R^n$; k is the number of clusters.

Output: a collection of k clusters.

Step:

1) Arbitrary select K samples from D as the center of initial cluster;
2) Repeat;
3) Calculate all the distance between each data sample and the center of the cluster;
4) Assign each object to the most similar cluster according to the above distance;
5) Calculate the mean of all the objects in each cluster and update the cluster mean;
6) Calculate the Squared Error Function;
7) Until the criterion function satisfies the threshold;

8) The algorithm terminates.

The K-Means algorithm attempts to determine the k divisions of the minimized Squared Error Function. When the cluster shape is compact, the difference between cluster and cluster is obvious, and size of all the clusters is similar, clustering result is ideal. The time complexity of the K-Means algorithm is O(NKt), where N is the sample set size, K is the number of clusters, and t is the number of times of iteration. [6] Specifically, the most of time, in the process of the K-Means algorithm's each iteration, spent on calculating the distance between each data set objects and calculating the Square Error Sum of all objects. Although the process of alloction each data object and the update of all k clusters center need to be executed many times, but the most heavy calculation in each time is to repeat the calculation of the Square Error Sum between data and different center points, and calculate the new center point and find the new center of each cluster. So, it can be separated into two single kernel functions. Then, it can be sent to the GPU processing core for parallel computing.

3 Parallel Design of K-Means Algorithm

First, this paper presents a GPU-based K-Means parallel algorithm--G-K-Means algorithm. The main idea of that algorithm is to improve the performance by moving the part which data is independent and computation is intensive in the traditional K-Means algorithm from the host to the GPU. Since the K-Means algorithm is an iterative convergence process which will calculate the distance between the data and the center of the cluster every time, the main parallel scheme includes the following two aspects:

(1) Parallel calculation of all the distance between data objects and cluster center point

In order to facilitate the data calculation on the GPU, we construct the data set matrix T[N][D], the center point matrix C[k][D] and the distance matrix Dis[N][k]. N is the size of the data set, k is the number of clusters to be classified, D is the dimension of the data sample, Dis[N][k] is the result from T[N][D] and C[k][D] set the C^T [D][k] matrix. Each row in the distance matrix Dis[N][k] represents the distance between a data object and center points of k clusters. This step can be transplanted to GPU, and use similar block matrix multiplication to parallel computing. Finally, it can improve the efficiency of distance calculation between the data samples.

(2) Parallel calculation of the Square Error Sum for all objects in the data set

In the process of the iterative convergence of the K-Means algorithm, each iteration needs to calculate the Squared Error Sum of all data objects in order to determine whether it is converge. First, for each object of each cluster, the operation of calculating the square sum of the distance from the object to its cluster center is independent, so parallelism can be achieved here. Second, the calculation of Square Error Sum for each object in each cluster is independent, parallelism can be achieved too. In the specific implementation, GPU grid is divided into N/1024 one-dimensional parallel blocks, each block has 1024 one-dimensional thread. Each thread corresponds to an object for calculating the Square Error Sum with its cluster center, and then use Reduction Thought to sum each thread result. During the Reduction, the thread in each block is first summed, and the Square Error Sum of the object in each block is obtained. Then, the same method is used to Reduction Sum each block and get the final result.

Although the calculation model of SIMD in GPU is good at parallel computing, the GPU-based K-Means algorithm has three important principles[7]. Firstly, GPU branch control and data cache mechanism are very weak, because a large number of computing processing unit occupies most of the space within GPU. Secondly, the data transfer rate between GPU and GPU's global memory is much slower than the data transfer rate between CPU and CPU cache, so with the appropriate thread block and thread bundle size, GPU can reflect powerful computing speed. Thirdly, the GPU-based K-Means algorithm increases the time when transfering data between GPU global memory and CPU memory compared to the traditional K-Means algorithm. Therefore, in order to optimize the performance of the algorithm, we must reasonably allocate the responsibilities of the host and the device, and design or implement the data storage and parallel computing model. The main flow chart of GPU-based G-K-Means algorithm is shown in Fig. 1.

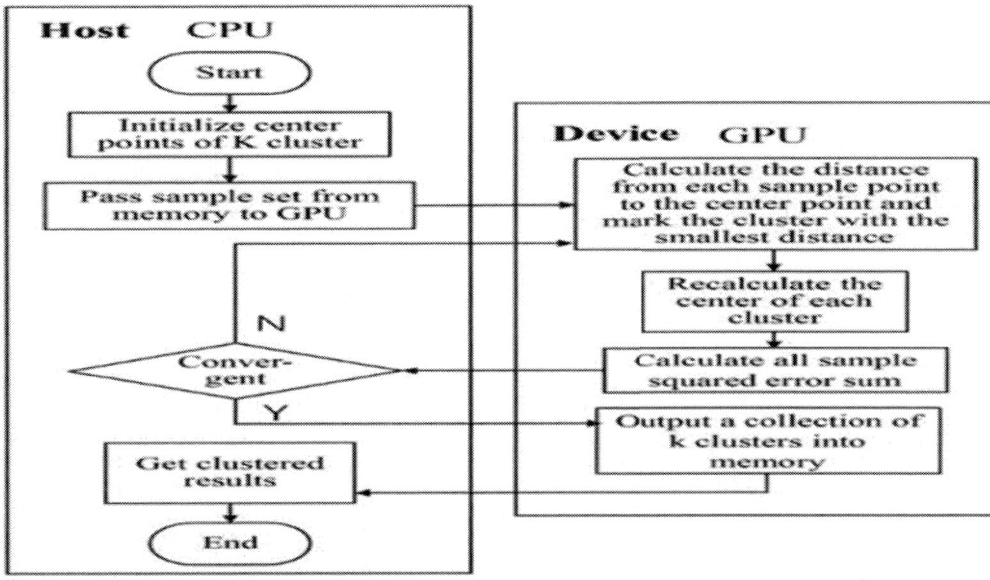

Figure 1. G-K-Means algorithm flow.

Algorithm process is as following:

1) Initialize the convergence threshold ε, the data set matrix $T[N][D]$ and the random selected k samples' central point matrix $C[k][D]$, where D is the data sample dimension. And calculate Squared Error Sum E_1;

2) Pass the matrix T and transposed C^T into the GPU;

3) In the GPU, use the sample matrix T and C^T to calculate the distance matrix $Dis[N][k]$ of each sample and center point in parallel by matrix operation;

4) According to the distance matrix $Dis[N][k]$, each data sample is marked to the smallest distance cluster, and the center point of each cluster is recalculated, and then the center point transpose matrix C^T is updated;

5) According to matrix $Dis[N][k]$ and matrix C^T, calculate the sample Square Error Sum E_2, then determine whether it is convergent, if $|E_2 - E_1| < \varepsilon$ is satisfied, then turn to 6), otherwise turn to 3);

6) Output cluster results then end.

4 Experiment and Analysis

The experimental data are randomly generated when comparing the GPU-based G-K-Means and the CPU-based K-Means. The experiment is divided into two groups. In the first group, data set T has a size N=100000, a data dimension D = 100.And in the other group, there are several data set ranging from hundreds KB to hundreds MB. Since the efficiency of the K-Means algorithm is affected by the value of k, the first group of tests is taken k from 2 to 1024, and the second group keep 128 as the value of k in order to observe the speedup ratio of parallel algorithm compare to serial algorithm.

In the experiment, the convergence threshold ε is 0.001 and the number of iterations is less than 500. Table 1 describes the results of the first set of experiments, including the convergence time of the two algorithms, the number of iterations and the speedup ratio. Table 2 describes the results of the second set of experiments.

Table 1. N=100000, D=100 G-K-Means&C-K-Means clustering time compare

K	time/s G-K-Means	K-Means	Iteration times	SpeedUp
2	11.386	11.186	133	0.98
4	15.446	24.914	177	1.62
8	19.089	55.645	222	2.92
16	12.339	67.049	141	5.43
32	13.236	136.298	148	10.30
64	12.580	268.150	149	21.32
128	8.307	330.629	93	39.80
256	5.61	417.006	58	74.33
512	3.607	527.611	36	146.27
1024	3.212	689.322	23	214.61

Table 2. k=128 G-K-Means&K-Means clustering time compare

	time/s G-K-Means	K-Means	Iteration times	SpeedUp
0.3	2.013	1.357	33	0.67
0.8	0.907	0.437	14	0.48
1.8	1.472	1.420	24	0.96
5.0	1.656	4.259	26	2.57
11.2	2.798	18.159	47	6.49
23.5	5.61	90.714	93	17.58
50.0	8.396	234.688	121	27.95
116.0	7.804	316.495	87	40.56
232.0	8.834	516.551	73	58.47

From the experimental results above, we can see that the clustering time of the algorithm is influenced by the value of k and the number of iterations. The G-K-Means parallel algorithm has a significant improvement over the clustering convergence rate compared with the K-Means algorithm. In particular, with the increase of k in clustering and the increase of clustering data, the speedup effect of parallel algorithm is more obvious. It can be seen from Fig. 2 that the clustering time difference between the two algorithms is very small when the value of k is small, and the advantage of G-K-Means algorithm is not obvious, but with the increase of k, the clustering time of G-K-Means algorithm increase slowly compared with the K-Means algorithm, and it converges slowly. When the k is 1024, G-K-Means algorithm achieves 214.64x faster than the K-Means algorithm. The K-Means algorithm has nothing to do with the parallel running time on the GPU and the K value.

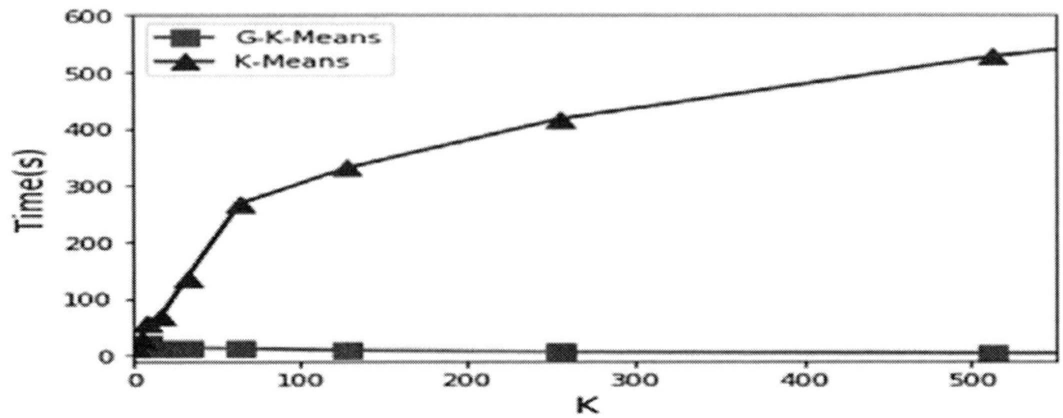

Figure 2. Clustering time comparing between G-K-Means&K-Means when N=100000,D=100-K-Means algorithm flow.

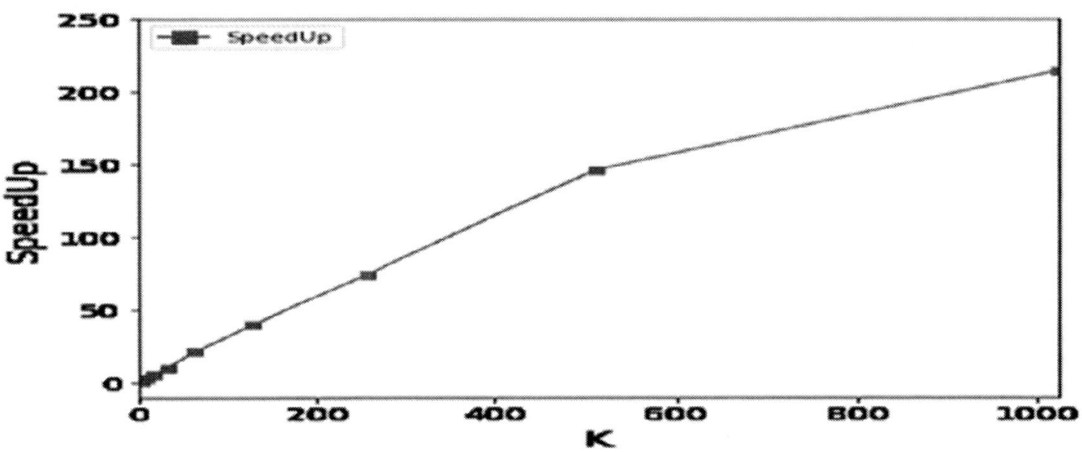

Figure 3. Algorithm Speedup when N=100000, D=100-K-Means.

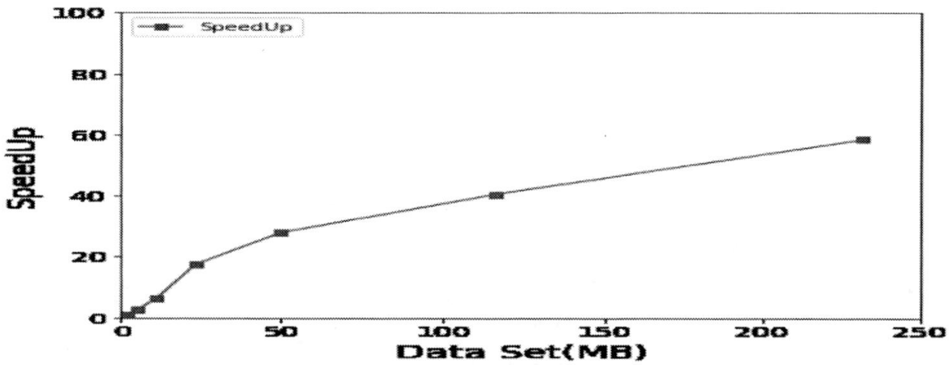

Figure 4. Algorithm Speedup for different dataset when k=128.

Fig. 4 depicts the clustering time comparison between the G-K-Means algorithm and the K-Means algorithm over a variety of data sets when k is 128. It can be seen that the acceleration effect of the G-K-Means algorithm on the smaller data set is not ideal, but with the increase of the data set, the clustering time of the G-K-Means algorithm is faster than that of the K-Means algorithm. When the set comes to 232MB, the acceleration ratio reached 58.47x.

The experimental results show that the G-K-Means algorithm, proposed in this paper, converts the process of multiple iterations and the updating process of k cluster centers to the GPU to improve the convergence speed of the algorithm. In particular, the greater the k value, the more obvious the effect of algorithm speedup. To illustrate the scalability of the algorithm, the experiment is carried out on a variety of data sets with different sizes. The results show that the speedup effect of G-K-Means parallel algorithm becomes more and more obvious as the data set scale increases.

5 Conclusion

In this paper, we deeply studied the parallelization of K-Means clustering algorithm of data mining. The experimental results show that GPU-based parallelization algorithm has greatly improved the efficiency when compares to the CPU-based serial algorithm. Especially, when data increase, the effect of acceleration becomes more obvious.

Acknowledge

This work was supported by Collaborative Innovation Center of Wireless Communications Technology and the National Natural Science Foundation of China (Grant No. 6157060279).

References

List and number all bibliographical references in 9-point Times, single-spaced, at the end of your paper. When reference

l footnote at the bottom of the column in which it was cite

1. Radiner L R.A tutorial on hidden Mardov model and selected applications in speech recognition[J].Proceedings of the IEEE,1989,77(2):257-286.
2. Rabiner L R,Juang B H.An Introduction to hidden Mardov models[J].IEEE ASSP Magazine,1986,3(1):4-16.
3. Dean J, Gheawat S. MapReduce: Simplified data processing on large clusters[J]. Communications of the ACM-50th Anniversary Issue: 1958-2008, 2008, 51 (1): 107-113.
4. Spark: Cluster Computing with Working Sets. Zaharia M, Chowdhury M, Franklin MJ, Shenker S, Stoica I. Technical Report No.UCB/EECS- 2010 -53 . 2010.
5. Han Jiawei, Kamber Micheline. Data Mining: Concepts and Techniques [M]. Second Edition. MingFan, Xiaofeng Meng translatrion. Beijing: Machinery Industry Press, 2007: p1-449.
6. M. Zechner and M. Granitzer, Accelerating K-Means on the graphics processor via CUDA, apr.2009, pp. 7-15.
7. Anguo Ma. Research on Key Technologies of High Performance GPGPU Architecture. National University of Defense Science and Technology. 2011:03-01.

DOI: 10.1051/itmconf/20171203049

Improving Property Service for the City Residential Community

Shou-Song JIN[a], Wei-Jun WU[b], and Xue-Mei HUANG[c]

Zhejiang University of Technology, Mechanical Engineering, Hangzhou, China
[a]jinshs@zjut.edu.cn, [b]1033049912@qq.com, [c]347517697@qq.com

Abstract: The city residential community tends to choose a property company to provide property services and the property company should provide satisfaction services to ensure it long employed in the residential community. To raise the property service quality for a city residential community, the demand indexes for the residential community wanting and the improvement measures for the property company adopting are designed based on relevant literature review and owner questionnaire survey. The analytic hierarchy process is used to determine the demand index weight. The improvement targets of demand indexes for the residential community are planned according to the demand indexes data obtained through questionnaire survey of some residential community owners and benchmarking residential communities. And the data of improvement measures is worked out by using the quality function deployment technology to keep a sense of proportion for improving the property service.

1 Introduction

As people living conditions and living standards continue to improve, urban residential district owners are generally willing to hire property companies to provide residential property services. For property companies, they can seize the property service market that make owners satisfied, so many property companies and related scholars have studied how to effectively improve the quality of modern residential property services. From perspective of customer satisfaction, Tian Fengcha and Wang Xumei and so on research evaluation index system of satisfaction for property management of urban residential area and performance assessment of services for property management companies [1-3].Cheng Hongqun and Zhu Jiaolan and so on carried out the residential district property service quality evaluation and investigation [4-5].Li Qingquan and He Ping and so on researches measures to improve service quality [6-7].Based on Quality Function Deployment (QFD), Li Suhua , Li Huaqiang and Diao Yu makes technological analysis into factors to influence service quality and puts forward improvement measures [8-9].But we haven't seen the reporters which apply QFD to improve the quality of residential property services. This article will act according to circumstances and learn widely from others' strong points to analyze a city residential area of property service improvement process.

2 Design Requirements Indicators and Improvement Measures

In order to improve the quality of urban residential district service, we must understand what the residential district needs and what property companies do. Refereed the relevant property services satisfaction research literature and the recent State Council issued the "Property Management Regulations", etc. Randomly asked many experienced management personnel, Invited behalf of the property management personnel and a number of owners to carry out brainstorming. Specifically, it was through the data analysis, expert interviews and owners survey, used 1-5 grade Likert scale method asked hundreds of owners on behalf of dozens of property management and several experts scoring, ignored the smaller indicators of accreditation listed in the research process and added indicators that the residential area considers to be important. Finally, we got six property service demand indicators that the residential property owners on the quality of property services which including Communication skills, maintenance efficiency, garbage removal, greening layout, traffic management and the elderly activities.

DOI: 10.1051/itmconf/20171203049

3 Determine the Weight of the Demand Indicator

In order to make the urban residential area owners feel satisfied, we need to improve the property needs of six demand indicators However, communication capacity (represented by CA), maintenance efficiency (ME), garbage removal (GR), greening layout (GL), traffic management (TM) and elderly activities (EA) of the six demand indicators on the degree of impact on the quality of service is different, and this difference can be expressed by the weight.

The weight calculation can be increased from 1 to 9 using the analytic hierarchy process of 1-9 scale. Invited hundreds of owner representative, dozens of physical management personnel and several experts to score for reducing the subjective influence of the individual. The importance of obtaining the six demand indicators by statistical processing is shown in TABLE 1. Used the two pairs of comparison method to fill the value of the ratio of TABLE 2, and TABLE 3. hierarchical analyzed of the root method to get the approximate weight value.

Table 1. Property Services Six Indicators Of The Importance Of Indicators

Demand Indicators	CA	ME	GR	GL	TM	EA
Importance	6.5	7.2	8.6	6.1	5.0	4.2

Table 2. Property Service 6 Comparsion Matrix of Demand Indicators

Demand Indicators	CA	ME	GR	GL	TM	EA
CA	1.00	0.90	0.76	1.07	1.30	1.55
ME	1.11	1.00	0.84	1.18	1.44	1.71
GR	1.32	1.19	1.00	1.41	1.72	2.05
GL	0.93	0.85	0.71	1.00	1.22	1.45
TM	0.77	0.69	0.58	0.82	1.00	1.19
EA	0.65	0.58	0.49	0.89	0.84	1.00

Table 3. Analytic Hierarchy Process

Demand Indicators	Multiply	Multiply6	Relative Weight
CA	1×0.90×0.76×1.07 ×1.30×1.55	1.30	1.55
ME	1.11×1×0.84×1.18 ×1.44×1.71	1.44	1.71
GR	1.32×1.19×1×1.41 ×1.72×2.05	1.72	2.05
GL	0.93×0.85×0.71×1 ×1.22×1.45	1.22	1.45
TM	0.77×0.69×0.58 ×0.82×1×1.19	1.00	1.19
EA	0.65×0.58×0.49 ×0.89×0.84×1	0.84	1.00
Total		6.20	1.00

According to the statistical criterion, the average randomness index RI standard value of 1.24 is obtained from the statistical standard, and the maximum characteristic root $\lambda = 6.06$, the consistency index CI = 0.012 and the consistency ratio CR = 0.01 <0.1 are obtained. The weight can be used as the weight of the property service demand index.

4 Demand Improvement Targets

Designed questionnaires by Using the 1-5 grade Likert scale method, requested the owners of residential quarters in accordance with the requirements of the questionnaire, the communication capacity of residential quarters, maintenance efficiency, garbage removal, greening layout, traffic management and elderly activities, the satisfaction is divided into very dissatisfied with 1 point, not satisfied with 2 points, the basic satisfaction of 3 points, more satisfied with 4 points, very satisfied with 5 points, examined the surrounding two famous residential district and grasped the corresponding demand indicators' data from its property company ,finally, through the statistical processing to obtain the residential quarters and benchmarking area of the property service demand index data TABLE 4 Talked into account the application of numerical practicality, the data collected by the survey in the table to the decimal after a data to 0 or 5 rounding treatment.

The satisfaction rate of six indicators of residential property service, maintenance efficiency, garbage removal, greening layout, traffic management and old age activities are obviously lower than those of benchmarking area. Through various comparative analysis, the improvement target as shown in TABLE 4 is planned value.

Table 4. Demand Indicators for Survey Data and Improvement Goals

Demand Indicators	CA	ME	GR	GL	TM	EA
Residential area	1.5	2.5	3.5	3.0	2.5	2.0
Benchmarking A	2.0	3.5	4.0	3.5	4.0	3.5
Benchmarking B	3.2	4.0	3.5	3.0	3.5	2.0
Planning objectives	2.5	3.0	4.0	3.5	3.0	3.0

5 Calculate the Importance of Improvement Measures

There is a causal relationship between the improvement measure value and the demand index value. By analyzing the improvement measures of the residential area, it can judge the importance of the improvement measures to improve the target. It is the process of applying the QFD quality meter to improve the importance of the improvement measures in Table 5. The improvement is the ratio to the expected improvement target and the residential area survey, and the importance of improvement is the percentage of the weight of the demand indicator and the product of the

DOI: 10.1051/itmconf/20171203049

improvement. According to the experience of the property management experts, the intensity of the correlation between the improvement measures and the demand indicators is determined by the grade of 4 to confirm the degree of correlation between the two, divided into strong correlation 3 points, moderate correlation 2 points, weak correlation 1, Not related to note 0 points. As there is no significant correlation between eight improvement measures such as property allocation, safety capability, established maintenance, complaint handling, environmental green, web construction, recreational facilities and traffic management, so ignore the quality table roof of the relevant types of analysis. Through the analysis of the improvement measures and the demand indicators, we can get the importance of the eight measures to improve the quality.

From Table 5, we can see the gap between the demand indicators and the improvement objectives, but also can see the improving measures that property companies need to focus on. According to the requirements of improvement target, the gap between communication skills and the improve target is the largest , the gap between traffic management and target is minimal, The most need to focus on the improvement measures is property configuration, security capacity only need a little improvement. Property company should be based on specific circumstances such as resource conditions, when it focused on the important improvement measures, the company should also be appropriate attention to non-significant improvement measures, and implement the improvement of property services.

TABLE V. THE IMPORTANCE THE IMPROVEMENT MEASURES TO IMPROVE THE OBJECTIVES

Demands \ Measures		Improvements								Plan the demand indicators to improve the target						
		Property Configuration	Security Capability	Timely Maintenance	Complaint Handling	Environmental greening	Web Construction	Recreational Facilities	Traffic management	Weights	Comparative Analysis			Improve goals		The importance of improvement
											Headquarters	Standard A	Standard B	Goals	Improvement	
Demand indicators	Communication Capacity	△			◎		◎			0.17	1.5	2.0	3.2	2.5	1.67	21.9
	Maintenance Efficiency	○		◎						0.19	2.5	3.5	4.0	3.0	1.20	17.6
	Garbage Removal	○								0.23	3.5	4.0	3.5	4.0	1.14	20.2
	Greening Layout					◎		○	○	0.16	3.0	3.5	4.0	3.5	1.17	14.4
	Traffic Management	○	○	△			△		◎	0.13	2.5	4.0	3.5	3.0	1.20	12.0
	Elderly Activities	○				△	○	◎		0.12	2.0	3.5	2.0	3.0	1.50	13.9
Measure of importance %		24.6	4.8	10.7	10.8	9.4	17.4	11.6	10.7	Correlation: ◎—3,○—2,△—1,□--0						

6 CONCLUSIONS

Urban residential district needs high-quality property services, property companies need a comprehensive system of property services to improve the ability. Property companies for residential property services to improve the measures can be related to access to literature, consult the owners and other residential property demand indicators and property companies to improve property services measures. Applicant Analytic Hierarchy Process to determine the weight of property services demand indicators, from the residential quarters questionnaire and benchmark survey data planning property services demand indicators to improve the target, and use the QFD analysis to obtain the importance of the property service improvement measures to achieve the demand target, and to consider how to improve the property service improvement measures according to the importance of the improvement measures.

DOI: 10.1051/itmconf/20171203049

References

1. Tian Fengcha. “Evaluation model of property management owners' satisfaction in small and medium - sized cities,” Science and Technology Information, vol. 8, Jun. 2011, pp. 114-115.
2. Wang Xuemei. “Study on Evaluation of Property Satisfaction of Xianhe Community”. China University of Petroleum, May.2012.
3. JHK Lai. “Comparative evaluation of facility management services for housing estates,” Building Services Engineering, vol. 35, Apr. 2011 , pp. 391-397.
4. Cheng Hequn,Qiu Huiling, etc. “Quality evaluation of residential property service,” Luojia Management Review, vol. 2, 2013, pp. 94-103
5. Zhu Lingjiao. “Investigation on Property Management Service Quality of Residential District in Zhuhai” Value Engineering, vol. 33, Nov. 2011, pp. 75-77.
6. Li Qingquan,ZhuWei.” Discussion on the improvement of property service quality based on service quality gap model”]. Property Research, vol. 11, 2012, pp. 113-116.
7. He Ping, Zheng Yizhong,Sun Yanhong. “Service Competitive Behavior Based on Service Quality and Price,” System Engineering Theory & Practice, vol.34, Feb. 2014, pp. 357-364.
8. Li Suhua. “Research on service quality system of automobile technology service enterprise based on QFD,” Value Engineering, vol.33, Nov. 2014, pp.145-147
9. Li HuaQiang, ZhangMeng “Research on QFD - based campus courier service quality,” Modern Business, vol. 15, May. 2015, pp. 258-259

Research on the Emergence Modeling of Equipment System

Xin-Hua He [1], Wei-Chao Zhang [2], Qiang Qu[3], Wan-Lin Lu [4]

[1] *Department of Information Engineering, Academy of Armored Force Engineering, Beijing, China*
[2] *Department of Information Engineering, Academy of Armored Force Engineering, Beijing, China*
[3] *Department of Information Engineering, Academy of Armored Force Engineering, Beijing, China*
[4] *Troop No.66133 of PLA, Beijing, China*
[1] *hxh717495@sina.com*, [2]*342722719@qq.com*, [3]*535565543@qq.com*, [4]*786164744 @qq.com*

Abstract: Under the conditions of information, the network-centric system and the confrontation in the system has developed into a major combat style. But the traditional line of sexual assessment method is difficult to accurately assess the information equipment system combat capability. Therefore, this paper studies the effective evaluation method of the operational capability of the information equipment system from the perspective of emerge. Based on the simulation modeling and evaluation method, building the capability model of the weapon equipment system to evaluate the operational capability of the information weapon weaponry equipment. Through the example analysis, the validity of the simulation model and the practicability of the evaluation system is analyzed by analyzing the examples.

1. Introduction

Weapons and equipment system is the basis of war-confrontation system, and it is also the basis of war system confrontation, its ability depends on the strength of the system's inherent combat capability, it is not only the sum of equipment and system combat capability, or the composition of the system structure and the composition of the interaction between the system [1], thus the emergence is the overall combat capability. However, the existing evaluation methods have many shortcomings in the evaluation of the overall emergence capability of the combat capability of the weapon equipment system. Therefore, this paper puts forward the main unit model of the combat capability of the equipment system by studying the theory of the combat capability of the weapon equipment system, by analyzing the method of multi-data association, the relationship between the principal units is judged, and building the weapon equipment system combat capability appearance model, evaluating the combat capability of it.

2. Information Weapon Equipment System Operational Ability

2.1 Brief Introduction to the Combat Ability of the Information Weapon Equipment System

Information-based weapons and equipment system combat capability is generated through the component system [2]. System within the various components of the system is a certain composition between the structure of interaction, resulting in the emergence of the effect form the whole. System combat capability is a new combat capability that emerges in this process, and these new combat capabilities are not equal to the linear sum of the original component system combat capability.

The information technology system is formed by the development of information network technology, its system combat capability generation has the characteristics of complexity, factor independence, factor synergy, overall emergence and so on.

2.2 Research Status of Combat Capability Evaluation of Weapon Equipment System

Since the birth of weapons and equipment, the calculation and evaluation of its combat capability has always been the command staff at all levels of attention. Many experts and scholars at home and abroad have made many pioneering researches on the evaluation of the combat capability of the weaponry and equipment system. In summary, the main methods of system combat capability assessment are divided into four categories: expert evaluation method, multi-index comprehensive method, test statistical method, modeling and simulation class method [3].

Expert evaluation method has the advantage of judging intuitive, less binding, easy to understand. The disadvantage is subjective and the evaluation results are not stable. The advantage of multi-index synthesis method is that the calculation model is clear、more scientific and reasonable, but the calculation model has few factors to consider, the lack of expression of the system. The advantage of the statistical method is that the evaluation results are more accurate, but it requires a large amount of statistical data to be analyzed. The advantage of the modeling and simulation method is that it takes into account the structure and interaction of the combat capability of the system, but the reliability of the simulation model is difficult to test and the computational complexity is high.

3. The Explanation of the Relevant Concept Of Emancipation

3.1 The Concept of the System Combat Capability Emerged

Emergence is a transition from low to high level [4], it is an overall emergence of the composition of the composition of the system in accordance with the structure of the interaction, and each complement, the effect is mutual restraint.

The emergence of combat capability means that the underlying combat capability is integrated and combined with a certain relationship form a new operational capability to meet the needs of operational using. It can get a higher level of combat capability through the ability of emerge, and it can also get the original capacity which not have some of the characteristics, these features will be more intuitive to show the strength of combat capability[5].

Therefore, we can give the definition from the combat capability of the weaponry and equipment system. Through the combination of the certain organizational structure and the certain level of the characteristics, the integration and combination of the combat capability of the weapon equipment system forms a new and value-added overall combat capability, so as to meet the needs of weapons and equipment system against combat.

3.2 The Mechanism of System Combat Capability Emerges

3.2.1 The Reason of System Combat Capability Emerges

The emergence of the three elements are a large number of the main body, the interaction between the main body, a group of simple rules of the conduct. The reason for the emergence of system combat capability is that in the equipment system with all kinds of equipment in the information system supports the battlefield situation sharing, coordination, interactive feedback of the system capacity.

3.2.2 The Manifestation of System Combat Capability Emerges

The operational elements within the equipment system are driven because of a common goal, dynamic, adaptive and interdependent to achieve the synergies, and the collaboration can improve the combat capability in a variety of ways. Combat elements of the coordination can be collaborative feedback. So System combat capability gets emerged in the form of performance for the combat capability of collaborative feedback, the formation is a new overall combat capability [6].

1) The Feature of System Combat Capability Emerges

Information ability is the basis of system combat capability. It is a variety of elements of centralized control, unified coordination, composed of a certain spatial structure to produce. So the interaction of a large number of elements is the reason of the emergence of system combat capability. and the performance of the system combat capability is the size and state of a factor's ability to have different degrees of feedback on the size and state of the associated factor ability.

3.3 Based on the Emerging System of Combat Capability Assessment Framework

The emergence of system combat capability is the ability of the system to a certain structural relationship. Therefore, the core of the model is to establish an effective system capacity model, unit structure model, and unit action model.

The system capacity model can reflect the characteristics of the system capacity and the process of system capacity generation. The unit structure model can accurately infer the structural relationship between the system capacity constituent elements, which indicates the occurrence of structural phenomena and the relationship between the emergence of the phenomenon. The model of unit action reflects the interaction between units, which makes the system capacity have different results.

4 Constructing The Main Unit Model Of The Bottom Combat Capability

4.1 Method of Building a Model

The main unit of the combat capability is the microscopic unit of the system combat capability, which is the foundation of the system to build the combat capability.

The method of constructing the main unit model of the bottom combat capability refers to the basic steps of constructing the required subject model and the core of the research problem. This paper refers to the CGF model, combined with the characteristics of the field of weapons and equipment system, and using a set of combat capability for its own characteristics of the main combat capability modeling method. The basic process is as follows:

Step 1: Define the domain and characteristics of the competency unit.

The ability of the main unit is an autonomous individual, characterizing a weapon equipment system combat capability behavior characteristic. These principal units generate system combat capability through cooperative relationships.

Step 2: Constructing the mapping relationship between the weapon system and capacity main unit.

From the composition of weapons and equipment

system to start, analyzing the system at all levels deeply, establish the weapons and equipment system structure to the combat capability of the main unit mapping.

Step 3: Constructing the hierarchy structure of the main unit of combat capability of weapon equipment system.

Capability unit hierarchy refers to the specific form of spatial arrangement and combination of the main body units within the system. Hierarchical combing system combat capability of the main unit, form a certain level structure.

Step 4: Judge capability unit associated structure.

The complex relationship between the elements of the equipment system is manifested as the complex relationship between the elements of the capacity. Analyze the relationship further between the main unit of the combat capability of the system, the network-like capacity of the main unit spatial structure.

Step 5: Inspection and evaluation.

To complete the establishment of a network-like system combat capability of the main unit spatial structure, inspection and correction of the main capacity of the main unit and the composition of the spatial structure of the actual impact of the actual using of weapons and equipment characteristics referring to the force drill data.

4.2 Determine the Relationship between the Main Unit of the Operational Capability of the System

The emergence of the system combat capability is the combat capability of the main unit with a certain composition and interaction of the resulting, so this article determines the weapons and equipment combat capability of the main unit relationship based on the SEM.

Step 1: Collect the sample size, the number of 10 times the unknown parameters

Step 2: Draw the RAM map, get the system combat capability of the main unit of the relationship by its topology. Then determine the estimator of the parameters in the model according to the *t* rule.

Step 3: By referring to the method of maximum likelihood method to estimate the association relation model, and then through the likelihood function $F_{ML} = \ln|\Sigma(\theta)| + tr\left[\Sigma^{-1}(\theta)S\right]$ to iterate a set of parameters θ which makes F_{ML} to reach the minimum value.

Step 4: Evaluate the model that has been obtained.

Step 5: Modify the association relationship model, modify the part that is not realistic.

5 Research on the Emergence Model Of Combat Ability of Weapon Equipment System

5.1 The Relationship Model of System Combat Capability

5.2.1 Correlation and Dynamics Model of System Combat Capability

Based on Kuramoto's coupled oscillator synchronization model to establish the system combat capability of the main unit combat collaborative dynamics model[8]:

$$\frac{d\theta_i}{dt} = \omega_i + c_{ij}\sum_{j=1}^{N} a_{ij}\sin(\theta_i - \theta_j), i = 1, 2, \cdots$$

The state of the combat capability subject unit i changing with time can be described by the phase parameter $\theta_i(t)$. Its operational command cycle is $T_i = 2\pi/\omega_i$, $A = (a_{ij}) \in R^{N\times N}$ is its adjacency matrix, if there is an association between the competency unit *i* and *j*, then $a_{ij} = a_{ji} = 1$; else $a_{ij} = a_{ji} = 0$, c_{ij} is the correlation strength between the capability main unit i and j.

5.2.2 System Combat Capability Correlation Relation Interaction *Model*

In the combat capability of the main unit weapons and equipment system shows that a combat capability of the main unit of another one of the gain or inhibition to the interaction relationship [9].According to the combat capability of the main unit of the feedback to characterize the impact of coordination on the system combat capability. When the combat capability C_1 and C_2 mutual get influence, the combat capability gets changed, the expression is as follows:

$$C_2' = \begin{cases} C_2 + \Delta t_1, \rho \geq \sigma_2 \\ C_2, \sigma_1 \leq \rho < \sigma_2 \\ C_2 - \Delta t_2, \rho < \sigma_1 \end{cases}$$

Where Δt is the relationship between the feedback effect, ρ is the degree of correlation between the ability of the main unit, Define the degree of association of the main unit of combat capability is $\rho_{ij}(t) = \langle\cos\left[\theta_j(t) - \theta_i(t)\right]\rangle, -1 \leq \rho_{ij} \leq 1, [\sigma_1, \sigma_2]$ is the degree of association. When the degree of association exceeds the threshold, the combat capability C_2 has an enhanced effect; otherwise, there is a decay effect, the degree of coordination in a range of combat capability C_2 remain unchanged.

5.2 A New Model that Similar to the Cellular Automata Model

On the basis of cellular automata, combined with the demand for the emergence of weapons and equipment system combat capability, make the finite discrete state setting extend to the continuous space, and an improved cellular automata model is established.

Define an improved continuous space cellular automata model, it can be represented by a five-tuple: $A^+ = (L, S_d, N^+, \theta, f)$, where L represents the set of cells in the spatial structure; S_d represents the continuous space of the cell state values. In the cellular automata, the cell state value is infinite continuous space, where *d* is the state space dimension; N^+ is the neighbor of the cell; θ is the phase of the cell; f is the state evolution function of the cell, cell's phase changed rules and cellular state transition rules.

Compared with the traditional cellular automata, the continuous space cellular automata redefine the spatial range of the cell neighbors, and extends to the infinite continuous space from the original mesh space, making it more suitable for the non-discrete system model establishment.

5.3 Emergence Model of Cellular Automata in Continuous Space

5.3.1 Cell's Unit

Definition: In the associated cell automata model which in the system combat capability emerges, the main unit of system combat capability is the system combat capability of the cells, C_i is the *i*th cell, and the cell space composed of all the cells is *L*, so $C_i \in L$, $i = 1, 2, \cdots$.

5.3.2 Cell's State

In the association automata model which is defined in this paper, the unit of the system combat capability is the individual of the cell, and the combat capability value is the state value of the cell. The cell state value is the continuous value in the one-dimensional space. Therefore, the state value of the main unit of the system combat capability is the cell state which is essentially the value of the combat capability, and S is the continuous space of all the cell states. In this paper, S takes the interval $[0,10]$.

5.3.3 Cell's Neighbors

The neighbors of the capability cells are associated with the cells' phase changed and the state transition has an impact on all cell sets, that are the combat capability of the main unit of the combat capability.

5.3.4 Evolution Rules of Cellular States

The evolution of the associated cell system requires two conditions: the initial state of the cell and the evolution rules. The following show the evolution of the state of the cells:

1. Changing rules of the cell's phase

$$\frac{d\theta_i}{dt} = \omega_i + c_{ij} \sum_{j=1}^{N} \sin(\theta_i - \theta_j), i = 1, 2, \cdots$$

In the formula, the phase value of cell i is θ_i, which is determined by the influence of its own operational command cycle $T_i = 2\pi/\omega_i$, and the influence of the relevant neighbor *N*. c_{ij} is the correlation intensity between cell *i* and *j*.

2.The transferring rules of cellular states

$$s_{t+1}^i = s_0^i + \sum_{j=1}^{N} \lambda_{ij} \rho_{ij}$$

In the formula, the state of cell *i* at time *t + 1* is determined by the correlation between its initial state s_0^i and its neighbor *N*. ρ is the degree of correlation between cell units , where $\rho_{ij}(t) = \langle \cos[\theta_j(t) - \theta_i(t)] \rangle$ and $-1 \le \rho_{ij} \le 1$, λ_{ij} is the correlation coefficient.

1) Evolution Rules of Cellular Systems

Continuous space cellular-automata simulation weapon equipment system combat capability according to the relationship between its neighbors, the specific process is as follows:

Step 1: Construct the cellular automata model, configures the spatial environment of the cell, set the neighbor of the cell and specifies the evolution rule of the cell's state.

Step 2: Initialize the initial state value of the cell's body.

Step 3: Define the end of the system evolution, and define the critical value σ.

Step 4: Set the initial time for the evolution of the system T_0.

Step 5: Calculate the state-value of the cell's state at a certain time according to the state evolution rule.

Step 6:Calculate the amount of change Δ in the state-value of a cell.

Step 7: Determine whether the system termination condition is less than σ, then jump to Step8, otherwise Step5.

Step 8: Stop the simulation of system, and output the combat capability cells' state-values.

6 The Effectiveness Validation Of The Emerging Model

6.1 Emergence Model of Cellular Automata in Continuo

Taking the weapon system of a military digitizer as an

DOI: 10.1051/itmconf/20171204001

example, through the decomposition of combat capability, the weapon system of the army digitizer is composed of the investigation intelligence system, command and control system, comprehensive security system, fire power system, tactical communication system, electronic warfare system. According to the steps of modeling the combat capability unit of weapon equipment system, construct the main unit model of combat, and the data processing software of SEM is used to process the data, then judge the relationship between the main elements of weapon equipment combat capability.

6.2 Simulation of the Model

6.2.1 Experiment 1: Compare with the Traditional Modeling Methods

Aiming at the change of the combat capability of the weapon system after the information transformation, and then evaluate the combat capability of the system by using the correlation model and the traditional non - emergence model, and then compare the evaluation results of the two methods. The following methods are used to assess the combat capability of the Army digitizer's weaponry system:

(1) Assess the combat capability of the information weapons and equipment system through the relationship between the emerging model;

(2) Assess the combat capability of the information weapons and equipment system through the traditional non - emerging model;

The concrete results are shown in the figure 1 and figure 2.

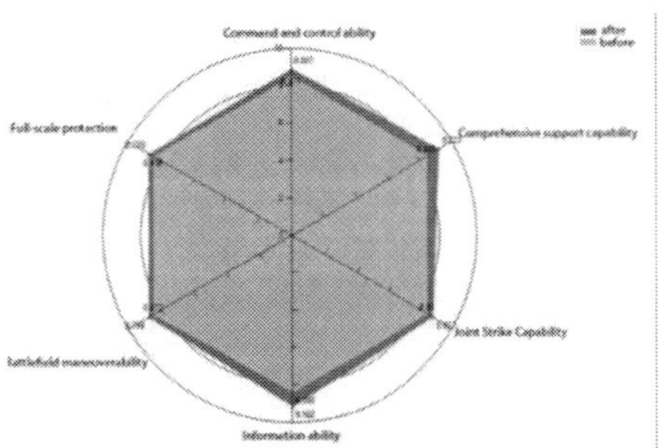

Figure 1. Combat capability contrast picture

Figure 1 shows the contrast of the system combat capability before and after the emergence. Figure 2 shows the compare of the ability of the weapons and equipment system before and after the emergence.

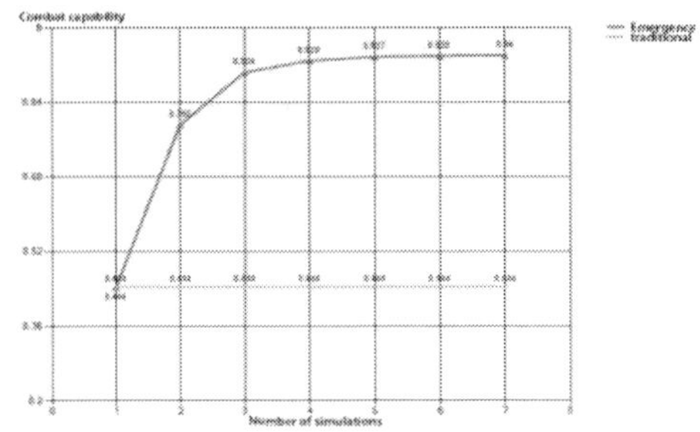

Figure 2. Combat capability contrast picture

It can be seen from Fig. 1 and 2 that the combat capability of the association model is higher than the traditional non-emerging model for the information weapon system. Therefore, information technology is helpful to improve the degree of combat capability, and the capabilities affect each other. So the model is used to evaluate the combat capability value higher than the traditional non-emerging model.

After the demand-demonstration and simulation-exercises of the weapons and equipment, the division of the weapons and equipment system combat capability is assessed as 9.461 by the experts. Using the traditional non-emergence model simulation, due to the neglect of the relationship between the system capacity and the lack of combat capability associated with the emergence of the assessment, the result is 8.479, the result of the association model presented in this paper is 9.201, which is more practical.

6.2.2 Experiment 2: Analyze the Sensitivity of the Key Combat Capability

Considering the characteristics of the information system combat capability, this paper analyzes the sensitivity of the key operational capability in the system, that is the impact of key operational capability on the overall combat capability of the system, which reflects the validity of the model, the following experiments were conducted:

(1) for the digital transformation of the weapons and equipment system, analysis the sensitivity of the command and control ability;

(2) for the digital transformation of the weapons and equipment system, analysis the sensitivity of the information ability.

The concrete results are shown in the figure 3.

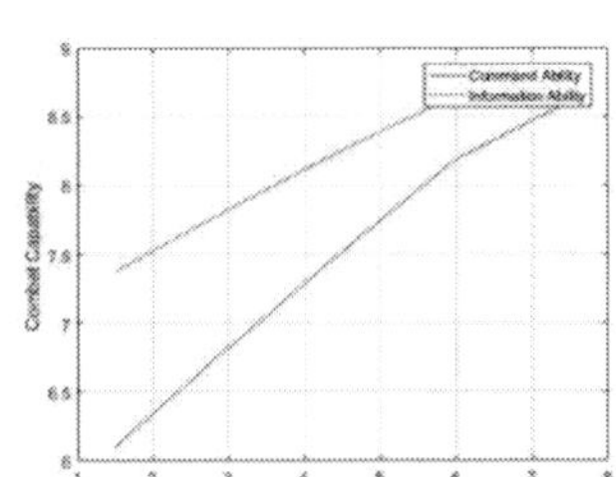

Figure 3. Analysis of sensitivity of key operational capability

From the experimental results of the two experiments, we can see that: to the overall combat capability of the system, is a non-linear relationship. Through the experimental data, we can find that the model of the correlation relationship in this paper considers the interaction between the combat capability of the system and it is a non-linear evaluation method. Therefore, the model of the correlation relationship proposed can reflect the characteristics truly of the combat capability of the weapon system and the real situation of the combat capability.

7 Conclusion

This paper takes the evaluation model of the combat capability of weapon equipment system as a research object, and establishes a model of combat capability based on an improved cellular automaton, and deeply studies the simulation of the operational capability of weapon equipment system, then builds the weapon unit system combat capability main unit model.

However, the model is a very complex problem, the emerging model of the operational capability of the system is only a meaningful exploration, there are many shortcomings, and is needed to continue to study the mechanism and the form of expression. The weapons and equipment system of information will consider more and more external factors and forms of expression, so as to further refine and understand the emerging phenomenon.

References

[10]-of-Systems[M], 2011: 1-16.

[1] Charles Domercant, Jean, Mavris, Dimitri N. Measuring the architectural complexity of military Systems-of-Systems[C]//Proceedings of IEEE Conference, 2011.

[2] Li Guoyi, Meng Fanliang, Dong Zhengbao, et al. Modeling for military system by weighted complex networks[C]//Proceedings of 2010 8th IEEE International Conference on Control and Automation(ICCA), 2010.

[3] Stenner Jr, Charles E. Command making progress toward achieving full operational capability[J]. Citizen Airman, 2011, 63(3): 2-2.

[4] John Holland. Emerging [M]. Shanghai: Shanghai Science and Technology Education Press, 2001.

[5] Charles Domercant, Jean, Mavris, Dimitri N. Measuring the architectural complexity of military Systems-of-Systems[C]//Proceedings of IEEE Conference, 2011.

[6] Albert Network Center Warfare and Complexity Theory [M]. Electronic Industry Press, 2004: 69-79.

[7] LUO Xiao-ming, ZHU Yan-lei, HE Rong. Study on Contribution Evaluation of Weapon Equipment Combat System Based on SEM [J]. Equipment College, 2015,26 (5): 1-6.

[8] Kalloniatis A, Fairbairn D E. A new paradigm for dynamical modelling of networked C2 processes[C]. Proceeding of the 13th International Command and Control Research and Technology Symposium. 2008: 17-19.

[9] Domercant J C, Mavris D N. Measuring the architectural complexity of military Systems

DOI: 10.1051/itmconf/20171204002

A Chinese Named Entity Recognition System with Neural Networks

[1]Hui-Kang Yi, [2]Jiu-Ming Huang, [3]Shu-Qiang Yang

[1]National University of Defense Technology School of Computer Science, Changsha, Hunan, 410073, China
[2]National University of Defense Technology School of Computer Science, Changsha, Hunan, 410073, China
[3]National University of Defense Technology School of Computer Science Changsha, Hunan, 410073, China
[1]huikangyi@gmail.com

Abstract: Named entity recognition (NER) is a typical sequential labeling problem that plays an important role in natural language processing (NLP) systems. In this paper, we discussed the details of applying a comprehensive model aggregating neural networks and conditional random field (CRF) on Chinese NER tasks, and how to discovery character level features when implement a NER system in word level. We compared the difference between Chinese and English when modeling the character embeddings. We developed a NER system based on our analysis, it works well on the ACE 2004 and SIGHAN bakeoff 2006 MSRA dataset, and doesn't rely on any gazetteers or handcraft features. We obtained F1 score of 82.3% on MSRA 2006.

1. Introduction

Named entity recognition (NER) is a subtask of Information Extraction (IE), and its performance is vital to the related tasks like entity coreference resolution and entity relationship extraction. These essential text processing tasks are import steps to deep language understanding systems.

NER task shares similar modeling approach with other sequential labeling problems (SLPs) like word segmentation, Part-of-Speech tagging (POS). a SLP system is to generate corresponding tag sequence giving the token sequences. Before the rise of Neural Networks, most popular SLP systems were modeled with probabilistic graph (statistical model), including hidden Markov modeling (HMM), maximum entropy modeling (ME), and conditional random field (CRF) [1]. For example, the widely-used Stanford NER kit [2] is trained at dataset CoNLL 2003 [3] with CRF. Most high-performance statistical models rely heavily on carefully hand-craft features, especially in Chinese files. And many of they are task-specific, so that they are difficult to adjust to new datasets or domains.

NER tasks is very challenging for two main reasons: 1) lack of well-tagged training data. the widely used NER benchmark CoNLL 2003 contains only 14,987 sentences, 204,567 tokens. 2) Comparing to other SLPs, the construct of an entity name is rather complicated. a name can be very long or very short; any word can be a name with few constraints. So NER systems normally gain lower F1 scores than word segmentation, POS tagging. And for Chinese NER task, the situation can be even more rough (see section II).

To overcome the limitation of well-tagged data, unsupervised learning methods are designed to give better generalization from small amounts of training data. As neural networks arise, SLP Modeling with neural networks draws people's attention. Collobert at al. [4] proposed a convolutional neural network (CNN) based models for SLPs. Also, recurrent neural networks (RNN) [5] and its variants such as long-short Term memory (LSTM) [6] are widely used in NLP tasks. LSTM can learn long distance dependencies for text processing. Huang et al. [7] developed a general sequential tagging model combining bidirectional Recurrent Neural Networks (RNNs) and CRFs, which achieves near state-of-the-art results on both POS and NER. Lample et al. [8] gives a more specific implementation of neural network model for NER tasks, their model introduced pretrained word embeddings from large corpus, and gives F1 scores of 90.97% on CoNLL 2003 dataset using no context features or spelling features. Ma et al. [9] combines Chiu's CNN model [10] and Lample's bidirectional LSTM-CRF model [8] for end-to-end SLPs. These models use neural networks strategies and/or pretrained word embeddings to give better generalization performance. And meanwhile, they show how far a NER system can go, without carefully designed hand-craft features.

In this paper, we mainly focus on two parts to adapt the neural network models for Chinese NER tasks: 1) discovery character level features for a word-level NER system; 2) train better word embeddings for Chinese NER tasks. We discussed details of Chinese NER systems (Section II) by comparing; how to train word embeddings (Section III) and use neural network and CRFs to model context dependencies.

2. Chinese Named Entity Recognition Tasks

A typical SLP, takes text sequence $\mathbf{X} = (x_1, x_2 \cdots, x_n)$ as input, and corresponding tag sequence $\mathbf{y} = (y_1, y_2 \cdots, y_n)$ as output. The goal of SLP is to establish the conditional probability model $\mathrm{P}(\mathbf{y}|\mathbf{X})$. For NER tasks, the output sequence $\mathbf{y}$ are the corresponding named entity types, such as *person, location, organization* and etc.

2.1 Challenges of Chinese NER

Comparing the English and other west languages, NER tasks for Chinese text face more challenges for some reason: 1) The concept of Chinese words is not clear and can't not be define with a universal standard. Chinese words are not separated by spaces; 2) English text have obvious features can indicate an entity name, like capitalized terms and different tense and article words, but Chinese words never change in all kinds of tense or part-of-speech; 3) Almost every Chinese character can be part of an entity name, so we can't build a vocabulary for each kind of entity type.

2.2 Word Segmentation and NER

Chinese character is the minimum lexical struct of texts. There are only 26 different English letters in total (regardless of case), but there are thousands of Chinese common characters. Chinese words, usually composed of several characters, that semantically related to the word. Take word "电脑" (computer) for example, character "电" means electricity or electronic and "脑" means brain. And the combination "电脑" (electronic brain) is used to describe the electronic machine that works like brains (computer). But for some words like transliterated words, their inner characters give mainly phonetic meaning and contribute no semantical features. Chinese word "巧克力" (chocolate) is a such typical transliterated word.

Chinese named entities are word-level. Normally, we perform word segmentation before. Word segmentation is also a SLP, and can be solved with similar model [11]. Ng et al. [12] discussed two approaches for the word segmentation issue in POS tasks: 1) performing NER tasks strictly after word segmentation (one-at-a-time); 2) performing word segmentation and NER tasks at same time (all-at-once). There are two challenges applying our model in character level regardless word segmentation: 1) an entity name can be much longer than a word in POS task; So high performance of parsing very long distance context dependencies required; 2) The ACE 2004 dataset, that we used for training, contains so many transliterated words; So character-based modeling is not suitable, instead, we considered introducing the character-level features in the word embedding layer.

3. Modeling

Our neural network modeling for named entity recognition task is similar to Lample et al. [8] and Chiu et al. [10]. We designed different heuristic function as loss of our model and compared two different word embedding model for Chinese NER dataset.

3.1 Word Embedding Layer

Pretrained word embeddings can improve model's performance comparing to random initial vectors [4]. Lample's [8] best results (F1 scores of 91.2 on CoNLL 2003 English training set) also generated with the model using pretrained word embedding from large corpus. In this part, we compared two different word embedding modeling approach: Skip-Gram [13] and CWE [14]. these two model improves performance significantly over randomly initialized vectors. CWE model is developed from the continuous Bag-of-Words model (CBOW), and it takes account the internal information of characters into Chinese words.

Chen [14] raised two challenges of character-word joint model for Chinese word embedding that could also happen in NER task: 1) A Chinese character might have various semantic meanings in different words; 2) Not all Chinese words are semantically compositional, such as transliterated words. In the area of similar tasks like POS, Ng et al. [12] found that character-based modeling slightly outperforms word-based ones and avoids biases introduced by word segmentation. But in our experiment, the character-based model didn't show its odds. We built our model in word-level and use pre-trained word embeddings trained by Skip-Gram model or CWE.

3.2 Neural Network for Encoding

Long short-term memory (LSTM), a kind of implementation RNN, is designed to combat the issue that RNN always fail to learn long dependencies in practice by introducing a memory-cell [6, 15]. Our encoding model is very close to Lample's [8]; a forward LSTM layer to encode input sequences from start to end and a backward LSTM layer to do the same in reverse. And for the concatenated outputs of LSTM layers, using another hidden layer before the next step (decoding) can improves performance obviously, see Figure. (1).

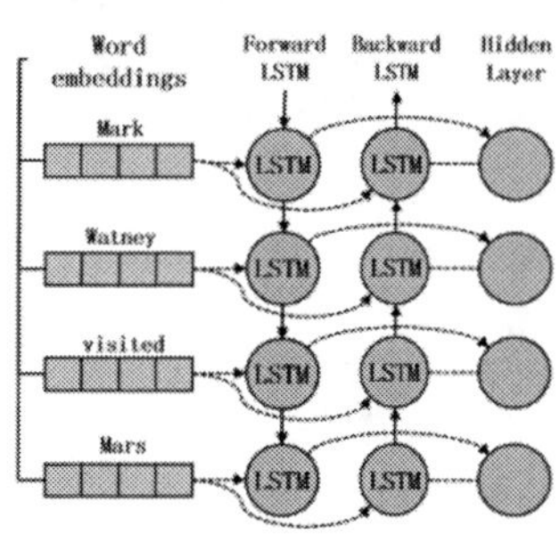

Figure 1. Bi-directional LSTMs with an extra hidden layer

3.3 Decoding Layer and Loss Function

We use Conditional Random Field (CRF) for decoding. For a input sentence

$$\mathbf{X} = (x_1, x_2 \cdots, x_n)$$

and a sequence of predictions

$$\mathbf{y} = (x_1, x_2 \cdots, x_n)$$

consider matrix **P** of size $n \times k$, where k is the number of distinct tags, $P_{i,j}$ corresponds to the score of the jth tag of the ith word in a sentence. And matrix **A** of size $k \times k$ is the matrix of transition scores, where $A_{i,j}$ represents the score of a transition from the tag i to tag j . We minimize the average log probability of the target words and log sum of transition costs:

$$\text{loss} = -\left(\frac{1}{N}\sum_{i=1}^{N} \ln P_{i,y_i} + c\frac{1}{N-1}\sum_{i=1}^{N-1} \ln A_{y_i,y_{i+1}}\right) \quad (1)$$

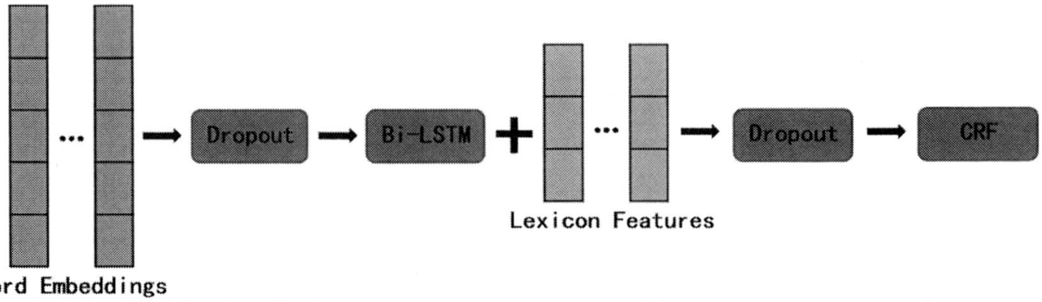

Figure 2. Order of Modeling Parts. Blue box represents process on the vectors; "+" means append a vector to another

In the experiment, we compared our loss function to the log
transition costs:

$$\text{loss} = -\left(\frac{1}{N}\sum_{i=1}^{N} \ln P_{i,y_i} + c\frac{1}{N-1}\sum_{i=1}^{N-1} \ln A_{y_i,y_{i+1}}\right) \quad (1)$$

In the experiment, we compared our loss function to the log likelihood function [1] Lample [8] used, our function gives better convergence efficiency. We also tested softmax function for decoding. in this way, only unary features are modeled, the loss function (equation. (1) becomes

$$\text{loss} = -\frac{1}{N}\sum_{i=1}^{N} \ln P_{i,y_i}$$

which is same as Mikolov et al. [13]. we use a simple greedy algorithm to get our prediction

$$y_i^* = arg \max_j P_{i,j}$$

and use viterbi algorithm to get prediction when using CRF to decode.

3.4 Lexicon Features

We didn't use any gazetteer to construct the lexicon features. Instead, we used the character-level statistics in training set only. We denote a Chinese character as c, a Chinese word as w , and w^j represents the jth character in the word w, function Tag(w) returns the entity type of word w. We count the how often every character that appears in different entity types k

$$Count_{k,j} = \sum_{c} \sum_{w, Tag(w)=k} Appear(c, w, j)$$

Where

$$Appear(c, w, j) = \begin{cases} 1, & if\ c = w^j \\ 0, & if\ c \neq w^j \end{cases}$$

then we use the sum of frequency of characters appearing in each tag as the lexicon features of words. We specified the offset of characters in a word, to expect giving more position related inner information to the model.

3.5 Order of Layers and Dropout

Technically, the word embeddings layer, bi-directional LSTM layer, lexicon features, are steps of feature modeling and they work independently. Word embedding gives semantic features; LSTM layer is used to modeling features of context dependency based on word embeddings; lexicon features is complement for character-level features. few experiments show that appending lexicon features between LSTM layer and decoding layer, out-performs other order of the feature processing layer. To avoid the model biases on one type of features over another, we apply a dropout mask before the LSTM layer and before the decoding layer. see Figure. (2)

3.6 Tagging Scheme

An entity mention refers to a single word or several continuous words in texts, so an informative tagging schemes is needed. Ratinov et al. [16] and Dai et al. [17] shows that, the schemes who give more information (BILOU for example), significantly outperforms BIO tagging scheme. But recent published NER systems include lamples' [8], did not observe a significant improvement from BIO to BILOU scheme. We accepted BILOU as our tagging scheme though all the experiments.

[1] provided by tensorflow 0.12.0

4. Experiment

4.1 Pretrained Word Embeddings

Based on the analysis in Section III, we use Wikipedia [18] as our backend corpus for training word embeddings. the original Wikipedia of articles include both simplified Chinese and traditional Chinese, we use *opencc* [2] to convert all the traditional Chinese text to simplified and deleted all the non-Chinese characters (most of they are reserved words of xml-format files). the Wikipedia dataset we used contains 260,969,652 characters, we filtered low-frequency words (mincount=5) and got a vocabulary of size 722,226. the embedding we used has dimension of 100.

the CWE model for word embedding requires a word list about transliterated words manually, we use the pre-trained embeddings (dimension=300) they provide instead.

4.2 Dataset Processing

The ACE 2004 dataset [19] consists news texts of three different languages: *Arabic, Chinese, English*. We use the Chinese data to evaluate our model. the original data (Chinese part) contains 314 files of broadcast news, 226 files of newswire and 106 files of Chinese Treebank. ACE 2004 dataset is for Automatic Content Extraction (ACE) technology evaluation. There are 6 types of named entities in ACE 2004: *FAC, GPE, LOC, ORG, PER, VEH*. We reorganized the data for NER tasks through few steps: 1) 1. get texts from *.xml* files and entity mentions and their offset; 2) use word segmentation tool [3] to get token sequence and get corresponding tag sequence; 3) let first 80% files be the training data, following 10% be the validation set, and last 10% be the test. By now, we obtained three different datasets *(bnews, Chinese Treebank, nwire)* for NER tasks.

We also tested our model on SIGHAN bakeoff 2006 Named Entity Recognition MSRA (MSRA 2006) task dataset. There are three types of named entities: *person, location, organization*. the training data of MSRA 2006 is well segmented but the test data is plain text. We rearrange the training data to plain text and applying *jieba* to segment the text (both training dataset and test dataset) into word sequence. So that our model would not biases by different word segmentation methods, since *jieba* tends to give slightly longer tokens.

And For all the data we used, we replaced all digits with zeros.

4.3 Traning Setting

For input data, we add two masks $<\mathrm{BOS}>$ (Beginning of sentence) and $<\mathrm{EOS}>$(end of sentence) to every sentence, so that $\mathbf{X}=(<\mathrm{BOS}>, x_1, x_2 \cdots, x_n, <\mathrm{EOS}>)$. the corresponding tag of the two mask are *U-BOS*, *U-EOS*. Then we concatenate these sentences to form our input data (A sequence of words) and cut the input sequence into lines with fixed length (=35). Our model was trained by these lines with a batch size of 20.

We compared two kinds of LSTM cells in the bi-directional LSTM layers: GRU [20], BasicLSTM [21]. Model with these two different cells give very close results, our conclusion results are all generated with a BasicLSTM cell. Increase number of layers in bidirectional LSTM doesn't improve the performance and cost more time, we use a single layer in bi-LSTMs. Before feeding word embeddings into LSTMs, we apply a dropout mask with a keep probability of 0.5.

Out model was built on Tensor flow (version=0.12.0)[4]. For all the data we used, we use *conlleval* [5] to evaluate our model in a word level.

The time for training a model is limited to 4 hours for ACE 2004 datasets and 6 hours for MSRA 2006, since we didn't observed improvement through long hours training. In fact, we found training with the loss function 1 gives same scores (statistically) comparing to log likelihood function [8] with much faster convergence efficiency.

4.4 Results

As a final experiment, we have trained our system on 4 different datasets for Chinese NER task.

Table I shows the results of different model on MSRA 2006. A single CRF parsing with only word embeddings gives poorly scores; But the CRF layer gives an increase of +3.13, while using bi-directional LSTM encoding to encode the word embeddings; Our lexicon features are extracted within the training data, it's boost to the performance is very limited. Using dropout resulted in a difference of +1.51. In fact, one dropout layer before the bi-directional LSTM layer can improve the scores significantly, we applied a dropout layer when join the lexicon features and outputs of LSTMs.

Table II shows our model's performance on different dataset. All three ACE 2004 datasets are from international political news. Our model could barely recognize the *WEA*s (weapon), especially on the Chinese treebank dataset whose size is smallest). but it achieved a F1 score of 89.87 recognizing *person* names on ACE 2004 *bnews* dataset.

Table1. Different Models on Sighan Bakeoff Msra 2006

Model	F1/dev	F1/test
CRF	57.33	56.22
Bi-LSTM+Softmax	77.81	76.94
Bi-LSTM+CRF	81.56	80.07
Bi-LSTM+Lexicon+CRF	81.13	80.79
Bi-LSTM+Lexicon+CRF+Dropout	82.42	82.30

[2] http://opencc.byvoid.com/

[3] Jieba: https://github.com/fxsjy/jieba. In this step, we applied word segmentation after we got the boundaries of entity mentions, so jieba won't bring any boundary error for the next NER task

[4] https://www.tensorflow.org

[5] http://lcg-www.uia.ac.be/conll2000/chunking/

 DOI: 10.1051/itmconf/20171204002

Table2. Full Model on Different Dataset

Dataset	Vocab	Tokens	F1
ACE2004 *bnews*	12,824	62,671	79.55
ACE2004 *Chinese Treebank*	5,857	24,688	78.79
ACE2004 *nwire*	12,662	61,070	79.48
MSRA 2006	72,821	1,240,945	82.30

5. Conclusion

In this Paper, we discussed details of applying a neural architecture for Chinese named entity recognition tasks. Comparing to English NER tasks, we dressed the issue of extracting Chinese character level features and compared with POS tasks. It is meaningful to model the characteristics and contexts with appropriate model and gradually abandon the handcraft features for NLP tasks such as named entity recognition. We presented a simple model for Chinese NER that combines recently published neural network models. And it doesn't rely on any hand-craft features. Several popular NER system for English [4, 8, 9, 10] uses CNNs or LSTMs to model character level features. In our next step, we will continue our study, from a linguistic point of view, on modeling Chinese characteristics with neural networks to improve our model's performance.

Acknowledgement

The work described in this paper is partially supported by The National Key Research and Development Program of China (2016QY03D0601, 2016QY03D0603) and National Natural Science Foundation of China (No.61502517, No.61672020, No.61662069).

References

[1] John Lafferty, Andrew McCallum, Fernando Pereira, et al. Conditional random fields: Probabilistic models for segmenting and labeling sequence data. In Proceedings of the eighteenth international conference on machine learning, ICML, volume 1, pages 282–289, 2001.

[2] Jenny Rose Finkel, Trond Grenager, and Christopher Manning. Incorporating non-local information into information extraction systems by gibbs sampling. In Proceedings of the 43rd annual meeting on association for computational linguistics, pages 363–370. Association for Computational Linguistics, 2005.

[3] Erik F Tjong Kim Sang and Fien De Meulder. Introduction to the conll-2003 shared task: Language-independent named entity recognition. In Proceedings of the seventh conference on Natural language learning at HLT-NAACL 2003-Volume 4, pages 142–147. Association for Computational Linguistics, 2003.

[4] Ronan Collobert, Jason Weston, Leon Bottou, Michael Karlen, Koray Kavukcuoglu, and Pavel Kuksa. Natural language processing (almost) from scratch. Journal of Machine Learning Research, 12(Aug):2493– 2537, 2011.

[5] Christoph Goller and Andreas Kuchler. Learning task-dependent distributed representations by backpropagation through structure. In Neural Networks, 1996., IEEE International Conference on, volume 1, pages 347–352. IEEE, 1996.

[6] Sepp Hochreiter and Jurgen Schmidhuber. Long short-term memory. ¨ Neural computation, 9(8):1735–1780, 1997.

[7] Zhiheng Huang, Wei Xu, and Kai Yu. Bidirectional lstm-crf models for sequence tagging. arXiv preprint arXiv:1508.01991, 2015.

[8] Guillaume Lample, Miguel Ballesteros, Sandeep Subramanian, Kazuya Kawakami, and Chris Dyer. Neural architectures for named entity recognition. arXiv preprint arXiv:1603.01360, 2016.

[9] Xuezhe Ma and Eduard Hovy. End-to-end sequence labeling via bidirectional lstm-cnns-crf. arXiv preprint arXiv:1603.01354, 2016.

[10] Jason PC Chiu and Eric Nichols. Named entity recognition with bidirectional lstm-cnns. arXiv preprint arXiv:1511.08308, 2015.

[11] Koth. kcws. https://github.com/koth/kcws, 2016.

[12] Hwee Tou Ng and Jin Kiat Low. Chinese part-of-speech tagging: Oneat-a-time or all-at-once? word-based or character-based? In EMNLP, pages 277–284, 2004.

[13] Tomas Mikolov, Kai Chen, Greg Corrado, and Jeffrey Dean. Efficient estimation of word representations in vector space. arXiv preprint arXiv:1301.3781, 2013.

[14] Xinxiong Chen, Lei Xu, Zhiyuan Liu, Maosong Sun, and Huan-Bo Luan. Joint learning of character and word embeddings. In IJCAI, pages 1236–1242, 2015.

[15] Yoshua Bengio, Patrice Simard, and Paolo Frasconi. Learning longterm dependencies with gradient descent is difficult. IEEE transactions on neural networks, 5(2):157–166, 1994.

[16] Lev Ratinov and Dan Roth. Design challenges and misconceptions in named entity recognition. In Proceedings of the Thirteenth Conference on Computational Natural Language Learning, pages 147–155. Association for Computational Linguistics, 2009.

[17] Hong-Jie Dai, Po-Ting Lai, Yung-Chun Chang, and Richard Tzong-Han Tsai. Enhancing of chemical compound and drug name recognition using representative tag scheme and fine-grained tokenization. Journal of cheminformatics, 7(1):S14, 2015.

[18] Wikipedia:Database download, 2017 (accessed April 4, 2017). https://dumps.wikimedia.org/zhwiki/latest/zhwiki-latest-pages-articles. xml.bz2.

[19] Shudong Huang Ramez Zakhary Alexis Mitchell, Stephanie Strassel. Ace 2004 multilingual training corpus ldc2005t09. Web Download., 2005.

[20] Kyunghyun Cho, Bart Van Merrienboer, Caglar Gulcehre, Dzmitry Bah- ¨ danau, Fethi Bougares, Holger Schwenk, and Yoshua Bengio. Learning phrase representations using rnn encoder-decoder for statistical machine translation. arXiv preprint arXiv:1406.1078, 2014.

[21] Wojciech Zaremba, Ilya Sutskever, and Oriol Vinyals. Recurrent neural network regularization. arXiv preprint arXiv:1409.2329, 2014.

Collective Entity Linking Method in Chinese Text Based on Topic Consistency

Yi Chen, Qingbo Wu, Yusong Tan, Wei Wang

School of Computer, National University of Defense Technology, Changsha, China 0731
chenyi15a@nudt.edu.cn, wuqingbo@ubuntukylin.com, tanyusong@kylinos.cn, wangwei15a@nudt.edu.cn

Abstract: Entity Linking refers to the task of linking entity mentions in the given text with their referent entities in a knowledge base, which is a key technology of knowledge base expansion. However, the performance of traditional Chinese entity linking methods are affected by the incomplete Chinese knowledge base. Also they rarely use the semantic relevance between entities. Therefore, we propose a Chinese collective entity linking method based on the consistency of the topic, which considers both the content similarity and topic relevance of the co-occurrence entities, and propose a method for calculating the topic consistency of entities. This method implements batch links for multiple ambiguous entities that appear in the same text, and reduces the reliance on the local knowledge base by using the combination of the local knowledge base and the external knowledge base. Experimental results show that our method performs well over the traditional methods. And it is potentially effective.

1. Introduction

Nowadays, we are in such an era of information explosion. How to effectively obtain valuable information from massive network data is a hot research problem in the field of Internet information extraction technology. The main problems are the diversity and ambiguity of natural language. The diversity of natural language refers to that the same meaning can be expressed in many different forms. This is due to the elasticity of expression of natural language. E.g., people call Kobe Bryant for Peter Pan, Ke God and so on. As for the ambiguity of the natural language, it means that the same word, phrase, or sentence have different meanings in different contexts. Because of the existence of ambiguity and ambiguity, it is difficult for the users to retrieve the relevant information of the target entity quickly and accurately when searching the information on the network [1].

Entity linking provides a solution for the both problems above. It mainly focuses on the representation of the entity in the text, and links the entity representation of the text in the natural language with the entries in the knowledge base [2]. If the page is pre-processed in the way of entity linking, the user can quickly and accurately find the relevant information of the corresponding entity. The application area of entity linking is relatively broad, and is applied to the knowledge base expansion, open field online knowledge question answering system, information filtering and information retrieval, machine translation and online advertising, etc [3] [4]. The existing research contributions of entity linking are mainly in English. In contrast, the development of Chinese entity linking technology is somewhat lagging behind. The main reasons are as follow. Firstly, the construction of Chinese open source knowledge base is in the initial stage, which restricts the development of Chinese entity linking work. Secondly, entity extraction technology is constrained by the word segmentation technology. Thirdly, as the Chinese grammar is more flexible, and the semantics is more abundant, which make Chinese entity disambiguation more difficult than English [5]. The current mainstream entity linking method is the context similarity between an entity reference term and its corresponding candidate entity, and the candidate entity with the highest similarity is the link target. This approach does not take into account the semantic relevance of the entities in the text, which leads to the waste of information and the decrease of the accuracy of entity linking.

In this paper, a Chinese collective entity linking method based on topic consistency is proposed. In our method we model each entity mention in the given text and its candidate entity as distinct nodes in a graph, and model topic consistency by links between nodes. We call this graph topic relation graph. For the entity mentions to be linked, we extract the topic of the contexts of the mentions. Finally, the candidate entities we choose are the most relevant to the topic of the given text. So we calculate the topic consistency between the context of the mention and the Baidu encyclopedia page of the candidate entity to determine the weight of the edge of mention to candidate entity firstly. And then we calculate the topic relevance between the candidate entities corresponding to different mentions. Finally, we transform the problem of entity linking into the topic consistency order problem of the candidate entity using the integration algorithm, and choose a set of candidate entities with the highest degree of topic consistency and content similarity as the target of entity linking.

The main contributions of this paper are summarized as follows. The topic relation graph we proposed takes into account both the content similarity and the subject relevance, and uses the collective algorithm of the batch link, to improve the accuracy and efficiency of the link. In the process of constructing the topic relation graph, for the construction of Chinese knowledge base incomplete problem, we combining the local knowledge with external knowledge to reduce the dependence on local knowledge base effectively. The experiment results show that our method achieve dramatic accuracy and recall rate. We conclude that the proposed entity linking method is potentially effective.

The rest parts are organized as follows: We introduce the related works in section 2. In section 3, we describe our linking method in detail, and provide the experimental results and evaluation in section 4. Section 5 is a conclusion.

2. Related Work

As an important basic research value for the expansion of knowledge base, entity linking technology has received extensive attention in academia in recent years. Early entity linking work is focused on a single entity. With the development of a series of collective entity linking methods, this method has become a research hotspot.

The idea of early entity linking research is to select the candidate entity with the largest similarity as the target object, by calculating the context similarity between the text of the entity mention and its corresponding candidate entity. The typical work is a computational model based on context similarity proposed by Bunescu, which has attracted much attention in the similarity computation method [6]. Nguyen adds the contextual characteristics and the page structure of the candidate entity in the Wikipedia page to calculate the similarity, thus effectively improving the accuracy [7]. However the accuracy of such algorithms is susceptible to lack of contextual information [8]. Zeng proposes the use of external knowledge to extend the eigenvector to improve the distinction between candidate entities [9]. Zhang uses the wiki concept similarity as a measure [10]. The main disadvantage of the similarity based method is to ignore the semantic correlation between entities, which is often helpful for distinguishing ambiguous entities. In addition, some scholars use the method of machine learning. For example, Zuo proposes a voting model [11]. The drawback of the machine learning methods is that the performance is subject to the quality and scope of the training corpus. Therefore, in order to overcome the shortcomings of these two kinds of methods, Kulkarni et al. have proposed the idea of collective entity linking [12].

The collective entity linking method solves the link problem of all entity mentions in the text at one time, avoiding the single-threaded processing mode in which the entities to be scanned and disambiguated. The basic idea is to build a graph model using the relationship between entities [13]. Han regards Wikipedia as a local knowledge base, treating entity references and candidate entities as vertices in the graph, establishing entity referent graph [14]. And then he uses the random walk algorithm to sort the candidate entities in the graph. On the basis of the above work, Ayman combines the context similarity and the popularity of the entity into the PageRank algorithm by modifying the initial probability value of the vertex [15]. However, the common problem of these methods is that they rely entirely on Wikipedia pages as the source of knowledge, and performs poorly on non-well-known entities. To solve this problem, Andrea utilizes the BabelNet semantic network to achieve the entity disambiguation by extracting the dense subgraph [16]. But the Babelfy algorithm relies too much on the local knowledge base.

3. Approach

In this section, we proposed our method which consists of three parts: candidate generation, relation graph construction, and candidate entities disambiguation.

3.1 Candidate Generation

The main function of the candidate entity generation module is to identify the entity mention for the given input text, and search the knowledge base to get the set of candidate entities corresponding to each entity mention.

In the first step, for the input text D, we use the toolkit THULAC issued by the Tsinghua University natural language processing and social humanities computing laboratory for word segmentation, and realize the entity recognition according to the output of the parting result. The principle of extraction is to extract only the named entities whose names are marked as people names, place names or institution names, and filter out the general term. Finally, we get the set of all the entity mention $M=\{m_1,m_2,\cdots,m_n\}$ in the input text D. The second step is to generate candidate entity sets. We search the knowledge base to find all the candidate entities that have the same name as the entity mention m_i in the knowledge base. All candidate entities corresponding to this entity mention are used as the initial candidate entity set $C_i=\{c_{i1},c_{i2},\cdots,c_{ik}\}$ for this entity. Where c_{ik} represents the kth candidate entity of the entity mention m_i. For the entity mention m_i that does not find the candidate entity in the knowledge base, we define that the candidate entity set C_i of m_i is null. Thus the initial candidate entity set of the entity mention set M is $C'=\{C_1,C_2,\cdots,C_n\}$.

We use Fudan CN-DBpedia Chinese knowledge map as the basis. This knowledge map now has 9,455,262 entities, and offers a full suite of APIs for free. As the

Chinese open source knowledge base construction in the initial stage, we use Baidu Encyclopedia as a supplement to make full use of Encyclopedia website knowledge update quickly to improve the accuracy. Baidu Encyclopedia is now the world's largest Chinese encyclopedia. As of March 2017, more than 1409,000 entries are collected by 124493000 multiple edits, and the content is updated very frequently. The ambiguous entities with the same name in CN-DBpedia have a suffix tag. For example, when we search for "Li Na" in CN-DBpedia, there are 27 objects with the same name. The suffix labels are Chinese women's tennis star, pop singer, Chinese stage director, and Guangxi Art Institute professor etc. It can be seen that the initial set size after the initial search may be too large. If the set of candidate entities is made too large, the calculation is more complicated, so the initial set must be filtered.

We use two steps to filter the initial set. Firstly, traversing each candidate entity set in the knowledge base to obtain the attributes of the candidate entity. Filtering out no attribute and uncommon entities to reduce the size of the initial set preliminarily. Then we calculate the cosine similarity between the input text D of the entity mention and the Baidu Encyclopedia page of the corresponding candidate entity as:

$$\text{Cos\_}Sim = \frac{m \cdot c}{|m||c|}$$

Where m represents the eigenvector of the text of the entity mention, an c represents the eigenvector of the encyclopedia page of the candidate entity. If the candidate entity does not have the corresponding encyclopedia page, the cosine similarity is defined as 0. The threshold τ =0.3 is defined by cross experiment. The candidate entity whose cosine similarity is less than the threshold is filtered to further narrow the candidate entity set size. So that we get the final candidate entity set $C = \{C_1, C_2, \cdots, C_n\}$.

3.2 Topic Relation Graph

In this section, we discuss the method of constructing an entity topic relation graph for the input text D to achieve the goal of a collective linking. The topic relation graph is an undirected graph $G = (V, E)$ with weight where V is the node set of the graph and E is the set of edges between nodes. The final result of the entity linking is based on the topology of the graph, and the quality of the graph affects the performance of the algorithm to a great extent. So the construction of entity relation graph is very important. We divide the graph into two parts: the outer circle graph and the inner circle graph. The part of all the entities mention is called the outer circle graph, while the part of all the candidate entities is called the inner circle graph. An example of a topic relation graph is shown in Fig.1.

Construct of vertex set: *Firstly, we construct the vertex collection. The* input *text D has a set of mentions* $M = \{m_1, m_2, \cdots, m_n\}$ *,while the set of candidates for the mentions are* $C = \{C_1, C_2, \cdots, C_n\}$. *So the vertex set V of the entity relation graph is defined as the union of the entity mention set M and the candidate entity set C. For the sake of convenience, we define the subset* $V_1 = \{m_i \mid \forall m_i \in M\}$ *as the vertex in the outer circle graph, and the subset* $V_2 = \{c_{ij} \mid \forall c_{ij} \in C_i, \forall C_i \in C\}$ *of V is the vertex of the inner circle graph.*

Construct of edges set: We construct the graph G as an undirected graph, which is divided into two kinds of edges. The first kind of edge is the edge of the entity mention and its corresponding candidate entity, that is, the connection between outer circle graph and the inner circle graph. The second is the edge of the interconnection between the candidate entities, namely the edge of inner circle graph. And the specific structure is as follows.

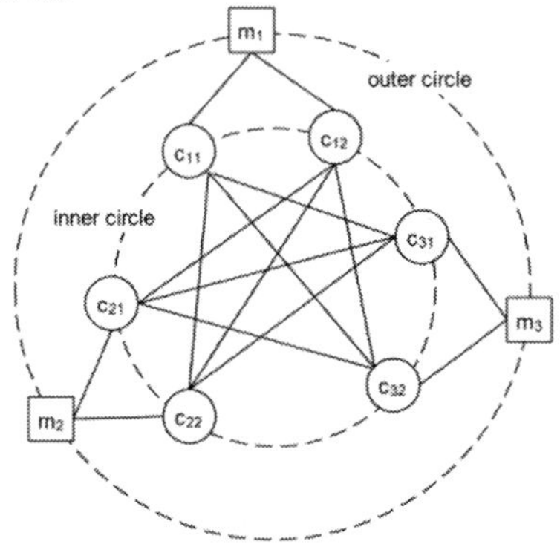

Figure 1. An example of topic relation graph.

The edge of the inner circle graph is called *Local Topic*. That is, the edge between an entity mention to be linked and one of its candidate entity. The value of local topic $Local(c_{ij})$ is calculated as: All the entities extracted from the input text D are formed as a vector $\vec{M} = \{m_1, m_2, \cdots, m_n\}$. For a candidate entity c_{ij} of one of the entity mention m_i , we grab the anchor text on the Baidu Encyclopedia page to form a vector $\vec{c_{ij}} = \{anchor_1, anchor_2, \cdots\}$. Then we use edit distance to calculate the number of the same items in the two vectors, and normalize the calculated values for all candidate entities of the same entity mention. In particular, for an entity that has only one candidate entity, the weight of the edge between them is 1, that is, the value of its local topic is 1. The value of local topic represents the relevance of the subject semantics of a candidate entity to its corresponding entity mention.

The edge of the inner circle graph is called *Global Topic*. If the vertexes in the set V_2 corresponding contents of the Baidu Encyclopedia page exist similarity, then there would be an edge to connect them in the graph. But in fact for the sake of calculation, we will be fully connected to the vertex in the construction phase of the inner circle graph. We use the weight 0 of the edge to determine whether the two vertices of the edge have a semantic association, and use the weight to determine the size of the semantic correlation between the two vertices. Particularly, there is no semantic correlation between candidate entities corresponding to the same entity mention. So we define that the weight of the edges between them are 0 to indicate that there is no association. The value of global topic is calculated by taking the candidate entity set of any two entity mentions m_s and m_t as examples. The candidate entity set of m_s is $C_s = \{c_{s1}, c_{s2}, \cdots, c_{sp}\}$, while the candidate entity set of m_t is $C_t = \{c_{t1}, c_{t2}, \cdots, c_{tq}\}$. Firstly, we initialize the topic relation graph. The vertices in C_s and C_t of the inner circle graph are fully connected, and the weight on the edges are set to 0. Secondly, we crawl the Baidu Encyclopedia pages of the vertex c_{s1} in the set C_s and the vertex c_{t1} in the set C_t separately. In order to determine the topic content of the page, all words in each page are weighted using the TF-IDF schema. Finding the keywords of the Baidu page where the two candidate entities are located, and making the collection of keywords which can represent the topic of each page. And then we generate their own word frequency vector, using the bag of words model to calculate the correlation of the two word frequency vector as the semantic relevance between c_{s1} and c_{t1}. If they are not related, the value is recorded as 0. Calculating the semantic similarity between c_{s1} and $c_{t1}, c_{t2}, \cdots, c_{tq}$ in turn to get q values, and then we normalize these q values to get the results as the global topic of c_{s1} and $c_{t1}, c_{t2}, \cdots, c_{tq}$, using $Global(c_{s1}, c_{tj})$ to express, where $j \in [1, 2, \cdots, q]$. The rest of the global topic values are calculated similarly. So the global topic of the vertexes between the set C_s and C_t are represented as $Global(c_{si}, c_{tj})$, where $i \in [1, 2, \cdots, p]$ and $j \in [1, 2, \cdots, q]$.

At this point, the vertices, edges and weights of the topic relation graph are constructed completely.

3.3 Collective Entity Linking

In this section, we propose a collective linking algorithm. The basic thought of the collective entity linking algorithm is to implement the one-time batch link for the multiple entities that co-occurrence in the given input text, using their semantic links and content dependency auxiliary disambiguation. The idea is to transform the entity linking problem into the rank of the topic consistency of candidate entities. According to the similarity obtained by section 3.2 and the collective entity linking algorithm introduced in the next step, we choose a set of candidate entities with the highest topic consistency of the entity mentions to be linked as the final link object. The process of collective entity linking algorithm consists of three steps.

First of all, for the entity relation graphs constructed in section 3.2, we perform the scoring calculation in the vertex set V_2 of the inner circle graph where $V_2 = \{c_{ij} \mid \forall c_{ij} \in C_i, \forall C_i \in C\}$. As for each $C_i \in C$, each time in the set C_i select and select only one vertex c_{ij}, where $i \in [1, n]$ and $j \in [1, length(C_i)]$. The inner circle graph score of c_{ij} is the score for the star chart with c_{ij} as the head node and the other selected nodes as component. Fig.2 is an example of star diagram. And the formula is as:

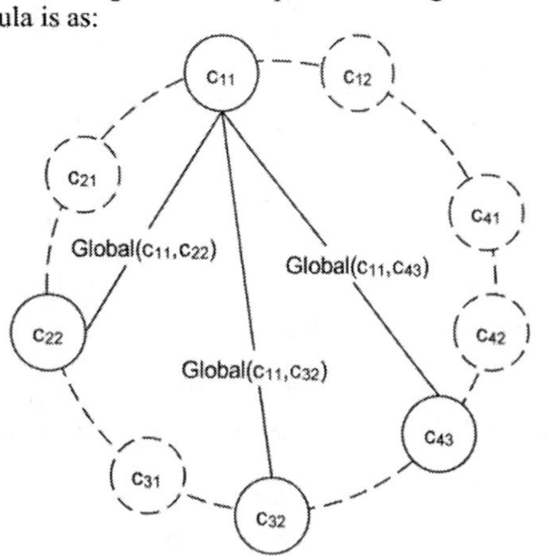

Figure 2. An example of star diagram in topic relation graph.

$$Trail(c_{ij}) = \max\{\sum_{k=1,k\neq i}^{n} Global(c_{ij}, C^{1}_{length(C_k)}C_k)\} \quad (2)$$

where $C^{1}_{length(C_k)}C_k$ represents a single vertex selected from the set C_k (except the set C_i) which is the only one vertex selected from set C_k at one time. And $Global(c_{ij}, C^{1}_{length(C_k)}C_k)$ represents the global topic of c_{ij} to these selected n-1 vertices, respectively. The n-1 global topic values are then added together, and the result is called a score of c_{ij}. We choose to record the maximum score of c_{ij} as the score $Trail(c_{ij})$ simultaneously.

Secondly, using the local topic between the entity mention and its candidate entity calculated in the section 3.2, and the trail value obtained in the previous step, we derive the semantic consistency score between the entity mention and the candidate entity by the following formula.

$$Consistency(m_i, c_{ij}) = Local(c_{ij}) + Trail(c_{ij}) \quad (3)$$

$Consistency(m_i, c_{ij})$ represents the whole topic consistency between entity mention m_i and its corresponding candidate entity c_{ij}, which is composed of the local topic score and the trail score. The value of $Local(c_{ij})$ indicates the relevance of the topic semantics between the encyclopedia page of the candidate entity

c_{ij} and the text where the entity mention m_i appears. $Trail(c_{ij})$ represents the context correlation score between candidate entity c_{ij} and other entities in the current text.

Finally, after calculating the topic consistency score between the entity mention and all of its candidate entities, the candidate entities are ranked according to the score from high to low. We choose the highest ranked candidate entity as the linking result of the entity mention. The linking result is as:

$$Link(m_i, result_i) = \arg\max_{c_{ij} \in C_i}(Consistency(m_i, c_{ij})) \quad (4)$$

where right side indicates that for a given entity mention m_i, the candidate entity c_{ij} with the highest score of the semantic consistency of m_i is selected from its candidate entity set C_i, and $Link(m_i, result_i)$ indicates that the pending entity mention m_i is linked to the candidate entity $result_i$ in the knowledge base finally. $result_i$ is the return value on the right side of the equation.

4. Experiments

In this section, we introduce the data set and baseline algorithm firstly, and then test the performance of our method and compare it with baseline algorithms.

4.1 Experiment Settings

In the experiment, we use CN-DBpedia as the local knowledge base. CN-DBpedia is a large-scale general field structured encyclopedia developed and maintained by Fudan University, which predecessor is Fudan GDM Chinese knowledge map. This map now has up to 9,455,262 entities, and offers a full suite of APIs for free. In order to make full use of Encyclopedia site knowledge update quickly to improve the accuracy, we use Baidu Encyclopedia as a supplement, which has been collected more than 14111 million entries.

We have selected two sets of public available corpus for performance testing of our collective entity linking algorithm based on content consistency.

The first group was compiled by NLP&CC 2014 Entity Linking contest. This test corpus includes 570 microblogging documents. Since the knowledge base that we use is not the NLP&CC Entity Linking contest, it is necessary to manually label the 570 micro-blog documents. And a total of 607 entities to be linked are marked.

The second group of data is a random crawl to 150 news texts from Phoenix News website information and Sina News, including military news, sports news, entertainment news, social news and other categories. Meanwhile we also manually extract the entity, and then label the extracted entities based on the local knowledge base. A total of 587 entities are marked.

4.2 Baselines

Champion_2014: This algorithm is an entity linking algorithm based on context similarity calculation, which integrates Sina microblogging user information based on the return of Baidu Encyclopedia.

Babelfy: This is an entity linking system based on graph which uses the BabelNet semantic network to disambiguate, and supports multi-lingual (including English, Chinese, Russian, etc.) entity disambiguation tasks. For the pending text, Babelfy first constructs its semantic relation graph based on semantic signature, and then discards the ambiguous entity by extracting the dense subgraph.

4.3 Evaluation Method

In order to evaluate the experimental results, we take the algorithm accuracy and performance metrics that include precision, recall and F_1-value as the criterions.

Firstly, we manually link the entity mentions to the corresponding entries in the knowledge base. Set M_E indicates the entity mention set, each entry of which can find the corresponding candidate entity in the knowledge base. For entities that are not linked in the knowledge base, they are marked as NIL manually. We call these entities as set M_N. Then we test the corpus using our proposed algorithm. Set R_E indicates the kind of entity mention set, each entry of which can find the corresponding candidate entity in the knowledge base by using proposed algorithm. The set R_N represents those entities that are not linked in the knowledge base by the outputs of the algorithm, that is, the set of entities labeled NIL. The accuracy rate indicates that how many results of our algorithm are the same as the results of manual labeling. The formula as:

$$Accuracy = \frac{|M_E \cap R_E| + |M_N \cap R_N|}{|M_E \cup M_N|} \times 100\% \quad (5)$$

Simply, the meaning of precision is the exact proportion of the linked entities, while the meaning of the recall is the proportion of all the exact entities being linked. In general, the increase in precision means a reduction in recall, so the F_1-value is used as a compromise. The formula is as follows.

$$Precision = \frac{|M_E \cap R_E|}{R_E} \times 100\% \quad .(6)$$

$$Recall = \frac{|M_E \cap R_E|}{M_E} \times 100\% \quad .(7)$$

$$F_1 = \frac{2 * Precision * Recall}{Precision + Recall} \times 100\% \quad .(8)$$

DOI: 10.1051/itmconf/20171204003

4.4 Evaluation Results

We test the performance of the algorithm that we proposed on the two corpus sheets. In contrast, we also test the algorithms Champion_2014 and Babelfy on the same data set. Table 1 shows the precision, recall and F_1-value of the algorithm Champion_2014, Babelfy and our method in NLP&CC 2014 corpus. Table 2 test results for the algorithm Champion_2014, Babelfy and our methods on the news texts which randomly crawl from the Phoenix information news website and the Sina News Network.

As seen from table 1, although our algorithm performs much higher than Babelfy in the accuracy, precision, recall and F_1 -value, but lower than Champion_2014 algorithm that has the best performance on NLP&CC 2014 entity linking contest. This is because the micro-blog short text is too short and has its own features, and the statements of users contain a variety of noise factors. However, our algorithm does not have the special treatment for micro-blog short texts as Champion_2014 algorithm does, which has a certain impact on our algorithm. Inspired by this, our next step is to consider how to reduce the impact of noise on our algorithm.

Table 2 shows that the accuracy, precision, recall, and F_1-value of our proposed algorithm in news texts are higher than Champion_2014 and Babelfy algorithms. The news texts have relatively less noise, which is conducive to our entity recognition. So we have better performance in the news texts than in the micro-blog texts. Although the Champion_2014 algorithm has a good performance in the micro-blog texts, but the performance of the algorithm model is highly dependent on the size and type of the samples, so the performance of the Champion_2014 algorithm in the news texts is lower than our method. Meanwhile, the performance of our algorithm in micro-blog texts is considerable in table 1, which indicates that our algorithm has good generalization performance. When compared with the representative work of the collective entity linking method Babelfy, our performance is significantly improved. This is because the performance of the Babelfy algorithm is highly dependent on the knowledge content of the BabelNet semantic network. For an entity that is not in the knowledge base, the Babelfy only assigns an abstract entity with no specific information. And our source of knowledge that combines the Fudan CN-DBpedia with the world's largest Chinese Encyclopedia Baidu encyclopedia, covering almost all areas, to provide effective support for the accuracy of entity linking.

In view of the Chinese word segmentation challenge, we use the THULAC word segmentation kit which is strong, and trained by the world's largest artificial word segmentation and POS tagging Chinese corpus (About 58 million words). Fig.3 shows the effectiveness of the word segmentation tool. We compare the performance of THULAC with the domestic representative of the word segmentation software: LTP-3.2.0, ICTCLAS and jieba. As seen from the Fig.3, the accuracy and F_1-value of the THULAC are higher than those of other three representative work in the test data of the news text corpus. It indicates that the use of THULAC toolkit for good word segmentation also improved our algorithm performance.

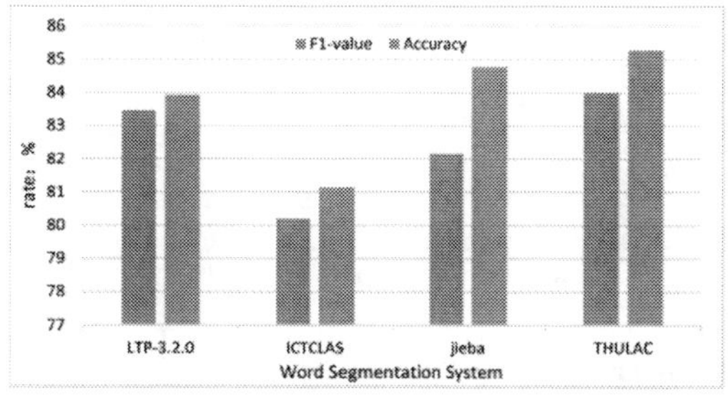

Figure 3. Effectiveness of the word segmentation tool.

Table1. Effectiveness on NLP&CC 2014 Corpus

System	Accuracy	Precision	Recall	F1-value
Champion_2014	86.82	80.78	85.98	83.30
Babelfy	71.82	70.36	75.71	72.93
Our method	82.37	79.88	82.69	81.26

Table2. Effectiveness on News Corpus

System	Accuracy	Precision	Recall	F1-value
Champion_2014	82.45	79.28	81.86	80.55
Babelfy	74.35	71.89	72.92	72.39
Our method	85.69	82.83	85.19	83.99

5. Conclusion and Future Work

In this paper, we propose a Chinese collective entity linking algorithm based on topic consistency and propose a method for calculating the topic consistency of the entity. For the entity mention to be linked, we extract the topic of its context. Finally, the candidate entity we choose is the most relevant to the topic of the context of the entity mention to be linked.

This method uses the combination of local knowledge base and external knowledge base to make up for the problem of imperfect Chinese local knowledge base and improve the accuracy. In addition, two layers of the selection method are used to control the size of candidate entities, and the computational complexity is reduced. Moreover, the computation of the correlation between the entity mention and the candidate entity takes full account of the topic relevance and the content relevance between the co-occurrence entities, which improves the precision and recall. Finally, using the semantic correlation between entities, we adopt the graph-based collective entity linking method to batch link the entity mention into the knowledge base. Our proposed method is refined, easy to accomplish and is effective from the experimental results. But the processing capacity for micro-blog and other social networking texts has yet to be improved. So in future work we intend to improve our algorithm for short texts and noise processing capabilities. In addition, in view of the inherent limitations of Chinese text processing, the next step is to explore more effective approach to further improve the accuracy, precision and recall.

Acknowledgment

This work was supported by National Core Electronic Devices, High-end Generic Chips and Basic Software (CHBS) Project "xx Mobile Terminal Operating System" under Grant No. 2016ZX01040101.

References

[1] M. Sozio and A. Gionis, "The community-search problem and how to plan a successful cocktail party," ACM SIGKDD International Conference on Knowledge Discovery and Data Mining, Washington, Dc, Usa,July,2010, pp. 939-948.

[2] W. Shen, J. Wang, and J. Han, "Entity linking with a knowledge base: Issues, techniques, and solutions," IEEE Transactions on Knowledge and Data Engineering, 2015, 27(2) , pp. 443-460.

[3] P. Fafalios, P. Papadakos, and Y. Tzitzikas, "Enriching textual search results at query time using entity mining, linked data and link analysis," International Journal of Semantic Computing, 2014, 8(04) , pp. 515-544.

[4] S. Guo, M. Chang, and E. Kiciman, "To Link or Not to Link? A Study on End-to-End Tweet Entity Linking," HLT-NAACL. 2013, pp. 1020-1030.

[5] W. Li, D. Qian, and Q. Lu, "Detecting, categorizing and clustering entity mentions in Chinese text," Proc. ACM SIGIR conference on Research and development in information retrieval, 2007, pp. 647-654.

[6] R. Bunescu and M. Pasca, "Using Encyclopedic Knowledge for Named entity Disambiguation," Eacl 2006, Conference of the European Chapter of the Association for Computational Linguistics, Proceedings of the Conference, Trento, Italy. DBLP, 2006, pp. 9–16.

[7] H. Nguyen and T. Cao, "Exploring wikipedia and text features for named entity disambiguation," Intelligent Information and Database Systems, 2010, pp. 11-20.

[8] S. Gottipati and J. Jiang, "Linking entities to a knowledge base with query expansion," Proceedings of the Conference on Empirical Methods in Natural Language Processing. Association for Computational Linguistics (ACL), 2011, pp. 804-813.

[9] Y. Zeng, D. Wang and T. Zhang, "Linking entities in short texts based on a Chinese semantic knowledge base," Natural Language Processing and Chinese Computing. Springer Berlin Heidelberg, 2013, pp. 266-276.

[10] T. Zhang, K. Liu and J. Zhao, "A graph-based similarity measure between Wikipedia concepts and its application in entity linking system," Journal of Chinese Information Processing, 2015, pp. 58-67.

[11] Z. Zuo, G. Kasneci and T. Gruetze, "BEL: Bagging for Entity Linking," International Conference on Computational Linguistics. 2014, pp. 2075-2086.

[12] S. Kulkarni, A. Singh and G. Ramakrishnan, "Collective annotation of Wikipedia entities in web text," ACM SIGKDD International Conference on Knowledge Discovery and Data Mining, Paris, France, June 28 - July. DBLP, 2009, pp. 457-466.

[13] Z. Guo and D. Barbosa, "Robust Entity Linking via Random Walks," ACM International Conference on Conference on Information and Knowledgemanagement, CIKM. ACM, 2014, pp. 499-508.

[14] X. Han, L. Sun and J. Zhao, "Collective entity linking in web text: a graph-based method," International ACM SIGIR Conference on Research and Development in Information Retrieval. ACM, 2011, pp. 765-774.

[15] A. Alhelbawy and R. Gaizauskas, "Graph Ranking for Collective Named Entity Disambiguation," Meeting of the Association for Computational Linguistics. 2014, pp. 75-80.

[16] A. Moro, A. Raganato, R. Navigli, "Entity linking meets word sense disambiguation: a unified approach," Transactions of the Association for Computational Linguistics, 2014, pp. 231-244.

Knowledge Reasoning Based on Neural Tensor Network

[1]Jian-Hui Huang, [2]Jiu-Ming Huang, [3]Ai-Ping Li, [4]Yong-Zhi Tong

[1]Massive Data Processing Lab National University of Defense Technology, Changsha, China
[2]Massive Data Processing Lab National University of Defense Technology, Changsha, China
[3]Massive Data Processing Lab National University of Defense Technology, Changsha, China
[4] Massive Data Processing Lab National University of Defense Technology, Changsha, China
[1]nudt_huangjianhui@163.com

Abstract: Knowledge base (KBs) is a very important part of applications such as Q&A system, but the knowledge base is always faced with incompleteness and the lack of inter-entity relationships. Knowledge reasoning is an important part of the construction of knowledge base, and is intended to find a way to supplement these missing relationships. This paper attempts to explore the model complexity of neural tensor network, a very important method of knowledge reasoning, and the reasoning accuracy. By increasing the number of slices in the tensor network layer, the number of parameters to be trained by the model is increased, thereby increasing the complexity of the model. The experimental results show that the number of slices is improved, which is helpful to increase the reasoning accuracy of the model, while the time consumption does not show obvious growth. The accuracy of the model on WordNet and FreeBase increased 2% and 3.2% respectively.

1. Introduction

The knowledge base is intended to store a large amount of information in a structured way, and the data is organized in a knowledge-dependent manner in which the nodes represent the entities and the edges correspond to the relationships among the entities. knowledge bases are considerably useful resource for many nature natural language processing tasks such as information retrieval, recommendation systems and so on. However, the knowledge base, including some well-known knowledge base such as Yago [3], WordNet [4] or the Google Knowledge Graph, suffer from incompleteness and a lack of auto reasoning capability. Hence, learning new facts based on the knowledge bases is an essential way to improve them. Much previous work (probability graph model and inductive logic programming and Markov Logic Network et al.) has focused on completing existing knowledge bases using patterns or classifiers applied to external large text corpora. However, not all common knowledge that is obvious to people which we called common sense, is expressed in Text. For example, we find a special bird, without special information, we know that it should have wings and will fly and other information, because these can be obtained through our common sense, without the need for additional text information Obtain. Therefore, learning new relations(triples) based on knowledge bases has been increasingly popular. Mukherjee .et al(2013)[5] used a matrix tri-factorization approach to reasoning new facts in knowledge bases. Socher et al.(2013)[1] introduced a neural tensor network to extracting common sense, which is the base of this paper . Guoliang Ji et al(2014)[2] applied a neural tensor network to reasoning over relations based on Chinese knowledge bases.

In this paper, I will explore the relationship between the number of slices and the reasoning accuracy of the model through specific experiments. NTN transforms the entities in the knowledge base into corresponding vectors , which can capture facts and their certainty about that entity ,to complete the initialization of the entity vectors. For sharing statistical strength among the entities that contain similar substrings, each entity is represented as the average of its word vectors. Each relation corresponds to a group of parameters of neural tensor networks. The entities and relationships can interact well through the tensor in the neural tensor layer of networks.

The main contribution of this paper is to explore the relationship between model complexity and reasoning accuracy through experiment, and to make a reference to the choice of model complexity when using this model to reason. The paper is organized as follows. Section 2 and section 3 introduce the Neural Tensor Network model and some related work respectively .Section 4 analyzes the model complexity. Section 5 reports the results of experiments. Section 6,I summarize my contribute and consider the further work directions.

2. Related Work

Here are the two parts involved in neural tensor networks and natural language processing: semantic vector space and depth learning.

2.1 Semantic Vector Space

Mapping the corresponding words to the low-dimensional vector semantic space is an important technique for natural language processing related tasks. It is also an important basis for other natural language processing tasks, such as POS tagging, naming entity recognition .Word vector related technology has been very mature. Neural language models (Bengio et ,2003; Collobert and Westion,2008) have been shown to be very powerful at language modeling, a task where models are asked to accurately predict the next word given previously seen words[7]. From the language model in 2003 to the 2008 word2vec and so on a series of word vector training technology development, makes the implied semantics of the word quite perfect.

2.2 Deep Learning

Deep learning technology in the visual and language technology has been quite mature, but in terms of text, relatively new. Deep learning technology in other aspects of the major achievements also makes the relevant personnel pay more attention to its natural language processing direction of the study. Nickle[6] applied a tensor factorizaton method for multi-relational learning, where a knowledge base was regarded as a three dimensional tensor. Bowman[7] introduced a recursive neural tensor networks model on a new corpus of constructed examples of logical reasoning in short sentences. Bordes et al [13] deal with the issue of weak interaction between entity vectors through multiple matrix products followed by Hadamard products.

3. Neural Tensor Network

This section introduces the neural tensor network model(NTN). NTN reasons over database entries which existed in knowledge base already by learning vector representations for each entity. We can see from Fig. 1, each relation triple is described as (e1,R,e2) and database entities are given as input to that relation's model. The model returns a high score if the relationship exist in database and a low one otherwise. This will answer any fact ,whether implicit or explicitly mentioned in the database, with a certainty confidence.

Next, I will introduce the model from two aspects: model structure, training goal.

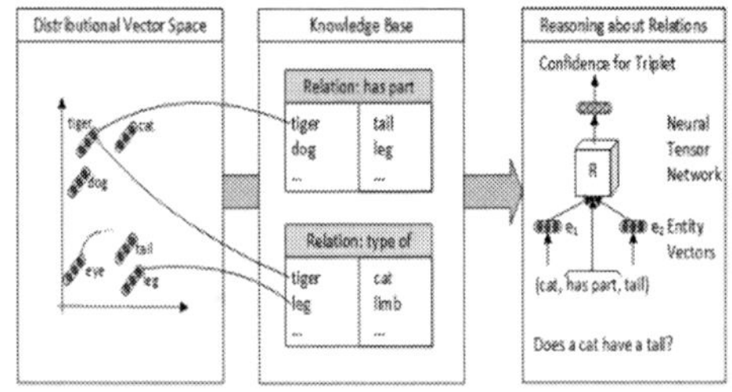

Figure 1. This figure shows how words in a knowledge base are mapped to a low-dimension vectors and averaged to construct entity vectors. Entity relation triples are inputted into a neural tensor network, which calculates the confidence that the two entities are in a relationship.

3.1 Model Structure

In this section, we introduce the NTN model structure. Firstly, we need to define some crucial parameters indexed by R for each relation's scoring function .If we use e1,e2 be the vector representations of any two entities in the database. Then the Neural Tensor Network (NTN) computes the confidence of a given triple (e1,R,e2) through a bilinear tensor layer which relates two entity vectors across multiple dimensions and the formula as follow.

$$score(e1,R,e2) = u_R^T f(e1^T W_R^{[1:k]} e2^T + V_R \begin{bmatrix} e1 \\ e2 \end{bmatrix} + b_R) \quad (1)$$

where f is a activation function, $W_R^{[1:k]} \in R^{d*d*k}$ is a tensor , the entity vectors e1,e2$\in R^d$,$V_R \in R^{k*2d}$, $b_R \in R^k$, $u_R \in R^k$.

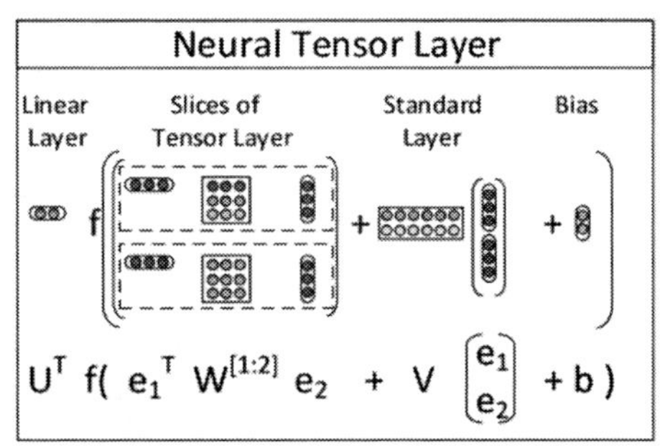

Figure 2. A visualization of the parameters of Richard Socher's Neural Tensor Network Model with k = 2 slices.

3.2 Training Objective

In the data set, the samples are represented in the form of triples. triple described as (e1,R,e2), where ei(i = 1, 2),R represent entities and relationship respectively, corresponds a tensor network whose inputs are ei(i = 1, 2). The main idea is that each triplet in the training set which be regard as positive samples and represent it with $T^R = (e1^R, R, e2^R)$, should receive a higher score than a triplet in which one of the entities is replaced with a random entity ,where there triplets are regards as negative samples

 DOI: 10.1051/itmconf/20171204004

and represent it as $T_c^R = (e1^R, R, ec^R)$. We minimize the objective as follow:

$$J = \sum_{i=1}^{N}\sum_{c=1}^{C} max\left(0,1 - score\left(T^{(i)}\right) + score\left(T_c^{(i)}\right)\right) + \lambda||\Omega||_2^2 \quad (2)$$

The loss function is a hinge-loss function and is followed by a regular term to prevent over-fitting. We denote the set of all relationships' NTN parameters by $\Omega = U, V, W, b, E,$ where U, V, W, b are model parameters and E is word vectors.

4. Analysis of Neural Tensor Network complexity

Some experiences of machine learning and deep learning tell us that it is possible to increase the complexity of the model and increase the performance of the model when the model is not over-fitting. Based on this argument, here I try to explore the model complexity and the reasoning ability of the neural tensor network model through experimental comparison .Here we assume that the word vector and the dimension of the entity vector take 200,$ei\epsilon R^{200}$. then the number of parameters of the neural tensor network layer is calculated as follows: The number of parameters of tensor $W_R^{[1:k]} \in R^{d*d*k}$ is 40000*k, the number of parameters in $V_R \epsilon R^{2*d}$ is 2*k. It can be seen that the most important factor affecting model complexity lies in tensor. The number of parameters that need to be trained in the model represents the complexity of the model. Equation (3) (4) shows the relationship between the total number of model parameters and the number of slices in the tensor network

$$N(k) = N(U) + N(W) + N(b) + N(V) + N(E) \quad (3)$$

$$N(k) = k + 200*200*k + k + 2*200*k + 400 \quad (4)$$

Table 1: The parameters of the model that need to be trained with the increase of the slice

Slices	3	4	5	6
Parameter(*10000)	12	16	20	24
Slices	7	8	9	10
Parameter(*10000)	28	32	36	40

5. Expriments

Experiments are conducted on both WordNet[1] and FreeBase[2] predict whether some relations hold or not using other facts in the database . Before reasoning with Neural Tensor Network, We have a very important step is to convert the entity into the corresponding entity vector. In this paper , I will use a simple random initialization method for entity Vector initialization.

5.1 Entity to Semantic Vector

Firstly, we simply initialize each word vector $x\epsilon R^{200}$ by sampling it from a zero mean Gaussian distribution : $x \sim N(0, \sigma^2)$. Next, the entity vector is converted to the average of the vector of the constituent words. On the right side of Figure 1, we can see that the entity vector of the input entity Bengal tiger is:

ς(Βεvγαλ τιγερ)=ς(Βεvγαλ)+ς(τιγερ) (5)

The advantage of doing so is that entities with the same substring can share the same part of the semantics. For example, Bengal tiger and South china tiger. The two entities have the same sub-string tiger, using the formula (5), can make two entities have the same semantic part.

5.2 Datasets

Table II is the data set used in this paper. For WordNet, I use 112,581 relational triplets for training. In total, there are 11 different relations which including 38,696 unique entities. In addition, the experimental will use 2609 relational triplets for validation , and use 10544 relational triplets for final test. For FreeBase ,I use 316232 relational triplets for training. In total, there are 75043 unique entities in 13 different relations. In contrast to the previous practice, some relationship of FreeBase is considered to be difficult to reason (such as place of birth, place of death, location, children, spouse, parents) has not been removed in this paper. Because the need to explore here is the relationship between model complexity and accuracy.

Table 2: The statistics for WordNet and Freebase including number of different relations #R.

Dataset	#R	#Ent	#Train	#Dev	#Test
WordNet	11	38696	112581	2609	10544
FreeBase	13	75043	316232	5908	23733

5.3 Environment of Experiment

Table III shows the operating environment on which this experiment relies. As the complexity of the model and the increase in the size of the data, the consumption of resources must be an important factor in our consideration. So it is necessary to discuss the environment in which the whole program is running. This paper will use the time as an important indicator to reflect the complexity of the model.

Table 3: The environment of experiments

Operating System	Win7_64bit
Language	Python2.7
Open Source Package	Numpy, Scipy
Memory of Computer	16G
Cpu	Core-i5-4460

DOI: 10.1051/itmconf/20171204004

5.4 Experimental Results

In this section, I will use the chart comparison and the use of python open source package matplotlib drawing way to visualize the results. In the first part, I will illustrate the complexity of the model through the entire program run time. Next, observe the change in the reasoning accuracy of the relationship reasoning in WordNet and FreeBase as the complexity of the model increases. In this paper, I will be the most common slice (slice = 3) as the baseline.

In table IV and table V ,I illustrate the complexity of the corresponding model by the number of slices, the total time consumed by the program run, and the number of model parameters .Where the reasoning accuracy is the average reasoning accuracy of all the relationships in the corresponding data set. Through the results in the table, we can see that with the increase of the number of slices, the running time of the model shows a linear increase rule. The accuracy of the reasoning is also changing. The reasoning accuracy of the FreeBase and WordNet are reach the peak when the slice is 6 and 7 ,respectively. the optimal reasoning results were 0.8242, 0.8532, compared to the baseline, respectively, increased 0.02 and 0.032. Then with the increase of the slice, the reasoning accuracy is reduced, which indicates that the model has been fitted.

Fig. 3 and Fig. 4 visualize the results by drawing, showing the specific changes in the reasoning accuracy of the various data relations in the two datasets as the model complexity changes .From Fig. 3 we can see that "similar to" and "domain topic" fluctuate the most, affected by the complexity of the model. It can be seen from Fig. 4 that the reasoning of "children", "place of birth", "place of death" and so on is still the least accurate. The greatest impact on model complexity is "children " and "place of birth".

Table 4: The relations between number of slices running time and reasoning accuracy (WordNet)

Slice	3	4	5	6	7	8	9	10
Para mete rs	120 000	160 000	200 000	240 000	280 000	320 000	360 000	400 000
Time (min)	125 3	147 5	180 0	232 9	241 3	253 6	288 0	302 0
Aver age Accu racy	0.8 045	0.8 081	0.8 036	0.8 242	0.8 168	0.8 101	0.7 918	0.7 803

Table 5: The relations between number of slices ,running time and reasoning accuracy (FREEBASE)

Slice	3	4	5	6	7	8	9	10
para mete r	120 000	160 000	200 000	240 000	280 000	320 000	360 000	400 000
Time (min)	232 0	257 8	286 6	300 4	315 9	340 0	362 5	378 5
Aver age Accu racy	0.8 213	0.8 236	0.8 320	0.8 403	0.8 538	0.8 440	0.8 220	0.8 102

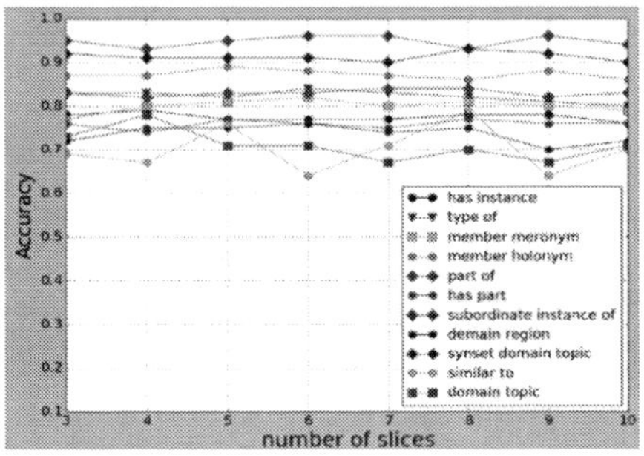

Figure 3. Changes of 11 relationships in WordNet

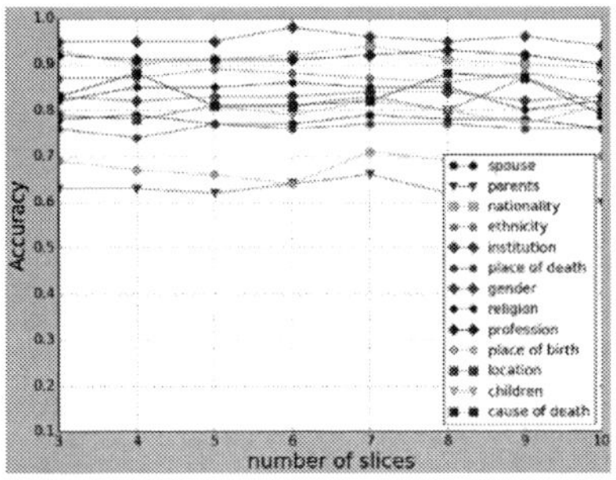

Figure 4 .Changes of 13 relationships in FreeBase

6. Conclusion

The complexity of the model can be determined by choosing the appropriate super-Parameters, and the appropriate complexity is helpful to improve the performance of the model. In the neural tensor network, the number of slices in tensor has the greatest influence on the complexity of the model. Hence, I started from the number of slices to explore the relationship between model complexity and model performance. Finally, through experiments, we know that the appropriate increase in the number of slices, is indeed conducive to improving the model of reasoning accuracy, of course, this also inevitably increases the program running time . The theme of this paper is to explore the effect of the complexity of the neural tensor network model on the reasoning accuracy ,So all of the entity vector initialization using a random initialization method .

Richard Socher in his paper [1] through the experimental show that the use of pre-training method to initialize the entity vector, is very helpful to increase of the reasoning accuracy .Using word2vec[8], glove even more complex language model, such as LSTM, for word vector pre-training, will become the focus of my next step.

Acknowledgment

The work described in this paper is partially supported by The National Key Research and Development Program of China (2016QY03D0601, 2016QY03D0603) and National Natural Science Foundation of China (No.61502517, No.61672020, No.61662069).

References

[1] R Socher., Chen, D., Manning, C.D., Ng, Y.: Reasoning With Neural Tensor Networks for Knowledge Base Completion. In: Advances in Neural Information Processing Systems 26 2013

[2] Guoliang Ji, Yinghua Zhang, Hongwei Hao, and Jun Zhao: Reasoning Over Relations Based on Chinese Knowledge Bases. Springer International Publishing,2014,8801:141-150

[3] F. M. Suchanek, G. Kasneci, and G. Weikum. Yago: a core of semantic knowledge. In Proceedings of the 16th international conference on World Wide Web, 2007.

[4] G.A. Miller. WordNet: A Lexical Database for English. Communications of the ACM, 1995.

[5] Mukherjee, T., Pande, V., Kok, S.: Extracting New Facts in Knowledge Bases:-A matrix trifactorization approach. In: ICML Workshop on Structured Learning:Inferring Graphs from Structured and Unstructured Inputs ,2013

[6] Nickel, M., Tresp, V., Chen, Kriegel, H.P.: A Three-Way Model for Collective Learning on Multi-Relational Data. In: Proceedings of the 28th International Conference on Machine Learning 2011

[7] Huang, E.H., Socher, R., Manning, C.D., Ng, Y.: Improving Word Representations via Global Context and Multiple Word Prototypes. In: Annual Meeting of the Association for Computational Linguistics, ACL ,2012

[8] Tomas Mikolov,Ilya Sutskever,Kai Chen,Greg Corrado,Jeffrey Dean. Distributed Representations of Words and Phrases and their Compositionality. arXiv:1310.4546 2013

[9] Y Goldberg , O Levy. Word2vec Explained: deriving Mikolov et al.'s negative-sampling word-embedding method. Eprint Arxi,2014

[10] R. Socher, B. Huval, C. D. Manning, and A. Y. Ng. Semantic Compositionality Through Recursive Matrix-Vector Spaces. In EMNLP, 2012.

[11] Danqi Chen, Richard Socher, Christopher D. Manning, Andrew Y. Ng. Learning New Facts From Knowledge Bases With Neural Tensor Networks and Semantic Word Vectors ICLR 2013

[12] A Bordes, J Weston, R Collobert, Y Bengio. Learning Structured Embeddings of Knowledge Bases. Aaai Conference on Artificial Intelligence,2011

[13] Xu Zenglin, Sheng Yongpan, He Lirong, Wang Yafang Knowledge Atlas Technology Journal of Electronic Science and Technology University, Vol. 45, 2016.7 page: 46-52

[14] R. Collobert and J. Weston. A unified architecture for natural language processing: deep neural networks with multitask learning. In ICML, 2008.

[15] Li Xiangyang, Miao Zhuang. Free text information extraction technology [J]. Information Science, 2004, 22 (7): 815-821

[16] LIU Qiao, LI Yang, DUAN Hong, LIU Yao, QIN Zhi-guang Overview of Knowledge Map Construction Technology University of Electronic Science and Technology Information and Software Engineering Institute of Computer Research and Development 2016 page: 582-600

[17] Lao N, Subramanya A, Pereira F, et al. Reading the web with learned syntactic-semantic inference rules[C]//Proceedings of the 2012 Joint Conference on Empirical Methods in Natural Language Processing and Computational Natural Language Learning. Association for Computational Linguistics, 2012.page:1017-1026.

[18] K. Bollacker, C. Evans, P. Paritosh, T. Sturge, and J. Taylor. Freebase: a collaboratively created graph database for structuring human knowledge. In Proceedings of the 2008 ACM SIGMOD international conference on Management of data, SIGMOD, 2008

The Design and Implementation of a Remote Fault Reasoning Diagnosis System for Meteorological Satellites Data Acquisition

Jie Zhu[1 2], Man-Yun Lin [1], Xian-Gang Zhao[1], Shu-Ze Jia[1]

[1]*National Satellite Meteorological Center, CMA, Beijing 100081*
[2] *Nanjing University of Information Science & Technology, Nanjing 210044*
[1]*juliet0411@126.com*

Abstract: Under the background of the trouble shooting requirements of FENGYUN-3 (FY-3) meteorological satellites data acquisition in domestic and oversea ground stations, a remote fault reasoning diagnosis system is developed by Java 1.6 in eclipse 3.6 platform. The general framework is analyzed, the workflow is introduced. Based on the system, it can realize the remote and centralized monitoring of equipment running status in ground stations, triggering automatic fault diagnosis and rule based fault reasoning by parsing the equipment quality logs, generating trouble tickets and importing expert experience database, providing text and graphics query methods. Through the practical verification, the system can assist knowledge engineers in remote、precise and rapid fault location with friendly graphical user interface, boost the fault diagnosis efficiency, enhance the remote monitoring ability of integrity operating control system. The system has a certain practical significance to improve reliability of FY-3 meteorological satellites data acquisition.

1. Introduction

FENGYUN3 meteorological satellites data acquisition network has four domestic ground stations, they are Beijing, Jiamusi, Urumqi, Guangzhou, and one oversea ground station in Kiruna, Sweden [1]. The data acquisition and transmission network was founded in 2008, and with the increasing complexity of the system, many factors, such as the diversity of device, decentralization of ground stations, different skill level between operators, have seriously restrict the improvement of fault diagnosis and removal efficiency, which greatly affects equipment MTTR (MTTR: Mean Time To Repair) [2], challenging the reliability and timeliness. Under the background of the trouble shooting requirements, it is necessary to develop a fault reasoning diagnosis system which has the functions of remote centralized monitoring and auxiliary precise fault reasoning for domestic and oversea ground stations, it has practical significance for improving data reception quality of meteorological satellites, and the similar systems are empty in China [3, 4, 5].

2. System Architecture And Function Design

Based on parsing the equipment quality logs, the system combines remote monitoring with fault reasoning, consisting of three subsystems, as shown in Figure 1, they are remote monitoring subsystem of equipment status、fault reasoning and diagnosis subsystem and report generation and release subsystem.

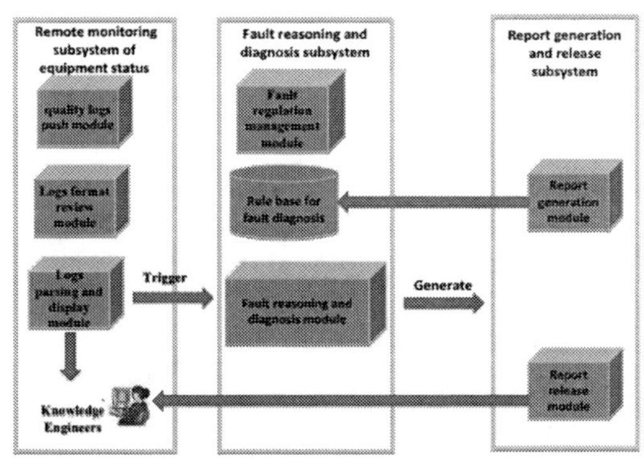

Figure 1. Framework of Remote Fault Diagnosis System

2.1 Remote Monitoring Subsystem of Equipment Status

Based on collecting and parsing of quality logs, the system can realize the remote centralized monitoring of the status of distributed ground stations data receiving devices automatically, consists of three modules: quality logs push module, logs format review module, logs

DOI: 10.1051/itmconf/20171204005

parsing and display module.

The quality logs (.REP) automatically record all working parameters of the ground data receiving devices in the form of text, which is the only valid and reliable data that reflects the real working state of the equipment, as the input of the fault diagnosis system. The file contains the following information: record time(UTC), elevating axis of the antenna, azimuth axis of the antenna, working status of the antenna(Standby, scan, command status, signal lock information, program tracking mode, auto tracking mode, test mode), signal level, antenna warning information(0 for normal and 1 for alarm), status end indication<CR>.

After every pass finished, quality logs(.REP) will be automatically push to integrated operation control center by FTP, after format review, subsequently, format review, only parsing and display correct logs.

2.2 Fault Reasoning and Diagnosis Subsystem

Fault reasoning and diagnosis subsystem is designed to an expert experience system, consists of fault regulation management module, rule base for fault diagnosis、fault reasoning and diagnosis module.

Fault regulation management module realize the increase, deletion, modification and inquiry function of the fault rules, fault rules dynamic update based on expert knowledge and practical experience.

Rule base for fault diagnosis is a database, which expert knowledge language is transformed into data language to store fault diagnosis rules.

Fault reasoning and diagnosis module has two ways to reasoning malfunction cause: automatic fault diagnosis and rule based fault reasoning.

2.3 Report Generation and Release Subsystem

Report generation and release subsystem generates the malfunction investigation report based on standard template, and through SMS, E-mail releases reports.

3. Design of Fault Diagnosis Rule Base

FENGYUN3 meteorological satellites data acquisition system consists of management & control subsystem (M&C), antenna subsystem, channel subsystem, storage and transmission subsystem, time calibration subsystem [6]. Among them, the M&C is the control center of the system, it assigns tasks to all data receiving devices based on the receiving timetable and prior agreement (including antenna polarization mode, converter frequency, demodulator parameter, etc.) , "guide" data reception and transmission automatically[7].

Fault diagnosis rule base related to all the malfunction all over the above subsystem, and can dynamic update based on expert knowledge and practical experience. The structure of fault diagnosis rule base as shown in Figure2. The structure of the fault tree as shown in Figure3.

The structure of fault diagnosis rule base

Num	Subsystem	Phenomenon	Cause	Solution	Frequency

Figure 2. The structure of fault diagnosis rule base

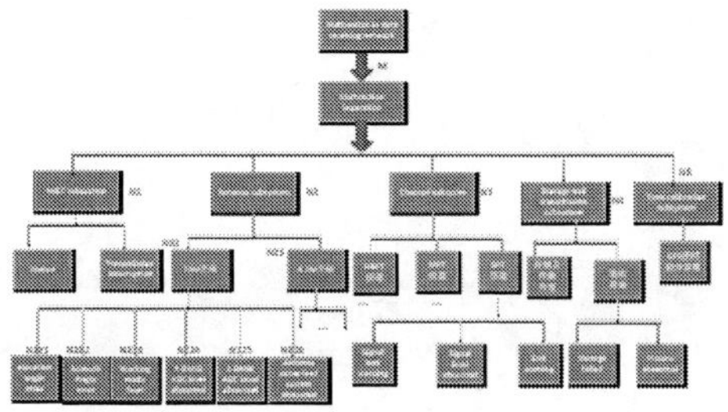

Figure 3. The structure of the fault tree

4. Design and the Implementation of Reasoning Machine

According to the symptom data provided by the user, reasoning machine adopts a certain strategy call the corresponding knowledge in the knowledge base [8], analyze and diagnose, until the root cause of the malfunction is located [9].

Reasoning machine has two ways to work, one is automatic fault diagnosis, and the other is rule based fault diagnosis.

(1) Automatic fault diagnosis

Defined a parent-node as a root node which has similar characteristics of the actual fault phenomenon, the leaf nodes are searched in their subtree by traversing the fault tree, retrieval based on the relationship between the root and leaf node fault feature, until the root cause is identified and located.

(2) Rule based fault diagnosis

Rule based fault diagnosis is suitable for the situation that fault related knowledge is clear and detailed, the reasoning engine will carry on comprehensive identification based on mathematical statistics and critical rules, a list of diagnostic results is given based on the available failure data, and find diagnosis result of the biggest certainty factor, that is look up the node in the knowledge base with closest to the fault tree leaf signatures, and as the result of fault diagnosis, improving the efficiency of fault diagnosis.

For example, as shown in Figure 4, after a rule matching based on fault symptom, the following situations will occur:

① If the match is successful only once, assuming the leaf N223, then the probabilities of nodes and leaves at each level

 DOI: 10.1051/itmconf/20171204005

are: $P(N223) = P(N22) = P(N2) = P(M) = 1$
(1)

The probability of the other nodes and leaves is:

$$P(X) = 0$$
(2)

Then the leaf N223 as the final result of fault diagnosis, located as root cause.

② If the match is successful many times, assuming the leaf N223、N224 and leaf N231 belong to node N23, then the probabilities of nodes and leaves at each level are:

$$P(M) = P(N2) = 1$$
(3)

$$P(N223) = P(N224) = P(N23) = P(N231) = \frac{1}{3}$$
(4)

$$P(N22) = \frac{2}{3}$$
(5)

The probability of the other nodes and leaves is:

$$P(Y) = 0$$
(6)

③ If none of the matches were successful, then the probabilities of nodes and leaves at each level are:

$$P(Z) = 0$$
(7)

After completing the above work, put the matching probability results in the statistical table, compare and find the biggest one as the result of the fault diagnosis.

5. Flow Diagrams of Algorithm

As shown in Figure 4:

① Open the file scanning process, monitoring the FTP folder of the fault diagnosis system, determine whether the device logs (.REP) is transferred.

② Check the format of the logs. Display the incorrect the file name on GUI (Graphical User Interface).

③ Display the details of the logs of correct format on GUI, including File type、Orbit number、Satellite name、start-time、end-time.

④ Triggering automatic fault diagnosis and rule based fault reasoning by parsing the equipment quality logs.

⑤ A list of diagnostic results is given based on the available failure data.

⑥ Finding the node of the biggest certainty factor.

⑦ Comprehensive analysis the result of automatic fault diagnosis and rule based fault reasoning, combining to final fault diagnosis report and push to GUI.

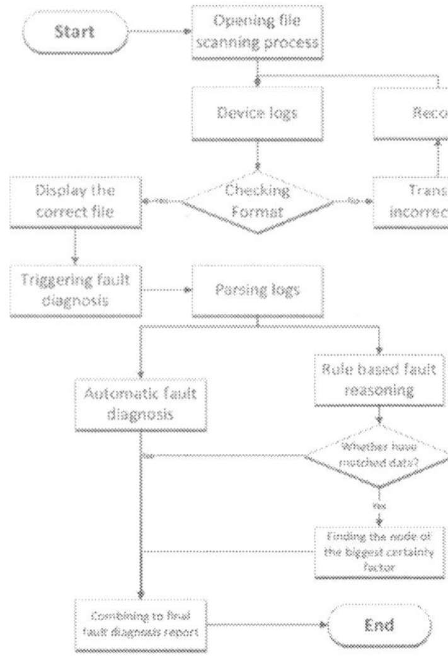

Figure 4. Flow diagrams of algorithm

6. Application Example

The practical effect of the fault reasoning diagnosis system is eventually demonstrated with application examples.

Based on java1.6, eclipse 3.6 platform, the fault diagnosis system is developed, for example, the antenna named NPSS1 in Kiruna ground station (Sweden) has broken down in March 29th,2016, the software interface of the fault diagnosis system(located in Beijing Integrated Operation Control Center) is shown in Figure 5. After receiving the device log and finished format checking, parsing the log and display it in two ways: text and graphics. It is found that the difference of the NPSS1 antenna azimuth angle between the command value and actual running angle was abnormal jump by rule based fault reasoning, the normal value should be 0[10], so the root cause was located: antenna azimuth mechanical fault. The diagnosis report generated by the system automatically.

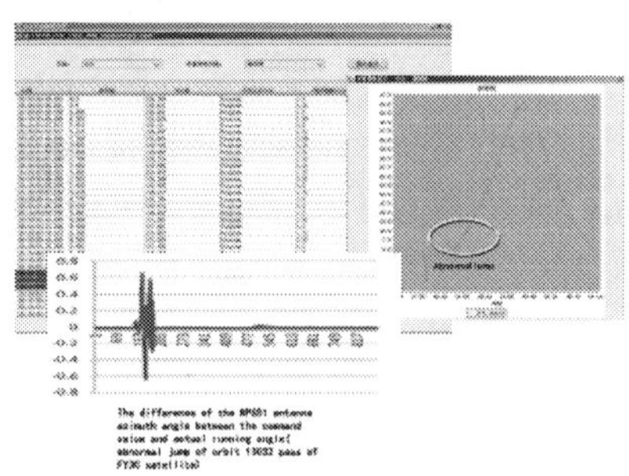

Figure 5 Example 1 of the fault diagnosis system

In our actual businesses, the fault diagnosis system effectively solves the contradiction between the increasing complexity of the distributed ground data receiving network of FY3 satellite and the lack of skilled operators, especially, it has unique advantages in remote reasoning for overseas ground station failures, make up for the language and time differences, effectively shorten the time of troubleshooting. Another example of the antenna stow because of strong wind in Kiruna (May 5th, 2017) as shown in Figure 6 and Figure 7. After the system working automatically, operators could start the backup mechanism immediately, effectively avoided further deterioration.

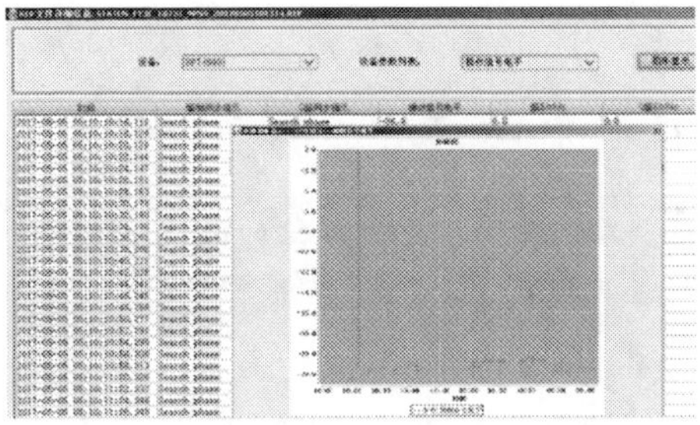

Figure 6 Example2 of the fault diagnosis system (signal level)

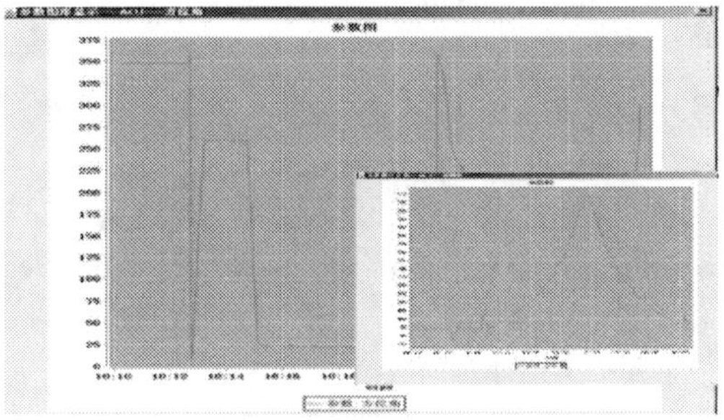

Figure 7 Example2 of the fault diagnosis system (antenna control unit)

7. Summary

Under the background of the trouble shooting requirements of FY3 meteorological satellites data acquisition in domestic and oversea ground stations, a remote fault reasoning diagnosis system is developed, triggering automatic fault diagnosis and rule based fault reasoning by parsing the equipment quality logs, generating trouble tickets and importing expert experience database. Through the practical verification, the system can run stably with perfect function and high security. It can provide remote, precise fault reasoning diagnosis, improved efficiency of troubleshooting, and provided a reference for other systems.

Acknowledgments

The work presented in this study is supported by National High-tech R&D Program (2011AA12A104).

Reference

[1] Lizi Xie, Xiangang Zhao, etc. Design and implementation on FENGYUN meteorological satellite key business point Computer Application, 2012, 32 (S2): 192-195,225

[2] Xiaogang Liu. Design and implementation of a Remote Maintenance and Test System for Lightning Location Finders. Meteorological Science and Technology, 2016, 44(4): 567-570

[3] Chengmao Wu. Design of Satellite Fault Expert Diagnosis System Based on Knowledge. Computer Measurement & Control.2010.04-0743-03

[4] Hairong Sun, James J. Han, Haim Levendel. Prioritized failure recovery in communication networks and its transient analysis. [J].Computer Communications, 2003, 26 (2):939-949

[5] Qing Zhou, etc. Evaluation on Maintenance Support Capabilities of Automatic weather station. Meteorological Science and Technology. 2012, 40(3):349:353

[6] Xiaoli Zhou. Fault Handling on FENGYUN meteorological satellite data receiving. Desert and oasis meteorology, 2009. 08 (3)

[7] Ying Wei. Trouble Shooting on FENGYUN meteorological satellite. Science and Technology Economic Guide 2016(08).

[8] Wen Zhao. Design of Ground Diagnosis System for Satellite in-orbit Fault. Spacecraft Engineering 201406, Vol.23 (03)

[9] Jin Luo. Development of Fault Diagnosis. Automation and Instrumentation 2003(02)

[10] Chuzhou Li, etc. The installation &calibration of receiving antenna for Fengyun-3 meteorological satellite. Meteo rological, Hydrological and Marine Instruments. 2009.06, No.2

 DOI: 10.1051/itmconf/20171204006

On the Construction of LCD Codes over F_5

Qian Song, Rui-Hu Li, Qiang Fu and Luo-Bin Guo

School of Science, Air Force Engineering University, Xi'an, Shaanxi 710051, P. R. China

Abstract. Recently, linear codes with complementary dual (LCD codes) are employed in direct-sum-masking technique for prevention of side channel attacks, which is another application on LCD codes out of data storage, communication system and consumer electronics. Follow on, they are also used to construct maximal entanglement entanglement-assisted quantum codes for protecting quantum information from noise. In this paper, by transforming known codes, some optimal LCD codes of short length with dimension 3 or 4 over F_5 are constructed, respectively.

1. Introduction

Let F_5^n be the n-dimensional row vector space over F_5, the finite field with five elements. A linear $[n,k]$ code C is a k-dimensional subspace of F_5^n. The weight $w(x)$ of $x\in C$ is the number of its nonzero coordinates, if the minimum weight of nonzero codewords in C is d, then C is denoted as $C=[n,k,d]$. The dual code $C^{\perp}$ of a linear code C is defined as

$$C^{\perp} = \{x \in F_5^n \mid x \cdot y = xy^T = \mathbf{0} \text{ for all } \mathbf{y} \in C\}. \quad (1)$$

Two codes C and C' are equivalent if one can be obtained from the other by permuting the coordinates and multiplying an monomial matrix, see [1]. A permutation matrix is a square matrix with exactly one 1 in each row and column and 0s elsewhere. A monomial matrix is a square matrix with exactly one non-zero entry in each row and column [1].

Cyclic LCD codes, called originally as reversible codes, were first introduced by Massey in 1964 [2]. After 28 years, Massey [3] then gave generalized definition of a linear LCD code as: C is said to be complementary dual if $C\cap C^{\perp}=\{\mathbf{0}\}$. He also showed that asymptotically good LCD codes exist and LCD codes can provide an optimum linear coding solution for the two-user binary adder channel.

In 2014, LCD codes were found to have an application against side-channel attacks in cryptography [4]. Since then, construction and applications on LCD codes were deeply and investigated [5-15] widely. For example, many maximal entanglement entanglement-assisted quantum codes were derived from good LCD codes [5-8]. Some optimal LCD codes are studied and constructed in the Refs. [6-15].

Ref. [2] gave equivalent conditions for an LCD code as follows:

Proposition 1.1. Let C be a linear code. Let G be a generator matrix of C and H a parity-check matrix. Then the three following properties are equivalent:

1. C is LCD.

2. The matrix HH^T is invertible.

3. The matrix GG^T is invertible.

Definition 1.2. An $[n,k]$ code C is called optimal if it has the highest weight among all the $[n,k]$ codes, such a code is denoted as $C=[n,k,d_O(n,k)]$, where $d_o=d_O(n,k)=max\{d \mid \text{there is an } [n,k,d]_q \text{ code}\}$. Denote $d_l = d_l(n,k)=max\{d \mid \text{there is an } [n,k,d]_q \text{ LCD code}\}$. If there is a $C=[n,k,d_l(n,k)]_q$ LCD code, we call C an optimal LCD code. If there is a $C=[n,k,d_l(n,k)-1]_q$ LCD code, C is called a near optimal LCD code.

In [15], for a given linear code C, the authors showed that there is an LCD code C' which is equivalent to C. Hence to construct optimal LCD codes one needs to give optimal linear codes and construct suitable equivalent transformations formed by coordinates permutation and monomial matrix.

The objective of this paper is to study construction of optimal LCD codes over F_5. In Section 2, we give will construct LCD $[n,k]$ codes with k=3, 4 from known codes obtained in the Database of Magma [16]. Section 3 gives discussions and the conclusion.

2. Construction of 3 and 4 Dimensional LCD Codes

In this section, we discuss construction of LCD codes from known linear codes, the results are provided in two subsections.

2.1 Construction of [*n*,3] LCD Codes

In this subsection, for length n with $3 \le n \le 62$, we present optimal $[n,3,d_o]$ linear codes and construct LCD $[n,3,d_l]$ codes with $d_o = d_l$.

The Database in Magma [16-18] give $[n,3,d_o]$ code for length n satisfies $3 \le n \le 62$, denote the generator matrix of the $[n,3,d_o]$ code as $G_{n,3}$. We check these 60 optimal codes and find that 33 of them are LCD codes. These 33 codes have the following lengths n, where $n=$ 3, 4, 7, 8, 10, 11, 14, 18, 19, 20-24, 26, 33, 34, 36-40, 42, 45, 47-49, 52-57. The remaining 27 codes can be used to construct optimal LCD codes by the following steps.

Step 1.1: If $n=$ 6, 12, 13, 15, 17, 28, 35, 41, 43, 46, 59, 60, for each $G_{n,3}$, we can change $G_{n,3}$ into $G'_{n,3}$ by diagonal transformation, where the columns of $G'_{n,3}$ are all monic vectors. Then $G' = G'_{n,3}$ satisfies

$$rank(G'(G')^T) = 3.$$

Hence $G'_{n,3}$ generate optimal LCD $[n,3]$ codes. Thus we can construct 13 optimal LCD codes.

For example, the matrix

$$G_{6,3} = \begin{pmatrix} 100223 \\ 010324 \\ 001434 \end{pmatrix}$$

We denote $G_{n,k}G_{n,k}^T = T_{n,k}$, where

$$T_{6,3} = \begin{pmatrix} 321 \\ 204 \\ 142 \end{pmatrix}$$

satisfies

$$rank\left(T_{6,3}\right) = 2$$

which implies $G_{6,3}$ generates a non-LCD code; using monomial matrix, we can change $G_{6,3}$ into a monic matrix $G'_{6,3}$, which generates LCD [6,3] codes as

$$G'_{6,3} = \begin{pmatrix} 100111 \\ 010413 \\ 001243 \end{pmatrix}$$

$$T'_{6,3} = \begin{pmatrix} 434 \\ 321 \\ 410 \end{pmatrix}$$

and

$$rank(T'_{6,3}) = 3.$$

Step 1.2: If $n=5,9,25,27,29,30,50,58$ for each $G_{n,3}$, we can permute one or two columns of $G_{n,3}$ and change it into $G''_{n,3} = (I_3 \mid P_{n\text{-}3})$. If $G_{n,3}$ has the form of

$$G''_{n,3} = (I_3 \mid P_{n-3}),$$

then no permutation is need. Now, let

$$\mathrm{I}_3 = (\alpha_1, \alpha_2, \alpha_3),$$

for

$$\alpha_1 = (1,0,0)^T,\ \alpha_2 = (0,1,0)^T,\ \alpha_3 = (0,0,1)^T,$$

then it is not difficult to check that

$$(3\alpha_1, 3\alpha_2, \alpha_3 \mid P_2),$$

$$(3\alpha_1, 3\alpha_2, 3\alpha_3 \mid P_6),$$

$$(3\alpha_1, \alpha_2, \alpha_3 \mid P_{22}),$$

$$\ldots,$$

$$(\alpha_1, 3\alpha_2, \alpha_3 \mid P_{55})$$

generate optimal LCD codes.
For example, the matrix

$$G_{5,3} = \begin{pmatrix} 10031 \\ 01013 \\ 00122 \end{pmatrix}$$

and

DOI: 10.1051/itmconf/20171204006

$$T_{5,3} = \begin{pmatrix} 113 \\ 113 \\ 334 \end{pmatrix}$$

satisfying

$$rank\left(T_{5,3}\right) = 2,$$

which implies $G_{5,3}$ generates a non LCD code; using monomial matrix, we can change $G'_{5,3}$ into a monic matrix $G''_{5,3}$ which generates LCD $[5,3]$ code, the reason is that

$$G_{5,3} = \begin{pmatrix} 10031 \\ 01013 \\ 00122 \end{pmatrix},$$

$$G''_{5,3} = (3\alpha_1 3\alpha_2 \alpha_3 | \; P_2),$$

$$T''_{5,3} = \begin{pmatrix} 101 \\ 024 \\ 141 \end{pmatrix},$$

and

$$rank(G''_{5,3} G''^{T}_{5,3}) = 3.$$

Step 1.3: If $n=$ 31, 32, 44, 51, 61, 62, for each $G_{n,3}$,we first change $G_{n,3}$ into $G'_{n,3}$ as we did in step 1.1, then permutation one or two columns of $G'_{n,3}$ as we did in step 1.2 and transform $G'_{n,3}$ into the form

$$G''_{n,3} = (I_3 | P_{n-3})$$

at last multiply the first three columns by suitable invertible diagonal matrix D, denote

$$G'''_{n,3} = (D | P_{n-3}),$$

then G''' gives an optimal LCD code. Thus we obtain 6 optimal LCD codes in this step.

For example, we first change $G_{31,3}$ into

$$G'_{31,3} = \begin{pmatrix} 1001111111100001111111111111111 \\ 0101324000011111324214334124231 \\ 0010000132413241324132413241324 \end{pmatrix}$$

then perform invertible diagonal matrix D, $G''_{31,3}$ is changed into $G'''_{31,3} = (3\alpha_1 3\alpha_2 \alpha_3 | \; P_{28})$,

$$T'''_{31,3} = \begin{pmatrix} 300 \\ 030 \\ 001 \end{pmatrix}$$

and $rank(T'''_{31,3}) = 3$.

Summarizing the previous discussion, the following theorem holds.

Theorem 2.1 If $3 \le n \le 62$, there exists an optimal LCD $[n,3,d]$ code.

2.2 Construction of [n,4] LCD Codes

In this subsection, for length n with $4 \le n \le 156$, we present optimal $[n,4,d_o]$ linear codes and construct LCD $[n,4,d_l]$ codes with $d_o = d_l$.

The Database in Magma [16-18] give $[n,4,d_o]$ code for length n with $4 \le n \le 156$. We checked these 153 optimal codes and found that 111 of them are LCD codes. These 111 codes have the following length n, where $n=$ 4, 6-9, 12-13, 17-27, 29-31, 34-38, 41-45, 47-48, 51-57, 59-61, 63-64, 66-67, 71-73, 77-81, 84, 86-88, 90, 93-97, 99, 103-105, 107, 109-113, 115-119, 123, 127-131, 133-138, 140-147, 149-153, 156. The remaining 42 codes can be used to construct optimal LCD codes by the following steps.

Step 2.1: If $n=$ 5, 10, 11, 14-16, 28, 32, 33, 39, 40, 46, 49, 50, 62, 65, 68-70, 74, 85, 91, 92, 98, 100-102, 106, 108, 114, 120-122, 124-126, 132, 139, 148, 154, 155, for each $G_{n,4}$, we can change $G_{n,4}$ into $G'_{n,4}$, where the columns of $G'_{n,4}$ are all monic factors. Then $G' = G'_{n,4}$ satisfies $rank(G'(G')^T) = 4$. Hence we can construct 36 optimal LCD codes in this way.

Step 2.2: If $n=$ 58, 75, 76, 82, 83, 89, for each $G_{n,4}$, we can permute one or two columns of $G_{n,4}$ and change it into $G''_{n,4} = (I_4 | P_{n-4})$.

Let

$$I_4 = (\beta_1, \beta_2, \beta_3, \beta_4),$$

where

$$\beta_1 = (1,0,0,0)^T,$$

$$\beta_2 = (0,1,0,0)^T,$$

$$\beta_3 = (0,0,1,0)^T,$$

DOI: 10.1051/itmconf/20171204006

$$\beta_4 = (0,0,0,1)^T$$

Then, similar to that we did in subsection A, it is not difficult to check that

$$(\beta_1, \beta_2, \beta_3, 3\beta_4 \mid P_{54}),$$

$$(\beta_1, \beta_2, 3\beta_3, \beta_4 \mid P_{71}),$$

$$(\beta_1, 3\beta_2, \beta_3, 3\beta_4 \mid P_{72}),$$

$$\cdots$$

$$(\beta_1, \beta_2, \beta_3, 3\beta_4 \mid P_{85})$$

generate optimal LCD codes.

For example, we change $G_{58,4}$ into $G'_{58,4} = (A \mid B)$, where

$$A = \begin{pmatrix} 1000321344203431424331242032101300313203 \\ 0100340434131024143402102423011034132303 \\ 0010011111111100000000011111111112222222 \\ 0003000000000011111111111111111111111111 \end{pmatrix}$$

and

$$B = \begin{pmatrix} 011142140233212002 \\ 212302410434032411 \\ 222333333333344444 \\ 111111111111111111 \end{pmatrix}.$$

Then

$$T_{58,4} = \begin{pmatrix} 0230 \\ 2300 \\ 3000 \\ 0003 \end{pmatrix},$$

we have $rank(T_{58,4}) = 4$. Hence, we have constructed an optimal LCD $[58,4,45]$ code.

Summarizing the previous discussion, the following theorem holds.

Theorem **2.2** If $4 \le n \le 156$, there exists an optimal LCD $[n,4,d]$ code.

3. Discussion and Conclusion

In this paper, we have studied the construction of LCD codes over F_5 from known linear codes by special transformations. Many $[n,3]$ and $[n,4]$ optimal LCD codes have been obtained from the Database of Magma and constructed via transformation technique. By the technique in this paper, one can construct many LCD codes with good parameters for some applications.

From [17-21], we know that existence of many optimal linear codes over F_5 are determined. Yet, it is not known whether these codes are LCD codes. Our future work concerns the constructions of LCD codes with larger lengths and higher dimensions. Hence, much work is needed in the future. The reader is thus cordially invited to uncover the world of LCD codes over F_5.

Acknowledgement

This work is supported by National Natural Science Foundation of China under Grant No.11471011 and Natural Science Foundation of Shaanxi under Grant No. 2017JQ1032.

References

1. W. C. Huffman, V. Pless, *Fundamentals of Error-Correcting Codes*, (Cambridge University Press, Cambridge, 2003).
2. J. L. Massey, Inform. Cont., 7, 369-380(1964).
3. J. L. Massey, Discrete Math., 106/107, 337-342(1992).
4. C. Carlet, S. Guilley, *Coding Theory and Applications, CIM Series in Mathematical Sciences*(Springer Verlag, 3, 97-105, 2014). See also : Adv. Math. Commun., 10, 131-150(2016).
5. J. Qian, L. Zhang, Design code. cryptogr.,77,193-202(2015).
6. L. Lu, R. Li, L. Guo, Q. Fu, Quantum Inf. Process, 14, 165–182 (2015).
7. K. Guenda, S. Jitman, T. A. Gulliver, Design code. cryptogr., (1-16) 2016. see also : arXiv: 1606.00134v1.
8. L. Lu, R. Li, L. Guo, Int.J. Quantum Inf., 14, 1750017 (2017) .
9. X. Hou, and F. Oggier, *IEEE International Symposium on Information Theory*, (1501-1505) 2016.
10. E. R. Lina, Jr. ,E. G. Nocon, *the DLSU Research Congress*, 4(2016).
11. K. Boonniyoma, S. Jitman, https: //arxiv. org/pdf/1605.06827.pdf.
12. S. Zhu, B. Pang,Z. Sun, arXiv:1610.08206v1 [cs. IT] 26 Oct 2016.
13. L. Jin, IEEE T. Inform. Theory, Doi 10.1109/TIT. 2016. 2644660, 2016.
14. B. Chen, H. Liu, arxiv.org/abs/1705.00770v1.
15. C. Carlet, S. Mesnager, C. Tang, Y. Qi, arXiv:1703.04346v2.
16. http://magma.maths.usyd.edu.au/magma/download/db/
17. M. Grassl, http: //www. codetables.de.
18. W. Bosma, J. Cannon, *Handbook of Magma functions*, (Sydney,1995).

19. Iliya Boukliev, Stoyan Kapralov, Tatsuya Maruta, Masaharu Fukui, IEEE T. Inform. Theory, 43,308-313(1997).
20. Tatsuya Maruta, Maori Shinohara, Ayako Kikui, Discrete Math., 309, 1255-1272 (2009).
21. Yuuki Kageyama, Tatsuya Maruta, *Seventh International Workshop on Optimal Codes and Related Topics*(Albena, Bulgaria, 2013).

DOI: 10.1051/itmconf/20171204007

Performance evaluation of AODV, DSR and DSDV in mobile ad-hoc network using NS-2

Fan-Shuo KONG, Bei-Bei CUI

School of Software Engineering, Beijing University of Technology, Beijing, China
e-mail: kongfanshuo0224@163.com, cuibeibeibatty@163.com

Abstract—Mobile ad-hoc network (MANET) is a set of movable hosts established without existing network infrastructure and can be self-organized dynamically. MANET protocols have faced big challenges due to dynamic changing network topology and asymmetric network link. In this paper, we simulate AODV, DSDV, DSR routing protocols in network simulator NS-2 and evaluate and compare the performance metrics for each routing protocol using packet delivery ratio, average end to end delay of packets and normalized routing overhead. We conduct the simulation by varying the sending rate of source node (2 packets/s and 4 packets/s) with different pause time using node movement model and cbr source traffic model.

1 Introduction

Ad hoc networks consist of hosts without existing network infrastructure and can be self-organized dynamically. The idea of mobile ad hoc network is to maintain strong and self-organized function in mobile wireless networks by incorporating routing functionality into movable nodes[1]. A lot of work has been done to develop and improve routing protocols in ad hoc networks[2]. In MANET, the mobile host need to communicate with other mobile hosts which may not in its radio transmission range, so it is essential for routing protocols to finish these following functions, determine network topology, maintain network connectivity, schedule transmission, and route packet. Routing protocols in ad hoc network were designed according to the goals of dynamic topology maintenance, minimal control overhead, minimal process overhead, multi hop routing ability, and loop prevention[3]. According to the strategy of routing, the routing protocols in ad hoc networks is categorized as table-driven(proactive) routing protocols and on-demand(reactive) routing protocols. The following figure 1 shows the classification of routing protocols. Each of these protocols performs differently in different wireless conditions. Hence it is necessary to analyze performance of these routing protocols to know its behavior and suitable working environment. Several factors may affect the overall performance of routing protocols in ad hoc network. For example, the link failures caused by node mobility will impact on packet transfer and quality of service (QoS). the internal characteristic of node itself like node speed or pause time, external factor like network size, traffic intensity will have a considerable impact on the overall performance of ad hoc network.

This paper is organized into five sections. The previous section covers the introduction of ad hoc network. Next section describes a detailed study on different types of MANET routing protocols. Section III describes the simulation methodology. Section IV describes performance metrics and result analysis, and the final section concludes the paper.

2 Literature Survey

2.1On-Demand routing protocol

On-Demand routing protocol first starts a process of path discovery and then transfers routing information when a path is required to get to the destination node.

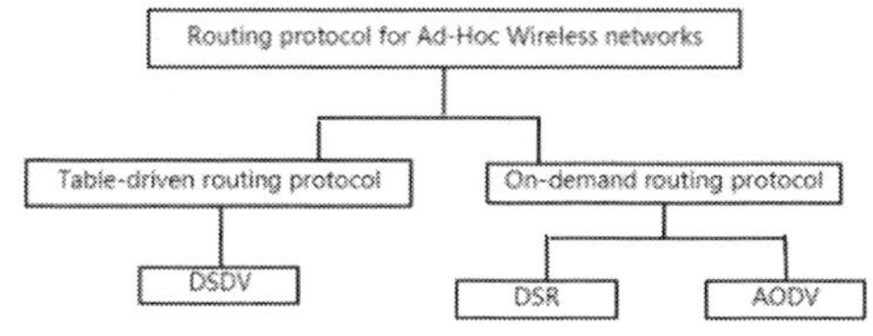

Fig. 1. Classification of routing protocols

2.1.1DSR

Dynamic Source Routing protocol is an on demand protocol, it overcomes the bandwidth consumption by removing periodic table update messages which is mandatory in table-driven approach[4]. DSR has two phases, Route Discovery phase to find a path and Route Maintenance phase to maintain a path. When there is a need to transfer packets to a destination, the source node will query available route from source to destination in its route cache, if no route is available, it will initialize a process of route discovery[5]. The request packet(RREQ) sent by source node includes the destination address at first, and the series of intermediate nodes' address will be added to the request packet through the broadcast flooding. When destination node receives RREQ packet, it will send back a route reply(RREP) packet to source node through the reverse path included by RREQ packet. After the establishment of route discovery, the data packet sent by the source carries complete ordered series of nodes which the packet must pass in packet's header, this could prevent the loop and eliminate the need of updating route information in the intermediate nodes which the packet is forwarded through. In route maintenance phase, once the link is broken between nodes, route error messages will be sent to all nodes in the network. Intermediate node use cache to maintain several routes to destination node, so sometimes if intermediate node gets the RREQ packet, it directly sends the path information to source node[5].

2.1.2AODV

Ad-hoc On-demand Distance Vector protocol is on-demand routing protocol[6]. When the source wants to transfer data, it will try to establish a path between itself and the destination. When a node wants to build a traffic connection, it first broadcast a request(RREQ) including the information of destination. The intermediate nodes process the RREQ, they record the reverse path to the source node in their route table, and then decide whether to broadcast the RREQ or not. When the node receives such a message, if it is the destination node itself or there is a route to the destination node in its route entry, it will send a reply(RREP) using the reverse route to the source node. The intermediate node will also record the reverse path to the destination when receiving the RREP. The source nodes then begin the process of sending data using the route entry which has the freshest sequence number of destination and minimum number of hops. The entries in the routing tables will be recycled in a regular interval. When the links is broken, the routing error packet(RERR) is flooded to the source node, and the process of route discovery restarts. Following figure 2,3 shows that how route will be established in AODV.

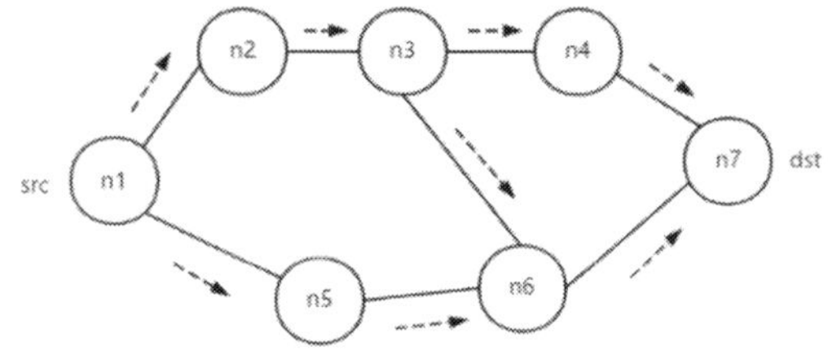

Fig 4. Route request broadcasting in AODV protocol

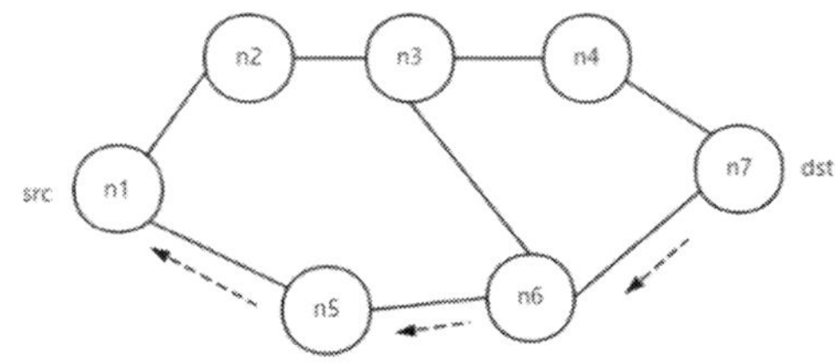

Fig 5. Route reply in AODV protocol

The main difference between DSR and AODV is in DSR, it carries complete ordered sequence of node path to be traversed in each data packet, while in AODV the source node and all intermediate nodes stores next hop information of each flow. Besides, DSR doesn't have beacon packets to tell neighbors of its existence, while in AODV, it requires periodic hello packet (beacon) transmission, which is used to inform its neighbors of its presence.

2.2Table-Driven routing protocol

Table-Driven routing protocols maintain a table about topology information of whole network in each node just like wired network routing protocol. In order to maintain accuracy and consistency of route table, nodes will update all tables frequently.

2.2.1DSDV

Destination Sequenced Distance Vector[7], is hop-by-hop distance vector routing protocol which requires each node to send routing updates in a regular interval. It is based on principles of classical Bellman-Ford Routing algorithm[8]. The routing table maintained by each node consists of records of the next hop for every reachable destination, the number of hops to destination and the sequence number assigned by destination. The sequence number is used to judge the freshness of route entry. If any change has occurred in its routing table from any received update, it will transmit its routing table update. The update is based on time-driven and event-driven, and "Full-dump" update or "incremental" update will be used to send the routing table updates.

DOI: 10.1051/itmconf/20171204007

3 Simulation Methodology

3.1Simulation Modeling

Simulation is the commonly used way to analyze the performance and behavior of wireless network before putting it in use in real application. Several network simulators can be used to simulate the scenario as accurate as in real time implementation. In this work, we used the discrete-event simulator NS2 (version 2.35) [9] to do the simulation, and conduct the performance analysis using AWK script[10]. we adopted several models integrated in NS2 simulator. We use IEEE 802.11 MAC model for MAC layer functionality. We adopt two Ray Ground propagation model for wireless signal propagation. For node mobility model, we use Random Waypoint Mobility model to implement dynamic network topologies. We use Radio Model for radio characteristics used by node with proper bandwidth and frequency. For Traffic Model, we use CBR, UDP Model for nodes to send traffic to destinations.

3.2Simulation Methods

The aim of our experiments is to quantify the effects of various factors and their impact on the overall performance in ad hoc networks. Each test of the simulation accepts a mobile scenario file and a traffic scenario file as input. The mobile scenario is created by a transcript program called cbrgen.tcl, which describes specific movement of each node with exact time the motion occurs or direction changes. The traffic scenario is created by the tool setdest, which describes the exact connection pairs initialized by particular nodes with exact time connection begins. To evaluate the performance of a specific factor, we take 5 runs of simulation to generate 5 different scenario patterns and the average of these 5 outputs is calculated to be the performance of the considered factor. For each factor, we adopted 7 sample points to compare three different ad hoc protocols, DSR, DSDV, AODV. Hence, 105 runs of simulation are conducted to analyze each factor for three protocols. Network layer characteristics is the factors to be observed, so only changes in the strategy of routing is observed and varied, while other characteristics of physical layer(ground propagation model), link layer(MAC 802.11), transport layer(UDP), application layer(CBR) stay fixed.

3.3Simulation Parameters

Simulation environment is in a 1000 * 300 square with total 50 mobile nodes with constant maximum speed 20 m/s. We set traffic pattern with maximum 20 UDP connections between mobile nodes. The mobility of all nodes is done with various pause times from 0 to 900s.The packets sending rate of each source varies from 2pkts/s to 4pkts/s. Simulation time is 900s. Detailed parameters are shown in table I.

TABLE I. SIMULATION PARAMETERS

Component	Type
Channel Type	Channel/Wireless Channel
Antenna Model	Omni Antenna
Radio Propagation Model	Two Ray Ground
Network Interface Type	Phy/ Wireless Phy
Mac Layer Protocol	IEEE 802.11
Interface Queue Type	Queue/DropTail/PriQueue
Number of Nodes	50
Pause Times	0, 150, 300, 450, 600, 750, 900
Number of Sources	50
Topology Size	1000m x 300m
Traffic Type	Constant Bit Rate (CBR)
Packet Size	512 Byte
Packet send rate	2pkts/s, 4pkts/s
Simulation Time	900 seconds
Simulation Tool	NS-2.35

4 Performance metrics and RESULT ANALYSIS

4.1Performance Metrics

The performance metrics reflects the Quality of Service (QoS) of the wireless network. The following three performance metrics are considered to characterize the performance and behavior of DSR, DSDV, AODV routing protocols: Packet delivery ratio (PDR), Average end-to-end delay of data packets and normalized routing overhead.

4.1.1Packet delivery Ratio

Packet Delivery Ratio (PDR) [11] measures the successful rate of packet delivery in ad hoc routing protocols. It is calculated that the total number of packets received by traffic destination divided by the total number of packets sent by traffic source.

$$\text{packet\_delivery\_ratio} = \frac{\sum CBR\_received}{\sum CBR\_sent} \quad (4\text{-}1)$$

where, $CBR\_received$ is the total number of CBR packets received from destinations, CBR_sent is the total number of CBR packets sent by sources.

4.1.2Average end-to-end delay of data packets

Average end-to-end delay[12] of data packets is defined as the average delay of received data packets within a network. End-to-end delay mainly includes propagation delay, transmission delay, queuing delay and processing delay. It is calculated that the sum of delay which cumulated by every successfully-arrived data packets divided by the total number of received data packets.

$$average\_end\_to\_end\_delay = \frac{1}{n}\sum_{i=1}^{n}(RT_i - ST_i) \quad (4\text{-}2)$$

where, n is the total number of received packets, RT_i is the received time of number i packet, ST_i is the sent time of number i packet, i varies from 1 to n.

4.1.3Normalized routing overhead

Normalized routing overhead[13] is defined as how many control packets consumed by one successfully-arrived data packet. It is calculated that the total number of control packets divided by the total number of received data packets.

$$\text{normalize route overhead} = \frac{\sum control\_packet\_sent}{\sum data\_packet\_received} \quad (4\text{-}3)$$

where, $control\_packet\_sent$ is the total number of control packets sent or forwarded by the nodes. $data\_packet\_received$ is the total number of data packets received from destinations.

4.2Result Analysis

4.2.1Packet Delivery Ratio:

Graphs in figure 4,5 shows packet delivery ratio of combination of DSR, AODV and DSDV. It can be seen when communication send rate is 2.0 or 4.0 packets/s, AODV and DSR routing protocol packet delivery ratio showed similarly satisfied results. No matter of the node is under the condition of weak mobility(low pause time), or strong mobility(strong pause time), the packet delivery rate is over 95%. However, packet delivery ratio of DSDV appears larger fluctuation with the change of the pause time, when the pause time equals to 0s, DSDV protocol packet delivery rate is lower than 80%. In general, In a short pause time(strong mobility), the performance of DSDV protocol is far less than AODV protocol and the DSR protocol.

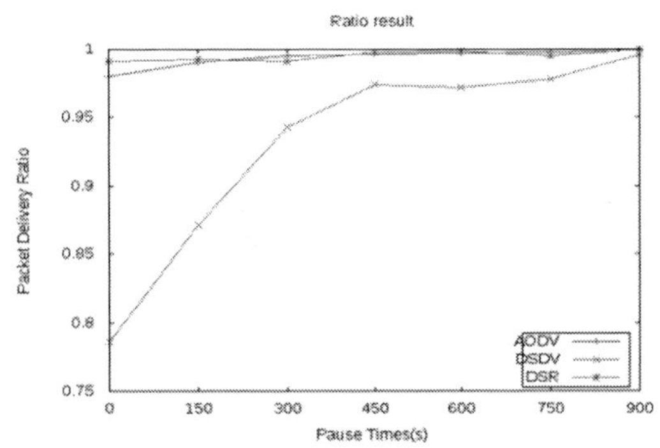

Fig.4. Packet Delivery Ratio of send rate 2 packets/s

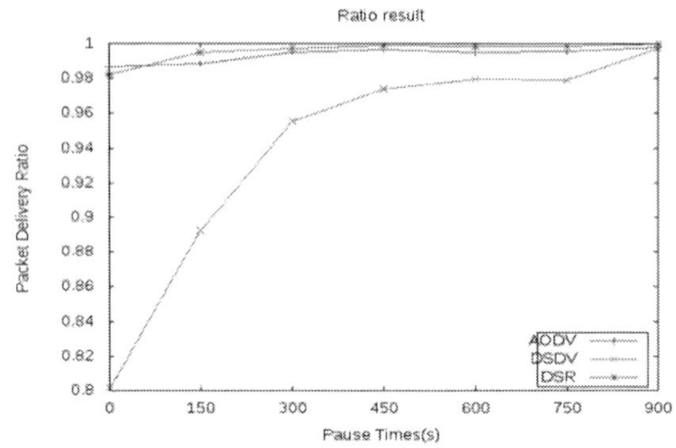

Fig.5. Packet Delivery Ratio of send rate 4 packets/s

4.2.2Average end-to-end delay of data packets:

As graphs shown in figure 6,7, it is observed that at all sending rate, the end-to-end delay gradually decreases for all protocols as node mobility becomes lower (pause time is longer). When the node mobility is frequent, AODV performs much better than DSR and DSDV.

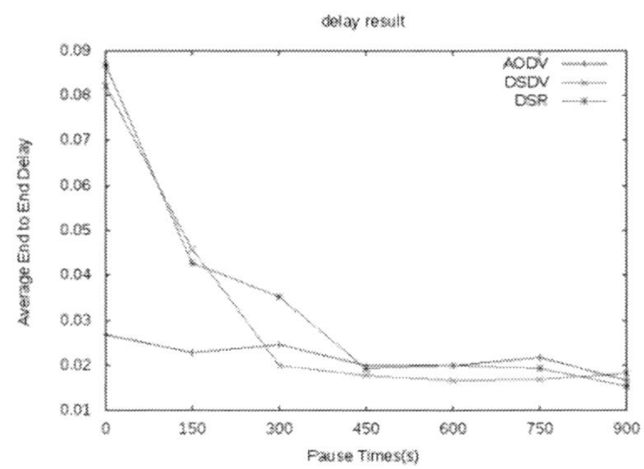

Fig.6. Average end-to-end delay of send rate 2 packets/s

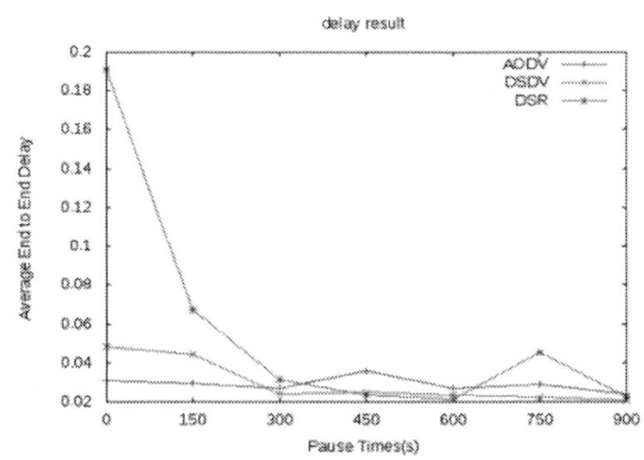

Fig.7. Average end-to-end delay of send rate 4 packets/s

4.2.3Normalized routing overhead:

Normalized routing overhead of DSDV protocol basically goes smoothly with the change of pause time and far more than that of AODV and DSR, that is because DSDV belongs to table-driven routing protocol, basically the routing overhead depicts small changes caused by network load and node mobility. While the AODV protocol and the DSR protocol is an on-demand routing protocol, the lower the mobility, the lower the normalized routing overhead is. Besides, in the same scenario, normalized routing overhead performance of DSR is always better than the AODV protocol, this is because the AODV protocol preserves only one routing entry for each destination node, when the link break, it will trigger a new round of routing discovery process. In general, DSR performs the best results than AODV and DSDV.

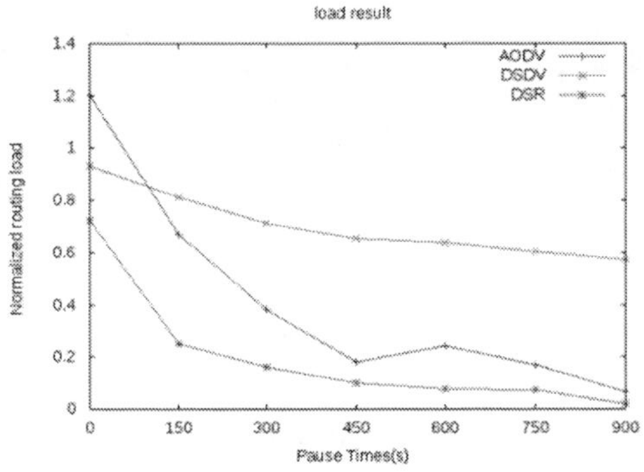

Fig. 8. Normalized Routing overhead of send rate 2 packets/s

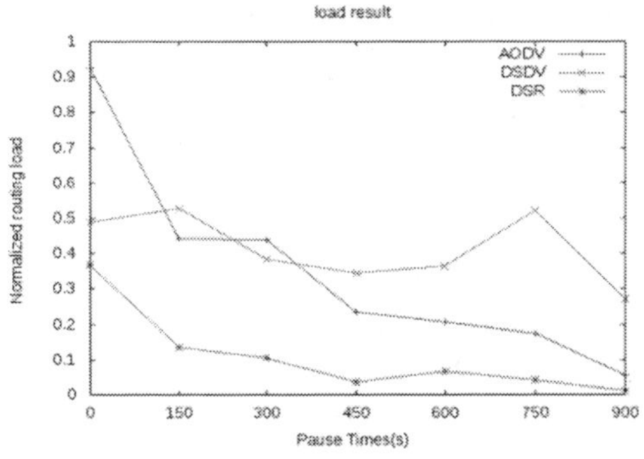

Fig. 9. Normalized Routing overhead of send rate 4 packets/s

Conclusion

This paper proposes an performance evaluation of three different routing protocols named as DSR, AODV, and DSDV. The process of the evaluation includes simulation of wireless network on platform in NS2. We analyzed them using three performance metrics named Packet Delivery Ratio, average end-to-end delay of data packets, and normalized routing overhead. From the simulation of these three routing protocols, we get the result as follows. For the result of packet delivery, DSR and AODV get the similarly better packet delivery ratio than DSDV. AODV get better performance in average delay than DSR and DSDV. DSR have minimum routing overhead than AODV and DSDV.

References

[1] Tonguz O and Ferrari G., "Adhoc Wireless Networks-A Communication -Theoritic Perspective, Wiley and Sons", 2009.

[2] Sarkar S, Basavaraju T.G. and Puttamadappa C., " Ad Hoc Mobile Wireless Networks: Principles, protocols and applications", Auerbach Publications, 2008.

[3] Royer E.M.and Toh C., "A review of current routing protocols for adhoc mobile wireless networks", IEEE personal communications,1999, pp. 46–56.

[4] D. B. Johnson and D. A. Maltz, "DSR : The Dynamic Source Routing Protocol for Multi-Hop Wireless Ad Hoc Networks," pp. 1–25.

[5] C. E. Perkins and E. M. Royer, "Ad Hoc On-Demand Distance Vector Routing," Proc. 2nd IEEE Wksp. Mobile Comp. Sys. and Apps., Feb. 1999, pp. 90-100.

[6] Perkins and Bhagwat "Highly Dynamic Destination Sequenced Distance-vector Routing (DSDV) for Mobile Computers, ACM SIGCOMM '94 Conference.

[7] The network simulator - ns-2. http://www.isi.edu/nsnam/ns/.

[8] Ould-Khaoua Ahmed and Al-Maashri. "Performance Analysis of MANET Routing Protocols in the Presence of Self-Similar Traffic". IEEE, ISSN- 0742-1303, First published in Proc. of the 31st IEEE Conference on Local Computer Networks, 2006.

[9] Performance Measurement of Various Routing Protocols in Ad-hoc Network, Rahman, Islam, Alex, International Conference of Engineers and Computer Scientists 2009, IMECS 2009, Hong Kong.

[10] Fasee Ullah, Muhammad Amin and Hamid ul Ghaffar,"Simulating AODV and DSDV For Adynamic Wireless Sensor Networks" IJCSNS International Journal of Computer Science and Network Security, VOL.10 No.7,July 2010

[11] Asma Tuteja , Rajneesh Gujrl and Sunil Thalia,"Comparative Performance Analysis of DSDV, AODV and DSR Routing Protocols in MANET using NS2",International Conference on Advances in Computer Engineering, 2010.

[12] Sapna S. Kaushik1 & P.R.Deshmukh2, "Comparison of effectiveness of AODV, DSDV and DSR routing protocols in Mobile Ad-Hoc Network" International Journal of Information Technology and Knowledge Management , Volume 2, No. 2, July-December 2009.

[13] S.Mohapatra, P.Kanungo , "Performance analysis of AODV, DSR, OLSR and DSDV Routing Protocols using NS2 Simulator," International Conference on Communication Technology and System Design 2011 ,SciVerse Science Direct, Procedia Engineering 30 (2012), pp69-76, doi:10.1016/j.proeng.2012.01.835.0

DOI: 10.1051/itmconf/20171204008

Design and Implementation of Movie Recommendation System Based on Knn Collaborative Filtering Algorithm

Bei-Bei CUI
School of Software Engineering, Beijing University of Technology, Beijing, China
e-mail: cuibeibeibatty@163.com

Abstract—In the spread of information, how to quickly find one's favorite movie in a large number of movies become a very important issue. Personalized recommendation system can play an important role especially when the user has no clear target movie. In this paper, we design and implement a movie recommendation system prototype combined with the actual needs of movie recommendation through researching of KNN algorithm and collaborative filtering algorithm. Then we give a detailed principle and architecture of JAVAEE system relational database model. Finally, the test results showed that the system has a good recommendation effect.

1 Introduction

With the rapid development of Internet technology[1], today's society has entered the era of Web 2, information overload has become a reality. How to find the required information in the mass of data has become a hot research topic. Movie is one of the main spiritual entertainment, also has the problem of information overload. In order to solve this problem, this paper put forward a proposal of personalized movie recommendation system[1,2].

Personalized recommendation try to know the characteristics and preferences of the user by collecting and analysing historical behavior to know what kind of person the user is, what kind of behavior preference the user has, what kind of things the user like to share and so on[3.4.5], and finally understand that user characteristics and preferences based on the rules of the platform and recommend the information and goods which the user interested[6.7]. Personalized recommendation system is a kind of information filtering technology. It is an integrated system which is a combination of a variety of data mining algorithms and user related information, to meet the interests or potential interests of users. The common recommendation system is categorized as content based recommendation system, collaborative filtering recommendation system, and hybrid recommendation system[9,10]. Each recommendation algorithm has different use range and use condition, it results in the use of different recommendation algorithm for the same information recommendation. In the actual application of recommendation system, the system tends to be a hybrid recommendation system. That is, to mix the advantage of each recommendation algorithm to the recommended process to effectively improve the recommendation effect.

In this paper, the key research contents is to help users to obtain user-interested movie automatically in the massive movie information data using KNN algorithm and collaborative filtering algorithm, and to develop a prototype of movie recommendation system based on KNN collaborative filtering algorithm.

2. Literature Survey

2.1KNN algorithm

KNN algorithm is called K nearest neighbor classification algorithm. The core idea of the KNN algorithm is: if the majority of the k most similar neighbors of sample in the feature space belongs to a certain category, then the sample is considered to belong to this category[8]. As shown in Figure 1, the majority of w's nearest neighbors belong to the x category, w belongs to the X category.

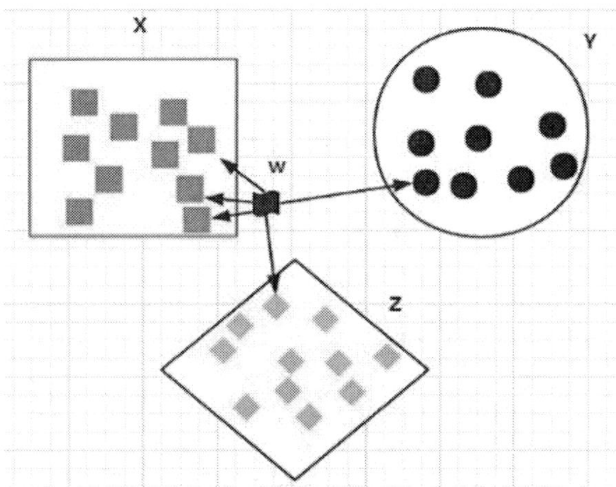

Fig. 1. example of KNN algorithm

2.2 Collaborative filtering algorithm

Collaborative filtering algorithm is categorized as user-based collaborative filtering algorithm[4] and project-based collaborative filtering. The basic principles of the two is quite similar, and this section mainly introduces the user-based collaborative filtering recommendation algorithm. The basic idea of collaborative filtering recommendation algorithm is to introduce the information of similar-interest users to object users[7]. As shown in figure 2.

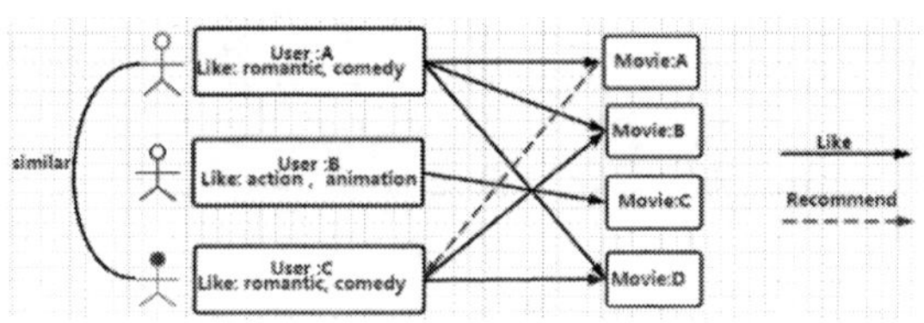

Fig. 2. example of UserCF algorithm

User A loves movie A, B, C, and user C likes movie B, D, so we can conclude that the preferences of user A and user C are very similar. Since user A loves movie D as well, so we can infer that the user A may also love item D, therefore item D would be recommended to the user. The basic idea of the algorithm is based on records of history score of user. Find the neighbor user as u\` who has the similar interest with target user u, and then recommend the items which the neighbor user u\` loved to target user u, the predict score which target user u may give on the item is obtained by the score calculation of neighbor user u\` on the item. The algorithm consists of three basic steps: user similarity calculation, nearest neighbor selection and prediction score calculation.

3 KNN collaborative filtering algorithm

KNN collaborative filtering algorithm, which is a collaborative filtering algorithm combined with KNN algorithm, use KNN algorithm to select neighbors. The basic steps of the algorithm are user similarity calculation, KNN nearest neighbor selection and predict score calculation[11.12].

3.1 User similarity computing

The similarity between users is calculated by evaluating the value of the items evaluated by two users.

Each user uses N dimension vector to represent item score, for example, to calculate of similarity of U1 and U3, first find out the set of films that they all scored as {m1, M2, M4, m5} and relative scores of these films. The score vector of U1 is {1,3,4,2}, and the score vector of U3 is {2,4,1,5}. The similarity of U1 and U3 is calculated by the similarity formula[13].

U\M	m1	m2	m3	m4	m5
u1	1	3	3	4	2
u2	3	1	4		
u3	2	4		1	5
u4	2		2		

Fig. 3. Calculating formula of users' similarity

The similarity of u and u' is denoted as $sim(u,u')$, the commonly used method of calculating user similarity are Cosine Similarity and Pearson Correlation similarity.

3.1.1 Cosine similarity

The method calculates the similarity between two users by calculating the cosine of the angle between the two vectors[2]:

$$sim(x,y')=\cos(\vec{X},\vec{Y})=\frac{\vec{X}\cdot\vec{Y}}{|\vec{X}|*|\vec{Y}|}=\frac{\sum_{s\in s_{xy}} r_{x,s}r_{y,s}}{\sqrt{\sum_{s\in s_{xy}}(r_{x,s})^2}\sqrt{\sum_{s\in s_{xy}}(r_{y,s})^2}} \quad (1)$$

Among them, $r_{x,s}$and $r_{y,s}$ are the score of goods s scored by user X and Y respectively. s_{xy} is the set of movies that user x and user y both scored on. In other words, $s_{xy}=\{s \in Items|r_{x,s} \neq \varepsilon \cap r_{y,s} \neq \varepsilon\}$[3]

3.1.2 Pearson correlation similarity

Pearson correlation similarity is a measurement of the linear relationship between two variables.

$$sim(x,y') = \frac{\sum_{s\in s_{xy}}(r_{x,s}-\overline{r_x})(r_{y,s}-\overline{r_y})}{\sqrt{\sum_{s\in s_{xy}}(r_{x,s}-\overline{r_x})^2}\sqrt{\sum_{s\in s_{xy}}(r_{y,s}-\overline{r_y})^2}} \quad (2)$$

Among them, $\overline{r_x}$ is the average score is x[3], the rest of the symbolic meaning is the same as formula(1).

3.2KNN nearest neighbor selection

After the calculation of similarity as $sim(u,u')$ between users, then the algorithm selects a number of users the highest similarity as the U's neighbor, denoted as u'. set a fixed value K for the neighbor selection, select only the most K high similarity as neighbors regardless of the value of the neighbor similarity of users. As shown in figure 4.

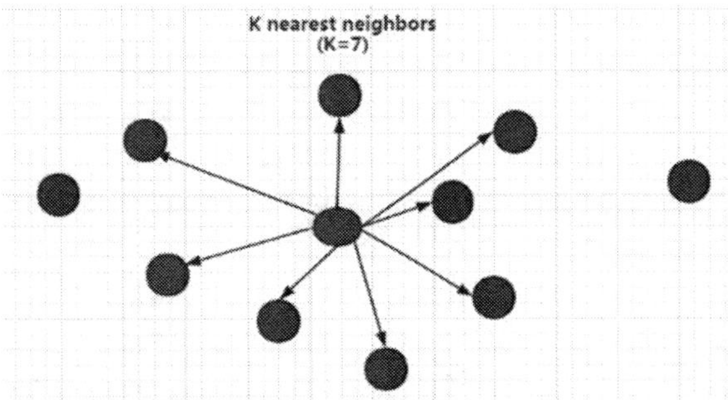

Fig.4. formula of K nearest neighbors when k=7

3.3Predict score calculation

After determining the user's neighbors, the score can be predicted according to the score of the neighbor to the item, The calculation formula is as follows:

$$r_{u,i}=\overline{r}_u+k\sum_{u'\in U} sim(u,u') * (r_{u',i} - \overline{r}_{u'}) \quad (3)$$

$$(k=1/\sum |sim(u,u')|)$$

$r_{u,i}$ was used to predict the score of user u to movie i[6].

To sum up, the process of calculating prediction score of user u for i is as follows:

Step1. Generate user - item two-dimensional matrix of score as Rmxn, where each score is $r_{u,i}$.

Step2: Use principle of cosine similarity or Pearson correlation similarity to calculate the similarity between each 2 users as $sim(u,u')$, and generate the user similarity matrix.

Step3: according to the results obtained by Step2, find K number of score which has the maximum weight, the corresponding K users is the neighbors of u.

Step4: Use formula 3 to calculate the predictive value of i for target user u.

In this way, we can calculate the prediction score of the target users for the non-scored movies, and the N movies with the highest score can be recommended to the user.

In this paper, KNN collaborative filtering algorithm based on user is used to implement the recommendation of movie[], and the collaborative filtering algorithm based on the project is used to implement the recommendation of the associated movie[5]. In addition, it can also recommend the movies to new users according to user registration information, and it can make new and unpopular movie recommendation according to the film's browsing and score[14].

4 Personalized recommendation system design

4.1architecture design

The system is based on B/S mode, uses JavaEE architecture, Tomcat server for system deployment, the architecture is shown in figure 5.

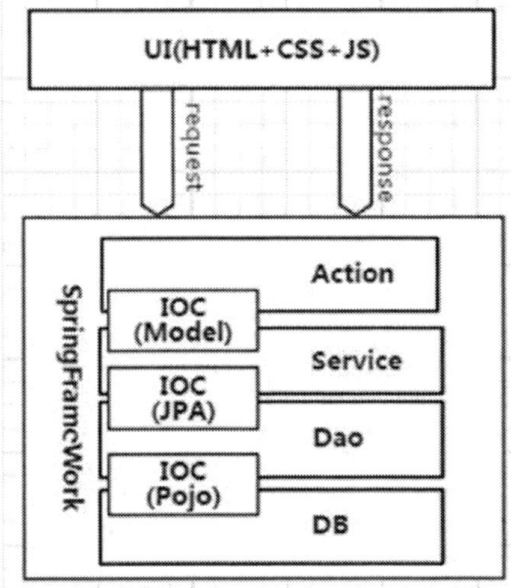

Fig. 5. System Architecture

Front view is implemented using HTML, CSS, JAVASCRIPT, the back end uses Struts2, Spring and Hibernate, the database uses MySQL for storage. The system is object-oriented to guarantee system of high cohesion and improve development efficiency using the SSH protocol[17]. Besides, it enhances the maintainability and scalability by separating Controller layer and View layer to reduce the degree of coupling between them, making it easier to maintain and modify the WEB application.

4.2Database design

Database is the basis of the system, this system uses MYSQL database, the overall database structure diagram is shown in the following figure 6, representing the integrity constraints between the data tables[18].

DOI: 10.1051/itmconf/20171204008

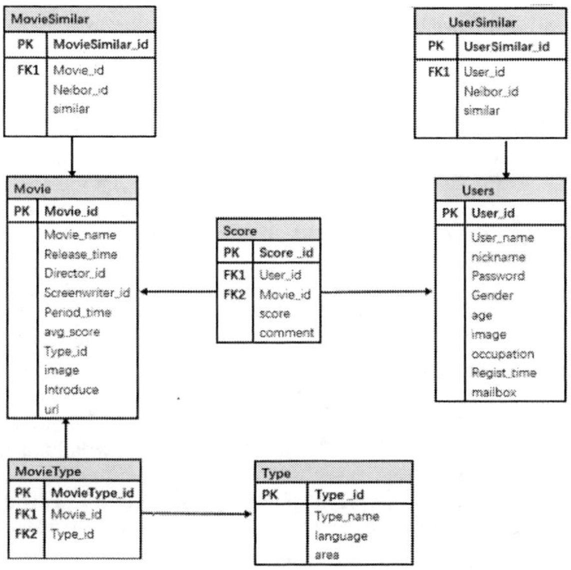

Fig. 6. Relational Model of Database

Table Users is the description of user information, including user ID, user name, password, registration time, etc. Table UserSimilar is the description of the user similarity information, including the user similarity ID, user ID, similar neighbor user ID, and the value of the similarity. Table Score is the description of users' rating information on the film, which is the direct information source of collaborative filtering algorithm, it includes the score ID, the user's ID who give the score ,the value of the score, content of comments. Table Movie is the description of the movie information, including the movie ID, movie name, director, movie URL, etc. Table MovieType is the description of type information of the movies, including the ID of movies' type, movie name, and type ID. Table MovieSimilar is the description of the movie similarity information, including the movie similarity ID, movie ID, the ID of highly similar neighbor, the value of similarity. Both the table UserSimilar and table Moviesimilar are the basis of the recommendation algorithm and system[15.16].

5 System operation effect

user registration system will capture the user's explicit and implicit behavioral characteristics and these characteristics is stored in the user database through the user login module. After logging in the system, the system will make the appropriate recommendation according to the user's information[19.20]. As shown in figure 7.

Fig. 7. the display of personal recommendation list

Conclusion

Under the condition of massive information, the requirements of movie recommendation system from film amateur are increasing. This article designs and implements a complete movie recommendation system prototype based on the KNN algorithm, collaborative filtering algorithm and recommendation system technology[10]. We give a detailed design and development process, and test the stability and high efficiency of experiment system through professional test. This paper has reference significance for the development of personalized recommendation technology.

References

[1] Peng, Xiao, Shao Liangshan, and Li Xiuran. "Improved Collaborative Filtering Algorithm in the Research and Application of Personalized Movie Recommendations", 2013 Fourth International Conference on Intelligent Systems Design and Engineering Applications, 2013.

[2] Munoz-Organero, Mario, Gustavo A. Ramíez-González, Pedro J. Munoz-Merino, and Carlos Delgado Kloos. "A Collaborative Recommender System Based on Space-Time Similarities", IEEE Pervasive Computing, 2010.

[3] Al-Shamri, M.Y.H.. "Fuzzy-genetic approach to recommender systems based on a novel hybrid user model", Expert Systems With Applications, 200810

[4] Hu Jinming. "Application and research of collaborative filtering in e-commerce recommendation system", 2010 3rd International Conference on Computer Science and Information Technology, 07/2010

[5] Xu, Qingzhen Wu, Jiayong Chen, Qiang. "A novel mobile personalized recommended method based on money flow model for stock exchange.(Researc", Mathematical Problems in Engineering, Annual 2014 Issue

[6] Yan, Bo, and Guanling Chen. "AppJoy : personalized mobile application discovery", Proceedings of the 9th international conference on Mobile systems applications and services - MobiSys 11 MobiSys 11, 2011.

[7] Davidsson C, Moritz S. Utilizing implicit feedback and context to recommend mobile applications from first use.

In: Proc. of the Ca RR 2011. New York: ACM Press, 2011. 19-22.http://dl.acm.org/citation.cfm?id=1961639[doi:10.1145/1961634.1961639]

[8] Bilge, A., Kaleli, C., Yakut, I., Gunes, I., Polat, H.: A survey of privacy-preserving collaborative filtering schemes. Int. J. Softw. Eng. Knowl. Eng. 23(08), 1085–1108 (2013)CrossRefGoogle Scholar

[9] Calandrino, J.A., Kilzer, A., Narayanan, A., Felten, E.W., Shmatikov, V.: You might also like: privacy risks of collaborative filtering. In: Proceedings of the IEEE Symposium on Security and Privacy, pp. 231–246, Oakland, CA, USA (2011)

[10] Research.ijcaonline.org

[11] Hu Jinming. "Application and research of collaborative filtering in e-commerce recommendation system", 2010 3rd International Conference on Computer Science and Information Technology, 07/2010

[12] www.pacis2014.org

[13] Xie HT, Meng XW. A personalized information service model adapting to user requirement evolution. Acta Electronica Sinica, 2011,39(3):643-648 (in Chinese with English abstract).

[14] Polat, H., Du, W.: Privacy-preserving top-n recommendation on distributed data. J. Am. Soc. Inf. Sci. Technol. 59(7), 1093–1108 (2008). http://dx.org/10.1002/asi.20831CrossRefGoogle Scholar

[15] Su, X., Khoshgoftaar, T.M.: A survey of collaborative filtering techniques. Adv. Artif. Intell, p. 4 (2009). http://dx.org/10.1155/2009/421425

[16] Yakut, I., Polat, H.: Estimating NBC-based recommendations on arbitrarily partitioned data with privacy. Knowl. Based Syst. 36(0), 353362(2012). http://www.sciencedirect.com/science/article/pii/S0950705112002031CrossRefGoogle Scholar

[17] Okkalioglu, M., Koc, M., Polat, H.: On the discovery of fake binary ratings. In: Proceedings of the 30th Annual ACM Symposium on Applied Computing, SAC 2015, pp. 901–907. ACM, USA (2015). http://doi.acm.org/10.1145/2695664.2695866

[18] Wang LC, Meng XW, Zhang YJ. A cognitive psychology-based approach to user preferences elicitation for mobile network services. Acta Electronica Sinica, 2011,39(11):2547-2553 (in Chinese with English abstract)

[19] Kaleli, C., Polat, H.: Privacy–preserving naïve bayesian classifier based recommendations on distributed data. Comput. Intell. 31(1), 47–68(2015). http://dx.org/10.1111/coin.12012MathSciNet CrossRefGoogle Scholar

[20] Munoz-Organero, Mario, Gustavo A. Ramíez-González, Pedro J. Munoz-Merino, and Carlos Delgado Kloos. "A Collaborative Recommender System Based on Space-Time Similarities", IEEE Pervasive Computing, 2010.

4g-Based Specialty Vehicles Real-Time Monitoring System Design and Implementation

Yu-Feng ZHUANG, Ke ZHANG

Logistics Department of Automation School ,Beijing University of Posts and Telecommunications Beijing, China
Email- zhuangyf@bupt.edu.cn,Email-mtt_zhangke@163.com

Abstract—In the future development of natural gas transportation industry, emerging ITS technology will be applied more and more, aiming at integrating precise positioning technology, geographic information system technology, database technology, multimedia technology and modern communication technology, sensor network technology and video capture technology, so as to achieve the transport steam (oil) vehicles in real time monitoring and management. The main research content of this paper is to design and research the monitoring and locating system of luck (oil) vehicle based on 4G on Android System. Real-time monitoring and alarming by sensor module, real-time video recording and uploading through camera module, real-time position recording and uploading through GPS module, vehicle navigation module and quick alarm module, which is composed of five parts. The system is the application of new intelligent transport technology in the field of special vehicle transport. It apply electronic information technology and internet of things technology to the vehicle system, so we can monitor natural gas and other special dangerous goods anytime, anywhere.

1 Introduction

With the development of natural gas transportation industry in the future, the emerging of the ITS (intelligent transportation system) technology will get more and more application, intended to reach the goal of monitoring and managing the steam (oil) transportation vehicles no matter where and how the weather is. The technology integrate many technologies, including precise positioning technology, geographic information system technology, database technology, multimedia technology and modern communication technology, sensor network technology, video technology, etc.

After investigation, the new generation of GPS vehicle monitor system should realize the collection and transmission of information of video, GPS, sensor, etc. The system plans to use 4G, for the system requires higher bandwidth of Internet access and the traditional GPRS data transmission cannot meet demand. In addition, the system plans to use advanced hardware platform and operating system for accommodating the trends and being competitive in the market of monitoring system. We have select Android as the operating system platform of this project, for Android system has advantages including strong portability, high openness, easy interaction, comprehensive functions, easy to be cut down, etc. Therefore, our system will be competitive at all aspects.

2 The System Overal Design

The main content of this paper is to realize the luck (oil) vehicle monitoring and locating system based on 4G network on the Android operating system. It mainly includes five parts: real-time monitoring and alarming through the sensor module, real-time video recording and uploading through the camera module, through the GPS module for real-time location recording and uploading, vehicle navigation module and alarm module.

The system is the application of the new intelligent transportation technology in the special transportation. It aims at applying the advanced electronic information technology to the vehicle system to realize the monitoring of the dangerous goods such as natural gas anywhere and anytime during the transportation. In this paper, we design a new real-time monitoring system, which should have the characteristics of the traditional vehicle monitoring system. Traditional monitoring system mainly consists of two parts: vehicle monitoring terminal and remote network server, that is, C/S architecture. Our system is still used in this design similar to the C/S architecture. The main tasks of the monitoring client include: collecting vehicle geographical location information and speed information, collecting the sensor information carried by the vehicle, locally processing and uploading the collected data in real time. The main tasks of the server include receiving the data sent by the client through the network and presenting it to the manager after

 DOI: 10.1051/itmconf/20171204009

processing. In the monitoring client design, we aim at special vehicles for the special design: In the information collection, in addition to carrying the usual GPS module we also added other sensors, including temperature sensors, air pressure sensors, concentration sensors, acceleration sensors; Network transmission using 4G and WIFI hybrid network alternative to the traditional GPRS; the system deployed four cameras to a more comprehensive and intuitive monitoring of the driver status, compartment conditions, road conditions; In addition, the client also integrated smart phone features (including SMS, telephone), in order to achieve the driver and the dispatch center in real-time communication. Due to the client equipped with a variety of sensors, including video sensors, the platform's data processing capabilities have higher requirements. So we chose Android operating system, designed specifically for embedded devices. In the server-side design, the work needs to be done include efficient and reliable real-time communication with multiple terminals; use of the database to store vehicle data; design UI; design automatic alarm rules based on vehicle sensor data; design based on real-time traffic Information optimization scheduling algorithm; vehicle driving information correction, preservation and display.

The overall design diagram as shown in Figure 1.

3 The System Hardware Design

The vehicle terminal is mainly composed of 6 modules, main control module with Android, communication module, GPS module, sensor module, power module, video modules. The design diagram of the terminal as shown in Figure 2.

4 The System Software Design

The vehicle terminal of this system uses Android, which is based Linux and not only free but also open source, as operating system. The Android is mainly used in portable devices, such as smart phones and tablets, for its high efficiency and openness, rich in interfaces and applications, easiness in human-computer interaction design, etc. Like other operating systems, Android utilizes layered architecture and is divided into 4 layers, which are Applications, Application Framework, Android Runtime and Linux Kernel from upper to lower.

According to the functional requirements of the monitoring system, the vehicle terminal has 4 modules, including sensor and alarm module, video recording and uploading module, GPS real-time location and navigation module, quick alarm and communication module.

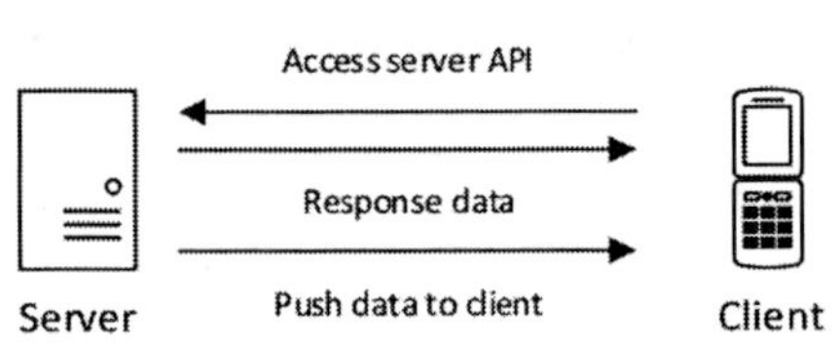

Figure 3. System workflow

4.1Sensor Monitoring Module

According to the literature survey and the actual site survey, we can see that the system needs to ensure the safety of the goods in the first place, so as to realize the real-time and Omni-directional monitoring of the goods and the vehicle itself to become an effective and reliable vehicle monitoring system. The main monitoring object of the monitoring system is natural gas or other dangerous goods the vehicles contained. Commonly used monitoring methods is using a variety of sensors to monitor. For liquefied natural gas, often use temperature sensors, gas concentration sensors, pressure sensors and level sensors to monitor. For other types of dangerous goods, although the monitoring indicators or parameters are different, the difference for our monitoring system design is only in the type and number of sensors. Sensor integration work also includes software integration, if we chose the direct connection program, we need to write the Android client sensor driver and sensor software control module. Therefore, the module's primary task is enabling multiple sensor devices to communicate with the Android operating system.

Secondly, after Android client obtained the data collected by multiple sensors, client needs to parse, process and save data in the local SQLite database, and upload data within a certain time interval to the server, in order to achieve real-time monitoring of vehicles. At the same time, the client will real-time detection of the data indicators, abnormal data in the case of alarm alerts, and upload alarm signals to the server, notify the management.

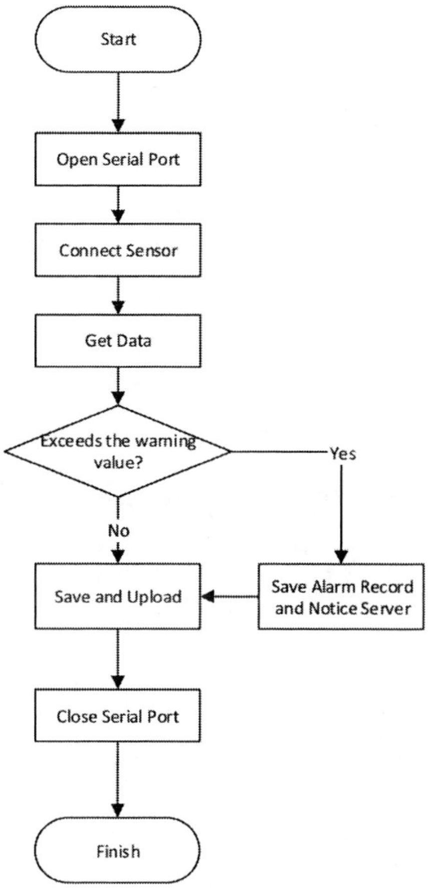

Figure 4. Sensor module flowchart

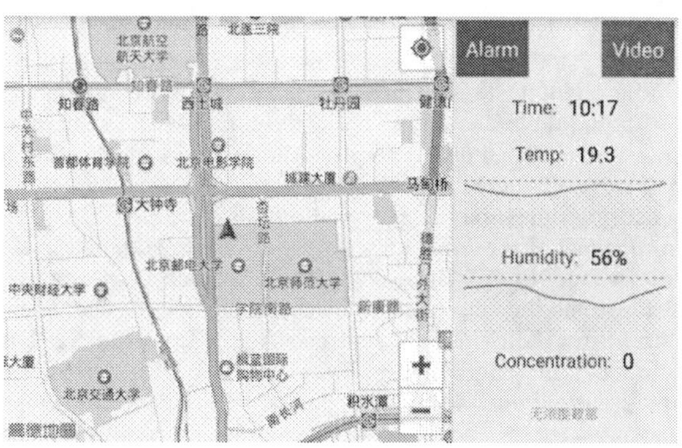

Figure 5. Effect picture (monitoring page)

4.2Video Monitoring Module

Compared with the traditional vehicle monitoring system, our system can monitor more comprehensive. Because there are more than kinds of sensors. The system has joined video monitor to meet the development of electronic information technology and the needs of social development.

Through layout multiple cameras and access Android terminal, the system can realize monitoring the vehicle in real time and at the same time monitoring video signal, saving in local and uploading. Although cameras are being considered as a kind of sensors, they are different in using and effect and the primary cause is the large amount of information they collect. Compared with general sensor's data which is far less than 1 KBPS, camera data is still likely to reach 1 MBPS per second after compression. As a result, cameras are not being considered as general sensors during design systems. We plan to use the camera of built-in encoding chip, because it could reduce resource which system cost in video transmission greatly. We plan to use standard H.264, which belongs to the highly compressed digital video codec standards. H.264 is an advanced technology on the video resolution and compression bit rate. For the vehicle terminal using Android, the library files and API for video decoding and displaying should have been integrated in the Android.

In addition to basic monitoring and controlling system with local monitoring, recording and alarming as previously described, the system has wireless Internet access to make special items could be monitored and record by the management system on the server during the transportation. The system and manager on the server could get all kinds of technical indices of dangerous goods or valuables during transportation, even monitor through the video. So as to achieve the goal of real "always" monitor.

4.3GPS And Navigation Module

According to the project requirements and relevant research, the information vehicle client upload should also contain the vehicle location information, so the system can also cooperate with the GIS system for real-time scheduling of special materials, or provide advanced services to other users. Android client powered by GPS chips, through the 4G module and WIFI network for secondary positioning, can quickly get to the vehicle's geographic location information and speed information. The obtained location information will be saved to the local SQLite database, and upload location information according to a certain strategy. The server side needs to correct the deviation of the uploaded data, save and show it in the right way. Managers can easily monitor and schedule each vehicle.

As a vehicle intelligent terminal, the system need to provide intelligent transportation services for local users, that is, drivers. The driver can obtain the navigation service or other POI search service through the system. The system is intended to integrate Amap Android navigation SDK, so we can quickly achieve vehicle navigation. At the same time the module integrates the voice synthesis function, we can achieve real-time voice broadcast to meet the driver's navigation needs.

 DOI: 10.1051/itmconf/20171204009

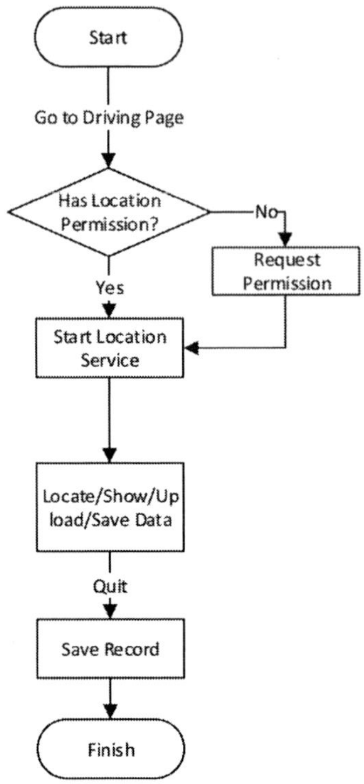

Figure 6. Location function flowchart

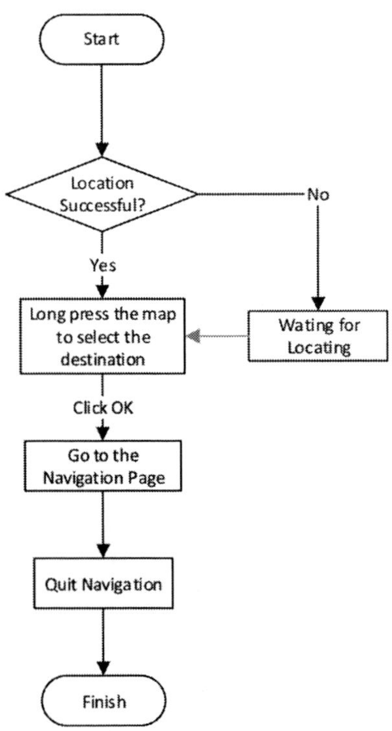

Figure 7. Navigation function flowchart

Figure 8. Effect picture (navigation page)

4.4Alarm And Communication Module

The system uses 4G network, can be convenient for telephone calls, send and receive text messages, access to the Internet and other functions. The system will store management center phone number, through the Android system Intent mechanism, to achieve quick alarm function, allowing users to quickly request assistance in case of emergency. At the same time, Android client can set the white list number. When managers call the client for emergency notification or emergency scheduling, no manual answer, we can connect the phone. In this way, save the emergency communication time, to protect the timely transmission of information and personnel safety.

This system adopts the common mode of vehicle monitoring system, namely "C/S" mode, which has the advantages of simple topology, easy expansion and low cost. Specifically, the system should be composed of a plurality of onboard clients and at least one server having a fixed IP. Android application will be developed in MVP mode, which separates the interface layer, Model layer and presenter of the whole system through reasonable layering, and realizes the whole client system by low coupling and high aggregation. Each module in the system will be separated from each other and work independently. Sensor module and video module will call the Android operating system API to achieve. Some sensor modules may need to write their own interfaces. The framework of the local network is to be implemented in the framework of OkHttp + Retrofit, which can quickly encapsulate the network framework and parse the data at the same time. GPS module will use Amap Location SDK to achieve high geographic location, the SDK in the traditional positioning interface on the packaging and optimization, faster and more accurate access to location information. Navigation module will use Amap Navigation SDK, we can achieve free integration and use of navigation. Quick alarm module will use the Android operating system API to achieve, while listening to incoming calls, emergency dispatching telephone free calls.

Conclusion

This paper designs a set of special vehicle monitoring system based on 4G. The system is the application of the new intelligent transportation technology in the special transportation. It aims at applying the advanced electronic information technology to the vehicle system to realize the monitoring of the dangerous goods such as natural gas anywhere and anytime during the transportation. We have accomplished the main functions of all modules. After the operation for some time, according to the feedback of the cooperative enterprise,this system is stable and reliable.

References

[1] Li Qiang, Construction of Mobile Library Service Platform Based on 4G, Heilongjiang University, 2012
[2] Yang Yang, Design and Research of Special Vehicle Monitoring System Based on 3G, Beijing University of Posts and Telecommunications, 2013
[3] Zhao Kun, Vehicle Locating and Monitoring System Based on GPSONE
in Open Vehicle, Xi'an University of Architecture and Technology, 2012
[4] Zhou Juan, Research and Realization of GPS / GPSONE Vehicle Monitoring and Location System, Xi'an University of Electronic Science and Technology, 2010
[5] Lin Ling, Research on the Application and Construction of Internet of Things Technology in Logistics, Beijing University of Posts and Telecommunications, 2011
[6] Liu Dongxu, Research and Development of Bar Code and RFID Integrated Terminal Based on Compound Communication Mode, Beijing University of Posts and Telecommunications, 2011
[7] Hou Yangjie, Research and Development of Central Monitoring Software for Vehicle Monitoring and Dispatching System, Tsinghua University, 2004
[8] She Fengya, Application Development of Mobile Phone Search and Positioning Based on, Beijing University of Posts and Telecommunications, 2010
[9] Li Wei, Mobile Video Surveillance System Based on Android Platform, Nanjing University of Posts and Telecommunications, 2013
[10] Ning Li, Design of Video Surveillance System Based on Android Platform, Beijing University of Posts and Telecommunications, 2011
[11] Liu Zhikai, Design and Realization of Intelligent Bus Terminal Based on ARM, Hebei University of Technology, 2010

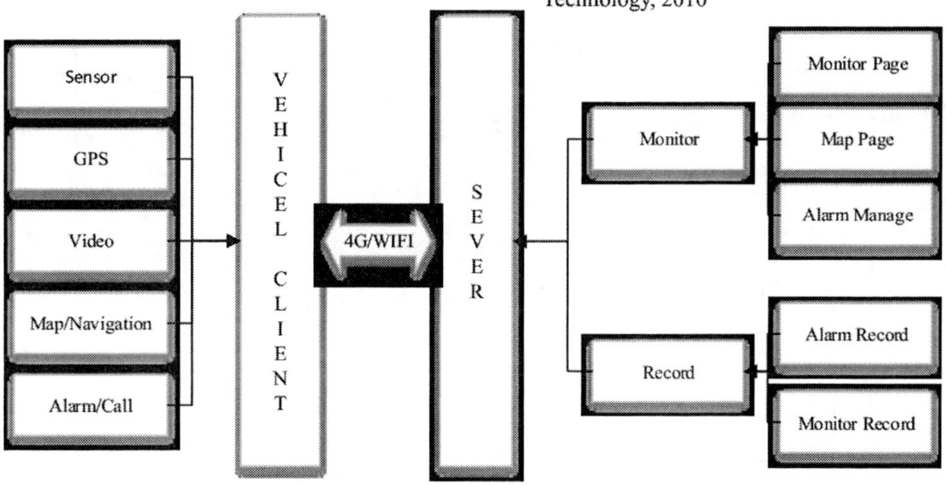

Figure 1. The whole design

DOI: 10.1051/itmconf/20171204009

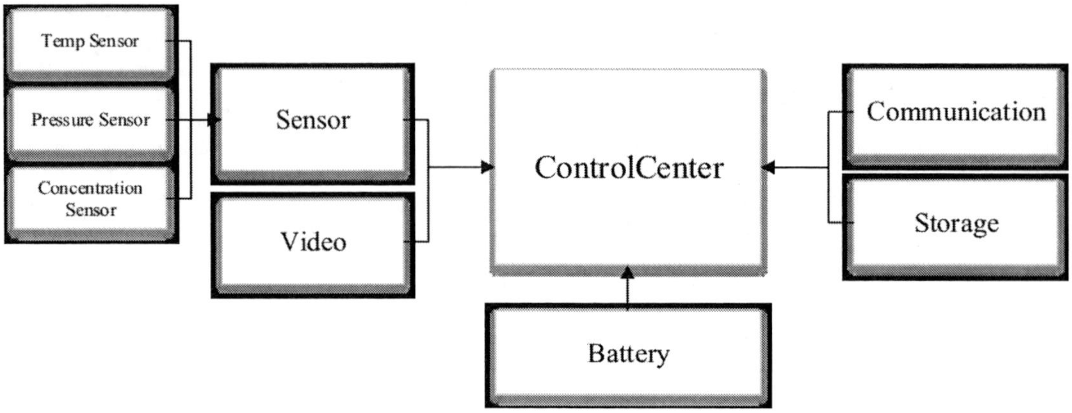

Figure 2. Hardware design

DOI: 10.1051/itmconf/20171204010

Collaborating Filtering Community Image Recommendation System Based on Scene

Tao HE, Ning ZHU, Gui-Xi XIONG, Zai-Rang ZHAO

Academy of Computer Science and Technology,Beihang university,Beijing, China
15801146625@163.com,zhuning730@qq.com,xiongguixi@buaa.edu.cn,zhaozairang@foxmail.com

Abstract—With the advancement of smart city, the development of intelligent mobile terminal and wireless network, the traditional text information service no longer meet the needs of the community residents, community image service appeared as a new media service. "There are pictures of the truth" has become a community residents to understand and master the new dynamic community, image information service has become a new information service. However, there are two major problems in image information service. Firstly, the underlying eigenvalues extracted by current image feature extraction techniques are difficult for users to understand, and there is a semantic gap between the image content itself and the user's understanding; secondly, in community life of the image data increasing quickly, it is difficult to find their own interested image data. Aiming at the two problems, this paper proposes a unified image semantic scene model to express the image content. On this basis, a collaborative filtering recommendation model of fusion scene semantics is proposed. In the recommendation model, a comprehensiveness and accuracy user interest model is proposed to improve the recommendation quality. The results of the present study have achieved good results in the pilot cities of Wenzhou and Yan'an, and it is applied normally.

1 Introduction

Internet information technology to guide the city to the direction of intelligent development, with the wisdom of the city to promote, urban transport, environment, security and other aspects to improve and enhance. Smart City's goal is to rely on information technology infrastructure, the use of Internet of things technology, data technology, mobile Internet technology research and application, so that urban residents to fully enjoy the wisdom of urban life brought about by information technology. As the basic unit of intelligent urban development, community management and service occupy a very important position, and directly relate to the daily life experience of urban residents. How to manage the community and how to provide community residents with information services is an important issue for community development.

During the construction of the intelligent community, the community managers and community residents have produced rich information data reflecting the community status through the camera equipment, the mobile terminal equipment and the community website. The information is mainly divided into three categories: text, image and video. text is simple, image is not likely to quickly access content in a short time; image expression information intuitive, visual impact, to meet people in a short time to master the information needs; video content expression information is full of vivid, but takes up the storage space big, and often needs to look from the beginning to the end, the time consuming, therefore the image data auxiliary with the text data becomes the community resident most willing to accept the information expression form. However, the content of the image data is difficult to access, and there is a semantic gap, the image association is low, and the low efficiency of image retrieval leads to the inability of the community residents to acquire the community image rapidly, so that they can not grasp or understand the community dynamics. With the popular web2.0, similar to Flickr, nice, in, ink weather such as picture sharing site has been popular, people began to use social labels to image tagging, image tag is between the image content and The granularity feature of image vision can solve the problem of "semantic gap" of image, and organize and manage the image with label. In the application of intelligent community, residents can use the mobile phone side of the community entities and community events anytime, anywhere to take pictures of the upload at the same time to help tag text information to describe the community image data, these community image data in the source, structure and type of decentralized But they often come with rich tag information and associated text information, but also have relevance in a certain time

DOI: 10.1051/itmconf/20171204010

and space, which provides a new idea for image management and service.

Information overload era, passive information retrieval is often replaced by active recommendation, the wisdom of the community building process is also true. Residents in the access to community information, image data retrieval is often unnecessary, the residents will not search for images to the picture, but the need for residents based on individual preferences or the popularity of the event, the initiative to reflect community image to residents to achieve community image data recommendation become an important business community services.

2 Community image scene semantic model

The semantic data of community image is multi-level. If all the semantic features of community image data are extracted at different levels, there are problems in the implementation of technology and application scenarios. Firstly, the features of community images are diverse, and different image features have different feature extraction algorithms, and some features of community images are high-dimensional, such as SIFT features, and require additional techniques to reduce dimensionality, resulting in community image semantic data access difficulties. Second, for the users' image acquisition needs, all of these features can not be one to one with the needs of users, it is difficult in the community to use the actual scene. Therefore, combined with community image scene elements and image tags, the community image scene-based semantic model is constructed to provide the foundation for community image acquisition service.

2.1Community Image Acquisition

In the intelligent community application, the community image data comes from two parts: the user upload pictures and Internet crawl pictures. The user perceives the community image through the mobile terminal, and generates the image data with the metadata description. The user uploads the picture data often has the controllable characteristic of the information format information, which can meet the requirements of community management and service. Network crawl technology, access to all types of Internet image data and related text description data, usually on the Internet to crawl the image type and information format is inconsistent, the lack of many other aspects of information, such as the lack of access to effective user information, picture utilization low.

2.2Community Image Scene Abstract Model

Community events reflect the status of the community, in time, space and subject have relevance, community image records of community events, is a more intuitive reflection of community status. Community image data reflects the state of the community, more intuitive than the text description credible, the same picture can also reflect the state of the community time information, spatial information, event information and even the nature of the event information. In this respect, community image data and community event scene information have great analogy, in order to make community residents a better understanding and master community dynamics, community image data and scene information associated with the use of community image is critical The meaning. Community image data scene provides a more simple and effective image content description method and community state expression mode, while the value of community image data is utilized, community residents and community managers can understand and master community dynamics.

$$S = \sum_{time\neq0} \sum_{place\neq0} I(time, place, theme, event, person, quality) \quad (1)$$

I representing an image data resource; $time$ representing a community event occurrence period label; $place$ representing an area label; $theme$ representing a subject representative of an image, selected by an uploader; $event$ representing an uploader or person involved in the image; $person$ representing an event reflected by the current picture; $quality$ representing the nature of the incident, that is, the severity of the event or the extent of the use of 5-point description.

Community Image Scene Abstract Model as follows, shows the image scene represent the community events.

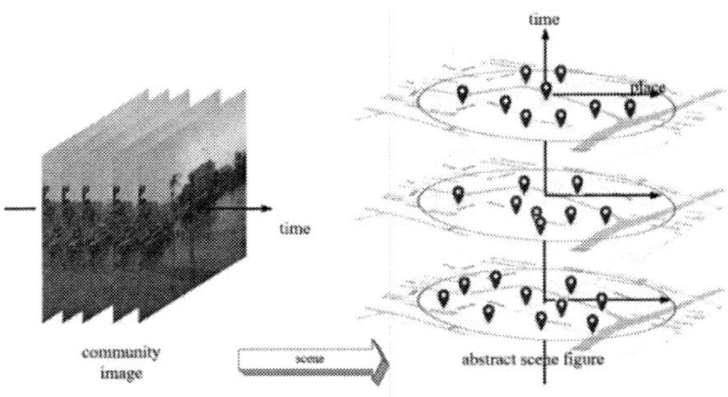

Figure 1. Community image scene abstract model.

2.3Community Image Scene Semantic Model

Based on the source of community image data, two kinds of data sources are studied. Under the support of tag semantic library and the model of community image abstraction, interaction between scene user and system and Internet image data based on link relation are used to crawl , To achieve tag recommendation, semantic annotation and scene semantic mapping, the formation of community image scene semantic model. The realization of the community image scene semantic model completes the document representation of the community image, and solves the difficult problem of the image representation. It is very important for the organization, management, retrieval and recommendation of the image.

Community Image Scenne Semantic Model as follows:

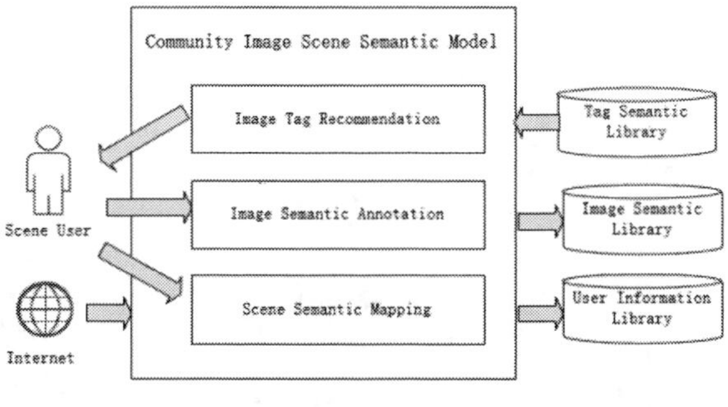

Figure 2. Community image scene semantic model.

The semantic model of community image scene includes the image tag recommendation, image semantic annotation and scene semantic mapping, and the image semantics and user information are stored in the database for the scene user uploaded image and the Internet crawling image.

2.3.1Image Tag Recommendation

In the mass annotation mode, the tag is the link between the image data and the user's link, the label can express the image content, can also represent the user's preference type. In order to accurately describe the image content and express the user's preference, the system is provided with the filter of the temporal and spatial theme scene elements. In order to provide a more accurate description of the image content and the expression of the user's preference, the system provides the content of the markup content to the same community events, different people's concerns, Label Recommendation. After the tagged image data is tagged, the tag vector set of tagged image resource is converted to a synonym word group, and the tags in the tag vector of each image resource are found corresponding to " Class, as a feature, a number of feature items constitute the feature space, statistical feature space set for each feature in the frequency of the emergence of the highest frequency of five features as the recommended candidate feature, and then statistical features of the highest candidate The five candidate label sets corresponding to the five candidate feature items are given.

When the scene user uploads a picture, it acquires the time-space scene element and the theme scene element, sets the scene factor filter condition, sets the time dimension to 30 minutes, the space dimension is 500m, the theme equals the user- The set of label vectors for all the tagged image resources can be represented in the following form.

$$S=\sum_{t=-15}^{t=15}\sum_{d=0}^{d=500}\sum_{i=1}^{n}I_i \quad (2)$$

S represents a collection of all image resources satisfying the scene filter condition. It is a set of label vectors. Each image resource in the set is represented by a series of labels, and the representation is as follows.

$$I_i=(tag_{i1},tag_{i2},..tag_{ij},...,tag_{im}) \quad (3)$$

A tag-based vector space model (VSM) is proposed for the tagged image resource set.

1. Select the feature

For the labeled resource set S, we need to fetch the feature item corresponding to each label by image resource, take the image resource as an example to select the feature item, and for every label of the image resource. The characteristic items are shown below.

$$\begin{aligned}&tag_{i1}=>X_{i1}\\&tag_{i2}=>X_{i2}\\&tag_{ij}=>X_{ij}\\&tag_{im}=>X_{im}\end{aligned} \quad (4)$$

2. Construct feature space

The construction of feature space is to transform the label vector of tagged image resource, to associate the tag with the synonym class information, and to count the number of tags contained in different feature items as the feature weight of each feature item. After the feature set is processed according to the selected feature, the feature set and the corresponding image label will be obtained.

$$\begin{aligned}&tag_1,tag_2,...,tag_x=>X\\&tag_1,tag_2,...,tag_y=>Y\\&tag_1,tag_2,...,tag_z=>Z\end{aligned} \quad (5)$$

The resulting feature space is as follows

$$K=\{(X,x),(Y,y)...,(Z,z)\} \quad (6)$$

Among them, X , Y , Z is the characteristic item, x , y , z , is the characteristic item weight.

3. Candidate feature items

The feature space model K is sorted according to the weight, and the five feature items with the highest weight are selected as candidate feature items

$$T=\begin{cases}X_1=x_{11},x_{21},...,x_{n1}\\X_2=x_{21},x_{22},...,x_{2n}\\X_3=x_{31},x_{32},...,x_{3n}\\X_4=x_{41},x_{42},...,x_{4n}\\X_5=x_{51},x_{52},...,x_{5n}\end{cases} \quad (7)$$

4. Candidate label set

For the candidate feature items, the labels in each feature item are statistically calculated, and a label with the highest number of occurrences in each feature item is selected to constitute the candidate label set, as shown below.

$$\mathrm{Re}commendTag=\{tag_1,tag_2,tag_3,tag_4,tag_5\} \quad (8)$$

DOI: 10.1051/itmconf/20171204010

2.3.2Image Semantic Annotation

This paper uses the mass annotation method to annotate the community image semantics. In the event of a community event, the user will select a system-recommended image tag and label the community image according to his preference and willingness to form the label semantics of the image data. The label semantics of the image data can be described as follows form.

$$I = (tag_1, tag_2, tag_3, \ldots, tag_n) \quad (9)$$

2.3.3Scene Semantic Mapping

The time field of the image data is usually presented in the form of year, month, day, minute, and second. The location field is presented as a GPS value. These specific time values and GPS values are the original scene semantics. There is no semantic feature. The user specific time for the image data Value and GPS value is not concerned, so the actual application of the project, the need to map the specific time value into the morning, noon, afternoon, evening and other semantic, the specific GPS values into a certain district, a certain road, Grid and so on. However, the semantic mapping rules of different scene elements under different topics are inconsistent, and the different vocabulary words are extended and classified, and the subject vocabulary is added to the different semantic map. The topic time vocabulary that should be added is breakfast, lunch and afternoon tea. The time vocabulary of the subject should be added, such as morning peak, day peak, afternoon peak and evening peak. , Dinner, supper and so on.

3 Community Image Recommendation model

The traditional collaborative filtering recommendation technique is based on the user-item scoring matrix to get the user information, and the other feedback information of the user, such as the user's feedback information, the user's feedback information, and the user's feedback information. In addition, the collaborative filtering recommendation algorithm is the most mature recommendation algorithm applied to complex objects such as images, Not taking full account of the user's interest will change over time and the user's location of the event is relatively fixed and fixed image data to produce these two issues, resulting in low efficiency of the recommendation. Aiming at the problems in the practical application of the intelligent city, this paper proposes a collaborative filtering image recommendation model which integrates the scene semantics, introduces the label semantics and the scene semantics of the image, filters out some image data which does not meet the condition, and combines the time scene semantic space scene Semantics to express the interest of the target user in a certain spatial region more accurately, and then use the collaborative filtering recommendation algorithm for image recommendation.

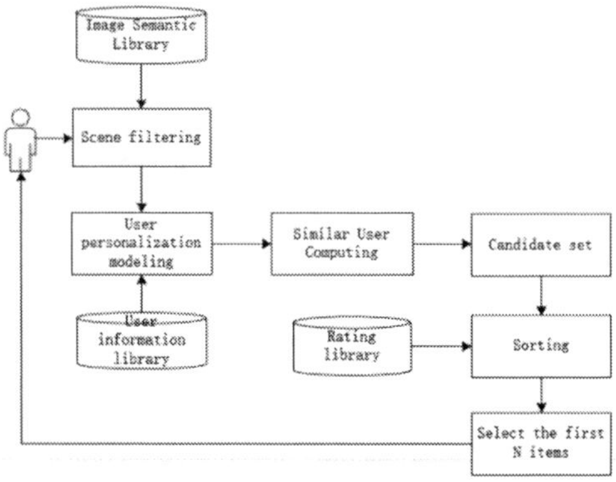

Figure 3. Community image recommendation model.

The synergistic filtering model of scene fusion semantics includes scene information filtering mechanism, user interest modeling, similar user acquisition and recommendation result generation. Scene information filtering mechanism mainly refers to the use of the current time and current location to filter away from here and now far image data, the remaining image data to better reflect the user's interest here and now preferences. User interest modeling is different from traditional scoring data modeling. In this paper, user interest preference based on scene information filtering mechanism is more accurate, and the user interest is represented by label and label weight information. Image recommendations The next steps are critical. Similar user acquisition refers to the similarity calculation between the user and the target user in the user space using the improved similarity calculation method, and selects the first k users to constitute the set of neighbors of the target user based on the similarity value sorting. Recommendation result generation refers to the evaluation of the images based on the uploaded records of the neighboring users of the target user, and generates the recommendation values, thereby recommending the ranking and generating the recommendation result.

3.1Scene filtering mechanism

Scene information includes temporal scene elements, spatial scene elements and so on. Both time scene elements and space scene elements are related to user's interests and preferences. User's interests will change with time. The same geographical elements also reflect the users' Of interest. Everyone's perception of things in a short time does not change too much, has a certain stability, and similar geographical location of the personal preferences of things similar, so you can according to a certain period of time within a certain location of the user's preferences to predict the user's preferences. This is the core idea of collaborative filtering. It is very important to perform scene-based resource filtering of image data resources before user personalized modeling and generating recommended images, in order to reduce the amount of computation and to express the interest in the most recent spatial range of user's most recent time, to improve the quality of image recommendation.

In the actual scene, the behaviors of similar users at different time and in different places affect the formation of user interest model. Adding scene information filtering mechanism can improve the accuracy of recommendation algorithm.

3.2User Interest Model

In the real life, the human forgetting curves exist objectively, and the user's preferences are changing constantly. The closer to the present time point, the closer the image is to the distance. Nowadays, the user interest model based on scene filtering is more realistic. Can change on behalf of the user's preferences. A user's interest in a particular area at this point in time is much greater than that of other similar users within the same time frame. User interest model needs to take into account the user's recent behavior changes, to reflect the user's recent hobbies. The user's interest vector is generated by using the tag information when the user uploads the image, not just the user interest model formed by monotonous user rating data.

The tag data at the time of image upload also represents the user's interest preference. The frequency and type of the tag use the user's hobby distribution to a great extent. The user personalized modeling is performed using the tag data generated by the user uploading the image data. First of all, for a target user who needs to be recommended, we need to obtain the time and space scene information, get the tagged data set of the tagged image in the scenario, and count the frequency of each tag. The tag data set represents the user's interest Type, label frequency represents the degree of user preferences. So the user interest model can be expressed as the following formula.

$$U=\{(tag_1,w_1),(tag_2,w_2)...,(tag_i,w_i)...,(tag_n,w_n)\} \quad (10)$$

The order of the labels is sorted according to the weight, that is, the more you can reflect the interests of the user preferences, on the contrary, the more the ability to reflect the user's interest in the weaker.

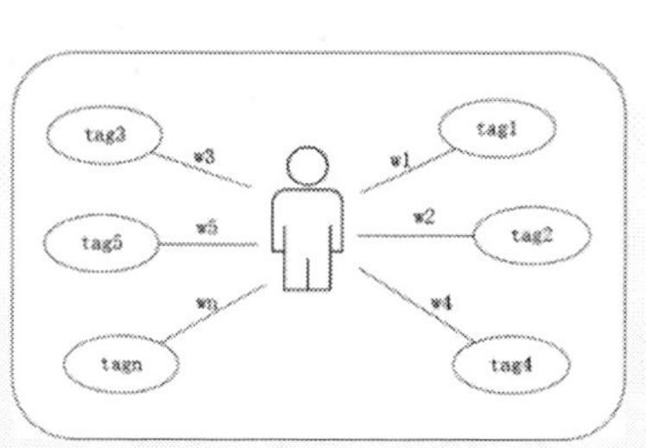

Figure 4. User interest model.

Compared with the traditional user interest model, the label information reflects the comprehensive user preference, and the tag weight information quantizes the user preference, so that the user's interest preference degree is expressed accurately.

3.3Similar User Acquisition

The similarity between the two users is the key step for the users to get. Considering the difference of different users, some users have high scores on the project and some users are generally low on the project. Another improved cosine similarity calculation method is shown below.

$$\mathrm{sim}(u_i,u_j)=\cos(u_i,u_j)=\frac{\sum_{k=1}^{n}\left(r_{i,k}-\bar{r}_i\right)\times\left(r_{j,k}-\bar{r}_j\right)}{\sqrt{\sum_{k=1}^{n}\left(r_{i,k}-\bar{r}_i\right)^2}\sqrt{\sum_{k=1}^{n}\left(r_{j,k}-\bar{r}_j\right)^2}} \quad (11)$$

3.4Sorting produces recommendations

The ranking is based on the likelihood that the target user will like a particular item he did not like, called the predictive score. The average weighting strategy is used to calculate the predicted score. Based on the historical score of the target user and the nearest user, The average weighting strategy is composed of two parts: the average score and the similarity value of the user, and the calculation method is as follows.

$$P_{u,i}=\bar{r}_u+\frac{\sum_{s=1}^{k} sim(u,u_s)\left(r_{s,i}-\bar{r}_s\right)}{\sum_{s=1}^{k} sim(u,u_s)} \quad (12)$$

Results

Because it is the actual project, the end result to the mobile side of the app and the Web version of the recommendation, in the wisdom of Yan'an and wisdom of Wenzhou have achieved effective results. The following are the results of Wenzhou.

DOI: 10.1051/itmconf/20171204010

Figure 5. User upload picture.

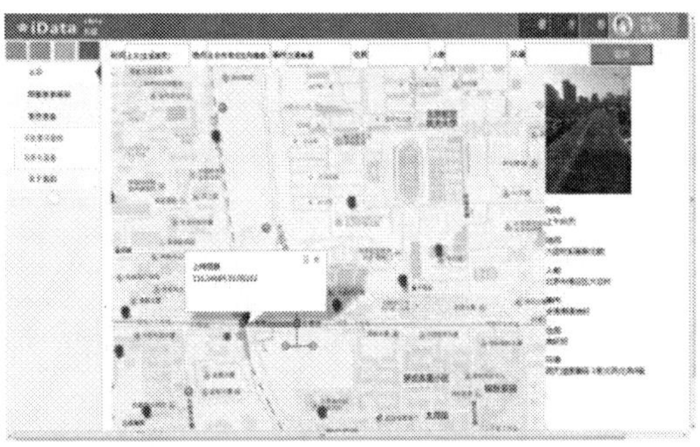

Figure 6. Community image shows in the map and its semantic.

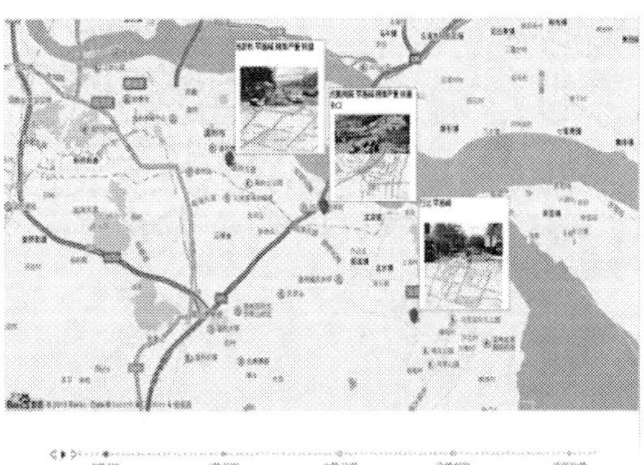

Figure 7. Community images shows the Wenzhou traffic dynamically change with the time and place.

The following are the results of Yan'an.

Figure 8. Yan'an picture wall by topic.

Figure 9. Map - based tourism image recommendation.

Conclusions

This paper mainly solves the following two problems, for the image data content is difficult to express, and the underlying eigenvalue for the user is difficult to understand and so on. Through the analysis of the community image scene, abstract the image elements, according to the specific scene to draw the image scene semantic formation process, constructs the community image scene semantic model. Based on the semantic model of community image scene, aiming at the problem that the interest of users in the traditional collaborative filtering changed with the passage of time, the user interest model of the fusion scene was proposed, and the good recommendation effect was achieved.

Acknowledgment

This research derived from National Natural Science Foundation of China whose name is : Large Data Computing Theory and Software Technology (61421003).

References

[1] J. Eakins, M. Graham, Content-based image retrieval, Technical Report, University of Northumbria at Newcastle, 1999.

[2] Bhusari P, Gupta R, Sinahal A. Personalized Image Search from Photo Sharing Websites Using Ranking Based Tensor Factorization Model (RMTF)[J]. International Journal, 2013, 3(8).

[3] Sharma S, Kaur D. Location based context aware recommender system through user defined rules[C]//Computing, Communication & Automation (ICCCA), 2015 International Conference on. IEEE, 2015: 257-261.

[4] Champiri Z D, Shahamiri S R, Salim S S B. A systematic review of scholar context-aware recommender systems[J]. Expert Systems with Applications, 2015, 42(3): 1743-1758.

[5] Zheng N, Li Q. A recommender system based on tag and time information for social tagging systems[J]. Expert Systems with Applications, 2011, 38(4): 4575-4587.

[6] Kim H N, Alkhaldi A, El Saddik A, et al. Collaborative user modeling with user-generated tags for social recommender systems[J]. Expert Systems with Applications, 2011, 38(7): 8488-8496.

[7] Tamura H, Yokoya N. Image database systems: A survey[J]. Pattern recognition, 1984, 17(1): 29-43.

[8] Szummer M, Picard R W. Indoor-outdoor image classification[C]//Content-Based Access of Image and Video Database, 1998. Proceedings., 1998 IEEE International Workshop on. IEEE, 1998: 42-51.

[9] Mori Y, Takahashi H, Oka R. Image-to-word transformation based on dividing and vector quantizing images with words[C]//First International Workshop on Multimedia Intelligent Storage and Retrieval Management. 1999: 1-9.

[10] Dye J. Folksonomy: A game of high-tech (and high-stakes) tag[J]. EContent, 2006, 29(3).

[11] Sun A, Bhowmick S S, Nguyen N, et al. Tag-based social image retrieval: An empirical evaluation[J]. Journal of the American Society for Information Science and Technology, 2011, 62(12): 2364-2381.

[12] Vadivu P S, Sumathy P, Vadivel A. Image Retrieval from WWW using Attributes in HTML TAGs[J]. Procedia Technology, 2012, 6: 509-516.

[13] Kantor P B, Rokach L, Ricci F, et al. Recommender systems handbook[M]. Springer, 2011.

[14] Pazzani M J, Billsus D. Content-based recommendation systems[M]//The adaptive web. Springer Berlin Heidelberg, 2007: 325-341.

ITM Web of Conferences 12, 04011 (2017) DOI: 10.1051/itmconf/20171204011
ITA 2017

Privacy Leaks through Data Hijacking Attack on Mobile Systems

Daojuan Zhang[1,2], Yuanfang Guo[1], Dianjie Guo[1] and Guangming Yu[3]

[1]*State Key Laboratory of Information Security, Institute of Information Engineering, CAS, Beijing, 100093, China*
[2]*University of Chinese Academy of Sciences, Beijing, 100049, China*
[3]*Chinese Research Institute of General Technology, Beijing, 100055, China*
Email: {zhangdaojuan, guoyuanfang, guodianjie}@iie.ac.cn, yuguangming2010@163.com

Abstract—To persistently eavesdrop on the mobile devices, attackers may obtain the elevated privilege and inject malicious modules into the user devices. Unfortunately, the attackers may not be able to obtain the privilege for a long period of time since the exploitable vulnerabilities may be fixed or the malware may be removed. In this paper, we propose a new data hijacking attack for the mobile apps. By employing the proposed method, the attackers are only required to obtain the root privilege of the user devices once, and they can persistently eavesdrop without any change to the original device. Specifically, we design a new approach to construct a shadow system by hijacking user data files. In the shadow system, attackers possess the identical abilities to the victims. For instance, if a victim has logged into the email app, the attacker can also access the email server in the shadow system without authentication in a long period of time. Without re-authentication of the app, it is difficult for victims to notice the intrusion since the whole eavesdropping is performed on other devices (rather than the user devices). In our experiments, we evaluate the effectiveness of the proposed attack and the result demonstrates that even the Android apps released by the top developers cannot resist this attack. Finally, we discuss some approaches to defend the proposed attack.

I. Introduction

Nowadays, the mobile device is extremely popular and has become a primary choice to store and handle the privacy data, e.g., SMS messages, contact information, etc. Unfortunately, the mobile devices also attract more attacks and the safety of these privacy data has received lots of concerns [11, 8, 13, 12, 14]. To steal the user privacy persistently, one of the common methods for the attackers is to obtain the elevated privilege of the user devices and inject the eavesdropping modules. During this process, the users are usually lured to install the malwares from the attackers, while some users become confused and grant the elevated privilege to the attackers. In addition, attackers can directly obtain the elevated privilege by exploiting the system vulnerabilities. Some spies can even access the devices of victims physically and then inject the eavesdropping modules. However, there are some limitations for the attackers. For example, they may only obtain the privilege temporarily because the malware is found and deleted by the user. Besides, by injecting the malicious modules into the user devices, it is easy for the attackers to expose themselves.

In this paper, we propose a new data hijacking attack for Android apps. By only obtaining the elevated privilege of the user device once, a long-time eavesdropping can be achieved by the attackers. The proposed attack is based on three facts. Firstly, mobile apps usually authenticate the users with passwords at the first time for convenience. The session keys are usually stored in data files for the future authentication. Secondly, data files of the mobile apps are jointly managed by the OS and can be located easily. Thirdly, for an account, multiple connections are usually allowed by the app servers at the same time, and these different connections cannot be distinguished whether they are from the same device. Thus, once the attackers obtain the elevated privilege, they can hijack the data files of users to construct a similar execution environment, named shadow system in this paper. If the users have logged into their apps at the attack moment, attackers will also be able to access the app server in the shadow system without authentication. As a result, the attack is still effective in the shadow system even if the elevated privilege of the user device expires. Besides, without re-authentication, it is difficult for the users to find the malicious behavior since the whole eavesdropping process is implemented on the

DOI: 10.1051/itmconf/20171204011

device of the attackers rather than the users. To evaluate the effectiveness of the proposed attack, we design a generic construction of the shadow system for Android apps and conduct the attack with 7 most popular real-world apps released by the top developers. The results show that the proposed attack can be conducted successfully even on Gmail, which are popular and downloaded more than one billion times.

In summary, our contributions of this paper are as follows.

- We propose a new data hijacking attack for mobile apps. By constructing the shadow system, we only need to obtain the elevated privilege once and can persistently steal the user privacies without any change to the user devices.
- We evaluate the effectiveness of the proposed attack by constructing a shadow system. The experimental results on the most popular Android apps indicate that most of the apps cannot resist the proposed attack.
- After the demonstrations of the proposed attack, we give some possible solutions to mitigate the data hijacking attack.

The rest of the paper is organized as follows. Section 2 introduces our motivation of this paper. The detailed data hijacking attack is described in Section 3. Section 4 presents the evaluation of the proposed attack on the popular Android apps. Solutions to resist the attack are discussed in Section 5. Finally, we conclude this paper.

2 Motivation

Since the security issues about the mobile devices are exposed frequently, we should be aware that mobile systems are not secure, especially for the Android system. According to a recent study [22], 73 Android vulnerabilities are collected and all of them can be exploited by the attackers to obtain the root privilege of the user devices. Some other researches such as [23] also reveal the severity of this problem that these vulnerabilities are exploited to achieve different activities by many malwares. Besides, even the regular app developers [1, 2, 3] exploit these vulnerabilities to help users to achieve a complete control of their devices. Once the attackers obtain the elevated privilege, numerous serious problems can be caused.

Since the system vulnerabilities may be fixed and the malware may be deleted, the elevated privilege may be obtained temporarily by the attackers. Besides, some spies can access the devices of victims physically, and do not intend to perform any change to the devices such that they can avoid being exposed. Thus, the user privacies on mobile devices can be stolen in a short period of time, but they are difficult to be eavesdropped persistently.

In this paper, a new data hijacking attack is proposed, and a shadow system is designed to steal the user privacies persistently and quietly. Via the attack practice, we hope to remind the app developers to design proper security mechanisms for protecting the users' data in an insecure execution environment, and also warn the users of the severe risks which can be caused by the abuse of elevated privilege.

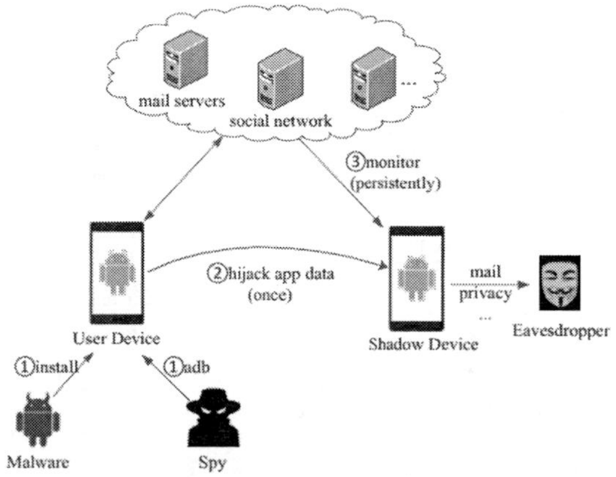

Figure 1. The process of the data hijacking attack.

3 The Proposed Data Hijacking Attack

3.1 Attack Process

As shown in Figure 1, the proposed data hijacking attack mainly consists of three steps.

Firstly, the attackers need to obtain the elevated privilege in the user devices. We assume that the privilege is obtained when the malwares are installed in the user devices or the devices are temporarily controlled by a spy. These approaches [22, 1, 2, 3, 4] can be employed to obtain the elevated privilege in the user devices.

Then, the attackers hijack the app data files in the user devices to construct the shadow system. In this phase, according to the information of the user device, a similar system (shadow system) is built and the same apps are installed by attackers. Besides, the app data files in the shadow system are replaced by the corresponding hijacked files.

Finally, in the shadow system, the attackers will have the same abilities as the victims at the attack moment. For example, if the users have logged in an app, the attackers can also access the app servers to view the user privacy such as email without authentication.

3.2 App Data Storage in Android

In order to implement the data hijacking attack, we firstly analyze the data storage of the app in the mobile system. Take Android as an example, the three critical locations for storing app data files or account data are as follows.

Private App Data. It is well-known that Android is constructed based on the Linux kernel. To isolate the apps, Android system creates different system users for the

TABLE I. The evaluation results on popular Android apps.

ID	Package Name	Category	Attack Requirements & Existing Defenses			Duration of Attack
			Unique ID	System	Protocol	
1	com.tencent.mobileqq	Comm	-	-	Single User Login	Fail in the first week
2	com.baidu.netdisk	Cloud	-	-	-	Persistent
3	com.sina.weibolite	Social	-	-	-	Persistent
4	com.netease.mail	Mail	-	-	-	Persistent
5	com.google.android.gm	Mail	-	Sync	-	Persistent
6	com.facebook.katana	Social	-	-	SMS verification	Incomplete verification
7	com.microsoft.skydrive	Cloud	-	Sync		Fail in the first week

installed apps with unique UID. For each app, there is a private directory in the system directory /data/data/ to store its private data files, which cannot be accessed by other unprivileged apps.

External Storage. Besides the private directory, the app data can be also stored in the external storage such as SDCard by an Android app. Files in the external storage can be accessed by all apps who have the permission *READ_EXTERNAL_STORAGE*. It is obvious that the critical data cannot be stored in external storages by the developers. In our experiment, this part of app data is not concerned.

Sync Adapter. The Sync Adapter [5] is a service provided by the Android system to transfer the data between the client and the server. Apps can store their account or session information based on this service. Thus, app data such as user contacts can be regularly synchronized with the cloud servers. The account information is stored in the system file */data/system/users/0/accounts.db*, which is a database file with SQLite format.

3.3 Differential Data Analysis

Although it is effective to directly hijack all the app data files into the shadow system, we introduce two differential data analyses to reduce the size of required files.

Firstly, when an app is installed in the different execution environments, many files such as the codes and resource files are identical. Assuming that the app P is installed in the device D, its data files are denoted as $F = \{f_1, f_2, \ldots\}$. Instead of hijacking all the files in F to the shadow system D', we install app P in D' and execute it to generate the files $F' = \{f'_1, f'_2, \ldots\}$. By computing the file signatures, only the different files $(F-F \cap F')$ are required to be hijacked. Thus, the size of the hijacked files can be reduced significantly.

Aiming at specific apps, the files related to the user account information can be located more accurately. Before attacking an app P, a legal account is registered in advance. And the files generated by the app before and after the user logging into the account are denoted as F_1 and F_2, respectively. Thus, the changed files $(F_2 - F_1)$ are related to the user account. However, although fewer files need to be hijacked by this approach, the apps may not be normally executed due to the lack of some critical files.

4 Evaluation

4.1 Environment Setup

We simulate the proposed attack with a real Android device and the corresponding shadow system is constructed by the Android emulator. The real device we used is Samsung Galaxy S6 with Android OS 5.1.1. Firstly, Android apps are installed in both the real device and the shadow system. Then, the account is registered and logged into the app in the real device. Finally, the different data files in the real device are copied to replace that in the shadow system.

Some aspects need to be noticed. When the data files are hijacked from the real devices to the shadow system, their permissions must be reset to ensure that the apps in the shadow system can be successfully executed. In our experiment, this process is automatically completed by a script program. Besides, since some account information of apps is stored into the SQLite database file (*accounts.db*) which may not be compatible for different systems, we write a JDBC program to transfer the data.

4.2 Experimental Results

As shown in Table I, 7 most popular Android apps released by the top developers are exploited to evaluate the effectiveness of the proposed hijacking attack. Our evaluation addresses the following two research questions:

- **RQ1** Can the apps discover the data hijacking attack and stop their services to the attackers?
- **RQ2** How long does the attack last if the app is attacked?

DOI: 10.1051/itmconf/20171204011

The results indicate that all the evaluated apps can be attacked. This experiment indicates that the user privacies can be accessed by the attackers in the shadow system without authentication. The QQ (*com.tencent.mobileqq*) is the most popular instant messaging app in China. Once the app is attacked, chat records can be accessed by the attackers. Thankfully, the app does not allow multiple users login to the app at the same time. If the attacker login the same account when the user is online, the attacker will be exposed. The Gmail (*com.google.android.gm*) and Microsoft OneDrive (*com.microsoft.skydrive*) manage their account connections by the Sync Adapter mechanism. To perform attack on these two apps successfully, the data in the system database file */data/system/users/0/accounts.db* needs to be hijacked. The left apps, such as *com.sina.weibolite* and *com.netease.mail*, can be simply attacked just by hijacking their app files. We persistently trace the user information for a month and only three apps re-authenticate their users. The QQ and Microsoft OneDrive correctly perform authentication and the attack fails in the first week, while the process of Facebook (*com.facebook.katana*) is incomplete. The Facebook server re-authenticates its user by sending the SMS verification code. If the code is not verified, both the user and the attacker cannot login to the app. However, once the user inputs the code, the attackers can also connect the app server in the shadow system again without authentication.

4.3 Case Study

Gmail is an email app developed by Google and downloaded more than 1 billion times. Figure 2 presents the result when the app data files of Gmail are hijacked. Gmail updates the email information based on the Sync Adapter mechanism. By replacing the system database *account.db* in the shadow system, our Gmail testing account can be logged in without authentication. The execution of Gmail depends on some other Google services such as Google Play Service and Google Framework Service. However, these services can be

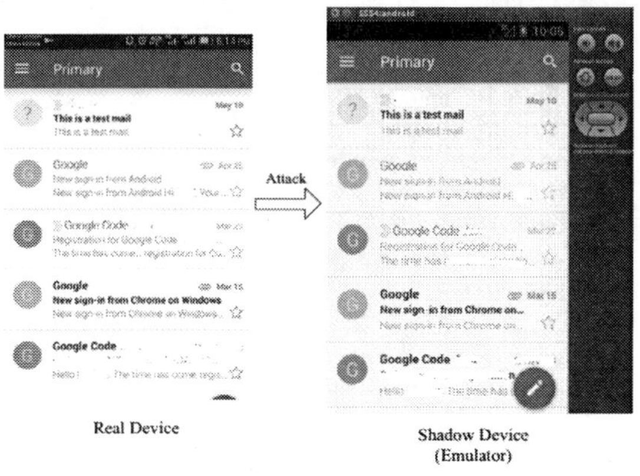

Figure 2. The attack example of Gmail.

directly installed in the shadow system and the attack is not affected. In our experiment, the emails in the shadow system can be read persistently for a month without authentication.

5 Possible Solutions

5.1 Android Emulator Detection

Since the Android emulator has low financial cost and simplifies the construction of the shadow system, detecting the Android emulator can help to defend the proposed attack. Basically, the emulators have different features with the real devices. For example, the contacts, inbox text messages and call logs are usually empty in the Android emulator. In addition, the feature of WIFI, GPS, and CPU can also be used for the Android emulator detection. Currently, some researches [21, 17, 19, 15, 18] have also stressed the Android emulator detection.

5.2 Security Protocol

When an app is developed, a reasonable timeout should be designed for the user authentication. If the users are not re-authenticated for a long period of time, the security risk will increase.

To avoid the inconvenience caused by the frequent authentications, some security tokens such as random numbers can be added in the network protocols. For each login, the app server allocates different security token and update it regularly. If an app returns an old token while the security token has been updated, the server will know that the user data is hijacked and need to re-authenticate the user. Therefore, the attackers have to analyze the complicated communication protocols and deploy a Trojan in the user devices for hijacking the token, which increases the attacking cost and the exposing probability.

5.3 Trusted Execution Environment

TrustZone is a hardware-based security extension technology incorporated with the ARM processors. Based on the TrustZone, the trusted execution environment (TEE) can be constructed [7]. The technique is effective to protect the core

TABLE II. The effectiveness and disadvantages of the solutions.

Solution	Effectiveness	disadvantage
Static Attribute	Weak	Easy to be Simulated
Security Protocol	Strong	Protocol Redesign
TEE	Strong	Hardware Support
Habit-based	-	Not Accurate

services in the mobile devices and some manufacturers have added this function into their newest smart phones. The isolation mechanisms of TrustZone ensure that the guest OS components cannot access the TEE's resources even though the attackers have the elevated privilege of OS. Meanwhile, the hardware-level authentication can ensure the uniqueness of devices and avoid the malicious attacks from the shadow system effectively.

5.4 Habit-based Authentication

Habit-based authentication is to find the attackers by learning the user history behaviors. For instance, if an app is used in a rare time period such as midnight or a rare network IP, the servers should re-authenticate their users actively. Based on the machine learning approach, even the operation habits such as rhythm click characteristics [10] can be considered as the features to distinguish different users. Some of recent researches [6, 16, 20, 9] also proposed the authentication on touch gesture-based behavioral biometrics. Actually, some apps such as QQ already have the functionality to prompt users that their accounts are logged in at another city according to the network IP.

Table II presents the effectiveness analysis of these solutions. Firstly, verifying static device attributes just increase the attack difficulty, and all these attributes can be simulated simply by the attackers. By comparison, the solutions based on the security protocols and the TEE is strong against the data hijacking attack, especially for the TEE. However, the technique of TEE depends on the hardware support. Finally, the authentication based on the user history behaviors may not be accurate at present. Most of these techniques are still being researched. On other hand, compared to the traditional computers, some information of mobile devices such as locations and networks are more variable. They are inaccurate and only auxiliary to the user authentications.

Conclusion

In this paper, we propose a kind of data hijacking attack for the mobile apps. By simply hijacking the data files of the apps to the constructed shadow system, the privacies of the victims such as emails can be accessed by the attackers persistently. We verify the effectiveness of the proposed attack with 7 most popular Android apps released by the top developers, and the results indicate that most of these apps do not provide strategies against this attack or their defense can be broken simply. Finally, we give some security suggestions to the users for defeating the proposed attack.

Acknowledgment

This work was supported by National Key Research and Development Program under Grant No.2016YFB0800603, National Natural Science Foundation of China (NSFC) under Grant No.61402477, Strategic Priority Research Program of the Chinese Academy of Sciences under Grant No. XDA06010703, and the National Key Research and Development Program of China under Grant No. 2016YFB0800403.

References

[1] 360 root. http://root.360.cn/.
[2] Baidu root. http://root.baidu.com/.
[3] How to root any device. http://www.xda-developers.com/root/.
[4] Jorrit chainfire jongma. how-to su: Guidelines for problem-free su usage. http://su.chainfire.eu/, 2014.
[5] Transferring data using sync adapters. http://developer.android.com/training/syncadapters/index.html.
[6] A. A. Alariki and A. A. Manaf. Investigation of touch-based user authentication features using android smartphone. In Advanced Machine Learning Technologies and Applications - Second International Conference, AMLTA 2014, Cairo, Egypt, November 28-30, 2014. Proceedings, pages 135–144, 2014.
[7] ARM. Trustzone. http://www.arm.com/zh/products/processors/technologies/trustzone/.
[8] S. Bugiel, L. Davi, A. Dmitrienko, T. Fischer, and A.-R. Sadeghi. Xmandroid: A new android evolution to mitigate privilege escalation attacks. Technische Universit¨at Darmstadt, Technical Report TR-2011-04, 2011.
[9] J. G. Casanova, C. S. ´Avila, G. Bailador, and A. de Santos Sierra. Authentication in mobile devices through hand gesture recognition. Int. J. Inf. Sec., 11(2):65–83, 2012.
[10] T. Chang, C. Tsai, Y. Yang, and P. Cheng. User authentication using rhythm click characteristics for non-keyboard devices. In Proceedings of the 2011 International Conference on Asia Agriculture and Animal IPCBEE, volume 13, pages 167–171, 2011.
[11] W. Enck, P. Gilbert, S. Han, V. Tendulkar, B. Chun, L. P. Cox, J. Jung, P. McDaniel, and A. N. Sheth. Taintdroid: An information-flow tracking system for realtime privacy monitoring on smartphones. ACM Trans. Comput. Syst., 32(2):5:1–5:29, 2014.
[12] W. Enck, P. Gilbert, S. Han, V. Tendulkar, B. Chun, L. P. Cox, J. Jung, P. McDaniel, and A. N. Sheth. Taintdroid: An information-flow tracking system for realtime privacy monitoring on smartphones. ACM Trans. Comput. Syst., 32(2):5:1–5:29, 2014.
[13] M. C. Grace, Y. Zhou, Z. Wang, and X. Jiang. Systematic detection of capability leaks in stock android smartphones. In 19th Annual Network and Distributed System Security Symposium (NDSS'12), San Diego, California, USA, Feb. 2012.

[14] L. Li, A. Bartel, T. F. Bissyand´e, J. Klein, Y. L. Traon, S. Arzt, S. Rasthofer, E. Bodden, D. Octeau, and P. McDaniel. Iccta: Detecting inter-component privacy leaks in android apps. In 37th IEEE/ACM International Conference on Software Engineering (ICSE'15), Florence, Italy, May. 2015, pages 280–291.

[15] F. Matenaar and P. Schulz. Detecting android sandboxes. http://www.dexlabs.org/blog/btdetect.

[16] Y. Meng, D. S. Wong, R. Schlegel, and L. Kwok. Touch gestures based biometric authentication scheme for touchscreen mobile phones. In Information Security and Cryptology - 8th International Conference, Inscrypt 2012, Beijing, China, November 28-30, 2012, Revised Selected Papers, pages 331–350, 2012.

[17] T. Petsas, G. Voyatzis, E. Athanasopoulos, M. Polychronakis, and S. Ioannidis. Rage against the virtual machine: hindering dynamic analysis of android malware. In Proceedings of the Seventh European Workshop on System Security, EuroSec 2014, April 13, 2014, Amsterdam, The Netherlands, pages 5:1–5:6, 2014.

[18] T. Petsas, G. Voyatzis, E. Athanasopoulos, M. Polychronakis, and S. Ioannidis. Rage against the virtual machine: hindering dynamic analysis of android malware. In Proceedings of the Seventh European Workshop on System Security, page 5. ACM, 2014.

[19] V. Rastogi, Y. Chen, and W. Enck. Appsplayground: automatic security analysis of smartphone applications. In Third ACM Conference on Data and Application Security and Privacy, CODASPY'13, San Antonio, TX, USA, February 18-20, 2013, pages 209–220, 2013.

[20] N. Sae-Bae, K. Ahmed, K. Isbister, and N. D. Memon. Biometric-rich gestures: a novel approach to authentication on multi-touch devices. In CHI Conference on Human Factors in Computing Systems, CHI '12, Austin, TX, USA - May 05 - 10, 2012, pages 977–986, 2012.

[21] T. Vidas and N. Christin. Evading android runtime analysis via sandbox detection. In 9th ACM Symposium on Information, Computer and Communications Security, ASIA CCS '14, Kyoto, Japan - June 03 - 06, 2014, pages 447–458, 2014.

[22] H. Zhang, D. She, and Z. Qian. Android root and its providers: A double-edged sword. In Proceedings of the 22nd ACM SIGSAC Conference on Computer and Communications Security, pages 1093–1104. ACM, 2015.

[23] Y. Zhou and X. Jiang. Dissecting android malware: Characterization and evolution. In Security and Privacy (SP), 2012 IEEE Symposium on, pages 95–109. IEEE, 2012

DOI: 10.1051/itmconf/20171204012

Scene Composition in Augmented Virtual Presenter System

Ting-Xi Liu[1], Yao Lu[2], Li-Jing Zhang[3], Zi-Jian Wang[4]

[1]*School of Computer Science, Beijing Institute of Technology, Beijing, China*
[2]*School of Computer Science, Beijing Institute of Technology, Beijing, China*
[3]*School of Computer Science, Beijing Institute of Technology, Beijing, China*
[4]*School of Computer Science, Beijing Institute of Technology, [4]China Central Television, Beijing, China*
[1]liutx@bit.edu.cn, [2]vis_yl@bit.edu.cn, [3]focus_zlj@163.com, [4]wangzijian@cctv.com

Abstract: In soccer match, presenters or commentators are needed to help the audiences understanding the match more clearly. For better visual effect, we design an Augmented Virtual Presenter System which can integrate presenter's image into the soccer field in match video. In fact, it is a scene composition process. In this paper, we will illustrate the structure and features of this system, and propose several solutions for the key problems. For scene composition, we design an algorithm consisting of automatic matting, localization, and occlusion processing. For occlusion problem, we propose a mixture solution including interactive and semantic segmentations for different scenarios.

1. Introduction

Soccer is one of the most popular games in the world. During the important soccer match events, such as FIFA World Cup or Euro Champions League, billions of fans will revel in it far into the night.

Most people enjoy soccer matches on TV because it is expensive and inconvenient for them to watch it in the stadium. The screen limits the information we could obtain from the match, so we need a commentator to narrate the game in the live. However, what a commentator could offer us is just voice. Obviously, it will be quite impressive for audiences if we let a presenter walk into the field, and describe the games or players more specifically and vividly.

For this purpose, we design an Augmented Virtual Presenter System. Virtual Presenter is a research hotspot in many fields. In [1] Noma et al create a virtual human presenter who accepts speech texts, and acts in real-time 3D animation synchronized with speech. [2] propose a method for modeling presentations in virtual environments, and [2] presents DynamicDuo, a system that uses an animated agent to help inexperienced speakers delivering their presentations in front of an audience.

Comparing with the systems mentioned above, it is not necessary for our system to model in 3D, and use real-human presenter instead. It will significantly reduce the complexity of the system, and enhance the reality of visual effect. Meanwhile, we propose a series of solutions to perform video synthesis automatically according to features of soccer match video.

The main functions of this system are matting presenter section in each frame of pre-recorded video, and inserting it into match video appropriately. We will illustrate the details of the system structure in next section.

There are two key problems in this system: scene composition and occlusion processing.

Scene composition: The match video and the presenter's video are obtained respectively. Therefore, how to synthesize scene with presenter's image and ensure the visual realism is the main problem to solve.

Occlusion processing: Generally, there are 22 players, 4 referees and other staffs in soccer field. So when the presenter is embedded in the ground, we need to deal with the occlusion problem in presenter's movements.

For scene composition, we propose a robust method to mat presenter from pure color background, then determine location and scale based on object detection using convolution neural networks.

For occlusion problem, we propose two kinds of solutions in different scenarios.

In close-up view, we use interactive image segmentation methods to segment the pixels of occlusion objects accurately;

In middle view or long view, we use semantic segmentation and matting methods to get coarse multi-object masks automatically.

 DOI: 10.1051/itmconf/20171204012

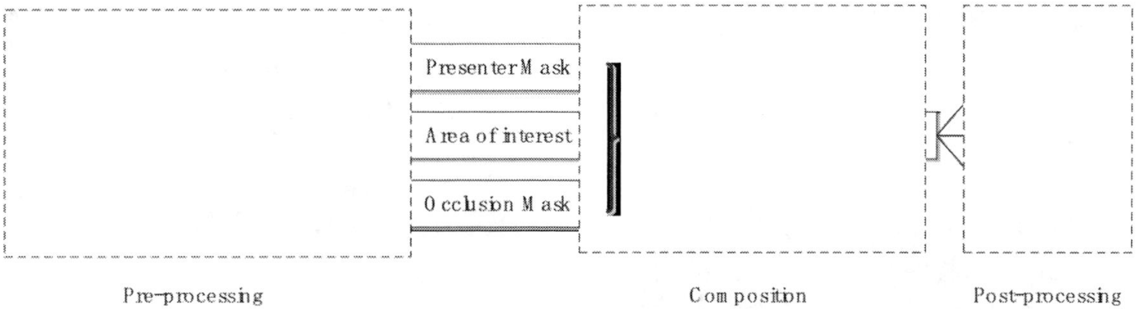

Figure1. Structure of Augmented Virtual Presenter System

In next section, we will introduce the structure of Augmented Virtual Presenter System. In section III and IV, we will illustrate the algorithms of scene composition and occlusion respectively. And section V will give a brief description of implementation details and results of our system.

2. Augmented Virtual Presenter System

The Augmented Virtual Presenter System (AVPS) integrates three modules, including pre-processing, composition and post-processing. The framework of AVPS is shown in Fig.1.

Pre-processing: This part accepts two video streams, presenter video and match video, as input.

For presenter video, we split it into frames and perform matting, store the masks and bounding boxes of presenter in each frame.

For match video, we perform localization and segmentation to obtain regions of interest and occlusion masks respectively.

Composition: With the information obtained above, we design a 3-layer composition hierarchy:

Layer-1: Specify scene from match video;

Layer-2: Insert the presenter's image into area of interest in Layer-1 using mask sequence from 1);

Layer-3: Cover the occlusion objects over Layer-2 by means of occlusion masks from 1).

Post-processing: In this part, we implement various of basic functions in video processing, e.g. video and audio editing (FFmpeg), simple animation effects (HTML5), and subtitle editing (FreeType).

3. Scene Composition

As we introduced in Section I, the match video and the presenter's video are obtained from different sources. The first key problem is how to merge the presenter's section into the scene in the match video appropriately.

For scene composition, we propose a two-step method:

Step1: Presenter image matting from pure color background to obtain a sequence of presenter's masks;

Step2: Localization based on object detection, to determine the coordinates and scales of presenter in match video.

3.1 Matting from Pure Color Background

There are many different matting approaches, e.g. Bayesian Matting [4], Poisson Matting [5], Closed-form Matting [6] and Robust Matting[7]. But these solutions cannot be applied in real-time video matting because of the complexity and demands of user interaction.

In order to obtain the presenter's section from video sequence in real-time automatically, we use a simple pure color background matting method.

We take several presenter's videos in front of a blue curtain background, which is not pure blue indeed. So we set a threshold, which is about 29~35 in our experiments. For each pixel in RGB color space, if both the value of blue component minus green and red are greater than the threshold, we consider it as a blue background point. After mask extraction by matting, we perform a Gaussian blur operation on the mask to smooth the border.

Algorithm 1 Pure Color Background Matting

Input: An image I with presenter in blue curtain background parameter $Thres$ is the threshold of background pixels

Output: Presenter's mask $Mask$

function PUREMATTING($I, Thres$)
  for each pixels I_i in I **do**
    $[R, G, B] \leftarrow I_i$
    if $(B - R) > Thres$ **and** $(B - G) > Thres$ **then**
      $Mask[i] \leftarrow 255$
    else
      $Mask[i] \leftarrow 0$
    end if
  end for
  $Mask \leftarrow$ GaussianBlur(Mask)
  return $Mask$
end function

The algorithm and result of matting are given in algorithm1 and Fig. 2.

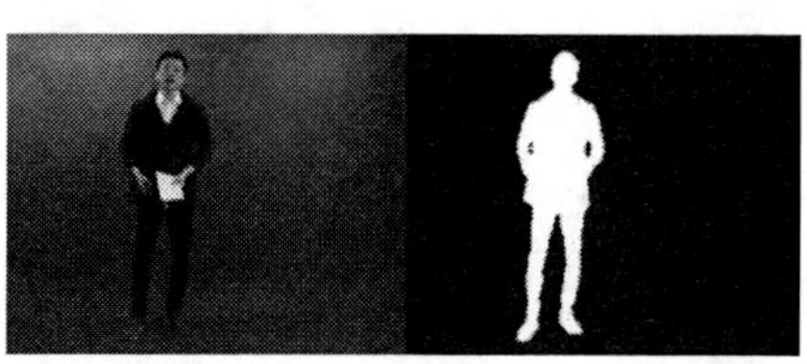

Figure 2. Result of Pure Color Background Matting

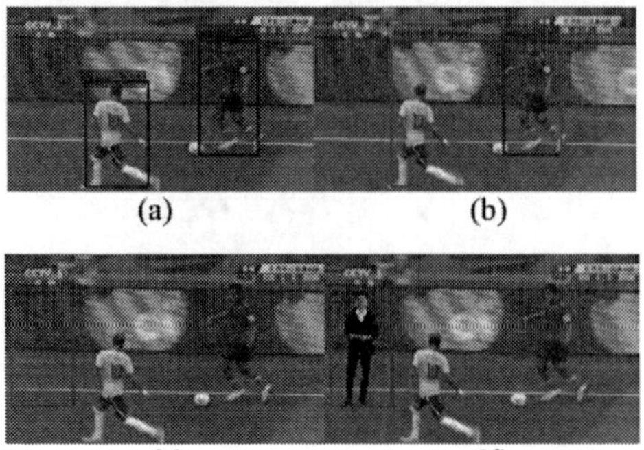

Figure 1. Procedure of localization. (a) shows the result of detection, (b) shows the region of interest (red bounding box), (c) shows the result of presenter's location and scale, (d) shows the composition result.

3.2 Localization By Object Detection.

In the first step we get a sequence of presenter's masks, and what's next is to insert the presenter into match video using these masks. Before that, a localization operation is needed to determine the locations and scales of presenter.

In order to perform localization automatically, we propose an algorithm based on object detection using convolutional neural network, to select the proper region for presenter according to the location of detected players. The localization operation consists of 3 steps:

Step1: Player detection.

Firstly, to get the players' attributes including locations and scales, we use a SSD (Single Shot MultiBox Detector)[8] model to perform detection. SSD is a method for detecting objects in images using a single deep neural network, it eliminates proposal generation procedure such as selective search in R-CNN[9] and region proposal network in Faster R-CNN[10]. This feature makes SSD easy to train and to be integrated into our system.

Step2: Selecting region of interest.

Based on the players' locations and confidences fetched in detection, we calculate the smallest bounding region that includes all important players, whose detection confidence is greater than a threshold (0.7 in our experiment).

Step3: Presenter localization.

In order to avoid crowding in visual effect, the presenter will enter from the side which is further to the region of interest. For example, in Fig. 3, the presenter enters the field from left. Then we set the corresponding edge (left in Fig. 3) as the far end of presenter's location, and determine the scale by the height of the player whose detected area is maximum in the image.

An example of the entire procedure is presented in Fig.3.

4. Occlusion Processing

As we know, in a soccer match, there are players, referees, staffs and other objects in the field. Our system

Figure 2. Accurate occlusion using interactive segmentation (GrabCut)

attempts to insert a presenter into the ground, and the presenter need to enter from the outside of the shot.

During the movements, the presenter should be occluded by some real players and objects in some case. Here we collectively define them as "occlusion objects".

For occlusion problem, we propose a framework which includes two processing method used in different scenarios:

Accurate extraction of occlusion objects for close-up view by interactive segmentation methods.

Automatic construction of occlusion hierarchies by pure matting or semantic segmentation for middle/long view.

4.1 Accurate Extraction of Occlusion Objects for Close-Up View

For close-up view, occlusion objects are too large to ignore the details in the border. In this case, we consider to apply interactive segmentation methods in accurate occlusion processing, e.g. GrabCut[11], Random Walk[12][13][14]. The result of accurate occlusion using GrabCut is shown in Fig. 4. This method acts better in the details compared with the automated approaches, but demands considerable user interactions.

4.2 Automatic Construction of Occlusion Hierarchies for Middle/Long View

For middle or long view, occlusion objects who occlude presenter are smaller. Under the case of low resolution, the details of these players and objects have little effect on visual effect. Meanwhile the number of objects are much more than that in close-up view, it's unreasonable to segment each objects manually by interaction methods.

The framework we propose for this case consists of two steps:

Step1: Generate complete, coarse masks of all occlusion objects in the field automatically;

Step2: Construct the occlusion hierarchies by footprint point.

Here we offer two alternative methods in step 1: 1) matting method, and 2) semantic segmentation using fully convolutional networks FCNs.

Method 1) is simple and efficient, can be used in scenarios that all the occlusion objects are in the green field area. It consists of 4 steps:

Step1: Use pure background matting to get green area as field;

(a) (b) (c)

Figure 3. Comparison of Matting method and Semantic Segmentation. (a) is the source image, includes 11 players, 1 referee and 1 staff. (b) shows the result of matting method. (c) shows the result of semantic segmentation using DeepLab model.

Step2: perform morphological transformation to remove the noise;

Step3: Find maximum contours, and fill the convex hull;

Step4: Perform pure matting in maximum contours to get occlusion masks of players.

The result of method 1) is shown in Fig.5(b).

Obviously, matting method is poor in robustness when the occlusion objects are not in the field entirely. For example, the goal keeper in Fig.5(a), whose body is not involved in green field, cannot be extract by matting method. So we consider applying semantic segmentation based on convolutional neural networks to extract masks of occlusion objects.

FCNs[15] is a method for semantic segmentation. It builds "fully convolutional" networks that take input of arbitrary size and produce correspondingly-sized output by transferring pre-trained classifier weights, fusing different layer representations, and learning end-to-end on whole images.

While what we used in this system is the improved approach DeepLab[16], which proposes atrous spatial pyramid pooling (ASPP) to robustly segment objects at multiple scales, and improves the localization of object boundaries by combining the responses at the final DCNN layer with a fully connected Conditional Random Field.

We integrate the DeepLab model in our system, considering all the players, referees and staffs as a semantic type 'people', and performing automated player segmentation. The result is shown in Fig.5(c).

Fig.5 shows the comparison of two methods. As we can infer from the result, the matting method acts slightly better than semantic segmentation in accuracy, but fails in matting objects who are not in the green field area (e.g. the goal keeper in Fig.5(a)), while semantic segmentation could roughly segment all the people in the image. So we offer both of these two alternatives, meanwhile manually fine-tuning operations are available too.

By means of occlusion mask obtained above, we can find contours to mark the location of each players and objects. Here we defined a footprint point for presenter and each objects, which equals the bottom point of their contours. If the footprint point of an object is lower than presenter's, we consider it as an occlusion object. The procedure is illustrated in Algorithm 2, and an example of automatic occlusion processing is shown in Fig.6.

5. Experiment

The main framework of the system is developed in C++, while modules using deep learning methods are based on Caffe and its Python APIs. Other development details are shown in Table 1.

We test our system in a Nvidia GTX Titan X GPU, with the support of GPU acceleration we could integrate deep learning models into the system. In detection task, the SSD300 (VGG16) model could reach 46 fps, and in semantic segmentation it takes about 1.54 seconds to perform segmentation in the resolution 1280×720.

Algorithm 2 Automatic Occlusion Processing

Input: Original image $\boldsymbol{Match}$, $\boldsymbol{Presenter}$
footprint point $\boldsymbol{Foot}$ of presenter
Output: Composed image $\boldsymbol{Result}$

function OCCLUSION($Match, Presenter$)
  $Mask_{all} \leftarrow$ SemanticSegment($Match$)
  $Contours \leftarrow$ findContours($Mask_{all}$)
  for each contour cnt **in** Contours **do**
    if $Foot_{cnt}.y > Foot_{pre}.y$ **then**
      $drawContours(Mask_{occ}, cnt)$
    end if
  end for
  $Layer1 \leftarrow Match$
  $Layer2 \leftarrow Presenter$
  $Layer3 \leftarrow Match(Mask_{occ})$
  $Result \leftarrow Merge(Layer1, Layer2, Layer3)$
  return $Result$
end function

Fig.6 shows a typical scenario of presenter with occlusion hierarchies. The two players whose footprint points are lower than presenter's are considered as occlusion objects.

Table 1. Implementation details of AVPS

Acceleration	CUDA 8.0
GUI	Qt 5.7
Image Processing	OpenCV 2.4.10
Audio	FFmpeg
Subtitle	FreeType 2.6
Animation	HTML5

Figure 4. A typical scenario of presenter with occlusion hierarchies

6. Conclusion

We develop an Augmented Virtual Presenter System and implement most of the modules and features. During the development, we propose a series of methods to perform video composition, and to solve key problems like occlusion. We apply matting, object detection, interactive and semantic segmentations for better visual effect and user experience.

The main contribution of the system is that we make it highly automated to present soccer match video. In the whole system, excepting for basic editing operations, manual inputs that we need to offer are just 1) interactions in accurate occlusion objects segmentation, and 2) manual adjustment to fix defects or refine the locations, etc.

Besides, most of the components in our system could be performed in real-time, which makes the system applicable in either live stream or analysis after the match.

Our system is developed for soccer match, but with the support of deep learning methods in detection and segmentation, we could easily transfer the system for other sports video such as volleyball, basketball, American football and so on, and many types of TV programs which need a presenter.

Acknowledgment

This work was supported by the National Natural Science Foundation of China (No. 61273273).

References

[1] Noma T, Zhao L, Badler N I. Design of a Virtual Human Presenter[J]. Computer Graphics & Applications IEEE, 2000, 20(4):79-85.

[2] Nijholt A, Welbergen V H, Zwiers J, et al. Introducing an Embodied Augmented Virtual Presenter Agent in a Virtual Meeting Room[J]. Acta Press, 2005.

[3] Trinh H, Ring L, Bickmore T. DynamicDuo:Co-presenting with Virtual Agents[J]. 2015:1739-1748.

[4] Chuang Y Y, Curless B, Salesin D H, et al. A Bayesian approach to digital matting[C]// Computer Vision and Pattern Recognition, 2001. CVPR 2001. Proceedings of the 2001 IEEE Computer Society Conference on. IEEE, 2001:II-264-II-271 vol.2.

[5] Jian S, Jia J, Tang C K, et al. Poisson Matting[J]. Acm Transactions on Graphics, 2004.

[6] Levin A, Lischinski D, Weiss Y. A Closed-Form Solution to Natural Image Matting[J]. IEEE Transactions on Pattern Analysis & Machine Intelligence, 2008, 30(2):228-242.

[7] Wang J, Cohen M F. Optimized Color Sampling for Robust Matting[C]// Computer Vision and Pattern Recognition, 2007. CVPR '07. IEEE Conference on. IEEE, 2007:1-8.

[8] Liu W, Anguelov D, Erhan D, et al. SSD: Single Shot MultiBox Detector[J]. 2015.

[9] Girshick R, Donahue J, Darrell T, et al. Rich Feature Hierarchies for Accurate Object Detection and Semantic Segmentation[C]// Computer Vision and Pattern Recognition. IEEE, 2013:580-587.

[10] Ren S, He K, Girshick R, et al. Faster R-CNN: Towards Real-Time Object Detection with Region Proposal Networks[J]. IEEE Transactions on Pattern Analysis & Machine Intelligence, 2015:1-1.

[11] Rother C, Kolmogorov V, Blake A. "GrabCut"[J]. Acm Transactions on Graphics, 2004, 23(3):309.

[12] Ju W, Xiang D, Zhang B, et al. Random Walk and Graph Cut for Co-Segmentation of Lung Tumor on PET-CT Images.[J]. IEEE Transactions on Image Processing, 2015, 25(3):1192-1192.

[13] Dong X, Shen J, Shao L, et al. Sub-Markov Random Walk for Image Segmentation[J]. IEEE Transactions on Image Processing, 2016, 25(2):516.

[14] Chefd'Hotel C, Sebbane A. Random Walk and Front Propagation on Watershed Adjacency Graphs for Multilabel Image Segmentation[C]// IEEE, International Conference on Computer Vision. IEEE, 2007:1-7.

[15] Long J, Shelhamer E, Darrell T. Fully convolutional networks for semantic segmentation[J]. IEEE Transactions on Pattern Analysis & Machine Intelligence, 2017, 39(4):640-651.

[16] Chen L C, Papandreou G, Kokkinos I, et al. DeepLab: Semantic Image Segmentation with Deep Convolutional Nets, Atrous Convolution, and Fully Connected CRFs[J]. 2016.

 DOI: 10.1051/itmconf/20171204013

A Data Forward Stepwise Fitting Algorithm Based on Orthogonal Function System

Han-Ju Li[1,a]

[1] *Dongguan Power Supply Bureau, Guangdong Power Grid Co., Ltd. Dongguan 523008, P.R.China*
99959828@qq.com

Abstract. Data fitting is the main method of functional data analysis, and it is widely used in the fields of economy, social science, engineering technology and so on. Least square method is the main method of data fitting, but the least square method is not convergent, no memory property, big fitting error and it is easy to over fitting. Based on the orthogonal trigonometric function system, this paper presents a data forward stepwise fitting algorithm. This algorithm takes forward stepwise fitting strategy, each time using the nearest base function to fit the residual error generated by the previous base function fitting, which makes the residual mean square error minimum. In this paper, we theoretically prove the convergence, the memory property and the fitting error diminishing character for the algorithm. Experimental results show that the proposed algorithm is effective, and the fitting performance is better than that of the least square method and the forward stepwise fitting algorithm based on the non-orthogonal function system.

1 Introduction

Data fitting or data approximation is an important and common technique in data mining [1]. Least squares method (LSM) is widely used in data fitting. But LSM has the following drawbacks: the solution may not exist; the number of parameters to be far less than the number of data, otherwise prone to over fitting; not successive approximation algorithm, the fitting error does not decrease with increasing complexity; do not have memory property, when increasing the base function, need to retraining parameters. In recent years, the paper [2-5] puts forward the method of piecewise linear fitting. In this method, the original data sequence is matched with the key points of the data sequence, which is used to compress the original sequence in order to get smaller storage and computation cost. However, this method cannot approach the original data sequence arbitrarily, and the fitting error is large. The orthogonal function system is an important set of functions. After completion, it can become the base of Hilbert space, which can be used to carry out the research of Fourier analysis, function approximation and data fitting. The orthogonal function system is easy to construct, and can be obtained by the implementation of the Schmidt orthogonalization method. The paper [6] gives some important orthogonal function systems. Because of the linear independence of the orthogonal function system, it can be used to extract the information of each vertical direction without overlapping. So the orthogonal function system is very suitable for data fitting. Based on LSM, the paper [7] uses a class of Orthogonal Spline Function GF system to fit the scattered data and the paper [8] uses the wavelet function to fit the discrete data. Based on the popular method of surface rendering, the paper [9] applies a complete orthogonal function system to fit the point cloud data. Because of the excellent properties of orthogonal function system, this paper adopts the linear combination of complete orthogonal trigonometric function on L^2 [0, 1] to fit the original data. However, the algorithm idea of this paper is different from the previous literature, but adopts the forward stepwise fitting strategy, and extracts the maximum residual information in each step. The algorithm proposed in this paper has some excellent properties, such as convergence, memory property, and gradual approximation.

2 Algorithm and Property

Set the data sequence is $\{y_1, y_2, \ldots$, given a positive integer M such that $N+M$ is odd, the data sequence is mapped to the plane of the data set

$$\left\{\left(\frac{1}{N+M}, y_1\right), \left(\frac{2}{N+M}, y_2\right), \ldots \left(\frac{i}{N+M} \quad\right) \ldots \left(\frac{N}{N+M} \quad\right)\right\} . \quad (1)$$

Let $f(x)$ be the original function of (1), i.e.

$$y_i = f\left(\frac{i}{N+M}\right), i = 1, 2, \ldots \quad .$$

Take the following orthogonal function system

---

[a] Corresponding author: 99959828@qq.com

$\{1, \cos 2\pi x, \sin 2\pi x, \cos 2\pi 2x, \sin 2\pi 2x, \dots$

in $L^2[0, 1]$ and use the additive model

$$f_n(x) = a_0 + \sum_{k=1}^{n} (a_k \cos 2\pi kx + b_k \sin 2\pi kx) \quad (2)$$

of the above orthogonal function system to fit $f(x)$. The n in (2) reflects the complexity of the model, in general, the bigger the n, the better the fitting, however, the more complex the model, prone to over fitting. The problem now is to give (1), how to learn the parameters of (2) and determine the appropriate complexity.

Given complexity n, we need to learn $2n+1$ parameters, denoted by $\gamma_n = (a_0, a_1, b_1, \dots$. Let $\mathbf{R}_{n+1}$ denote the residual vector of $f(x)$ and $f_n(x)$ in (1), i.e.

$$\mathbf{R}_{n+1} = \left(y_1 - f_n\left(\frac{1}{N+M}\right), y_2 - f_n\left(\frac{2}{N+M}\right), \dots \quad \left(\frac{N}{N+M}\right)\right). \quad (3)$$

LSM is to obtain the parameters such that the mean square error $\text{MSE}(\mathbf{R}_{n+1})$ minimum, i.e.

$$\gamma_n = \arg\min_{\gamma_n} \text{MSE}(\mathbf{R}_{n+1}) = \arg\min_{\gamma_n} \frac{1}{N} \sum_{i=1}^{N} \left(y_i - f_n\left(\frac{i}{N+M}\right)\right)^2.$$

In this paper, the forward stepwise fitting strategy is adopted. Defining basis functions

$\beta_k(x) = a_k \cos 2\pi kx + b_k \sin 2\pi kx$, $k = 0, 1, \dots$, where $\beta_0(x) = a_0$.

The idea of the algorithm is to use the basis function $\beta_k(x)$ to fit the residual vector $\mathbf{r}_k$ produced by the last basis function $\beta_{k-1}(x)$, which makes the mean square error $\text{MSE}(\mathbf{r}_k - \boldsymbol{\beta}_k)$ minimum, where

$$\boldsymbol{\beta}_k = \left(\beta_k\left(\frac{1}{N+M}\right), \beta_k\left(\frac{2}{N+M}\right), \dots \quad \left(\frac{N}{N+M}\right)\right), \mathbf{r}_k = (r_{k1}, r_{k2}, \dots$$

and $\mathbf{r}_0 = (y_1, y_2, \dots$.

That is to solve the following optimization problems

$$(a_k, b_k) = \arg\min_{a_k, b_k} \text{MSE}(\mathbf{r}_k - \boldsymbol{\beta}_k) = \arg\min_{a_k, b_k} \frac{1}{N} \sum_{i=1}^{N} \left(r_{ki} - \beta_k\left(\frac{i}{N+M}\right)\right)^2.$$

In the following we solve the above optimization problem.

If $k = 0$, $\mathbf{r}_0 = (y_1, y_2, \dots$, $\boldsymbol{\beta}_0 = (a_0, a_0, \dots$, then we have

$$a_0 = \arg\min_{a_0} \text{MSE}(\mathbf{r}_0 - \boldsymbol{\beta}_0) = \arg\min_{a_0} \frac{1}{N} \sum_{i=1}^{N} (y_i - a_0)^2 = \frac{1}{N} \sum_{i=1}^{N} y_i. \quad (4)$$

If $k \ge 1$, denote $L(a_k, b_k) = \text{MSE}(\mathbf{r}_k - \boldsymbol{\beta}_k)$, let

$$\frac{\partial L(a_k, b_k)}{\partial a_k} = 0, \quad \frac{\partial L(a_k, b_k)}{\partial b_k} = 0,$$

and solve the above equations, and then we have

$$a_k = \frac{\begin{vmatrix} \sum_{i=1}^{N} r_{ki} \cos\frac{2\pi ki}{N+M} & \sum_{i=1}^{N} \cos\frac{2\pi ki}{N+M} \sin\frac{2\pi ki}{N+M} \\ \sum_{i=1}^{N} r_{ki} \sin\frac{2\pi ki}{N+M} & \sum_{i=1}^{N} \sin^2\frac{2\pi ki}{N+M} \end{vmatrix}}{\begin{vmatrix} \sum_{i=1}^{N} \cos^2\frac{2\pi ki}{N+M} & \sum_{i=1}^{N} \cos\frac{2\pi ki}{N+M} \sin\frac{2\pi ki}{N+M} \\ \sum_{i=1}^{N} \cos\frac{2\pi ki}{N+M} \sin\frac{2\pi ki}{N+M} & \sum_{i=1}^{N} \sin^2\frac{2\pi ki}{N+M} \end{vmatrix}}, \quad (5)$$

$$b_k = \frac{\begin{vmatrix} \sum_{i=1}^{N} r_{ki} \sin\frac{2\pi ki}{N+M} & \sum_{i=1}^{N} \cos\frac{2\pi ki}{N+M} \sin\frac{2\pi ki}{N+M} \\ \sum_{i=1}^{N} r_{ki} \cos\frac{2\pi ki}{N+M} & \sum_{i=1}^{N} \cos^2\frac{2\pi ki}{N+M} \end{vmatrix}}{\begin{vmatrix} \sum_{i=1}^{N} \cos^2\frac{2\pi ki}{N+M} & \sum_{i=1}^{N} \cos\frac{2\pi ki}{N+M} \sin\frac{2\pi ki}{N+M} \\ \sum_{i=1}^{N} \cos\frac{2\pi ki}{N+M} \sin\frac{2\pi ki}{N+M} & \sum_{i=1}^{N} \sin^2\frac{2\pi ki}{N+M} \end{vmatrix}}. \quad (6)$$

Using (5) and (6), we obtain the following algorithm.

Algorithm A (Data forward stepwise fitting algorithm based on orthogonal trigonometric function, OTFS-DFSFA).

Input: data sequence $\{y_1, y_2, \dots$ and Complexity n;

Output: $f_n(x) = a_0 + \sum_{k=1}^{n} (a_k \cos 2\pi kx + b_k \sin 2\pi kx)$.

Step1. Mapping data sequence into (1);

Step2. According to (4), calculate a_0, get $\beta_0(x) = a_0$ and calculate $\mathbf{r}_1 = \mathbf{r}_0 - \boldsymbol{\beta}_0$;

Step3. For $k = 1, 2, \dots$,

1) According to (5) and (6), calculate a_k and b_k, and get basis function $\beta_k(x) = a_k \cos 2\pi kx + b_k \sin 2\pi kx$;

2) Update residual vector $\mathbf{r}_{k+1} = \mathbf{r}_k - \boldsymbol{\beta}_k$;

Step4. Output $f_n(x) = \sum_{k=0}^{n} \beta_k(x)$.

Algorithm A has the following properties.

Proposition B. $\mathbf{R}_{n+1} = \mathbf{r}_{n+1}$.

Proof. It follows from Step3 *2)* in Algorithm A that

$$\mathbf{r}_{n+1}(i) = \mathbf{r}_n(i) - \boldsymbol{\beta}_n(i) = \mathbf{r}_{n-1}(i) - \boldsymbol{\beta}_{n-1}(i) - \boldsymbol{\beta}_n(i)$$
$$= \cdots \quad \cdots$$
$$= y_i - \left(a_0 + \beta_1\left(\frac{i}{N+M}\right) + \beta_2\left(\frac{i}{N+M}\right) + \cdots \quad \left(\frac{i}{N+M}\right)\right)$$
$$= y_i - f_n\left(\frac{i}{N+M}\right) = \mathbf{R}_{n+1}(i), \quad i = 1, 2, \dots$$

Proposition C. The coefficient vector γ_{n-1} of (2) with complexity $n-1$ and the coefficient vector γ_n of (2) with complexity n satisfy

$$\gamma_{n-1}(i) = \gamma_n(i), \; i = 1, 2, \dots \quad 2n-1.$$

Proof. It follows from (5), (6) and step2, step3 in Algorithm A.

Proposition C shows that the algorithm has memory property. The model of high complexity inherits corresponding position coefficient of the model of low complexity. Note that LSM does not have such property.

Proposition D. $\text{MSE}(\mathbf{R}_{n+1})$ is a decreasing function on n.

Proof. By Proposition B we have $\text{MSE}(\mathbf{R}_{n+1}) = \text{MSE}(\mathbf{r}_{n+1})$. By Step3 2) in Algorithm A we have

$$\text{MSE}(\mathbf{r}_{n+1}) = \text{MSE}(\mathbf{r}_n - \boldsymbol{\beta}_n),$$

where $\boldsymbol{\beta}_n$ is obtained by Step3 *1)* in Algorithm A, i.e.

$$(a_n,b_n)=\arg\min_{a_n,b_n}\mathrm{MSE}(\mathbf{r}_n-\boldsymbol{\beta}_n)=\arg\min_{a_n,b_n}\frac{1}{N}\sum_{i=1}^{N}\left(r_{ni}-\beta_n\left(\frac{i}{N+M}\right)\right)^2$$
$$=\arg\min_{a_n,b_n}\frac{1}{N}\sum_{i=1}^{N}\left(r_{ni}-a_n\cos\frac{2\pi ki}{N+M}-b_n\sin\frac{2\pi ki}{N+M}\right)^2$$

Therefore

$$\mathrm{MSE}(\mathbf{r}_{n+1})=\mathrm{MSE}(\mathbf{r}_n-\boldsymbol{\beta}_n)=\frac{1}{N}\sum_{i=1}^{N}\left(r_{ni}-a_n\cos\frac{2\pi ki}{N+M}-b_n\sin\frac{2\pi ki}{N+M}\right)^2$$
$$\le\frac{1}{N}\sum_{i=1}^{N}\left(r_{ni}-0.\cos\frac{2\pi ki}{N+M}-0.\sin\frac{2\pi ki}{N+M}\right)^2=\mathrm{MSE}(\mathbf{r}_n).$$

Note that LSM does not have Proposition D.

3 Convergence of the Algorithm

Theorem E. Algorithm A is convergent.

Proof. It suffices to proof that the denominator of formula (5) and (6) is not equal to 0, i.e.

$$\left(\sum_{i=1}^{N}\cos^2\frac{2\pi ki}{N+M}\right)\left(\sum_{i=1}^{N}\sin^2\frac{2\pi ki}{N+M}\right)-\left(\sum_{i=1}^{N}\cos\frac{2\pi ki}{N+M}\sin\frac{2\pi ki}{N+M}\right)^2\neq 0.$$

In fact, by Cauchy inequality we have

$$\left(\sum_{i=1}^{N}\cos^2\frac{2\pi ki}{N+M}\right)\left(\sum_{i=1}^{N}\sin^2\frac{2\pi ki}{N+M}\right)-\left(\sum_{i=1}^{N}\cos\frac{2\pi ki}{N+M}\sin\frac{2\pi ki}{N+M}\right)^2\ge 0.\quad(8)$$

So we only need to prove that the equality sign of (8) not occur. A necessary and sufficient condition for the equality sign of (8) occur is

$$\cos\frac{2\pi ki}{N+M}=0, i=1,2,\ldots \text{ or } \sin\frac{2\pi ki}{N+M}=K\cos\frac{2\pi ki}{N+M}, i=1,2,\ldots \quad ,\quad(9)$$

Where K is a constant. First it follows from the first item of (9) that there exits integer m_i such that

$$\frac{2\pi ki}{N+M}=m_i\pi+\frac{\pi}{2}, i=1,2,\ldots \quad .$$

This implies $4ki=(2m_i+1)(N+M)$, $i=1,2,\ldots$ .However, the above equation is not valid. In fact, the left side of the equation is an even number, and the right is an odd number. So $\cos\frac{2\pi ki}{N+M}\neq 0$ for some $i=1,2,\ldots$. So the first item of (9) is not established. Second it follows from the second item of (9) that

$$\tan\left(\frac{2\pi ki}{N+M}\right)=\sin\frac{2\pi ki}{N+M}/\cos\frac{2\pi ki}{N+M}=K, i=1,2,\ldots \quad .$$

The function $\tan\left(\frac{2\pi kx}{N+M}\right)$ is periodic with $\frac{N+M}{2k}$, and is strictly monotonically increasing function in a cycle. It follows from $\tan\left(\frac{2\pi ki}{N+M}\right)=\tan\left(\frac{2\pi k(i+1)}{N+M}\right)$ that there exists an integer m such that $\frac{2\pi k(i+1)}{N+M}-\frac{2\pi ki}{N+M}=\frac{(N+M)m}{2k}$, i.e. $4\pi k^2=(N+M)^2m$. This is a contradiction because the left of the upper equation is an irrational number, and the right is an integer. Therefore, (9) does not hold and (8) cannot take equal sign, so the denominator of (5) and (6) is not zero.

4 Model Selection

The canonical method of model selection is regularization method. Regularization usually has the following form:

$$\min_{f\in\Omega}\frac{1}{N}\sum_{i=1}^{N}L(y_i,f(x_i))+\lambda J(f),\quad(10)$$

Where the first term measure the capacity of model fitting the training data, and the second is the regularization term, which reflects the complexity of the model structure. The relative importance of model fitting accuracy and structure complexity is controlled by regularization parameter $\lambda\ge 0$. Data fitting is usually transformed into an optimization problem with loss function and regularization term, in which parameter λ play a tradeoff between loss and over fitting risk. The literature [10] has carried out a thorough study on this problem.

Given complexity n, because of the memory property of Algorithm A, Algorithm A can learn n models, and the complexity of these models from 1 to n. The question now is how to choose the right model from these models. According to (10), the following specific regularization forms are adopted.

$$\min_{k\in\{1,2,\ldots}\frac{1}{N}\sum_{i=1}^{N}\left(y_i-f_k\left(\frac{i}{N+M}\right)\right)^2+\lambda\|\boldsymbol{\gamma}_k\|_2^2,\quad(11)$$

Where $\boldsymbol{\gamma}_k=(a_0,a_1,b_1,\ldots$ and $\|\boldsymbol{\gamma}_k\|_2^2=a_0^2+\sum_{i=1}^{k}(a_i^2+b_i^2)$. According to Proposition B and Proposition D, the first term of (11) is equal to $\mathrm{MSE}(\mathbf{r}_{k+1})$, and decreases as the k increases. When the complexity is changed from k to $k+1$, we analyze the change of the two terms of (11). The first item of (11) decrease from $\mathrm{MSE}(\mathbf{r}_{k+1})$ to $\mathrm{MSE}(\mathbf{r}_{k+2})$, the decrease is $\mathrm{MSE}(\mathbf{r}_{k+1})-\mathrm{MSE}(\mathbf{r}_{k+2})$, and the second item of (11) increase from $\lambda\|\boldsymbol{\gamma}_k\|_2^2$ to $\lambda\|\boldsymbol{\gamma}_{k+1}\|_2^2$, and the increase is $\lambda(a_{k+1}^2+b_{k+1}^2)$. If

$$\mathrm{MSE}(\mathbf{r}_{k+1})-\mathrm{MSE}(\mathbf{r}_{k+2})\le\lambda(a_{k+1}^2+b_{k+1}^2)$$

Then when the complexity is changed from k to $k+1$, the value of (11) becomes larger. According to the above discussion and the memory property of Algorithm A, the following over fitting criteria are obtained:

If complexity k satisfies

$$\mathrm{MSE}(\mathbf{r}_k)-\mathrm{MSE}(\mathbf{r}_{k+1})\le\lambda(a_k^2+b_k^2),\quad(12)$$

Then $f_m(x)$ is over fitting for all $m\ge k$, where λ can be adjusted according to practical problems.

5 Experiments

5.1 Experimental data

The data used in the experiment comes from the Dongguan statistical survey information network, which records the monthly electricity load in Dongguan from

DOI: 10.1051/itmconf/20171204013

January 2011 to May 2016 (unit KWH), with a total of 65 records. Take and get the following data set.

Table 1. Monthly load data

time(x)	load(y)	time(x)	load(y)	time(x)	load(y)	time(x)	load(y)
1/66	47.06	18/66	53.56	34/66	53.09	50/66	26.47
2/66	36.17	19/66	54.32	35/66	50.46	51/66	48.80
3/66	32.31	20/66	58.16	36/66	50.60	52/66	53.32
4/66	44.61	21/66	61.04	37/66	39.80	53/66	59.02
5/66	46.10	22/66	53.85	38/66	34.12	54/66	65.30
6/66	48.07	23/66	50.23	39/66	51.20	55/66	69.44
7/66	52.13	24/66	42.14	40/66	50.95	56/66	69.33
8/66	56.05	25/66	51.01	41/66	58.20	57/66	61.98
9/66	59.34	26/66	44.25	42/66	63.31	58/66	56.03
10/66	50.88	27/66	26.21	43/66	70.87	59/66	53.55
11/66	48.76	28/66	46.67	44/66	68.62	60/66	52.96
12/66	45.21	29/66	47.67	45/66	64.08	61/66	49.41
13/66	45.02	30/66	58.59	46/66	56.73	62/66	28.66
14/66	29.76	31/66	63.33	47/66	51.17	63/66	53.54
15/66	39.81	32/66	62.87	48/66	51.92	64/66	52.67
16/66	46.19	33/66	57.99	49/66	50.66	65/66	62.43
17/66	47.09						

5.2 Comparison of the fitting performance with the least square method

First, this experiment compares the descending speed of MSE with LSM. Given complexity n, the fitting degree of the algorithm is measured by $\mathrm{MSE}(\mathbf{R}_{n+1})$, where $\mathbf{R}_{n+1}$ is determined by (3). Taking complexity from 1 to 45, we get the contrast graph of the MSE descending speed of the two algorithms. As can be seen from Figure 1, $\mathrm{MSE}(\mathbf{R}_{n+1})$ of the LSM does not tend to zero as the complexity increases, and $\mathrm{MSE}(\mathbf{R}_{n+1})$ of the forward stepwise fitting algorithm tends to zero as the complexity increases.

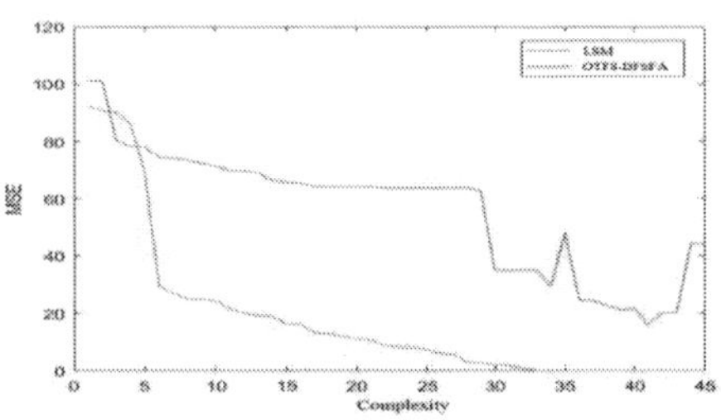

Figure 1. Comparison of the two algorithms for MSE descent speed.

Secondly, complexity 5 and 20 are taken respectively to compare the actual fitting effects of the two algorithms. The experimental results are shown in figure 2.

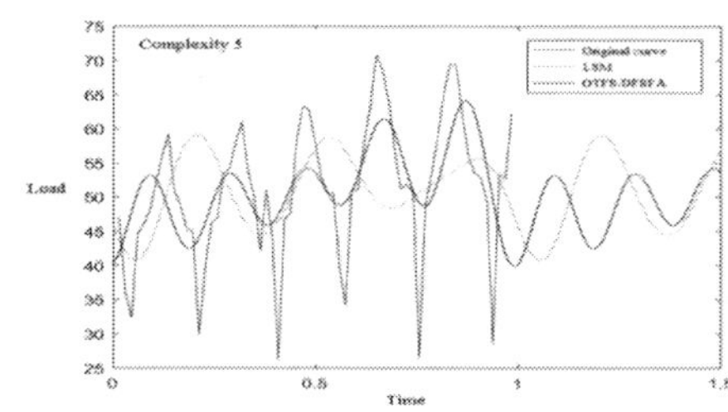

(a) Complexity 5

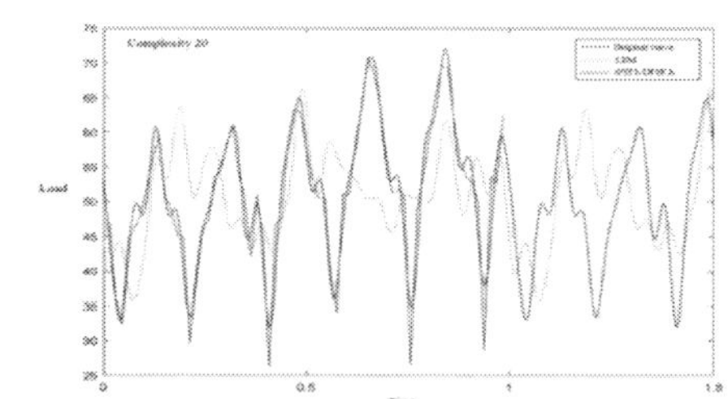

(b) Complexity 20

Figure 2. Fitting effect diagram for the two algorithms .

5.3 Comparison of fitting performance with non-orthogonal function system

This experiment adopts the following non-orthogonal function system

$$\{1, x, \cos 2\pi x, x^2, \cos 2\pi 2x, \ldots \quad \ldots\}.$$

The forward stepwise fitting algorithm which is similar to algorithm A is adopted to compare the fitting effects of two different functional systems. First, compare the MSE's descent rate, taking the complexity from 1 to 45, and get the contrast chart of the following MSE descent speed in figure3.

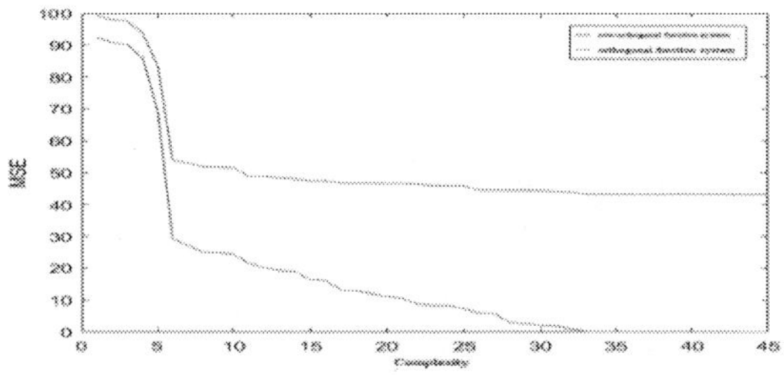

Figure 3. Comparison of the two functional systems for MSE descent speed.

Secondly, complexity 5 and 20 are taken respectively to compare the actual fitting effects of the two functional systems. The experimental results are shown in figure 4.

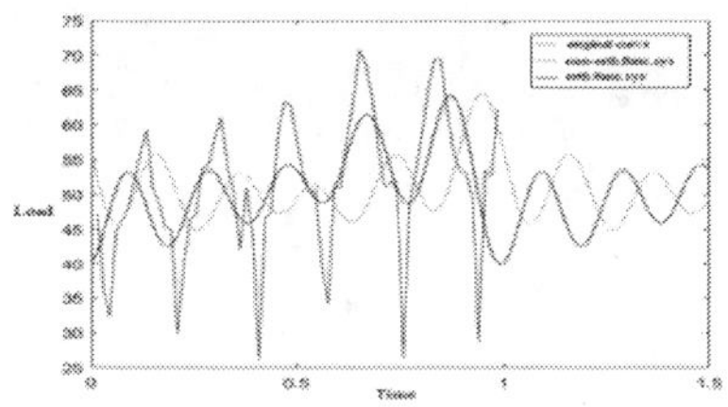

(a) Complexity 5

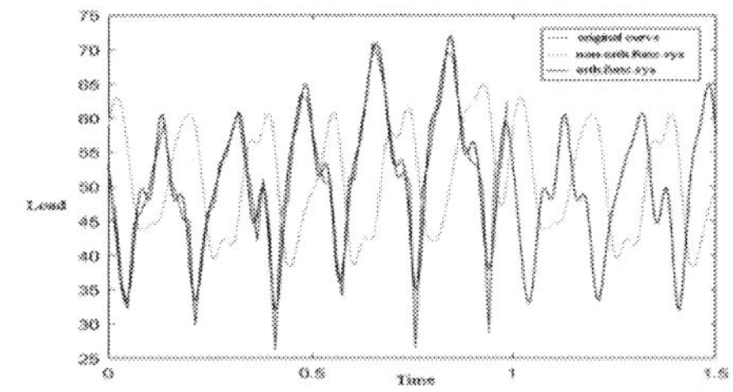

(b) Complexity 20

Figure 4. Fitting effect diagram for the two functional systems.

5.4 Model selection and over fitting decision

Taking complexity 34, by the memory property of the algorithm A, we get a total of 34 models with complexity from 1 to 34, and take $\lambda = 1/65$ to compute the regularization formula (11) and the over fitting condition (12) of each model. The calculation results are as follows.

As can be seen from above table, if $k = 32$, then $\mathrm{MSE}(\mathbf{r}_{k+1}) + \lambda\|\gamma_k\|_2^2$ is minimal. Therefore, the optimal complexity of the model is 32. If $k = 33$, then

$$\mathrm{MSE}(\mathbf{r}_k) - \mathrm{MSE}(\mathbf{r}_{k+1}) < \lambda(a_k^2 + b_k^2) .$$

So, $f_n(x)$ is over fitting for all $n \geq 33$. In the following the fitting effect of the models are given in figure 3 where complexity is 32 and 33.

Table 2. Model selection calculation process

k	$\mathrm{MSE}(\mathbf{r}_k)-\mathrm{MSE}(\mathbf{r}_{k+1})$	$\lambda(a_k^2+b_k^2)$	$\mathrm{MSE}(\mathbf{r}_{k+1})+\lambda\|\gamma_k\|_2^2$	k	$\mathrm{MSE}(\mathbf{r}_k)-\mathrm{MSE}(\mathbf{r}_{k+1})$	$\lambda(a_k^2+b_k^2)$	$\mathrm{MSE}(\mathbf{r}_{k+1})+\lambda\|\gamma_k\|_2^2$
1	10.251	0.3114	93.416	18	0.1563	0.0047	16.5497
2	1.5381	0.0477	91.926	19	1.0096	0.0306	15.5708
3	0.7125	0.0219	91.235	20	0.8475	0.0258	14.7491
4	4.1539	0.1298	87.211	21	0.5502	0.0167	14.2156
5	16.685	0.5155	71.042	22	1.8056	0.0549	12.4648
6	39.905	1.2366	32.373	23	0.4944	0.0152	11.9856
7	2.2415	0.0686	30.201	24	0.0228	0.0007	11.9635
8	2.0925	0.0644	28.173	25	0.9756	0.0297	11.0176
9	0.0653	0.002	28.120	26	1.3258	0.0411	9.733
10	0.5375	0.0164	27.589	27	0.3139	0.0095	9.4286
11	2.7816	0.0866	24.894	28	2.7799	0.0844	6.733
12	1.4559	0.0441	23.482	29	0.2114	0.0065	6.5282
13	0.9028	0.0278	22.607	30	0.5797	0.0177	5.9661
14	0.2252	0.0070	22.389	31	0.1792	0.0056	5.7925
15	2.6388	0.0806	19.830	32	0.8889	0.0274	4.931
16	0.2561	0.0078	19.582	33	0.8519	1.35e+24	1.35e+24
17	2.9715	0.0908	16.701	34	2.93e-04	9.16e-06	1.35e+24

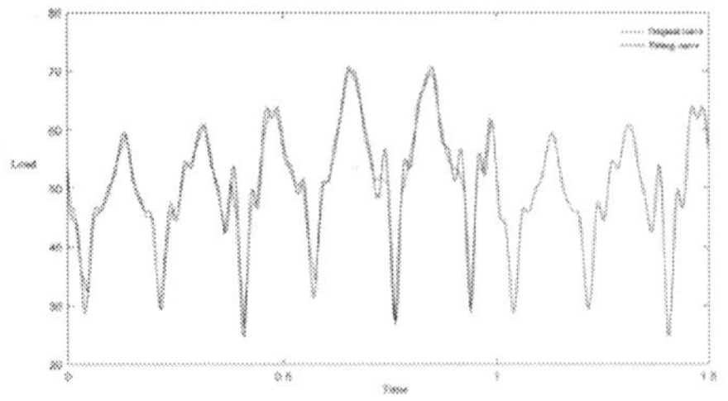

(a) Complexity 32

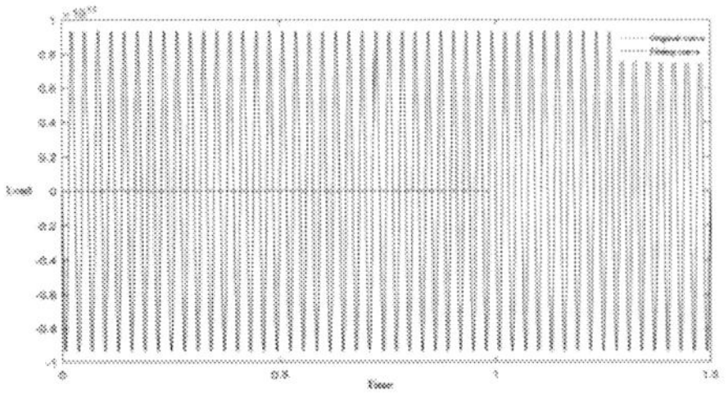

(b) Complexity 33

Figure 5. The best fitting effect diagram and the over fitting effect diagram.

6 Conclusion

In this paper, a data forward stepwise fitting algorithm based on orthogonal function system is proposed. The algorithm has memory property, and the time complexity of the algorithm is less than that of LSM when learning multiple models. The algorithm has gradual approximation property, and the fitting error decreases as the complexity of the model increases. The experimental results show that the performance of the proposed algorithm (MSE dropping speed and fitting accuracy) is better than that of LSM and the forward stepwise fitting algorithm based on the non-orthogonal function system. At the same time, the optimal model selection method and over fitting criterion are given. The experiment shows that the model selection method and the over fitting criterion are effective and have practical significance.

Acknowledgment

This paper is supported by the innovation project (no: 031900KK52170031) of Guangdong Power Grid Co.

References

1. J.O Ramsay, B.W Silverman. *Applied functional data analysis: methods and case studies* (Springer, New York ,2002)
2. T Pavlidis, S.L Horowitz.Segmentation of plane curves.IEEE Trans.Com 23, 8(1974): 860- 870
3. Kevin B Pratt, Eugene Fink.Search for patterns in compressed time series.Inter.J.Ima.Grap 2,1 (2002): 89-106
4. Sanghyun Park, Dongwon Lee, Wesley W Chu.Fast retrieval of similar subsequences in long sequence data bases.*Proceedings of the 1999 Workshop on Knowledge and Data Engineering Exchange* (IEEE. Computer Society, Washington,1999)
5. L.J Yu,J.T Li,Y.D Zhang.Fast picture and macro block level adaptive frame/field coding for H.264. *Proceedings of IEEE Asia Pacific Conference on Circuits and Systems* (IEEE Press, 2006)
6. R.X Song.J.Sys.Sci& Math.Sci 28, 8 (2008):949-960
7. Z.C Cai,W Chen.Least square approximation and analysis for scattered data based on orthogonal GF system.Act.Scienti.Natur.Univ.Suny 52, 5 (2013):73-77
8. X.K Liang.Fitting method of data based on wavelet function.Com.Appl.Soft 20, 4 (2003):3-4
9. Y.Y Liang,R.X Song.Complete orthogonal function system V and points cloud fitting.J.Sys.Simu 18, 8 (2006):2109-2113
10. L Wang,W.J Wang,G.X Jiang.Optimization for smoothing parameters in process of data fitting. Com.Sci 42, 9 (2015):226-229

[a] Corresponding author: 99959828@qq.com

Research on the Index System of Coordination Effectiveness for Equipment System-of-System based on Information Measurement

Zheng Wang

College of Information System and Management, National University of Defense Technology, Changsha, Hunan
joshuakai900901@163.com

Abstract: Through physical domain, information domain and cognitive domain are involved in the analysis of coordination effectiveness evaluation for equipment SOS, the index design method based on information measurement is used to design the index system of coordination effectiveness for equipment SOS.

1. Introduction

Research on coordination effectiveness evaluation method of equipment SOS is an important part of demonstration of equipment SOS, while optimal selection of index system is a key to coordination effectiveness evaluation of equipment SOS [4]. Generally, information measurement is defined as evaluation and measurement on the amount of information. Theory on information measurement provides new technical support for the research on the index system of coordination effectiveness evaluation for equipment SOS. On the basis of difficulties and characteristics of the index system selection of equipment SOS effectiveness, the index system of coordination effectiveness evaluation for equipment SOS based on information measurement is established [5].

2. Principles Development on the Index System of Coordination Effectiveness Evaluation For Equipment F

Evaluation index is a basic principle to measure combat effectiveness of equipment SOS, has an important directive, normative and tractive effort on military struggle preparation and army construction. When developing the evaluation index, if many problems cannot be solved effectively, such as more subjective qualitative evaluation indexes, fewer objective quantitative evaluation indexes, more single evaluation tests, less system matched evaluation, much static single inspection examination, and less dynamic overall inspection, inspection and evaluation are difficult to truly reflect combat capability of forces. Under conditions of informationization, when developing the combat effectiveness evaluation index, high efficiency and accuracy are required as follows:

2.1 Evaluation Index Must Be Consistent with Actual Combat Requirement

Actual combat is the basic standard to examine the combat capability of forces. Inspection and evaluation of combat effectiveness for equipment SOS should objectively response to the combat capability of forces, and develop the evaluation index of coordinative combat effectiveness for equipment SOS in accordance with actual combat standards.

2.2 Evaluation Index Must be Reasonable and Scientific.

Coordinative combat of equipment SOS is a complex system integrated comprehensively by various capabilities. Each capability contains several specific capabilities. Therefore, when determining evaluation index, the level should be divided reasonably at first. According to each specific capability required to perform combat mission under conditions of informationization, decomposition is made around combat element, combat unit, combat system, combat SOS and combat direction, key link and key element are chosen to reflex each capability to the greatest extent, weight values of quantification are established scientifically, and quantification evaluation of coordinative combat effectiveness is achieved.

2.3 Evaluation Index Must be Comprehensive and Measurable.

Related factors involved in coordinative combat effectiveness of equipment SOS have many types and high correlation. Firstly, when developing the evaluation index, it must be relatively complete and systematic, both comprehensively reflex the combat level of equipment SOS and take care of important factors to influence the combat effectiveness of system. Secondly, you should try to select the evaluation index that can go through direct measurement, be obtained by statistics, and be easy to quantification processing, so the influence of human factor is reduced and objectivity, authenticity and operability of evaluation is improved.

2.4 Evaluation Results Should be Comparable.

Whether the evaluation index of coordinative combat effectiveness for equipment SOS is reasonable, concerning whether to scientifically measure the gap between combat capability and wining standard by evaluation, compare the combat capabilities under different conditions, evaluate capabilities required to execute different missions by the same force. Therefore, the evaluation index framework needs to be widely recognized and normative. On this basis, detailed index system is developed in accordance with equipment type, mission type, etc.

3. Evaluation Index System Framework of Coordination Effectiveness For Equipment SOS

Evaluation index of equipment's combat effectiveness can be progressively analyzed layer-by-layer in four aspects, from bottom to top:

Capability measurement of equipment sub-system;

Single effectiveness measurement: relationship is built with capability index, capability index with same or similar attribute is integrated as a single effectiveness index;

System effectiveness measurement: under certain combat environment, evaluation is made on system effectiveness of key links at every combat stage;

SOS (system-of-system) effectiveness measurement: effectiveness index is determined by comprehensively considering mission and task of equipment SOS, combat scenario, combat unit and other factors between system effectiveness and SOS effectiveness [6].

Layered architectural diagram of combat effectiveness evaluation index system is shown as Figure 1.

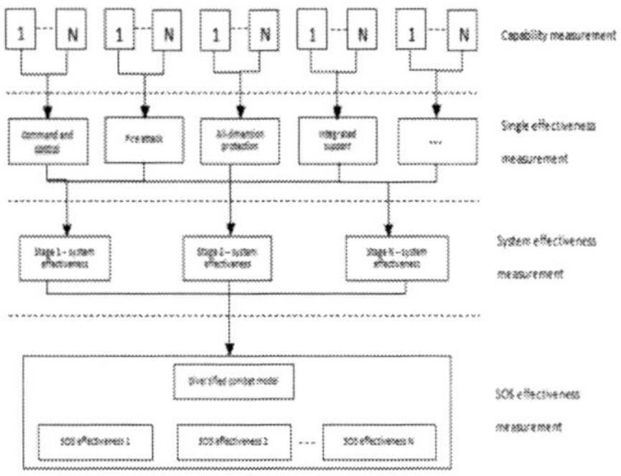

Figure1. Layered architectural diagram of combat effectiveness evaluation index system

Combat effectiveness index measures the size of combat effectiveness, and reflects the implementation extension of combat mission. Selection of effectiveness index affects the validity of combat effectiveness evaluation analysis. When making combat effectiveness evaluation analysis, it is required to reasonably choose combat effectiveness index, sort out relationship between indexes, and establish combat effectiveness index system. Currently, there isn't a set of unified combat effectiveness index to establish rules. Different combat effectiveness indexes can be used by different researchers under different combat scenarios. For example, indexes are presented in terms of deployment maneuver capability, command and control capability, strike and assault capability, defense and survival capability, sustainable combat capability; indexes are presented at the aspect of command information, fire application, battlefield maneuver, comprehensive protection, equipment support, man-machine integration. Some researches on comprehensive evaluation index of combat effectiveness for equipment SOS mainly investigate the following aspects and establish corresponding indexes:

3.1 Evaluation Index of Intelligence Reconnaissance Capability

Intelligence reconnaissance is defined as an activity to obtain Intelligence required by military struggle. Evaluation of intelligence reconnaissance capability should make comprehensive survey around whether quantity and types of early-warning and reconnaissance equipment are within a complete range, whether configuration of early-warning and reconnaissance equipment is reasonable, whether detection range can be connected effectively, whether reliability and timeliness of various intelligence obtained by early-warning and reconnaissance forces meet requirements, whether intelligence required by superior leaders can be provided in time, and whether anti-jamming capability of various early-warning and reconnaissance equipments and their working performance and operator proficiency under various complex meteorology and hydrology conditions and complicated electromagnetic environment satisfy requirements, etc.

3.2 Evaluation Index of Command and Control Capability

Command and control is a key factor to decide whether the combat is won or not. Its evaluation index should be determined from three main aspects - control coordination structure, control coordination approach and autonomous coordination capability:

Control coordination structure mainly depends on perfection degree of structure establishment, definition degree of duties segregation, smoothness degree of control coordination mechanism, and improvement degree of control coordination efficiency.

Control coordination approach can primarily be measured in two aspects. One is hardware facilities, the other is software facilities. The index of hardware facilities contains the complete extent of information network used to control coordination, the number of distributed integrated information processing center, interconnection extent between each sensor unit and data processing center, networked level between each distributed information processing center, the average number of high-performance military computer used for information processing, average networked level of computers in information processing center, digitized degree of each information carrier, average data storage capacity of each information processing center, etc. The index of software facilities contains the type of application software system for special information processing, the grade of application software system for special information processing, the number of special basic combat database, the application degree of advanced information processing technology, etc.

Autonomous coordination capability is mainly the efficiency of autonomous coordination mechanism between each service force on the basis of mandatory control coordination [7].

3.3 Evaluation Index of Fire Strike Capability

This index development mainly considers the following aspects: able to give full play to the performance of weapon and equipment; able to apply tactics flexibly based on the change of battlefield situation and complete combat mission in accordance with specified time; suppressive fire, air defense fire, anti-tank fire, anti-ship fire, anti-submarine fire, to-space fire, to-air fire, to-earth fire, and to-sea fire can exert each advantage to strike against enemy accurately and effectively; whether the probability of damage meets specified requirements, etc.

3.3.1 Evaluation Index of Stereoscopic Maneuver Capability

It consists of air maneuver capability, sea maneuver capability, ground maneuver capability. Evaluation of stereoscopic maneuver capability should develop evaluation index in terms of scramble, rapid maneuver, engagement preparation, adaptability at random, etc. Evaluation index of scramble contains whether to be able to achieve combat readiness transfer within specified time, whether real time of scramble can meet requirements, and whether sortie rate of staff and weapon equipment can meet standards; Evaluation index of rapid maneuver contains whether matching transportation scheme is sophisticated and reasonable, all kinds of situation disposal in the march is effective in time, whether safe protection measures are efficient, and whether staff and equipment van reach specified location and forceful situation is established against enemy; Evaluation index of engagement preparation contains whether force assemble and deployment can meet tactical requirements, whether to perform combat marshalling and organize combat mobilization in accordance with combat requirements, and whether everything is ready for operation within specified time; Evaluation index of adaptability at random contains whether quick response can be made at any time in accordance with the change of battlefield situation, whether disposal is timely and effective, whether redeployment is rapid and concealed, etc.

3.3.2 Evaluation Index of Information Attack Capability

Evaluation index can be divided into quantity, quality and applied level of offensive equipments in various information war. Specific index contains quantity and performance of ground fixed electronic interference station in the battlespace, quantity and performance of aircraft in electronic warfare into which combat controls can be put, quantity and performance of anti-radiation UAV, proportion of satellite communications jamming equipment, quantity and performance of equipment in tactical electronic warfare, average quantity of ship-based electronic jamming equipment, quantity and performance of ship-based acoustic jamming equipment, means of network attack against enemy, able to identify jamming characteristics of enemy timely and accurately, and probability of destroying communication system of enemy, etc.

3.3.3 Evaluation Index of All-Dimension Protection Capability

It should cover defensive reconaissance and surveillance, air defense anti-missile, information defense and other protective action. Evaluation index of air defense anti-missile mainly contains whether various air defense forces allocations are reasonable, and can form long-range, mid-range and short-range, high-altitude, mid-altitude and low-

 DOI: 10.1051/itmconf/20171204014

altitude air defense anti-missile system, early-warning detection distance, range, probability and time of air strike forces against enemy and incoming missile, response time of air defense anti-missile troops, resist capability of air strike forces against enemy and incoming missile, etc. Index of information defense capability mainly contains physical protective capability, technology protective capability, and safe management capability index [8].

3.3.4 Evaluation Index of Integrated Support Capability

Evaluation mainly contains three aspects - combat support, logistics support and equipment support. Evaluation index of combat support, logistics support and equipment support should mainly assess whether support force is grouped uniformly and used scientifically, whether support task allocation is reasonable, whether support relationship is clear, whether support plan is sophisticated, whether various support material, weapon equipment, ammunition and storage can achieve specified index, whether support method is applied flexibly, whether support is real-time, timely and effective, etc.

3.3.5 Evaluation Index of "Three-War" Capability

It mainly contains whether advocacy is achieved timely and effectively to make friendly forces maintain morale high; whether to go to psychological warfare widely in order to break down the morale of enemy effectively; whether various media and information resources can be used effectively to make friendly forces maintain advantageous position in public opinion and to make hostile forces passive position in public opinion; whether to make full use of international law, law of war and other favorable conditions to disclose various illegal behaviors and ways of enemy in the war; whether legal basis is chosen to be good for friendly forces to go to war in existing international law, law of war and other international regulations, etc.

3.4 Index System of Coordination Effectiveness for Equipment SOS based on Information Measurement

3.4.1 Information Conversion in Equipment SOS.

Logically, structure of equipment SOS contains three domains: Physical Domain, Information Domain and Cognitive Domain, as shown in Figure 2. Physical Domain mainly contains combat force of both sides, various combat platforms and geographic space, etc. Information Domain contains various sensors used to detect information about enemy, fusion devices used to deal with information, and communication network used to transfer information [1]. Cognitive Domain contains command and control device used to make decision by commander and assistant commander. Main work performed in three domains is as follows:

Physical Domain is used to describe battlefield facts, including objective physical object – weapon system, topographic features, troops, etc. Physical Domain also contains intangible content, such as combat intention and combat plan of both sides [3].

Information Domain deals with data from Physical Domain, form and distribute Common Relevant Operating Picture (CROP). Three main functions are achieved: collection of data from sensor; generation of CROP by fusion processing; distribution of CROP to all friendly forces.

Cognitive Domain is the cognitive process of CROP. Individuals receive CROP and generate situation awareness of individuals, and form shared situation awareness and make decision by teamwork. Its workflow is: the objective battlefield information from Physical Domain is used to detect, integrate, comprehensively deal with, transfer and generate CROP in Information Domain; commander cognizes CROP, forms situation awareness, makes decision in accordance with battlefield situation, and commands and controls troops.

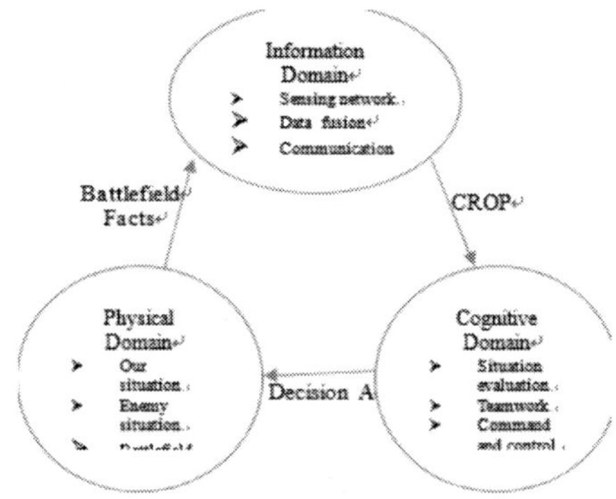

Figure.2. System structure diagram of equipment SOS

Coordination combat of system is mainly defined that all sub-systems coordinate with each other by electronic information system, the key point of which is quality of information transferred between electronic information systems, mainly including six steps:

Battlefield facts reception: weapon battlefield facts are received from Physical Domain;

Data acquisition: sensor network is used, battlefield space entity is detected, and related battlefield facts data is acquired;

Data fusion: at the first stage, data is transferred to the fusion device to deal with various intelligence; at the second stage, fused data of each fusion system is transferred to central processing device to generate CROP;

Network distribution: according to demands of troops, different versions of CROP are transferred to user by network;

DOI: 10.1051/itmconf/20171204014

Individual awareness: each user recognizes and understands received CROP to get certain battlefield situation awareness. CROP is explained alone, whose quality is affected by technology and capability of individuals;

Shared awareness: battlefield situation facts are perceived between individuals by coordination improvement, finally shared situation awareness is formed [2].

Above processes are linked to obtain the information conversion link of information system, as shown in the figure. Hierarchical conversion is described in Figure 3, whose emphasis is placed on quality of processes instead of processes themselves. Two in Information Domain, while three in Cognitive Domain, described as follows:

The first conversion describes the impact of sensor capability on quality of information acquired by sensor. The change in information quality of sensor described in figure can be gained by changing comprehensive degree and characteristic parameters of sensor network.

The second conversion represents quality of information from sensor group. Quality of CROP is formed after fusion. Fusion index refers to information fusion level of battlefield entity by fusion device.

During the third conversion, CROP generated by fusion is distributed to user to observe CROP quality via network. Observable CROP quality depends on communication network of information transmission. Different versions of CROP are distributed to different users, which depends on demands of end-users.

The fourth conversion is that the information is transferred to Cognitive Domain, the relationship between observable CROP and individual awareness is described, and the quality of individual awareness depends on capability level of individuals.

The fifth conversion describes the relationship between individual situation awareness and shared situation awareness. Situation awareness serves as dependent variable to replace information quality. This is the beginning of teamwork. Coordination capability relies on several factors, such as team experience, teamwork time, personality of members, etc.

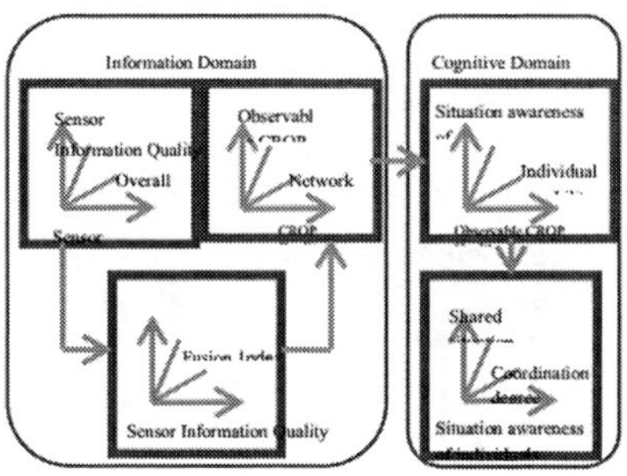

Figure.3. Links diagram of system information conversion

3.4.2 Evaluation Index System Based On Information Superiority

Above all, information superiority of system is measured by analyzing the quality of each information conversion process in equipment SOS, to evaluate the coordinative combat effectiveness of equipment SOS. Information superiority reflects contrast results of information countermeasure capability of two sides in the information countermeasure process of information system, finally it is reflected in the quality of shared situation awareness generated in information system, so the quality of available information quantitatively describes information superiority. Due to different forms of information conversion in Information Domain and Cognitive Domain, the quality of information conversion mainly relies on objective factors in Information Domain, such as information acquisition capability, information distribution capability, information defense capability, etc. However, the quality of information conversion mainly relies on subjective factors in Cognitive Domain, such as information processing capability, information sharing degree, decision-making time, etc. Therefore, evaluation indexes of information superiority measurement are different in these two domains. Specific indexes are shown in Figure 4, as indicated below:

Information superiority index

It contains information acquisition capability, information distribution capability, information processing capability and information defense capability. Information acquisition capability is defined as the capability to obtain information from Physical Domain based on the capability of sensor. Information distribution capability is defined as the capability to transfer information in Information Domain based on the quality of network connections. Information processing capability is defined as the capability to do information fusion in Information Domain based on fusion index. Information defense capability is defined as the anti-jamming capability of information conversion device in Information Domain. commanding and decision-making capability index

It contains the quality of situation awareness, the degree of information sharing, the index of decision-making time, etc. The quality of situation awareness is defined as the quality of shared situation awareness after individual awareness is summarized in accordance with the degree of coordination, one of conclusive indexes based on information superiority. The degree of information sharing is defined as the coordinative degree in Cognitive Domain. The index of decision-making time is defined as absolute time of commanding and decision-making. combat capability index

It contains battle damage, combat achievement, etc. Battle damage is defined as quantity and types of our battle damage units in a simulation countermine experiment. Combat achievement is defined as quantity and types of enemy's battle damage units in a simulation countermine experiment.

DOI: 10.1051/itmconf/20171204014

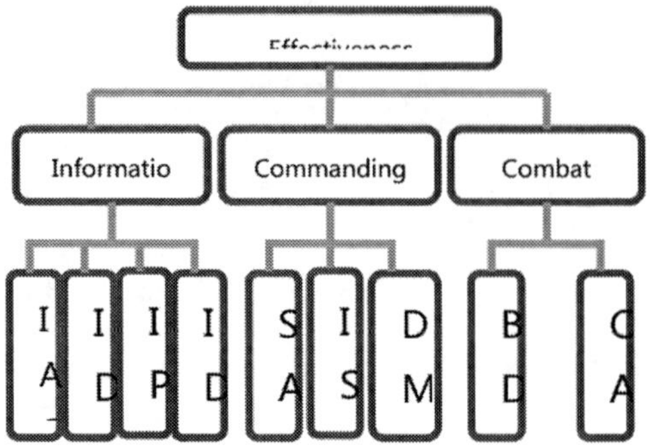

Figure .4. Index system of effectiveness evaluation based information superiority

Notes:IAC- Information acquisition capability; IDC- Information distribution capability; IPC- Information processing capability; IDC - Information defense capability; SAQ- Situation awareness quality; ISD- Information sharing degree; DMT- Decision-making time; BD - Battle damage; CA - Combat achievement

4. Case

Above evaluation index system based on information superiority designs a set of simple air combat simulation experiment. Its combat scenario is that: blue side is equipped with a piece of fighter in combat, while red side has the following two schemes.

Table1. Formation scheme of red side

Type / Scheme	Early warning aircraft（pcs）	Fighter（pcs）
Scheme 1	1	3
Scheme 2	0	4

Evaluation index system based on information superiority is used to analyze the index of combat effectiveness of red and blue sides in above schemes. According to suggestions of domain expert, information acquisition, processing, distribution, and defense capabilities, the quality of situation awareness, and the degree of information sharing are taken value in [0,1]; decision-making time is taken value in (0,1), the shorter the decision-making time is, the higher the value is; combat achievement and battle damage are taken value in [0,1]. In addition, when performances of fighters of red and blue sides are close, evaluation is made on all basic capability indexes of red and blue sides, as follows.

Table2. Combat effectiveness of red and blue sides

Side / Effectiveness	Red Side Scheme1	Red Side Scheme2	Blue Side
Information acquisition capability	0.6	0.2	0.2
Information processing capability	0.5	0.3	0.2
Information distribution capability	0.5	0.2	0.2
Information defense capability	0.5	0.2	0.2
Situation awareness quality	0.7	0.3	0.4
Information sharing degree	0.7	0.8	1
Decision-making time	0.5	0.5	0.8
Combat achievement	0.7	0.9	0.5
Battle damage	0.7	0.6	0.7
Overall effectiveness	0.009	0.00016	0.00018

It can be seen that each single effectiveness of red side is superior to that of blue side in scheme 1; in scheme 2, only combat capability of red side is superior to that of blue side, and others are close to those of blue side, but its situation awareness quality and decision-making time are lower than those of blue side due to the needs of coordination. Calculation of single effectiveness and SOS effectiveness can use method of weighting, multiplicative method, additive method, etc. In this case, multiplicative method is used, i.e. each single effectiveness is multiplied to get system effectiveness, each system effectiveness is multiplied to get SOS effectiveness(certainly, different evaluation methods of SOS effectiveness can be chosen in accordance with different needs of system evaluation.). In case 1, case 2 and case 3, computed SOS combat effectiveness of red side is 0.009, 0.00016 and 0.00018 respectively. This shows that in computed coordinative effectiveness evaluation based on information measurement, the effectiveness of one fighter is higher than that of multiple fighters.

The above discussion can be verified in the following X-sim simulation. As shown in Figure 5, 6, 7, 8, under certain conditions, if red side encounters with blue side in accordance with scheme 1, before blue side discovers red side's warplane, red side's early warning aircraft have discovered blue side's warplane, finally blue side's warplane is shot down under the coordination between early warning aircraft and fighter and our warplane is not damaged.

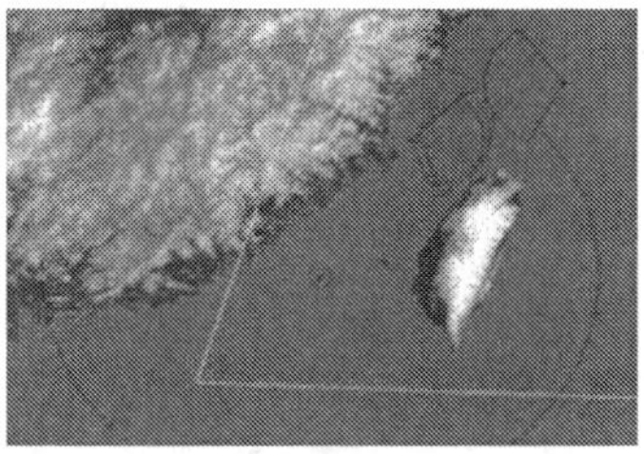

Figure.5. Scheme 1-intial battlefield

DOI: 10.1051/itmconf/20171204014

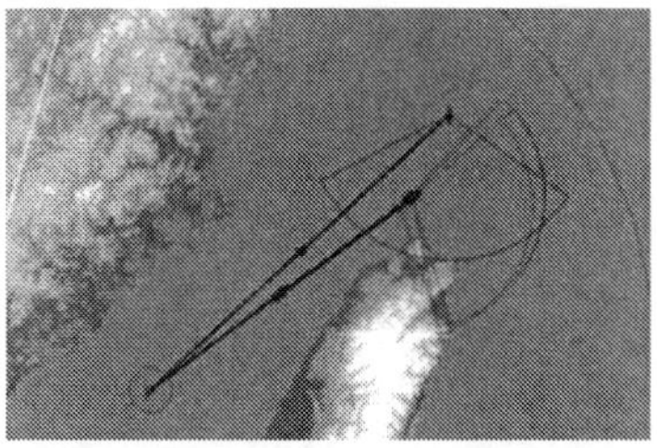

Figure.6. Scheme 1-enemy aircraft detected by early warning aircraft

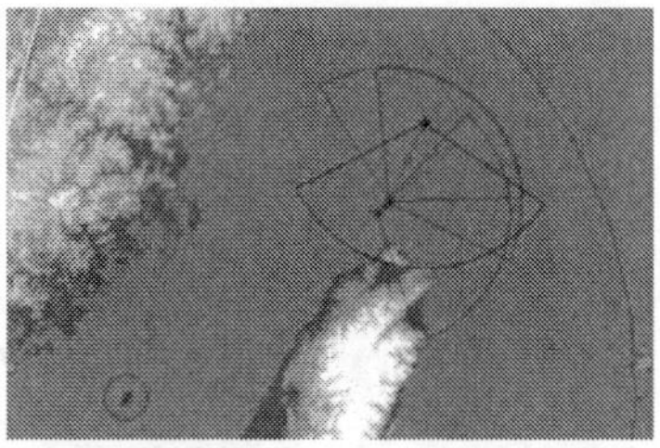

Figure.7. Scheme 1- coordinative operation between early warning aircraft and fighter

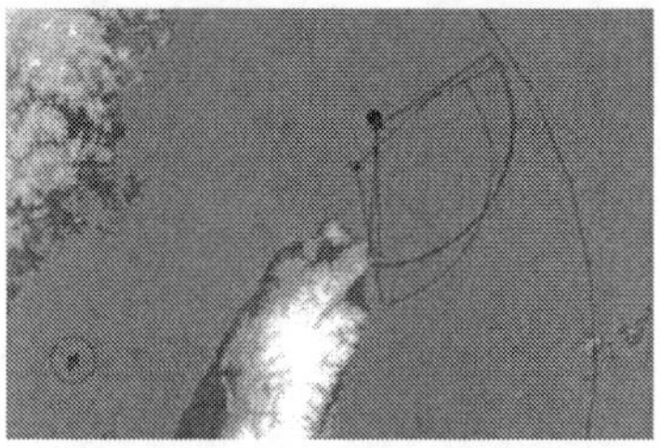

Figure.8. Scheme 1-Blue warplanes are shot down

Under the same conditions, if the formation of red side is based on scheme 2, due to the heading, red side passes blue side and doesn't discover blue side; however, blue side has detected red side and comes round to the back of red side for surprise attack; finally, blue side's warplane is shot down, as shown in figure 9-14.

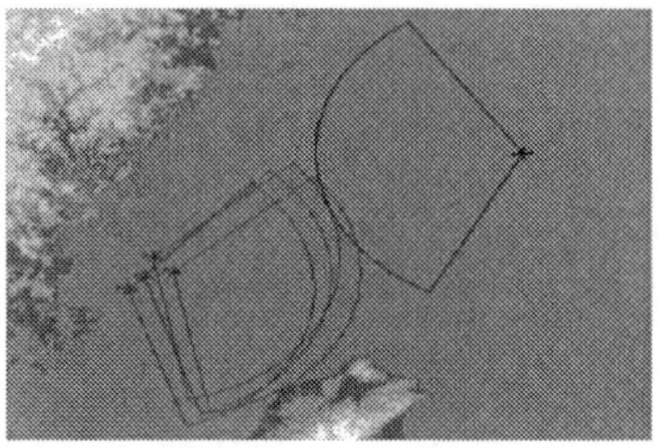

Figure.9. Scheme 2-initial battlefield

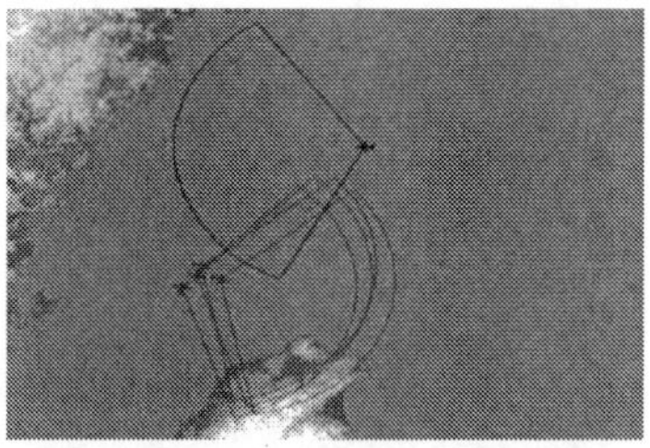

Figure.10. Scheme 2- red side encounters with blue side

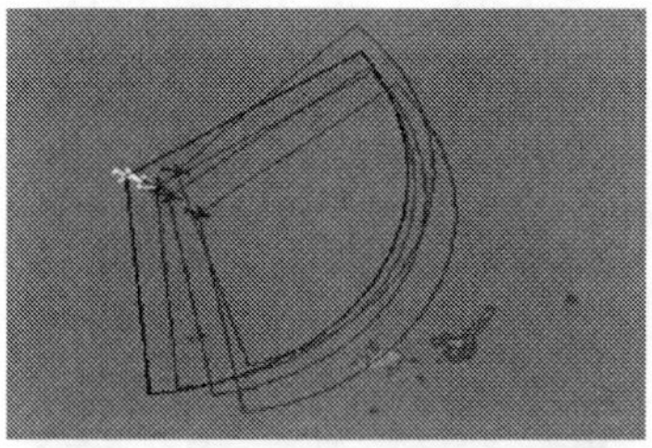

Figure. 11. Scheme 2-surprise attack of blue side from the rear

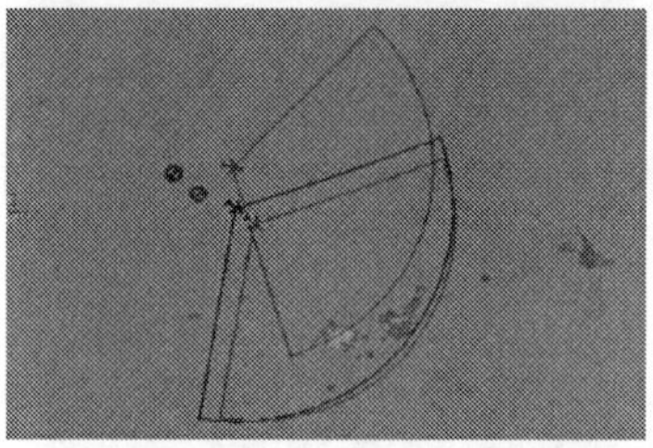

Figure.12. Scheme 2-two red aircraft are shot down

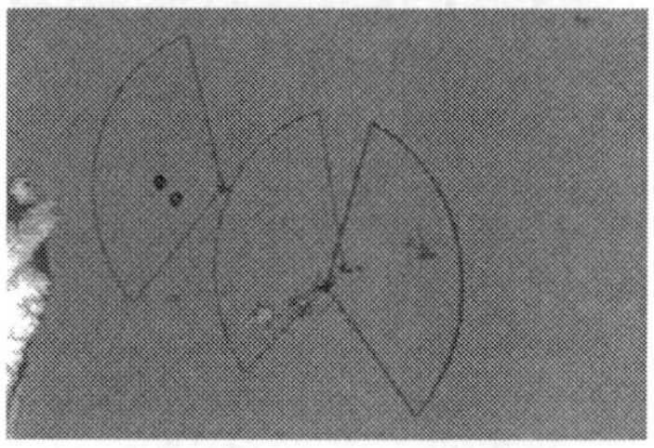

Figure.13. Scheme 2-meeting engagement of red side and blue side(the first warplane is not shot)

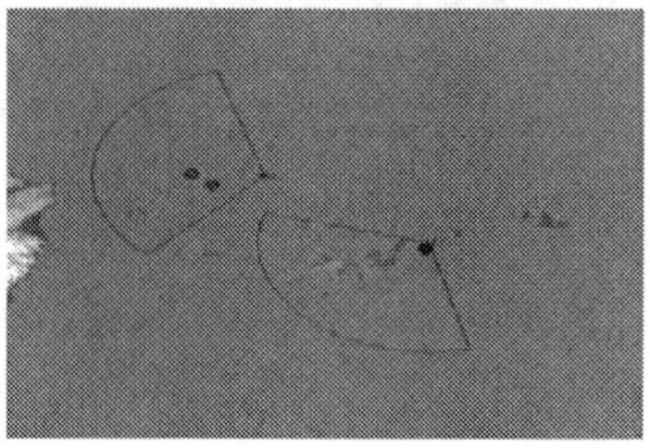

Figure.14. Scheme 2- meeting engagement of red side and blue side(blue side is shot down)

Above simulation results verify the formation mode of red side in scheme 1, which has better operational effects. Therefore, the index of coordinative effectiveness for equipment SOS based on information measurement has a certain practical significance for the simulation of equipment SOS.

5. Follow-On Work

Discussion is made on the selection principles of the index of coordinative effectiveness for equipment SOS. On this basis, it proposes and verifies a index system of coordinative effectiveness for equipment SOS based on information measurement. At the aspect of specific index classification for above index system, it also needs further standardization studies. Meanwhile, conversion rules between different-level indexes also need to be improved further.

References

[1] Zhi Qunceng, Zhang Letian, Li Zhendong. Information measurement model research based on the state of time dimension [J]. National Defense Science & Technology, 2015(01):35-39. (*references*)

[2] Xu Jianfeng, Tang Jun, Ma Xuefeng et al. Objective information model and measurement [J]. SCIENCE CHINA Information Sciences, 2015(03):336-353.

[3] Wang Huanchen. System information measure [J]. Journal of University of Shanghai for Science and Technology, 2011(06):631-640.

[4] Liu Xing, Zhao Min. The measurement of information and knowledge [J]. Command Information System and Technology, 2013(05):39-45.

[5] Walter Perry, Robert W Button, Jerome Bracken et al. Measures of Effectiveness for the information-age navy : The Effects of Network-centric Operations on Combat Outcomes [R] . RAND, 2002.

[6] Tong Huan, Wang Jianzhong, Duo Yinxian, Combat Effectiveness Evaluation of Firearms system based on MMESE, International Conference on Information, Network and Automation, 2010.

[7] Zheng Xuebing, heng Jinjin, The fuzzy Synthetic Evaluation of Combat Effectiveness for Avionics System based on Rough set Theory,International Forum on Information Technology and Applications,2009

[8] Jerry Wightman, The Role of Modeling and Simulation in the Evaluation of FCS: OneSAF, NETS, and DETES, 2008.4.9.

***** Formatting Issue - Best Available Paper/Graphic *****

Controllable and Anonymous Authentication Scheme for Space Networks

Zhi-Yan Hu[1], Xue-Hui Du[2], Li-Feng Cao[3]

[1]*State Key Laboratory of Mathematical Engineering and Advanced Computing Zhengzhou, China*
[2]*State Key Laboratory of Mathematical Engineering and Advanced Computing Zhengzhou, China*
[3]*State Key Laboratory of Mathematical Engineering and Advanced Computing Zhengzhou, China*
[1]*huzhiyan1234@126.com*, [2] *dxh37139@sina.com*, [3]*caolf302@sina.com*

Abstract: This paper analyzed the existing anonymous authentication schemes which have the weakness of high calculation and communication cost and weak security. So we designed a secure and efficient anonymous authentication scheme to meet the need of the space network, which has the characteristic of resource limited, high exposure and intermittent connectivity. At first we proposed a signature algorithm based on certificateless public key cryptosystem and one-off public key, and then presented an anonymous authentication scheme according to the proposed signature algorithm, it needs two message interaction to complete the mutual authentication and key agreement. When the user has the illegal behavior, the service provider can reveal the illegal user's real identity through cooperation with the trusted center. Compared with the similar literature, the proposed scheme achieves high security with low computation and communication cost. (Abstract)

1. Introduction

The space network structures with double plane of heaven and earth, which is based on the ground network and expanding with space-based network. The network consists of space-based backbone network, space-based access network, ground-based node network [1], so it has characteristics of heterogeneity, intermittent connectivity and high exposure. Compared with the traditional network, the space network is more easily attacked by eavesdropping, tampering and replay attack. The deployment of access authentication and privacy protection for the security of the space network is essential [2]. The space network of highly exposure makes it necessary for user real identity authentication when it needs to use the space network service. At the same time, network authentication needs to achieve anonymity and traceability in order to prevent the disclosure of privacy. What's more, it is necessary to reduce the computational overhead of the user and service provider for the resource limited space networks [2]. Last but not the least, the need to reduce the message length and minimize the number of interactions should also be considered for the characteristics of intermittent connectivity.

Scholars at home and abroad have done a lot of research on anonymous authentication in the wireless networks. Liu et al. [3] proposed an anonymous authentication scheme using certificateless public key cryptosystem to achieve mutual authentication using MAC, and it used bilinear pairing to build the user index to achieve the connection between user identity and the index. Shim[4] presented a signature algorithm for vehicular sensor networks based on bilinear pairings, and a mutual authentication scheme was presented based on the algorithm, but it still required a large amount of calculation and had the key escrow problem. Hsieh et al. [5] proposed an anonymous protocol using self-certified public key technology and bilinear pairing for mobile user, the user and the service provider needed three message interaction to realize authentication and key agreement, but a lot of calculation was required. Amin et al. [6] pointed out the shortage of Hsieh's protocol that cannot resist the server spoofing attack and unable to hide the true identity of the user, but Amin's scheme needed a trusted third party in the authentication process. He et al. [7] used self-certified public key mechanism to realize the anonymity of user authentication, and mutual authentication was achieved by verifying the non-forged messages, but the scheme did not achieve malicious user identity tracking and recovery, and the three information interaction increased the communication pressure. Zhou et al.[8] proposed a controllable roaming authentication protocol for heterogeneous wireless network which achieved anonymity, authentication and user tracking using one-off public key and signature algorithm, but using bilinear to track the true identity of the user required a large amount of computational overhead. Wan et al.[9] proposed an anonymous authenticated key agreement protocol based on trusted computing, the user

DOI: 10.1051/itmconf/20171204015

***** Formatting Issue - Best Available Paper/Graphic *****

constructed dynamic identity using random number to realize the anonymity and untraceability every time, but it is essential to use smart card and biometric information to design the protocol. Zhou et al. [10] designed an anonymous authentication scheme that a server needs 1 rounds of message exchange to authenticate the user's real identity, the scheme can track the true identity of the illegal user with the help of home server, but there are complex certificate storage and calculation pressure using mobile trusted module technology to verify the trusted terminal.

Aimed at the problems of the existing anonymous authentication scheme, this paper proposes a secure and efficient anonymous authentication scheme which is suitable for the space network. It uses the certificateless public key cryptosystem to overcome the key escrow problem, and designs a one-off public key signature algorithm to realize efficient authentication, uses pseudonyms to achieve anonymous authentication, and tracks the true identity of the illegal user through the interaction with the trusted center.

2. Preliminaries

2.1 Bilinear Maps

Let l be a security parameter, q is a prime number of $l-bit$, G_1 represents a cyclic additive group of order q, G_T represents a cyclic multiplicative group of the same order, P is a generator of G_1, Q is a generator of G_1, we call map $e: G_1 \times G_1 \rightarrow G_T$ a bilinear map if the following properties are satisfied:

(1) Bilinearity: for all $a,b \in Z_q^*$, such that $e(aP,bQ)=e(P,Q)^{ab}$;

(2) Non-degeneracy: exist $P,Q \in G_1$, such that $e(P,Q) \neq 1$;

(3) Computability: $\forall P,Q \in G_1$, it's efficient to compute $e(P,Q)$.

2.2 System Model

In space networks, the system model is composed of space-based access network, space-based backbone networks, ground-based node network and base station (BS). As shown in Figure 1. The base station completes the work of system setup and key generation. Ground nodes makes an anonymous access request to the space-based network nodes when it's in the space-based network node's coverage range. Then ground nodes and space-based network nodes can communicate safely with each other after mutual authentication and key establishment.

3. One Signature Algorithm Based on Certificateless Cryptosystem and One-Off Public Key

3.1 Algorithm Design

Our algorithm contains 5 polynomial time algorithms including system setup, partial private key generation, user key generation, sign and verification.

3.1.1 System Setup

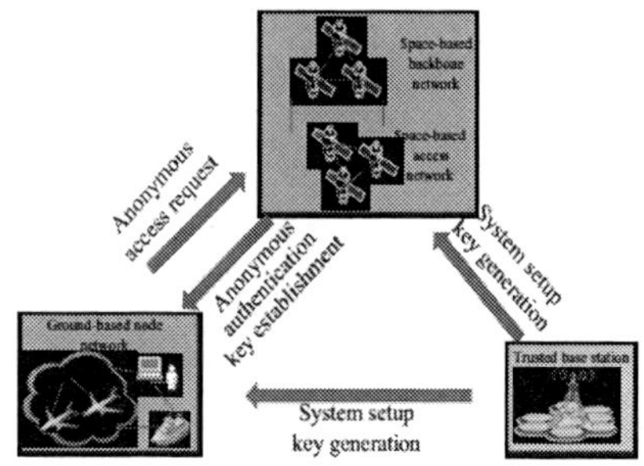

Figure 1. Anonymous authentication model for space networks

The trusted center KGC generates cyclic additive group G_1 and cyclic multiplicative group using security parameter k, and bilinear mapping $e: G_1 \times G_1 \rightarrow G_2$. It chooses $\lambda \in Z_q^*$ randomly as the master key and the generator $P \in G_1$, computes $P_{pub}=\lambda P$ .The KGC selects two secure hash functions $H_0:\{0,1\}^* \rightarrow Z_q^*, H_1:\{0,1\}^* \rightarrow Z_q^*$. In the end, the KGC makes system parameters set $paras=(G_1, G_2, e, P, P_{pub}, H_0, H_1)$ public and keeps the master key λ secret.

3.1.2 Partial Private Key Generation

The user A has the real identity of RID_A, A randomly selects $x_A \in Z_q^*$ and computes $R_1 = x_A P$, and transmits RID_A and R_1 to KGC through secure channel. Then it chooses $y_A \in Z_q^*$ randomly and computes $R_2 = y_A P$ and $R_A = R_1 + R_2$. The pseudonym is $PID = RID \oplus H_0(\lambda R_A, T_{ID})$ while T_{ID} represents valid period of the pseudonym. The KGC builds the connection between PID and RID, and then computes the partial private key $D_A = y_A + \lambda PID$. In the end, the KGC transmits (R_A, D_A, PID) to the user A through the secure channel.

***** Formatting Issue - Best Available Paper/Graphic *****

3.1.3 User Key Generation

The user A generates the whole private key (x_A, D_A) when it received the massage transmitted from the KGC. And then A check the equation $(x_A + D_A)P = R_A + P_{pub} \cdot PID$ to verify the correctness of the private key. After verification user A randomly chooses $z \in Z_q^*$ and sets $P_1 = z(x_A + D_A)P$, $P_2 = zR_A$ and $P_3 = z \cdot PID \cdot P$. User A transmits (P_1, P_2, P_3) to other side B.

3.1.4 Sign

The user A randomly picks $a \in Z_q^*$ and computes $N = aP$, $h = H_1(N, M)$, $S = h(x_A + D_A)z + a \cdot h$, $M \in \{0,1\}^*$ represents the message. The user A transmits $\sigma = (N, S)$ and M to the other side B.

3.1.5 Verification

B checks the equation $e(P_1, P) = e(P_2, P)e(P_3, P_{pub})$ to verify the validity of one-off public key, as a result of

$$e(P_1,P) = e(z(x_A + D_A)P, P) = e(z(x_A P + y_A P + PID \cdot P_{pub}), P)$$
$$= e(zR_A + z \cdot PID \cdot P_{pub}, P) = e(P_2, P)e(P_3, P_{pub})$$

The user A is a legal user verified buy the trusted center who has the system master key after the verification. And then it computes $h = H_1(N, M)$ and verifies the validity of signature through $S \cdot P = h(N + P_1)$, if the equation holds, outputs true, otherwise false.

3.2 Security Analysis

3.2.1 Anonymity

At first, the public key and signature contain user's pseudonym other than the real identity of user at the interactive process of algorithm to ensure the anonymity of the algorithm. Secondly, in the process of the one-off public key, the user uses random selection of data to build the public key, so the attacker cannot connect the public key with the user. The algorithm achieves complete anonymity.

3.2.2 Traceability of Anonymous User

Assuming that the user is compromised by the adversary into a malicious user, the other party B can communicate with the trusted center KGC to achieve the tracking of malicious users A. B transmits the pseudonym of user A PID to the KGC, KGC can recover the real identity of malicious through $RID = PID \oplus H_0(\lambda R_A, T_{ID})$. The algorithm can achieve efficient revocation of the real identity of malicious users.

3.2.3 Key Escrow

The algorithm is based on certificateless public key cryptosystem, the user's full private key consists of (x_A, D_A), x_A is generated by the user, D_A is generated by the KGC. KGC gets x_A through $R_1 = x_A P$ is equivalent of solving discrete logarithm problem on elliptic curve group, so the KGC cannot get the full private key of user achieving the security of no key escrow.

3.2.4 Unforgeability

At first, the legal user can not forge the public key and signature. After the public key verification, the public key is proved to contain the system master key. After the signature verification, it is proved that the signature contains the system master key, so the signature is legal and cannot be forged. Secondly, the one-off public key cannot be forged. The signature cannot pass the verification if P_1 is forged, it cannot pass the public key verification if P_2, P_3 are forged.

The illegal user can not forge the public key and signature. The illegal user randomly picks $b \in Z_q^*$, sets $P_1' = bP_1$, $P_2' = bP_2$, $P_3' = bP_3$. Obviously it can pass the public key verification, but it cannot get legal private key (x_A, D_A) to compute the signature. As a result of getting $(x_A + D_A)$ through $P_1' = bz(x_A + D_A)P$ as well as getting a through $N = aP$ is equivalent of solving discrete logarithm problem on elliptic curve group. The illegal user can not compute valid signature. Furthermore, the illegal user randomly chooses $a, b \in Z_q^*$ and sets $P_1' = aP_{pub} + bP$, $P_2' = bP$, $P_3' = aP_3$, obviously it can pass the public key verification, but it cannot construct valid signature through the forged private key. We can draw the conclusion that whether legal users or illegal users can not forge valid public key and signature.

4. Authentication scheme for the space network

4.1 Certificateless Anonymous Authentication Scheme

We propose an anonymous authentication scheme for space networks based on certificateless cryptosystem and one-off public key, as shown in Figure 2. The trusted base station completes system initialization and key generation in advance, then the user completes mutual anonymous authentication process with the access service satellite.

*** Formatting Issue - Best Available Paper/Graphic ***

4.1.1 System Setup

The base station BS (the trusted center) generates system parameters according to Section 3.1, defines 4 hash functions $H_0:\{0,1\}^*\times G_1 \to Z_q^*$, $H_1:\{0,1\}^* \to Z_q^*$, $H_2: Z_q^* \to Z_q^*$, $H_3: G_1 \to \{0,1\}^*$, and publish system parameter set $paras=(G_1,G_2,e,P,P_{pub},H_0,H_1,H_2,H_3)$, keeps system master key λ secret.

4.1.2 Key Generation

The user A in space networks communicates with the trusted base station BS according to partial private key generation and user key generation algorithm descripted in section 3.1 , and verify the full private key (x_A,D_A) of the user A, which $D_A=y_A+\lambda PID$, $PID=RID\oplus H_0(\lambda R_A,T_{ID})$. The BS saves (R_A,PID) . The access service satellite randomly picks $v\in Z_q^*$ as the private key and sets $P_{AS}=vP$ as the public key.

4.1.3 Access Authentication

The first step, the user A in the space network randomly picks $z\in Z_q^*$, and computes the one-off public key $P_A=(P_1,P_2,P_3)$ which $P_1=z(x_A+D_A)P$, $P_2=zR_A$ and $P_3=z\cdot PID\cdot P$. Then A gets the current timestamp T_A , and randomly chooses $a\in Z_q^*$, computes $L_0=H_2(a)$, $k=H_3(aP_{AS})$, $\omega=k\oplus L_0$, $N=aP$, $h=H_1(N,T_A,L_0)$ and $S=ah+z(x_A+D_A)h$. The user A sends the signature $\sigma=(N,S)$, ω , T_A and P_A to AS.

The second step, the AS verifies the validity of timestamp when it receives the message. If the timestamp is fresh, then AS verifies the validity of the public key according to section 3.1. After verification the AS computes $k=H_3(vN)$, and gets $L_0=k\oplus\omega$. Then the AS computes $h=H_1(N,T_A,L_0)$ and verifies the validity of the signature through $S\cdot P=h(N+P_1)$. And then the AS creates the repeated authentication list $L_{RA}=\{PID,L_i,Num,T_{die}\}$ which $L_i=H_2(L_{i-1})$ and Num represents authentication times, T_{die} represents expiration time. In the end, the AS randomly picks $b\in Z_q^*$ and computes $M=bP$, the session key is $K_{AS-A}=bN=abP$. After that AS gets current timestamp T_{AS} , uses symmetric encryption algorithm to compute $EM=E_k(P_A,M,T_{AS})$, and sends T_{AS} and EM to the user A.

The third step, the user A verifies the freshness of the timestamp. After verification it decrypts the message EM using k. By comparing T_{AS} to prevent the message from being tampered, by comparing P_A to verify the identity of AS. After that the session key is $K_{A-AS}=aM=abP$.

4.2 Repeated Authentication and Key Update

When the same user makes the access request to the same access service satellite, they realize fast and efficient authentication and update the session key according to the following steps.

The first step, the user A in the space network randomly picks $a'\in Z_q^*$, computes $N=a'P$, $L_i=H_2(L_{i-1})$, $k=H_3(aP_{AS})$ and $\omega=k\oplus L_i$, and then sends $E_k(\omega,PID_i,T_A)$ to the AS.

The second step, the AS computes $k=H_3(vN)$ when it receives the message, and decrypts the message to verify the freshness of the timestamp. If the timestamp is invalid, rejects, otherwise it can get $L_i=k\oplus\omega$, and uses PID_i and L_i to check the repeated authentication list L_{RA} whether exists the corresponding item, if there is one item in the list, the AS checks the T_{die}. If all these verification pass, the user A passes the authentication. The AS updates the list $L_{RA}=\{PID,L_i,Num,T_{die}\}$. And then AS randomly chooses $b'\in Z_q^*$, computes $M=b'P$, so it can get the session key $K_{AS-A}=b'N=a'b'P$. In the end, the AS gets the current timestamp T_{AS} and uses symmetric encryption algorithm to compute $EM=E_k(P_A,M,T_{AS})$, sends T_{AS} and EM to the user A.

The third step, the user A verifies the freshness of the timestamp at first. After that it decrypts the message EM using k . By comparing T_{AS} and P_A to verify the AS. If it passes, updates the session key $K_{A-AS}=a'M=a'b'P$.

4.3 Security Analysis

4.3.1 Traceability of Malicious User

In the process of access authentication, the access service satellite can recover the real identity of the malicious user through the communication with the trusted base station when it finds the malicious behavior of the user, so our scheme realizes the traceability of the malicious user. The AS sends the identity PID to the BS, the BS can get the real identity through $RID=PID\oplus H_0(\lambda R_A,T_{ID})$.

***** Formatting Issue - Best Available Paper/Graphic *****

4.3.2 Anonymity

In the entire process of authentication, the user's pseudonym is transmitted other than the real identity, so our scheme realizes user identity privacy protection.

4.3.3 Mutual Authentication

In the first access authentication process, the AS can verify the user A through the one-off public key verification and signature verification to avoid forgery attack. The user A decrypts the message $EM = E_k(P_A, M, T_{AS})$, and verifies the AS through comparing T_{AS} and P_A as a result of only legal AS can decrypts the message through computing $k = H_3(vN)$. In the process of repeated access authentication, only the legal user A can compute $L_i = H_2(L_{i-1})$ through L_{i-1} that can pass the repeated authentication list.

4.3.4 Session Key Security

In this scheme, the intermediate parameters have strong timeliness and the session key is independent and unique which determined by both sides of communication using random number, the attacker cannot obtain session key information from the previous message, so our scheme achieves forward security, known session key security and key control security, and this scheme realizes no key escrow based on certificateless cryptosystem.

5. Performance Comparison

This paper compares the first authentication scheme, the repeated authentication scheme and some existing authentication schemes in authentication efficiency (as shown in Table 1) and security (as shown in Table 2). Compared with [5] [6], our scheme has lower computational overhead, the interaction time is less, and the communication cost is relatively lower. In terms of security, the [5] scheme cannot resist identity guessing attack, and a trusted center is not able to achieve recovery of the real identity of the user in the two schemes. Compared with the literature [7], although our authentication scheme has more multiplication in group, there is no exponentiation operation, so the total computational cost is relatively low, and the message interaction time is less leading to low communication overhead. In terms of security, our scheme realizes traceability. There is a large number of hash operations in the [8], and the scheme needs to consume 2n bilinear pairing operation to realize the recovery of the malicious user in the worst case (n is the number of registered users in the trusted center). Although our scheme's computational overhead is relatively large in the first authentication, there is no need to construct one-off public key and signature algorithm in the repeated authentication, and requires only one hash operation in the realization of a malicious user identity tracking which greatly reduces the computational overhead, and computational overhead of user is less than the server. All these properties meet the characteristics of resource limited for the space network. In terms of communication cost, our scheme only needs two interactive messages, and the message length is short which suitable for the characteristics of intermittent connectivity. In terms of security, our scheme achieves user anonymity, key escrow security and mutual authentication which can protect the communication security in the space network of highly exposure.

Table1. Efficiency comparison of authentication scheme

Operation	**Literature [5]**		**Literature [6]**		**Literature [7]**		**Literature [8]**		**Our scheme-1**		**Our scheme -2**	
	User	*Server*	*user*	*server*	*user*	*server*	*user*	*server*	*user*	*server*	*user*	*server*
Scalar Multiplication in group(M)	7	5	4	7	2	2	6	5	6	5	3	3
Scalar addition in group (A)	1	1	4	4	1	0	0	1	0	1	0	0
Map-to-point(P)	1	1	2	0	0	0	0	0	0	0	0	0
Hash(H)	7	2	9	8	8	5	5	5	3	3	2	1
Bilinear pairing (BP)	0	2	0	2	0	1	1	4	0	3	0	0
exponentiation (E)	0	2	0	0	2	4	0	0	0	0	0	0
Signature length	-		-		-		Z_q^*		$G_1 \times Z_q^*$		-	
Interaction times	3		4		3		2		2		2	
User identity recovery	×		×		×		2BP		1H		1H	

*** Formatting Issue - Best Available Paper/Graphic ***

Table2. Security comparison of authentication schemes

Scheme	Anonymity	Traceability	Mutual authentication	No key escrow	Session key security
Literature [5]	N	N	Y	Y	Y
Literature [6]	Y	N	Y	Y	Y
Literature [7]	Y	N	Y	Y	Y
Literature [8]	Y	Y	Y	Y	Y
Our scheme	Y	Y	Y	Y	Y

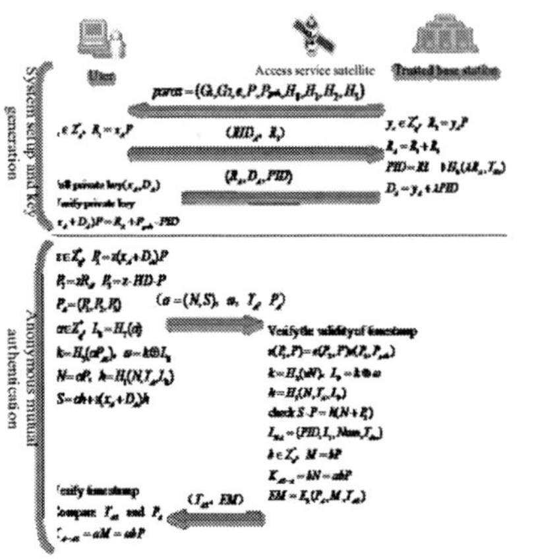

Figure 2. Anonymous authentication scheme

6. Conclusion

Most of the existing anonymous authentication schemes are aimed at heterogeneous wireless networks and vehicular ad hoc networks which cannot meet the requirements of high security and low power consumption. In this paper, we design a one-off public key and signature algorithm based on certificateless cryptography, and propose an efficient secure anonymous authentication scheme according to the proposed algorithm. It needs two message interaction between the user and the access satellite and one signature algorithm to complete the first authentication, and uses repeated authentication list to achieve efficiently repeated authentication. What's more, our scheme can realize anonymity revocation of malicious user through interaction with the trusted center. Comparative results show that our scheme achieves high efficiency while ensuring anonymity, mutual authentication, no key escrow, traceability and session key security which is more suitable for deployment in highly exposed and resource limited space networks.

Acknowledgment

This paper is supported by the National Key Research and Development Program of China (No.2016YFB0501900), the National Programs for High Technology Research and Development of China (No.2015AA016006) and the National Natural Science Foundation of China (No.61502531).

References

[1] FH Li, LH Yin, W Wu, LJ Zhang, and GZ Shi, "Research Status and Development Trends of Security Assurance for Space-ground Integration Information Network," Journal on Communications, vol. 37, Nov. 2016, pp. 156-168, doi:10.11959/j.issn.1000-436x.2016229.

[2] C Lin, Y Dong, and Z Shan, "Research on Space Internetworking Service Based on DTN," Journal of Computer Research & Development, vol. 51, May. 2014, pp. 931-943, doi: 10.7544/issn1000-1239.2014.20130769

[3] J Liu, Z Zhang, R Sun, and K S Kwak, "An Efficient Certificateless Remote Anonymous Authentication Scheme for Wireless Body Area Networks," Proc. EEE International Conference on Communications (ICC 12), IEEE Press, 2012, pp. 3404-3408, doi: 10.1109/ICC.2012.6363786.

[4] K A Shim, "An Efficient Conditional Privacy-Preserving Authentication Scheme for Vehicular Sensor Networks;" IEEE Transactions on Vehicular Technology, vol. 61, May. 2012, pp. 1874-1883, doi: 10.1109/TVT.2012.2186992.

[5] W B Hsieh and J S. Leu, "An Anonymous Mobile User Authentication Protocol Using Self-certified Public Keys Based on Multi-server Architectures," The Journal of Supercomputing, vol. 70, Oct. 2014, pp. 133-148, doi: 10.1007/s11227-014-1135-8.

[6] R Amin and G P Biswas, "Design and Analysis of Bilinear Pairing Based Mutual Authentication and Key Agreement Protocol Usable in Multi-server Environment," Wireless Personal Communications, vol. 84, May. 2015, pp. 439-462, doi: 10.1007/s11277-015-2616-7.

[7] D He, S Zeadally, N Kumar, and W Wu, "Efficient and Anonymous Mobile User Authentication Protocol Using Self-Certified Public Key Cryptography for Multi-Server Architectures," IEEE Transactions on Information Forensics & Security, vol. 11, Sep. 2016, pp. 2052-2064, doi:10.1109/TIFS.2016.2573746.

[8] YW Zhou, B Yang, and WZ Zhang, "Controllable and Anonymous Roaming Protocol for Heterogeneous Wireless Network," Chinese

*** Formatting Issue - Best Available Paper/Graphic ***

Journal of Electronics, vol. 44, May. 2016, pp. 1117-1123, doi: 10.3969/j.issn.0372-2112.2016.05.015.

[9] T Wan, ZX Liu, and J F Ma, "Authentication and Key Agreement Protocol for Multi-Server Architecture," Journal of Computer Research and Development, vol. 53, Nov. 2016, pp. 2446-2453, doi: 10.7544/issn1000-1239.2016.20150107.

[10] YW Zhou, B Yang, and WZ Zhang, "Secure and Efficient Roaming Authentication Protocol with Controllable Anonymity for Heterogeneous Wireless Network," Journal of Software, vol. 27, Feb. 2016, pp. 451−465, doi:10.13328/j.cnki.jos.004840.

Autonomous Recognition System for Barcode Detection in Complex Scenes

Chen Chen[1], Bing-Wei He[2], Li-Wei Zhang[3], Pei-Qing Yan4

[1] *School of Mechanical Engineering Fuzhou University, Fuzhou, China*
[2]*School of Mechanical Engineering Fuzhou University, Fuzhou, China*
[3]*School of Mechanical Engineering Fuzhou University, Fuzhou, China*
[4] *School of Mechanical Engineering Fuzhou University, Fuzhou, China*
[1] *chenpartydouble@163.com,* [2] *mebwhe@fzu.edu.cn*

Abstract: Linear barcode technology has been widely used in our common life, such as in logistics, retailed products and many other applications. Many researches and smart applications focus on how to decode the barcode so that it is difficult to locate precisely when the background becomes very complex. Moreover, many smart apps need human interaction to make sure the detected region is in a correct position of the screen. This paper presents an effective approach to locate the barcodes in real-time without manual disturbing. Basic morphological operations and Parallel Line Segment Detector (P-LSD) are applied to achieve the legal block of barcodes. Our method has been evaluated by a standard database and the experimental results show that our approach is more robuster than other earlier methods.

1. Introduction

Linear 1D barcodes are now present on the packaging of almost all retail products. Additionally, they are also widely used in the express logistic just as more and more people purchase their desirable items online. The barcodes are one-dimensional series of parallel lines that carry alphanumeric information which can be read using laser scanner, computers, cell phones etc [1]. The alphanumeric Information are encoded in bars and spaces of varying widths along with redundant information for error correction, which is the main principle behind barcodes. These are a very advantageous and an efficient method of data representation. Obviously, the existing of barcodes can be of very big help in today's world where large amount of information is increasing exponentially [2]. In order to precisely analysis the potential information of barcodes, we need to localize the barcodes quickly and robustly from the image captured by the camera.

Localizing barcodes means finding or locating barcodes in simple or complex images. It is mainly based on two main properties of barcodes. The main character of the barcode that many methods utilize during the barcode localization is that a barcode contains many parallel edges. The other property of barcodes indicates that it has a strong directional continuity. It is obviously means that barcodes have very strong continuity at one particular orientation and very low in all other orientations [4].

Many apps are currently available in many mobile application store which is a conveniently and helpfully way to read the barcode in people's common life. However, the current techniques also have many disadvantages that limit their usability, and similarly, their use in industry area. The main flaw of present system is that it is need for clean, close to the target images as much as possible, well framed. Moreover, present techniques expect the scanned region to look more like the flat bed. Additionally, they assume a human operator has already known the particular area of interest. In other word, current techniques do not localize them in large pictures, they only read them.

In this paper, we propose a new real-time method based on morphological operations and Parallel Line Segment Detector (P-LSD) for linear barcode detection of camera-captured images in the wild. We use the basic morphological operations to split the potential block which contains the area of barcodes. The tolerance will be occurred inevitably under adopting the preceding step as it is sensitive to light condition and blur and the loose value of threshold. Parallel Line Segment Detection, a fast method for barcode cropping, is proposed to modified this problem. We make sure the system is low computation and our plan achieves state-of-art results on the public datasets.

2. Previous Work

Many existing methods for Barcode Localization can roughly be divided into four forms in the image

DOI: 10.1051/itmconf/20171204016

processing techniques field. These forms contain the techniques based on the basic morphological operations, image scanning, distance transforms and bottom-hat filtering [2]. Some of which come under Frequency Domain Methods while others come under Spatial Domain Methods. In the following paragraphs we will discuss previous approaches proposed to locate the barcode.

Methods based on Spatial Domain are those that search for set of dark lines on white background and that also have strong directional continuity at a specific angle so as to locate barcodes [3]. Katona et al. [5] detected the barcodes based on the basic morphological. They also present another skill for both 1D and 2D barcode detection by using the space domain of parallel stripes in another paper. Other approaches like Tuinstra's using basic morphological operations to localize barcodes are relied on the fact that the bars can be highlighted by gradient calculation using sobel kernel due to high intensity difference between bars and the background [6].

Juett and Qi's method using primitive operators is based on Bottom- Hat filtering instead of edge detection. However, it takes more time than the previous method and this method needs a human interaction that it needs manually input optimal parameters although its results are more accurate [4]. Telkin and Coughlan's method is based on scanning the image in four directions. It was designed mainly for blind people so as to` help them in their routine tasks [7].

Methods using wavelet transformation to look at images for barcode like appearance by a cascaded set of weak classifiers are based on Frefuency Domain Methods [8]. Each classifier works in wavelet domain by searching for areas where may contain barcodes. Most of the currently available barcode reading applications identify, thus they usually require human to place the barcodes in a correct position within the camera screen. A. K. Jain and Yao Chen's proposed to use multi-channel Gabor filtering technique to locate barcodes at any orientation. This method can also locate them on both planar and curved surfaces.

3. Barcode Location

In this research work, our goal is to implement a barcode localization method which works well under different imaging conditions and for different test images. We use a different way based on detecting, filtering and line segmentation in this paper. On the top of that, we take advantage of Line Segment Detector introduced by [10]. Various steps of our method are given in order. Fig.1 is the framework of our method for detecting barcodes.

3.1 Barcode Estimation Using Morphological Operation

As proved in section 2, the texture information of a barcode is the most distinctive feature which can summarized by three descriptors: contrast, coarseness and directionality. Candidate area estimation based on the descriptor of contrast is realized in four steps: image preprocessing, segmentation and filtering, directional image open operation and candidate pickup.

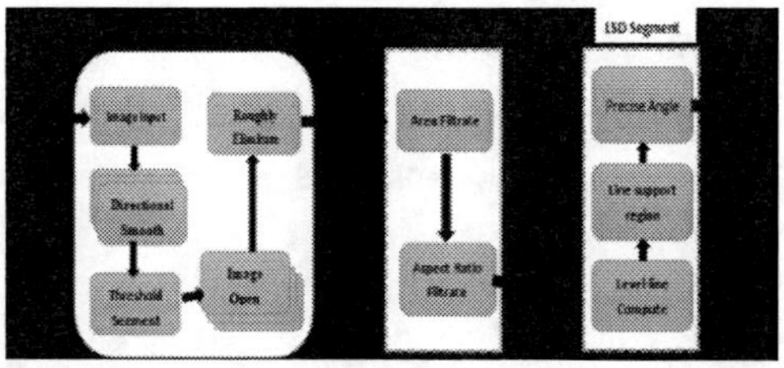

Figure1. The Framework of our method for barcode location.

3.3.1 Image Preprocessing

In this step, the main tasks are to convert the input image into greyscale intensity image and to highlight the barcode bars against its background. GSF filter is applied to smooth the initial image which can remove the noise due to external factors.

3.3.2 Segmentation

Image segmentation is a common and traditional problem in the field of image processing. However, we adopt conventional thresholding segmentation instead of other progressive algorithm to find the possible block which contains barcode, as it is an easily and helpful way to get the interesting area if the background is distinct from foreground. In order to avoid the error, we pick up a weit threshold comparatively. After the above operator, we will achieve the potential area.

3.3.3 Directional Image Open Operation

In the case with complex background, segmentation results still contain many isolated edges in similar orientation. We use 5×5 square structuring element to perform dilation operator so as to merge the nearby areas so that a region contains the barcodes will be formed.

3.3.4 Candidate Pickup

These operators above will segment a huge number of candidate regions. We start eliminating the obvious false positives based on the aspect of the area and the aspect ratio of each blob. Each candidate block has its width w_i, its height hi, Note that if the proportion and its height h_i are too much smaller than the ordinary values we remove this potential region.

 DOI: 10.1051/itmconf/20171204016

3.4 PLSD - Parallel Line Segment Detector

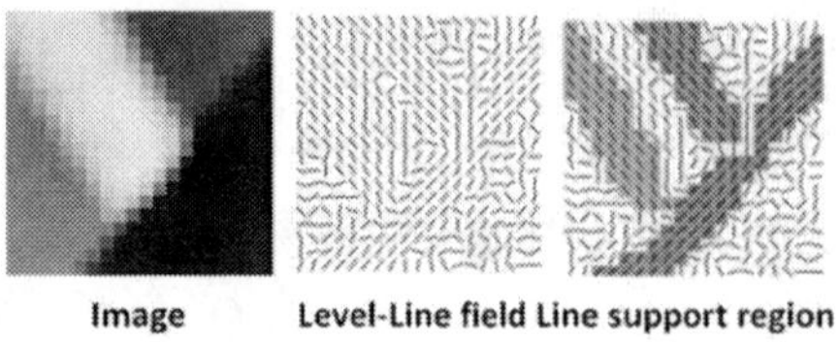

Figure2. The core concept of Line Segment Detector (LSD)

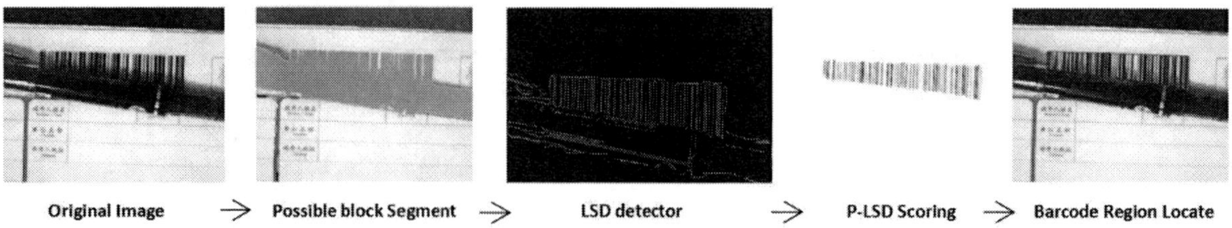

Figure3. Workflow of our method for locating possible barcode region

After determining the potential blocks, precise barcode regions should be picked up using P-LSD similar to the Line Segment Detector by [10]. The main feature of a barcode that we utilize during the barcode detection/localization stage is that a barcode contains many parallel edges and no other edges. In this paper, we first use LSD to segment the parallel edges. The simple progress of this method is showed in Fig.2 [10]. In the first step, this method is using a 2×2 mask to compute the image gradient and its level-line angle(LLA) to segment the level-line field. Let (xi,yi) be the any point of the input image, the image gradient is computed as

$$g_x(x,y)=\frac{i(x+1,y)+i(x+1,y+1)-i(x,y)-i(x,y+1)}{2}$$

(1)

$$g_y(x,y)=\frac{i(x,y+1)+i(x+1,y+1)-i(x,y)-i(x+1,y)}{2}$$

So the level-line angle is computed as

$$LLA(\partial_i)=\arctan\left(\frac{g_x(x,y)}{-g_y(x,y)}\right) \tag{2}$$

It is worth mentioning that the computed value corresponds to the image gradient at coordinates (x+0.5,y+0.5) and not (x,y). To produce coherent results, half-pixel offset is added to the output rectangles coordinates. This simple process will highlight a large number of the central pixels which have the highest gradient magnitude that is denoted as

$$G(x,y)=\sqrt{g_x^2(x,y)+g_y^2(x,y)} \tag{3}$$

Pseudo-ordering is conducted to sort the pixels to look for the line segments with higher gradient magnitude which is manually splitted into 1024 bins between zero and the largest observed value on the image. In order to improve the efficiency of the straight line detection algorithm, pixels with gradient magnitude smaller than β are rejected directly.

$$\beta=\frac{q}{\sin\tau} \tag{4}$$

Where q is a bound of gray quantization error, τ is the angle tolerance to be used in the line-segment support region.

A region growing algorithm is utilized starting from a pixel in the ordered list of the pixels which are produced by previous operators to produce a line-support region. It is obvious that the segmented line support regions are intuitive representation of lines we want to get. So the region of pixels is interpreted as a solid object and its smallest surround rectangle needs to be found to form the line. (c_x, c_y), the center of the rectangle which is also the center of the line, is set to

$$c_x=\frac{\sum_{k\in R}G(k)\cdot x(k)}{\sum_{k\in R}G(k)}$$

$$c_y=\frac{\sum_{k\in R}G(k)\cdot y(k)}{\sum_{k\in R}G(k)} \tag{5}$$

Where G(k) is the the gradient magnitude of pixel k, R is the representation of line support region. The main rectangle's angle corresponding to the angle of the line is set to the angle of the eigenvector associated with the smallest eigenvalue of the matrix

$$M = \begin{pmatrix} m^{xx} & m^{xy} \\ m^{xy} & m^{yy} \end{pmatrix} \quad (6)$$

With

$$m^{xx} = \frac{\sum_{k\in R} G(k)\cdot(x(k)-c_x)^2}{\sum_{k\in R} G(k)},$$

$$m^{yy} = \frac{\sum_{k\in R} G(k)\cdot(y(k)-c_y)^2}{\sum_{k\in R} G(k)}$$

(7)

$$m^{xy} = \frac{\sum_{k\in R} G(k)\cdot(x(k)-c_x)(y(k)-c_y)}{\sum_{k\in R} G(k)}$$

Many legible lines will be displayed after conducting the above steps. In this paper, we do not adopt the primary method to verify the validity of the lines. LSD method will outputs five parameters of segmented line, the start point, the end point, the width w_i, the angle precision p_i and the NFA[10].

Normal

Overexposure

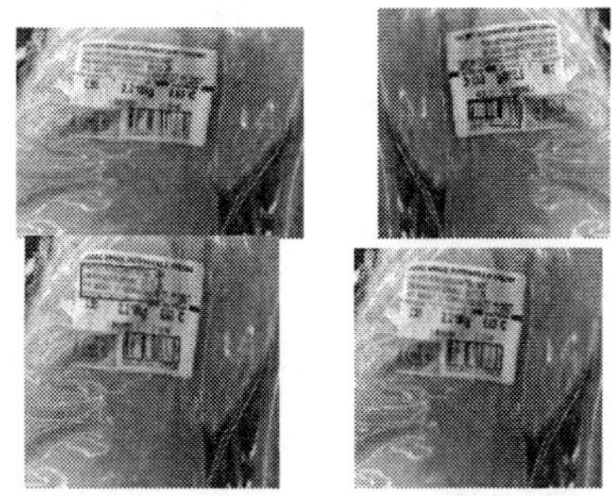

Curved

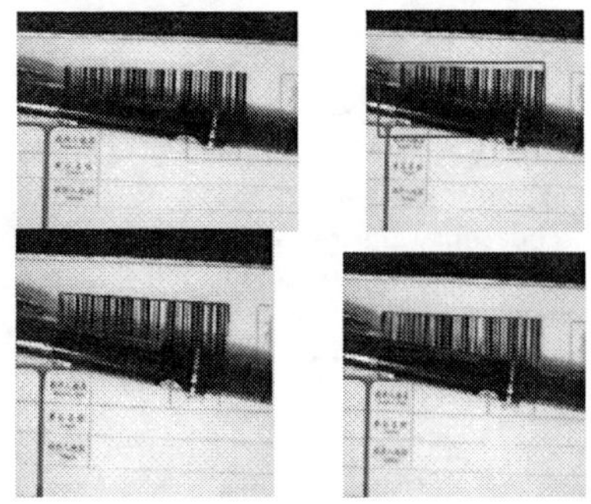

Occlusion (a) (b) (c)

Figure 4. Comparison of experimental results with different approaches

In this paper, we use the angle precision p_i to distinguish the illegality of lines which is based on the main character that barcode has many parallel line edges. In the first step, we create a integer array ε to be used to store the angle parameter p_i of each illegal line corresponding to the segmented block. The angle α of barcode's segmented edges is achieved by ranking and simple math statistics. Obviously, the segmented support region should have roughly the same angle and the distance between each other should not be too wide, so that a support score s_i is computed for each segmented block.

$$s_i = s_m^{\partial_i} + s_m^{d_i}$$

(8)

s^{α}, s^{d} represent the score of angle and distance conditions respectively.

$$s_m^{\partial_i} = \begin{cases} 1, & if \partial_i = \partial_\Delta \\ 0, & otherwise \end{cases} \quad (9)$$

$$s_m^{d_i} = \begin{cases} 1, & if D_m^{d_i} < T^d \\ 0, & otherwise \end{cases}$$

DOI: 10.1051/itmconf/20171204016

where D is a basic function corresponding to the distance we denote and T is a setting threshold for judging.

Finally, the bounding box covering the segment region is computed. So the barcode is defined as the oriented bounding box centered in the rectangle center, with the width of rectangle as width and the height of rectangle as height. Fig.3 shows the process of our method.

4 Experiments and Results

4.3 Datasets

In this section, we use a standard 1D barcode dataset, the WWU Muenster Barcode Database [11] to evaluate the performance of our proposed model. WWU has 1055 barcode images acquired by a Nokia N95 mobile phone and the size of the image is 640×480 pixels.

4.4 Results

Fig.4 shows the results by different methods for detecting barcodes on original datasets. The first column is the original image, (a) column is Zamberletti's, (b) column is Tekin's, (c) is our result. We have designed a framework and developed a system to implement our method in real-time. The desktop PC has an Intel Core i5-4670t CPU and 12 GB RAM, with Windows 7 system. The detailed performance results are shown in Table I and Table II. The accuracy of our approach for detecting barcode is 98.69 % and the consuming time is significantly reduced when compared to different methods in the WWU Muenster Barcode Database. We can see that our methods perform better than other methods whether the background is normal or complex. The methods of Tekin and Zamberletti are relied on the results of the Hough transform. In the presence of a more text intensive area, the performance of these methods will be in poor. Our methods has better robustness and can locate barcodes faster than the method of Refs [7][11].

5 Conclusion

We have presented an effective system to detect the region of the barcode and proved its effectiveness by using the standard dataset- WWU. The approach we proposed uses basic morphological operations and a Line Segment Detector to find the regions of barcodes. The experiment results show that our approach is accurately to detect the barcodes whether the background is complex or not. Moreover, our method is verified to have the character of angle invariance. At the same time, the accuracy of location using our method is higher than other approaches applied in earlier research.

Table1. Comparison of Recognition Occupancy

DATASE T	Approaches And Results		
	Ref [7]	*Ref [11]*	*Ours*
Muenster [11]	90.13 %	93.23 %	98.69 %

Table2. Average Time Cost In Seconds

DATASE T	Approaches And Results		
	Ref [7]	*Ref [11]*	*Ours*
Muenster [11]	0.142	0.130	0.112

Acknowledgment

This work was supported by the National Natural Science Foundation of China (Project No. 61473090).

References

[1] Bodnar, P., and L. G. Nyul. "Improving Barcode Detection with Combination of Simple Detectors." Eighth International Conference on Signal Image Technology and Internet Based Systems 2012:300-306.

[2] Creusot, Clement, and A. Munawar. "Real-Time Barcode Detection in the Wild." Applications of Computer Vision IEEE, 2015:239-245.

[3] Kutiyanawala, Aliasgar, X. Qi, and J. Tian. "A simple and efficient approach to barcode localization." International Conference on Information, Communications and Signal Processing IEEE, 2009:1-5.

[4] Juett, Xqj, and X. Qi. "Barcode localization using bottom-hat filter." Nsf Research Experience for Undergraduates (2005).

[5] Katona, M, and L. G. Nyul. "A Novel Method for Accurate and Efficient Barcode Detection with Morphological Operations." International Conference on Signal Image Technology & Internet Systems 2012:307-314.

[6] Tuinstra, Timothy R. "Reading Barcodes from Digital Imagery." (2006).

[7] Tekin, E, and J. M. Coughlan. "An algorithm enabling blind users to find and read barcodes." Applications of Computer Vision IEEE, 2009:1-8.

[8] Bodnar, P., and L. G. Nyul. "Improving Barcode Detection with Combination of Simple Detectors." Eighth International Conference on Signal Image Technology and Internet Based Systems 2012:300-306.

[9] Kaur, Savreet, and R. Maini. "Implementation of Barcode Localization Technique using Morphological Operations." International Journal of Computer Applications 97.13(2014):42-47.

[10] Gioi, Rafael Grompone Von, et al. "LSD: A line segment detector." Image Processing on Line 2.4(2012):35-55.

[11] Zamberletti, A., et al. "Neural Image Restoration for Decoding 1-D Barcodes using Common Camera Phones. " Visapp 2010 - Proceedings of the Fifth International Conference on Computer Vision Theory and Applications, Angers, France, May DBLP, 2010:5-11.

[12] Wachenfeld, Steffen, S. Terlunen, and X. Jiang. "Robust 1-D Barcode Recognition on Camera Phones and Mobile Product Information Display."Mobile Multimedia Processing: Fundamentals, Methods, and Applications DBLP, 2008:53-69.

Dependent Space and Attribute Reduction on Fuzzy Information System

Chang SHU, Zhi-Wen MO

College of Management Science, Chengdu university of technology, Chengdu, Sichuan, 610059, P. R. China
Collegeof Mathematics and Software Science, Sichuan Normal University, Chengdu, Sichuan, 610066,P.R.China
E-mail:20812229@qq.com ,E-mail: mozhiwen@263.net

Abstract: From equivalence relation R_B^δ on discourse domain U, we can derive equivalence relation R^δ on the attribute set A. From equivalence relation R^δ on discourse domain A, we can derive a congruence relation on the attribute power set $P(A)$and establish an object dependent space. And then,we discuss the reduction method of fuzzy information system on object dependent space. At last ,the example in this paper demonstrates the feasibility and effectiveness of the reduction method based on the congruence relation T^δ providing an insight into the link between equivalence relation and congruence relation of dependent spaces in the rough set. In this way, the paper can provide powerful theoritical support to the combined using of reduction method, so it is of certain practical value.

1. Model Basis

Definition 1 Suppose that (U,A,F) is a fuzzy information system,where U is a limited object discourse domain, A is a limited condition attribute set, F is a mapping set. $f \in F, f : U \times A \to V, V \in 2^{[0,1]}, 2^{[0,1]}$ represents $[0,1]$ power set. $\tilde{R}$ is a fuzzy equivalence relation on the discourse domain U, $\tilde{R}: U\times U \to [0,1]$. Suppose that it has the following attributes:

1) $\tilde{R}(x_i,x_i)=1$;

2) $\tilde{R}(x_i,x_j)=\tilde{R}(x_j,x_i)$;

3) $\tilde{R}(x_i,x_j)\geq \tilde{R}(x_i,x_k)\wedge\tilde{R}(x_k,x_j)$

Definition 2 Let $\tilde{R}$ be a fuzzy equivalence relation on the discourse domain U, the cut relation of the fuzzy equivalence relation is defined as:

$$R_\delta = \{(x_i,x_j)|\tilde{R}(x_i,x_j)\geq \delta\} \quad (0\leq\delta\leq 1).$$

Theorem1 Let $\tilde{R}$ be a fuzzy equivalence relation on the discourse domain U, $R_\delta = \{(x_i,x_j)|\tilde{R}(x_i,x_j)\geq \delta\} (0\leq\delta\leq 1)$ is an equivalence relation, and (U,R_δ) is a approximation space.

Proof . First ,it is obvious that R_δ has reflexive and symmetric;

The following lines show the transitivity of R_δ:

If $(x_i,x_k)\in R_\delta,(x_k,x_j)\in R_\delta$,

Then $\tilde{R}(x_i,x_j)\geq \tilde{R}(x_i,x_k)\wedge\tilde{R}(x_k,x_j)\geq\delta$, where means $(x_i,x_j)\in R_\delta$,

Then R_δ has transitivity and R_δ is an equivalence relation,(U,R_δ) is approximation space.

Definition 3 Suppose that $(S,\circ)$ is a semi-lattice, $C: S\to S$ is a closure operator, if the following conditions hold for $\forall x,y\in S$:

1) $x\leq C(x)$;

2) $x\leq y \Rightarrow C(x)\leq C(y)$;

3) $C(C(x))=C(x)$.

Theorem 2 Let R_δ be an equivalence relation on, $P(U)/R_\delta$ is a division of $P(U)$(discourse power set). Suppose that (U,A,F) is a fuzzy information system, B is the attribute subset of attribute set of A ,i.e. $B\subseteq A$, the subset of the discourse domain U ,i.e. $X\subseteq U$, denote $C(R_\delta)$ on $(P(U),\cup)$ as:

$$C(R_\delta)(X)=\cup\{Y|Y\in P(U)/R_\delta, X\cap Y\neq\phi\}$$

then $C(R_\delta)$ is a closure operator.

Proof. It is obvious from the definition that

1) $X \subseteq C(R_\delta)(X)$ holds;

2) Suppose $X_1 \subseteq X_2$, we still need to prove that $C(R_\delta)(X_1) \subseteq C(R_\delta)(X_2)$.

It means that $\forall Y \in C(R_\delta)(X_1) \Rightarrow Y \in P(U)/R_\delta \Rightarrow X_1 \cap Y \neq \phi$; because $X_1 \subseteq X_2$, so

$X_2 \cap Y \neq \phi \Rightarrow Y \in C(R_\delta)(X_2)$, from the arbitrariness of Y we can derive $C(R_\delta)(X_1) \subseteq C(R_\delta)(X_2)$;

3) From the conclusions of 1) and 2) it is obvious that $C(R_\delta)(X) \subseteq C(C(R_\delta))(X)$;

We still need to prove that $C(R_\delta)(X) \supseteq C(C(R_\delta))(X)$.

For $\forall Y \in C(C(R_\delta))(X) \Rightarrow Y \in P(U)/R_\delta \Rightarrow Y \cap C(R_\delta)(X) \neq \phi$, from the definition of operator we can derive $Y \cap X \neq \phi \Rightarrow Y \in C(R_\delta)(X)$, from the arbitrariness of Y we can derive $C(R_\delta)(X) = C(C(R_\delta))(X)$.

2 Model of Depedent Space

Theorem3 Let (U, A, F) be a fuzzy information system , B is the attribute subset of attribute set A ($B \subseteq A$) and R_δ is a equivalence relation on U, then $R_B = \{(x, y) | X, Y \in P(U), C(R_\delta)(X) = C(R_\delta)(Y)\}$ is a congruence relation on the semi-lattice $(P(U), \cup)$.

Proof. First, it is obvious from the definition that it is an equivalence relation.

Next, let $X_1, X_2, Y_1, Y_2 \in P(U), (X_1, X_2) \in R_B, (Y_1, Y_2) \in R_B$,

From $C(R_\delta)(X_1) = C(R_\delta)(X_2)$, $C(R_\delta)(Y_1) = C(R_\delta)(Y_2)$ we know, for $\forall Z \in P(U)/R_\delta$

$Z \cap (X_1 \cup Y_1) \neq \phi \Leftrightarrow Z \cap (X_2 \cup Y_2) \neq \phi$, $C(R_\delta)(X_1 \cup Y_1) = C(R_\delta)(X_2 \cup Y_2)$ holds,

It means that $(X_1 \cup Y_1, X_2 \cup Y_2) \in R_B$, it proves that R_B is a congruence relation on U.

Theorem 4 Let (U, A, F) be a fuzzy information system , B is the attribute subset of attribute set A ($B \subseteq A$) , R_δ is a equivalence relation on U and $R_B = \{(x, y) | X, Y \in P(U), C(R_\delta)(X) = C(R_\delta)(Y)\}$, then (U, R_B) is an object dependent space on U.

Proof . From theorem 3 we know that R_B is a congruence relation on U, from definition 3 we can easily know that (U, R_B) is object dependent space on U.

Definition.4 Let the (U, A, F) be a fuzzy information system , $\widetilde{R}$ is fuzzy equivalence relation on discourse domain U, $\widetilde{R}: U \times U \rightarrow [0,1]$, define the relation:

$$R_B^\delta = \{(x_i, x_j) | \widetilde{R}_l(x_i, x_j) \geq \delta, a_l \in B, B \subseteq A, x_i, x_j \in U\} 0 \leq \delta \leq 1.$$

Theorem5 Let the (U, A, F) be a fuzzy information system , $\widetilde{R}$ is a fuzzy equivalence relation on discourse domain U, $\widetilde{R}: U \times U \rightarrow [0,1]$,

$R_B^\delta = \{(x_i, x_j) | \widetilde{R}_l(x_i, x_j) \geq \delta, a_l \in B, B \subseteq A, x_i, x_j \in U\} (0 \leq \delta \leq 1)$ is an equivalence relation about attribute set B on the discourse domain U.

Proof.

1) Reflexivity: From the definitions of R_B^δ and $\widetilde{R}$, it is obvious that $(x_i, x_i) \in R_B^\delta$;

2) Symmetry: $(x_i, x_j) \in R_B^\delta \Rightarrow (x_j, x_i) \in R_B^\delta$;

3) Transitivity: $(x_i, x_j) \in R_B^\delta$, $(x_j, x_k) \in R_B^\delta \Rightarrow \widetilde{R}_l(x_i, x_j) \geq \delta, \widetilde{R}_l(x_j, x_k) \geq \delta$, from the theorem.1 we know that $\widetilde{R}_l(x_i, x_k) \geq \widetilde{R}_l(x_i, x_j) \wedge \widetilde{R}_l(x_j, x_k) \geq \delta \Rightarrow (x_i, x_k) \in R_B^\delta$

Theorem 6 Let (U, A, F) be a fuzzy information system, $\widetilde{R}$ is fuzzy equivalence relation on discourse domain U , $\widetilde{R}: U \times U \rightarrow [0,1]$, denote $R^\delta = \{(X, Y) | R_X^\delta = R_Y^\delta, X, Y \subseteq A\}$, then R^δ is equivalence relation on A.

Proof . From the definition, it is easy to know that R^δ is equivalence relation on A.

Theorem 7 Let (U, A, F) be a fuzzy information system, $\widetilde{R}$ is a fuzzy equivalence relation on discourse domain U ($\widetilde{R}: U \times U \rightarrow [0,1]$, $C(R^\delta)(X) = \cup\{Y | Y \in A/R^\delta, X \cap Y \neq \phi\}$), then $C(R^\delta)$ is a closure operator on $(P(A), \cup)$.

Proof.1) Law of increasing: for $X \in P(A), x \in X$, then $[x]_{R^\delta} \cap X \neq \phi \Rightarrow x \in [x]_{R^\delta} \subseteq C(R^\delta)(X) \Rightarrow X \subseteq C(R^\delta)(X)$;

2) Monotonicity : Let $X, Y \in P(A), X \subseteq Y$, if $x \in C(R^\delta)(X) \Rightarrow [x]_{R^\delta} \cap X \neq \phi$, then $[x]_{R^\delta} \cap Y \neq \phi \Rightarrow x \in [x]_{R^\delta} \subseteq C(R^\delta)(Y)$;

3) From 1) and 2) we know, for $\forall X \subseteq A, C(R^\delta)(X) \subseteq C(R^\delta)(C(R^\delta))(X)$; On the other hand:

$x \in C(R^{\delta})(C(R^{\delta}))(X) \Rightarrow [x]_{R^{\delta}} \cap C(R^{\delta})(X) \neq \phi$, from the definition we know $[x]_{R^{\delta}} \subseteq C(R^{\delta})(X)$,

It mea $x \in C(R^{\delta})(X)$,thus $C(R^{\delta})(C(R^{\delta}))(X) \subseteq C(R^{\delta})(X)$,which means $C(R^{\delta})(C(R^{\delta}))(X) \subseteq C(R^{\delta})(X)$. Thus this law is proved.

Theorem 8 Let (U, A, F) be a fuzzy information system, $\tilde{R}$ is fuzzy equivalence relation on discourse domain U ($\tilde{R}: U \times U \to [0,1]$), then $T^{\delta} = \{(X, Y) | C(R^{\delta})(X) = C(R^{\delta})(Y), X, Y \in P(A)\}(0 \leq \delta \leq 1)$ is congruence relation on semi-lattice $(P(A), \cup)$.

Proof . First, from the definition it is easy to know that T^{δ} is equivalence relation.

Next,let $X_1, X_2, Y_1, Y_2 \in P(A), (X_1, X_2) \in T^{\delta}, (Y_1, Y_2) \in T^{\delta}$, then $C(R^{\delta})(X_1) = C(R^{\delta})(X_2)$, $C(R^{\delta})(Y_1) = C(R^{\delta})(Y_2)$, therefore $\forall Z \in P(A)/R^{\delta}, Z \cap (X_1 \cup Y_1) \neq \phi \Leftrightarrow Z \cap (X_2 \cup Y_2) \neq \phi$, so $C(R^{\delta})(X_1 \cup Y_1) = C(R^{\delta})(X_2 \cup Y_2)$, it means $(X_1 \cup Y_1, X_2 \cup Y_2) \in T^{\delta}$, thus it is proved that T^{δ} is a congruence relation on semi-lattice $(P(A), \cup)$.

Since T^{δ} is congruence relation on semi-lattice $(P(A), \cup)$, (A, T^{δ}) is called the attribute dependent space on attribute set A.

Note: The above deduction demonstrates that the closure operator on limited semi-lattice and congruence relation can determine each other.

3 Attribute Reduction Based On Dependent Space

It is feasible to discuss the issue of reducing attribute of fuzzy information system based on the attribute dependent space (A, T^{δ}) built on attribute set A. The following is some basic knowledge of reduction theory.

(A, T^{δ}) is an attribute dependent space on the attribute set A and T^{δ} is congruence relation on semilattice $(P(A), \cup)$,we denote a division of attribute power set $P(A)$ formed by congruence relation T^{δ} as $P(A)/T^{\delta} = \{[x]_{T^{\delta}} | x \in P(A)\}$ where $[x]_{T^{\delta}} = \{y | y \in P(A), (x, y) \in T^{\delta}\}$,

Then $[x]_{T^{\delta}}$ is called x-contained congruence class of congruence relation T^{δ}.

Theorem 9 We define a binary operator $\vee$ on the non-empty set $P(A)/T^{\delta} = \{[x]_{T^{\delta}} | x \in P(A)\}$ as: $[x]_{T^{\delta}} \vee [y]_{T^{\delta}} = [x \cup y]_{T^{\delta}}$, then $(P(A)/T^{\delta}, \vee)$ is a semi-lattice.

Proof. For $\forall [x]_{T^{\delta}}, [y]_{T^{\delta}} [z]_{T^{\delta}} \in P(A)/T^{\delta}$

1) Idempotent law: $[x]_{T^{\delta}} \vee [x]_{T^{\delta}} = [x]_{T^{\delta}}$;

2) Law of commutation: $[x]_{T^{\delta}} \vee [y]_{T^{\delta}} = [x \cup y]_{T^{\delta}} = [y \cup x]_{T^{\delta}} = [y]_{T^{\delta}} \vee [x]_{T^{\delta}}$;

3) $[x]_{T^{\delta}} \vee ([y]_{T^{\delta}} \vee [z]_{T^{\delta}}) = [x]_{T^{\delta}} \vee ([y \cup z]_{T^{\delta}}) = [x \cup y \cup z]_{T^{\delta}} = ([x]_{T^{\delta}} \vee [y]_{T^{\delta}}) \vee [z]_{T^{\delta}}$

Definition 5 We define a binary relation $\leq$ on the non-empty set $P(A)/T^{\delta} = \{[x]_{T^{\delta}} | x \in P(A)\}$ as: $[X]_{T^{\delta}} \vee [Y]_{T^{\delta}} = [Y]_{T^{\delta}}$, then denote it as $[X]_{T^{\delta}} \leq [Y]_{T^{\delta}}$,

Theorem 10 $(P(A)/T^{\delta}, \leq)$ is a join semi-lattice.

Proof . First, the binary relation $\leq$ satisfies reflexivity, anti-symmetry and transitivity, so the binary relation $\leq$ is a partial ordering relation on $P(A)/T^{\delta} = \{[x]_{T^{\delta}} | x \in P(A)\}$, then $(P(A)/T^{\delta}, \leq)$ is a partial ordering set.

Second, it is obvious that $[x]_{T^{\delta}} \leq [x]_{T^{\delta}} \vee [y]_{T^{\delta}}$, $[y]_{T^{\delta}} \leq [x]_{T^{\delta}} \vee [y]_{T^{\delta}}$, if $[x]_{T^{\delta}} \leq [z]_{T^{\delta}}, [y]_{T^{\delta}} \leq [z]_{T^{\delta}}$, then $[x]_{T^{\delta}} \vee ([y]_{T^{\delta}} \vee [z]_{T^{\delta}}) = ([x]_{T^{\delta}} \vee [y]_{T^{\delta}}) \vee [z]_{T^{\delta}} = [x]_{T^{\delta}} \vee [z]_{T^{\delta}} = [z]_{T^{\delta}}$, i.e. $[x]_{T^{\delta}} \vee [y]_{T^{\delta}} \leq [z]_{T^{\delta}}$, therefore there exists a least upper bound about $\leq$ in $\{[x]_{T^{\delta}}, [y]_{T^{\delta}}\}$, the theorem is further proved using arbitrariness.

Definition 6 Let (U, A, F) be a fuzzy information system, $T^{\delta_1} and T^{\delta_2}$ are two congruence relation on the attribute power set $P(A)$. if the resultant congruence classes have the relation $[x]_{T^{\delta_1}} \subseteq [x]_{T^{\delta_2}} (x \in P(A))$, then we say that the congruence relation T^{δ_1} is finer than T^{δ_2}, denoted as $T^{\delta_1} \leq T^{\delta_2}$.

Different thresholds $\delta(0 \leq \delta \leq 1)$, a number of sets formed under the congruence relation T^{δ} constitute a hierarchical congruence structure of the attribute power set $P(A)$, which is $\{[x]_{T^{\delta_i}} | 0 \leq \delta_i \leq 1\}$.

To better prepare the attribute reduction for information system, we need to define an order relation on the semi-lattice $(P(A), \cup)$ and create a combined semi-lattice.

Theorem 11 Let $(P(A), \cup)$ be a semi-lattice on an

attribute power set. We define an order relation $\leq_{\vee}$ on $P(A)$ as:

For $\forall x, y \in P(A), x \leq_{\vee} y \Leftrightarrow x \cup y = y$,

$(P(A), \leq_{\vee})$ is a join semi-lattice.

Proof . From the definition of $\leq_{\vee}$, it is easy to verify that the set satisfies reflexivity, anti-symmetry and transitivity, so $\leq_{\vee}$ is a partial order relation on $P(A)$, and $(P(A), \leq_{\vee})$ is a partial order relation. For $\forall x, y \in P(A)$, there exists $\sup\{x, y\}$, which means $x \vee y = x \cup y$. Thus it is proved that the partial order set $(P(A), \leq_{\vee})$ is a combined semi-lattice.

Theorem 12 Let (A, T^{δ}) be an attribute dependent space, T^{δ} is a congruence relation on the semi-lattice $(P(A), \cup)$, then for

$$\forall X \in P(A)/T^{\delta}, \text{ let } X = \{x_1, x_2, \cdots x_n\}, \text{ then}$$

$$x_1 \cup x_2 \cup \cdots \cup x_n \in X.$$

Proof. Since $X = \{x_1, x_2, \cdots x_n\}$, so for $\forall i, j \in 1,2,\cdots n.$, $(x_i, x_j) \in T^{\delta}$ holds. From the definition of congruence relation and idempotent law, $(x_i, x_1 \cup x_2 \cup \cdots \cup x_n) \in T^{\delta}$ holds, so it is proved that $x_1 \cup x_2 \cup \cdots \cup x_n \in X$.

Corollary1 Supposes that (A, T^{δ}) is a dependent space, T^{δ} is a congruence relation on the semi-lattice $(P(A), \cup)$, then there is a biggest element in each congruence class (equivalence class) $[x]_{T^{\delta}}$ of the congruence relation T^{δ} related to $P(A), x \in P(A)$.

Proof. Suppose congruence class (equivalence class) $[x]_{T^{\delta}}$ of the congruence relation T^{δ} related to $P(A)$is: $[x]_{T^{\delta}} = \{x_1, x_2, \cdots, x_n\}$, from the theorem 12, we can derive that $x_1 \cup x_2 \cup \cdots \cup x_n \in [x]_{T^{\delta}}$. Because $(P(A), \leq_{\vee})$ is a combined semi-lattice, therefore $x_1 \vee x_2 \vee \cdots \vee x_n = x_1 \cup x_2 \cup \cdots \cup x_n \in [x]_{T^{\delta}}$, $x_1 \vee x_2 \vee \cdots \vee x_n$ is the biggest element in $[x]_{T^{\delta}}$.

Note: The corollary1 indicates that for different congruence structures, there is always a biggest element in each congruence class. This provides a theoretical basis for finding attribute reduction method using congruence relation.

Theorem 13 Let (A, T^{δ})be a dependent space, where T^{δ} is a congruence relation on the semi-lattice $(P(A), \cup)$. For $\forall x \in P(A)$, then $C(T^{\delta})(x) = \cup [x]_{T^{\delta}}$ is a closure operator on $(P(A), \cup)$.

Proof . The method is similar to the proof of theorem 7.

Definition.7 Let (A, T^{δ})be a dependent space, where T^{δ} is a congruence relation on the semi-lattice $(P(A), \cup)$, $C(T^{\delta})$ is a closure operator on $(P(A), \cup)$, denote the set made up of all $C(T^{\delta})$ closure elements in $P(A)$ as $C_{T^{\delta}}$, then

$$\forall x \in C_{T^{\delta}} \Rightarrow C(T^{\delta})(x) = x$$

Theorem 14 Let (A, T^{δ})be a dependent space, where T^{δ} is a congruence relation on the semi-lattice, $(P(A), \cup)$ denote

$$T_{\delta}^{L} = \{(x, y) | x, y \in P(A), \forall z \in C_{T^{\delta}}, x \leq_{\wedge} z \Leftrightarrow y \leq_{\wedge} z\}, \text{ where}$$

T_{δ}^{L} is a congruence relation on semi-lattice $(P(A), \cup)$, and $T_{\delta}^{L} = T^{\delta}$.

Proof. Since $|C_{T^{\delta}}| = |P(A)/T^{\delta}|$, and $\forall z \in C_{T^{\delta}}, z$ is the biggest element in the congruence class T^{δ} related to $P(A)$, so $\forall x, y \in P(A) \Rightarrow (x, y) \in T^{\delta} \Leftrightarrow (x, y) \in T_{\delta}^{L} \Rightarrow T_{\delta}^{L} = T^{\delta}$, thus we prove that it is a congruence relation.

In the following discussion, $\sigma(D)$ represents the smallest algebraic unit created by dividing D.

Theorem 15 Let (U, A, F) be a fuzzy information system, there is an attribute dependent space (A, T^{δ}), $\forall x, y \in A$, $\forall X \subseteq A, B \subseteq U$, the following conclusions can be drawn:

1) $(x, y) \in R^{\delta} \Leftrightarrow (\{x\}, \{y\}) \in T^{\delta}$;

2) $X \in A/R^{\delta} \Rightarrow X \in C_{R^{\delta}}$;

3) $C_{R^{\delta}} = C_{T^{\delta}} = \sigma\left(A/R^{\delta}\right)$.

Proof.

1) Because $(x, y) \in R^{\delta} \Leftrightarrow [x]_{R^{\delta}} = [y]_{R^{\delta}} \Leftrightarrow C(R^{\delta})(\{x\}) = C(R^{\delta})(\{y\}) \Leftrightarrow (\{x\}, \{y\}) \in T^{\delta}$;

2) From the definition of closure operator, it is obvious that the conclusion holds;

3) Prove $C_{R^{\delta}} = C_{T^{\delta}}$ at first:

Suppose $X \in C_{R^{\delta}}, \forall Z \in P(A)$, if $X \subset Z$,

$$C(R^{\delta})(X) = \cup\left\{Y \middle| Y \in A/R^{\delta}, Y \cap X = \phi\right\} = X$$

There exists $Y \in A/_{R^\delta}$, thatmakes $Y \cap (Z-X) \neq \phi$, it leads to $C(R^\delta)(Z) = \cup\{Y | Y \in A/_{R^\delta}, Y \cap (X \cup (Z-X))$

$$\neq \phi\} = X \cup (\cup\{Y | Y \in A/_{R^\delta}, Y \cap (Z-X) \neq \phi\}) \neq X$$

, so, for $\forall Y \in [X]_{T^\delta}, Y \subseteq X$, it leads to

$X = \cup [X]_{T^\delta} \in C_{T^\delta}$, thus $C_{R^\delta} \subseteq C_{T^\delta}$;

Next we prove $C_{R^\delta} \supseteq C_{T^\delta}$ .Suppose $X \in C_{T^\delta}$, because $X = \cup [X]_{T^\delta}$, so X is the biggest element in the congruence class $[X]_{T^\delta}$, suppose there exists $Y \in A/_{R^\delta}, Y \not\subset X, Y \cap X \neq \phi,$ which means $Y \subseteq C(R^\delta)$ (X).

Therefore there exists $Z \in P(A), Z \not\subset X$ that makes $C(R^\delta)(X) = C(R^\delta)(Z)$, this means $Z \in [X]_{T^\delta}$, this is contradictory to the statement that X is the biggest.

So for

$\forall Y \in A/_{R^\delta}, Y \cap X \neq \phi$ C_{R^δ}, then $Y \subseteq X$, that means $X = \cup\{Y | Y \in A/_{R^\delta}, Y \cap X \neq \phi\} \in C_{R^\delta}$,

So $C_{R^\delta} \supseteq C_{T^\delta}$. Thus $C_{R^\delta} = C_{T^\delta}$ is proved.

Next we prove $C_{R^\delta} = \sigma\left(A/_{R^\delta}\right)$.

From $C_{R^\delta}(A) = A$, it is easy to get to $A \in C_{R^\delta}$. Suppos $X, Y \in C_{R^\delta}$, then

$$X \cup Y = \{\cup\{Z | Z \in A/_{R^\delta}, Z \cap X \neq \phi\}$$

$$\cup(\cup\{Z | Z \in A/_{R^\delta}, Z \cap Y \neq \phi\}) = \cup\{Z | Z \in A/_{R^\delta}, Z \cap (X \cup Y) \neq \phi\} = C(R^\delta)(X \cup Y) \in C_{R^\delta}$$

, further $\forall Y \in A/_{R^\delta}, Y \cap X \neq \phi \Leftrightarrow Y \subseteq X \Leftrightarrow Y \cap \sim$ X$=\phi$,which means $Y \cap \sim X \neq \phi \Leftrightarrow Y \cap X = \phi$.

Therefore $C(R^\delta)$ ($\sim$ X)=

$$\cup\left\{Y | Y \in A/_{R^\delta}, Y \cap (A-X) \neq \phi\right\} = \cup\{Y | Y \in A/_{R^\delta}, Y \cap X = \phi\} = \sim$$

X$\in C_{R^\delta}$, so C_{R^δ} is the smallest algebraic unit generated by $A/_{R^\delta}$, thus the equation is proved.

Next, we discuss dependent relation which is unique in attribute dependent space.

Definition.8 Given a fuzzy information system (U, A, F), for attribute dependent space (A, T^δ), for $X \subseteq A$, if $C(T^\delta)(A) \subseteq C(T^\delta)(X)$, we say that the attribute set A is dependent on the attribute subset X, denoted as $(A, X) \in dr$ (i.e. A is dependent on X).

Definition 9 Let (A, T^δ) be an attribute dependent space, we call $X \subseteq A$ is the reduction set of A. If the following conditions are satisfied:

1) $(A, X) \in dr$;
2) $\forall Y \subset X, (A, Y) \notin dr$.

Theorem 16 Let (U, A, F)be a fuzzy information system , for attribute dependent space (A, T^δ) and $X \subseteq A$, if $(A, X) \in dr$, then the smallest set X (based on set inclusion relation) that satisfies $(A, X) \in dr$ is the reduction set of the attribute set A.

Proof . Because $\forall X \subseteq A$, so $(A, X) \in dr \Leftrightarrow C(T^\delta)(A) = C(T^\delta)(X) \Leftrightarrow (A, X) \in T^\delta$, thus the theorem is proved.

Definition 10 Let (U, A, F)be a fuzzy information system , for attribute dependent space (A, T^δ), if $(A, X) \in dr$, then $dd = \dfrac{|C(T_B^\delta)(A)|}{|C(T_B^\delta)(X)|}$ is the degree of dependence of the attribute set A on attribute subset X, where $|\bullet|$ represents the number of set elements.

The degree of dependence describes the degree to which the attribute set A depends on the attribute subset X. The degree of dependence has the following characteristics:

1) $0 \leq dd \leq 1$;
2) The bigger the dd is, the higher the degree to which the attribute set A depends on the attribute subset X , indicating that the attribute subset X is more important. The smaller the dd is, the lower the degree to which the attribute set A depends on the attribute subset X , indicating that the attribute subset is less important.

We can see from this that the reduction of the attribute set A can also be described as finding the attribute subset that makes the degree of dependence $dd \in (0,1)$ reach the maximum value.

Next, given the congruence relation in the attribute dependent space, a system of attribute congruence classification (division) as well as a theory about attribute reduction and some reduction methods will be put forward.

Definition 11 Let (U,A,F) be a fuzzy information system , and (A,T^{δ}) an attribute dependent space , where T^{δ} is a congruence relation on the attribute power set $P(A)$, $M \in P(A)$ is the smallest element (based on set inclusion relation) in $[X]_{T^{\delta}}$, then M is T^{δ} representative element in $[X]_{T^{\delta}}$, the set made up of all representative elements of congruence class as $E(T^{\delta})$.

Lemma 1 Let (U,A,F) be a fuzzy information system , attribute dependent space (A,T^{δ}), T^{δ} is a congruence relation on the attribute power set $P(A)$, for $X,Y \in P(A)$, if $Y \subseteq X$, and $X \in E(T^{\delta})$, then $Y \in E(T^{\delta})$.

Proof . If $Y \notin E(T^{\delta})$, then $Y \neq X$, and $\exists Z \in [Y]_{T^{\delta}}, Z \in E(T^{\delta})$, then $Z \subseteq Y, Z \neq Y$, from $(Z, Y) \in T^{\delta}$, then $(Z \cup (X-Y), X) = (Z \cup (X-Y), Y \cup (X-Y)) \in T^{\delta}$. Moreover, because $Z \cup (X-Y) \subseteq X, Z \cup (X-Y) \neq X$, is contradictory to $X \in E(T^{\delta})$, thus the lemma is proved.

Definition 12 If $Y \subseteq A$, $(Y,A) \in T^{\delta}$,and $\forall y \in Y$, then $(Y-y,A) \notin T^{\delta}$. We call Y as a T^{δ} – reduction of attribute set A .

The question now is to choose an attribute reduction that satisfies the conditions from all the subsets of the attribute set A. We know if there are N attributes in the attribute set A, then the number of its non-empty subsets is $2^{N}-1$, because the attribute set is a limited set, so the reduction set can be found for certain using definition 12. However, usually there are multiple reductions.

All the T^{δ} – reduction sets $\{Y_i : i \le l\}$ of A are denoted as $reduct(A,T^{\delta})$. If the intersection set of all T^{δ} – reduction sets of A $Y = \cap\{Y_i\}$ is non-empty, we call Y the core attribute in the attribute set A, denoted as $CORE(A)$. But usually the core attribute does not constitute the reduction of attribute. All reductions contain core attribute, therefore core attribute is absolutely necessary. The attributes in $\cup\{Y_i\} - \cap\{Y_i\}$ do not appear in all reductions therefore they are relatively necessary. The attributes in $A - \cup\{Y_i\}$ do not appear in any reduction therefore are absolutely unnecessary.

4 Methods And Examples Of Attribute Reduction

	x_1	x_2	x_3	x_4
a	0.5	0.6	1	1
b	1	0.7	0.9	0.9
c	0.7	1	1	0.9
d	0.5	0.5	0.1	0.1

The procedure of attribute reduction for fuzzy information system under the dependent space model is as follows:

Step 1 Work out the congruence relation T^{δ} based on the given fuzzy information system (U,A,F) and choose the threshold δ (the method of choosing δ is the same as the method in example 1 where F distribution is used).

Step 2 Work out the congruence classification $P(A)/T^{\delta}$ of $P(A)$ based on the chosen congruence relation.

Step 3 Find out the smallest element set $M(T^{\delta})$ (based on smallest elements with inclusion relation) of each congruence class in all congruence classes.

Step 4 Write out the set made up of all T^{δ} – reduction sets $reduct\text{-}(A,T^{\delta})$.

Step 5 Work out the intersection set of all reduction sets. If the intersection set is not empty, it is the core attribute set $CORE(A)$. If the intersection set is empty, there is no core attribute.

Example 1 The table below defines a fuzzy information system

Table 1 fuzzy information system

Let $\delta_1 = 0.1, \delta_2 = 0.5, \delta_3 = 0.6, \delta_4 = 0.7, \delta_5 = 0.9, \delta_6 = 1$, we can obtain the cut relation matrix and the equivalence classes of the attribute set A :

$$\begin{pmatrix} 1 & 1 & 1 & 1 \\ 1 & 1 & 1 & 1 \\ 1 & 1 & 1 & 1 \\ 1 & 1 & 1 & 1 \end{pmatrix} \delta_1 = 0.1,\ A/R^{\delta_1} = \{abcd\},\ \begin{pmatrix} 1 & 1 & 1 & 1 \\ 1 & 1 & 1 & 1 \\ 1 & 1 & 1 & 1 \\ 1 & 1 & 0 & 0 \end{pmatrix}$$

$\delta_2 = 0.5$, $A/R^{\delta_2} = \{abc, d\}$

$$\begin{pmatrix} 0 & 1 & 1 & 1 \\ 1 & 1 & 1 & 1 \\ 1 & 1 & 1 & 1 \\ 0 & 0 & 0 & 0 \end{pmatrix} \delta_3 = 0.6, \; A/R^{\delta_3} = \{a, bc, d\},$$

$$\begin{pmatrix} 0 & 0 & 1 & 1 \\ 1 & 1 & 1 & 1 \\ 1 & 1 & 1 & 1 \\ 0 & 0 & 0 & 0 \end{pmatrix} \delta_4 = 0.7, \; A/R^{\delta_4} = \{a, bc, d\}$$

$$\begin{pmatrix} 0 & 0 & 1 & 1 \\ 1 & 0 & 1 & 1 \\ 0 & 1 & 1 & 1 \\ 0 & 0 & 0 & 0 \end{pmatrix} \delta_5 = 0.9, \; A/R^{\delta_5} = \{a, b, c, d\},$$

$$\begin{pmatrix} 0 & 0 & 1 & 1 \\ 1 & 0 & 0 & 0 \\ 0 & 1 & 1 & 0 \\ 0 & 0 & 0 & 0 \end{pmatrix} \delta_6 = 1, \; A/R^{\delta_6} = \{a, b, c, d\}$$

In the equivalence classes of the attribute set: $A/R^{\delta_1} = \{abcd\}$, $A/R^{\delta_5} = \{a,b,c,d\}$, $A/R^{\delta_6} = \{a,b,c,d\}$ are either put into a single class or treated as a separate class therefore there is no practical meaning. So, for threshold values of $\delta_2 = 0.5$, $\delta_3 = 0.6$, $\delta_4 = 0.7$, the beset threshold $\delta_3 = 0.6$ can be identified using the F statistics. With this threshold, the attribute set A is classified $\{\{a\},\{b,c\},\{d\}\}$.Next, we will use congruence relation T^{δ_3} to find out the attribute power set

$$P(A) = \left\{ \begin{array}{l} \{\phi\},\{a\},\{b\},\{c\},\{d\},\{a,b\},\{a,c\},\{a,d\},\{b,c\},\{b,d\},\{c,d\}, \\ \{a,b,c\},\{acd\},\{bcd\},\{abd\},\{abcd\} \end{array} \right\}$$

.

Its congruence classification is: $P(A)/T^{\delta_3} = \{\{\phi\},\{a\},\{b,c,bc\},\{d\},\{ab,ac,abc\},\{ad\},\{bd,cd,bcd\},\{acd, abd,abcd\}\}$. According to the reduction algorithm in attribute dependent space, the smallest set congruent to the attribute set A is the attribute subsets $\{acd\}$ and $\{abd\}$, therefore both of them are the reduction of the attribute set. The absolute necessary attribute set i.e. core attribute set $\{ad\}$ can be found by calculating the intersection set.

In the end, we wish that this article can provide beneficial theoretical and applied contributions finding better, faster, more effective method of attribute reduction for the fuzzy information system .

Acknowledgements

This study was supported by the national natural science fund project(No.61203285),the education Department of Sichuan Province (No.14ZB0065) , Key projects in Si Chuan province department of education(No.12ZA138) and Science and Technology Project funds (No.K33).

References

[1] Liu Qing: *Rough Inference* [M], Beijing Science Press, 2005(3): 20-67.
[2] Wang Reng, Miao Duoqian etc.: *Summary of Theory of Rough Set and Its Application* [J]. Pattern Recognition and Artificial Intelligence, 1996(6): 337-344.
[3] Zhang Wenxiu, Liang Yi, Wu Zhiwei: *Information System and Knowledge Discovery* [M]. Science Press, 2003.
[4] Novotny, M., Pawlak, Z. *On a Problem Concerning Dependence Spaces* [J]. Fundamental Informaticae, 1992 (16):275-287.
[5] Novotny M. *Dependence Spaces of Information Systems* [M]. In: Ortowska E.(ed) Incomplete Information Rough Set Analysis, Physica-Veolag, 1998:193-289.
[6] NovotnyM. *On Dependence in Will's Contexts* [J]. Fundamental information, 1993(19):343-353.
[7] E.Lois and M. Benedicty. *Mappings Dependence Spaces* [m]. Pittsburgh (Pennsylvania), March 1970.
[8] Cheng Tao, Huang Xiaokun: *Attribute Reduction of Information System Based on Dependent Space* [J]. Honghe University News, 2012(10): 26-28.
[9] Pawlak Z, *Rough Sets* [J]. International Journal of Computer and Information Science, 1982, 11(5): 341-356.
[10] Z.Pawlak: *Rough Sets: Theoretical as Pects of Reasoning about Data* [M]. Kluwer Academie Publishers, Boston, 1991.
[11] Andrew Kusiak*, Anoop Verma: *Analyzing Bearing Faults in Wind Turbines: A Data-mining Approach* [J]. Renewable Energy, 2012(48): 110-116.
[12] Alex Betphen J Smith: *Data Warehousing, Data Mining, &OLAP* [M] . New Yor k: McGraw - Hill Bo ok Co. , 1999.

An Enhancing Security Research of Tor Anonymous Communication to Against DDos Attacks

Tao FENG*, Ming-Tao ZHAO

College of Computer and Communication, Lanzhou University of Technology, Lanzhou 730050, China
zhaomingtao1226@163.com
**Corresponding author: fengt@lut.cn*

Abstract: Tor (The Second Onion Router) is modified by the first generation onion router and known as the most prevalent anonymous communication system. According to the advantage of low latency, high confidentiality of transmission content, high security of communication channels and et al., Tor is widely used in anonymous Web browsing, instant message and so on. However, the vulnerability and blemish of Tor affect system security. An identity and Signcryption-based concurrent signature scheme was used to prevent the behaviors of attackers from inserting controlled nodes and conspiring to make DDos attacks. The integrated security of Tor system was enhanced in our scheme. In addition we have proved the scheme.

1 Introduction

Anonymous communication can hide the telecommunication relationship in the business flow without changing the existing network protocol and complete the protection of the privacy information such as the user's identity. Consequently, the eavesdropper cannot directly or indirectly infer the telecommunication relationship and the identity of communications [1]. According to the advantage of simple configuration and excellent performance, the third system of Tor anonymous communication system has been developed quickly. Tor can resist the attack from listening and flow analysis, which is currently one of the most widely, used anonymous communication system on the Internet [2].

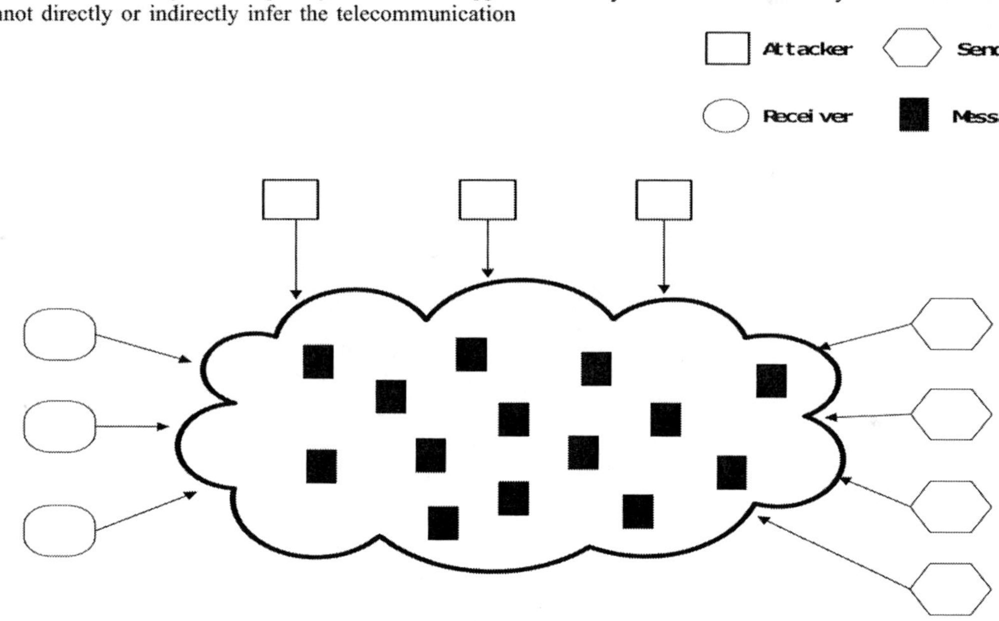

Figure 1. Traditional network model

 DOI: 10.1051/itmconf/20171204018

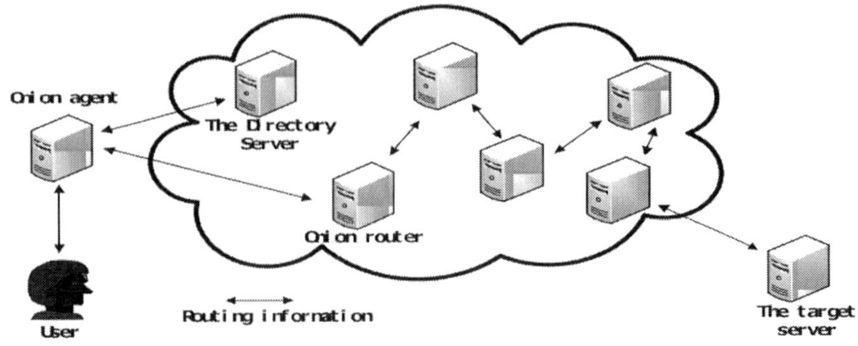

Figure 2. Tor network model

Compared with the traditional network communication, Tor can withstand strong flow analysis. So, Tor can guarantee the anonymity and security of the communication better. What's more, Tor can coordinate with existing many applications, so Tor has better flexibility and extensibility [3]. As one large-scale application anonymous communication system, in the design of Tor, performance, user demand and other factors have been considered. In the realization of the specific function, some unsafe strategy were adopted which exposed the vulnerability. In order to a low delay, Tor does not have completely anonymous, plus with lack of user access certification, which have has provided the favorable natural conditions for the attacker to DDos attacks[4].

In order to improve the security of Tor anonymous communication system, a new kind of anonymous communication scheme is proposed by Zhou et.al [1], the scheme make up the deficiency of the traditional Tor anonymous communication system in some extent. However, the scheme increases time. Based on the technology signcryption, Zheng et.al [4] proposes a node authentication mechanism, which is realizes a third party certification between TTP and node and among nodes by introducing the authority of the third party (TTP).

In the present study, a concurrent signature scheme based on identity authentication and signcryption[5] were adopted. The scheme can Verifies the reliability of accessed Tor nodes eliminate the false nodes. In the stage of middle volunteer node (OR) added to the Tor network, confirm the identity of the both sides through mutual authentication, and use signcryption to ensure the authentication information are unforgeable in the validation process. Through the authentication mechanism of the directory server and nodes, and between nodes, the scheme can effectively improve the reliability of system Tor nodes, prevent malicious nodes got into the system to improve security and effectiveness.

2 Prepared Knowledge

2.1 Bilinear Maps

Let G_0 and G_1 be two multiplicative cyclic groups of prime order p. Let g be a generator of G_0 and e be a bilinear map, $e{:}G_0 \times G_0 \rightarrow G_1$. The bilinear map e has the following properties:

(1) Bilinearity: for all $u, v \in G_0$ and $a, b \in Z_p$, we have $e(u^a, v^b) = e(u, v)^{ab}$.

(2) Non-degeneracy: $e(g, g) \neq 1$.

We say that G_0 is a bilinear group if the group operation in G_0 and the bilinear map $e{:}G_0 \times G_0 \rightarrow G_1$ are both efficiently computable. Notice that the map e is symmetric since $e(g^a, g^b) = e(g, g)^{ab} = e(g^b, g^a)$.

2.2 Tor System Basic Model

The Tor system is a distributed global network, using a centralized directory management structure. The entire Tor network consists of seven parts [6]:

(1) User Clients(User): A computer that communicates anonymously with the outside world through onion routing networks, usually the user needs to connect to the Tor network with an onion proxy.

(2) Onion Proxy: Responsible for the establishment of data transmission channel, receive TCP data stream, and sends the data stream to the established transmission channel.

(3) Onion Router: To establish an anonymous communication link and to forward data.

(4) Entry Node: The first onion router on the path, which communicates directly with the user.

(5) Exit Node: Refers to the last onion router on the path that communicates directly with the target server.

(6) Middle Node: Means an onion router on a path other than the ingress and egress nodes.

(7) The Directory Server: Mainly responsible for the collection, management, storage of all OR information and node exit and join the network-related operations.

Onion routing system can be roughly divided into three stages which are establishing connection, transferring data and closing connection [7].

2.3 Establishment of Anonymous Communication Link

First, Alice's onion proxy sends a "Create" command packet to the first onion router OR1 which is chosen. This "Create" packet, let C_{AB} represent the CircID between Alice and Bob, and also includes the first half of the Diffie-Hellman handshake information (g^{x1}), then use Bob's public key encryption. Bob returns a Created packet, which contains the latter half of Diffie-Hellman handshake information (g^{y1}) and the hash value $H(\mathrm{K}_1)$ of the session key K_1 (g^{x1y1})[8]. Once the link is established, Alice and Bob can send forward packets. The forwarded packets are encrypted with their negotiated session key K_1.

If you want to expand this virtual circuit, Alice sends an Relay Extend packet with K_1 encrypted to Bob, which contains the encrypted information g^{x2} and the next-hop onion router address (Known as Carol).Bob builds a "Create" packet. Use C_{BC} to represent the CircID between Bob and Carol, also contains the half of the handshake information g^{x2}, then encrypted with Carol's public key and sent to Carol. Carol returns a "Created" packet, which contains the latter half of Diffie-Hellman handshake information (g^{y2}) and the hash value $H(\mathrm{K}_2)$ of the session key K_2 (g^{x2y2}). When Bob receives the Carol response message, Bob encrypts a Relay Extended packet with the session key K_1 between it and Alice (contains g^{y2} and $H(\mathrm{K}_2)$), then send it back to Alice. Now, the link to Carol, Alice, and Carol's session key is K_2[9].

Alice just need repeats the process, it can gradually expand the length of the virtual circuit, and finally to establish a connection with the destination node (Figure 3 Tor link establishment process).

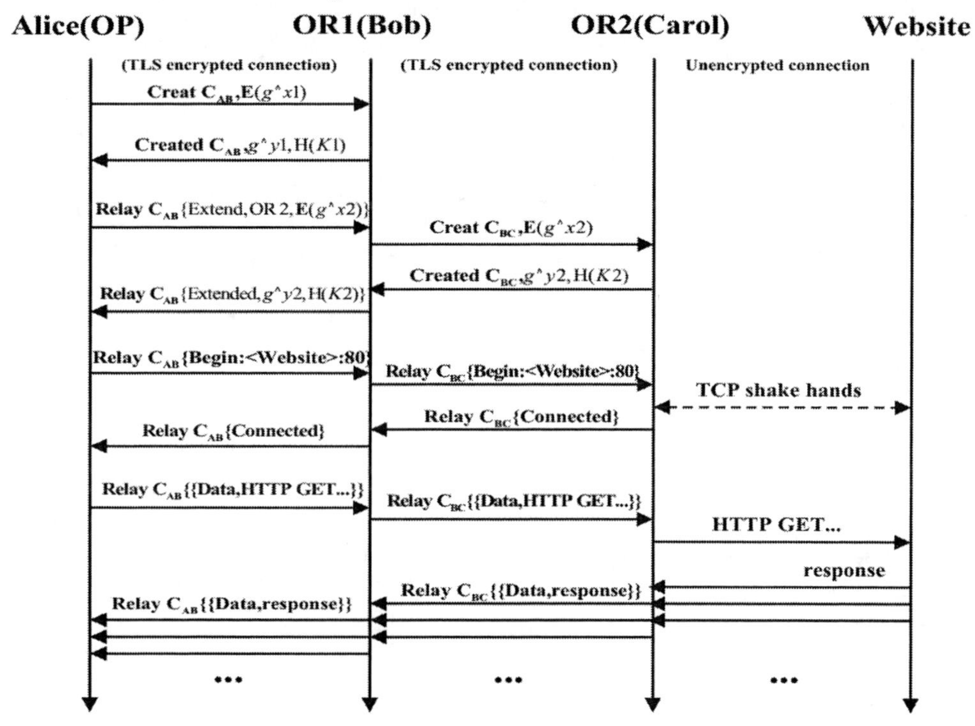

Figure 3 . Tor link establishment process

2.4 The Data Transfer Process of Tor

OP sends the encrypted packet to the OR node of next-hop. Theoretically, each node on the Tor rerouting path is randomly selected by the user. But in practical application, the OR nodes responsible for forwarding are randomly selected by Tor. In Figure 4, we choose a client OP, three OR nodes to form an anonymous communication link. Shows the transfer of data from the OP to the server E [10].

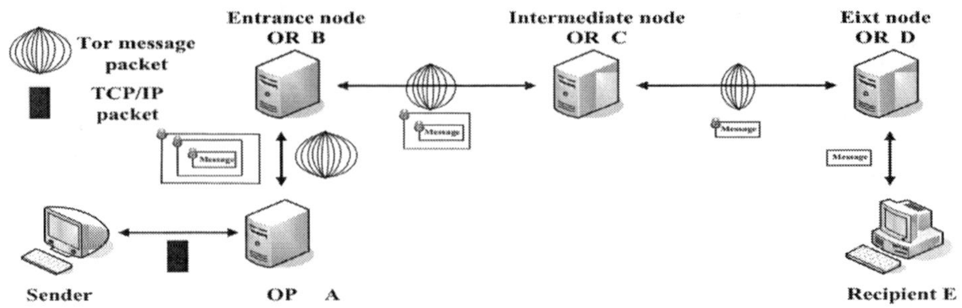

Figure 4. Tor data transfer process

As can be seen from the figure, the link establishment procedure from A to E, need to go through B, C, D three forwarding nodes (Relay). Corresponding to each forwarding node, before the transmission, communication data was also encrypted from the back to front by onion agent according to its public key, which passed Tor nodes, and formed a recursive hierarchical data structure called the onion package [11]. Thus, the communication usually uses Onion to replace the usual TCP / IP packets. This ensures that each onion router only knows the onion router that passes it data and the next-hop onion router it wants to pass data to, without knowing all the onion routers that are going to pass between the sender and the receiver. So as to achieve the purpose of hiding routing information and resist traffic analysis. In the sending process, the message packets are decrypted one layer while passed an onion routing node. Until after routing node D export of Tor network, the sending information is restored to the plain text message. In the whole link, the forwarding node only needs to know the nodes of the next hop and the next hop. Thus ensuring the security of the identity information of the two sides of communication [12].

3 An Identity and Signcryption-based Concurrent Signature Scheme

User A represents the initial signer, and user B represents the matching signer. The signcryption algorithm in the scheme is mutual. A and B each run this algorithm once. In this scheme, i is the signer and j is the matching signer, $i, j \in \{A, B\}$ the scheme includes the following algorithm:

(1) System establishment:

G_1 is a q-order cyclic additive group, q is a prime number, p is the generator of G_1; G_2 is a g-order cyclic multiplicative group. PKG(Private Key Generator)randomly selects the master key $s \in Z_q^*$, calculate $P_{pub} = s^P$ as the public key of PKG. Select two secure Hash functions: $H_0:\{0,1\}^* -> G_1, H_1:\{0,1\}^l \times G_T -> \{0,1\}^*$ G_1 Z_q^* ,l is the length of the plaintext to be encrypted. PKG public system parameters $\pi = \{q, G_1, G_2, e, l, P, P_{pub}, H_0, H_1\}$.

(2) Key extraction: using A,BID: ID_A, ID_B, PKG calculate $S_A = sQ_A$, $S_b = sQ_B$, and $Q_A = H_0(ID_A)$, $Q_B = H_0(ID_B)$. The public key of A and B is: Q_A, Q_b, and private keys is S_A, S_B.

(3) keystone mapping(Footprint):The input parameter of this algorithm is (β, k_i), and $\beta \in G_1$, $k_i \in Z_q^*$, k_i is the keystone selected by the signer. Calculate $f_i = \beta + H_0(k_i)$, output f_i.

(4) Signcryption: the input parameter for this algorithm is $(ID_i, ID_j, Q_i, Q_j, S_i, f_i, m_i)$, the algorithm runs as follows:

①selected randomly $a_i \in Z_q^*$, Calculate $U_i = a_i P$, $w_i = e(P_{pub}, Q_j)^{ai}$.

②let $R_j = f_i$, Calculate $h_i = H_1(m \| R_j \| ID_A \oplus ID_B)$.

③selected randomly $r \in rZ_q^*$,calculate

$$\begin{cases} R_i = rQ_i - R_j - h_j Q_j \\ h_i = H_1(m \| R_i \| ID_i \oplus ID_j) \\ V = (h_i + r)S_i \end{cases}$$

④Calculate: $c_i = m \oplus w_i$, is the ciphertext after encrypts, output signcryption $\sigma_i = \{c_i, V, R_A, R_B\}$.

(5) Designcrypt: This algorithm is matching signers restore the ciphertext to plaintext. The input parameter is (c_i, U_i, S_j), Calculate: $m = c_i + e(U_i, S_j)$ output m.

(6) Mutual authentication (Averify): This algorithm is mutual authentication between A and B. It is used to verify the validity of the received signature and the plaintext obtained in the previous algorithm. The input for this algorithm is $\sigma_i = \{c_i, Q_A, Q_B, m\}$. First calculate:

$$h_A = H_1(\mathrm{m} \| \mathrm{R}_A \| \mathrm{ID}_A \oplus ID_B)$$
$$h_B = H_1(\mathrm{m} \| \mathrm{R}_B \| \mathrm{ID}_A \oplus ID_B)$$

Then, verify if $e(\mathrm{P}_{pub}, \mathrm{R}_A + \mathrm{h}_A Q_A + \mathrm{R}_B + h_B \mathrm{Q}_B) \overset{?}{=} e(\mathrm{P}, \mathrm{V})$. If it is true, output accept, else output reject.

(7) Third-party authentication (Verify): This algorithm is implemented after the respective keystone is released. The role is that any third party can confirm who is the signer by this algorithm except the both parties involved in this scheme, so that binding signature to signer's identity is realized. The input of this algorithm is $(\sigma, \mathrm{Q}_A, \mathrm{Q}_B, \mathrm{m})$, and σ may be the signcryption of A or the signcryption of B. If $R_B = H(\mathrm{k}_A)$, and Averify$(\sigma, \mathrm{Q}_A, \mathrm{Q}_B, \mathrm{m})$ = accept, then σ is the signcryption of A; If $R_A = H(\mathrm{k}_A) + \mathrm{H}(\mathrm{k}_B)$, and Averify $(\sigma, \mathrm{Q}_A, \mathrm{Q}_B, \mathrm{m}) = \mathrm{accept}$, then σ is the signcryption of B.

4 The Authentication Process of Tor Node

The directory server in the Tor network is used as a third-party authentication authority. If OR node $R_i = (1, 2, 3 \ldots \mathrm{n})$ wants to join the Tor network, which must register with the directory server. The directory server then checks the performance of the OR, including uptime, bandwidth, and so on. OR needs to be authenticated to confirm its reliability when it joins the Tor network. In order to prevent the information from being falsified and tampered with during the verification process, we combine identity-based signcryption. Increased node reliability through directory server and node, node-to-node authentication mechanisms. The authentication procedure is shown in Figure 5 and Figure 6:

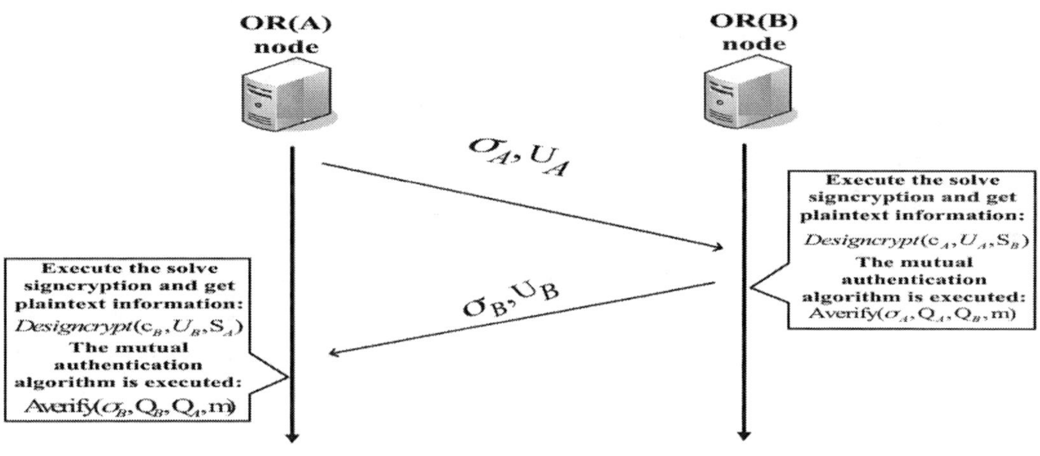

Figure 5. Mutual authentications between the Tor nodes

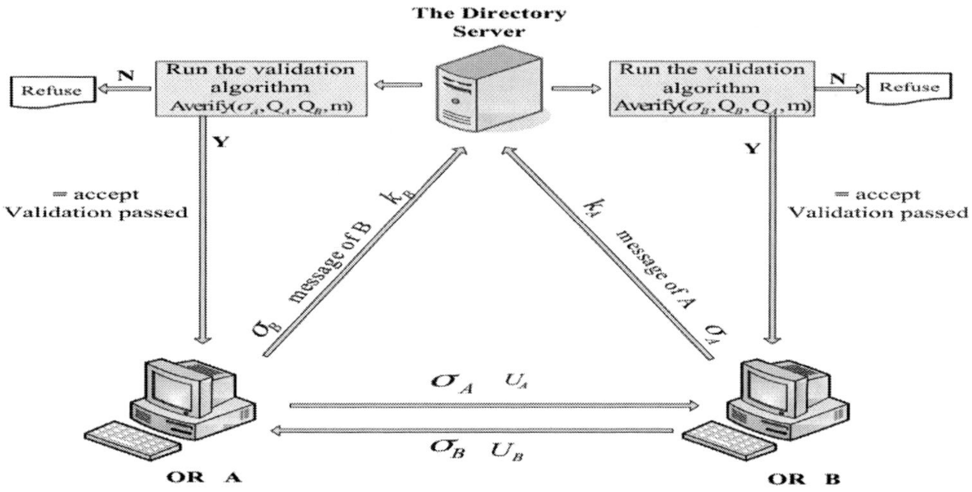

Figure 6. Third-party authentications for the Tor directory server

Specific operations are as follows:

The parameters in Fig. 6 are explained as follows: σ_A is the signcryption generated by the OR (A) node; σ_B is the signcryption generated by the OR (B) node; U_A is the secret key to decode the signcryption from node of OR (A); similarly, U_B with OR (B) node; k_A is the keystone of OR (A); k_B is the keystone of OR (B).

(1) In the Tor network node A wants to communicate with node B, node A can generates a set of information m containing time parameters and partial identity information. Node A will randomly select $k_A \in Z_q^*$, k_A will be used as its keystone.

if node A send message to node B
then
do $f_A = Footprint(0, k_A)$
$\sigma_A = signcrypt(ID_A, ID_B, Q_A, Q_B, S_A, f_A, m)$
node A send σ_A, U_A to node B
else
$\sigma_A = signcrypt(ID_A, ID_B, Q_A, Q_B, S_A, f_A, m)$ Will not be performed
node A don't send any message to node B
end if

(2) After node A sends message to node B:
if node B received node A message
then
do $m = Designcrypt(c_A, U_A, S_B)$, and do $Averify(\sigma_A, Q_A, Q_B, m)$
if $Averify(\sigma_A, Q_A, Q_B, m) = reject$
then
The identity of the node A will be questioned by node B
node B not to provide any services to node A
else
if $Averify(\sigma_A, Q_A, Q_B, m) = accept$
then
continue with step 5
end if
else
node B continue to wait node A message

(3) In the Tor network node B wants to communicate with node A, node B can generates a set of information m containing time parameters and partial identity information. Node B will randomly select $k_B \in Z_q^*$, k_B will be used as its keystone.

if node B send message to node A
then
do $f_B = Footprint(f_A, k_B)$
$\sigma_B = signcrypt(ID_B, ID_A, Q_B, Q_A, S_B, f_B, m)$
node B send σ_B, U_B to node A
else
$\sigma_B = signcrypt(ID_B, ID_A, Q_B, Q_A, S_B, f_B, m)$ Will not be performed
node B don't send any message to node A
end if

(4)After node B sends message to node A:
if node A received node B message
then
do $m = Designcrypt(c_B, U_B, S_A)$, and do $Averify(\sigma_B, Q_B, Q_A, m)$
if $Averify(\sigma_B, Q_B, Q_A, m) = reject$
then

The identity of the node B will be questioned by node A
node A not to provide any services to node B
else
if $Averify(\sigma_B, Q_B, Q_A, m) = accept$
then
continue with step 6
end if
else
node A continue to wait node B message

If it has already been validated that what B print is indeed the signcryption of A, then the verification from B to A will pass.

(5) After node B verifies the node A:
if $Averify(\sigma_A, Q_A, Q_B, m) = accept$
then
node B send node A's message m、signcrypt σ_A and node A's keystone k_A to The DirecTory Server
do $Verify(\sigma_A, Q_A, Q_B, m)$
if $R_B = H(k_A)$
then
node B to node A's verify will be passed
else
The identity of the node A will be questioned by node B
else
The identity of the node A will be questioned by node B

(6) Similarly, after node A verifies the node B:
if $Averify(\sigma_B, Q_B, Q_A, m) = accept$
then
node A send node B's message m、signcrypt σ_B and node A's keystone k_B to The DirecTory Server
do $Verify(\sigma_B, Q_B, Q_A, m)$
if $R_A = H(k_B)$
then
The verification from node A to node B will be passed.
else
The identity of the node B will be questioned by node A
else
The identity of the node B will be questioned by node A

5 Proof of Signcryption-based Concurrent Signature Scheme

$$c_i \oplus e(U_i, S_j) = c_i \oplus e(a_i P, sQ_j) = c_i \oplus e(sP, Q_j)^{a_i} = c_i \oplus e(P_{pub}, Q_j)^{a_i} = m$$

As shown in the above equation, as long as the encryption algorithm is executed correctly, the decryption algorithm solves the encrypted plaintext in the encryption algorithm.

5.1 Proof of Correctness

(1) Proof of Decryption:

(2) OR nodes are mutually authenticated

The OR (B) node verifies the signature of the OR (A) node:

$$e(P_{pub} R_A, h_A Q_A + R_B + h_B Q_B) = e(P_{pub}, rQ_A + h_A Q_A)$$
$$= e(sP, (r + h_A)Q_A) = e(P, (r + h_A)S_A) = e(P, V)$$

The OR (A) node verifies the signature of the OR (B) node:

$$e(P_{pub} R_A, h_A Q_A + R_B + h_B Q_B) = e(P_{pub}, rQ_B + h_B Q_B)$$
$$= e(sP, (r + h_B)Q_B) = e(P, (r + h_B)S_B) = e(P, V)$$

As shown in the above equation, If the OR (A), OR (B) node's signcryption algorithm is executed correctly, then the Averify algorithm will return the accept result.

5.2 Proof of Safety

Through the Tor anonymous network mechanism combined with the identity-based concurrent signature technology, the middle volunteer node join the Tor network must to authenticate the identity. The OR (A) node sends the attribute information to the OR (B) node, include σ_A, U_A. Between the OR (A) and OR (B) nodes, if there is an attacker Bob, Bob must be informed $e(P_{pub}, Q_B)^{a_A} = e(s a_A P, Q_B)$ about identity information. Since Bob cannot know the private key S_B of OR (B), Bob must have the contents of $s a_A P$. Because $s, a \in Z_q^*$, given $(P, sP, a_A P) \in G_1^3$, so to calculate A is obviously B's CDH problem. The middle attacker Bob can't decrypt the content (σ_A and U_A) transferred from node OR(A) to node OR(B), even though he intercepts it. So the mutual authentication process between OR nodes is confidential.

5.3 Proof of Anti-collusion

In the entire Tor network, the directory server managers all OR nodes added and exit. The entire Tor network is also composed of many relay nodes. As shown in Figure 7.

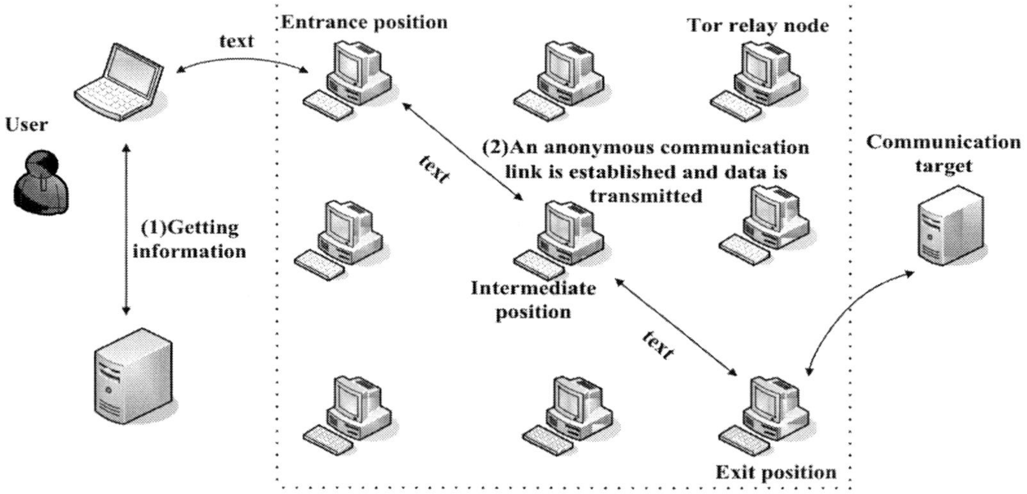

Figure 7. Tor network structure diagram

As shown in Figure 7above, in the first phase of the entire Tor network (The joining phase of the volunteer node). Through this program can guarantee that each legitimate relay node to join Tor to form the entire Tor network system, When the user wants to communicate with the target node, users are required to apply to the Tor directory server. The Tor directory server randomly selects the Tor relay node among the valid nodes that pass the audit and thereby establishing a communication link. The number of relay nodes in a Tor network is very large and the relay nodes before and after the link are randomly selected by the directory server. There is no interaction between the relay nodes during the link establishment phase. When the link is established, at the time of information transmission, the transmission of the message packets takes place in one direction. The message packet passes through each onion routing node, it will decrypt a layer to get to the next hop address, and the onion packet is then passed to the next node. Do not know the entire onion router between the senders to the receiver to go through. When this transmission is complete the link will be destroyed, so as to avoid the DDos attack initiated by OR nodes in the process of information transmission.

In the Tor network, in the volunteer node to join the stage if not legitimate certification, most illegitimate volunteer nodes can be disguised as legitimate nodes to join the Tor network. If the number of these illegal relay nodes occupies more than half of the legitimate relay nodes, when the link is established, the false probability of a randomly selected relay node of the directory server is extremely large. Multiple false nodes in the current link collusion before data communication get the private key of other false nodes that Decrypt the layer of their own. At the time of data transmission, a fake node obtains the onion packet because it owns the private key of a number of other false nodes; this onion packet security will have a great threat. The scheme adopted in this paper can authenticate the identities of the relay nodes that join the Tor network. Greatly reducing the possibility of false nodes joining the Tor network, which greatly reduces the DDos behavior that launched by the false nodes in the link.

5.4 Proof of High Efficiency

The same signcryption technology is used to prevents the insertion of malicious managed nodes into the Tor network, The literature [4] is aimed at the user in the establishment of the anonymous link stage. The reliability, stability and reliability of the intermediate nodes of the Tor network are evaluated by a trusted third-party authority. Issue a reliable certificate for the Verifies OR node which has passed and generates a public-private pair for the OR node. By verifying each other's trusted certificate to determine each other's identity and a signcryption technique is used to ensure the unforgeability of the trusted certificate. The concurrent signature scheme in this paper does not require the third authority to issue trusted certificate, therefore part of the time overhead of issuing trusted certificate can be saved.

In this paper, the signature scheme based on signcryption technique is less expensive than the scheme in [4]. The specific operation situation is shown in Table 1.

Table 1. The scheme of this paper is compared with the literature

Operation	The program of literature		The program of this paper	
	Signcryption	Decryption	Signcryption	Decryption
Exponent	0	0	1	0
Bilinear pairings	1	1	1	1
Hash	2	2	2	0
multiplication	3	1	3	0

From Table 1 can be drawn the scheme adopted in this paper has different degree of reduction in the decryption link Hash, multiplication operation. In addition, the scheme adopted in this paper is carried out in the OR node adding to the Tor network phase, without involving other time cost. The scheme adopted in [4] is carried out in the link establishment phase of the Tor network, which involves the fusion of original keys with OR nodes. So the scheme of this paper is more efficient than the literature [4].

6 Conclusion

The present concurrent signature scheme does not need a third authority party to issue a trusted certificate, save the overhead. Compared with [4], the present program has different degrees of reduction in decryption link Hash and multiplication operation. Proved from security, unforgeable and collusion-resistance, the present concurrent signature scheme has the advantage of safe, unforgeable and collusion-resistance. So the scheme can effectively resist the collusion DDos attack behavior of attacker from the very great degree in the Tor network insert controlled node.

Acknowledgement

This work is supported by the National Nature Science Foundation of China (No.61462060).

References

1. Yanwei Zhou,Qiliang Yang,Bo Yang,et.al. A Tor Anonymous Communication System with Security Enhancements[J]. Journal of Computer Research and Development, 2014,51(7):1538-1546(in Chinese).
2. Bo Wang. How to use Tor network safely [J]. Computer and Network, 2015, 41(14):37-37 (in Chinese).
3. Yong Zhou. Research on Anonymous Communication Based on TOR[D].Xidian University, 2013 (in Chinese).
4. Guang Zheng. Security analysis and research of Tor anonymous communication system.Shanghai Jiao Tong University, 2011 (in Chinese).
5. Kui Liu, Xiangqian Liang, Xiaolin Li. Concurrent signature scheme constructed by identity-based ring signcryption[J]. Journal of Computer Applications, 2013, 33(5):1386-1390 (in Chinese).
6. Chengqiang Huang. Research on Tor-based Construction Technique for Backward Anonymous Channels[D]. Xidian University, 2014 (in Chinese).
7. Xin Liu, Neng Wang. Research on Anonymous Communication Based on Tor Network[D], Shanghai: East China Normal University, 2011 (in Chinese).
8. Yue Han, Tianbo Lu. Tor Hidden Service Scaling[J]. software, 2016(2) (in Chinese).
9. Qi Liang, Shiti Li. Design Principles and Implementation Analysis of Anonymous network Tor[J]. Information & Communications, 2016(3):130-131 (in Chinese).
10. Ling Z, Luo J, Yu W, et al. 1 Extensive Analysis and Large-Scale Empirical Evaluation of Tor Bridge Discovery[J]. Proceedings-IEEE INFOCOM, 2015, 26(7):2381-2389.
11. Eltschinger S, Loewith R. TOR Complexes and the Maintenance of Cellular Homeostasis.[J]. Trends in Cell Biology, 2016, 26(2):148-159.
12. Sankar S, Chopra R, Xu W, et al. Identification of Lkb1 Mutation as a Predictive Biomarker for Sensitivity to Tor Kinase Inhibitors: US, EP2992878[P]. 2016.

Social Relationship Discovery Via Call Records

Wen-Zhe ZHAO [1,a], Ping-Jian ZHANG [2,b]

[1]School Of Software Engineering, South China University of Technology, Guangzhou, China
[2]School Of Software Engineering, South China University of Technology, Guangzhou, China
[a]392767725@qq.com, [b]pjzhang@scut.edu.cn,

Abstract: Telecom users constitute a huge, but relatively sparse social network. Community discovery has been a research topic of data mining. Traditional algorithms are greatly influenced by outliers. This paper presents a new algorithm based on social triangle theory. Experiments show that the new algorithm is effective.

1 Introduction

Short messages and call records are an important part of social media network. One needs to dig out the various social relations among users or the behavior habit of the users from the call and SMS records, to develop more suitable pricing or business package politics for users, and to provide users with better service to attract more users.

To achieve the above objectives, the community partition of telecommunication users is a prospective direction. Before the birth of Internet, people began to study the structure of networked community, such as early biomedical research on the protein structure [1]. The division of community structure is closely related to the segmentation of images in computer science and the hierarchical clustering in sociology [2]. This paper utilizes the idea of social triangle theory and proposes a community discovery algorithm based on the improved triangle theory, and designs and conducts some experiments to demonstrate its effectiveness.

2 Related Work

2.1 Hierarchical Cluster Algorithm

Here we will introduce the splitting algorithm. The most representative splitting algorithm in the community algorithm is GN algorithm[3]. The basic idea of the GN algorithm is to find the largest edge in the network, and delete it. GN algorithm steps are as following:

Step1: find the betweenness of the entire network.

Step2: find the edge which has the highest betweenness, remove it.

Step3: repeat the step 2 until all notes are degenerated into a community.

The GN algorithm solves the problem that the Laplace bisection algorithm must know the number of nodes in the community in advance. In order to get better clustering, Newman et al. proposed a standard for measuring the quality of community division-modularity. Modularity is used to represent the ratio of the number of edges connecting two different communities to all edges in the network. The specific formula of the modularity is shown as follow:

$$Q = \frac{1}{2m}\sum_{ij}(A_{ij} - P_{ij})\delta(C_i, C_j) \qquad (1)$$

where m represents the sum of the number of edges in the network. A_{ij} represents the value of the i-th row and the j-th column element in the adjacency matrix. The matrix P is an adjacency matrix used to store the relationship between the original nodes, and P is the node i and j correspond to the value of the element ij. If the two nodes belong to the same community, ie $c_i = c_j$, then $\delta(ci, cj) = 1$, otherwise $\delta(ci, cj) = 0$.

In the pseudo-random network mentioned above, when the nodes i, j point to each other, said node i, j connected. Assuming that the degree of the two nodes in the network (including the out-degree and in-degree) were k_i and k_j. For the network with m sides, we can define $p_i = \frac{k_i}{2m}$ as the connection probability of i to j. $p_j = \frac{k_j}{2m}$ as the connection probability of j to i. Define any element in P is $P_{ij} = 2mp_ip_j = \frac{k_ik_j}{2m}$, then the Q can be rewritten as following:

$$Q = \frac{1}{2m}\sum_{ij}(A_{ij} - \frac{k_ik_j}{2m})\delta(C_i, C_j) \qquad (2)$$

According to the modularity theory, we can see that the closer the Q is to 1, the more obvious the community structure is, and the Q found in the actual network community is often located between 0.3 and 0.7 [4].

3 Community Discovery Alogorithm Based On Improved Triangle Theory

3.1 Triangle Theory

In real society, the relationship among people is complicated, for example, A and B are good friends, B and C are also good friends, so are C and A. Thus, the relationship among them constitutes a triangle shown as below.

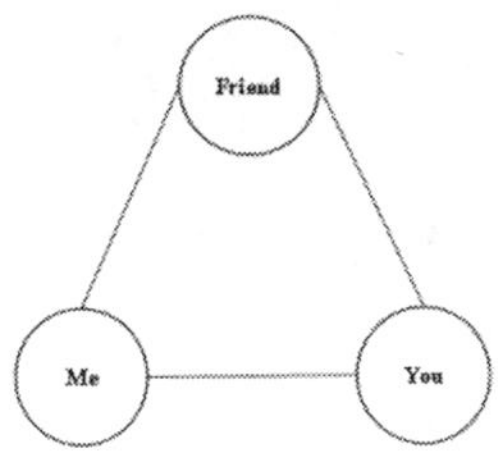

Figure 1. Simple social triangular structure diagram.

For members of the same social triangle, we can classify them as a unified community. Since there is such a social triangular relationship exists in the network, the network diagram given in the above can be extended to build a complex display society, as shown in Figure 2.

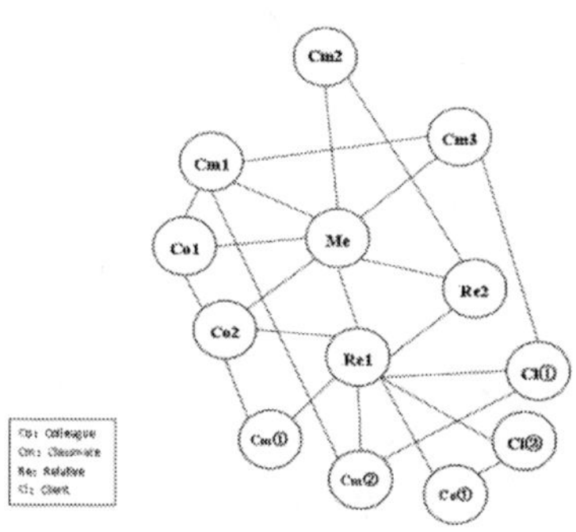

Figure 2. Complex social triangle group structure diagram

4 Design Of Triangle Community Division Algorithm

4.1 The Initial Community To Determine

We first determine the threshold ε of the good acquaintance, and then find out all the links and the similarity between nodes. Points with similarities larger than ε are grouped into a triangular group as the initial community.

4.2 The Algorithm Flow

Algorithm 2: Community Discovery Algorithm Based on Triangle Theory

Input: The structure of social network (diagram)
Output: Each community and the members of community
Steps:
//Step1: Find the initial triangular group.
Set ε = value;
for every node v_k in V **do**
  if v_k can make a triangle with other 2 nodes (v_i, v_j) (or more nodes)
  then
   generate new cluster_ID;
   insert v_k, v_i, v_j ......into queue Q_k
  else insert v_k into queue Q_{res}
  delete v_k form V;
until every node was assigned.
//Step2: Traverse all the initial societies and merge the initial communities containing the public triangles;
for j1=0 to k-1 **do**
  for j2=j1+1 to k
   if count $(v(Qj1 \cap Qj2)) >= 3$
    Merge (Q_{j1}, Q_{j2})
//Step3: To find structure-accessible point which is not distributed based on the new community composition obtained by step2
for every node v in Q_k do
  for every node u in Q_{res};
   if max($v \rightarrow u$)
    assign u to Q_k which most similar to u;
  delete u form Q_{res};

5 Experimental Design and Result

5.1 Experiment Result and Analysis

The algorithm designed in this paper is based on the clustering theory. The calculation process of this paper is actually a complex network clustering process, in the process of trying to find the optimal clustering results for the known clustering structure data We often use the

DOI: 10.1051/itmconf/20171204019

accuracy rate, recall rate and F value to evaluate the effect of clustering [6].

Table 1. Accuracy and recall rate analysis table

	Assigned correctly	Assigned wrongly
Detected	T1	F1
Undetected	T2	F2

1) The first step is to perform an initial triangular search in all nodes. In the second step, the upper triangular group is merged and the members of the triangle are expanded by searching for the structural community as the initial community. Finally, three societies along with two outliers are detected. Since one of the three societies contains only three nodes, the three nodes are treated as incorrectly assigned nodes when calculating the accuracy rate. In this test, the similarity threshold is chosen to be 0.1. The final result is shown in table 2.

Table 2. clustering based on triangle improved algorithm result

Clustering Based on Triangle Improved Algorithm						
category	pi	pj	pi∩pj	Accuracy rate	Recall rate	F value
Associa-tio n1	15	16	15	1	0.938	0.968
Associa-tio n2	14	18	14	1	0.778	0.875
The average				1	0.858	0.922

Where pi represents the number of algorithm allocations and pj represents the number of original network members, pi∩pj represents the number of members of the algorithm that are overlapped with the original association.

The GN algorithm result is shown in table 3.

Table 3. GN algorithm clustering result

Clustering GN algorithm clustering						
category	pi	pj	pi∩pj	Accuracy rate	Recall rate	F value
Associa-t ion1	16	16	16	1	1	1
Associa-t ion2	13	18	13	1	0.722	0.839
The average				1	0.861	0.92

In the US political book network dataset, The similarity threshold is chosen to be 0.3 in this test. In this experiment, the algorithm proposed in this paper divides the whole network into five communities, and the GN algorithm divides into six communities, where the nodes with lower coverage are regarded as outliers. The specific experimental results are shown in Table 4 and Table 5.

Table 4. Clustering based on triangle improved algorithm result

Clustering Based on Triangle Improved Algorithm						
category	p_i	p_j	pi∩pj	Accuracy rate	Recall rate	F value
Associ-ation1	8	13	14	0.500	0.308	0.381
Associ-ation2	40	49	35	0.875	0.714	0.787
Associ-ation3	36	43	32	0.889	0.744	0.810
The average				0.755	0.589	0.659

Table 5. GN algorithm clustering result

Clustering GN algorithm clustering result						
category	pi	pj	pi∩pj	Accuracy rate	Recall rate	F value
Association1	7	13	3	0.429	0.231	0.300
Association2	45	49	41	0.911	0.837	0.872
Association3	42	43	35	0.833	0.814	0.824
The average				0.724	0.627	0.665

The results are depicted as follows:

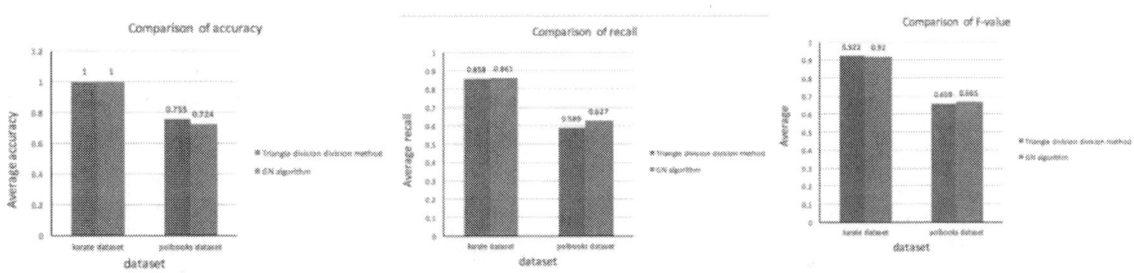

Figure 1. Comparison of Different Parameter of Triangle Sociology and GN Algorithm in Two Data Sets

Combining the above results with GN algorithm, it can be seen that the algorithm designed in this paper can reach the level of traditional excellent community division algorithm.

6 The Application Of Triangle Algorithm In Telecommunication Network Division

In the experiment, about 20,000 call records among 524 users are extracted. The triangular community division algorithm and the GN algorithm are compared and analyzed respectively. The Dunn index is picked to evaluate the effect of clustering[5], whose expression is as formula.

$$D = \min_{i=1,\dots,g}\{\min_{j=i+1,\dots,g}(\frac{d(C_i,C_j)}{\max_{k=1,\dots,g}(diam(C_k))})\} \tag{3}$$

Where $d(C_i,C_j)=\min_{x\in C_i,y\in C_j}\{d(x,y)\}$ represents the distance between two different clusters, $diam(C_i)=\max_{x,y\in C_i}\{d(x,y)\}$ indicates the maximum distance between members of the cluster. The larger the D is, the larger the cluster is. The results are shown in Figures 7.

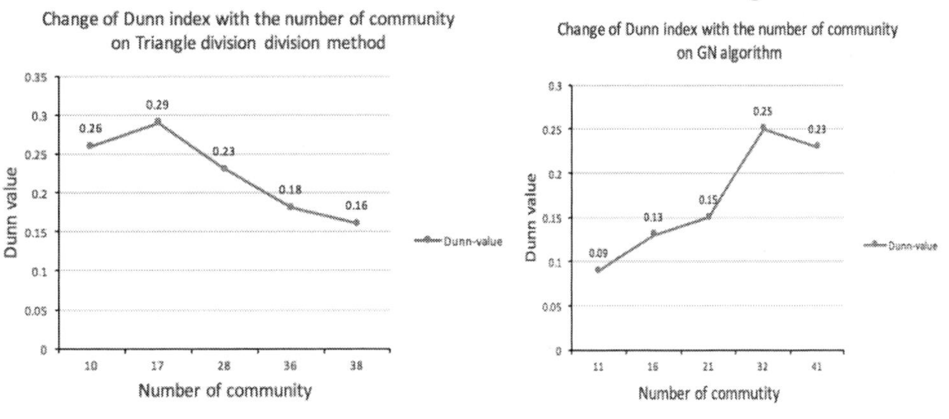

Figure 2. Diffrent method Dunn index changes with the number of community

The maximum value of Dunn index is 0.29, which is larger than the maximum value of Dunn index of traditional GN algorithm. This indicates that the triangular community division algorithm is better than GN algorithm when the number of community is kept at a certain value.

As a traditional community network division algorithm, GN algorithm for outlier detection and the capacity of processing telecom networks is relatively weak. The triangulation division algorithm is mainly based on the similarity of triangular relationships among node. If a user can not build a triangular relationship with other users, none of the structural reachable point of the user appears in a triangular group. The algorithm will treat it as an outlier. Due to the exclusion of a large number of outliers, the maximum value of the Dunn index of the triangulation method is higher than that of the GN algorithm, and the clustering efficiency is better than the GN algorithm.

Summary

In the paper, existing community discovery algorithms are reviewed. Then, a triangle community division algorithm based the social triangular theory is proposed and implemented, and validated using standard data set. The new algorithm is then compared to the GN algorithm using the telecommunication call record data set. Experimental results show that the new is algorithm is more effective.

Acknowledgement

This work is supported by the Guangzhou Science Technology and Innovation Commission (Grant No. 201604010099).

References

1. Li Haiyan. Study on Protein Folding with Complex Networks [D]. Beijing: Beijing University of Posts and Telecommunications, 2009, 18-21.
2. Girvan M, Newman M E J.Community structure in social and biological networks [J]. Proc Natl Acad Sci USA, 2002, 99:7821-7826.
3. ZHENG Feng-ni.Study on discovery method of network community based on node similarity clustering in complex network [J] .Computer & Modernization, 2013,5: 231-233.
4. PAN Gao-feng, WANG Xing-hua et al.Application of community discovery method in complex network partition identification [J]. Power System Protection and Control, 2013,41 (13): 116.
5. LUO Zhi-gang, DING Fan, et al.New Advances in Research on Complex Network Community Discovery Algorithm [J].Journal of National University of Defense Technology, 2011,33 (1): 47-51.
6. Fan Ming, Meng Xiaofeng. Concept and Technology of Data Mining [M]. Machinery Industry Press, 2012.7.
7. Pei Weidong, Xia Wei, et al.Analysis of Evolutionary Model for a Class of Triangular Structure Dynamic Complex Networks [J]. Journal of University of Science and Technology of China, 10 (11), 2010.
8. Lancichinetti A, Fortunato S, Kertesz J. Detecting the overlapping and hierarchical community structure of complex networks[EB/OL].2009.
9. Lü Tianyang, Zheng Weimin et al. Evaluation Index of Weighted Complex Network Society and Its Discovery Algorithm [J], Acta Physica Sinica, 2012,61 (21).
10. Statistical.Pattern.Recognition, Andrew.R.Webb, Keith.D..Copsey, 3ed, Wiley, 2011: 543-545.

Using Non-symmetry and Anti-packing Representation Model for Object Detection

Fei Xiao[1], Jin-Wen Tian[1], Guang-Wei Wang[2], Chang-Qing Chen[3,a]

[1]*School of Automation, Huazhong University of Science and Technology, Wuhan, 430074, China;*
[2]*School of Computer and Information Science, Hubei Engineering University, Xiaogan, 432000, China*
[3]*School of Software, Huazhong University of Science and Technology, Wuhan, 430074, China;*
[a]*ccqclczy@163.com*

Abstract: In this paper, we present a non-symmetry and anti-packing object pattern representation model (NAM) for object detection. A set of distinctive sub-patterns (object parts) is constructed from a set of sample images of the object class; object pattern are then represented using sub-patterns, together with spatial relations observed among the sub-patterns. Many feature descriptors can be used to describe these sub-patterns. he NAM model codes the global geometry of object category, and the local feature descriptor of sub-patterns deal with the local variation of object. By using Edge Direction Histogram (EDH) features to describe local sub-pattern contour shape within an image, we found that richer shape information is helpful in improving recognition performance. Based on this representation, several learning classifiers are used to detect instances of the object class in a new image. The experimental results on a variety of categories demonstrate that our approach provides successful detection of the object within the image.

1 Introduction

In this paper we consider the problem of detecting and localizing object of a generic category, such as horse or car in static images. This is a difficult problem because objects in a category can vary greatly in shape and appearance. Variation arise not only from changes in illumination, occlusion, background clutter and view point, but also due to non-rigid deformations, and intra-class variation in shape and other visual properties among objects in a rich category.

How do we deal with the variation, especial the intra-class and pose variability of object? Most of the current researches have focused on modeling object variability, including several kinds of deformable template models [1, 2], and a variety of part-based, fragment-based models [3,4,5,6,7,8,9]. There are several possibilities to represent object classes. A star shape model [10, 11] can be easily trained and evaluated in contrast to the constellation model [12] or complex graphical models [13]. It allows using as many parts as required, since the complexity scales linearly. Moreover, this model is flexible enough to deal with large variations in object shape and appearance of rigid and articulated structures.

The method of Leibe*etal*.[14] give a highly flexible learned representation for object shape that can combine the information observed on different training examples. Opelt, *et al.*[9] explore a similar geometric representation to that of Leibe*et al.* [14] but use only the boundaries of the object, both internal and external (silhouette).

The pictorial structure models [5, 15] represent an object by a collection of parts arranged in a deformable configuration, where the deformable configuration is represented by spring-like connections between pairs of parts. Crandall *et al.* propose k-fans model [16] to study the extent to which additional spatial constraints among parts are actually helpful in detection and localization. The patchwork of parts model from [6] is similar, but it explicitly considers how the appearance model of overlapping parts interacts to define a dense appearance model for images. It is proved that adding spatial constraints gives better performance.

Another way is to develop a feature set [17, 18, 19, 20] that is robust to variable local shape and the wide range of poses. Lowe [17] proposed a scale invariant feature transform (SIFT), which combines a scale invariant region detector and a descriptor based on the gradient distribution in the detected regions. Geometric histogram [21] and shape context[18] compute a histogram describing the edge distribution in a region. These descriptors were successfully used, for example, for shape recognition of drawings for which edges are reliable features. HOG [22] is similar to that of edge orientation histograms[19, 20], scale-invariant feature transform descriptors [17], and shape contexts [18], but differs in that it on a dense grid of uniformly spaced cells and uses overlapping local contrast normalization for improved accuracy.

Our approach has two methods to deal with the variation of object, both global and local. Firstly, we propose a non-symmetry and anti-packing object pattern representation model (NAM) to represent an object category. The NAM object model consist of several local parts, we call it sub-patterns. The model codes the global geometry of generic visual object categories with spatial relations linking object pattern to sub-patterns.

Secondly, the proposed descriptors of sub-pattern can deal with the local variation of object. Shape based information have been selected as a key component of local features. After reviewing exist edge based descriptors, we show experimentally that grids of Histograms of Edge Direction (G-HED) descriptors significantly outperform existing feature sets for shape class detection. Contour shape have been used in object recognition to a certain extent: Shotton*et al.*[23] and Opelt*et al.* [9] use boundary fragments to represent an object and use boundary matching method to detect object.

The proposed framework can be applied to any object that consists of distinguishable parts arranged in a relatively fixed spatial configuration. Our experiments are performed on images of side views of horses; therefore, this object class will be used as a running example throughout the paper to illustrate the ideas and techniques involved.

The rest of the paper is organized as follow. Section 2 describes the non-symmetry and anti-packing model. Section 3 introduces the sub-pattern descriptor. Section 4 and 5 presentthe framework of our approach. In section 6, experiments on real images show that the model is effective for object detection.

2 Description of Non-symmetry and Anti-packing Pattern Representation Model

The non-symmetry and anti-packing object pattern representation model (NAM) is an anti-packing problem. The idea of the NAM can be described as follows: Given a packed pattern and n predefined sub-patterns $\{p_1, p_2, \cdots, p_n\}$, pick up these sub-patterns from the packed pattern and then represent the packed pattern with the combination of these sub-patterns.

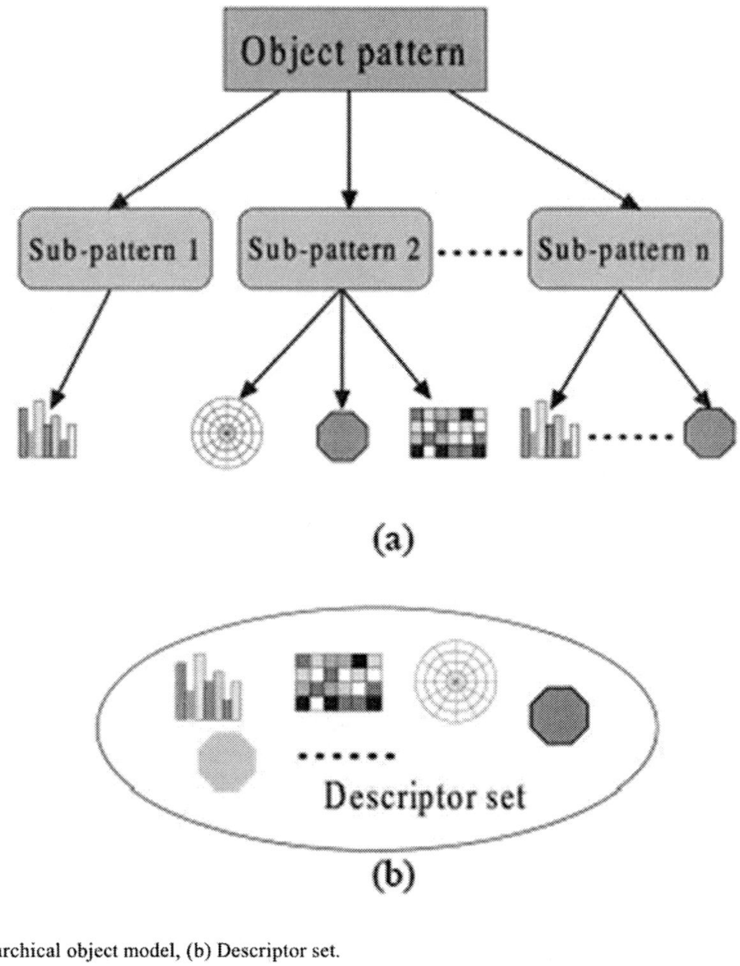

Figure 1..(a)Our hierarchical object model, (b) Descriptor set.

The object pattern representation method is a hierarchical model that codes the global geometry and local appearance of generic visual object categories with spatial relations linking object pattern (top level) to sub-patterns (second level), and local feature cues linking sub-pattern (second level) and local feature class (third

DOI: 10.1051/itmconf/20171204020

level). See Fig. (1) (a), the object pattern is at the top level, the second and third level is the sub-patterns and local feature descriptors of sub-pattern respectively. Fig. (1) (b) presents the sub-pattern descriptor.

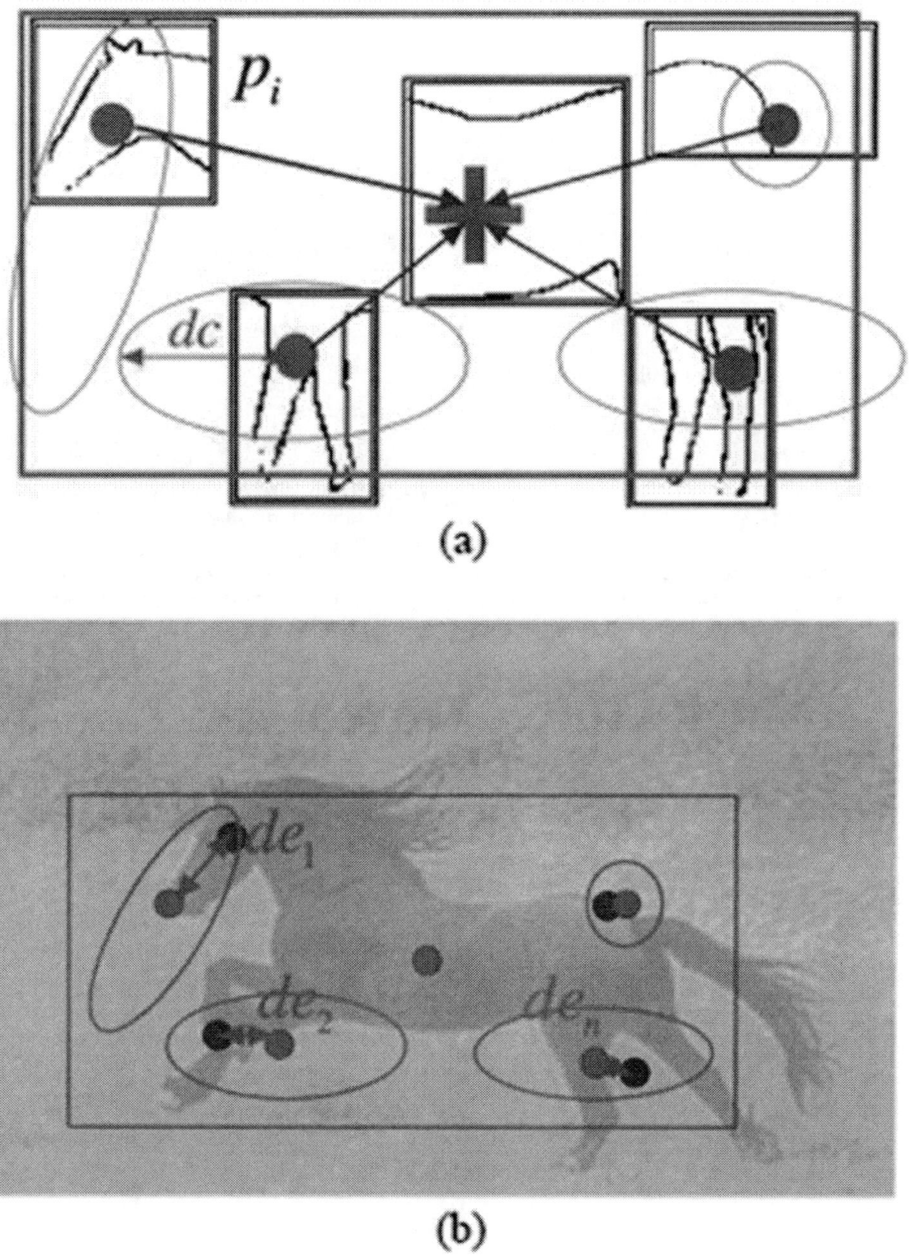

Figure 2. (a)Global spatial structure. Sub-patterns p_1 (black box) are arranged within the bounding box (red). Small red circles show the optimal position and blue ellipses the spatial uncertaintydc. (b)To code the pose variation of a side view horse using global spatial structure. Green arrows show the deviation distancede.

Global Spatial relation: The spatial relations between top level and the second level can be described by global spatial structure. Fig. (2)presents an example of the global spatial structure for horse class.

Local feature encoding: Sub-patterns can be described by a rich set of cues (such as shape, color and texture) inside them. Between second level and third level, we capture different sub-pattern cues from the sub-pattern window, each type of cue is encoded by using an appropriate descriptor, and these encoded information concatenated into a feature vector. In this paper, we use shape information to represent the sub-patterns and edge direction histogram (EDH) to describe the shape information. The detail of encoding sub-pattern feature have presented in Section 3.

Here, we use an object pattern Γto describe an object

category. The object pattern that consists of n sub-patterns p_i can be defined by the following expression:

$$\Gamma = \bigcup_{i=1}^{n} p_i(x, r, de, w, \phi(x,r) | \{f_1, f_2, \cdots, f_{m_i}\})$$

Where x is a two-dimensional vector specifying an "anchor" position for sub-pattern p_i relative to the object pattern position; $r$represent the scale of the sub-pattern; de is a deviation vector; w shows the discriminative weight of the sub-pattern. $\phi(x,r))$ denote a feature vector for the i^{th}sub-pattern and $f_j(1 \leq j \leq m_i)$ is one of the feature descriptors.

The non-symmetry relationship between sub-patterns describes the global structure information of object category and is designed to decouple variations due to affine warps, pose variability and other forms of shape deformations. Anti-packing is a procedure that finding sup-patterns in query images, combining them into an object pattern and classifying.

3 Sub-pattern Description

Sub-pattern can be described by a rich set of cues inside them, such as shape, color and texture. Based on the observation that for a wide variety of common object categories, shape [9, 24, 25] matters more than local appearance [26, 27]. In this paper we use shape information as a key component for object detection.

Since edge points are related to shape information closely, the local shape can often be characterized rather well by the distribution of edge directions. The proposed descriptors are inspired by edge orientation histogram [28, 29, 30, 31, 32], Histograms of Oriented Gradients [22, 33] and shape contexts [18]. They use only edge pixel counts with the direction histogram and they are computed on dense overlapping grids that make the performance so affect.

The implementation of our descriptor combines many of these ideas from early work and more recent contributions.

We first obtain the sub-pattern edge map by using a Canny edge detector and remove spurious edges using a grouping technique inspired by Mahamudet al. [34].

Next, a sub-pattern window is subdivided into a$\kappa\times\kappa$grid ("cell"), for each cell accumulating a local 1-D histogram of edge direction over the pixels of the edge within the cell. This step is very similar to region description in [35].

Finally, we accumulate a measure of local histogram over somewhat larger spatial regions ("blocks") and use the results to normalize all of the cells in the block. We refer to the normalized descriptor blocks as grid of Histogram of Edge Direction (G-HED) descriptors.

We now give details of our G-HED implementations and the effects of the various choices on detector performance.

In our experiments reported, we usually use square G-HED's, i.e., $\kappa\times\kappa$ grids block of $\eta\times\eta$ pixel cells each containing direction binsγ, where$\kappa\eta,\gamma$ are parameters. The sub-pattern window is 64×64 pixel and it is divided into 4×4 grid, e.g.,$\kappa = 4$. The various choice of block size ζ is also very important for detector performance. In our experiments, 2×2 grid blocks perform best for sub-pattern detection. The stride (block overlap) is fixed at half of the block size (e.g. a cell).

The edge pixel direction is generated by using two 3×3 masks of Sobel operators, e.g., vertical edge mask and horizontal edge mask. For each edge pixel$p_{(i,j)}$, its edge vector can be represented with the vector $D = \{dx_{i,j}, dy_{i,j}\}$, where $dx_{i,j}$ and $dy_{i,j}$ are obtained by using the vertical edge mask and horizontal edge mask on the location $p_{(i,j)}$ of sub-pattern window respectively. Each edge pixel direction is calculated with the equation$\theta_{i,j} = \tan^{-1}\left(\frac{dy_{i,j}}{dx_{i,j}}\right)$. The direction bins are evenly spaced over ("unsigned") or ("signed"). Using 9 bins (e.g. 20° per bin) can obtain better performance.

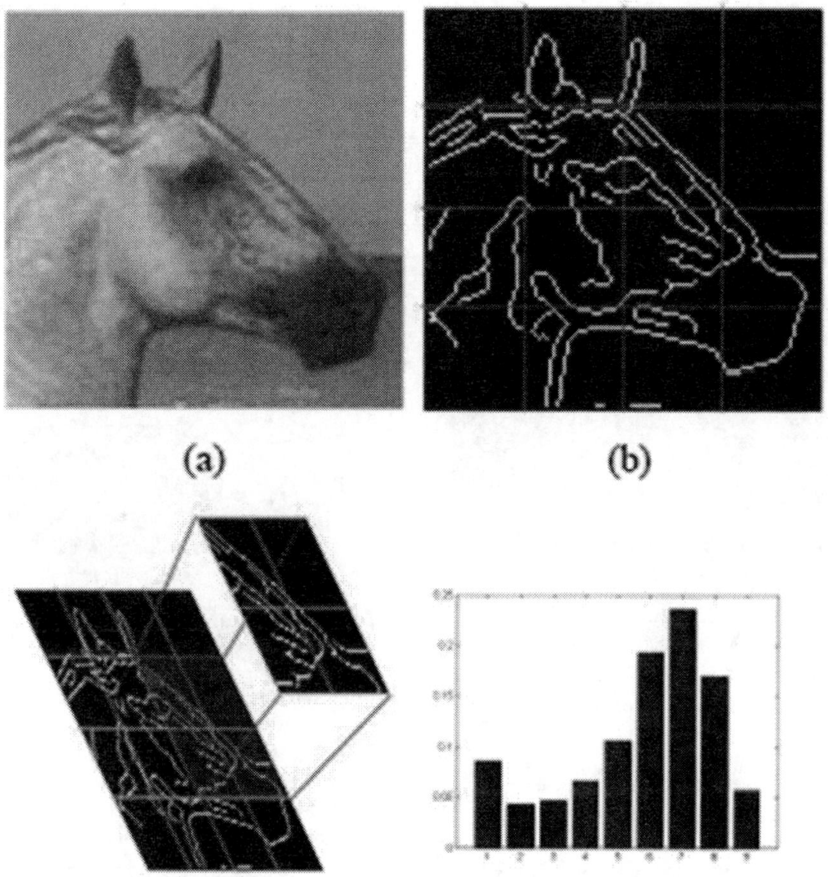

Figure 3. The contour shape descriptor. (a)Original image, (b)Edge map, (c) 4×4 grid on edge map, (d)Edge direction histogram of one block containing 4 grids.

A global direction histogram of a sub-pattern would average too much spatial information to infer pose. Here, we adapt the method of [35] for describing sub-patterns. A sub-pattern is subdivided evenly its bounding box into $n \times n$ grid, and accumulating a local 1-D histogram of edge direction over the edge pixels within the 2×2 grid, as illustrated in Fig.(3). In the experiments reported, we use$n = 4$. The combination of these histograms then represents the descriptor.

4 Detection

The pipeline of our detection framework as follow: first, training a classifier for each sub-pattern. Next, using one classifierto detect hypothesis of object location, i.e., initial detection. After that, a verification scheme is applied to the hypothesis to obtain final detection.

4.1 Learning Classifiers

The task of learning is to establish n classifier $\{Cf_1(\cdot), Cf_2(\cdot), \cdots, Cf_n(\cdot)\}$ for an object pattern with n sub-patterns; each classifier is corresponding to a sub-pattern. Take a classifier for example, given a set of training image windows labeled as positive (object) or negative (nonobjective), each image window is converted into a feature vector as described above. These vectors are then fed as input to a supervised learning algorithm that learns to classify an image window as member or nonmember of the object pattern. In our experiments, two-class LIBSVM had been used for classification (For details of LIBSVM see [36]).

4.2 Detection Hypothesis Using One of the Learned Classifiers

Sliding window classification [25] is a simple, effective technique for object detection. The initial detection problem is to determine whether the query image contains instances of sub-pattern and where it is. Having trained a SVM window classifier, we can detect and localize novel object instances in a test image using a simple sliding-window mechanism [22, 37]. Here, we select the jth sub-pattern $p_j$as an initial detected sup-pattern. The classifier $Cf(\cdot)$ corresponding to sub-pattern p_j is applied to fix-sized windows at various locations in the feature pyramid, each window being represented as a feature vector $\phi(x, r)$, where x specifies the position

DOI: 10.1051/itmconf/20171204020

of the window in the image, and r specifies the level of the image in pyramid. The following expression represents the classifier $Cf_j(\cdot)$ at one of the sliding windows.

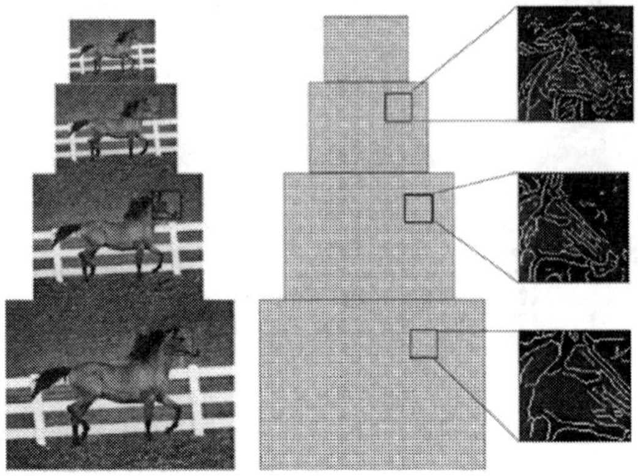

Figure 4. Image pyramid (Left), feature pyramid (Middle) and exampleof feature windows (Right).

A threshold α is introduced to determine whether the window is positive or contain an instance. If $s_{p_j} > \alpha$, then,the window is positive, $h_j = (x, r)$ is a hypothesis and we put the h_j into the sub-pattern hypothesis set $H = \{h_{j,1}, h_{j,1}, \cdots, h_{j,k}\}$. Lowering the threshold increases the correct detections but also increases the false positives; raising the threshold has the opposite effect. In our experiment, we use$\alpha = 0.5$.

The feature pyramid illustrated in Fig.(4), which is similar to [33], specifies a feature map for a finite number of scales in a fixed range. In practice we compute feature pyramid by computing a standard image pyramid via repeated soothing and subsampling, and then computing a feature map from each level of the image pyramid. A test image is scaled to sizes ranging from 0.48 to 1.2 times the original size, each scale differing from the next by a factor of 1.2.

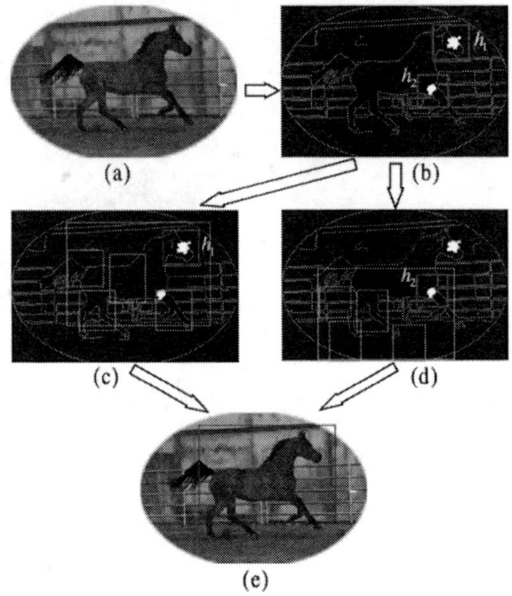

Figure 5. Initial detection and verification. (a)Query image, (b) Hypothesis set of initial detection $\{h_1, h_2\}$, (c)Process of verification for h_1,(d)Process of verification forh_2 and (e)Final result.

5 Verification

These hypothesis are then refined through a verification scheme to obtain final detection result. Fig. (5) introduces the process. The first step is to generate a hypothesis h_Γ of the object pattern Γ by applying a transformation $T(\cdot)$ to $h_j$andΓ. Fig.(5) (b) illustrate the transformation procedure.$h_j$is one of hypothesis in set H . The transformation $T(\cdot)$ exploits the rough localization provided by the spatial relationship between the sub-patterns and the object pattern. Then the transformation for the hypothesis h_j and object patternΓ is characterized by:

$$Sp_i = Cf_i(\emptyset(L_i))$$

Where $L_i = (x_i, r_i, de_i)(1 \le i \le n)$ is the expected location of sub-patterns besideh_j. This transformation provides not only position x_i, scale estimation r_i but also deviation de_i of sub-patterns in the object pattern.

Next, classifier$Cf_i(\cdot)$ is applied to the corresponding window at location L_i.

Where s_{p_j} is to determine that whether location L_i contains sub-pattern p_j . The overall verification score$S_{ver}(h_\Gamma)$for object pattern$\Gamma$is a combination of the sub-patterns detection result s_{p_i}:

$$S_{ver}(h_\Gamma) = \sum_{i=1}^{n} (w_i \cdot s_{p_i} - de_i)$$

wherew_i is the discriminative weight of sub-pattern p_i , de_i is the deviation of sub-pattern from the optimal position. The verification of object pattern was illustrated in Fig.(5)(c) and (d). When the value of the S_{ver} is above a threshold β, the hypotheses position $h_\Gamma$contains an instance of the object pattern.

6 Experiments

We present extensive experimental evaluation, involving several existing data sets covering eight diverse shape-based object classes for a total of more than 900 test images.

6.1 Evaluation Criteria

In this section, we investigate the performance of our system under the PASCAL criterion. For a detection to be marked as correct, its inferred bounding box b_{inf} must agree with the ground truth bounding boxb_{gt} based on an overlap criterion as $\frac{b_{inf} \cap b_{gt}}{b_{inf} \cup b_{gt}} \geq 0.5$. Each b_{gt} can match to only one b_{inf} , and so spurious detections of the same object count as false positives

Table 1. Performance of our detection system on INRIA horse data set, containing 170 positive images and 170 negative images.

β	No. of correctdetections TP	No. of falsedetections FP	RecallRTP/170	PrecisionPTP/(TP+FP)
20	152	110	0.8941	0.5802
30	138	107	0.8118	0.5633
40	130	98	0.7647	0.5702
50	126	86	0.7412	0.5942
60	121	74	0.7118	0.6205
80	110	53	0.6471	0.6748
100	103	45	0.6059	0.6959
120	87	39	0.5118	0.6905
150	67	26	0.3941	0.7204
180	41	14	0.2412	0.7455
210	23	7	0.1353	0.7667

Table 2. Performance of our detection system on WEIZMANN horse data set.

β	No. of correctdetections TP	No. of falsedetections FP	RecallRTP/328	PrecisionPTP/(TP+FP)
20	299	36	0.9144	0.8925
30	294	34	0.8991	0.8963
40	289	31	0.8838	0.9031
50	283	28	0.8654	0.9099
60	266	24	0.8135	0.9172
80	229	17	0.7003	0.9309
100	206	11	0.6299	0.9493
120	185	8	0.5657	0.9585
150	149	6	0.4557	0.9612
180	106	4	0.3242	0.9636
210	62	2	0.1896	0.9688

When a detection system is put into practice, we are interested in knowing how many of the objects it detects, and how often the detections it makes are false. This trade-off is captured more accurately by a variation of the recall-precision curve, where

$$Recall = \frac{TP}{nP}$$

$$Precision = \frac{TP}{TP + FP}$$

whereTP is the number of true positives, FP is the number of false positives and nP the total number of positives in data set. The first quantity of interest, namely, the proportion of objects that are detected, is given by the recall. The second quantity of interest, namely, the number of false detections relative to the total number of detections made by the system, is given by

$$1 - Precision = \frac{FP}{TP + FP}$$

Plotting recall versus (1-precision), therefor, expresses the trade-off.

Performance is also evaluated by plotting detection rate (DR) versus the incidence of false positives (false positives per image (FPPI)) while varying the detection threshold, where

$$Detection\ rate = \frac{TP}{nP}$$

$$Fals\ positives\ per\ image = \frac{FP}{nN}$$

Where nN is the total number of images in data set. Comparison between different methods is mainly based on two points on the DR/FPPI plot, at 0.3 and 0.4 FPPI.

6.2 INRIA Horse and Weizmann-Shotton Horse

INRIA horse [38]. This challenging data set consists of 170 images containing one or more horses, seen from the side, and 170 images without horses. Horses appear at several scales and against cluttered backgrounds.

Weizmann-Shotton horse [23]. Shotton*et al.*propose another horse detection data set, composed of 327 positive images containing exactly one horse each and 328 negative images.The INRIA and Weizmann are very challenging data sets of horse images, containing different breeds, colors, and textures, with varied articulations, lighting conditions, and scales.

We present our results in Table 1 and 2. The different detection results are obtained by varying the threshold parameter β as described in Section 4.3.

We compare our method with Dalal*etal.*[22] and Ferrari *etal.* [25] on the INRIA and Weizmann horses data sets. We randomly select 100 training images per category in Caltech101 and Google images to train classifiers. Dalal's method is currently the state of the art in human detection and has proven very competitive on other classes as well. The object detection method by Ferrari *etal.* achieved considerable gains on many object categories. Like ours, their object detectors are based on sliding a window subdivided into tile but uses different feature descriptors.

The results are displayed in Fig.(6). Our detector achieves a substantially higher performance than HOG. Compared to [25] our method achieved same fine performance. However, their criterion (a detected bounding box is considered correct if it overlaps$\geq$ 20%) is rather loose, and it might consider as correct also rather inaccurate detections.

6.3 ETHZ Shape Classes

The ETHZ shape database(collected by V. Ferrari *et al.*[39]) consists of five distinctive shape categories (apple logos, bottles, giraffes, mugs and swans) in a total of 255 images. All categories have significant intra-class variations, scale changes, and illumination changes. Moreover, many objects are surrounded by extensive background clutter and have interior contours.

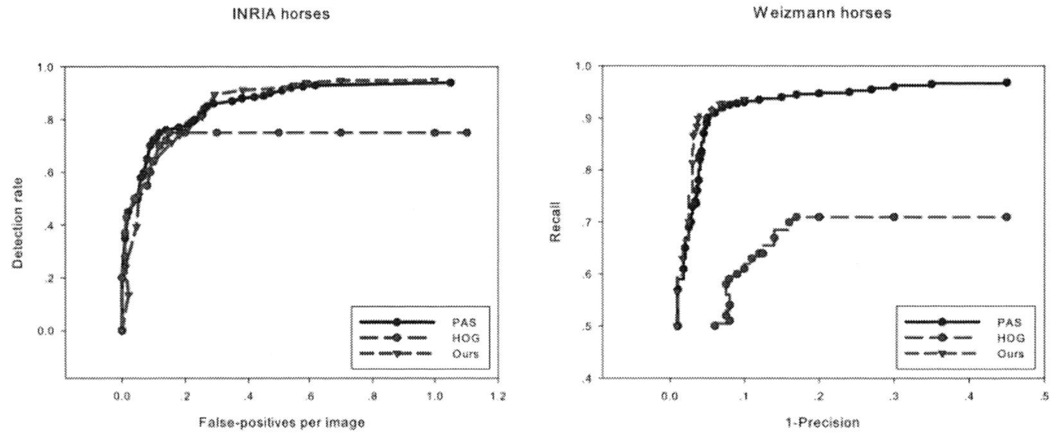

Figure 6..Comparison between our detector, Ferrari *et al*: [25] PAS-based one and Dalal*et al*: [22] HOG-based one.

Table 3. Comparison of detection performance with [Ferrari et al., 2007] on the ETHZ shapedata set at 0.4 FPPI.

	Apple	Bottle	Giraffe	Mug	Swan	average
Our	88.6	83.4	83.9	83.5	87.5	85.4
Fritz	89.9	76.8	90.5	82.7	84.0	84.8
Ferrari	83.2	83.2	58.5	83.6	75.4	76.8

We compare to [39] and [40]} on the ETHZ shape database. Experiments are conducted in 5-fold cross-validation. We split the entire set into half training and half test for each category, and average performance from 5 random splits is reported. This is consistent with the implementation in [39, 40] which reported the state-of-the art detection performance on this data set. Table 3 shows our comparison to [39] on each of the categories. Average over all categories we improve the performance of [39] by 8.6% to 85.4%. On apple logos, giraffes and swans, we improve the performance by 5.4, 25.3 and 12.1% respectively. On bottles and mugs, our approach performs comparable. We account the performance on the bottles and mugs to the shape which is less discriminant with respect to the background. As the data set was designed to test shape-based approaches, the improvements obtained by our approach underlines the versatility and adaptively of the hierarchical representation.

Figure.7.. Detections for INRIA and Weizmann horses data sets when the value of threshold is 50. In the middle row, the rightmost imageshows a missed detection.

7 Conclusion

We have proposed a non-symmetry and anti-packing object pattern representation model (NAM) to represent a object category. This model can effectively codes global structure of object. The object pattern model consists of several part sub-patterns. Each sub-pattern is represented by a rich set of image cues(shape, color and texture). One sub-pattern descriptor can incorporate several feature descriptors. We selected appropriate feature descriptor for the sub-pattern to deal with the local variation. In our work, the edge direction histogram descriptor introduced to describe the shape information of sub-patterns. Based on this representation, several learning classifiers were trained to detect sub-pattern instances. The proposed framework can be applied to any object category that consists of distinguishable parts arranged in a relatively fixed spatial configuration.

8 Conflict of Interest

This article content has no conflict of interest

Acknowledgement

The authors wish to acknowledge the support of the National Natural Science Funds of China under Grant No. 61370092, Natural Science Funds of Hubei Province under Grant No. 2013CFC005, and Hubei Engineering University Teaching Research Project (Grant No. 2015A38).

References

1. T.F. Cootes, G.J. Edwards, and C.J. Taylor.Active appearancemodels.IEEE Trans. Pattern Analysis and Machine Intelligence,pages 681–685, 6 2001.
2. J. Matthews and S. Baker. Active appearance models revisited.International Journal of Computer Vision, 63(6):135–164,2004.
3. R. Fergus, A. Perona, and A. Zisserman.A sparse object categorymodel for efficient learning and exhaustive recognition.In IEEE conf. on Computer Vision and Pattern Recognition,2005.
4. S. Agarwal, A. Awan, and D. Roth.Learning to detect objectsin images via a sparse, part-based representation.IEEE Trans.Pattern Analysis and Machine Intelligence, pages 1475–1490,2004.
5. P.F. Felzenszwalb and D.P. Huttenlocher.Pictorial structuresfor object recognition. International Journal of ComputerVision, pages 55–79, 2005.

6. Y. Amit and A. Trouve. Pop: Patchwork of parts models forobject recognition. International Journal of Computer Vision,pages 267–282, 2007.
7. L. Kyoung-Mi. Component-based face detection and verification.Pattern Recognition Letters, pages 200–214, 2008.
8. H. Schneiderman and T. Kanade. Object detection using thestatistics of parts. International Journal of Computer Vision,pages 151–177, 2004.
9. A. Opelt, A. Pinz, and A. Zisserman.A boundary-fragmentmodelfor object detection. In European conf. on Computer
10. Vision, 2006.
11. J. Shotton, A. Blake, and R. Cipolla.Contour-based learningfor object detection.In International conf. on Computer Vision,2005.
12. B. Leibe, E. Seeman, and B.Schiele.Pedestrian detection incrowded scenes. In IEEE conf. on Computer Vision and PatternRecognition, pages 878–885, 2005.
13. R. Fergus, P. Perona, and A. Zisserman. Object class recognitionby unsupervised scale-invariant learning. In IEEE conf.on Computer Vision and Pattern Recognition, pages 264–271,2003.
14. E. Sudderth, A. Torralba, W. T. Freeman, and A. Wilsky.Learning hierarchical models of scenes, objects, and parts.In International conf. on Computer Vision, pages 1331–1338,2005.
15. B. Leibe, A. Leonardis, and B. Schiele.Robust object detectionwith interleaved categorization and segmentation. InternationalJournal of Computer Vision, pages 259–289, 2008.
16. P. Felzenszwalb, D. McAllester, and D. Ramanan.A discriminativelytrained, multiscale, deformable part model. In IEEEconf. on Computer Vision and Pattern Recognition, pages 151–168, 2008.
17. D. Crandall, P. Felzenszwalb, and D. Huttenlocher. Spatialpriors for part-based recognition using statistical models.InIEEE conf. on Computer Vision and Pattern Recognition, 2005.
18. D.G. Lowe. Distinctive image features from scale-invariantkeypoints. International Journal of Computer Vision, 60(2):91–110, 2004.
19. S. Belongie, J.Malik, and J. Puzicha.Matching shapes. InInternational Conference on Computer Vision, pages 454-461,2001.
20. W. T. Freeman, K. Tanaka, J. Ohta, and K.kyuma. Computervision for computer games. In 2nd International Conferenceon Automatic Face and Gesture Recognition, pages 100–105,1996.
21. W. T. Freeman and M. Roth. Orientation histograms for handgestrue recognition.In Intel. Workshop on Automatic FaceandGesture-Recognition, pages 296–391, 1995.
22. A. Ashbrook, N. Thacker, P. Rockett, and C. Brown.Robustrecognition of scaled shapes using pairwise geometrichistograms. In Proc. Sixth British Machine Vision Conf., pages503–512, 1995.
23. N. Dalal and B. Triggs. Histgrams of oriented gradients forhuman detection.In IEEE conf. on Computer Vision andPattern Recognition, 2005.
24. J. Shotton, A. Blake, and R. Cipolla. Multi-scale categoricalobject recognition using contour fragments. IEEE Trans.Pattern Analysis and Machine Intelligence, 2008.
25. J. Sullivan, O. Danielsson, and S. Carlsson. Exploiting partbasedmodels and edge boundaries for object detection.InDigital Image computing, 2008.
26. V. Ferrari, L. Fevrier, F. Jurie, and C. Schmid. Groups of adjacent contour segments for object detection. IEEETransaction on MAMI, 2008.
27. G. Bouchard and B. Trigs.Hierarchical par-bbased visualobject categorization.In IEEE conf. on Computer Vision andPattern Recognition, 2005.
28. L. Zhu, Y. Chen, A. Yuille, andW. Freeman. Latent hierarchicalstructural learning for object detection.In IEEE conf. onComputer Vision and Pattern Recognition, 2010.
29. F. Mahmoudi and J. Shanbehzadeh. Image retrieval based onshape similarity by edge orientation autocorrelogram. PatternRecognition, pages 1725–1736, 2003.
30. D. Tao, X. Tang, X. Li, and X. Wu. Asymmetric bagging andrandom subspace for support vector machines-based relevancefeedback in image retrieval. IEEE Trans. Pattern Analysis andMachine Intelligence, pages 1088–1099, 2006.
31. T. Dacheng, T. Xiaoou, and L. Xuelong. Which components areimportant for interactive image searching? IEEE Transactionson Circuits and Systems for Video Technology, 2008.
32. G. Xinbo, X. Bing, T.Dacheng, and L. Xuelong. Imagecategorization: Graph edit distance + edge direction histogram.Pattern Recognition, pages 3179–3191, 2008.
33. K. Young-Woo and O. Il-Seok.Watermarking text documentimages using edge direction histograms. Pattern RecognitionLetters, pages 1243–1251, 2004.
34. Pedro F. Felzenszwalb, Ross B. Girshick, D. McAllester, andD.Ramanan. Object detection with discriminatively trained partbased models. IEEE Trans. Pattern Analysis and MachineIntelligence, 2010.
35. S. Mahamud, L. R. Williams, K. K. Thornber, and K. Xu.Segmentation of multiple salient closed contours from realimages.IEEE Transaction on MAMI, 2003.
36. ChunhuiGu, J. J. Lim, P. Arbelaez, and J. alik. Recognitionusing regions.In IEEE conf. on Computer Vision and PatternRecognition, pages 1030–1037, 2009.
37. Chih-Chung Chang and Chih-Jen Lin. Libsvm: a libraryfor support vector machines. Software available athttp://www.csie.ntu.edu.tw/_cjlin/libsvm, 2001.
38. P. Viola and M.jones.Rapid object detection using a boostedcascade of simple features. In IEEE conf. on Computer Visionand Pattern Recognition, pages 1–8, 2001.

DOI: 10.1051/itmconf/20171204020

39. A. Opelt, A. Pinz, M. Fussenegger, and P. Auer.Generic objectrecognition with boosting.IEEE Trans. Pattern Analysis andMachine Intelligence, pages 516–431, 2006.
40. V. Ferrari, L. Fevrier, and C. Schmid. Accurate object detectionwith deformable shape models learnt from images. In IEEEconf. on Computer Vision and Pattern Recognition, pages 564–571, 2007.
41. M. Fritz and B. Schiele. Decomposition, dscovery and detectionof visual categories using topic models. In IEEE conf. onComputer Vision and Pattern Recognition, pages Part I:511–518, 2008

DOI: 10.1051/itmconf/20171204021

Organizational Resilience: The Theoretical Model and Research Implication

Lei XIAO[a], Huan CAO[b]

Economic and Business School, University of Electronic Science and Technology of China, Chengdu, China
[a]xiaolei@uestc.edu.cn, [b]caohuan@uestc.edu.cn

Abstract: Organizations are all subject to a diverse and ever changing and uncertain environment. Under this situation organizations should develop a capability which can resist the emergency and recover from the disruption. Base on lot of literature, the paper provides the main concept of organizational resilience; construct the primary theoretical model and some implications for management.

I Introduction

In recent years, the management of crises and disasters has become a key topic of concern for both practitioners and academics. Natural disasters, pandemic disease, terrorist attacks, economic recession, equipment failure and human error can all pose both a potentially unpredictable and severe threat to the continuity of an organization's operation.（Bhamra et al., 2011[1], Zolli & Healy, 2012[2]）. The annual number of these high-risk events worldwide has steadily increased from around 350 in 1980 to almost 1000 in 2014 and the direct loss increased by $ 250 billion from $ 50 billion (UN, 2015). Different organizations have different reaction when facing these destructive dangerous situations, some organizations have been successfully adjusted and continue to grow and some organizations are lack of response and eventually closed down.

Crises may precipitate form a number of sources, but regardless of their severity or intensity, the challenges crises need for varying approaches to deal with them. In the attack of disruptive environment, why some organizations succeed while others failed? Coutu (2002) [3], Hamel & Välikangas (2003) [4] presented the "Organizational Resilience" in Harvard Business Review. In recent years, the literatures about organizational resilience have increased in academic journals.

What is the organizational resilience, which elements it consists, and how its management implications and such as a series of questions are mentioned on the research agenda. This article summarizes the existing organizational toughness literature, firstly we review the concept and factors of organizational resilience, then the paper propose a theoretical model of organizational, the last is the implication to management research.

2 The concept of Organizational Resilience

The term "resilience" comes from the Latin word "resilire" (which means to leap or jump back). In the academic community Resilience first produced in the field of ecology. Holling (1973) [5] considered that Resilience determines the persistence of relationships within a system and is a measure of the ability of these systems to absorb changes of state variables, driving variables, and parameters, and still persist. After then, resilience has been developed in many areas such as ecology (Walker et al. 2002[6]), engineering (Hollnagel et al., 2006[7]), psychology（Powley, 2009[8]), organization management （Weick, 1993[9] ; Gilbert, Eyring, & Foster, 2012[10]). At present, there has no an uniform definition of organizational resilience（Linnenluecke,2017[11]）.Scholars give the conception from the system point social, psychological point and strategic management point of view. Sutcliffe and Vogus (2003)[12] argue that resilience is an organizational level phenomenon as the power of organizational units to resume, rebound, bounce back, or positively adjust untoward events. Lengnick-Hall et al.(2011)[13] defined organizational resilience as a firm's ability to effectively absorb, develop situation-specific responses to, and ultimately engage in transformative activities to capitalize on disruptive surprises that potentially threaten organization survival. Annarelli and Nonino(2016)[14] think resilience is a capability to face disruptions and unexpected events in advance thanks to the strategic awareness and a linked operational management of internal and external shocks. The research on resilience has experienced high reliability organization, positive organizational behavior, business model, and supply chain stages.

The organizational resilience is different from adaptability, agility, flexibility, improvisation, recovery, redundancy and robustness. Resilience involves the reaction of the organization under destruction, which emphasizes the ability of recover and develops in a state of uncertainty, discontinuity, and emergency.

In this paper, we define organizational resilience as

DOI: 10.1051/itmconf/20171204021

organization's ability to restore to the original state even develops a new skill in disruptive conditions. In particular, organizational resilience has the following characteristics

1) Resilience is a capability under discontinuous, emergent internal and external environment. The organizational resilience is a potential capacity which cannot be perceived in operation activities of organization. But when the environment becomes disruptive and emergent, organizational resilience can take advantage for organization.

2) Resilience emphasis on survival, adaptability, bounce back and development under disruptive situation. Organizational resilience is recovery ability after destruction rather than a resistance to unexpected event. Organization with high resilience can adjust timely and shape a new capacity confronted with a variety of dramatic changes.

3) Organizational resilience is a multi-level conception and related to the organizational resources, routines and process. Resilience across levels including individuals, groups and organizations and depends on the interactions among different levels. Meanwhile, resilience is a process which affected by resources and routine of organization.

3 The Factors of Organizational Resilience

Some literatures put forward the factors and specific measurements of organizational resilience in various angles, this paper only list few representative ones. In a system viewpoint, Tierney (2003) [15] dimensionalizes the construct with four dimensions of robustness, redundancy, resourcefulness and rapidity. Deniz and Arzu (2015) [16] developed three dimension structure of organizational resilience: robustness, agility and integrity. In strategic viewpoint, McManus (2008) [17] think that a resilient organization should need situation awareness, management of keystone vulnerabilities and adaptive capacity. Akgün, A. E., & Keskin, H. (2014) [18] considered lots of elements including competence orientation, deep social capital, original/unscripted agility, practical habits, behavioral preparedness and broad resource networks. In psychology and organizational behavior, Weick (1993) [9] provides that ability to improvise, virtual role systems, organizational wisdom and respectful individual and social interactions have great impact on organizational resilience.

Another representative article is Lengnick-Hall et al. (2011) [13], which divided organizational resilience into cognitive dimensions, behavior dimensions, and context dimensions. In other words, a resilient organization needs to express resilience completely in these three aspects. Cognitive resilience is a conceptual orientation that enables an organization to notice, interpret, analyze, and formulate responses in ways that go beyond simply surviving an ordeal. Behavioral resilience is the engine that moves an organization forward. This property enables a firm to learn more about the situation and to fully use its own resources and capabilities through collaborative actions. Contextual resilience provides the setting for integrating and using cognitive resilience and behavioral resilience. Contextual resilience is composed of connections and resources.

E. Cunha et al. (2013) [19] deconstructed organizational resilience from three levels: individual level, group level, and organizational level. The employee is the basic elements of organization system and the individual resilience is the main source of organizational resilience. Individual has resilience does not mean that groups or organizations he or she belongs to also have such characteristics, there need some process to realize it.

4 The Theoretical Model of Organizational Resilience

Organizational resilience is a newer tradition in organizational theory that incorporates insights form both coping and contingency theories. Although some literatures have analyzed the concept and measurement of organizational resilience, there is still a lack of integrative construct. The empirical research is also difficult due to the unpredictability of crisis disasters and the lack of samples. Some scholars thought that organizational resilience is contextual which means a resilience specific to a certain situation. It is important to realize that resilience arises from a complex interplay of many factors at different levels of analysis (Van Der Vegt et al., 2015[20]).

DOI: 10.1051/itmconf/20171204021

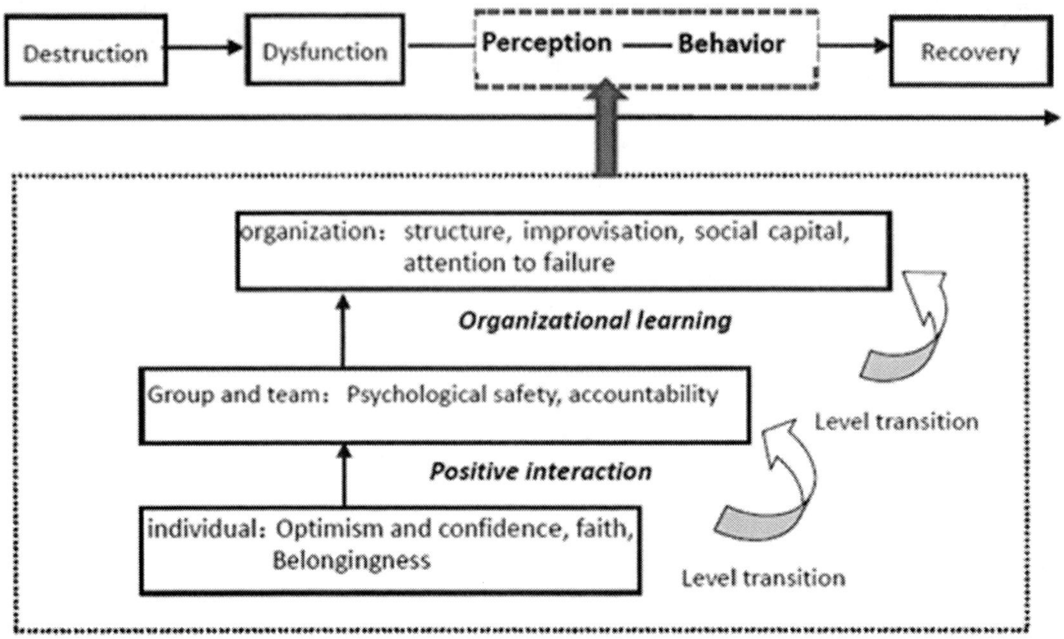

Figure 1. Theoretical model of organizational resilience

Combined with the work of Lengnick-Hall et al. (2011[13]) and Cunha et al. (2013) [19], this paper regard that organizational resilience is influenced by many factors, many levels. We try to construct a multi- level and multi-factors model in Figure 1.

The paper think an organization need become resilient at individual level, group level and organization level. The factors of every level are different. Resilient individuals as part of the whole organizational system are expected to be a positive factor for organizations to develop their resilience capacity. The Personal character such as confidence, optimism, faith and belongingness are contributed to individual resilience (Luthans et al., 2006[21]; Cunha et al., 2013[19]). Resilient groups developed the capacity to see failures and imperfections as sources of learning and progress. Edmonson (2007) [22] thought that a combination of psychological safety and accountability are critical ingredients for the group level. For the organizational level, the adaptive structures, improvisation, social capital and the attention to failure are the main factors.

In addition, there is a mutual influence between different levels. We think there is a "level transition" phenomenon from the low level to high level. The relation interaction between members can promote group resilience and organizational learning can help group to form organizational resilience.

The above model is only a preliminary idea, especially the impact of each dimension factors need to be determined, the overall follow-up also needs to be adjusted and improved in next work.

5 The Quest for Management Research

Resilience is generally seen as a desirable characteristic for an organization. More and more publications were found in academic journals, but there are lots of works to accomplish in management research.

1. The research of resilience need be strengthened. The academic community is already aware of the urgency of resilience and has some development in this area. However, there is a lack of research on the measurement, the realization mechanism and the relationship with other organizational variables, the advanced discussions of the organization's resilience developed slowly (Vegt et al. 2015) [20]. Linnenluecke (2017) [11] pointed out that the context of resilience, organizing for resilience, measuring resilience and multi-level and cross disciplinary work are the primary research in future.

2. Combination of resilience and traditional problems. The other management research topics such as organizational culture, organizational structure, collective mind, social capital, psychological safety, supply chain and so on are relevant with organizational resilience. Once academia get consensus on the concept, measurement, model and mechanism of organizational resilience, lots of valuable problems can be studied.

3. Organizational resilience and the management practice. How to become a resilient organization? Especially under the crisis and disaster situations, utilize the organizational resilience theory to makes organizations overcome adversity. Resilience capacity can be developed and managed. For example, in the human resources management, managers can take specific HR principles and HR policies to enhance the employees and the overall organizational resilience.

6 Conclusion

Organizational resilience has been considered as an

DOI: 10.1051/itmconf/20171204021

important field in management. This research give the concept, measures and integrated model of organizational resilience. The model includes lot of factors, relations and mechanisms. We find that there is great potential for future research within the area of resilience. For enterprises, they should be aware of the challenges of uncontinuous and disruptive environment and build resilience capability or prepare to do something in advance.

Acknowledgement

This paper was supported by Chinese Higher-education Institution General Research and Development Funding (ZYGX2015J161, ZYGX2014J101) and Ministry of Education in China, Humanities and social science projects (14YJC630001).

References

1. Bhamra, R., Dani, S., & Burnard, K. (2011). Resilience: the concept, a literature review and future direction. International Journal of Production Research, 49(18), 5375-5393.
2. Zolli, A., & Healy, A. M. (2012). Resilience: why things bounce back, Simon and Schuster.
3. Coutu, D. L. (2002). How resilience works. Harvard Business Review, 80(5), 46-56.
4. Hamel, G. and Välikangas, L. (2003). The quest for resilience. Harvard Business Review 81(9), 52–63.
5. Holling, C.S (1973). Resilience and stability of ecological systems. Annual Review of Ecology and Systematics, 4, 1-23.
6. Walker, J., & Cooper, M. (2011). Genealogies of resilience from systems ecology to the political economy of crisis adaptation. Security dialogue, 42(2), 143-160.Ali E.
7. Hollnagel, E., Woods, D. D., & Leveson, N. (2007). Resilience engineering: concepts and precepts. Ashgate Publishing, Ltd..
8. Powley, E. H. (2009). Reclaiming resilience and safety: resilience activation in the critical period of crisis. Human Relations, 62(9), 1289-1326.
9. Weick, K. E. (1993). The collapse of sensemaking in organizations: the Mann Gulch disaster. Administrative science quarterly, 38(4), 628-652.
10. Gilbert, M. Eyring, M. & Foster, R.N. (2012). Two routes to resilience. Harvard Business Review, 90(12), 65-73.
11. Linnenluecke, Martina K. (2017). Resilience in business and management research: a review of influential publications and a research agenda. International Journal of Management Reviews, 19(1), 4-30.
12. Sutcliffe, K. M., & Vogus, T. J. (2003). Organizing for resilience. Positive organizational scholarship, 94-110.
13. Lengnick-Hall, C. A., Beck, T. E., & Lengnick-Hall, M. L. (2011). Developing a capacity for organizational resilience through strategic human resource management. Human Resource Management Review, 21(3), 243-255.
14.]Alessandro Annarelli, & Fabio Nonino (2016). Strategic and operational management of organizational resilience: current state of research and future directions. Omega, 62, 1-18.
15. Tierney, K. J. (2003). Conceptualizing and measuring organizational and community resilience: lessons from the emergency response following the September 11, 2001 attack on the World Trade Center, Univ. of Delaware, Newark, DE.
16. Deniz Kantur, Arzu İşeri -Say (2015). Measuring organizational resilience: a scale development. Journal of Business, Economics & Finance, 4(3), 456-472.
17. McManus, S. (2008). Organisational resilience in New Zealand, Ph.D. thesis, University of Canterbury, Christchurch, New Zealand.
18. Akgün & Halit Keskin (2014). Organizational resilience capacity and firm product innovativeness and performance. International Journal of Production Research, 52(23), 6918–6937.
19. E. Cunha, M. P., Castanheira, F., Neves, P., Story, J., Rego, A., & Clegg, S. (2013). Resilience in organizations. Working paper
20. Van Der Vegt, G. S., Essens, P., Wahlström, M., & George, G. (2015). Managing risk and resilience. Academy of Management Journal, 58(4), 971-980.
21. Luthans, F., Avey, J. B., Avolio, B. J., Norman, S. M., & Combs, G. M. (2006). Psychological capital development: toward a micro-intervention. Journal of organizational behavior, 27(3), 387-393.
22. Edmondson, A. C. (2007). The competitive imperative of learning. Harvard business review, 86(7-8), 60-67.

DOI: 10.1051/itmconf/20171204022

Characteristic Analysis of Sandstorms in Taklamakan Desert

Teng-Ling LUO[1,2,a], Wei-Ming ZHANG[1,b], Qun-Bo HUANG[1,2,c], Yi YU[1,2], De XING[1,2,d], and Xiang XING[1,2,d]

[1]*Academy of Ocean Science and Engineering, National University of Defense Technology, Changsha, China*
[2]*College of Computer, National University of Defense Technology, Changsha, China*
[a]*luotl17@163.com*

Abstract: Firstly, the annual variation of sandstorm and strong sandstorm weather process in China from 2000 to 2012 is analyzed according to the"Sand-Dust Weather Yearbook" (2012). Secondly, based on the ERA-Interim Reanalysis from ECMWF and MISR data from the Terra satellite, we investigate the correlation between different dust weather process and land meteorological elements. Finally, the temporal and spatial distribution features of the aerosol optical depth (AOD) in the Taklamakan Desert is studied. And we compare the Taklamakan Desert AOD with nationwide AOD. The results show that: (1) the frequency of sandstorm and strong sandstorm has shown a downward trend and the occurrence of sandstorm decreases more in recent years. (2) In the Taklamakan Desert, the number of sandstorm is positively correlated with the surface temperature, meanwhile, negatively related to the surface relative humidity. (3) In all seasons, the average of AOD in Taklamakan Desert is higher than that of the whole country, and there are obvious differences among the four seasons.

1 Introduction

Sandstorm is a weather phenomenon that strong wind blows dust on the ground, making the air turbid and causing the level of visibility less than 1km 1. When sandstorms happen, sand will be blown up to the troposphere and above under the influence of turbulence or cyclones 23. In the atmosphere, lofted dust is a kind of aerosol which can act as cloud condensation nuclei and ice nuclei. And the dust in the air can scatter and absorb solar radiation, which may influence the radiation energy budget. Besides, Sandstorm can cause huge damage to the society, politics and economy of a country or a district. Nowadays the adverse effects of sandstorm have caught more attention from the Chinese government.

The Taklamakan Desert is the largest desert in China which covers an area of 270000km^2 of the Tarim Basin. As the major source of dust in China, it is necessary to analyze the characteristics of sandstorm in the Taklamakan, in order to provide a theoretical basis for the prevention and control of sandstorm.

Many researchers have done much work about sandstorm in China. Qiu et al. suggested that China's sandstorm mainly occurred in the southern and northern of desert in Xinjiang and its surrounding areas, Gansu Hexi Corridor, dry desert in Inner Mongolia and Qinghai Qaidam Basin and other places 4. Wang et al. analyzed the characteristics of dust circulation in the north of China 5. Wang et al. investigated the path of dust transmission 6. Shi et al. studied the relationship between the sandstorm in China and the global environment 7. Wang et al. used the climate model to predict the abnormal climate and sandstorm 8.

Since the occurrence of sandstorm is directly affected by the surface meteorological elements, it is essential to find out the relationship between the surface meteorological elements and the frequency of sandstorms. In the paper, we try to discuss the characteristics of sandstorms based on the temporal and spatial distribution features of AOD and the land meteorological elements. We hope to offer a better understanding of the causes of sandstorm in the Taklamakan area.

2 Data Sets

In this paper, we have three data sources. The first data is the production of multi-angle imaging spectrometer (MISR) on the satellite "Terra". During the daytime the Terra passes over the equator at 10:45 LT. And the MISR on the Terra has a push-broom camera to measure the Earth at nine different along-track view angles. Besides, MISR can retrieve aerosol properties and it can produce aerosol optical depth (AOD) globally. In this paper we used Level 3 aerosol optical depth (AOD) data from January 2000 to December 2012 with the resolution of 0.5° by 0.5°.

The second data comes from the ERA-Interim Reanalysis data of ECMWF which provides data from 1979 to the present. With the help of model improvements, Substantial improvement have been archived in ERA-Interim Reanalysis data. The ERA-Interim products have a variety of 3-hourly surface parameters, land-surface conditions. Here we mainly use the surface temperature and surface relative humidity with the resolution of 1° by 1°.

The last one is the "Sand-Dust Weather Yearbook" (2012) which is published by China Meteorological Administration. The "Sand-Dust Weather Yearbook" (2012) recorded sandstorms that occurred from 2000 to 2012 in China and provided basic information of sandstorm. In this study, we selected 29 sandstorms from 2000 to 2012 as the research objective to study the characteristics of ground meteorological elements during the period of sandstorms.

3 The Basic Analysis of Sandstorm in the Taklamakan Desert

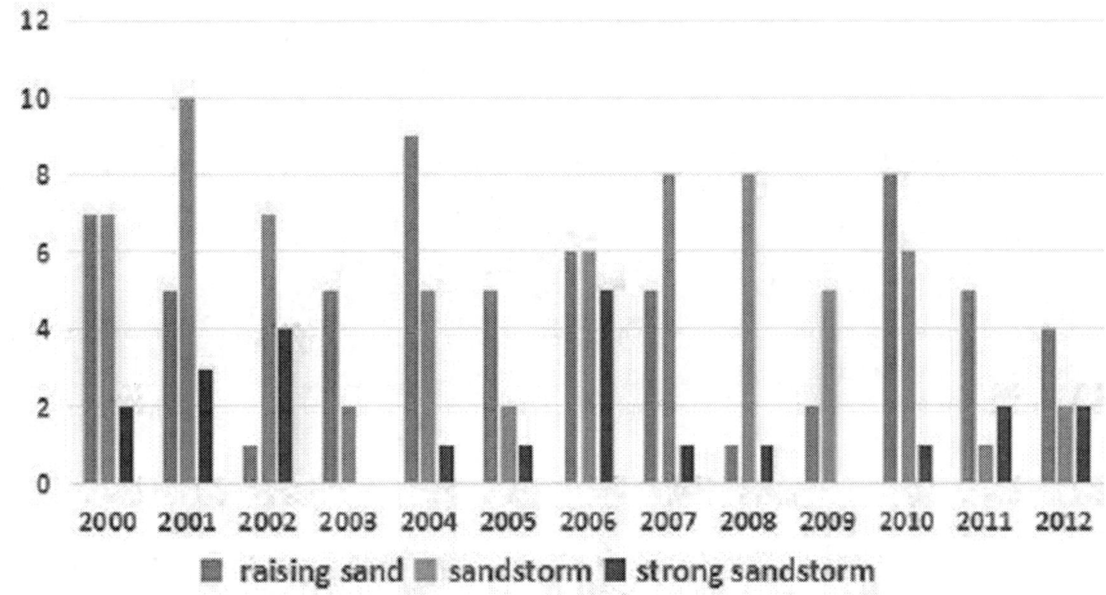

Figure 1. The number of sandstorms occurred in the spring

Figure 1 shows the statistics of sandstorms in the Taklamakan Desert during the spring of 2000 ~ 2012. The data is picked out from the "Sand-Dust Weather Yearbook" (2012). We record the number of raising sand, sandstorm and strong sandstorm in the Taklamakan Desert. It can be seen that raising sand and sandstorms appear more than strong sandstorm. Raising sand occurs most (9 times) in the year of 2004 while the least occurrence (only once) happens in 2002 and 2008.The sandstorm happens most (10 times) in 2001, but the least number is merely once in 2011. The number of strong sandstorms in 2006 is the highest (5 times), while the least occurs in 2003, and there is no strong sandstorm in this year.

DOI: 10.1051/itmconf/20171204022

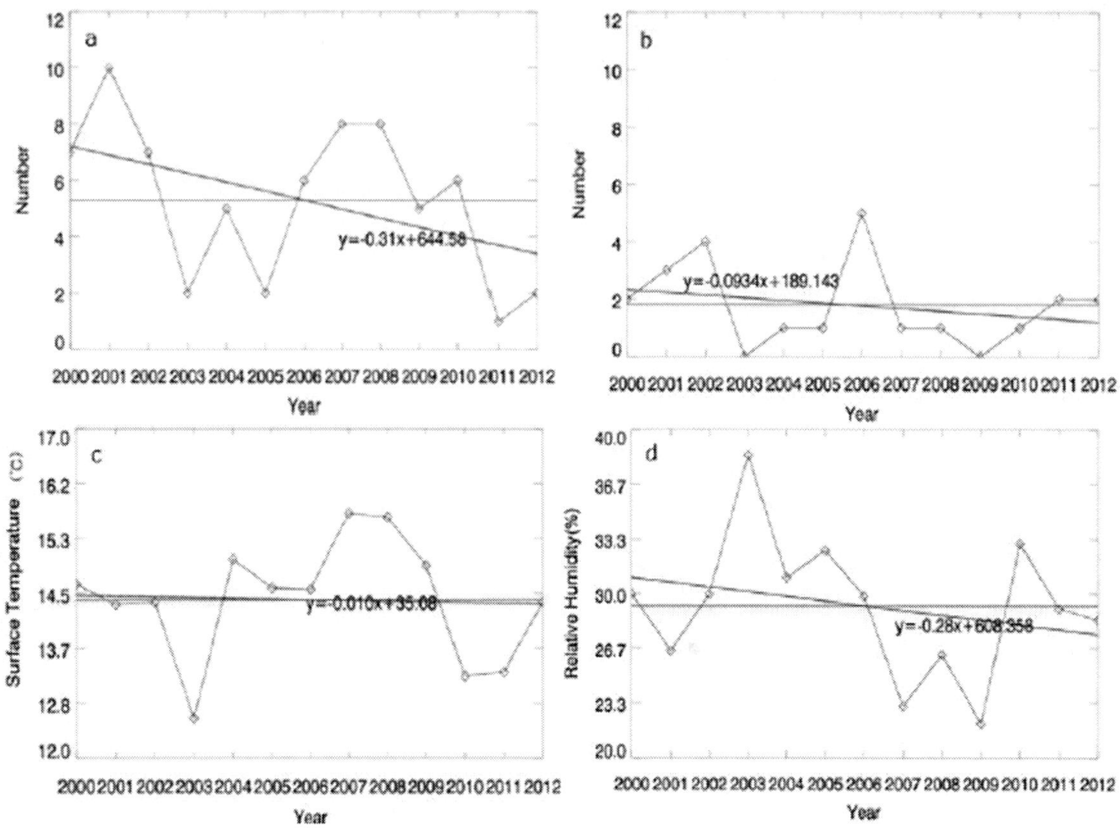

Figure 2. Statistical analysis of changes for the year 2000 through 2012 (a) sandstorm (b) strong sandstorm (c) surface temperature (d) surface relative humidity

Figure 2a shows a significant decline of the annual occurrence frequency of sandstorm in the Taklamakan Desert. Similarly, there is also a downtrend in the happening of strong sandstorm in Figure 2b. It can easily conclude that the frequency of sandstorm has a larger drop than the strong sandstorm from 2000 to 2012 in the Taklamakan Desert by comparing Figure 2a and Figure 2b.

From Figure 2a and Figure 2c, we can infer a positive relationship between the appearance of sandstorm and the land surface temperature. As we can see, when the surface temperature is higher in the year of 2006 to 2009, the sandstorm also happens more in those years. On the contrary, there are fewer sandstorms from 2002 to 2004 when the surface temperature is lower. The reason of this positive relationship may be that high temperature will produce updrafts, resulting in the decrease of the atmosphere stability and leads to sandstorm.

In the same way, we can infer that there is a negative correlation between the occurrence of sandstorm and the surface relative humidity. From the figure 2a and Figure 2d, when the surface relative humidity is higher in the years of 2003, 2004 and 2005, sandstorms happen fewer. However, sandstorms occur more in 2007 and 2008 when the surface relative humidity is lower. This negative correlation may be caused by the fact that the drier of the sand, the easier it will be lofted by wind, which produces the sandstorm.

Table 1 shows the correlation coefficients of two types of sandstorms and the two kinds of surface meteorological elements. According to the data, the correlation coefficient between the frequency of sandstorm and the surface temperature is as high as 0.526 and pass the significant test, which confirms our inference above. Nevertheless, the correlation between the strong sandstorm and land surface temperature is not supported. The coefficient is only 0.044, which fails the significant test.

Table 1. Coefficient of correlation between meteorological element and type of sandstorm

Type of sandstorm / Meteorological elements	Sandstorm	Strong sandstorm
Surface temperature	0.526	0.044
Surface relative humidity	-0.471	-0.042

The relationship between the frequency of sandstorms and surface relative humidity is also verified, with a high coefficient -0.471. However, the correlation between the surface relative humidity and the number of strong sandstorms is also not significant, and the correlation coefficient is only -0.042 without passing the significance test.

The probable reason of the weak link between the surface temperature, surface relative humidity and the strong sandstorms is that the strong sandstorm is mainly affected by the weather process rather than the others.

4 The temporal and spatial distribution features of AOD in the Taklamakan Desert.

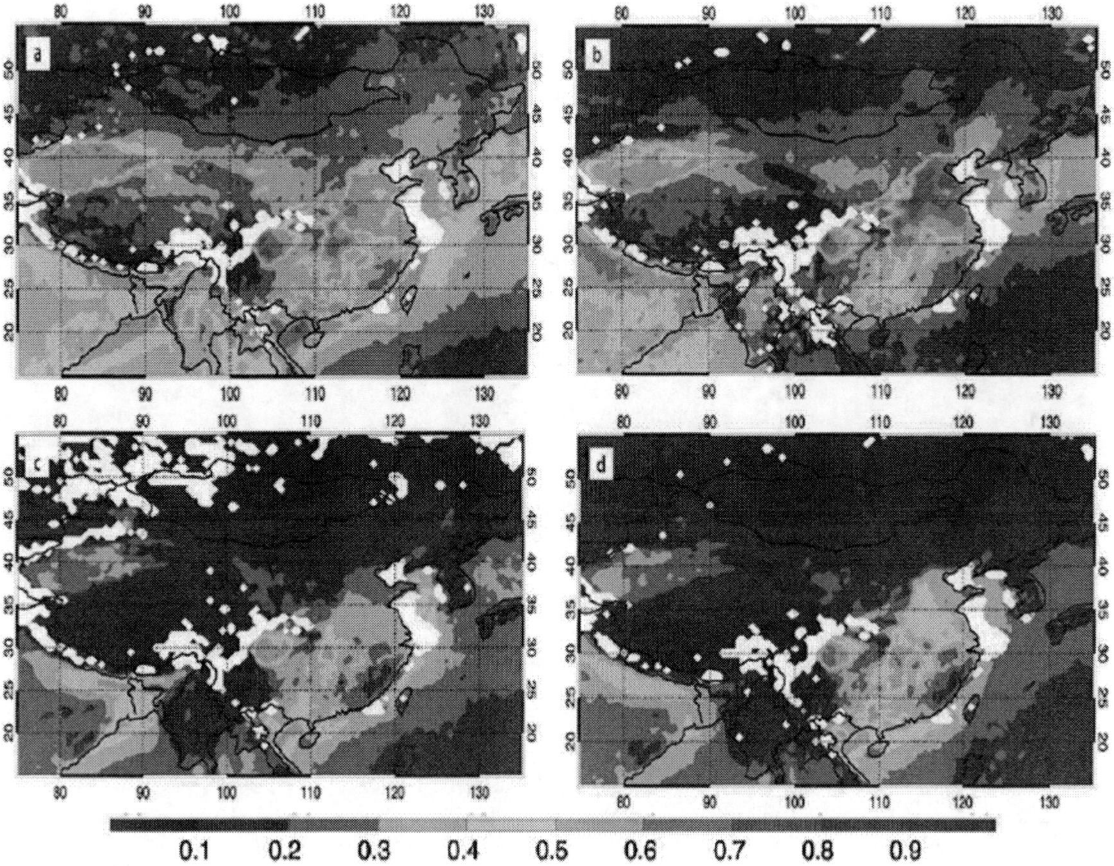

Figure 3. Seasonal mean AOD in China. (a) spring (b) summer (c) autumn (d) winter

Figure 3 shows the temporal and spatial distribution features of AOD in the Taklamakan Desert from 2000 to 2012. In the spring, there is a high value center in the Aksu and Korla areas, north of the Taklamakan Desert and near the Ruoqiang in the east, with a maximum optical thickness of 0.7. In the summer, the frequency of sandstorms decreases without the effects of cold front. And the value of the overall level of the AOD in summer is lower than that in spring, but there is also a high value (0.7) in the southern part of the Taklamakan Desert. However, in autumn and winter, there is almost no sandstorm. So the optical thickness of the AOD reduces rapidly, with a maximum value of 0.3.

Overall, there is thicker AOD in the southern and northern regions of the Taklamakan Desert, which means these two areas tend to experience more sandstorms than other places. There may be a reasonable explanation to this phenomenon: the Kunlun Mountain and the Tian Mountain locates in the south and north of the Taklamakan Desert respectively. This kind of terrain may enhance the wind speed on the ground, leading to sandstorms.

5 Comparative Analysis of Aerosol Optical Depth (AOD) of China and Taklimakan Desert

We further compared the frequency of AOD in China and the Taklimakan Desert. Figure 4a shows the average AOD of the Taklimakan Desert is 0.4 in the spring, much higher than the average AOD of the China over this period of 0.12. This phenomenon indicates that sandstorms are strong in the spring in the Taklimakan Desert. Figure 4b presents that the average of AOD in the Taklimakan Desert fell to 0.3 in the summer as the frequency of sandstorms decreasing. It is found that the average AOD in the Taklimakan Desert fell again and remained at around 0.2, and the average of the nationwide AOD remained at around 0.1, for there is little sandstorm in autumn and winter (Figure 4c, 4d).

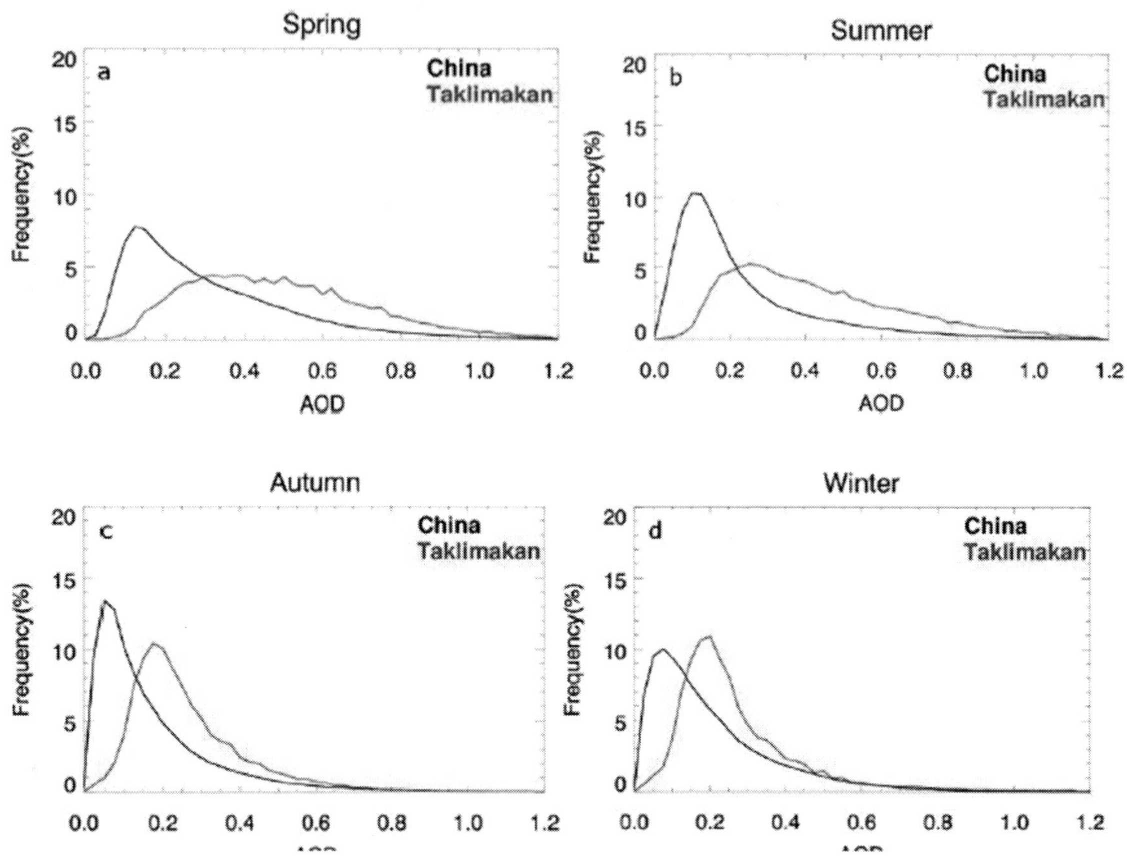

Figure 4. Probability distribution function (PDF) of AOD. (a) spring (b) summer (c) autumn (d) winter

In summary, the AOD in spring and summer is higher than that in autumn and winter, which indicates that sandstorms mainly occur in spring and summer. In all seasons, the average AOD in the Taklimakan Desert is greater than that of the nationwide AOD.

6 Discussion and Conclusion

We used the "Sand-Dust Weather Yearbook" to make basic analysis of sandstorms in the Taklamakan desert, and we also used ERA-Interim Reanalysis data to have correlative analysis of meteorological elements and sandstorm. The AOD data of MISR from 2000 to 2012 were used to study the characteristics of AOD in the Taklimakan Desert.

Results show that the frequency of sandstorm and strong sandstorm in recent years has shown a downward trend and the occurrence of sandstorm decreases more. The number of sandstorm is positively correlated with the surface temperature, while negatively related to the relative humidity. MISR data shows that the AOD is higher in the spring and summer than that in the autumn and winter, which indicates that sandstorms occur mainly in spring and summer. In all seasons, the average of AOD in Taklamakan Desert is higher than that of the whole country and the difference among the four seasons is obvious.

Although we have analyzed the correlation among sandstorms and surface temperature and surface relative humidity, we still have a long way to go. There are many other factors affecting sandstorms, such as polar vortex, evaporation rate and precipitation. Besides weather situation, atmospheric stability and wind field characteristics may be also important factors causing to sandstorms, which should also attract our attention in the future.

Acknowledgment

The work was supported by the Natural Science Foundation of China (Grant No. 41375113).

References

1. China Meteorological Administration. Sand-Dust Weather Yearbook [M], 2014.6
2. Kaufman, Y. J., D. Tanre, and O. Boucher (2002), A satellite view of aerosols in the climate system, Nature, 419, 215–223.
3. Rosenfeld,D.,Y. Rudich, and R. Lahav(2001),Desertdust suppressing precipitation: A possible desertification feedbackloop, Proc. Natl. Acad.Sci. U.S.A., 98, 5975–5980.

4. Qiu X F, Zeng Y, Miaq Q L. Temporal-spatial distribution as well as tracks and source areas of sand-dust storms in China[J]. Acta Geographica Sinica, 2001(3).
5. Wang K, Jiang H, Hong W U. Circulation Dynamical Structure in Course of Dust Storm Occurrence in North China in Spring of 2001[J]. Plateau Meteorology, 2002.
6. Wang Shigong, WANG Jinyan, ZHOU Zijiang. Regional Characteristics of Dust Events in China[J]. Acta Geographica Sinica, 2003, 58(2):193-200.
7. Shi Y. Discussion on The Present Climate Change from Warm-day to Warm-wet in Northwest China[J]. Quaternary Sciences, 2003, 23(2):152-164.
8. Wang H, Lang X, Zhou G, et al. A Preliminary Report of the Model Prediction on the Forthcoming Winter and Spring Dust Climate over China[J]. Chinese Journal of Atmospheric Sciences, 2003, 27(1):136-140.

Employee Turnover Prediction Based on State-transition and Semi-Markov- A Case Study of Chinese State-owned Enterprise

Ming FANG[a], Jia-Hao SU[b], Tao WANG[c*], and Ren-Jie HE[d]

College of Information System and Management, National University of Defense Technology, Changsha, China
[a]mingxfz@gmail.com, [b]sujiahao15@nudt.edu.cn, [c]wangtao@nudt.edu.cn, [d]839434993@qq.com
**corresponding author: wangtao@nudt.edu.cn*

Abstract: As a main direction of Human Resource Management, employee turnover can provide decision support for managers. In this paper, we aim at predicting the turnover amount of employee on condition of different variable values. The properties of employee and job position are formulated as two variables, where the value of variable varies according to the the state of properties. Additionally, state-transition model is applied to describing employee's job-state as well as the turnover type. Subsequently, we proposed a semi-Markov model to calculate the conditional turnover amount of employee. Then, we provide a dataset of employee records to illustrate how these models work in reality. Finally, it is proven that the proposed method in this paper is with great significance for managers to develop recruitment plans, promote rules, and retire regulations

1 Introduction

Employee turnover is the leaving act of employee in a workforce. In the study of improving employee satisfaction and decreasing the staff cost for workforce such IT [1,27], tourist [2] and hospitality [3], employee turnover is of particular importance for managers to predict organization structure and develop employee transfer plan.

Employee turnover has long been the focus of Human Resource Management (HRM). Turnover management can provide decision support of managers. Actually, before the turnover behavior happens, an employee first forms an intention to leave the organization. Employee turnover intention is a conscious and deliberate willingness to leave one's formal organization of employment [4,5]. Various potential factors may have influence on turnover intention, then contribute to turnover behavior.

Turnover intention always comes from individual factors [6,7], organizational factor [8,9] and environmental factors [10,11] Individual perception is an important factor to the turnover phenomenon, which is a subjective measure of oneself, e.g. how easy it would be to find a new job [12]. The inducement-contribution balance developed from organizational equilibrium theory is touted as the one of the most influential factors of turnover. Employee would like to stay in current position only if the inducement of this organization is greater than or equal to the contribution asked by managers. [4,13] In addition, employee turnover is often influenced by economics, the rate declines during economic recessions [14], while it increases during economic rebound [15].

Afterwards, researchers start to find the connection of turnover intention with turnover behavior [16-18], and the result suggests that the longer the elapsed time between the measurements of intention and behavior, the lower is the correlation [19].

Based on turnover intention, extensive studies have been made on modeling and predicting the turnover. For instance, [20] studies twenty variables to build a turnover prediction model, and only six variables are found effective by stepwise logit analysis; [21] provides a dataset of life insurance company to find the effects of prior absenteeism and performance rating on voluntary turnover; [28] propose a forecast model based on neural network to predict the impact of employee turnover on the performance; recently, machine learning has been applied to turnover prediction by [22].

The turnover can cause serious loss and difficulty because of the leaving of employees who have relatively high human capital [23]. Thus HRM strategies are developed to facilitate the retention of employees [24-26].

Nevertheless, little attention has been paid to Chinese enterprise as well as the internal transfer within organization. In this paper, we propose employee turnover as the combination of inter-organization turnover and internal transfer, with inter-organization turnover denoting recruit, retire, resign and deposal, while internal transfer denoting training on current job position, exchange to fellow position and promote to higher position. In addition, we propose state-transition model to describe the properties related to employee turnover, and employee are classified to deferent groups according to their state properties. Subsequently, conditional semi-Markov (CSMK) model is proposed to predict the turnover on condition of different constraints. Based on CSMK, transition amount can be calculated for each turnover type, then the employed amount can be predicted for each employee group. Lastly, a case study of Chinese state-owned enterprise is provided to illustrate how state-transition and CSMK work in reality. These models are proven to be available to predict the structure of an organization, which is with great significance for managers to develop recruitment plans, promote rules, and retire regulations. This turnover prediction method can be generalized to any organization that with similar structure and employee rules.

2 Modeling Based on State-transition Mode

Turnover of employee always contributes to the change of the employee property and the organization structure. Make an assumption that there is an employ-position system that contains both the property of employee and job position. Then, we can define job-state to describe the state of this system. The job-state will transfer to another state if system property changes, because of employee turnover, and this process can be described by state-transition to classify the turnover type. Therefore, we claim that the state-transition mode can be applied to predict the employee turnover.

2.1 Formulating the Properties about Employee Turnover

Job position are classified into i grades according to their authority and function; the bigger the grade is, the higher the position level is. Let a and b be the property of job position and employee respectively; both a and b are related to employee turnover, where $a=(a_1,a_2, ...,a_s,...,a_n)$ and $b=(b_1,b_2, ...,b_l, ...,b_m)$. For a job position, a_s denotes the sth ($s=1,2, ...,n$) property and it has P_s values, *i.e.* $A_s = (a_{s1}, a_{s2}, ...,a_{sp_s}, ...,a_{sP_s})$ and $a_s \in A_s$. While $a_s = a_{sp_s}$, it means that the sth property of this position equals to the pth value of A_s. Similarly, b_l denotes the lth ($l=1,2, ...,m$) property of employee and it has Q_l values, *i.e.* $B_l=(b_{l1},b_{l2}, ...,b_{lq_l}, ...,b_{Q_l})$, $b_l \in B_l$ and the lth property of employee equals to the qth value while $b_l = b_{lq_l}$.

Subsequently, a_j and b_k are developed to describe states that contain all property values of a position or an employee. Position states are distinguished by their subscript j that denotes the sequence number of position states, where $a_j=(a_{1p_1},a_{1p_2}, ...,a_{sp_s}, ...,a_{np_n})$ and $a_j \in A$. Similarly, employee states are distinguished by k, $b_k=(b_{1q_1},b_{2q_2}, ...,b_{lq_l}, ...,b_{mq_m})$ and $b_k \in B$. j and k are calculated as (1) and (2).

$$j = \sum_{s=1}^{n-1}((p_s-1)\prod\nolimits_{r=s}^{n} P_r) \quad p_n. \tag{1}$$

$$k = \sum_{l=1}^{n-1}((q_l-1)\prod\nolimits_{r=l}^{m} Q_r) \quad q_m. \tag{2}$$

Then, ρ is proposed to measure the property of manning quotas. As is shown in (3), ρ describes 4 position states about employee turnover.

$$\rho = \begin{cases} 0 & \text{on guard} \\ 1 & \text{overstrength} \\ 2 & \text{vacancy} \\ 3 & \text{opening \& overstrength} \end{cases} . \tag{3}$$

Based on the definition of these properties, we can define the employee job-state as a triple (ijk), or a tetrad ($ijk\rho$), to describe state-transition mode. The system state will be changed, when there is any transition happens to position state or employee state. It should be note that the total number of I, j and k are I, J and K, respectively.

2.2 Classifying State-transition of Employee's Turnover

In this paper, state-transition is a formal expression of employee's turnover, describing the transition among job-states. Without considering the property of manning quotas (ρ), state-transition of employee can be described by three-dimensional state (ijk), then all these states can make up a set, Ω_0, whose element corresponding to employee group. This group is denoted by U_{ijk}, to group employees with different state-transition. Similarly, the employee's turnover of retire, deposal, resign, recruit and training are denoted by Ω^r, Ω^d, Ω^{rs}, Ω^{rc}, and Ω^t, where $\Omega^r=\{(ijk)^r \mid i\in I\}$, Ω^d, $=\{(ijk)^d \mid i\in I\}$, $\Omega^{rs}=\{(ijk)^{rs} \mid i\in I\}$, $\Omega^{rc}=\{(ijk)^{rc} \mid i\in I\}$, and $\Omega^t=\{(ijk)^t \mid i\in I, j\in J, k\in K\}$. As in (4), all the state and turnover can be merged into a set Ω, $\omega\in\Omega$.

$$\begin{gathered} \Omega = \Omega_0 \cup \Omega^r \cup \Omega^d \cup \Omega^{rs} \cup \Omega^{rc} \cup \Omega^t \\ \omega = ((ijk),(ijk)^r,(ijk)^d,(ijk)^{rs},(ijk)^{rc},(ijk)^t). \end{gathered} \tag{4}$$

Then, take $(ijk)\rightarrow(ijk)'$ as the employee's transition from current state to objective state. This transition process can be formulated as (5). Note that $i'= i^+$ or $i'= i^{++}$ when employee is promoted gradually or leapingly; $j'= j$, when employee exchanges to another position that with the same property as current position; $k'=k+1$ after training on current positon, without any transition of i and j; $(ijk)'=ijk$ after recruit of new employee, initializing the job-state. Specially, the transition is denoted as $(ie)^t\rightarrow(ijk)$ when an employee is recruited as a freshman, where e (e=0,1,2,3) denotes the employee's education degree is bachelor ($e=1$), master (e=2) doctorate (e=3), or else ($e=0$).

$$(ijk)' = \begin{cases} i^+ j' k & \text{promote} \\ ij'k & \text{exchange} \\ ijk^{r/d/rs} & \text{retire/disposal/resign} \\ ijk' & \text{train} \\ ijk & \text{recruit} \end{cases} \tag{5}$$

While manning quotas is taken into consideration, the transition can be denoted as $(ijk\rho)\rightarrow(ijk\rho)'$. These four-dimensional states ($ijk\rho$) makes up the set, $\Omega_{(ijk\rho)}$. The transition of i, j and k follows the same rule as the three-dimension state (ijk). What should be noted is that manning quotas transfers between on guard (ρ=0) and vacancy (ρ=2), or between overstrength (ρ=1) and open & overstrength (ρ=3). ρ' equals *2* or *3* when employee leave his/her current position where ρ equals *0* or *1*, meaning that these transitions provide an open job-state (ρ=2,3) for other employee to replenish while the objective state (ρ=0,1) becomes busy for its occupied by this employee, such as retire, deposal and resign. As is

 DOI: 10.1051/itmconf/20171204023

demonstrated in the following table, ρ' equals *0* or *1* when employee is recruited, and ρ' maintains *0* or *1* after employee's attending training.

Table 1. Table Type Styles

$(ijk\rho)'$	ρ	ρ'	**Transition**	**Open**	**Busy**
$i^{+}j'k\rho'$	0/1	2/3	promote	$ij\cdot\rho'$	$i^{+}j'\cdot\rho$
$ij'k\rho'$	0/1	2/3	exchange	$ij\cdot\rho'$	$ij'\cdot\rho$
$ijk\rho'$	0/1	2/3	retire/deposal/resign	$ij\cdot\rho'$	--
$ijk'\rho$	0/1	0/1	training	--	--
$ijk\rho'$	2/3	0/1	recruit	--	$ij\cdot\rho'$

NOTE: a. Instead of *k*, '·' in column Open and Busy denote that there is no constraint on employee properties.

Actually, each of the state-transitions in TABLE 1 is a combination of two turnover processes, e.g. promote equals to both retire/deposal/resign from current position and recruit to another position with higher grade, as demonstrated in (6).

$$(ijk\rho \to i^{+}j'k\rho') \Leftrightarrow (ijk\rho \to ij\cdot\rho')\&(i^{+}j'\cdot\rho' \to i^{+}j'k\rho). \quad (6)$$

3 Employee Turnover Prediction Based on Conditional semi-Markov Model

Employee turnover prediction is the prediction of employee's turnover probabilities to next job-state, on condition of various influence factor, at different times. As demonstrated in Section II, the 6 subsets (Ω^{r}, Ω^{d}, Ω^{rs}, Ω^{rc}, and Ω^{t}) of Ω are mutually exclusive and complete. Additionally, the three-dimensional states (*ijk*) of employee are with conditional homogeneity. Thus semi-Markov can be applied to modeling state-transition, and predicting employee turnover.

3.1 Conditional Semi-markov Model

The transfer of employee's job-state over time can be abstracted as a stochastic process, $\{X(t),\ t\geq 0\}$. In this process, τ and c are provided as variables to classify the job-state of employee, $\tau=(\tau',ĭ)$. The adjoint variable, τ, is provided to describe employee state, where τ' is a natural factor denoting properties such as gender and native place, while ĭ (ĭ=ĭ^{a},ĭ^{w},ĭ^{g}) is an adjoint factor, whose elements, ĭ^{a}, ĭ^{w}and ĭ^{g}, denote the age, working age and grade age at the beginning of current job-state, respectively. Another variable is c, the environment to describe properties of job-state group (U_{ijk}), such as age, education degree and manning quotas.

Let ω' be the objective state of ω for employee's turnover, $\omega'\in\Omega$. Thus the transfer probability of sate-transition from ω to ω' can be denoted as $P_{\omega\to\omega'}|\tau,c$, and (7) is the constraint on condition of τ and c. When there is a given ω', the interarrival time distribution can be defined as $F_{\omega\to\omega'}(t|\tau,c)$, as demonstrated in (8). Therefore, $\{X(t),\ t\geq 0\}$ is the CSMV process of employee turnover, with variables of τ and c.

$$\sum\nolimits_{\omega'\in\Omega} P_{\omega\to\omega'}|\tau,c = 1. \quad (7)$$

$$F_{\omega\to\omega'}(t|\tau,c) \equiv \Pr(t_{n+1}-t_{n} \leq t | X_{n} = \omega, X_{n+1} = \omega', \tau, c). \quad (8)$$

3.2 Conditional Calculation of State-transition

Based on the definition of CSMV process, we propose (9), function $T_{\omega\to\omega'}(t|\tau,c)$, to demonstrate how transfer probability changes over time. It's apparent that employee's turnover depends on transfer probability among states as well as the distribution of interarrival time. Equation (10) and (11) reveal the connection of T with P and F, where $T_{\omega\to\omega'}(t|\tau,c)=0$ on condition of $P_{\omega\to\omega'}|\tau,c$. Then, T can be derived as (12), the multiplication of P and F.

$$T_{\omega\to\omega'}(t|\tau,c) \equiv \Pr(X_{n+1} = \omega', t_{n+1} - t_{n} \leq t | X_{n} = \omega, \tau, c). \ (9)$$

$$P_{\omega\to\omega'}|\tau,c \equiv \Pr(X_{n+1} = \omega' | X_{n} = \omega, \tau, c) = \lim_{t\to\infty}(T_{\omega\to\omega'}(t|\tau,c)). (10)$$

$$F_{\omega\to\omega'}(t|\tau,c) = \begin{cases} \dfrac{T_{\omega\to\omega'}(t|\tau,c)}{P_{\omega\to\omega'}|\tau,c} & if\ P_{\omega\to\omega'} > 0 \\ 1 & if\ P_{\omega\to\omega'} = 0 \end{cases}. \quad (11)$$

$$T_{\omega\to\omega'}(t|\tau,c) = (P_{\omega\to\omega'}|\tau,c)\,F_{\omega\to\omega'}(t|\tau,c). \quad (12)$$

Assume that the state-transition cycle is one year, then ω denotes job-state at the beginning of this year. Let d ($d=0,1,2,\ ...$) be the duration time of ω at the beginning of this year, then the transfer probability to ω' within this year can be derived as (13), with variables of τ and c. Let $N_{d}^{\omega}(\tau)$ be the amount of employee whose duration time of ω is exactly d, then in (14), $N^{\omega}(\tau)$ denotes the amount of employee whose job-state is ω; in (15), the amount of employee whose job-state transfer to ω' on condition of is calculated by multiplying employee amount on ω and transfer probability from ω to ω'. Therefore, the total amount of employee whose job-state transfer to ω' can be calculated as (16), and $N_{t+1}^{\omega'}$ is the amount of employee on state ω' at the beginning of next year. In (17), it should be noted that $\in\Xi$ denotes an accessible process, e.g. in $\omega\in\Xi\omega'$, ω is the current job-state whose objective state is ω'.

$$T_s^{\omega\to\omega'}(\tau,c)=\Pr(X_{n+1}=\omega',d_n<t_{n+1}\ \ t_n-d_{n+1}\le|X_n\ \ \omega,\tau,c)$$
$$=T_{\omega\to\omega'}(d_{n+1}|\tau,c)-T_{\omega\ \ \omega'}(d_n|\tau,c). \quad (13)$$

$$N^{\omega}(\tau)=\sum\nolimits_s N_s^{\omega}(\tau). \quad (14)$$

$$N^{\omega\to\omega'}(\tau)=N^{\omega}(\tau)T_s^{\omega\to\omega'}(\tau,c)=\sum\nolimits_s N_s^{\omega}(\tau)T_s^{\omega\to\omega'}(\tau,c). \quad (15)$$

$$N^{\omega\to\omega'}=\sum\nolimits_\tau N^{\omega\to\omega'}(\tau). \quad (16)$$

$$N_{t+1}^{\omega'}=N_t^{\omega'}+\sum_{\omega\in\Xi\omega'}N^{\omega\to\omega'}-\sum_{\omega'\in\Xi\omega''}N^{\omega'\to\omega''}. \quad (17)$$

These calculations have been specifically given in Fig.1, which displays the transition among groups as well.

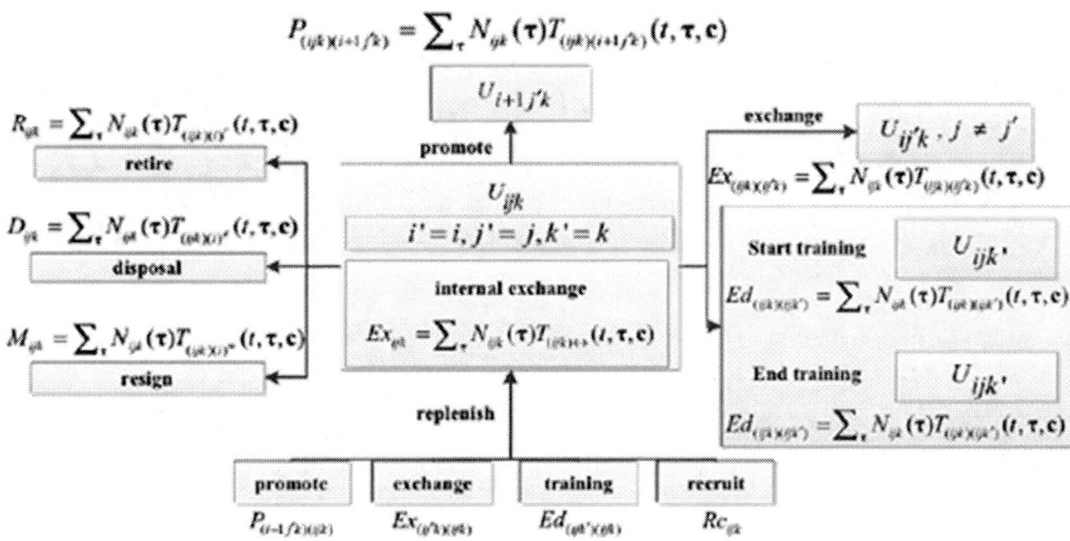

Figure 1. State-transition based on employee's transifer.

3.3 Variable adjustment

After state-transition in this year, variables and the structure of groups will be changed next year, thus we propose variable adjustment to reset τ and c at the beginning of next year.

As a natural factor of τ, τ' is constant no matter the job-state transfers or not. On the contrary, $\tilde{\iota}$ will change as job-state transfers. In this section, turnover means promote, exchange or training instead of recruit, retire, resign or deposal; the reason is that recruit is a initialization of job-state and there is no objective state of retire, resign or deposal. Thus, both $\tilde{\iota}^a$ and $\tilde{\iota}^w$ will be increased by s at the beginning of next year if employee turnover occurs in this year. For $\tilde{\iota}^g$, it will be zeroed if the turnover is promote; its value will be kept if the turnover is exchange or training for there is no influence on position grade of these two.

As for the environment variable, c will be reset for each job-state group, which can be calculated according to the employee amount of each state-transition.

In summary, there are 5 steps of employee turnover prediction, as shown in Fig.2.

- Step1: Group the employee data according to job-state, construct hierarchical work of employee turnover, and distinguish state-transition among groups.
- Step2: Calculate environment variable for each group, count employee amount on condition of natural factor, and count employee amount of each group, based on statistics of employee data.
- Step3: Use state-transition function to predict the amount of employee transfers among groups on condition of adjoint variable.
- Step4: Calculate the employee amount, employee amount of each group and the employee amount on condition of adjoint variable, and update the environment variable for each group, based on current employee amount and the prediction of employee turnover.
- Step5: Repeat step *3* and *4* to predictive the employee structure of next year.

DOI: 10.1051/itmconf/20171204023

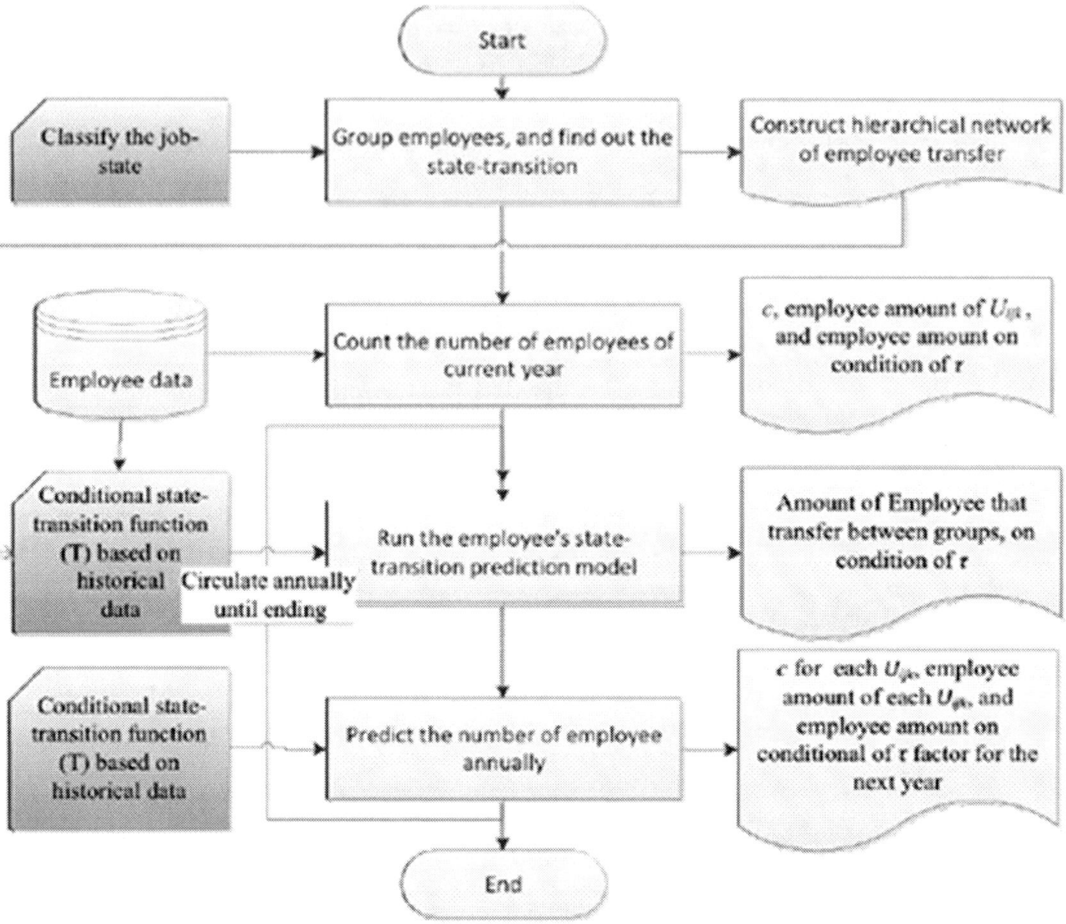

Figure2. Flow chart of prediction model

4 Case Study for A State-owned Enterprise

In order to demonstrate how state-transition and CSMK work in reality, here we provide a case study of Chinese state-owned enterprise. We select the employee data in recent 11 years, from 2006 to 2016, within nearly 6 million state-transition records. All properties (*i, j, k, τ, c* and *d*) mentioned in Section III can be acquired directly or calculated indirectly. Additionally, the true employee amount of each state group (U_ω) has been involved in these dataset, denoted as $N^{(\omega)}$.

Based on the employee turnover rules of this organization, job-state groups are classified as Fig.3, where $I=8$ $(i=0,2, \ldots,7)$. Actually, there is a limitation that some turnover could only occur on several grades. To be specific, as in (18), retire and deposal only occurs when $i=(6,7)$, recruit occurs only when $i=(0,1,\ldots,4)$.

Subsequently, state-transition and CSMK are applied to predict employee turnover according to the 5 steps of prediction, then we can get the predicted employee amount of each job-state group. And the prediction result is demonstrated as Fig.4 and Fig.5.

$$\begin{aligned}
\Omega^{I} &= \{(ijk)^{I} \mid i \in I\} \\
\Omega^{rs} &= \{(ijk)^{rs} \mid i \in I\} \\
\Omega^{r} &= \{(ijk)^{r} \mid i = 6,7\} \\
\Omega^{d} &= \{(ijk)^{d} \mid i = 6,7\} \\
\Omega^{rc} &= \{(ijk)^{rc} \mid i = 0,1,\mathrm{L}\ ,4\}.
\end{aligned} \tag{18}$$

 DOI: 10.1051/itmconf/20171204023

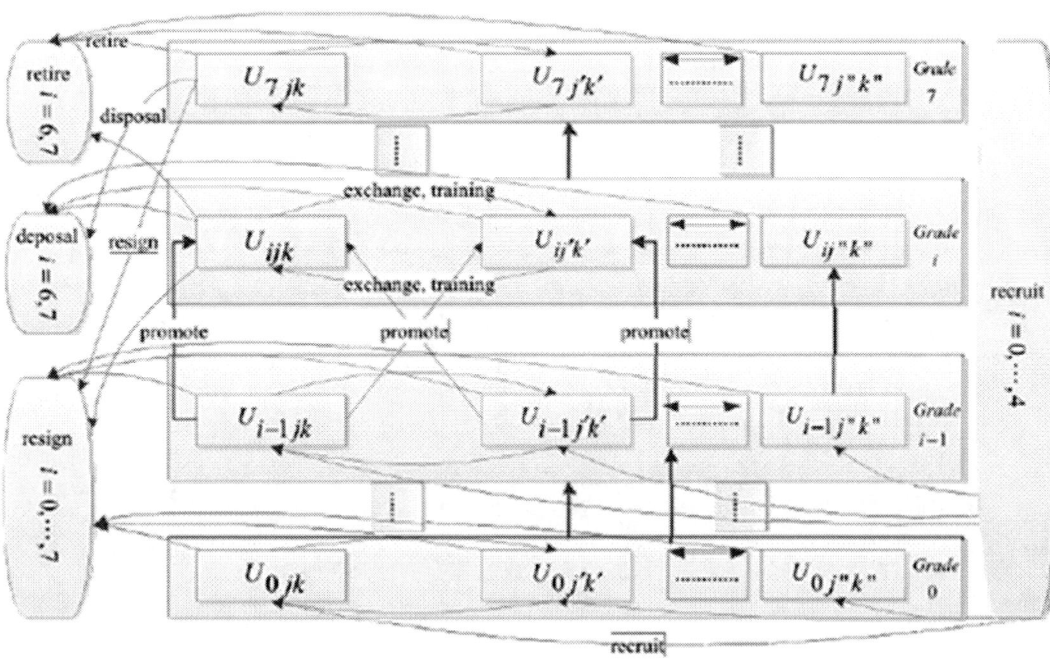

Figure3. Groups of job-state based on employee turnover rules.

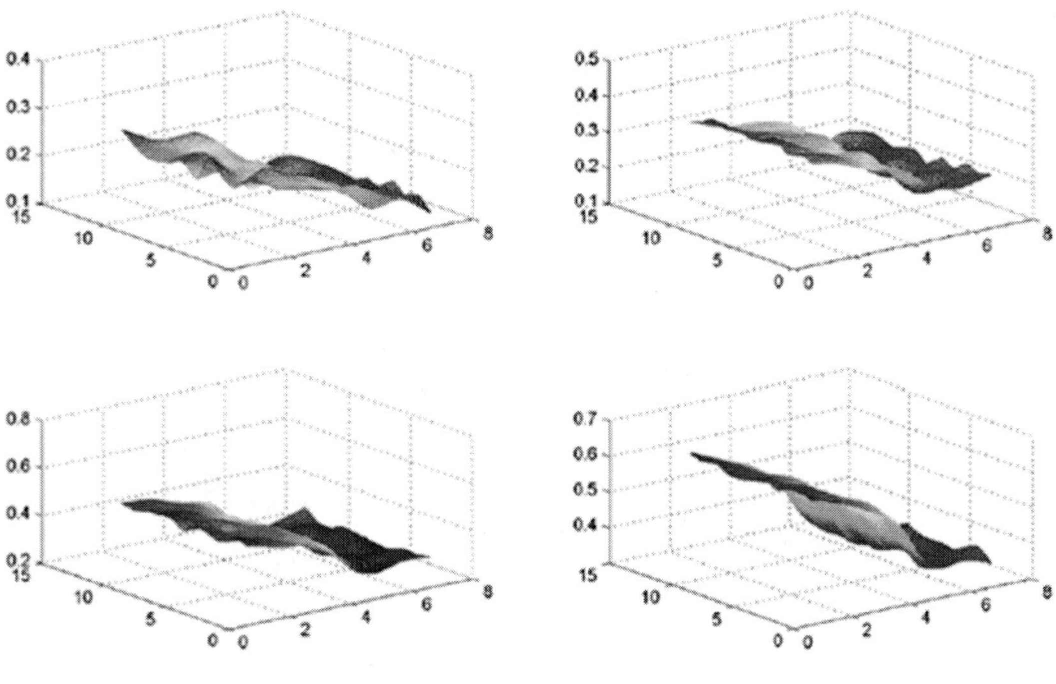

Figure4. Transfer probabilites among job position grades on condition of education degrees.

In Fig.4, we provide the transfer probabilities among different job grades (from 0 to 7), on condition of different education degrees. As for this four subfigures, degree equals to *0*, *1*, *2* and *3*, from left to right and then from top to bottom, respectively. It apparent that the transfer always decrease slowly when $i \leq 3$ or $i \geq 5$, while it decrease rapidly when $3<i<5$. In addition, when $i \leq 5$, the higher the degree is , the higher the transfer probability. Specially, when $e=0$, the employee's education degree is lower than bachelor ($e=1$). Thus we can conclude that transfer probabilities decrease as position increase, and the employ are always with higher promote probability on lower or higher position, while the employee on medium position transfers less frequently.

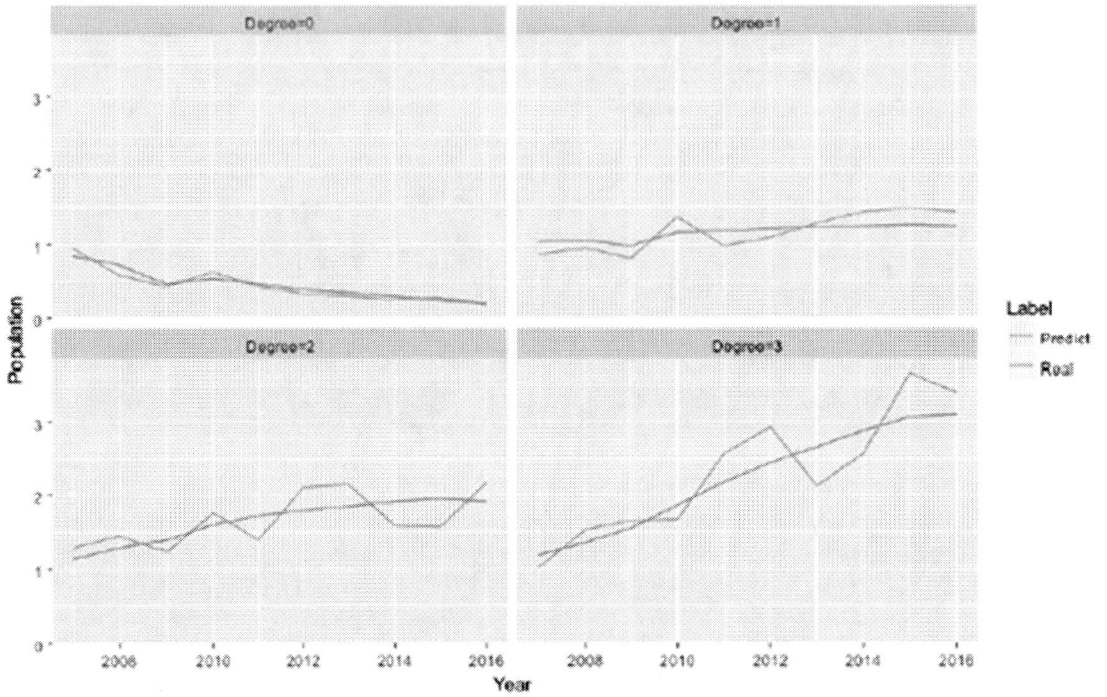

Figure 5. Comparison of predicted amount with the real amount of employee on condition of education degrees

In the line chart of Fig.5, we compare our predicted amount with the real amount of employee on condition of education degrees, from 2006 to 2016. The employee amount of each group (degree) in different years has been normalized according to the amount of 2016. It comes to conclusion that the amount of employee with higher education degree ($e \geq 1$) increases over time, and the increase rate is positively relative to their degree. But the amount of employee with lower degrees decrease rapidly. Which suggests that the education level of the employee structure tends to be higher and higher. The average prediction accuracy is calculated as 0.855.

The case study proves the effect of our proposed method of turnover prediction.

5 Conclusion

There have been large amount studies on employee turnover, including its influence factors, modeling and prevent strategies. However, little attention has been paid to Chinese enterprise as well as the internal transfer within organization. Therefore, we propose the models of state-transition and CSMK to describe the turnover as well as to predict the turnover. These methods have been proved effective in reality by a case study of the employee records data, from 2006 to 2016, provided by a Chinese stated-owned enterprise.

Our study makes a primary contribution to predicting employee turnover of Chinese enterprise, both the inter-organization and the internal transfer. For managers, especially managers of Chinese enterprise, proposed method provides effective supports of developing recruitment plans, promote rules, and retire regulations. This turnover prediction method can be generalized to any organization that with similar structure and employee rules. In our prediction model, we didn't consider the turnover demotion, which will be an interesting direction. And more influence factors should be considered in our further study, which might be individual, organizational or environmental.

Acknowledgment

This work is supported by the Natural Science Foundation of China (grant nos. 71522014, 71301165, 71690233, 71331008, 71671186 and 61473301).

References

1. J. Dittrich, J. Daniel and R. Zawacki, "Perceptions of equity, job satisfaction, and intention to quit among data processing personnel", Information & Management, vol. 9, Sep. 1985, pp. 67-75, doi: 10.1016/0378-7206(85)90028-X.
2. J. Yang, C. Wan, and Y. Fu, "Qualitative examination of employee turnover and retention strategies in international tourist hotels in Taiwan", International Journal of Hospitality Management, vol. 31, Sep. 2012, pp.837-848, doi: 10.1016/j.ijhm.2011.10.001.
3. F. DeMicco and J. Giridharan, "Managing Employee Turnover in the Hospitality Industry", Hospitality Review, vol. 5, 1987.
4. J. March and H. Simon, "Organizations", American Journal of Sociology, vol. 65, 1959, pp.105-132.
5. R. Tett and J. Meyer, "Job satisfaction, organizational commitment, turnover intention, and turnover: Path analyses based on meta-analytic findings", Personnel Psychology, vol. 46, Jun. 1993, pp. 259–293, doi: 10.1111/j.1744-6570.1993.tb00874.x.
6. M. Hunter, F. Tan and B. Tan, "Voluntary turnover of information systems professionals: A cross-cultural investigation", Journal of Global Information Management, vol. 16, 2008, pp. 46-66, doi: 10.4018/jgim.2008100103.
7. J. Hackman and G. Oldham, "Work redesign", Nursing Management, vol. 25, 1994, pp. 12, doi: 10.5465/AMR.1981.4285748.
8. M. Igbaria and S. Siegel, "The reasons for turnover of information systems personnel", Information & Management, vol. 23, Dec. 1992, pp.321-330, doi: 10.1016/0378-7206(92)90014-7.
9. D. McKnight, B. Philips and B. Hardgrave, "Which reduces IT turnover intention the most: Workplace characteristics or job characteristics?", Information & Management, vol. 46, Apr. 2009, pp. 167-174, doi: 10.1016/j.im.2009.01.002.
10. M. Tan and M. Igbaria, "Turnover and remuneration of information technology professionals in Singapore", Information and Management, vol. 26, Apr. 1994, pp. 219-229, doi: 10.1016/0378-7206(94)90094-9.
11. J. Quan and H. Cha, "IT certifications, outsourcing and information systems personnel turnover", Information Technology & People, Vol. 23, 2010, pp.330-351, doi: 10.1108/09593841011087798.
12. S. Patrick, "The theory of planned behavior", Organizational Behavior and Human Decision Processes, vol. 50, 1991, pp. 137-44
13. D. Joseph, K. Ng, C. Koh and S. Ang, "Turnover of Information Technology Professionals: A Narrative Review, Meta-Analytic Structural Equation Modeling, and Model Development", MIS Quarterly, vol.31, Sep. 2007, pp. 547-577.
14. T. Willoughby, "Computing personnel turnover: A review of the literature", Proceedings of the 1977 annual conference, ACM Press, vol. 7 Oct. 1977, pp. 211-214, doi: 10.1145/800179.810204.
15. R. McLaughlin, "That old bugaboo, turnover", Datamation, vol.25, Oct. 1979, pp. 97–101.
16. K. Bartol, "Turnover among DP personnel: a casual analysis", Communications of the ACM, vol.26, Oct. 1983, pp.807-811, doi: 10.1145/358413.358433.
17. J. Thatcher, L. Stepina and R. Boyle, "Turnover of Information Technology Workers: Examining Empirically the Influence of Attitudes, Job Characteristics, and External Markets", Journal of Management Information Systems, vol.19, Dec. 2002, pp.231-261, doi: 10.1080/07421222.2002.11045736.
18. M. Dinger, J. B. Thatcher, L. P. Stepina and K. Craig, "The Grass is Always Greener on The Other Side: A Test of Present and Alternative Job Utility on IT Professionals' Turnover", IEEE Transactions on Engineering Management, vol. 59, Aug. 2012, pp. 364-378, doi: 10.1109/TEM.2011.2153204.
19. M. Fishbein and A. Icek, "Attitudes and voting behavior: An application of the theory of reasoned action." Progress in applied social psychology, vol.1, 1981, pp. 253-313.
20. K. ANG, C. GOH and H. KOH, "AN EMPLOYEE TURNOVER PREDICTION MODEL: A STUDY OF ACCOUNTANTS IN SINGAPORE", Asian Review of Accounting, Vol. 2, 1994, pp.121-138, doi: 10.1108/eb060649.
21. P. Morrow, J. McElroy, K. Laczniak and J. Fenton, "Using Absenteeism and Performance to Predict Employee Turnover: Early Detection through Company Records ☆ ", Journal of Vocational Behavior, vol.55, Dec. 1999, pp. 358-374, doi: 10.1006/jvbe.1999.1687.
22. R. Punnoose and P. Ajit, "Prediction of Employee Turnover in Organizations using Machine Learning Algorithms" International Journal of Advanced Research in Artificial Intelligence(IJARAI), vol. 5, 2016, pp. 22-26, doi: 10.14569/IJARAI.2016.050904
23. M. Zhang and D.Zhang, "The new development of voluntary turnover model", J. Econ. Manage. Abroad, vol. 25, 2006, pp. 24-28.
24. T. Ferratt, R. Agarwal, C. Brown and J. Moore, "IT Human Resource Management Configurations and IT Turnover: Theoretical Synthesis and Empirical Analysis", Information Systems Research, vol. 16, Sep. 2005, pp. 237-255, doi: 10.1287/isre.1050.0057.
25. S. Ang and S. Slaughter, "Turnover of information technology professionals: The effects of internal labor market strategies", ACM SIGMIS Database, vol. 35, Jun. 2004, pp. 11-27, doi: 10.1145/1017114.1017118.
26. T. Lee and S. Maurer, "The retention of knowledge workers with the unfolding model of voluntary turnover", Human Resource Management Review, vol. 7, Aut. 1997, pp. 247-275, doi: 10.1016/S1053-4822(97)90008-5.
27. M. Zhang, D. Zhang and S. Li, "An Empirical Study on a Path Model of Turnover Intention among Technical Staff in IT Enterprises", Nankai Business Review, vol. 4, Jun. 2003, pp. 12-20, doi: s10.3969/j.issn.1008-3448.2003.04.003.

DOI: 10.1051/itmconf/20171204023

28. H. Yang, "Simulation of Prediction Model of Employee Turnover Influencing", Computer Simulation, vol. 30, Jul. 2013, pp. 200-203, doi: 10.3969/j.issn.1006-9348.2013.07.04

Analysis on the Influence of Shortwave Communication in Different Ground Forms

Qian-Bo ZHUANG[a], Ming-Ming CUI[b], and Xi-Liang LIN[c]

China Satellite Maritime Tracking and Control Department, Jiangyin, China
[a]nwy1986@163.com, [b]nwy1986@163.com, [c]dylxl9123@sina.com

Abstract: The reasons for the different size of the transmitting power and the different effects of different ground forms on the signal power loss are analyzed in detail. A shortwave communication device includes first and second carriers are given respectively. With the flexible connecting portion, relative position of the first and second carriers can be changed freely to expand the transmission range and enhance the transmission.

1 Introduction

In shortwave communication we must use the 1000W radio transmitter, because the power of 125W radio is too small to meet our needs [1-4]. In the East China Sea, 125W radio is also fully able to meet the communication needs, and most of time we just need turn to 1/2 POWER FULL [5-6]. Why do we ask the power of 125W radio to be smaller when we are farther away from the seaboard [7-12]. According to the analysis, we believe that this phenomenon is mainly caused by the different multi-hop ground reflection loss that is due to the different forms of the ground. Here we will explain it from three aspects.

2 Theory Analyses

2.1 Short Wave Propagation

Shortwave communication uses a radio frequency of 1.5 to 30MHz. Short wave propagation mainly divided into two types, ground wave and sky wave. Sky wave can achieve long distance communication with ionosphere reflection, and ground wave spread along the earth's surface, and the surface of the earth is a conductor resistance, when traveling waves in it, there is a part of the electromagnetic energy is consumed, and with the increase of frequency, wave loss increases gradually. Because the ground large attenuation on shortwave, so ground wave only a short distance.

So, the spread of shortwave is mainly dependent on the sky wave propagation, which mainly depends on the ionosphere communication. In this propagation process, short wave can be transmitted to the receiver by one hop, which means one reflection by the ionosphere. And it also maybe pass to the receiver with two hops, which means first reflection by the ionosphere, second reflection by the ground and third reflection by the ionosphere again. Even with three hops or four hops, the short wave can reach the receiving end. According to statistics, with three hops are the most situations.

2.2 The Transmission Loss of Shortwave Channel

In the short wave radio transmission, energy loss mainly comes from three aspects:

Propagation loss in free space

Ionosphere absorption loss

Multi-hop ground reflection loss.

The loss of free space propagation is due to the fact that the radio waves are gradually moving away from the emission point, and the energy is growing in the space, so that the electric field strength of the receiving point is weakened as the distance increases.

The ionosphere absorption loss is due to the fact that the ionosphere absorbs a portion of the energy during the reflection of short wave through the ionosphere to the receiving point, and the signal is depleted. The absorption loss of the ionosphere is related to the electron density and the gas density. The greater the electron density is, the more the probability of electrons colliding with the gas molecules will become, so the greater the energy is absorbed. The greater the density of the gas is, the more the number of collisions per electron per unit of time will become, so the greater the loss increases. In addition, the absorption loss is also related to the frequency of the radio wave. The higher the frequency is, the smaller the absorption loss will become. The lower the frequency is, the greater the absorption loss will become.

As mentioned above, in the propagation of the sky wave, the radio waves need multiple reflections, and in the mode of multi-hop propagation (i.e., two or more reflections), the propagation loss not only takes into account the fact that the radio waves enter the ionosphere twice, but also consider the loss of ground reflection. A large number of experimental data show that this kind of signal loss due to ground reflection is related to the polarization of the radio waves, operating frequency, ray elevation and geological conditions. And when the ground form is sea water and land, the difference of the surface conductivity σ is great.

It can be seen that in these three aspects of energy loss, the first two is not much different in shortwave communication of different waters.

Considering that the ship is mainly located in the marine area, we will do analysis over the land and the ocean. Combined with the above analysis, we can conclude that the transmission power required for short wave communication when the ship is in the sea area is smaller than that when the ship drove out the East China Sea. This is mainly due to different ground forms, the seawater and the land, leading to different multi-hop ground reflection loss.

2.3 The Comparison of the Multi-Hop Ground Reflection Losses Caused By Two Different Ground Forms

In the engineering calculation of multi-hop ground reflection loss, it can be assumed that the incident wave is messy polarization wave, and the energy of radio wave is evenly distributed on the horizontal polarization and the vertical polarization. According to these contents, the formula is calculated as follows [13].

$$L_g = 10\lg\left(\frac{|R_V|^2+|R_H|^2}{2}\right) \quad (dB) \tag{1}$$

Where R_V denotes the reflection coefficient of the vertical polarization, and R_H is the reflection coefficient of the horizontal polarization.

R_V and R_H can be calculated by the following formula:

$$R_V = \frac{\varepsilon_r' \sin\delta - \sqrt{\varepsilon_r' - \cos^2\delta}}{\varepsilon_r' \sin\delta + \sqrt{\varepsilon_r' - \cos^2\delta}} \tag{2}$$

$$R_H = \frac{\sin\delta - \sqrt{\varepsilon_r' - \cos^2\delta}}{\sin\delta + \sqrt{\varepsilon_r' - \cos^2\delta}} \tag{3}$$

where δ denotes the Ray elevation, ε_r is the Relative complex dielectric constant of the ground ($\varepsilon_r' = \varepsilon_r - j60\lambda\sigma$), σ is the Ground conductivity $(\Omega\bullet m)^{-1}$, and λ is the Wavelength (m).

Considering that the ship is mainly located in the marine area, the ground forms are set to sea water and dry soil. The values of and in the case of several ground forms are shown in the table below.

Table 1. The values of ε_r and σ in the case of several ground forms

Ground form	The range of values		Average values	
	ε_r	$\sigma/(\Omega\bullet m)^{-1}$	ε_r	$\sigma/(\Omega\bullet m)^{-1}$
Sea water	80	1~4.3	80	4
Fresh water in Rivers or Lakes	80	10^{-3}~2.4×10^{-2}	80	10^{-3}
Wet soil	10~30	3×10^{-3}~2.4×10^{-2}	10	10^{-2}
dry soil	3~4	1.1×10^{-5}~2×10^{-2}	4	10^{-3}

The relevant values are substituted into the formula to calculate the multi - hop ground reflection losses in two different ground forms of seawater and dry soil, and compare them.

In the vertical direction of the antenna, the angle between the maximum radiation direction and the ground is called the vertical emission direction or the elevation angle of the antenna. The directional pattern of the logarithmic cycle antenna is approximately independent of the operating frequency.

Let us suppose that, elevation angle $\delta = 30°$, and wavelength λ = 30m. The values of ε_r and $\sigma/(\Omega\bullet m)^{-1}$ are set to their average values. After calculation, it is of the form of sea water.

$$|R_V| \approx 1, |R_H| \approx 1, \frac{|R_V|^2+|R_H|^2}{2} \approx 1 \tag{4}$$

And in the form of dry ground, it is expressed as follows.

$$|R_V| \approx \frac{\sqrt{73}}{73}, |R_H| \approx \frac{8}{13}, \frac{|R_V|^2+|R_H|^2}{2} = \frac{1}{5} \tag{5}$$

According to the parameter hypothesis above, in the formula of the multi-hop ground reflection loss can be obtained.

$$L_g = 10\lg\left(\frac{|R_V|^2+|R_H|^2}{2}\right) \quad (dB) \tag{6}$$

DOI: 10.1051/itmconf/20171204024

During which the value of $\frac{|R_V|^2 + |R_H|^2}{2}$ is 1 and 0.2 in the two ground forms of seawater and dry soil. And this formula represents the ratio of the reflected radio signal power to the incident radio signal power. Although some simplification has been made in the calculation process, it is still possible to see that the multi-hop ground reflection loss in the form of dry ground is much greater than that in the form of seawater.

3 Simulating

According to table 1, it is easily to find that the number of ones in the sequence is about 50% not related to the lengths of the sequences. The time domain properties and auto-correlation characteristics of the physical random sequence and sequence after spreading are described in Figure 1.

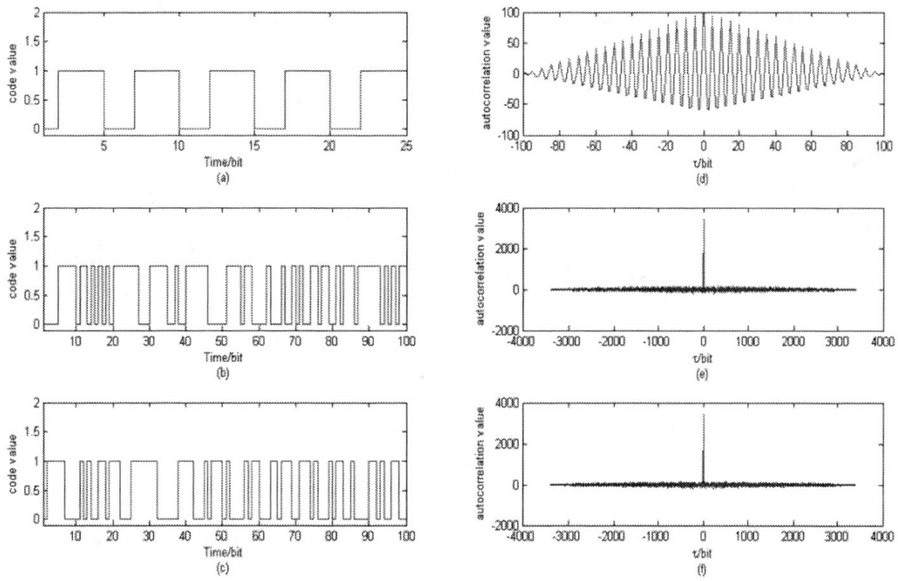

Figure 1. The time domain properties and auto-correlation characteristics of the physical random sequence before and after spreading

Through the analysis above, it is concluded that the difference of the multi-hop ground reflection loss in different ground forms is the main reason for the large difference of the transmission power required for shortwave communication in different sea areas.

4 Conclusions

In this paper, we mainly analyze the reasons for the different size of the transmitting power, and focus on the different effects of different ground forms on the signal power loss. Testing results proved the physical random sequence spreading sequence has the same autocorrelation properties as the physical random sequence itself not related to the periodicity of t In this paper, we mainly analyze the reasons for the different size of the transmitting power, and focus on the different effects of different ground forms on the signal power loss he plaintext though the time waveform has significant difference, which proves that physical random sequence can effectively realize the information spreading.

Acknowledgment

The preferred spelling of the word "acknowledgment" in America is without an "e" after the "g". Avoid the stilted expression, "One of us (R.B.G.) thanks." Instead, try "R.B.G. thanks". Put applicable sponsor acknowledgments here; DO NOT place them on the first page of your paper or as a footnote.

References

1. Wang Y, Tao T. Shortwave communication technology. National Defense Industry Press. 2002; 2(1).
2. Zhang X, Li N. New Technology of Shortwave Communication. People 's Liberation Army Press. 1997; 12(1).
3. Rong D, Jin F. Modern wireless communication. Electronic Industry Press. 2007.
4. Qin T, Zhao M. The Principle, Technology and Application of Wireless Local Area Network. Xi'an University of Electronic Science and Technology Press. 2004.
5. Wang T, He B. Short distance wireless and mobile communication network. Electronic Industry Press. 2006.

6. M. K. Simon, J. K. Omura, R. A. Scholtz, et al., Spread Spectrum Communications Handbook, Beijing: Post & Telecom Press, 2002.
7. G. Xao, C. Liang, Y. Wang, Pseudorandom Sequences and Applications, Beijing: National Defence Industry Press, 1985: 167-183.
8. M. Stipcevic and R. Ursin, An On-Demand Optical Quantum Random Number Generator with In-Future Action and Ultra-Fast Response, Scientific reports, 5:1-8, 2014.
9. A. Figotin, A random number generator based on spontaneous alpha-decay, PCT patent application WO0038037A1.
10. M. Stipcevic and B. Medved Rogina, Quantum random number generator based on photonic emission in semiconductors, Rev. Sci. Instrum. 78, 045104:1–7 (2007).
11. J. G.Rarity, P. C. M. Owens and P. R. Tapster, Quantum random-number generator and key sharing, J. Mod. Opt. 41, 2435–2444 (1994).
12. A. Stefanov, N. Gisin, O. Guinnard, et al., Optical quantum random number generator, J. Mod. Opt. 47, 595–598 (2000).
13. W. Li, I. Reidler and Y. Aviad, Fast Physical Random-Number Generation Based on Room-Temperature Chaotic Oscillations inWeakly Coupled Superlattices, Physical Review Letter, 111, 044102, (2013)

ITM Web of Conferences 12, 04025 (2017) DOI: 10.1051/itmconf/20171204025
ITA 2017

Corporate Governance and Bidder Abnormal Returns in M&A

Yao CHENG

Business School, Beijing Language and Culture University, Beijing, China
chengyaoblcu@163.com

Abstract: we examine how corporate governance influences long-term and short-term bidder returns from China's domestic mergers and acquisitions during 2010-2016. This paper examines a range of corporate governance measures while controlling for bidder and deal characteristics. Our long-term regression analyses show that the positive impact of executive ownership remains. Independent directors record a negative effect on abnormal returns.)

1 Introduction

Mergers and acquisitions (M&As) is one of the most thoroughly and extensively researched topics in finance due to its profound implications for wealth on the part of all parties involved. Research evidence suggests that target firm shareholders earn positive and significant returns around announcement date while bidder firm shareholders obtain at best negligible positive, zero or negative returns (Sudarsanam and Mahate, 2013). Fuller et al. (2002) associate positive returns to the resulting combination with the transfer of wealth from bidders to targets. There is, however, no evidence to suggest that M&As create value for shareholders in the long run (Sudarsanam and Mahate, 2006).

It is in this context that the present study seeks to examine the impact of corporate governance mechanisms on bidder abnormal returns. This study examines shareholders wealth effects and the role of corporate governance in the M&A decisions in an emerging economy: China. China is a special case for an investigation of this relation due to its increasingly active M&A activities and unique market characteristics (Kakabadse et al., 2010).

Unprecedented economic growth and the promulgation of the corporate law in the early 1990s have resulted in rapid development of financial markets and phenomenal growth of M&A activities. A report by Baird and Company (2012) shows that from the year 2001 to 2009, China's M&A increased at the speed of 20.5% compounded annual growth rate. The report also shows that in 2010 domestic M&A deals rose by 12% over 2009, reflecting healthy economic fundamentals and a slightly larger risk appetite among bidders. Despite the rapid growth and the importance of M&A activities in the real economy, there has been a dearth in literature on the M&A market in China.

2 Literature Review and Hypotheses Development

2.1 Wealth Effects around M&A Announcement Date

Most research on M&A in China is limited and inconclusive or is based on small sample size. Li and Chen (2002) find positive returns for bidder firms, which they attribute to state intervention in the process and the private firm liquidity discount. Similarly, Zhang and Wang (2006) report positive earnings for bidder firms and attribute that to insider trading and the fact that M&A transactions were still a new phenomenon in China.

Again, Song et al. (2008) record positive and significant returns around announcement date from a study of 23 acquisitions announced between 1998 and 2007. Chi et al. (2011) examine the performance and characteristics of bidding firms on 1148 Chinese acquisitions from 1998 to 2003, and find positive abnormal returns of 0.27% over a three-day event window. Chi et al. (2011) research also highlights that the political advantages of bidding firms have a significantly positive impact on the bidders' performance, while the economic advantages do not. By contrast, Zhang (2003) find negative returns and conclude that hubris and agency hypotheses explain why bidding companies lose value. Given that the Chinese government is heavily involved in the M&A process as both owner and regulator and the private firm liquidity discount, it is hypothesised, in its null form, that:

H1: Bidder abnormal return around M&A announcement date are positive and significant.

2.2 Corporate Governance and Bidder Returns

A number of studies have tested corporate governance mechanisms within the M&A context. Previous research highlights the importance of the ownership structure in determining bidder abnormal returns around M&A announcement (Shim and Okamuro, 2011). Specifically, Megginson and Netter (2007) note that state ownership has an impact on firm performance especially in emerging countries. The association between state ownership and investment decisions is generally not sufficiently explored and particularly in China. There are studies that criticise state ownership of firms because of political intervention and the need to help achieve government objectives instead of profitability (Sun and Tong, 2003; Wei et al., 2005).

However, Chen et al. (2009) findings support Stiglitz (1999) results that market- oriented state shareholders may be the most suitable controlling owners of firms in countries with weak institutional environments. Additionally, Chi et al. (2011) suggest that state ownership is not necessarily associated with negative bidder abnormal returns. Given that state ownership has been associated with neglecting profitability objectives in favour of social objectives, it is hypothesised stated in its null form, that:

H2.1: There is a significant and negative relationship between state ownership and bidder returns around M&A announcement.

Agency theorists prefer a board dominated by independent non-executive directors. They argue that boards dominated by non-independent directors have less incentive to monitor management (Mallin, 2010). Prior research highlight that the presence of independent directors on the board of directors plays an important role in monitoring managers' decision- making process (Fama and Jensen, 1983).

In support, Byrd and Hickman (1992) find that tender offer bidders are best served when outsider representation is close to 60% of the board. Additionally, Kroll et al. (2008) and Masulis et al. (2007) find similar results. There are no direct studies on China. Existing evidence from corporate governance and firm performance is mixed (Yang et al., 2011). Given the evidence from Qui and Yao (2009) in the Chinese context, it seems reasonable in spite of the mixed results on the relationship between independent directors and bidder returns to hypothesise, stated in its null form, that:

H2.2: There is a significant and positive relationship between board independence and bidder announcement returns.

2.3 Control Variables

Our study controls for a number of bidder specific and deal specific characteristics which are expected to influence the bidder returns.

Bidder characteristics

This study controls for firm specific characteristics including Tobin's q, leverage administration, transactions and size, of which are measured at the end of the year prior to the announcement date.

Deal characteristics

The study also controls for deal characteristics including method of payment, listing status of the target firm, value of the transaction, diversifying or focusing acquisition and previous M&A experience.

3 Data and Methodology

3.1 Sample Selection

Our study focuses on domestic M&A deals between January 2010 and December 2016 by Chinese listed firms. The initial data set is obtained from the China Stock Market and Accounting Research (CSMAR) database. It comprises 26,763 deals.

The bidder is a Chinese firm with Class 'A' shares traded on the Shanghai or Shenzhen Stock Exchange, while the target firm can be a listed public firm or a private firm (Cosh et al., 2006).The status of the deal must be successful with the deal value disclosed. To avoid the results generated by very small transactions (Fuller et al., 2002), the amount paid for the target should be at least 1 million Chinese Yuan. M&A involving firms in the financial industry are excluded, because they are subjected to special accounting and regulatory requirements. To ensure that the movement in the share price is due to the M&A announcement and not to other confounding events, we controlled for confounding events by removing announcements with such events as share splits, dividend and earnings announcements, and executive changes within the event window from the sample. Our final sample comprises 1,921 M&A transactions.

3.2 Sample Characteristics

Table 1 presents an overview of the final sample of M&A deals.

Panel A shows the distribution of M&A deals by the year of announcement. The general trend that has characterised the Chinese M&A market over the last decade: increase in both the number of deals and the value of the transactions over time as indicated by rising average deal values. Cash payment dominates both the number of deals (90.06%) and the total value of transactions (58.84%). However, on average very large deals tend to be paid by stock or mixed payment methods. The average size of deals paid with equity was CNY1630 million and paid by a combination of methods was CNY1180 million. The average size of deals paid in cash are relatively small at CNY180 million. This is consistent with Boateng and Bi (2010) who note that bidder firms in China prefer to finance M&As by cash because they have large cash holdings and Chinese firms still prefer to deal with business transactions in cash.

Panel B shows the distribution of M&A deals by bidder industry. 96.77% of the announced M&A deals are negotiated. This is consistent with findings from Tuan et al. (2007) where the bidding firm takes over the target firm by negotiating with the major shareholders. Negotiated equity transfer accounts for 63.35% of the deals while 33.42% are negotiated asset transfer. There are 60 debt restructuring cases accounting for 3.12% and only 2 tender offer announcements accounting for 0.10%. However in terms of deal value, tender offers are conducted in the largest scale recording an average deal value of CNY886 million, which is followed by asset transfer with CNY419 million.

3.3 Methods

We employ the bidder abnormal returns around the announcement date and post-M&As as the dependent variables and corporate governance mechanisms as the key explanatory variables. We use bidder characteristics and deal characteristics as control variables.

Bidder abnormal returns post-M&A

To calculate BHAR, firstly, the returns of the firms and benchmark returns (market returns) are compounded individually. Secondly, the difference between the returns of the bidding firms and the returns of the equally weighted market returns is calculated to derive the BHAR.BHAR is calculated for a 24-month post-acquisition period, starting with one month after the announcement date.

Multivariate analysis

We also control for deal specific characteristics such as listing status of the target firm, diversifying acquisitions, method of payment, the deal value and repeat bidders. Specifically, public target is a dummy variable equal to 1 if the target is listed on the stock exchange or 0 otherwise. Diversifying acquisition is a dummy variable equal to 1 for diversifying acquisition or 0 otherwise.

Two methods of payment indicators are created for all cash-financed and all stock-financed deals. All cash equals to 1 when the M&A transaction is fully financed with cash or 0 otherwise. All stock equals to 1 when the M&A transaction is financed fully with stock or 0 otherwise. The deal value is measured as the log transformation of Chinese Yuan value of the M&A deal. Repeat bidder is a dummy variable equal to 1 if the bidder is engages in more than one deal or 0 otherwise. To capture the effects of the ownership status of the target firm, the target variables are interacted with the method of payment variables to create the mutually exclusive and exhaustive deal categories.

To avoid the problems of multicollinearity, the dummy construction rule is applied and therefore only public target x all cash, private target x all stock and private target x all stock variables will be used in hypothesis testing.

4 Empirical Results

4.1 Descriptive Statistics

Table 2 presents the summary statistics of the corporate governance, bidder specific and deal specific characteristics variables. The results show some of the salient features of the Chinese board structure and composition.

On average, the total number of directors in a board range from 5 to 19, the figures recommended by the Chinese Company Law guidelines. An average board size is 9.22 with a median of 9. This reflects full compliance by the Chinese listed firms with the regulation and is consistent with prior studies (Huyghebaert and Wang, 2010).

The results also show the continued downward trend in CEO/Chairman duality with 13.1% of the firms whose CEOs still hold the dual positions. Currently the CSRC requires that the number of independent directors sitting on a board should be at least 0.33 of the total number of directors. On average, the results from the sample show that 80.1% of the sample firms are complying with the regulations. By comparison, companies have a board more than half of the board to comprise of independent directors in mature markets.

Table 2 further shows 90.2% of the bidding firms engage in diversifying deals. This suggests the possibility that firms attempt to achieve risk diversion through engaging inM&A across different industries. On average, the value of the transaction is CNY 142 million with the values ranging between CNY 1.0 million (which is the selection criteria minimum cut-off value) and CNY 32,800 million and a median of CNY 38.9 million. These statistics imply that there are some very large deals. The values also vary considerably given a very high standard deviation of CNY 1,460 million. The results show that 73.0% of the M&A transactions in the sample are by repeat bidders.

4.2 Robustness Tests

To ensure the reliability of our results, we conduct robustness checks for the multivariate analysis. For robustness tests, we calculated bidder abnormal returns in the short-term using the market adjusted returns model where abnormal returns is the difference between the stock returns and the market index returns. The results are are consistent with market model.

Finally, we conducted diagnostic tests on the regression results. High levels of correlations between independent variables can inflate standard errors resulting in less-efficient parameterestimates. To assess this possibility, we conducted two tests of multicollinearity. First, we checked correlations among independent variables using the correlation matrix. The correction between variables ranges between 0.01 and 0.64, none exceeding the 0.80 threshold. Second, we conducted a variance-inflation-factor (VIF) test. The values rangebetween 1.04 and 3.51 and none of them is above the VIF threshold of 10. The two tests thus provide evidence that multicollinearity is not a problem.

5 Conclusion

We study the shareholder wealth effects of China's domestic mergers and acquisitions in the period of 2006-2010. Specifically we examine how corporate governance influences both short-term and long-tem bidder abnormal returns. We demonstrate that market responses differ in ways which suggest a difference in how the market's assessment of share price from the perspectives of short run and long run. The results demonstrate that bidder firms experience wealth gains in the short run but lose value in the long run.

This paper shows that corporate governance structure

play an important role in shareholders abnormal returns, there are several points that limit its scope.

First, measures of stock performance are sensitive to the methodology and choice of variables. Indeed, our review of the literature highlights that existing studies produce varying and sometimescontradictory outcomes.

Second, our study examines a sample from a particular country over a particular period and therefore its generalizability may be limited given the unique China's market environment.

Third, studies on this subject suffer from low explanatory power of theindependent variables as they are so many variables that influence decision making and this study is no exception.

We therefore recommend further research employing different approaches and more variables to shed new light on these issues. Future research could useother stock performance measures such as operating performance and calendar time approach. The attitude with respect to whether the deals are hostile or friendly is also an interesting topic worth investigation. Given the scarcity of literature on emerging markets, we recommend similar studies on other emerging markets for comparative purposes.

Finally, we recommend studies that consider both qualitative and quantitative methodologies when examining corporate attitude towards M&As and its interaction with corporate governance.

References

1. Agrawal, A. and Jaffe, J. F. (2000). The post-merger performance puzzle. Advances in Mergers and Acquisitions, Vol. 1, p. 7–41.
2. Alexandridis, G., Petmezas, D. and Travlos, N. G. (2010). Gains from mergers and acquisitions around the world: New evidence. Financial Management, Vol. 39(4), p. 1671–1695, Winter.
3. Barber, B. M. and Lyon, J. D. (1997). Detecting long-run abnormal stock returns: The empirical power and specification of test statistics. Journal of Financial Economics, Vol. 43, p. 341-372.
4. Baird, R .W. and Company (2011). China M&A Market: 2010 Review and Outlook for 2011 and Beyond. M&A Market Analysis and Capital Markets Update, February 2011.
5. Bartholdy, J., Olson, D. and Peare, P. (2007). Conducting event studies on a small stock exchange, European Journal of Finance, Vol. 13(3), p. 227–252.
6. Bauguess, S. and Stegemoller, M. (2008). Protective Governance Choices and the Value of Acquisition Activity. Journal of Corporate Finance, Vol. 14(5), pp. 550-566.
7. Bhagat, S. and Bolton, B. (2009). Corporate Governance and Firm Performance: Recent Evidence. Available from (Accessed 26.06.2009).
8. Campa, J. M. and Hernando, I. (2004). Shareholder Value Creation in European M&As. European Financial Management, Vol. 10(1), p. 47-81.
9. Chi, J., Sun, Q. and Young, M. (2011). Performance and characteristics of bidding firms in the Chinese stock markets. Emerging Markets Review, Vol. 12(2), p. 152-170.
10. Deloitte. (2010). A long path to better corporate governance: 2010 China listed companies corporate governance survey. Deloitte Touché Tohmatsu CPA Ltd
11. Fama, E. F., Fisher, L., Jensen, M.C. and Roll, R. (1969). The adjustments of stock prices to new information. International Economic Review, Vol. 10 (1), p.1-21.
12. Gao, L. and Kling, G. (2008). Corporate governance and tunnelling: Empirical evidence from China. Pacific-Basin Finance Journal, Vol. 16, p. 591-605.
13. Jensen, M. C. and Ruback, R. S. (1983). The market for corporate control: The scientific evidence. Journal of Financial Economics, Vol. 11, p. 5–50.
14. Kato, T. and Long, C. (2006). Executives compensation, firm performance and corporate governance in China: Evidence from Firms listed in the Shanghai and Shenzhen stock exchanges. Economic Development and Cultural Change, Vol. 54(4), p. 945-983.
15. Li, L. and Naughton, T. (2007). Going Public with Good Governance: Evidence from China, Corporate Governance: An International Review, Vol.15(6), p.1190-1202.
16. Lieberman, M. B. and Asaba, S. (2006). Why do firms imitate each other? Academy of Management Review, Vol. 31(2), p.366–385.
17. Sudarsanam, P. S. (2003). Creating Value from Mergers and Acquisitions: The Challenges, An Integrated and International Perspective. FT Prentice Hall Harlow.
18. Wei, Z., Xie, F. and Zhang, S., (2005). Ownership structure and firm value in China's privatized firms: 1991–2001. Journal of Financial and Quantitative Analysis, Vol. 40 (1), p. 87–108.
19. Pangarkar, N. (2000). What drives merger behaviour of firms? Strategic Momentum vs. Bandwagons. International Journal of Organization Theory and Behaviour, Vol. 3(1&2), p.37-72.
20. Rui O., Firth, M. and Fung, P. (2012). Corporate Governance and CEO Compensation in China, (September 2012).
21. Sudarsanam, P. S. (2003). Creating Value from Mergers and Acquisitions: The Challenges, An Integrated and International Perspective. FT Prentice Hall Harlow.
22. Tao, L. and Fie, X. (2014).The payment pattern of merger and acquisition: An empirical analysis from China's listed companies. Advanced Management Science (ICAMS), 2010 IEEE International Conference, Vol.3, no., p.575-581, 9-11 July 2010.
23. Uddin, M. and Boateng, A. (2009). An analysis of short run performance of cross-border mergers and acquisitions: evidence from the UK bidding firms. Review of Accounting and Finance , Vol. 8, p.431-453.

Yang, J., Chi, J. and Young, M. (2011). A review of corporate governance in China. Asian-Pacific Economic Literature, Vol. 25(1), p. 15–28

Table 1. Distribution of M&A deals by year and bidder industry
(Panel A: Distribution of M&A deals by year of announcement)

Year	Mean deal value (CNY millions)	Number of deals	Number of deals (%)
2007	68	41	2.13
2008	105	105	5.47
2009	119	139	7.24
2010	87	184	9.58
2011	268	165	8.59
2012	309	163	8.49
2013	338	328	17.07
2014	331	285	14.84
2015	322	257	13.38
2016	398	254	13.22
All	276	1,921	100.00

(Panel B: Distribution of M&A deals by bidder firm industry)

Bidder industry	Mean deal value (CNY millions)	Number of deals	Number of deals (%)
Agriculture	70	46	2.39
Mining	502	59	3.07
Manufacturing	189	1,071	55.75
Utility	459	104	5.41
Construction	489	39	2.03
Transportation	830	86	4.48
Information technology	651	102	5.31
Retail and wholesale	309	110	5.73
Real estate	308	97	5.05
Service	141	64	3.33
News and media	55	7	0.36
Miscellaneous	120	136	7.08
All	276	1,921	100

DOI: 10.1051/itmconf/20171204025

Table 2. Summary statistics

Independent variable	Count	Mean	Median	Std. Dev.	Minimum	Maximum
Governance variables						
State shares	1921	0.287	0.282	0.259	0.000	0.863
Legal person shares	1921	0.189	0.075	0.226	0.000	0.903
Board size	1921	9.397	9.000	2.142	5.000	19.000
Board independence	1921	0.801	1.000	0.399	0.000	1.000
CEO duality	1921	0.131	0.000	0.338	0.000	1.000
Executive shares	1921	0.009	0.000	0.051	0.000	0.638
Executive pay (CNY thousands)	1921	819.972	568.000	880.812	14.000	10500.000
Bidder characteristics						
Tobin's q	1921	2.338	1.795	2.286	0.680	48.088
Leverage	1921	0.143	0.114	0.123	0.000	0.788
Administration	1921	0.735	1.000	0.442	0.000	1.000
Related transaction	1921	0.605	1.000	0.489	0.000	1.000
Firm size (CNY millions)	1921	7390.000	1850.000	40700.000	14.800	994000.000
Deal characteristics						
Public target	1921	0.062	0.000	0.242	0.000	1.000
Diversifying acquisition	1921	0.902	1.000	0.298	0.000	1.000
All cash	1921	0.901	1.000	0.299	0.000	1.000
All stock	1921	0.044	0.000	0.205	0.000	1.000
Deal value (CNY millions)	1921	276.000	38.900	1460.000	1.000	32800.000
Repeat bidder	1921	0.730	1.000	0.444	0.000	1.000

Hydrophobic Lurylamine Modified Heteropoly Acid as an Efficient and Recyclable Catalyst for the Hydrolysis Reaction in Aqueous Solution under Microwave

Lin WU[a], Bian-Jiang ZHU, and Yin-Feng WU

Qingdao Technical College, Qingdao, Shandong Province
[a]wul@qtc.edu.cn

Abstract: A new modified phosphotungstic acid (HPW) catalyst (HPW-catal) was synthesized b y a simple mixing method under ambient atmosphere and evaluated for the hydrolysis of sucrose and ethyl acetate under microwave irradiation. The as-synthesized catalyst was characterized by X-ray diffraction (XRD), Fourier transform infrared spectroscopy(FTIR), and NH3-TPD, which proved that HPW was sucessfully modified with lurylamine and the catalyst still remains the Keggin structure. Significantly, the HPW-catal showed excellent catalytic hydrolysis perforance for the sucrose and ethyl acetate under microwave irradiation. Both of the reactions were studied over other solid acid catalysts, such as AM-15 and ZSM-5. At mild tempretures, the sucrose and ethyl acetate could be hydrolyzed into corresponding products. The maximum glucose yield and alcohol could reach 100% and 95%, respectively. The HPW-catal can be recycled and reused. The HPW-catal will provides new ideas for the modifying of heteropoly acids.

1 Introduction

Mineral acids (H_2SO_4, HCl and HNO_3) are essential in many industrially reactions such as alkylation, esterization and isomerization. Although these acid catalysts always exhibit high activity, they are typically associated with serious problems of high toxicity, corrosion, production of waste, difficulty of separation and recovery. From the viewpoint of "green chemistry" and "green technology",[1] production methods should be refined so as to minimize adverse effects on the environment or human health. Therefore, the search for more environmentally friendly solid acid catalysts had extraordinarily been paid attention.[2, 3] Among these solid acids, Heteropoly acids (HPAs) stand out due to their strong Bronsted acidity and fairly high thermal stability in the solid state.[4-6] As a consequence, several new industrial processes based on HPAs, such as hydration of olefins, oxidation of methacrolein, and polymeriztion of tetrahyrofuran, have been developed and commercalized.[7] Additionally, HPAs catalysed Fries rearrangement of phenyl acetate,[8] and Friedel–Crafts acylation of phenol[9] and oxidation of alcohols[10] have also been reported. Therefore, HPAs are excellent heterogenous solid acid catalyst in the catalytic system of solid-gas reaction or hydrophobic solvent.

On the other hand, the catalytic reactions in aqueous systems have interesting advantages including low cost, nontoxicity, availability, and safety. HPAs were also employed as homogeneous catalysts to accomplish a series of reactions in aqueous solution with relative high performance due to their high solubility in the polar solution. For example, in the hydrolysis of cellulose, $H_3PW_{12}O_{40}$ (HPW) exhibited high yield and selectivity of glucose (50.5% and >90% separately) due to its strong Bronsted acid strength and high hydrothermal stability.[11] The effects of Bronsted and Lewis acidity on the activity and selectivity of the HPA-based catalyst for the hydrolysis of cellulose were also discussed in another reports.[12] HPAs together with supported ruthenium catalysts showed not only high activity but also remarkable selectivity to sugar alcohols reaching up to 81% yield of C4 to C6 sugar alcohols in aqueous phase with 7 h at 160 °C.[13] Although the HPAs are unique acid catalysts in the aqueous reaction, the high solubility in polar reaction media largely hinder their practical utilizations. So far, some efforts that impregnating HPAs onto or encapsulating it into porous carriers with high surface areas, such as silica, active carbon, zeolite,[14-17] and partially exchanging protons of the parent HPA with large inorganic cations like Cs^+, K^+, Rb^+ and NH_4^+,[18, 19] have been made to separate the HAPs and reused them. Unfortunately, these methods were seldom successful. So, it is very desirable to develop an efficient and recyclable HPAs catalystic systmem to solve the separation and recycle issues of HPAs catalyst. In our opinion, an ideal catalyst in aqueous solution should mix and contact very well with reactant and separate spontaneously from the system after reaction.

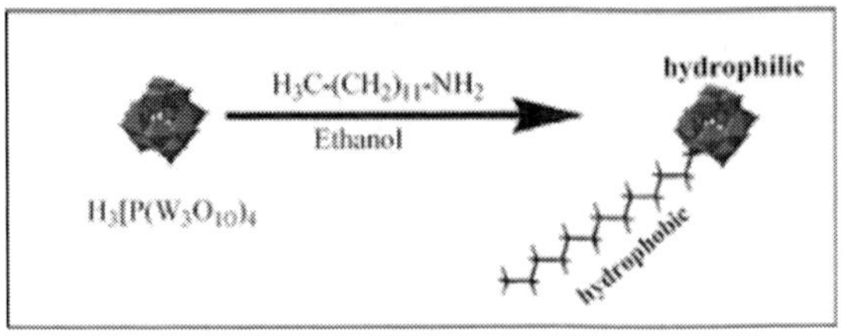

Figure 1. Synthesis of modified HPW catalyst

In this study, a much more environmentally benign and safe process for the hydrolysis of ethyl acetate and sucrose with luryamine modified heteropoly acid is reported. Most importantly, it's much easier than other typical HPAs to separate the catalysts with the products as they exists in different phases. What's more, the modified heteropoly acids showed stable and high catalytic activity. As far as we know, this is the first report of successful heteropoly acid catalyst modified in this way aiming to change its hydrophobicity which still has excellent catalytic acivity.

2 Experimental

2.1 Materials

Lurylamine(Tianjin Guangfu Fine Chemical Research Institute, lurylamine content ≥ 99 %), H3PW12O40 (Sinopharm Chemical Reagent Co., Ltd, AR), alcohol (Sinopharm Chemical Reagent Co., Ltd, AR), ethyl acetate (Sinopharm Chemical Reagent Co., Ltd, AR), sucrose (Tianjin Guangcheng Chemical Reagent Co.,Ltd, AR), concentrated sulphuric acid (Sinopharm Chemical Reagent Co., Ltd, AR), dilute sulphuric acids (0.1 mol/L, 0.3 mol/L, 0.5 mol/L, self-made by diluting concentrated sulphuric acid with a certain amount of water), Amberlyst®-15 (Abbr.Am-15, SIGMA-ALDRICH), HZSM-5 (Nankai University, silicon / aluminum ratio is 50), ammonium phosphotungstate (Abbr.AWP, Chengdu Kelong Chemical Reagent Factory, AR), distilled water.

All the other assistant chemicals were purchased from Sinopharm Chemical Reagent Co., Ltd, and used as received.

2.2 Modified HPW Catalysts Preparation

Under the ambient tempreture, 2 mmol lurylamine was dissolved in 10 mL alcohol and 1mmol HPW was dissolved in 2 mL, then mixed them in a 50 mL vessel, the mixture was stirred magnetically for 2 h before adding distilled water to generate white precipitatation. Then the white precipitatation were washed with distilled water for several times using centrifuge and dried overnight at 100 °C in an oven. The resultant powders were target catalysts called HPW-catal.

2.3 Catalytic Experiments

The hydrolysis of ethyl acetate: The reaction was carried out in a CEM Discover microwave synthesis reactor (CEM corporation, USA), after 0.3 g HPW-catal, 0.3 mL ethyl acetate were added into 15 mL distilled water, the solution was heated in 70 °C and the reaction was stopped after 0.5 h, 1 h, 1.5 h, 2 h, 2.5 h, respectively. In comparison to HPW-catal, the hydrolysis of ethyl acetate catalyzed by 0.3 g AM-15, 0.3 g ZSM-5, 0.3 g AWP, 0.1 mol/L H_2SO_4, 0.3 mol/L H_2SO_4, 0.5 mol/L H_2SO_4 were also conducted in the same condition as HPW-catal. What's more, the traditional hydrothermal reaction experinments were also performed, in this condition all of the reaction systems were performed in 70 °C and the time lasted for 1 h, 3 h, 5 h, 8 h, 10 h, respectively.

The hydrolysis of sucrose: In this experiment, 0.02 g HPW-catal, 0.02 g sucrose and 1 mL H_2O were mixtured which were heated at different temperatures for different reaction time under the microwave reactor mentioned above. The performance of other catalysts in the same condition were also tested.

The repeatability test: Both of the hydrolysis reactions above were used to test the repeatability of HPW-catal. The former reaction, after 0.3 g HPW-catal, 0.3 g ethyl acetate were added into 15 mL distilled water, the solution was heated in 70 °C holding for 1.5 h. After the reaction, HPW-catal were separated from the solution, washed with distilled water for several times, and dried in oven. The resulted HPW-catal were used to catalyze again as the same condition above, repeat four times. The later reaction, 0.02 g HPW-catal, 0.02 g sucrose and 1 mL H_2O were mixtured, then the mixture was heated in 75 °C holding for 2 h. then the similar operation as the former reaction were carried out.

2.4 Product Analysis

Samples in the hydrolysis of ethyl acetate were filtered through 0.22 μm-pore-size filters (Membrana) prior to analysis. The products in resultant solutions after reaction were identified by gas chromatograph (GC, 7890A, Agilent, USA). The temperature of injection was at 260 °C. Nitrogen was used as the carrier gas, and its flow rate was 1 mL/min. The injection volume was 1 μL and the split ratio was 20 : 1. The temperature program for the column was held at 60 °C for 1 min and programmed to 120 °C at a ramping rate of 25 °C/min, to 135 °C at a ramping rate of 30 °C/min, then to 180 °C at a ramping rate of 15 °C/min with a hold time of 3 min.

Samples in the hydrolysis of sucrose were also filtered through 0.22 μm-pore-size filters (Membrana) prior to analysis. The yield of glucose in resultant solutions was measured by Glucose biosensor (SBA-40E, Institute of Biology, Shangdong Academy of Science,China). Take 1 g/L of glucose solution as standard liquids in order to calibrate the glucose content.

Products yield of the two kinds of reactions were calculated by the following equation:

Products yield = np/nr * 100 %

where np is amount of substance of products quantified in this work and nr is amount of substance of reactants.

2.5 Catalyst Characterization

FT-IR spectra were recorded on Thermo Electron Fourier transform infrared spectrophotometer (FT-IR) Nicolet 6700. The sample was pelletized with KBr and used to record the infrared spectra, ranging from 4000 to 400 cm−1. Powder X-ray diffraction data (XRD) were recorded at a scanning rate of 0.02°/s using a Bruker D8 ADVANCE X-ray diffractometer at 40 kV and 40 mA with monochromatized Cu Kα (λ = 1.5418 nm) radiation. N_2 adsorption–desorption experiments were performed with a Micromeritics ASAP 2020 M+C surface area and porosity analyzer. The samples were outgassed for 10 h under vacuum at 100°C prior to adsorption. NH_3-TPD experiments were performed with a Micromeritics Autochem II chemisorption analyzer.

3 Results and Discussion

The FT-IR spectra method used to determine the change of groups on the samples before and after synthesis. FT-IR spectra of HPW, HPW-catal, lurylamine were shown in Fig. 2. The Keggin structure of both HPW and HPW-catal was identified by four characteristic absorption bands appearing at (i) 1080 cm^{-1} (stretching frequency of P–O_a in the central PO_4 tetrahedron), (ii)983 cm^{-1} (terminal bands for WO_d in the exterior), (iii)895 cm^{-1} (stretching vibration of W–O_b–W bridges between corner sharing octahedras) and (iv)799 cm^{-1} (stretching vibrations of W–Oc–W bridges between edge sharing octahedras) as described elsewhere.[20, 21] In spite of the decrease of peak intensities and slight shift of peak positions, the four peaks appeared distinctively, which indicates that the Keggin structure of heteropolyanion was well reserved after the protons in the HPA were substituted by the organic cations. What's more, the another powerful evidence was shown that there were three ranges of Keggin structure feature peaks at 7~9°, 18~21°, 26~29°, respectively in XRD pattern , although some peaks became weak and absence due to the reaction between the lurylamine and HPA (in Figure. 3). [22] The two elliptic dotted lines stand stretching vibration and bending vibration of C-H respectively, indicating the sucessful introduction of carbon chain into the HPW-catal. The stretching vibration of OH for HPW-catal became weak compared with HPW because of the effects of hydrophobic nature of HPW-catal.At the same time, the vabrication of -NH_3^+ between 3100-3335 cm^{-1} appears after modification, which also indicated that the HPW has been modified by lurylamine. Based on above analysis, the lurylamine molecue has been incorporated onto the structure of HPW. The hydrophobic character of the HPW-catal also can prove this.while the NH stretching vibration blueshifts because of the effect of modification.

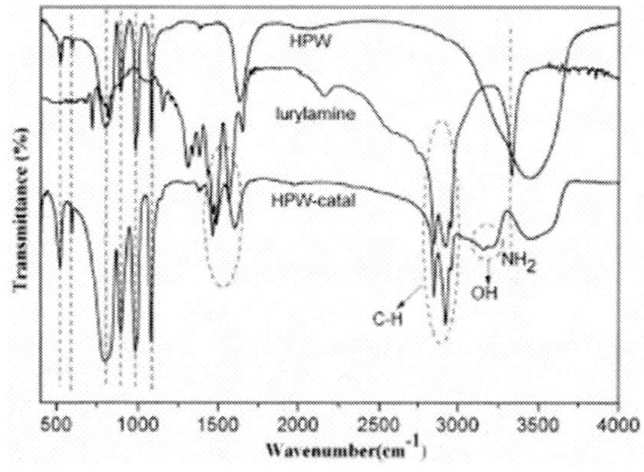

Figure 2. FT-IR spectra of HPW, lurylamine, HPW-catal

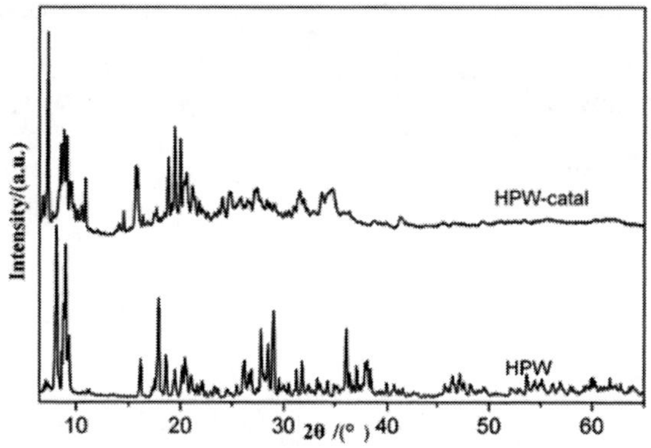

Figure 3. Powder X-ray diffraction patterns of HPW and HPW-catal

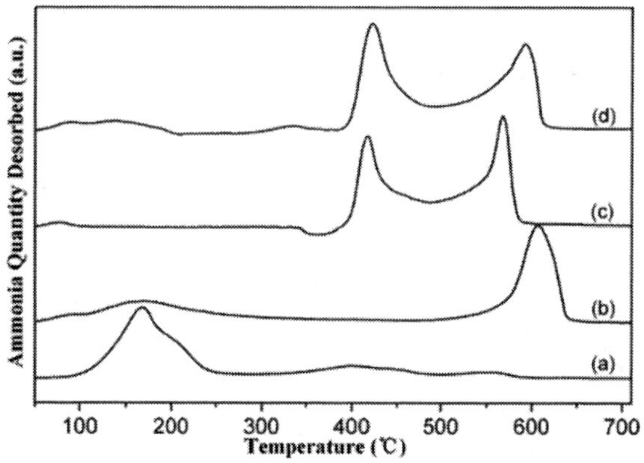

Figure 4. No-NH3-TPD profiles of HPW(a) and HPW-catal(c), NH3-TPD profiles of HPW(b) and HPW-catal(d)

In order to analyse the catalyst further, the NH_3-TPD was empolyed to detect the acid sites on the catalyst. Before the experiments, the TPD was carried out without NH_3(No-NH_3-TPD). It is found that the HPW shows an obvious peak before 200°C attributed to the presence of water. The HPW-catal shows an weak peaks before 200°C due to its hydrophobic nature and a strong peak between 550-640°C contribute to the destructure of lurylamine. For the NH_3-TPD analysis, HPW exibits two peaks around 400 °C and 600 °C which was attributed to mediate strong acid site and a strong acid site respectively. Judging from the area of the peaks, the amount of mediate acid sites is relative equal to the strong one. Intrestingly, after the modification, the HPW-catal also show two obvious peaks atrributed to mediate strong acid site and strong acid site. Combined with the analysis of No-NH_3-TPD, the HPW-catal shows more mediate strong acid sites after modification due to the reaction between the strong acid site and HPW. The EA analysis was empolyed to evaluate the amount of the organic molecule in the structure of HPW-catal. It is turned out that the nitrogen content was about 0.593 mmol/g. By theoretical caculation, the nitrogen content of HPW-catal should be 0.329, 0.614, 0.871 mmol/g corresponding to 1:1, 2:1, 3:1 reactant ratio for lurylamine/HPW. That is to say, to react with the proton of 1mmol HPW, at least, it needs 3 mmol lurylamine. So, in our experiments, the accounts of HPW were excess, which should explain the strong acid site of HPW-catal since only part of H^+ ions in HPW had combined with lurylamine.

To evaluate the catalytic performance of the lurylamine modified heteropoly acid in the water, the hydrolysis reaction of sucrose and ethyl acetate was carried out. For the hydrolysis of sucrose(Figure 5), two kinds of products (glucose and fructose) were generated.the yield of glucose was used to measure the catalytic activity. The results of glucose yield for the hydrolysis of sucrose catalyzed by HPW-catal, AWP, AM-15 and HZSM-5 were summarized in Table 1. It is found that the glucose yield of 76% can be obtained after 0.5 h and 100 % is got after 2h, when the HPW-catal served as the catalyst and the reaction temperature was75°C (Table 1, entry 1-5).The temperture effect on the reactions was also evaluated in the experiments (Table 1, entry 6-10). The results indicated that the optimal conditions of sucrose hydrolysis over HPW-catal was 2h, 75 °C with 100 % glucose yield under microwave. It should be pointed out that no glucose yield was obtained for the reaction without any catalysts (Table 1, entry14) under such that conditions, which indicated that the HPW-catal indeed served as catalyst during the reaction. For the comparation, the catalyst of AWP, AM-15 and HZSM-5 were also employed to catalyse the reaction under the same condition. The results showed that the glucose yield was 4%, 100% and 56% respectively (Table 1, entry12-14). That is to say the activity of HPW-catal is the same as commercial AM-15, and higher than AWP and HZSM-5.

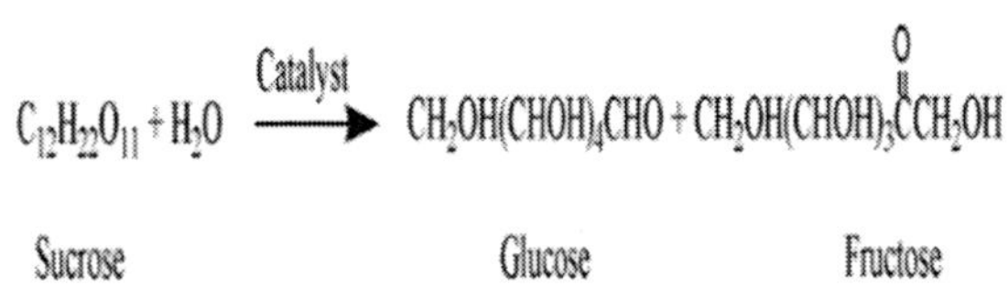

Figure 5. Process for the hydrolysis of sucrose

Table 1. Results of sucrose hydrolysis over catalysts under microwave condition

Entry	Catalyst	Time /(h)	Temperature /(°C)	Glucose yield /(%)
1		0.5		76
2		1		88
3		1.5		94
4		2	75	100
5		2.5		100
6		2	60	22
7		2	65	56
8		2	70	88
9		2	75	100
10		2	80	100
11	AWP	2	75	4
12	AM-15	2	75	100
13	HZSM-5	2	75	56
14	-	2	75	0

The hydrolysis of ethyl acetate in the aqueous solution was also employed to evaluated the performance of catalyst (Table 2). Alcohol yield of 95% can be obtained within 1.5 h at 70°C under the microwave for the HPW-catal. As comprison, AWP, AM-15, HZSM-5 and dilute sulphuric acid were also used to catalyzed the reaction(Table 2, entry 6-11). Under the same condition the alcohol yield for the calalyst of AM-15, HZSM-5 and AWP is 89.7%, 80.4% and 2.8%. Interestingly, the HPW-catal showed higher activity on hydrolysis of ethyl acetate than HZSM-5, AWP and even AM-15. The most important reason is believed that hydrolysis of ethyl acetate catalyzed by HPW-catal in water is a homogenous reaction while others were heterogenous reactions. It should be note that the hydrophobic HPW-catal can be dissolved in ethyl acetate before reacting. In the water reaction system, the ethyl acetate is a separation phase due to the hydrophobic nature. During the reaction, the HPW-catal mixs very well with ethyl acetate, when the hydrolysis takes place, the products alchohol and acetic acid will get into water directly, the equilibrium of reaction will change. When the reaction reached equilibrioum, the ethyl acetate was almost used out, the HPW-catal was automatically separated due to its hydrophobic nature. It is well known that the inorganic miner acid such as sulphuric acid can also give a high conversion of hydrolysis of ethyl acetate. But the seperation and recycle problems for H_2SO_4 was still not solved, while HPW-catal precipitated from the system spontaneously after reaction and could be used repeatedly.

Figure. 6 shows the plots of alcohol yield versus time for the hydrolysis of ethyl acetate at 70 °C catalyzed by the HPW-catal under microwave irradiation and conventional heating (oil bath), rspectively. Evidently, compared with the conventional heating, the microwave

DOI: 10.1051/itmconf/20171204026

irradiation significantly accelerated the hydrolysis reaction and increased the yield of alcohol. Under conventional heating, the maximum yield of alcohol was 63 % after 5 h for reaction, while the alcohol yield of about 75 % can be obtained under microwave irradiation for only 0.5 h. Additionally, the maxium yield of 95% can be reached after irradiation of 1.5 h. The rate of ethyl acetate hydrolysis under the microwave irradation is estimated to be much more 5 times than that under converntional heating. It was believed that the microwave irradiation might activate the participating molecules in the reaction, and improve the effective contraction among molecules, which lead to the acceleration the hydrolysis process.

Table 2. Results of ethyl acetate hydrolysis over catalysts under mcrowave conditions

Entry	Catalyst	Time /(h)	Temperture /(°C)	Alcohol yield /(%)
1		0.5		75.1
2		1		83.5
3	HPW-catal	1.5		95
4	AM-15	1.5	70	89.7
5	HZSM-5	1.5		80.4
6	AWP	1.5		2.8
7	1mlH_2SO_4	0.5		100
10	3mlH_2SO_4	0.5		88.5
11	5mlH_2SO_4	0.5		86.6

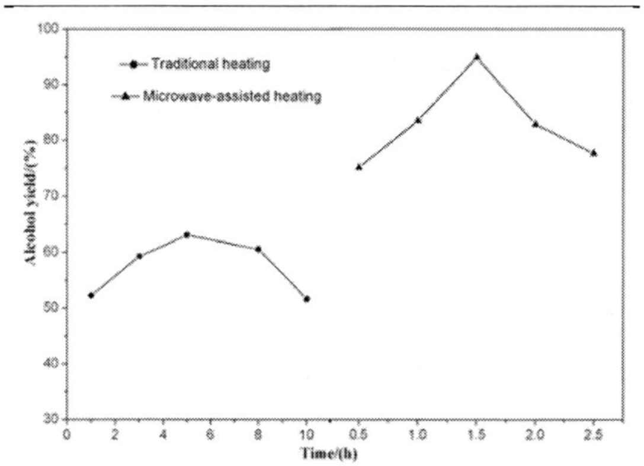

Figure 6. The contrast of alcohol yield between the condition of traditional heating and microwave-assisted heating at 70 °C.

In the aqueous reaction system, the HPW-catal can be recycled easyliy due to the hydrophobic nature. The catalyst was repeated 5 cycles for the hydrolysis of sucrose and ethyl acetate (Figure. 7). It can be seen that after 5 recycles the HPW-catal can still performed high activity on both of the reactions.

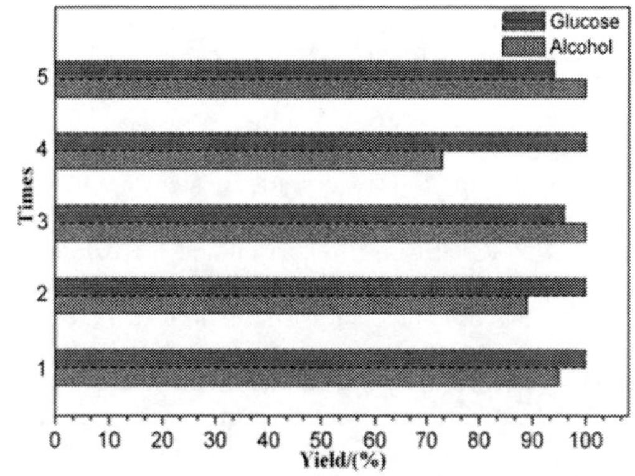

Figure 7. Results of HPW-catal repeatability tested on the two reactions

4 Conclusions

In summary, we have demonstrated that a new HPW modified catalyst not only was hydrophobic but maintain high catalytic activity. In the hydrolysis reaction of ethyl acetate, alcohol yield of 95% was obtained. It's worth mentioning that HPW-catal was soluble in ethyl acetate which was different from other solid acid, so the solution was emulsion with magnetic stirring during the reaction, but precipitated from the system spontaneously after reaction and could be used repeatedly. Glucose yield of 100% was got by using HPW-catal in the hydrolysis of sucrose, which is same as using AM-15. Additionally, the HPW-catal catalyst showed a stable catalytic activity and can be reused after reaction. Due to the satisfactory catalytic performance, easy availability and its special in dissolubility, HPW-catal shows encouraging prospects for practical uses in hydrolysis reactions.

References

1. A. Takagaki, C. Tagusagawa, S. Hayashi, M. Hara and K. Domen, "Nanosheets as highly active solid acid catalysts for green chemical syntheses", Energy Environmental Science, 2010, vol. 3, pp. 82-93.
2. A. Corma "Inorganic solid acids and their use in acid-catalyzed hydrocarbon reactions", Chemical Reviews, 1995, vol. 95, pp.559-614.
3. T. Okuhara, "Water-Tolerant solid acid catalysts", Chemical Reviews, 2002, vol. 102, pp.3641-3666.
4. I. V. Kozhevnikov, "Catalysis by heteropoly acids and multicomponent polyoxometalates in liquid-phase reactions", Chemical Reviews, 1998, vol. 98, pp.171-198.
5. T. Okuhara, "New catalytic functions of heteropoly compounds as solid acids", Catalysis Today, 2002, vol. 73, pp. 167-176.
6. I. Kozhevnikov, "Heterogeneous acid catalysis by heteropoly acids: Approaches to catalyst deactivation", Journal of Molecular Catalysis A: Chemical, 2009, vol. 305, pp. 104-111.

7. M. Misono,N. Nojiri, "Recent progress in catalytic technology in japan", Applied catalysis, 1990, vol. 64, pp. 1-30.
8. E. F. Kozhevnikova, E. G. Derouane and I. V. Kozhevnikov, "Heteropoly acid as a novel efficient catalyst for Fries rearrangement", Chemical Communications, 2002, pp. 1178-1179.
9. J. Kaur, K. Griffin, B. Harrison and I. Kozhevnikov, "Friedel–Crafts acylation catalysed by heteropoly acids", Journal of Catalysis, 2002, vol. 208, pp. 448-455.
10. H. Firouzabadi, N. Iranpoor and K. Amani, "Solvent-Free and selective oxidation of hydroxy groups to their corresponding carbonyl functions with ferric nitrate activated by heteropoly acids", Synthesis, 2003, pp. 408-412.
11. J. Tian, J. H. Wang, S. Zhao, C. Y. Jiang, X. Zhang and X. H. Wang, "Hydrolysis of cellulose by the heteropoly acid $H_3PW_{12}O_{40}$" Cellulose, 2010, vol. 17, pp. 587-594.
12. K.-i. Shimizu, H. Furukawa, N. Kobayashi, Y. Itaya and A. Satsuma, "Effects of Brønsted and Lewis acidities on activity and selectivity of heteropolyacid-based catalysts for hydrolysis of cellobiose and cellulose", Green Chemistry, 2009, vol. 11, pp.1627-1632.
13. R. Palkovits, K. Tajvidi, A. M. Ruppert and J. Procelewska, "Heteropoly acids as efficient acid catalysts in the one-step conversion of cellulose to sugar alcohols", Chemical Communication (Camb), 2011, vol. 47, pp. 576-578.
14. Q. Y. Liu, W. L. Wu, J. Wang, X. Q. Ren and Y. R. Wang, "Characterization of 12-tungstophosphoric acid impregnated on mesoporous silica SBA-15 and its catalytic performance in isopropylation of naphthalene with isopropanol", Microporous and Mesoporous Materials, 2004, vol. 76, pp. 51-60.
15. S. Mukai, L. Lin, T. Masuda and K. Hashimoto, "Key factors for the encapsulation of Keggin-type heteropoly acids in the supercages of Y-type zeolite" Chemical Engineering Science, 2001, vol. 56, pp. 799-804.
16. F. Marme, G. Coudurier and J. C. Védrine, "Acid-type catalytic properties of heteropolyacid H3PW12O40 supported on various porous silica-based materials", Microporous and Mesoporous Materials, 1998, vol. 22, pp. 151-163.
17. M. E. Chimienti, L. R. Pizzio, C. V. Cáceres and M. N. Blanco, "Tungstophosphoric and tungstosilicic acids on carbon as acidic catalysts", Applied Catalysis A: General, 2001, vol. 208, pp. 7-19.
18. W. G. Klemperer,C. G. Wall, "Polyoxoanion chemistry moves toward the future: from solids and solutions to surfaces", Chemical Reviews, 1998, vol. 98, pp. 297-306.
19. J. Tian, C. Fang, M. Cheng and X. Wang, "Hydrolysis of cellulose over CsxH3–xPW12O40 (X = 1–3) heteropoly acid catalysts", Chemical Engineering & Technology, 2011, vol. 34, pp. 482-486.
20. L. Zhang, Q. Jin, L. Shan, Y. Liu, X. Wang and J. Huang, "H3PW12O40 immobilized on silylated palygorskite and catalytic activity in esterification reactions", Applied Clay Science, 2010, vol. 47, pp. 229-234.
21. Y. Leng, J. Wang, D. Zhu, Y. Wu and P. Zhao, "Sulfonated organic heteropolyacid salts: Recyclable green solid catalysts for esterifications", Journal of Molecular Catalysis A: Chemical, 2009, vol. 313, pp. 1-6.
22. M. T. Pope, Y. Jeannin and M. Fournier, Heteropoly and isopoly oxometalates, Springer-Verlag Berlin, 1983.

Empirical Research on the Impact of Agriculture Technique on Agricultural Output

Peng JIANG[1, a], Ai-Sheng REN[2, b]

[1]Institute of Agricultural Information and Economics, Beijing Agriculture and Forestry Academy of Science, Beijing ,China
[2]Institute of Agriculture and Economic Development, Chinese Academy of Agriculture Science, Beijing, China
[a]jiangpeng0451@126.com
[b]17125661@qq.com

Abstract: Due to the issues of the current agriculture technique relating to agriculture output, as well as its mutual relationship between both factors, this paper was set up from the interactions among capital input, labor input and technical input of agricultural sectors and modern industrial sectors, agricultural output. Through a production model constructed by agricultural technique and agricultural output, it can be illustrated from the co efficiency regression that agricultural technique progress had a positive relationship with agricultural output. At last, based on the issues reflected from model, some countermeasures were promoted accordingly.

1 Introduction

A great deal of practice shows that the development of agricultural technology is the first impetus to promote agricultural production. Agricultural technology progress has become the power of agricultural production, and plays an important role in the agriculture production in Agricultural developed countries. In the early 1970 of the 20th century, 60%-80% of the growth in agricultural productivity in the world's major developed countries was achieved by technological progress. In 1929-1972, 81% of U.S. agricultural growth and 71% per cent of productivity growth were attributed to agricultural technological advances. From the practice of China's agricultural development, according to the Chinese Academy of Agricultural Sciences, in 1972-1980, 27% of China's output increment was obtained by agricultural technology progress. In the , agricultural output increased by 35% and 40% respectively in the 6th Five-Year Plan and the 7th Five-Year Plan. After more than 20 years of efforts, the contribution rate of agricultural technology development to agricultural growth in China has exceeded 45%.

Since the opening-up policy, China's agricultural production has made considerable progress. In the background of large-scale labor outflow and the shrinking of arable land, the development of agricultural technology provides guarantee for sustained production of agricultural products. February 1, 2012, the CPC Central Committee issued a "state Council to accelerate the promotion of agricultural science and technology innovation to continuously enhance the supply and security of agricultural products in several views", it presents that Agricultural science and technology innovation needs to be accelerated and it plays an important role in the popularization of agricultural technology led by government and the increase of agricultural output. As a large population of developing country, in the case of shortage of arable land resources and insufficient investment in agriculture, speeding up the innovation of agricultural technology is of great significance to guarantee sustainable development of agricultural production. By using time series data to test the influence and size of agricultural technology on China's gross agricultural product since 90, the paper further verifies the importance of agricultural technology to agricultural production.

2 Research Methods

2.1 Assumptions

According to the method of urban and rural dualistic economy, there are four hypotheses:

1) There are two sectors in the economy: traditional agriculture sector and modern industry sector, the output level of the two departments is determined by the production factors and technical level of each input. The input elements of traditional agriculture sector are capital (mainly land), labor and technology (simple technology), and the input elements of modern industry sector are capital, labor and technology (modern technology).

2) The development of urban economy has reached saturation; the capital supply of modern industry sector and the supply of urban labor are invariable.

3) The scale of the traditional agricultural sector and the modern industry sector pay unchanged.

4) The labor and capital elements can flow freely between the two sectors and the rural labor force can be transformed into modern industrial labor.

2.2 The Model of Agricultural Technology's Influence on Agricultural Production

According to the above assumptions, the C-D production function of the agricultural sector and the modern industry sector can be expressed as follows:

$$Y(t)_1 = F[A(t)_1, L(t)_1, K(t)_1] = A(t)_1 L(t)_1^{\alpha} K(t)_1^{1-\alpha} (0 < \alpha < 1) \quad (1)$$

$$Y(t)_2 = F[A(t)_2, L(t)_2, K(t)_2] = A(t)_2 L(t)_2^{\beta} K(t)_2^{1-\beta} (0 < \beta < 1) \quad (2)$$

In Eq.(1), $Y(t)_1$ represents the output of the agricultural sector, $K(t)_1$ indicates the amount of capital invested in the agricultural sector, $L(t)_1$ is the variable to proxy for the number of labor inputs in the agricultural sector, $A(t)_1$ Represents the technical level of the agricultural sector, which reflects the effectiveness of agricultural labor input. In Eq.(2), $Y(t)_2$ represents the number of capital inputs in the modern sector, $K(t)_2$ indicates the amount of capital invested in the modern sector, $L(t)_2$ is the variable to proxy for the number of labor inputs in the modern sector, $A(t)_2$ indicates the technical level of modern industry in urban area, which reflects the effectiveness of modern industrial labor input. In Eq.(1) and Eq.(2), α and β are the labor output elasticity of two sectors respectively. The profit function of the agricultural sector can be expressed as:

$$r_1 = TR_1 - C_1 = A(t)_1 P(t)_1 L(t)_1^{\alpha} K(t)_1^{1-\alpha} \quad W(t)_1 L(t)_1 \quad Z(t)_1 K(t)_1 \quad (3)$$

In Eq.(3), r_1 is the profit of agricultural production, TR_1 is the total income of agricultural production, C_1 is the total cost of agricultural production, $P(t)_1$ is the price of selling agriculture, since agriculture belongs to the necessities of life, its price is controlled strictly by the state, the change range is small, we assume it is unchanged. $W(t)_1$ is the wages in agricultural production, $Z(t)_1$ is the rental of capital in agricultural production. The labor, capital and the rents of capital are respectively calculated first-order bias and made equal to zero in Eq.(3).Based on profit maximization, and we can get wages engaged in agricultural production and rents for agricultural productive capital:

$$W(t)_1 = \alpha A(t)_1 P(t)_1 L(t)_1^{\alpha-1} K(t)_1^{1-\alpha} \quad (4)$$

$$Z(t)_1 = (1-\alpha) A(t)_1 P(t)_1 L(t)_1^{\alpha} K(t)_1^{-\alpha} \quad (5)$$

Eq.(4) by dividing Eq.(5), the following results are obtained:

$$K(t)_1 = \frac{(1-\alpha) W(t)_1 L(t)_1}{\alpha Z(t)_1} \quad (6)$$

Substituting (6) for (1), the following results are obtained:

$$L(t)_1 = \frac{Y(t)_1}{A(t)_1} \left[\frac{\alpha Z(t)_1}{(1-\alpha) W(t)_1} \right]^{1-\alpha} \quad (7)$$

We assume that $TL(t)_1$ is the total agricultural production of labor force, then the number of surplus labor in agriculture ($L(t)_3$) can be provided for the modern industrial sector of the rural labor force:

$$L(t)_3 = TL(t)_1 - L(t)_1 = TL(t)_1 - \frac{Y(t)_1}{A(t)_1} \left[\frac{\alpha Z(t)_1}{(1-\alpha) W(t)_1} \right]^{1-\alpha} \quad (8)$$

Similarly, the profit function of the modern industry sector can be expressed as:

$$r_2 = TR_2 - C_2 = A(t)_2 P(t)_2 L(t)_2^{\beta} K(t)_2^{1-\beta} \quad W(t)_2 L(t)_2 \quad Z(t)_2 K(t)_2 \quad (9)$$

In Eq.(9), r_2 is the profits for the modern industrial sector, TR_2 is the total income for the modern industrial sector, C_2 represents the total cost of the modern industrial sector, $P(t)_2$ is the price of products for the modern industrial sector, $W(t)_2$ is the wages for the modern industrial sector, $Z(t)_2$ is the rent of capital. Likewise,

$$L(t)_2 = \frac{Y(t)_2}{A(t)_2} \left[\frac{\beta Z(t)_2}{(1-\beta) W(t)_2} \right]^{1-\beta} \quad (10)$$

This paper assumes that the total urban labor force is $TL(t)_2$, the modern industrial sector needs rural labor force is $L(t)_4$:

$$L(t)_4 = L(t)_2 - TL(t)_2 = \frac{Y(t)_2}{A(t)_2} \left[\frac{\beta Z(t)_2}{(1-\beta) W(t)_2} \right]^{1-\beta} \quad TL(t)_2 \quad (11)$$

$L(t)_3$ equals $L(t)_4$ when the supply and demand balance is available, according to Eq.(8) and Eq.(11) we can get that:

$$TL(t)_1 - \frac{Y(t)_1}{A(t)_1} \left[\frac{\alpha Z(t)_1}{(1-\alpha) W(t)_1} \right]^{1-\alpha} = \frac{Y(t)_2}{A(t)_2} \left[\frac{\beta Z(t)_2}{(1-\beta) W(t)_2} \right]^{1-\beta} - TL(t)_2 \quad (12)$$

For easy analysis, this paper assumes that α equals β, and according to Eq.(12), we can get the salary in a balanced state:

$$W = \left[\frac{\frac{Y(t)_1}{A(t)_1} \left[\frac{\alpha Z(t)_1}{1-\alpha} \right]^{1-\alpha} + \frac{Y(t)_2}{A(t)_2} \left[\frac{\alpha Z(t)_2}{1-\alpha} \right]^{1-\alpha}}{TL(t)_1 + TL(t)_2} \right]^{\frac{1}{1-\alpha}} \quad (13)$$

Because $L(t)_3$, $L(t)_4$ and L_m are equal in equilibrium state , L_m indicates the number of rural labor outflow, according Eq.(8) and Eq.(11) we can get that:

$$L_m = \frac{TL(t)_1 \frac{Y(t)_2}{A(t)_2}\left[\frac{\alpha Z(t)_2}{1-\alpha}\right]^{1-\alpha} - TL(t)_2 \frac{Y(t)_1}{A(t)_1}\left[\frac{\alpha Z(t)_1}{1-\alpha}\right]^{1-\alpha}}{\frac{Y(t)_1}{A(t)_1}\left[\frac{\alpha Z(t)_1}{1-\alpha}\right]^{1-\alpha} + \frac{Y(t)_2}{A(t)_2}\left[\frac{\alpha Z(t)_2}{1-\alpha}\right]^{1-\alpha}} \tag{14}$$

The relationship between the output of the agricultural sector and the outflow of rural Labor can be derived according to Eq.(14):

$$Y(t)_1 = \frac{Y(t)_2 A(t)_1 \left[\frac{\alpha Z(t)_2}{1-\alpha}\right]^{1-\alpha}}{A(t)_2 \left[\frac{\alpha Z(t)_1}{1-\alpha}\right]^{1-\alpha}} \times \frac{TL(t)_1 - L_m}{L_m + TL(t)_2} \tag{15}$$

According to 5 and 4,

$$Y(t)_1 = Y(t)_2 \frac{[A(t)_1]^{\alpha}}{A(t)_2} \left\{ \frac{Z(t)_2 [K(t)_1]^{\alpha}}{P(t)_1 [L(t)_1]^{\alpha}} \right\}^{1-\alpha} \times \frac{TL(t)_1 - L_m}{L_m + TL(t)_2} \tag{16}$$

According to Eq.(16), the technical level of the Shan agricultural sector is positively correlated with the agricultural production, this means that the higher the level of agricultural technology, the more agricultural production. The same conclusion was reached by Huang Tikun and Rozelle by establishing a model of crop production and supply.[Huang Tikun, Rozelle. China's food economy [m]. Beijing: China Agriculture Press, 1998].Therefore, the innovation of agricultural science and technology will improve the efficiency of agricultural production and increase the output of agricultural products. The reasons are as follows: First, the popularization of advanced agricultural technology can improve the level of agricultural scale, the change of decentralized operation, small-scale management, reduce the number of abandoned, to improve the productivity of agricultural land and labor efficiency; Second, the popularization of information technology helps farmers to obtain product and price information in time, expand the sales and service radius of agricultural products and agricultural commodities, Facilitate the Organization and scale of agricultural trade which is decentralized, small and single, promote the transformation of agricultural product supply and sale, solve the problems encountered in the process of agricultural products circulation and sales effectively and improve farmers ' enthusiasm for agricultural production; Third, the popularization of advanced agricultural technology is helpful to attract capital to agriculture, strengthen the enthusiasm of foreign capital to agriculture, increase the input of agriculture, and improve the production efficiency of agriculture. The technical level of modern industry sector is negatively correlated with agricultural production, that is, the higher the level of modern industrial sector, the smaller the agricultural production. Possible reasons are as follows:

First, the higher the level of modern industrial sector leads to the higher quality of labor force in modern industrial sectors, and it may cause a large number of rural high quality labor force to flow out, the shortage of high quality labor required for agricultural production, and may reduce agricultural production efficiency, and then lead to lower agricultural production; Second, the improvement of technical level of modern industrial sector will accelerate the development of modern industry in urban areas, and the rapid development of urban areas will increase the demand for rural labor force, under the premise of low agricultural comparative income, it will induce the outflow of rural labor force, and then cause the labor shortage necessary for agricultural production. Third, the improvement of modern industrial sector technology will have an alternative effect on the labor force and reduce the use of labor. And it may inhibit the outflow of rural labor, hinder the large-scale development of agriculture, reduce efficiency of agricultural production, and decline the production of grain.

3 Variables and Data Description and Regression Equation

The analysis shows that capital investment, rural labor force, level of agricultural technology and area of cultivated land are the direct and main factors affecting output. Agricultural Science and technology innovation is very important to improve agricultural production efficiency in the condition that the land resources are not changed or even reduced, and the rural labor force outflow. Is the above conclusion in line with China's actual situation? This paper will use the time series agricultural output, input of agricultural labor force , agricultural fixed capital, agricultural technology level, the total area of crop sowing in Statistics Yearbook of China (1990-2012), China Rural Statistical Yearbook (2012) and China Fixed Assets Investment Statistics Yearbook (2012) Related statistic data (table 1) to verify the conclusions. Since agricultural technology is a broad concept, it is difficult to define its specific content in statistics. Because the level of agricultural mechanization has played a leading or decisive role in other agricultural technologies, and other agricultural technologies will be difficult to be applied in agricultural production without the widespread use of advanced agricultural machinery, and taking into account the availability of data, we take the total power of agricultural machinery instead of agriculture. Therefore, we use the regression equation for empirical testing. The model is as follows:

$$AP = CI^{\gamma_1} AL^{\gamma_2} AT^{\gamma_3} SA^{\gamma_4} \tag{17}$$

This paper takes logarithm of all variables to eliminate the effect of variance between variables.

$$Ln(AP)_t = C + \gamma_1 Ln(CI)_t + \gamma_2 Ln(AL)_t + \gamma_3 Ln(AT)_t + \gamma_4 Ln(SA)_t + \varepsilon_{it} \tag{18}$$

The investment of agricultural material capital is measured by the stock of fixed capital of agriculture which is calculated with total agricultural capital formation minus fixed assets depreciation. This paper uses the depreciation rate of fixed assets in the agricultural sector as the agricultural economic depreciation rate in the basic fixed assets depreciation rate of the enterprise, and it is 4.24%.In order to eliminate the impact of inflation, the 1990-year-old agricultural fixed asset investment price index should have been used to calculate the actual physical capital stock, but this index is difficult to construct because of the lack of agricultural fixed assets Investment Price index data. Price index of agricultural production materials indicates the relative degree of price change trend and degree of agricultural means of production in a certain period. Therefore, this paper uses the National agricultural production material Price index to replace the agricultural fixed asset price index;

The data of agricultural output, agricultural labor input, total power of agricultural machinery and farm sown area are from the annual Rural Statistical Yearbook of China; ε_{it} represents other factors those are not to be considered.

4 Empirical Results and Analysis

Table 1. Elements of agricultural inputsand output of agricultural inputs from 1990 to 2012

year	Agricultural output (hundred million RMB)	**Stock of fixed capital in agriculture (hundred million RMB)**	**Total power of agricultural machinery (hundred million RMB)**	**Input of agricultural labor force (ten thousand)**	Total area of agricultural sowing (thousand hectare)
1990	7662.1	2590.3	2870.8	38914	148362
1991	8157.0	2805.1	2938.9	39098	149586
1992	9084.7	2930.2	3030.8	38699	149007
1993	10995.5	3151.9	3181.7	37680	147741
1994	15750.5	3317.9	3380.3	36628	148241
1995	20340.9	3593.7	3611.8	35530	149879
1996	22353.7	3827.9	3854.7	34820	152381
1997	23788.4	3980.7	4201.6	34840	153969
1998	24541.9	4083.7	4520.8	35177	155706
1999	24519.1	4124.3	4899.6	35768	156373
2000	24915.8	4146.4	5257.4	36043	156300
2001	26179.6	4253.8	5517.2	36513	155708
2002	27390.8	4339.4	5793	36870	154636
2003	29691.8	4411.6	6038.7	36546	152415
2004	36239.0	4636.6	6402.8	35269	153553
2005	39450.9	4766.3	6839.8	33970	155488
2006	40810.8	4927.7	7252.2	32561	152149
2007	48893.0	5107.8	7659	31444	153464
2008	58002.2	5239.0	8219	30654	156266
2009	60361.0	5404.4	8749.6	28890	158614
2010	69319.8	7587.2	9278	27931	160675
2011	81303.9	8440.5	9734.7	26594	162283
2012	89453.0	8622.2	10255.9		160866

NOTE: The data is from the annual "China Statistical Yearbook", "China Rural Statistical Yearbook", "China Fixed Assets Investment Statistics Yearbook."

Table 2. Regression results

Variables	**Coef**	**Sign of T**	**R-squared**	**Adjusted R**	**F**	**Pr>F**
CI	0.756825	1.461030·	0.960414	0.951100	103.1121	<0.001
AL	-0.706029	-0.241293				
AT	1.001170	4.047169··				
SA	-0.657432	-0.241293				

NOTE: The results are calculated by EVIEWS6.0 software. *** Indicates that the estimated value in the single tail test in the 10%, 5% of the confidence level is significantly non-zero.

As can be seen from table 2, the linear equations have higher R value and f value, which shows that the regression equation based on the theoretical model is well fitted.

Based on the regression results, we can draw conclusions as follows:

*1)*Agricultural technology level (AT) has a significant positive impact on agricultural production,1% per cent increase in agricultural technology will increase agricultural production by 1.001%,it means that the higher the agricultural technology, the higher the gross agricultural product. And there are two possible causes are as follows: First, since the 1990s, the development of urban non-agricultural industry and the outflow of large numbers of young adults in rural areas lead to shortage of labor force and increasing abandoned of arable land. And romoting agricultural science and technology innovation can effectively counteract this effect and increase the output of agricultural production. Second, due to the accelerating progress of urbanization and industrialization, the fluctuation of agricultural sown area is more frequent, and in the case of arable land scarcity, it is necessary to rely on technological innovation to improve the production.

2) The effect of agricultural fixed capital investment (CI) on output is not significant, which shows that the impact of agricultural fixed capital investment on agricultural production is not obvious.

3) The regression coefficient of agricultural labor input (AL) is negative, which means that the increase in the labor force in agricultural production will reduce the output. This shows that in the case of limited arable land, the current total agricultural labor force in rural areas is surplus. To some extent, this problem hinders the transfer of farmland and the scale of operation, it also restrains the agricultural technology progress and popularization and reduces the labor productivity, which indicates that promoting the integration of urban and rural areas, developing non-agricultural industries and transferring agricultural labor force is of great significance to the improvement of agricultural production. And this conclusion is with Chen Yuanji ET (1994) [Chen Giyuan, Hu Piliang. The three-dimensional economic structure of China and the transfer of agricultural surplus Labor [j]. Economic Studies, 1994 (4)], Wu (2002) [Wu. The transfer of rural surplus labor and the problem of "three agriculture" [J]. Macroeconomic studies, 2002 (6)] are basically consistent. However, the impact on agricultural production is not significant; indicating whether agricultural labor input in the end has a negative impact on agricultural production is not obvious.

4) The regression coefficients of agricultural sown area (SA) are negative. However, the impact on agricultural production is not significant, indicating that the impact of agricultural acreage on agricultural production is not very obvious, which means that increasing or reducing agricultural acreage, does not necessarily lead to a rise or fall in the total value of agricultural products. As the same time ,it is difficult to determine the increasing agricultural acreage to increase agricultural output in the case of a shortage of arable land per capita in China, and to reduce agricultural acreage in the context of the continuous development of agricultural technology will not necessarily reduce agricultural output.

5 Research Conclusions

According to the above results, the level of agricultural science and technology has a positive effect on agricultural production, which means that the higher the level of agricultural production, the corresponding increase in the total value of agricultural products .With the progress of urbanization, the rapid development of non-agricultural industry and large rural labor force has transferred into the urban non-agricultural sector with higher wage rate. At the same time, agricultural science and technology innovation hedge the negative impact of rural labor force, and ensure the safety of agricultural production. Secondly, the influence of agricultural fixed capital investment on agricultural production is insignificant. Thirdly, there is a negative correlation between agricultural labor input and agricultural output, and the increase of agricultural labor force will lead to the decrease of agricultural output. At present, the agricultural production in China is constrained by the arable land, the agricultural science ,technology input and production level ,and the increase of scientific and technological input and production level in agriculture has replaced the rural labor force to some extent. The liberated labor force or the surplus labor force in the countryside will hinder the circulation of farmland in rural areas, and it will inhibit the upgrading and localization of agricultural technology and reduce agricultural productivity and reduce agricultural output. Finally, there is no obvious positive correlation between agricultural sown area and agricultural production, and their changes will not have a significant impact on the other variable, regardless of sown area or agricultural output.

Fund Projects

Beijing Academy of Agriculture and Forestry Special Fund for Scientific and technological innovation capacity (NO.KJCX20150203)

References

1. [1] Huangyuxiang etc. agricultural mechanization and the transfer of rural labor force [J]. Agricultural mechanization in China, 2005 (2): 7-10.
2. [2] Yu Qingdong, Li Yaixia. Study on agricultural mechanization and the transfer of rural labor force [J]. Agricultural mechanization Research, 2007 (4): 198-201.
3. [3] Mao Fei, Kong Xiangzhi. General situation and future orientation of China's agricultural modernization [J]. Reform, 2012 (10): 9-21.
4. [4]Koppel and Hawkins.Rural Transformation and the Future of Work in Rural Asia Economic Development and Cultural Change,1991,42(4),788-805.
5. [5] Shongjiang, Zhang. On the loss and prevention of rural excellent labor force in the process of urbanization [J]. Journal of Jinan Socialist College, 2001 (4): 87-90.
6. [6] Fan Decheng, Wang Zhihua. A study on the role of agricultural scale management in promoting urbanization from the perspective of rural labor force transfer [j]. Economic restructuring, 2011 (6): 81-84.
7. [7] Kiang Minglun etc. Stage characteristics, development trend and countermeasures of agricultural rural development in China [J]. Economist, 2012 (9): 81-90.
8. [8] Yang Minli, White Park. Analysis of the relationship between total power and influencing factors of agricultural machinery [J]. Agricultural Mechanization Research, 2004 (6): 45-47.
9. [9]Hayami Yujiro,God Yoshihisa .Agricultural Economics [M]. China Agriculture Press, 2003

ITM Web of Conferences **12**, 04028 (2017) DOI: 10.1051/itmconf/20171204028
ITA 2017

Short-term Forecast Model of Vehicles Volume Based on ARIMA Seasonal Model and Holt-Winters

Zhi-Hui WANG[1, a], Chen-Yang LU[2, b], Bin PU[2, c], Gui-Wen LI[1, d], and Zhen-Jiang GUO[1, e]

[1]*Intelligent Center, Yunnan Science Research Institute of Communication & Transportation, Kunming, China*
[2]*National Pilot School of Software, Yunnan University, Kunming, China*
[a]*937140839@qq.com*, [b]*luchenyanglcy@163.com*, [c]*937140839@qq.com*, [d]*344294117@qq.com*, [e]*3811247@qq.com*

Abstract: In order to alleviate the urban traffic congestion and ensure traffic safety, we need to do a good job in urban road traffic safety planning, make the real-time analysis and forecast of urban traffic flow to detect changes of current traffic flow in time, make scientific planning of roads and improve the road service ability and the transport efficiency of freight vehicles. The data of short-term vehicles volume is characterized by uncertainty and timing correlation series. Given this, the ARIMA seasonal model and the Holt-Winters model are used to establish a forecasting model for the short-term vehicles volume of the city. Finally, we compare the model with predictions.

1 Introduction

City vehicles volume is one of the important basis for the preparation of urban development planning, and it is also an important basic data for economic evaluation and post evaluation of urban construction projects. For the accurate forecast of vehicles volume, it can help transport the traffic control department of scientific management, to ensure the traffic safety. Short-term forecast of vehicles volume is mainly based on a period or even the daily traffic flow changes at the start, to study the short-term variations in the flow of goods vehicles. The short-term vehicles volume is a non-stationary time series[2] with both seasonal and periodic trends[1] and with some diversification.

Because of these attributes, the two typical time series prediction models of ARIMA and Holt-Winters are used to forecast the vehicles GPS data between October 20, 2015 to November 06, 2015 of Kunming, Yunnan Province to analysis and processing.

Traditional predictive methods must collect significant amounts of data, synthesize the various factors that affect the volume of the vehicle collecting data are difficult[3]. This type of forecasting method's hard to model. Sometimes the model can be successfully established, but the model parameters are lacking the necessary data and can't be reasonably estimated[4]. Because there are two significant characteristics of urban vehicles volume: Firstly, the data varies with the seasons and has a certain periodicity; Secondly, the series formed by the volume of the urban vehicle can be treated as a random series. We can use the ARIMA and Holt-Winters prediction model to approximate the series. When the random series matches the prediction model, the future value can be predicted by the time series and the current value[5]. Therefore, we build the forecasting model of urban vehicles volume to improve the accuracy of forecasting. Aim to plan the road traffic system scientific and improve the transportation efficiency of vehicles.

2 Data Source

The establishment of this model mainly selects the GPS data of vehicles in Yunnan Province from October 20, 2015 to November 16, 2015. Obtained the hourly vehicles volume data of 19 major cities in Yunnan Province after data preprocessing and preliminary statistical analysis. Choicing the 18 days vehicles volume data of city ID as 01 of Kunming to construct the model.The data example shown in Table 1:

Table 1. Vehicles Volume Data Example

Data	Time Period	City ID	Vehicles Volume
20151120	0	01	328
20151120	1	01	130
20151120	2	01	34
20151120	3	01	42
20151120	4	01	82
20151120	5	01	149

3 Model Overview

During the period from October 20, 2015 to November 06, 2015 the volume of the total vehicle of Kunming shows a significant fluctuation. And seasonal characteristic was more significant. The seasonal cycle is the 24 hours a day.

The peak and troughs of the volume of the vehicle at each time of the day are very stable. The peak of the volume of the vehicle appears at 9 o'clock to 10 o'clock every day, the trough of the volume of the vehicle appears at 3 o'clock to 4 o'clock every day. The random error is tested by Ljung-Box test, and the P value of random error white noise test is 0, indicating that the original data has sufficient seasonal and the random error has little effect.

3.1 ARIMA Seasonal Model

ARIMA seasonal model is a form of ARIMA model. For non-stationary time series with seasonal and trendy urban vehicles volume, the stationary time series can be obtained by periodic series difference and seasonal series difference. ARIMA seasonal model can extract the time series characteristics of seasonal, trend and random errors in the vehicles volume series.

Through the timing diagram and the result of difference operation[6], the vehicles volume predict model was determined as the $ARIMA(p,d,q)\times(P,D,Q)[S]$ initially, the p is the degree of nonseasonal autoregressive[7], d is the number of differentials, q is the moving average order[8]; P is the seasonal automatic regression order[9], D is the seasonal time differences, Q is the seasonal moving average order; S is the seasonal period[10]. The complete structure of the ARIMA seasonal model is as follows:

$$\nabla^d\nabla_S^D Y_t = \frac{\theta(x)\theta_s(x)}{\phi(x)\phi_s(x)}\varepsilon_t \quad (1)$$

Among them,

$$\begin{cases} \theta(x) = 1-\theta_1 x - \ldots - \theta_q x^q \\ \phi(x) = 1-\phi_1 x - \ldots - \phi_p x^P \\ \theta_s(x) = 1-\theta_1 x^s - \ldots - \theta_1 x^{QS} \\ \phi_s(x) = 1-\phi_1 x^s - \ldots - \phi_P x^{PS} \end{cases} \quad (2)$$

Y_t is the non-stationary time series at time t, ε_t is the white noise process, s is the cycle step, the study of the vehicles volume sequence has obvious cyclical and using the hourly data as the unit of seasonal data, so the $s = 24$, x is the hysteresis operator. $\theta(x)$ is the moving average coefficient polynomial of degree q , $\phi(x)$ is the autoregressive coefficients polynomial of degree. $\theta_s(x)$ is the moving average coefficient polynomial of degree Q, $\phi_s(x)$ is the autoregressive coefficients polynomial of degree P [11].

ARIMA seasonal model establishment steps:

- Test series smoothness. By observing the time series scatter plot, check whether the unit root exists and the ACF, PACF graph to determine whether the sequence is smooth. For the non-stationary sequence, it can be smooth by difference operation.
- Model identification and parameter fitting. According to the time series ACF graph and PACF graph to select the appropriate parameters of the seasonal ARIMA model to fit.
- Parameter estimation. Using the AIC criterion to determine the model parameters, compare the AIC values of each parameter model, select the model with the smallest AIC value as the optimal model.
- Model test. The residuals white noise test of the constructed model to determine whether the model is feasible.
- Model prediction. Use the established model to predict future time series.

3.2 Holt-Winters Model

Holt-Winters model is based on the statistical time series forecasting model, which can predict the time series with no distinct function rules but does correlate and seasonal trend. The time series of seasonal fluctuation, random variation and linear trend are decomposition, combined with exponential smoothing method to estimate the amount of decomposition and establish the prediction model.

The Holt-Winters seasonal model based on the addition is added to the horizontal component and the seasonal component[12]. The complete definition of the model is as follows:

$$\begin{cases} l_t = \alpha(y_t - s_{t-m}) + (1-\alpha)(l_{t-1} + b_{t-1}) \\ b_t = \beta(l_t - l_{t-1}) + (1-\beta)b_{t-1} \\ s_t = \gamma(y_t - l_{t-1} - b_{t-1}) + (1-\gamma)s_{t-m} \\ \hat{y}_{t+h} = l_t + hb_t + s_{t-m+h} \end{cases} \quad (3)$$

The t is the time of the time series. l_t is the horizontal component, b_t is the trend component, s_t is the seasonal component, m is the set seasonal period, h is the prediction period, the constant α, β, γ is the smoothing coefficient.

The Holt-Winters seasonal model based on multiplication is the horizontal component multiplied by the seasonal component. The complete definition of the model is as follows:

$$\begin{cases} l_t = \alpha\frac{y_t}{s_{t-m}} + (1-\alpha)(l_{t-1} + b_{t-1}) \\ b_t = \beta(l_t - l_{t-1}) + (1-\beta)b_{t-1} \\ s_t = \gamma\frac{y_t}{l_{t-1} - b_{t-1}} + (1-\gamma)s_{t-m} \\ \hat{y}_{t+h} = (l_t + hb_t)s_{t-m+h} \end{cases} \quad (4)$$

The t is the time of the time series. l_t is the horizontal component, b_t is the trend component, s_t is the seasonal component, m is the series seasonal period, h is the prediction period, the constan α, β, γ Holt-Winters seasonal is the smoothing coeffcient.

DOI: 10.1051/itmconf/20171204028

4 Experimental Results

4.1 ARIMA Experimental Results

Perform the white noise test on the original sequence; The results shows the , indicate that the original sequence is a non-white noise sequence[13], which has the significance of the research.

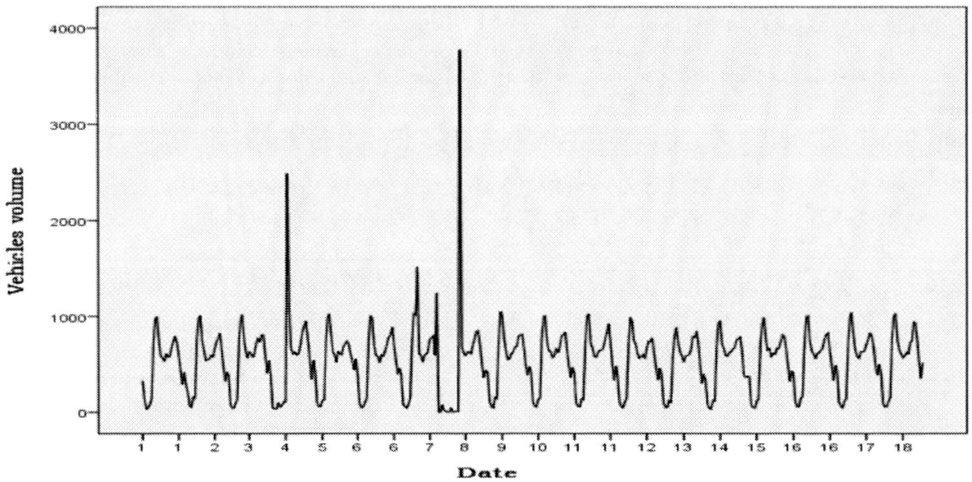

Figure 1. Original data time series graph

The vehicles volume shows the significant seasonal characteristics by per hour in Kunming. Tested by ADF, getting the probability of corresponding statistics is 0.01, Rejecting the assumption that the original sequence is a non-stationary series, the result shows that the vehicles volume time series are stationary, which consistent with the observations observed in Figure 1.

Table 2. Adf Checklist

Dicke y-Fuller	*Lag order*	*P-value*
-8.7814	7	0.01

By observing the autocorrelation, partial autocorrelation and ADF test result of Figure 2, the original sequence was diagnosed as a trend stationary, seasonal non-stationary series[14,15]. So we make the one-degree difference to the series. So the $d = 0$, $D = 1$. Through the autocorrelation graph and partial autocorrelation graph, we can obtain the p and q value in the $ARIMA(p, d, q) \times (P, D, Q)[S]$. The parameter q of the $MA(q)$ can be determined by the truncation of the AC, the parameter p of the $AR(p)$ can be determined by the truncation of the PAC. From the Figure 2 we can do analysis that it could be possible the value of p could be 0 or 1, the value of q could be 0 or 1, the value of P could be 0 or 1, the value of Q could be 0 or 1.

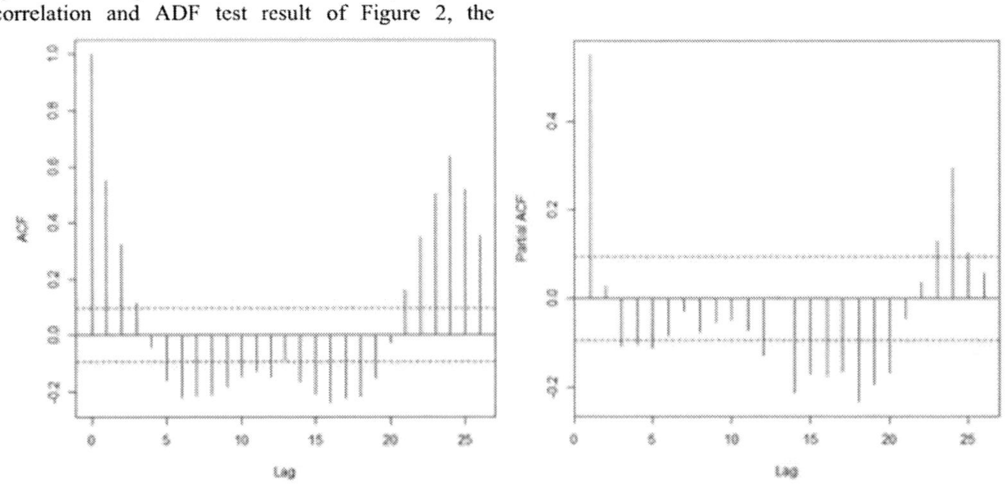

Figure 2. ACF,PACF graph

DOI: 10.1051/itmconf/20171204028

The $ARIMA(p,d,q)\times(P,D,Q)[S]$ model may have a lot of combination results. For these combination results, the optimal model can be determined by the AIC, SBC and AICC principle. The R model is used to determine the model as the optimal model according to the AIC criterion. We use the R modeling,determine the $ARIMA(1,0,0)\times(0,1,1)[24]$ as the optimal model according to the AIC criteria.

At the same time, the residuals of the model are tested, and the results show that the $p=0.01$, $\chi^2=9.106$, which demonstrate that the series information of vehicles volume has been fully extracted, and the series model residuals are white noise series. The final model is identified as the optimal model[16].

Table 3. Combination Of Arima Seasonal Model

Model	*AIC*	*AICc*	*BIC*
ARIMA（1,0,0）(0,1,1)[24]	5565.81	5565.87	5577.84
ARIMA（1,0,0）(0,1,2)[24]	5566.64	5566.74	5582.68
ARIMA（1,0,0）(1,0,0)[24]	6029.76	6029.86	6046.04
ARIMA（1,0,1）(1,0,0)[24]	6031.71	6031.85	6052.05
ARIMA（1,0,2）(1,0,0)[24]	6032.20	6032.4	6056.61
ARIMA（1,0,3）(1,0,0)[24]	6005.18	6005.44	6033.66
ARIMA（1,0,0）(0,0,1)[24]	6069.37	6069.47	6085.65
ARIMA（1,1,0）(0,1,1)[24]	5750.95	5751.01	5762.98

Predict Model use the $ARIMA(1,0,0)\times(0,0,1)[24]$ to predict the volume of the vehicle of the next 48 hour in the Kunming. The prediction results are shown in Table □, R^2 is 0.987, indicated that the model is highly fitted.The data fit graph is shown in the blue section of Figure 3. The model residual graph is shown in Figure 4.

Table 4. Arima Seasonal Model Fitting Degree Statistics

Sufficiency	*Average*
Stationary R square	0.987
R Square	0.990
RMSE	36.067
MPAE	9374.087

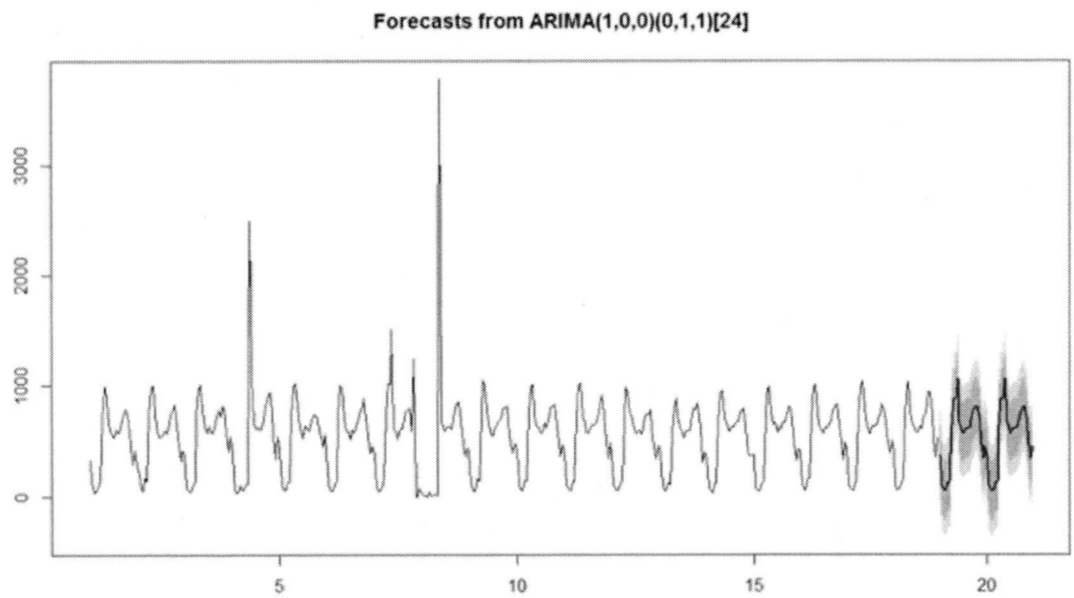

Figure 3. ARIMA Seasonal Model predict results graph

DOI: 10.1051/itmconf/20171204028

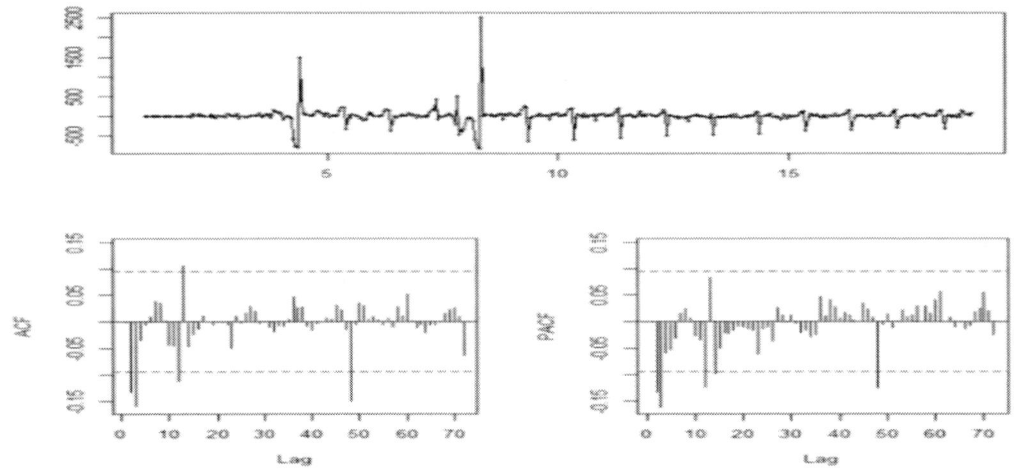

Figure 4. ARIMA Seasonal Model residual graph

4.2 Holt-Winters Experimental Results

The parameter alpha, beta and gamma of Holt-Winters Exponential smoothing model associated with the level, trend and the seasonal factors. The estimated value of alpha, beta and gamma are 0.0025, 0.2046 and 0.0734 respectively. The estimate of Alpha is 0.0025, indicating that the estimates at the current series time point balance the historical observations and the most recent observations substantially. The estimate of beta is 0.2046, indicating that the slope of the estimated Holt-Winters trend is stable over the entire time series substantially. The estimate of gamma is 0.0734, which is very high, indicating that the seasonal part of the forecast at the current time point is based on historical observations, and the forecast results are shown in Figure 5.

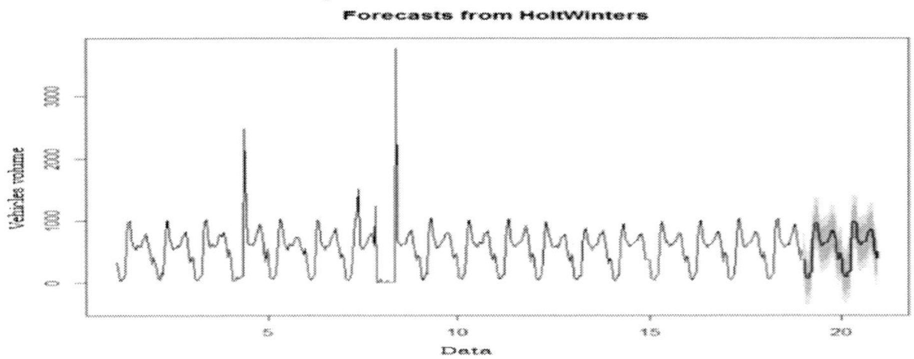

Figure 5. Holt-Winters forecast result graph

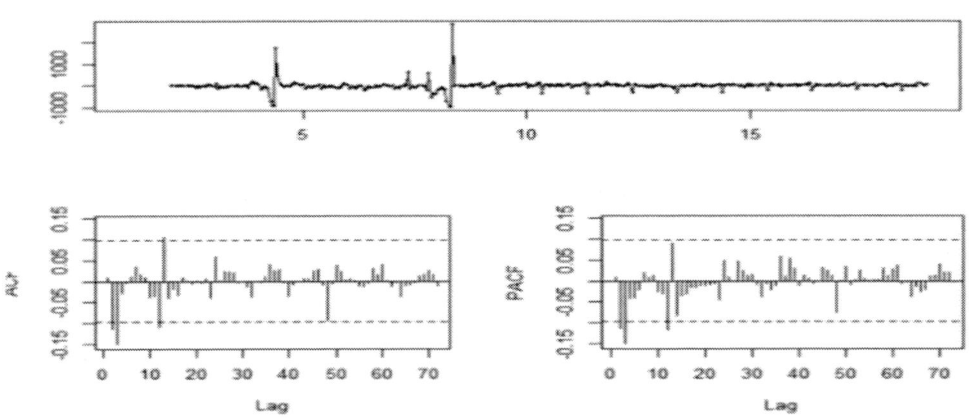

Figure 6. Holt-Winters residual Graph

DOI: 10.1051/itmconf/20171204028

Table 5. Holt-Winters Model Fitting Degree Statistics

Sufficiency	***Average***
Stationary R square	0.745
R Square	0.673
RMSE	197.419
MPAE	119.188

Table 6 shows the experimental comparing result of the ARIMA and Holt-Winters. The ARIMA seasonal model has the higher predictability of vehicles volume data, and the predicted mean square error and mean error also lower than the Holt-Winters model.

Table 6. Model Fitting Degree Statistics

Model	***Stationary R square***	***RMSE***	***AAD***
ARIMA seasonal model	0.987	64.481	0.099
Holt-Winters	0.745	90.884	0.101

5 Conclusion

The ARIMA seasonal model and the Holt-Winters model are used to forecast vehicles volume of Kunming in Yunnan Province. The forecast value was compared with the actual value, we can conclude that the ARIMA seasonal model is used to predict the volume of the vehicle are better than Holt-Winters model, and the ARIMA seasonal model has a higher fitting degree and better forecasting error. Due to limited data, and there are many factors that affect the volume of the short-term vehicle, the forecast model has some errors. Other factors should be considered in the actual application.

Acknowledgment

This work has been supported by the Open Foundation of Key Laboratory in Software Engineering of Yunnan Province under Grant NO. 2017SE204.

References

1. HongMeng Ji. Analysis on Passenger Transport Requirment and Passenger Volume Forcast of High Speed Railway[D].Beijing Jiaotong Universit,2015.
2. Diongue A K, Diop A, Ndongo M. Seasonal fractional ARIMA with stable innovations[J]. Statistics & Probability Letters, 2008, 78(12):1404-1411.
3. Wang Y, Wang J, Zhao G, et al. Application of residual modification approach in seasonal ARIMA for electricity demand forecasting: A case study of China[J]. Energy Policy, 2012, 48(3):284-294.
4. ZhenLong Wang. Time series analysis[M]. BeiJing: China Statistics Press, 2000.
5. Kalekar P S. Time series Forecasting using Holt-Winters Exponential Smoothing[J]. Kanwal Rekhi School of Information Technology, 2004.
6. ChingFu Chen, YuHern Chang, YuWei Chang. Seasonal ARIMA forecasting of inbound air travel arrivals to Taiwan[J]. Transportmetrica, 2009, 5(2):125-140.
7. Montanari A, Rosso R, Taqqu M S. A seasonal fractional ARIMA Model applied to the Nile River monthly flows at Aswan[J]. Water Resources Research, 2000, 36(5):1249-1259.
8. Mohan S, Vedula S. Multiplicative seasonal Arima model for longterm forecasting of inflows[J]. Water Resources Management, 1995, 9(2):115-126.Article in a journal:
9. Diongue A K, Diop A, Ndongo M. Seasonal fractional ARIMA with stable innovations[J]. Statistics & Probability Letters, 2008, 78(12):1404-1411.
10. Aston J A D, Findley D F, Mcelroy T S, et al. New ARIMA Models for Seasonal Time Series and Their Application to Seasonal Adjustment and Forecasting[J]. Journal of Official Statistics, 2007(1).
11. Kim B S, Hossein S Z, Choi G. Evaluation of temporal-spatial precipitation variability and prediction using seasonal ARIMA model in Mongolia[J]. KSCE Journal of Civil Engineering, 2011, 15(5):917-925.
12. Chatfield C. The Holt-Winters Forecasting Procedure[J]. Journal of the Royal Statistical Society, 1978, 27(3):264-279.
13. Chatfield C, Yar M. Holt-Winters Forecasting: Some Practical Issues[J]. Journal of the Royal Statistical Society, 1988, 37(2):129-140.
14. Kalekar P S. Time series Forecasting using Holt-Winters Exponential Smoothing[J]. Kanwal Rekhi School of Information Technology, 2004.
15. Chatfield C, Yar M. Prediction intervals for multiplicative Holt-Winters[J]. International Journal of Forecasting, 1991, 7(1):31-37.
16. Roberts S A. A General Class of Holt-Winters Type Forecasting Models[M]. INFORMS, 1982.

ITM Web of Conferences **12**, 04029 (2017) DOI: 10.1051/itmconf/20171204029
ITA 2017

Analysis and Forecast of Traffic Accident Big Data

Chen CHEN

Tunnel Traffic Engineering Design Office, Yunnan Province Transportation Planning and Design Institute, Kunming, China
522253113@qq.com

Abstract: Nowadays, as traffic accidents keep happening, traffic safety has become a major focus of contemporary social issues. Many factors account for traffic accidents, such as accident location, time period, driver's feelings, weather and other uncertain complex factors. As a result, the occurrence of traffic accidents is nonlinear, so it is necessary to explore the correlation between the data from many different aspects so as to avoid risks. By analyzing traffic data and graphics, R language shows how the data is related. After data preprocess, data selection by using R language Remap package remapB and remapH function, we get the locations of the accidents and the accident thermal chart, where you can find high- frequency accident locations. Besides, we employ decision tree, linear regression, random forest algorithm to model the data. According to the actual results, we can verify the correctness of the model and get the most accurate model and it can help us to predict this model with similar data in the future. The ultimate goal of data analysis is to choose the most accurate model after validating the model, analyzing the characteristics of the data and the relationship between the model and the data.

1 Introduction

1.1 Research Background

At present, China's national economy develops rapidly. Motor vehicle ownership, driving numbers, and road traffic flow continued to rise. Road traffic plays a more and more significant role in promoting economic and social development. The next traffic safety problem has become a key factor which can influence lives and property's safety of people, affecting and restricting the benefits of social and economic development. Road traffic safety is the result of the interaction of many non-deterministic factors such as people, cars, roads and the environment[1]. We need to analyze the road safety accident factors from many aspects and multi-level of the road. According to the characteristics such as accident occurrence, ambiguity and multi- factors, excavating such as the relationship, law, and features between all kinds of historical accident data. Our major cities facing a major problem is the safety of road traffic accidents. The analysis and forecast of large traffic data are conducive to planning transportation and improving the transport facilities significantly. Timely and accurate access to traffic accident data, analysis rapidly and establish the correct model become the primary requirements of large data traffic accident analysis.

The development and progress of road traffic have brought great convenience to human society, economic benefits and social prosperity. At the same time, the recurrence of traffic accidents has brought great disaster to human society. Traffic accidents have become a major public hazard in today's society. According to the traffic sector statistics, in 2011, road traffic accidents involved 210812 casualties, resulting in 62,387 people died and caused economic losses of 1078.73 million yuan directly. China is one of the countries which has the largest number of global traffic accidents.

In 2011, after the ban on drunk driving, the ownership of country car was 78 million, road traffic accidents were 210,812, the death toll as high as 62387. Comparing with Japan, the ownership of country car was more than 7,000, traffic accidents up to three times in China, while the death toll was only 4611 people. In the United States across the Atlantic, the ownership of the car was 285 million, the number of car accidents killed only 42,000 people[2]. China's road traffic development is facing the bottleneck period. There is still a huge gap between China and developed countries in traffic safety. Such as the development and enforcement of traffic regulations and the safety awareness of traffic drivers and the quality of the drivers themselves. We need to solve the problem of road traffic from a new perspective and direction in China.

Traffic accident with large data has the following characteristics:

Firstly, It has the amount of data and traffic is related to every citizen. Every day it will produce a lot of data.

Secondly, The data is incredibly complex, and it has a significant amount of data. The data attributes are complex, and garbage data occupy most of the need for a large number of data screening, deleting, and selecting[3]. To reduce the complexity of the data needs to obtain valid data efficiently.

Thirdly, for the data processing requirements quickly, high traffic accident data timeliness, and let the data more accurate, we need to process time efficiently.

The era of extensive data has come, intelligent traffic has become a major component of our daily life. More accurate traffic accident data and faster processing have emerged as a goal which data analyst pursue on.

1.2 Research Purposes

Large data has been into all aspects of traffic management deeply. It has a significant role especially in traffic accidents. In traffic trips, people are most concerned about traffic safety. So it has great significance to analyze the big data of traffic accidents. Traffic accidents have great importance on whether it is for people to travel recommendations, or the transport sector takes a reasonable and practical way to ease the traffic.

In this paper, the data is analyzed and processed, the invalid data is deleted, the dirty data is removed and the data of the traffic accident are analyzed, modeled, forecasted and verified. After the data is cleaned, the correctness of each model is verified and the data is displayed on the map. Find the law between the potential of data, through the adaptive method to choose a high degree of correctness model. Forecast the severity of traffic accident which occurred at a particular time and place to improve the effectiveness of the data.

1.3 Related research

Traffic big data as the emerging research areas, many scholars have a discussion on its origin and development status. Liu Youyuan (2009) discussed the data collection and analysis of traffic accidents in Australia. Meng Xiaofeng (2013) introduced the application and challenge of large data. Chen Mei (2012) discusses the use of large data in the transportation system. Tennessee patrols in the United States used IBM's predictable technology for traffic accidents, which introduced the system's CRASH version in 2014 (historical data collision reduction analysis). The state began deploying the system after installing the CRUSH from IBM and ESRI at the Memphis Police Department. After the police had deployed the system, it captured 70 violations within two hours, and 70 violations were usually the number of times that police trapped by the traditional way a week. By using the system, Tennessee road patrols provide the results show that the accuracy rate of up to 72% within the pilot range of 6 months.

Also, there is a P4S system developed in cooperation with the United States. The system is developed by SLD and basic road data and accident data and traffic environment data. It includes three levels of data analysis; one is the basic data analysis, the formation of the required frame; the other is developing the analysis tool by mining the primary data; the last one is application level, including traffic diagnosis, economic analysis, and traffic forecasting decisions. Using visual analysis to the traffic big data, and display the accident data on the map. After the data preprocessing (Filtering missing values, filtering data subsets, converting data types...), to compare the different data modeling algorithms. Using the vrious algorithms to build the model for the train set , and to pretic the results by the test set data. The prediction results of each model are compared with the actual data results, and the confusion matrix is given to compare the accuracy of each model with the kappa value (the fit between the observers).

2 Data Preprocessing

The data used in this paper is derived from the sample data of traffic accidents in Shanghai Public Security Bureau. The collection time of data is from July 2015 to April 2016 in the month, all of them is about the traffic accident. The total amount of data is more than 2000; the data contains four attributes, namely accident number, accident type, accident location and accident time. Analyzing the above data, among them the accident number is the character type, the type of error is text type, the accident location is text type and the time of the accident is time type. There is a missing value in the data, and the text data is not easy to handle.

2.1 Geographic Location is Converted to Latitude and Longitude

For the accident location attribute in the data, because of its value is the particular geographical area, it is necessary to transform the text type accident site into the numerical coordinate position[4]. Using Remap which is an interactive dynamic map data visualization tool based on the Echarts(a JS plugin made by the Baidu Company), proceed as follows:

Step 1, apply for Baidu map ak (that is, access to Baidu map API key), if you don't have Baidu account, you are required to register Baidu account access key.

Step 2, spelling http request url, pay attention to use the first step to apply for ak.

Step 3, after receiving the http request, you should return the data (json and xml format are supported).

Step 4, parse the data returned before (here using json format).

Step 5, convert and save the required data.

The following is an example of the conversion data, where Address is the address given in the original data, longitude latitude is the latitude and longitude after conversion:

Address: Shanghai Zhongshan South Road into the East Road, about 200 meters west

Longitude latitude: 121.4616653 31.19660184

Address:50 meters west of Tongren Road, Beijing West Road, Shanghai

Longitude latitude: 121.4565581 31.23211911.

2.2 Numerical Analysis

Preprocessing the data, analyzing the maximum and minimum values of the data, the mean, the distribution, and the overall impression of the data[5]. Including the handling and filling of missing values. In the analysis, it was found that there were six missing values in the type

DOI: 10.1051/itmconf/20171204029

attribute, and the missing values were interpolated. The analysis of the position can see the following minimum and maximum distribution.

Lowest:[Jiading] Ring Road Jihang Road East about 10 meters

[Jiading] Ring Road Jia Tang Road East about 30 meters

Edison Road into Zhang Heng Road NATO about 60 meters

An Bo Road Yingkou Road East about 30 meters Anhe Road New Land Road West About 2 meters

Highest: Zhuguang Road will be about 50 meters northbound Zhuo Road

Zhuguang Road into Songze Avenue NATO 100 meters

Zhuting Road into the Shanfang Road about 3000 meters north

Zhuting Road into the Yuanmen Road about 5 meters east

The west of the Zhu Fei Road connects with the Shangfei base secondary river bank road.

2.3 Consolidate Data

In this case, it is necessary to integrate the data that has been processed before. The text-type accident location in the original data is merged with the geographical coordinates of the site, that is latitude and longitude, it becomes a new data frame, which is used for the database. The values type of accident in the four essential attributes of the data is slight, general, significant, converting to numerical data according to the severity of the accident, the corresponding values are 1, 2, 3, and then the numerical type of a factor as a classification attribute. The time type in the data is converted to numeric data. Examples of processed data are as follows:

1 Shanghai City [Jiading] Ring Road, Jiaxing Road East about 10 meters 3.1e +15

1 2015/8/16 16:29 121.2516 31.39889.

3 Incident Data Visualization

3.1 Draw the Accident Map

The accident map is used to display the location of the accident distribution; It's the test data used to show the occurrence of traffic accidents in Shanghai. The data for this part is a randomly selected traffic accident location from July 2015 to April 2016.

Firstly, we get the map of Shanghai and then superimposed the traffic accident data into the map of Shanghai to get the following figure. Figure 1 is the map of Shanghai, Figure 2 is the accident distribution map.

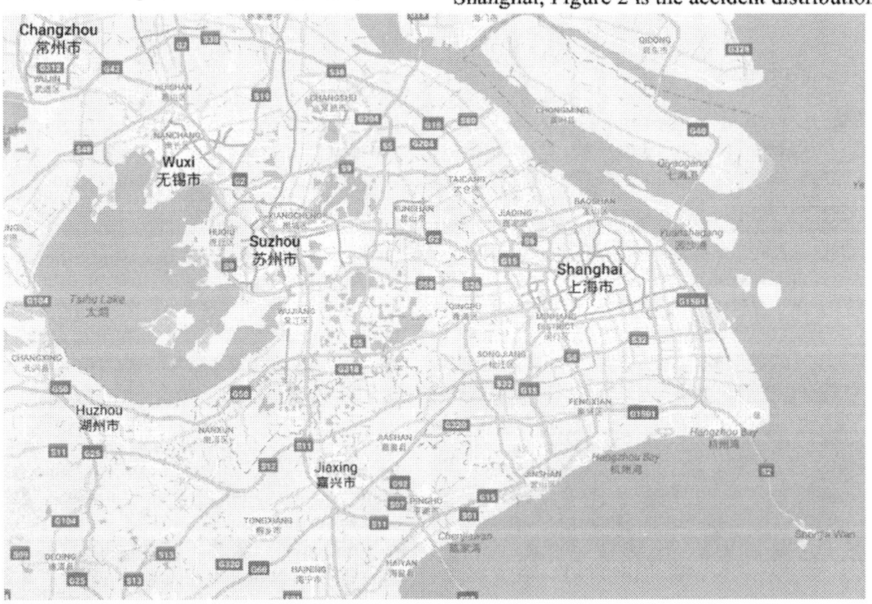

Figure 1. The map of Shanghai

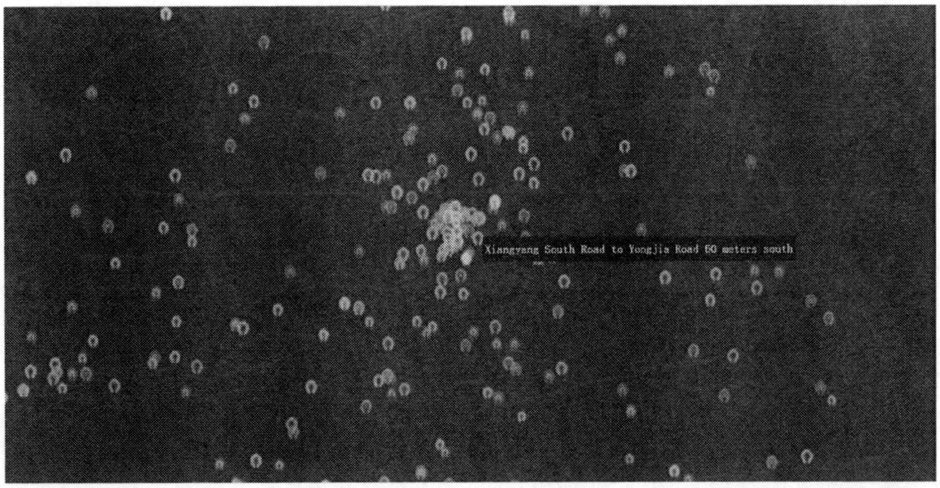

Figure 2. The Accident Map

3.2 Draw the Accident Heat Map

The accident heat map is used to show the traffic accident density in Shanghai. The data used is also derived from the previous test data that been randomly selected, It is the traffic accidents occurred in Shanghai from July 2015 to April 2016.

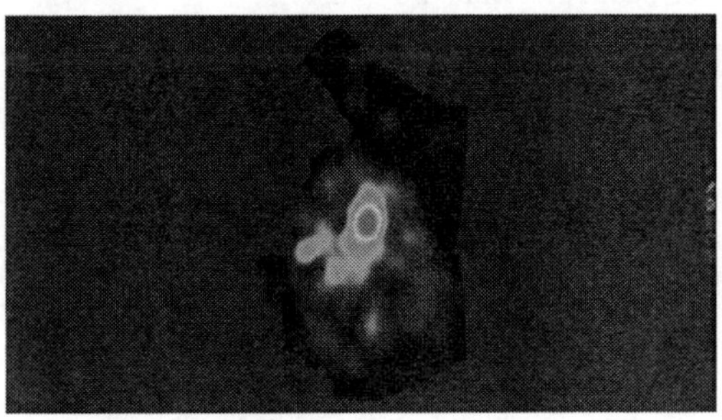

Figure 3. The Accident Heat Map

From the heat map, we can see that the distribution of accidents is centralized, combined with the numerical analysis of II.B , you can see the hot spots are mainly gathered in the accidental high incidence area around, which can be analyzed from data.

4 Modeling Prediction

This paper mainly uses the numerical types of the accident type as 1, 2 and 3 as the classification attributes to predict the different types of accident occurrence probability. The validation of the model uses K-fold cross validation. In the experiment, we use the 70% of the random data as the training data and the remaining 30% of the data as test data.

4.1 Fisher Linear Discriminant (FLD)

Fisher Linear Discriminant (FLD) is the classical algorithm in pattern recognition, which was used in pattern recognition and artificial intelligence field by Belhumeur in 1996[6]. The FLD algorithm project the high-dimensional pattern samples into the best discriminant vector space, to achieve the effect that extracting the classification information and compressing the feature space dimension. To guarantee the model samples have the largest outer-class distance and the minimum inner-class distance in the new subspace after projection, which requires that the pattern has the best separability in the current space. As an effective feature extraction method[7], it is possible to ensure that the next projection model has the smallest intraclass distance and the largest interclass distance in the new space, that is, the pattern has the best separability in the space.

4.2 Random Forest

Random forest is to build a forest as the random method. The forest consists of many decision trees, there is no association between each decision tree in the random forest. After getting the random forest, let the forest in each of the decision trees separately to make judgments when there is a new input sample into the forest[8]. Look at what kind of class this sample should belong to (for the classification algorithm), and then look at which kind of class was choice at most, to predict the sample is that class.

In the process of establishing each decision tree. There are two points to note: sampling and entire division. Firstly, it's the two random sampling process, the random forest needs to take a sample from the rows and columns of the input data. For row sampling, using the way that takes the back sampling methods, which means in the sampling set of samples, there are may be duplicate samples. Assuming that there are N input samples, then the sampling is also N samples. This situation makes it possible for each tree using not all of the samples when it's training, making it not easy to appear over-fitting relatively. And then column sampling, select m ($m << M$) from the M features[9]. The sampling data is used to establish a decision tree in an entirely split way. So that

DOI: 10.1051/itmconf/20171204029

the decision tree can not continue to divide or all the samples inside are pointing to the same one category. In general, many decision tree algorithms have an important step-pruning, But there's no need to do that because the two previous random sampling process ensured the randomness, so even if not pruning, it will not appear the over-fitting.

The experiment result of the random forest algorithm: Each decision tree is a skilled expert in a small field (because m features was chosen from M functions to train the each tree) So that there are many experts in various areas in the random forest. For a new question (new input data), data can be analyzed it from different aspects. By using the results of the random forest function prediction, there were 89 cases was predicted as 1 (the minor accident) and 4 cases were predicted as 2 (the general accident). There error predict result cases: there are one sample was predicted as the 1.0009203, but the actual result should be 1 (minor accident); there are 22 samples was predicted as the 2 (general accident), but the actual result should be 1 (minor accident); there are two samples was predicted as the 3 (major accident), but the actual result should be 1 (general accident); there are six samples was predicted as the 1 (general accident), but the actual result should be 2 (general accident).

4.3 Bagging Decision Tree

Decision Tree is based on the known of the probability of occurrence at the various situation, the probability that the expected value of the present value is greater than or equal to zero which obtained by constructing a decision tree to evaluate project risk, judge the feasibility of the decision analysis method. It is an intuitive graphical method of the probability analysis. Because this decision branch is painted like a tree branch, it is the called the decision tree.In the machine learning, the decision tree is a forecasting model, which represents a mapping between object attributes and object values. Entropy is the messy system degree, the ID3, C4.5 and C5.0 spanning tree algorithms using the entropy[10]. This measure is based on the concept of entropy in informatics theory.

A decision tree is a tree structure, which each internal node represents a test on an attribute value, each branch accounts for a test output, and each leaf node accounts for a category.

A decision tree is a very common classification method. It is a supervised learning method; the so-called supervised learning is given a bunch of samples, each sample has a set of attributes and a category, these categories are determined in advance, then we can get a classifier through the learning, the classifier will give the correct classification to the new samples. This machine learning method is called supervised learning.

Bagging:

Bagging algorithm- Creating a combined classification model for the learning strategy, where each model gives equal weight prediction.

Input:

D: d training tuples

K: the number of models in the combined classifier

A learning method (Decision tree algorithm, Backward propagation algorithm etl.)

Output: combined classifier-compound model MA

Method:

For i=1 to k do //Create K models;

Create a self-help sample Di by returning samples to D;

Using Di and the learning method to derive model Mi;

End for

Using the combined classifier to classify the tuple X: K models classified x, and return the majority of votes.

There are K training sets, and these training sets have the returning samples to create K models so that for each sample, every sample can be chosen[11]. The advantages of the bagging algorithm: 1. the accuracy rate of the combined model is significantly higher than any single classifier of the combined model. 2. For the larger noise, the performance will not be poor and has the robustness; 3.It's not easy to cause the over-fitting.

The correct result of the bagging algorithm: The result 1 (Minor accident) has 86 samples, the result 2(General accident) has four samples. The error result of the bagging algorithm: there are 8 samples was predicted as the 1 (Minor accident), but the actual result should be 2 (General accident); there are one sample that the real result should be 3 (Major accident); there are 22 samples was predicted as the 2(general accident), but the actual result should be 1(minor accident), there are 2 samples was predicted as the 3(Major accident), but the actual result should be 1(minor accident).

5 Experiment Analysis

By using LDA (linear judgment) function to build the model, and compare the predicted result with the actual result the result shows that the correct results have 95 cases. Even though the examination found, but the actual results are 1 (Minor accidents), but predicted to 1.00092 have one case, there are 26 cases of 2 (general), there are 2 cases of 3 (major) are wrong results.

The result of random forest, there are 89 cases was predicted to be 1 (Minor accident), there are 4 cases predicted to be 2 (General accident). The error predict result: there is one sample was predicted as the 1.0009203, but the actual result should be 1 (Minor accident); there are 22 samples was predicted as the 2 (General accident),but the actual result should be 1(Minor accident); there are 2 samples was predicted as the 3(Major accident), but the actual result should be 1(General accident); there are 6 samples was predicted as the 1(General accident), but the actual result should be 2(General accident).

The predicted result of tree bag function, the correct result: there are 86 cases of 1(Minor accident), 4 cases of 2 (General accident). The error predict result: there are 8 samples was predicted as the 1(Minor accident), but the actual result should be 2 (General accident), there are one sample that the actual result should be 3 (Major accident); there are 22 samples was predicted as the 2, but the actual result should be 1(Minor accident); there are two samples was predicted as the 3(Major accident), but the actual result should be 1(General accident).

In this paper, the predictive analysis of three algorithms is carried out to evaluate the accuracy of the model and the Kappa value (two observers fitting degree). From the minimum, quartile, mean and maximum values to compare the accuracy and Kappa values of the model(two observers fitting degree), the closer the accuracy of 1, the better the predicted result.

The Kappa value is between -1 to 1, but usually between 0 ~ 1. This is divided into five groups to represent different degree of consistency: 0.0 ~ 0.20 is the very low consistency, 0.21 ~ 0.40 is the general consistency, 0.41 ~ 0.60 is the moderate consistency , 0.61 ~ 0.80 is the high degree of consistency , 0.81 ~ 1 is the completely consistency.

To compare data from the accuracy and Kappa value, we can know the actual performance of the model, the graphic display is as follows.

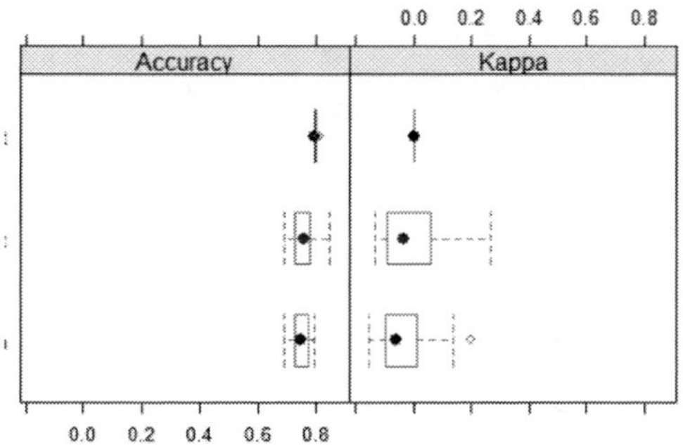

Figure 4. Compare results

6 Conclusion

From the above, we can find that the FLD algorithm has the best predict result from the accuracy aspect, the Bagging decision tree has the best predict result from the Kappa value, the random forest has the best predict result from the integrated effect. The experiment also reflects the characteristics of the three algorithms. Therefore, we can use the linear judgment analysis as the model, with the least error value when we the accuracy is more important; we can use the bagging decision algorithm when the appropriate degree is more important; we can use the random forests as the mode when the integrated effect is more important. The appropriate model should be determined by the different usage. Of course, this paper only uses three methods; we don't rule out the existence of other better models. For the current application model, linear judgment is the most suitable for traffic accident data prediction.

Acknowledgment

This work has been supported by the Open Foundation of Key Laboratory in Software Engineering of Yunnan Province under Grant NO. 2017SE204.

References

1. Qiao X M, An X U, Wei S. Developing tendency forecast of road traffic accident in China[J]. Journal of Changan University, 2004, 24(6):64-66.
2. Li G, Huang T Y, Yan H, et al. Grey residual error model of highway traffic accident forecast[J]. Journal of Traffic & Transportation Engineering, 2009, 9(5):88-93.
3. Qian W D, Zhi-Qiang L L, Prof. Road Traffic Accident Forecast Based on Gray-Markov Model[J]. China Safety Science Journal, 2008, 18(3):33-36.
4. Dong S H, Zhuo-Shen A P. Study on Road Traffic Accident Forecast Based on BP Neural Network[J]. China Safety Science Journal, 2010, 20(9):15-20.
5. Vuyst F D, Ricci V, Salvarani F. Nonlocal Second Order Vehicular Traffic Flow Models And Lagrange-Remap Finite Volumes[M]// Finite Volumes for Complex Applications VI Problems & Perspectives. Springer Berlin Heidelberg, 2011:781-789.
6. Quinlan J R. Induction on decision tree[J]. Machine Learning, 1986, 1(1):81-106.
7. Friedl M A, Brodley C E. Decision tree classification of land cover from remotely sensed data[J]. Remote Sensing of Environment, 1997, 61(3):399-409.
8. Quinlan J R. Bagging, Boosting, and C4.5[C]// Thirteenth National Conference on Artificial Intelligence and Eighth Innovative Applications of Artificial Intelligence Conference, AAAI 96, Iaai 96, Portland, Oregon, August 4-8. DBLP, 1996:725-730.
9. Wang H, Jiang Y, Wang H. Stock Return Prediction Based on Bagging-Decision Tree[C]// 2009 ieee international conference on the grey system and intelligent services. 2009:1575-1580.
10. Tu M C, Shin D, Shin D. A Comparative Study of Medical Data Classification Methods Based on Decision Tree and Bagging Algorithms[C]// Eighth IEEE International Conference on Dependable, Autonomic and Secure Computing. IEEE Computer Society, 2009:183-187.
11. Oza N C. Online bagging and boosting[C]// IEEE International Conference on Systems, Man and Cybernetics. IEEE, 2006:2340-2345 Vol. 3.

Feature Fusion Based on Convolutional Neural Network for SAR ATR

Shi-Qi CHEN, Rong-Hui ZHAN, Jie-Min HU, Jun ZHANG

Automatic Target Recognition Laboratory,National University of Defense Technology,Changsha, China
chenshiqi12@nudt.edu.cn. zhanrh@nudt.edu.cn,hujiemindawang@163.com,zhj64068@sina.com

Abstract—Recent breakthroughs in algorithms related to deep convolutional neural networks (DCNN) have stimulated the development of various of signal processing approaches, where the specific application of Automatic Target Recognition (ATR) using Synthetic Aperture Radar (SAR) data has spurred widely attention. Inspired by the more efficient distributed training such as inception architecture and residual network, a new feature fusion structure which jointly exploits all the merits of each version is proposed to reduce the data dimensions and the complexity of computation. The detailed procedure presented in this paper consists of the fused features, which make the representation of SAR images more distinguishable after the extraction of a set of features from DCNN, followed by a trainable classifier. In particular, the obtained results on the 10-class benchmark data set demonstrate that the presented architecture can achieve remarkable classification performance to the current state-of-the-art methods.

1 Introduction

As a kind of active microwave imaging radar with all-day, all-weather and long-range detection capabilities, synthetic aperture radar (SAR) has occupied a leading role in areas such as early warning, surveillance and guidance, of which the most extensive application is in automatic target recognition (ATR).

With the emergence of well-performed classifiers such as support vector machine (SVM) [1], k-nearest neighbor (KNN) [2] and AdaBoost [3], machine learning technology has attracted much attention in SAR ATR studies. However, most of the work in machine learning approaches focus on designing a set of feature extractors. In SAR ATR field, the existing technique lacks the ability of extracting effective features and fusing them. Recently, a newly-developing learning method called convolutional neural networks (CNN) have been successfully applied to many large scale visual recognition tasks such as image classification [4]-[6], object detection [7][8]. Motivated by the model of mammal's visual system, CNNs consist of many hidden layers with the convolution operations which extract the features in the image and achieve state-of-the-arts results on the visual image data set such as ImageNet [4]. In this way, we consider employing CNN in SAR ATR field by means of designing reasonable network structure and optimizing training algorithms.

Generally, the architecture of CNNs can be interpreted as a two-stage procedure in image classification tasks. Unlike the previous methods which heavily rely on handcrafted features with human intervention, the training process in CNN automatically find appropriate features in search space, which are sent into trainable classifiers in the second stage, and thus to avoid the complexity of pre-processing and feature selection.

A variety of works have been done to achieve better performance in the past decades, however, it still remains a challenging task since modern advanced techniques require tens of thousands of examples to train adequately. Robert Wang [9] has augmented dataset to test the the adaptability on subsets under different displacement and rotation settings. Furthermore, the training based on very deep networks still faces problems for the reason that the stacking of non-linear transformations in typical feed-forward network generally result in poor propagation of activations as well as vanishing gradients. Hence it remains necessary to modify the architecture of deep feed-forward networks.

Owing to the background speckles all over the SAR images and the irregular distributions of strong scattering centers, SAR ATR is of great complexity especially when the networks get deeper. To enable the feasibility of training deeper network with limited data, we adopt CNN architectures which fuse the features extracted from different branches and these structures tends to perform well in maximally exploiting the input data and improving classification accuracy.

The remainder of this paper is organized as follows. Section II discusses the basic components of the CNN network as well as the training method. Section III gives an introduction into the two feature fusion categories and how they are constructed in the proposed networks. Experimental results conducted from SAR imagery are analyzed in Section IV to identify the desirable performance of the novel network architectures. Finally, we summarize this paper.

2 Structure And Training of Cnns

Among various of deep learning methods, CNN is an effective model which considers the dependencies between pixels in an image. The CNN consists of consecutive layers of neurons with learnable weights and bias, where the concept of perceptive field is applied. In this scenario, we will give a detailed description of the basic operation modules in CNN.

2.1Convolution Layer

Each CNN layer can be visualized as a 1-dimensional (1D) stack of 2-dimensional (2D) filters. Meanwhile, a subset of a layer's neuron works as receptive fields for the layers next to it.

The fundamental operation underpinning a CNN is the 2D convolution. In the convolution layer, we define the input feature maps of the previous layer as $O_m^{(l-1)}(m=1,...M)$ which are connected to the output feature maps $O_n^{(l)}(n=1,...N)$. $O_m^{(l-1)}(x,y)$ and $O_n^{(l)}(x,y)$ represent the unit of the mth input feature map and the nth output feature map at position (x,y) respectively. Each unit in the convolution layer is computed as:

$$O_n^{(l)}(x,y)=\sigma(\sum_{m=1}^{M}\sum_{p,q=0}^{F-1}k_{nm}^{(l)}(p,q)O_m^{(l-1)}(x-p,y-q)+b_n^{(l)}) \quad (1)$$

where the convolution kernel $k_{nm}^{(l)}(p,q)$ denotes the trainable filters, while other terms $b_n^{(l)}$ and σ represent the bias of the nth output feature map and the nonlinear activation function.

2.2Activation Function

To form a highly nonlinear mapping relationship between the input image and the output label, a proper activation function is added at each convolution layer [10]. Since a hyperbolic tangent function or a sigmoid function [11] may get trapped into saturating nonlinearities during the gradient propagation process, a piecewise linear function which does not suffer from vanishing gradients is introduced to make the computation more efficient. The rectified linear unit (ReLU) activation function [12] is defined as:

$$f(x)=\max(0,x) \quad (2)$$

2.3Pooling Layer

Pooling layers are introduced in CNN to reduce the resolution of images between successive layers. By either using averaging or choosing maximal value neuron in the group, pooling layers largely reduce the amount of computation through lessening the parameters. These layers also make CNN better at translation, shift and distortion invariance. We assume that each feature map in a convolution layer corresponds to a single map in the associated pooling layer. For example, the max pooling operation [13] is defined as

$$O_m^{(l+1)}(x,y)=\max_{p,q=0,...K-1} O_m^{(l)}(x\cdot s+p,y\cdot s+q) \quad (3)$$

where K is the pooling size, and s is the stride which indicates the internals between adjacent pooling windows.

2.4Error Function

As a training method for neural networks, the back propagation (BP) [14] algorithm in CNN uses the categorical cross entropy as the object function, which aims to measure the consistency between the prediction of network outputs and the truth labels.

Softmax layer [15] is a commonly used multi-classification layer in which the output probabilities over each class is computed at the final stage of the CNN architecture.

Given a training set $\{(x^{(i)},t^{(i)});i\in 1,...,N,t^{(i)}\in 1,...,T\}$, where $x^{(i)}$ is the ith input image, N is the number of examples, and $t^{(i)}$ refers to the target label among T classes. The prediction $y_j^{(i)}$ of jth class for ith input is passed through softmax function to yield a normalized probability distribution over classes. The softmax layer operation takes the form as [15]:

$$p_j^{(i)}=\frac{e^{y_j^{(i)}}}{\sum_{j=1}^{T}e^{y_j^{(i)}}} \quad (4)$$

We use the softmax output layer in conjunction with the categorical cross-entropy error function. With that as the background, the error function E is defined as:

$$\mathrm{E}=-\frac{1}{N}[\sum_{i=1}^{N}\sum_{j=1}^{T}1\{t^{(i)}=j\}\ln p_j^{(i)}] \quad (5)$$

2 Feature Fusion in Cnn

The combination of a variety of convolution layers and pooling layers plays an influential role in learning robust feature representations. Unlike natural image datasets, SAR images are more complex due to its complicated imaging mechanism. Even when the images are obtained from different azimuth angle, the consequent shapes of targets from the same type vary a lot. Furthermore, the speckling noise in SAR images makes it tougher to interpret each target.

DOI: 10.1051/itmconf/20171205001

Although CNN works as a good feature extractor, how to make use of multi-dimensional features and fuse them together still deserves exploration. To increase the diversity of extracted feature and understand the interactions between them, we formulate two patterns of feature fusion. Since the targets in SAR images may not be square shaped, use of convolution kernels sharing the same size are restricted to learn more adequate features, hence the inserted convolution kernels are modified as that with rectangular shape.

3.1Feature Fusion under Concatenation Pattern

Usually, the original convolution layer contains several square kernels, in this pattern we replace them with two convolution branches arranged by concatenation. This mode of feature fusion on convolution level is referred to as "conv-fusion" module. The concrete structure of its elements is demonstrated in Figure 1, where a represents the equivalent kernel size in standard CNN structure while n denotes the adjustable kernel size. Here, the convolution marked with S are same-padded while V signifies that are valid-padded.

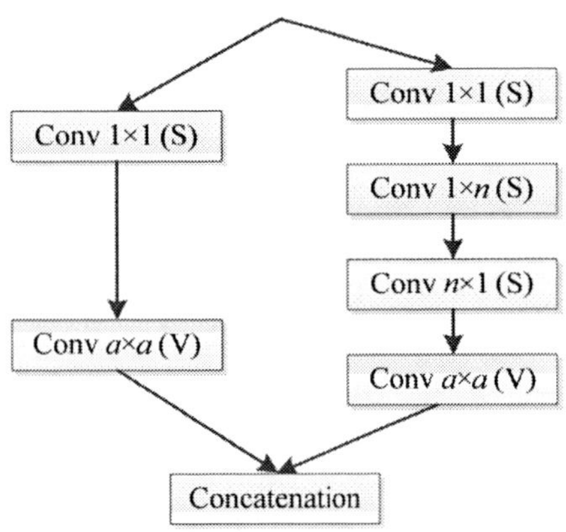

Figure 1. Conv-fusion module

Different from general convolution, S indicates that the size of the output grid is identical with that of input feature map. For the purpose of getting a same output size from two branches, the convolution operation under same mode is utilized to ensure the input and output dimension match. That is to say, when the feature map with size $m \times m$ is transferred into the module, the size of output feature map is $(m-a+1) \times (m-a+1)$.

In this module, the 1×1 convolutions placed before convolution operation of other sizes function as dimension reduction module [5], which allow for expanding the depth and width of CNN without increasing the computational complexity.

3.2Fusion under Summation Pattern

Deep networks stacked by several layers are usually tracked in degradation problem. Enlightened by the deep residual learning framework [16], we design the second pattern of feature fusion. Formally, the expected underlying mapping also known as unreferenced mapping is represented as F(x). H(x) denotes the residual mapping consisting of two consecutive convolution layers. When each convolution only computes corrective terms $H(x) = F(x) - x$ rather than the entire approximation F(x), the thought of shortcut connection which means skipping several layers is realized. By adopting the summation mechanism between layers, the information from previous layer flow more smoothly to the next layer without attenuation and the layers can learn the difference from the input feature map. Additionally, considering the ability of asymmetric kernels in extracting features with various scales and structures, we propose a new conception called asymmetric shortcut connection block (ASCB) as shown in Figure 2.

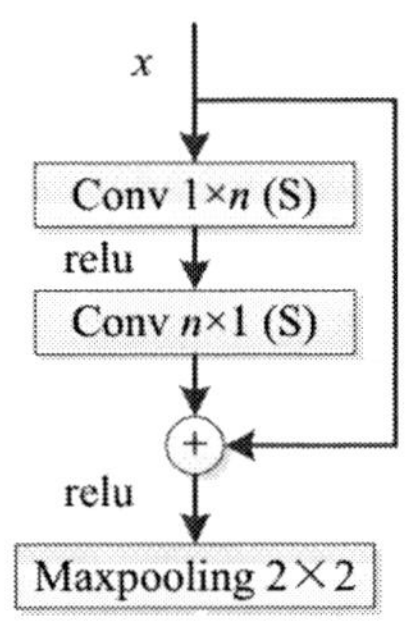

Figure 2. Asymmetric shortcut connection block

This means the untransformed input of previous layer can be propagated to the output and the feature maps between adjacent layer can be joined, hence making the deep network easier to be optimized and more efficient to be trained. To ensure that transformed output feature maps match the input size, we use two consecutive convolution operations under "same" mode.

Since the convolution kernel size differs in each layer with the deepening of networks, multi-scale features can be potentially extracted under the multi-level fusions, which intensify the links between features from adjacent layers and make them more adaptable to train deep networks.

3 Experiment Results

To design the appropriate number of feature maps and filter sizes used in convolutional layers as well as down sampling rates and numbers of stacking layers, several CNN architectures were tested. As the operations of forward and backward propagation are highly parallelizable, we utilize GPU processing based on deep CNN implementation to accelerate the testing process.

4.1Data Description

The CNN structure in this paper is applied to address the problem of SAR ATR for MSTAR dataset. The MSTAR benchmark data act as a standard data set to test and evaluate the performance of recognition algorithms. In our experiment, images for training are captured at 17 degree depression angle and that for testing are captured at 15 degree. The proposed algorithm is evaluated on the ten-target classification problem, and the corresponding number of images for training and testing are listed in Table I.

4.2Training Details

As has been presented in previous work, the implementation details play a decisive role in recognition

TABLE I. NUMBER OF TRAINING AND TESTING IMAGES FOR THE EXPERIMENTS

Target Types	No. Testing	No. Training
BMP2(9563)	195	233
BMP2(9566)	196	
BMP2(C21)	196	
T72(132)	196	232
T72(812)	195	
T72(S7)	191	
BTR70	196	233
BTR60	195	256
BRDM2	274	298
ZSU	274	299
T62	273	299
ZIL	274	299
2S1	274	299
D7	274	299
Total	3203	2747

performance. We aim to derive a set of best CNN structures both concerning low computation cost and high accuracy constraints towards the application of limited labelled SAR data. Except for some hyper parameters determined in CNNs, other details such as weight initialization, learning rate also count.

To improve the training speed as well as prevent the network from becoming trapped in local minima, a set of fine-tuning methods have been applied to various of recognition tasks. Based on the gradient descent method, Adam [17] algorithm can dynamically adjust the updating amount of each parameter according to the moment estimation and thus achieve the efficiency and stability of CNN. In view of this, we chose the Adam technique as a substitute for normal mini-batch SGD using the given default value set in $\eta = 0.001$, $\beta_1 = 0.9$, $\beta_2 = 0.999$ [17].

Additionally, several subsets of training data are chosen stochastically from the whole data set as mini-batch and all the models are trained under a 50-element batch size.

As for weight initialization, the weights of all the layers are sent into an initializer [18] with uniform distribution $(-\sqrt{6/(fan\_in + fan\_out)}, \sqrt{6/(fan\_in + fan\_out)})$, where fan_in and fan_out represents the number of input units and output units respectively.

4.3Experiments on Different Network Configurations

Here, we present the general layout of our baseline convolutional neural network (BCNN) and then describe the details of components used in BCNN. The schematic view of BCNN is depicted in Figure 3. To reduce the feature dimension, each convolution layer is followed by a pooling layer with the 2×2 pooling size and a stride of 2 pixels.

To avoid a fair amount of redundancy and spilling over of local information brought by relatively large receptive fields in each convolution layer, we choose convolution kernel size smaller than 7. In the structure, the fully connected layer is replaced by the global average pooling (GAP) layer since the correspondence between feature maps and categories is strengthened and no parameters need optimizing [19].

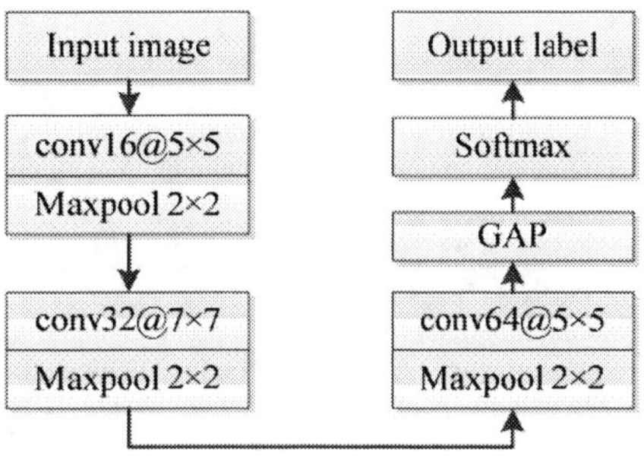

Figure 3. Overall architecture of BCNN (conv. (kernel depth) @ (kernel size))

For MSTAR dataset, the recognition accuracy on BCNN is obtained by the above hyper parameter setting. Next, the feature-fusion patterns are introduced into the BCNN and all these CNN-based methods share the same parameter setting except for different framework. The relevant composition of transformed conv-fusion CNN is listed in Table II.

TABLE II. COMPOSITION OF CONV-FUSION CNN

Layer name/Type	Output size	Filter size	Left Branch Filter size	Right Branch Filter size
Input image	64×64×1	/	/	/
Conv-fuse1	60×60×16	/	5×5	1×3 / 3×1
Maxpool1	30×30×16	2×2	/	/

DOI: 10.1051/itmconf/20171205001

Conv-fuse2	24×24×32		7×7	1×5 / 5×1
Maxpool2	12×12×32	2×2	/	/
Conv-fuse3	8×8×64		5×5	1×7 / 7×1
Maxpool3	4×4×64	2×2	/	/
GAP	64	2×2		

We have to mention that in the conv-fusion module, the number of feature channels from two branches are defaulted as the same. Hence, the feature map number of the merged convolution layer becomes twice.

As for the second pattern of feature fusion, an asymmetric shortcut connection block is inserted into the network between each convolution layer and pooling layer, with different asymmetric convolution set in each block. The whole network is called Module-residual CNN. Here we chose 1×3 / 3×1, 1×5 / 5×1, 1×7 / 7×1 kernel size in an ASCB and obtain an improvement in classification accuracy. Figure 4 is a flow chart of the proposed network.

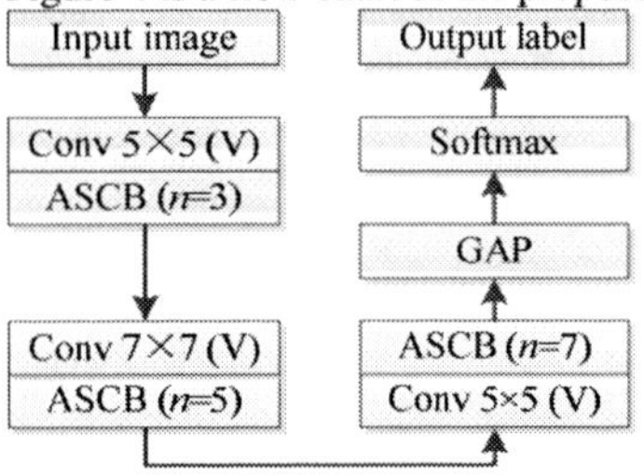

Figure 4. An Illustration of The Proposed Network

TABLE III. THE CONFUSION MATRIX UNDER CONCATENATION PATTERN

Target Types	Recognition Result										Accuracy (%)
	BMP2	T72	BTR70	BTR60	BRDM2	ZSU	T62	ZIL	2S1	D7	
BMP2(9563)	195	0	0	0	0	0	0	0	0	0	100.00
BMP2(9566)	195	0	0	0	1	0	0	0	0	0	99.49
BMP2(C21)	189	4	0	0	3	0	0	0	0	0	96.43
T72(132)	1	195	0	0	0	0	0	0	0	0	99.49
T72(812)	5	183	0	1	0	0	6	0	0	0	93.85
T72(S7)	8	177	0	1	0	0	4	0	1	0	92.67
BTR70	0	0	196	0	0	0	0	0	0	0	100.00
BTR60	0	0	7	188	0	0	0	0	0	0	96.41
BRDM2	1	0	0	0	272	0	0	1	0	0	99.27
ZSU	0	0	0	0	0	274	0	0	0	0	100.00
T62	0	1	0	0	0	1	271	0	0	0	99.27
ZIL	0	0	0	0	0	0	1	273	0	0	99.64
2S1	1	0	3	0	1	0	0	0	269	0	98.18
D7	0	0	0	0	0	0	0	0	0	274	100.00
Global Accuracy (%)	98.38										

TABLE IV. THE CONFUSION MATRIX UNDER SUMMATION PATTERN

Target Types	Recognition Result										Accuracy (%)
	BMP2	T72	BTR70	BTR60	BRDM2	ZSU	T62	ZIL	2S1	D7	
BMP2(9563)	195	0	0	0	0	0	0	0	0	0	100.00
BMP2(9566)	191	3	0	0	2	0	0	0	0	0	97.45
BMP2(C21)	189	2	2	1	1	0	0	0	1	0	96.43
T72(132)	0	196	0	0	0	0	0	0	0	0	100.00
T72(812)	2	190	0	0	0	0	3	0	0	0	97.44
T72(S7)	6	183	0	0	0	0	2	0	0	0	95.81
BTR70	0	0	194	1	1	0	0	0	0	0	98.98
BTR60	0	0	4	191	0	0	0	0	0	0	97.95
BRDM2	0	0	0	0	274	0	0	0	0	0	100.00
ZSU	0	0	0	0	0	274	0	0	0	0	100.00
T62	0	3	0	0	0	0	270	0	0	0	98.90
ZIL	0	0	0	0	0	1	0	273	0	0	99.64
2S1	0	2	0	0	1	0	3	0	268	0	97.81
D7	0	0	0	0	0	0	0	0	0	274	100.00
Global Accuracy (%)	98.72										

TABLE V. THE CONFUSION MATRIX OF UNDER DECISION-LEVEL FUSION

Target Types	Recognition Result										Accuracy (%)
	BMP2	T72	BTR70	BTR60	BRDM2	ZSU	T62	ZIL	2S1	D7	
BMP2(9563)	195	0	0	0	0	0	0	0	0	0	100.00
BMP2(9566)	195	0	0	0	0	1	0	0	0	0	99.49
BMP2(C21)	195	1	0	0	0	0	0	0	1	0	99.49
T72(132)	0	196	0	0	0	0	0	0	0	0	100.00
T72(812)	1	190	0	1	0	0	4	0	0	0	96.94
T72(S7)	4	187	0	0	0	0	0	0	0	0	97.90
BTR70	0	0	196	0	0	0	0	0	0	0	100.00
BTR60	0	0	3	192	0	0	0	0	0	0	98.46
BRDM2	0	0	0	0	274	0	0	1	0	0	100.00
ZSU	0	0	0	0	0	274	0	0	0	0	100.00
T62	0	0	0	0	0	0	273	0	0	0	100.00
ZIL	0	0	0	0	0	0	0	274	0	0	100.00
2S1	0	0	1	0	0	0	0	0	273	0	99.64
D7	0	0	0	0	0	0	0	0	0	274	100.00
Global Accuracy (%)	99.42										

To visually understand the intermediate state in the ASCB block and verify the reasonability of feature fusion, we display a set of hierarchical features learned from CNN. For instance, a BMP2 image is randomly chosen from the training dataset then the forward propagation process in each stage is visualized. In Figure 5, several output grids of size 8×8 in the second ASCB are displayed.

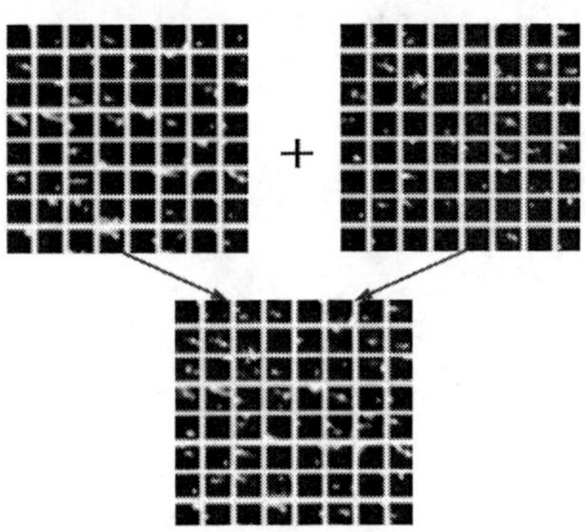

Figure 5. Visualization of 8×8 feature map in ASCB (n=7)

We can see from the figure 5 that the loss of visual information is suppressed after the last output map is fed through the block. By exploiting the complementarity of each map aggregated to the next stage, our proposed CNN structure can learn more specific and abstract features.

The recognition results for different CNN structures are shown in Table III, IV, V, where each row denotes the real target type and each column denotes the predictive label.

As we can conclude from the table, the overall accuracy of the two proposed architectures can reach 98.38% and 98.72% respectively. Whilst variations exist in testing set, the lowest accuracy is 95.81% for T72 in the second pattern feature fusion. For the targets without variants, the totally precise accuracy obtained in BMP2, T72, BRDM2, ZSU and D7 illustrates the effectiveness of our algorithms.

Since each CNN architecture extracts global and local features transmitted into classifier, we integrate three network architectures and make decision-level fusion of which we choose the largest posterior probability, a decision-level recognition rate of 99.42% can be obtained.

4.4Comparison with Previous Methods

To evaluate the feature extraction and fusion capability of the proposed CNN, we compare it with some widely cited methods including support vector machine (SVM) [20], Adaptive Boosting technique [21], polynomial kernel PCA (KPCA) [22], sparse representation based on monogenic signal (MSRC) [23] and Iterative graph thickening model of image representations (IGT) [24]. The recognition accuracies of these algorithms are shown in Table VI. Experiments conducted by Jun Ding [25] also suggest a typical CNN architecture but comparatively lower classification rate with data augmentation for this method.

TABLE VI. CLASSIFICATION RESULTS OF OTHER METHODS

Method	Accuracy (%)
SVM [20]	86.73
Adaptive Boosting [21]	92.70
KPCA [22]	92.67
MSRC [23]	93.66
IGT [24]	95.00
CNN with data augmentation [25]	93.16
BCNN	97.39
Conv-fusion CNN	98.38
Module-residual CNN	98.72

 DOI: 10.1051/itmconf/20171205001

Decision fusion CNN	99.42

It is desirable that the feature fusion CNNs show the ability of classifying ten-class targets regardless of the existence of variants. Meanwhile, neither increasing the width of network nor the complexity of architectures, the excellent combination of high-level feature representations and learning of potential invariant feature can achieve particularly good performance even when the labelled training data is limited.

4 Conclusion

Understanding the multi-scale and hierarchical features learned by CNN and then dig thoroughly into the discriminative features help us finish target recognition task. In this paper, we first constructed novel CNN architectures which contain two independent modules called "conv-fusion" module and asymmetric shortcut connection block, then fined tune the hyper parameters in the deep CNN in the second stage and finally applied them to address the problem of recognition using SAR images. Experimental results indicate that the proposed network can gain superior performance compared with other state-of-the-art methods by extracting forceful feature representations. Furthermore, the CNN approach presented in this paper can be revised or extended to other practical applications and thus provide insightful points in the recognition tasks aimed at small dataset.

Acknowledgment

The research work is supported by the National Natural Science Foundation of China under grant No.61471370.

References

[1] Q. Zhao and J. C. Principe 2001. "Support vector machines for sar automatic target recognition," IEEE Transactions on Aerospace & Electronic Systems, vol. 37, no. 2, pp. 643–654.

[2] Guo, G., Wang, H., Bell, D., Bi, Y., & Greer, K. 2003. Knn model-based approach in classification. Lecture Notes in Computer Science, 2888, 986-996.

[3] Y. Sun, Z. Liu, S. Todorovic, and J. Li 2007. "Adaptive boosting for sar automatic target recognition," IEEE Transactions on Aerospace & Electronic Systems, vol. 43, no. 1, pp. 112–125.

[4] A. Krizhevsky, I. Sutskever, and G. Hinton 2012. "ImageNet classification with deep convolutional neural networks," in Proc. Adv. Neural Inf. Process. Syst., pp. 1106–1114.

[5] C. Szegedy et al. 2015. "Going deeper with convolutions," in Proc. IEEE Computer Vision Pattern Recognition, Boston, MA, USA, Jun. 8–10, pp. 1–9.

[6] K. Simonyan and A. Zisserman 2015. "Very deep convolutional networks for large-scale image recognition," presented at the Int. Conf. Learning Representations. [Online]. Available: http://arxiv.org/abs/1409.1556

[7] R. Girshick, J. Donahue, T. Darrell, and J. Malik 2014. "Rich feature hierarchies for accurate object detection and semantic segmentation," in Proc. IEEE Computer Vision Pattern Recognition. , pp. 580–587.

[8] X. Chen, S. Xiang, C. Liu, and C. Pan 2014. "Vehicle detection in satellite images by hybrid deep convolutional neural networks," IEEE Geoscience Remote Sense Letter, vol. 11, no. 10, pp. 1797–1801.

[9] Du, K., Deng, Y., Wang, R., Zhao, T., & Li, N 2016. Sar atr based on displacement- and rotation-insensitive cnn. Remote Sensing Letters, 7(9), 895-904.

[10] Chen, S., Wang, H., Xu, F., & Jin, Y. Q. 2016. Target classification using the deep convolutional networks for sar images. IEEE Transactions on Geoscience & Remote Sensing, 54(8), 1-12.

[11] Y. Lecun, L. Bottou, Y. Bengio, and P. Haffner 1998. "Gradient-based learning applied to document recognition," Proc. IEEE, vol. 86, no. 11, pp. 2278–2324.

[12] V. Nair and G. E. Hinton 2010. "Rectified linear units improve restricted boltzmann machines," in ICML.

[13] Y. LeCun, K. Kavukcuoglu, and C. Farabet 2010. "Convolutional networks and applications in vision," in Proc. IEEE International Symposium Circuits System, pp. 253–256.

[14] Y. L. Cun, B. Boser, J. S. Denker, R. E. Howard, W. Habbard, L. D. Jackel, and D. Henderson 1990. "Handwritten digit recognition with a backpropagation network," in Advances in Neural Information Processing Systems, pp. 396–404.

[15] C. M. Bishop 2006 Pattern Recognition and Machine Learning. New York, NY, USA: Springer-Verlag.

[16] He, K., Zhang, X., Ren, S., & Sun, J. 2015. Deep residual learning for image recognition. 770-778. .

[17] D. P. Kingma and J. Ba 2014. "Adam: A method for stochastic optimization," Computer Science.

[18] K. He, X. Zhang, S. Ren, and J. Sun 2015. "Delving deep into rectifiers: Surpassing human-level performance on ImageNet classification," in Proc. Int. Conf. Comput. Vis., pp. 1026–1034.

[19] Lin, M., Chen, Q., & Yan, S. 2013. Network in network. Computer Science.

[20] Bengio Y, Nicolas Boulanger-Lewandowski, Razvan Pascanu 2013. "Advances in optimizing recurrent networks," IEEE International Conference on Acoustics, Speech and Signal Processing, 8624-8628.

[21] Sun, Y., Liu, Z., Todorovic, S., and Li, J. 2007. "Adaptive boosting for sar automatic target recognition," Aerospace and Electronic Systems, IEEE Transactions on 43, 112–125.

[22] Mishra, A. K., & Motaung, T. 2015. Application of linear and nonlinear PCA to SAR ATR. Radioelektronika.IEEE.pp.349-354..

[23] D. Ganggang, W. Na, and K. Gangyao 2014. "Sparse representation of monogenic signal: With application to target recognition in sar images," vol. 21, no. 8, pp. 952–956.

DOI: 10.1051/itmconf/20171205001

[24] S. Umamahesh, M. Vishal, and R. Raghu, G. 2014. "Sar automatic target recognition using discriminative graphical models," vol. 50, pp. 591–606.
[25] D. Jun, C. Bo, L. Hongwei, and H. Mengyuan 2016. "Convolutional neural network with data augmentation for sar target recognition," in IEEE Geoscience and remote sensing letters, vol. 13, no. 3, pp. 364–368.

A Relevance Vector Machine Prediction Method Based on the Biased Wavelet Kernel Function

Fang LIU[1], Fei ZHAO[1], Zhen-Hao YU[1], Cui ZHANG[1]

[1]*National Engineering Laboratory for Fiber Optic, Sensing Technology, Wuhan University of Technology, Wuhan, China;*
School of Computer Science and Technology, Wuhan University of Technology, Wuhan, China;
Key Laboratory of Fiber Optic Sensing Technology and Information Processing of Ministry of Education, Wuhan University of Technology, Wuhan, China
fangliu@whut.edu.cn, Knight_zf@126.com

Abstract—Relevance Vector Machine (RVM) is an important learning method in the field of machine learning for its sparsity, global optimality and the ability to solve nonlinear problems by using kernel functions. In this paper, a family of biased wavelets was used to construct the kernel functions of RVM. Biased wavelet have adjustable nonzero mean which makes the kernel of RVM more flexible. With the kernel method of the Centered Kernel Target Alignment (CKTA), the biased parameter was selected to improve the prediction performance of RVM model. The algorithm based on the biased wavelet kernel showed an increased prediction accuracy compared to using wavelet kernel and Cauchy kernel. In short, Relevance Vector Machine with the biased wavelet kernel is a flexible prediction algorithm with high prediction accuracy.

1 Introduction

RVM proposed by Tipping [1] is a Bayes probability model, and its kernel does not need to satisfy the Mercer conditions [2]. Based on the favorable features including its sparseness, Bayesian properties, and kernel characteristics [3], RVM is one of the famous sparse Bayesian learning models [4, 5]. Similar to the support vector machine (SVM) model [6], the effect of the RVM depends on the kernel function and kernel parameters [7]. At present, the methods for choosing an effective kernel function and reasonable kernel parameters are still imperfect [8, 9].

The kernel matrix can be learned from data via semi-definite programming (SDP) techniques in [10]. Cristianini, Shawe-Taylor, Elisseeff and Kandola [11] proposed a quantity measure named as 'kernel target alignment' (KTA) to adapt the kernel matrix to sample labels, and a series of algorithms are derived for clustering, transduction, kernel combination [12] and kernel selection [13]. However, KTA is only a sufficient condition to be a good kernel matrix, but not a necessary condition. It is possible for a kernel matrix to have a very good performance even though its KTA is still low [14]. CKTA proposed by Marina [15] is better than KTA with several experiments.

Based on the characteristics of the biased wavelet, it is suitable to be the kernel function of RVM. Wavelet analysis, which can efficiently overcome the shortcomings of Fourier analysis and other analysis tools, is becoming a focus point of many sciences. The zero-mean characteristic of wavelets often drives the phenomenon that a large number of multiresolution levels are needed to reduce the L^2 norm of the approximation error. In order to reduce the redundancy, biased wavelet was proposed by Galvao [16].

In this paper, the biased wavelet was constructed as the kernel function of RVM. CKTA was used to optimize the biased parameters with a fixed scale parameter. We evaluated the prediction accuracy with the biased wavelet kernel, Cauchy kernel and wavelet kernel by using the data from fiber Bragg grating (FBG) temperature sensor system.

With a short introduction of RVM and biased wavelet, the biased parameters were filtrated by CKTA to build the biased wavelet kernel in section 2. Experiments are presented in section 3 and the conclusions in section 4 concludes the paper.

2 Methods

RVM is a fully probabilistic framework and introduce a prior over the model weights governed by a set of hyperparameters, one associated with each weight, whose most probable values are iteratively estimated from the data.

DOI: 10.1051/itmconf/20171205002

Let x be the input data and y the output data. A point $y(x)$ can be predicted by:

$$y(x)=\sum_{i=1}^{n} w_n \cdot k(x,x_n)+w_0 \quad (1)$$

Where $\{w_n\}$ is the weight vector and $k(x,x_n)$ is a kernel function. n is the length of weight vector and w_0 the measurement noise.

The noise vector w_0 is assumed to be normally distributed with zero mean and a variance of σ^2. Using Bayes' rule, the posterior distribution of w, α, σ^2 with y can be computed:

$$P(w,\alpha,\sigma^2|y)=\frac{P(y|w,\alpha,\sigma^2)P(w,\alpha,\sigma^2)}{P(y)}=\mathrm{N}(\mu,\Sigma) \quad (2)$$

Where

$$\mu=\sigma^{-2}\Sigma\Phi^T y \quad (3)$$

$$\Sigma=\left(A+\sigma^{-2}\Phi^T\Phi\right)^{-1} \ \text{ωιτη} \ A=diag(\alpha) \quad (4)$$

The parameters a corresponds a zero-mean Gaussian distribution over w, which avoids overfitting. The hyperparameters (α and σ^2) is optimized iteratively by maximizing the posterior probability $P(w,\alpha,\sigma^2|y)$.

After learning the mean and variance, the results of (3) is applied to (1):

$$\hat{y}=\mu^T\Phi \ , \ \hat{\sigma}^2=\sigma_{MP}^2+\Phi^T\Sigma\Phi \quad (5)$$

The predicted variance $\hat{\sigma}^2$ is the sum of the variance caused by the measurement noise σ_{MP}^2 and the uncertainly in the prediction of w.

Kernel functions are important for prediction performance. Methods of selecting the kernel functions, such as experience [17], comparison [18] and multi-kernels [19, 20], have been developed in practical application.

Due to the characteristics of the biased wavelet, it can describe the whole data, as well as the details. Therefore, when the biased wavelet is used as a kernel of RVM, the feature space is able to be close to the target space by dynamically adjusting the biased parameters for different types of data, which can improve the prediction accuracy of the RVM model.

A biased wavelet function u satisfying

i. $u\in L^2(R)$

ii. $u(0)\neq 0$

iii. $u(\tau)$ is rapidly decreasing to zero when $\tau\to\infty$

iv. $\hat{u}(\omega)$ is rapidly decreasing to zero when $\omega\to\infty$

In this paper, we used the third type of the biased wavelet (6) and the Mexican Hat (7) as the mother wavelet.

$$u(x)=\exp\left(-\frac{x^2}{2}\right) \quad (6)$$

$$\psi(x)=\frac{2}{\sqrt{3}}\pi^{-1/4}\left(1-x^2\right)\cdot\exp^{-x^2/2} \quad (7)$$

Then, a set of biased wavelet kernels was defined by

$$k(\tau,\mathrm{b})=|\sigma|^{-1/2}\left[\psi\left(\frac{\tau-\mathrm{b}}{\sigma}\right)+cu\left(\frac{\tau-\mathrm{b}}{\sigma}\right)\right] \quad (8)$$

Where σ is scale parameter, b is translation parameter, c is biased parameter and τ is a continuous real variable.

Since there is no explicit form for the mapping function, the learning algorithm of RVM get the information of the feature space, model, the training data and their relationship from the Gram matrix. KTA based on Gram matrix is considered as an effective way to filter biased parameters.

Let $X=\{x_k\}_{k=1}^N$ be the input data and the corresponding output data was $Y=\{y_k\}_{k=1}^N$. The range of the index was $i,j\in[1,N]$ and the Gram matrix of kernel was defined by

$$[MK]_{i,j}=k(x_i,x_j) \quad (9)$$

The target matrix was defined by

$$[\mathrm{Y}]_{i,j}=y_i\cdot y_j \quad (10)$$

KTA was defined by

$$A(MK,Y)=\frac{\langle MK,Y\rangle_F}{\sqrt{\langle MK,MK\rangle_F\cdot\langle Y,Y\rangle_F}} \quad (11)$$

Where

$$\langle MK, Y\rangle_F = \sum_{i,j=1}^{n} MK(x_i, x_j) Y(x_i, x_j) \quad (12)$$

The purpose of the KTA is to calculate the degree of alignment between the Gram matrix and the target matrix. However, if, in the feature space, the origin is far away from the convex hull of the data, then the elements of MK have about the same value and, as a result, the matrix MK is ill-conditioned. Therefore, CKTA, a better method, was proposed by Marina.

From given kernel k, the centered kernel was defined by

$$k_C(x_i, x_j) = \left\langle \Phi(x_i) - \frac{1}{n}\sum_{i=1}^{n}\Phi(x_i), \Phi(x_j) - \frac{1}{n}\sum_{j=1}^{n}\Phi(x_j) \right\rangle$$

$$= k(x_i, x_j) - \frac{1}{n}\sum_{i=1}^{n} k(x_i, x_j) - \frac{1}{n}\sum_{j=1}^{n} k(x_i, x_j) \quad (13)$$

$$+ \frac{1}{n^2}\sum_{i,j=1}^{n} k(x_i, x_j)$$

The centered Gram matrix was defined by

$$[MK_C]_{i,j} = k_C(x_i, x_j) \quad (14)$$

Similar to KTA, CKTA was defined by

$$A(MK_C, Y) = \frac{\langle MK_C, Y\rangle_F}{\sqrt{\langle MK_C, MK_C\rangle_F \langle Y, Y\rangle_F}} \quad (15)$$

Compared with KTA, CKTA has the advantage of solving the problem of unbalanced data and the invariance of the linear transform.

Based on CKTA, the filtering strategy of biased parameters was shown in Fig. 1. The target biased parameter of the maximum CKTA was used to construct the final selected kernel. Our experiments showed that the relationship between biased parameters and values of CKTA was not monotonic, which meant that the target biased parameter could be found within a certain range.

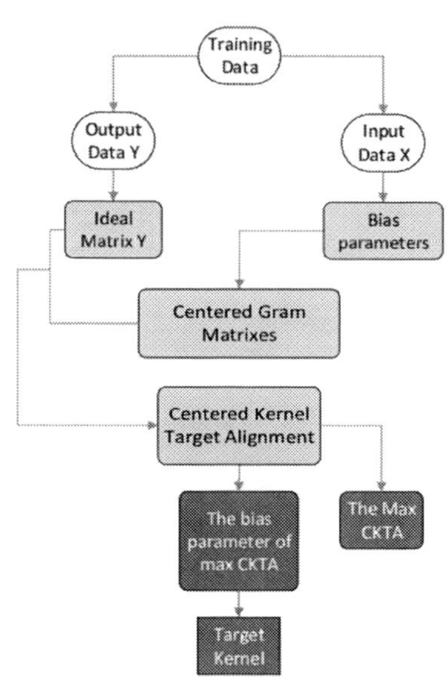

Figure 1. Flowchart representation of the selection of the bias parameter

3 Experiments

3.1 Data Set and Error Measures

The dataset contains 1440 instances from 120 hours of responses from FBG temperature sensor system for the Second Yangtze River Bridge in Wuhan.

The prediction algorithms were evaluated with respect to the mean relative error (MRE), the mean absolute error (MAE) and the root-mean-square error (RMSE).

$$MRE = \frac{1}{n}\sum_{i=1}^{n}\frac{|y_i - \hat{y}_i|}{|y_i|} \quad (16)$$

$$MAE = \frac{1}{n}\sum_{i=1}^{n}|y_i - \hat{y}_i| \quad (17)$$

$$\text{RMSE} = \sqrt{\sum_{i=1}^{n}\frac{(y_i - \hat{y}_i)^2}{n}} \quad (18)$$

where y_i is the true value, $\hat{y}_i$ is the predictive value and n is the length of test samples involved.

DOI: 10.1051/itmconf/20171205002

3.2Selection Method of Biased Wavelet Kernel

The wavelength responses from sensors were selected as the output data, and time series were the input data.

Fig. 2 showed the relationship between the CKTA value and biased parameters c, when 48 hours of data were used as the training data and the next 50 samples were test data. It could be seen from the figure that the CKTA reached its maximum when the Biased Parameter was -1.3. Because of the monotonic of the connection, the best biased parameter was generally found in the range $[-10,10]$. Therefore, the target biased wavelet kernel was filtered out.

Compared with the biased wavelet kernel, Cauchy kernel and the Wavelet kernel by using the Mexican Hat (7) as the mother wavelet, TABLE I. listed the prediction results of the MAE, MRE and RMSE with different length of training set from 96 hours of data. The next 50 samples after every length of training set were taken as test set. Test responses indicated that performance enhancement could be obtained by using the biased wavelet kernel.

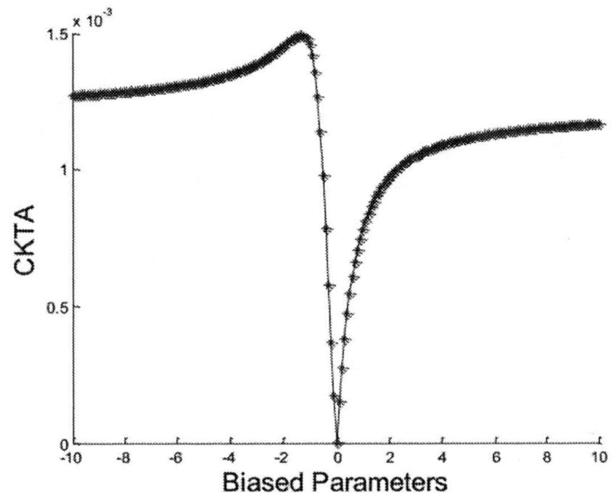

Figure 2. The connection between CKTA and values of biased parameters.

TABLE I. Wavelength variation estimation performances of rvm models

Hours		24h	48h	72h	96h
CKTA	Wavelet	6.842e-06	3.305e-06	2.384e-06	1.847e-06
	Cauchy	2.664e-03	1.111e-03	6.460e-04	4.809e-04
	Biased Wavelet	2.820e-03	1.495e-03	6.836e-04	5.094e-04
MAE (pm)	Wavelet	35.699	9.077	4.186	4.534
	Cauchy	13.016	7.541	4.148	2.587
	Biased Wavelet	10.407	6.861	3.738	2.555
MRE (pm)	Wavelet	0.143	0.036	0.019	0.012
	Cauchy	0.051	0.030	0.017	0.011
	Biased Wavelet	0.041	0.027	0.015	0.010
RMSE (pm)	Wavelet	36.820	9.305	5.359	3.475
	Cauchy	14.755	7.776	5.009	2.958
	Biased Wavelet	12.229	7.042	4.389	2.948

Conclusions

In this paper, the kernel function of RVM was constructed by biased wavelet and the optimization of the kernel parameters was investigated. For the adjustable nonzero mean of biased wavelet, the biased wavelet kernel is a flexible function. The CKTA method was used to optimize the parameters of RVM kernel. The biased wavelet kernel function can be adjusted by changing the parameters to maximum the CKTA. Experimental results showed a higher prediction accuracy by the biased wavelet kernel function.

Acknowledgment

This work was supported by the National Natural Science Foundation of China (No. 61402345). This work was supported by the Fundamental Research Funds for the Central Universities (WUT:2017IVB072).

References

[1] Tipping M E. Sparse bayesian learning and the relevance vector machine[J]. Journal of Machine Learning Research, 2001, 1(3):211-244.

[2] Vapnik, V.N. The Nature of Statistical Learning Theory,2nd ed. ; Springer; New York, NY, USA, 2000.

[3] Son Y, Lee J. Active Learning Using Transductive Sparse Bayesian Regression[J]. Information Sciences, 2016, 374:240-254.

[4] Wu Y, Breaz E, Gao F, et al. Nonlinear Performance Degradation Prediction of Proton Exchange Membrane Fuel Cells Using Relevance Vector Machine[J]. IEEE Transactions on Energy Conversion, 2016:1-1.

[5] Lin Y, Xia K, Jiang X, et al. Landslide Susceptibility Mapping Based on Particle Swarm Optimization of Multiple Kernel Relevance Vector Machines: Case of a Low Hill Area in Sichuan Province, China[J]. 2016, 5(10):191.

[6] Wang X Y, Liang L L, Li W Y, et al. A new SVM-based relevance feedback image retrieval using probabilistic feature and weighted kernel function ☆[J]. Journal of Visual Communication & Image Representation, 2016, 38:256-275.

[7] Fei S W. Kurtosis prediction of bearing vibration signal based on wavelet packet transform and Cauchy kernel relevance vector regression algorithm[J]. Advances in Mechanical Engineering, 2016, 8(9).

[8] Close R, Wilson J, Gader P. A Bayesian approach to localized multi-kernel learning using the relevance vector machine[C]// Geoscience and Remote Sensing Symposium (IGARSS), 2011 IEEE International. IEEE, 2011:1103-1106.

[9] Gönen M, Alpaydın E. Localized algorithms for multiple kernel learning[J]. Pattern Recognition, 2013, 46(3):795-807.

[10] Lanckriet G R G, Cristianini N, Bartlett P, et al. Learning the Kernel Matrix with Semi-Definite Programming[J]. Journal of Machine Learning Research, 2002, 5(1):323-330.

[11] Cristianini N, Shawe-Taylor J, Elisseeff A, et al. On kernel-target alignment[C]// International Conference on Neural Information Processing Systems: Natural and Synthetic. MIT Press, 2001:367--373.

[12] Lei Y. A Relevance Vector Machine Prediction Method Based on Adaptive Multi-kernel Combination and Its Application to Remaining Useful Life Prediction of Machinery[J]. Journal of Mechanical Engineering, 2016, 52(1):87.

[13] Trafalis T B, Malyscheff A M. Optimal selection of the regression kernel matrix with semidefinite programming[M]// Frontiers in Global Optimization. Springer US, 2004:575-584.

[14] Nguyen C H, Ho T B. An efficient kernel matrix evaluation measure[J]. Pattern Recognition, 2008, 41(11):3366-3372.

[15] Marina M A. Data Centering in Feature Space[J]. Ninth International Workshop on Artificial Intelligence & Statistics, 2002.

[16] Galvão R K H, Yoneyama T, Rabello T N. Signal Representation by Adaptive Biased Wavelet Expansions[J]. Digital Signal Processing, 1999, 9(4):225-240.

[17] Fei S W, He Y. Wind speed prediction using the hybrid model of wavelet decomposition and artificial bee colony algorithm-based relevance vector machine[J]. International Journal of Electrical Power & Energy Systems, 2015, 73:625-631.

[18] Zhao C H, Zhang Y, Wang Y L. Relevant Vector Machine Classification of Hyperspectral Image Based on Wavelet Kernel Principal Component Analysis[J]. Dianzi Yu Xinxi Xuebao/journal of Electronics & Information Technology, 2012, 34(8):1905-1910.

[19] Nen M, Alpayd&#, Ethem N. Multiple Kernel Learning Algorithms[J]. Journal of Machine Learning Research, 2011, 12:2211-2268.

[20] Li D, Wang J, Zhao X, et al. Multiple kernel-based multi-instance learning algorithm for image classification[J]. Journal of Visual Communication & Image Representation, 2014, 25(5):1112-1117.

A Reliable And Efficient Data Migration Method Based On GlusterFS

Li Li, Gang Yin, Tao Wang

Computer Science, National University of Defense Technology,Changsha, China
dylan-lili@foxmail.com,jack_nudt@163.com,taowang.2005@outlook.com

Abstract— Big data storage and high speed data access have become the main performance bottleneck for many big data applications. The higher speed data access and lower cost for storage must be required than some applications having small-scale data. Distributed hierarchical storage provides a good storage way to speed data access and lower cost. But it a data migration method which you choose decide the performance of distributed hierarchical storage system because data migration occurs frequently in hierarchical storage systems. There are many data migration methods, which most of those cannot ensure data utterly integrity after data migration. In this paper, we invent a reliable and efficient data migration method to ensure the utterly integrity of migrated data by MD5 checksum and improve performance of data migration by the pipeline technology. Through adjusting parameters, we get the best performance of data migration by using pipeline in our storage system which is a hierarchical storage system based on GlusterFS.

1 Introduction

In recent years, with the rapid development and popularity of computer science and information technology, the scale of the industry application system expands rapidly and the industry application data is generated by explosive growth. For example, the US New York Stock Exchange generates about 1TB transaction data every day, the Internet archives store about 2PB data, and increasing at a rate of at least 20TB every mouth [1]. Different periods of data have different meanings for application having massive data. The data of newly generated have the much higher frequency to access than the older data [2]. According to statistics, 80% of the disk data is not often accessed, but which is very important and must be completely stored. How to store these data in order to achieve the requirements of higher speed data access and lower cost.

At present, SSD (Solid State Disks) and HDD (Hard Disk Drives) are the main storage devices. The SSD have high data access speed, but the price of unit storage is very expensive and the lifespan is short. Though the price of unit storage is much cheaper and the lifespan is longer for the HDD disks, they cannot meet performance requirements because of the low speed of the data access for the application having massive data. Hierarchical storage [3] can be a good balance of storage costs and the speed of data access as application needed. The data is not accessed for a long period of time which is stored in the HDD and the frequently accessed data is stored in the SSD. Since only a small amount of data needs to be accessed frequently over a period of time, a small amount of SSD are required and the most of data is stored HDD. The hierarchical storage strategy have a good performance in accessing data with almost cost of HDD.

For the application having massive data, it's necessary to use the distributed storage to store massive data because a single disk storage capacity should be insufficient.

GlusterFS [4] proposed by Z RESEARCH Company is an open source distributed file system, which is widely used in cloud storage system. GlusterFS has PB class file cluster storage capacity by linking to many kinds of cheap x86 hosts with Infiniband RDMA [5] or TCP/ IP [6] protocol to a large-scale parallel network file system. In view of the large differences in data access frequency between different data, GlusterFS is used to build a hierarchical distributed storage cluster. A few SSD and a lot of HDD with different access speeds disks are connected into a cluster. The online volume having high speed of data access is created on the SSD and the offline volume having low unit storage costs is created on the HDD disks. In this way, the storage cluster provide good performance of data access under constraints of storage capacity and hardware costs.

In this distributed hierarchical storage system, data access frequency is dynamic. In order to enable the system to provide better performance all the time, we need to migrate frequently data between different storage devices. There are many methods to migrate data between offline volume and online volume, the most commonly used way is to migrate data file for offline database. But statistics show that large data file migration maybe fail or migrated data is not available because of various types of problems. For example, unexpected computer downtime during migration, or varying degrees of data loss will result in inconsistent data [7]. Therefore, in order to ensure data availability before and after large data file migration, data file must be verified after data migration.

At present, there are two main aspects to ensure the data availability after migration. One is comparing some specific data consistence before and after data migration by using spot checks and partial statistics [8]. It is a sampling approach, which can only ensure the sampling part of the data consistency, not all data. Another way is ensuring the data consistency in transfer process by using SHA1 [9], MD5 checksum [10] or other data verification method. This approach can ensure all data integrity after data migration because each bit of all data is checked in data transfer. However, it takes much more time to verify the data compared to the only migration data.

In this paper, we using a parallel method to verify and migrate data with pipelining. We want to take a little extra time to finish verify data available and integrity. Under the condition of ensuring data available and integrity, our method can significantly enhance the migration efficiency.

2 Related Work

2.1 GlusterFS

GlusterFS is mainly composed of storage server (brick server), client and NFS/Samba storage gateway. Obviously, there is no metadata server component in the GlusterFS architecture, which is largest design advantage than other file system. It is a decisive significance for improving the performance, reliability and stability of the entire system. GlusterFS builds a storage cluster through TCP/IP and InfiniBand RDMA high-speed network interconnection. The client can access data through the native Glusterfs protocol by using the FUSE (File System in User Space) module mount GlusterFS storage cluster into local file system [11]. So it is easy to access data stored in GlusterFS cluster by mount point in local file system.

2.2 MD5 Checksum

The MD5 checksum checks the correctness of the data by performing a hash operation on the received transmission data because arbitrary two strings should not have the same hash value (i.e., it is strong possibility that hash value is not the same, and it is difficult to create artificially two hash values of the same string). An MD5 checksum verifys the correctness of the data by performing a hash operation on the received transmission data. The hash value is calculated by received data is compared to the hash value transmitted with the data. If the two values are the same, which indicates that the transmitted data is intact and not been tampered (The hash value has not been tampered on the premise); if not, which indicates that the migration is fail and remove the destination file. Therefore, MD5 checksum can be used in data files migration to ensure the consistency of data.

2.3 The Traditional Method of Verifying data

There are two main aspects to ensure the data consistency and availability after data migration. Someone verify data consistency based on guard [12], which has three main steps. Firstly, some specific data is added into data as the guard data. Then, we check the consistency of the guard data after data migration. We regard as this data migration is successful if the guard data is complete. If not, this process of migration must result in some data was lost. But it is not always right this data migration is successful if the guard data is complete, because we verify the specific data not the whole data and some data maybe be lost aside from guard data. Therefore, we do not use this way to verify the migrated data for our migration method.

The people named Bin Wei Tennyson X. Chen [13] verify every bytes of migrated data by MD5 checksum. They use the popular MD5 algorithm to generate the hash codes with every bytes of source data before it be migrated. And then, the data migration is started. The MD5 checksum of migrated data is generated and compared with source data hash codes when the process of data migration is finished. They regard as this data migration is successful if their MD5 checksum were same. If not, this process of migration must be failed because the data is inconsistency. This way certainly ensure the data consistency, but the cost is very high and it is almost three times higher than only data migration. If we need to migrate the very large data, the time spent cannot be accepted.

From the above, we need to a data migration method which not only ensure the data consistency after data migration but also have a better efficiency.

3 Our method

In this section, we design a reliable and efficient data migration method based on distributed hierarchical storage system with GlusterFS. We improve the method of data migration, in order to greatly increase efficiency of data migration under the condition of ensuring the data available and integrity after migration.

3.1 A reliable data migration frame

Our method is used to big data frequent migration which has a strict requirements about data consistency from one storage cluster to another storage cluster. Our purpose is to ensure data consistency and provide a good performance. In order to

achieve that aim, the source data is split into many pieces to execute the migration and verification in parallel.
Firstly, we split the source data into many pieces, and then a piece of source data is migrated and another is verified at the same time. We will try to design parallel steps as much as possible to improve efficiency.

3.2 Mathematical expression of the improved method

The traditional method of data migration from source data files to destination path with MD5 checksum verifying data, which can be divided into the following three serial steps:

- Step 1: Obtain the MD5 checksum of the source data file;
- Step 2: Copy the source data file to the destination path;
- Step 3: Obtain the MD5 checksum of the destination data file, then compare it with the MD5 checksum of the source data file in step one. If they are the same, the migration succeeded and the destination data is available. Otherwise, the data is invalid, delete the destination data file to avoid produce dirty data.

For large data files, time consumption mainly includes reading the source file I/O time T1 and the CPU time T2 of calculating the MD5 checksum of the source file contents in step 1, the time T1 of reading the source file and writing destination file I/O time T3 in step 2, read the destination file I/O time T4 and the CPU time T5 of calculating the MD5 checksum of the destination file contents in step 3, so the total time consumption is:

$$All\_Time=T1+T2+T1+T3+T4+T5 \quad (1)$$

According to the study of the serial migration method mentioned above, we found that step 2 which is copying the source data file to the destination path contains reading the source file into buffer and then writing buffer contents into the destination file, the step 3 which is obtain the MD5 checksum of the destination data file contains reading the destination file into buffer and then calculating the value of destination file MD5 checksum. It is worse for efficiency that the contents of the destination file exists in the buffer twice in step 2 and step3, so we can optimize this method by calculating the value of destination file MD5 checksum when it is in buffer in step 2 and removing the step 3. The step 2 is changed to step 2' which contains reading the source file into buffer, writing buffer contents into the destination file and then calculating the value of buffer contents MD5 checksum. This approach can reduce the time consumption of T3 in step 3, which is the time of reading the destination file, so the total consumption of improved method becomes:

$$All\_Time=T1+T2+T1+T3+T5 \quad (2)$$

T2 and T5 are the time of calculating the value of source file and destination file MD5 checksum. Normally, the source file and the destination file are the same, so T2 = T5 and this formula can be written as:

$$All\_Time=T1+T2+T1+T3+T2 \quad (3)$$

We cannot read all the contents of large file into buffer because it will result in memory overflow and performance degradation. We should read and process a segment contents of large file until the end of the file. Definition t1 is a part of T1 which is the time of reading a segment file into buffer, similarly, t2 is a part of T2 which is the time of calculating the value of buffer contents MD5 checksum and t3 is a part of T3 which is the time of writing buffer contents into file. Therefore, the time consumption of step 1 should be written as:

$$T1+T2=t1+t2+t1+t2+\cdots \quad (4)$$

Similarly, the time consumption of step 2 ' should be written as:

$$T1+T3+T2=t1+t3+t2+t1+t3+t2+\cdots \quad (5)$$

According to the improved method, we found that reading a segment source file into buffer and calculating the value of buffer contents MD5 checksum use different computer resource the disk and CPU in step 1. So, we can makes two-stage pipelining [14] optimization step 1. Similarly in step 2', the three substeps that reading the contents of the source file into buffer with I/O resource, calculating the value of buffer contents MD5 checksum with CPU resource and writing the buffer contents into the destination file with I/O resource. Because migration occurs between different speed volumes of data access in this storage cluster, reading file and writing file are executed on different disks, we can makes the three-stage pipelining optimization in step 2'. Therefore, the total time with pipelining is:

$$All\_Time=\max(T1, T2)+\max(T1, T3, T2)+\vartheta \quad (6)$$

The max (T1, T2) represents the maximum value of T1 and T2, max (T1, T3, T2) represents the maximum between T1, T3 and T2, and ϑ represents the additional time between processes switch.

3.3 Software implementation

The data migration method have two parts which one is calculating the source data checksum and the other part is data migration and verify the consistency of data. In order to migrate data with pipelining, we split the source data into many parts to make the migration and verification parallel.

Figure 1 shows the flow diagram of the reliable migration software, the main steps are as follows.

Symbol definition:

- Q1, Q2: The symbol of Q1 and Q2 denote two fixed size buffer queue to cache the unit buffer. Q1 store the available buffer objects. Q2 store the some parts of source data read into memory.

- Bi (B1, B2, B3 ...): Bi denotes the unit buffer object to store the piece of data. It is one of Q1 or Q2 elements.
- P1, P2: P1 and P2 denote two process of reading the source data into buffer and calculating their checksum.
- Similarly, the symbol of q1, q2, bi, p1, p2, p3 denote the same things in second part of migration process.
- S: S denotes the source data.
- D: D denotes the destination data.
- Bi<-Qi or bi<-qi: These denote polling an item from queue named Qi or qi as Bi or bi.
- Bi->Qi or bi->qi: These denote add the item Bi or bi into the Qi or qi queue.
- Pi~: The symbol Pi~ indicates that the process Pi has ended.
- Qi=0: This indicates that the queue Qi is empty.

Step 1: Obtaining the value of source data file MD5 checksum with pipelining.

The fixed size of the two buffer queues Q1 and Q2 is initialized and then Q1 is filled with unit buffer object Bi of constant size. The buffer queues is used for recycling the buffer object to avoid requesting and releasing frequently buffer resulting in performance degradation. The two threads P1 and P2 are executed in parallel to obtain the MD5 checksum of source data file. The thread P1 is a loop which reads the segment contents of source data file into buffer object B1 fetched from the Q1 queue until the end of source data file. The thread P2 is also a loop which calculates the value of the MD5 checksum of the contents of the buffer object B2 fetched from the Q2 queue until the end of thread P1.

Step 2: Copying source data file to destination and obtaining the MD5 checksum of destination data file.

Similarly, the fixed size of the three buffer queues q1,q2 and q3 is initialized and then q1 is filled with unit buffer object bi f constant size which is denoted as q1 (b1, b2, b3 ...). The three threads p1, p2 and p3 are executed in parallel to copy file and obtain MD5 checksum of destination file. The thread p1 and p3 are similar function to P1 and P2 in step 1. The thread p2 is a loop which writes the contents of buffer object b2 fetched from the Q2 queue into destination file until the end of thread p1.

3.4 Parameter Optimization

Buffer is used to improve performance by realizing the parallel optimization. Several buffer queues is used to avoid requesting and releasing frequently buffer resulting in performance degradation in software implementation. There are two parameters impacting obviously performance which are the unit buffer size and queue size. The unit buffer size represents how much contents is processed at a time, such as how much file contents is read into the buffer once and how much contents of buffer is handle to calculate MD5 checksum once. The unit buffer size too small to improve performance because it needs too many times loop for large files. If the unit buffer size increases to a threshold, the performance is not improved as the unit buffer size get bigger because it is limited by other conditions. Meanwhile it not only wastes computer resources, but also decline a little performance because of dealing with large buffer.

The size of the buffer queue is the maximum times of one thread executed continuously. A single process can be executed several times without switching process, to avoid thread switching frequently caused performance degradation. For example, if the buffer queue size is equal to 1, all threads are executed serially. So, if it is too small, the processes switch frequently resulting in time of switch processes increase and performance degradation because of the resource blocking. The time of processes switch reduces as the buffer queue size get bigger. However, if the buffer queue size increases to a threshold, the performance is not improved as it get bigger, because it is limited by other conditions. Therefore, in order to achieve the best performance, these two parameters that unit buffer size and buffer queue size must be adjusted according to the environment.

4 Experiments Design

In this section, we describe the experiment questions, experiment dataset and environment as well as the corresponding evaluation metrics.

4.1 Experiment Questions

In order to explore the efficiency of our improved data migration method. We focus on the following three experiment questions.

- Q1: How to adjust the parameter of buffer queue size and unit buffer size to optimize our data migration method in our specific experiment environment?
- Q2: How much efficiency of our method is improved than original method under migrating data from online volume to offline volume?
- Q3: How much efficiency of our method is improved than original method under migrating data from offline volume to online volume?

For experiment question Q1, we use the way of controlling variables to optimal the two parameters. At the same time, we fix one parameter and change another step by step to get the optimum value when the migration speed get best. For Q2 and Q3, under the optimal parameters conditions, we compare migration speed of our method with original method in different size file. So we can analyse the efficiency of our data migration method.

4.2 Dataset and experiment environment

To address the above research questions and validate our approach, we build the experiment environment which include four computers with different hardware and choose some different size files ranging from 1M to 20G as dataset.

1) Experiment Dataset: We create some different files ranging from 1M to 20G as dataset, because we need to validate our method efficient in different size files. In order to get the best parameters of buffer queue size and unit buffer size, we set the buffer queue size value from 1 to 100 and unit buffer size from 1K to 16M.

2) Experimental Environment:

The experimental environment is a GlusterFS cluster which consists of two servers configured as shown in Table 1 and four servers configured as shown in Table 2 by Gigabit Ethernet network connection. The high-speed data volume is created which contains two nodes configured in Table 1 and named “online volume”. The low-speed data volume is created which contains the four machines configured in Table 2 and named “offline volume”.

TABLE I. high-speed data volume server configuration

Hardware	Configuration
CPU	8 Core Intel(R) Xeon(R) CPU E5-1620 0 @ 3.60GHz
Memory	DDR3 1600 MHz 48G
Hard Disk	Samsung SSD 840 EVO 250GB
Network Card	Intel Corporation Ethernet Controller 10-Gigabit X540-AT2
Software	Ubuntu 14.04 LTS, GlusterFS 3.8.1

TABLE II. low-speed data volume server configuration

Hardware	Configuration
CPU	8 Core Intel(R) Xeon(R) CPU E5-1620 0 @ 3.60GHz
Memory	DDR3 1600 MHz 48G
Hard Disk	Western Digital Caviar Green (AF, SATA 6Gb/s) 2TB
Network Card	Intel Corporation Ethernet Controller 10-Gigabit X540-AT2
Software	Ubuntu 14.04 LTS, GlusterFS 3.8.1

4.3 Evaluation Metrics

Our method verify the every bytes of data with MD5 checksum, so the migrated data must be available and integrity. We evaluate the method with efficiency which is migration speed.

5 Experiment Result

In this section, we first build the experiment environment which it creates a GlusterFS storage cluster and then creates two data volume as online data volume and offline data volume to migrate data from one to another. We adjust the parameters of unit buffer size and buffer queue size until our migration method is the fastest speed. Then we compare the efficiency of our migration method with traditional method and analyze the experiment result.

Figure 2 shows the speed of migrating the file that size is equal to 2GB with different unit buffer size and buffer queue size in my experimental environment plotted by the speed of data migration on the horizontal axis and the buffer queue size on the vertical. In the case of constant unit buffer size and the buffer queue size being less than 55, as the buffer queue size increase, the process switching times will reduce and the speed of migration will increase. But when the buffer queue size exceeds 55, as the buffer queue size increase, the speed of migration will decrease slowly. So, in the case of constant unit buffer size, when the buffer queues size is equal to 55, the speed of migration will get fastest.

Similarly, in the case of constant buffer queue, as the unit buffer size increase, the speed of migration will increase, but the increase rate of migration speed decreases. As we can see in Figure 3, the migration speed is roughly same when the unit buffer size equals 8M and 16M. However, the unit buffer size equals 16M that is used much more computer memory resources than the unit buffer size being 8M. So, in the case of constant buffer queue size, when the unit buffer size is equal to 8M, the speed of migration will get fastest. To sum up, under current environment, when the unit buffer size equals to 8M and the buffer queue size is equals to 55, the migration software will get the best performance.

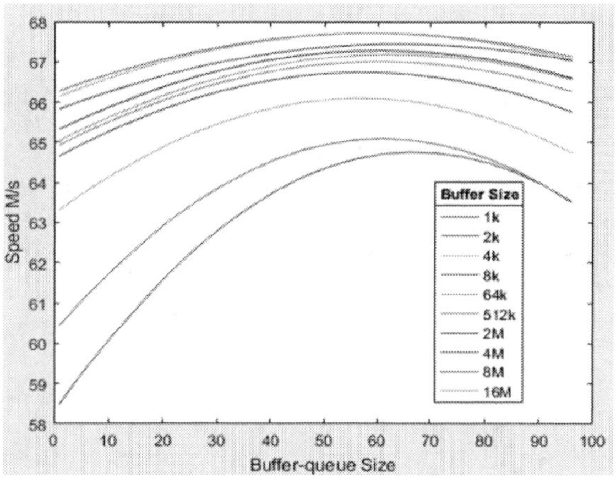

Figure 2. Optimal Parameter

Data migration mainly occurs when the data access frequency changes significantly; for example, data will be frequently accessed and then the data will migrate from the Offline-Volume to Online-Volume, if the Online-Volume storage space is insufficient and then the data that is accessed unlikely for the next period of time is migrated to the Offline-Volume to ensure that Online-Volume has enough space.

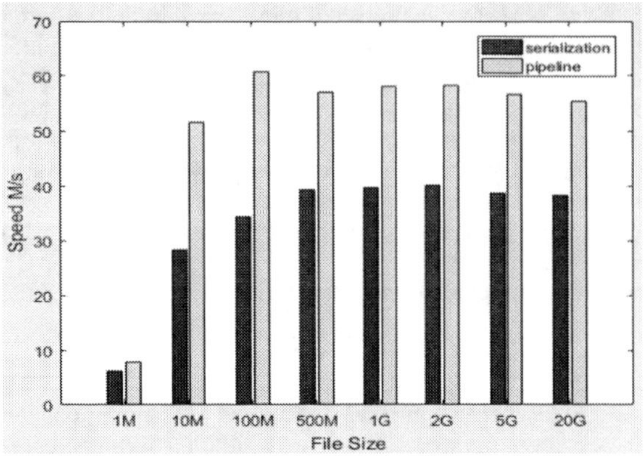

Figure 3. Data of Online-volume migrate to Offline-volume

Figure 3 shows the comparison of the efficiency of serial migration and pipeline migration which migrate data files of different size from online data volumes to offline data volumes and Figure 4 shows the comparison of the efficiency of serial migration and pipeline migration which migrate data files of different size from offline data volumes to online data volumes, which plotted by the speed of data migration on the horizontal axis and the file size on the vertical.

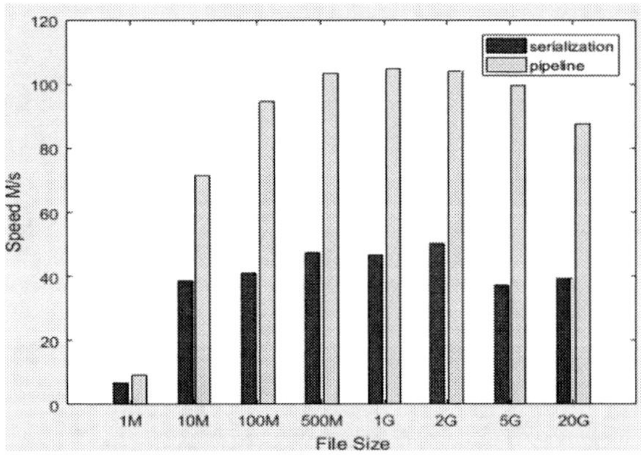

Figure 4. Data of Offline-volume migrate to Online–volume

Conclusion

This reliable data migration method is very important for data migration. It can be used to judge the integrity and availability of the migrated data accurately and quickly. It has a good application prospect for the application of high data integrity. At the same time, the pipeline migration method can greatly enhance the efficiency of data migration. In this experimental environment, the pipeline migration method efficiency of migrating the large data files over 500M from high-speed data volumes to low-speed data volumes can always is higher 2.5 times than the serial migration method from Figure 3. The migration files over 500M can also is higher 1.5 times than the serial migration method even from low-speed data volumes to high-speed data volumes from Figure 4.

References

[1] White T. Hadoop: The definitive guide[M]. 2st edition. " O'Reilly Media, Inc.", 2012.

[2] Song L, Dai H, Ren Y. A Learning Method of Hot-Spot Extent in Multi-Tiered Storage Medium Based on Huge Data Storage File System[J]. Journal of Computer Research & Development, 2012.

[3] Ao L, Yu D, Shu J, et al. A tiered storage system for massive data: TH-TS[J]. Journal of Computer Research & Development, 2011, 48(6):1089-1100.

[4] Gluster Inc. An Introuduction to Gluster Architecture. 2011.

[5] Liu J, Jiang W, Wyckoff P, et al. Design and Implementation of MPICH2 over InfiniBand with RDMA Support[M]. arXiv, 2003.

[6] Socolofsky T J, Kale C J. TCP/IP tutorial[J]. Technology, 1991.

[7] Wang G, Wang D, Li W, et al. Data Migration Technology Research Based on Big Data Environment[J]. Microcomputer Applications, 2013.

[8] DING Jian hua YAO Pei fu DONG Wei Yunnan Copper Industry Group. Technique and Implementation of Data Migration and Its on Storage Systems[J]. Computer Development & Applications, 2014.

[9] Eastlake Rd D, Jones P. US Secure Hash Algorithm 1 (SHA1)[M]. RFC Editor, 2001.

[10] Rivest R L. The MD5 message-digest algorithm. RFC 1321[J]. 1992.

[11] LengZhiJiang. The Research and Implementation of a Scal-out Cloud Storage Based on Distributed File System GlusterFS [D]. Fudan university, 2014.

[12] Schneider W A. Integral Formulation for Migration in Two and Three Dimensions[J]. Geophysics, 1978, 43(43):49.

[13] Wei, Chen, T.X. Verifying data migration correctness: The checksum principle[J]. 2014.

[14] Stone H S. High-performance computer architecture[J]. 1987.

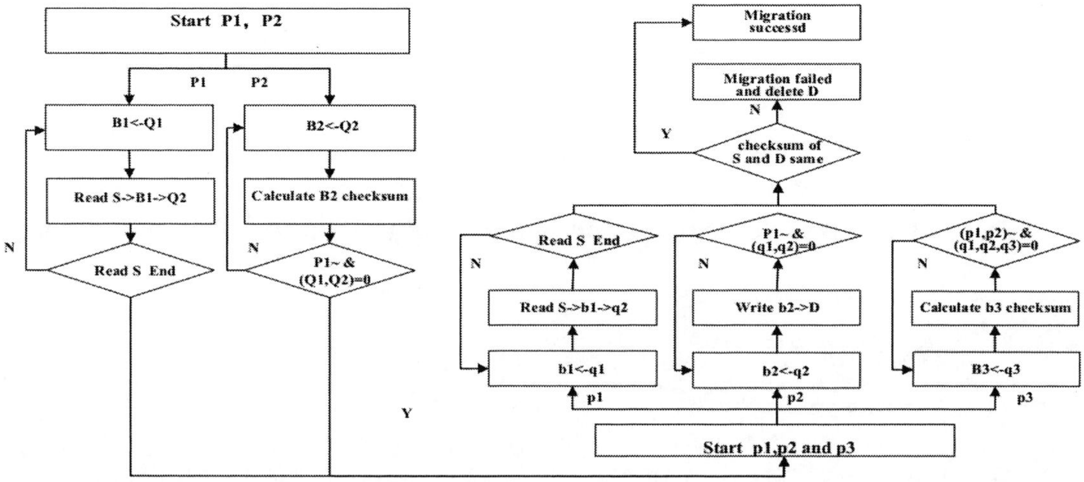

Figure 1. Flow chart of reliable migration method with pipelining

DOI: 10.1051/itmconf/20171205004

A Novel Fuzzy Data Association Approach for Visual Multi-object Tracking

Liang-Qun* LI, En-Qun LI, Wen-Ming HE

ATR Key Laboratory, Shenzhen University, Shenzhen, Guang Dong ,China
Shenzhen Chichen Cloud Net Co., LTD, Shenzhen, Guang Dong ,China
Shenzhen Pan Go Microsystems Co.,LTD, ,Shenzhen, Guang Dong ,China
e-mail: lqli@szu.edu.cn,67327301@qq.com,18900058@qq.com

Abstract—Multiple object tracking (MOT) is one of the most important research areas in visual surveillance. However, some practical challenges remain to be overcome for implementing this technology, such as occlusion, missed detection, false detection, and abrupt camera motion. In this paper, to the visual multi-object tracking, a novel fuzzy data association algorithm is proposed. In order to incorporate expert experience into the proposed algorithm, a fuzzy inference system based on knowledge is designed, and the fuzzy membership degrees are used to substitute the association probabilities between the objects and observations. The experiment results on several public data sets show that the proposed algorithm has advantages over other state-of-the-art tracking algorithms in terms of efficiency.

1 Introduction

The objective of multi-object tracking is to estimate the current states of objects based on previous visual measurements up to the current time in a video sequence, such as positions, size, identification (ID), etc. It is very important for many computer vision tasks with applications such as automated surveillance, traffic safety, vehicle navigation, human computer interaction, and robotics [1], [2]. With the development of the detection technology of object, detection-based multi-object tracking methods have been extensively studied [3].

A key problem of the tracking-by-detection approach is that of the data association between visual measurements and multiple objects. In order to solve the data association problems, many data association approaches have been proposed in recent decades. To obtain the global optimal solution or sub-optimal solution, Park et al.[1]proposed a binary integer programming formulation for a data association problem which pursues the minimum cost data associations among target measurements via one-to-one, one-to-m, and m-to-one associations. Milan et al. [4] used gradient descent to find strong local minima of complex nonconvex energy that captures image evidence and various physical constraints for tracking. Leibe et al. [5] proposed to perform coupled multiple-object detection and tracking by applying the minimum description length principle, formulate it as a QBP, and solve it by expectation maximization (EM) method. Benfold and Reid [6] employed MCMC to track multiple heads where motion is exploited to detect false positive (FP) detections. Bae et al.[7] proposed a data association with a track existence probability by incorporating the detections into tracks to solve partial occlusions, and a track management method was used to deal with track initialization, link and termination, which can associate terminated tracks for linking tracks fragmented by long-term occlusions.

In this paper, a novel fuzzy logic data association method for online visual multi-object tracking is proposed. The error and the change of error of motion, shape and appearance models are used to construct the fuzzy input variables and fuzzy inference system. In the fuzzy inference system, the association probabilities between observations and objects are replaced by the fuzzy membership degrees, which can incorporate reasoning based on the fuzzy rule base in the same sense as human reasoning.

The rest of this paper is organized as follows. Section 2 describes the proposed multi-object tracking algorithm. Experiment results that compare the performances of all algorithms are presented in Section 3. Finally, some conclusions are provided in Section 4.

2 Proposed Multi-Object Tracking Algorithm

2.1 Fuzzy Logic Data Association

To calculate the fuzzy association probabilities $\mu_{i,j}(k)$ between the objects $\{\hat{x}_{k-1}^{i}\}_{i=1}^{m}$ and observations $\{z_k^j\}_{j=1}^{n}$ (or detection responses), a fuzzy inference system (FIS) is designed based on the affinities of motion and appearance. The FIS contains four basic elements: fuzzifier of input variables, fuzzy knowledge-base, fuzzy inference engine, and defuzzifier.

2.2System variables

Suppose that the predicted state of object i at the kth frame is $X = \{\hat{x}_i(k)\}_{i=1}^{m}$,where $\hat{x}_i(k) = (x_i(k), v_{x_i}(k), y_i(k), v_{y_i}(k))$. $x_i(k)$ denotes the x-coordinate of the object's prediction position, $y_i(k)$ denotes the y-coordinate of the object's prediction position, $v_{x_i}(k)$ and $v_{y_i}(k)$ denote the corresponding velocities of object, respectively i .

Given detection responses, we denote the set of all observations at the frame k as $Z = \{z_j(k)\}_{j=1}^{n}$, where $z_j(k) = (z_x^j(k), z_y^j(k))$, $z_x^j(k)$ and $z_y^j(k)$ denote the x-coordinate, y-coordinate of the observation j respectively. The rules of the fuzzy data association approach are expressed in terms of two input variables and an output variable. The input variables $E_{i,j}(k)$ and $\Delta E_{i,j}(k)$ are defined in terms of the prediction errors and change of errors of motion and appearance models. Firstly, the normalized prediction errors of motion model is defined as follows:

$$E_{i,j}^{M}(k) = \begin{cases} 1, & If \left\| z_j(k) - \bar{z}_j(k) \right\|_2 > \left\| z_j(k) - H_k \cdot \hat{x}_i(k-1) \right\|_2 \\ \rho_M \cdot \dfrac{\left\| z_j(k) - \bar{z}_j(k) \right\|_2}{\left\| z_j(k) - H_k \cdot \hat{x}_i(k-1) \right\|_2}, & If \left\| z_j(k) - \bar{z}_j(k) \right\|_2 < \left\| z_j(k) - H_k \cdot \hat{x}_i(k-1) \right\|_2 \\ 0, & If \left\| z_j(k) - \bar{z}_j(k) \right\|_2 = \left\| z_j(k) - H_k \cdot \hat{x}_i(k-1) \right\|_2 \end{cases} \quad (1)$$

where $\bar{z}_j(k) = H_k \cdot A_k \cdot \mathbf{\hat{x}}_i(k-1)$ denotes the predicted observation. In this paper, H_k^i is an 2×4 observation transition matrix, F_k^i is 4×4 state transition matrix.

Appearance is an important cue for the data association in MOT. In order to make the appearance model robust, the RGB color histogram is used to capture the statistical information of object region. To satisfy the low-computational cost imposed by real-time processing discrete densities, m-bin histograms should be used. Then, we have

Appearance model of object i: $\hat{H}(x_i) = \{H_m(x_i)\}_{m=1,2,\ldots,N}$

Appearance model of observation j: $\hat{H}(z_j) = \{H_n(z_j)\}_{n=1,2,\ldots,N}$

where $H_m(x_i)$ is the number of pixels of object i in the mth color bin, $H_n(z_j)$ is the number of pixels of observation j in the nth color bin. In order to estimate the similarity between object i and observation j, we employ the correlation coefficient method to calculate the prediction error of appearance model.

$$E_{i,j}^{A}(k) = \rho_A \cdot \frac{\sum_{m=1}^{N} (H_m(x_i) - \overline{H}_1)(H_m(z_i) - \overline{H}_2)}{\sqrt{\sum_{m=1}^{N} (H_m(x_i) - \overline{H}_1)^2 \sum_{n=1}^{N} (H_n(z_i) - \overline{H}_2)^2}} \quad (2)$$

where

$$\overline{H}_1 = \frac{1}{N} \sum_{m=1}^{N} H_m(x_i), \quad \overline{H}_2 = \frac{1}{N} \sum_{n=1}^{N} H_n(z_j)$$

and their values lie in [-1,1], Based on $E_{i,j}^{M}(k)$ and $E_{i,j}^{A}(k)$, the change errors $\Delta E_{i,j}^{M}(k)$ and $\Delta E_{i,j}^{A}(k)$ can be defined as follows:

$$\Delta E_{i,j}^{M}(k) = \begin{cases} \dfrac{\Delta E_{i,j}^{M}(k) - \Delta E_i^{M}(k-1)}{\Delta E_i^{M}(k-1)}, & if \left| E_{i,j}^{M}(k) - E_i^{M}(k-1) \right| < \left| E_i^{M}(k-1) \right| \\ \dfrac{\Delta E_{i,j}^{M}(k) - \Delta E_i^{M}(k-1)}{\left| \Delta E_{i,j}^{M}(k) - \Delta E_i^{M}(k-1) \right|}, & if \left| E_{i,j}^{M}(k) - \Delta E_i^{M}(k-1) \right| > \left| E_i^{M}(k-1) \right| \\ 0, & if \left| E_{i,j}^{M}(k) - E_i^{M}(k-1) \right| = \left| E_i^{M}(k-1) \right| \end{cases} \quad (3)$$

and

$$\Delta E_{i,j}^{A}(k) = \begin{cases} \dfrac{\Delta E_{i,j}^{A}(k) - \Delta E_i^{A}(k-1)}{\Delta E_i^{A}(k-1)}, & if \left| E_{i,j}^{A}(k) - E_i^{A}(k-1) \right| < \left| E_i^{A}(k-1) \right| \\ \dfrac{\Delta E_{i,j}^{A}(k) - \Delta E_i^{A}(k-1)}{\left| \Delta E_{i,j}^{A}(k) - \Delta E_i^{A}(k-1) \right|}, & if \left| E_{i,j}^{A}(k) - \Delta E_i^{A}(k-1) \right| > \left| E_i^{A}(k-1) \right| \\ 0, & if \left| E_{i,j}^{A}(k) - \Delta E_i^{A}(k-1) \right| = \left| E_i^{A}(k-1) \right| \end{cases} \quad (4)$$

As a result, we define $E_{i,j}(k)$ and $\Delta E_{i,j}(k)$ to be

$$E_{i,j}(k) = \sqrt{\frac{E_{i,j}^{M\,2}(k) + E_{i,j}^{A\,2}(k)}{3}} \quad (5)$$

$$\Delta E_{i,j}(k) = \sqrt{\frac{\Delta E_{i,j}^{M\,2}(k) + \Delta E_{i,j}^{A\,2}(k)}{3}} \quad (6)$$

2.3Membership Functions (fuzzifier)

The crisp values are mapped into some fuzzy sets defined in the universe of discourse of input and output. Generally, the more numbers of fuzzy sets we made, the more accuracy of output we got. But more numbers of fuzzy sets will increase the computation load of the algorithm. Usually, the number of fuzzy sets will be decided by experience. In the fuzzy inference system, five fuzzy sets that are labeled in the linguistic terms of zero (ZE), small positive (SP), medium positive (MP),large positive (LP), and very large positive (VP), are specified for each crisp input ($E_{i,j}(k)$and $\Delta E_{i,j}(k)$). These membership functions of each crisp input are shown in Fig.3.

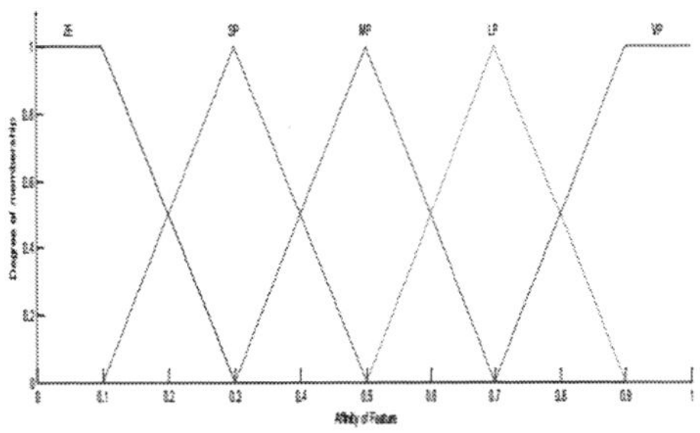

Figure.2 Membership functions for the fuzzy sets of $E_{i,j}(k)$and $\Delta E_{i,j}(k)$

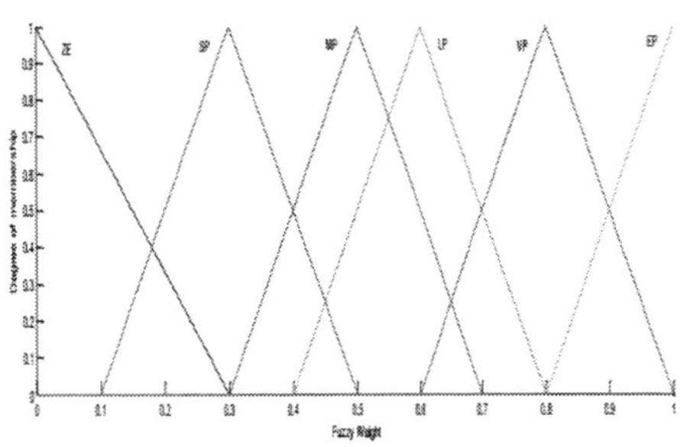

Figure.3 Membership functions for the fuzzy sets of $\mu_{i,j}(k)$

Unlike that of the input data, the output data have six fuzzy sets labeled in the linguistic terms of ZE, SP, MP, LP, VP and extremely large positive (EP). The membership functions of the fuzzy sets are defined by the triangular functions and the core of these fuzzy sets are not equally spaced. The membership functions of output are shown in Fig. 4. According to the input and output defined above, the fuzzy rules can be expressed by employing fuzzy IF-THEN rules as follows:

TABLE I. Fuzzy rule base for $\mu_{i,j}(k)$

$\mu_{i,j}(k)$		$E_{i,j}(k)$				
		ZE	SP	MP	LP	VP
$\Delta E_{i,j}(k)$	ZE	EP	VP	LP	SP	SP
	SP	VP	LP	MP	SP	SP
	MP	LP	MP	MP	SP	ZE
	LP	MP	MP	SP	SP	ZE
	VP	SP	SP	ZE	ZE	ZE

Tables 1 show the fuzzy rules of fuzzy inference system for the fuzzy association probability $\mu_{i,j}(k)$ .The output of the weight membership functions which are used to evaluate the crisp outputs through the Max–Min compositional rule of inference technique and center of gravity (COG) defuzzification.

2.4Overall the Proposed Algorithm

According to the derived results mentioned above, the structure of the proposed online visual multi-object tracking algorithm can be summarized as follows.

Algorithm: Online multi-target tracking based on fuzzy Logic Data Association(PROPOSED ALGORITHM)

1. **Initialization**
Applying the offline-trained detector based on aggregated channel features [8] to obtain the observations (detection responses) $\{z_k^j\}_{k=1:T}^{j=1:n}$ at the current frame.

2. **State estimation**
For k=1,2,…
- Data association: Find the best association pairs $\{(\hat{x}_{k-1}^i, z_k^j)\}$between the objects $\{\hat{x}_{k-1}^i\}_{i=1}^m$ and observations $\{z_k^j\}_{j=1}^n$ by using the fuzzy logic data association algorithm described in Section 2.1.
- State update: Update the object states with the associated measurements by using the Kalman filtering.

End For

3 Experiment Results

We tested our algorithms on various publicly available sequences as shown in Table 2, including PETS.S2L1 dataset and PETS.S2L2 dataset.

the information of the used datasets

Name	FPS	Lengt h	Resolution	Trajectories
PETS.S2L1	7	795	768×576	19
PETS.S2L2	7	436	786×576	42

Comparisons with several state-of-the-art algorithms were made. Both qualitative analysis and quantitative evaluations were presented to show the effectiveness of our algorithms. The widely used CLEAR MOT metrics was employed to evaluate the proposed algorithm[7]. In order to compare the performance of the proposed algorithm with other multiple tracking algorithms, we chose two reported state-of-art trackers, such as Bae et al's proposed method[7] and OM+APP[4].

Table 3 shows the comparison results for all metrics on all three sequences individually. Firstly, the tracking results for the PETS.S2L1 data set are compared. This data set is widely used in multi-object tracking literatures. Because the human density is low, though the dataset includes some nonlinear motion of objects and some proximity objects, all algorithms can track these objects with high tracking accuracy. Fig.4 shows the results of the proposed algorithm. From Table 6 and Fig.4, we can see that the tracking accuracy (MOTA) of the proposed algorithm is higher than that of both [7].

Secondly, the tracking results for the PETS.S2L2 data set are compared. In this dataset, the human density is higher than the PETS.S2L1, and the objects are frequently occluded. Fig.5 shows the results of the proposed algorithm.

Conclusion

In this paper, we proposed a new fuzzy data association approach for visual multi-object tracking. By incorporating fuzzy logic into multi-object tracking system, the association probabilities are allowed to be adjusted dynamically based on the conclusions of a set of fuzzy rules. Finally, experimental results show that the proposed algorithm provides much better performance than other state-of-art algorithms.

Acknowledgement

This work was supported by the National Natural Science Foundation of China (61301074, 61271107, and 61375015), Natural Science Foundation of the Guangdong Province of China (S2012010009417).

References

[1] Chiwoo Park, Taylor J. Woehl, James E. Evans, and Nigel D. Browning. Minimum Cost Multi-Way Data Association for Optimizing Multitarget Tracking of Interacting Objects. IEEE Transactions on Pattern Analysis and Machine Intelligence. 37 (2015)611-624.

[2] Lu Wang, Nelson Hon Ching Yung, LishengXu. Multiple-Human Tracking by Iterative Data Association and Detection Update, IEEE Transactions On Intelligent Transportation Systems. 15(2014)1886-1899.

[3] Shu Tian, Fei Yuan, Gui-Song Xia. Multi-object tracking with inter-feedback between detection and tracking, Neurocomputing, 171(2016) 768-780.

[4] A. Milan, S. Roth, and K. Schindler. Continuous energy minimization for multi-target tracking, IEEE Trans. Pattern Anal. Mach. Intell. 36(2014)58–72.

[5] B. Leibe, K. Schindler, N. Cornelis, and L. Van Gool, Coupled object detection and tracking from static cameras and moving vehicles, IEEE Trans. Pattern Anal. Mach. Intell.,30(2008)1683–1698.

[6] B. Benfold and I. Reid. Stable multi-target tracking in real-time surveillance video, in Proc. IEEE Conf. Comput. Vis. Pattern Recog., 2011, pp. 3457–3464.

[7] Seung-Hwan Bae, Kuk-Jin Yoon. Robust Online Multiobject Tracking With Data Association and Track Management,IEEE TRANSACTIONS ON IMAGE PROCESSING, 33(2014)2820-2833.

[8] P. Dollár, R. Appel, S. Belongie, et al. Fast feature pyramids for object detection. IEEE Trans. Pattern Anal. Mach. Intell., 36(8)(2014)1532-1545.

Performance Comparison of Tracking Results on Two Different Datasets

Sequence	Method	MOTA	MOTP	IDS	MT	ML	FG
PETS.S2L1	Bae et al.[7]	83.0	69.6	4	100	0	4
	OM+APP[4]	90.6	80.2	11	21	1	6
	Proposed Algorithm	86.2	65.4	11	15	0	58
PETS.S2L2	Bae et al.[7]	30.2	69.2	284	2.4	19.0	499
	OM+APP[4]	56.9	59.4	99	28	12	73
	Proposed Algorithm	51.5	66.1	154	11	3	362

Figure.4. Results of the proposed algorithm on PETS.S2L1 dataset

Figure.5. Results of the proposed algorithm on PETS.S2L2 dataset

ITM Web of Conferences **12**, 05005 (2017) DOI: 10.1051/itmconf/20171205005
ITA 2017

Classification of Desired Motion Force Based On Cerebral Hemoglobin Information*

Yan-Xiang Sui[1], Chun-Guang Li [2], Hong-Miao Zhang[3], Juan Li[4]

[1]*School of Mechanical and Electric Engineering, Soochow University, Suzhou, China*
[2]*School of Mechanical and Electric Engineering, Soochow University, Suzhou, China*
[3]*School of Mechanical and Electric Engineering, Soochow University, Suzhou, China*
[4]*School of Mechanical and Electric Engineering, Soochow University, Suzhou, China*
[1]*suiyanxiang@163.com*, [2]*lichunguang@suda.edu.cn*, [3]*zhanghongmiao@suda.edu.cn*, [4]*lijuan@suda.edu.cn*

Abstract: Strength training using patients' desired force level is helpful to improve training effect and promote rehabilitation. Generally, force levels are recognized by applying EMG or biomechanical information, these methods were not suitable for patients who lost important muscle groups or have weakened muscle functions. This paper proposed a method for identifying force level based on cerebral hemoglobin information, rather than the information depending on limbs. Ten subjects performed pedaling movement in three force levels. Features were extracted in both the time-domain and frequency-domain, with deoxygenated hemoglobin (deoxy) and the difference between oxygenated hemoglobin (oxy) and deoxy as parameters. Important frequency bands (0.01-0.03Hz, 0.03-0.06Hz, 0.06-0.09Hz, 0.09- 0.12Hz) were confirmed by performing power spectrum density analysis. And significant measure channels were selected by performing one-way analyses of variance on three time periods around the start of movement. Force level was recognized by applying extreme learning machine (ELM). The corresponding precision rate was up to 78.7%. The proposed identification method was not restricted to the existence of limbs or the strength of limb information. It was realized based on brain information recorded in a real movement environment; it is helpful to realize the desired force level of subjects and to provide a control command for rehabilitation training equipment.

1. Introduction

Recently, the number of people with motor dysfunction in lower limbs has been increasing rapidly because of natural disasters, injuries, accidents, diseases, and so on. In order to improve the training effect and the efficiency of recovery, patients' resistance training and active participation is very important and necessary. Thus, there is a great need to control rehabilitation device by patients' motion states of force level.

Generally, EMG and other biomechanical information were used to recognize motion states [1-3]. However, many patients lost important muscles or have little muscle functions, and thus EMG or biomechanical information was not enough to identify motion states for these patients. Recently, brain information obtained by using EEG and fMRI technology has been very popular around the world [4-6]. Dario Farina, et al. classified four actual cycling torque motion by EEG information, and the recognition rate was around 50.8% [7]. Dong-Eun Kim, et al. also applied EEG to classify the three grades (25%, 50%, 75%) of hand grip MVC (Maximum Voluntary Contraction), and the result was about 52.03% for left hand and 77.7% for right hand [8]. However, the above research had strict restrictions on testing environment and subjects. By contrast, functional near infrared spectroscopy (fNIRS) is a suitable tool to record brain information. Baolei Xu, et al. classified the speed and force clench imagination by support vector machine (SVM), the accuracy results was 72% [9]. Yunfa Fu, et al. combined the features of NIRS and EEG to recognize three levels of imagined force (at 20/50/80 % MVGF (maximum voluntary grip force)) and speed (at 0.5/1/2 Hz) of hand clenching by SVM. The average classification accuracy was 72% [10]. Xuxian Yin, et al. used concentration changes of oxy in the left hemisphere as input features to classify the imagined hand force and speed levels, and the recognition rate was around 75% [11]. However, similar research to identify motion states of lower limbs is very few. Studies [12-13] identified spontaneous motion states of lower limbs by using fNIRS. It confirmed the feasibility and advantage of fNIRS technology, especially for recognizing spontaneous motion states.

It is very important for patients to train the strength of lower limbs during the process of rehabilitation training. Moreover, controlling the resistance of lower limbs' movement by patients spontaneously is also necessary for promoting recovery. Therefore, the paper proposed a method to recognize the indented resistance of lower limbs' movement by applying fNIRS technology. Pedaling movement in three-class force levels was performed, and motion was controlled by the subjects themselves. Since Zengyong Li, et al [14] observed the meaningful features from prefrontal lobe in subjects at risk of stroke by spectral analysis, features in both the time-domain and the frequency-domain were considered in the paper. In addition, in order to reduce regional location error of individuals, information in the channels of interest rather than regions were analyzed. It was supposed that time-frequency features in the channels were preferable for recognizing motion states of spontaneous movements.

2. Experiments

2.1 Subjects

Ten right-handed healthy participants (10 male, age: 21±2 years old) at Soochow University participated in riding bicycle experiment. None of them had a history of neurologic, psychiatric or other related disease. All the participants were informed of the test procedure before the experiment.

2.2 Instruments

A FORIE-3000 optical topography system (Shimadzu Corporation, Kyoto, Japan) [15] was used to measure concentration changes of oxygenated hemoglobin (oxy), deoxygenated hemoglobin (deoxy), and total hemoglobin (total). The distance between each pair of detector and emitter was 3 cm. The sampling period of hemoglobin signals was 0.13s. An experimental diagram of riding bicycle is shown in Fig. 1 (a). Pedaling force was recorded by the rehabilitation bicycle device.

One set of 3×5 parietal flash holder was applied to fix emitters and detectors. In the experiment, 15 probes (7 detectors and 8 emitters) were used to collect cerebral activation data in a 3×5 area (Fig. 1 (b)). Based on the international 10-20 system [16-17], the probe holder was placed on the top of the head , and detector 7 was placed in the straight ahead of Cz portion with a distance of 3 cm. 22 channels are presented with digital numbers in Fig. 1 (b). The motor-related regions of interest included prefrontal cortices (PFC: channels 1, 2, 3, 4, 5, 6 and 7), supplementary motor areas (SMA: channels 14, 16, 17, 19, 21 and 22), premotor cortices (PMCL: channels 13 and 18 in the left hemisphere; PMCR: channels 15 and 20 in the right hemisphere). These regions have been proved to play an important role in controlling force [18]. The frontal eye cortices (FEC: channels 8, 9, 10, 11 and 12) was not the region of interest in our study.

2.3 Motion task

Pedaling task was performed in three levels of force (low resistance: 0N, medium resistance: 30N, and high resistance: 50N). Fig. 1 (c) illustrates the temporal sequence of the task design. Force movement task were first executed after a pre-rest period, and there was a rest between every two force tasks. As for each motion state, the task were performed two times. The start and end times of each task, as well as the time duration of each rest, were controlled by the subjects spontaneously. But the subjects were informed in advance to rest enough with a period not less than 25 seconds. The subjects were familiar with this time interval by exercising 2-3 times before the experiment. During the experiment, the start and end of each task were recorded with a mark by an experiment operator. The hemoglobin concentration of the subjects was recorded simultaneously in the whole process of the test.

3. Analysis Methods

The concentration changes in the difference between oxy and deoxy, and that in the deoxy were analyzed. And the information in time-domain and frequency-domain were both analyzed for extracting hemoglobin features.

Firstly, power spectrum density analysis was carried out to observe principal frequency ranges of the data in different force levels. And based on spectral distribution characteristics, Chebyshev filtering method was used for performing band- pass filter.

Secondly, in order to avoid negative effects caused by bad data in baselines during the whole experiment, the change rate of oxy and deoxy (oxy_rate and deoxy_rate) in each concerned channel were calculated. The interval number of five was selected to calculate change rate. And as for each channel, the deoxy_rate and the difference between the means of oxy_rate and deoxy_rate (oxy_rate - deoxy_rate) were both calculated.

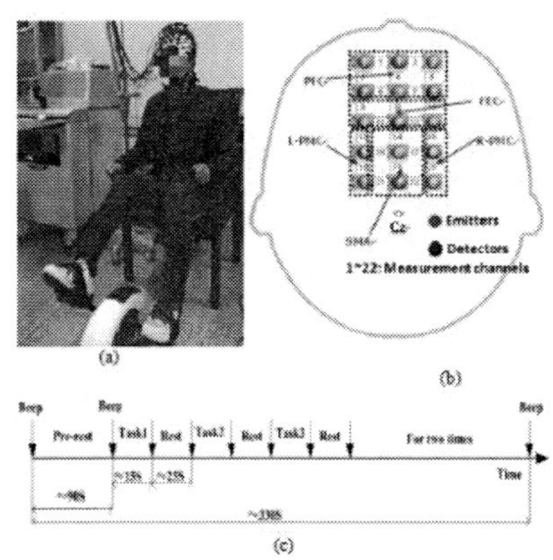

Figure. 1. (a) The experimental setup. (b) Distribution of the detected channels in motor-related region.(c) The task design. Task1: pedalling task with low force. Task2: pedalling task with medium force.Task3: pedalling task with high force.

Thirdly, to confirm the difference of frequency bands among the three force levels, average "oxy_rate-deoxy_rate" in all the channels were carried out for each sampling point. One ANOVA1 analysis on different frequency bands with the average values of "oxy_rate-deoxy_rate" in the period of T3 (nine points after the start mark were recorded as T3) was performed. Statistical significance of the task was set at $P<0.05$.

Fourthly, to confirm the important channels in the time domain, as for each channel (exclude the channels of FEC), mean values of nine points before and after the motion start mark were recorded as T2 and T3, and

DOI: 10.1051/itmconf/20171205005

mean value of nine points in front of T2 was recorded as T1. A one-way analysis of variance (ANOVA1) on 'time (T1, T2, T3)' was performed for each channel. The Fisher least significant difference test was used as a post hoc test. Statistical significance of the task was set at $P<0.01$. Since the head size of subjects were not the same, the channels in the adjacent position of two regions may have some kind of positioning error. And the channels in each region may have opposite channel information. That is why the information in each channel rather than the average hemoglobin in each region was analyzed in our research.

At last, ELM recognition algorithm was adopted for distinguishing force levels. The algorithm solved the major bottleneck of feed-forward neural networks in learning speed, and provided a good performance at extremely fast learning speed [19]. In addition, ELM algorithm is easily implemented and less sensitive to specified parameters [20]. In this study, the number of hidden neurons in ELM was selected from100 to 2000, the step of 50 was selected.

4. Results

According to the feedback of investigation report written by subjects and the preliminary observation of data, all the subjects' data were chosen for analysis.

Based on power spectrum density analysis, the frequency corresponding to the power spectrum's peak of the concerned channels were presented in Fig. 2.

It is found that the main frequency bands in different force levels were different. In level of 0N, the main frequency in each channel was almost below 0.03Hz. In the level of 50N, the main frequency in most channels was between 0.03Hz and 0.06Hz. The results were consistent with the conclusion of the paper written by Z. Li [21]. He has proved that the oscillation in interval between 0.02–0.08 Hz was considered to reflect the neurogenic activity in the vessel wall. In order to avoid losing some useful information, the analyzed frequency range was increased to 0.01-0.12Hz. Band-pass filter with four bands (I: 0.01-0.03Hz, II: 0.03-0.06Hz, III: 0.06-0.09Hz, IV: 0.09-0.12Hz) was performed respectively. By performing one-way analysis on the four frequency bands with the average " oxy_rate-deoxy_rate" in T3, it is found that the main frequency bands in different force levels were significantly different. The results are given in Fig. 3. During the low force motion, band IV was lower than others ($P=0.000$) and the band I was larger than band II ($P=0.002$). As for the medium force, there are no significant characters. At the high force, band I was lower than band II ($P=0.01$), and band III ($P=0.016$) and IV was larger than others ($P=0.000$).

To confirm the important channels during each task with the mean values of T1, T2 and T3. When the mean value in T3 was obviously larger or smaller than those in both T1 and T2, and simultaneously, and the two means in T1 and T2 have no significant difference, the channel was selected as an important one. The deoxy and "oxy_rate-deoxy_ rate" were both used for selecting important channels.

0N: as shown in Fig. 4, "oxy_rate-deoxy_ rate" of channel 11 in T3 was significantly lower than those both in T2 and T1 ($P=0.001$). And the values of deoxy in T3 were obviously different from those both in T2 and T1 for the channels 2 ($P=0.000$) and 3 ($P=0.000$). Thus, the channels of 2, 3, and 11 were considered as important channels for recognizing low force level.

30N: As for the medium force level (Fig. 5), there was not any important channel being selected with the values of "oxy_rate-deoxy_ rate". As for deoxy, the values of channel 8($P=0.000$) in T3 was greatly larger than those in T1 and T2 .

50N: As for the high force level (Fig. 6), "oxy_rate-deoxy_rate" of channels 11, 12 ($P=0.000$), 13 ($P=0.000$), 17 ($P=0.000$), 21 ($P=0.004$) in T3 was obviously larger than those in the T1 and T2. And deoxy of channel 2 ($P=0.000$), 4 ($P=0.003$) in T3 was also selected by the same method. The above channels were useful for recognizing high force level.

Overall, all the important channels (eight channels: 2,3,4,8,11,12,13,17,21) in the three force levels were chosen for reorganizing force levels, as summarized in TABLE I. And the four frequency bands were all selected. For each important channel, the average values in T3 were carried out for each frequency band. Thus, there was 36 feature vector (4 frequency bands × ("oxy_rate-deoxy_rate" in 11,12,13,17,21 + "deoxy_rate" in the channels of 2,3,4,8)). The format of training set and test set were listed in TABLE II. As for ten subjects, the 16 rows represented the characters of eight training subjects (8 subjects × 2 times) in each force level. rows of the test set were corresponding results of other two subjects (2 subjects × 2 times × 3 force levels).

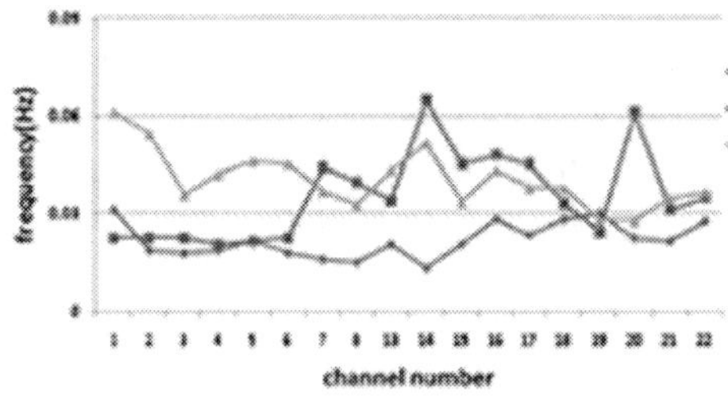

Figure. 2. The power spectrum's peak of the concerned channels (except for channels in FEC) in different force levels.

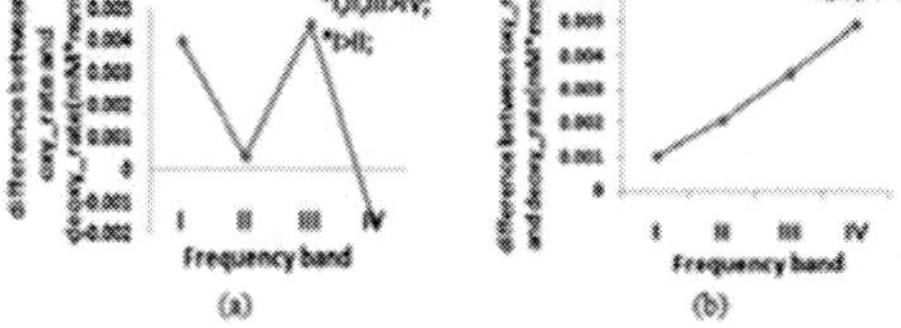

Figure. 3. (a) Characters of frequency bands in low force level. (b) Characters of frequency bands in low force level. Medium force level was not found significant characters. I, II, III, and IV represent the frequency band of 0.01-0.03Hz, 0.03-0.06Hz, 0.06-0.09Hz, and 0.09-0.12Hz, respectively. Significant difference level: *$p<0.05$.

DOI: 10.1051/itmconf/20171205005

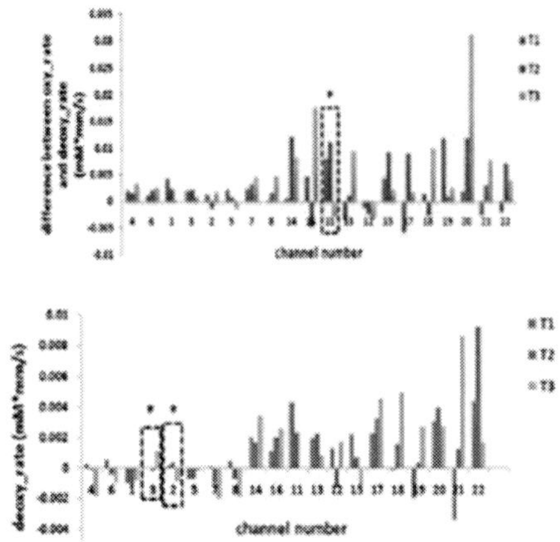

Figure. 4. 0N force level: (a) the average the difference between oxy and deoxy in the period of T1, T2 and T3. (b) the average deoxy in the period of T1, T2 and T3. When T3 was significantly larger or lower than T1 and T2, and T1 and T2 have no significant difference, the channel were marked with black dotted box. Significant difference level: *P<0.01.

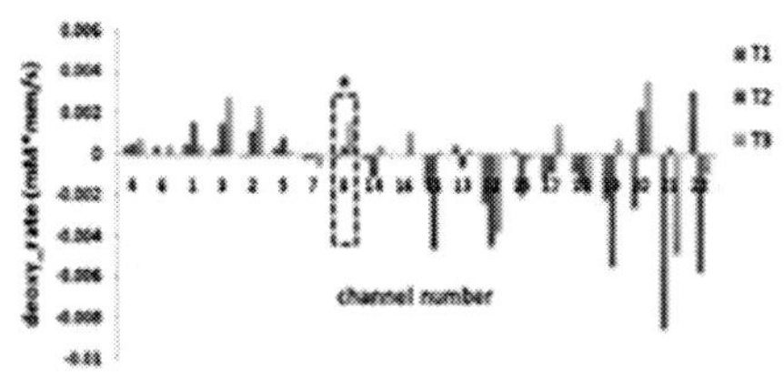

Figure. 5. 30N force level: the average deoxy in the period of T1, T2 and T3. When T3 was significantly larger or lower than T1 and T2, and T1 and T2 have no significant difference, the channel were marked with black dotted box. Significant difference level: *P<0.01.

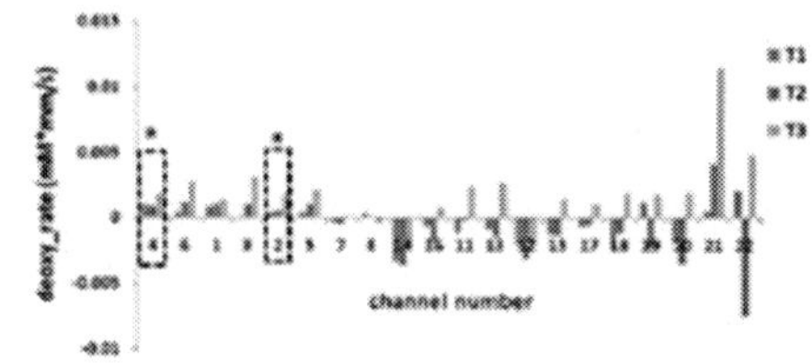

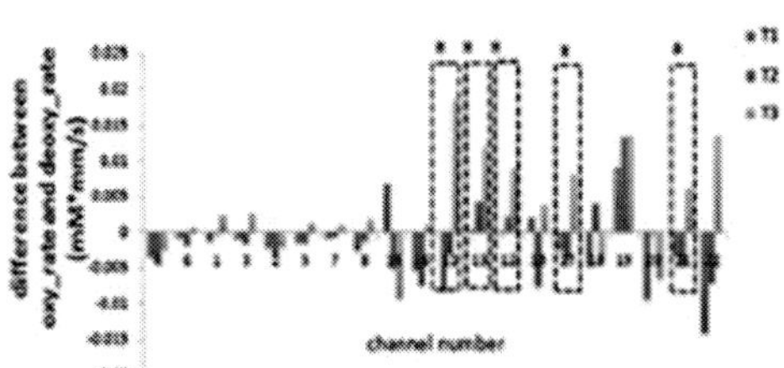

Figure. 6. 50N force level: (a) the average the difference between oxy and deoxy in the period of T1, T2 and T3. (b) the average deoxy in the period of T1, T2 and T3. When T3 was significantly larger or lower than T1 and T2, and T1 and T2 have no significant difference, the channel were marked with black dotted box. Significant difference level: *P<0.01.

Table1. Channels of Interest during EachForce Level

	The channel number of interest channels (deoxy/the difference of	
	Increasing	*Decreasing*
Low force	3 / none	2 / 11
Medium force	8 / none	none
High force	2,4 /	none

Table2. ELM: Training Data and Testing data

task	Characters (four frequency bands and eight channels)
Low Force	16 rows×36 characters [a]
Medium speed	16 rows×36 characters [b]
High Force	16 rows×36 characters [c]
Testing	12 rows×36 characters [d]

a. Training data in low force motion of eight subjects.
b. Training data in medium force motion of eight subjects.
c. Training data in highforce motion of eight subjects.
d. Testing data in low force motion of two subjects.

The best number of hidden neurons in ELM was 150 in this study. The mean of identification rates were 78.9%, 80%, and 77.3% respectively for the 0N, 30N and 50N force levels. The average precision rate was up to 78.7%.

5. Discussion

The paper introduced a method to identify force level of pedaling based on cerebral hemoglobin information. The information in time-domain and frequency-domain were analyzed to extract features. Additionally, information in the channels of interest rather than regions were analyzed to reduce regional location error of individuals. ELM method was applied for classification with a recognition rate 78.7% being achieved. The proposed identification method is favorable to identify motion states of lower limbs in a real environment, and further to improve the effect of rehabilitation training.

Currently, there are many methods to select optimal features for pattern recognition. The paper [22] investigated different time window combinations during the task period. The optimal time was selected to achieve a better accuracy. The identification rate of right and left motor imagery was 75.6%. Vikas, et al. presented a classification-guided (wrapper) method for extracting NIRS feature in time-domain, and then to classify left and right hand movements. The identification rate can achieve 100% [23]. Based on univariate and multivariate ranking and sequential forward and backward selection, four different wrapper methods and three different classifiers (k-Nearest neighbor, Bayes, and Support Vector Machines) were studied. The above researches considered features in time-domain only. In our study, the information in time-domain and frequency-domain were both analyzed, and the features in frequency-domain provided characteristic differences additionally. Parameters of nine important channels in the four independent frequency bands were selected as input features. And a relatively good recognition rate of 78.7% was achieved for spontaneous motion states without evoked stimulation.

At present, the researches on identifying motion states of lower limbs are very few. The study [24] combined EEG and NIRS for some actual motion (right/left arm and hand task) identification. Their accuracy of identifying right and left motion was 72.2%, and the accuracy of classifying arm and hand tasks was 79.9%. The study [25] used EEG–fNIRS feature for decoding motor imagery of both force and speed of hand clenching, it achieved an accuracy of 89% ± 2%. In comparison, by using fNIRS technology alone, our proposed method identified force levels of lower limb with an accuracy of 78.7%. This is meaningful for controlling rehabilitation device relatively simple. Overall, the current result lays a foundation of realizing autonomous control of rehabilitation training equipment and it may be great benefit for the research on rehabilitation robots. This will be more preferable to motivate patients' active participation and enhance training effect.

Acknowledgment

This work was supported by a grant from the national high technology research and development program (863 Program: 2015AA042301), China Postdoctoral Science Foundation (2015M580461).

References

[1] S. Lee, "Power assist control for walking aid with HAL-3 based on EMG and impedance adjustment around knee joint. "in Proc. IEEE/RSJ Int. Conf. Intelligent Robots and Systems (IROS 2002), Lausanne, Switzerland, pp. 1499–1504, 30 Sep.–4 Oct, 2002.

[2] T. Kagawa, "A human interface for stride control on a wearable robot. "in Proc. IEEE/RSJ Int. Conf. Intelligent Robots Systems (IROS 2009), St. Louis, MO, USA, pp. 4067–4072, 11–15 Oct., 2009.

[3] T. Hayashi., "Control method of robot suit HAL working as operator's muscle using biological and dynamical information."in Proc. IEEE/RSJ Int. Conf. Intelligent Robots and Systems (IROS 2005), pp. 3063–3468, 2–6 Aug, 2005.

[4] Farwell, "Talking off the top of your head: toward a mental prosthesis utilizing event-related brain potentials."Electroencephalography and clinical Neurophysiology 70(6), pp.510-523, 1988.

[5] Weiskopf, Nikolaus, et al. "Principles of a brain-computer interface (BCI) based on real-time functional magnetic resonance imaging (fMRI)." IEEE transactions on biomedical engineering 51(6), pp. 966-970, 2004.

[6] Serruya, "Brain-machine interface: Instant neural control of a movement signal." Nature 416(6877), pp.141-142, 2002.

[7] Farina, D., Optimization of wavelets for classification of movement-related cortical potentials generated by variation of force-related parameters. Journal of neuroscience methods, 162(1), pp.357-363,2007.

[8] Kim, Dong-Eun, et al. "EEG analysis following change in hand grip force level for BCI based robot arm force control." Journal of Korean Institute of Intelligent Systems 23.2 (2013): 172-177.

[9] Xu, B., Fu, Y., Miao, L., Wang, Z., & Li, H. (2011, December). Classification of fNIRS data using wavelets and support vector machine during speed and force imagination. In Robotics and Biomimetics (ROBIO), 2011 IEEE International Conference on (pp. 1224-1229). IEEE.

[10] FU Yun Fa. "Recognition of Actual Grip Force Movement Modes Based on Movement-related Cortical Potentials." Acta Automatica Sinica6,2013, pp:1045-1057.

[11] Yin, X., Xu, B., Jiang, C., Fu, Y., Wang, Z., Li, H., & Shi, G.. Classification of Hemodynamic Responses Associated With Force and Speed Imagery for a Brain-Computer Interface. Journal of medical systems,39(5), pp.1-8,2015.

[12] Li, C. (2015). Identification of motion trend of lower limbs based on near-infrared spectroscopic technology. Advances in Mechanical Engineering, 7(3), 1687814015575979.

[13] Li, C., Li, J., Hu, H., Li, W., Ren, Z., & Qu, W.. Adjustment of Intention to Start a Motion of Lower Limbs Based on Cerebral Hemoglobin Information. In Intelligent Human-Machine Systems and Cybernetics (IHMSC), 2015 7th International Conference on Vol. 1, pp. 568-573. IEEE, 2015, August.

[14] Li, Zengyong, "Spectral analysis of near-infrared spectroscopy signals measured from prefrontal lobe in subjects at risk for stroke." Medical physics39(4), pp.2179-2185, 2012.

[15] Shimadzu Corporation, Kyoto, Japan, Instruction manual for functional optical imaging system FOIRE-3000 series, Manual No. : M587-E005, Rev. B, Oct. 2010.

[16] Okamoto, Three-dimensional probabilistic anatomical cranio-cerebral correlation via the international 10–20 system oriented for transcranial functional brain mapping. Neuroimage, 21(1),pp. 99-111,2004.

[17] D. Tsuzuki, "Virtual spatial registration of stand-alone fNIRS data to MNI space, " NeuroImage, vol. 34, pp. 1506–1518, 2007.

[18] N. Picard, "Imaging the premotor areas." Current opinion in neurobiology 11(6), pp.663-672,2001.

[19] Huang, G. B., Zhu, Q. Y., & Siew, C. K.. Extreme learning machine: theory and applications. Neurocomputing, 70(1), pp.489-501,2006.

[20] Huang, "Extreme learning machine for regression and multiclass classification." IEEE Transactions on Systems, Man, and Cybernetics, Part B (Cybernetics) 42(2), pp. 513-529, 2012.

[21] Li, Zengyong, et al. "Wavelet analysis of skin blood oscillations in persons with spinal cord injury and able-bodied subjects." Archives of physical medicine and rehabilitation 87.9 (2006): 1207-1212.

[22] Hong, "Classification of prefrontal and motor cortex signals for three-class fNIRS–BCI." Neuroscience letters 587, pp, 87-92. 2015.

[23] Gottemukkula, "Classification-guided feature selection for NIRS-based BCI." International Ieee/embs Conference on Neural Engineering IEEE, 2011:72-75.

[24] Buccino, "Hybrid EEG-fNIRS Asynchronous Brain-Computer Interface for Multiple Motor Tasks." PloS one 11(1), pp.e0146610, 2016.

[25] Kai, Keng Ang, J. Yu, and C. Guan. "Extracting effective features from high density nirs-based BCI for assessing numerical cognition." 22.10,2012, pp:2233-2236.

[26] Zikai Yi, "statically stable walking gait planning of a kind of exoskeleton walking aid robot". Journal Of Mechanical Transmission (J), 40(1), pp. 48-53,2016.

ITM Web of Conferences 12, 05006 (2017) DOI: 10.1051/itmconf/20171205006
ITA 2017

A Replacement Algorithm of Non-Maximum Suppression Base on Graph Clustering

Xin Zhao[1], Yue-Qing Wang[2], Yong Dou[3]

[1]*National Laboratory for Parallel and Distributed Processing, National University of Defense Technology, Changsha, China*
[2]*National Laboratory for Parallel and Distributed Processing, National University of Defense Technology, Changsha, China*
[3]*National Laboratory for Parallel and Distributed Processing, National University of Defense Technology, Changsha, China*
[1]*zhaoxin15a@nudt.edu.cn*, [2]*yueqingwang@nudt.edu.cn*, [3]*yongdou@nudt.edu.cn*

Abstract: Non-maximum suppression is an important step in many object detection and object counting algorithms. In contrast with the extensive studies of object detection, NMS method has not caused too much attention. Although traditional NMS method has demonstrated promising performance in detection tasks, we observe that it is a hard decision approach, which only uses the confidential scores and Intersection-over-Unions (IoUs) to discard proposals. By this way, NMS method would keep many false proposals whose IoU with the ground truth proposal is smaller than the threshold, which indicates that NMS may not suitable for counting the object number in images. To eliminate the limitation on object counting task, we propose a novel algorithm base on graph clustering to replace the NMS method in this paper. Experiments on faster-rcnn and SSD show that our algorithm achieves better performance than that of NMS on the object counting task.

1. Introduction

Object detection has been extensively studied and applied to a variety of real tasks recently [5], [11]. All of these algorithms provide and score a set of object proposals, and then use the Non-Maximum Suppression (NMS) method to decide which proposals need to be removed, so NMS is considered as an important part of all object detection algorithms. The NMS method greedily merges the higher scoring proposals with lower scoring ones when the IoU between them is large enough (e.g. IoU > 0.5). Classical NMS method contains the following five steps: 1) sort scores in descending order; 2) select the proposal box with the maximum score; 3) calculate the IOUs between the selected proposal box and other ones; 4) remove the proposals whose IoUs are bigger than the IoU threshold; 5) repeat from step 2 to 4 until there is no proposal boxes in the residual set. NMS method is simple, fast, effective and easy to implement, so it is very popular. NMS can also be applied to object counting task. Compared to object detection task, the object counting task not only detects the objects, but also reports the number of objects.

Although the NMS method can efficiently remove some overlapping proposals and achieve promising performance on object detection tasks, we observe that: i) NMS method is a hard decision approach which only uses the confidential scores, IoUs and a threshold value to remove the overlapping proposals; ii) NMS may keep many false proposal boxes which have no real objects in them. These issues limit the development of NMS method, and further adversely affect the performance of object counting task.

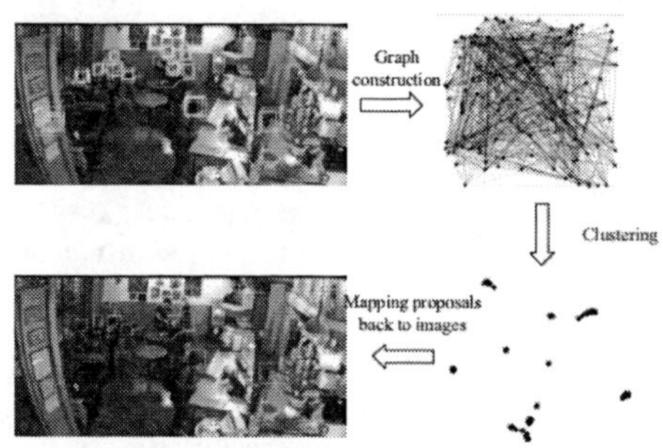

Figure 1. The framework of our approach. We first construct the graph using proposals and IoUs in one image, then cluster all proposals, and finally choose one proposal in each cluster as the final results.

To address these issues, we propose a novel algorithm based on graph clustering to replace NMS method. Compared to the NMS method, our algorithm significantly reduces the false proposals, and is more suitable for object counting task. As is shown in Figure 1, our algorithm first builds a graph which regards the proposals as vertexes, and IOU between proposals as the edges. After that, our algorithm performs a clustering method on all vertexes. Finally, for each clustering center, we choose the proposal with the highest score as the final kept proposals.

In addition, we find that the widely used criterions: MAP (Mean Average Precision) and recall are not suitable for evaluating the performance of object counting task. In fact, when there are many false proposals at last, the MAP and recall might be high, while the number of objects might be considerably different from the number of real objects. For evaluating the performance of object counting task more precisely, we also propose a new criterion.

Extensive experimental results show that our algorithm achieves better performance than NMS on object counting tasks, which indicates our new method is effective.

2. Related Works

There are only a few studies focus on the NMS method. In this section, we will give a brief introduction about these works. They can roughly be grouped into three categories.

The first category mainly concerns the running time of NMS, so they propose several methods to speed up the NMS method. In specific, Alexander Neubeck et.al. proposed several ways to speed up 1D and 2D NMS [7]. Their work shows that the dependency of the neighborhood can be reduced, and the number of comparisons can be pushed down. The work in [8] speeds up the classical NMS method using general purpose GPU on embedded architecture.

The second category focus on the replacement methods of NMS method. Mean-Shift [6] is widely used in the field of clustering [1], image smoothing, image segmentation, and especially object tracking. Li et.al. [14] speed it up on the GPU platform. Affinity propagation clustering algorithm (APC) [9] also needs not to know the number of clustering centers previously. In [11], Rothe etc. announce a new novel method which is an adapting APC method. The new method reduce the limitation of traditional NMS method on object detection task.

The third category tries to use a neural network to simulate the NMS process. In [3], Wan etc. integrate convolutional network, the deformable part model and NMS method into a single model. In [4], Hosang et.al. propose a convolutional neural network to replace NMS, called Tnet. Different from [3], [4] trained separately.

Although achieving promising performance, the above mentioned algorithms only focus on the object detection task, while ignore the object counting task. In our paper, we propose a novel algorithm based on graph clustering to replace the NMS method, which is suitable for the object counting task.

3. Our Approach based on Graph Clustering

In this section, we present the details of our approach based on graph clustering.

Our approach can be split into three stages. By regarding the proposal boxes and the IoU as the vertexes and the edges respectively, our approach firstly construct a graph for each image. After that, we design a novel algorithm to cluster the vertexes in each graph, and group these vertexes into several clusters. Finally, we choose one vertex for each cluster. Note that if the score of the chosen proposal is too low, we would regard the chosen proposal as the background, and discard it.

Algorithm 1: Our approach based on graph clustering.

```
Input: {score_i}_{i=1}^N, E(i,j), i,j ∈ {1,···,N}, ε η
Output: V_keep
Add all proposal id into V_unprocess;
V_final ← [];
k ← 1;
repeat
    Sort scores of V_unprocess in a decrease order;
    Choose the V_i with the highest score;
    Assign k to be the label of V_i;
    for j = 1; j <= length(P_unprocess); j++) do
        if E(i,j) > ε then
            Add V_j into V_keep;
            Set k to be the label of V_j;
            Delete V_j from V_unprocess;
    k ← k + 1
until V_unprocess == [];
for k = 1; k ≤ C; k++ do
    for j = k; j ≤ C; j++ do
        if d(k,j) < η then
            Merge two clusters.
```

We show our clustering method in Algorithm 1. In Algorithm 1, the $V_{unprocess}$ means the vertex set waiting for processing, $E(i,j)$ indicates the IoU between the proposal i and proposal j, and the V_{keep} is the output of our clustering method, which records the vertexes need to be kept in the image. At first, we add all vertexes into $V_{unprocess}$, and initialize V_{keep} to empty. Next, we sort the $V_{unprocess}$ in a decrease order, and choose the V_i who has the highest score. Then, we regard the V_i as the kth clustering center, and find other proposals whose IoU with V_i is bigger than another threshold, and add these vertexes into cluster k. The algorithm would repeat these steps until $V_{unprocess}$ is empty. After that, the algorithm would merge the clustering centers if they are too close to separate. Finally, we would keep one vertex for each cluster, and map these vertexes into proposals. By this way, our method can reduce the false proposals significantly compared with NMS.

4. Experiment

To test the performance of our method, we test our method on four datasets. To evaluate the effectiveness of our approach, we choose two famous object detection frameworks: Faster-RCNN [10] and SSD [5], to produce the proposals and their scores. We only replace the NMS method of these two frameworks using our new method, and test the overall performance. The data sets used in our experiment is shown in Table 1, which includes one scene of the brainwash data set and three scenes in PDL data set. The Brainwash dataset is introduced by Stewart etc. in [12], which is collected from a busy cafe, containing 10461 images: 9977 images for training and 484 image for testing. PDL dataset is collected by ourselves using several different cameras. Our data set would be opened up in the future.

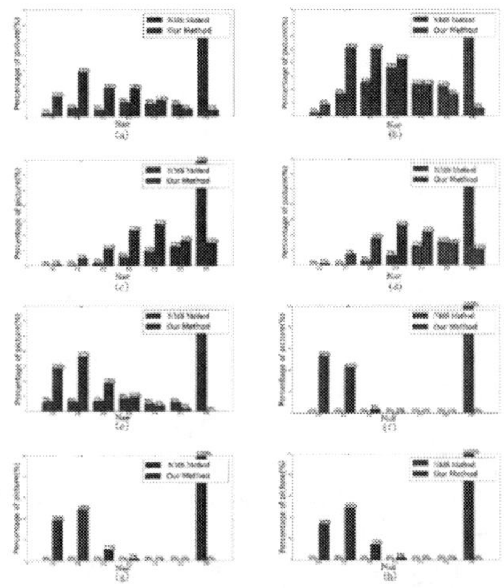

Figure 2. The performance of original method NMS method and our method. These subfigures present the performance of two methods a) in Faster-RCNN framework on brainwash dataset, b) in Faster-RCNN framework on PDL_scene1, c) in Faster-RCNN framework on PDL_scene2, d) in Faster-RCNN framework on PDL_scene3, e) in SSD framework on brainwash, f) in SSD framework on PDL_scene1, g) in SSD framework on PDL_scene2, h) in SSD framework on PDL_scene3.

Table 1. The Data Sets Used In Our Experiments.

Dataset	Testing samples	Training samples	All samples
Brainwash	484	9977	10463
Pdl_scene1	293	0	293
Pdl_scene2	515	0	515
Pdl_scene3	498	0	498

To initialize our object detection model, we use the pre-trained model on ImageNet [15] as the initial model, and then fine tune the pre-trained model using our data sets. After the training process, we obtain the well trained model, and then we use the model to test on all test images.

Figure 3. Final proposals kept by NMS method and our method. a) The final proposals of NMS on one image of Brainwash data set. b) The final proposals of our method on the same image of Brainwash data set. c) The final proposals of NMS on one image of PDL_scene1. d) The final proposals of our method on the same image of PDL_scene1.

To report the performance of object counting task, we use an new criterion, called N_{diff}. Note that a smaller N_{diff} permits a better performance. For example, when N_{diff} equals to 0, it means the number of objects detected by the method matches the number of the real objects. In specific, we first calculate the difference between the number of real objects and number of detected objects for each image, and compute the absolute value of the difference: $N_{diff} = abs(N_{real} - N_{detected})$. As is described, if the method can correctly count the number of objects in one image, the N_{diff} would equal to 0. After that, we statistic the percentage with different N_{diff} in the test data set. For convenience, we record the percentage with different N_{diff} as P_0, P_1, ... , P_6, where P_i means the percentage of images when N_{diff} equals to *i*. Note that P_7 is the percentage of images whose N_{diff} is larger than 5.

From the definition of these criterions, we can conclude that P_0 means the percentage of images whose real number of objects equals to the detected number. Therefore, the larger the P_0, the better the performance.

In addition, we also report the typical criterion used in object detection MAP of the NMS and our replacement method.

The MAP of classical NMS method and our method are reported in Table 2. As is shown in Table 2, our method achieves comparative MAP on pdl_scene1 and pdl_scene2 compared to the NMS method. However, on other data sets, NMS achieves better MAP than our method because the calculation of MAP does not consider the influence of false proposals.

Table 2 the map of nms and our methods in two object detection frameworks on four data sets.

MAP	Faster-RCNN		SSD	
	NMS Method	Ours	NMS Method	Ours
brainwash	0.76	0.69	0.71	0.65
pdl_scene1	0.90	0.89	0.77	0.70
pdl_scene2	**0.83**	**0.83**	0.72	0.64
pdl_scene3	**0.85**	**0.85**	0.75	0.66

The P_i (i =1, 2, 6) of the two method are shown in Figure 2. As can be seen from Figure 2, the P_0 of our method equals to 13% for faster-rcnn and 26% for SSD, which is significantly larger than that of traditional NMS method on Brainwash data set. This means our method could count the objects in one image more accurate. Therefore, our method is more suitable for object counting task.

To compare the performance of the NMS method and our method more vividly, we draw the final proposals on the original images and choose several images to display the results. Figure 3 draws the final proposals of our method and NMS method. It can be seen from Figure 3 that: i) our method can count the number of objects more precisely, for example, in the PDL scene, the true number of people is 4, the number counted by our method is correct, while that of NMS is larger than 30; ii) the locations of the final kept proposals are more accurate than that of NMS method. We conclude from these results that NMS always keeps many false proposals, so it cannot count the objects correctly in the image. By contrast, our clustering method can count the objects more precisely.

5. Conclusion

In this paper, we propose a novel method based on graph clustering to replace traditional NMS method, and apply this method on the object counting task. Our approach can be split into three stages. By regarding the proposal boxes and the IoU as the vertexes and the edges respectively, our approach firstly construct a graph for each image. After that, we design a novel algorithm to cluster the vertexes in each graph, and group these vertexes into several clusters. Finally, we choose one vertex for each cluster. Experiments on faster-rcnn and SSD show that our algorithm achieves better performance than that of NMS on object counting tasks.

References

[1] Mean Shift, Mode Seeking, and Clustering. page 10, 1995.

[2] Adrien Descamps and Cyril Carincotte. Counting people in the crowd using a generic head detector 1 Introduction 2 Previous Work 3 Overview of our approach.

[3] David Eigen. "End-to-End Integration of a Convolutional Network , Deformable Parts Model and Non-Maximum Suppression," (September 2010):5540096, 2011.

[4] Jan Hosang, Rodrigo Benenson, and Bernt Schiele. "A convnet for non- maximum suppression," pages 1–14, 2015.

[5] Wei Liu, Dragomir Anguelov, Dumitru Erhan, Christian Szegedy, and Scott Reed. "SSD: Single Shot MultiBox Detector," Arxiv, pages 1–15, 2015.

[6] Peter Meer. Mean Shift Analysis and Applications.

[7] Alexander Neubeck and Luc Van Gool. "Efficient non-maximum suppression. Proceedings," International Conference on Pattern Recognition, 3:850– 855, 2006.

[8] David Oro, Xavier Martorell, and Javier Hernando. "WORK-EFFICIENT PARALLEL NON-MAXIMUM SUPPRESSION FOR EMBEDDED GPU".

[9] ARCHITECTURES Carles Fern Herta Security , Barcelona , Spain Uni- versitat Polit ' ecnica de Catalunya , Barcelona , Spain Barcelona Super-computing Center Email : david.oro@hertasecurity.com. Icassp 2016, pages 1026–1030, 2016.

[10] Michael Pfeiffer. Clustering by Passing Messages between Data Points.2007.

[11] Shaoqing Ren, Kaiming He, Ross Girshick, and Jian Sun. "Faster R- CNN: Towards Real-Time Object Detection with Region Proposal Networks," Nips, pages 1–10, 2015.

[12] Rasmus Rothe, Matthieu Guillaumin, and Luc van Gool. "Non-maximum suppression for object detection by passing messages between windows," Lecture Notes in Computer Science (including subseries Lecture Notes in Artificial Intelligence and Lecture Notes in Bioinformatics), 9003:290–306, 2015.

[13] Russell Stewart and Mykhaylo Andriluka. "End-to-end people detection in crowded scenes," Arxiv, page 9, 2015.

[14] Li P, Xiao L. "Mean Shift Parallel Tracking on GPU[C]," Iberian Conference on Pattern Recognition and Image Analysis. Springer-Verlag, 2009:120-12

[15] J. Deng, W. Dong, R. Socher, L.-J. Li, K. Li, and L. Fei-Fei. "ImageNet: A Large-Scale Hierarchical Image Database," In CVPR09, 2009

A Weight-Based Clustering Method

Zhao-Yu Wang[1], Shie-Jue Lee[2], Shing-Tai Pan3

[1]*Department of Electrical Engineering, National Sun Yat-sen University, Kaohsiung, Taiwan*
[2]*Department of Electrical Engineering, National Sun Yat-sen University, Kaohsiung, Taiwan*
[3]*Department of Electrical Engineering, National University of Kaohsiung, Kaohsiung, Taiwan*
[1]*zywang@water.ee.nsysu.edu.tw*, [2]*leesj@mail.ee.nsysu.edu.tw*, [3]*stpan@nuk.edu.tw*

Abstract: This paper proposes a weight-based self-constructing clustering method for time series data. Self-constructing clustering processes all the data points incrementally. If a data point is not similar enough to an existing cluster, then (1) if the point currently does not belong to any cluster, it forms a new cluster of its own; (2) otherwise, the point is removed from the cluster it currently belongs to before a new cluster is formed. However, if a data point is similar enough to an existing cluster, then (1) if the point currently does not belong to any cluster, it is added to the most similar cluster; (2) otherwise, it is removed from the cluster it currently belongs to and added to the most similar cluster. During the clustering process, weights are learned and considered in the calculations of similarity between data points and clusters. Experimental results show that our proposed approach performs more effectively than other methods for real world time series datasets.

1. Introduction

Clustering is an unsupervised classification technology, with a purpose of forming meaningful clusters for the objects under consideration. Usually, similar objects are grouped in the same cluster, and different objects are grouped in different clusters. Clustering techniques play a very important role in the field of artificial intelligence [1] [2][3][4]. In particular, they are widely applied in times series data analysis in a variety of areas, such as bioengineering [5], environmental monitoring [6], economic applications, and so on. In the process of clustering time series data, using the same weight for each dimension may cause bad effects. To deal with this difficulty, Huang et al. proposed TSKmeans [7], which is K-means with weights, to assign different weights to different dimensions of the data. A similarity measure based on the weighted Euclidean distance was adopted. Through quadratic programming, smooth subspace in time stamps can be produced. It was shown that TSK means can result in better clusters than the original K-means for time series data.

This paper proposes another weight-based clustering method for time series data. Instead of using K-means, an iterative self-constructing clustering method is adopted. The method performs several rounds of clustering until convergence is reached. In each round, all the data points are processed incrementally. If a data point is not similar enough to an existing cluster, then (1) if the point currently does not belong to any cluster, it forms a new cluster of its own; (2) otherwise, the point is removed from the cluster it currently belongs to before a new cluster is formed. However, if a data point is similar enough to an existing cluster, then (1) if the point currently does not belong to any cluster, it is added to the most similar cluster; (2) otherwise, it is removed from the cluster it currently belongs to and added to the most similar cluster. During the clustering process, weights are learned and considered in the calculations of similarity between data points and clusters. If the cluster assignment of one instance has been changed in the current round, the next round of clustering continues. Otherwise, the cluster assignments are stable and the whole clustering process stops with a desired number of clusters.

The rest of this paper is organized as follows. TSKmeans is briefly reviewed in Section II. Our proposed method is presented in Section III. Experimental results are shown in Section IV. Section V gives a conclusion.

2. Related Work

Many clustering methods have been proposed for time series data [8] [9][10][7]. Among them, TSKmeans [7] is the most recently published. TSKmeans is a K-means incorporated with weights. It tries to make the distance between the data points contained in a cluster and the center of the cluster small through the use of weights of

DOI: 10.1051/itmconf/20171205007

time stamps. Given X = $\{X_1, X_2, \ldots, X_n\}$ is a set of n time series patterns. Each pattern $X_1 = \{x_{i1}, x_{i2} \ldots, x_{im}\}$ is the ith pattern characterized by m values, i.e., m time stamps. The membership matrix U is a n × k binary matrix, k is the total number of clusters, with $u_{ip} = 1$ indicating that X_i belongs to cluster p and u_{ij} , j ≠ p, is 0. The centers and weights of clusters are represented by two sets of k vectors Z = $\{Z_1, Z_2, \ldots, Z_k\}$ and W = $\{W_1, W_2, \ldots, W_k\}$, with w_{pj} being the weight of the jth time stamp for the pth cluster. The purpose of TSKmeans is to minimize the following objective function:

$$P(U, Z, W) = \sum_{p=1}^{k} \sum_{i=1}^{n} \sum_{j=1}^{m} u_{ip} w_{pj} \left(x_{ij} - z_{pj}\right)^2 + \frac{1}{2} \alpha \sum_{p=1}^{k} \sum_{j=1}^{m-1} \left(w_{pj} - w_{p,j+1}\right)^2 \quad (1)$$

Subject to

$$\begin{cases} \sum_{p=1}^{k} u_{ip} = 1, \ u_{ip} \in \{0, 1\} \\ \sum_{j=1}^{m} w_{pj} = 1, 0 \leq w_{pj} \leq 1 \end{cases} \quad (2)$$

by the application of quadratic programming. Using these weights in each iteration of Kmeans until convergence is reached. At the beginning, TSKmeans generates randomly the centers of clusters and sets initial values for the weights of clusters. Then the following three steps are done iteratively:

◎ Step 1. For each pattern Xi, compute the distance Dpi between it and cluster p by

$$D_{pi} = \sum_{j=1}^{m} w_{pj} (x_{ij} - z_{pj})^2 \quad (3)$$

for 1 ≤ p ≤ k, 1 ≤ i ≤ n. A pattern is assigned to the cluster with the smallest distance. If pattern i is assigned to cluster p, then u_{ip} is set to 1 and u_{ij} is set to 0, j ≠ 0.

◎ Step 2. Update the centers of all clusters by

$$Z_p = \frac{\sum_{x_i \in \, cluster\ p} x_i}{total\ number\ of\ patterns\ in\ cluster\ p} \quad (4)$$

for 1 ≤ p ≤ k.

◎ Step 3. Use known U and Z to update W by applying quadratic programming to Eq.(1) with

$$\alpha = \sum_{i=1}^{n} ||X_i - \frac{\sum_{j=1}^{n} X_j}{n}||^2 \quad (5)$$

If clusters have changed in the current iteration, then go back and Steps 1–3 are performed again. Otherwise, TSKmeans stops. However, TKmeans suffers from the same problem as K-means does. The number of clusters has to be specified in advance. Our proposed approach can overcome this shortcoming.

3. Proposed Method

We propose a self-constructing clustering (SCC) method which does not require the number of clusters to be specified by the user in advance. We describe the clustering in detail. Also, we improve the method by incorporating weights in the calculation of similarity, just as TKmeans does to K-means. SCC performs several rounds of clustering until convergence is reached. In each round, one full training cycle on the training set of N patterns $X^{(1)}, X^{(2)}, \ldots, X^{(N)}$, is done. Let K be the number of existing clusters. Each cluster C_p, 1 ≤ p ≤ K is characterized by its center Z_p, deviation V_p, size S_p, and weight W_p. Initially, K is 0. Suppose we are in the rth round, r ≥ 1. For pattern i, $X^{(i)}$, 1 ≤ i ≤ N, we calculate the similarity between $X^{(i)}$ and each existing cluster by

$$\mu_p(X^{(i)}) = \prod_{j=1}^{m} \exp[-w_{pj} (\frac{x_j^{(i)} - z_{pj}}{v_{pj}})^2] \quad (6)$$

for 1 ≤ p ≤ K. Two cases are considered:

Case 1. If

$$\mu_p(X^{(i)}) < \epsilon \quad (7)$$

for 1 ≤ p ≤ K, we do the following:

1) If $X^{(i)}$ currently does not belong to any cluster, it forms a new cluster C_{K+1} of its own. And we have K = K + 1, $Z_K = X^{(i)}$, $V_K = \{v_0, v_0, \ldots, v_0\}$, $S_K = 1$, and W_K containing m randomly generated numbers.

2) If $X^{(i)}$ currently belongs to cluster Ca, we remove $X^{(i)}$ from Ca and update the characteristics of Ca. And a new cluster C_{K+1} containing only $X^{(i)}$ is created as previously.

Case 2. If

$$\mu_p(X^{(i)}) \geq \epsilon \quad (8)$$

for some existing clusters, we do the following:

1) If $X^{(i)}$ currently does not belong to any cluster, it is added to the most similar cluster, say C_t , and the characteristics of C_t are updated by

$$Z_t^n = \frac{S_t^o Z_t^o + X^{(i)}}{S_t^o + 1} \quad (9)$$

$$v_{aj}^{n\,2} = \frac{1}{S_a^o} \{(S_a^o - 1) v_{aj}^{o\,2} + S_a^o z_{aj}^{o\,2} + x_j^{(i)2} - (S_a^o + 1) z_{aj}^{n\,2}\} \quad (10)$$

$$S_a^n = S_a^o + 1 \quad (11)$$

2) If $X^{(i)}$ currently belongs to cluster Ca, we remove $X^{(i)}$ from Ca, updating the characteristics of Ca, and we add $X^{(i)}$ to the most similar cluster Ct as before.

After all the patterns are considered, if none of the cluster assignments has changed, SCC stops with K clusters. If the cluster assignments of some patterns have changed, we update the weights W by minimizing the objective function of Eq.(1). Then we proceed with the next round of clustering.

4. Experimental Results

In this section, we present and compare the experimental results of several clustering methods on six real world time series datasets: SynControl, Trace, CBF, ECGFiveDays, FaceFour, and OliveOil [11]. For convenience, our proposed method is called SCC with weights, abbreviated as SCC-W. The characteristics of the six datasets are listed in Table I. In this table, column 1 indicates the name of the dataset, and the remaining columns indicate the number of instances, the number of features, and the number of classes, respectively, in each dataset. Note that these datasets are single-labeled, i.e., an instance belongs to only one class.

Table I
DESCRIPTIONS OF DATASETS

Dataset	# instances	# features()	# classes
SynControl	600	60	6
Trace	200	275	4
CBF	930	128	3
ECGFiveDays	884	136	2
FaceFour	350	112	4
OliveOil	60	570	4

Table II
PERFORMANCE COMPARISONS

Dataset	Algorithm	Fscore	RI	NMI	#clusters	CPU time
CBF	SCC	0.5451	0.5526	0.2240	3	0.03
	SCC-W	**0.7452**	0.6899	**0.4834**	3	1.70
ECGFiveDays	SCC	0.5454	0.5020	0.0040	2	0.03
	SCC-W	0.555	0.5058	0.0094	2	1.25
FaceFour	SCC	0.5977	0.5842	0.4524	4	0.01
	SCC-W	**0.7967**	**0.8379**	**0.6954**	4	1.10
SynControl	SCC	0.5254	0.6813	0.5759	6	0.03
	SCC-W	0.6544	0.8262	0.7480	6	0.60
Trace	SCC	0.6070	0.7505	0.5613	4	0.01
	SCC-W	**0.6393**	**0.7610**	**0.5844**	4	0.63
OliveOil	SCC	0.5532	0.468	0.3356	4	0.01
	SCC-W	**0.8679**	**0.8847**	**0.7460**	4	2.30

For the sake of fairness in comparison, a method was applied on every dataset ten times and the average of the results of the ten runs is then presented. To evaluate the effectiveness of these methods, the following performance measures are adopted [12]: Fscore , RI and NMI . All these measures have a common property: a higher measure indicates a better clustering performance.

The results after clustering are shown in Table II. It can be seen that SCC-W outperforms SCC for all the six datasets. However, more CPU time is required SCC-W.

5. Conclusion

We have presented a weight-based self-constructing clustering method for time series data. Self-constructing clustering processes all the data points incrementally. If a data point is not similar enough to an existing cluster, then (1) if the point currently does not belong to any cluster, it forms a new cluster of its own; (2) otherwise, the point is removed from the cluster it currently belongs to before a new cluster is formed. However, if a data point is similar enough to an existing cluster, then (1) if the point currently does not belong to any cluster, it is added to the most similar cluster; (2) otherwise, it is removed from the cluster it currently belongs to and added to the most similar cluster. During the clustering process, weights are learned and considered in the calculations of similarity between data points and clusters. Experimental results have shown that our proposed approach performs more effectively than other methods for real world time series datasets.

References

1. S. Haykin. 1999. *Neural Networks – A Comprehensive Foundation.* Upper Saddle River, NJ, USA: Prentice-Hall.
2. D. L. Olson and Y. Shi. 2007. *Introduction to Business Data Mining*, vol. 10. McGraw-Hill/Irwin Englewood Cliffs.
3. C.-S. Ouyang, W.-J. Lee, and S.-J. Lee. 2005 .A TSK-type neurofuzzy network approach to system modeling problems. *IEEE Transactions on Systems, Man, and Cybernetics, Part B (Cybernetics)*, 35(4):751-767.
4. S.-J. Lee, C.-S. Ouyang, and S.-H. Du. 2003. A neuro-fuzzy approach for segmentation of human objects in image sequences. *IEEE Transactions on Systems, Man, and Cybernetics, Part B (Cybernetics)*, 33(3):420-437.
5. T.-Y. Chiu , T.-C. Hsu , C.-C. Yen , J.-S. Wang. 2015. Interpolation based consensus clustering for gene expression time series. *BMC bioinformatics*, 16(1):117.
6. B. DeVries , J. Verbesselt , L. Kooistra , M. Herold. 2015. Robust monitoring of small-scale forest disturbances in a tropicalmontane forest using landsat time series. *Remote Sensing of Environment*, 161:107-121.
7. X. Huang , Y. Ye , L. Xiong , R.Y. Lau. , N. Jiang , S. Wang. 2016 . Time series k-means: A new k-means type smooth subspace clustering for time series data. *Information Sciences*, 367:1-13.
8. L. Rabiner , B.-H. Juang. 1993 . *Fundamentals of speech recognition*. Prentice hall.
9. Y. Chen , M. Nascimento , B.C. Ooi , A.K. Tung . 2007. SpADe: On shape-based pattern detection in streaming time series. *Proceedings of the 23rd IEEE International Conference on Data Engineering*, pages 786-795, IEEE.
10. T. W. Liao.2005. Clustering of time series data—a survey. *Pattern recognition*, 38(11):1857-1874.
11. Y. Chen, E. Keogh, B. Hu, N. Begum, A. Bagnall, A. Mueen, G. Batista. 2015.The UCR time series classification archive.
12. X. Huang , Y. Ye , H. Guo , Y. Cai , H. Zhang , Y. Li. 2014. DSKmeans: a new kmeans-type approach to discriminative subspace clustering. *Knowledge-Based Systems*, 70:293-300.

DOI: 10.1051/itmconf/20171205008

An Accurate Topic Mining Algorithm Based on Business Dictionary

Zhi Yang*, Feng Lin, Mu Hu, Qing-Qiang Meng, Hao-Quan Zheng

NARI Group Corporation /State Grid Electric Power Research Institute, Nanjing, China
* *yangzhi1@sgepri.sgcc.com.cn*

Abstract: The text mining is an important branch of data mining. Many scientific research institutions and teams are actively exploring and putting forward algorithms. Because of industry and scene difference, it is difficult to use the common analysis algorithm of log to mine the potential information accurately. For example, a topic is given in one scene, how to find the main related words is not easy. To deal with the problem, this paper provides the accurate topic mining algorithm based on business dictionary. In the algorithm, segmenting with business dictionary is achieved in the document set after screening the valid documents. In this step, the document set is split into professional terms and then the invalid words are removed. Finally, the qualitative analysis is transformed to quantitative analysis. With the relevance index, the relevance degree of every word is computed. The relevance matrix is returned to the user to analyze the relevance of the words and topic. The algorithm has been applied to PMS and the validation result shows the main related factors can be analyzed accurately.

1. Introduction

With the expansion of breadth and depth of data, the potential value of data, which can create wealth, is cognized by more and more enterprises, governments and other research communities [1]. As the key step of data knowledge discovery [2], data mining [3, 4, 5, and 6] is one of the research focuses. Text mining [7, 8] is an important branch of data mining. Nowadays, many algorithms have been proposed to solve data analysis in the text scenario. However, in electric power, there are too much related equipment, inconsistent statement, unfixed topics and many related fields in the descriptions of power operation and maintenance log. It is difficult for the existing text mining algorithms to find out its maximum value. How to achieve accurate data mining is becoming one of research hotspots.

In text mining, the text data is stored in the database or file in the form of semi-structured or unstructured data. It is difficult to dig out its value because of semantic information hidden in it. At present, there are many scientific research institutions and teams to provide algorithms. There are mainly two types. The first is text cluster [9-14]. The cluster analysis [9] is one of important method to realize text mining. The literatures [10, 11] provide two fuzzy cluster methods based on weighted characteristic. In them, the feature weight vector, which reflects the internal structure of data set, is obtained by using the supervised or unsupervised learning process. Then the distance function of weighted characteristic comes into being. Another representation method is automatic weighted characteristic technique [12, 13]. In the K-Means or FCM, the feature weight vector indicates importance of each feature on the whole data set. Besides, the literature[14]proposes the fuzzy clustering algorithm by integrating the feature weighting metric into the framework of soft subspace learning. In these algorithms, because that there are different key words in different topic and the descriptive ability of each key word for topic is different, it is difficult to find out the best feature vector and weight.

Another is topic mining [15-24]. In the PLSA (Probabilistic Latent Semantic Analysis) model [17, 18], the probability is related with special documents. So, there are some defects for dealing with new documents. In addition, over-fitting comes into being easily. The most famous topic model is LDA (Latent Dirichlet Allocation) [19, 20, and 21]. In the model, the document set is input. By setting the appropriate parameters, the final multiple topics and word-distribution in each topic could be obtained. On the basis of LDA, The extended LDA models (Twitter-LDA [22], Labeled-LDA [23], MB-LDA [24], etc.) are used for some scenarios. In these algorithms, the topic mining can be achieved and topic-related words are enumerated. However, business experts need to take time to analyze what is the topic and whether these words are related with the topic. Furthermore, the flexibility of algorithm is low and the topic-related words cannot be got for random topic.

The above algorithms can solve many text mining problems, but don't satisfy the text mining demand of electric power. In the scene of text mining, the log data is stored in the semi-structured database and in every

ITM Web of Conferences 12, 05008 (2017) DOI: 10.1051/itmconf/20171205008
ITA 2017

description of log, operation and maintenance information of power network equipment and systems (for example, equipment failure, maintenance procedure, etc.) are stored. The demand is that for given topic, the semantic-related words can be found out. At the same time, the semantic correlations of words are got. The potential value of data can be used for design and planning of power network. But, the above algorithms could not dig out the accurate result.

To address the aforementioned problems, we provide the topic mining algorithm with business dictionary to precisely find out the log value. In the algorithm, on the basis of the theory of topic mining, according to the process of document-word, by using the natural language semantic segmentation technology, the semantic impact factor of words are computed. Then, with the help of business dictionary, the accurate semantic-related words are returned to business expert. It is convenient for them to find out the potential knowledge.

The advantage of this algorithm lies in:

Search topic-related words with semantic technology. For the given topic, by use of semantic theory, conditional probability and business dictionary, the semantic-related words are found out accurately.

Precisely dig out the words with the business dictionary. In this case, the interference of large number of unrelated words is avoided. The time and energy to search the business words from all the words can be economized.

Reduce the number of documents with topic. Using the topic, the irrelevant documents can be excluded. So, the efficiency is improved obviously.

This paper is organized as follows. Section 2 states the topic mining theory and evaluation criterion. The topic mining algorithm with business dictionary is proposed and analyzed in section 3. Section 4 verifies this system solution in the PMS. The last section draws to a conclusion.

2. Topic Mining Theory and Evaluation Criterion

2.1 Topic Mining Theory

In the scene of given topic, the ultimate objective of topic mining is that the optimal semantic-related word set can be found out. Because that actually the semantic-related words often exist in the sentence with topic word, the conditional probability is used for computing the semantic-related degree of word-topic.

In the document set, it is rare that there are different words in different topic. Usually, the words belong to two or more topics shown as figure 1. Because that it is simple that different words are in different topics, in this paper, it is discussed that the words belong to more topics. When In one sentence word A and word B appear together, they are described as co-occurrence.

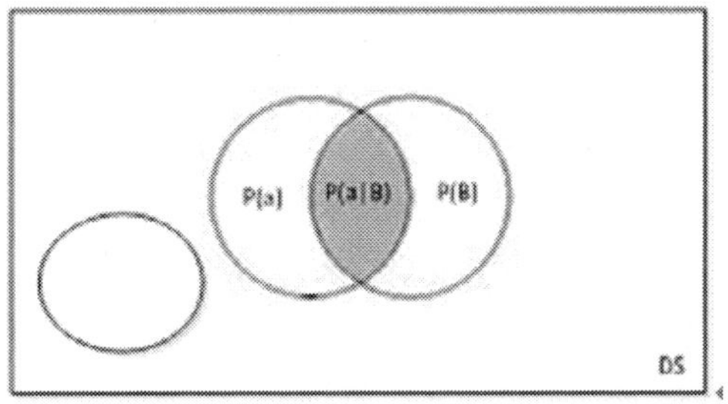

Figure 1. semantic-related probability

In the document set DS, there are many sentences S which describe one or more topics. In every sentence, there are many words W. From the above figure, we can see that there are some words a in the topic B. $P(a)$ is made up of many topic-related $\mathrm{P}(a_i)$. For the given topic B, the $P(a \mid B)$ is semantic-related degree.

The mathematical formula of semantic-related degree set is:

$$S = \{O_i\}, i = 1,2,3,... \tag{1}$$

In which, the O_i indicates the semantic-related degree of every word. Its mathematical formula is:

$$O_i = P(A_i \mid B) = P(A_i B) / P(B), i = 1,2,3,... \tag{2}$$

In which, $P(A_i B)$ indicates the co-occurrence probability of B and A_i in the document set. $P(B)$ Indicates the occurrence probability of topic B. $P(A_i B)$ indicates the occurrence probability of A_i under the premise of topic B.

The higher semantic-related degree is, the higher the O_i is. For the words with which the topic isn't together, the O_i is zero.

2.2 Evaluation Criterion

For the given topic, we can obtain many words from the above algorithm. There is different contribution of every word for the topic. The contribution of all words is 100%. For user's threshold, the fewer words, the better the effect. In this case, proportionality index is used to describe it.

$$proportionality = numP / numA$$

In the formula, the $numP$ indicates word number of cumulative sum of contribution is greater the threshold. The $numA$ indicates the number of all the word number.

The proportionality is qualitative analysis index. The index cannot indicate the final result is good or not.

Combined with the actual business situation, user evaluates it.

3. Topic Mining Algorithm with Business Dictionary

The general principle of the algorithm is that the original data cannot be changed and disturbing by man-made factors should be avoided. Based on it, the topic mining algorithm is designed.

By using the topic set, the total amount of documents is reduced and topic-related documents are kept. Then, by means of business dictionary, the accurate words can be searched and saved. Finally, on the basis of relevance index, the semantic-related of word-topic can be obtained. The sorted result can be returned to user.

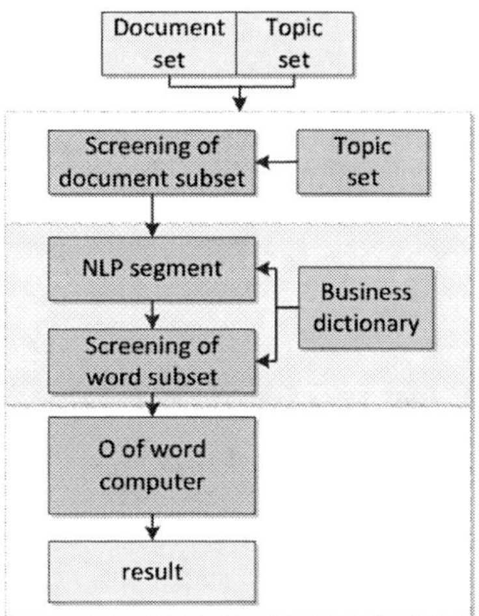

Figure 2. The process of algorithm

There are three steps in the algorithm.

The first step: Screening of document set

There are many topics in the document set. When one or more topics are analyzed, the related documents need to be filtered out. In this way, the analysis scope can be reduced to improve efficiency. The filtering method is that on the base of topic (or related topic) set, the fuzzy search can be used to traversal of all documents. When the topic is contained in the document, the document is related, otherwise it is independent. According to the topic set, the irrelevant documents are taken away.

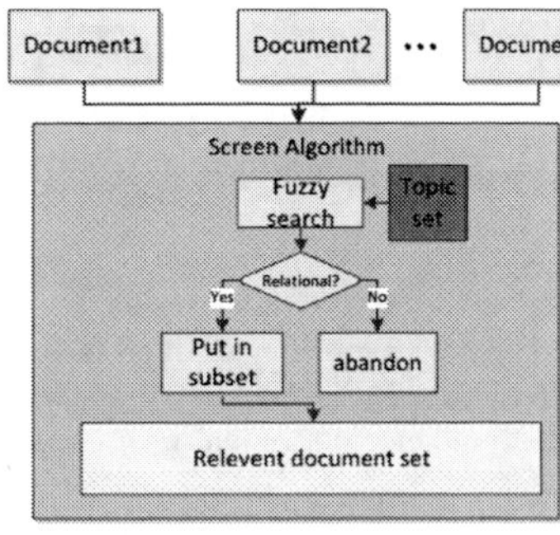

Figure 3. The process of screen algorithm

The documents of subset are related to topic. When there are none in the subset, it indicates there is no document related to topic.

The second step: Segment with business dictionary

There are different technical terms in different industries. In the same industry, there are some specific terms in different scenarios. If these terms, which are not included in the general dictionary, cannot be identified, the valid information hidden in the documents will be lost and some data value cannot be found. So, in order to avoid the loss of useful information, the defect can be remedied in the stage. The business dictionary depends on specialized person. There are industry term, special scene term and some common term. The segment process with business dictionary is that segmenting word to split document set, then, filtering out the form word, figure, and so on. The reserved word set is effective which the base for precise theme mining is.

The detailed procedure is as follows:

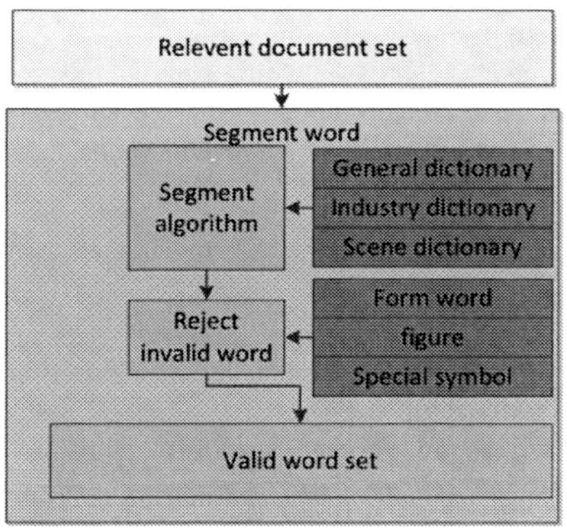

Figure 4. The process of segmenting word

The third step: relevance index computing

Because the words and topic appear in the same document, the words describe the topic from different aspect or angle. The correlation degree of different word and topic is different. The higher the correlation, more intimate the word and topic. In this case, the accurate characterization can be got from the word set. The related words reflect the customer's focus to a certain degree. In the paper, the relevance index is used to describe the relationship. The relevance index is illustrated with the ratio of word frequency and topic frequency.

The formula to compute the relevance is as follow:

$$R = {WF}/{TF} = {\sum w_i}/{\sum t}, i = 1,2,3,... \quad (3)$$

In the formula, the R indicates the relevance. The WF indicates the word frequency. The TF indicates the topic frequency.

After computing R of all words, a data matrix is formed which describes the relevance of each word and topic.

The data matrix as result is returned to the user. On the base of the data matrix, the data can be displayed with network diagram etc.

The algorithm analysis:

By appoint the topic and analyze the topic in the document set, the user can obtain the relevant words. In this case, the relationship between the topic and related words is shown accurately. At the same time, it is avoided that the minor topic is ignored.

In the algorithm, there are no all the topics but appointed topic. So, the workload can be saved to improve efficiency.

By use of business dictionary, the specific business words can be retained. It is very good to grasp the topic accurately. At the same time, the high frequency and not related words are removed. In this case, the related words are focused.

Using the relevance index formula, the relevance of topic and word as qualitative analysis index is used for the user to support making the policy decision.

4. Experiment and Analysis

The above solution has been applied to the power production management system (PMS) of State Grid of China.

The PMS is the most advanced power production management system in the world. It is one of SG186 engineering applications, which is one of the most massive and complex applications. The investment of PMS1.0 is over billion. The investment of PMS2.0 is much larger than PMS1.0. Including in the low pressure data, the total amount of data of PMS2.0 is over 150 billion. In these data, the log is very large and contains much information such as grid operation and fault information. In the log, there is a lot of implicit information which are not found. In this paper, the fault data is selected to verify the above algorithm.

In the PMS of some province, there is a lot of fault and defect data of main transformer, line, tower and other equipment in the log. The log describes the related equipment, phenomenon, process, consequence and failure analysis. From the data, we can analyze the main factor and secondary factor. The direct or indirect causes may be obtained.

In the R language [25] environment, based on the real data, the verification can be achieved. The main analysis process is as follows:

4.1 Preprocess Stage

The fault log is stored in the structured database. So, three fields are selected to analyze the algorithm. The three fields are as follow:

Table1: the description of three fields

No	Field name	Description
1	DSMCE	city name
2	JSYC	reason of failure
3	GZQFK	The description information of failure

In the selected log data, because that the null value is no influence to analysis result. So, all the null values are deleted.

In order to determine the topic set, the categorical data (JSYC) is analyzed. From the data, the "40499" value is selected as analysis object. Then, the data about it is analyzed with word cloud algorithm. The biggest words are selected as topics. The topic set is:

{ "switch trip" , "phase fault" , "Lightning" }

4.2 Verification Process

First step: screening of the document set. Using the topic set, all the documents are filtered with the fuzzy algorithm. In the fuzzy algorithm, the filter condition is "like". If the document contains the topic, the document is remaindered. The remainder is the valid data which number is 4528.

Second step: segment with business dictionary. According to the state grid and the fault scenario, the professionals can formulate the business dictionary.

In the result of segmenting, there are many invalid words. There are many form words, single letters, and figures, and so on in the invalid words which are shown as following.

{ A,C,B,Q,30,23,64,5,7,17,... }

Without the business dictionary, it is difficult to find out the main factor.

Because there are a lot of words after segmenting, some words, which frequency is higher, are selected to show word frequency chart. The top 150 words are related in every chart. From the chart, we can see that with the business dictionary, it is easy to see the main factor set which is { "switch trip" , "phase fault" , "Lightning" }.

Third step: with the above formula (3), the topic one by one is used to analyze the related words. The relevance index of every word can be computed. The user's threshold is 90%. With the help of the evaluation criterion formula, we find out the proportionality of top 10 is more than 90%. So, the top 10 is selected to analyze. For example, the result of the topic "switch trip" is shown as following.

Fail to coincide	0.37
Line protection action	0.26
Overcurrent I share protection action	0.24
Red two, 203 lines	0.24
Advanced 609 wire	0.22
Bump	0.21
crack of needle bottle	0.21
Zhoucun 634 line	0.2
Unsuccessful Reclosing	0.18
phase fault	0.18

Figure 5. The related words of topic "switch trip"

From the figure, we can see that the word frequency of "Fail to coincide" is closest to topic "switch trip". The result is returned to the user. Based on the result, the algorithm plot in the igraph package is used to show the result. The result is shown as follow.

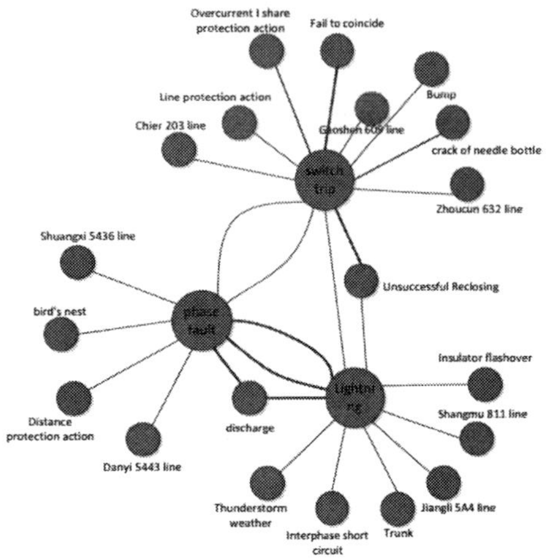

Figure 6. Relevance chart of related words and topic

In the figure, the wider circles are topics, the smaller circles are related words. The connection line between the big circle and small circle indicates relation of related words and topic. The thickness of the connection indicates relevance degree.

The business professional can analyze real influence factors. For example, there are several lines relating the topic "switch trip". It indicates these line faults often cause the topic" switch trip".

Analysis

Based on the algorithm, the most relevant words with topic can be shown with the thick line. In this case, it is convenient to the business workers to analyze the main factors and secondary factors accurately.

Screening the document set with the topic set can reduce the amount of documents. So, the efficiency of topic analysis in small document set is improved evidently.

Segment with business dictionary can retain more potential information about documents. By the help of it, the professional may analyze the relevant words accurately.

Using the relevance index, the qualitative analysis is transformed into the quantitative analysis. On the base of this, the relevant degree can be described accurately.

5. Conclusion

Because that it is difficult to accurately analyze the related words to document set from the log data, this paper provides the accurate topic mining algorithm based on business dictionary. In the algorithm, firstly, with the topic set, the valid document set can be filtered with fuzzy algorithm. After creating the industry and scene business dictionary, the documents are segmented into a lot of words. In this case, the invalid words are removed. At last, by using the relevance index, the relevance of every word can be computed. The qualitative analysis is transformed into quantitative analysis. The algorithm is applied to PMS. The validation result shows the main related factors of topic can be analyzed accurately.

Although the algorithm can solve the problem of analyzing the log data accurately, when drawing up the business dictionary, the business expert must be need. The quality of the business dictionary is constrained by business expert ability. Furthermore, it is the research direction in the future how to improve the efficiency of the algorithm in the distributed environment.

References

[1] Jiawei Han,Micheline Kamber,Jian Pei.Data Mining Concepts and Techniques Third Edition. Ming Fan, Xiaofeng Meng.China Machine Press,2015.7

[2] Luo, Qi.Advancing knowledge discovery and data mining.Proceedings-1st International Workshop on Knowledge Discovery and Data Mining,WKDD,pp:3-5,2008

[3] Mehmed Kantardzic.Data Mining:Concepts,Models,Methods,and Algorithms, Second Edition. Xiaohai Wang,Zhigang Wu.Tsinghua University Press,2014.12

[4] Yu Wu.Accurate Data Mining For Big Data.Chemical Industry Press.2014.3

[5] Mhamdi Faouzi1,Elloumi Mourad1.A new survey on knowledge discovery and data mining.Proceedings of the 2nd International Conference on Research Challenges in Information Science,RCIS 2008, pp:427-432

[6] Tang Zhihang,Li Zhenhui,Yang Baoan.Knowledge discovery and data mining to assist natural language understanding.Journal of Computational Information Systems, v5, n1, pp:317-322, February,2009

[7] Al Fawareh, Hejab Ma'azer,Jusoh, Shaidah,Osman, Wan Rozaini Sheikh.Ambiguity in text mining.Proceedings of the International Conference on Computer and Communication Engineering 2008, ICCCE08: Global Links for Human Development, pp:1172-1176

[8] Roncero, V.G., Costa, M.C.A., Ebecken, N.F.F..Text mining on a grid environment.WIT Transactions on Information and Communication Technologies, v 42, p 13-21, 2009

[9] Bezdek J C . Pattern Recognition with Fuzzy Objective Function Algorithms . New York : Plenum Press, 1981

[10] Wang Li Juan, Guan Shou Yi, Wang XiaoLong, Wang XiZhao. Fuzzy C Mean algorithm based on feature weights Chinese Journal of Computers , 2006, 29(1D) : 1797—1803(in Chinese)

[11] Li Jie, Gao XinBo, Jiao LiCheng. A new feature weighted fuzzy clustering algorithm. Acta Electron Sinica, 2006, 34(1),pp:89—92(in Chinese)

[12] Huang J Z,Ng M K, Rong H, Li Z. Automated variable weighting in k-means type clustering. IEEE Transactions on Pattern Analysis and Machine Intelligence, 2005, 27(5),pp:1—12

[13] Wang Qiang, Ye Yunming, Huang J Z. Fuzzy k-means with variable weighting in high dimensional data analysis/Proceedings of the 9th International Conference on Web—Age Information Management. Zhangjiajie, China, 2008,pp:365—372

[14] WANG Jun, WANG Shi—Tong, DENG Zhao—Hong.A Novel Text Clustering Algorithm Based on Feature Weighting Distance and Soft Subspace Learning.chinese journal of computers,Vol.35 No.8,2012,pp:1655-1665

[15] Lu Ming-Yu,Yao Xiao-Na,Wei Shan-Ling.BBS hot topic mining algorithm based on fuzzy clustering.Dalian Haishi Daxue Xuebao/Journal of Dalian Maritime University, v34,n4, pp:52-54+58,2008

[16] Zhang Chenyi,Sun Jianling,Ding Yiqun.Topic mining for microblog based on MB-LDA model.Jisuanji Yanjiu yu Fazhan/Computer Research and Development, v48, n10, pp:1795-1802,October,2011

[17] Steyvers M,Griffiths T.Probabilistic topic models.Handbook of latent semantic analysis,2007,427(7),pp:424-440

[18] Sethi A,Upadrasta B,Bangalore K.Introduction to Probabilistic Topic Modeling.2012

[19] Wainwright M J,Jordan M I.Graphical models,exponential families,andvariational inference.Foundations and Trends in Machine Learning,2008,1(1-2)pp:1-305

[20] Heinrich G.Parameter estimation for text analysis.Technical report,Technical report,2005

[21] Blei D M,Jordan M I,et al.Variational inference for Dirichlet process mixtures.Bayesian analysis,2006,1(1),pp:121-143

[22] Zhao W X,Jiang J,Weng J,et al.comparing twitter and traditional media using topic model[M].Advances in information Retrieval.Springer Berlin Heidelberg,2011,pp:338-349

[23] Ramage D,Hall D,Nallapati R,et al.Labeled LDA:A supervised topic model for credit attribution in multi-labeled corpora[C].proceedings of the 2009 comference on Empirical Methods in Natural Language Processing:Volume 1-Volume 1.Association for Computational Linguistics,2009,pp:248-256

[24] Zhang Chenyi,Sun Jianling,Ding Yiqun.Topic Mining for Microblog Based on MB-LDA Model.Joural of Computer Research and Development,48(10),pp:1795-1802,2011

[25] R https://www.r-project.org/

A Multi-Source Data Aggregation and Multidimensional Analysis Model for Big Data

Pan LIU, Lin CHEN

School of Computer, National University of Defense Techonology ChangSha, China
1185307014@qq.com,agnes_nudt@qq.com

Abstract:With the rise of Internet applications such as search engines, social networks, and e-commerce, the amount of data in the Internet is rapidly expanding. There are a lot of data generated every moment, and the global information is also increasing. Therefore, the big data is driven by the Internet industry, and it is also a subversive technological innovation compared to the cloud computing and Internet of things. How to carry on the fast retrieval in the massive and different types of data? How to discover potential associations between different data? How to mining the potential value of the data? And how to create a multidimensional view of the data? These urgent problems need to be solved. In this paper, a multi-source data aggregation and multidimensional analysis model for big data (DAM_AM) is proposed. The model adopts the hierarchical structure and introduces data aggregation mechanism, multi-source processing mechanism, object and association mapping mechanism, and "walk" mechanism. Using these mechanisms, multi-source data is normalized to a coherent and consistent representation pattern. And then the fields that represent a class of entity in the representation pattern are aggregated into a set of fields. By mapping different field sets into different objects and associations and combining with the time dimension and space dimension, we can build a multifaceted visual model. Through the concrete case analysis and verification, it indicates that the DAM_AM model can analyze the data from multidimensional and multi-level, and shows the potential correlation between different data. The model not only has high computational efficiency and has high scalability, but also shows the analysis results clearly and intuitively.

1 Introduction

With the rise of Internet applications such as search engines, social networks, and e-commerce, the amount of data in the Internet is rapidly expanding. According to incomplete statistics, Google's daily processing of data amounted to 20PB [1]; Facebook 's user data has reached 15PB and grows at a rate of 60TB per day; Taobao's data center stores at least 14PB of data[2]. International Data Corporation(IDC) predicts that the global information will reach 35ZB [3] in 2020. How to deal with the large-scale data and extract the value from the large-scale data has become an urgent problem. Therefore, The big data is driven by the Internet industry, and it is also a subversive technological innovation compared to the cloud computing and internet of things.

Compared with the traditional data, the characteristics of big data can be summarized as [4]: huge data volume, variety , data update fast, high uncertainty . these features make big data processing face enormous challenges: data volume increases ceaselessly; data in various forms; the authenticity and quality of data is uncertain. In response to these difficulties and challenges, different platforms of big data processing have been introduced. At present, platforms of big data processing are divided into four categories: batch computing platform, flow computing platform, interactive computing platform and graph computing platform.

The representatives of batch computing platform are the Apache Hadoop [5] and Microsoft Dryad. The Hadoop is the open source implementation based on the MapReduce programming model, and it is established as a open source project in 2006.

The representatives of stream computing platform are Twitter's Storm and Yahoo's S4. In Storm, the processing logic of a Storm application is encapsulated into an object named Topology which is composed of several message source components named Spout and message handler named Bolt, and the processing logic is presented in the form of a directed graph. Storm uses the master / slave architecture.

Interactive computing is the feature of database system (DBMS, Database Management Systems) . Users enter a SQL query command at the database system terminal, the database system will return the search results [6]. The first interactive computing platform is Google's Dremel [7], which is an extensible interactive data query system for read-only nested data. Dremel is able to perform aggregated queries on the table including trillions rows in seconds by using service tree and column storage technology of data.

At present, the major graph computing platforms are Apache's Giraph [8] , GraphX [9] developed by the University of California at Berkeley, and the GraphLab[10] developed by Carnegie Mellon University .

Through studying on the interactive computing and the graph computing, we find that the interactive computing can get query results efficiently from large-scale data, but it is difficult to deal with different types of data, and the results are not intuitive enough because the results are always presented in the form of table. Thus it is not easy to find data association in deep level. The graph computing displays the results of calculation and query in a graphical way. Although the results are very clear and intuitive, the computational efficiency is not as good as the interactive computing. In this paper, we propose and design a multi-source data aggregation and multidimensional analysis model for big data (DAM_AM). Not only can the the model deal with different types of data by normalizing the data in several formats into the same representation pattern, but also makes the final results display more intuitive and clear by creating different views to display the results of querying and matching. The DAM_AM model not only has higher efficiency of calculation and query, and compared with the graph computing, the analysis architecture has a strong scalability. Instead of rebuilding a new model , the new data can be directly updated to the existing models based on new data and previous data,

2 A Multi-Source Data Aggregation and Multidimensional Analysis Model for Big Data

2.1 Model Concepts

Definition 1 Object: A specific instance of a type. An object can be a specific type, node, or entity and it is uniquely defined by the key and described by attributes.

Definition 2 Association: A relationship between two objects. Associations are directional, and it is uniquely defined by the key and described by attributes.

Definition 3 Key: A unique data that identifies an object or association and can vary based on context.

Definition 4 Attribute: Data that describes an object or association and shows features of an object or association. Attribute can be used for searching, detailing, grouping the objects and describing associations and objects.

In the DAM_AM model, objects and associations have types to organize and classify the data. the creation of an object or association is based on a combination of key and type. Different object types can be created to support different types of analyses. Any attributes that are used for searching or querying should have an index put on the corresponding database fields to speed up the results and they do not necessarily need to be "real" values queried from the underlying database.

2.2 The DAM_AM Model Description

The framework of the DAM_AM model is divided into three layers: data resource layer, model layer and data presentation layer. The overall framework is shown in Fig. 1.

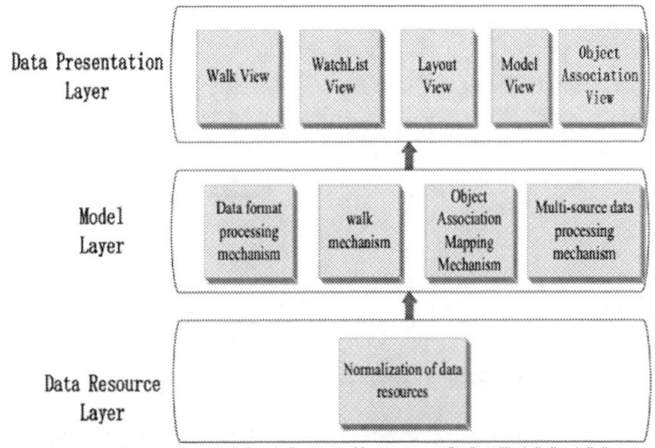

Figure 1. The hierarchical frame diagram of the DAM_AM model

The data resource layer normalizes the different types data which can be accessed and read from different data sources. Only after normalization can you map objects and associations correctly from The set of fields to be aggregated.

The model layer is used to deal with problems when we create the analytical model and map objects and associations from tables. This layer contains multi-source data processing mechanism, walk processing mechanism, object and association mapping mechanism and data format processing mechanism.

The data presentation layer is used to visualize the DAM_AM model and the results of searching and querying. It can display the associations between different objects in a more intuitive way. It contains object and association view, walk view,"WatchList" view, layout view, model view and so on.

2.3 Key Technologies of the DAM_AM Model

1) Data Resource Aggregation Mechanism

Data resource layer first to access and read data from different data sources, These data formats are different, such as the data formats may be csv, xls, xml or database tables and so on. These data must be brought together into a common representation format so that they have a consistent and coherent presentation pattern. And then the fields that represent a class of entity in the representation pattern are aggregated into a set of fields. There may be intersections between different sets of fields, but the key used to identify the entity in sets of fields can not be crossed, and the other fields that used as the attributes of the entity can be crossed. The DAM_AM model maps different sets of fields into different objects and associations according to the needs of the analysis. The data resource aggregation is shown in Fig. 2.

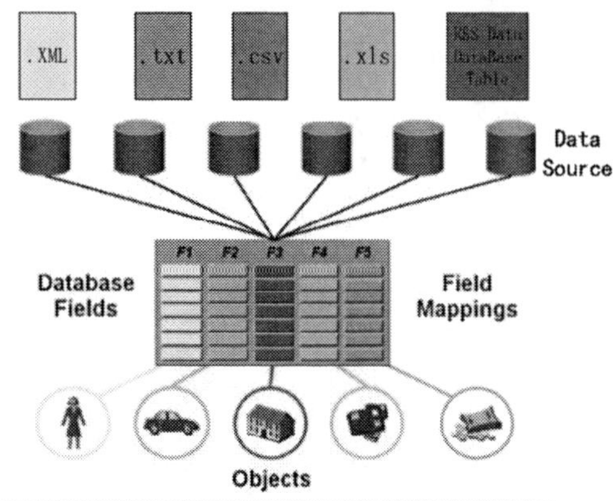

Figure 2. Data aggregation display

2) *Format Processing Mechanism*

The reliability and quality of the data directly affects the creation of the analysis model. So it is necessary to deal with the data before creating the analysis model. We found that the problems of data can be divided into four areas: value errors, data missing, unreasonable data structure, incomplete formats. show in Fig. 3.

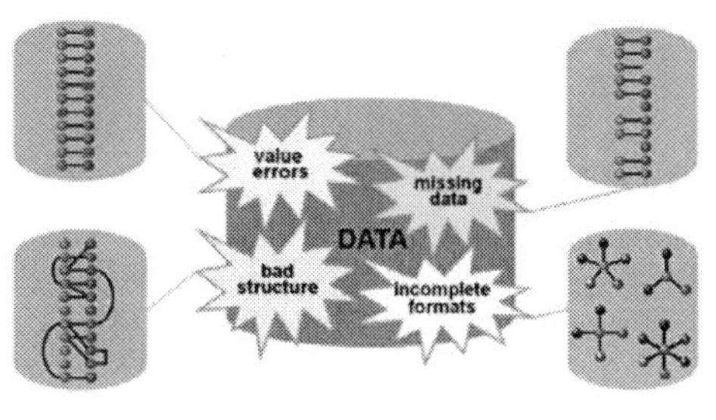

Figure. 3. Classification of data problems

In order to avoid data format errors and data inconsistencies, the data format processing mechanism will deal with the data properly, such as concatenating field values , representing names as SMITH/JOHN/Q and do not break the name into separate fields, uppercasing all values, removing extra spaces as well as representing dates differently.

3) *Multi-Source Data Processing Mechanism*

When you create a DAM_AM model, you must be aware of the correspondence between the model you are creating and the existing data sources. When there are multiple data sources, the correspondence between the model and the different data sources can be roughly divided into three categories (show in Fig. 4). On the basis of that, we analyze the conditions for generating these three modes in detail.

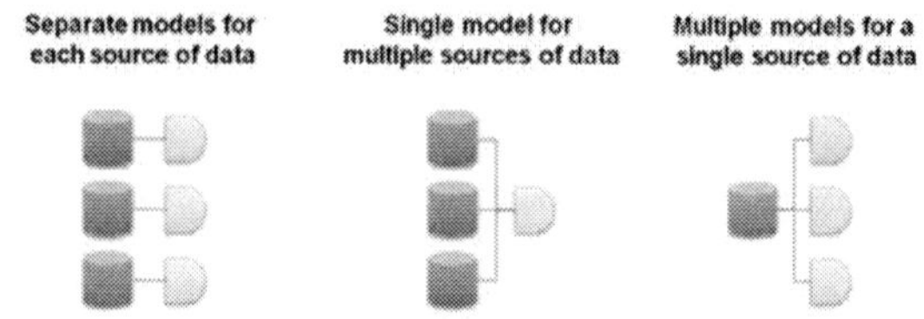

Figure 4. Corresponding modes between multi-sources and models

Separate models for each source of data. the conditions for generating this mode includes: When there aren't any common keys between any of the data sources; When there aren't any common values between any of the data sources; When the sources are very dissimilar to each other – even if there are common values; When each data source can provide its own unique set of patterns and trends.

Single model for multiple sources of data. the conditions for generating this mode includes: When only attribute values can be derived from a source; When there are limited numbers of associations between objects in the data; When there aren't any patterns independently contained within any single source of data.

Multiple models for a single source of data. the conditions for generating this mode includes: When different viewpoints on the data are needed for exposing different analytical situations; When there is more than one way to model the data set; When the data source is very complex - containing multiple tables/fields for the primary objects

4) *Object and Association Mapping Mechanism*

The object and association mapping mechanism is the basis for building a DAM_AM model. Because the process of establishing a DAM_AM model is to map the fields and tables in the database into the objects and associations. For this reason, we must understand the concepts of fields and tables in the database schema before building the model. In addition, we should know the SQL syntax such as Select, Join and Where clauses, because all the objects in the DAM_AM model are created through Select statements , and Select statements is a very fast database operations.

Before you building any model, you should first get familiar with the database and need to understand the structure of the database (tables/fields) as well as review the data to determine which fields are populated. An example of creating objects and associations is shown in Fig. 5.

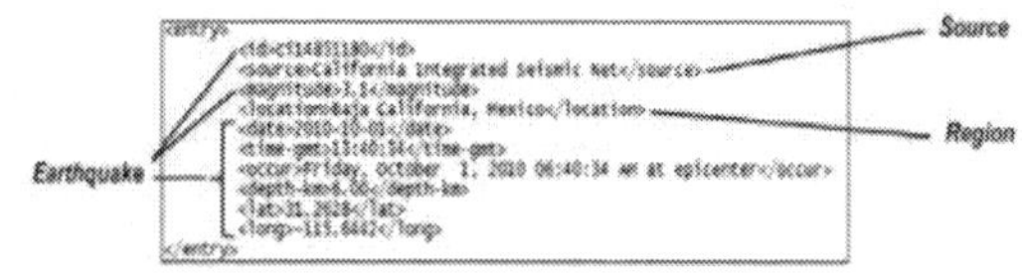

Figure 5. Example of creating objects and associations

Through the analysis of the original XML data, it can be seen that an event entity should consist of three objects: Earthquake , Region and Source. These three objects can represent the event of earthquake clearly. Therefore, we need to create these three objects which mapped from the original data. In the process of creating the objects, we also need to set the names, keys, attributes, icons, and related descriptive labels for different objects. Three objects are created, and the next step is to create associations between the objects. Since the original file is in XML format, this raw data need to be normalized to the table representation via the data resource layer. Association is mapped based on the tables. so as long as the two keys of objects exist in the same table, the association between the two objects can be established. Association are also directional. Before you establishing the association, you need to determine the "FromObject" and "ToObject" to ensure there is a directional association between two different objects. You also need to set key, attributes, and the color of the wires for the association. As shown in the figure above, we can establish the association between Earthquake and Source, and we can also establish association between Region and Earthquake.

5) Walk Processing Mechanism

Walk processing mechanism is to "walk" the objects in the same model or different models. In the association processing mechanism, we propose the concepts of "walk" and level. "walk" refers to an in-depth search on the specified object which based on associations between different objects. A level which equals to 1 means that only "walk" the objects which are directly associated with the specified object. We can "walk" from one object to other objects, and so on, until find the target object. The whole process of the "walk" completely shows the relevancy between objects at different layers, which helps to analyze and find the potential association between different data. In addition, the walk processing mechanism can also cross-search between different models, as long as the keys of the objects in different models are same.

3 Case Analysis and Validation

In this section, we will use the DAM_AM model to analyze and model the example, and show the results of the analysis. Firstly we read four tables named as tblTelephone, tblSuspect, tblOrganization and tblSuspect_tblOrganization from a database. The tblOrganization table includes fields such as name, organization_id and classfiction and so on. The tblSuspect table includes fields such as suspect_id, first name, last name and sex and so on. The tblTelephone table includes fields such as start time ,end time, duration,from number and to number and so on. The tblSuspect_tblOrganization table includes fields such as unique_id, suspect_id and organization_id and so on.

These four tables will be normalized into a unified representation pattern by the data resource layer. The data is formatted to exclude some wrong format, such as the data with the date type, which does not need to display a specific time, will be dropped time. Since these four tables are all read from the same data source, we select the separate models for each source of data. The next step is to use object and association mapping mechanism to create the corresponding objects and associations. Analysis of the different fields of the table, we can see the "FromNumber" field and the "ToNumber" field in the tblTelephone table can be used as different keys to create two objects. And they represent the caller phone and callee phone respectively. On the basis of the analysis, we create two objects. These two objects are both named Phone .The keys of these two objects are not same but types of these two objects are the same. According to the definition of the object for the third quarter, they should be the same object. Thus, these two objects in the model are the same icon and have the same name. In the DAM_AM model, such objects are referred to as merged object.

And then we set the key, attributes, and icon for these two objects whose object types are both Phone. On the basis of that, we establish the association of these two objects based on the tblTelephone table. And in order to set the direction of the association, we set "FromObject" to the Phone object whose key is "FromNumber" and set the "ToObject" to the Phone object whose key is ."ToNumber". Finally, we set the key of the association and the color of the connection line. Similarly, analysis of the fields for the remaining three table, it is noticeable that tblSuspect table can create Suspect object and tblOrganization table can create Organization object. And then the association between the Suspect object and the Phone object can be established based on the tblTelephone table. Then again, the association between the Organization object and the Suspect object can also be established based on tblSuspect_tblOrganization table. The steps about creating the new objects and establishing the new associations are the same as for creating a Phone object, so we will not repeat them again.

Each time a new object and association is added to the same model, the model will update. We can see the model update process (show in Fig. 6) after these three objects and associations are created.

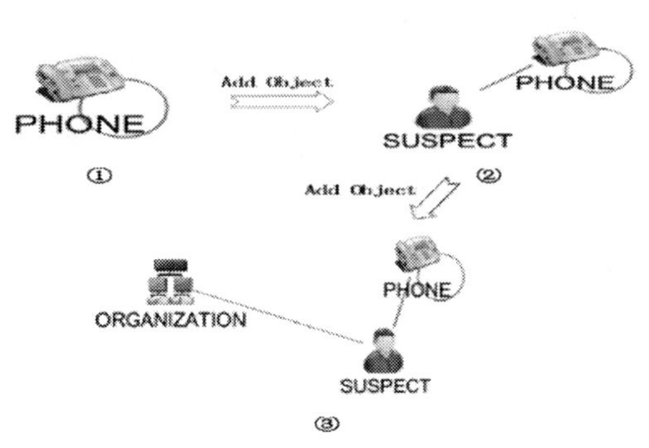

Figure 6. The update process of the DAM_AM model

From the view of the model update, we can see that ① denotes a self-linked object, ② denotes the transition

 DOI: 10.1051/itmconf/20171205009

model, ③ denotes the final DAM_AM model. Open the object and association view of this model to see the Fig. 7.

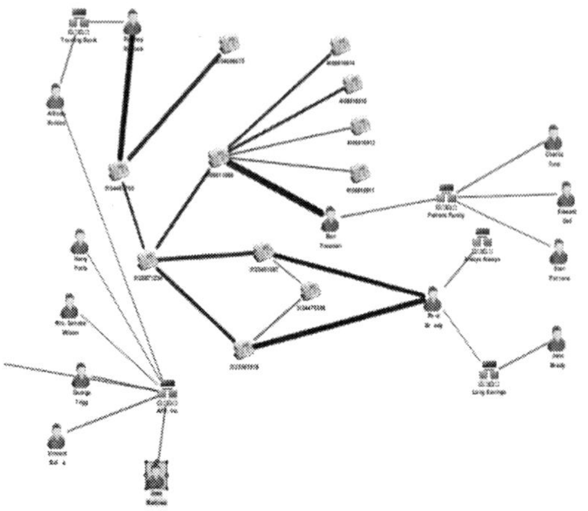

Figure 7. Object and association view

Through the analysis of the object and association view, we can see clearly which two Phone objects have made a phone call, and the thickness of connecting lines represents the number of calls. the thicker the connecting lines, the higher the frequency of calls. Similarly, we can see which Suspects are included in Organizations.

After creating the DAM_AM model, we can create a "WatchList" file. To match the contents of the "WatchList" file in the DAM_AM model ,and then the matched objects will be marked in a special icon in the view. In order to obtain the relationship between the two special Suspect objects and other objects in the model, You can select these Suspect objects and "walk" them. Finally we can see the relationship between these two objects and other objects in the view. Show in Fig. 8~10.

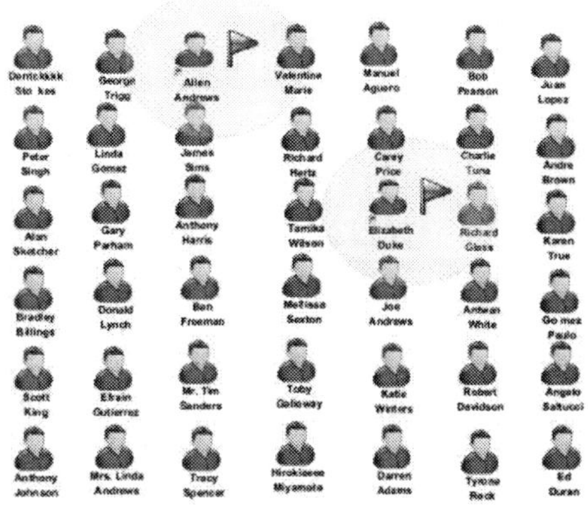

Figure 8. "WatchList" view

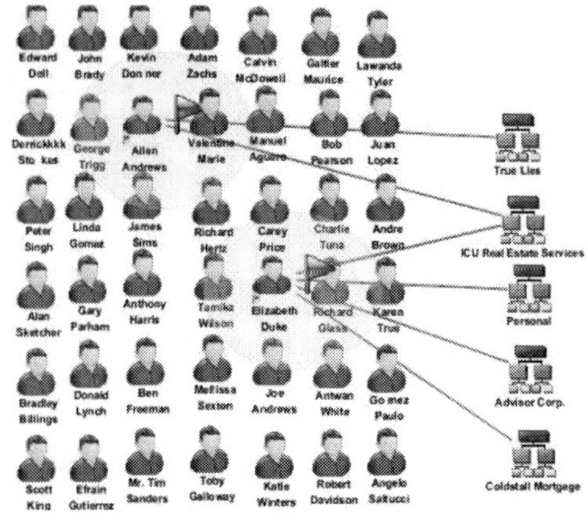

Figure 9. "walk" view

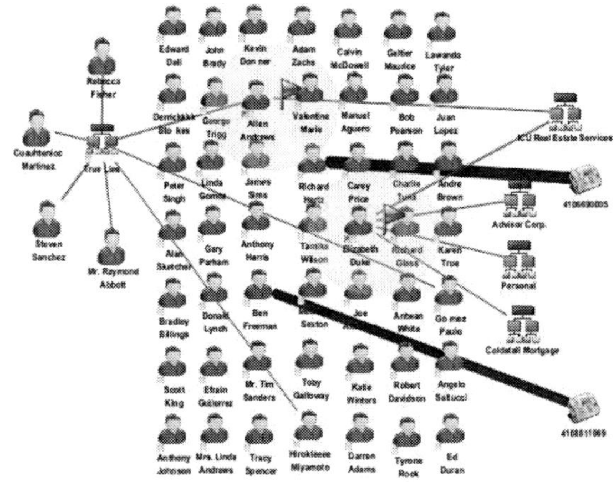

Figure 10. "walk" view

4 Conclusion

In this paper, we design a multi-source data aggregation and multidimensional analysis model for big data (DAM_AM). The model adopts the hierarchical structure and introduces data aggregation mechanism, multi-source processing mechanism, object and association mapping mechanism, and walk mechanism. Using these mechanisms, multi-source data is normalized to a coherent and consistent representation pattern. And then the fields that represent a class of entity in the representation pattern are aggregated into a set of fields. By mapping different field sets into different objects and associations we can build a multifaceted visual model. The DAM_AM model is further improved and enriched the model by putting forward some new concepts such as merged object, "WatchList", and "walk". the DAM_AM model can analyze the data from multidimensional and multi-level and shows the potential correlation between different data. The model not only has high computational efficiency and has high scalability, but also shows the analysis results clearly and intuitively.

DOI: 10.1051/itmconf/20171205009

References

[1] Dean J, Ghemawat S. MapReduce: simplified data processing on large clusters.Communications of the ACM. 2008, 51 (1): 107–113.

[2] Gantz J, Reinsel D. The digital universe in 2020: Big data, bigger digital shadows,and biggest growth in the far east. IDC iView: IDC Analyze the Future. 2012, 2007: 1–16.

[3] China Computer Society Big Data Expert Committee China Big Data Technology and Industry Development White Paper, 2013.

[4] Barwick H. The" four Vs" of Big Data. Implementing Information InfrastructureSymposium, 2012.

[5] Apache Hadoop MapReduce. https://hadoop.apache.org.

[6] Pavlo A, Paulson E, Rasin A, et al. A comparison of approaches to large-scale dataanalysis. In Proceedings of the 2009 ACM SIGMOD International Conferenceon Management of data. 2009: 165–178.

[7] Melnik S, Gubarev A, Long J J, et al. Dremel: Interactive Analysis of Web-ScaleDatasets. In Proc. of the 36th Int'l Conf on Very Large Data Bases. 2010:330–339.

[8] Apahce Giraph. http://giraph.apache.org/.

[9] Xin R S, Gonzalez J E, Franklin M J, et al. Graphx: A resilient distributed graphsystem on spark. In First International Workshop on Graph Data ManagementExperiences and Systems. 2013: 2.

[10] GraphLab: A New Parallel Framework for Machine Learning. http://www.select.cs.cmu.edu/code/graphlab/.

PtmxGuard: An Improved Method for Android Kernel to Prevent Privilege Escalation Attack

Bin Kong[1, 2], Ying LI[3, 4, *], Lu-Ping Ma[3]

[1]*National Secrecy Science and Technology Evaluation Center, Beijing, China*
[2]*School of Economics and Management, Beijing Jiaotong University, Beijing, China*
[3]*Institute of Information Engineering, Chinese Academy of Sciences, Beijing, China*
[4]*School of Cyber Security, University of Chinese Academy of Sciences, Beijing, China*
Email: liying@iie.ac.cn

Abstract—Vulnerabilities in Android kernel give opportunity for attacker to damage the system. Privilege escalation is one of the most dangerous attacks, as it helps attacker to gain root privilege by exploiting kernel vulnerabilities. Mitigation technologies, static detection methods and dynamic defense methods have been suggested to prevent privilege escalation attack, but they still have some disadvantages. In this paper, we propose an improved method named PtmxGuard to enhance Android kernel and defeat privilege escalation attack. We focus on a typical attack pattern that attacker hijacks the control flow of Android kernel to modify process credentials by corrupting critical global function pointers. PtmxGuard enforces Code Pointer Integrity to Android kernel, checks the accuracy and reliability of those pointers when they're triggered by related system calls, and intercepts the system calls when attack activities are detected. Experiment result demonstrates that PtmxGuard can defense privilege escalation attack effectively.

1 Introduction

Android has become the most popular operation system applied to smart mobile device [1]. Android smart device facilitates people's work and life. Meanwhile, it stores a massive amount of personal privacy and sensitive information, which makes it a preferred target for attacker.

However, vulnerabilities in Android system give opportunity for attacker to damage the system security. Vulnerabilities in Android kernel are considered to be the most dangerous bugs, since kernel is a part of the trusted computing base of Android system [2]. Taking advantage of kernel vulnerabilities, attacker acquires the ability to bypass system protection mechanisms and carry out some malicious behavior, such as gain root privilege and steal personal data. Privilege escalation attack, also known as root exploit, is the process of exploiting kernel vulnerabilities to obtain the highest privilege [3]. If a process gains the root privilege, it has access permission to access any data and obtains control over the whole system.

Many efforts have been made to mitigate kernel vulnerabilities and prevent privilege escalation attack. Security-Enhanced Linux (SELinux), Data Execution Prevention (DEP), Privileged eXecute Never (PXN) and Address Space Layout Randomization (ASLR) have been introduced to enhance Android system and raise the difficulty of vulnerability exploit. However, SELinux can be broken through by corrupting the security identifier and security context of process credentials, and real attacks show that mitigation technology can be bypass by other exploit technology, e.g. Return-Oriented Programming (ROP) [4-9]. Some researchers suggested static detection methods to recognize privilege escalation attack [10, 11], but they all rely on the source code and predefined features. There are some other dynamical approaches to defeat privilege escalation attack, such as PREC, RGBDroid and Security Identifier Randomization [12-16]. Although they have contributed significant improvement on protecting Android kernel, they also have some certain limitations, which are described in Section II..

In this paper, we presented an improved method to enhance Android kernel and defense privilege escalation attack. Firstly, we studied on a number of attack instances and find out a typical attack pattern that attacker tampers critical global pointers, hijack the control flow of kernel and finally modify the process credentials. Secondly, we proposed an improved method named PtmxGuard to protect Android kernel from privilege escalation attack. PtmxGuard enforces Code Pointer Integrity to Android kernel. We specifically focus on the critical global function pointers defined by ptmx driver, which are most likely to be utilized by privilege escalation attack. PtmxGuard verifies the accuracy and reliability of those pointers when they are triggered by related system calls, and intercepts root exploit as soon as it detected attack activity. Finally, experiment result shows that PtmxGuard can defense privilege escalation attack effectively.

The paper is organized as follows. Related work is discussed in Section II. In Section III, we explain that the aim of privilege escalation attack is tampering the UID of malicious application to zero. We summarize a typical pattern of privilege escalation attack and introduce how to trigger a function pointer by related system call. Section IV shows the proposed improved method named PtmxGuard and presents the details of how to defense privilege escalation attack on the base of Code Pointer Integrity. Experiment and result of the proposed method is shown in Section V. Conclusion is made in Section VI.

2 Related Work

Many efforts have been made to mitigate Android kernel vulnerabilities and protect the system against privilege escalation attack.

SELinux has been introduced into Android kernel and has been enforced since Android version 4.4 [4]. Instead of Discretionary Access Control (DAC), SELinux adopts flexible Mandatory Access Control (MAC) mechanisms to provide fine-grained authorization according to pre-configured security policy. However, an attacker can tamper the process's security identifier and security context, and break through the restriction of SELinux's policy. DEP technique enables the kernel to mark certain areas of memory as non-executable, such as Dalvik heap, which can limit executing injected malicious code [5]. PXN has been introduced into Android system to prevent the kernel return to user space to execute untrusted instructions [6]. Unfortunately, real attacks show that DEP and PXN can be fully bypassed by code reuse attack, such as ROP, which leverages existing native code in memory as shellcode payload instead of injecting custom malicious instructions [7, 8]. ASLR is supported since Android kernel version 2.6.35 [9]. It allows the kernel to randomize the stack address, heap address, the location of shared libraries and other key memory areas. ASLR makes it probabilistically hard for attacker to locate key variables. The vulnerability mitigations above enhance the system's ability to resist privilege escalation attack. Adding mitigation techniques makes kernel vulnerabilities more difficult to exploit than they would be without mitigations. However, they can't prevent privilege escalation attack completely.

Some methods have been proposed to detect and resist privilege escalation attack. Won-Jun Jang et al. suggested a mechanism to detect rooting attack by monitoring inter process communication, extracting the characteristics of decompiled code and recognizing abnormal activities [10]. However, this mechanism may produce false alarm, as the rooting attack features it identified is too broad. DroidExec is a root exploit malware recognition by feature matching based on similarity calculation [11]. The recognition rate relies on decompile technology and the predefined features. Those two method perform static detection. In contrast, PtmxGuard is able to detect privilege escalation attack dynamically.

PREC is a light-weight framework to dynamically identify system calls originated from third-party native code, and execute them within isolated threads [12]. PREC defeats privilege escalation attack by slowing down the execution frequency of those system calls. It focuses on those malicious activities that repeat high-risk system calls for many times in a short time interval. Yeongung Park et al. proposed a security enhancement framework for Android kernel. It introduces three mechanisms to limit untrusted programs with root privilege to access protected critical system resources and user's private data [13-15]. However, the framework takes effect when an attack program has obtained root privilege illegally and is trying to access some critical and privacy data. In contrast, PtmxGuard doesn't give an attacker a chance to get root privilege. PtmxGuard intercepts the privilege escalation attack, as soon as it detected those malicious behaviors. Lifeng Wei et al. proposed an improved method to enhance Android kernel. By replacing the ways of allocating security identifier from sequential allocation to randomized allocation, it becomes hard for attacker to determine the security identifier of root user [16]. However, the protection may be compromised by exhausting the value of security identifier.

3 Privilege Escalation Attack

3.1 Android User ID

Android system allocates a distinct system identity called User ID (UID) to each application, and Android kernel regards each application as a unique Linux user. Application Sandbox Mechanism isolates each application in its own process space and restricts access to resources by UIDs, prevent applications from interfering with each other at run time.

Generally, the UIDs of user applications are always greater than 10,000. Android kernel retains certain fixed UIDs for system applications, e.g. 1000 for system server process. In particular, a zero UID is associated with the root user, who is unconfined and owns the highest access permissions in Android kernel. Thus, the aim of privilege escalation attack is tampering the UID of malicious app to zero.

3.2 Android Process Credential

In Android kernel space, each process is associated with a structure of process credential named cred. It stores all security attributes of the corresponding application process, including four pairs of UIDs/GIDs: the real (*uid/gid*), the saved (*suid/sgid*), the effective (*euid/egid*) and the filesystem's (*fsuid/fsgid*). If SELinux is configured in kernel, cred will include a *security* pointer points to the structure *task_security_struct*, which contains the SELinux security context (e.g. *sid* and *osid*) of the process.

Android system provides a kernel stack for each process in order to maintain some necessary information when the process switches to kernel space via system call and runs in kernel mode. A process's kernel stack and its process control block *thread_info* store in a union and share the same memory area, which is normally 8KB aligned. The structure *thread_info* has fixed size and stores at the beginning of the shared memory. It contains a *task* pointer points to the process descriptor *task_struct*. The structure *task_struct* includes a *stack* pointer points to the start of the shared memory. There are also two critical pointers *cred* and *real_cred*, and they both point to the structure *cred*. Fig. 1 shows the relationship between several data structures mentioned above.

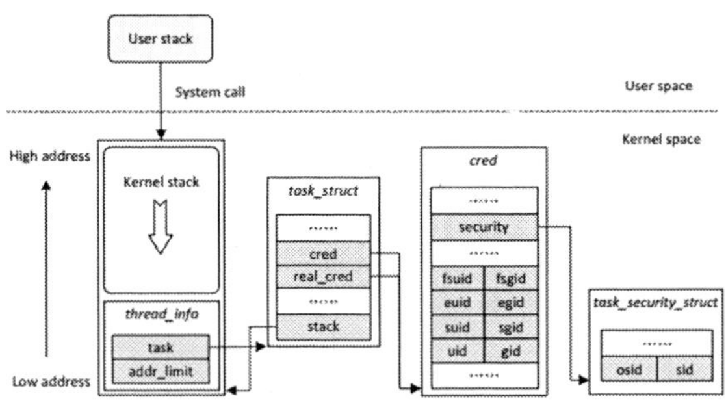

Figure 1. Android process credential

3.3 Typical Pattern of Privilege Escalation Attack

The aim of privilege escalation attack is tampering the UID of malicious app to zero, which represents the root user of Android kernel. However, user application is not allowed to modify variables of process credentials saved in kernel space. Therefore, attacker exploits kernel vulnerabilities to achieve privilege escalation.

Attacker usually carefully construct input parameters of vulnerability function to overwrite something critical, e.g. global function pointers in the kernel, manipulate them to his liking and hijack the control flow of kernel by triggering pointer.

After studied a number of root exploits, we include a typical pattern of privilege escalation attack, as shown in Fig. 2.

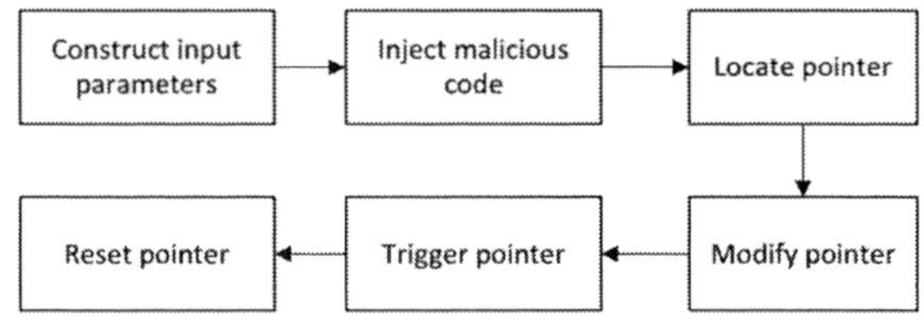

Figure 2. Typical pattern of privilege escalation attack

Firstly, construct input parameters and pass them to the vulnerability function. Crafting input data allows manipulating the target memory region to an expected state. Secondly, allocate an executable memory region and inject malicious code. The injected code is used to modify security attributes (e.g. *uid, sid*) stored in the process credential of the attack application. Thirdly, find an available function pointer in kernel space and get its position. Available function pointers have the ability to manipulate kernel's execution flow. Then, exploit the vulnerability and modify the function pointer to point to the injected malicious code. After that, trigger the function pointer by related system call. The kernel function associated with the function pointer will be performed, and the kernel is hijacked and turns to execute the injected code. Finally, reset the function pointer if necessary to avoid unexpected situation.

The most commonly used pointers is *fsync* of the structure *ptmx_fops*, which is a global structure in the kernel symbol table. Due to the way the binary kernel image is loaded, all global items in the kernel symbol table have the same static address, even if the system reboots.

3.4 Android System Call

The key step to execute the injected malicious code is triggering the modified function pointer by related system call. Android system call is a set of standard interface providing by kernel for restricted communication between user space and kernel space. Applications in user space switch to kernel model to access kernel resource by system call.

As shown in Fig. 3, application in user space invokes system-call interface wrapped by C/C++ library and pass necessary parameters. Then, the system-call interface invokes the intended system call in kernel space. After that, system call invokes kernel function associated with the modified function pointer to access resource, and return states or values to the upper level.

DOI: 10.1051/itmconf/20171205010

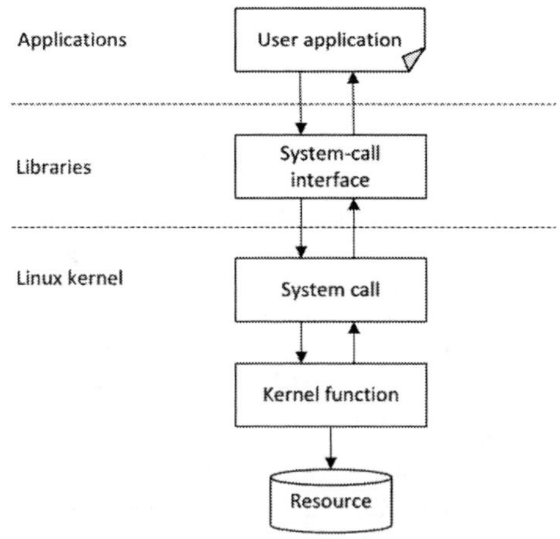

Figure 3. Procedure of system call

4 Design and Implement

According to the typical attack pattern mentioned above, attacker gains privilege escalation by corrupting critical function pointers, and hijacking the control flow of Android kernel to execute injected malicious code. After modifying function pointer, attacker retrieves it and triggers the pointer by related system calls. Therefore, triggering function pointer by related system call is the key to achieve hijack. Hence, we introduce Code Pointer Integrity when triggering the pointer to resist this type of privilege escalation attack.

4.1 Framework Design

An improved method PtmxGuard is introduced into Android kernel to defense privilege escalation attack. PtmxGuard enforces Code Pointer Integrity when triggering critical function pointers, checks whether they are accurate and reliable. If not, PtmxGuard will recognized it as an attack and intercept it.

Fig. 4 shows the framework of the proposed PtmxGuard. It contains five function modules: the monitor module, the sensitivity check module, the integrity verification module, the attack detection module, and the intercept module. There are also two data sets: the sensitive function set and the attack feature set. The sensitive function set includes critical kernel functions, which are most likely to be utilized by privilege escalation attack. And attack feature set defines some typical features extracted from real privilege escalation attack instances.

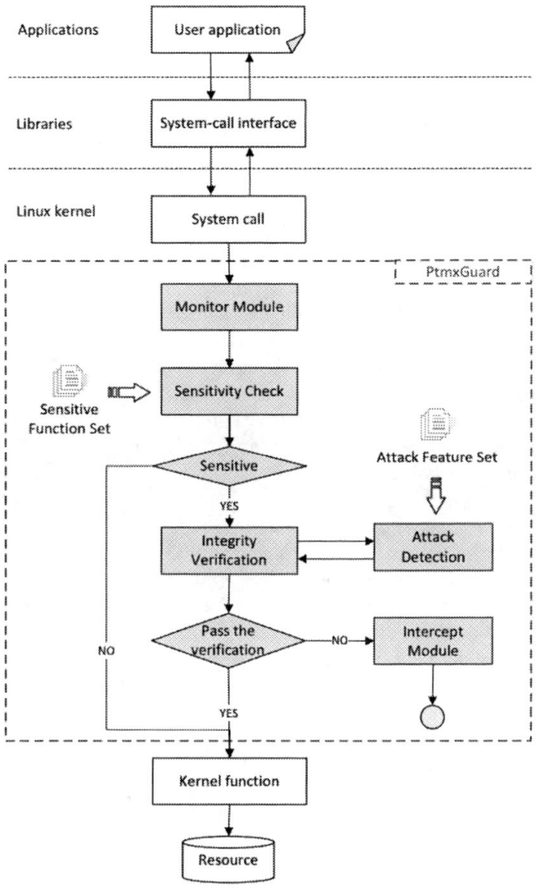

Figure 4. Framework of the proposed PtmxGuard

When an attacker tries to trigger the modified function pointer and invoked corresponding kernel function by related system call, the monitor module will detect the behavior dynamically and the sensitivity check module will retrieve the sensitive function set to check whether the corresponding kernel function is sensitive. If not, PtmxGuard allows the system call to invoke insensitive kernel function. Otherwise, the integrity verification module will retrieve the value of function pointer and pass it to the attack detection module to match the attack feature set. If the memory region where the function pointer points to fits the attack features, it will not pass the verification. PtmxGuard regards it as an attack and the Intercept Module will send a warning and intercept the system call.

4.2 Implement Details

PtmxGuard contains five function modules and the implement details are shown in below.

1) Monitor Module

Using hook technique to monitor system calls and check whether they intend to invoke kernel functions. When detecting the behavior, it delivers to the next module.

2) Sensitivity Check Module

Query the sensitive function set to judge whether the intended kernel functions are sensitive and associated with privilege escalation attack. If not, allow system calls to invoke kernel functions directly. Otherwise, go to the next module.

We define the kernel functions related with the *ptmx* driver as sensitive functions and include them into the sensitive function set. The driver *ptmx* is defined in Android kernel and represented by a kernel-level file structure *ptmx_fops*, which holds pointers to functions defined by the driver. Function pointers within *ptmx_fops*, particularly the pointer *ptmx_fops.fsync*, are preferred targets for attacker, since the values of most entries within *ptmx_fops* are 0 by default, except the pointer *ptmx_fops.open*. Therefore, reset pointer is relatively uncomplicated and only requires writing the value 0 back to the corrupted pointer location.

We define the sensitive function set as shown in TABLE I, which includes sensitive kernel functions and corresponding function pointers.

TABLE I. Sensitive Function Set

Kernel Functions	**Function Pointers**
ptmx_fops->fsync()	ptmx_fops.fsync
ptmx_fops->llseek()	ptmx_fops.lseek
ptmx_fops->read()	ptmx_fops.read
ptmx_fops->write()	ptmx_fops.write
ptmx_fops->ioctl()	ptmx_fops.ioctl

3) Integrity Verification Module

PtmxGuard monitors system calls and determines that one of which is trying to invoke sensitive kernel function. After that, this module verifies the integrity of corresponding function pointer. It firstly gets the function pointer from the sensitive function set, retrieve its value and check whether it is empty. The values of all pointers in Table 1 are set to NULL or 0 by default. If not, we think it is occupied and pass the value of pointer to the attack detection module for further verification and obtain the return result. If the return result implies that the pointer is accurate and reliable, PtmxGuard allows the system call to invoke sensitive kernel function. Otherwise, deliver it to the intercept module.

4) Attack Detection Module

The module is responsible for attack detection. It fetches instructions in the memory region where the function pointer points to, and checks whether they match the features according to the attack feature set.

We extract three attack features from real privilege escalation attack instances as follows:

- The function pointer points to user space. Kernel function pointers are restricted within kernel space in consideration of system security. Pointing to user space is regarded as dangerous, since user space is free for user applications but out of control of Android kernel. The address range of user space is from 0x00000000 to 0xbfffffff.
- The function pointer points to the heap memory region. Heap memory is marked as non-executable by default because of Android Data Execute Prevention. Kernel function pointers will not point to non-executable memory region unless they are tampered.
- The instructions in where the function pointer points to have the ability to modify security attributes of process credentials. The most common instruction is *commit_creds(prepare_kernel_cred(0))*, which allocates a *cred* struct with full privileges as the same as root user and then applies it to the current process.

New attack feature will be added to improve the proposed PtmxGuard, if new type of privilege escalation attack appears.

5) Intercept Module

If system call fails to pass the integrity verification, this module will log related information, intercept the system call and reset the occupied pointer to empty value in order to avoid unexpected situation.

5 Experiment

In order to prove the defense effect of PtmxGuard, we conduct experiment in Android virtual device. We choose LG Nexus 5 for experiment. The detail of experiment environment is shown in Table II.

TABLE II. Experiment Environment

Hardware Configuration	Model	LG Nexus 5
	CPU	Goldfish 3.4
	ROM	2GB RAM, 16GB ROM
	Architecture	ARMv7
Software Configuration	Android Version	4.2.2
	Kernel Version	3.4.67

We pick the kernel vulnerability CVE-2013-6282 as example. It's a typical privilege escalation vulnerability exposed in Linux kernel and also applicable for Android

DOI: 10.1051/itmconf/20171205010

kernel. By exploiting the vulnerability, attack modifies the pointer *ptmx_fops.fsync*, and hijack kernel to execute injected code to gain privilege escalation by invoking corresponding kernel function *ptmx_fops->fsync()*.

We develop an exploit program named put_user_exploit to prove the defense effect. Before introducing the proposed PtmxGuard, the exploit program succeeds in privilege escalation and sets the *uid* of current process to 0, as shown in Fig. 5. After implementing PtmxGuard, the exploit program fails to get root privilege, because the malicious behavior of put_user_exploit is detected and intercepted by PtmxGuard, as shown in Fig. 6.

Fig. 7 shows the log information recorded by PtmxGuard. In this figure, the value of the sensitive function pointer *ptmx_fops.fsync* is 0x84cc, which locates in user space instead of kernel space. Therefore, it can't pass the integrity verification and intercepted by PtmxGuard.

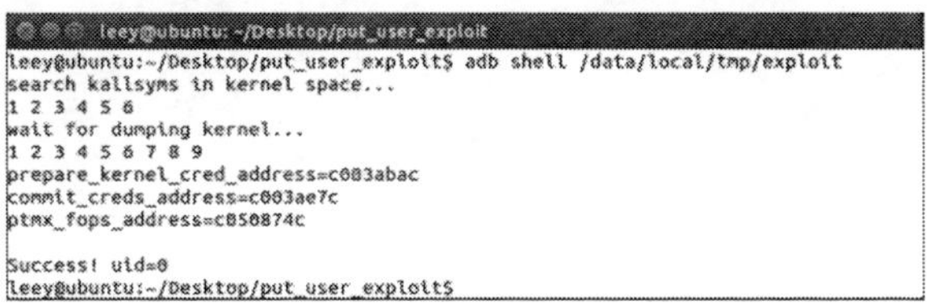

Figure 5. Succeed in privilege escalation without PtmxGuard

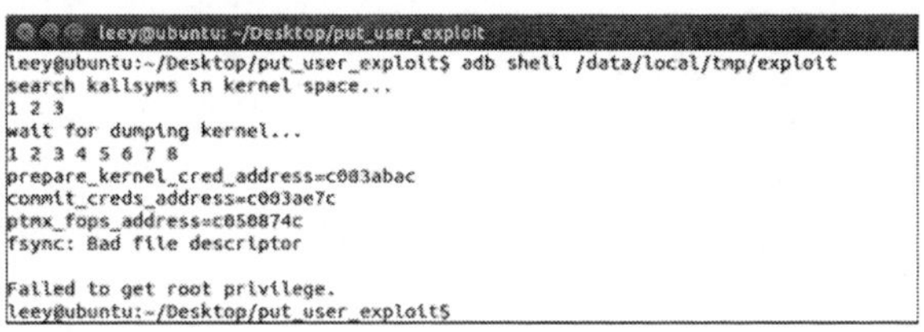

Figure 6. Fail to get root privilege with PtmxGuard

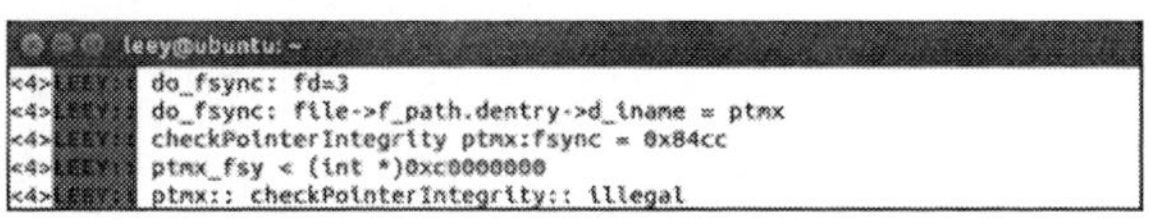

Figure 7. Log information of PtmxGuard

Conclusion

In this paper, we propose an improved approach named PtmxGuard to enhance Android kernel and defeat privilege escalation attack. We focus on a typical attack pattern that attacker hijacks the control flow of Android kernel by corrupting critical global function pointers, and force the kernel to modify security attributes of process credentials. PtmxGuard enforces Code Pointer Integrity to Android kernel, checks whether they are accurate and reliable when triggered by related system calls, and intercepts those system calls when attack activities are detected. Experiment result shows that PtmxGuard can defense privilege escalation attack effectively.

References

[1] Gartner. Gartner Says Five of Top 10 Worldwide Mobile Phone Vendors Increased Sales in Second Quarter of 2016[EB/OL]. [2017-01-12]. http://www.gartner.com/newsroom/id/3415117.

[2] Chen H, Mao Y, Wang X, et al. Linux kernel vulnerabilities: State-of-the-art defenses and open problems[C]. Proceedings of the Second Asia-Pacific Workshop on Systems. ACM, 2011: 5.

[3] Vidas T, Zhang C, Christin N. Toward a general collection methodology for Android devices[J]. digital investigation, 2011, 8: S14-S24.

[4] Smalley S, Craig R. Security Enhanced (SE) Android: Bringing Flexible MAC to Android[C]. NDSS. 2013, 310: 20-38.

[5] Drake J J, Lanier Z, Mulliner C, et al. Android hacker's handbook[M]. John Wiley & Sons, 2014.

[6] Xu W, Fu Y. Own your android! yet another universal root[C]. 9th USENIX Workshop on Offensive Technologies (WOOT 15). 2015.

[7] Kanonov U, Wool A. Secure Containers in Android: the Samsung KNOX Case Study[J]. arXiv preprint arXiv:1605.08567, 2016.

[8] Davi L, Dmitrienko A, Sadeghi A R, et al. Privilege escalation attacks on android[C]. International Conference on Information Security. Springer Berlin Heidelberg, 2010: 346-360.

[9] Liebergeld S, Lange M. Android security, pitfalls and lessons learned[M]. Information Sciences and Systems 2013. Springer International Publishing, 2013: 409-417.

[10] Jang W J, Cho S W, Lee H W, et al. Rooting attack detection method on the Android-based smart phone[C]. Computer Science and Network Technology (ICCSNT), 2011 International Conference on. IEEE, 2011, 1: 477-481.

[11] Wei T E, Tyan H R, Jeng A B, et al. DroidExec: Root exploit malware recognition against wide variability via folding redundant function-relation graph[C]. 2015 17th International Conference on Advanced Communication Technology (ICACT). IEEE, 2015: 161-169.

[12] Ho T H, Dean D, Gu X, et al. PREC: practical root exploit containment for android devices[C]. Proceedings of the 4th ACM conference on Data and application security and privacy. ACM, 2014: 187-198.

[13] Park Y, Lee C, Lee C, et al. Rgbdroid: a novel response-based approach to android privilege escalation attacks[C]. Proceedings of the 5th USENIX conference on Large-Scale Exploits and Emergent Threats, LEET. 2012, 12: 9-9.

[14] Park Y, Lee C, Kim J, et al. An Android security extension to protect personal information against illegal accesses and privilege escalation attacks[J]. Journal of

DOI: 10.1051/itmconf/20171205010

Internet Services and Information Security (JISIS), 2012, 2(3/4): 29-42.
[15] Lee C, Kim J, Cho S, et al. Unified security enhancement framework for the Android operating system[J]. The Journal of Supercomputing, 2014, 67(3): 738-756.
[16] Wei L, Zuo Y, Ding Y, et al. Security Identifier Randomization: A Method to Prevent Kernel Privilege-Escalation Attacks[C]. 2016 30th International Conference on Advanced Information Networking and Applications Workshops (WAINA). IEEE, 2016: 838-842.

DOI: 10.1051/itmconf/20171205011

Motion Learning Based on Bayesian Program Learning

Meng-Zhen CHENG, Quan-Hua TANG, Long-Jun HUANG

School of Software,Jiangxi Normal University,Jiangxi, China
e-mail: 1538801696@qq.com,593913588@qq.com,huanglong98614@163.com

Abstract:The concept of virtual human has been highly anticipated since the 1980s. By using computer technology, Huma n motion simulation could generate authentic visual effect, which could cheat human eyes visually. Bayesian Program Learning train one or few motion data,generate new motion data by decomposing and combining.And the generated motion will be more realistic and natural than the traditional one.In this paper, Motion learning based on Bayesian program learning allows us to quickly generate new motion data, reduce workload, improve work efficiency, reduce the cost of motion capture, and improve the reusability of data.

1 Introduction

In 2009, the special effects of the movie-Avatar caused a burst of viewing boom. The vivid Na'vi people, all kinds of creatures, magnificent scenes in the movie all show the magic of computer animation technology. Among them, the movements of Na'vi people refers to the movements of actors and completes by using the late processing simulation through computer technology. All of these are done through computer graphics technology, the usage of this technology has a lot of work, such as Toy Story Mania, Cars, Spiderman and so on. These films have many effects, such as toys and cars could walking, jumping and moving, express emotions and so on. With the de-velopment of computer animation, it is a challenge that how to become more natural to liquidate the body posture and varieties of movements. The Na'vi is a virtual pers-on, human motion simulation is a technology that compu-ter could build a virtual person to simulate human behavi-or in a natural world.

Machine learning[1] is the way your computer using experience to optimize system performance, it is an important branch of artificial intelligence. Machine learning is the study of how to make the computer simulation process of human learning knowledge, innovation and reconstruction of the existing knowledge in order to improve the system's ability to deal with problems ,we also call it optimize performance. Artificial neural network and Bayesian learning are the focus of research in machine learning, but also the two field of in-depth study.

Bayesian Learning was derived from the proof of a special case of the British mathematician, Thomas, in 1763, in the case of a book on the theorem of the author of the book of letters by the author of the book. Bayesian learning is one of the main algorithms to solve machine learning problems. Bayesian learning provides a solution for the study of uncertain expression, while but the real world and mankind itself have their own uncertain problems, artificial intelligence solves how to answer these uncertainties, thus the Bayesian learning show the advantages compared to other algorithms. Algorithm of Bayesian learning compared to other learning algorithms, better able to ignore the impact of the error data, and can handle incomplete data.[2-4]

Bayesian program learning[5] been presented in the study of human level concept learning based on Bayesian programming learning by Brenden M. Lake et al from three schools in North America,breaking the barriers that the traditional machine learning to thousands of examples to train.It marks a big step in the field of machine learning.In this paper, based on the Bayesian program learning method, only one or few examples can be used to make the virtual person learn the abstract concept of motion, so as to achieve the effect of simulation, and even generate additional examples.

2 Related Notion

2.1 Human model

Human motion simulation is the use of computer simulation of virtual human behavior in the natural world of technology, in order to make the virtual human action realistic, it is necessary to fully simulate the human bones, muscles and other elements. Therefore, there are many models to simulate human motion, such as surface model, solid model, multilevel model and rod like model (skeletal model). No matter what kind of model is the study of the geometric characteristics of the human body and the use of geometric characteristics to establish the model of the response characteristics. Because of this study is using the method of Bayesian learning process of learning and human motion simulation, and the main elements to support human motion is the bones and muscles are attached to the bones, with the skeletal motion and change the form of the human motion, learning is the learning of the movement of the human skeleton, so this article uses stick to show the human motion model[6].

Stick Model (Skeleton Model). The rod model is composed of joints and stick to a simple graphical representation of the human body model, through joint torsion and mobile graphics bar to show the movement of the human body, its complexity to be decided by the joint. This model of data storage is small, easy to edit, simple a variety of body posture, but because of rod like graphics, only describe the skeletal structure, this model can represent human motion when reverse action, realistic vision of the weak.[7]

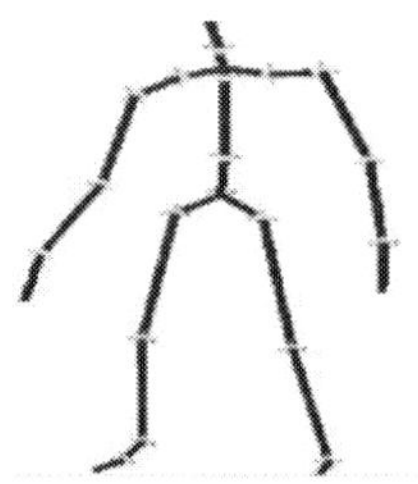

Figure 1. stick model (skeleton model)

2.2 human motion data

The human body is composed of 206 bones, 639 muscle tissue composition, the structure is very complex, and the movement of the human body is actually human bones and muscles, so the human motion description is very complicated, a slight movement is likely to involve multiple bone and muscle tissue movement. How to simulate the movement of the human body more realistic and smoothly becomes a great challenge to the research of virtual human. Motion capture technology is the process of recording the human motion by the sensor, and converting it into the data information of human motion. Because this method can effectively capture the real human motion data, mapping the motion of virtual human is a real human motion, so the effect of real human motion is very similar, and this technique can simulate complex movements.

This study is based on the motion capture, however, due to the high cost of motion capture data, this paper use Biovision company to carry on the research of human motion data to research the BVH file format.Finally, the generated data is stored in BVH format.

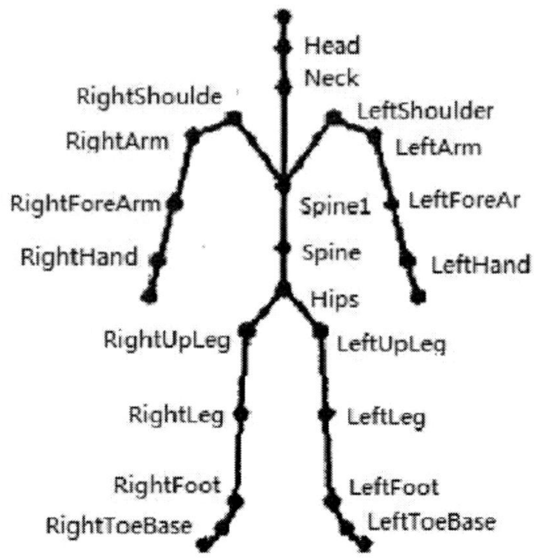

Figure2. Human skeleton structure model

2.3 Bayesian program learning

In 2004, Lebeltel et al. Proposed the concept of Bayesian program for solving the problem of robot uncertainty for the first time.This concept is based on Bayesian reasoning and Bayesian learning, the aim is to calculate the P(Y|X, Data, Knowledge), is the use of a simple target concept (things to do), the motion data and motion data have been inferred to infer the motion data of the next step, we get the target concept of motion data.The core idea of the Bayesian program is to convert the target into a number of conditional probability distributions function using the Bayesian's law and the chain rule.The Bayesian program can reaffirm many of the classical probability models such as Bayesian Network (BN), Hidden Markov Model (HMM), and so on.The main goal of the Bayesian program is to effectively control the robot to complete a complex action, greatly improving the performance of the robot work for the robot to contribute more intelligence to a force. And after the in-depth study of experts and scholars in each country, people on the Bayesian program of artificial intelligence learning methods and further research results.

In 2015, Brenden.M.Lake et al. Proposed a Bayesian learning procedure based on the concept of human level--Bayesian Program learning, the robot uses 50 character sample automatic analysis reasoning wrote a number of new characters, in which the robot learn to draw inferences and the like.And these new characters passed the Turing test, people can not distinguish people write and the robot write from the many characters.Previous machine learning methods require a large amount of sample data to support, but people does not need to learn a lot of learning samples, people can learn from a few or even a sample of knowledge.Brenden and others believe that a man has such a strong learning ability is because the human is able to analyze things, extract feature rich and representative from a single object, and use these features to construct other examples,then,this knowledge is acquired.Bayesian learning to simplify the concept of rich things, and uses probabilistic semantics to deal with the noise and capture the abstraction of the accidental structure, and then construct a procedure under the Bayesian criterion. In this paper, we will study the simulation of human motion by means of Bayesian programming,make a virtual person able to simulate a new action through one or more actions..

3 Motion learning

3.1 Technology Roadmap

Motion learning based on Bayesian program learning using the method of Bayesian program learning to learn the human motion data, and generate new motion data.The Bayesian program learning framework enables virtual humans to learn abstract concepts from a few or even a sample, as humans do, and to learn other instances independently from these abstract concepts.The following is the sequence diagram of motion learning.

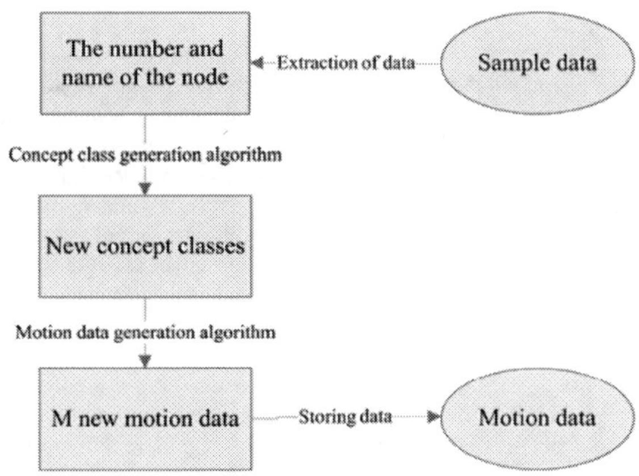

Figure3.Sequence diagram of motor learning

3.2 Concept class generation algorithm

In the motion learning based on Bayesian program learning, the input motion data is analyzed and reorganized to obtain the new concept class Ψ .After analysis, virtual human will be divided into 5 parts, namely the left hand, right hand, the left leg, right leg and spine; according to the storage of human skeletal structure in the BVH file that the first joint point of each part is the parent node of the lower joint. Therefore, it is necessary to study the relationship between the first joint and the root node of each component.

Ψ={H， S， R} is composed of the location of the root node, the 5 parts S={S1， S2， ...， S5}, and the location relationship between them and the root node R={R1 ， R2， ...， R5}.

$$P(\psi) = P(H)\prod_{i=1}^{5} P(S_i)P(R_i \mid S_1,\dots,S_{i-1}) \quad (1)$$

The Si is composed of N joint {si1， si2， ...， sin}, sij={xij， yij， zij}, zij is the name of the joint; yij is the maximum rotation angle of each joint point, and with the parent node location close relationship; xij is the joint point around the X axis and Y axis, Z axis angle.

$$P(Si) = \prod_{j=1}^{n} P(x_{ij} \mid z_{ij})P(y_{ij} \mid z_{ij}) \quad (2)$$

Among them, P （ xij|zij ） accord with Gauss distribution, P（yij|zij）accord with Gamma distribution.

Algorithm description:

Function GenerateType：
{
for i = 1 to 5 do //Analysis of virtual human 5 parts
Get the joint n and z for the first i parts
Get parts Si
Through the empirical analysis of the sample data, calculate the relationship Ri between the part Si and the root node
end for
New concept class Ψ={H， S， R}
}

After the calculation of the concept class generation algorithm, a new concept class Ψ is obtained. This concept class is a study of the existing concepts, abstracting the existing sample data, and obtaining the most empirical and probabilistic calculation. The appropriate one, will be extracted, the combination, and obtained.But this is only the extraction of abstract concepts, and did not generate new sports data, the following will be a detailed description of the generation of motion data.

3.3 Motion data generation algorithm

Get a new concept class, and then generate a new sports data is simple, and everyone's movement is basically similar,the difference is that each person's small habits will lead to different forms of motion and amplitude.For the human body movement simulation is the joint position and rotation angle of the different.As long as the new concept of the class to add a number of motion variables, that is, the joint point of the position and rotation angle to add some noise, it can produce a number of new motion, that is, a number of motion data frames.

Therefore, after getting a new concept class, the new motion data is generated by the following steps:

The initial position of each part of the human body is sampled in the motion data.Li(m) is obtained by calculating the joint distribution of parts S1(m), ..., Si-1(m) and Ri(m) that obtained by the sampling of the position relationship between the first joint point of each part and the root node.

$$L_i^{(m)} = P(L_i^{(m)} \mid R_i^{(m)}, S_1^{(m)}, ..., S_{i-1}^{(m)}) \quad (3)$$

Among them, Ri (m) through clustering the Ri of each part in the sample, to add noise points to the new concept of the class Ri.

二、Scaling the rotation angle of each joint point in the component,the rotation angle of each joint node in the sample data and the position relation of the parent node are clustered respectively,adding the noise points to the angle of rotation xij and the location relationship with the parent node yij.

$$x_{ij}^{(m)} = P(x_{ij}^{(m)} \mid x_{ij}) \quad (5)$$

$$y_{ij}^{(m)} = P(y_{ij}^{(m)} \mid y_{ij}) \quad (6)$$

三、Through the above two steps, Li(m),xij(m) and yij(m)constitute a deterministic function of F, each Si (m) is a deterministic function.Thus,obtained m new component S(m)={S1(m), S2(m), ..., S5(m)} with different trajectories and shapes.

$$S_i^{(m)} = f(L_i^{(m)}, x_{ij}^{(m)}, y_{ij}^{(m)}) \quad (7)$$

Algorithm description:

```
Function GenerateData:
{
  for i = 1 to 5 do
        Calculate the distance with Ri and save it to r[]
     end for
   Divide the smallest of r [] to Ri(m)
   Determine m starting positions Li (m)
     for j = 1 to n do //n is the total number of joints

   Calculate the nearest xij(m) with xij distance,calculate the nearest yij(m)with yij distance
     end for
   Get the data of each component Si(m)
  end for
  NDatas get new motion data NDatas
}
```

4 Experimental and Evaluation

The experimental data of the BVH format file as input, the motion data in each frame for analysis, analysis of the components as shown in the following figure:

Figure4.Each part

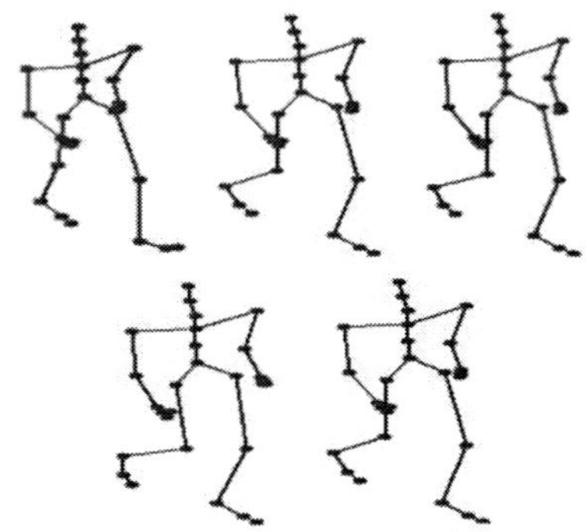

Figure5. New motion

Using Matlab to map the acquired motion data to a virtual person, the virtual human action is obtained. First, the action is compared with the real movement of human beings, and the virtual human movement is evaluated from the perspective of the authenticity of the virtual human m-ovement and the nature.Virtual human action is more natural, in line with the rules of human m-ovement, more real.Then, the new motion data obtained by the experiment was fitted with the bvh format data captured by Biovision's motion,and the similarity was 79.64%.From the above two points, we can know that the algorithm gen-erated by the algorithm is more consistent with the real human movement data, but in the futureresearch there is still much room for improvement.

Conclusion

This article provides an effective way to learn about sports. In this paper, our study includes two algorithms: concept class generation algorithm, motion data generation algorithm. After research, the generated data and motion capture data similarity is higher, but in the future work study will be further research..

Conclusion

This work was supported by the Science and Technology Research Project of Jiangxi Provincial Department of Education (GJJ13232).

References

[1] Tom M. Mitchell .Machine Learning [M].Machinery Industry Press,2004.
[2] Lebeltel O,Bessière P,Diard J,et al.Bayesian robot programming[J].Autonomous Robots, 2004,16(1): 49-79.
[3] Diard J,Bessiere P,Mazer E.A survey of probabilistic models using the bayesian programming methodology as a unifying framework[C].2003.
[4] Russell S,Norvig P. Artificial intelligence: a modern approach[J].1995.
[5] Brenden M.Lake,Ruslan Salakhutdinov,Joshua B.Tenenbaum.Human-level concept learning through probabilistic program induction. Science,2015,11: 1332-1338.
[6] Fua P. Plänkers R,Thalmann D.Realistic Human Body Modeling[C].In Fifth International Symp- osium on the 3-D Analysis of Human Movement, Chattanooga, TN, 1998, 5(1): 360~372.
[7] Thalmann D.Human Modelling and Animation[R].Eurographics'93 State-of-the-Art Reports, Chapter 7,2004, 18(2): 49-54.

Ship Detection and Classification on Optical Remote Sensing Images Using Deep Learning

Ying LIU [1], Hong-Yuan CUI [1], Zheng KUANG [1], Guo-Qing LI [1]

[1] *School of Computer and Control Engineering, University of Chinese Academy of Sciences, UCAS ,Beijing, China;*
Beijing University of Posts and Telecommunication, BUPT,Beijing, China;
Institute of Remote Sensing and Digital Earth Chinese Academy of Sciences, CAS,Beijing, China
yingliu@ucas.ac.cn, hongyuancui@163.com,kuangzheng2013212987@bupt.edu.cn, ligq@radi.ac.cn

Abstract—Ship detection and classification is critical for national maritime security and national defense. Although some SAR (Synthetic Aperture Radar) image-based ship detection approaches have been proposed and used, they are not able to satisfy the requirement of real-world applications as the number of SAR sensors is limited, the resolution is low, and the revisit cycle is long. As massive optical remote sensing images of high resolution are available, ship detection and classification on theses images is becoming a promising technique, and has attracted great attention on applications including maritime security and traffic control. Some digital image processing methods have been proposed to detect ships in optical remote sensing images, but most of them face difficulty in terms of accuracy, performance and complexity. Recently, an autoencoder-based deep neural network with extreme learning machine was proposed, but it cannot meet the requirement of real-world applications as it only works with simple and small-scaled data sets. Therefore, in this paper, we propose a novel ship detection and classification approach which utilizes deep convolutional neural network (CNN) as the ship classifier. The performance of our proposed ship detection and classification approach was evaluated on a set of images downloaded from Google Earth at the resolution 0.5m. 99% detection accuracy and 95% classification accuracy were achieved. In model training, 75× speedup is achieved on 1 Nvidia Titanx GPU.

1. Introduction

Ship detection and classification in remote sensing images is of vital importance for maritime security and other applications, e.g., traffic surveillance, protection against illegal fisheries and sea pollution monitoring. With the increasing volume of satellite image data, automatic ship detection and classification from remote sensing images is a crucial application for both military and civilian fields. However, the detection systems are faced with the need to process massive amounts of incoming data and the requirement of nearly real-time capacity of reaction. Many valuable studies have been carried out in this field, but these typical algorithms are usually effective only for common image analysis, not for the task of ship detection and classification in remote sensing images which often contains vast data and many background noises. Most of the conventional methods face difficulty in accuracy, performance and complexity.

In recent years, deep learning, or deep neural network has shown great promise in many practical applications. State-of-the-art performance has been reported in several domains, ranging from speech recognition [1], visual object recognition [2] to text processing [3]. In fact, it could be argued that the network's learning ability has been a crucial factor in the recent success of pattern recognition applications. It has also been observed that increasing the scale of deep learning with respect to the number of training examples or the number of model parameters, or both, can drastically improve ultimate classification accuracy [2]. Subsequently, the use of GPUs [1,2,4] is a significant advance in recent years that makes the training of modestly sized deep networks practical. Since the early work of ship detection and classification, it has been known that the variability and the richness of image data make it almost impossible to build an accurate detection and classification system entirely by hand.

In terms of the sparseness of ship distribution on the sea, regions of ship targets are small parts in remote sensing images. In this paper, ship candidates are coarsely extracted by image segmentation methods first, then actual ships are detected from all the ship candidates and finally classified into 10 different ship classes by deep learning. The proposed method consists of preprocessing (ship candidates extraction), ship detection and ship classification model training. The specific contributions of this paper are as follows: 1) Cohen-Daubechies-Feauveau 9/7 (CDF 9/7) wavelet coefficients were extracted from the raw images and then ship candidates were extracted from the LL subband by conducting image enhancement, target-background segmentation and ship locating based on shape criteria; 2) a CNN model was implemented for ship detection and 99% accuracy was achieved; 3) for ship classification, using the proposed model, 95% accuracy was achieved; 4) up to 75× speedup was achieved on a server with a GTX Titanx GPU. The flow diagram of the proposed ship detection and classification approach is shown in Figure 1.

The reminder of this paper is organized as follows. Section II overviews the related work about this research; section III describes the processing of ship candidates extraction; section IV explains our proposed CNN model for ship detection and classification; section V demonstrates the experiments and analysis about the results; section VI conducts this paper.

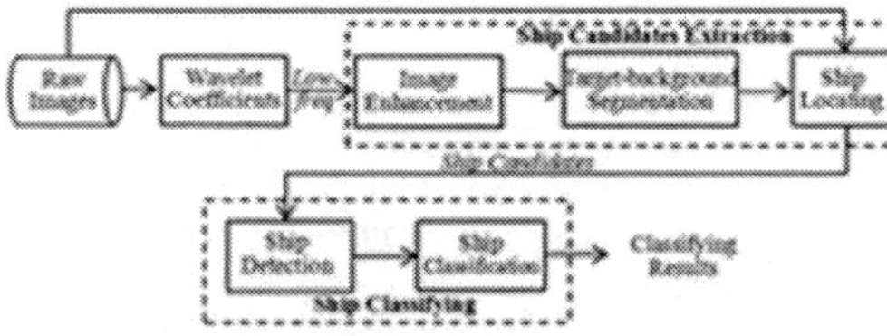

Figure 1. Flow diagram of the proposed ship detection and Classification approach.

2. Related Work

As SAR images have advantages which mainly include relatively little influence of weather and time, ship detection in SAR images has extensively been studied [5~9]. The most common algorithms of ship detection are based on a constant false-alarm rate (CFAR) detector with a certain SAR images' background distribution such as Gauss distribution [6], k-distribution and Gamma distribution [8] or other combination [9]. Han and Chong [5] took a brief review of ship detection algorithms in polarimetric SAR images. Greidanus et al. [7] compared the performance of eight ship detection systems based on spaceborne systems by running a benchmark test on RADARSAT images of various modes. However, ship detection based on SAR has limitations. First, with a limited number of SAR satellites, the revisit cycle is relatively long and it cannot meet the needs of the application of real-time ship monitoring. Second, the resolution of most satellite SAR images is often not high enough to extract detailed ship information.

For ship detection and classification on optical images, traditional methods were widely studied [10~13]. Zhu [10] and Antelo et al. [11] extracted manually designed features from images such as shapes, textures and physical properties while Chen [12] and Wang [13] exploited Dynamic Bayesian Network to classify different kinds of ships, however, they cannot overcome the images' variability and big volume problems. Recently, as the emergence of deep learning architectures, an autoencoder-based deep neural network combined with extreme learning machine was proposed [14] and it outperformed some other methods in detection accuracy. Tang [14] used SPOT-5 spaceborne optical images for ship detecting to verify this idea and achieved relatively satisfying results. However, it has some limitations: 1) as the image resolution is 5m, the extracted features are good enough to detect ships from waves, clouds and islands. But higher resolution is needed for recognizing different types of ships and the model should be expanded to improve its feature-representing ability which will need much more

computation; 2) as autoencoder model uses full connection totally which leads to a large number of nodes and large computation; 3) autoencoder-based deep learning has no concept of local features, so it cannot extract enough detail features when the model is expanded; 4) research indicates that autoencoder-based deep learning is more appropriate for speech recognition [18], hand-writing recognition [19] and texture classification [20]. It only works with simple image data set, so cannot satisfy the requirement of real-world applications.

3. Ship Candidates Extraction

Ship candidates extraction is the first step of our proposed method which preprocesses the raw images and extracts all ship candidates. First of all, CDF 9/7 wavelet coefficients are extracted from images. Instead of reducing processing time by passively cutting an image into tiles or scaling to a low-resolution version, extracting wavelet features can impressively increase the detection efficiency. After a 2-D discrete wavelet transform (DWT), the original image is decomposed into a low-frequency subband (denoted as LL) and horizontal/vertical/diagonal high-frequency subbands (denoted as LH, HL, and HH). The wavelet coefficients in different subbands tend to reflect different properties of the original image. Generally speaking, the low frequency contains most of the global information, while the high frequency represents local or detail information. Ship candidates are extracted from the low-frequency subband LL by conducting image enhancement, target-background segmentation and shape criteria-based ship locating.

3.1 Image Enhancement

In image enhancement, in order to remove uneven illumination, a morphological operator, i.e., top-hat transform (THT), is used for ship candidates extraction and background suppression. As ships are usually brighter than their surroundings, the white THT is employed in the proposed work [shown in Figure 2(a)]. The mathematical definition of white THT is as follows [14]:

$$Tw(f) = f - f \circ b \quad (1)$$

where f is the input LL coefficients of the original image, $\circ$ denotes opening operation, and Tw is the enhanced image. In the simulations, b is set as a circular structuring element with a radius of 12.

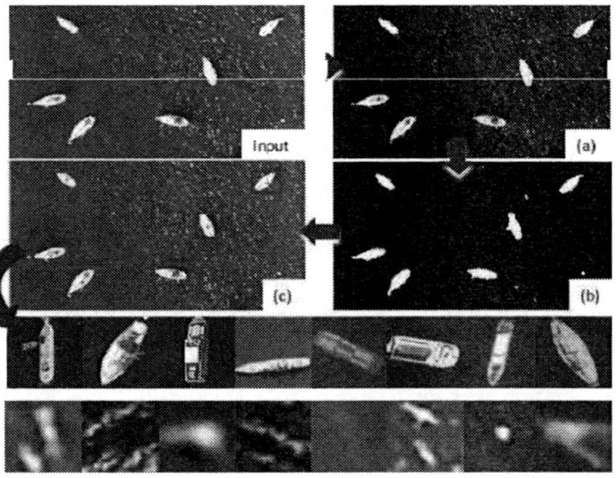

Figure 2. The process of ship candidates extracting.

3.2 Target-Background Segmentation

In target-background segmentation, each input image is binarized by the Otsu algorithm [15]. Otsu is a widely used method to automatically perform clustering-based image thresholding. The algorithm assumes that the image contains two classes of pixels following bi-modal histogram (foreground pixels and background pixels), then it calculates the optimum threshold to separate the two classes so that their combined spread (intra-class variance) is minimal and their inter-class variance is maximal. After that, connected regions are labeled. As the binarized image usually remains small holes in the sea waves or clouds, then the median filtering, morphology dilation and erosion (circular structuring element with a radius of three) are applied to fill the isolated holes. Finally, the masks of sea waves, clouds, islands and ship candidates are segmented [shown in Figure 2(b)]. In the following, ship candidates will be further extracted by using the unique shape properties of ships.

3.3 Ship Locating

In ship locating, the ship candidates are further extracted by using the unique shape properties of ships, including the area, the major minor axis ratio and the compactness [14]. Area equals the number of pixels in the corresponding connected region. Area is used to cut off the clouds, sea waves and other obviously large/small false targets. Major minor axis ratio is defined as

$$R_{ls} = \frac{L_{axisL}}{L_{axisS}} \quad (2)$$

where L_{axisL} and L_{axisS} are the length of long and short axes of the bounding rectangle, respectively. Compactness measures the degree of circular similarity, and it is defined as

$$Compactness = \frac{Perimeter^2}{Area} \quad (3)$$

By using these shape criteria, we can obtain the coarse locations of ship candidates [shown in Figure 2(c)].

In the experiments, the size of the testing images is about 1000×1000 (in pixels) with resolution 0.5m. The size of ship candidates is supported to be larger than 20 in pixels. In this case, the regions with area smaller than 20 would be removed. Moreover, as the long axis of ship should be longer than the minor axis, the major minor axis ratio is selected as 1.2. Compactness is set as 80 to exclude the regions which are obviously irregular. Note that some of the pseudo-targets may be included in the extracted regions; however, they can be removed in the process of ship detection by CNN in Section Ⅳ.

4. Ship Detection and Classification by CNN

Ship detection by deep learning is the next step of our proposed method. It detects actual ships from all the ship candidates and then the actual ships are classified into different types by CNN.

The state-of-the-art ship detection approaches extract features using feature operators or feature descriptors, then use traditional machine learning methods for detection. Features extracted by these methods generally have some fundamental limitations in practical applications. For example, they may have poor performances when the images are corrupted by blur, distortion, or illumination which commonly exist in remote sensing images. So the processed images may contain various pseudo-targets, e.g., islands, clouds, sea waves, etc. Traditional machine learning algorithms, e.g., support vector machine (SVM), may have difficulties in efficiently handling such highly varying inputs. When dealing with highly variant conditions, the

 DOI: 10.1051/itmconf/20171205012

computation is exponentially increased. Relatively, automatically learned features by deep learning from images can help to tackle these issues. Recent works have shown that the features extracted by deep learning outperform those manually designed ones on target detection.

4.1Convolutional Neural Networks

CNN is a kind of deep learning networks and it combines three architectural ideas to ensure some degree of shift, scale and distortion invariance: local receptive fields, shared weights and spatial or temporal sub-sampling. With local receptive fields, neurons can extract elementary visual features such as oriented edges, end-points and corners. These features are then combined by the subsequent layers in order to detect higher-order features. Units in a layer are organized in planes within which all the units share the same set of weights. The set of outputs of the units in such a plane is called a feature map. Units in a feature map are all constrained to perform the same operation on different parts of the image. A complete convolutional layer is composed of several feature maps (with different weight vectors), so that multiple features can be extracted from each location. An implementation of a feature map is equivalent to a convolution, followed by an additive bias and squashing function, hence the name convolutional neuron networks.

Once a feature has been detected, its exact location becomes less important. Only its approximate position relative to other features is relevant. Not only are the precise positions of each of those features irrelevant to identify the pattern, it is potentially harmful because the positions are likely to vary for different instances. A simple way to reduce the precision with which the positions of distinctive features are encoded in a feature map is to reduce the spatial resolution of the feature map. This can be achieved with the so-called pooling layers (or sub-sampling layers) which perform a local averaging or maximizing and a sub-sampling, reducing the resolution of the feature map, and reducing the sensitivity of the output to shifts and distortions. Successive layers of convolution and sub-sampling are typically alternated.

Since all the weights are learned with back-propagation, CNNs can be seen as synthesizing their own feature extractors. The weight-sharing technique can reduce the number of free parameters, thereby reducing the gap between test error and training error.

4.2Training for Ship Detection and Classification

In training, firstly, we solve a two-class (ship and non-ship) classification problem. We constructed a CNN consisting of four convolutional, three max-pooling and a fully-connection layer with a final 2-way softmax classifier for ship detection. Its structure is shown in Figure 3, where 64×64 is the size (in pixels) of each input image with RGB three channels, 5×5, 5×5, 3×3 and 3×3 are the sizes of convolution kernels, 30×30, 13×13 ,11×11 and 4×4 are the sizes of feature maps in each convolutional layer, 64, 128, 256 and 384 are the numbers of feature maps in each convolutional layer, 512 is the number of output units of fully-connection layer and the number '2' at the right end is for the 2-way softmax classifier in detection. After ship detection, all the actual ships are detected. To classify all the ships into 10 different types, this model is used for ship classification by changing the number '2' to '10' at the right end.

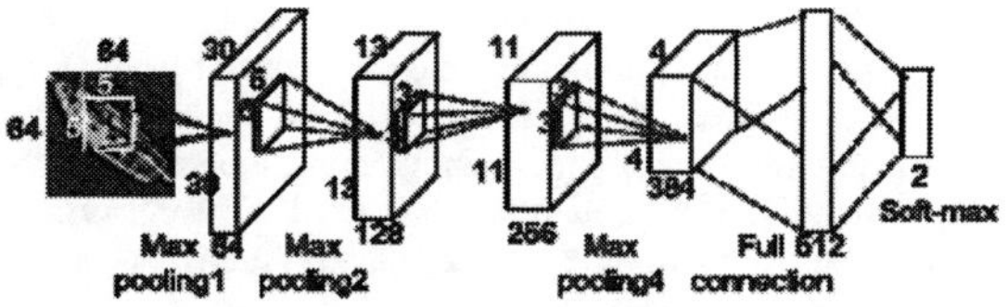

Figure 3. Our proposed CNN model.

The standard way to model a neuron's output f as a function of its input x is with $f(x) = \tanh(x)$ or $f(x) = (1+e^{-x})^{-1}$. In terms of training time with stochastic gradient descent, these saturating nonlinearities are much slower than the non-saturating nonlinearity $f(x) = \max(0, x)$. Following Nair and Hinton [16], we refer to neurons with this nonlinearity as Rectified Linear Units (ReLUs). Deep CNNs with ReLUs train several times faster than their equivalents with tanh units.

In order to reduce test errors, combining the predictions of many different models is a very successful way. But it appears to be too expensive for big neural networks. However, there is a very efficient version of model combination that only costs about a factor of two in training. The recently introduced technique, called 'dropout' [17], works by setting the output of each hidden neuron to zero with probability 0.5. The neurons which are 'dropped out' in this way do not contribute to the forward pass and do not participate in back-propagation. So every time an input is presented, the neural network samples a different architecture, but all these architectures share weights. At test time, we use all the neurons but multiply their outputs by 0.5, which is a reasonable approximation to taking the geometric mean of the predictive distributions produced by the exponentially-many dropout networks. Without dropout, our network exhibits substantial overfitting. Dropout roughly doubles the number of iterations required to converge.

For the other configurations of the network model, we trained our models using stochastic gradient descent with a batch size of 20 examples, momentum of 0.9, an equal learning rate 0.001 for all layers and weight decay of 0.0005.

5. Experiments

5.1 Platform Description

We conducted the training on a server with Intel Core i5-4460 CPU @3.20GHz, 8.00GB RAM and GTX TitanX card. Matlab2014a and cuda 7.0 were used.

5.2 Data Sets

Images shown in Figure 4(1) were downloaded from Google Earth and after ship candidates extraction, a dataset consisting 1200 images (containing ships, clouds, sea waves and islands) was obtained and used for performance evaluation each in 64 × 64 pixels, 4/5 used for network training and 1/5 for testing.

In order to be more convincing, another dataset shown in Figure 4(2), consisting 1500 images (10 categories of ships) each in 256 × 64 pixels with higher resolution was also downloaded and used for performance evaluation.

(1) (2)

Figure 4. Datasets.

5.3 Experiment and Results

An equal learning rate 0.001 is used for all layers, meanwhile, values of the batch size, momentum and weight decay are set as 20, 0.9, 0.0005 correspondingly. 'Dropout' regularization method is used to reduce over fitting in fully-connected layers. This depth of the model seems to be important: we found that removing any convolutional layer resulted in inferior performance. Eventually, 99% detection accuracy and 92% classification accuracy were achieved in dataset (1), which is comparable with some state-of-the-art algorithms, such as SVM. In dataset (2), even higher classification accuracy 95% was achieved, which is closely related to the higher spatial resolution. Classifying error rate of each type of ship by CNN is shown in TABLE Ⅰ. Seventy-five times (75×) speedup was achieved on a GTX TitanX card.

TABLE I. CLASSIFYING ERROR RATE OF EACH TYPE OF SHIP BY CNN ON DATASET (2)

Ship class	C0	C1	C2	C3	C4	C5	C6	C7	C8	C9
Error rate	13%	6.5%	3.3%	10%	10%	6.5%	3.3%	0%	3.3%	3.3 %

As a comparison, Support Vector Machine (SVM) and Neural Network (NN) were used for classification on dataset (2), and achieved 87% and 81% accuracy respectively shown in TABLE Ⅱ.

TABLE II. CLASSIFYING ACCURACY ON DATASET (2)

Method	CNN	SVM	Neural Network
Accuracy	95%	87%	81%

6. Conclusion

Ship detection and classification is a widely studied topic both in civilian and military applications. Environmental complexity of marine makes it hard to extract ships from remote sensing optical images both effectively and efficiently. In this paper, we proposed a ship detection and classification method on remote sensing optical images. Firstly, CDF 9/7 wavelet coefficients were extracted from the raw images and the LL subband was used in ship candidates extraction to reduce the processing time. Then ship candidates are extracted by conducting image enhancement, target-background segmentation and ship locating based on shape criteria. Note that there are still nonship targets in the ship candidates, so in the next step a CNN was trained to detect actual ships from all candidates. Finally, using the CNN model, we classified all the actual ships into different ships. The model was trained on remote sensing images downloaded from Google Earth. Eventually, 99% detection accuracy and 95% classification accuracy were achieved, which is comparable with some state-of-the-art algorithms. Experiments showed that CNN, as a deep neural network is a good model for automatically feature learning and extraction. And up to 75 × speedup was achieved on a server with a GTX TitanX GPU which indicates its potential for real-time processing.

References

[1] G. Dahl, D. Yu, L. Deng, and A. Acero, "Context-dependent Pre-trained Deep Neural Networks for Large Vocabulary Speech Recognition," IEEE Transactions on Audio Speech & Language Processing, vol. 20, Jan. 2012, pp. 30-42, doi: 10.1109/TASL.2011.2134090.

[2] D. C. Ciresan, U. Meier, L. M. Gambardella, and J. Schmidhuber, "Deep Big Simple Neural Nets Excel on Handwritten Digit Recognition," CoRR, vol. 22, Nov. 2010, pp. 3207-3220, doi: 10.1162/NECO_a_00052.

[3] R. Collobert and J.Weston, "A Unified Architecture for Natural Language Processing: Deep Neural Networks with Multitask Learning," International Conference on Machine learning (ICML 08), ACM press, Jul. 2008, pp. 160-167, doi: 10.1145/1390156.1390177.

[4] R. Raina, A. Madhavan, and A. Y. Ng, "Large-scale Deep Unsupervised Learning Using Graphics Processors," International Conference on Machine Learning (ICML 09), ACM press, Jun. 2009, pp. 873-880, doi: 10.1145/1553374.1553486.

[5] Z. Y. Han and J. S. Chong, "A Review of Ship Detection Algorithms in Polarimetric SAR Images," International Conference on Signal Processing (ICSP 04), IEEE press, vol. 3, Sept. 2004, pp. 2155-2158, doi: 10.1109/ICOSP.2004.1442203.

[6] K. Eldhuset, "An Automatic Ship and Ship Wake Detection System for Spaceborne SAR Images in Coastal Regions," IEEE Transaction on Geoscience and Remote Sensing, vol. 34, Jul. 1996, pp. 1010-1019, doi: 10.1109/36.508418.

[7] H. Greidanus, P. Clayton, N. Suzuki, and P. Vachon, "Benchmarking Operational SAR Ship Detection," International Geoscience and Remote Sensing Symposium (IGARSS 04), IEEE press, vol. 6, Dec. 2004, pp. 4215-4218, doi: 10.1109/IGARSS.2004.1370065.

[8] C. C. Wackerman, K. S. Friedman, and X. Li, "Automatic Detection of Ships in RADARSAT-1 SAR Imagery," Canadian Journal of Remote Sensing, vol. 27, Jul. 2014, pp. 568-577, doi: 10.1080/07038992.2001.10854896.

[9] D. J. Crisp, "The State of the Art in Ship Detection in Synthetic Aperture Radar Imagery," Organic Letters, vol. 35, May 2004, pp. 2165-2168.

[10] C. Zhu, H. Zhou, R. Wang and J. Guo, "A Novel Hierarchical Method of Ship Detection from Spaceborne Optical Image Based on Shape and Texture Features," IEEE Transactions on Geoscience and Remote Sensing, vol. 48, Sept. 2010, pp. 3446-3456, doi: 10.1109/TGRS.2010.2046330.

[11] J. Antelo, G. Ambrosio, and C. Galindo, "Ship Detection and Recognition in High-resolution Satellite Images," International Geoscience and Remote Sensing Symposium (IGARSS 09), IEEE press, vol. 4, Feb. 2010, pp. 514-517, doi: 10.1109/IGARSS.2009.5417426.

[12] H. Chen and X. Gao, "Ship Recognition based on Improved Forwards-backwards Algorithm," International Conference on Fuzzy Systems and Knowledge Discovery (FSKD 09), IEEE press, vol. 5, Dec. 2009, pp. 509-513, doi: 10.1109/FSKD.2009.336.

[13] Q. Wang, X. Gao, and D. Chen, "Pattern Recognition for Ship Based on Bayesian Networks," International Conference on Fuzzy Systems and Knowledge Discovery (FSKD 07), IEEE press, vol. 4, Aug. 2007, pp. 684-688, doi: 10.1109/FSKD.2007.447.

[14] J. Tang, C. Deng, G.H. Huang, and B. Zhao, "Compressed-Domain Ship Detection on Spaceborne Optical Image Using Deep Neural Network and Extreme Learning Machine," IEEE Transactions on Geoscience and Remote Sensing, vol. 53, Jul. 2014, pp. 1174-1183, doi: 10.1109/TGRS.2014.2335751.

[15] R. C. Gonzalez and R. E. Woods, "Digital Image Processing," 3rd ed. Knoxville: Gatesmark, 2007, pp. 742-745.

[16] V. Nair and G. E. Hinton, "Rectified Linear Units Improve Restricted Boltzmann Machines," International Conference on Machine Learning, (ICML 10), Proc icml, Jun. 2010, pp. 807-814.

[17] Krizhevsky A, Sutskever I and Hinton G, "ImageNet classification with deep convolutional neural networks," In NIPS, 2012.

[18] J. Gehring, Y. Miao, and A. Waibel, "Extracting Deep Bottleneck Features Using Stacked Auto-encoders," International Conference on Acoustics, Speech and Signal Processing (ICASSP 13), IEEE press, vol. 32, Oct. 2013, pp. 3377-3381, doi: 10.1109/ICASSP.2013.6638284.

[19] P. Vincent, H. Larochelle, and Y. Bengio, "Extracting and Composing Robust Features with Denoising Autoencoders," International Conference on Machine Learning (ICML 08), ACM press, Jul. 2008, pp. 1096-1103, doi: 10.1145/1390156.1390294.

[20] M. Chen and Z. Xu, "Marginalized Denoising Autoencoders for Domain Adaptation," International Conference on Machine Learning (ICML 12), Computer Science, 2012.

ITM Web of Conferences 12, 05013 (2017) DOI: 10.1051/itmconf/20171205013
ITA 2017

Optimised Selection of Stroke Biomarker Based on Svm and Information Theory

Xiang WANG, Wei SHI, Xiao-Cui WANG, Tao WANG

School of Electronic and Information Engineering, Beihang University, Beijing, China
wxiang@buaa.edu.cn,littlestone_buaa@163.com,wangxc1992@buaa.edu.cn,wt860122@buaa.edu.cn

Abstract—With the development of molecular biology and gene-engineering technology, gene diagnosis has been an emerging approach for modern life sciences. Biological marker, recognized as the hot topic in the molecular and gene fields, has important values in early diagnosis, malignant tumor stage, treatment and therapeutic efficacy evaluation. So far, the researcher has not found any effective way to predict and distinguish different type of stroke. In this paper, we aim to optimize stroke biomarker and figure out effective stroke detection index based on SVM (support vector machine) and information theory. Through mutual information analysis and principal component analysis to complete the selection of biomarkers and then we use SVM to verify our model. According to the testing data of patients provided by Xuanwu Hospital, we explore the significant markers of the stroke through data analysis. Our model can predict stroke well. Then discuss the effects of each biomarker on the incidence of stroke.

1 Introduction

Nowadays, stroke has become one of the most prevalent and deadly diseases worldwide, both the occurrence rate and the mortality rate remain at a high level. For instance, approximately 6.9 million people had an ischemic stroke and 3.4 million people had a hemorrhagic stroke in 2013[1]. Between 1990 and 2010 the number of strokes which occurred each year decreased by approximately 10% in the developed world and increased by 10% in the developing world [2]. In 2013, stroke was the second most frequent cause of death after coronary artery disease, accounting for 6.4 million deaths (12% of the total) [3]. Because symptoms of lung cancer resemble those of other diseases such as phthisis or pulmonary infection, it is possible to misdiagnose clinically and even to lose the optimal opportunity for the treatment. So far, conventional detecting methods includes chest CT examination, Magnetic Resonance Angiography and Digital subtraction angiography, requiring high testing costs and expensive apparatuses. And the treatment of stoke are mostly surgical operation. All these methods rely on doctors' judgment based on experiments, and are time and money consuming to some extent. This current situation calls for new technologies to realize more efficient and accurate lung cancer detection, and the development of genetic circuit meets this need.

Marker detection has become a hit idea in achieving early-stage prediction and treatment of various diseases. It is an indicator of physiological and pathological state, produced by the illness itself or by the body in response to diseased tissue's growth. Compared to the traditional detection methods which usually have considerable experimental requirements and costs, markers can not only explore the pathogenesis at the molecular level, but also have unique advantages in accurate and sensitive evaluation of early, low levels damage, which provides an early warning of the disease [4]. Many markers such as, s100 and GFAP, have been found to play important roles in the diagnosis, treatment and prognosis of stroke [5-6]. Thus, taking advantage of the genetic circuits inside cells, we can achieve more sensitive and economical marker detection with good real-time performance.

Support Vector Machine (SVM), based on the statistical theory of VC dimension theory and Structural Risk Minimization Theory (SRM), is a specifically designed machine learning algorithm for small sample data processing. SVM shows many unique advantages in solving the problem of pattern recognition of small sample, nonlinear and high dimensional data, so SVM method has been widely used in many fields including pattern recognition, regression estimation, probability density function estimation, character recognition, speech recognition, text classification, signal processing and other fields [7].

In recent year, the biomarker testing of stroke has attracted more and more attention to help make the early diagnosis of stroke or make an evaluation of relent patients.

For acute stroke, the biologist cannot find out one single, effective biomarker to predict the condition, except use multiple markers to finish the analysis. In this paper, we focus on filtering and detecting the stroke markers so as to realize efficient and accuracy detection of stoke. The former part, based on the data provided by Xuanwu Hospital, is proposed to figure out the significant markers of the stroke through data analysis. The second part is provided to analyze the importance of each marker in stroke prediction or diagnosis.

2 Screening of biomarkers

Nowadays, in order to detect the acute ischemic stroke patients, we have to perform multiple biochemical examination such as routine blood test, threshold function test and blood fat and blood sugar examination. Plenty of biomarkers are in tests, however some of these biomarkers are useless and duplicate. At the same time, there will be some overlap of information between biological markers with similar biological function, increasing the test cost. In order to detect the acute stroke quickly and effectively, we first screen the biomarkers of acute stroke.

The experiment data set contains leukocyte, APOA and other biomarkers (24 species all in all). We conducted a total of 500 sets of experimental data processing, corresponding to 500 patients sample. We treat 3/4 as a training set, and the rest as validation set in order to verify our model.

2.1 Mutual information analysis

Because the mutual information does not need to presume the distribution type of data, it can effectively capture the nonlinear correlation of variables. The relationship between stroke markers and the prevalence of stroke is not simple linear. Therefore, we use mutual information as the correlation analysis method to screen the unrelated markers [9].

The mutual information of two discrete random variables X and Y can be defined by Eq.1:

$$I(X;Y)=H(X)-H(X|Y) \\ =\sum_{y\in Y}\sum_{x\in X}p(x,y)\log(\frac{p(x,y)}{p(x)p(y)}) \quad (1)$$

Where $p(x,y)$ is the joint probability distribution function of X and Y , $p(x)$ and $p(y)$ are the marginal probability distribution functions of X and Y respectively. The mutual information satisfies $0\leq I(X;Y)\leq H(X)$ .The lower bound is reached if and only if X and Y are independent. The upper bound is achieved when Y fully determine X . Hence, the larger the mutual information, the more close the relation between X and Y is to a one-to-one relation. Treat multiple biomarkers as $x_1,x_2,x_3...$, and treat The sick(1) or not(0) as a Y variable, calculate the mutual information between X and Y , respectively, we can get the relationship between each biomarker and stroke, shown in table 1.

Through the results, we can see that Fib, Cholesterol, uric acid and several biomarkers of stroke has a high MI [10]. From the pathogenesis of stroke, these markers has a close relationship with acute stroke. The serum level of UA increasing slightly is relevant to the increasing cerebral ischemia pathological load. Fib can promote vascular smooth muscle cells, ultimately affect the blood viscosity. Cholesterol will make the blood pressure change and bring about acute stroke [11]. In order to detect the acute ischemic stroke patients accurately and efficiently, we take 0.02 as the threshold.

TABLE I. THE RESULT OF MUTUAL INFORMATION

Biomarker	***MI***	***Biomarker***	***MI***
platele	0.0241	High Density Lipoprotein	0.0137
red blood cell	0.0082	Low density lipoprotein	0.0372
leukocyte	0.0239	APOA	0.0157
blood sugar	0.0147	APOB	0.0270
Glycosylated Hemoglobin	0.0169	Fib	0.0582
HCY	0.0197	CRP	0.0207
creatinine	0.0183	anti-thyroglobulin antibody	0.0111
BUN	0.0236	TSH	0.0276
uric Acid	0.0707	T3	0.0245
triglyceride	0.0136	T4	0.0189
Cholesterol	0.0406	FT3	0.0294
		FT4	0.0110

2.2 Principal component analysis

The performance of the model is closely related to its structure, and the computational efficiency of the model is determined by the complexity of the structure [9]. There are complex relationships among the 12 high correlation biomarkers we screen out by mutual information. If all of them are adopted as inputs, it will directly increase the complexity of the model structure, and redundancy problems may be passed to the output of the model, which would cause serious influence on the detection performance.

Principal component analysis (PCA) is a statistical procedure that uses an orthogonal transformation to convert a set of observations of possibly correlated variables into a set of values of linearly uncorrelated variables called principal components [9]. This transformation is defined in such a way that the first principal component has the largest possible variance (that is, accounts for as much of the variability in the data as possible), and each succeeding component in turn has the highest variance possible under the constraint that it is orthogonal to the preceding

DOI: 10.1051/itmconf/20171205013

components [8]. The resulting vectors are uncorrelated orthogonal basis set.

High dimensional data are often transformed into lower dimensional data via the principal component analysis where coherent patterns can be detected more clearly. Thus it could decrease the complexity of the procedure and cut down the time consume.

The linear combination of the n variables $x_1, x_2 ... x_n$, can be composed of up to n integrated variables, listed in

$$\begin{cases} f_1 = a_{11}x_1 + a_{12}x_2 + ... a_{1n}x_n = \mathbf{a}_1^T\mathbf{x} \\ f_2 = a_{21}x_1 + a_{22}x_2 + ... a_{2n}x_n = \mathbf{a}_2^T\mathbf{x} \\ ... \\ f_n = a_{n1}x_1 + a_{n2}x_2 + ... a_{nn}x_n = \mathbf{a}_n^T\mathbf{x} \end{cases} \quad (2)$$

For each $i(i = 1, 2, ... n)$,it meets the conditions of standardization(3) and non-related conditions(4).

$$\mathbf{a}_i^T\mathbf{a}_i = \alpha_{i1}^2 + \alpha_{i1}^2 + ... \alpha_{in}^2 = 1 \quad (3)$$

$$\mathrm{cov}(f_i, f_j) = 0 \qquad j < i, j = 1, 2 ... n \quad (4)$$

Under the premise of satisfying these two conditions, the variance $\mathrm{var}(f_i)$ reaches the maximum, then the comprehensive variable f_i is the first i principal component of the overall x .Principal component analysis can achieve data compression, and achieve the purpose of revealing the intrinsic relationship between variables and statistical interpretation.

TABLE II. CUMULATIVE VARIANCE CONTRIBUTION OF EACH MARKER

Component number	*Eigen value*	*Cumulative variance contribution/%*
1	2.986	24.882
2	2.253	43.653
3	1.634	55.543
4	1.354	65.978
5	1.212	77.197
6	1.010	86.828
7	0.886	89.075
8	0.730	91.133
9	0.487	94.838
10	0.281	97.179
11	0.148	98.996
12	0.120	100.000

Formula (1) and (2) are used to measure the information ratio and variance contribution rate of the original independent variables contained in the principal components.

$$\gamma_i = \mathrm{var}(f_i) / \sum_{k=1}^{p} \mathrm{var}(f_k) = \lambda_i / \sum_{k=1}^{p} \lambda_k \quad (5)$$

$$\eta_m = \sum_{k=1}^{m} \gamma_k = \sum_{k=1}^{m} \lambda_k / \sum_{j=1}^{p} \lambda_j \quad (6)$$

The ETA _m determines the size should be to replace the original variables with the number of principal components, usually when the value of _m reached 70%~90%, while the rest of the main points can be omitted, thus completing the dimensionality reduction function. Table I shows the result of PCA.

2.3Total variance explained of PCA(principal component analysis)

The scree plot can be used to determine the best number of principal component. The abscissa plot in the diagram stands of principal components, and the vertical plot represents for the eigenvalue, so the steep part of the connection of principal component and eigenvalues would be the right number of principal component we take. In this study, the eigenvalue bigger than 1 is investigated and the scree plot and variance contribution ratio are both considered to determine the optimal principal component. From figure2, it can be seen that the eigenvalues of the first six principal components are larger, and the line is steep, so the first six principal components make the greatest contribution to the explanatory variables. From table 2, the first six principal components' eigenvalues are bigger than 1, and it is proper to extract six principal components and the cumulative variance contribution rate is 86.56%, which concentrates the most information of the acute cerebral stroke.

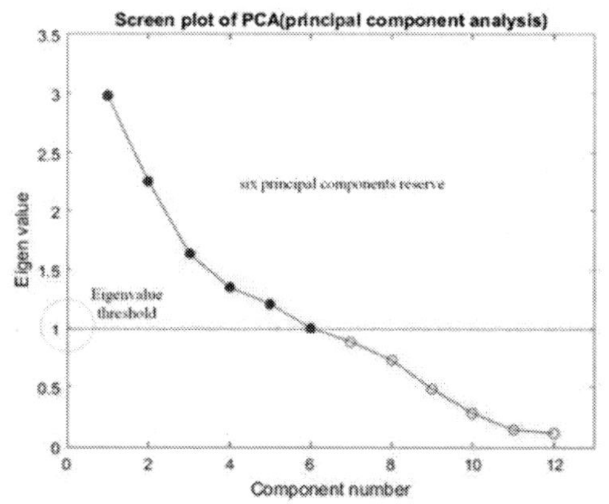

Figure 1. Screen plot of PCA (principal component analysis)

DOI: 10.1051/itmconf/20171205013

After the rotation of the load matrix of the principal component, the load factor is closer to 1 or -1, so the principal component can explain the named variable better. Table 3 shows that the first principal component f_1 mainly integrated the information of Cholesterol, low density lipoprotein and APOB. These three biomarkers are related to the body fat content, so f_1 is named as fat factor.

The second principal component f_2 mainly shows the information of CRP, and this protein value can be a good indication of acute stroke, so we name f_2 as protein factor. The third principal component f_3 mainly contains the information of T3, FT3. Both of these two are T3, but their forms are different, so f_3 is named as T3 factor. The fourth main component integrates two kinds of human metabolite, which characters the body's metabolic information, so we name it as the metabolic factor. The fifth principal component mainly reflects the content of TSH and Fib. The internal connection between the two is not clear, but they performs the same importance, so f_5 is named TSH-FIB factor. The sixth principal component mainly integrates the information of platelet and leukocyte, and the former is in the negative direction of the sixth principal component. The platelet is produced from a giant cell, and the giant cell and leukocyte are both belong to the human body cells, so we name f_6 as the cell factor.

TABLE III. ROTATED COMPONENT MATRIX OF PCA(PRINCIPAL COMPONENT ANALYSIS)

Biomarker	f_1	f_2	f_3	f_4	f_5	f_6
platele	0.170	0.237	0.420	-0.055	-0.077	-0.530
leukocyte	0.134	0.321	0.075	0.542	0.072	0.398
BUN	0.142	0.288	0.359	0.139	-0.400	-0.329
uric Acid	-0.118	-0.128	0.129	0.751	0.077	-0.081
Cholesterol	0.457	-0.304	0.171	0.029	0.030	0.152
Low density lipoprotein	0.482	-0.263	0.125	0.040	0.002	0.043
APOB	0.439	-0.252	0.138	-0.081	-0.061	0.223
Fib	0.127	0.356	0.320	-0.298	0.375	0.187
CRP	0.085	0.501	0.032	-0.017	0.290	0.254
TSH	0.178	-0.107	-0.190	0.119	0.726	-0.499
T3	-0.314	-0.252	0.512	-0.092	0.225	0.072
FT3	-0.363	-0.248	0.454	0.006	0.128	0.133

These six factors are set as the input of the next level of acute stroke screening process, and the results of the test will verify the rationality of the combination of selected biological markers.

3 Diagnosis and prediction of stroke

3.1 SVM(support vector machine) background

In order to extract enough information from the data to determine and predict the acute stroke, we use support vector machine to diagnose and predict. SVM (support vector machine) is a new kind of machine learning based on statistical learning theory, a technique for pattern recognition and classification in a variety of applications for its ability for detecting patterns in experimental databases [7]. First define the training and validation set in this paper.

The training set

$$S=\{(x_i,y_i),\ldots(x_l,y_l)\}\in(X*Y)^l \quad (7)$$

The validation set

$$T=\{(x_{l+1},y_{l+1}),\ldots(x_n,y_n)\}\in(X*Y)^{n-l} \quad (8)$$

where $x_i\in X=R^n, y_i\in Y=\{0,1\}(i=1,2,\ldots n)$. n is the total number of stroke set, l is the number of training set. And we assume R^n represents the multidimensional space of the biomarker, x_i represents each of these biomarkers. y is a label to characterize the presence or absence of disease, 0 represents no stroke, 1 represents stroke. In the distinction between hemorrhagic stroke and ischemic stroke identification process, the result set Y is $\{2,3\}$, 2 represents hemorrhagic stroke, 3 represents ischemic stroke.

In this paper, RBF is adopted as kernel function in SVM to map the input variables into the high-dimensional Hilbert space by non-linear mapping. We assume

$$K(x_i,x'_j)=e^{\left\{\frac{-\|x_i,x'_j\|^2}{2\sigma^2}\right\}} \quad (9)$$

$$K(x_i,x'_j)=\phi(x_i)\cdot\phi(x'_j) \quad (10)$$

Thus, the corresponding classification function given in

$$f_{(x)}=\operatorname{sgn}[w.\phi_{(x)}+b]=\operatorname{sgn}[\sum_{j=1}^{l}x'_i\alpha_i K(\mathbf{x}_i,\mathbf{x}'_j)+b] \quad (11)$$

Thus, nonlinear SVM is the optimization problem of the following equation.

$$\begin{cases}\min\phi_{(w)}=\frac{1}{2}(w.w)+c\sum_{j=1}^{l}\xi_i \\ s.t x'_i((w.\phi_{(x_i)})+b)\geq 1-\xi_i\geq 0,\xi_i\geq 0,i=1,2\ldots l\end{cases} \quad (12)$$

3.2Combined detection

It is important to determine the exact location and extent of the injury before and after the treatment, which is important for deciding what treatment strategies to take. For example, before a proper treatment is performed, a physician must quickly determine the type of stroke, ischemic stroke or hemorrhagic stroke, because different types of stroke treatment strategies are very different. In order to obtain the complete diagnostic information, the need for the following tests to assess the risk of stroke or stroke: CT scan magnetic resonance (MRI), magnetic resonance angiography (MRA), transcranial Doppler (TCD), carotid artery ultrasound.

At present, most of the instruments are used to diagnose the type of stroke, which can be distinguished by the image or cell metabolism. These advanced detection means, but the high cost, while the popularity of these detection equipment is not high, the general hospital may not have such conditions, we can also achieve the goal of the traditional biochemical testing.

Although the clinical results of ischemic stroke and hemorrhagic stroke are similar, but the process is very complex, there are overlapping factors, there are more obvious factors. In modeling, the input variables are usually chosen as input variables of the model. However, many of the original input variables detected by modern instruments, there will be some factors and the results do not matter, if these factors into it, the model will not be accurate. Although some factors are related to the dependent variables, there is a redundant relationship between each other. Therefore, we need to filter out irrelevant factors and reduce the redundant variables.

3.2.1The detection of normal people and patients

Accurate and rapid determination of the exact location and size of the lesion is needed before treatment, and it is important to determine what treatment strategies are required. For example, a doctor must quickly determine the type of stroke before the appropriate treatment is performed, ischemic stroke or hemorrhagic stroke, because the different types of stroke treatment strategies are different. Thus we take steps to diagnose and predict stroke.

The first step is to distinguish patients from patients and normal people. Once the result is stroke, SVM is performed for further judgement of its type. The experiment result proves that SVM can achieve higher prediction results through the six factors of joint detection.

From Fig. 3 we can see that in the combined detection it can distinguish patients from normal people perfectly. And in the second step, it also has a high rate of distinguishing between ischemic stroke and hemorrhagic stroke. Thus combined detection has a good result of experiment.

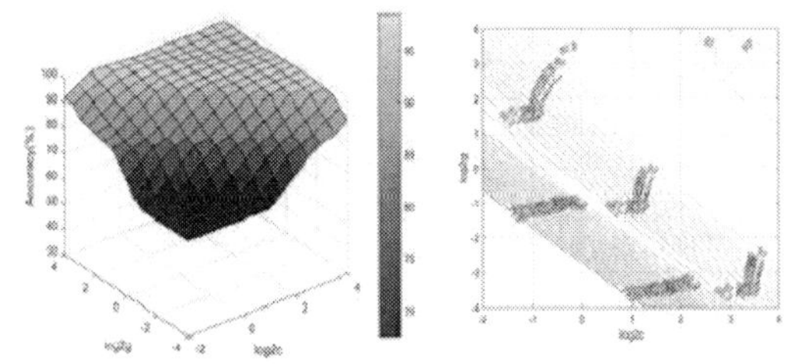

Figure 2. Learning process of the first step(between normal people and patients)

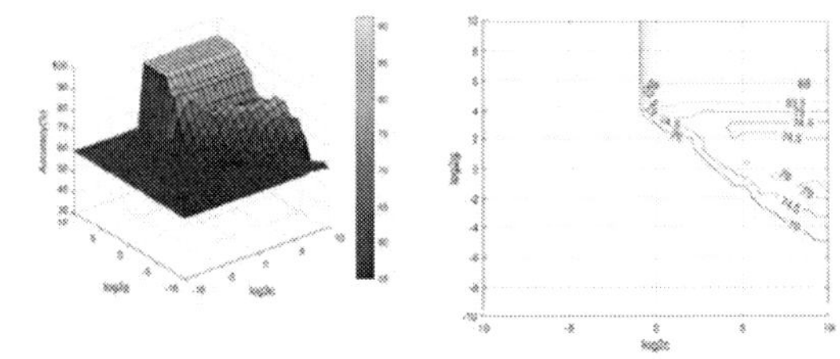

Figure 3. Learning process of the second step(between hemorrhagic and ischemic stroke)

TABLE IV. PREDICTION ACCURACY OF THE SVM

step	specificity	sensitivity	Correct index(specificity+ sensitivity-1)
The first step	100%	100%	100%
The second step	88.89%	92.59%	81.48%

3.2.2 Single biomarker detection

Then we analyze each marker's effect on the stroke based on the SVM model. For related biomarker such as: C-reactive protein, FIB, HCY, etc., the predicting accuracy rate is below 80%, compared with of joint detection of several kinds of markers, the detection accuracy is greatly reduced, which cannot meet the requirement of detection discrimination.

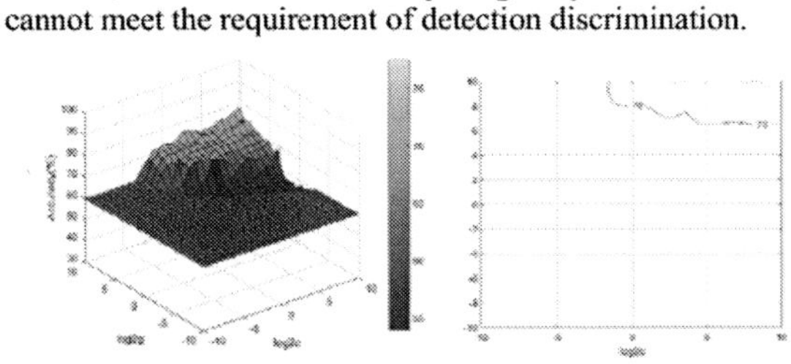

Figure 4. Learning process of HCY

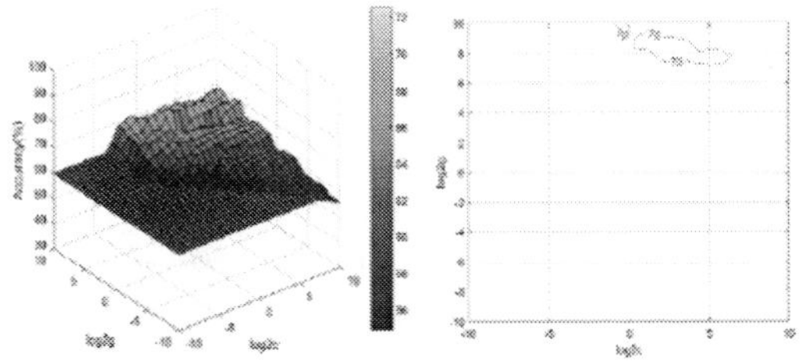

Figure 5. Learning process of FIB

According to simulation result, we can analyse each factor's effect on the onset of stroke. From figure 6-11, it can be concluded that HCY has the biggest influencing, it can achieve over 70% accuracy rate during the studying process. FIB and BUN also have a higher influence and the average rate of simulation perforation is 60 percent or more, followed by triglyceride and CRP. Blood sugar, general below 60% accuracy, is the lowest of the six. That is to say, Blood sugar could hardly distinguish between ischemic stroke and hemorrhagic stroke. It is a consistent biomarker of acute stroke and it can't be used to distinguish these two type of acute stroke.

From the forecasting result, we can also see that when only using single index detection, the correct rate of prediction low, which indicates that when using a single index, it can't be used to identify the different forms of stroke. The use of combined detection can greatly improve the prediction efficiency and accuracy.

TABLE V. SPECIFICITY OF THE BIOMARKER ON JUDGING STROKE

Biomarker	hemorrhagic stroke	ischemic stroke	Correct index(specificity+ sensitivity-1)
HCY	0%	100%	0%
FIB	27.78%	92.59%	20.37%
BUN	0%	100%	0%
triglyceride	0%	100%	0%
CRP	5.56%	96.30%	1.86%
sugar	5.56%	100%	5.56%

Conclusion

Due to the low cost and the development of Bioinformatics, machine learning draws an increasing attention to many countries and plays an important role in the diagnosis and prevention of various diseases. This paper demonstrates the biomarkers of stroke. First, six comprehensive and independent indexes are got by pre-treated data with the mutual information analysis and principal component analysis. A SVM-based approach is proposed to distinguish patients from patients and normal people. The validation results of the SVM method yields up to 85% classification accuracy with high sensitivity and specificity. Further, we analyse the importance of each marker in stroke prediction or diagnosis.

Acknowledgment

This research is supported by the National Science Foundation of China (Grant No. 81571142), the National Science Key Foundation of China (Grant No. 61232009), the National Science Foundation of China (Grant No. 60973106), Astronautic support Fund (Grant No. 374007), and National 863 Project of China (Grant No. 2011AA010404). Thanks to Xuanwu hospital for data support and assistance.

References

[1] Vos T, Barber R M, Bell B, et al. Global, regional, and national incidence, prevalence, and years lived with disability for 301 acute and chronic diseases and injuries in 188 countries, 1990–2013: a systematic analysis for the Global Burden of Disease Study 2013[J]. Lancet, 2015, 386(9995): 743-800.

[2] Feigin V L, Forouzanfar M H, Krishnamurthi R, et al., "Global and regional burden of stroke during 1990–2010: findings from the Global Burden of Disease Study 2010". Lancet, 2014,383(9913): 245-254.

[3] Collaborators M C O D. Global, regional, and national age–sex specific all-cause and cause-specific mortality for 240 causes of death, 1990–2013: a systematic analysis for the Global Burden of Disease Study 2013[J]. Lancet, 2015, 385(9963):117-171.

[4] Jimeno A, Hidalgo M. Molecular. "biomarkers: their increasing role in the diagnosis, characterization, and therapy guidance in pancreatic cancer". Molecular Cancer Therapeutics, 2006, 5(4): 787-96.

[5] De Rubertis G, Davies S W. Genetic. "circuit design from an electronics perspective". Molecular, Cellular and Tissue Engineering, 2002. Proceedings of the IEEE-EMBS Special Topic Conference on IEEE, 2002: 145-146.

[6] Brophy J A, Voigt C A., "Principles of genetic circuit design. Nature Methods", 2014,11(5): 508-520.

[7] Wu Zhao,Hong Chen,Longfeng Xiang,Xiaomei Xie,Min Chen,Zuli Zhao,Qi Li."passive acoustic detection of diver based on SVM".Proceedings of 2016 IEEE, 2016: 623-628

[8] LI TianJiang, DU Qiang, "Abstract principal component analysis". science china, 2013, 56(12): 2783-2798

[9] Thomas M.Cover,Joy A.Thomas."elements of information theory(second edition)", A john wiley&sons, inc., 2006: 19-22

[10] LIN Ri-wu,CHEN Zao-shu,XU Yi-ye, "research on correlation of random blood clucose, CRP, FIB after the first acute stroke and atroke", modern preventive medicine,2012, 39(3): 759-760

[11] LI Zijian, "Recent advance in early diagnostic biomarkers of ischemic stroke", China science and technology information,Jan, 2014: 140-141

Algorithm of search and track of static and moving large-scale objects

Anatoly Kalyaev[1,a], Maxim Khisamutdinov[1]

[1]*SRI MCS SF, Taganrog, Russia*

Abstract. We suggest an algorithm for processing of a sequence, which contains images of search and track of static and moving large-scale objects. The possible software implementation of the algorithm, based on multithread CUDA processing, is suggested. Experimental analysis of the suggested algorithm implementation is performed.

1 Introduction

The problem of search and track of static and moving large-scale objects is needed in many areas of human activity such as astronomy, aviation, medicine, etc [1-7] (Fig 1,2). The problem implies processing of a single image or a sequence of images for detection coordinates of static and moving large-scale objects.

We propose new method based on calculation of the descriptors of the image frame using a graphic subsystem and comparing it with the preliminarily trained matrix of objects by means of an artificial neural network model.

Figure 1. Detecting and tracking of static large-scale objects.

The method of large-scale object search consists of 3 steps:

• preliminary processing of an image of a video sequence (conversion to monochromatic, reducing noise with the help of median filtering, increasing contrast, selection of visibility region);

• detection of the point features of the image (calculation of descriptors) (Fig. 3);

• comparison of the point features with a template (comparison of the detected point features of the image with template features of possible objects) (Fig. 4).

Figure 2. Detecting and tracking of moving large-scale objects.

[a] Corresponding author: anytroll@gmail.com

Figure 3. All points and parameters of potential targets.

Proposed algorithm is pretty hard to calculate that is why we decided to aim it at parallel computing system realization. For analysis of the suggested algorithm we have developed software implementation based on multithread loading of the CUDA-calculator.

Figure 4. Filtered results with real target.

2 Algorithm

At figure 5 you can see the structure flow chart of the developed algorithm. Let's describe it in details. At first blocks of flow-chart we show input data of the algorithm: the next frame frame of the video sequence, the vector of parameters opt_flow of the optical flow, the matrix of training descriptors sum_descr and the vector vPoints of the points, which correspond to the desired targets.

The algorithm starts with calculation of the descriptors descriptors_1GPU of the image frame using a graphic subsystem. Then the obtained descriptors are compared with the preliminarily trained matrix sum_descr by means of an artificial neural network model. Operation of the model is described in the next section of the paper.

The output results of the artificial neural network model are the matrices trainIdx, distance, matches. Further on, we select the descriptors of the vector descriptors_1GPU which most exactly coincide with the matrix sum_descr according to the maximum distance criterion MAX_DISTANCE. The next step of the algorithm consists in transformation of the obtained descriptors good_matches into the items of the vector vPointsBig. Coordinates of each group of the vector vPointsBig are averaged by means of a special algorithm. The rest items of the vector vPointsBig are added to the vector vPoints with the help of the algorithm of point adding to the vector vPoints, which is similar to the algorithm of new points adding for point targets. The vector vPoints, which now contains some added items, is updated with the help of the correspondent algorithm, similar to the algorithm of the vector vPoints update for point targets. The last step of the algorithm is output of the suspected targets obtained by analysis of the vector vPoints.

3 Implementation

For analysis of the suggested algorithm we have developed software implementation [8]. For faster execution of our software tool we use multithread loading of the CUDA-calculator (see Fig.6).

Since new versions (higher than 4.0) of the CUDA platform follow the rule "one CUDA context for one process in the system", certain complications, concerning software implementation of multithread loading of the CUDA-calculator, become a problem. It is possible to avoid such limitation, using API CUDA and generating virtual CUDA contexts for one thread in RAM. Owing to such approach, we have no limitations concerning the rule "one CUDA context for one process", and each thread will have its CUDA context. In this case, the only imitation is available RAM of the computer device.

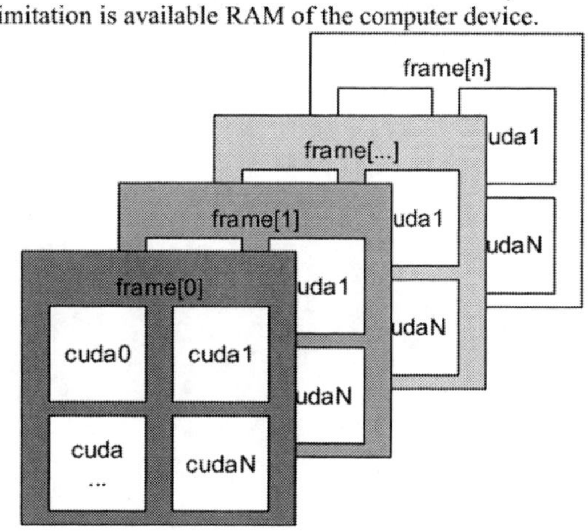

Figure 6. Multithread loading of the CUDA-calculator.

The main idea is loading a group of images into video memory and data-intensive processing of image fragments (the image is equally divided among threads). The number of threads (cuda1 ... cudaN) is chosen experimentally according to the characteristics of the used video card and the size of available RAM of the computer system (recommended utilization of the graphics processor (GP) is not more than 80%). It is necessary to take into account utilization of the graphics processor, not the top temperature limit of the core.

To analyse the execution time of our software implementation of the suggested algorithm with multithread programming of the CUDA-calculator we used the following test [9-10]. The number of used threads is 1-8, the input number of images is 2-64. If we use 1 thread and 64 images, then utilization of the graphics processor does not exceed 10%, and if we use 8 threads and 64 images, then GP utilization is 80%. Table 1 shows the testing results. The first column contains the number of images in the sequence. The first line contains the number of threads. The execution time is measured in seconds.

DOI: 10.1051/itmconf/20171205014

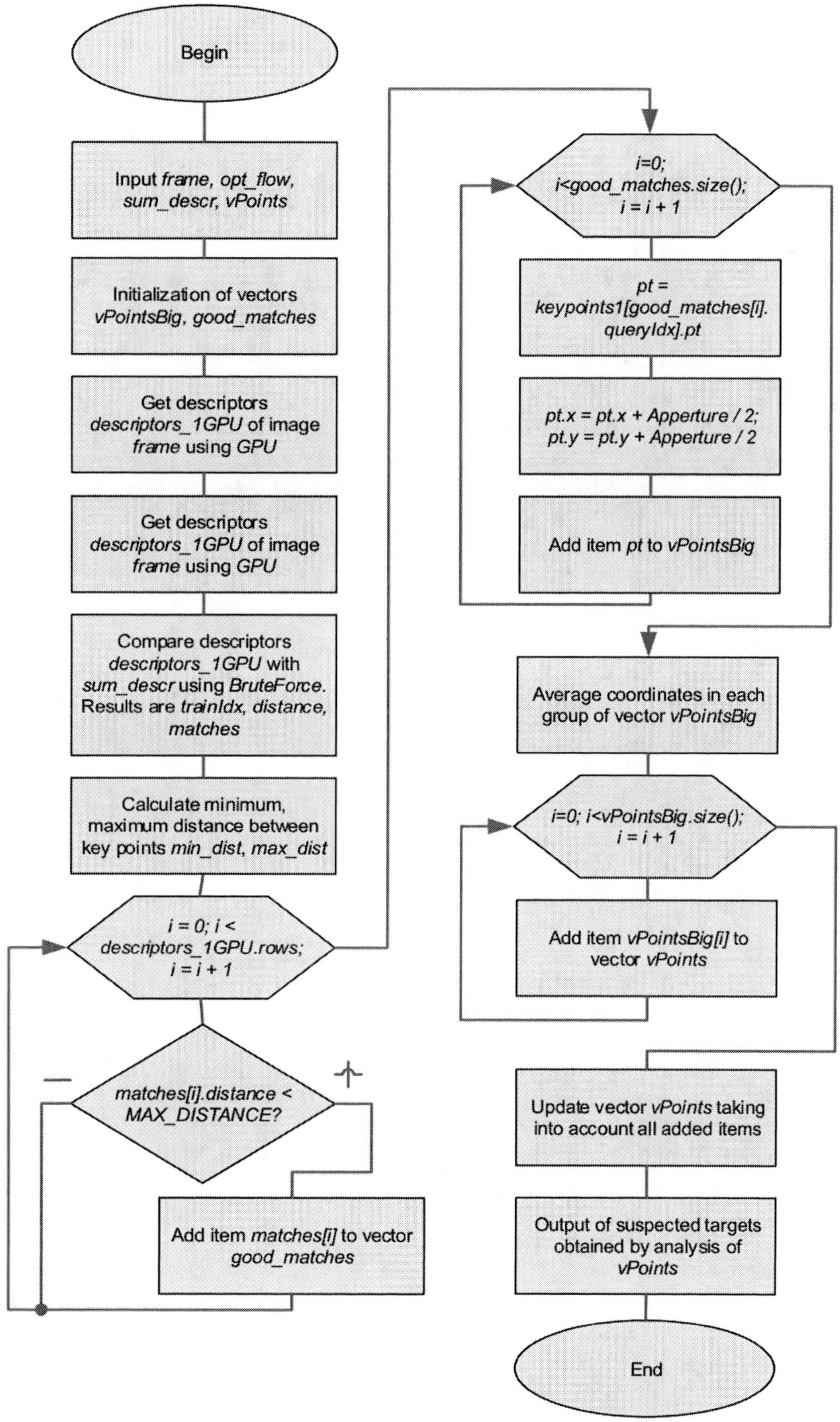

Figure 5. The structure flow chart of the algorithm of large-scale object search and detection from complex background.

Table 1. Testing results of the execution time.

	1	**2**	**4**	**8**
2	1.2	0.8	0.45	0.22
4	3.4	2.3	1.2	0.55
8	5.9	3.3	1.59	0.79
16	12.8	7.1	3.8	1.7
32	24.5	13.5	7.6	3.4
64	97.3	51.8	26.1	13.5

As you can see from the table, owing to use of multithread loading of the CUDA-calculator it is possible to reduce time costs proportionally to the number of used threads.

Acknowledgment

The project is supported by the Grant of the President of Russian Federation № MK-5463.2016.9.

References

1. Herbert Bay, Tinne Tuytelaars and Luc Van Gool, "Speeded-up robust features (SURF)," Computer vision and image understanding, vol.110, No.3, 2008, pp. 346-359. [8] M. Calonder, V. Lepetit, C. Strecha, and P. Fua. "BRIEF: Binary robust independent elementary features," In European Conference on Computer Vision, 2010.
2. Image Matching Using SIFT, SURF, BRIEF and ORB: Performance Comparison for Distorted Images (PDF Download Available). Available from: https://www.researchgate.net/publication/292157133_Image_Matching_Using_SIFT_SURF_BRIEF_and_ORB_Performance_Comparison_for_Distorted_Images [accessed Jun 14, 2017].
3. B. Shan, "A Novel Image Correlation Matching Approach," JMM, vol. 5, no. 3, 2010.
4. I.S. Korovin, M.G. Tkachenko, M.V. Khisamutdinov, A.I. Kalyaev, Artificial intelligence hybrid methods application in the task of the heavy oilfields profitability increase / Source of the Document Neftyanoe Khozyaystvo - Oil Industry (1), pp. 106-109 (2016).
5. A.I. Kalyaev, I.A. Kalyaev, Method of multiagent scheduling of resources in cloud computing environments / Source of the Document Journal of Computer and Systems Sciences International 55 (2), pp. 211-221 (2016).
6. I. Kalyaev, A. Kalyaev, I. Korovin, Decentralized approach to control of robot groups during execution of the task flow / Lecture Notes in Computer Science (including subseries Lecture Notes in Artificial Intelligence and Lecture Notes in Bioinformatics) **98**, 12, pp. 48-54 (2016).
7. Ya.S. Korovin, A.I. Kalyaev, Methods and algorithms of improving the efficiency of data transmission systems in oil corporations' enterprise networks. / Neftyanoe khozyaystvo - Oil Industry (9), pp. 96-100 (2013).
8. A. Kaliaev, Multiagent approach for building distributed adaptive computing system / Procedia Computer Science 18, pp. 2193-2202 (2013).
9. I.S. Korovin, M.V. Khisamutdinov, A.I. Kalyaev, Data Mining Methods Application to the Problem of Handling Corporative Dataset on Heavy Oil Production // Proceedings of the 2016 International conference on intelligent control and computer application. ACSR-Advances in Comptuer Science Research (30) p.387-389, (2016).
10. I.S. Korovin, A.I. Kalyaev, M.V. Khisamutdinov, Using a dynamic model of technological processes to reduce the cost of heavy oil extraction // Conference: 2nd Information Technology and Mechatronics Engineering Conference (ITOEC) p.21-22, (2016).

A Visual Attention Based Object Detection Model beyond Top-Down and Bottom-up Mechanism

Du-Zhen Zhang[1], Chuan-Cai Liu [2]

[1]*School of Computer Science and Technology, Jiangsu Normal University, Xuzhou 221116, Jiangsu, P.R. China*
[2]*School of Computer Science and Engineering, Nanjing University of Science and Technology, Nanjing 210094, Jiangsu, P.R. China*
[1]*zhduzhen@aliyun.com*

Abstract: Traditional saliency-based attention theory supposed that bottom-up and top-down factors combine to direct attentional behavior. This dichotomy fails to explain a growing number of cases in which neither bottom-up nor top-down can account for strong selection biases. Thus, the top-down versus bottom-up dichotomy is an inadequate taxonomy of attentional control. In our previous study, we presented a general computational framework for detecting task-oriented salient objects in images beyond top-down and bottom-up mechanism. It possesses three parts: selection history, current goal and physical salience. Selection history is integrated with current goal and physical salience to compose an integrative framework. In this extended version, our ameliorated model is applied to face and car detection and simulates task-dependent reasonable eye trajectories (visual scan paths). Experimental results demonstrate that selection history (reward) is shown to influence saccade trajectories. Our findings support the idea that attention and gaze can be directed voluntarily to regions of interest (by selection history and current goal) and can be captured by local features of an object that stand out from the background (by physical salience).

1. Introduction

Visual search plays a key role in our everyday activities; the visual system pays attention to the salient objects for efficient search. Visual saliency plays important roles in natural vision in that saliency can direct eye movements, deploy attention, and facilitate tasks like object detection and scene understanding. Attention determines which among multiple competing stimuli are represented in the brain. There are two conventional categories of factors that drive attention: bottom-up and top-down factors [11]. Bottom-up factors are derived solely from the visual scene. Regions of interest that attract our attention are in a bottom-up way and the responsible feature for this reaction must be sufficiently discriminative with respect to surrounding features. Top-down methods [14] [23] are task-driven or goal-driven. Top-down and bottom-up factors should be combined to direct attentional behavior. Many models have been built to compute saliency maps. A recent review of attention models from a computational perspective can be found in [6] [7]. Saliency models have been developed for eye fixation prediction and salient object detection. The former focuses on identifying a few fixation locations on natural images, which is important for understanding human attention. The latter, also called salient object segmentation, is used to accurately detect where the salient object should be, which is useful for many high-level vision tasks [24] [6].

Recently, the theoretical dichotomy of attentional control between top-down and bottom-up is challenged. The dichotomy fails to explain a growing number of cases in which neither bottom-up nor top-down can account for strong selection biases [4]. Thus, the top-down versus bottom-up dichotomy is an inadequate taxonomy of attentional control. A wealth of research has demonstrated that reward information provides a third source of input to the attention system. When a large reward is received, attention is strongly primed to select the rewarded target [12] [10].

Awh et al. [4] proposed selection history (including two classes of 'history' effects, i.e., selection and reward history) as a third category of control by explicitly distinguishing current goals from selection history effects. A 'priority map' which they still highlighted integrates three distinct categories of selection bias: the observer's current selection goals, selection history, and physical

DOI: 10.1051/itmconf/20171205015

salience of the items competing for attention. Acknowledging selection history as a third category of control can clarify many ongoing debates and can make clear large swaths of selection phenomena that are unrelated to current selection goals and physical salience. This concept model is a breakthrough to traditional prominent models of attentional control.

In the paper [25], we proposed a general computational framework for detecting specific salient objects in images beyond top-down and bottom-up mechanisms and verified qualitative and quantitative effects of current selection goals and selection history in our experiments. Salient objects are detected by directly measuring the saliency of an image window in the original image and the well established sliding window based object detection paradigm is adopted. Our experimental results on challenging object detection datasets demonstrate that physical salience generates a bottom-up saliency map for highlighting the salient regions of an image. The main effect of the selection history is to concentrate on salient objects, the current goal has a strong effect in detecting correct salient objects. Experiments also indicate that there is competition among selection history, current goal and physical salience to detect correct salient objects.

In this paper, we will extend our previous work. Our model is applied to salient object detection and generates task-dependent eye trajectories.

The rest of this paper is organized as follows. Section II introduces related works. Our extended computational framework is described in Section III. Experimental results and comparisons are presented in Section IV, and conclusions are given in Section V.

2. Related Works

The objectness measure [2] quantifies how likely an image window contains an object of any class. Each outputting image window is endowed with an objectness score to measure how likely this window contains a salient object. It uses several existing image saliency cues (including a novel 'superpixels straddling' cue to capture the closed boundary characteristic of objects), and greatly reduces the number of windows from an image according to their objectness distribution. We use it to generate physical salience and quantify how likely an image window contains a salient object [25].

LabelMe [16] is a web-based image annotation tool that is used to label the identity of objects and where they occur in images. We use the HOG (Histograms of Oriented Gradient) descriptor from the LabelMe toolbox and extend it to extract image features of current goal, selection history and sampled image windows.

Fig. 1 is a schematic diagram of our framework [25]. Selection history, physical salience, and current goal are three distinct sources of selection biases to accomplish salient object detection. Our primary goal is to present a general computational framework for detecting salient objects in images. Selection history is integrated with current goals and physical salience to compose an integrative framework.

1) *Selection history*. This category of control is intended to represent 'history' effects which shape the overall landscape of the observer's selection biases. Umemoto et al. [21] demonstrated that likely targets are more likely to be encoded into working memory, even when observers lack explicit knowledge of this contingency. We extract the mean HOG features of a specific image class as the selection history used to indicate reward.

2) *Physical salience*. This category represents the fact that selection is sometimes biased in a manner that depends only on the properties of the stimulus display itself, it has been described as a 'bottom-up' (stimulus-driven) process. In our study, we use the objectness measure [2] to generate physical salience and quantify how likely a sampled image window contains a salient object.

3) *Current goal*. This category of attentional control acknowledges the critical role of goal-driven selection, it has been described as a 'top-down' (goal-driven) process. Whenever there is a search task, goal-driven processes tend to dominate guidance, as indicated by attention being systematically biased toward image features that resemble those of the search target.

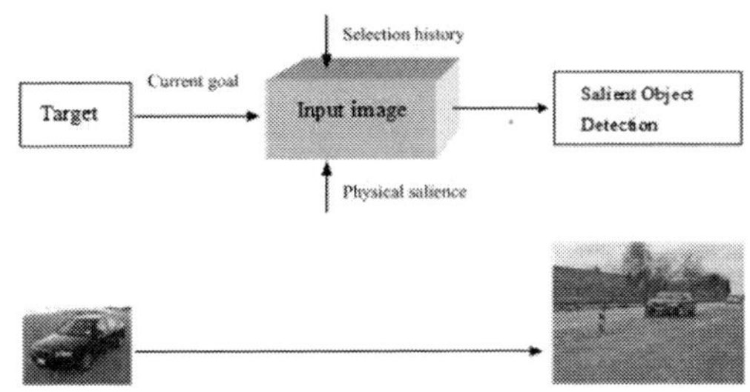

Figure 1. A schematic diagram of our framework [25].

In the present study, we devise a computational model of visual attention during search in complex scenes based on similarity between the target and regions of the search scene. Similarity is defined using a histogram-matching technique.

An image window saliency is defined as the objectness score of the window [2]. The objectness measure [2] is executed and outputs a number of windows.

The most promising candidate window is defined as:

$$\max_{score} \min_{w} (\| f_{in} - f_{w} \|)^{\| f_{w} - f_{h} \|} \quad (1)$$

DOI: 10.1051/itmconf/20171205015

Where f_{in} , f_w and f_h denote the features of target (current goal), sampled window and selection history respectively, $\|\bullet\|$ is *L-1* norm of features.

If there is no target, the most promising candidate window is defined as:

$$\max_{score} \min_{w}(\| f_w - f_h \|) \tag{2}$$

We use (2) to verify the effect of selection history.

Each image may have several objects of the same class, we output the best 4 detected windows in our experiments.

Fig. 2 is an example for image detection results using our detector. On each image the best 4 detected windows are superimposed, brighter windows have higher objectness and saliency.

Fig. 2(b) shows that the history has a strong influence on deployment of attention. The selection history biases the characteristic of visual attention during search toward scene regions that resemble target features. This is in line with the research by Umemoto et al. [21]. Fig. 2(c) demonstrates that the task has a strong influence on deployment of attention too. The salient object within the image is correctly detected.

Figure 2. (best viewed in color) Example detection results using objectness [2] and our detector. On each image the best 4 detected windows are superimposed, brighter windows have higher objectness. From left to right: (a) objectness [2] based detetctor, (b) history effect, (c) our integrative detector [25].

3. An Extended Algorithm Implementation for Salient Object Detection

The limitations of the model are unsteady and time-consuming due to objectness [2]. In this extended version, objectness [2] is superseded by the algorithm LARK (Locally Adaptive Regression Kernels) proposed by Seo and Milanfar [19].

LARK is a generic detection/localization algorithm capable of searching for a visual object of interest without training. The proposed method operates using a single example of an object of interest to find similar matches, does not require prior knowledge (learning) about objects being sought, and does not require any preprocessing step or segmentation of a target image either. LARK is based on the computation of local regression kernels as descriptors from a query (target), which measure the likeness of a pixel to its surroundings. Salient features are extracted from said descriptors and compared against analogous features from the target image.

The detection framework of LARK can also be useful for solving the bottom-up saliency detection [18]. Therefore, the schematic diagram of our framework modified as shown in Fig. 3.

The most promising candidate window is defined as:

$$\min_{w}(\| f_{in} - f_w \|)^{\| f_w - f_h \|} \tag{3}$$

Where f_{in} , f_w and f_h denote the features of target (current goal), sampled window and selection history respectively, $\|\bullet\|$ is *L-1* norm of features.

If there is no target, the most promising candidate window is defined as:

$$\min_{w}(\| f_w - f_h \|) \tag{4}$$

We use (4) to verify the effect of selection history.

Each image may have several objects of the same class. The number of the detected objects m satisfies:

$$D_m < 1.5\bar{D}_n = \frac{1.5}{n}\sum_{i=1}^{n} D_i \tag{5}$$

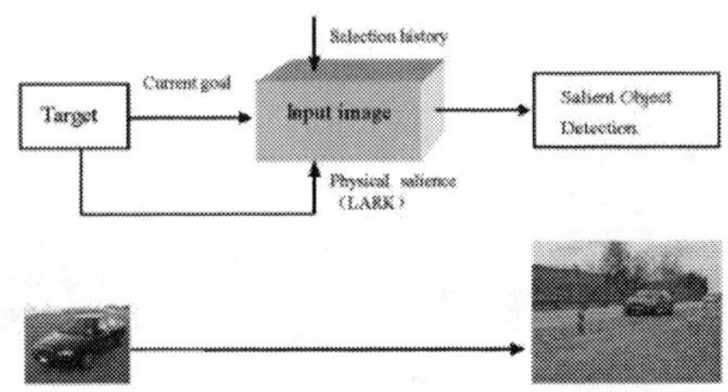

Figure 3. A modified schematic diagram of our framework.

where $D = (\| f_{in} - f_w \|)^{\| f_w - f_h \|}$, n is the number of output windows running LARK.

4. Experimental Results

Attention and saliency play important roles in visual perception. Fixations were found around faces, cars, and text [8] [13]. In our experiments, the model is applied to face and car detection and generate task-dependent eye trajectories.

Dalal and Triggs [9] showed that HOG descriptors significantly outperformed existing feature sets for human detection. In our experiments, HOG descriptors [15] are extracted from current goal, selection history and sampled image windows.

4.1 Face Detection and Task-Dependent Eye Trajectories

We extract mean HOG descriptors as the selection history from the ORL face database provided by Samaria and Harter [17]. There are 10 different images of 40 distinct

DOI: 10.1051/itmconf/20171205015

subjects. For some of the subjects, the images were taken at different times, varying lighting slightly, facial expressions (open/closed eyes, smiling/non-smiling) and facial details (glasses/no-glasses). All the images are taken against a dark homogeneous background and the subjects are in up-right, frontal position (with tolerance for some side movement). The size of each image is 92x112, 8-bit grey levels. Fig. 4 shows images of faces randomly selected from the ORL face database.

Figure 4. Example images randomly selected from the ORL face database.

Fig. 5 shows our result on the image from Seo and Milanfar [19]. Eye trajectory (visual scan path) is superimposed on the image. Red represents higher resemblance.

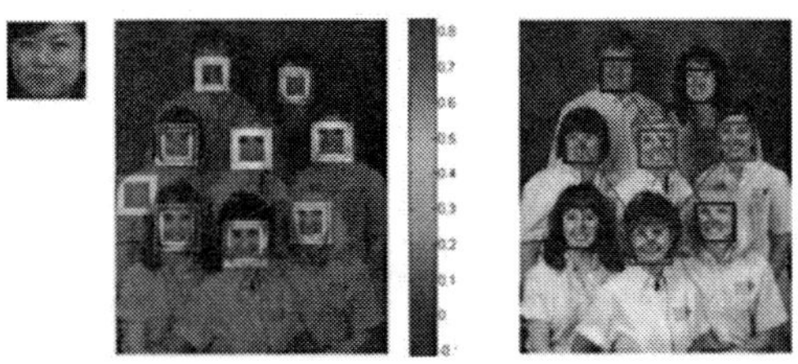

Figure 5. (Left) The original query. (Middle) The LARK detection result by Seo and Milanfar [19]. (Right) Our result. Eye trajectory superimposed on the image (solid line).

From Fig. 6, it can be seen that selection history (reward) guides search automatically and interferes with the performance of a specific visual search task. It has a direct, non-volitional impact on human perception and attention that is independent of its impact on endogenous attentional control. The anterior cingulate cortex (a cortical expression of the mesolimbic dopamine system) plays a crucial role in this source of attentional control [12]. The results demonstrate that selection history acts to change visual salience and thus plays an important and undervalued role in attentional control. A recent review by Anderson [3] also demonstrated that learned value plays a distinct role in the guidance of attention (referred to as value-driven attention).

The more similar matches have higher priority to attend to and have higher reward. Eye trajectories generated by our model are consistent with the study assuming that eye movements are selected to maximize reward by reducing uncertainty that could result in suboptimal actions and that framing the decision about where to look in terms of uncertainty reduction has been effective in explaining aspects of static scene viewing as well as dynamic scene viewing [20].

Fig. 7 illustrates the comparison between our results and [22]. It is obviously that our model have better effect on face detection and eye trajectories.

Figure 6. (Left) Query. (Middle) Only query effect. (Right) Only history effect. Eye trajectories superimposed on the images (solid line).

Figure 7. (Left) Query. (Middle column) Salient objects segmentation results and scan paths are generated using the latest version of the saliency tool box downloaded from http://www.saliencytoolbox.net using the default parameters. Full details of the model can be found in [22]. (Right) Our result eye trajectories superimposed on the images (solid line).

4.2 Car Detection on the UIUC Car Dataset

The UIUC car dataset [1] consists of learning and test sets. The learning set contains 550 positive (car) images and 500 negative (non car) images. The test set is divided into two parts: 170 gray-scale images containing 200 side views of cars of size 100*40, and 108 gray-scale images containing 139 cars at various sizes with a ratio between the largest and smallest cars of about 2.5. We use only one query image at a time from the 550 positive examples and extract mean HOG descriptors as the selection history. Fig. 8 shows images of cars randomly selected from the UIUC car dataset.

Fig. 9 shows our results of correct detections on the UIUC car test set. Eye trajectory is superimposed on the image (solid line) if the image has more than one car. We compute detection precision as:

$$Precision = \frac{TP}{TP + FP} \tag{6}$$

where TP is the number of true positives, FP is the number of false positives.

The overall detection precision improvement of our proposed method over LARK [19] is from 71.7% to 79.5% on the UIUC car test set. Our method increases 8% by using (5) to filter out false positives.

Figure 8. Example images randomly selected from the UIUC car dataset.

Figure 9. Examples of correct detections on the UIUC car test set. Eye trajectories superimposed on the images (solid line).

4.3 Discussions

LARK is a powerful training-free nonparametric object detection framework by employing local steering kernel (LSK), which well captures image underlying structure, and by using the Matrix Cosine Similarity (MCS) measure [19]. The method can automatically detect in the target image the presence, the number, as well as location of similar objects to the given query image. To deal with more general scenarios, accounting for large variations in scale and rotation, multiscale and multirotation approach were also proposed. It is faster (3.655 second per image of our integrative detector MATLAB implementation on the UIUC car dataset with Intel(R) Core(TM) i3-2330 2.2 GHz CPU and 4GB RAM), while objectness [2] is time-consuming. In this study, objectness [2] is superseded by the algorithm LARK and (5) is used to filter out false outputs.

We apply our model to face and car detection and generate task-dependent eye trajectory. Experimental results demonstrate that selection history (reward) is shown to influence saccade trajectories. This is consistent with the study by Belopolsky [5].

As in [19], the performance of our method is little affected by the choice of similar query images. Semantic feature extraction and semantic similarity measure will be employed to further depress the effect in our future study.

5. Conclusions

Attention is a central question for vision science. The traditional theory of top-down versus bottom-up is an inadequate taxonomy of attentional control. In our previous study [25], we presented a general computational framework for detecting salient objects in images beyond top-down and bottom-up mechanism. Its three parts (selection history, current goal and physical salience) are integrated to compose an integrative framework. We verified qualitative and quantitative effects of current selection goals and selection history in experiments. Experimental results suggest that physical salience generates bottom-up saliency maps for highlighting the salient regions of images. The main effect of the selection history is to concentrate on salient objects although this might cause errors. The current goal has a strong effect on detecting correct salient objects. Our experiments indicated that there is competition among selection history, current goal and physical salience to detect correct salient objects. The limitations of the model are unsteady and time-consuming due to objectness [2]. In this extended version, objectness [2] is superseded by the algorithm LARK. Our ameliorated model is applied to face and car detection and simulates task-dependent reasonable eye trajectories. Experimental results demonstrate that selection history (reward) is shown to influence saccade trajectories. Our findings support the idea that attention and gaze can be directed voluntarily to regions of interest (by selection history and current goal) and can be captured by local features of an object that stand out from the background (by physical salience).

The main contributions of this study are our integrative computational framework and experimental conclusions. Our combined computational model currently remains limited to processing of low-level features, and as such it is unable to reflect eye movement influences that depend on higher-level visual features (such as objects). Our current detector implementation is simple and there is much room for improvement, e.g., using more sophisticated visual features.

Acknowledgment

The authors would like to thank the reviewers for their constructive comments and suggestions. This work is supported by the National Natural Science Fund of China (Grant Nos. 61373063, 61373062), the project of Ministry of Industry and Information Technology of China (Grant No. E0310/1112/02-1), and the Natural Science Fund of JSNU (Grant No. 15XLA09).

References

[1] Agarwal, S., Awan, A. and Roth, D., "Learning to Detect Objects in Images via a Sparse Part-Based Representation," IEEE Trans. Pattern Analysis and Machine Intelligence, 26(11), pp.1475-1490, 2004.

[2] Alexe, B., Deselaers, T., and Ferrari, V., "What is an object?" In Proc. IEEE Conf. on Computer Vision and Pattern Recognition (CVPR), pp. 73–80, 2010.

[3] Anderson, B. A., "A value-driven mechanism of attentional selection," Journal of Vision, vol. 13, no. 3, pp. 1–16, 2010.

[4] Awh, E., Belopolsky, A. V., and Theeuwes, J., "Top-down versus bottom-up attentional control: A failed theoretical dichotomy," Trends in cognitive sciences, 16(8), pp.437–443, 2012.

[5] Belopolsky, A. V., "Common priority map for selection history, reward and emotionin the oculomotor system," Perception, vol. 0, no. 0, pp.1–14, 2015.

[6] Borji, A., Sihite, D. N., and Itti. L., "Salient object detection: a benchmark," In Proc. European Conf. on Computer Vision (ECCV), pp.414–429, 2012.

[7] Borji, A., and Itti, L., "State-of-the-art in Visual Attention Modeling," IEEE Trans. Pattern Anal. Mach. Intell., PAMI 35(1), pp.185–207, 2013.

[8] Cerf, M., Harel, J., Einhauser, W., and Koch, C., "Predicting human gaze using low-level saliency combined with face detection," Neural Information Processing Systems, vol. 20, pp. 241–248, 2007.

[9] Dalal, N., and Triggs, B., "Histograms of oriented gradients for human detection," In Proc. IEEE Conf. on Computer Vision and Pattern Recognition (CVPR), Vol. 1, pp. 886-893, 2005.

[10] Della Libera, C., and Chelazzi, L., "Visual selective attention and the effects of monetary reward," Psychological Science, vol. 17, pp. 222–227, 2006.

[11] Desimone, R., and Duncan, J., "Neural mechanisms of selective visual attention," Annual Reviews of Neuroscience. 18, 193–222, 1995.

[12] Hickey, C., Chelazzi, L., Theeuwes, J., "Reward changes salience in human vision via the anterior cingulated," The Journal of Neuroscience, 30(33), pp.11096-11103, 2010.

[13] Judd, T., Ehinger, K., Durand, F., and Torralba, A., "Learning to predict where humans look," in Proceedings of the IEEE 12th International Conference on Computer Vision (ICCV '09), pp.2106–2113, Kyoto, Japan, September 2009.

[14] Liu, T., Yuan, Z., Sun, J., Wang, J., Zheng, N., Tang, X., and Shum, H., "Learning to detect a salient object," Pattern Anal. Mach. Intell. PAMI 33(2), pp.353–367, 2011.

[15] Ludwig, O., Delgado, D., Goncalves,V., Nunes, U.,"Trainable Classifier-Fusion Schemes: An Application To Pedestrian Detection," in: 12th Internat. Conf. on Intelligent Transportation Systems, pp.432-437, 2009.

[16] Russell, B. C., Torralba, A., Murphy, K. P., and Freeman, W. T., "LabelMe: a database and web-based tool for image annotation," International Journal of Computer Vision, 77(1-3), pp.157-173, 2008.

[17] Samaria, F., Harter, A., "Parameterisation of a stochastic model for human face identification," in 2nd IEEE Workshop on Applications of Computer Vision December, Sarasota (Florida), 1994.

[18] Seo, H. J., Milanfar, P., "Static and Space-Time Visual Saliency Detection by Self-Resemblance," J. Vision, vol. 9, no. 12, pp. 1-27, 2009.

[19] Seo, H. J., Milanfar, P., "Training-free, generic object detection using locally adaptive regression kernels," Pattern Analysis and Machine Intelligence, IEEE Transactions on, 32(9), pp. 1688-1704, 2010.

[20] Tatler, B. W., Hayhoe, M. M., Land, M. F., et al.. "Eye guidance in natural vision: Reinterpreting salience," Journal of Vision, 11(5), pp. 1–23, 2011.

[21] Umemoto, A., Scolari, M., Vogel, E. K., and Awh, E., "Statistical learning induces discrete shifts in the allocation of working memory resources," Journal of Experimental Psychology: Human Perception and Performance, 36(6), pp.1419-1429, 2010.

[22] Walther, D., Koch, C., "Modeling attention to salient proto-objects," Neural Networks, vol. 19, pp.1395–1407, 2006.

[23] Yang, J., and Yang, M., "Top-down visual saliency via joint crf and dictionary learning," In Proc. IEEE Conf. on Computer Vision and Pattern Recognition, pp. 2296–2303, 2012.

[24] Yang, C., Zhang, L.H, Lu, H.C, & Ruan, X., "Saliency detection via graph-based manifold ranking," In: Proc. IEEE Conf. on Computer Vision and Pattern Recognition, pp.3166–3173, 2013.

[25] Zhang, D. Z., Liu, C. C., "A salient object detection framework beyond top-down and bottom-up mechanism," Biologically Inspired Cognitive Architectures, vol.9, pp. 1-8. 2014.

ITM Web of Conferences **12**, 05016 (2017) DOI: 10.1051/itmconf/20171205016
ITA 2017

Online Active Learning with Drifted Data Streams Using Paired Ensemble Framework

Ji-Cheng Shan[1a], Wei-Ke Liu[2], Chen-Xi Chu[3], Chao-Fan Dai[1], and Qing-Bao Liu[1]

1Science and Technology on Information Systems Engineering Laboratory, National University of Defense Technology, 410073 Changsha, China
2College of Atmospheric Sciences, Lanzhou University, 730107 Lanzhou, China
3Sino-Dutch Biomedical and Information Engineering School of Northeastern University, 110819 Shenyang, China

Abstract. In learning to classify data streams, it is impractical and expensive to label all of the instances. Online active learning over streaming data poses additional challenges for its increasing volumes and concept drifts. We propose a new online paired ensemble active learning framework consisting of a stable classifier and a timely substituted dynamic classifier to react to different types of concept drifts. Classifiers are built in block based way and will learn new instances incrementally online. According to a combination strategy of uncertainty strategy and random strategy, the decision whether to label the incoming instance for the updating of the stable classifier and the dynamic classifier will be made. Experimental evaluation results on real datasets show the advantage of the proposed work in comparison with other approaches.

1. Introduction

Data streams are widely produced in areas such as financial activities, traffic flow, sensor networks and web applications with the development of storage technology and networking architecture [1]. In these dynamic environments, data streams are massive, temporally ordered, fast changing and potentially infinite [2].

In classification domain for data streams, usually unlabelled data is massive while labelled data is limited. Mostly it will be costly and time consuming to obtain labels of the instances in data streams due to oracle cost. Real time data streams can hardly provide sufficient labelled instances, restricting the generalization capability and predicting accuracy. Therefore, active learning focuses on how to label instances selectively to maximize the prediction accuracy as possible with limited label budget. Based on some criteria, active learning method selects the most representative and informative instances interactively [3]. Usually the representativeness of an incoming instance can be measured by its uncertainty according to the classifier model trained from the labelled instances [4]. Therefore, how to design appropriate metrics to assess the representativeness of an incoming instance becomes important concern [5].

In the scenario of data streams, classifiers need to make the decision whether to request the class label for every incoming instance immediately with no re-access as the data continuously arrive in real time [6]. Due to the non-stationary nature of data streams, concept drift, which refers to changing relations between the input attributes and the target labels, tend to often emerge over time. Moreover the decision threshold or a region of uncertainty cannot be kept fixed as concept drift negatively impacts the accuracy of the model that learned from the past training instances.

Usually concept drifts can be divided into sudden, gradual, or recurring drifts. Typical approaches that deal with concept drift mainly include: sliding window methods, new online means, special detection techniques, and adaptive ensembles [7]. Adaptive ensembles generate base classifiers sequentially from fixed size blocks of training examples called data chunks [8]. However, once the chunk size is too big the ensembles may react too slowly for sudden drifts as old classifiers still have remain weights. It can offer partly help in detecting sudden changes to use small size chunks, while this may also damage the stability and computational costs performance of the ensemble. Simple incremental learning [9-14] keeps sensitivity to sudden changes to make self-adaption timely but is not enough for coping with gradual drifts as forgetting history data and sharp adaptation to newest status. In order to adapt to both sudden and gradual changes, it could be suitable to combine significant features from block-based ensembles and incremental learning approaches.

In this paper, a new online paired ensemble active learning framework consisting of a stable classifier and a timely substituted dynamic classifier is proposed to react to different types of concept drift better. Classifiers are built using block based method. Once built, the two classifiers predict and learn from incoming instances in an online incremental way. The stable classifier will make suitable reactions to gradual changes; meanwhile the dynamic classifier keeps sensitivity to sudden changes.

The rest of the paper is organized as follows. Section II briefly reviews the related work. Section III presents the online paired ensemble active learning framework in detail. Experimental results and analysis are discussed in Section IV, and conclusion is given in Section V.

2. Related Work

In stream data classification, a set of infinite instances $S=\{(x_t,y_t)|t=1,\ldots,T\}$ appear with time flowing, where x_t is a vector for attribute values, y_t is the class label satisfying $y_t \in \{c_1,..,c_K\}$, and t indicates the time sequence. The active learning is to selectively label instances and build a classifier L from them to predict class labels for the future instances.

Žliobaitė et al. [15] presents a generic framework for active learning incrementally from drifting data streams. Several active learning strategies are incorporated into the framework. The strategies are equipped with mechanisms to control and distribute the labelling budget over time for learning more accurate classifiers adapted to changes. The three new proposed effective active learning strategies include *Variable Uncertainty Strategy* (*VarUn*), *Uncertainty Strategy with Randomization* (*RanVarUn*), and *Split Strategy* (*Split*). As discussed in the paper, different strategies perform best in different situations. Usually *RanVarUn* and *Split* strategies work well as they combine the uncertainty strategy and random strategy so that they will label the instances that are close to the decision boundary more often, but occasionally they will also label some distant instances. However with single classifier to learn incrementally, the combination strategy may still miss concept drifts occur in short period or even suffer accuracy decay as the drifted distribution differs from the historical trend. Xu et al. [16] adopts paired learning framework to cope with concept drift, and incorporates hybrid active learning strategies to identify both the most valuable instances and the potential changes in data streams. The stable classifier predicts based on all available labelled instances, while the reactive one predicts based on a window of recent instances from random strategy. So the reactive classifier is trained with instances uniformly distributed in the whole space, while the stable classifier is trained with instances mainly around the decision boundary. Whenever the reactive classifier has a better accuracy, the stable classifier is replaced by the reactive one, and the reactive classifier is reset. This replacing way makes both classifiers forget distributions of instances far away from the current window as the reactive classifier pay more attention to instances labelled in the window. Therefore it weakens the ability of the stable classifier to detect gradual drift. It may also cause late reaction to real drift as the replacement always happens after drift having been detected. So the framework may be over fit to sudden or local drifts and cannot deal gradual and recurring drifts well. To make the classifier be sensitive to both sudden and gradual drifts, this paper consider combining significant features from paired ensembles and incremental learning approaches.

3. Online Paired Ensemble Active Learning Framework for Drifted Data Streams

In this section, the new online paired ensemble active learning framework is described in detail. The main procedure is shown in Fig. 1. A circular array structure buffer window with the block size is used to cache incoming stances. When the window gets filled for the first time, the stable classifier and the first dynamic classifier will be built, as show in Fig. 2. Instances in the window will be accessed in order and be selected to learn according to the uncertainty strategy and random strategy as instances continue to be read from the stream. The new coming instance will replace the instance that has just been processed, as shown in Fig. 3. A new dynamic classifier will be built once the window is fulfilled by new instances again. Along with the building and updating of the new dynamic classifier, the stable classifier will incrementally learn from new instances online.

Algorithm 1: Online Paired Ensemble Active Learning Framework
Input: *S*: incoming data streams with unknown label, *x*: new instance *W*: chunk size to build new classifier *C*: circular array of W size to cache instances *p*: counter for processed instances, initialized with 0 Objective: build C_d and update C_s from *S* to classify instances as accurate as possible.

```
While (S hasNext) do
  x = S.nextInstance
  p=p+1
  If (p < W)                  //filling the first chunk
    C[p] = x
  Else If (p == W)
    C[p]= x                   //first chunk fulfilled
    CreateNewDynamicClassifier()
  Else       //p > W
    DealInstance(x)   // deal incoming instances after
                      //first chunk fulfilled
  End If
End While
For each instance I in C      //the chunk C still have
                              //W instances to deal
   DealInstance(I)
End For
```

Figure 1. Online paired ensemble active learning framework.

```
Algorithm 2: CreateNewDynamicClassifier()
L_n ← Randomly label a tiny portion of instances from chunk C
Build new classifier C_d from L_n
Update the stable classifier C_s with L_n
```

Figure 2. Procedure to build new dynamic classifier.

```
Algorithm 3: DealInstance(x)
Initialization: i=0, i is the index for the instances to be processed and cached
instance I_x =C[i]   //new instance comes, get cached
                     //instance to from chunk C
labelling=uncertaintyStrategy(I_x)
If labelling=true, then
  label I_x, then update C_s and C_d with labelled I_x
Else
  labelling =randomStrategy(σ)
  If labelling=true, then
    label I_x, then update C_s and C_d with labelled I_x
  End If
End If
C[i]= x  //the new instance will be cached in position
         // i to overwrite I_x
i=(i+1)%W
If i==0 then   // new instances fulfil the chunk again
  CreateNewDynamicClassifier()
End If
```

Figure 3. Algorithm to deal new instance.

When processing instances in the cache window, uncertainty strategy and random strategy are used in order. If an instance $\boldsymbol{x}$ is chosen to be labelled for its high uncertainty, the true class label of the instance $\boldsymbol{x}$ will be requested. If uncertainty strategy is failed to be satisfied, the algorithm then using random strategy to decide whether this x should be labelled. The uncertainty strategy is presented in Algorithm 4. It takes the instance $\boldsymbol{x}$, the ensemble classifier $\boldsymbol{E}$, the uncertainty threshold $\boldsymbol{\theta_m}$ and the adjustment step for threshold $\boldsymbol{s}$ as input. The algorithm calculates the margin for instance $\boldsymbol{x}$ using ensemble classifier $\boldsymbol{E}$ built by the stable classifier $\boldsymbol{C_s}$ and the dynamic classifier $\boldsymbol{C_d}$. Then, it compares the margin of $\boldsymbol{x}$ with threshold $\boldsymbol{\theta_m}$ If $margin(x)<\boldsymbol{\theta_m}$, then instance $\boldsymbol{x}$ is requested for labelling (*labelling=true*) and the threshold $\boldsymbol{\theta_m}$ will be adjusted. Otherwise, instance $\boldsymbol{x}$ should not be labelled according to the uncertainty strategy (*labelling=false*). A margin-based metric to measure the uncertainty of an instance considers both the maximum a posteriori probability and the second most probable class label. The margin for instance x is defined as in (1)

$$margin(x)=P_L(\hat{y}_{c_1}|x)-P_L((\hat{y}_{c_2}|x), \quad (1)$$

where $\hat{y}_{c_1}$ and $\hat{y}_{c_2}$ are respectively the class with the maximum posteriori probability and the second most posteriori probability [17] [18], $\boldsymbol{L}$ is the ensemble classifier used. The margin-based metric is prone to select instances with minimum margin between posteriori probabilities of the two most likely class labels. The random strategy is the same with that used in [16] because of its concision.

```
Algorithm 4: uncertaintyStrategy(x)
input:  x: incoming instance,
        E: ensemble classifier built with C_s and C_d
        θ_m =0.6/numberOfClasses ,uncertainty threshold
        s=0.1, step to adjust threshold θ_m
output: boolean variable labelling indicates whether to
        request the true label of I_x.
margin(x)=P_E(ŷ_c1|x)-PE(ŷ_c2|x);
If (margin(x)< θ_m) then
  θ_m =θ_m * (1 - s/numberOfClasses);
  return labelling=true;
Else
  return labelling=false ;
End If
```

Figure 4. Uncertainty active learning strategy algorithm.

4. Experimental Evaluation

In this section, the proposed online paired ensemble active learning framework (*OnPEAL*) is empirically evaluated on real streaming classification problems. *OnPEAL* is compared with the paired ensemble framework for active learning (*PEFAL*) presented in [16] and three representative active learning strategies described in [15], including *Variable Uncertainty Strategy* (*VarUn*), *Uncertainty Strategy with Randomization* (*RanVarUn*), and *Split Strategy* (*Split*). All the experiments are performed using the MOA data stream software suite [19]. MOA is an open source software environment for stream data mining, including evaluation measures and a collection of implemented algorithms. For comparison, the *PEFAL* algorithm is implemented using MOA according to the procedure described in [16] and the active learning classifier using those strategies has already been integrated into MOA by authors of [15]. All algorithms use Hoeffding tree as base classifier to perform the classification and to produce the maximum a posteriori probability.

4.1 Datasets

In the experiments, four real world public datasets referred in [12] are used: Airlines [20], Cover Type [21], Electricity [22], and NSL-KDD [23]. The characteristics of each dataset are listed in Table 1. Detailed information for the datasets can be referred to [12].

Table 1. Dataset characteristics

Dataset	Number of Instances	Number of Attributes	Number of Classes
Airlines	539383	7	2
Cover Type	581012	54	7
Electricity	45312	8	2
NSL-KDD	148517	41	2

 DOI: 10.1051/itmconf/20171205016

4.2 Accuracy Evaluation

In this subsection, the accuracy on different datasets with labelling budget varying from 0.1 to 0.5 is evaluated. Fig. 5 plots the accuracy of different methods as a function of the labelling budget. The results show that *OnPEAL* obtains better accuracies on all the four datasets with limited labelled percentage. For Airlines, the accuracy improvement of the *OnPEAL* is clear when labelled percentage arises. For Cover Type and Electricity, the accuracy is relatively stable with small improvement trend with the labelled percentage increasing. As for the NSL-KDD dataset, the accuracy of *OnPEAL* is stable and the difference between *OnPEAL* and Split is slight when the labelled percentage is higher than 0.2. *OnPEAL* gets high accuracy on all the datasets when the labelled percentage is low and the accuracy keeps stable with improvement trend when the labelled percentage arises. In *OnPEAL* framework, the stable classifier can follow the long-time trend of the instance space and the dynamic classifier keeps sensibility to sudden changes. Therefore the online paired ensemble framework can make adaptive adjustment to drifts in data streams.

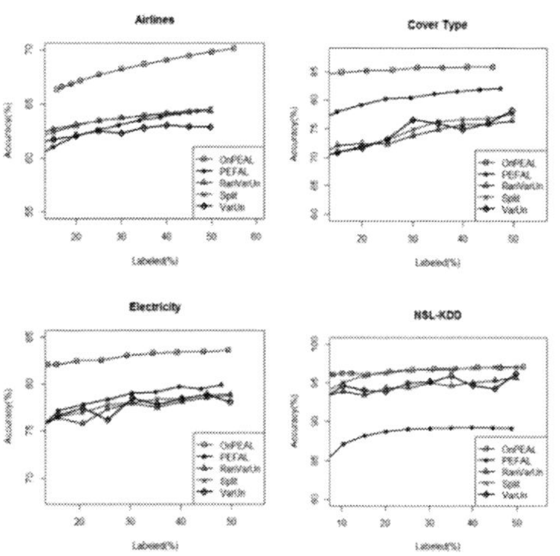

Figure 5. Accuracy on evaluation datasets with different labelled percentages.

4.3 Sensitivity to Parameters

The impact of the window size W over the accuracy and labelled percentage of *OnPEAL* is experimentally evaluated in this subsection. The initial random selection percentage when building new classifier using block based method is set at 0.3 to control the active labelled percentage in certain region. As shown in Table 2, both the accuracy and labelled percentage are relatively stable for Cover Type and NSL-KDD datasets. Airlines gets stable accuracy and decreasing labelled percentage with window size increasing. However, both the accuracy and labelled percentage reduce when window size improves for Electricity. This may be caused by the small amount of Electricity data and its continual drift changes.

Table 2. Accuracy and labelled percentage for different window sizes

	Airlines		Cover Type	
Window Size	Accuracy (%)	Labelled (%)	Accuracy (%)	Labelled (%)
100	69.232	54.738	85.239	35.797
150	69.332	50.924	86.055	35.956
200	69.415	48.371	86.001	36.009
250	69.463	46.511	85.958	36.014
300	69.429	45.102	85.713	35.979
350	69.451	44.024	85.608	35.94
400	69.474	43.099	85.224	35.922
450	69.491	42.33	84.975	35.884
500	69.476	41.705	84.8	35.897
	Electricity		NSL-KDD	
Window Size	Accuracy (%)	Labelled (%)	Accuracy (%)	Labelled (%)
100	85.748	41.121	96.650	36.679
150	84.7	40.759	96.569	36.539
200	84.012	40.167	96.545	36.466
250	83.712	39.867	96.576	36.308
300	83.294	39.467	96.895	36.185
350	83.482	39.017	96.720	36.063
400	82.483	38.736	96.789	35.992
450	82.33	38.301	96.615	35.945
500	82.285	38.258	96.762	35.870

5. Conclusion

Cost limitation of labelled instances and the potential concept drifts have posed significant challenges on stream data classification in practice. Therefore a new online paired ensemble framework for active learning with drifted data streams using combination labelling strategies is proposed. The ensemble classifier consists of a long stable classifier built since beginning and a timely substituted dynamic classifier. Two different active learning strategies, uncertainty strategy and random strategy, are incorporated into the framework in order to find out the most informative instances without missing the potential changes happened anywhere in the instance space. Experimental results on real world datasets demonstrated that the novel approach gets good prediction accuracy. For future work we would like to investigate the ensemble framework and active learning strategies in more detail.

References

1. J. Gama: Knowledge Discovery from Data Streams, 1st ed. Chapman & Hall/CRC (2010).
2. P. Domingos, G. Hulten.: Mining high-speed data streams. Proc. 6th ACM Int. Conf. on Knowledge Discovery and Data Mining, pp. 71–80 (2000).

3. X. Zhu, P. Zhang, X. Lin, Y. Shi.: Active learning from stream data using optimal weight classifier ensemble. IEEE Transactions on Systems, Man, and Cybernetics, Part B: Cybernetics, vol. 40, pp. 1607–1621 (2010).
4. J. Attenberg, F. Provost.: Online active inference and learning. Proc. 17th ACM Int. Conf. on Knowledge Discovery and Data Mining, pp. 186–194 (2011).
5. D. Cohn, L. Atlas, R. Ladner.: Improving generalization with active learning. Mach. Learn 15(2), 201–221 (1994).
6. L. I. Kuncheva.: Classifier ensembles for detecting concept change in streaming data: Overview and perspectives. in Proc. 2nd Workshop SUEMA 2008, pp. 5–10 (2008).
7. D. Brzezinski, J. Stefanowski. Reacting to different types of concept drift: the accuracy updated ensemble algorithm. Neural Networks & Learning Systems IEEE Transactions on, 25(1), 81-94 (2014).
8. H. Wang, W. Fan, P. Yu, J. Han.: Mining concept-drifting data streams using ensemble classifiers. in Proc. KDD, pp. 226–235 (2003).
9. R. Elwell, R. Polikar.: Incremental learning of concept drift in nonstationary environments. IEEE Transactions on Neural Networks, vol. 22, pp. 1517–1531 (2011).
10. A. Bifet et al..: Leveraging bagging for evolving data streams. in Proc. ECML/PKDD, Part I, pp. 135–150 (2010).
11. L. L. Minku, X. Yao.: DDD: A new ensemble approach for dealing with concept drift. IEEE Transactions on Knowledge and Data Engineering, 24(4), pp.619–633 (2012).
12. N. C. Oza, S. J. Russell.: Experimental comparisons of online and batch versions of bagging and boosting. in Proc. 7th ACM SIGKDD Int. Conf. Knowledge Discovery Data Mining, pp. 359–364 (2001).
13. J. Z. Kolter, M. A. Maloof.: Dynamic weighted majority: An ensemble method for drifting concepts. J. Machine Learning Research, vol. 8, pp. 2755–2790 (2007).
14. R. Kirkby.: Improving Hoeffding trees. Ph.D. dissertation, Department of Computer Science, University of Waikato, (2007).
15. I. Zliobaite, A. Bifet, B. Pfahringer B.: Active learning with drifting streaming data. IEEE Transactions on Neural Networks and Learning Systems, vol. 25, pp. 27–39 (2014).
16. W. Xu, F. Zhao, Z. Lu. "Active learning over evolving data streams using paired ensemble framework." Eighth International Conference on Advanced Computational Intelligence, pp.180-185, (2016).
17. Y. Fu, X. Zhu, B. Li, "A survey on instance selection for active learning," Knowledge and Information Systems, vol. 35, pp. 249–283 (2013).
18. D. Ienco, B. Pfahringer, I. Zliobaite, "High density-focused uncertainty sampling for active learning over evolving stream data, " Proc. 3rd Int. Workshop on Big Data, Streams and Heterogeneous Source Mining: Algorithms, Systems, Programming Models and Applications, pp. 133–148 (2014).
19. A. Bifet, G. Holmes, R. Kirkby, B. Pfahringer.: MOA: Massive online analysis. Journal of Machine Learning Research, vol. 11, 1601–1604 (2010).
20. E. Ikonomovska, J. Gama, S. Dzeroski.: Learning model trees from evolving data streams. Data Mining Knowl. Discovery, 23(1), 128–168 (2011).
21. A. Frank, A. Asuncion. (2010). UCI machine learning repository [Online]. Available: http://archive.ics.uci.edu/ml
22. M. Harries, C. Sammut, K. Horn.: Extracting hidden context. Machine Learning, 32(2), 101–126 (1998).
23. M. Tavallaee, E. Bagheri, W. Lu.: A detailed analysis of the KDD CUP 99 data set. Proc. 2nd IEEE Symposium on Computational Intelligence for Security and Defence Applications, pp. 1–9 (2009).

Improved SURF Algorithm and Its Application in Seabed Relief Image Matching

Hong-Mei ZHANG[1], Le YANG, Ming-Long LI[1]

[1]Department of Automation, School of Power and Mechanical Engineering
Wuhan University, Wuhan, China, e-mail: le_yang@whu.edu.cn

Abstract— The matching based on seabed relief image is widely used in underwater relief matching navigation and target recognition, etc. However, being influenced by various factors, some conventional matching algorithms are difficult to obtain an ideal result in the matching of seabed relief image. SURF(Speeded Up Robust Features) algorithm is based on feature points pair to achieve matching, and can get good results in the seabed relief image matching. However, in practical applications, the traditional SURF algorithm is easy to get false matching, especially when the area's features are similar or not obvious, the problem is more seriously. In order to improve the robustness of the algorithm, this paper proposes an improved matching algorithm, which combines the SURF, and RANSAC (Random Sample Consensus) algorithms. The new algorithm integrates the two algorithms advantages, firstly, the SURF algorithm is applied to detect and extract the feature points then to pre-match. Secondly, RANSAC algorithm is utilized to eliminate mismatching points, and then the accurate matching is accomplished with the correct matching points. The experimental results show that the improved algorithm overcomes the mismatching problem effectively and have better precision and faster speed than the traditional SURF algorithm.

1 Introduction

AUV (Autonomous Underwater Vehicle) is a type of unmanned underwater vehicle (UUV), Because of its high autonomy, passivity, invisibility, it has been widely used in the field of marine science and military[1]. With the development of the AUV, the image-matching algorithm based on seabed relief also becomes the research hot spot [2]. Image matching algorithm is a key part of image matching navigation, and robust image matching algorithm is the basis of safe navigation. Under the influence of various factors, the conventional matching algorithm is prone to mismatching in seabed relief image matching, which brings security flaws to navigation, so it is of great significance to study the reliable image-matching algorithm.

Among the image matching algorithms, SURF algorithm as an improved algorithm of the SIFT (Scale-invariant feature transform) algorithm, first proposed by Bay in 2006, due to its high efficiency and good robustness to rotation and scale, SURF is widely used in object recognition, 3D reconstruction and image matching[3-6]. Many scholars have studied the image matching algorithm based on SURF, Xie Yulai proposed underwater images real-time registration method based on SURF[3]; SU Kexin presented anti-viewpoint changing image matching algorithm based on SURF[4]; Yanwei Pang used fully affine invariant SURF for image matching[5]; ZHAO Lu-lu proposed an images matching algorithm based on SURF and fast approximate nearest neighbor search for that nearest neighbor matching of high-dimensional feature vector was low[6]. The SURF algorithm has achieved good results in a specific application. Accurate extraction of the image feature points is the key to ensure successful matching. However, in the practical application, the traditional SURF algorithm is prone to mismatching, especially in the area where the seabed features are not obvious.

RANSAC algorithm is a model parameter estimation method, first proposed by Fischler and Bolles in 1981[7], which can be used to deal with outliers in the data, and widely used in the purification of data. Qu Tianwei's research confirms that the RANSAC algorithm can reduce the interference of outliers and improve the matching effect [8]. In order to reduce the error matching, improve the performance of the SURF algorithm, and ensure the correct matching of the seabed relief image, comprehensively utilize the advantages of SURF algorithm and RANSAC algorithm to present an improved SURF algorithm. First, the matching image and reference image is preprocessed, then use the SURF algorithm to extract their feature points and pre-match, finally, the RANSAC algorithm is used to

DOI: 10.1051/itmconf/20171205017

eliminate the mismatching points, and on this basis, the fast and accurate image matching is realized.

2 Traditional SURF algorithm and RANSAC algorithm

2.1 SURF Algorithm

Hessian matrix has good performance in experiment speed and precision. This matrix is widely used to determine the specific location and size of the scale, and SURF algorithm uses Hessian matrix as feature extractor. For any point $X=(x,y)$ in the image I that needs to be matched, the Hessian matrix $H(X,\sigma)$ is defined by vector σ as:

$$H(X,\sigma)=\begin{bmatrix} L_{xx}(X,\sigma) & L_{xy}(X,\sigma) \\ L_{xy}(X,\sigma) & L_{yy}(X,\sigma) \end{bmatrix} \quad (1)$$

Among them, $L_{xx}(X,\sigma)$ is the convolution of point X in matching image I and the value of second-order Gaussian Filter $\partial^2 g(\sigma)/\partial^2 x$; the meaning of $L_{xy}(X,\sigma)$ and $L_{yy}(X,\sigma)$ is similar to this.

Bay et al. [9] proposed a box type filter approximate to second order Gauss filter, and then use the integral image to expedite the convolution speed, and reduce the computational work. For a gray image, the value of any point (x,y) in the integral image refers to the sum of the gray values of all the points in the rectangle region, which is formed from the upper left corner of the image to this point.

$$I_{\Sigma}(x)=\sum_{i=0}^{i\le x}\sum_{j=0}^{j\le y} I(i,j) \quad (2)$$

In the original image, expand the size of the box to get a different scale image pyramid, template filtering as shown in Figure 1.

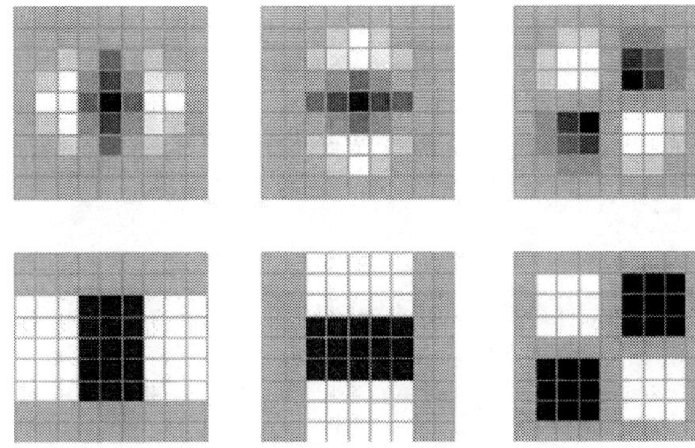

Fig.1 Box Filter

Box type filter in Figure 1 corresponds to second order Gauss filter, the value after Box filtering template respectively convoluting with the image is D_{xx} 、 D_{yy} and D_{zz} . The value of the Hessian matrix for each point in the scale space of the SURF operator, Bay et al. give an approximate formula as shown in formula (3).

$$delta = D_{xx}D_{yy}-(0.9D_{xy})^2 \quad (3)$$

If the filter template size is $N\times N$, then the corresponding scale $s=\sigma=1.2\times N/9=1.2$. After using the Hessian matrix to find the extreme value, the non-maxima suppression is carried out in the $3\times3\times3$ three-dimensional domain. Only the feature points are larger or smaller than the 26 neighborhood values around the previous scale, then the next scale and current scale can be treated as candidate feature points, make a interpolation operation in scale space and image space to get stable feature points location and the scale value.

2.2 RANSAC algorithm

RANSAC algorithm is a resampling method, with minimal observation points to estimate the basic model parameters. For the basic assumption of the algorithm is: sample contains the correct data (inliers and can be described by the model of data), also contains abnormal data (outliers, deviated very far from the normal range, unable to adapt to the mathematical model of the data), that the data set contains noise. These abnormal data may be due to errors in measurement, incorrect assumptions, calculation and so on. In addition, RANSAC also assumes that, given a right set of data, there is a method to calculate the model parameters consistent with the data [10].

Its basic idea can be described as follows:

STEP1 : Randomly select the required minimum number of samples that can determine the model parameters.

STEP2: Calculate the model parameters.

STEP3: Determine the number of points from all points that are in accordance with the prescribed tolerance.

STEP4: If the number of the correct points in the point set is more than the predetermined threshold value τ , then use the determined interior points to re-estimate the model parameters.

STEP5: Otherwise, repeat 1 to 4 steps (up to N times).

Select enough number of iterations N to ensure that at least one random sample set does not contain abnormal data and the probability $p \geq 0.99$. If it is assumed that the probability of any selected data point is the correct data for u, then $v = 1 - u$ indicates the possibility of containing abnormal data. The minimum number of points required for the N iterations is assumed to be m, then

$$1 - p = \left(1 - u^m\right)^N \quad (4)$$

Transform to be

$$N = \frac{\log(1-p)}{\log\left(1-(1-v)^m\right)} \quad (5)$$

3 The improved SURF algorithm

3.1The Principle of Improved Algorithm

The improved algorithm utilizes the advantages of the SURF algorithm and RANSAC algorithm, firstly, the feature points are extracted and pre-matched by SURF algorithm, then use RANSAC algorithm to eliminate the false matching points, lastly on this basis to carry on precise-matching. The principle of the algorithm is shown in Figure 2.

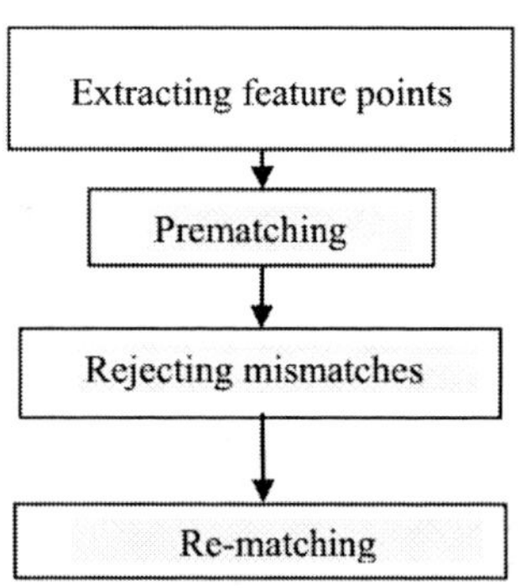

Fig.2 Improved algorithm principle diagram

4 Experiment and analysis

4.1Experimental image acquisition

First, using side-scan sonar system to obtain seabed relief image, and the original image is preprocessed to obtain high-quality seabed relief image for subsequent experiments.

Figure 3 (a) is the preprocessed image. In order to carry out the matching experiment, select the background image (a) in the black box as part of the target image to be matched, as shown in Figure 4 (b)

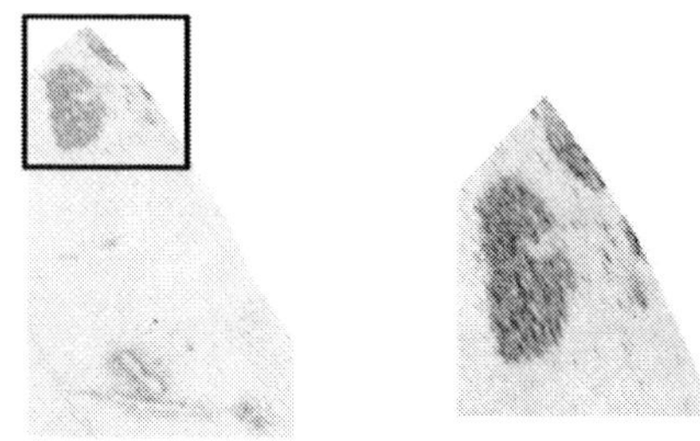

(a) background image (b) target image

Fig.3 Experimental image selection

4.2SURF feature extraction

Using Hessian matrix to extract the image's feature points, as shown in Figure 4.

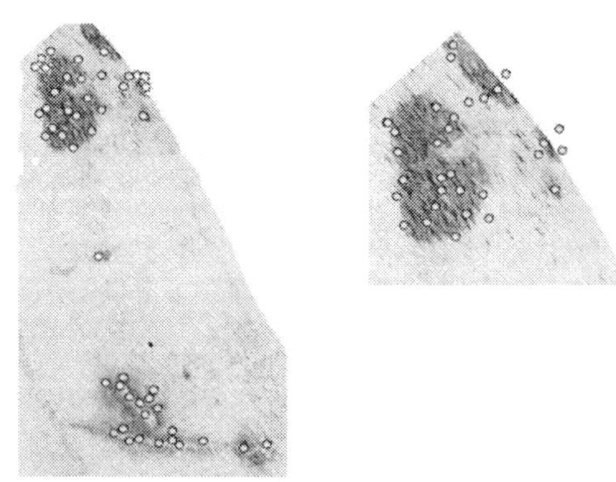

Fig.4 Image feature point extraction

It can be realized from Figure 6 that the Hessian matrix can effectively detect and extract the feature points in the area with high contrast and obvious features.

4.3 Main direction determination

In order to distinguish the obtained feature points, the SURF algorithm uses the main direction of the feature points to describe the feature points.

In order to guarantee the rotation invariance, in SURF, there is no statistics of its gradient histogram, but the Haar wavelet features within feature point neighborhood are counted. That is feature points as the center, in the neighborhood of the calculated radius of 6S (S is the scale value where the feature points lie.), the sum of the Haar wavelet responses of all points in the 60-degree sector in the X and Y directions is statistically analyzed (Haar wavelet length is 4S). And the response value is assigned to the Gauss weight coefficient,which makes the response near the feature points is large, and the response far away from feature points is small, then use the response in the range of 60 degrees to form a new vector, traverse the entire circular area, the direction of the longest vector is selected as the main direction of the feature points. In this way, through the feature point calculation one by one, to get the main direction of each feature point, the process is shown in Figure 5.

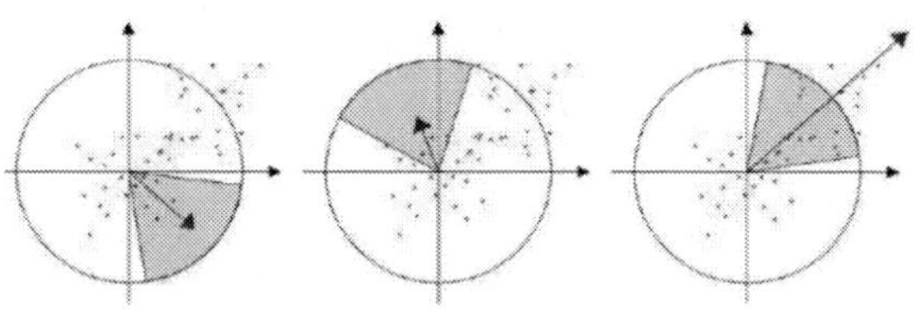

Fig.5 Determination of principal direction based on Haar wavelet

4.4Descriptor generation

Feature point as the center, axis is fixed to the main direction of the main position, according to the main direction of the selected length for 20s square area, and it was divided into 4×4 sub regions. In each sub region, some simple features are calculated. Now d_x is defined as the Haar wavelet response in the horizontal direction, d_y is the Haar wavelet response in the vertical direction. In order to enhance the robustness against the geometric deformation and the location error, a Gauss weight is added to the Haar wavelet response d_x and d_y at the feature points. Finally, the response of d_x and d_y in horizontal direction and vertical direction are accumulated separately in each sub region, then, $|d_x|$ and $|d_y|$ are accumulated separately to obtain the polarity of the intensity variation. The basic intensity image of each sub region is described by the following vector:

$$V=(\sum dx,\sum dy,\sum|dx|,\sum|dy|) \tag{6}$$

So,the length of descriptor vector formed by 4×4 sub region is 64, and call this to be feature point's SURF descriptor.

4.5Feature matching

The SURF descriptor of the feature point in the target image is pre-matched with the SURF descriptor of the corresponding block feature point in the background image [11]. Since the extracted feature points may be noise or non-feature points, the initial match may not be correct. The matching result is presented in Figure6:

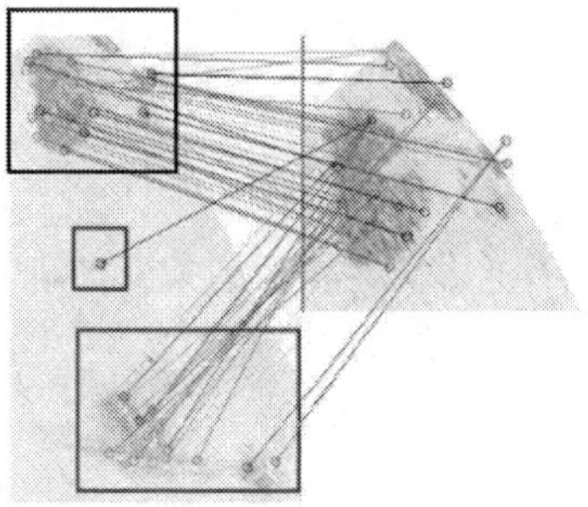

Fig.6 Feature points matching of SURF algorithm

In Figure 6, the black box part on the left side is the correct matching area, and the red box circle part is the mismatching area. Obviously, during the image matching process, the feature points in the red box will affect the success probability. For this reason, use RANSAC algorithm to remove the mismatching points, as shown in figure 7:

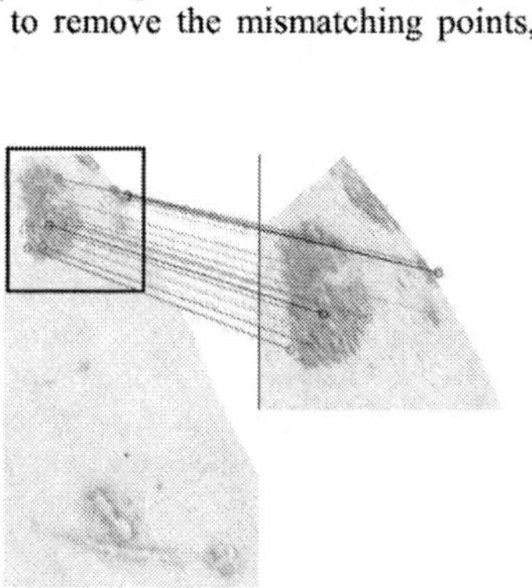

Fig.7: RACSAC algorithm removes the mismatching points

4.6Matching verification

Randomly choose three pairs from the correct matching points to estimate the affine transformation matrix of feature

DOI: 10.1051/itmconf/20171205017

point sequence. In this paper, RANSAC algorithm is used to estimate the affine transformation matrix H:

$$H=\begin{bmatrix} h_{11} & h_{12} & h_{13} \\ h_{21} & h_{22} & h_{23} \\ h_{31} & h_{32} & h_{33} \end{bmatrix} \quad (7)$$

Then the affine transformation matrix H is used to test whether the difference of each characteristic point position and the estimated position is within the tolerance range [12]. As follows:

$$\left(x_i' - \frac{h_{11}x_i + h_{12}y_i + h_{13}}{h_{31}x_i + h_{32}y_i + h_{33}}\right)^2 + \left(y_i' - \frac{h_{21}x_i + h_{22}y_i + h_{23}}{h_{31}x_i + h_{32}y_i + h_{33}}\right)^2 < \delta \quad (8)$$
$$i = 1, \ldots, n$$

When the number of matching points fit formula 8 is bigger than threshold m and the difference between the feature point's position and the estimated position is less than the threshold $d_{\max}$, and then believe the matching is successful. Otherwise, repeat the above procedure and re estimate the matrix H. If the number of corresponding feature points is less than four, or the matrix H is re-estimated to be 100 times and there is no a constraint fits formula 8, then the image matching is considered to be failure.

In Figure 6, the black box part on the left side is the correct matching area, and the red box circle part is the mismatching area. Compared with Figure 7, it can be found that there is no mismatching phenomenon after using the improved algorithm. The improved SURF algorithm uses SURF algorithm to extract feature points and pre match, and then use the RANSAC algorithm to eliminate the false matching point pairs, and on this basis to achieve precise matching. During the matching process, this method filtrates a large number of image's feature points, and rejects the mismatching points. The improved algorithm not only solves the mismatching problem in the traditional SURF algorithm, but also improves the problem of traditional SURF algorithm needs to match a large number of feature points. The simulation results show that the improved SURF algorithm has greatly improved the image matching accuracy. At the same time, compared with the traditional SURF algorithm, the matching error, matching efficiency and real-time performance are significantly improved. The performance comparison between the improved algorithm and the original algorithm is shown in Table 1.

Tab.1 Performance Comparison Before And After Improvement

Traditional SURF algorithm	Improved SURF algorithm	
	Number of feature points	53
Matching method and performance	Number of mismatching feature points	19
	Match time/s	25.21
	Number of feature points	15
	Number of mismatching feature points	0
	Match time/s	3.11

It can be seen from the Table 1 that whether in matching accuracy or matching time, the improved algorithm is better than the traditional SURF algorithm. The matching time is reduced to 12%, and the matching efficiency is increased to 100%.

Conclusions

SURF algorithm uses the concept of Haar feature and integral image, which can greatly speed up the matching speed; RANSAC algorithm can calculate the model parameters of the point set according to a set of sample points with abnormal data, and get the effective sample data. Due to the traditional SURF algorithm is prone to mismatching in the seabed relief image matching, the paper proposes an improved algorithm based on SURF algorithm and RANSAC algorithm, and applies it to the seabed relief image matching. The improved algorithm combines the advantages of SURF algorithm and RANSAC algorithm to improve the accuracy and robustness of the simulation, and the simulation results verify the effectiveness of the algorithm.

Acknowledgment

This work is partially supported by the National Natural Science Foundation of China (41376109) and National High Technology Research and Development Program of China (863 Program) (2009AA12Z311).

References

[1] Bo XU, Bai J L, Hao Y L, et al. The Research Status and Progress of Cooperative Navigation for Multiple AUVs[J]. Zidonghua Xuebao/acta Automatica Sinica, 2015, 41(3):445-461.
[2] Zhang H M, Zhao J H, Shao N. Underwater Match Navigation Based on Characteristic Seabed Relief Image[J]. Measurement & Control Technology, 2011, 30(11):96-226.
[3] Xie Y, Li X, Lu J, et al. Underwater Images Real-Time

Registration Method Based on SURF[J]. Journal of Computer-Aided Design & Computer Graphics, 2010, 22(12):2215-2220.

[4] SU K, HAN G, SUN H. Anti-Viewpoint Changing Image Matching Algorithm Based on SURF[J]. Chinese Journal of Liquid Crystals and Displays, 2013, 4: 034.

[5] Pang Y, Li W, Yuan Y, et al. Fully affine invariant SURF for image matching [J]. *Neurocomputing*, 2012, 85: 6-10.

[6] Zhao L L, Geng G H, Kang L I, et al. Images matching algorithm based on SURF and fast approximate nearest neighbor search[J]. Application Research of Computers, 2013, 30(3):921-923. (in Chinese)

[7] M.A. Fischler and R.C. Bolles. Random sample consensus: A paradigm for model fitting with applications to image analysis and automated cartography. Communications of the ACM, 24(6):381–395, 1981.

[8] Wenchao L, Guodong L, Haiyan Y. Application of SIFT and advanced RANSAC algorithm on image registration[J]. Computer Engineering and Applications, 2013, 49(15): 147-149.

[9] Bay H, Tuytelaars T, Van Gool L. Surf: Speeded up robust features[M].Computer vision–ECCV 2006. Springer Berlin Heidelberg, 2006: 404-417.

[10] Zhang H, Shao N, Meng X, et al. 2010. Fast Image Matching Method and Its Applications in Underwater Positioning[J]. Electrical and Control Engineering (ICECE), International Conference on, 2010: 970 - 973.

[11] Tao W, Zhao J, Liu J, et al. Study on the side-scan sonar image matching navigation based on surf[C].Electrical and Control Engineering (ICECE), 2010 International Conference on. IEEE, 2010: 2181-2184.

[12] Chen F X, Wang R S. Fast RANSAC with Preview Model Parameters Evaluation[J]. Journal of Software, 2005, 16(8).

ITM Web of Conferences 12, 05018 (2017) DOI: 10.1051/itmconf/20171205018
ITA 2017

Mining based on Extraction and Importance Evaluation Using Multi-Measures Methods for Electronic Documents

Wen XIONG, Zi-Hui DING

China Great Wall Computer Shenzhen Company Limited, China Electronics Corporation,Beijing, China
xiongwen@greatwall.com.cn

Abstract—Mining the implicit knowledge in the electronic documents is a critical task in text analysis and data mining. To attain a knowledge-based view of the electronic documents, the clustering method based upon the topic cannot only be used, but also that based upon the extraction can be done. Therefore, a novel method for the clustering of the electronic documents, summarizing of the full text based on the extracted segments, and an evaluation using multi-measures for the importance to the document were presented. In the method, eighteen kinds of named entities and two kinds of syntactical phrases were extracted, and exploited for the text clustering. Then, a novel similarity equation was proposed for the calculation about the extractions. Meantime, three measures for the importance to the document were proposed, which provided a different view for the document's content, and recommended a prior checking for the users. Therefore, the method can improve the efficiency of the knowledge discovery, and enhance the management of the document on the large scale of document collection.

1 Introduction

Along with the increases of the tremendous volume of the computer server, and the popularizing of the fast application of the cloud computing, many organizations have been accumulating more and more of the electronic documents. Mining the commercial value and the implied knowledge in the set of the electronic documents becomes an incremental market demand. The common methods in the text analysis and text mining include text classification, text clustering, named entity recognition (NER), information extraction (IE), text summary, document recommendation, etc.

From the angle of information retrieve (IR), a way of obtaining the information from a set of the documents is to index the full text of each document in the set based on words first, then, to use a search engine and some keywords to sort the relevant documents by calculating the similarity, and then, to return a sorted list to the user. The user will further examine the content of the documents, and locate the similar paragraphs. The result of the retrieve depends on the distribution of the keywords on the set of the documents.

Alternative methods from the text mining (TM), e.g. document clustering, calculate the document similarity according to the word morphologies and their distribution, which cluster the documents into some relatively independent classes according to the similarity rule, which can be used for analyzing the implied knowledge in the electronic documents. Both procedures above can be regarded as a pre-process, which are based on words, and extract the words' distribution, such as term frequency, term frequency and inverse document frequency (TF-IDF), etc.

However, there are many extractable segments instead of words, such as named entities (NE) and phrases, which represent the characteristic of the electronic documents, and their distributions in the documents represent the originality, and the quality. The finance relevant enterprises have a superior requirement to the active information, such as the stock, the events of corporation combination, the company's announcement, etc. E.g. the competitive companies care the commercial activity from the competitors, such as the fund invested to certain domains, the amount of money from the trade, and business show at certain localities in a special time. In addition, the jargons and phrases belong to the technology appeared at the interview of the competitors express the interests of the research and development (R&D) on the current or in the future.

Therefore, those named entities will be analyzed and extracted, such as company, location, people, time, money, number, and quantity. In addition, grammar chunks, such as the long verb phrases (VP) as the semantic of the activity, and the long noun phrases (NP) as the technical content of the R&D, will also be done.

Clustering and categorization for the documents often need to apply the feature reducing due to the high dimension

DOI: 10.1051/itmconf/20171205018

of the word features in the document set. The common distribution of these words decides the inherent division of the document set. The result of the clustering only discloses the topic-level knowledge, which means the user cannot find the extraction-level knowledge intuitively from it, and the further process will be needed for text extraction. Therefore, the text extraction can be regarded as another pre-process different from that based on words mentioned above. Then, the text clustering and text classification based upon the extraction will provide other different viewpoints to the user, according to the kinds of the extractions and their similarity as the document features for the analysis, which exhibits the knowledge views of the document set, and therefore, have a special application value.

For the long documents, the summarizing for the full text provides a useful and a meaningful method. Generally speaking, it calculates the importance in the sentence based upon the importance in the words, then, it extracts the abstract by the importance in the sentence. Some named entities are ignored in the procedure, and time, number, and quantity are insensitivity. Therefore, it cannot satisfy the user's requirement from the angle of the IE, although this kind of summary can effectively shorten the content browsed by the user, and provide an abbreviate view of full text. On the other hand, the summarizing for the full text composed by the sentences based on the extraction segments will provide a new user view, which directly take the content extraction as the user's requirement, and form an important complement and an intuitionist expression for the abbreviated view of the full text, having a special application value.

Based on the above starting points, this paper presents a novel method for the clustering of the electronic documents, summarizing for full text based on extracted segments, and an evaluation using multi-measures for the document importance, which can be used for the analysis, mining, summary, evaluation, and recommendation for the electronic documents of the organizations.

The rest on the paper is organized as follows: first, in Section 2, the new method for mining and evaluation based on extraction is proposed; then, in Section 3, the related work in the mining and analysis of the documents is introduced in brief; in addition, in Section 4, the detail about the experiments is described; finally, in Section 5, conclusions are reached from the above discussion.

2 Methods

2.1Text Clustering Based on Extraction Information

To attain the cluster knowledge in the document set, we exploited the extracted information, such as named entities and grammar phrases. The former includes eighteen classes, such as Person, Facility, Geo-Political Entity (GPE), Product, Word of Art, Language, Time, Money, Ordinal, Nation or Region Politic (NORP), Organization, Location, Event, Law, Date, Percent, Quantity, and Cardinal. The latter includes two classes, i.e. long NP and long VP.

We can express the document as twenty variable-length vectors, which correspond to the eighteen classes of *NE*s and two classes of grammar phrases, and formulated the similarity of the documents as follows.

$$S(u,v)=\sum_{i=1}^{20}\max_{\substack{j=1,\dots,n1\\k=1,\dots,n2}}\{S'(u_{ij},v_{ik})\}$$
$$s.t.\ S'(u_{ij},v_{ik})=\begin{cases}|q_j=q_k|,\ i=Quantity\\|c_j=c_k|,\ i=Money\\|t_j\cong t_k|,\ i=Time,Date\\u_{ij}==v_{ik},i=Ordinal,Cardianl,Percent\\N-ed(u_{ij},v_{ik}),\ i=other.\end{cases}\tag{1}$$

Where: $ed(,)$ is the Levensthein edit-distance [1], and q for quantity, c for currency, t for time unit, and N for constant. Then, we adopted centroid-based clustering algorithms, e.g. K-Means to form the knowledge clusters.

2.2 Summarization for full text based on the adjoined position of the extracted information

Different from summarization for full text based on word importance, that based on the adjoined position of the extracted information needs to iterate each sub-clause of each sentence, and outputs the sentences and sub-clauses in the original order if they hit an extraction, which provides a view based on the extractions.

2.3 The importance evaluation for electronic documents using multi-measures integration

In the technical articles, a concept is more original when it was proposed early, or it was mentioned by the technical articles published after it. This typical phenomenon is appeared in the scientific papers and the patent texts [2]. Therefore, the paper proposes a measure for the originality of the documents, which reflects the original importance in the importance evaluation in the background set of documents as follows.

$$O_1=\sum_{i=1}^{n}O(T_i)$$
$$s.t.\ \mathrm{O}(T)=max(\frac{sup(T)-2}{\text{age-in-days}(T)+1},0).\tag{2}$$

Where: $sup(T)$ is the support degree, and $\text{age-in-days}(T)$ is the number of the days when T appeared. The document is more important when the score of the document is bigger according to it.

The writing features are more complex when the number of the different words, named entities, long VP, and long NP is bigger. This typical phenomenon is also appeared in the scientific papers and patent texts [3]. Therefore, the paper presents a measure for the writing quality of the documents, which reflects the quality importance in the importance evaluation in the background set of documents as follows.

$$C = IOWA_w(<v_1, a_1>, \ldots, <v_{10}, a_{20}>) \\ = \sum_{i=1}^{20} w_i a_{\sigma(i)} \\ s.t. <v_1, \ldots, v_{20}> = <1, 2, \ldots, 20>. \tag{3}$$

Where: $IOWA$ is the Induced Ordered Weighted Averaging operator, and w_i is the weight of a_i, corresponding to the twenty extractions; v_i is the induced variable. The document is more important when the score of the document is bigger according to it.

The concepts are often distributed widely when they are appeared in more articles in the background set of documents, which expresses they can be widely supported by other articles according to the extractions. Therefore, the paper proposes a measure for the concept distribution of the documents, which indicates the importance to the concept aspect in the importance evaluation in the background set of the documents as follows.

$$D_i = \sum_{\substack{i=1 \\ i \neq j}}^{n} S(u_i, u_j). \tag{4}$$

Where: u is the vector expression of the document mentioned at sub-Section II.A, and S is the similarity measure in the (1). The document is more important when the score of the document is bigger according to (4).

Meantime, the paper presents an integration evaluation using the *IOWA* operator on the above three measures as follows.

$$C = IOWA_w(<u_1, b_1>, <u_2, b_2>, <u_3, b_3>) \\ = \sum_{i=1}^{3} w_i b_{\sigma(i)} \\ s.t. <u_1, u_2, u_3> = <3, 2, 1>. \tag{5}$$

Where: the three measures are normalization according to the maximum and minimum scores, and b_i corresponds to the originality, the concept distribution, and the complexity scores of the document. w_i is weight of b_i, and u_i is the induced variable. Finally, the C value in the (5) is projected into the range of [0, 100] according to user's custom.

3 Related Work

Yu and Hsu [4] proposed a mining method based on content for the retrieve of the Computer-Aided Design (CAD) documents, which extracted the key phrases from the query and these documents according to the external knowledge base of the phrases, and modified the TF-IDF to express the weight of the key phrases, and to form the CAD-VSM (Vector Space Model). Then, the CAD document with maximum similarity of the query was returned, which indicated the effectiveness of the similarity calculation based on extracted information.

A dynamic semantic text clustering method was presented in [5], which used the extracted frequent items and named entities to express the document, and clustered the documents according to the expression. It reduced the dimensions of the document expression effectively due to the use of the extracted info.

To improve the clustering quality and the interpretation of the clustering results, a hierarchical clustering using *NE*s as privilege information was presented in [6], which can power the clustering solution. In our case, long *VP*s and long *NP*s are utilized besides the *NE*s.

An *NE* shared measure (NESM) was presented in [7], which was competitive to the standard similarity measure. Especially on the news documents, the *NESM* performed better than the standard measure.

4 Experiments

We carried out the experiments on the Chinese corpus [1], which needed the processes of the Chinese segmentation, the part of speech (POS), the named entity recognition, the component syntactic analysis, etc. We utilized the free ICTCLAS [8] tool due to its mature performance, and the free NiuParser [9] tool due to its sophisticated models based on the statistic, such as Conditional Random Fields, Average Perceptron, Maximum Entropy, and Recurrent Neural Network.

We executed a post-process on the results generated by the above tools, and extracted the useful knowledge. To illustrate the procedure of the post-process, we invented a commercial event with the correct expression as follows

"ZaiXiangGangALiBaBaChuXiHuoDongDeALiBaBaGaoGuanWangShaoHuaYu 2017Nian2Yue28RiFanHuiBeiJing, BingDaiLaiLiao5QianWanYuanRenMinBiDe TouZiXiangMu, ZaiDaYue3000PingMiDeGongYeYuanQu, ZhuanLiFaMingJiShu JiangTongGuoTouZiZhuanHuaWeiShiJiDeGongYeChanPin."

Figure 1. Example of a commercial event.

After the Chinese segmentation and the POS tagging, the sentence was changed as follows.

[1] http://www.nlpir.org/download/tc-corpus-answer.rar

"Zai /p XiangGang /ns ALiBaBa /ns ChuXi /v HuoDong /vn De /u ALi /ns BaBaGao /a Guan /v Wang /nr ShaoHua /nr Yu /p 2017Nian /t 2Yue /t 28Ri /t FanHui /v BeiJing /ns , /w Bing /c DaiLai /v Liao /u 5Qian /m Wan /m Yuan /q RenMinBi /n De /u TouZi /vn XiangMu /n , /w Zai /p DaYue /d 3000 /m PingMi /q De /b GongYe /n YuanQu /n , /w ZhuanLi /n Fa Ming /vn JiShu /n Jiang /d TongGuo /p TouZi /v ZhuanHua /v Wei /v Shi Ji /a De /u GongYe /n ChanPin /n . /w"

Figure 2. Example after the component syntactic analysis.

We merged the adjoining words with the appropriate POS tags to form the extractions. The result was as follows.

Organization: ″XiangGangALiBaBa″ ; *Location*: ″BeiJing″ ; *GPE*: ″XiangGang, BeiJing″ ; *Person*: ″WangShaoHua″ ; *Quantity*: ″3000PingMi″ ; *Money*: ″5QianWanYuanRenMinBi″ ; *Date*: ″2017Nian2Yue28Ri″.

Then, we utilized the NiuParser tool for the component syntactic analysis (CSA) to extract the long *NP*s, and the long *VP*s with a verb. The segmentations after the CSA were as follows.

(VP (VV ChuXi) (NP (NN HuoDong))),
(VP (VV FanHui) (NP (NR Beijing))),
(VP (VV DaiLai) (AS Liao) (NP (QP (CD 5QianWan) (CLP (M Yuan))) (NP (NN RenMinBi))),
(NP (NN TouZi) (NN XiangMu)),
(NP (NN GongYe) (NN YuanQu)),
(NP (NN ZhuanLi) (NN FaMing) (NN JiShu)),
(NP (NN GongYe) (NN ChanPin)).

Figure 3. Example after the component syntactic analysis.

Thereafter, we extracted the long *VP*s and the long *NP*s as follows.

Long *VP*s: ″ChuXiHuoDong, FanHuiBeiJing″ ; ″DaiLaiLiao5QianWanYuanRenMinBi″ ;

Long *NP*s: ″TouZiXiangMu, GongYeYuanQu″ ; ″ZhuanLiFaMingJiShu, GongYeChanPin″.

The number of the clusters in Sub-Section (II.A) can be given by the prior experience or by trial to obtain a satisfied effect (e.g. 5).

The weight vector for the twenty dimensions in (3), and the weight vector for the three dimensions in (5) can be obtained by the prior experience, or by training from the corpus tagged manually. Feasible values for the two vectors can be illustrated as follows.

$$< w_1, w_2, ..., w_{20} > = < 0.05, 0.05, ..., 0.05 > ;$$

$$< w_1, w_2, w_3 > = < 0.6, 0.3, 0.1 > .$$

5 Conclusions

Mining the implied knowledge in the document set, we cannot only use the clustering method based on the topic, but also use that based upon the extraction. In addition, text summary based on the adjoining positions of the extractions was also used besides that based upon the sentence weight was done by use. The importance evaluation for electronic documents using multi-measures integration was adopted, which considered the document's originality, writing quality, and concept distribution. Those measures reflected the importance to the document by the views from the special angle, and an IOWA operator was used for integrating them into a final measure. In our internal testing, the earlier feedback from the users about the method was positive.

For future work, we will use the lexicon of the synonym for increasing the hitting score of the similarity between two documents, such as the abbreviation of the locations, and organizations. And more precise weights in the IOWA operators will be adopted by supervisor learning. Moreover, to benefit the model of the traditional topic-level, a hybrid similarity equation integrated with VSM of word weights and that of extractions with the extraction-level bias will be explored.

Acknowledgment

We used the ICTCLAS and the NiuParser for the Chinese segmentation, POS tagging, and syntactic parsing. Here, we express our thanks to the researchers for their mature open-source software, and our thanks to the reviewers for their review of the paper.

References

[1] V. I. Levenshtein, Binary Codes Capable of Correcting Deletions, Insertions and Reversals. Soviet Physics Doklady, 1966, 10:707-710.

[2] M. A. Hasan, W. S. Spangler, T. Griffin, and A. Alba, "COA: finding novel patents through text analysis," in KDD'09: Proceedings of the 15th ACM SIGKDD international conference on Knowledge discovery and data mining. New York, NY, USA: ACM, 2009, pp. 1175-1184.

[3] X. Jin, et al., "Patent Maintenance Recommendation with Patent Information Network Model." IEEE, International Conference on Data Mining IEEE, 2011: 280-289.

[4] Yu, Wen Der, and J. Y. Hsu. "Content-based text mining technique for retrieval of CAD documents." Automation in Construction 31.5 (2013):65-74.

[5] Yafooz, Wael M. S., et al., "Dynamic Semantic Textual Document Clustering Using Frequent Terms and Named Entity." IEEE, International Conference on System Engineering and Technology IEEE, 2013:336-340.

[6] Roberta A, Sinoara, et al., "Named entities as privileged information for hierarchical text clustering." International Database Engineering & Applications Symposium ACM, 2014:57-66.

[7] Montalvo, Soto, R. Martínez, and V. Fresno, "NESM: a named entity based proximity measure for multilingual news clustering." Procesamiento Del Lenguaje Natural 48(2012):81-88.

[8] H. P. Zhang, et al., "HHMM-based Chinese lexical analyzer ICTCLAS." Sighan Workshop on Chinese Language Processing Association for Computational Linguistics, 2003: pages. 758-759.

[9] J. Zhu, M. Zhu, Q. Wang, T. Xiao, Niuparser: A Chinese Syntactic and Semantic Parsing Toolkit, in: Proceedings of the 53rd Annual Meeting of the Association for Computational Linguistics and the 7th International Joint Conference on Natural Language Processing: System Demonstrations, 2015, pp. 145–150.

Exponential Synchronization of the Hopfield Neural Networks with New Chaotic Strange Attractor

Zhan-Ji GUI, Kai-Hua WANG*

Department of Software Engineering, Hainan College of Software Technology ,qionghai, 571400, P.R. China
School of Mathematics and Statistics, Hainan Normal University, Haikou, Hainan, 571158, P.R. China
** Corresponding author: kaihuawang@qq.com*

Abstract—This paper studies the problems of exponential synchronization for the Hopfield neural networks with impulsive effects and Gui chaotic strange attractor. By employing the Lyapunov functional method of impulsive functional differential equations, some criteria for synchronization between two impulsive neural networks are derived. An illustrative example is provided to show the effectiveness and feasibility of the proposed method and results.

1 Introduction

Recently, the issue of controlled synchronization in complex dynamical networks has become a rather significant topic in both theoretical research and practical applications [1–3]. It is known that in theory and practice, impulsive control has been widely used to stabilize and synchronize chaotic systems. For example, Yang and Chua derived some sufficient conditions for the stabilization and synchronization of Chua's oscillators via impulsive control[4]; Xie, Wen and Li obtained sufficient conditions for the stabilization and synchronization of the Lorenz system via impulsive control with varying impulsive intervals[5]. The Hopfield neural networks with impulse effect are studied, where the criteria on the existence, uniqueness and global stability of periodic solution are obtained. Further, Gui chaos strange attractor was also found[6-10].

Motivated by the above discussions, the aim of this paper is to study the synchronization of Hopfield neural networks with a Gui chaotic strange attractor. By employing the Lyapunov-like stability theory of impulsive functional differential equations, some criteria for synchronization of Hopfield neural networks are derived.

The remainder of the paper is organized as follows: Section 2 describes the issue of synchronization of coupled impulsive systems with a Gui chaotic strange attractor. In Section 3, some sufficient conditions for the synchronization are derived by constructing suitable Lyapunov-like function. In Section 4, an illustrative example is given to show the effectiveness of the proposed method. Conclusions are given in Section 5.

2 Preliminaries and Problem Formulation

In this paper, we consider the following nonautonomous Hopfield neural networks model with impulses

$$\begin{cases} \dot{x}_i = -a_i x_i(t) + \sum_{j=1}^{n} b_{ij} f_j(x_j(t)) + c_i(t), \\ \qquad t > 0, t \neq t_k, \\ \Delta x_i(t_k) = x_i(t_k^+) - x_i(t_k^-) = -\gamma_{ik} x_i(t_k), \\ \qquad t > 0, t = t, \end{cases} \tag{1}$$

where $\Delta x_i(t_k) = x_i(t_k^+) - x_i(t_k^-)$ are the impulses at moments t_k^+ and $t_1 < t_2 < \cdots$ is a strictly increasing sequence such that $\lim_{k\to\infty} t_k = +\infty$; $x_i(t)$ corresponds to the state of the ith unit at time t, a_i is a positive constant set; b_{ij} denotes the strength of the jth unit on the ith unit at time t, $c_i(t)$ denotes the external input on the ith neuron and $f_j(x_j(t))$ denotes the output of the jth unit at time t.

As usual in the theory of impulsive differential equations, at the points of discontinuity t_k of the solution $t \to x_i(t)$ we assume that $x_i(t_k) \equiv x_i(t_k^-)$. It is clear that, in general, the derivatives $x_i'(t_k)$ do not exist. On the other hand, according to the first equality of (1) there exist the limits $x_i'(t_{k_k}^{\mp})$.

According to the above convention, we assume $x_i'(t_k) \equiv x_i'(t_k^-)$.

Throughout this paper, we assume that:

(H₁) Functions $f_j(u)$ satisfy the Lipschitz condition, i.e., there are constants $L_j > 0$ such that

$$|f_j(u_1) - f_j(u_2)| \le L_j |u_1 - u_2|,$$

for all $u_1, u_2 \in R = (-\infty, +\infty)$.

(H₂) There exists a positive integer p, such that

$$t_{k+p} = t_k + \omega,\ \gamma_{i(k+p)} = \gamma_{ik},$$

$i = 1, 2, \cdots, n,\ k = 1, 2, \cdots$

(H3) $a_i > 0, c_i(t)$ are all continuous ω-periodic functions.

As is known to all that (1) can exhibit chaotic phenomenons [6-10]. In order to show it clearly, we give the following example.

Example 1. Consider a two-dimensional neural network with impulsive effects, which can be described by the following impulsive differential equations:

$$\begin{cases} \dot{x}_1 = -2x_1(t) + 0.56 f_1(x_1(t)) + 0.48 f_2(x_2(t)) \\ \quad + c_1(t), \quad t > 0, t \ne nT, \\ \dot{x}_2 = -2x_2(t) + 0.61 f_1(x_1(t)) + 0.3 f_2(x_2(t)) \\ \quad + c_2(t), \quad t > 0, t \ne nT, \\ x_1(nT^+) = (1-\gamma_1)x_1(nT),\ n = 1, 2, \cdots, \\ x_2(nT^+) = (1-\gamma_2)x_2(nT),\ n = 1, 2, \cdots, \end{cases} \tag{2}$$

where $f_j(x_j) = 0.5(|x_j + 1| - |x_j - 1|)$. Obviously, $f_j(x)$ satisfy (H₁). Now we investigate the influence of the period T of impulsive effect on the system (2). Set

$$c_1(t) = 2 - 0.5\cos(1.5t),$$

$$c_2(t) = 2 + 0.5\sin(0.5t),$$

$$T = 0.4\pi,\ \gamma_1 = 0.35,\ \gamma_2 = 0.2.$$

According to Theorems 1 and 2 in [6], the cellular neural network model (2) has a unique 2π-periodic solution with 5-impulses in a period.

Furthermore, if $T = 1$, then (H₂) isn't satisfied. Periodic oscillation of system (2) will be destroyed by impulses effect. Numeric results show that system (2) still has a global attractor which can be a Gui chaotic strange attractor. Every solutions of system (2) will finally tend to the new chaotic strange attractor which is useful in exponential synchronization (see Fig.1-3). □

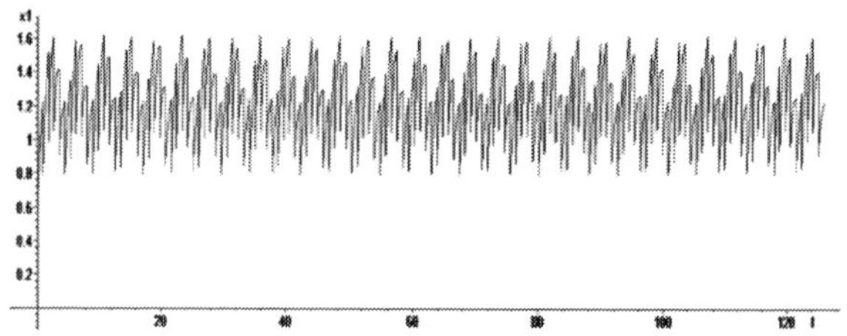

Figure 1. Time-series of the $x_1(t)$ of system (2) with $T = 1$

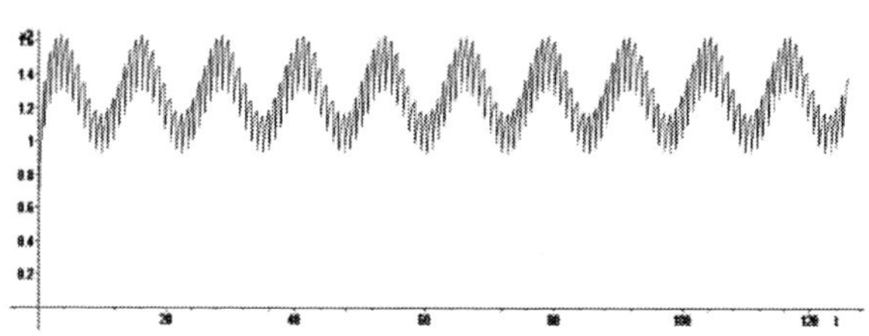

Figure 2. Time-series of the $x_2(t)$ of system (2) with $T = 1$

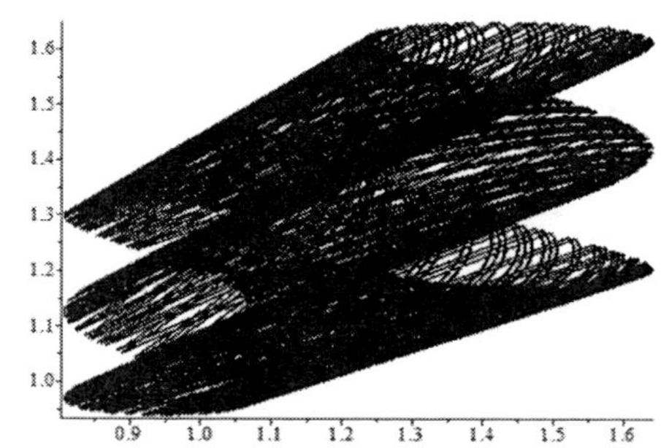

Figure 3. Phase portrait of Gui chaotic strange attractor of system (2)

For the purpose of synchronization, we introduce the response system that is driven by (1) via a set of signals

$$\begin{cases} \dot{y}_i = -a_i y_i(t) + \sum_{j=1}^{n} b_{ij} f_j(y_j(t)) + c_i(t), \\ \quad t > 0, t \ne t_k, \\ y_i(t_k^+) = x_i(t_k^-) - \gamma_{ik} y_i(t_k^-), \\ \quad i = 1, 2, \cdots, n,\ k = 1, 2, \cdots, \end{cases} \tag{3}$$

Let $e_i(t) = y_i(t) - x_i(t)$ be the synchronization error, $x_i(t)$ and $y_i(t)$ are the state variables of drive system (1) and response system (3). The error system of the impulsive synchronization is given by

$$\begin{cases} \dot{e}_i = -a_i e_i(t) + \sum_{j=1}^{n} b_{ij}(e_j(t)), & t > 0, t \neq t_k, \\ e_i(t_k^+) = -\gamma_{ik} e_i(t_k^-), & i = 1,2,\cdots,n, k = 1,2,\cdots, \end{cases} \tag{4}$$

where $g_j(e_j(t)) = f_j(y_j(t)) - f_j(x_j(t))$. Note that the origin is the equilibrium point of system (4). If $e_i(t)$ tends exponentially to origin in evolution, exponential synchronization between two systems would be realized. Our aim is to find some criteria on the impulsive gains γ_{ik} such that drive system (1) and respond system (3) are exponentially synchronized for any initial condition.

According to the assumption (H₁), $g_i(\cdot)$ possesses the following properties:

$| g_j(e_j(t)) | \le L_j | e_j(t) |$, and

$g_j(0) = 0, \quad j = 1, 2 \ldots, n.$

Throughout the paper, we denote

$$\|y(t) - x(t)\| = \sum_{j=1}^{n} | y_j(t) - x_j(t) |^r .$$

Definition 1. Systems (1) and (3) are said to be exponentially synchronized if there exist constants $M \ge 1$ and $\eta > 0$ such that

$$\|y(t) - x(t)\| = M \|y(0) - x(0)\| e^{-\eta t},$$

for any $t \ge 0$. Constant η is said to be the degree of exponential synchronization.

Lemma 1. Assume that $x > 0, y > 0, p > 1, q > 1$, $1/p + 1/q = 1$, then the inequality

$$xy \le \frac{1}{p} x^p + \frac{1}{q} x^q$$

holds (the inequality is called as Young inequality).

3 Main results

In this section, we investigate the exponential synchronization of system (1) and (3) by using Lyapunov like functional method.

Theorem 1. Under the assumption **(H₁)**, **(H₂)** and **(H₃)**, the system (1) and (3) are exponentially synchronized, if there exist positive constants $r > 1$, $w_i > 0$ and $\sigma_{ij} \in R$ $i, j = 1, 2, \cdots, n.$ such that

$$-ra_i + (r-1)\sum_{j=1}^{n} L_j^{r(1-\sigma_{ij})/(r-1)} | b_{ij} |^{r(1-\sigma_{ij})/(r-1)} + \sum_{j=1}^{n} \frac{\lambda_j}{\lambda_i} L_i^{r\sigma_{ji}} | b_{ji} |^{r\sigma_{ji}} < 0, \quad i = 1, 2, \ldots, n. \tag{5}$$

Proof. By inequality (5), choose a small $\varepsilon > 0$ such that

$$r(\varepsilon - a_i) + (r-1)\sum_{j=1}^{n} L_j^{r(1-\sigma_{ij})/(r-1)} | b_{ij} |^{r(1-\sigma_{ij})/(r-1)} + \sum_{j=1}^{n} \frac{\lambda_j}{\lambda_i} L_i^{r\sigma_{ji}} | b_{ji} |^{r\sigma_{ji}} < 0, \quad i = 1, 2, \ldots, n.$$

Consider the following Lyapunov function:

$$V(e(t)) = \sum_{i=1}^{n} \lambda_i | e_i(t) |^r e^{r\varepsilon t}. \tag{6}$$

Calculating the upper right dini-derivative D^+V of V along the solution of system (4) at the continuous points $t \neq t_k, t \ge 0$, we have

$$\begin{aligned} D^+V(e(t)) &= \sum_{i=1}^{n} \lambda_i \Big[r\varepsilon e^{r\varepsilon t} | e_i(t) |^r + re^{r\varepsilon t} | e_i(t) |^{r-1} \cdot D^+ | e_i(t) | \Big] \\ &= \sum_{i=1}^{n} \lambda_i \Big[r\varepsilon e^{r\varepsilon t} | e_i(t) |^r + r\,\mathrm{sign}(e_i(t)) e^{r\varepsilon t} \cdot | e_i(t) |^{r-1} \Big(-a_i e_i(t) + \sum_{j=1}^{n} b_{ij} g_j(e_j(t)) \Big) \Big] \\ &\quad + r\sum_{j=1}^{n} | b_{ij} || e_i(t) |^{r-1} \left| g_j(e_j(t)) \right| \Big]. \end{aligned}$$

By Lemma 1, we have the following inequalities:

$$\begin{aligned} D^+V(e(t)) &\le \sum_{i=1}^{n} \lambda_i e^{r\varepsilon t} \Big[r(\varepsilon - a_i) | e_i(t) |^r + (r-1)\sum_{j=1}^{n} L_j^{r(1-\sigma_{ij})/(r-1)} | b_{ij} |^{r(1-\sigma_{ij})/(r-1)} | e_i(t) |^r + \sum_{j=1}^{n} L_j^{r\sigma_{ij}} | b_{ij} |^{r\sigma_{ij}} | e_j(t) |^r \Big] \\ &= \sum_{i=1}^{n} \lambda_i \Big[r(\varepsilon - a_i) + (r-1)\sum_{j=1}^{n} L_j^{r(1-\sigma_{ij})/(r-1)} \cdot | b_{ij} |^{r(1-\sigma_{ij})/(r-1)} + \sum_{j=1}^{n} \frac{\lambda_j}{\lambda_i} L_i^{r\sigma_{ji}} | b_{ji} |^{r\sigma_{ji}} \Big] | e_i(t) |^r e^{r\varepsilon t} \le 0, \\ &\quad t \ge 0, t \neq t_k. \end{aligned}$$

Also, we can calculate right limits of Lyapunov-like function $V(e(t))$ at impulsive moments t_k as follows

DOI: 10.1051/itmconf/20171205019

$$\begin{aligned} V(e(t_k^+)) &= \sum_{i=1}^{n} \lambda_i \,|\, e_i(t_k^+) \,|^r\, e^{r\varepsilon t_k^+} \\ &= \sum_{i=1}^{n} |\, 1-\lambda_i \,||\, e_i(t_k) \,|^r\, e^{r\varepsilon t_k} \\ &\le \sum_{i=1}^{n} \lambda_i \,|\, e_i(t_k) \,|^r\, e^{r\varepsilon t_k} = V(e(t_k)), \end{aligned}$$

which implies that

$$\begin{aligned} V(e(t)) \le V(e(0)) &= \sum_{i=1}^{n} \lambda_i \,|\, e_i(0) \,|^r \\ &= \sum_{i=1}^{n} \lambda_i \,|\, y_i(0) - x_i(0) \,|^r \\ &\le \max_{1\le i\le n}\{\lambda_i\} \left\| y(0) - x(0) \right\|, \\ &\text{for} \quad t \ge 0. \end{aligned} \tag{7}$$

According to (6), we have

$$\begin{aligned} V(e(t)) &\ge \min_{1\le i\le n}\{\lambda_i\} \sum_{i=1}^{n} |\, e_i(t) \,|^r\, e^{r\varepsilon t} \\ &\ge \min_{1\le i\le n}\{\lambda_i\} e^{r\varepsilon t} \,\|\, y(t) - x(t) \,\|. \end{aligned} \tag{8}$$

From (7) - (8), we can obtain

$$\|\, y(t) - x(t) \,\| \le M \,\|\, y(0) - x(0) \,\|\, e^{-r\varepsilon t}.$$

where $M = \max_{1\le i\le n}\{\lambda_i\} / \min_{1\le i\le n}\{\lambda_i\} \ge 1$. According to Definition 1, we conclude that the drive system (1) and the response system (3) are exponentially synchronized. This completes the proof. □

4 A Simulation Example

In this section, we give an example to illustrate the effectiveness of the results obtained in the previous sections. Consider a two-dimensional neural networks with impulsive effects.

Taking (2) as the drive system in Example 1. The response system is constructed as follows:

$$\begin{cases} \dot{y}_1 = -2y_1(t) + 0.56 f_1(y_1(t)) \\ \quad + 0.48 f_2(y_2(t)) + c_1(t), \quad t \ne nT, \\ \dot{y}_2 = -2y_2(t) + 0.61 f_1(y_1(t)) \\ \quad + 0.3 f_2(y_2(t)) + c_2(t), \quad t \ne nT, \\ y_1(nT^+) = x_1(nT^-) - \gamma_1 y_1(nT), n = 1,2,\cdots, \\ y_2(nT^+) = x_2(nT^-) - \gamma_2 y_2(nT), n = 1,2,\cdots. \end{cases} \tag{9}$$

Then the error system of drive system (2) and respond system (9) is constructed as follows:

$$\begin{cases} \dot{e}_1 = -2e_1(t) + 0.56 g_1(e_1(t)) + 0.48 g_2(e_2(t)), \\ \dot{e}_2 = -2e_2(t) + 0.61 g_1(e_1(t)) + 0.3 g_2(e_2(t)), \\ \qquad t \ne nT, \\ e_1(nT^+) = -\gamma_1 e_1(nT^-), \quad n = 1,2,\cdots, \\ e_2(nT^+) = -\gamma_2 e_2(nT^-), \quad n = 1,2,\cdots. \end{cases} \tag{10}$$

Numeric results show that system (9) still has a Gui chaotic strange attractor[6-10]. The phase plot of Gui chaotic strange attractor of response system is shown in Fig. 4. It is easy to check the conditions in Theorem 1 are satisfied. Therefore, systems (2) and (9) exhibit exponential synchronization. Define $e_i(t) = y_i(t) - x_i(t)$ and the errors (10) between systems (2) and (9) are depicted in Fig. 5.

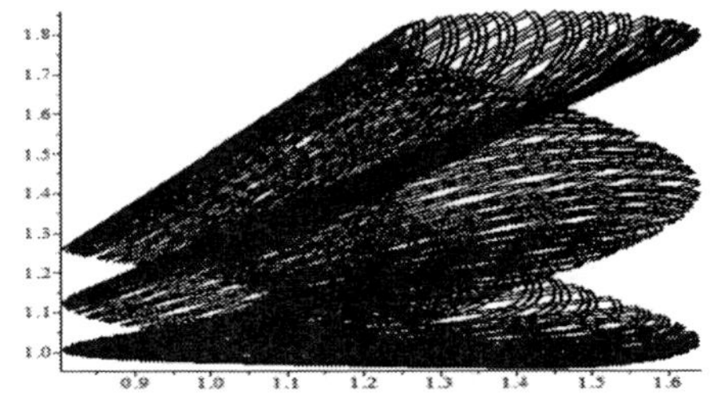

Figure 4. Phase portrait of Gui chaotic strange attractor of system (9)

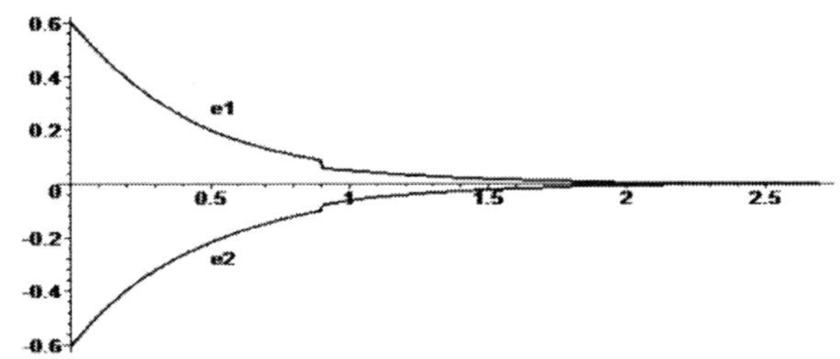

Figure 5. Synchronization errors between drive system (2) and response system (9)

Conclusions

In this paper, the conditions for the exponential synchronization of a class of neural networks with impulsive effects are derived by utilizing Lyapunov functional method. A numerical simulation is given to show the effectiveness and feasibility of the proposed method. As far as we know, there is no paper to deal with such a problem.

Acknowledgments

This research was jointly supported by the Nature Science Foundation of Hainan Province under Grant No. 117164, 117097 and Foundation of Hainan Educational Committee under Grant No. Hnky2017ZD-10.

References

[1] T. Hayakawa, W.M. Haddad, K.Y. Volyanskyy. Neural network hybrid adaptive control for nonlinear uncertain impulsive dynamical systems, Nonlinear Anal. Hybrid Syst. 2(2008):862–874.

[2] G. Agranovich, E. Litsyn, A. Slavova. Impulsive control of a hysteresis cellular neural network model, Nonlinear Anal. Hybrid Syst. 3(2009):65–73.

[3] J. Zhou, L. Xiang, Z.R. Liu. Synchronization in complex delayed dynamical networks with impulsive effects, Physica A. 384(2007):684–692.

[4] T. Yang, L.O. Chua . Impulsive stabilization for control and synchronization of chaotic system, IEEE Trans. Circuits Syst. I. 44(1997):976-988.

[5] W. Xie, C. Wen, Z. Li.Impulsive control for the stabilization and synchronization of Lorenz system, Phys. Lett. A. 275(2000): 67-72.

[6] Z.J. Gui, W.G. Ge. Existence and uniqueness and periodic solutions of nonautonomous cellular neural networks with impulses, Phys. Lett. A. 354(2006): 84-94.

[7] J. Zhang, Z.J. Gui. Existence and stability of periodic solutions of high-order Hopfield neural networks with impulses and delays. Journal of Computational and Applied Mathematics. 224(2)(2009): 602-613.

[8] J. Zhang, Z.J. Gui. Periodic solutions of nonautonomous cellular neural networks with impulses and delays. Nonlinear Analysis: Real World Applications, 10(3)(2009):1891-1903

[9] Z.J. Gui, W.G. Ge. Periodic solution and chaotic strange attractor for shunting inhibitory cellular neural networks with impulses. In Chaos. 16 (2006): 33116-1-10.

[10] Z.J. Gui, W.G. Ge. Impulsive effect of continuous time neural networks under pure structural variations.In International Journal of Bifurcation and Chaos. 17(2007): 2127-2139.

DOI: 10.1051/itmconf/20171205020

Study on the Ecological Environmental Protection System of Songjiang District

Guo-Dong YAN[1,a], Ya-Nan CAI[1,b], Guo-Wei YAN[2,*], and Shuang-Shuang LIU[1,c]

[1]*School of management, Shanghai University of Engineering Science, Shanghai International Cruise Business Institute NO,333 Longteng Road, Shanghai, China.*
[2]*shanghai Lixin University of accounting and finance,NO 2800 Wenxiang Road, Shanghai, China*
[a]*Yanguodong@163.com,*[b]*3295229749@qq.com,*[c]*nanluk@qq.com*
**Corresponding author: 15618592002@163.com*

Abstract: For Strong and Optimize Shanghai Ecological Environmental System. Shanghai has increased its investment in ecological environmental protection. Songjiang ranks the first in terms of environmental quality in all districts for 8 consecutive years. All the above achievements are due to the efficient and fast optimization and upgrading in its ecological environmental system. This paper focuses on analyzing the features of the ecological environmental protection system of Songjiang, clarifying clarifies the main bottlenecks, and puts forward corresponding countermeasures and suggestions to provide references for relevant government departments.

1 Introduction

Strong and Optimized Shanghai Ecological Environmental System. Shanghai has increased its investment in ecological environmental protection. Spending on energy conservation and environmental protection projects has accounts for 70% of the overall budget of Shanghai Municipal Environmental Protection Bureau. In 2003, Shanghai Environmental Protection and Coordination Committee were set up with seven special working groups and 10 operation mechanisms were established. In 2008, the Special Fund for Energy Conservation and Emission Reduction was established in Shanghai. The document of Several Suggestions on Establishing the Sound Ecological Compensation Mechanism which was established in 2009 explicitly adopted the basic principles of "Government takes the main responsibilities while the market takes the auxiliary responsibilities." Through analyses, it is found that during the five rounds of the Shanghai environmental protection three-year plans, policy mechanism accounts for growing proportions of the total projects in recent years. The fifth round of policy mechanism projects accounted for 17.91% of the total projects. A number of subsidy policies were adopted by the Municipal finance on the basis of environmental protection infrastructure projects.

Remarkable Achievements were made by Songjiang District in Ecological Environmental Protection. Songjiang District successively won the honorary titles such as the "International Garden City", "National Sanitary District", "National Green City Model ", "Chinese Inhabitable Environment Model", "Top Ten Leisure Cities of China", etc. Songjiang ranks the first in terms of environmental quality in all districts for 8 consecutive years. All the above achievements are due to the efficient and fast optimization and upgrading in its ecological environmental system. This paper focuses on analyzing the features of the ecological environmental protection system of Songjiang, clarifies the main bottlenecks, and puts forward corresponding countermeasures and suggestions to provide references for relevant government departments.

2 Features of the Ecological Environmental Protection System of Songjiang District

The Ecological Environmental Protection System is vigorously promoted. To effectively promote the regional environmental protection work, the Songjiang Environmental Protection and Coordination Committee was established in 2002, ensuring the smooth implementation of the Three-year Environmental Protection Plan. In 2013, Songjiang Afforestation and City Beautification Administration approved the establishment of the Federation of City Beautification, Environment Protection and Sanitation. In June 2013, the township simple garbage enclosures were all demolished, and RMB 5580 per Chinese mu were compensated according to the storage area. Songjiang implemented the "Green Account" step by step in four streets, and 6 street towns including Jiuting, Xinqiao, etc.

Residents are encouraged and subsidized to sort dry and wet garbage, and scan the bag bar codes when discarding garbage. In 2014, Shanghai Afforestation and City Beautification Administration assigned the administrative rights of "Urban Life Garbage Commercial Cleaning Service" to districts and towns.

Sound Long-term Management Mechanism. Songjiang District has set up a sound long-term management mechanism. Established the work mechanism of information interaction and joint law enforcement and publicity, and effectively improved the administrative management efficiency. The Social Public Participation Mechanism was established and the "Environmental Protection Guardian" teams were established covering all 16 streets and towns in the district, such as the "Environmental Protection Volunteer" team, Citizen Patrol team, Community Red Armbands, Patriotic Sanitary Inspectors, etc. The "Microblog Netizen Patrol Team" was recruited publicly by Songjiang Afforestation and City Beautification Administration Bureau.

Integrated Joint Mechanism of Environmental Administrative Localization Administration In 2012, Suggestions on the Administrative Localization Implementation of the Songjiang District Afforestation & City Beautification, and City Administration, and its supporting implementation proposals, evaluation methods and detailed rules were drafted and put into operation by all streets and towns on January 1st, 2014. Through administrative localization, unified rights and responsibilities, urban integration, and classified implementation, the government coordination functions are strengthened, the administrative function of government departments are transformed, the administrative localization efficiencies are deepened, the urban administration focus is continuously promoted towards a downward direction, and the new urban administrative framework is actively built featuring "clear responsibilities, joint interaction, comprehensive management, scientific efficiency".

Regulation Inspection and Reinforce Monitoring of Environmental Quality. The establishment of Songjiang Beautification, Environmental Protection, and Sanitation Comprehensive Evaluation System focuses on joint interactions between the district and subsidiary towns. "Daily Patrol, Night Inspection, Weekly Supervision, and Quarterly Evaluation" in terms of environmental protection and sanitation are carried out in 16 street towns (parks), full-day and all-round quality inspections are implemented to realize efficient supervision featuring "timely discovery, fast treatment, effective resolution, and forceful inspection". In 2013, based on the unified quality inspection platform of the city, Songjiang Environmental Protection authority carried out all-day, and all-round effective inspections on 1573 samples in the district. The Laboratory Information Management System (LIMS) was officially approved in 2013, and the third party evaluation was introduced into the environment and sanitation inspection. 7 sub-systems under Songjiang Environmental Protection Bureau were integrated to form the Songjiang Pollutant Inspection Platform, which was officially accepted by Shanghai Environmental Protection Bureau on Dec 21st, 2012.

3 Dilemma of Songjiang Ecological Environmental System

Law Enforcement Supervision and Responsibility Mechanism are yet to be perfected. The current law enforcement supervision mechanism is imperfect. The environmental protection department and the other functional departments are peer government departments, therefore work coordination and supervisory management are unable to be effectively carried out. The comprehensive environmental law enforcement performances are inadequate. Besides the hot and difficult problems coordinated and resolved by city (district) government, the environmental protection authorities lack coordination capacity. Weaknesses existing in the law enforcement and inspection mechanism: there are difficulties existing in the coordination between the environmental protection authorities and other functional departments, especially in inspection implementation; there are no clearly identified methods on supervision in laws and regulations. Weaknesses existing in the law enforcement responsibility system: there are no concrete implementations on the Mayor and District Mayor Accountability System. Weaknesses existing in government employee performance assessment mechanism: the assessment is GDP oriented with low-level of citizen participation.

The Ecological Construction Mechanism is yet to be perfected. First, the financing of ecological compensation mainly relies on government transfer payments and special funds. Second, the department oriented ecological compensation lacks explicit responsibility body and clear work divisions, so that there are overlapped administrative responsibilities. Third is the over narrow scope and low standard of ecological compensation. Fourth, there is insufficient stability in the "Engineering Project" compensation mode.

4 Discussion on Optimization of the Ecological Environment Protection System of Songjiang District

Optimize the Property Right System of Resources and Environment. We should optimize the mechanism of ecological compensation. First is to accelerate the process of ecological compensation legislation, further clarify the funding sources, key areas, compensation methods, and compensation standards, and define the rights and obligations between relevant stakeholders and the guarantee measures; Second is to increase the fiscal transfer payments from the Central and Shanghai governments; Third is to speed up the reform on resource taxes, timely impose environment tax, and provide stable funding sources for ecological compensation; Fourth is to broaden the financing channels, and encourage social capitals to participate in the ecological environment construction and maintenance. We should improve the system of resource property rights. First is to optimize the resource property right system, and establish the system of resource paid usage; Second is to reconstruct the system of resource taxes and environmental taxes; Third is to speed up the reform on market structures of resource industry; Fourth is to optimize the means of price control, and establish the mechanism for the government to appropriately intervene price regulations of resource products. Fifth is to increase the prices of resource products, reduce the prices of renewable resources, and raise up the waste discharge costs.

Establish a Comprehensive Decision-making Mechanism on Environment and Development . We should improve the decision-making mechanism of multiple participation. We should build up the policy oriented department coordination mechanism, and implement the veto mechanism on policies and planning failed to pass the environmental impact assessment; We should suspend the approval of new construction projects with new pollutants in areas exceeding the total pollutant emission standards; We should suspend the approval of construction projects with relatively great ecological impact in severely polluted areas or areas without completing the task of ecological recovery. We should highlight the environmental impact assessment system. First is to carry out environment evaluations targeting high energy consuming and highly polluting industries, industrial parks, and hydropower bases; Second is to perfect the corresponding management mode connecting new project examination and approval with pollution emission reduction, according to the regional and industrial planning environment examination regulations; Third is to advance the separation between environmental protection composition institutions and examination and approval authorities, and set up independent legal environment protection agencies; Fourth is to clearly define the responsibilities of all parties, and increase penalties on legal violations. The public participation mechanism should be promoted. First is to enrich the ways of environmental publicity and education; Second is to define decision-making participation rights, environmental supervision and environmental litigation rights of non-governmental organizations and individual citizens; Third is to strengthen environmental information disclosure, according to the potential pollution degrees and levels to the environment caused by enterprises, and conduct classification management; Fourth is to formulate and perfect the NGO environmental laws and regulations as soon as possible.

Strengthen the Supervision and Management Retroactive Mechanism . The punishment mechanism on environmental damage activities should be established. First is to raise the charging standards according to the principle of "Making discharge standard higher than governance cost"; Second is to greatly increase the penalty on illegal behaviors; Third is to innovate the punishment methods on environmental damage behaviors, according to the uncapped "daily penalty"; Fourth is to improve the environmental pollution accident investigation system, the environmental pollution damage compensation system and the system of environmental public interest litigation. The environment related law enforcement capacity should be strengthened. First is to establish and perfect the environment law enforcement agencies, and form the provincial, county and township level environmental law enforcement supervision network; Second is to increase investments in the environmental law enforcement, and improve the level of law enforcement equipment; Third is to strengthen the construction and training of the environmental law enforcement teams; Fourth is to standardize the procedures of the environmental law enforcement system; Fifth is to strengthen cooperation between departments, and innovate the mechanism of law enforcement. Supervisions on ecological civilization construction should be strengthened. First is to strengthen the supervision of various levels of the National People's Congress on ecological civilization construction; second is to strengthen the judicial supervision, and actively promote the implementation of the "Environmental Impact Assessment System"; Third is to strengthen social supervision.

Deepen the Reform on the Resource and Environment Administrative System. The inter-departmental coordination mechanism should be built. We should set up Songjiang Leadership Group for Ecological Civilization Construction, organize Songjiang environmental protection joint meetings, and conduct resource and environment administrative system reform step by step. The establishment of primary level environmental protection agencies should be strengthened. We should flexibly adopt the local environment management systems and advocate vertical management in accordance with the principle of "matching rights with responsibilities and delegating rights to lower levels". We should set up local offices of township environment protection bureaus in key towns of Songjiang, receiving vertical administration from the district environment protection bureau, or set up special positions responsible for environment protection work in township governments. Joint prevention and control mechanism targeting air pollution should be promoted. We should carry out "smog" treatment accountability mechanism, set up corresponding air pollution control and prevention regulations. The environmental law enforcement authorities should eliminate the negative interference of local interests, according to the vertical management mode, expand the PM10 and PM2.5 particles disclosure channels, and establish and perfect the accountability system for excessive discharge of atmospheric pollutants.

Acknowledgement

This research was financially supported by the Shanghai government decision-making consultation project of Research on the path of making cruise supporting industrial park relying on the Wusong International Cruise Port (2015/2016-Z-J03), We are grateful for their valuable comments.

References

1. Johan Jansson & Agneta Marel. Green Consumer Behavior: Determinants of Curtailment and Eco-innovation Adoption. Journal of Consumer Marketing Vol. 27, 2010
2. Xiangrong Liu, in:Ecological Civilization Development Strategy Study,People's Publishing House, Beijing,2013.
3. Yuanchun Peng, in: Unban Residents' Environmental Behavior Study, Guangming Daily Press, Beijing,2013.
4. Dayong Hong, in: Empirical Research on Chinese Residents' Concern and Behavior Based on the Environment-friendly Society, China Renmin University Press,Beijing,2012.
5. Ecology Civilization Research Center of Beijing Forestry University, in:Chinese Provincial Eco-civilization Construction Evaluation Report,Social Sciences Academic Press, 2013.
6. Lang Zhang:The Change of Shanghai Ecological Resources Use Mode Promote Green Space System Mutation. Territory & Natural Resources Study.(2013)

Empirical Research on the Topological Properties of Internet+ Information Resources Network Nodes

Bin WU[1,a], Ping WU[2,*], Ji-Tao MA[3,a], Ting-Ting GUO[3,a], Jun LI[3,a], and Wei LIU[3,a]

[1]*No. 542, Beijing Rd. Kunming, Yunnan Province, PRC*
[2]*No.246 East Renming Rd. Kunming, Yunnan Province PRC*
[3]*No. 542, Beijing Rd. Kunming, Yunnan Province, PRC*
[a]*star_amethyst@qq.com*
* *Corresponding author: 138087273@qq.com*

Abstract: The "Internet+" is the product of the Internet development, and its network topology isn't the same as the traditional Internet. The relevance of the average daily visiting data and the daily page viewing data are studied empirically, the rich-club coefficient and the node access probability are redefined, and the topological entropy model to measure the degree of nodes information aggregation is built by using the entropy theory. The experimental results showed that the calculation model scaled the degree of information aggregation of the nodes in the "Internet+" topology efficiently. It provides an available computational model for the observation of resource access behaviors in the "Internet+" network.

1 Introduction

Internet network topology can draw the evolution trend of the dynamic characteristics of Internet users' behavior, it is helpful to understand the interaction mechanism among the participants on the network limited resources, and then to design a theoretical tool to avoid network congestion and get a more reasonable method to use the network information resources. At present, the main idea of Internet topology research is to abstract Internet into complex network to deal with, the known research results include small world network[1,2], scale free network[3,4], weighted directed network and its derivative[5,6,7,8].

In recent years, in order to simulate the dynamic changes more realistically in Internet topology, to understand and grasp the characteristics of the dynamic evolution of the Internet, many scholars have conducted a detailed study of Internet topology, by which some of the newer results have been achieved. From the view of the "like attracts like" partial connection phenomenon, someone has studied the network node connection status and internal LAN connection preferences, designed a new network topology model, and reflected the characteristics of small world and aggregation better than the BA model and the GLP model[9]. Garcia Robledo and others have analyzed the linear relationship of multiple complex network test indicators to select a non-redundant set based on the Internet evolution characteristics and the unsupervised machine learning technique, and that the Internet topology structure will be analyzed accurately with these non-redundant indicators[10]. Chai, He and colleague have designed a network cache gain algorithm with the concept of complex network betweenness, it shows that the algorithm not only has the capable of quickly delivering contents, but also reflects the power-law distribution characteristics of Internet topology intuitively[11]. Bo J and Ying Z have studied the spectrum stability of the network nodes interact growth based continuous data snapshots of Internet network topology and found the mapping relations between topology spectrum ranges and values of the network indicators[12]. Holbert B and Tati S have construct a network component of the estimated virtual topology through reasoning the real topology with partial route information, it resolves the problem of network topology detection failure caused by the incomplete route tracking information[13]. Liu Xiao and Zhao Hai have selected topological data (such as ipv4, ipv6 and internet AS) to compare and analyze structure indicators, found the linear relationship among the network structure order, the network scale and the network basic connectivity, and have gotten a result that the internal of the Internet is a dissipative structure[14].

In order to study the real network topology of Internet more deeply, the current research mainly focuses on the aspects of the network connection structure, the measurement index and the characteristic information of the network. However, the "Internet+" is a new form of the development of the Internet, the information content of network information resource stored in the nodes has the characteristics of polymerization and coordination, and the similar

DOI: 10.1051/itmconf/20171205021

resources is provided by nodes existed in the information resources network[15]. Therefore, the degree distribution of a single node in the information resources network is different from that of in the traditional Internet.

2 Network Node Topological Properties of the "Internet+"

2.1 Analysis of Network Nodes

Because the news content is very similar in the Internet, the same content may appear in multiple news sites in the same day[16]. It means that news nodes are similar in the network topology, so these nodes had been selected as a study object to grasp topological properties. The data, used for an empirical analysis, comes from the China Internet Data Platform(CNIDP), including QQ News, Phoenix News, Netease News and other domestic well-known Chinese news sites, and the time span is from January to August in the year 2015. First, a set of statistical charts of unique visitors(UV) and page views(PV) has been drawing after data-cleaned、data-indexed and other data processing steps (see Figure 1.a and Figure 1.b). As shown in figures 1.a & 1.b, UV and PV of news sites have a near linear relationship and the Phoenix New has the maximum UV and the maximum PV.

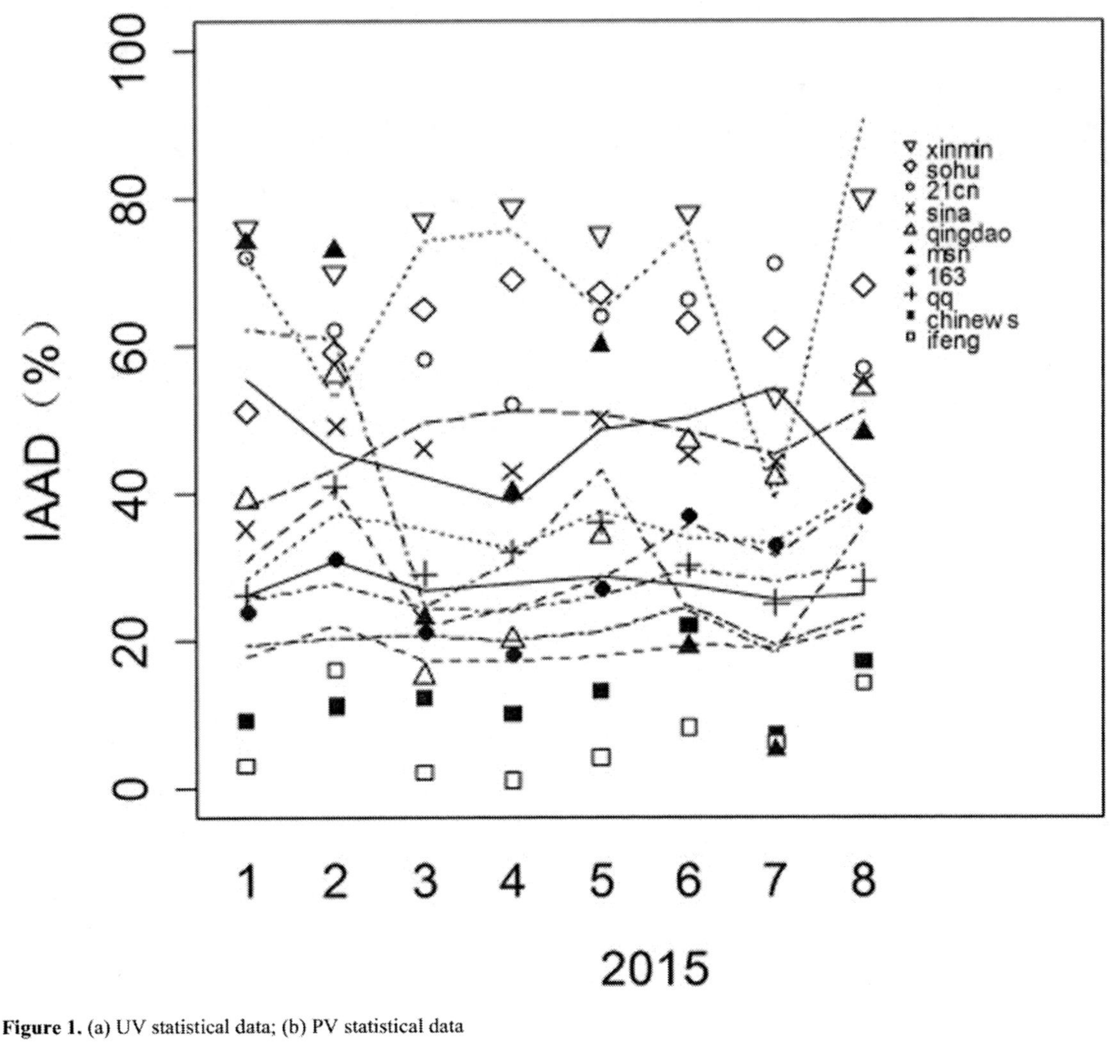

Figure 1. (a) UV statistical data; (b) PV statistical data

For a better observation on the accessing frequency of information resource on a node, the information average access density (IAAD), calculated by PV divide UV, is provided to present the sparse degree of information- accessed. IAAD curves have been drawn to show a reverse trend (see Figure 2) that a site (Xinmin News) with the lowest UV and the lowest PV has the largest IAAD, and a popular site(Phoenix News) has the minimum IAAD value.

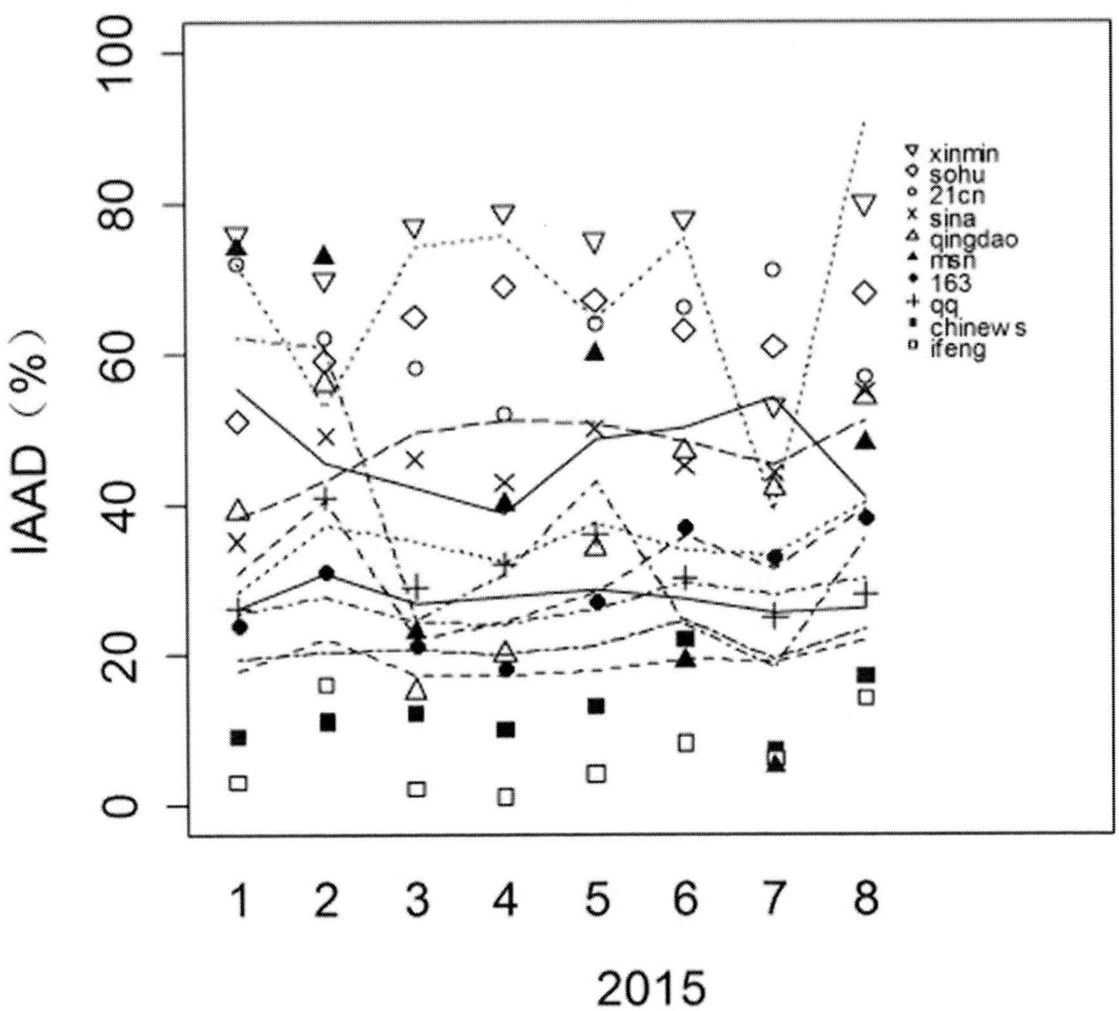

Figure 2. News sites with the information average access density curve in the year of 2015

The traceability of data has been analyzed to find that Shanghai Municipal Committee is in charge of the site of Xinmin News, the information with the site needs to be strictly audited prior to publication, the credibility of information content is high. As a result, the IAAD value and the probability that each message is viewed in the site are higher. In contrast, because the Phoenix News belongs to the Phoenix New Media consulting company, so the audit information has more lenient conditions, the IAAD and the probability is lower correspondingly. However, the Phoenix News average daily traffic is about 40 times the Xinmin News that it is not effective to explain the phenomenon of the "Internet+" network structure based on the topological measure of nodes and edges. In order to describe the "Internet+" network node topology effectively, it is necessary to analyze the rich-club and information aggregation properties of the network nodes.

2.2 The Rich-club Attribute of Network Nodes

Colizza and colleges, who analyzed the rich-club phenomenon of Internet, believe that the rich-club coefficient Φ can more effectively reflect the strength of the network traffic and the interaction process of network nodes. According to the definition of the rich-club coefficient, $\Phi=2l/r(r-1)$, where the l is the actual number of edges of neighborhood service node and the r is the number of nodes in the neighborhood. By definition, the Φ coefficient reflects the intensity of the surrounding nodes connected adjacent points directly. As an independent information node, it is unable to effectively estimate the Φ by computing the number of links directly-connected routers. To effectively reflect the rich-club attribute of network nodes, it's assumed that the Φ is the ratio of the number of actual accesses and the number of possible accesses in the unit time.

Definition 1 The concurrent access of information network node per unit time is li, the maximum number of concurrent is C, then$\Phi= li/C$. Considering the number of concurrent users and the service response time is a near linear relation, the rich-club coefficient is calculated as follow:

$$\varphi_i = \frac{t_i - \alpha}{\beta \cdot C} \quad (1)$$

As the formula (1) shows, the φ_i is equal to the ratio of the network node response time and the maximum response delay time. That is to say, the longer response delay, the greater the load of the network nodes, the higher the number of concurrent. When the network node is full load, the number of concurrent is the highest, and the service response delay is at maximum.

So, the formula (1) can be approximated equivalent to:

$$\varphi_i = \bar{t}_i / t_{\max} \quad (2)$$

In the formula, the t_i is the average response time of nodes, and the t_{max} is the maximum response time among nodes.

2.3 The Information Aggregation Attribute of Network Nodes

With the widespread use of cloud computing technologies, the nodes in the Internet+ network will show the aggregation phenomenon[18]. Namely, with the same time interval t, the larger the arrivals number of the node, the higher the information-viewed probability of the node, which means network structure has an obvious aggregation attribution. In order to evaluate the attribute value of information aggregation quantitatively, it's assumed that the similar news content is evenly distributed on all nodes, the network transmission delay of all nodes is shorter than a timeout length, and the nodes can accept all requests without discard actions.

Definition 2 The information-viewed number in the node is defined the p_i, the arrivals number of the node is n_i, and the average information-viewed number is calculated by $c_i=n_i/p_i$, which represents the sparse degree that each message is viewed in the node. The information-viewed probability is defined as follow.

$$\rho_i = \frac{c_i}{\sum c_i} \quad (3)$$

Taking into account the rich-club attribute of the news network topology, and each node stores a large number of similar information, so the possibility of a node being accessed has a relationship with the information-viewed probability and the number of instant access concurrency. If the node access probability is high, the concurrency is low, which means that the value of the information stored in the node is not high, then the degree of the information aggregation is low. Thus, the degree of the information aggregation of nodes ξ_i should be related to the information-viewed number ρ_i and the number of instant access concurrency l_i.

$$\xi_i = f(l_i, \rho_i) \quad (4)$$

3 "Internet+" Network Topology Modeling

3.1 The Network Topological entropy Based on the Information Aggregation

"Internet+" is essentially an extension of the application of Internet, so the network structure also has the scale-free characteristic. Meanwhile, a large number of similar information may be spread on a number of nodes, on which there are different access probabilities. As a result, the network topology will have a certain order, and the topological entropy can be used to model the topology.

According to the definition of entropy, the topological entropy of the network node is given in formula (5):

$$H = -\sum_{i=1}^{n} \xi_i \ln \xi_i \quad (5)$$

In order to simplify the process of modeling the "Internet+" network topology, it is assumed that the t_{max} value of all nodes in the "Internet+" network is not obvious, and then the entropy of a single node is derived as follow.

$$p_i = l_i \cdot t = \frac{C \cdot \bar{t}_i}{t_{\max}} \cdot t$$

$$\Longrightarrow$$

$$\frac{\bar{t}_i \cdot n_i}{p_i \cdot t_{\max} \sum_i c_i} = \frac{n_i}{t \cdot C \sum_i c_i}$$

$$= \rho_i \cdot \frac{p_i}{t \cdot C} = \rho_i \cdot l_i / C$$

$$\Longrightarrow$$

$$H_i = -\frac{\rho_i \cdot l_i}{C} \ln \frac{\rho_i \cdot l_i}{C}$$

$$= -\frac{\rho_i \cdot l_i}{C} (\ln \rho_i + \ln l_i - \ln C)$$

$$= \alpha_i \Delta \rho_i + \beta_i \Delta l_i - \xi_i \Delta C$$

The α and β are coefficients of linear regression equation, $l_i=\alpha+\beta \cdot C$. From the derivation formula of the topological entropy, it is known that the topological entropy of a single node is approximately equal to sum of the topological entropy of the concurrent connection and the topological entropy of the information-viewed probability, and minus the topological entropy of the maximum concurrency in the node.

3.2 Computation of the Minimal Entropy of "Internet+" Network

For measuring the topology of the "Internet+" effectively, first of all, it's assumed that the probability distribution of information-viewed among nodes remains almost unchanged in a unit of time, entropy derivation formula is showed as follow:

$$\frac{dH_i}{d\xi_i} = \alpha_i \frac{d\Delta\rho_i}{d\xi_i} + \frac{d\alpha_i}{d\xi_i}\Delta\rho_i + \beta_i \frac{d\Delta l_i}{d\xi_i} + \frac{d\beta_i}{d\xi_i}\Delta l_i - \Delta C \qquad (6)$$

In the formula 6, α_i=l_i/C and β_i=ρ_i/C.

At second, it's assumed that the concurrent number of all nodes keeps a stable value when the probability distribution of information-viewed is invariable. At then, the topological entropy of a single node has a minimum value with $d\Delta\rho_i/d\zeta_i$=0 and $d\Delta l_i/d\zeta_i$=0, so the formula is simplified as follow.

$$\frac{d\xi_i}{d\rho_i\, dl_i} = \ln C^{-1}\left(\frac{1}{(\rho_i \ln\rho_i)^{-1} d\rho_i} + \frac{1}{(l_i \ln l_i)^{-1} dl_i}\right) \qquad (7)$$

The information aggregation degree(IAD) of the node is calculated by integrating on both ends of the formula 7:

$$\xi_i = \frac{l_i \cdot \rho_i \ln(l_i \cdot \rho_i)}{C \ln C} + \lambda \qquad (8)$$

The λ is a integration constant.

4 The Topology Model Test

In general, the clusters of the news site have capable of processing 1 million requests per second at least, so the minimum threshold is taken. The integration constant λ is zero for calculation simplicity. The IAD can be approximately calculated by formula 9.

$$\overline{\xi_i} = \frac{\overline{l_i} \cdot \overline{\rho_i} \ln(\overline{l_i} \cdot \overline{\rho_i})}{C \ln C} \qquad (9)$$

Experimental data comes from the daily statistical average number of the ten major news networks, from January to August in the year of 2015. After steps of data cleaning, data sorting and data calculating by using Rstadio tools, the 3-dimension graphical of the IAD is showed as figure 3

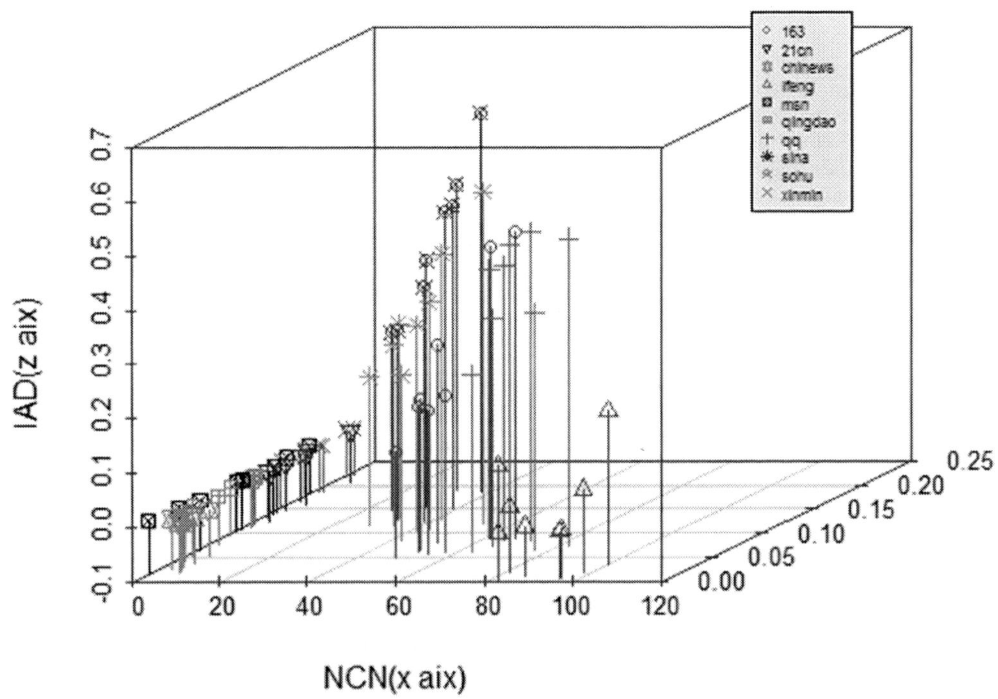

(Note: The NCN stands for node concurrent number and the IPD stands for information-viewed probability distribution.)

Figure 3. The AID distribution of news sites

From above the figure, it is concluded that the IAD of the Sohu News is highest(0.388), follow by the Sina News(0.383) and the QQ News(0.296), and the Phoenix News with the highest UV is about 10 times lower than the Sina News and the QQ News. This result shows that although the daily visits of Phoenix News is larger, but the extent of the use of information in the site is not higher than the Sina News and the QQ News. Furthermore, the Xinmin News with the highest IAAD has a negative IAD value(-0.013), it says that every information stored in the site has a higher frequency to be viewed.

In summary, the model can be simple to evaluate the information aggregation degree of all nodes from the information-viewed number and the number of the instant access concurrency.

5 Conclusion

Through the relationship analysis of the News site's PVs and UVs in the "Internet+" structure, a phenomenon has been found that the site with a lower value of PV and UV has the larger IAAD value, and the phenomenon can't be explained effectively by the conventional complex network theories. In order to explain this phenomenon reasonably, the rich-club attribute of the "Internet+" node is analyzed at first, then the information-viewed probability is defined, and the model for calculating the IAD is established finally based on the topological entropy theory.

The experimental result shows that the proposed model can be used to evaluate the information aggregation degree in the "internet+" network, which provides a new evaluation for the analysis of the "Internet+" network structure.

Acknowledgement

This paper was supported by the *Applied Basic Research Key Program of Yunnan Province* (2012CC031), with the project named as The *Cloud Key Technology and its Applicable Research for Scientific and Technical Resources Public Service.*

References

1. Watts D J, Steven H S. Collective dynamics of 'small-world' networks. Nature, 1998,393(6684):440-442.
2. Strogatz, Steven H. Exploring complex networks[J]. Nature, 2001, 410(6825):268-276.
3. Barabási A L, Réka A. Emergence of scaling in random networks. Science, 1999, 286(5439):509-512.
4. Réka A, Barabási A L. Statistical mechanics of complex networks. Reviews of modern physics, 2002, 74(1):47.
5. Boccaletti S, Latora V, Moreno Y, et al. Complex networks: Structure and dynamics. Physics reports, 2006, 424(4):175-308.
6. Barrat A, Barthélemy M, Pastor S R, at el. The architecture of complex weighted networks: Proceedings of the National Academy of Sciences of the United States of America,2004. Boston:pnas, 2014, 101(11):3747-3752.
7. Antal T, Krapivsky P L. Weight-driven growing networks. Physical Review E, 2005, 71(2): 026103.
8. Dorogovtsev S N, Mendes J F. Minimal models of weighted scale-free networks. 2004, arXiv:cond-mat/0408343. http://arxiv.org/abs/cond-mat/0311416.
9. LIANG S, LI M, LEUNG K, et al. An Experimental Study of Response Times of Web Applications. Journal of Computer Research and Development, 2003, 40(7): 1076-1080.
10. Garcia-Robledo A, Diaz-Perez A, Morales-Luna G. Correlation analysis of complex network metrics on the topology of the Internet. Emerging Technologies for a Smarter World (CEWIT), 2013 10th International Conference and Expo on. IEEE, 2013: 1-6.
11. Chai W K, He D, Psaras I, et al. Cache "less for more" in information-centric networks (extended version). Computer Communications, 2013, 36(7): 758-770.
12. Bo J, Ying Z, Jing D, et al. Study on the stability of the topology interactive growth mechanism using graph spectra. Communications, IET, 2014, 8(16): 2845-2857.
13. Holbert B, Tati S, Silvestri S, et al. Network Topology Inference With Partial Information. Network and Service Management, IEEE Transactions on, 2015, 12(3): 406-419.
14. LIU X, ZHAO H, WANG J, et al. Dissipation Analysis of Internet Topology Structure. Journal of Northeastern University(Natural Science),2015, 36(9): 1237-1241.
15. LU X, WANG H, WANG J. Virtual Computing Environment iVCE:Concept and system structure. Science in China(Series E:Information Sciences), 2006, 10:1081-1099.
16. LIANG H. A Similarity Detection System of Network News. JILIN: JILIN University, 2011.
17. Calvert K L, Doar M B, Zegura E W. Modeling internet topology. Communications Magazine, IEEE, 1997, 35(6): 160-163.
18. LIANG S, LI M, LEUNG K, et al. An Experimental Study of Response Times of Web Applications. Journal of Computer Research and Development, 2003, 40(7): 1076-1080.

Big Data Drive Tourism Enterprises Integration Innovation

Guo-Hong CHEN

Management College, Shenyang Normal University, Shenyang,110034/Huang He Bei Street No.253, China
guohong_c@sina.com

Abstract: Big data affects the integration of innovative products and services of tourist enterprises. Tourist enterprises are in urgent need of integration innovation as it becomes the source of competitive advantage. In the era of big data, integration innovation in tourist enterprise can impacted from several factors: large data mining analysis, strategy of tourist development, integration of innovative resources and capabilities, etc. Tourism enterprises should leverage big data to build a large tourist data analysis system, by focusing on integration of large data and valuation and exploring internal and external models tourist enterprises.

1 Literature Review

The concept of big data was originated by Peter (1960) as data science. Toffler (1980) predicted in "Third Wave" that society will enter the era of big data. Bill (1990) proposed the concept of "massive data". In twenty-first century, big data is getting more attention[1-3]. A report from McKinsey (2011) suggests that big data has penetrated into every field of industries and business functions and is becoming an important factor for productivity[4]. Research from Brown (2011) pointed out that big data can bring game-changing impact[5]. Christina (2013) believes that big data has the power of creative destruction for current business model. Rapid development of big data reflects part of human's continuous exploration process[6].

Integration innovation was first introduced by Rosenberg (1963), who noted that integration innovation takes place when similar technologies are applied across different industries. Greenstein (1998) categorized integration innovation into three modes, i.e. replacement, complementary and combination. Morgan (2004) proposed a model to combine internal and external technology integration.

China scholars have also conducted in-depth research in this area. Zhang Yanxing (1996), Meng Qingwei (2003) and Hu Chunxiang suggested that integration innovation, i.e. introduction, digestion, absorption and recreation, is the key processes by which an enterprise obtain and consolidate external advanced technology and experience. Liu Xin (2006) concluded that integration innovation focuses more on the impact of innovation and its long term competitiveness. Li Ping (2013) proposed that integration innovation can be defined as combining new technologies from different fields for the development process of new technology and process and system.

Big data and integration innovation have made a huge impact the supply and demand balance of tourist industry. Olsen, Moore (1998), Law (2000) Buhalis (2002) have shown that big data technology and information is changing function of tourist distribution channels by providing value-added services. Fesenmaier (2000) and Frew (2004) believe that big data can help tourist enterprises with a wide range of promotional activities to supplement offline promotion activities. Xu Hong and fan Qing (2008) pointed out that innovation is the driving force for the convergence of tourist industry. Liu Yuqing (2009) proposed that deep penetration of big data into the tourist enterprises has changed the management mode. Ma Xue Feng (2010) proposed integration is to actively introduce relevant technology from other industries with technical advantages into tourist enterprises. Liu Xueting (2011) believes that technology integration is an important catalyst for tourist enterprise integration and innovation. Yang Yanfeng (2012) believes that big data is driving the integration of tourism industry. Gao Lingjiang and Xia Changjie (2012) also believe that technology innovation brings system management and product market innovation into tourist enterprises and eventually change the mode of tourist enterprises development.

In practice, although experts and scholars proposed various definitions, description, concept, and impact of big data and integration innovation, current research focuses more on qualitative analysis on macroscopic scale. Microscopic quantitative research on the impact of big data and integration innovation is limited. There is a lack of research on the impact of big data on the nature of integration innovation. For many tourist enterprises, the interest in big data remains as abstract and theoretical; therefore it is either lack of practical operation or applicable to only specific cases. The absence of systematic research leads to the fact that limited research has had very little impact in guiding the introduction and innovation of tourist product and services. Potential impact of big data on tourist product and service needs to be explored, in particular in conjunction with integration innovation, so that forward-looking principles can be established to guide tourist enterprises. It is also important to reveal these principles with the power of big data to identify hidden characteristics and trends that are common to tourist enterprises.

2 Tourist Enterprises Based on Big Data and Integration Innovation

2.1 Analysis of Large Data Mining in Tourist Enterprises

Acquisition and analysis of big data for tourist enterprises is closely related to business process such as product design, channel selection, price formulation, and strategy. Tourist enterprises can collect and analyze consumer information to extract information on consumer need, consumer concern and hot topics, and specifics such as consumption and spending behavior. Further analysis of consumer behavior can lead to potential new customer, design and development of tourism products, marketing and sales activities.

For example, construction of high-speed rail in a city provides a quick and easy way of transportation. Neighboring cities can now be connected with the high-speed rail, and tourist flow between these cities will be impacted. Studies using spatial econometric model shows that construction of high-speed rail can have spatial spillover effect on neighboring cities. A spatial spillover effect is defined as the impact of social and economic activity of one city on surrounding cities. High speed rail has positive spatial spillover effect as it facilitates long-distance travel and promotes long distance tourism. However, a negative spatial spillover effect exists if there is competition for tourist flow between these cities. As such tourist enterprises can analyze tourist information in real time to identify and develop marketing strategy to deal with positive or negative spillover flow.

2.2 Development Strategy of Tourist Enterprises

With big data processing technology becoming more and more mature and perfection, tourist enterprises should get better at using big data for reform and innovation. New business models such as Ctrip, LY, Piaoguanjia are being introduced by large and medium-sized tourist enterprises via leveraging large data collection, intelligent tourism and industry restructuring. In the era of big data, the tourist enterprises can objectively analyze consumer behavior with high accuracy. At the same time, tourist enterprises can depend on big data analysis to support enterprise strategy development to adapt to change.

In the process of formulating development strategy, on the one hand, the tourist enterprises can perform consumer data mining with special focus on tourist demand, consumption need, interconnectivity, and consumer feedback. The enterprise can make decision about tourist consumption behavior and value orientation. On the other hand, in marketing and sales process, tourist enterprises can use big data to monitor corresponding attention, interest, active contraction, action and sharing strategy. Big data analysis can guide tourist business strategy to better serve consumers and expand market share.

2.3 Integration Innovation Resources and Capabilities for Tourist Enterprise

Tourist market information is an important resource for the integration innovation. Tourist enterprises face the new challenge of how to use of these resources to promote growth and integrate innovation for decision-making. By analyzing and understanding the dynamics of market trend, tourist enterprises can better forecast tourist market, preferences and spatial distribution of tourist flow, and facilitate the restructuring and combination for upstream and downstream integration. Since big data can provide comprehensive historical and cross-border perspective, it is advantage to use the data as a platform to create value and expand market and enhance services. Through the analysis of consumer behavior and tourist psychology, future tourist industry can be expected to provide corresponding products and services.

Comparing with traditional tourist enterprise data analysis and management, big data analysis is more focused on the extension of the external data, overall market trend analysis and prediction, and these can positively affect the tourist enterprise information system, data processing ability, management mode and so on. At the same time, the value of isolated data is far less than that of widely correlated data; the value of collective data is far greater than that of a single type of data.

3 Strategies for Integration Innovation

3.1 Construction of Large Tourism Data Analysis System

3.1.1 Macro environment of tourist industry

First, it begins with data collection and analysis on external tourist environment data, including external macro economy, regional development, tourism consumption patterns, and tourism competitiveness. Secondly, it includes comparison of area traffic, such as mode of transportation by aviation, railway, waterway and highway. Furthermore, it is clearly advantageous to include quantitative analysis of regional tourist characteristics, climate information, and other tourist resources. Finally, it must include tourist resource, core tourist market, potential market status, analysis of regional competition.

3.1.2 Regional tourist market segmentation

Analysis includes tourist age, gender, education level, occupation, income, behavior. Distribution of tourist information, behavior, collection mode, attention to special location, time duration at scenic spots, travel related dynamic machine, etc.

3.1.3 Supervision system of tourist market

Supervision system include monitoring regional tourist market, tourist flow, early warning, hot spots, hot search, tourist flow prediction, hot spots distribution; Public opinion to scenic tourist reputation evaluation, emotional volatility, positive and negative feedback, public opinion warning mechanism.

3.2 Integration and Valuation of Big Data

3.2.1 Integration of big data

Correlation analysis by integration of big data from different industries can promote the development of cross-border tourism and accelerate the pace of integration innovation. Tourist enterprises and enterprises from related industries can share information and resources for in-depth analysis of market information to understand consumption pattern and tourists preference for market trend forecast. For example, by integrating real estate development and seals information with local tourist market data, tourist products and market development can be designed to meet the needs and preferences of new households.

3.2.2 Valuation of blg data

Big data is an important cornerstone for innovative products and innovative business models. Big data helps building new business models. Tourist enterprises value big data as a capital of the enterprise and use large data analysis to forecast tourist business model innovation and to create new profit growth. Unlike typical corporate valuation, the data information is enterprise resources and capital and has market value. Economists agree that big data is an intangible asset.

The commercial value of big data includes two aspects. First it can help tourist enterprises to reduce cost and improve productivity. Secondly, it helps tourist enterprises to better segment and position tourist market, such as data analysis, product design, better meet customer need, improving core competitiveness, value creation.

4 Integration Innovation System of Tourist Enterprises

Using big data allows construction of a new type of tourist enterprises completely. Internally, tourist enterprise can qualitatively predict market trend by changing from traditional upstream and downstream organization to integration of various different industries sharing and analyzing the data on product design. Tourist enterprises themselves are transformed into consumer and supplier of big data. Externally, in the Internet era, the emergence of a large number of online tourist enterprises and open platform, such as Ctrip, Tuniu, extends the conventional definition of tourist enterprises and place more emphasis on use of big data mining to meet customer need and provide better service.

At the same time, the tourist industry itself is a boundary-less industry. Big data allows the industry to grow in multiple directions on multiple platforms with multiple integrations. "Internet +" is a thought process of promoting the formation of cross-border and mutual integration and innovation. When creating integration innovation based with big data industry, tourist enterprises play the main role to support for the development of related industries and fields, identify new spaces for the development of tourist enterprises.

References

1. Frankel F, Reid R. Big data: Distilling meaning from data, J. Nature, 2008, 455(7209):30-30.
2. Anderson C. The end of theory: The data deluge makes the scientific method obsolete, J. Wired Magazine, 2008, 16:1-3.
3. Donovan S. Dealing with data, J. Science, 2011, 331(6018):639-806.
4. James Manyika, Michael Chui. Big Data: The Next Frontier for Innovation, Competition and Productivity, J. McKinsey Quarterly, 2011, 5:38-47.
5. Brown, Brad, Chui, Michael, Manyika and James. Are You Ready for the Era of "Big Data", J. McKinsey Quarterly, 2011, 4:129-137.
6. Jeanne E. Johnson. Big Data + Big Analytics = Big Opportunities, J. Financial Executive,2012,7.

DOI: 10.1051/itmconf/20171205023

Color Image Inpainting By an Improved Criminisi Algorithm

Yu-Ting HE[a,1], Xiang-Hong TANG[b,1,2]

[1]*School of Communication Engineering, Hangzhou Dianzi University, Hangzhou, China*
[2]*School of information Engineering, Hangzhou Dianzi University, Hangzhou, China*
[a]*1689238330@qq.com*, [b]*tangxh@hdu.edu.cn*

Abstract: Due to the incorrect filling order and the fixed size of patch, the traditional examplar-based image inpainting algorithm tends to cause the image structure fracture, texture error extension and so on. So in this paper, it proposes an improved Criminisi algorithm with adaptive adjustment with gradient variation to color image inpainting algorithm. Firstly, to overcome the discontinuity of the edge structure caused by the incorrect filling order, using curvature of isophotes to constraint the filling order. Secondly, in order to solve the lack of the step effect in rich texture region, it adaptively adjusts the sample patch size according to the variation of local gradient. Finally, the local search method is used to find the best matching patch. The experimental results show that the proposed algorithm's PSNR increased by 1-3dB and obtain better results in terms of different types of images.

1 Introduction

Digital image restoration is a process of filling unknown area according to the information of known area of the image in a visually plausible way. One of the most representative algorithms is the exemplar-based image inpainting algorithm proposed by Criminisi et al. [1]. In recent years, many scholars have put forward different improvement methods aiming at the deficiencies of the Criminisi algorithm [2-8]. Xiang et al. [4] inducted the curvature to the data item so that the information could be extended along the direction of the isophotes, and introduced the matching method based on matrix similarity into image restoration to solve the image visual discontinuity problem caused by error matching. Qi et al. [5] changed the priority function to the weighted sum of the terms, avoiding the order of error filling when the data item is zero; Considering the existence of some mistakes between the patch to be repaired and the matching patch, the algorithm improved the update of confidence . The improved algorithm had a better repair for the image structure, but in the rich texture region produced block effect. Yin et al. [6] added the curvature of the isophotes to the calculation of the priority function, and led the curvature term into the search matching, which had a better restoration effect on the image with single structure, but it was not ideal for image with complex structure and texture. Deng et al. [7] completed the image restoration in phases by defining a new priority function, and searched for the matching patch using local search to find the best matching patch to reduce the repair time. Wang et al. [8] used the adjustment factor to determine the priority of each patch and added a normalized cross-correlation function (NCC) to the matching condition to scale the similarity between the source patch and the target patch.

However, these algorithms rarely take into account the impact of the priority calculation when the data item becomes zero in the priority function and the influence of curvature on the filling order, which is easy to produce the wrong filling order during the restoration process. Moreover, most of them use a fixed sample patch size to search for the best matching patch, thus in the rich texture region it will produce the staircase effect. So in this paper, the curvature of the isophotes is introduced as a cofactor into the calculation of the priority function to make the filling order more accurate and to prevent the error extension or discontinuity of the image structure. In addition, the algorithm adaptively adjusts the sample patch size according to the local gradient variation of the image. Finally, the local search is used to replace the global search in traditional inpainting algorithm. The improved algorithm makes the entire repair order more reasonable, which has better repair effect of the image structure, especially on the curve part.

DOI: 10.1051/itmconf/20171205023

The paper is organized as follows. Section 2 introduces the Criminisi algorithm, analyzes the shortcomings of the traditional algorithm and proposes an improved algorithm. Section 3 gives the comparison of experimental results between the improved algorithm and other algorithms. Finally, the conclusion is described in section 4.

2 An Improved Criminisi Algorithm

2.1 Criminisi Algorithm

The Criminisi algorithm [1] is an exemplar-based image inpainting algorithm, which combines the characteristics of transmission structure and texture synthesis. As shown in Fig. 1, assuming that the target region is indicated by Ω and

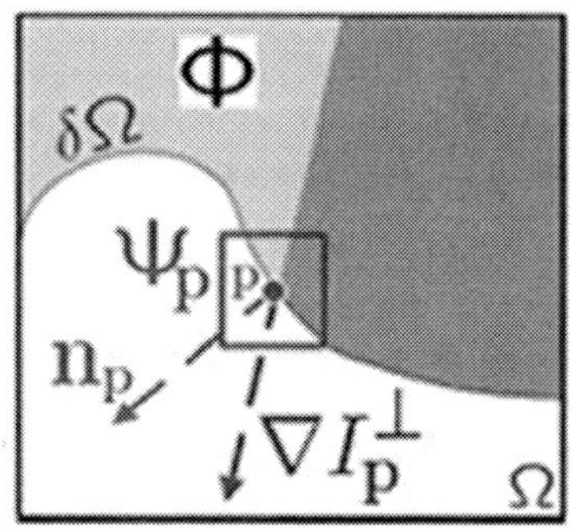

Figure 1. Schematic diagram of Criminisi algorithm

its contour by $\delta\Omega$, the source region is Φ, ψ_p is the target patch, which centred at the point p for some $p \in \delta\Omega$. The Criminisi algorithm contains the following three steps [1] :

First, the priority function $P(p)$ of target patch ψ_p is the product of two terms: the confidence item $C(p)$ and the data item $D(p)$. They are defined as follows respectively:

$$P(p) = C(p) \cdot D(p) \tag{1}$$

$$C(p) = \sum_{q \in \psi_p \cap \Phi} C(q) / |\psi_p| \tag{2}$$

$$D(p) = |\nabla \mathbf{I}_{\mathbf{p}}^{\perp} \cdot \mathbf{n}_{\mathbf{p}}| / \alpha \tag{3}$$

Where, p is a point on the fill front $\delta\Omega$, $|\psi_p|$ represents the area of ψ_p, α is the normalization factor. $\mathbf{n}_{\mathbf{p}}$ stands for the unit normal vector at point p orthogonal to the fill front $\delta\Omega$, $\nabla \mathbf{I}_{\mathbf{p}}^{\perp}$ is isophotes vector at point p. The initial value of $C(p)$ is set to:

$$C(q) = \begin{cases} 0, \forall q \in \Omega \\ 1, \forall q \in \Phi \end{cases} \tag{4}$$

Second, when all priorities of target patch on the fill boundary have been completed, it looks for a patch $\psi_{\hat{p}}$ with the maximum priority, and then uses the global search to find the most similar sample patch $\psi_{\hat{q}}$ in the source area.

$$\psi_{\hat{q}} = \arg \min_{\psi_q \in \Phi} d(\psi_{\hat{p}}, \psi_q) \tag{5}$$

$$d(\psi_{\hat{p}}, \psi_q) = \sum_{i=1}^{n} \left[(I_R - I_R^{'})^2 + (I_G - I_G^{'})^2 + (I_B - I_B^{'})^2 \right] \tag{6}$$

Where, $d(\psi_{\hat{p}}, \psi_q)$ represents the sum of squared differences (SSD) of the known pixels in the corresponding patches. I、I' respectively represent the color values of corresponding known pixel points of $\psi_{\hat{p}}$ and ψ_q.

At last, when the patch $\psi_{\hat{p}}$ is filled, the fill front have changed. The confidence of all points in the $\psi_{\hat{p}}$ need to be updated:

$$C(p) = C(\hat{p}),\ p \in \psi_{\hat{p}} \cap \Omega \tag{7}$$

Repeat the above steps until the pixels of the area to be repaired are filled completely.

2.2 The Priority Improvement

In the practical application, it is found that when the data item of some pixels may be zero in the filling process, its priority value are also zero, which leads to incorrect filling order and affects the repair effect to a certain degree. In addition, the curvature of the isophotes [9] as a second order differential is one of the most important descriptions of the morphological features of the isophotes reflecting the local characteristics of the image [10]. However in the algorithm [7], they did not take into account the above problems when calculating the priority. Therefore, this paper adds the curvature of the isophotes as a cofactor to the calculation of the priority function. On the one hand, the structural information of the image can be extended along the direction of the isophotes so that the structural part can be repaired better, which can prevent the error extension or discontinuity of the image structure. On the other hand, when the data item of some pixels are zero, it can avoid the wrong filling order. The improved priority function is defined as follows:

$$P(p)=\begin{cases}\alpha\cdot D(p)+\beta\cdot|K(p)|, & T\le T_{\Omega_s}\\ C(p) & ,T>T_{\Omega_s}\end{cases}\tag{8}$$

Where $K(p)=\nabla\cdot[\nabla \mathbf{I_p}/|\nabla \mathbf{I_p}|]$ is the curvature of the isophotes at the center pixel p, $\nabla \mathbf{I_p}$ is the gradient at pixel p. α、β are the weights of data item and confidence item, let $0\le\alpha$、$\beta\le 1$, $\alpha+\beta=1$. In this paper, $\alpha=0.6$, $\beta=0.4$. T is the number of current repair for the damaged image; T_{Ω_s} is the total number of repairing edge structure, and it is defined as [7]:

$$T_{\Omega_s}=18\cdot\frac{A_{E_\Phi}A_\Omega}{A_\Phi A_{\psi_p}}\tag{9}$$

Where, A_{E_Φ} is the quantity of edge pixels in the source region Φ, which can be obtained by Canny operator; A_Ω is the number of pixels in the target area Ω; A_Φ represents the number of pixels in the source area Φ; A_{ψ_p} is the area of the patch ψ_p to be repaired.

When the priority function $P(p)$ takes the weighted sum of the data item $D(p)$ and the curvature term $|K(p)|$, it mainly completes the restoration of the image structure. When it is determined by the confidence term $C(p)$, it achieves the inpainting of the texture part of the image. At this time, the initial value of $C(p)$ is still set according to (4).

2.3 Adaptive Adjustment of Sample Patch Size

For the traditional exemplar-based image restoration algorithm, a fixed-size sample patch is used to search for the best matching patch. However, an image usually contains different edge structures and texture features, if using the same size of sample patch for image restoration, it will greatly affect the overall image restoration effect. In order to overcome this shortcoming, this paper adaptively adjusts the sample patch size by using the gradient change of the local area of the image. If the image has complex background, in order to prevent the wrong extension of the edge structure, using a smaller sample patch to search for the best matching patch. When the image of the texture area is relatively flat, then using a larger sample patch to avoid the staircase effect. The specific implementation method is as follows:

Firstly, assuming that the number of pixels of the color damaged image is M, and convert the color image to the gray-scale image I according to (10):

$$I=(Red+Green+Blue)/3\tag{10}$$

Where $Red, Green, Blue$ respectively represent R, G, B three color components values.

Secondly, calculating the gradient value $grad$ of the gray-scale image I:

$$grad=\sqrt{I_x^{\,2}+I_y^{\,2}}\tag{11}$$

Where, $I_x=\partial I/\partial x$, $I_y=\partial I/\partial y$ are the gradient of the pixels at x and y directions respectively.

Then, calculating the gradient mean and gradient variance of the gray-scale image I:

$$mean=\sum_{i=1}^{M} grad(p_i)/M\tag{12}$$

$$\text{var}=\sum_{i=1}^{M}(p_i-mean)^2/M\tag{13}$$

Where, the pixel $p_i\in\Phi\cup\Omega$.

Finally, the size W of the patch $\psi_{\hat{p}}$ with the highest priority is determined by (14).

$$W=\begin{cases}11\times 11, & |G_p|\le \text{var}\\ 9\times 9, & \text{var}<|G_p|\le(mean+8\cdot\text{var})/2\\ 5\times 5, & |G_p|>(mean+8\cdot\text{var})/2\end{cases}\tag{14}$$

Where, $|G(p)|$ is the average gradient value of the known pixels in the patch $\psi_{\hat{p}}$.

$$|G(p)|=\sum_{i=1}^{N} grad(q_i)/N\tag{15}$$

Where, the pixel $q_i\in\psi_{\hat{p}}\cap\Phi$, N is the number of known pixels for $\psi_{\hat{p}}$, and the initial size of W is 9×9.

2.4 The New Searching Strategy

According to the neighborhood of the image with the similarity principle, the proposed algorithm uses local search method to determine the best matching patch in order to improve the inpainting efficiency. The main idea is as follows: at the center of the pixel p with the maximum priority, expanding Z pixels through up and down, left and right. That is, it forms a relatively large patch, which size is $(2Z+1)\times(2Z+1)$. Then the best matching patch $\psi_{\hat{q}}$ of the target patch $\psi_{\hat{p}}$ is searched in this relatively large patch. In this paper, the value of Z is mainly determined by the size of the image damaged region and the complexity of the image structure which can be reflected by the variance.

$$Z = \begin{cases} \sqrt{num/11}, & \text{var} \le 0.0020 \\ \sqrt{num/11}+15, & 0.0020 < \text{var} < 0.0042 \\ \sqrt{num/11}+40, & \text{var} \ge 0.0042 \end{cases} \quad (16)$$

Where num is the total number of pixels of damaged area.

As described above, the steps of the improved algorithm are as follows:

1) Select the target area Ω, and marks the area with a specific color.

2) Determine the fill front $\delta\Omega$ of the target area Ω, when $\delta\Omega = \phi$, the algorithm ends and outputs the restored image.

3) Convert the color image to the gray-scale image I according to (10).

4) According to (8), calculate the priority $P(p)$ of each point on the fill front $\delta\Omega$, and find the patch $\psi_{\hat{p}}$ with the highest priority.

5) Adaptively adjust the size of the target patch $\psi_{\hat{p}}$ according to (14).

6) In each component of the image to be repaired, the point p is taken as the center, and the best matching patch $\psi_{\hat{q}}$ is searched in the size of $(2Z+1)\times(2Z+1)$ of the local known area.

7) Copy the image information of the best matching patch $\psi_{\hat{q}}$ to the target patch $\psi_{\hat{p}}$.

8) Update the confidence value according to (7).

9) Repeat 2) to 8) until all the target region to be filled.

3 Experimental Results and Analysis

In order to verify the effectiveness of the proposed algorithm, the simulation experiment is realized with Matlab R2011 on the computer with the 3.30 GHz processor and the 2GB memory.

Fig. 2 shows the results of using the Criminisi algorithm, the algorithm [6], the algorithm [7] and the improved algorithm to restore the Barb image. As show in Fig. 2(c), 2(e) and 2(f), these three algorithms have better repaired results for pure texture regions. In algorithm [6] and this paper, the curvature of the isophotes is added to calculate the priority. So there is no structural discontinuity at the junction of the arms and knees in Fig. 2(d) and Fig. 2(f). While the algorithm [7] and the Criminisi algorithm doesn't introduce the curvature into the priority. Therefore by comparison of the inpainting results can be obtained that introducing the curvature of the isophotes will be more accurate to calculate the priority function. Moreover, the inpainting result of the proposed method provides better visual quality and the PSNR value increases by about 3dB compared to other algorithms.

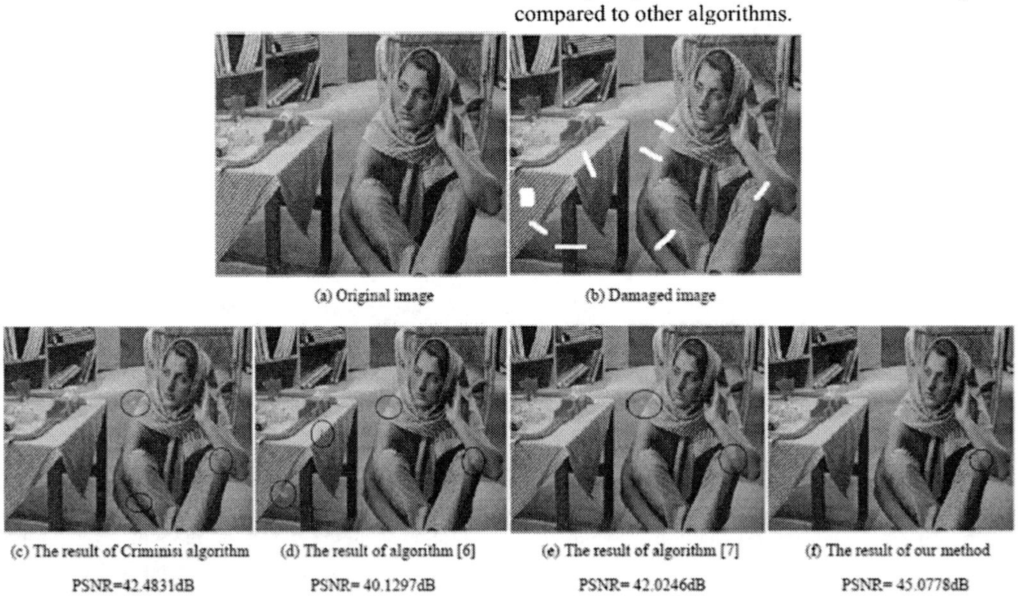

(a) Original image (b) Damaged image

(c) The result of Criminisi algorithm PSNR=42.4831dB (d) The result of algorithm [6] PSNR= 40.1297dB (e) The result of algorithm [7] PSNR= 42.0246dB (f) The result of our method PSNR= 45.0778dB

Figure 2. Barb image inpainting results

DOI: 10.1051/itmconf/20171205023

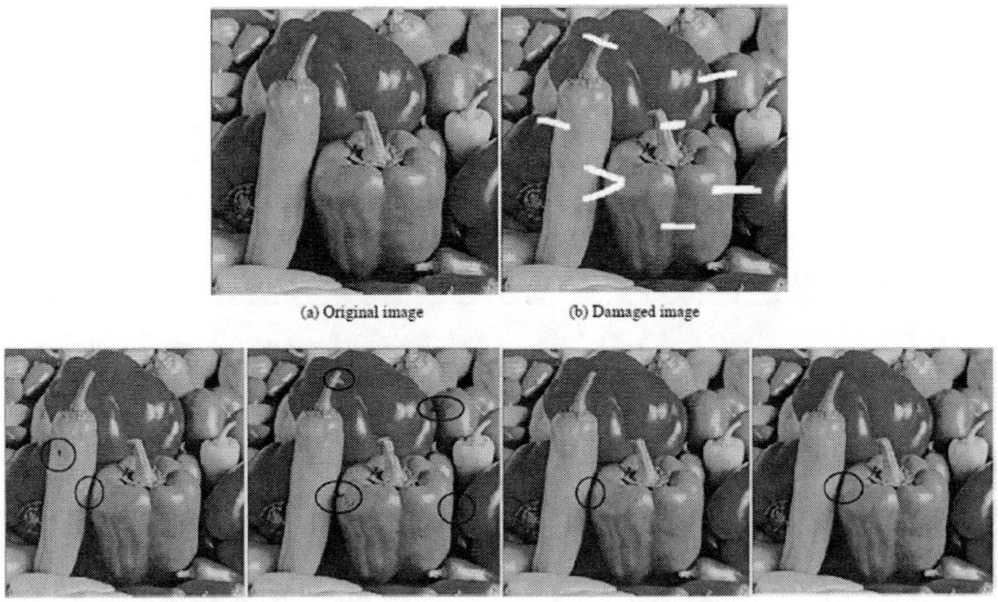

(a) Original image (b) Damaged image

(c) The result of Criminisi algorithm PSNR=40.1561dB

(d) The result of algorithm [6] PSNR=35.0995dB

(e) The result of algorithm [7] PSNR= 40.7769dB

(f) The result of our method PSNR=42.9921dB

Figure 3. Peppers image inpainting results

(a) Original image (b) Damaged image

(c) The result of Criminisi algorithm PSNR=34.2760dB

(d) The result of algorithm [6] PSNR=35.2091dB

(e) The result of algorithm [7] PSNR=36.0592dB

(f) The result of our method PSNR=36.3165dB

Figure 4. Carriage image restoration results

Table 1. Comparison of the PSNR values (dB) of this algorithm with other algorithms

Damaged image	Algorithms			
	Criminisi algorithm	**Algorithm [6]**	**Algorithm [7]**	**Proposed algorithm**
Barb (671 × 531)	42.4831	40.1297	42.0246	45.0778
Peppers (512 × 512)	40.1561	35.0995	40.7769	42.9921
Carriage (512 × 512)	34.2760	35.2091	36.0592	36.3165

.

Fig. 3 shows the inpainting results of the Peppers image. As show in Fig. 3(c), the Criminisi algorithm has some small flaws in the inpainting process. In Fig. 3(d), the algorithm [6] is not good for the restoration of the edge structure of the image, which appears obvious structural discontinuity. While the results of the image inpainting between the algorithm [7] and the improved algorithm is much better than the algorithm [6].

Fig. 4 presents the comparison of the restoration results for text removal. From the results of the restoration, it can see that when the image with complex background structure is repaired, the inpainting effect of this algorithm is visually better and without the wrong texture filling.

Table 1 shows the comparison of the PSNR value of the proposed algorithm and other algorithms. From Table 1, the proposed algorithm's PSNR value has increased significantly than other algorithms and has a better visual effect.

4 Conclusion

Owing to the incorrect filling order, the traditional examplar-based image inpainting algorithm leads to the image structure fracture and texture error extension. In this paper, an improved color image restoration algorithm is proposed based on the Criminisi algorithm. Firstly, the curvature of the isophotes can be used to characterize the local information of the image. Therefore, the curvature is used as a new control factor to redefine the priority of the block, so as to ensure that the filling order is more accurate and avoid structural information error extension and enhance the continuity of the image structure. Secondly, by using the local gradient and combining with the mean and variance of the gradient of the image, the size of the sample patch is adaptively adjusted to overcome the staircase effect caused by the fixed size sample patch. Finally, in order to improve the overall efficiency of the image restoration, this paper uses local search method to find the best matching patch. The experimental results show that the proposed algorithm can effectively overcome the shortcomings in the traditional algorithm, and achieve better restoration effect for the damaged area of different degrees of image, especially for the damaged image with obvious structural changes. Since the proposed algorithm uses adaptive adjustment of the sample patch size, the running time has increased compared to the Criminisi algorithm.

References

1. Criminisi A, Perez P, Toyama K. Region filling and object removal by exemplar-based image inpainting [J]. Image Processing IEEE Transactions on, 2004, 13(9):1200-12.
2. Zhou Y, Li L, Xia K. Research on weighted priority of exemplar-based image inpainting [J]. Journal of Electronics (China), 2012, 29(1):166-170.
3. Zhai D H, Yu J, Duan W X, Xiao J. Image inpainting algorithm based on partition block of damaged region [J]. Joumal of Image and Graphics, 2014,19(6):835-842 (in Chinese).
4. Xiang C, Duan P, Cao Y, et al. An improved exemplar-based image inpainting algorithm [C]. Canada: International Conference on Comp-uter Science & Education, 2014:770-775.
5. Qi M, Zhao Z Y, Xu Y L, et al. Image inpainting algorithm based on exemplar structure characteristics [C]. Sapporo, Japan: International Conference on Information Science, Electronics and Electrical Engineering, 2014:1932-1935.
6. Yin L, Chang C. An effective exemplar-based image inpainting method [C]. Chengdu, China: IEEE, International Conference on Communication Technology. 2012:739-743.
7. Deng L J, Huang T Z, Zhao X L. Exemplar-based image inpainting using a modified priority definition[J]. Plos One, 2015,10(10):e0141199.
8. Wang J, Lu K, Pan D. Letters: Robust object removal with an exemplar-based image inpainting approach[J]. Neuro computing, 2014,123:150-155.
9. Chan T F, Shen J. Nontexture inpainting by curvature-driven diffusions[J]. Journal of Visual Communication & Image Representation, 2001,12(4):436-449.
10. Zhu Xuan, Zhou Mingquan, Zhu Chunxiang. Image filtering by combination of the curvature-driven and edge-stopping nonlinear diffusion [J]. Acta Photonica Sinica, 2008,37(3):609-612 (in Chinese).

AUTHOR INDEX

AUTHOR INDEX

AUTHOR INDEX

AUTHOR INDEX

EDP Sciences – Web of Conferences
17, Avenue du Hoggar
Parc d'Activité de Courtabouf
BP 112
F-91944 Les Ulis Cedex A
France

ISBN 978-1-5108-4742-2
9 781510 847422